*The Letters of*
ROBERT DUNCAN *and* DENISE LEVERTOV

*The Letters of*

# ROBERT DUNCAN

*and*

# DENISE LEVERTOV

*Edited by*
ROBERT J. BERTHOLF
*and*
ALBERT GELPI

STANFORD UNIVERSITY PRESS
*Stanford, California 2004*

Stanford University Press
Stanford, California

© 2004 by the Board of Trustees of the
Leland Stanford Junior University.
All rights reserved.

Printed in the United States of America
on acid-free, archival-quality paper.

Library of Congress Cataloging-in-Publication Data

Duncan, Robert Edward, 1919–
    The letters of Robert Duncan and Denise Levertov /
edited by Robert J. Bertholf and Albert Gelpi.
        p.   cm.
    Includes bibliographical references and index.
    ISBN 0-8047-4568-4 (alk. paper) —
ISBN 0-8047-4569-2 (pbk. : alk. paper)
    1. Duncan, Robert Edward, 1919—Correspondence.
2. Levertov, Denise, 1923—Correspondence.
3. Poets, American—20th century—Correspondence.
I. Bertholf, Robert J.   II. Gelpi, Albert.   III. Title.
PS3507.U629 Z485   2004
811'.54—dc22                              2003016976

Original Printing 2004
Last figure below indicates year of this printing:
13   12   11   10   09   08   07   06   05   04

Designed by James P. Brommer
Typeset in 11/14 Garamond

Frontis and title page image:
Drawing by Denise Levertov from the
limited edition of *A Tree Telling of Orpheus*
(Los Angeles: Black Sparrow Press, 1968)

# CONTENTS

Acknowledgments    *vii*

Introduction: The "Aesthetic Ethics" of the
    Visionary Imagination    *ix*
    ALBERT GELPI

Editorial Note    *xxxiii*


PART ONE        1953–1959                                    I

PART TWO        1960–1963                                  229

PART THREE      1964–1968                                  437

PART FOUR       1969–1988                                  627


Appendix    *727*

Glossary of Names    *757*

Brief Chronology of Duncan and Levertov    *791*

Books in Letters    *797*

Notes    *799*

Index    *837*

# ACKNOWLEDGMENTS

Denise Levertov's letters are in the Poetry/Rare Books Collection, University of Buffalo, the State University of New York, and Robert Duncan's letters are in Special Collections at Green Library, Stanford University. The librarians in both institutions were indispensable in making the documents available for transcription so that the process of editing and collation could begin. Albert Gelpi would also like to thank Peter Mallios, Deanne Williams, and Douglas Kerr for assistance at various stages in preparing the texts of the Levertov letters. Robert Bertholf would like to thank Roumiana Velikova and Elizabeth Null for assistance in preparing the typescript. Finally, we are deeply grateful to Helen Tartar and to Tim Roberts for the alert editorial eye and the guiding editorial hand that helped us shape our transcriptions into this edition.

# INTRODUCTION: THE "AESTHETIC ETHICS" OF THE VISIONARY IMAGINATION

*Albert Gelpi*

> "the special view we have . . . of why and what
> the poem is"
> —Robert Duncan to Denise Levertov,
>   July 17, {18,} 1959

> "in the formation of what I think of as 'aesthetic
> ethics' . . . Duncan became my mentor."
> —Denise Levertov, "Some Duncan Letters"

## I

By almost any measure, the correspondence between Robert Duncan and Denise Levertov constitutes the most important exchange between two American poets in the second half of the twentieth century. To begin with, it is voluminous; there are over 450 letters, written between 1953 and 1985, and the body of letters on both sides seems to be virtually complete. Both Levertov and Duncan took care to keep each other's letters as vital documents in their poetic lives; the confluence between them confirmed, as nothing else did, the integrity of what they had written and inspired new creative expression. So energetically did their poems and letters spring from the same source that on a few occasions a letter moved spontaneously into verse. What gives the correspondence historic as well as personal importance is the fact that its consistent and even obsessive concerns help to map the contested terrain of American poetry since mid-century.

Donald M. Allen's landmark anthology, *The New American Poetry* (New York: Grove Press, 1960), first designated the various groups that began experimenting with different kinds of open-form verse during the 1950s in reaction to the dominance of the New Criticism and the different kinds of closed-form poetry it fostered in the academy and in literary journals. The Black Mountain group made up Section I of the anthology and included generous selections from Charles Olson, Robert Duncan, Denise Levertov, and Robert Creeley—the four central figures—as well as from Paul Blackburn, Larry Eigner, Jonathan Williams, and Edward Dorn. The clustering of poets and their "Statements on Poetics" defined not just the group identities but their differences as poets of open form. Where New York poets like John Ashbery and Frank O'Hara allied their experimentation with abstract expressionist painters and where Beats like Jack Kerouac and Allen Ginsberg undertook a Whitmanian fusion of Transcendentalist idealism and popular culture, the Black Mountain poets sought explicitly to extend into postwar American poetry the Modernist experimentation that Ezra Pound and William Carlos Williams had instigated earlier—first through the Imagist program and later (with Louis Zukofsky and George Oppen) through the Objectivism of the 1930s.

Black Mountain was a small, experimental liberal arts college founded in the North Carolina hills during the 1930s. It was already in serious financial difficulty when Olson became its rector during the five years before its doors closed in 1956. But Olson's energy and will drew not just Creeley and Duncan but Buckminster Fuller, John Cage, Merce Cunningham, Franz Kline, M. C. Richards, and others to mingle with the handful of remaining students in an extraordinary carnival of the arts. During those same years, Olson's 1950 essay "Projective Verse" became the manifesto that gave the Black Mountain poets their program and identity, and their association became a matter of public record through their appearance together in print: first in Cid Corman's *Origin* and then in *The Black Mountain Review*, edited by Creeley at Olson's instigation and running from 1954 to 1957. Indeed, since Duncan and Creeley were associated with the college faculty only briefly and Levertov never even visited the campus, the *Review* rather than the college is the more accurate locus for the group designation.

The Black Mountain poets remained a visible group through the 1960s, but a widely dispersed group, since its nucleus coalesced through a series of intersecting friendships and crisscrossing sets of correspondence. Olson began writing to Duncan in 1947 and to Creeley by spring 1950, before they had met in person. At the same time, but separately, Levertov and Creeley became friends in the early 1950s while living with their families as near neighbors in southern France. Duncan initiated correspondence with Levertov (now back in New York) in 1953; they met for the first time in New York in 1955 when he was passing through on his way to Europe, whereupon she arranged his meeting with Creeley (now in Mallorca). Personal meetings between pairs of correspondents occurred but were rare occasions, both infrequent and precious. Levertov arranged for a joint reading with Duncan and Creeley at the Guggenheim Museum in New York in April 1964, but she saw Olson only a couple of times at public performances. Indeed, the only occasion in which all four participated was the three-week Vancouver poetry festival at the University of British Columbia in the summer of 1963.

Their collective identity, therefore, lay in a poetic stance, summed up as "composition by field," the central tenet of "Projective Verse." What's more, their geographical separation—Olson at Black Mountain and then in Gloucester, Creeley in New Mexico and on the road, Levertov in Manhattan and Mexico, Duncan in San Francisco and Stinson Beach—worked to a certain advantage. Since they were peculiarly dependent on letters, the copious epistolary record of their principles and practice in relation to their contemporaries constitutes a major chapter in the literary history of the period. At the same time, as the letters also show, the central four poets were already pursuing divergent courses before Olson's death in 1970, so that the full account of Black Mountain poetry must include not just what drew them together but—just as importantly—what made for their individual paths of development in the 1970s and after. In the descent from Black Mountain, the account of the long, close, almost symbiotic association between Duncan and Levertov and its sudden rupture tells a particularly dramatic and revealing story.

Olson wrote "Projective Verse" to formulate the poetic agenda talked out in his intense and extended correspondence with Creeley, and the group positioned itself in a constellation around the kinetically capitalized program of "COMPOSITION BY FIELD," wherein "FORM IS NEVER MORE THAN AN EXTENSION OF CONTENT. (Or so it got phrased by one, R. Creeley . . . )" (*The New American Poetry*, 387). The page was a field on which the poem was composed, and that linguistic field arose from and remained in dynamic interaction with the entire field of the poet's experience. Necessarily, then, as Pound and Williams had shown, the poem found its form not by fixed conventions of meter and stanza but in a spatial arrangement of phrases and lines on the page improvised so as to graph or score the measured movement of consciousness in the process of articulation. Moreover, the poem —far from being "autotelic," to use Eliot's word for the Modernist ideal of the self-contained art-object disjunct from inchoate experience—emerged in and through the engagement with the whole field of experience: material and psychological and verbal. For all people, but for poets in a more self-conscious way, language is an element within the total field, but its particular mode of participation is to construct images of the field into evolving forms that then enter the field as new elements within the ongoing processes of intersection and mediation. As the mediating and signifying function of language became more contested in modern consciousness—Romanticism, Modernism, and Postmodernism are markers in that contest—the function of the mediating signifier became all the more a conscious concern and issue.

The field of experience—and of language as its mediating element—is, then, infinite and all-inclusive; it incorporates and articulates physics and metaphysics, history and psychology, religion and myth, anthropology and politics. At the same time, the poet's engagement with the field in and through language is individual and local, informed by his or her temperament and consciousness and circumstances. And therein lie the individuating terms of the engagement that produce different poetries—even within a group committed to composition by field. One way to begin to track those differences is at the point of origin and descent from Pound and Williams. To make some initial distinctions: where Olson and Duncan drew on the example of the Pound of *The Cantos* and the Williams of *Paterson*, Levertov and Creeley drew on the Imagist Pound but more particularly on the Williams of the short lyrics.

Thus, despite the fevered early correspondence between Olson and Creeley, which produced "Projective Verse," their poetries took on, from the start, different shapes and intentions. Where Olson was the epic poet of the macrocosm, Creeley remained resolutely the poet of the personal microcosm. Where the expansive Olson, combining the example of *Paterson* and the *Pisan Cantos*, made his Gloucester an epitome of history and the cosmos, Creeley the agnostic Puritan concentrated on testing the ironic dislocations and slippages whereby words sought and failed to mediate perception of the present moment and memory of the past. As for Levertov and Creeley, Williams hailed them as the two poets of the postwar generation who understood and pursued his demands for poetic form: diction, colloquial yet precise and concise, measured by rhythmic structure and line breaks. Nevertheless, though the letters between Creeley and Levertov acknowledged their grounding in Williams, their poetries pointed them in different directions; her awed attendance on the mystery of things moved to the opposite end of the spectrum from his skeptical and scrupulous minimalism.

On the other hand, what drew Levertov to Duncan was precisely what drew Duncan and Olson to Pound: the mystique and metaphysics of the visionary imagination. Or, as Levertov later put it, "the tradition of magic and prophecy and song" (*New and Selected Essays*, 196). For all these Black Mountain poets except Creeley, the mythopoeic power of the imagination constituted the supreme cognitive faculty to grasp the mystery and inner reality of phenomenal experience, and Levertov and Duncan in particular based their poetics on the visionary character of the creative process. Duncan insisted that what we call Modernism was really an extension of Romanticism, and Levertov acknowledged her grounding in nineteenth-century poetry. As the letters demonstrate, they assimilated their reading of Wordsworth, Coleridge, Emerson, and Whitman with their reading of Pound and Williams and Stevens. They located the continuity between Romantics and Modernists in the strenuous effort to validate and exercise the imagination as a faculty of perception in a culture that increasingly experienced itself as spiritually and politically bereft of ordering structures and convictions. For Levertov and Duncan, the imagination could, even despite the havoc of two world wars, yield insight into the reality of the particular as well as intimations of the coherence of the whole. The notion of the creative process that they shared was essentially (but, as we shall see, differently) religious, and what bonded them was the effort to invest the kinds of formal experimentation they learned from Pound and Williams with something of the metaphysical aura and mystique of the Romantic imagination.

Given the dynamic of the Black Mountain group, therefore, differences in content and outlook led Levertov and Creeley into such different poetic spaces that their correspondence dwindled in the seventies without any break in their acknowledgment of each other's poetic integrity. But the more remarkable and revealing development was that the very strength of the association between Levertov and Duncan brought them, also in the early 1970s, to a devastating contestation on the very issues that they had thought bound them in spiritual as well as poetic communion. The close exchange of letters between Levertov and Duncan develops their convictions and notions about the visionary imagination and the creative process in rich and copious detail over many years of their friendship. Harder to discern and delineate are the causes of the rupture.

## II

The correspondence between Robert Duncan and Denise Levertov began in May 1953, when he was moved to send her a fan letter that consisted solely of the text of "Letters for Denise Levertov: An A Muse Ment." The poem was intended as homage to poems of Levertov, particularly "The Shifting," which Duncan had marveled at in the pages of *Origin*. ("For a Muse Meant" was the title when it became the lead poem in *Letters*, Duncan's collection of poems to his friends.) When Levertov opened the envelope in New York, with no identification or explanation other than the San Francisco postmark and the cryptic initials R. D. at the end of the typescript, she found the text so puzzling in its verbal wit and oblique assertions that she took it as sly amusement at the expense of her poems. Could R. D., she wondered, possibly be Robert Duncan, whose verses she had chanced upon several years before in a review of Duncan's first book, *Heavenly City, Earthly City*? She had read those passages with such quickened excitement that they remained etched on her memory. But "For a Muse Meant," written during the period of Duncan's imitations of Gertrude Stein, presented itself in a poetic manner so different from and even at variance with her own and with what she had read of his own that in her puzzled and offended reply she wondered why, if R. D. were indeed Robert Duncan, he had undertaken to mock her.

The misunderstanding precipitated an embarrassed exchange—assurances on his side, apologies on hers—that quickly cleared up the awkward failure of communication and affirmed their admiration for each other. However, the seemingly minor episode is significant in retrospect as a foreshadowing of future trouble; after all, their first encounter produced what Levertov even at the time called "a spectacle of crosspurposes" (Letter 3) about the purpose and meaning of a poetic text. The differences foreshadowed but quickly passed over in this initial exchange would run under the surface of their correspondence and break into the open again at the end. Levertov would never share Duncan's fascination with Stein's kind of language games nor play as he did with verbal slippages and ambiguities. It is no accident that the "Language" poets of the 1970s and 1980s could read Duncan selectively and view him (somewhat to his own dismay) as a precursor, while Levertov rejected "Language" poetry as a perversion of the poetic ethos she had shared with Duncan.

In 1953, Duncan and Levertov were separated by residence on opposite coasts and were occupied with settling into their own poetic careers and personal circumstances. Duncan had begun his lifelong partnership with the painter Jess Collins in January 1951 and was a central figure in complex confluences of poets that made for the San Francisco Renaissance. Levertov, English-born but married to the American writer Mitchell Goodman in 1947, had come to New York the following year and was excitedly adapting to the American poetic and cultural scene. As a result, the exchange between the two poets did not really take off until after their first brief meeting—and instantaneous bonding—in New York in February 1955. Once that vital connection was made, however, the correspondence took off dramatically; they wrote to each other regularly, for much of the time at least once a month, with many periods when the letters were flying back and forth even more frequently.

Though the correspondence does give vivid anecdotal impressions of individual poets and of the opposing camps of the 1950s and 1960s, its distinctive importance lies in these two poets' fierce and unswerving focus on the essential issues motivating their poetic practice. The matters that they reflected on again and again were the character of the imagination, the nature of the creative process, the sources, means, and ends of poetry. All the while they were sending each other new poems, and each analyzed the other's work empathetically but unsparingly, sometimes word by word and line by line. For they were not just fellow poets; they functioned for each other as muse and critic, inspiriter and judge, *anima* and *animus*. And though their meetings on either coast were occasions of special joy and satisfaction, the fact that their meetings were relatively infrequent (especially in view of the depth of their relationship) meant that they lived it all out, spelled it all out in their correspondence.

Their preciously hoarded letters, they both assumed, were signs and measures of their unshakable correspondence ("co-respondence," she once called it) on a profound psychological and spiritual as well as aesthetic level.

*Anima* and *animus*: Levertov fully endorsed Duncan's celebration of their friendship as "the happy conjunction of the two of us, where sympathies and differences shld give rise to a dialectic" (Letter 395). Their exchange makes clear that within that co-respondence their different qualities of mind and sensibility served as stimulus and challenge. Repeatedly Levertov noted Duncan's wide reading and eclectic learning, his intellectual energy and his power of abstraction as resources she needed and drew upon. On his side, Duncan again and again tells her that she gives him a sense of the concrete particular, the intense emotion of embodied existence that he lacks and yearns for. Responding to Levertov's "Note on the Imagination," Duncan (adapting the terminology in Pound's 1914 "Vortex") distinguished between a perceptual imagination like hers and a conceptual imagination like his (Letter 143); for her part, as the younger poet and a woman, she tended to defer to the "higher order" of the conceptual imagination and even gendered it as masculine in contrast to the more intuitive and feminine character of her imagination (Letter 182). Their mutually empowering sense of co-respondence, acknowledged and cherished again and again in the letters, makes its fracture in the early 1970s all the more shocking.

The wedge that drove them apart came with their responses to the Vietnam War: the question of how the imagination can and should address violence, how poetry can and should engage politics. Suddenly and unexpectedly, in ways that they found appalling but irresistible, they were forced to recognize their fundamental disagreement. At first, in the late 1960s, they tried to stave off admission of their widening differences, but they were too true to themselves as poets to dissemble or evade. All the accumulated weight of their years of intimate and shared trust invests with excruciating poignancy and force the final barrage of letters in which they stood, toe to toe, and battled it out till their long friendship lay in irreparable ruins about them.

The source of the misunderstanding, first and last, was their different religious backgrounds and upbringing and the different religious assumptions and values that consequently informed their adult sensibilities. Born in Oakland in 1919, Duncan was adopted as an infant by theosophical parents, in fact was chosen for adoption through consultation of the astrological charts. He grew up (first in Oakland and then in Bakersfield) in a household and extended family steeped in various occult traditions and surrounded by the texts of Mme. Blavatsky and Hermes Trismegistus, alchemy and astrology, Rosicrucianism and the Kabbala. Though as an adult he took all symbolic systems not so much as matters of metaphysical belief but rather as metaphors of the activity of consciousness, his consciousness was thoroughly hermetic, imbued with the gnosticism at the heart of the various occult symbologies. Jess would paint a portrait of Duncan as the "Enamourd Mage," writing his poetry at a desk fronted by hefty hermetic volumes with their titles fully legible. Citing the sources of his poetry in 1953, Duncan spoke of "the secret doctrine" that offers "the Gnosis of the modern world." Thus for him the activity of imagination in language was a kind of "magic," and the poem was "an occult document," a spell of initiation, a rite of passage into metamorphosis and mystery (*A Selected Prose*, 13–14). The open sequence that was the major labor of the last twenty-five years of his life is called "Passages": verbal passages exploring the secrets of his consciousness, mapping the maze of his heterodox imagination.

Levertov was born in Ilford, on the eastern periphery of London, in 1923, and she too traced her mystical and visionary inclinations, more orthodoxly rooted in the Judeo-Christian tradition, to her parents and her education at home (she and her older sister Olga never went to school). Her father was a Hasidic Jew from Russia who converted to Christianity, married a Welsh woman and emigrated to England, where he was ordained an Anglican priest and became a scholarly and active participant in Jewish-Christian dialogue in the years between the two world wars. Levertov's Welsh ancestors numbered a couple of visionaries well known in their day. She was not a practicing member of the Christian church at the time she began her friendship with Duncan any more than he belonged to any particular cult. However, from the outset her early poetry shimmered with an experienced conviction of the almost sacramental mystery of each perceived object: a perception that turns the poem into an epiphany. So in her widely cited essay "Some Notes on Organic Form" (1965), she invokes Gerard Manley Hopkins's notions of "inscape" and "instress" to describe the psychological and spiritual dynamics of perception and expression, and she goes on to define organic poetry as "a method of ap-perception, i. e., of recognizing what we perceive, . . . based on an intuition of an order, a form beyond forms, in which forms partake, and of which man's creative works are analogies, resemblances, natural allegories. Such poetry is exploratory" (*New and Selected Essays*, 67–68).

From the beginning, then, the poetic explorations of Duncan and Levertov were pointed in directions more divergent than they could acknowledge: the poem exploring hermetic gnosis, and the poem exploring natural allegories. Though they wanted to see their distinctive orientations as complementary —and they did function so for more than a decade—in point of fact their grounding in different theological traditions accounts for the differences in politics and ethics that began to surface in the letters of the late 1960s. Gnos-ticism is hermetic and platonist; radically dualistic in its conception of physi-cal, moral, and spiritual life, it assumes as first principle the irreconcilable op-position between spirit and matter, good and evil. In the various formulations of different hermetic cults, gnosis—a special spiritual insight open only to a gifted elite of initiated individuals—reveals spirit as fallen into material bodies, trapped in mortal flesh and threatened constantly by physical and moral corruption, so that spirit must strive to hold itself untainted by physical existence until death releases it back into immortality. Since Duncan was a naturalist as opposed to a supernaturalist, he adapted the gnosticism he learned at home to his own humanist purposes, eliding the agon of spirit into the agon of consciousness: "Consciousness is God, the occult tradition says" (*A Selected Prose*, 147). For him, then, theology reveals not the transcendent Godhead but the godly or godlike powers of the human, as consciousness strives to rise above the embroiling contentions of the material, temporal world by creating its own apotheosis in and through the realizations and intimations of language. Duncan's 1953 formulation cites Plato and St. Augustine (who was himself steeped in Manicheism before his conversion to Christianity) and says for himself: "Soul is the body's dream of its continuity in eternity—a wraith of mind. Poetry is the very life of the soul: the body's discovery that it can dream. And perish into its own imagination" (*A Selected Prose*, 14). Out of the dispirited and dispiriting travail of modern existence the "gnosis of the ancients" can still be attained in "the poem as a supreme effort of consciousness" (*A Selected Prose*, 3).

In contrast to gnosticism, the Judeo-Christian tradition proclaims not just a personal God but God-with-us: Emmanuel, incarnate in flesh, immersed in human history, engaged in material and social existence. In that mythos God-with-us signifies the always already achieved reconciliation of matter and spirit, a reconciliation that nonetheless has to be made manifest and realized again and again. It is the human responsibility, generation by generation and person by person, to make His immanence imminent. In the Judeo-Christian tradition, therefore, reconciliation is not reserved for the isolated individual or the privileged elite but is open to and required of the whole people in communion. From Adam on, human fallibility has meant that we find completion not in self but in relationship, not in independence but in interdependence. The body is a social body, and in community the people support each other in overcoming the capacity for evil and manifesting God-in-us. During the stresses of the 1960s Levertov did not belong to a religious community, Jewish or Christian. However, in rallying the poetic community to oppose the war and in joining the larger community of resisters, she found herself justifying her ethic of collective action by recourse to assumptions rooted in her religious upbringing at home. So much so that in "A Poet's View," published in 1984, she looks back to describe how she had come, in the intervening years, to ground both her politics and her sacramental sense of nature in a reaffirmation of Christian belief and practice, which led to her reception into the Catholic Church.

Politics did not enter the letters or impinge on Levertov and Duncan's discussion of the creative process and the visionary imagination until the prolongation of the war forced the issue to the center of their interchange. They were in immediate agreement that the Vietnam War represented the aggressive policy of a capitalist system bent on oppression at home and imperialism abroad; but by the late 1960s they could no longer ignore the differences in their responses. Duncan's outrage erupted into the poetry first; a number of "Passages" were published separately under the title *Of the War: Passages* 22–27 (1966). But even earlier "The Fire: Passages 13" had already admitted Duncan's dilemma in responding to the war. The first part of "The Fire" cites the Renaissance Neoplatonists "Pletho, Ficino, Pico della Mirandola" to invoke the "magic" of art, its hermetic power to cast a "spell that binds / the many in conflict in contrasts of one mind." The poem then describes Piero di Cosimo's painting *A Forest Fire* in detail as a demonstration of how the magic of the visionary imagination can in fact suffuse the violent painting with a "charmd" and glowing "stillness." In Duncan's presentation, Cosimo's technical mastery of the paint medium provides the imaginative detachment to assimilate or sublimate the terrified flight of humans and animals into stillness sustained "in the light of his vision." But "The Fire" calls into question whether Duncan has the technical mastery to attain this visionary perspective: "Do you know the old language? / I do not know the old language." And the second half of the poem demonstrates that lapse in the adequacy of language and imagery by contrasting Cosimo's "vision" of catastrophe with Duncan's own grotesque cartoons of the modern war makers like Johnson and Nixon and Goldwater. Convinced that his own rage at the war, however morally justified, implicated him in the violence and betrayed his deepest responsibilities as a visionary artist, Duncan chose, after 1966, to maintain an anarchist detachment from the war zone for the sake of his life in poetry.

Duncan's antiwar poems—the second part of "Earth's Winter Song" and "UpRising," to give other examples—are just as shrill and didactic, just as filled with images of violence, as the poems of Levertov he would later condemn. In fact, it was she who first criticized him on precisely those grounds. She told him that "The Fire" was "poetry of tremendous power" (Letter 322). However, a year and a half later she objected to "Earth's Winter Song" for the distorted and scatological depiction of Vice President Humphrey's collusion in the war. Was she being "priggish," she asked him, in charging him with judgmental "self-righteousness" (Letter 363)? But the reversal of roles was right around the corner. This same letter mentions "Life at War," completed that very day—but, oddly enough, with no premonition Duncan would soon be citing it as evidence of the disastrous effects of self-righteous politics on her poetry.

She was vulnerable to his accusations; she soon found herself alarmed that the rhetoric of suffering and resistance was sapping her capacity for visionary wonder. Yet at the same time that Duncan retreated from the polemics of "UpRising," so that Cosimo-like he could absorb the conflict into his imaginative vision, she found herself impelled, against the ingrained inclination of her imagination, to join other protesters in public demonstration and to lend her powers of speech to oppose and denounce the evil. In Cosimo's painting Duncan saw that the animal-faced humans and the human-faced animals instinctively knew enough to flee the scene of the conflagration. However, when he read Levertov poems like "Life at War," "Advent 1966," and "Tenebrae," and then the book-length journal-poem in *To Stay Alive*, he saw his *anima*-muse perversely rushing into the conflagration that he was sure would consume her.

Gnostic dualist as he was, he warned her that war was the unceasing and inevitable condition of mortal life: "THERE HAS BEEN NO TIME IN HUMAN HISTORY THAT WAS NOT A TIME OF WAR" (Letter 449). He might shrink from the war as evil but also thought it unwinnable because inherent in the dialectical law of nature and human nature: "I see the Vietnamese War (as I saw the Second World War) as a revelation of the truth of the potential evil of 'America'— . . . a revelation of the truth of American Karma" (Letter 409). For anyone aware of life as war, and particularly for the individual gifted with gnosis, self-preservation and individual realization are the primary responsibilities. He did not need Vietnam to make him conclude: "We no longer live within a possible history, I think" (Letter 273). So in "Adam's Song," written before he knew Levertov, the speaker instructs his Eve: "The war is all about us"; and then draws her into the mind's hermetic garden:

> It is as if the garden were
> always there, even where we are,
> here,   where war is,   the certain
> end,   the paradise.

When Duncan saw Levertov leaving the vision of paradise they had shared to enter the war zone, he issued increasingly sharp warnings. After she sent him "Advent 1966" in December of that year, this single, spinning sentence, with all its modifying phrases and explanatory clauses, twists torturously around the dilemma of preserving the imagination from the war's devastation:

> Denny, the last poem brings with it an agonizing sense of how the monstrosity of this nation's War is taking over your life, and I wish that I could advance some—not consolation, there is none—wisdom of how we are to at once bear constant (faithful and ever present) testimony to our grief for those suffering in the War and our knowledge that the government of the United States is so immediately the agency of death and destruction of human and natural goods, and at the same time continue as constantly in our work (which must face and contain somehow this appalling and would-be spiritually destroying evidence of what human kind will do—for it has to do with the imagination of what is going on in Man) now, more than ever, to keep alive the immediacy of the ideal and of the eternal (Letter 383).

Duncan added that "Jess and I have decided that we will wear black arm-bands" to register their witness of dissent, but even so he was careful to distinguish acts of protest from the poetic act: "Even 'Up Rising' is not this kind of witness; for ultimately it belongs to the reality of that poem and a vision of Man. And I do not answer for myself in my work but for Poetry" (Letter 383). The capital P for Poetry elevated it above the human contention into "a vision of Man." By this point, however, Levertov was convinced that more active resistance to the war and to the system that drove the war was a moral obligation. In the margins of a letter about the "outrage and grief of this war" that she received from Duncan soon after the one cited above, she wrote: "I took refuge in action, & so was less ravaged by the war than he . . . " (Letter 386).

Levertov's instincts, formed by her religious and moral education at home, told her that evil was not inevitable and invincible, but privative: not a constitutive reality, as Manichaean dualism supposed, but instead the rectifiable and reversible failure on our part to be what we should and can be. Evil was not a constitutive element of life but the failure to realize goodness in the choices and determinations of individual and collective will. So she responded to Duncan that she could not compartmentalize her life, personal from public, even at the risk of inner vision. The war could be won—not, admittedly, by any isolated and fallible individual, but by a mutually supportive community committed to advancing good against evil; she saw no moral choice but to commit herself to a group like "Resist." She had no utopian illusions about her compatriots, she told him, but they were the active resistance on the ground, and with them she found a shared compassion and will that were changing the terms by which she lived and, yes, wrote.

By 1968 they had reluctantly to acknowledge the gap widening between them not despite their shared opposition to the war but, appallingly, within it. So, "just here where we might be thought to be in agreement," Duncan felt increasingly compelled "to drive thru to the doubts I have in the area of agreement." The widely publicized trial of Mitchell Goodman (along with Doctor Benjamin Spock and three others) for conspiracy against the draft law fueled Duncan's effort to win her over from "the very courage of your convictions" to his gnostic anarchism: "I draw back from commanding conscience, as I wld avoid whatever tyranny of the will." Against her notion of conscience as "moral imperative," Duncan proposed instead "the conscience to stand by the individual life, to go underground, evade or escape the conscription." Such a conscience seeks instead "creative permission": an "inner knowing what we have to do" in order to make imaginative order out of the condition of war. Even Christ's "writing in the place of 'Thou shalt not kill' his 'Thou shalt love,'" Duncan declared, bound the individual volition into a coercive morality which said that "no man is free until *all* be free; no man has life until *all* have life." For him, "free immediate individual" self-determination had to take precedence over the Christian commandment of love and community. (The phrases quoted throughout this paragraph come from Letters 409 and 410.)

By 1971 Duncan was so appalled by what seemed to him the "totalitarian" intransigence of her moral certitude that he derided her self-righteous pronouncements as self-deluded, sentimental "Polonius pieties" and in opposition declared himself a moral "pluralist" of "Heraclitean opposites": "Within the plurality of forces the Heraclitean opposites have the drama and pathos of a heightened figure upon a ground in which a multitude of figures appear" (Letter 452). In Duncan's construction the embattled forces become imagined as "a multitude of figures," metaphors in the "heightened figure" or meta-metaphor, as in the aestheticized and sublimated "drama and pathos" of the scurrying figures in Cosimo's *Forest Fire*.

In Duncan's eyes, an image of her, filmed as a speaker at an antiwar rally and shown on the television news, exposed the capitulation to violence masking as resistance. In her tirade, he told her, she looked not like a moral reformer but like Kali, the Hindu goddess of destruction, triumphant in the spectacle of death. And he wrote that charge into Part III of "Santa Cruz Propositions," dated October 28, 1968: "*SHE* appears, Kālī dancing,   whirling her necklace of skulls, / trampling the despoiling armies and the exploiters of natural resources / under her feet.   Revolution or death!" (*Ground Work: Before the War*, 45). Hurt and angry, Levertov tried to explain in the long letter of October–November 1971 that her agitation had come from the circumstances of the rally. Some of the more moderate organizers had perceived her as radical and wanted to keep her from speaking, but suddenly she was thrust onto the platform and told that she had only three minutes to blurt out the seven minutes of remarks she had written for delivery. As for "Revolution or death," the refrain Duncan had excerpted from her journal poem "Staying Alive" for his own purposes, the phrase represented "neither 'threat' nor 'vow' nor 'ultimatum' but just a statement of the problem": namely, her troubled conviction that "the one chance . . . of the world/(earth) I love being saved from annihilation lay in the forces for radical political/societal change" (Letter 453). Unpersuaded, Duncan insisted on the Kali image as evidence of the neurotic basis of Levertov's protest.

The single sentence that perhaps best distinguishes the ethical consequences of their positions is Duncan's injunction that "the poet's role is not to oppose evil, but to imagine it" (Letter 452). Imagining evil is hermetic: a private act of consciousness that can be assimilated into the larger dualisms of his vision. Duncan's platonic purpose is clear in the line that he chose to write as an epigraph in my copy of *Bending the Bow*: "In the War now I make a Celestial Cave." The capitals designate the gnostic poles of his making—War versus Celestial Cave; on the field of battle he makes his visionary poetry. In my copy of "Of the War," the pamphlet with the "Passages" that grew out of the Vietnam crisis, he inscribed this gnostic line as a charge to himself: "in the slaughter of man's hope distil the divine potion that stirs sight of the hidden."

War versus vision: Duncan titled one of his important and revealing essays "Man's Fulfillment in Order and Strife." Strife is the condition of material nature and so of human existence; the search for order is, as for Blake, the function of spirit—that is to say, of the imagination. Thus, where Levertov's war poetry showed her overwhelmed by the violence without and within, he was resolved to assimilate the recognition of evil into a subsuming vision: "The outrage of 'Up Rising'" would be "reveald in other lights in the course of other poems" (Letter 370) in *Bending the Bow* (1968). In contrast to imagining evil in this way, opposing evil as Levertov had done in her recent poetry constituted a public and political act—in his view, an act of self-deluded and self-destructive folly in a hopeless cause. The only resolution, he argued, was imaginative and poetic, not political and social; ethics were aesthetic.

Inevitably, their argument uncovered differences about the nature of poetry itself and about the relationship of language to meaning. In the last battery of letters Duncan insisted strenuously that form and content were synonymous in the poem so that there was no meaning or purpose extrinsic or prior to the creation of meaning and the discovery of purpose in the evolution of the poem. For that reason poetry could make no claims about absolutes but must instead register the revisions and subversions that would occur; the "open universe" he posits is a Heraclitean and pluralist universe (*A Selected Prose*, 6). A poem like "The Law I Love Is Major Mover" reiterates the point: order in disorder, disorder in order. The law that impels life and poetry is a search for momentary consonances in a flux of dissonances. In *Trilogy*, H. D., who shared Duncan's gnostic sense of radical doubleness, wrote, thinking of Hermes at the crossroads, that "gods always face two-ways."

Duncan, like H. D., identified Modernism with Romanticism, as in her own way did Levertov. However, Duncan's and Levertov's different inflections of Romanticism pointed them in opposite directions, and their readings of Emerson, the arch American Romanticist, epitomize the divergence. In "Notes on Organic Form" Levertov quotes Emerson to corroborate her sense that "man's creative works are analogies, resemblances, natural allegories": "Emerson says in his essay 'Poetry and Imagination,' 'Ask the fact for the form'" (*New and Selected Essays*, 68, 71). In her Duncan essay of 1975, Levertov still designated Duncan's "romanticism" as a link between them, but Duncan's 1983 essay "The Self in Postmodernist Poetry" makes a point of saying that "I read my Emerson dark"—less as the exemplar of Romantic synthesis than as the unwitting exemplar of the Romantic dissolution that opened the way to modern dissonance. For that reason, Duncan's Romanticism turns on the cusp from Modernism to Postmodernist deconstruction: "What I would point out in my work as one of its underlying currents is the weaving of a figure unweaving, an art of unsaying what it says, of saying what it would not say" (*Fictive Certainties*, 226, 231). Levertov's Emerson posits a poetry integral to the truths of nature; Duncan's more Poe-like Emerson adumbrates instead a poetry integrated by the play of its own self-inversions and self-reflexivities. Levertov came to see that in the contention between dark and light "it was Duncan's apparent belief that the dark side was 'more equal' . . . that I could not stomach" (*New and Selected Essays*, 207); Duncan called his last book *Ground Work: In the Dark*.

Inescapably, their metaphysical and ethical differences forced them to acknowledge different conceptions of the relation between form and truth in the poem. When Duncan read Levertov's essay on his early poetry, collected later in her first book of essays, *The Poet in the World*, he responded warmly to her enthusiasm but stuck on one point. He was concerned about her sense of "the truth of the poem," especially in light of "my own uneven relation to truth"; he saw his commitment rather in being "true to the object," to "the statement of the poem," to "what the form will be" (Letter 141). By 1966 Duncan was warning that there was no truth anterior or exterior to the realization of poetic form: "[protest] is either futile or, succeeding, belongs to a complex of political meanings that can have no 'truth in itself.' This is of the nature of all acts in so far as they are *means*, i.e. not identical with their own intent. Like lines or images of a poem that are not felt as immediacies of 'form' but as means toward an end of the poem" (Letter 380). In the final exchange he made his point bluntly: "we do not say something by means of the poem but the poem is itself the immediacy of saying—it has its own meaning" (Letter 452).

In retrospect we can see that Levertov had dissented from Duncan's self-reflexive hermeticism as early as 1959: "god knows I love craft but there must (mustn't there) first be the *happening*, before which one is swept headlong" (Letter 136). So in the final exchange she drove her point home with a bluntness to match his:

> To me it *does* mean that "one says something by means of the poem"—but not in the sense of "using" (exploiting) the poem: rather that the writer only fully experiences his "content" (that which he is impelled to say by means of the poem) through the process of writing it. . . . Which is to say that the poem reveals the content, which is apprehended only dimly (in varying degrees) till that revelation takes place. If it (the poem) "has its own meaning" it is only that the revelation is not only the realization, concretization, clarification, affirmation, of what one knows one knows but also of what one didn't know one knew. I do not believe, as you seem to, in the *contradictory* (& autonomous) "meaning" of a poem. (Letter 453)

In terms of the literary and philosophical history of the last two centuries, Levertov read Romanticism and Modernism without Duncan's sense of Postmodernist deconstruction. When Levertov began formulating her notion of an organic poetry, citing Romantics like Emerson, Duncan acknowledged her position but saw his primary base in language as making him more a "linguistic" than an organic poet: "the linguistic follows emotions and images that appear in the language itself as a third 'world'; true to what is happening in the syntax as another man might be true to what he sees or feels" (Letter 290). It is in statements like this one that Duncan can be seen as a precursor of the Language poets of the 1980s. But for Levertov language constituted the instantiation of subject and object, mind and world—not a separate "third 'world.'" Against Duncan's sense of the poem as a hermetically self-enacting semiotic event in which form and content arise simultaneously, she cites Emerson's assertion in "The Poet" that, while the finished poem does indeed fuse form and content, the processes of poetic genesis and creation arise out of the urgencies of experience prior and extrinsic to the poem. As she read them, Emerson's injunctions about a "metermaking argument" and "asking the fact for the form" were consonant with Williams's "No ideas but in things."

Not surprisingly, then, Levertov's "Some Notions of Organic Form" (1965) revises the capitalized dictum of "Projective Verse"—"THE FORM IS NEVER MORE THAN AN EXTENSION OF CONTENT"—into her own understanding: "Form is never more than a *revelation* of content" (*The New American Poetry*, 387; *New and Selected Essays*, 73). The italicizing of "*revelation*" underscored her revision of the Black Mountain aesthetic. At the time of the 1965 essay she thought that she was expressing an aesthetic understanding she shared with Duncan, but by 1971 she knew that she had to capitalize the distinction between "extension" and "revelation": "Form is never more than the REVELATION (not extension) of content" (Letter 453). After the breakup her 1975 essay on Duncan reiterated the point: "the 'veracity of experience' does not come into being only in the course of the poem, but provides the ground from which the poem grows, or from which it leaps (and to which it fails to return at its peril)" (*New and Selected Essays*, 213).

The same letter of 1971 counters Duncan's concept of the self-creative individual in a tragically dualistic universe with the Christian notion of redemption of the individual in and through community: "'We are members one of another.' I've always believed that even if it was St Paul, whom I dislike on many counts, who said it"; "The concept of the Incarnation is the concept of Man's redeemability, however fallen into corruption, for man was made in God's image. Even sceptics and atheists cannot help being culturally affected by that concept" (Letter 453). Duncan had served as "mentor" in formulating "what I think of as 'aesthetic ethics'" (*New and Selected Essays*, 205); however, "A Poet's View" (1984) traces the evolution in her aesthetic ethics "over the last few years from a regretful skepticism which sought relief in some measure of pantheism (while it acknowledged both the ethical and emotional influence of my Jewish-Christian roots and early education) to a position of Christian belief" (*New and Selected Essays*, 241–42).

The 1971 salvo of letters dredges from the years of "happy conjunction" a tangled mesh of differences that were present but unregarded from the start. To sum them up in terms that put the differences as sharply as possible within the dialogic co-respondence between the poets: where Duncan was metaphysically platonist and gnostic, religiously polytheist, morally manichaean and pluralist, psychologically individualist, politically anarchist, and linguistically self-reflexive, Levertov was metaphysically incarnationalist, religiously monotheist and Christian, psychologically communitarian, politically socialist, and linguistically referential. The difference between a notion of identity as essentially self-creating and a notion of identity as essentially relational imbued their divergent notions of the visionary imagination and their divergent notions of poetry. As Duncan's poetry revealed ever more unmistakably its hermetic character, Levertov's revealed ever more unmistakably its sacramental character. The divergence is that between a gnostic theology and an incarnational theology.

## III

By November 1971, Duncan and Levertov were "wounded veterans" of their battle about their "political/ideological/philosophical/aesthetic differences" (Letters 451 and 464)—a conflict between friends in which there could be no simple victor. Their relationship was severely strained but, as each assured the other, reparable. Levertov proposed a "halt" or "truce" in their discussion of poetry and politics for "a year and a day" so that on a personal level they could "try to just be friends again in a new way" (Letter 456): "Live & love & be well—I'm the same Denise as ever" (Letter 463). The epistolary exchange slowed markedly but continued, with a subdued Duncan regretting the ferocity of his attack. Then there occurred the episode that wrecked the friendship beyond repair. James Mersmann's *Out of the Vietnam Vortex: A Study of Poets and Poetry against the War* (Lawrence: University Press of Kansas, 1974) contained major chapters on Levertov and Duncan. In his fundamentally sympathetic discussion of Levertov's antiwar poetry, Mersmann paraphrased (and questioned) Duncan's judgment that for Levertov "the war is really only an irritant that knocks the scabs from already present psychological sores" (93). Those words are Mersmann's, but a footnote cites Duncan's own from an interview with Duncan conducted in May 1969.

Duncan had proposed what he saw as the neurotic motive behind Levertov's protest poetry as early as 1966. "Life at War," he told her, was "the clotted mass of some operation . . . having what root in you I wonder" (Letter

370). Quoting his query, she answered: "Consciously the history of the poem is this: looking at the fragile beauty of human bodies I was struck afresh by the extreme *strangeness* of men actually *planning* violence upon each other" (Letter 371). "Consciously" acknowledges his suspicion of unconscious motivation, but in her long letter of late 1971 she insisted to him again that the depiction of violence, sometimes in horrific anatomical detail, represented in no way some "perverse gratification (as you seem to think)" but on the contrary her effort to imagine the war, to break through "white middleclass skin," including her own, to grasp "what is really going on, even if through small analogies" (Letter 453).

Less than a year before the publication of *Out of the Vietnam Vortex* Duncan seemed to want to reassure her: "I would plead that you might have my trust that eventually (meaning: once the sequence of events has at last been realized) I will rearrive at what I feel to be a just reading, a reading in which all the work of these years must prove good—be made good" (Letter 468). She was stunned, therefore, to find in Mersmann's book the extended footnote with Duncan deriding her war poems as displaced eruptions of her own sexual neuroses. The offending passage reads:

> There's another field of feeling that frequently comes up when she means to write a protest feeling, and that is her own sadism, and masochism, and so the war becomes like, becomes a not gloating but almost as fierce an expression as the fantasies of Dickey. She'll be writing about the war and suddenly—in one of the earlier poems that's most shocking ["Life at War"]—you get a flayed penis, and . . . when she reads it you get an effect and tone of disgusted sensuality. And when you look at her poetry it tells more to look at that flayed penis and realize that her earlier poems are talking about stripped stalks of grass! She's got one that loves peeling [perhaps the "Pleasures" poem quoted above]. Suddenly you see a charged, bloody, sexual image that's haunting the whole thing, and the war then acts as a magnet, and the poem is not a protest though she thinks she's protesting. (94; the second bracketed insertion is Mersmann's)

Levertov made it clear that such an unwarranted attack, personal and public, went unpardonably beyond their legitimate disputes and required his disavowal or rescission.

Despite this affront Levertov responded the next year to an invitation to contribute to a collection of essays about Duncan's work called *Scales of the Marvelous* (edited by Ian Reid and Robert Bertholf and published in 1979). "Some Duncan Letters—A Memoir and a Critical Tribute," written in 1975, is a warm and generous homage to her old mentor—but also a memorial to their friendship. Reviewing his old letters for the essay, she wrote to tell him of feeling the throb of their old co-respondence yet felt constrained by honesty to herself to add: "I was all set to write to you, Robert, a year or so? ago, when lo, that book by James Mersmann arrived with its long quote from an interview with you. . . . I hoped you'd write and apologize and perhaps print a retraction some place, but there was never any word from you & so I felt our friendship twice broken, deeply betrayed" (Letter 469).

It was three years before Duncan addressed her accusation. He meant the letter he wrote as a rapprochement but made no reference to the Mersmann interview. Instead he praised her new collection, *Life in the Forest* (1978). Reading those poems "enabled me at last to break the bonds I had wound around my feeling for you" and to recognize that the "range" of her recent work had been "won in just those 'War poems' I took even rancorous exception to" (Letter 472). The letter enclosed the text of "The Torn Cloth," written, he told her, in November or December of 1975 (though he did not explicitly connect its composition with the arrival of her last letter). "The Torn Cloth" puns on the reversibility of "reaving" and "weaving" and muses about "re-weaving" their friendship:

> We       reaving
> —"re-weaving"    I had meant
>         to write,
> (*Ground Work: Before the War*, 137)

In words quoted earlier but written in 1983, in which Duncan described his poetry as "the weaving of a figure unweaving, an art of unsaying what it says, of saying what it would not say" (*Fictive Certainties*, 231), he was perhaps thinking, among other things, of Levertov and of "The Torn Cloth." But Levertov, while thanking him for his comment on *Life in the Forest*, could not respond to the poem as he seemed to wish: "your letter came *at least* 2 years too late. I don't find it in me to respond with the warmth & gladness you expected. There can be a statue of limitations on emotional commitments" (Letter 475).

Levertov's letter of February 19 replaced another, longer response to Duncan, dated February 1, 1979, but marked later in her hand at the top: "(Not Sent)." There she elaborated her feelings more fully here: "Gradually my love for you dwindled, until I cannot honestly say I feel it any more. I wish I could. I *don't* mean I feel some other, negative emotion in its place. I don't even feel angry. How could I, so long after?" (Letter 474). For all intents and purposes their correspondence ends with these February letters. She wrote in 1984 expressing sorrow after hearing about the illness—kidney failure, later discovered to be complicated by heart problems from high blood pressure—that would kill him four years later. That brief letter noted the bitter-sweet irony of their being honored jointly but so much after the fact by *Poetry* magazine: "felicitations on the $1/2$ a Shelley prize—I expect they told you I am getting the other $1/2$!" (Letter 476). This time his reply was never mailed.

The unmailed letters, included here among the others, are a sign, though none is needed, of lost connections—all the more heartbreaking because these were in fact love letters of a special kind. After their first meeting in 1955 Levertov wrote Duncan: "If I were to *really* write to you it wd. be a real crazy letter— something like a loveletter, tho' not that—dominated by some image of the moon, a full moon" (Letter 4). In fact, the letters did spell their particular love out within (but without ever putting at risk) Duncan's lifelong partnership with Jess and her marriage to Mitch Goodman. (The Goodmans' divorce in 1974 had nothing to do with the now-estranged Duncan.) At the same time, the particular intensity between Levertov and Duncan stemmed, in all its in-flections, from the fact that their relationship transpired in their minds and imaginations and in their written words. Their love for each other was a love of the language they shared: "I can't separate always the . . . ¿but what is the sepa-ration there? the love of everything you write and that I love you. . . . But love is nature to nature and your being is what sustains me there" (Letter 80); "I can't say what I feel about your poems, usually, any more than I can say what I feel about you as a presence, except to say I love you" (Letter 220). Levertov ended her poem-letter of April 1966 with the following prescient recognitions. Because external commitments to witness against the war were making them "silent to one another,"

> I send you therefore
> as if on a seagull's wing
>
> one word—
>
> what word shall it be?—
>
> 'Love'?—I love you but
> I love
>       another, as you do.
> Love I send, but I send it
> in another word.
>           Longing?
>              Poetry.
>
> (Letter 367)

The terms of their love suited them well, but it cast them in certain speci-fied and (for the time) complementary roles. He was her *animus*: "You are more the Master, a Master poet in my world" (Letter 376). And she in turn was his *anima*:

> You see you have three presences for me, Denny, that touch the deepest life feeling. One is the Denise I have been able openly to speak of, the companion in art—where in certain poems of yours, by grace of your "poet," I am brought into

that heart of life that poetry opens: then this poet you are I love because you are
most true. No . . . it seems more that through loving this you so I come to love
what is most true. And then, sometimes you are a poetic conscience for me.
Not that my truth will be like yours—but that just where I fail my own *poet*,
I betray this love.

　　Then there is, related, another presence: an idea of you or something you
mean to me—yet it also seems to be really *you* and to reach the heart. . . .

　　The third is just your real actual presence, where I have never felt these ghosts
of conscience. (Letter 226)

"The companion in art," "the idea of you or something you mean to me,"
"your real actual presence": it is noteworthy which Denise comes last in Dun-
can's declension. By the early 1970s, however, the real, actual Denise had
painfully to acknowledge that she had outgrown his idea of her and so had to
reject him as her Master in poetry, and Duncan, in fidelity to "my own *poet*,"
had painfully to exorcise her as his poetic companion and conscience. His first
words to here were "An A Muse Ment"; now that she claimed a separate po-
etic stance, he could not simply let her go; his own stance meant that he had
to drive her out.

　Duncan's description of Levertov's "presences for me" comes near the end
of an exchange with her about H. D. and her longtime friend and "Patroness"
Bryher. Duncan had introduced Levertov to a deep reading of H. D.'s work.
In the late 1950s and early 1960s, he was launched on *The H. D. Book* and
sending segments for approval and comment. Through him Levertov met
H. D. in New York, and the two women began a warm and admiring corre-
spondence, terminated before long by the stroke that would end H. D.'s life
in September 1961. As poetry editor of *The Nation*, Levertov asked Duncan to
review *Helen in Egypt*, in part as a final tribute to the stricken poet. H. D. they
shared, writing poems to and about her. But they found themselves strangely
at odds about Bryher's role in H. D.'s life. Levertov wrote Duncan that when
she met Bryher in a Manhattan hotel just a few months after H. D.'s death,
she was chilled by what seemed Bryher's selfish callousness to her friend's fi-
nal plight. And she was chilled too by the tone of Duncan's response that,
while admitting Bryher's ruthlessness, tried to explain if not excuse it. "Surely,"
Levertov countered, H. D. "would have been as much a poet" without Bry-
her's patronage, but Levertov leaves the sentence hanging with a question
mark (Letter 225). Toward the end of Duncan's response the repressed point
of this exchange suddenly surfaces. His defensiveness stems from the shadow
identification of himself with Bryher as possessive patron and of Levertov
with H. D. as victimized recipient: "Say I was to prove as dreadful as we now
see Bryher can be, then will you, Denny, not be loyal but see me in truth, yet
somehow love me?" (Letter 226).

　The combined threat and plea in Duncan's question went unnoticed in his long letter, ending with a cadenza about their love calling them to their true selves. Levertov replied: "I keep all yr letters but that letter I'll keep apart from the others especially" (Letter 228). But as the decade proceeded, there were other occasions when Duncan's attack on poets outside his circle but associated with her struck home as displaced criticisms of her. When she became an editorial adviser for Norton in the mid-1960s and expanded Norton's poetry list to include, among others, Adrienne Rich, Margaret Avison, Hayden Carruth, and Ronald Johnson, Duncan's response was cool and condescending about what he called the "genteel" conventionality of the new poets she favored. Affronted, Levertov asked if his censure were aimed really at her, and the full text of a sentence quoted in part earlier moves from acknowledging his mastership to registering her growing resistance to his prescriptions: "You are more the Master, a Master poet in my world, not less, just because I feel that the only emulation of such a master is to be *more oneself*" (Letter 376).

Perhaps Duncan caught the telltale elision from "the Master" to the less exclusive "a Master" and then to the uncapitalized "a master." In any case he went out of his way in a 1969 piece for the journal *Stony Brook* to single out Hayden Carruth and Adrienne Rich, two close and admired poet-friends of Levertov outside his circle, for an intemperate and unprovoked attack, without even warning Levertov of his diatribe beforehand ("A Critical Difference of View," *Stony Brook* 3/4 [Fall 1969]: 360–63). He insisted to Levertov that his quarrels with Carruth and Rich were not personal but formal and aesthetic, but she heard nasty personal animus: "I feel it was an attack not only factually unjustified and quite disproportionately contentious, but humanly a very thoughtless & cruel act" (Letter 440). There were vital issues at stake, and their political and aesthetic differences were to boil to the surface before the end of the next year. But in the end what brought their relationship to the breaking point was the very force and intensity of their love for each other— or for the image of each in the other's imaginative life.

In her unsent letter of 1979 Levertov wondered if on some unplanned occasion she and Duncan might meet by chance and spontaneously resume their friendship on some new plane. That occasion never came in life, but her elegy "To R. D., March 4th, 1988" recounts a dream that came to her "exactly a month" after his death. In the poem he appears to her in a cathedral sonorous with organ music, and they clasp hands wordlessly—beyond those words that parted them but within the words of the new poem. Later she wrote that the dream "left me with a strong feeling that we were, in fact, truly reconnected. I sent [the poem] to Jess, who assured me that Robert's affection for me had remained intact" (*New and Selected Essays*, 229). A little over a year before her own death from cancer on December 20, 1997, Levertov wrote me about the rift with Duncan: "Retrospectively, I feel I was too stubborn & should have forgiven him when I received the words about *Life in the Forest*—

it was unChristianly stiff-necked of me. But at that time I was not able to think that way" (September 23, 1996).

I saw Duncan last in March 1985 at a reading he gave at the end of a Bryn Mawr conference on H. D. and Marianne Moore. He was already ill and exhausted by the conference, but in a brilliant reading he prefaced "The Torn Cloth" with an admission of his responsibility in tearing his friendship with Levertov apart. He had been possessed and driven, he said, by a "daemon" to push matters to the breakpoint, but his primary commitment to his inner life compelled him to let the daemon run its course. His imagination had required her as *anima*: "You stand behind the where-I-am./ The deep tones and shadows I will call a woman" (*Bending the Bow*, 7). But on his terms—as she came to recognize for herself, he had to make her submit: "poet to poet I do want to win assent to my concept of the poem" (Letter 457). "Win" is the vocabulary of war, the word of the would-be victor; but the strategy had the opposite effect on her: contention with so strong an *animus* only served to clarify her own position. What was in contention between them was what they had both assumed they shared—namely, a poetics. In Duncan's phrasing, their differences in the "concept of the poem" were rooted in "your not believing [as he did] in the primary meaning of the art of the poem itself" and, instead, her "thinking of the poem as communication of meanings whose primacy was posited outside the art, in 'Life' or social realities" (Letter 462).

The elegy to Duncan is her belated response to "The Torn Cloth." Its opening lines unweave their long friendship before reweaving it in the dream-epiphany of reconciliation:

> You were my mentor. Without knowing it,
> I outgrew the need for a mentor.
> Without knowing it, you resented that,
> and attacked me. I bitterly resented
> the attack, and without knowing it
> freed myself to move forward
> without a mentor.
> (*A Door in the Hive*, 4)

The mutually empowering "dialectic" that they had joyously entered at the outset of their association had taken a disastrous turn that neither of them foresaw or could forestall. Their letters are the testament of their co-respondence and estrangement in the tangled configuration of postwar American poetry.

# EDITORIAL NOTE

The correspondence between Robert Duncan and Denise Levertov, running from the early 1950s into the 1980s, begins with his sending her a poem in homage, "For A Muse Ment," and her mistaking it for criticism; and the correspondence fades out after a bitter dispute over their poetic responses to the Vietnam War. The intervening letters record the long, close, and extraordinarily rich friendship between these two important poets and chart the growth of their closely related but finally divergent poetics, in which points of shared assumption and points of difference are equally telling.

In the letters Levertov and Duncan engage in intense examination of the creative process and the character of the imagination, and they test and illustrate their poetics by detailed commentary on their own practice. All the while on the more personal level they discuss domestic matters, recount anecdotes about friends and other artists, and engage social and political issues. The editors have presented the full text of all the letters (including a few written but not mailed) in order to preserve the integrity and complexity of the personal and poetic association. Because the letters turn on poems (and even occasionally turn into poems), we have included texts of poems sent as they appear in the letters, even though the poems, sometimes with changes in the text, are available in published collections of their work. Moreover, in a separate appendix (this was Levertov's own suggestion shortly before her death) we have gathered the most salient poems and passages not fully cited in the letters that became the ground of increasingly sharp contention during the late 1960s and the early 1970s.

Because the range of reference in the letters is enormous, we have provided needed information at the back of the volume: in endnotes to individual letters; in a glossary of people, places, and events that recur in the letters more than once or twice; and in a chronology of relevant biographical data for both poets. The intention of this apparatus of notes, appendix, glossary, and chronology is to create a readily available contextual frame so that the letters can be read easily and can speak for themselves.

On both sides the letters are for the most part but not entirely handwritten, though Duncan often follows the practice of typing in quoted passages in prose or verse before resuming in script. The headings provide date and place (that is, city or town) of writing, expanding, if need be, on what is given in the original letter. Otherwise, addresses are given as the poets wrote them. When, toward the end of the correspondence, Levertov sometimes writes on her personal stationery, the printed name "Denise Levertov Goodman" is not included; and when on a few occasions the poets write on other stationery, those letterheads are omitted as unnecessary or, in one or two cases, misleading as to where the letter was actually written. Salutations have always been put on a separate line, whether or not they so appear in the letters, and closings are similarly always rendered as two lines.

The poets indicate paragraph breaks in various but inconsistent ways: often by the customary indentation of the new paragraph, but sometimes by a solidus (especially Duncan) or a long blank space (especially Levertov) or by dropping down a line and starting again without indentation. For ease and flow of reading, paragraph breaks have here been normalized with indentations. Both Duncan and Levertov regularly employ square brackets for asides or interpolations of their own, and so we used {curved brackets} for our own editorial insertions. Dashes of whatever length in the letters have been normalized to the conventional em dash. Ellipses have also been normalized: three spaced dots if the ellipsis represents an elision within a quoted sentence, four spaced dots if the ellipsis comes at the end of a quoted sentence, the fourth dot being the period. In a very few places six spaced dots reflect multiple dots in the holographs. Terminal punctuation with quotations has been normalized to American style. Levertov tended to use single quotation marks in the British manner, but in the printed letters the usage has been made consistent with the American use of double quotation marks.

We have striven to render accurately the words written on the page. For that reason we preserve certain characteristic writing and spelling habits, particularly but not exclusively on Duncan's part, that were part of the texture of their language, such as "thot" for "thought," "shld" for "should," "tho'" or "tho" for "though," "dont" for "don't," and past tenses (mostly by Duncan) such as "faild" for "failed," "launcht" for "launched," or "workt" for "worked." We have, however, corrected misspellings, slips of the pen, and typing errors that might be distracting or confusing to the reader. Both poets used initials as shorthand for the names of people whom they knew the other would recognize, such as "M" for Levertov's husband Mitchell Goodman or "JW" for "Jonathan Williams," but when the identity of the person might be unclear, we provided the names in curved brackets. Both poets often interpolate words, phrases, even sentences in the texts of their letters. Levertov in particular made insertions, sometimes between the lines, sometimes up the margins and running around the edges of the pages, occasionally upside down. We have, of course, included the insertions by both poets, but for ease of reading we have not tried to reproduce them typographically but have placed them at the end of the paragraph into which they were interpolated. The exception to this practice is that comments occasionally made before the salutation and after the signature appear in the printed texts where they were written.

Because the circumstances of their lives made personal meetings between Levertov and Duncan comparatively rare, their intensely close and sustained friendship was conducted almost completely through letters. The frequency of their communication back and forth gives the correspondence something of the sustained power of an epistolary narrative. The correspondence is so regular and so copious that headnotes were not necessary for continuity; however, as mentioned above, the notes, glossary, and chronology provide contextual and biographical information. Our editorial practice has the single and simple intention of allowing the reader to enter that narrative and follow it through.

*Robert J. Bertholf & Albert Gelpi*

*The Letters of*
ROBERT DUNCAN *and* DENISE LEVERTOV

# PART ONE   1953–1959

Denise Levertov in Greenwich Village, 1958. Photograph by Jonathan Williams.

Letters for Denise Levertov : An A Muse Ment[1]

1

{June 1953

San Francisco}

•  in
    spired / the aspirate
    the aspirant almost
    without breath
it is a breath out
    breathed spiraling—    An aspiration
pictured as the familiar spirit
    hoverer
    above
    each loved each
a word giving up its ghost
memorized as the flavor
    from the vowels / the bowels /
    of meaning
be still thy braith and hear      hesitate as if the bone-
    them speak:           cranium-helmut in-
voices; ? ; images ? essences ?   hearing;) clearing
    as only in               old graym attar.
Yeat's "desolation of reality."

•  specialization, yes. Better to stumb-
ll to it.• You cld have
knockd me over with a feather-weight
of words.    The sense
    sleight but absolute.
Nock, nock, nock sum sense into me head.
    O.K.
better awake to it. For one
    eyes-wide-open vision
    or fotograph
than ritual.

specialization, yes—even if the old ritual
is lost.
I was completely lost and saw the sign
without meaning to.
This was not the design—

A great effort, straining, breaking up
all the melodic line (the lyr-
ick strain?) Dont
hand me that old line we say
you dont know what yer saying.

Why knot ab stract
a tract of mere sound
is more a round
of dis ab con
    traction
a deconstruction
for the reading of words.

Lists of imaginary sounds, I mean sound signs I mean things designd
in themselves I mean boundary marks I mean
abounding memorizations I mean a memorial rising,
I mean a conglomeration without rising.

1. a dead camel
2. a nude tree
3. a hot mouth (smoking)
4. an old saw (rusty edge)
5. a copy of the original
6. an animal-face
7. a broken streetcar

8. a fake cigar
9. papers
10. a holey shawl
11. the addition of
    the unplanned for
    interruption: a
    flavor stinking coffee
    pot (how to brew
    another cup in
    that Marianne Moore, Pound,
    Williams, H.D., Stein, Zukofsky,
    Bunting, S. J. Perse, surrealist
    Dada staind pot)
12. A table set for break-
    fast.
    A morning lang
wuage—ai ai wailing
    the failing.

        song of the languagers
What are the signs of life? the breath, pulse,
   the constant
sloughing off of old disguises in
   creasing, increasing—
Notes— to hesitate, retract:
   step by step— to be idiot-awkward
   with it— to take care
by the throat & throttle it—
   bottle that genius
for mere magic or intoxic
   vacation.
it is sober he stumbles
   on truth? Hell, no—

this he sober gnaws
the inconsequential
   eternity of his skull.

His appetite is not experimental.


dear Denise Levertov—

2

{27 June, 1953
San Francisco}[1]

No no no—not at all "adversely." The abyss, that everything about your poems (the possibilities arising to mind) that excited my more than admiration about then my own aesthetic is I see *not yours*. But in, in a large measure, having freed the language for yourself (—that is, getting the feel of the language) you free it too from "originality" and "the greatest."

And then, from there the "Letters" are *for* you not about you. They are reflections upon and from *my* aesthetics (which is proper to a degree) and it is not at all necessary to presume they are reflections upon or from *yours*.

Written in part because I felt that—my rapport with these latest poems (and, for instance, also with Olson's) was such—there might be (another possibility) of an understanding of what I am after. And there is the abyss-mal, the gap.

More simply:
Particulars—

1) The *strain*—what one is after is the tensions in meanings—Confucius names "the effort" as one of three supreme virtues in living. The other two—not to be "great" (to be an "unknown" in all its meanings, not to know) and (2) to have friends visit from afar (to be understood? with the reality—the distance, the visiting, recognized). So—the "strain"— to acclaim the *strain* itself; the I can hardly do it so easily. "No more difficult than walking/this talking" But walking is (this complicated "learnd" motion of muscles) is inherently "difficult." The conscious mind wld. stumble.

2. A flavor stinking coffee—staind pot.
   Well, here again how far off can I be. What I mean is that *I* (and I hoped you—not because it wld mean you were a better poet for it, but because it wld. mean you might understand what I am searching out). But I didn't didn't didn't mean either

   a) that not being original or being derivative was *your* quality. But I did write eagerly of *my* beloved coffee pot that you might share the dismay/delight of origins—what most excites me, the predicament of poetry. My titles now for volumes of poetry are: IMITATIONS, and DERIVATIONS. "originality" is *NOT* either interesting or available to me.

    b) that "stinking" meant *bad*. I took delight in "stinking"—again the predicament of flavour.

*You* stuck the dirty in.
But I have (in "Domestic Scenes"[2]) already given "stinking" its tone "the stink of the real."

So I too (as you—at my response) am caught in the dismay of misunderstanding. I write you "it"; some of the figures (and rips) in the carpet and you find it not "the least like Duncan." Can misapprehensions be greater.

    My praise is your abuse—

all regards<br>Duncan

The Yeats poem is

---

**3**

{June–July, 1953
New York}

Dear Robert Duncan,

    I'm abashed at my stupidity—blundering into yr. poem with my defensive misconceptions. If you still have my other letter, you might send it to Cid {Corman} because there's a certain sad interest in such a spectacle of crosspurposes. Maybe we're all at crosspurposes oftener than we think.

    You still don't say what you meant by "specialization" & I still don't know. Please tell me.

    I certainly am glad you admire my poems because I've been admiring yours for 4 years now, since I found a copy of *Heavenly City, Earthly City,* on Cornelia St. When I said that it didn't sound like Duncan I meant, not like that Duncan, & really not like yr. *Origin* poems either. But I guess I also said it from shyness, i.e. I imagined some grotesque scene, R.D. saying to Robert Duncan (whom he knows slightly, meets at a party) "Ha, ha, someone mistook me for you," & both laughing with raucous disgust.

    Thanks for the Yeats poem. I like that about "the effort"—yes, that's exactly it. I have a poem you might like, which Cid is printing in #10, that relates.[1] If I can find it I'll enclose it. I hope Cid is doing some more of yours. I'd like to see them, where else do you have some?

    Can you see, given my original wrong angle, how yr. Letters fitted together almost point by point as a deploring?

    "You cld. have/knocked me over with a feather-weight/of words" was a reproach, etc. etc. Don't be mad at me for not understanding yr poem, & thank you.

Denise Levertov.

Dear Robert,

I've wanted to write ever since you left but I wished to write such a special kind of letter—something befitting the effect on me of your visit—that I put it off, to save for a special day.[1] But now I want to send you some poems so I'll write anyway.

If I were to *really* write to you it wd. be a real crazy letter—something like a loveletter, tho' not that—dominated by some image of the moon, a full moon, for some reason—I suppose because of that poem of yours, the moon at the window—no indeed, I just realized that what I've been wanting to write wasn't a letter at all but a poem. So in the meantime: how was the voyage, how do you & Jess like Mallorca, and Creeley, have you ever read Blaise Cendrars' *African Saga* (*L'Anthologie Nègre*) (some of it sounds like yr. "Early History")—I guess that's all the questions.[2] Mitch finally finished all that revision & synopsis & sent it off; ran himself down and has been ill with some virus since, but life is more relaxed—now we're waiting to hear from the publisher. Lee's {Leland Bell} show is on & is terrific; he has sold 2 paintings too & got some good reviews. Louisa {Mattiasdottir} Bell has 2 new paintings I wish you'd seen. We were to have visited M C Richards this weekend but Mitch and Nik weren't well. Thanks very much for sending those poems, it was good of you to think of it in the rush of departure. Love to Jess—we loved his collage—love from

Denise.

4

March 31ˢᵗ, {19}55
{New York}

dear Denise & Mitch:

We are settled in, with more space than we have ever had before. It is the apartment which the Creeleys had here last year. Somewhat settled in that is, beds and mattresses do not arrive from Palma until Tuesday. And when in the world does the Spanish tongue arrive? Here I am an old gabbler in a town of continual gabble, about anything, and I can only really say goodday. We have still another month before the Creeleys come out to Bañalbafur—during which time we are the unique foreigners. The townspeople are generous (always giving more than the weight, but also—both Madelena our housekeeper and the Fonts our grocers—adding unexpected presents: some fresh lemons, or a handful of garlic, or cookies) and friendly (as talkative people must be, and these people play at words like monkeys or birds—pajaritos wld. avoid the rime).

I can't restrain myself from a comment or two on the Creeleys. Bob we both like very much indeed. I am glad that I was quite sure of his stories before I met him, for I certainly would have been won over to them by

5

April 16, {19}55
{Bañalbufar,
Majorca}

*him*—and that is always confusing. But what must be sketched in is that she isn't really likeable. She is embitterd—and while one can piece together why—what has that to do with it as Jess says. Plenty of unembitterd people have all the why in the world. And then she is, I am afraid, stupid. And that is a dreadful opinion to hide—as we must. None of this has outed. But we stayd three days while buying furniture, and her censorship of him (prose commentary and even poems are subject to her judgment) reveald the worst—and her censorship of Blackburn, Corman and Dahlberg. Well— Jess commented that her face caught unawares was obstinate (I had seen it as "embitterd")—the thing is a situation. It means we must be distant in order to be friendly and that we must witness without comment her badgering him. Dahlberg blew up outrageously and violated all guest-rights—saying to her face that she was stupid and shld. shut-up. So one must add to the fact that she is obstinate the fact that she is pathetically vulnerable. There is a weakness in the resisting.

Bob cannot see why he quarreld with Blackburn but he (Bob) couldn't stand his (Paul's) wife. However, I came dangerously close to the margin when I encouraged Bob to try to get Blackburn back into the magazine. He wrote a letter to Blackburn and decided to print an article which he had not printed in the last issue. It was Ann then that was outraged that the gesture was made toward Paul. As if Bob had promised not to have anything to do with Paul again.[1]

So I sketch out for you, because I gather you will understand that situation, that we will be living here subject to our repression of many feelings. I need both of you as confidantes and as your forebearance. Some part of corresponding I can see will be to size up in conversation how things are going and then to let off steam, where I can. Of course, Jess more than helps, he is so patient. But that only means his blowing up point is at some more decisive point.

Ann's criticism is, however, related to another point. We had been talking about printing a journal of arts—well, broader—of ideas and anything. A sort of "newspaper"—with unedited correspondents. Creeley had written a piece on "Letters to the Editor" and Ann objected to it. After he had spent an hour getting her to forgive him the piece, he suggested at lunch that I shld. be entirely the editor of the journal—which negated her hold over it.

Well, out of that comes plans for an eight page sheet open for letters, commentaries, news, photos, drawings, comic strips, advertisements, recipes, stories and poems. I wld. like both of you to be correspondents in full standing. That is, edit yourselves and send me just what you want to go in the newspaper. We have already a piece from Olson—whom Robert wrote right away—and I am writing today to those I know.

We will have one of the stories from Creeley's children's book—the story the Cat told.

I want to sketch out thru the journal the broadest range of intelligence.

love
Robert

dear Denise:

6

April 20, 1955
{Bañalbufar}

Yr letter sent the 5th arrived from Palma today. Now that I have a typewriter and can send some mss. to you of things unprinted. Only one new poem—which springs up after days of Jess's reading haikkus out {of} Blyth's book[1]—and so a poem in Japanese spirit to reflect Jess reading the book with amusement and impatience alternating at Blyth's fulsome explications of the poems. *Origin* XV arrived two days ago from Creeley— and I have read and re-read the Blackburn poems. My pleasure is never untainted with envy at the first getting at poetry like this. It always seems when there, right there, are pages of poems that that writer Blackburn, or you, or Olson must live continually in that realm—as if none of you ever saw dully. But to have poetry I am eager to read! like I am eager to read any new work of Pound or Marianne Moore or Williams. And there are four of you now—as exciting, however it is, as Surrealism! "The Innocent Cat" is a pure joy! It is only a sly afterthot that "guilty" is not necessary, & doesn't cover those "unguilty" cruel human eyes for whom the cat is also cruel. Why do I want to interfere. A pure joy! and let poems be absolute as a cloud. As they will. I instruct myself. Jess sez he likes it stet; that the "guilty" is a flourish; and besides that gilt is hidden in guilt.

I, among with other what stars, have passd a place of arrival and will as always write letters back. In earlier days something wld. have seemd lost to me, regret for what one has passd have colord the sentences. But now, it is like a happy fate; a natural wonder one acknowledges. And lays claim to. If this were 1855, we cld write without chagrin of kindred souls. But rightly we want not the sentiments of it, but its powers. And I keep for 1955—the kin; as a communal recognition secret to us even as we recognize it—and so "a cloud!" Surrounded by its own intense blue which you, I, we know rightly is (as in *The Cantos*) "of Heaven." And so, not ours. But of us. Pronouns. I must sometime dispel them and see then what the language sez. I hope the *journal* we plan can include that blue I mentioned. What a long way from e. e. c{ummings}.'s "squeeze yr nuts & open yr face." But each poet in his own time.

I am sending off "unsolicited" copies of eight poems and of the prose pieces I read to Corman. The Blackburn issue incited me. Donahoe don't emit light to me.[2] Nor absorb light (as dark poetry does). Ah! but the angelus, just now. I was unprepared that the nightingale wld. be as insistent a monotone as water dripping, and that the angelus wld. be an alarum (as it is here) against the invading night. I shall mail off this effusion to you— which *is* another part of that eventual love letter; and return to bring in wood and help prepare dinner.

Love,<br>Robert

## 7

Dear Robert

My mother arrived 2 weeks ago and has been ill most of the time since so I've had no time or concentration for letters.[1] But I do have 3 poems. Damn it, ever since you were here I've felt as if I cd. do so much with just a bit more time & quiet to get hold of things, & I've been snowed under with housewifery. Though sometimes I wonder if I don't tend to produce more under pressure. I'm not sure. As far as personalities, all in one house, are concerned, it is going to be O.K.—she & Nik get along wonderfully, also she & Mitch. But she probably will have to have an operation so I'm likely to have a summer of nursing, more or less. We may be able to get up to Burlington Vt. anyway, they have a good hospital there.

I'm sending some things for your paper—it's strange, I had had just about the same idea at the same time, & wrote to Bob about it—did he show you the letter? I'm not sure if these are the kind of things you'd want— if not, it doesn't matter. But please be sure to send back the page from a children's book—doesn't it sound like G. Stein? The book is a miscellany I had & always kept, called *The Golden Cushion*—no date on it but the clothes in some of the pictures look like about 1918–19.[2] I'd like the picture of the stone head back too but it's not important. Mitch sends the Private Slovik ad. with a note appended.

Kenneth {Rexroth} broadcast the tape I made & as a result Weldon Kees wrote & said he'd like to publish them or at least get Adrian Wilson (someone who just did a book for him, it seems) to do so. Also Kenneth wants me to apply for a Guggenheim—I'm sure I'll never get one but I'm going to take a shot at it anyway, with his name, & perhaps W. C. W. {Williams}'s, also Herbert Read—maybe that "Sir" will fetch 'em. Ha!

All you said of Ann comes as no surprise because she was just about like that in N.H. in 1950 & in France a year or so later—except that then one could hope it was something temporary (in N.H. that she was pregnant, in France the sudden change in environment etc.) but now it's a set pattern. In France I did feel I'd arrived at a sort of uneasy friendship with her, i.e. we

went to Aix together a couple of times & she loosened up a bit & was almost
confidential, but that was so long ago, or seems so. Did you know she was in
an orphanage & was adopted, or taken for adoption, several times, & each
time ignominiously taken back? So I do feel very sorry for her. But what is
really lousy is that this business of censoring people's work etc seems to
have grown or be growing—I don't believe that used to be. And then the
economics of it—that makes it extraordinarily complex. I've so often wished
I had a few bucks so that Mitch could write only & not have to scramble for
a living most of the time—but I guess it's better this way really.

Mallorca sounds lovely & if in a year or 2 we were to get some sort of a
break financially—enough to live there for a year or so—maybe we'll go
there, if Nik seems stable & my mother is well. I used to think we'd just
have to stay here for years in order not to disrupt Nik's life but that has
begun to seem too rigid an attitude—if there were a few English or
American kids to play with he'd be alright I think. He probably wouldn't
learn Spanish easily as he's too shy to try.

I'm reading *The World Is Round* to him & he likes it a lot.[3] Thank you
for sending the little poem about the nightingales.

Is Jess painting? Give him our love please.

I was sorry not to feel, when I finally saw them, as enthusiastic over
Blackburn's poems as you did. They are more accomplished in a way than
earlier poems of his I've seen, like "Death & the Summer Woman" & the
one about the birds; but I didn't like them as much. There seems to be
something spurious, something slick about them—he's 'learnt' from Olson,
Creeley, & those *they* learnt from but he hasn't *really* absorbed it, he hasn't
really learnt from them, but cleverly—very cleverly—picked up appearances
from them. It's not that I object to 'influences' being apparent—I took in
what you said about that & I think you are right—but there's a subtle
difference between the frank acknowledgment of influences & the clever
picking up of ways that give at first a dazzling impression of individuality,
originality, or whatever. Or maybe it's to do with content—i.e. his quality
as a man isn't of sufficient strength, or interest, to carry—his proficiency has
shot ahead of him. It's hard for me to figure how much of my feeling comes
from knowing him. I always like seeing him, got along with him (& even
with silly little Freddy)—certainly never quarreled with him—but I don't
think I have really much respect for him. He has charm—& that can always
work on me, to temporary enthusiasm. And he has quick wits, & once read
me a poem of my own (15th St) so completely as I wanted it that I'll always
be grateful for those few moments—But tho' he has brains 10 times better
than mine, there's something adolescent about him which bores me. I know
what it's like—(in his poems I mean)—a child prodigy of marvellous
technique *imitating* deep emotion in his playing. Maybe I'm completely

wrong & if I ever come to feel so I'll tell you. I don't mean it as cattiness & I really do wish I didn't feel this way, I'd much sooner like them very much, it seems ungracious not to. Well. O, but I forgot—I don't feel all that at all about "Here is a marriage." I also like the "Storm" but it seems to me very much like Enslin, whom everyone but Cid seems to despise. Yes, I like that one very much.

Wade Donahoe's letter seemed awfully stuffy.[4] I like some of his poetry tho'.

If the note on what you've said about revising seems platitudinous to you just throw it away. I wd. never send any such thing to a regular magazine— yr. paper sounded casual enough for it tho'. When do you expect to get the 1st one out?

I'm very glad you like Bob, & that he likes you.

*Tues.* Since beginning this letter my mother has been rushed off to the hospital in an ambulance. That was yesterday. 'Condition fair' they said on the phone just now. Tonight the doctor will tell the results of the Xrays etc. She is much better but will have to have an operation.

Some of the material I mentioned I can't enclose as I've not been able to prepare it. Will send later.

Love—from Denise. And love to Jess.

P.S. Sunday 22d.

The poems are not for the magazine. (I'm sending them to Cid as I haven't sent him any lately).

Among the things that recently arrived from England was my wormeaten copy of Peter Heylins' *Cosmographie* (1665) (but written earlier) which was given me when I was 11 by a Mr. Bull, a plumber & carpenter, who'd found it in the belfry of a church. I hope I can show it to you & to Jess some day.

---

**8**

May 25, 1955

{Bañalbufar}

dear Denise—

The sun left sunny Mayo in sunny Mallorca it was now ten days, of dreary grey and even rain some; then today, in the afternoon the sun came; I struggled somewhat alive from a three days malaise; and Jess painted a painting of a young woman seated at a table with coffee service, her head resting upon one hand and arm propped at table, in a garden, or a woods. But the real character of the painting, or part of it I see now, is the opaque lights, the transparent lights, the opaque darks, the transparent darks. The title was *The Nasturtium that Dissolved the World.* But the woman was exactly you, and Jess saw it as I exclaimd it—so it is a portrait of Denise which I received today as a present for the spirits. And it hangs where I have only to glance up into it as I write—across the room—a canvas about three feet by two feet. If it is only fancy that makes the likeness, my fancy is as persistent as a scholar's facts—or I am lost! But this afternoon also there was much time for writing and difficult mixtures of impulses—some half guessd, some only to be discoverd out of the work as I did it—and then I find that recent reading of "critical prose" which I had for a long time denied myself leads me to expound where I mean to suggest, to belabor distinctions that had I managed the discretion of art I would have barely allowd for. But out of two lengthy entries it is one which is a prose commentary as continuum of a poem with which the entry commences.

I was in a mixture of joy and, because I had liked the possibility of appearing in companion volume in the Divers series, of regret:[1] at the news via Creeley of an offer from {Adrian} Wilson in San Francisco. It wld. mean a beautiful book indeed. Send me notice as soon as any decision is made and I will subscribe immediately—

Love,
Duncan

May 26th—today your letter arrived, with materials etc. The children's page of book is wonderful—and Nik's poem also, which I shall want to use for the children's page. But I do not like labelling the poem "by Nik Goodman aged 4" (and hence not responsible for his madness, or "do infants work better than they know") since R. D., aged 36 is equally, in the best of any poem, equally unresponsible and knows not what, etc. or else R.D. aged 36 dont do so good. So Nik Goodman will join anonymous, and R. Creeley, to hold it, as it must—the poem, that is. As any one does. But I will write more later—the journal can get into production only in July (since I can't pay for it until after July 1st). I think I will plan a section *POETICS*, with reading lists; my Maximus essay Part I which is on the physiology of poetry; your note on revisions and invite notes from Olson, Creeley, Zukofsky perhaps.

I sent off a great amount of work to Corman—but that must have been told in my last letter.

There is so much writing accumulating now which I want to share with you; I am sometimes aghast at the mechanism that goes faster than I could think it out to write it out, so that I read myself as I write to find out what I am saying!—the fantastic simultaneities of the brain. I will type up sections and send them as I can, with or without other communication; and maybe catch up with myself.

Thanks to both you and Mitch—

RD

dear Denise/

Right at the moment I have reachd a point of negation in regard to attempting printing *Correspondences*—it's the damnd business of money and when I face the reality of it Jess and I have the choice of using what we save out of our hundred a month for that—or for getting to London in December —and it's the latter that becomes more persuasive as time goes on. The craving for the society of English speech grows. My notebooks are becoming deformd by the "ideas" which ordinarily I throw away into talk, invaluable talk for a head like mine that no wastebasket could keep clear for a poem. I can more than understand dear old Coleridge who grew up to be a boring machine of talk; I can fear for my own poor soul. And, isolated from the city of idle chatter, here, my head fills up, painfully, with insistent IMPORTANT things-to-say. I toss at night, spring out of bed to sit for hours, crouchd over a candle, writing out—ideas, ideas, ideas. Solutions for the universe, or metaphysics of poetry, or poetics of living. Nor does my reading matter help—I have deserted Cocteau for a while because his ratiocination was perhaps the contagion; and the *Zohar* which irritates the cerebral automatism.

Calling up too conflicts of poetry or too—impulses toward extravagant fantasy, my attempt to reawaken the "romantic" allegiances in myself—to Poe, or Coleridge, or Blake—are inhibited by a "modern" conscience; I grow appalld at the diffusion of the concrete. It's I suppose an impatience with my inabilities more than a conflict. The hardest struggle is to give up achievement; well, this seeming achievement (as for instance "Africa Revisited" is something I would not be able to write today, and so, reading it I feel deprived of poetic imagination). The desire to have imagination freed again, with the preconceptions from the ways it was free before. It's to give that up; to be willing not to have the power; and to explore then, powerless to be willing to work. This, anyway, the mood too of the day.

I send two ballads written for Helen Adam, efforts at the romantic style. To do it I have to will to be depraved in the modern sense—to "derive" in so wholesale a fashion—and then the devil of the first poem and the green lady of the second are hardly rare—when compared with the old African of the revisited poem.[1] This is a mood of impatience with the old bag of tricks which the magician has to work with. And then, "It is time for painting to be a minor art" Stein sez in *How to Write*.[2] How to be a minor artist is another part of the task. And a puzzling one. But it seems to me that the poet has an exaggerated repute still—he is, or else, a major artist or a major man. And how to void the importance of the writing in living? How to idle rather than creating? to have the splendors of a shell or a stone or a cloud rather than of a cathedral or a monument—

R.D.

Dear Robert,

A note only—to say I'm confused at this point about what I sent you for yr. paper—but anyway if "Nik's poem" that you speak of is the one I made by linking one of his sayings with one by a little girl he knows, that wasn't sent for the paper—Cid is doing it with some others in *Origin* 17 or 18.[1]

Will write soon. Do you want more things? Clippings? Quotes? I'd like to have a better idea what *kind* of things you'd like.

Things about the same here. No more word from W{eldon}. Kees.

Virginia came over the other night.

Love to Jess.

Love
from D.

**10**

7<sup>th</sup> June. {1955}
249 W. 15<sup>th</sup>
{New York}

Martha, 5, scrawling a drawing, murmurs
"These are two angels. These are two bombs. They
are in the sunshine. Magic
is dropping from the angels' wings."
Nik, at 4, called
    over the stubble field, "Look,
the flowers are dancing underneath the
tree, and the tree
    is looking down with all its apple-eyes."
Without hesitation or debate, words
used and at once forgotten.

D. L.

Love to Jess

P. S. Do you know Sir John Davies' "The Dance"?

Robert, Robert, how are you? It was very hot here and I went into a deep faint which frightened Mitch and when I came out I was lying on the kitchen floor surrounded by Mitch, Lee Bell, and 2 policemen, all very tall, wondering about me whether I was epileptic. But I had chickenpox. Believe me, chickenpox is not funny. But the days ran into one another and I had leisure to dream. Last Thursday afternoon I woke up after a dream and wrote it down. Mitch is bored by people telling their dreams usually but he liked this one so I thought perhaps it would not bore you:

Strange horsemen in the night. High on the flat space behind (just at the side of ) the pediment of a white columned building a woman has come out to look into the night—she has heard them, she wants to see them. She is a woman alive now but looks like a greek terracotta in dress & hair. It is

**11**

{early July, 1955}
249 W. 15<sup>th</sup>
N. Y. 11

moonlight around her & she looks down into the dark tangible almost castle-shaped (pinnacled) mass of dark city to see them—and they almost appear—don't they?—for a moment. Charioteers. I look down to see, then back to her, and in that instant she has changed into an old frail man in dapper evening dress. His attitude is the same as hers and his purpose. Now to the hills we look—he in the scene, I somewhere without—to see them, if they glimmer of shields and raging wheels in the thunderspaces of the woods half-burnt on the mountaintops. And last, looking back, now to the background of the writhing castle-city (now grown smaller & less significant) that background, night itself, is seen to be a density of green and purple flowers, ordered as a tapestry or a carving—and it has been there all along, as if with a grim smile. But the horsemen seem to have gone, further off, with their gleaming wheels.

That was it. I guess you & Jess will miss Bob. What d'you think is up? He wrote that you, and John Altoon, had made "a huge difference," but that "even so he couldn't make it."

What's Altoon like? I spoke to him on the phone, in N.Y., once or twice. I can't see that cover of his for *BMR* {*Black Mountain Review*} at all—just another piece of fad.[1] If you like it I wish you'd explain why.

Did you ever read *Rootabaga Country* by Carl Sandburg?[2] I've been enjoying it, reading it to Nik, and he liked it and said was it written by the same one as the one about the girl Rose & the boy Willy (*The World is Round*).

I don't really understand your ballads, why you are writing that way. It doesn't seem the right direction for you. It seems wasteful both of yourself and in general (like writing sonnets). Or do you think I'm too narrow-minded? Perhaps it is a way to something for you. But when I remember what else you have written, even long since, as well as of late especially, I can't quite believe that. They are more like something you might have written very long ago. But I expect in all these weeks since you sent them you've almost forgotten them, so enough.

Jonathan Williams was here a few weeks ago with Ed and Helène Dorn. This weekend Sy Gresser is here. It's like a hotel as we don't see much of our guests but I like having visitors anyway. We've been planning on going to Mexico to live, in the fall, but my mother is having another op. next week so I don't suppose we'll make it. Also the school, for Nik, turns out to be damn expensive. But maybe in the spring.

I wrote something about Louisa Bell's paintings, did Bob show it to you?

No, hell where did that no come from? 4 small boys are playing here now.

No poems since the last I sent you—too much to cope with, current events. Sometimes I feel wasteful or wasted (in that sense) but damn it if

I can't make something in spite of, or out of, all that, I don't care to anyway. I just have to, that's all. But we might get to live somewhere easier.

My love to you,<br>D.

Did you ever hear "Toccata for Percussion" by Carlos Chavez?

P.S.

I was happy to read your things in *BMR*.[3] They are what I look for first. As one looks for any news of someone one loves but hardly knows. And despite what I say about the ballads I actually let all that you write just happen to me—as years ago with my beloved Keith Sawbridge, with the face of Rembrandt's son. Why shd. I think of him? He wasn't a poet—never made it, I guess, any way.

But he had some quality you have—I'm not sure what it was, but anyway all he did (tho' other people, in his case, despised it, and him) had for me a crazy exalted validity, *no matter what.* He disappeared into some dreary London hinterland long ago and I suppose for ever. A Rimbaud too late.

I liked yr. Max Ernst a lot, as it happened I had just had that Ernst book out of the library. Did you ever read a DHL story called "The Border Line."[4] A terrific story.

dear Denny—

If Bob did not bring your page from the Reader with him, I will get it in Palma when I go in and send it on to you. He is going to use it in *BMR* 6— which is shaping up wonderfully; toward the wonderful that is: an issue with a more other worldly brew. And I have set me to the what-would-this-world-be-if-it-were-another, or this person if he were another. Or Blake set me to it. And Cocteau. What does their necessity mean? Notes, anyway, on the imagination as Jacob wize it struggles with the angelic madness. To have a moon of one's own! . . .

And he will bring you his news too. His life sets right now on his back, that Old Man of the "Domestic" Sea. But not *domus,* that is the damnd thing of it. What is hard for him to see—¿even impossible? is how much Ann had set the whole thing against him. Against the art, certainly. But I have written that all to you as we saw it in the beginning. What does this will against joy mean? It strikes an old terror in the heart—yet not the tragic terror. Because she is so set to it, and not nobly. Praise beloved Ibsen that he spoke for the free spirit.

I have abandond *CORRESPONDENCES* to the excitement of preparing a new volume of my own work 1949–1950 which will be out in September

**12**

13 Julio {19}55<br>{Bañalbufar}

with 17 collages by Jess, a preface and four poems as illustrations of collages added. Much of the excitement comes for me in finally accepting these poems at all. It isn't that they were poorly done. But they are so unredeemd. I had felt in recent years uneasy indeed at these self-lacerations. But I see them now as a spectacle of it, and present them so. A measure in what scale?

Once *Caesar's Gate* is out, I will be only five years behind myself in publication. . . . It is the collages that transform the book, and where I can—in the Preface and the illustrational poems—that I try to *place* the book. The collages make it more expensive than other Divers Press books— but I hope that by having a limited edition of 10 copies with special collages and poems added (that is, composing a new collage and a new poem for each of the ten) the price of the subscription to the regular editions may be kept down to $2 a copy. Certainly any orders before the book is out can be taken at $2. We are going to have to borrow the money to put it out and I want some assurance that it can be paid back. Amen. So be it, as Williams says. So be it to money.

And *he* {W. C. W.} comes thru to us again with the second part of the "Asphodel" poem—these works are seductively beautiful; as if, I mean, I could borrow his grace.[1] So hard won—and the urgency of its winning is the grace. But hallelujah for wisdom. For the painful knowledge and the joyful knowledge of the poem.

Have you read George MacDonald's *Lilith*? It is reprinted now, along with his first novel *Phantastes*? Helen Adam has sent us another MacDonald book *Malcolm* which already provides the world. It is the *romance* that engages me mind.

Love
Duncan

---

**13**

16 July, {19}55
{Bañalbufar}

dear Denny—

Your letter arrived today and set me right down here to respond. A bit, well, about ballads, and *no matter what*, and dreams, and then—since you ask so, altho I wld. leave seeing to the act of seeing, about the cover and from that to maybe painting but back to writing certainly. The two ballads were in part of origin a gift for Helen Adam who herself writes nothing but ballads which horrify all aesthetic sense and subvert because they appeal to something just long enuf ago to have preceded values—and then I do not know why we are ashamed of fancy. Has imagination really won the battle? So: there was another determination in yielding to these pseudo-ballads, for the freedom itself from my own technical pride. Yet there is no pure invalidity possible. And both ballads in spite of my concept return like crows to the corpse of some experience. My sense for it is anyway to let the writing loose from its moorings if need be but to allow range; and now where it might happen above or below, nobly or ignobly to disrupt the personal. When you ask why I am writing that way or is it the right direction that all belongs to the *me* who is shaped, impelld, made as I make the poem. But the words and the poem are also all other and less or more than what we use them for or how we are used by them. The Ballads are no more nor less than a nurse reading by a fireside, a simple minded bogey rime. Almost immoral when we are lined up in the Armageddon of verse conventions against form or poetry. But I don't believe in this battle of the species. It is not a question of "no matter what" any more than any *interest* is; and it is the interest in, not the faith, that I wld. take as my clue. Ideally that we might be as readers or spectators of poetry like botanists—who need not tell themselves they will accept no matter what a plant is or becomes; or biologists—who must pursue the evidence of what life is, haunted by the spectre of what it ought to be as they might be. As *makaris* we make as we are, O.K., and how else? It all however poor must smack of our very poorness or however fine of our very fineness. Well, let me sweep out the old validities: and readdress them. They are inventions of an order within and out of nonorders. And it's as much our life not to become warriors of these orders as it is as our life to realize what belongs to our order in its when and who we are and what does not. I can well remember the day when Chagall and Max Ernst seemd bad to me, I was so the protagonist of the formal (like Arp or Mondrian) against the illusionary. The paintings have not changed. Nor is it that I have *progressd*, or gone in a direction. But my spiritual appetite has been deranged from old convictions.

It's with all this relativity, to use the word, as it is vulgarly used; that I can *practise* austerity, a mode, a measure. And the measure is all important to us if we work at all. "Awareness restful & fake is fatiguing" Pound sez. And since I don't like the idea of "fake"—well, that is a fake mountain means something —its made of papier maché etc.—but what the hell is fake writing??? a fake Shakspere means he didn't writ it. But what is a fake emotion? "Faked" love reads evidently clearly like "faked love"—a given emotion. What is fatiguing? What dont be understood I takes it. Or what doesn't *belong*?

Anyway my sense of what belongs rests me. And from it I can venture— how does this belong? Certainly *no matter what* is a needless burden to carry. It isn't that it is *fake* that makes for my not getting much of what is printed—its that it doesn't concern me. I am impatient with Conrad Aiken, but why be patient. . . . he's a chipmunk and this biologist is interested in beetles. At least I know that he isn't a first, second or any class beetle. Blake got me off onto the ballad, and Coleridge (we read Lowes's *Xanadu* here for the first time).[1] It was the concern returning for the Mariner or Cristabel. To explore what it was.

I cannot put myself together as a direction (like say E. P. directing the language, conquering the line from the pentameter) or an integration (as Rexroth sees poetry). I am of all a mind not to put myself together. And then to have been barely consequent.

O! Altoon's cover and your piece on Louisa Bell's paintings which I liked and the photographs of Louisa Bell's paintings which I didnt like.[2] It's only by keeping in mind that whatever I do is a "fad" and a "fake" that I manage to work at all against my fear of being found out. What the hell do we live in— an aesthetic as severe as ever Calvinism and if we are to live radiantly must tell ourselves like poor Cowper that we are damnd. Is it really less rooted in our seeing that a smear of ink on a paper not be another shape than that a smear be reminding us of other things? But the smear is an act of smearing, the wildest gesture of pretense is a human declaration of pretense, and valued if we valued smearing, or the witness, nervous and almost hysterical, of a happening. A deliberated mereness again. Not a defense of the cover but how to explain the continued interest in it. Beyond that he has a flair, the thing is "knowing"—and ¿does it show off a bit? Rexroth wrote to me that he could never be interested in "this adolescent truculence" (he meant Creeley's poetry). We are surrounded by sins of puerility or senility, of default; of fad or fake, of not belonging to an order of things. Of being of the moment.

It's that a thing can have no values outside of itself; this particular so-shaped stone, or that a human being might surpass expression—a no matter which is a what.

I try to make the description of how I feel without including its particu-larity. But it is particular. And singular. It's the declaration of and embodied freedom in how it is painted . . . and then that the forms themselves happen so, and almost are not integrated, that the artist addresses himself to a discomposition . . . but he fails! unless someone like you wonder what or why, he fails. With me, who rejoice, he fails because it is seen (composed) to my eye. It's the free movement of the mind thru the time of the poem, and the lively everywhere possible charge of it, that delights me. Which exercises just the old validities I was going to sweep aside. You see, the ballads, or art like Altoon's—whatever it is where I have my sure response in spite of my known aesthetics gives freedom—*is* freedom of movement. But you are more than right, the art of Kline, or Altoon, or Twombly etc. is the ruling art of the day. I do not rejoice that there is a ruling art; and I certainly do not rejoice that this art which I respond to is a *fad*. Like there is a *fad* for a kind of writing growing out of Williams and Pound.

(Monday)

I let this sit over night, to read it this morning and see if I said anything at all more than reaction. And then there are a few words to say about

Altoon's cover (rather than about why I like it); and they have again to do with the question of where the word *fad* came in. My first guess is that by *fad* you meant to protest against the dominant style of the day, which Abstract Expressionism of America really is. In this same sense, in their time Cubism, Constructivism, Expressionism, Surrealism were all "fads" in a way that more ordinary painting never is. Today, for instance, the Art Nouveau and the painting of the Nabis (Vouillard and Bonnard, Roussel, and Denis) has been reborn as a fad. Gertrude Stein, or Ezra Pound, or Mary Butts, John Donne or Chris Smart, Edith Sitwell or Henry Miller may be a fad— but I seem to have selected my own fads, those I adore—any old one is a fad provided only that he be not in the midstream, the region without excess. Where, I grant you, it would seem to be rarer that a distinction can be wrought. But this word under which I smart so—this "fad" is but other brother to an accusation often brought to my door of cultism. Admired by a clique, who clique-claque cultivate their taste to an act they would not naturally ordinarily take up. In the Workshop which I attended in San Francisco I was frequently accused of reading things into Williams that weren't there. Of the fallacy of the importance of wheelbarrows. The cult of the unimportant object.

But Altoon's cover was derived from one of a series of drawings in the dominant style—and hence from a "fad"—and here my sword of his *freedom* is double edged for, like us (in relation to Williams or Pound or (particularly for me) H. D. etc.) he conforms to a mode rather than inventing one. What happend next wld make for still an other sense of the cover's being a fad, for he used the drawing (which however else it had been done had not been *calculated*) to calculate a cover. Here his—but a different of him—nice sense of chic, his elegant temper took over the play; and the thing was composed, cut, adjusted, calculated in relation to the shape and size of the magazine, became, what it is, a little triumph of the ruling taste (as for instance Kitasono's cover was in a ruling taste).[3] So where first, as the original drawing was conceived, its expressive inarticulateness related to a fad; second, as it was used, its decorative articulateness related to another fad.

But I imagine some of the problem for you comes from the New York environment where the competitive struggle has set artist against artist, painter against his eyes etc. We found the evening at Lee Bell's lively enough in one way—that could lead to some appreciation of Balthus or Giacometti —and could open my eyes out of an old resistance to Helion's work. But when one came nearer to the New York scene—there was only the necessity to put down or put in its place work which to our uncompeting eyes had had its own free wonders—of Hoffmann, or Larry Rivers, of Kline or Dubuffet, Pollock or Still. Even dear old Matisse must be somehow in the wrong direction; or our liking or disliking him be more pertinent than our seeing him. The point is not that one not make his ideogram of it; have his great design of what belongs and what has been discarded; but that in this environment the designs are not great nor determined by the eye but ambitious and determined by the market. Of some kind of luck the freedom of one's love of art or the bigotry of one's aesthetic has little or nothing to do with working in an art. So Blake—and no one in N.Y. could rival him for his life-long hatred of Titian, Rembrandt and Rubens—or Pound—and who can rival his love affairs with Homer, Brancusi, Beardsley, Dowland, Bartok, Iamblichus and Gesell for a wide flung ideogram with Kung and Frobenius to hold the structure—are—the one a great "painter" for all his hatred of painting, and the other a great artist for all his cultivation of taste in art.

Your piece on Louisa Bell's painting I liked very much, because you led the eye to the color and thru it to the shared seeing of life. But it was all the color that was the key for you and it was, once stripped by the black and white camera of its color, something else that one *saw*—something that did not inform the eye of the same world that the color must have. Another meaning, and a poorer one, for the cats and people so congeald in the schoold composition. But principally that I couldn't get the challenge of a thing being made from them—

love,
Duncan

## 14

Dear Robert,

I've had your book several weeks now and not written. I hope you werent hurt. I was tremendously pleased to get it from Bob, and hardly a day has gone by since but I've looked into it, sometimes to read, sometimes just to handle it & look, too excited to read. I've also brought up here with me the book with the Venice poem and all the TSS you've sent.[1] What a marvellous past that is beginning (or not beginning for it begins before that really) "who go about the town" . . . For me it is incredibly evocative and precise—as if it had been written for me, which I suppose will seem strange to you, but it is so.

We got up here 2 weeks ago, delayed by Nik getting mumps, just to cap off the chickenpox. We have a pleasant shabby 1/2 a house with a large green garden. I remember one terribly cold spring day in Florence seeing in a bookshop window a book of poems (I forget by whom—not Toller—) at a page where it said:

Über meinen grünen Garten
Flügeln die Schwalben

(Over my green garden
fly the swallows . . . )

and how I was restored and believed at once that spring was about to become.

There are lake beaches on the sands where almost no-one goes; trees & a narrow strip of sand or stones. The lake water is clear & often so shallow that one can walk out a long way on the smooth sandy floor of it—a strange pleasant feeling. I walk out till it's almost to my shoulders then turn & swim back. Sometimes there are quite big waves, and it doesn't have the insipidity of some lakes.

Back of where we live, (on the ridge, not close to the lake) the country begins.

We have an extra child, a friend of Nik's called Paul. (5½) And my mother finally got out of hospital & convalescent home & is here too. She makes up wonderful stories for the two little boys—a kind of serial story about 2 boys on the Welsh mountains, half invention & half memories.

Sometimes I come across some scrap that looks to me like part of a collage, and I've wondered if I could save them & send them to Jess in case he could make use of them. But perhaps that's not how it is done, perhaps he has to have found them himself? Would you please tell me? Give him my love. There was a kid on the bus yesterday who looked like him.

I have no new poems to send you, all the domestic crises of the last few months have driven me under and I'm only beginning to feel properly alive again. It was very good to see Bob, we had a good evening together—Mitch and Nik were in Brooklyn. Mitch had seen him while I was out there with Nik, then we changed places so that I had a chance to see Bob. Mitch had a violent argument in the Cedar bar with and about Franz Kline and in defense of Lee Bell and Louisa Matthiasdottir.

It is too bad those photos weren't better—did you see them? The university library up here is not bad; uneven but one never knows what one may find. Bob promised to send me a reading list you had given him but we[2]

dear Denny/

You will be getting not only this letter but—it seems harder to mail a letter than to write one—a long letter I wrote in July,[1] left evidently at the Creeley's house and found only yesterday when I was in town and had gone there to try to find my uncollected works (which I had lent Bob just before he left, and which has evidently been "mislaid"). Well, from the way I feel it will be two long ones. But how puzzled I was when I got your letter just before I left for Palma with its asking if I had seen Louisa Bell's painting in the reproductions, etc. I had had a swift thought that the Spanish mails were not to be trusted. Then, when I found this first long letter I thought that I would just put it aside or throw it away, but upon reading it, it does get said

## 15

24 agosto {19}55
{Bañalbufar}

what I would like to say. And for the qualifications I can make them here. Or "it" here—because from your letter ("Mitch had a violent argument in the Cedar bar with and about Franz Kline and in defense of Lee Bell & Louisa Mattiasdottir") I see that what I suspected is more than true, that the issues of New York's cold war in the arts are involved in whether I like or dislike Altoon's cover (in the dominant and now under attack style) and whether I like or dislike the reproductions of Louisa's paintings. But let you and me put aside the battle for survival as far as they go. Kline's work I find magnificent indeed—quite of a company in the Guggenheim museum with the Chagalls and Brancusis and the beautiful Bonnard. But I can name any number of painters in the American expressionist school, or rather have seen any number, who are ordinary and uninspiring indeed. For the other side of the fence, neither Bell nor Mattiasdottir it seems to me are very pretentious painters, they hardly aim at the magnificent. What a derangement then that a question of either/or could come up between them and a painter in the grand manner. My not liking (and even this was that my response was so vague to the photographs that I suggested they were not exciting) was hardly like my not liking—say De Kooning, which I dont, but the painting remains to worry me, my distaste corrodes at my aesthetics, and now I find myself wishing I could see canvasses to find out what is so persistent about his work. You see, I would like to be free in response from the damnable war in which their response can be used. Because I have discoverd new responses (and then responsabilities) in myself thru Kline's work—O for such great bold sweeping containd statements contemplating themselves!—need I or must I argue with (I am more than sure that such great bold sweeping containd statements sweep out whole marvellous realms of seeing from their maker's eyes—as Pound cannot hear Milton, as Epstein thinks Mondrian a fake, as the youthful Henry James was scornful of Walt Whitman, as D. H. Lawrence found James Joyce obscene) Kline or the Cedar bar enthusiasts. To violate my sense of his painting.

Your note on Louisa's work does remain in my mind, to make me wish I had seen the paintings themselves—tho imaginary paintings of objects, of fresh simplicities and morning warmths leap into mind. In *How to Write* Stein writes: "Painting now after its great moment must come back to be a minor art." You are in the note so beautifully free from the war—it is simply the reality of the paintings that you reveal.

---

I have been reading Rexroth's *The Dragon and the Unicorn* and am almost on the brink of being able to write about it—especially to note the music of the poem which will need a difficult analysis of *how*, of the structure; but to the ear it comes as changes in tone, reading aloud ones voice is compelled to change tone. Changes so wedded to the change in address, from the travel diary to the metaphysics that at first I was not aware how subtly it had been wrought—I was taking it for granted. And then I find out all over again from reading the poem here how thoroughly I adore Kenneth.

Zoroaster long ago
Said poetry presents us
With apparent pictures of
Unapparent realities.

The sleep . . .

The man so measuring tempo, step and thought, so wedded echoing sound and pace—the all but invisible caesura that gives the contour to Said poetry; or the progression (with the *P* of poetry just beginning its theme) between "Zoroaster" and "Said poetry".

---

Meanwhile it is something else that I have got on my mind, and I think that I went on so insistently about the painting and responding because it postponed my attempting to describe the nightmare of the Creeley household here since he left. Jess and I did not like Ann Creeley at all, we had found her affair with Victor Kalos only proof of her obsession with punishing Robert and an evidence of how demoralized she was that she would use herself as a means.[2] So we have never been to visit her since he left. But her neglect of the children and her misuse of them has been the subject matter for the gossip of the circle about her.

I take pen in hand—whatever the economy for weight in mailing. This is the first attempt to send news of this situation and two things haunt my attempt to write it. First is that my sense of her being bad for herself and then everything around her is inseparable from my dislike and we have both prayed that Bob would be free—but how can he be when the children remain victims now of her inability to live and her emotional self-destruction. Second is that it will be necessary to tell Bob at some point and all my instincts are against it. I am hardly a disinterested newsman. And I dread the thot of his not being out of it. Malice and gossip are freakd twins—were there any good will it would have a hard time surviving the ravages of the Americans abroad in Palma, a regular Greek chorus brings news of omen after omen. Its a sullen and miserable stormhead brewing. Jess and I by removing ourselves from all direct knowledge have only had the more of the group fantasy that surrounds that house. Well, and not only among the Americans but, now that we draw into the Mallorcan community of the town which had adopted the children as their own we find another force of watchers. It's this picture of a girl, perhaps more stupefied than stupid, but with a will of her own now against the goods of the heart or mind, with good will gone then, surrounded by the psychic human wolf and hyena pack, that little clump of woe-diggers that howls along in *The Women of Trachis* or carries the news of Agave's derangement, waits for Clytemnestra's bloodbath. And unarmed now by any love for the girl, disarmd by my sense of her outrage (the *hubris* I had seen earlier in her sneering at—O but I hate the word sneering and it was only or all of a willful contempt, as if she knew she was facing something in her contempt—for *Wuthering Heights* "a silly book" she had calld it; or in her avoidance of the cathedral which is the one evidence of a human spirit contradictory to meanness in the city), I find myself howling about the wolf pack, certainly a troubled part of me ravening for the bits and scraps of the kill.

I think the center of the storm however is the children. Bob's relation to them is not that of father—but that of a fond older brother. Had he been *pater familias* he would have been a home maker which he wasn't (his idea was that the woman made the home), and a bread winner—that is, he would have labored to build a home. The gatherd chorus is of men without children: Austryn Wainhouse who believes in the virtue of sterility and the vice of fertility (translator of de Sade, Wainhouse is excited by the idea of the extinction of the human race);[3] John Altoon who has hidden within his war psychosis (he dwells on a terror threshold, in speech and reactions, thrashing about like a mouse in a jar of oxegyn) I have begun to suspect, another breakdown—his rejection of his Armenian family, ambivalently subscribing on the one side to a shame of his race and on the other to the shame of dishonoring family—the crisis then again of being against family; "they should never have given birth to me, if they were not *American*"; and Jess and myself, being Sodomites, are profoundly not *parents*. The difference between Bob and Ann is not that between a good father and a wicked mother; but between a fond but self-centered older brother and an angry (certainly ambivalent, for even earlier we witnessd deliberate "punishments" which were arbitrary thinly disguised attacks upon the children) harassd older sister. The *hubris* at root then is of childbearing out of parenthood. The women too of the chorus are childless. That there is not a parent on the scene is one of the omens. As if the chorus that moves to speak before Medea had had no hearth nor children of their own.

Second—and a factor of environment—is that these Americans aboard are Americans (except for Jess and myself) without hearth. The Creeley household because of the absence of *care* is the victim of sullen and slovenly housemaids—the current one only more neglectful than the last who was an evil sprite in the house. I have been only once to the house, which was on this last visit to Palma, because a manuscript had been left there. Well, Ann was not home; I couldn't find the manuscript; and sat amidst the alternately eagerly playful—(puppy-children)—and quarrelsome children. Charlie, the littlest, is still immune from the infections of the house; and has her inner radiance, face begrimed and hair uncombd as she was, with a stye beginning on one eye. But Tommy and David dwell in the thick of the infections, of tears and blows, climaxed by a savage kick from Tommy at David's head while he was lying on the floor. The whole role for the visitor being to ward off some new savagery among them, to divert them and to attempt some amelioration of woes deeper than any visitation could reach.

We learnd from the maid that Ann was not expected home for some time, and left the disorderd house as always to its fate.

What fascinates me tho is the physical setting, the stage-directions that dramatize not the mere absence of homelike feeling but the wreck of the house. At Altoon's he has lived for four months, as if it were a joke of the inevitable, with broken plumbing and a tyrannous housemaid, without learning even the few words of Spanish that might repair his situation.

The *hubris* of the Creeleys was to have children without the precincts of parenthood, and the chorus is of those who self-exiled or excluded from the precincts of parenthood who have not commited the act which would define their *hubris*. That is, if any of us had children, we would explore our unfitness. It was Jess who pointed out that the chorus of a Greek play is the vehicle not of the divine action but of the divine consciousness—and thus gave me a key to unlock this description as best I could. The act is committed by the "victims" of the *hubris*, which becomes a tragedy when the actors become aware of their act (at this point, previously without consciousness, they come to *actual experience* which is the apotheosis of their act and the consciousness of the watchers). The actors commit what the chorus recognizes. The culpability for the one is human and felt as a miserable confusion mounting to an agony. The culpability for the other is divine and felt as an approaching thunderstorm, a *tormenta* as the Spanish so wonderfully call it, mounting to a divine wrath of justice. When Prometheus or Oedipus or Agave come to their *own*—and the prototype for me is Agave's awakening and seeing what she has done—they come to their individual culpability, to self-knowledge which is character and in which they can like Prometheus or Oedipus or Agave come to a realization instead of a ruin from the contest with the divine reality.

I do not see Ann coming to any self-knowledge any more than does Lulu or Madam Bovary and whatever her end might be it will be as a victim. But what might happen is that if the terrible breaks loose (and it is that that threatens) Bob will come to the self-knowledge, come belatedly into the holy precincts of parenthood or of marriage (which as sacraments exclude the pride or the possession) and there to tragic knowledge. It is before that that all of us who love him might come to the knowledge of what that love might mean. It is not of parenthood or of marriage or of tragic knowledge I pray he be free, but of all participation in the actual sacrilege in sentimental parenthood or marriage.

Love,
Robert

**16**

Sept. 15, 1955
{Bañalbafur}

dear Denny/

In the midst of the rats nest of my desk yesterday I found two beginnings of letters to you—that wanderd off into cul-de-sacs of subject matter. It's that I happen upon just those moments often when if I were near I would come to visit you and that would need no subject matter; but now I start out boldly and am soon listening to only my own voice. I need a space

for you to have been present in. And I reply eagerly; or move about the room a bit. The cats endearing every day and now soon we must leave them. To go to Paris! perhaps. We just finished James Stephens's *Demi-Gods* and are now reading Virginia Woolf's *The Years* aloud which Jess has never read before.[1] And now the year has suddenly turnd a corner into Autumn—a little early for it's the 21st isn't it when officially this new slight edge of a winter is scheduled to appear.

Both the neglected letters began with book lists. I note: Jess and I read both *Rootabaga Stories* and *Rootabaga Pigeons* and forgave Sandburg all his mortal sins . . . almost were tempted but didnt have faith enuf to go back over his poetry and see if any of it could be rescued. If you do not know them already tour with Nik thru George MacDonald's *The Princess and the Goblins, The Princess and Curdie*, and *At the Back of the North Wind.* Then see if you can find, or have some friend in England search out for you *The Light Princess and Other Tales.* And Oz books if you have not been already abroad in them. Another one of Stein's to follow up *The World is Round* is *A First Reader.* H. D. wrote a beautiful book for Bryher's little girl—calld *The Hedgehog.*[2] And E. Nesbitt we liked very much.

re: your subscript "Do you know Sir John Davies' "The Dance"? No, I don't. And I would be eager for knowing—if you could type a copy.

A great wind has come up—and on the radio paroxysms of *Tristan . . .* or now, it is, Jess tells me, *Tannhäuser.* No—it turnd out to be *Tristan.*
. . . . . .

*Caesar's Gate* is well under way—the plates for the collages are done, and the written texts (prologue & poems written here) and half of the printed text was proof read today and returnd to the printer. I hate the *business* of the book and it does seem in spirit counter to the generosity of writing which has nothing to do with subscriptions and editions. Yet even these proof sheets delight me—almost make up for this business of financing the printing.
. . . . . .

Some neglected contemporary poetry—

| Parker Tyler, | *The Granite Butterfly* |
| Louis Zukofsky, | *55 Poems* |
| | *Anew* |
| Basil Bunting | *Poems 1950* |

| Laura Riding | *Collected Poems* |
| | *A Progress of Stories* |
| Gertrude Stein | *Bee Time Vine.* |

Love
Robert

For Oz books—all of Baum's are wonderful—also his other books—and the first eight or so of Ruth Plumly Thompson's.[3]

An affectionate P.S. to send greetings & to protest Robert's revealing my mistakes in Wagnerian dimensions. Also to add that you should keep an eye peald for *Little Pictures of Japan,* a beautiful children's book of translated poems.

Jess

**17**

October 11th {1955}
249 W. 15th St.
N. Y. 11

The picture is reproduced from "Dances of Spain & Italy" by Mabel Dolmetsch, & is from a treatise prepared, 1463, by Guglielmo Ebreo for the Duke of Milan.

Dear Robert,

Just a note to send you these poems and to tell you that I am reading *Robert Falconer* (MacDonald) to myself (an old paperback copy, 1907, that came in my mother's boxes—I remember seeing it years ago but I'd never read it) & *The Princess & the Goblin* to Nik (with the Arthur Hughes pictures —that I never read either—tho I do remember reading perhaps *The Princess & Curdie* when I was 8, staying at an old vicarage in Gloucestershire—& *At the Back of the North Wind* I read several times before I was 12).

Mitch is in Europe! in Scandinavia. He went all in a rush to do an article for *Atlantic Monthly,* with a free ticket from Scandinavian airlines. It was very exciting and I feel I can enjoy it vicariously. He'll be gone a month. I miss him but I'm glad he could go.

Did I write to you about that modern dance class I went to in Vermont where everyone improvised (on a certain night) and it *worked*? If not I'll try to describe it, it was something quite important for me.

I'm copying out that Sir John Davies poem for you & Jess—was not going to write till I had it finished but it will be a few nights more before that, and meanwhile you must wonder what's become of me.

I have started a weekly ballet class & have 5 pupils that pay & 2 free, so far. At one point I felt deadly scared of the whole thing but in the end I was glad I hadn't backed out.

Of Bob I'll write another time. And I haven't made a reply to your letter about painting either. I've nothing to say at the moment about that except that I'd like you not to think of me as embroiled at all in a war of N.Y.

painters because in fact I hadn't even heard of it till the night we were at Lee's with you, & then some more when Jonathan {Williams} was here, & then as hearsay, from you, from Bob a little, & that's about it. I don't see many people actually & have been in that Cedar Bar twice in my life, & both times it was almost empty & no-one mentioned painting. Of course I now know there are sides taken etc. etc. but I didn't;—& don't much care now that I do.

Do you know a Rousseau called (I think) *Carnival Night*? I love it. And last week I saw a painting by Vivin that impressed me very much too. A small blue & green painting of trees & still river water with yellow weed on the water—completely hallucinatory. I'll write more when I send the Sir John Davies poem.

Love—
Denny

P.S.

I expect you heard about Weldon Kees. I felt pretty badly about it as you might imagine—he having written me such a letter not long before.

Lawrence Ferlinghetti has written to say he'd like to do a book for me. I'm very pleased. Do you know him? I'd only heard his name for the first time a few days before his letter.

Jonathan has also come up with a sort of offer but I don't know that I'd have enough poems for both. Maybe. There were some other things I was going to tell you but I must go to sleep. D.

> "We soon found ourselves in Holborn, & my companion led the way towards the City. The evening was sultry & close.
>
> 'Nothing excites me more,' said Mr. Falconer, 'than a walk in the twilight through a crowded street. Do you find it affect you so?'
>
> 'I cannot speak as strongly as you do,' I replied. 'But I perfectly understand what you mean. Why is it, do you think?'
>
> 'Partly, I fancy, because it is like the primordial chaos, a concentrated tumult of undetermined possibilities. The germs of infinite adventure and result are floating around you like a snowstorm. You do not know what may arise in a moment & colour all your future. Out of this mass may suddenly start something marvellous, or, it may be, something you have been looking for for years.'"
>
> (From *Robert Falconer* by George Macdonald.)

**18**

October 15th {1955
New York}
2d letter.

Dear Robert and Jess,

I didn't mail the other because I hadn't copied the 2 poems, so here are all together. I wish I had the whole of "Orchestra" and mean to look for it on 4th Ave or at least at the 42d St library but have had no time at all. I'm sorry it looks so messy—a labour of love should surely have a better appearance but it was done late at night or at odd moments and my writing is ugly as you know, anyway.

Meanwhile, I've received the collage, Jess; thank you *very* much. It came as a wonderful antidote to a certain tameness of life that I feel just now, with Mitch away, keeping house with Nik & my mother, such a well-behaved life without any wildness at all. Not that I'm exactly *wild* when Mitch is home—but this way the responsibility for everything is on me & makes me feel confined (when I have time, as now, to think about it).

I don't even lose my temper with anyone. Probably I'll explode if this keeps up! No. I don't really feel depressed, or oppressed, or repressed, at all, but it was a pleasure to get that collage, in any case.

About Bob—the last day of his stay here (he stayed at 15th St this time) he met Cynthia again and all that had happened since they parted cleared away and he was very happy to have found her again. But he hasn't written since so I don't know more. I daresay you've heard this from him tho'.[1]

c/o James Broughton, Regents Hotel
44 rue Madame, Paris VIe

dear Denny,

Your letters and poems enclosed arrived today, just as I was trying to decide whether to write to you now or wait until we got to Paris which is a week off. I am sending off to you a typescript of work done in notebooks these last six months; most of it before Bob left. I hardly know what I have done since—tho I finishd my rug which I thot I never would do. And Jess and I have read three of George MacDonald's scotch romances: *Malcolm*, *Sir Bibbie*, and *Alec Forbes of Howglen*, and *The Hobbit* by Tolkien, four E. Nesbit books we hadn't read before, out of one of which (*The House of Arden*) I got "the Time you're in tells you what to do";[1] and I read Darwin's *Origin of Species* out of which I got:

> I look upon the geological record as a history of the world imperfectly kept, and written in a changing dialect; of this history we possess the last volume alone, relating only to two or three countries. Of this volume, only here and there a short chapter has been preserved; and of each page, only here and there a few lines. Each word of the slowly changing language, more or less different in the successive chapters, may represent the forms of life which are entombd in our consecutive formations, & which falsely appear to us to have been abruptly introduced.

What if poetry were not some realm of personal accomplishment, open field day race for critics to judge, or animal breeding show— . . . but a record of what we are, like the record of what the earth is is left in the rocks,

**19**

{late November, early December, 1955 Bañalbafur}

left in the language? Then what do we know of poetry at all compared to this geology? and how silly we must look criticizing . . . as if geologists were to criticize rather than read their remains. The "only here and there a few lines" is certainly the sense of all one accomplishes. Take the "Venice Poem" . . . a part of some line that I will never quite make clear. ¿but if the poet makes the fragment clear, the Reader can see?

• And we read aloud too Dostoyevsky's *Crime and Punishment*, and Conrad, Virginia Woolf (*The Years*) . . . a partial catalogue only to show that Bañalbafur is blissful for reading. Tho I still hear far away ghosts of my mother's reproofs against idle reading whenever I curl up with a book; and at more neurotic times feel as if I were "wasting myself" and growing pale and listless. Whereas I am growing fat and ruddy.

I think we will go to England for a month in the winter—January perhaps. Is there anyone I ought to see? Robert Payne gave me a letter to Herbert Read.[2] You know him, should I send the letter on and write myself? But thots of England are beyond the brink of Paris . . . which is the brink of dreams and confusions, and fears about money and cold, and the trials of wanting elegances. Tho some elegances we *have* got. For we both had suits made and of the best, beautiful Spanish flannel.

For your wreath, I thank thee. It's another ghost that goes into, because I want to take it so into, my heart. That bright sea is cold, I think; at least here where it is not cold at all I always hesitate as if it were cold. Tho all the sea of childhood was cold . . . that sea that I used to picture then rising in a single mountain high wave and sweeping me and old Atlantis into its rush. That is also your Sir John Davies' daucning.

"The Way Through" is a beauty.[3] Keying in with the passage from *Robert Falconer*. And with the modern daunce. droping by words. rain And out of a tedium. It sings in my head. I need these poems to start me, and they spring as I need them. What I was going to write now and not wait was just—send a poem—send something to let me write a poem, for you, for a poem. And you did.

love,
Robert

**20**

{January, 1956}
Guadalajara, Mexico

Dear Robert,

It was specially good to hear from you as I felt I'd lost touch with you, through my own fault really. I couldn't write, these last months. Something has been happening to me. I fell in love, with someone who loves me and had loved me a long time without my knowing it.[1] For a few weeks we managed to see each other every day—somehow. Every day the departure for Mexico came nearer. I loved & do love Mitch, and then there's Nik. And I feel deeply committed to my marriage. So there was the last day, and a day later I was in Mexico City, & now here. There was no alternative, obviously, and no doubt with my resilience, which frightens me sometimes, I'll live through it. But I'm still in a daze of misery and confusion.

Forgive me for unburdening myself to you, but when I got your letter yesterday I wanted so much to write to you & I just can't write a different kind of letter at the moment. I've not written to anyone else at all since coming to Mexico, except a couple of postcards.

Please let me know when you leave Bañalbufar. And I'll soon write a regular letter. Write soon—

   to: c/o Poste Restante,
     Guadalajara,
     Jalisco, Mexico.

Love from
Denise

We have found a house and move in Saturday and Nik will start school next week. Mitch was sick for a few days with the "turista" and is now better. Things in general are pretty good. Will write about Mexico, etc. soon.

dear Denise—

I sit huddled over the gas jet, with the pipes frozen and too cold to sit at the table. By next Friday we must leave London—which I could love; but even leaving this early there will only be two hundred and fifty dollars left. Paris and London have eaten it all and my mind is quite divided between the sense of having wasted time and space—to its all being so unrealized. And then I had come like a moth sick with a romance, a pilgrimage which I never had courage or madness to make. I wanted solitude for one thing—feard it; and brought with me all the paraphernalia of my domestic scene. In another month Jess will be on his way back to San Francisco—and there is a slim chance that I may remain here until the end of the summer; more likelihood I too must go back. In the fall I have a job with the Poetry Center in S.F. which may make things easier for me than they were before. Only one poem in these last two months—and only one section of that I find "true"—to the mark. It began with a fierce scene I had with John Davenport at the end of an evening at G.S. Fraser's over Pound.[1] And now Pound's *Rock Drill*, "Cantos 85–95," come with revelations painful for me that it has not been put all together. It is a failure of imagination (of creating the image) so that some of the poet's voices ascend in ecstatic evocations

**21**

3 February 1956
{London}

By the nymphs        and have ecstasy, sober
and that the universe is alive;

and there is a brief, beautiful prayer for compassion ("Canto 93"); and the great bell-tones of ideograms ring *sensibility, foundations*, and the days of the four seasons with the four suites of the deck of 52 cards.

But another voice goes on, insistent, pouring out an old man's references and bile.

And here, where all might, must have been riskd, for some ridiculous divine vision—some whatever it might be. But he's so uninspired worrying the money thing, and his sudden outburst—the word: *kikery*: is only too much like the mean of my mind these days stuck in the mire of money / what I mean is that this dwelling is a settling into the LIE. Hence in the *Cantos* / a falsification?

---

Yes, a falsification; as I find I am willing to falsify. It is only when the voice in writing lifts into the language itself speaking that the truth of the made-thing presides. The feeling of what is false for me is the evident *use* of language to persuade. When we are not persuaded it is easy to see that there is no poetry, devotion to making;

---

By the 15th of February we must leave Paris. And our address then will be as before Bañalbufar, Mallorca.

love
Robert

---

**22**

dear Denise/

I had hoped that I wld. see you in N.Y.—but maybe after Mexico you will try San Francisco in the Fall. We are in throws of leaving—it is only a week off. Olson has askd me to Black Mountain to take over Bob's work until Sept. when I will go on to San Francisco. Our address there is: Black Mountain College. Which is almost our "sign" these days. #6 of the *Review* is generously provided with both my work and Jess's.[1] • Under separate cover I am sending the sketch book for you—it may provide some interest. And I'll write again. If Lisboa seems as wonderful as it did the first time I'll write from there before we sail (which will be some time between the 10th–17th of March). If not, then I'll write from Black Mountain.

Is falling in love a particular weather of loving? It always throws me back upon a state of being that is heart's freedom and solitude . . . but "falling" is not of our will or pleasure as loving is; and then rare; then, an epiphany. I suppose we do well enough to meet it and admit it at all. Longing for freedom and solitude is anyway for me bound up with falling in love . . . all the familiar world becomes so a saturation with myself—the household, or circle of friends, becomes a stage of self-realization. And then something I did not realize . . . and "falling in" then to love. Luckily we are not overwhelming conquerors—even of our own households. And fragments unrealized remain.

But it's now just a year ago when I having fallen in love ran away from it, set out for Europe and my own confusions. "It is because I know I will never see you again that I praise Love's power."

I have an offer from the Poetry Center to be Assistant Director—but now further correspondence reveals that they hope to pay $100 a month; which is just too little to take the work without taking additional employment. I will have time however to decide. It would be about three days a week. • I have written a preface for a small book using this summer's "ballads"—and quote yr objections.[2] I'll send you a copy of same to get your approval for quoting.

Hopes for some kind of another play for this Fall. . . . Did you hear anything about the Guggenheim? Did you apply? This next year I am going to compel myself to apply for aid everywhere.

Love
Robert

Dear Robert,

I think it's a long time since I sent you any poems. And it's a long time since you sent me any—that is, I've had the printed ones, which is wonderful too, but I'd like the immediacy of typed recently-written ones please.

Here are some. All except "Something to Wear" (which I'm not sure if I sent you or not—it's from December) are from Mexico all in March except "Tomatlan," which is just done; and except also for "Homage" which I sent you before but which looked not as I wished it when I read it & which I then re-wrote, adding a word & re-lining it. I hope you think it's better—anyway it is now what I wanted.[1]

We are going to move in a few weeks to Oaxaca wh. sounds better in every way. Guadalajara isn't cheap and worse than that it is booming in a rather American way—a tremendous amount of building going on, v. modern—some of it v. imaginative in a way, but empty, a shell, for *money* only to live in—for there is no quality of grace or feeling to inform it, in the lives of the prosperous people who will occupy these houses—the arts unknown, their acceptance of the architects' imagination an acceptance of fashion merely. There are a few people I will be sorry not to know longer, among them John

23

April 23[d] '56
Calle Florencia 1915
Guadalajara, Jalisco,
Mexico.

Herrman, the one Williams writes of in his autobiography. But I'm always obliged to move away from people, it seems—and I like to move, too; this time, anyway.

Oaxaca, from Mitch's letters (he's been there 10 days, coming back tonight) sounds like a place you wd like. Wd. there be any chance of your getting down here, say between leaving B.{lack} M.{ountain} & going to S.F.? I know it's a long way & a question of money but someone might be driving down or something—who knows? Anyway it wd. be very wonderful if you could. Bob was going to come but as you know, no doubt, he's gone to San Francisco at present instead.

I didn't get the Guggenheim. I don't think I'll apply again this year, too much tiresome work. You say you quote my objections to yr ballads. God knows whether I feel the same any more—I doubt it—& don't remember exactly what I did say. So please—let me see first? Don't forget—I am abashed. Because after all why the hell not (the ballads, I mean). If that were all, maybe yes, it wd. be a regression of a kind; but I'm sure it's *not* all (only you haven't been sending me what else, you know) &—well, basta.

But the events of my own life of late have changed me & made me more open, I believe—there's room for it *all, all,* anything—no matter—if life informs it. Now I understand better (I think) many things that you have said. So if you want to use that either leave out my name or, better, add something of what I say now. Except that, I realize, it's not well enough said. But if you'll send me the other, maybe I cd. add a line or two from now. Seems a lot of fuss to be making but truly I'm abashed to have what I then said given permanence by your quoting it.

Mitch & I went to the Pacific (sans famille) for 4 days. The sea I feel always as a life-giver—& the whole landscape was in tune with the sea, as it often is not; a paradise. And somehow I was restored to myself, & we to each other. But the ache remains—& I wouldn't have it otherwise—without it I'd be a monster—with it I know forever how alive I am.

I had an idiotic letter from poor Cid. I cd. shake him. I defend him to other people & then he goes & makes me ashamed of him with his pomposity. Oh well.

A knifegrinder goes by here some mornings, blowing on a panpipe. Papageno.[2] It's the gayest little scale, up & down—light, gay, & almost wistful.

I'm confused about Bob's address—he gave me Ed Dorn's address to write to, but it wasn't the same one Ed had given me in a letter only 2 days before. If you write soon (I hope you will) wd. you please tell me what his address now is?

Also, when the new *BMR* goes out, wd. it be possible to have someone send me the last issue also? I haven't got a copy any more.

Love to Jess, please.

What are you reading? Do you like being at Black Mountain?

I *wish* I could see you—letters are fine but I'd like to listen to you.

Love from

Denise.

dear Denise,

Joyful morning, prolongd by your letter, by you! I pour myself another cup of coffee. If you have been waiting, as I find I have been waiting, for correspondence . . . how niggardly I have been. I wanted anyway to have a copy of a poem I wrote in London which is beginning note of these new ones: and yesterday the trunk came with mss; today your sheaf. ¿Can I read these poems as rapidly as I attempt to consume them? a hungry man. I let them leap up, knowing—¿isn't it the virtue of the art? that however consumed they leap on the page. Mine now to return to. "The mirror caught in its solitude / cannot believe you as I believe." And "I am afraid / not to be beautiful."[1] Credo! they come of benedictions that love makes upon all . . . and upon me then and increase the day. I should not want to shake off whatever foolishness of spirit might persist from these: but take them as law. Wordsworth whom I am beginning to read was haunted by the fact that Nature (he was a Forest and hence—: had hidden glades, where her Beauty was—acknowledged by all. But I thot: it takes this that "I cannot see nor know" what glade of myself the forest wanderer may discover as his own. But all the vague thing I was trying to read out of him seems now an insufficient "cannot believe you as I believe."

Yet all, all, these songs are songs I would sing. "They have / a great space of dark to / bark across. The rabbits / will have their teeth at / the spring moon."[2] And then my eye finds it is gazing at this beautiful Mexican stamp *Danza de la Media Luna*. Last night was full of the moon, we saw at the window.

The red-eyes of rabbits and red flowers . . . and the "I want your red to anger me" come as ghostly correlations of that taunt the sentence dictated to me: "Do I not withhold the penetrations of red . . . " But not *ghostly*— vivid.[3] Make authentic.

Do not then be abashd, for it is part of the *all*,[4] it is unabashd, the generosity. That you askd "it doesn't seem the right direction for you" of the ballads. As I had courage then not to be abashd—or to be more than abashd. But I send along with these recent poems—the "Preface." Wouldn't it be the false place for your YES (which is, to me, so present in your quoted letter that it is an act of triumphant egotism to begin there: that your concern, like mine, demands both *test* and *all*)?

\*   \*   \*   \*

Charles provides a Spring Song:

Bud pink enclosing
apple White

bud-white, bud-white,
the tree sang,
red-apple, red-apple

with a drawing of a tree, in exchange for Jess's gift of a red cardinal upon his limb "emblazoned." And last night (Charles) talkd about Eliot: how "Christ the Tiger" has come to inhabit the spring." Tho he was not sure of what poem, he recited the passage. From "Gerontion" I thot—isn't it? I have no text on hand to verify. But it is beautiful, as white burgeoning boughs now (barks and bows), when poetry we do not always acknowledge insists upon its place. "In the juvescence of the year". . . . April is his in some peculiar (but he staked his claim there) way. But it *was* hosts of actual daffodils that sent me to my present puzzled search of Wordsworth.

{6 daffodils drawn across the page}

All the windows open to the sun, with clouds of spring and palest watery-wash of blue for sky. The ink of your letter just such a blue
And I offer my sheaf that it come to you as yours has to me.

*con amore*
Robert

---

## 25

June 3/{19}56
{Black Mountain
College}

[This never-maild letter at last maild]

dear Denise—

Yes, I realize that I did not include in the last letter the Introduction to the "Homage"—so here with.[1] In the intervening month or so I have written or finishd writing "The Origins of Old Son" which has some nice songs and to my ears right now one beautiful speech partial dythyrambic.[2] But perhaps the busy inertia of the classes in poetics—well, "busy inertia" could also be "disturbing excitement of" because in the process I am stultified by wrestling with tekniks beyond my own practice: that: and the disturbances even here, especially here, thrown up by Creeley's charge upon the Rexroth household—these have left me confused as to *tone*, as to tuning in to the feel of the language again. I was the idiot anyway who said to Bob that what he needed was a woman—like Rexroth had been blessd with one. This ¿with a sense that Marthe's particular forces were specifically *it*? But no, I had only in mind that she had made along with Kenneth the feeling of a household. Right now Kenneth writes that Marthe has returnd to him;

and Creeley writes that Marthe has returned to S.F. only for the month needed to gather her things and children and join him in Taos. One sees only consequences, and nowhere the joy or liberation of self that the discovery of love brings. In the last year Creeley has made many declarations of love; and started with each only to find the default. Which I take it lies with him in good part—and the women are not always in the most familiar pattern of being wives or mistresses or beloveds of "best friends" or men he respected. To case, here in Black Mountain, was Harriett a young girl who thru Creeley made her rite of passage to womanhood: tho even here, where she was virginal, there was a boy in love with her whom Creeley *over-reachd*. Harriett is still in love with Creeley and, since no more than Bob does she observe the testimony of facts, feels *she* is the one Creeley loves. Anyway, right now Marthe is the real one. And poor Kenneth has the burden of the testimony of facts.

But I am numb before all this right now. From whatever source or weather, numb. And can here hear mere talk circling around it, with the shock of the design, the compulsion triumphant over spirit. O when the human force so various is restricted to these funnels: the difference between the delighting course of the stream (even polluted, as factories and sewers use the water way) and the stream diverted by human cunning to irrigate, piped to your own faucet. And this analogy that ¿was promising? again proves to be numb.

I'ze reduced to stupidity when I'ze reduced to judgment.

But I wld. love another letter from you—especially I want your new address before I get the Review in the mails for you. But no, I'll get it maild off to the old one & trust to its being forwarded.

love
Duncan

Dear Robert,

Your letter and the poems you sent me were such a wonder—but somehow though I did respond to them directly I didn't have it in me to respond anything like adequately in a letter. So forgive my silence.

What I love about you specially is your capaciousness—(I love you for reading Wordsworth now for instance). Without having anything like your deep understanding and grip of things I do have the same kind of zest for many different kinds of things, different worlds really, and I only know one other person besides you (David Mitchell in England) who has it too.

As for Wordsworth, (while lots of him seems dull & pompous), things like the skating at sunset & just after, the part, also from the *Prelude*, about St Batholemews Fair—the phantasmagoria ("the silver-collar'd Negro with his

## 26

June 16th {1956}
Calle Florencia 1915
Guadalajara, Jalisco

timbrel") and . . . "the face of every one / That passes by me is a mystery!"—
and lines like

> "the sounding cataract
> haunted me like a passion"

and

> . . . "Once again I see
> These hedgerows, hardly hedgerows, little lines
> Of sportive wood run wild. . . . "

—I get as much from them now as when I was 13 or 14—and somehow
almost everyone I know who goes on to read more contemporary or more
sophisticated writers seems to lose any feeling they had for someone like
Wordsworth. But not you—you're constantly discovering and rediscovering
with beautiful humility and arrogance. Lovely, lovely, your fearless appetite—
how timid it makes most people's responses seem!

Here are 1 or 2 poems. I have terrible Mexican cramps in my stomach
this morning and can't finish this letter.

Could you get someone to send me *B.M.R.* please? Larry Eigner
mentioned having received it and I'm dying to see it.

Do you know Whitman's "This Compost"? With love

from<br>Denise

P.S.

Nik was 7 last Monday. He got a magnifying glass, some carpentry tools,
a compass—Had a good time.

---

## 27

I have some share in Hell. Anyway I resolved or askd for a dream on Lammas
Eve [July 31] and struggled up from the nightmare above with the conviction
that everything in my life was *really* the dark underground station of de-
formities and/or mutilations; and lay in the dark for some time in the toils of
that revelation. Only when I started working the poem did I see the puns in
the object that I couldn't decide was a sink strainer or stopper. The Prince's
words at the close belong to the poem and not the dream (and contain as best
I can the revelation) (I mean as far as I can see it must be true.)

2. Now after typing the mss. for you. And hence typing them out of
previous mss for myself too. The morning which was all sun has gone into
a late afternoon which is all dark clouds as if for rain. Bird flutes and twitters.
And a cock crows. Must be late indeed. I shall wander up toward Olson's
with your poems in hand. And return after supper or tomorrow morning
before mail goes out to converse again. The two I showd him: "The
Springtime" which I knew he would relish, the "sad golden village"; and the

which he did. But then that's a sure thing, with vatic quality. And the other "The Lovers" he said no, it was love not poetry that was speaking. "Laying the Dust," when he took the rest, he saw as measured, "made." But then there was the problem of whether or no you had let it go easy. Such the difficulties of bring{ing} a horse to poems; yet I, who have my own liking for independence, always am trying it. The thing about a lover not being a poet talking I thought interesting; along the line of a talk he had had with me re: my own—that I did not purify to the formal thing.

It has something to do with keeping style? Yet your poetry as a "room of thinking and knitting . . . cats and woman" is perhaps a counter-style just there to "cars and people" and what do we refine thru style or however? Sometimes I search out to refine or to gain greater intensity of feeling for the poem itself, or more often for the loved language. An infuriatingly stupid book on Aesthetics by Richards & Ogden quotes George Eliot: "a mode of amplifying experience and extending our contact with our fellow-men beyond the bounds of our personal lot."[2] Which is beautiful— and *love* then too isn't it of the will to extend life, ¿how separable from poetry, from making life? Style is certainly a part of the whole act—not the whole. Style whatever it may be, may be also so general as to transcend identity. The particular of style that gives signature or value, I think courage might disregard and even, outgrow. You know, the Olson-thing; or the Duncan-thing or the Levertov-thing. We can certainly and do if we are passionately moved confound aesthetics.

---

Morning note: There is courage in Da Vinci and Rembrandt to seek in art to render and incorporate fleeting significant personal expression. The human smile! it needed the most ardent eye during the time of painting, and then constant, to draw out of this most evasive of human sentiments a passionate reality. We see Da Vinci wavering this side or that side of failure—a grimace of "sweetness," overdone. The miracle among other miracles of Rembrandt is that he suffuses such human transient quality; the personal enters the radiance. Sweetness, sadness—he dares telling expressions.

---

Note: Bob's address: c/o Dorn 1478 Grove St. SF. Thing is that Dorn just moved to that address. Bob hasn't written yet; tho Ida Hodes writes he has been there for a week.

Dear Robert,

We finally heard from Bob in Taos, about Marthe Rexroth.

I feel very sad about Kenneth. He always wanted children so much & now that he has them he loses them. And to someone he disliked long before he knew him!

# 28

July 16th {1956}
Calle Florencia 1915
Guad. Jal. Mex.

He hasn't written to me for some time—I guess he thinks of me as such a partisan of Creeley's that he feels mad at me too. I want to write to him but am afraid of saying something tactless.

Have you heard from him?

Are those paintings in *The Artist's View*, #8, Jess's own?[1] I am always poring over it & each time I find something more.

No, that poem "Laying the Dust" wasn't measured out, it was written all in one go.* About "The Lovers" I know exactly what Olson means but I have tried to give it sober consideration & I don't think it is true of this poem.[2]

*But yes, it does *sound* a bit careful somehow.

I made the following cuts in that one called "Tomatlan" wh. I think I sent you:

> #I
> Cut 1st line
> #II
> Cut last 4 words
> #III
> read the end as follows:
>> screws them, until they
>> are blue flames, green
>> smoke, and
>> screws them again
>>> (5 words cut, the lines adjusted).

What you last sent I liked very much and reread often. To think of them is an excitement—a constriction in the breast as when one thinks of whatever is irrevocably lost, loved, poignant or possible—

We are having torrential rains and also slow drenching drizzly rains & fierce hailstorms. The house is slowly disintegrating around us.

How is B. Mountain for you? Who mails off *B.M.R.*s? Wd. you please ask them to send me one soon? I'm absolutely pining for it.

With love from
Denise

**29**

July 18, {19}56
{Black Mountain
College}

dear Denise—

Yesterday I wrappd and prepared for the mail your two copies of *BMR*—and so was ready in some conscience to write to you today. And now a letter from you and a new poem which prepares me to write a new poem. I have been entirely the damnable delay on your getting the magazine: first putting it off on rumors of your moving—but today or tomorrow it will actually be in the mail (I have to mail mags from Asheville, because Black Mountain post questions if it really is a book or not—and as *not* charges some fantastic mailing fee)—

I have been the tactless one in the Rexroth-Creeley rounds: writing to forestall if I could Marthe's decision to go to Taos, and at the same time knowing—as Jess reassures me, as well as others on the San Francisco scene—that Kenneth had made it quite impossible for Marthe to choose to go on with him. Now, I would clear the air of my charges: for once she has made the decision, for the children and for Marthe and Bob there must be all the clearing for a new life. It sticks in my craw that life is not cleard nor new just like that, and rises from my heart that it must be. Can we have regard for some particular one when we do not have it then everywhere? I am more a partisan of the household, the things loved, than of starting all over again. And so have a disrelation too to the situation.

I am partisan of Bob because I think of him as tougher and of him as independent; and antagonist of Bob because I think of him as keeping double accounts, embezzling with the funds of the actual. And so: the real is sentimental in part. But this is substantially Kenneth too. He is self-unprepared for this actual and real loss.

. . .

BELOW: But searching for ms. for ms. For "A Poem Slow Beginning" I found (these pages had been forwarded to me in N.Y. during vacation interim and only read then once) the second ms. of "Tomatlan"—all is clear now.

I am perplexd in trying to correlate your revisions with the poem "Tomatlan" I have. You say: (1) cut first the line of # I

    [At the touch]————————cut
    of the sea wind
            the palms
    etc.

(2) cut last 4 words of #II

        rustling fingers—
    flames of desire and pleasure.
    [the sea wind that]————————cut

O.K. both of these seem to bring us by cut more directly into the poem. But what I can't relate to # III is: does the

    screws then, until they
    are blue flames etc.

follow "voluptuous"
or/but what 5 words are cut, what lines adjusted?

This whole group of Mexican poems has rich interplay now—and as new bits arrive I have the lovely occasion of reading thru a growing book of the intense scene. And become impatient with my own present practice, tempted to draw upon, read the landscape. I set my "meanings" class to drawing upon the dense foliage of light and air moved and moving forest outside the classroom.

Myself, I am still reading, in little islands of tolerance, Nietsche's *Zarathustra* and have in mind continuing the "Structure of Rime" as such a "learning," an evocation of teachers and receiving of counsels. Enclosed: III of same, a snake-daemon speaking.

With two other pieces in progress: the self-singing poem opening passage of which I send here too; and a new play which starts out from early acts of Jason and Medea where ever hither bound.[1]

My teaching schedule is heavy this summer—with two full courses of study. And a third full course in reading Rimbaud's *Illuminations* or How to Make one's way as an amateur in the French Language.

The morning has hurried away: and the hour for my afternoon class advances. I will spend some time at the typewriter now preparing sample texts for you.

With love and my regards to Mitch and Nik.

Robert[2]

---

**30**

{July 1956
Guadalajara, Mex.}

Dear Robert,

"Tomatlan" goes like this:

I

The sea quiet, shadow-colored and
without shadows.
From which shall rise
the sea wind, moving
swiftly towards the
steep jungles. The sea wind
the awakener.

II

The sea wind is
a panther moving
swiftly towards the
mountain jungles.
Its silky fur
brushes me.

III

The green palmettos of the
blue jungle

shake their
green breasts, their stiff
green hair—
the wind, the sea wind is come
and touches them
lightly, and strokes them, and
screws them, until they
are blue flames, green
smoke, and
screws them again.

     IV
At the touch
of the sea wind
    the palms
shake their green breasts, their

    rustling fingers—
flames of desire and pleasure.
The sea wind that

    moves like a panther
blows the spray inland.
    Voluptuous

and simple—the world is
larger than one had thought.
It is a

new peace
shades the mind here
with jungle shadows
    frayed by the
sea wind.

I guess I sent you only part of it or something. Enclosed also is another new one.

The quote about yr. ballads thank god is not so embarrassing as I'd feared & yr. preface is damned interesting.

I wrote to Kenneth finally—my impulse to do so was too keen to withstand & so I can't regret it even if he doesn't take it right. I just said I felt anxious about him, having heard (then) the bare rudiments of what had happened, & knowing how he felt about his children.—Sent my love, & hoped he would write when he could. The thing is, that makes me feel so sad, that long ago (before I met Mitch) when K. heard I had had an abortion under very unhappy circumstances, quite a story, he was so distressed & said why hadn't I told him, I cd. have come to S. F. & had it, he wd. have helped me, & that he himself had always wanted children but his 1st wife feared insanity and his 2d apparently couldn't have any. Of course it was an impossible idea even if it had not been too late but I was much affected by his letter wh. was true and wistful.

Anyway, I hope it works for Bob—tho' I'd have said what he needed was not a woman but to stand alone without a woman for a while, so that when he found one, later, maybe, there wd. be some more voluntary meeting between him & her, not the close dependence of a—I think it's called a demand-need?

John Herrmann (you know who that is? if not, see W. C. W. autobiography —tho that gives a very incomplete idea of him) who's been living here for 7 yrs & for longer than that hasn't written a word, has bought a typewriter & is renting a room & is going to work again. We are very happy about that.

"A Poem Slow Beginning" is very beautiful, with many depths and sur-faces, having in common with what George MacDonald I have read, that its simplicities are complex—not casuistry, not deceptions, but retaining their integrity as what at first they seem, while being *as well* other than what they seem—like the Hasidic *counterparts*, too.[1]

I imagine Coleridge to have been very like you in many ways. But he lost himself ? as he grew older, & you won't.

Those kids at Black Mountain are very lucky, to be studying with you. For that I wish I were there—tho' everything else I've heard about the place assures me I wouldn't thrive there at all.

Thanks very much for sending off the *B.M.R.*'s. I'm looking forward to them.

I'm waiting now to hear from Ferlinghetti, which poems he wants, so that I can select for Jonathan.[2]

Love from
Denise.

---

**31**

August 7th {1956
{Guadalajara, Mex.}

Did I send you a poem called "The Bird"?

Dear Robert

Thanks very much for the *B.M.R.*'s. Jess' translations are the end. Enclosed is a small present for him.

We went to Mexico City for a few days, and saw Al's {Albert Kresch} paintings & pastels in the gallery at wh. Gogo Nesbitt works. They looked terrific and we felt proud of him. And there were also some good paintings by an older man in N.Y. Earl Kerkham I think his name is and a magnificent large painting of a waterfall, having a relationship I thought to the best of Courbet but iridescent in color, by one André Vandenbroek who turned out to be the same André Al had spoken of, and husband to Gogo. We went to visit them in a wonderful old house in an old suburb. But I didn't like Gogo. She's a fox. And a poseuse. At least so she impressed me. There was a time during the evening when I was liking her but as the time past what I'd liked seemed false.

Mitch is in the W. Indies for 3 wks on a job for *Atlantic Monthly*. I was going to go but in the end it wasn't possible. I was disappointed but not too badly.

I keep buying a paper game they sell in the market here to send you because the figures look as if they may have originated in something like Tarot, but Nik always uses them first, thinking they are for him. Next week.

Enclosed also are some poems.

Love
from Denise.

Dear Robert,

The mailman's horn sounded—I flew out to the gate—he handed me the package with a special smile as if he knew what was in it—and there was the book of drawings,[1] which I unwrapped between the gate & the door!

I think that's just the loveliest thing to do. I never had a present that made me happier.

That night I started writing something quite different from anything I'd ever done before. I don't know if it'll come off, but it's a direction anyway. Started by the book of drawings.

*Thank you.*

I had such a nice letter from Mike McClure. It ended, "Yesterday Jess read us Robert's *Medea* in a beautiful park." I didn't know there was a *Medea*. That's something to look forward to.

When I was packing I put *Faust* by mistake among the things I was putting away instead of with what I was bringing, damn it. Reading over *My Life in Art* (Stanislavsky) recently I've been thinking a lot about the theatre (also because of WCW's letter about *Waiting for Godot*.)[2] My ballet class is beginning rehearsals of Swan Lake for a festival but I can't take part because I can't get to 3 rehearsals a week. They're in the evenings & as I go to 2 classes a week anyway it wd. mean too much time away from Nik at bedtime. I'm disappointed because I seem to have stage fever. Did you know Gordon Craig is still alive—84, lives at Vence. There was an interview with him in the London *Observer*.[3]

With love—
Denise

**32**

September 9 {1956}
Guadalajara, Mex.

**33**

dear Denise/

*The Field* or perhaps *The Opening of the Field*—the book that will follow *Letters* is under-way; as this morning I devoted to typing up manuscripts to date on it. "The Structure of Rime" I plan to be a long work, in-folded in the book. Nietzsche's *Zarathustra* gave me the start: I shall leave the form of the poem open, theoretically without end. Returning to it, I think, thruout the book. But allowing that there will be another year's work before I actually compose the book, I have been almost unwisely bold in declaring its existence this early. Some of these poems, all of these poems? you have already. This ms. anyway to bring them together in a tighter sequence.

Jess and I found the best apartment we have had yet. And both Kit Kat and Pumpkin are back with us; I have a beautiful little writing desk, made for writing letters—so perhaps I shall fulfill its promise. The augurs predict exhaustion and oppression; the light contradicts the portent. The augurs may be right, for I have been exhausted so far by anything, by often dubious tasks in my job as Assistant Director on the Poetry Center, by smoking, by people . . . there seem to be too infrequent idle moments that permit idling. And then I want luxuries of books, records and painting extravagantly. I sent the *Homage to Coleridge* off to Caetani, maybe she will want the whole, and there will be money someday.[1] I am going to send "The Dance," "The Structure of Rime," and "A Poem Slow Beginning" to *Poetry New York London,* for the chance that they might buy something, but my doubts grow. DBTS for debits and doubts.

Paradise of San Francisco! I shall never leave again. Marthe is still with Kenneth. Tho Kenneth's moods are shifty and often unpleasant. Bob sent some small poems from Albuquerque. The *Ark* is out.[2] Black Mountain College suspended operations. *The Maiden Head* may be done here—I will send a typescript in a few days-daze.[3]

Love
Robert

**34**

Dear Robert,

Thank you for the *Field.* Yes I'd seen almost all, but not all, & in any case to read them in their order is different. I wont comment for fear of sounding trite. Except to say it all bears the print of your hand which to me is a master hand.

Did you ever get the letter in which a little print was enclosed for Jess? And the letter I wrote when the drawing-book came? I'm glad you like being back in S.F. And that you got your cats back alright. Our Hawthorn got lost soon after we left, alas. Here we have none but there's a very nice dog who visits sometimes.

We received *Howl* a few days ago. It seems to us very impressive—
Jonathan had written disparagingly of it but having seen it I think he was
just being petty. It has the strength & truth of a man's real voice—nothing
put-up, contrived, smoothed to please—yet it has variety within itself—it's
not a strident complaint—there's a non-sugary sweetness (honey) in a line
like "The kindly search for growth, the gracious desire to exist of the
flowers . . . "—akin to Whitman's "Tall sunflower creaking on its stalk"—
but it's with Smart he belongs much more than with Whitman. Anyway,
with the exception of some of the earlier things at the end these poems live
in themselves & are undeniable.

I think it exceptionally petty of J. to say " . . . might titillate Poetry
Lovers at an Intimate Reading" . . . "fortissimo" . . . etc. That little boy at
heart likes a nice tidy little artwork I suspect & no loose ends. I'm going to
tell him too.

Moreover, I'm shocked to see Cid's jealousy of Jonathan, Jonathan's of
Ferlinghetti—Wow!

I took my mother on a trip to Michoacan (Morelia—Patzuaro—the small
island of Janitzio) & saw wonderful country, Tarascan Indians, pots, copper
pans, & many lovely things; maybe I'll try to describe some in my next letter.
Sometimes I feel I cd. spend the rest of my life in Mexico. Not here tho'.

Love—
D.

dear Denise,

At last—a ms of the first *Medea* play for you! Caetani askt to see it for
*Botteghe Oscure*—if she would take it, it would mean a good sum of money
to tide me over. But I have major doubts. So far, given her choice she has
selected the periphery and rejected all central work. And this one—at the
heart—no, I cannot believe she will take it.

But typing the manuscript for the possibility gave me a copy for you—
and that is a great reward for me.

Off we must go to town, to post office—

love,
Duncan

Dear Robert,

We had a 2 day visitation here—Allen Ginsberg, Gregory Corso, Peter &
Lafcadio Orlovsky.[1] Corso, among a welter, had some good poems to show,
Allen only a pretty depressing notebook. There was a kind of gentleness
among/between them that I liked. But the aftertaste of their visit isn't too

## 35

{October 1956
San Francisco}

## 36

November 12th {1956}
Florencia 1915
Guadalajara, Mex.

good. How the hell do they manage to be quite so young? At first I responded to it, being impressionable, by feeling & acting young myself. But by the end I was feeling a little bored & about 80 yrs old.

I tried to get news of you but they clammed up for some reason.

Do you know a Corot called *Le Pont de Mantes*? I have a black & white reproduction of it from the Mondadori edition open on my desk.[2] It represents a world, a view of the world (a little bit of it) that I feel I can realize. When they say to me I should take marijuana, peyote, etc, & see the natural world enlarged & intensified I look at that, or at a preColumbian pot or warrior, or out of the window, & I feel no yen to see this other world mechanically introduced to the perceptions—that is, from curiosity I'd like to see it but I don't feel a longing for it. I want much more to make something of what I have. It's like finishing what you have on your plate before you ask for more.

And then, the making of a mystique out of what they (individually & collectively) are; that seems to me adolescent. One wants to relate one experience to another, to perceive one's experience {so} that it fulfills its weight & meaning—but they go beyond that & make every experience have more importance than it can carry.

It seems not necessity but loneliness that makes them elevate necessities into virtues. Well, & loneliness is unavoidable; & they love each other & have this gentleness. But they *cultivate* loneliness & all else, till qualities lose their original wild robust character; lose their scent as some flowers do when gardenbred. Now I'm writing at random to see what I think—

They tasted the splendours & miseries of adolescence & wish to maintain the sensation when they should be growing older. Perhaps.

Nik fell for Peter in his red hat, who came & played in the garden with him & the other kids & told about carton houses he'd built as a kid with real rooms in them—you cd. crawl from room to room if you were small enough—

Mitch is going to a small place on the coast with John Herrmann to work undisturbed—Nik & I will go for Xmas. Bob may come down then—we just had a good letter from him.

What's *Ark* like? I've not seen it yet. Are you in it? Write soon—

Love from
Denise

**37**

November 15, {19}56
{San Francisco}

dear Denise/

Re: the poetry of Ginsberg, I haven't replied to it as I will: his sense of life when he is at his best (in a recent poem "At Sather Gate" for instance) is *finer* than his idea of *person* allows. He pushes his poetry—almost as his generation push their drugs and sex. It is only the pushing that alienates me. But then it is quite a lot of "only" that only. And I think I am reticent about making it clear to Allen that he has a spirit I like at work: because this other organiser Ginsberg would use such an admission. The group were a little like political ward workers and I excused myself from every participation. Corso's folk poems (like "I Married the Pig's Daughter" which might take an equal stand with immortal Mother Goose) are good indeed again; but he flatterd and threatend (if you are with us you are *great*; if you aren't . . . —a terrible either/or) and so little respected my reserves that I ended by quite disliking him. Jess who is more seriously alarmed by public-mindedness than I am, and by the assaults of "brotherhood" threw Ginsberg and Peter out of the house when they came to see me, and made it clear that:[1] but we had both decided in Europe that when I took the job at the Poetry Center the household would be kept for friends. I do not believe that one can close one's doors to the demand—whatever, without a cost in closing doors to life: but I am willing to undertake the cost in homage to the household which I worship and draw from.

The painful thing for me is that Jess has turnd against Bob—but he must have been opposed in some way from the first. Jess and I so much see in common: but my love for Bob deepens—as the love for his poetry deepens by sympathies that I would be happier if they were shared. Well, they are shared by Madeline Gleason who shows an understanding of Bob—a recognition. And oddly enuf, I find Rexroth's respect for the quality persists. Tho the personal sense is—I might say *of course*—wildly distorted by fantasies.

In Jess's case I recognize that a decision was made—a decision that has some seeds of the fantastic: that someone might come as Bob did to Kenneth's household and bring the Storm.

But I proclaim the Storm. It has been here since the beginning. And if Jess had doubt of my love for him I have none.

But poor dear Bob! His poems show a real longing for Marthe. And Kenneth has never allowd that they might have been in love. It mars the fine thing—the green tip for feeling. And I feel horribly betrayd at having flown to the protection of Kenneth's household—it was the sense of the children who do seem to me to have so much in him.

It is some other letter I wanted to write—about some new poets here. About your beautiful "Pepper Trees."[2] But I shall write soon; not *reactions*— (this seems almost wearily reaction above) but realities. I am slowly finding time to type out the play for you and for Bob—maybe now that he will be visiting you I can send the one carbon for all to read and have the other for sending to a magazine or two.

Love
Duncan

and now Denise . . . a full month later but I shall go ahead by pen—which I prefer: and then, it is a late hour to be pounding the machine-writer. Why didn't I send off this letter of November 15 when I wrote it? Perhaps that I felt talking about "my love for Bob" etc. was un-measured. And I mistrust the effusion of it which is not the ring of the actual thing. Well, now I send it however it rings. The measured holding feeling I have is reading new poems as in *If You* which arrived a week ago.[1] And that writing to Bob like writing to you has for me a special field: in which I can range whole heartedly. Within my range—that one can be "ranged" as differing from being "de-ranged."

There is a promise at least of a new packet of my work to appear in a San Francisco collection to be done by Grove Press—they askd for ten to fifteen poems: I sent eleven sections from 1946—each year thru 1956, a poem per year—of work that has not been publishd and that won't be in books forthcoming. It's a good solid selection—once I set about it and composed it, I was (am) enthusiastic. There had been a promise when Laughlin wrote asking for work for *New Directions*—I sent sections from *Writing Writing*. I wanted it most to go along with, as counterpoint to, *Letters*. But Laughlin, Kenneth tells me, did not like the work at all. These are all, right now, distractions from the new play which has me in its grips. It's like being on the scent, the very lure: I am in the thick of excitement (worry) of realizing the thing. And what bursts it gives me—of freshets long pending.

And for Christmas, for Christmas I must have conquerd the one small first act scene before which I am stoppd (it needs some reconception and I have not the courage)—then the rest is so beautifully just what I would live by.

Jonathan writes go ahead on the drawings for *Letters*—I have them completed, a sequence of my *Ideal Reader*—who is a little old woman quite at the heart of nature who knows and drinks up so much more of lore and life than I do—and graces me by reading, as she graces a bird by listening or a landscape by recognizing. There she sits reading or listening or thinking: watering her garden or holding her cat. And what cares she of what she knows of my possible career—of whether there is to be an anthology or a book or a review: she reads me thru and thru as she reads all the writing of the world for the world in it or thru it. Shall she be W. C. W.'s "so be it?"

December 17—morning/with good winter sunlight to write a little further by, and a sink cleard of last night's and breakfast's litter and washd down behind me; and assignments before me of finding a goose for Xmas and getting mail out. The Poetry Center job gnaws away at my freshness. This coming year I've scheduled Charles, Robert Lowell and Marianne Moore—all of whom I would stand by (tho I haven't read *The Mills of the Kavanaughs*—Lowell's later work, the fervor of the earlier poetry moved me).[2] But *essentially* the concept of a civic activity I cannot stand by. At every point I am liable to betray my contempt. And today I am somehow or anyhow over filld with it. "Lose their original wild robust character, lose their scent as some flowers do when garden bred" you write of the cultivated. It is beautiful warning. I can take it from its application to the Ginsberg exploitation of loneliness, and transfer it to my dangerous excitement at points of exaltation: for I might have my cultivations. And no wonder then I am revolted by all this promotion of, cultivation of Poetry, until one craves a colossal scorn that would put it all down.

Yet Rexroth who does put it down seems both right and in a deeper sense wrong. With the prospect of Charles—he is vilifying him and I cannot find words that would stop it—stop Kenneth before my feeling for him shrinks to a sentimentality. And he has a program of a kind against what he calls the "vulgarity" of Marianne Moore's last book. What can or doesn't this word "vulgarity" mean? But spite seems paramount in these campaigns of Rexroth's and spite is a shriveld reasoner indeed. And concerning me thus—with continued blasts against Bob, Charles or Miss Marianne Moore, he is so clearly knifing the heart of me: that my closest concerns are bound up with these is daily evidence.

Now, if ever this is to fly directly to you I must put this in an envelope— search for perhaps a poem to enclose and send to you and Mitch our greetings for the turn of the year and Christ's celebrated birthday—

love
Robert

dear Denise,

This is one of those impulsive mornings—and this poor little yellow sheet must be scrawld over because it is I myself who would like to be stepping out of an envelope to say hello—to be there; or, for I am tenaciously at home, to be here. Return postage guaranteed then. To say hello, and ¿what? I don't know. I am filld with arguments this morning. I read poor (but "poor" as it betokens also deprived of riches) old Yvor Winters in the *Hudson Review*, chewing the ulcer-haunted cud of "Whither ye poets and ye professors"?[1] And I've to declare for New Year's resolution one to resign from the Poetry Center sinecure or I wither. [As in a story of M. P. Shiel's a lost man in a bottle-cave befouls his own air, over years.][2] And the ear for its delight craves the clearest disinterested air, for spontaneous passion in response. I wish I were shy or incapable of seeing a crowd of human virtues.—but it's just the degenerating fact that I can attend to poems which in any natural course of events would never come my way that makes one useful to the P. C. Away with it all, then.

## 39

December 31, {19}56
{San Francisco}

I have learnd to cheer myself up and clear a way by writing "gift" poems, not for ever publication. Perhaps going so long unpublishd at all makes me "odd" about that activity—and in most terms I'm still not legitimately botherd by publication. But here is one, the first in "A Little Buk of Songs and Pictures for Jess" for the lares of the household and the counsel of friends:

To Pumpkin-Cat

Grey guide, dear gay
   solemn heart's messenger,
Pumpkin we calld you—Oz
was first Heaven—and like
   Jack Pumpkinhead
you are perpetually fond and
   foolish-wise.

Go before us, where you are
we are,
   heart's[3] furrd, purring silver spirit,
delight indwelling in your smile
as if carved by your nature
   for our thot.

And we will remember. A magic
is happiness that
   —evasive but faithful—
household elf-cats, selves,
painted landscapes and faces,  songs
   celebrate; that this
great reality is most Oz     and you
     continually poet thereof.

love
Duncan[4]

---

**40**

January 15th {1957
Guadalajara, Mex.}

Bob was down here 3 days. It was good.

Dear Robert

Thanks—for Xmas card, letters, poems. Got back from the beach yesterday & have umpteen yearly Xmas letters from dear but un-writing friends—friends from other times & places—to answer so I'll get that done before I write properly to you. Love to Jess.

Love from
Denise

I was going to write to you from among the coconut palms but I got malaria & afterwards just vegetated.

P.S.

*Here & Now* came from Ferlinghetti at last—on the anniversary of the day I parted—I suppose for ever—from John Day on the corner of Christopher St. & 7th Avenue W.—(Next day we left N.Y. and came to Mexico)—indeed it must be forever: it has taken me all of a year to give new life to my marriage & to Mitch. It has seemed often like a denial of life itself, yet I find myself no less alive—only older. And happy enough to find myself wanting another child—but I don't think we will be having one. The book is a nice green—alder or willow—but the poems abash me somewhat—it all seems small & weak—but I'll be sending you your copy as soon as I get them (I have only the one advance copy as yet, which Mitch & I will keep.)

Meanwhile Jonathan seems to be going ahead on the other book.[1] Wish I could find even one poem of his that I could honestly say I liked—so far no, I can't abide 'em, & it makes me feel guilty towards him, wishing there were more mutual admiration between us.

Love—

D.

Dear Robert,

I wish you could indeed, as you say, step out of an envelope. I put off writing to you because of all the Xmas letters & things I wanted to get out of the way first—now it seems there are things I wanted to write about that are already half-forgotten. For instance the way the sea was on one side of the sandbar, & on the other the lagoon, so different, only a 100 yards or so apart (except that I dont really know how far 100 yards is—if you were here I could say, only as far as that wall from here). And the armadillo. And the patterns of the coconut-palm jungle. And many other things. I have poems about 1 or 2 things wh. I will send.

Meanwhile I am concerned lest I've hurt Mike McClure's feelings in a letter I sent him giving my reactions to his poems. I'd be sorry anyway to have done so, but am all the more so because he's a friend of yours. I've sent him another note to say I was sorry if I'd stepped over decent bounds—I don't set up to be a critic, in fact I distrust the very idea of criticism in some ways, but he asked for my reactions; now his silence (before that he had been bombarding me with letters) makes me feel I said more than was useful.

I get an idea of what you must have felt about Ginsberg from a letter he wrote me from N.Y. describing his "planned rape of the city" e.g. seeing Laughlin, Grove Press, ed. of *Mlle.*, etc etc, but *everybody*—in a word,

## 41

February 1 {1957}
Florencia 1915
Guadalajara, Jalisco
Mexico.

hustling like mad. He's apparently been hustling on my behalf as well as on his own & Corso's which is very kind of him I think but hell, how is he going to survive as a person & as a poet if he carries on that way. He seems also to have "discovered" O'Hara, Ashbery et al., a group I regard with great suspicion. So; I don't like all that. But he has something very nice about him too.

Are you quitting the Poetry Center job then?[1] I shd. think you had had enough of it. How to live, what to do. Have you any available alternatives? Good to quit, anyway.

I think I told you Bob spent 3 days at the sea with us? It was good. And today a letter came in which he sounds refreshed & cheerful, new events having again changed things for him—but I won't tell you his news, no doubt he has told you himself, or will. All you say of yr. play, and other work, makes me long for the time to come when I can see it. I often wish I cd. come to S. F. & have a week's feast of reading, listening, looking.

But what I want most is to re-establish here the kind of rhythm I had in the spring of last year, that broke when Nik's school vacation began; keep a notebook & write with almost regularity. I learned that I could do it, as I had believed; but once interrupted it's hard for me to get back to it.

Re. publication (also about translations), of wh. you speak in a December letter, here's a quote from a letter of Edwd. Fitzgerald "I hardly know why I print any of these things, which nobody buys; & I scarce now see the few I give them to. But when one has done one's best, & is sure that that best is better than so many will take pains to do, though far from the best that *might be done*, one likes to make an end of the matter by Print. I suppose very few People have ever taken such Pains in Translation as I have: though certainly not to be literal. But at all Cost, a thing must *live*: with a transfusion of one's own worse life if one can't retain the Original's better. Better a live Sparrow than a Stuffed Eagle."[2]

---

Have been reading some novels of Elisabeth Madox Roberts—*The Time of Man* & *Black is My True Love's Hair*—She had her own proper voice,[3] a prose with its own melodic line & distinctive harmonies, not often seeming merely a manner, no, mostly living its life quite undeniably, with force, dignity, flexibility, & zest. It seems she was a southern woman, had a hard life, published nothing till 40 or more—but I know almost nothing about her. She died 10 or so years ago.

Thank you for the poems—("To Pumpkin Cat," & 3 poems from a birthday book.)[4] Thank you also (differently) for mentioning me to Donald Allen (Evergreen) who wrote to me recently. I also had a nice letter from a friend of yours, Robin Blaser—I hope he got my reply alright.

Love to Jess.

Love from
Denise

dear Denny/

I've a cold cup of coffee, a cigarette and a rainy day! And a kitchen table to sit at and an opulent begonia plant to sit under to write letters. And an afternoon to work on manuscripts (to get some off to you and Bob and Robin Blaser in Boston) and only one nightmare—the Poetry Center where I must see the fact of poetry exploited and promoted until I sicken on the vine—but that nightmare I push this morning back, back into some corner as best I can to see if I can recover a bit of grace.

There's been the sheaf of poems from you. This clean direct line lifts me. Those "Pepper Trees" and now "The Departure"[1]—it's the non-dream day light facts of the imagination. And if it survives, if there is an element—this water is specific. How nervous my tensions seem to me compared! I have further still to go I think in struggling (intellectualizing) with metrics—but I would have a prayer that it might soon drop away, the armor of it, and only the natural skeleton remain: showing in such ease the deepest (deformations) incisions of style only. It's things like:

" . . . nowadays. And for god's sake
    don't let's leave in the end. . . . "

                            that I'd like to come to my hand-ear-eye. These poems are seeds of content. Both Jess and I spent a bright morning yesterday—and we send on a sheaf to entertain in return.

After months of hearing all—and there is such a muchedumbre of poets—the readings here, discrimination or discretion is a paramount emotional necessity. Tolerance is fatal—I want only now what I can love and let the rest go. There are old claims to disclaim. For years I have, if remotely in the last years—but still by hoping—been involved with Jack Spicer's work: but it is a poetry used for inflicting miseries that proliferate from masturbation fantasies (the more painful because he projects now a poetry of the wet-dream)—And at last I find that {I} can no longer question my disaffection. Jess says beautifully that he (Spicer) gains one's attention by promising to amuse or excite and then abuses the promise: the listener entertains his poem—and his poem transgresses guest rights, proves not to be a poem but a personal whine.

As, again, I find un-truth in Rexroth's Marthe poems—mixd with true feeling—and the more terrible for that—sentimentalities—his self image—and avoidance of reality.[2] He defaults from moral knowledge of himself. And in that—where he can speak of many qualities—he can not speak (or perhaps see) her moral knowledge. If the poem is to be personal it needs in addition to the personality (the self-image), the measure of emotional fact. I dislike the self-image of oneself as hero (but can we escape it? I don't worry *that*) and the projection of all debility, coldness, degeneration upon the "they."

**42**

February 12, 1957
{San Francisco}

It don't ring true.

I assent to Arthur in *The Maiden Head* who cries out: "I have come to loath all person." . . . that obscures what the man is. Paramount now that the poem not excite admiration or disgust for the author—but be made a *thing*—an object bearing only necessary trace that we might infer from the working of the worker.

Do you have a long-play phonograph? I have a good record made from a broadcast on KPFA of recent work that I'd like you to have if you can play it. I've decided—with the reaction to the Poetry Center on my heart—not to read in "public." There is an actual number of those who want to hear ones work. Which makes the false culture-centerd audience the more repugnant. In the worst attack of my disgusts (at the nadir of a bout with the flu almost a month ago) I even wrote a letter asking for *Letters* back from Jonathan because I felt used there somehow. The tone—whiskey-glass in hand, *Gentry* Magazine—of his spring announcements belie my work. But I didn't mail it: I did write a letter later of disaffections—with the language; and with his linking Patchen with Blake which can only be done in ignorance of Blake. In my introduction to Jonathan's poems I think I anticipated the disabilities as well as the virtues. He has enthusiasms but not passions. He collects experience; don't undergo the world. I don't think that what you want in a poem is there at all. I like resistant style and clever invention even divorced from necessary powers: is one a little sad that there is no ear for the spirit that moves a music, that the eye is so satisfied with the effect? And so misses Ginsberg who eschews the clever—who goes as a spirit moves him. Or as Jonathan writes when I objected to his saying Nobody he knows reads Lowell—that he still can't find anything in it.—if I am to get to manuscripts . . . I close abruptly—

love
Robert

**43**

March 1, {19}57
{San Francisco}

dear Denny/

Tonight I shall have your book in my hands! And then there will be as there was with Bob's *If You*, must be, the time for all that full response I wait for—the flood-out of energies.

Right now this letter only to accompany this poem I am mid-way on: "The Propositions." That springs into itself from the excitements, tunings up, resistance and confirmations of Olson's visit here—still in progress. Tonite is the last of five evenings where he has given his "Special View of History."[1]

But let the long letter come this week-end. And this note exclaim! As if by design these longd-for full-fillings between now having heard (over three public readings, not duplicating) and four "lectures" a book of Charles's unprinted poems. And together gatherd your collection. Which sometimes (dreams I would read,) so waited for it to appear.

love
Robert

Dear Robert,

44

March 7th {1957}
{Guadalajara, Mex.}

Too bad you got the book before I could send it you—but will be sending a copy anyway when it comes, shd. be in a day or 2 now. I'm afraid it will have been a disappointment because just about all the poems must be familiar & a number of them are not recent—but I feel I stand by it & so I hope you will have liked it anyway.

The other morning I woke straight from a dream which I here transcribe, I think in the exact words of the dream, tho' of course the pictures which the narration accompanied I can't reproduce.

"Once there was a bear; and as he went through the woods he saw a tree, and climbed it, its leaves as he thought looking fair and very fine to eat—being like bears, like dogs or the ears of dogs, like gods. But alas it was the wicked tasman tree, & once up in its boughs the bear was captured, finding himself half-bear, half-boughs. 'Ach, how bad it is up here,' he would cry out, 'with the tree's mocking voice calling out *Dinner? Dinner?*" all day long.' But at nights he would become all bear again, & wander freely in the woods; & that was good."

I didn't answer your earlier letter because Mitch has been sick with hepatitis & I've been running up & down stairs with trays, shopping for pills & special food, phoning the doctor etc. & also feeling inordinately tired. You said some things, especially about "The Departure," for which I thank you with joy. And you sent poems—among them that wonderful "Mrs. Noah" (which by the way I read to Nik, who was spellbound & wanted *more*.) And Jess's nightjar! And now this new one with the quick action of the cook & Old Man River & the interaction of its parts—something that even tho' I haven't gotten a proper hold on it in my mind strikes me as having much more substance than the E. Sitwellian "Ballad of the Enamourd Mage," which seems selfindulgent in a way I cannot care for. Or inbred; or self-generating.[1] I'm not sure what word to use. It is perhaps a failure of response in me only, connected with my distrust of E. Sitwell especially in her later poems. I don't think any poet, however different in kind, can afford to forget the words "No ideas but in things."[2] And yet there are such moving (moving) lines in the poem. And yet the total effect distresses me. And yet (I want you to know) because to me you are one of the great, as well as belov'd, I have never & will never speak "critically" of you to anyone but yourself. It is a liberty I take but I think you will forgive it. And it is so rarely I don't like whatever comes from you.

No, we don't have a record player unfortunately. But we know someone here who does—they are not the perfect people in whose company to listen to the record but they wouldn't be bad either—so if you cd. send it I would be very very glad.

Wish I could have heard Olson.

We are moving to Oaxaca in June but already some sense of departure has hold of me. This place is changing rapidly & losing some of the poignant qualities that made the landscape interchangeable with my feelings last spring. So I welcome the prospect of change, even tho' there's that feeling of its taking me even further away from everyone I know & love except my immediate family.

Enclosed are a few poems from the last few weeks.

With love<br>from Denise.

I guess you know the poem called "Homage" (in the book) is for you. I was never sure if you liked it or not, or if is was good enough, but now I see it in print I don't feel ashamed of it, and it is yours.

---

**45**

March 9 {10}, 1957
{San Francisco}

dear Denise/

Yes, I knew the poem "Homage" was for me; and I was shy of it. Truth trembles in ardor. You, I, the great, all the living must tremble if the life (isn't it the livingness that we do homage to, we have the homage to make for) is, where it is touchd. I write that there be there in the poem, somewhere in the total work passages of "the great": but when you recognize that (as the urgencies of belief, of love command) I would let it be. And then the Beloved and the great are of the human thing. Before which the person is rightly shy, rightly less. Truth rightly trembles. As does my reticence mislead (where in the letter to you it was misunderstood—I had that all so proceeded so from my discovery of closest kinship). That your poems move awareness in me, give life. But I would be shy, "speechless" there too, about the hidden thing that "deep" is. "Great" and "Beloved" are such used words that it needs the full focus of powers to give definition. That would be secret to all that does not recognize. There. That is it, your recognition is always present to me. Because of that recognition, the distress at the Mallorca ballads or the Mage is true for me. I obey whatever leads me into the act of writing. There are particular forms that demand most of me, where I recognize strength. In the sheer indulgence of fantasy there are unmanifest (bodiless) powers that strength (definition) does not overtake. I have dis-appointments as well as appointments with the real; and let them be. Or, rather, go with them as far as I can. (As going with Edith Sitwell I have found in-substantial grandeurs that ask substance; it is not distrust of the unreal, but love of the real that moves me to search elsewhere: that makes Williams substantially "great" for me). I shall never select for you—I want all to be given—because you will demand the real. It is my homage to you.

Here are two more sections of "The Propositions." Charles's lectures led me back to *Leaves of Grass* (where I had rememberd his "noiseless patient spider")—and then in one evening—after writing Homage à Whitman section 5—I read, finding the two other poems I will send on with this.

Well, then—it is early dark morning; and I shall go to bed, read on in *Leaves*—with the touch of your letter still vivid—-

love
Robert

March 10 {19}57

McClure gave me *Origin* XX with the Wade Donahoe letter to read[1]— but the disturbing twist of that letter is not Donahoe's animimadversion in writing of my work—but Corman's malice that would use a cat's paw. He had the best material from *Letters* submitted in answer to his request for something for XX (this in Europe). That he rejected it was statement of one thing (as Olson told me only that he, I, Creeley and then I noticed Blackburn were not included)—but the parting gesture to leave if it were possible the picture of me construed with lifted eyebrows, pseudo-feminine (¿effeminate?), Pound-posteuring—is another thing. A gratuitous effort.

(As submitting *Black Mountain Review* to whatever parting swipes; or the condescending appraisal of Bob—not-entirely disposable but we must get in "I wish he would grow up")—Are we being paid back for a disregard. I think so. But all my efforts to regard Corman where I could—in the poetry—were met with letters that discouraged all reading.

When I sent the Letter to you to *Origin*—Corman forwarded it to Olson with the query "Why is Duncan making fun of, ridiculing, you?"[2] and had it not been for love there that held thru Olson's reading the poem as that, and bellowing with the outrage, I should have lost all. Olson took the hurt (as it came from Corman) and I knew nothing of that testing until I read Charles's letters to Bob—but what fearful malice that would bring such trials to joy. Hofmannstahl writes "There are no two people on this earth who could not be turnd into deadly enemies by a devilishly contrived indiscretion." (from the Book of Friends) and now that I have gone there to look the aphorism up.[3] Another—

> The next of kin see in a person's attitudes towards the world the intentions, which are usually the purer part; those more distant see the realization into which many impure, even evil things have often enterd.[4]

of the book—after the elation of these poems being brought together: the regret that they were selected; that the work is split into two books that is one. And then that you should have composd the book (the primary composition I take it to be the chronology; there is a revelation in the actual sequence—in the book we want to come into the working processes of *poetry*. As in the single poem, in its sequence of lines we are in the processes. Then, there is—in *Letters*—a deliberated order of relationships that dictates disturbances within the actual order of chronology). As one might arrange a family by affinities felt for a photograph. That, your hand there, I miss. For me it will take the Jargon book, with this one to bring the poems together fully (I miss as much as I rediscover in *Here and Now*; and must go back to your manuscripts for poems that ask to accompany these.

But even with this regret—I do love the solid print. One sees again, meets the poem anew (as if the typescripts then are suddenly freshend too—a book springs to the imagination)—

And after Whitman's Spider (which poem was calld up in response to Olson's saying the Primordial was Spider: we faced Chaos, first things and that all last things, orders where the web, the past, the rested upon: from which we must spin out—there was your own spider:

> "to go / just that much further, beyond the end / beyond whatever ends: to begin, to be, to defy"

and my joyful, ravenous spider was there[5]

## 46

26th March {1957}
Florencia 1915
Guadalajara, Mex.

Dear Robert

Your Whitman poem is very lovely, I think it some of yr. best work. Thanks (as always) for sending it. And the Whitman itself is a wonder too—there's another Whitman poem I want to send you but must get it from the library first, I can't remember what it is called.

Were you affected by the earthquakes? I was frightened when I saw the headline, but they said no-one was badly hurt. What was it like? There is a deep thrill (if one can use that poor word after its terrible experiences in our lifetime) in the idea of the earth's inward tensions & passions, isn't there?—forgotten most of the time—

And now the *Medea* has come. I'll begin it tonight. Good! Thank you very much indeed.

Yes, that Wade Donahoe letter, & indeed the whole paltry issue, was shameful. I wrote Cid one hell of a letter about it, I wonder if friendly relations will ever exist between us again. However, I must say I think he was not malicious so much as obtuse. On the whole he has I believe a good heart but he can be most horrendously stupid. If malice *was* operating he will come to be very sorry & ashamed in time, I'm sure. Meanwhile the only way to make reparations wd. be to run a special issue, "post-ultimate," with only you & Bob & Olson in it. The parents of Stuart Perkoff were here last night; said you had liked his work in S.F.

I don't know him but they are friends of a friend of ours here.

No poems to send you this time—I'm in the dumps, rather. But I have your play to read tonight.

Love—
D.

P.S.

What's become of Jonathan {Williams}? Is he on tour? Haven't heard a word of late.

Dear Robert,

It was entirely an experience of feeling to read your play—that is, I still have very little idea "intellectually" what it is "about" but I did have a strong sense of what it *is*—a journey into a world of dark perspectives like a night-moth forest—riven with fleecy golden glitters like Jove as a shower-of-gold—lovely & terrifying. I've been sick with something that made everything spin around all the time, as in an awful hangover—it was an inflammation of the inner ear.

A kid called Gavin Douglas turned up here, that is he's in a hospital with a broken leg but gets out tomorrow & will be around on crutches for a while. He sends you his greetings & apologies for not having written. Will send you some poems next time (as soon as I copy them out.)

Love—
Denise

**47**

{April 1957
Guadalajara, Mex.}
*Easter Monday*

Gavin lent me the Wittenborn Dada book & we have been reading it all these Easter days.[1]

Bob may come down in June when we move to Oaxaca, and Al Kresch too perhaps.

Do you still say "Paradise of San Francisco! I shall never leave again"?

**48**

Dear Robert,

We were lucky enough to meet James {Broughton} in the inn at Guanajuato.

So I send these by hand even tho' it takes longer, because that way they come straight from me to you. Also a picture, in which I cheated by taking off my glasses.

We'll be in Oaxaca by June 20th—Crespo #19, Oaxaca, Oax., Mexico.

With love—
Denise.

**49**

dear Denny/

I have been the last month or so at preparing a collection of poems (1942–1952) for Grove; that, prune as much as I can, is an unwieldy unlikely large "selection" when I notice how slim their volumes of poetry are. I have had the title for any such a collection for several years: *Derivations*. It's because I am such a hermit crab of a poet—if one may think of a hermit crab scuttling from shell to shell of everything that seems wonderful to him in poetry. How it all or any of it is somehow *mine* I don't know. Any way— this not being an original is a kind of sport I can have with the times. There are so many ungenerous derivations. With me, it is my love of shells. An occultist aunt of mine told me, in the beginning, that I was cheating to be a poet. "You were a poet before," she told me, "and it will just come easy for you. It isn't what you really have to do."[1]

And over that information to strive toward the art. As if, "easy," one were not still far short of a demanding never-to-be achieved thing. Tho I must drive myself not to exploit felicities. Rereading, turning this same period, *Personae*, and Lawrence's poems which are in print now in England and which I got complete (O what a field of contemplation for a bee), the greatest learning out of these is the casual (aesthetically) deliberate poem. Almost shell-less? I am dependent upon a certain intoxication either of rhapsody or of form (later). We all are! so that poems are all at a certain intensity. "Laughter," Lawrence writes:

Listen to people laughing
and you will hear what liars they are
or cowards.

We are never quite so at ease, a possibility of free verse short of poetry, the made thing. Or, viz. Plato, strain toward idea and leave no background of opinion. Pound is more willing just to do it somehow; Lawrence at home with ordinary verses: from which the lovely intense things, or in which they are, where they are. With a dimension.

Both, over-ridden by their opinions? and we, by will (and horror of, rightly, what all unmeasured feeling is—the twist in sights of hatreds divorced from their impulse—meaning), demand focus.

"Is hatred a sin?" Jess askd. Well, no—but such a blast (like love), such a storm that need be brought longest to the crucible. My hatreds and loves come all mixd with debris and such a cloud that needs clarifying, to see, for a vital force. Certainly not—as you said of Ginsberg's *loneliness*, another mixture—cultivation.

What amazes me is that these poems of Lawrence's with their blindness drawn to attack blindness: "The stone-blind bourgeois, and the stone-blind bolshevist"—no more true, as true as, newspaper editorials—give environment of truth. We know what he is talking about.

Yet I, perhaps because of "unnatural vices," cannot but imagine man as everywhere natural. Termites, too, involved in blind pursuits of life's demands render about them "mechanical traffic streams" of life.

\* \* \*

I have not written, have I? since Broughton brought your sheaf of poems back from Mexico, and the photograph which stands propd up facing me in the morning when I write at this desk. From the Crucible "A Stir in the Air," and "Sunday Afternoon" kept to the measure. And the others—the other thing I like so in reading *Personae* and Lawrence the verse permitted "of another nature." I send the last poem I've done "Xs of Harmony & Disharmony" perhaps—I don't remember—I sent you the opening movement when I wrote it.

This is a summer full of publications—*Botteghe Oscura* had "Hero Song," "Of the Art," and "The Green Lady." *The Evergreen Review* has "This Place, Rumord to be Sodom," "The fear that precedes changes of heaven," and the seven sections done to date on "The Structure of Rime." *Measure* (publishd by John Wieners in Boston) is printing "The Propositions" and in the second issue "The Dance" and "The Maiden."

I promised Wieners I would write you and ask you to send work to *Measure*—33 S. Russell Street. Boston 14, Mass. He consistently welcomes the best from me. It's a magazine, potentiality, which might give us all field for appropriate flowering.

Then, on top of these, and Grove asking to see a book I have started sending poems out to test the scene. *Poetry, Chicago* took five poems from 1948 and 1949.[2] "A rich choice" wrote Rago: and him turning down some of the best work when I sent it to him before going to Europe. Chaque à son gout.

Anyway, I've sent groups of five poems to all the places that pay. I hope to catch more "fish" on the line. With my little pink poems alive squirming on the hook.

Now, I must up and type a copy of "X's"; and maybe to find a picture I like for you

love
Robert

---

dear Denise/

A packet of poems—had I sent "Crosses of Harmony & Disharmony"? It seems so long since I have written. There was almost a month preparing a manuscript for Grove Press, which hangs fire now in New York; but I am uplifted by having got it composed—to fill in the continuum between *Caesar's Gate* and *Letters* (which Jonathan W. assures me now shld be ready by December). Do you have a typescript of *Letters*? It turns out that the printer Robertson had lost his script and so I have to prepare a new triplicate copy (essential for accurate proof-reading that I have a carbon of the copy in the printer's hands) so I could send you my present copy as soon as I have prepared the new script for the new printer. The book is to be done by Fredericks, once of Banyon Press.

The Grove book is titled *A Book of Resemblances* and will collect, along with much else (particularly my *Writing Writing* pieces, some of which Laughlin turnd down), the work that appeard in *Origin. Poetry* (Chicago) took five poems from the 40s, and I have from them too the H. D. *Selected Poems* to review.

Enclosed too, notes on three poems in *Measure*,[1] first engagements with Marshall and Dorn, and a first effort to get at the rewards of Eigner's work. First, I say: because clarification will yield a simpler observation. I get so wound up, in order to come upon any perceptions at all. After reading over and typing last nites notes on Eigner's "Brink," I thot isn't it a simpler process at work in his art—one has only to indicate that a close sequence in measure provides more subtle adjustments; and that—I do get that right— reestablishing himself (his line) in each line, he has the aesthetics of keeping the syllable-count freely variable. No primitive or psychotic, he is secure (disciplined) in a voluntary movement (needs not, that is, have any schematic reiteration in order to achieve equilibrium). And most restfully exciting to me—who must forever perhaps keep a rhetoric at work, "a little contrived" as John Crowe Ransom wrote in rejecting some recent work (see—"Poetry, A Natural Thing").[2] • Olson is preparing a volume of Eigner's poetry—for Jargon? But that takes so long. I have been working at Don Allen, an editor of Grove who is here for the summer, to get him to see Eigner. But fruitlessly. Perhaps my rhetoric is to catch the eye of such? Sadly enuf, it does. And the beautiful straight thing excites only the poet. I regret not having visited Eigner as you once urged me to; again I don't regret it, for I did not see his work then as I do now. I shld. have been intruding. A file of *Origin* enables me to go back, unearth texts where there are no books. Isn't there promise that *Measure* might give us a working-ground again, where there will be some circulation of what we are doing? I still ask of *Measure* that it not divide writing into Poetry and that other thing, prose. And agree with Jess who mistrusts the total absence of anything womanly there (in the first issue): it excludes the manly. And leaves a frantic mood, where in individual works it is not so.

Love,
Robert

Dear Robert,

    I owe you a real letter—which this is not. But there've been lots of obstructions. This is a note only: Jonathan wants some sort of blurb or statement (in a hurry) for front inside flap of *Overland to the Islands*. I have absolutely nothing to say. Do you think you'd have time to make a couple of sentences? If you don't feel like it, please don't feel bad—only let me know fast, & I'll ask Bob. If I had the immodesty I'd quote one of W. C. W.'s letters to me but I just can't. I don't see why there has to be anything, actually. Poems shd. be let to speak for themselves. But J. seems determined to have something.

    So—if you could I'd be very grateful.

Love—
Denise

**51**

Thurs. October 3ʳᵈ
or 4ᵗʰ {1957}
Crespo #19
Oaxaca {Mex.}

dear Denny/

    Here's the paragraph I send

    Of *Overland to the Islands*, Robert Duncan writes:

    Denise Levertov in these poems brings me again and again to the most intense thing, to that crossing of the inner and the outer reality, where we have our wholeness of feeling in the universe. She catches it as only the craftsman devoted to the language can catch it that has also her genius there so that the thrill of adrenaline comes at the nape of the neck. She has no superior in this clarification of a scene—-moving traffic, Mexican girls after First Communion kicking a baseball, or the arrival of sharks off shore at sundown—-and we recognize there "like the lights just now/in the thunderstorm—-the balance/is that fine" that the world contains exact

**52**

October 7, 1957
{San Francisco}

images of our terrors and joys. In the dance of word and phrase to express feeling, in the interior music of vowels, in subtlety of changing tempo within the form, in the whole supple control in freedom, she excells.

but how difficult to write a "blurb" where I owe so much more. It's you, Creeley and Olson that always are there for me, from whom I backslide into the inner unrooted in the outer, or the outer unrooted in the inner; and whom I imagine when the best is there, when the poem turns one of its wonderful clear things for me, as sharing my joy in the thing made.

Then, with you—as in other ways with them—there are the things in your work that have given my life strength, "kept the home fires burning{.}"

In a book I am just reading for the first time of Jane Harrison's, her *Epilegomena* I find:

> . . . In Orlagau in Thuringia the custom is calld "whipping with fresh green," and the spoken words tell the same tale: "Good morning! Fresh green! Long life! You must give us a bright thaler." All is to be fresh, new, bright, living. It is the induction by contagion of new vitality and fertility. . . . Leaping over a bonfire, dancing round it, is still by the peasantry of modern Europe supposed to bring fertility, or as they wld say "Good luck," to man and beast and crops. . . . Here we have it would seem pure *im*pulsion, the bringing in of good. But behind lurks *ex*pulsion. The word "bonfire" is not, as used to be held, *bon-feur*, good fire, *feu de joie*; it is bane or bone fire, a fire for burning up old bones and rubbish. Purification and the rubbish-heap first, and only later, because of the splendid blaze, a glow like the life-giving sun, jollification, fertility, impulsion. . . . Aristotle . . . said that poetry had two forms: *praise* which issued in hymns and heroic poetry (enkomia), *blame* which yielded iambic satire. . . . We analyze and distinguish but at bottom is the one double-edged impulse, the impulse toward life.

Well, the poem "The Lovers" has kept something alive for me. And "A Stir in the Air" or "The Sharks" keep disturbances alive, tune one to come alive there; as "The Departure" keeps a delight for me alive. In the scene, as if it were mine, where you brought the goods home.[1] What a blaze for me this evening, with the duty to do, re-reading these poems.

I've just finishd notes on Marianne Moore that I liked; I'll send you a copy as soon as I get some from the Poetry Center.[2] And a review of H. D.'s *Selected Poems* which will come out in *Poetry*.[3] Who wrote that the 5 poems in the current issue had received an award and sent a check for $100.[4] Which has me still in the giddy impression of unlimited wealth. And Jonathan writes *Letters* is at the printers, and *Overland to the Islands* awaits only its covers to be on hand!

In all this abundance, might there be help for those obstructions? Is there anything I might do?

I have named you as a reference in applying for a Guggenheim and am fearful now that I have added to the impossible. But I wanted to have the configuration there, among the references, of my closest contemporaries. But if I should get the fellowship—I wld like to visit Mexico . . . if . . . even that would be late next spring or summer. That goes by so quickly and arrives so slowly.

And now, I don't remember when I wrote last, what poems I have sent. Did you have "Keeping the Rhyme" or the "Song of Fair Things"? They were both weeks ago.[5] With no poems since. And that recurring feeling now of being on the verge.

love
Robert

Dear Robert,

bless you, & I thank you. I had been (for no special reason but a caprice of memory) remembering an evil deed of my 18th or 19th year—wondering if like in *Faust* part II any ditchdigging could tilt the balance—well, such praise is an easy way, the acceptance of it, to forgive oneself—but still when one person is drawn to speak so, (the whole letter (that with O. & R. C. I'm "there for you"), not only the paragraph for the book) it can't but be that guilt flies out the window & courage & gladness to be me well up in its place.

The obstructions to writing letters were: a long household disorder here—Mitch upset by it & unable to work—then I persuaded him to take off to N.Y. (while things straightened out a bit here) & renew himself at its dirty but energizing springs—& that worked: 6 weeks later he's back & beginning a new book that really has his attention—also cleared up a number of practical problems. But while he was away Nik had amoebic dysentery & had to undergo an unpleasant cure—then he had 2 weeks of midterm vacation on top of that—& I fired a horrid maid whose sulky personality was weighing me down, & so for 10 days was without any help as well as having Nik completely on my hands (& without US gadgets & things (I mean, washing machines & supermarkets) that's pretty tough)— & all the while the maddening delay on getting the house finished—daily noise of workmen, the patio a mass of rubble etc etc. I did write 3 or 4 poems during this period, thanks to the evenings, Nik asleep & me quite alone, but knocked myself out staying up too late every night so that the very day (last week) that Mitch returned I got sick. However the house (inside—they're still messing around outside) is the best ambience, in itself,

53

Saturday
October 12[h] {1957
Oaxaca, Mex.}

I've ever had—something I made really—. But we're leaving in January as Nik is really just not happy (in Guadalajara he was, but Mitch was not—so it goes). But I'm glad. I feel now that I've had enough of Mexico, it is no longer stimulating to me. I'm not interested in description at this point & there seems nothing more here in the way of symbolic equivalent for me. If there's really a chance you might come to Mexico I'll be desolated to have gone before you came but otherwise I know it is time to be going. My fears of N.Y. have diminished—partly because Mitch is not at this point worried about money, feels he can make out well enough for our purposes, partly because I'm in a mood to welcome a fight with something connected with one (as Mexico can never be), partly because I *know* Nik will be better off (& therefore easier for me to live with) and perhaps most of all because we are going to spend all our weekends hunting for a place to live up the Hudson Valley, an inspiration that has come to us—a locality that has a very strong appeal to us for all sorts of reasons & where after years of defeatist fancying that only rich people cd. live there, we've suddenly become sure there must be bakers & green-grocers & carpenters etc etc & therefore must also be places which we cd. afford.

The quote from Jane Harrison is a most terrific discovery, thanks so much for it. God, if they wd only stop bashing & hammering out there. My head. Do you know the *Wonderful Adventures of Nils* by Selma Lagerlöf? Just read it to Nik. I've always loved *Gösta Berling's Saga* {illegible} about the {illegible} prize—that's really nice. $100 is a $100. It was foolish of you to put me in yr. Gugg. application because you know they're only a bunch of businessmen at heart and sincerity will count for nothing with them. But good luck.

I want to write to you about Eigner, with whom I've corresponded quite a bit, & am glad you like so much now. But must look back at his things & again at what you wrote about him.

P.S.

Thanks for the "Song of Fair Things"—close-knit & of insidious presence —by insidious I mean it creeps over one's resistance to rhythms & names that seem too far from the present & establishes itself, its hold, within one, slowly & without hesitation.

The last you sent were the one with the splendid moose in it,[1] & the other of new grass—"Keeping the Rhyme." And too—"Crosses of Harmony & Disharmony," and "Songs for an Evening's Singing."

---

By the way, I was unable to admire or enjoy a single one of Jimmy Broughton's poems which made it very hard to thank him for his kind thought in sending the book, without either being hypocritical or hurting his feelings.

Am suspicious of that *Measure*—for me anyway. I guess because Wieners, who came once to 15th St., seemed a petulant feeble child.

Saw *The Evergreen Review*,[2] with yr. picture but aside from yr work & Rumaker's it fell pretty flat—too much whooping up of—what? It has absolutely nothing to do with you for instance—geographical lumping together becomes tiresome.

dear Denise,

Of Broughton's book—I wonder if it is kindness where one is not certain of the reader's affinity to ask that a book be received. And in my case (tho I am more responsive than you) James had askd for a review of the *Unicorn* which I overdid (as once, hired as kitchen help in a summer hotel and orderd to kill a chicken, panickd I tore the bird to pieces) and sought to penetrate below the level at which a distaste lay—and I was caught because the thing held in reserve there was *mea culpa* a social betrayal. Whatever critical responses I have are hopelessly entangled with my knowledge of the personal use poetry has there in Broughton's work.

Now, after a successful review of H. D.'s *Selected Poems*, I have a request from Rago, wld. I have a go again at the *Unicorn*; and I've to hack about at the undergrowth to see if I can do it straight on.[1] What I dread putting on record is the obvious: that the poems are carelessly done, and that there are technical inabilities.

But what excites me is that I may be able to do your new book (taking, in retrospect the *Here and Now*); and Creeley's "The Dress" and *The Whip*;[2] Grove plans to bring out a Selected Olson in the spring. But right now the challenge lies in how to register the muddled appreciation. I wish the *Unicorn* were true from false or false from true; that it furnish forth the whatever that lead{s} us not to its author but to its world. Amen. But it does eat away at me unkindly; as if askd to substantiate a friend who has not had the concern for substance that would resist. It slides out from under. I find I don't like or dislike excellence in a poem: I recognize it, or it challenges me, may be over there beyond my liking or disliking. As how beside the point: do I like the house, or Jess or the begonia plant or Pumpkin or Kit Kat. These things give me substance, and I can even in horror of the real see them as goods short of the Good. The image of the Good springs from them, a dissatisfied ideal might gnaw away there. As I value your dissatisfaction where I detour from here and now, and the trial you take, and I take with you in such as "The Enamored Mage." I return again and again to the sentence as, by some nature (temperament) to the questionable region—that is insidious.

The paragraph for your bookblurb over-reaches: its a bastard genre where I haven't the place to discover the nature of the response, nor to find perspectives on the work. What is left is true as I could make it. I had the physiological fact to go on—the adrenaline shots; and to sketch in where that applies.

Let guilt fly out the window
Let shame and pride go
Where they will, for our deeds are
world wanderers. Turnd
out of house, let them
not return to us, but go
hoboing. See—there is your old evil
that was once eighteen
abandond wench!
cooking her pot of scraps in a ditch,
has she taken to drink?
to live it out bleary-eyed?
Old malice, bitch, on your way!
Out the window! out of the house!

Nov 6/ But there two weeks or so have gone by/ and clearing my desk after at last! completing the review of the Broughton and managing to get at some of what fails there, and to find that there is some I can recommend— but enuf! I find this letter and start out here. To enclose a recent poem. Writ homage à Pound.[3] And from Eigner's comment on my notes—re: "Brink." Much to the point.

*All that syllable-word count.? How might it not have been otherwise? although it would be different if so—-in a number of places these aren't the first words, in BRINK, thought of—-or anyway some lines were interpolated, certainly. The count lends ballast to the discussion? huh? . . . How do you contrive, or come close to it? writing long things or short ones. Only way I can tell is to do the best you can think of, that sounds best. And the best gets you immediacy and force, which involves obscurity as soon as you bring in another reader (with a listener you can offer "notes" without losing force much) And so community between millions is blocked in this instance too, in language itself. But immediacy (which includes detail) and force are paramount in life, I guess. . . .

I had meant by contrivance I think that often I let the feel of the line be confused with possible effect. But I can't carry this ball too far; for I am always dependent upon the felt pattern from which the words wove.

Here a poem.[1] I would have come to Mexico only to visit you—and now might, if I shld get the Guggenheim, pay a visit East. But would you and Mitch consider visiting San Francisco before you go back to New York? Is it too impractical? There would be a strong interest here in having you read— which would mean some money; surely $100 in all. Anyway—If you might and let me know, I would work on it.

Robert

**55**

{October 1957
San Francisco}

(Guy Fawkes' Day in England! Ah, what memories of delicious firework smells, of creepy Guys propped on their homemade wagons in the fog by Ilford Station—& lighting the fireworks—"Golden Rain" lit down near the peartree at the bottom of the garden & falling in the sky.

Dear Robert

**56**

November 5th {1957
Oaxaca, Mex.}

I received the form from the Gugg. Foundation & here is a carbon of what I have sent them. God knows what will go down well with the unknown quantities, probably very academic people, who will read it. Hope it helps not hinders anyway.

The cat was returned by a nice old fat Lola. So now we have two, having acquired a little all black guttersnipe in the meantime! They are funny to watch. The bigger one is an aristocratic type, a perfect lady, & really shd be called Charlotte—is in fact named Sylvester, but is known as Big Minou—while little Minou, so easy to please, with her loud purr, is a gamine.

Have been reading Kerouac's *On the Road*—at first I felt well, tho' this is fun to read, & has a Huck Finn fascination (geographical) etc, it doesn't really amount to much because it's a flood of personal reminiscence & keeps repeating the same thing over & over—but having finished it & thought about it a couple of days I see something else. That the repeated movement —OUT on a wave of zest, & back, blue & worn—OUT & back, OUT & back, is just exactly the point, the American rhythm, the raison d'être of the book at all. As for the similarity of J.K.'s piled up adjective style & Ginsberg's, that bothered me till I reflected that if one took it from the other it was most likely Allen that took off from Kerouac—this novel was written 10 years ago. Enclosed is a new poem the title & content of which were given me in a dream.

Love from
Denny

If you get the Gugg. & come East for a while—how exciting! But this week of dances makes me wonder if you ought not to go to Mexico anyway. There is a lot here. And yet often nothing, nothing.

P. S. Do you think you cd. get someone to send me a copy of *Measure*?

Dear Robert

That poem "The Question" seems to me one of the best things you've ever done. I keep reading it & I think more of it each time. And it may be Hommage à EP in content but is not at all an imitation—very much yours. Thanks for sending it.

Abt. coming to S.F., we talked about it but much as I'd like to it doesn't seem possible, because Mitch has already wangled free transportation for us to N.Y.; also—less important but still a factor—such a visit wouldn't be much fun with Nik—we can't drag him around to a lot of grownup places nor can we just keep dumping him with people he doesn't know, & so we'd have to keep taking turns staying with him, etc. If ever we can do it from N.Y.—get a ride with someone or something like that—he could stay with his grandparents in Brooklyn (if it were during a vacation wh. it wd. have to be) & then, we could enjoy it & keep what hours we liked, etc. But thanks for suggesting it and I very much regret that it can't be.

All this week there has been a wonderful festival of Indian dances from all over Mexico here in Oaxaca. What variety of styles & costumes, what vitality, what seriousness, what basic & moving music, what a sense of what dancing is—a basic human activity. Most were danced by kids from the government boarding schools—they are country children from areas where there are no schools to speak of—& though the academic curriculum is poor & dry there is this one terrific thing, that they don't separate them from their own traditions but foster them—how well, the complete seriousness and devoted enthusiasm of the boys (rarely girls, who are excluded from most of the dances) demonstrates. There was no feeling of their having "learnt it in school"—it was evidently a living tradition. For the State of Oaxaca dances, groups of adults from various villages participated. If you care to look up in a library Frances Toor's *Treasury of Mexican Folkways* you'll find descriptions of some of the best dances.[1] The Venado (Deer Dance) or the Huichols, & the Conchesos—but we saw many she doesn't mention. No doubt there is some more scholarly book on the subject but she is not bad.

Mitch is reading Jaime de Angulos' *Indian Tales* to Nik & they are both enjoying it very much. I haven't read it yet but there's another of the same kind that we read over & over which I think you wd. like—*Nine Tales of Raven* by Fran Martin, published by Harper.

Had such a nice letter from James Broughton all of a sudden. He says

Kenneth has reviewed *H & N.* in *Poetry*—I haven't seen it but I guess Ferlinghetti will send me one.[2]

Thank you for your exorcism. Funny that our letters crossed, mine with the Gugg. thing speaking of incantation, and yours with that. Only it didn't quite work because of the words "abandond wench," since the wickedness I was recalling concerned an unkindness—no, cruelty—to my sister's children and the spirit that dominated me at that time was so far from being an abandond wench. Without that line it's for me.

Where are you doing the reviews?

Larry's {Eigner} note was very interesting. I have an idea about him which I dont know quite how to express—I don't mean in any way to denigrate his work, but I think his illness plays a very large part in shaping it. As physically he shakes & jerks & has no coordinating power, & is deprived of many experiences, so in his poetry there are breaks, and incomplete apprehensions of physical objects or of the connexion between them, and irrelevancies or superficially apparent irrelevancies. Sometimes his letters to me are really chaotic—I don't think either that I suffer from a rigid sense of order that makes me see them so, they really are incoherent—But what is miraculous and beautiful is that he makes his deprivations & disabilities into the very ground for his poetics—he never imposes an order there that he cannot experience in his body—so that when he succeeds (not in every poem I think but in very many & in as much of his prose) one sees a kind of mythic picture of chaos fruitful, chaos making. Have you thought of him along these lines at all? Do you think I'm wrong?

I sowed grass-seed & some of it has begun to come up in spite of no rain, 2 cats, several visiting birds (a kind of tiny dove couple & their child, principally) & kids. I water it daily with great pleasure—the thin young blades look elfin. I'm reading *The Brothers Karamazov.* Wouldn't G. Mac-Donald have loved Dostoyevsky.

> Love—write soon—
> Denise.

Dear Robert,

A change of plan!! At least, maybe. It's like this: Mitch thinks he may be able to get a refund on the plane ticket he has. Then we'd have the possibility of going to N.Y. via the W. Coast. *BUT* since the total cost (not all of which either way would be covered by the ticket) wd. be greater that way, it cd. only be done if the $100 you spoke of from readings cd. actually be guaranteed. What do you think? Do you really think that between what you cd. arrange & possibly Ferlinghetti arranging something too, I could make *not less than*

## 58

Nov. 29 {1957}
Crespo 19
Oaxaca {Mex.}

$100 or up to $150? (I'm writing to him too.) As for the problem of Nik, I now have a friend from Guadalajara & her 9 yr old boy, Nik's friend, living in S.F., so he cd stay with them a lot of the time—she is very hospitable & warmhearted so it wd. be O.K.

I must say I find it hard to believe I cd. make that much money but I guess in San Francisco anything {words illegible} . . . What we wd. do wd. be, go to Tijuana by plane & take the bus from there to LA, where we have friends who would put us up, & again bus to SF where we wd. stay about a week—if in addition to the $ for reading a few people give us free meals! Tho' actually I think Maybelle Beim[1] (the one with the little boy) will want to do all that, she did already ask me. Well, anyway, let us know as soon as possible what you think, remembering that a) it has to be definite and b) that meanwhile Mitch will be finding out about the refund, bus fare, & all that side of it, & that if that is not feasible it wd. be off anyway. (M. says it almost certainly will be O.K. tho.) If it all works out I'll take a nip of something before I read & try to do it really well & not sound shyly ladylike the way I did on that tape a few years ago.

Love from<br>Denise

P.S.

The week we could make it wd. be approx. Jan 18–25th

---

**59**

Nov. 30, 1957
{San Francisco}

dear Denise/

Your sense of Eigner's work is pretty much what I feel in reading him. You talk earlier about the folk dances—well, in the dance of the poem there are involuntary areas which he must use as gesture, like the involuntary cessations of thot must be used as direction or pattern. I am not, for instance (with the exception of the visual displacement) usually conscious at the level of effort of the organic information and coordination involved in picking up a cup from a table . . . Well . . . tho I take it there is some organic difficulty to make the right estimation mean so much to me. And I find it particularly exciting that there are calculations and exactnesses involved . . . "by the numbers." Mightn't a spastic disorder force Eigner (it's an unconscious cerebration involved) into a kind of either between the mathematic and the chaos. I get anyway the impression that he is either clear or he misses: and admire him that he has learnd his nature must take the chance.

---

I've begun work toward an essay on *Here and Now* and *Overland to the Islands* . . . which means letting my mind rove over the poems feeding where it will and gazing off into whatever spaces. No, I don't want to pin the poems down, classified and analyzed; nor to dissect my own relations there but to tell the story of particular clovers writ by a bee. That's tonite's mood as it goes.

Reading currently Eliot's essays *On Poetry and Poets* where I find him often keen. I think there is even something in his conservative doctrine of the language that appeals to me. "first to preserve and second to extend and improve"—tho his championing of culture and his mistrust of experience is not always illuminating. But take this passage for the function of the writer:[1]

> "In expressing what other people feel he is also changing the feeling by making it more conscious; he is making people more aware of what they feel already, and therefore teaching something about themselves . . . new variations of sensibility which can be appropriated by others."

And in this passage he seems to be describing a process I often find myself involved in in a poem:

> "The poet may be concernd solely with expressing in verse—using all his resources of words, with their history, their connotations, their music— this obscure impulse. He does not know what he had to say until he has said it. . . . " or earlier in the same essay. "He has something germinating in him for which he must find words; he connot identify this embryo until it has been transformd into an arrangement of the right words in the right order. When you have the words for it, the 'thing' for which the words had to be found has disappeard, replaced by the poem."[2]

dear Denise & Mitch/

60

Dec. 3, 1957
{San Francisco}

I can guarantee that Denise won't make less than $100, and I'm pretty sure of at least $150. Let's say the hundred is underwritten for sure, as the fee for one reading downtown—and if I can raise more than that in sub- scriptions it will all be to the good. With that as the basic reading, I have written to the Poetry Center that a reading cld. be arranged at the College for a fee of fifty dollars. I will cover University of California at Berkeley possibilities this coming week: three readings in a week is about the limit of what would be pleasant. If they all came thru they would certainly bring in more than the $150 you find "incredible." I will get together with Ferlinghetti right away to work on one plan. Rexroth will be solidly for your reading here and that shld mean some radio publicity; but since I have six months ago broken all relations with him and do not intend to repair them, he is just as sure to kick up the mud over however it is plannd.

Your problem won't be where to find "free meals" but where to find a meal free. The McClures, the Duerdens, (if the Poetry Center schedules you at this late date), Ruth Witt, Rexroth, Ferling and *we*—will want you whenever and however much you can accept. And I want to arrange a dinner and evening at the Roth's. If your friends with small son come thru and have room, it will be an advantage, since your staying in "neutral" environs will leave you free in arranging your stay. But remember forwarnd, Jess and I can set up beds in the front studio. Bathrooms etc. are arranged so that there is a reasonable amount of privacy: no body has to troop thru the studio etc.

The McClures certainly wld. have room.

---

I just phoned Ida Hodes to enquire about State College schedule—the Spring semester begins the last week in January as I understand it, and prospects for a campus reading don't look so good. As, damn it, the first of the semester wld be poor across the bay too.

Ferlinghetti is, I think, slow on the up-take. But I arranged to see him the beginning of next week to make plans. He was surprised that one could get the fee underwritten and pessimistic about a subscription.

---

News from Bob that they had a baby (girl) last week, and application form for me to recommend him to John Hay Whitney Foundation which I take it gives special grants to handicapped and underprivileged artists. Just being addicted to poetry seems to be a certain handicap.

I seem to have pressed successfully for Olson to be poet in residence (the first) at the Poetry Center next summer.

*MEASURE* I am sending by the same mail—

love
Robert

---

**61**

Dec. 7$^h$ {1957}
Crespo 19
Oaxaca {Mex.}

Dear Robert

Thanks v. much for your letter & all the work involved & especially for your assurances of welcome.

We are uncertain what the situation is because tho' the 1st part of the letter is very optimistic the 2d. seems to contradict it but no doubt you will explain next time. Our confusion largely stems from not knowing what you mean by "downtown," e.g. is it one & the same as the Poetry Center or does it refer to some other place? Please excuse us.

I've heard from Mae Belle Beim & she definitely wants to have us stay with her & she has a car too. But for one or two late nights maybe we could stay with you & Jess and Nik would be happy over there with them. About the fare: Mitch is working on that & I think it will work out OK but I don't want to count on any of it yet in case not.

How many poems (remembering that most of mine are not very long) does the average reader read in an evening?

If there were 3 readings would I have to have 3 completely different programs? Because if so I don't have enough, & will have to execute a Russian gopak and 3 conjuring tricks to eke out. Please provide 3 white rabbits, one lizard, and a bolony sausage. The hat we will procure. But O brethren let us pray that this will not be necessary.

Mitch has gone to Chiapas for a week because he's on tenterhooks waiting for some news—any news—from the damn agent. It certainly is time he had some good news.

Do you think K{enneth} R{exroth} will be more offended if I do or do not write to him (I mean, if we really do come to SF.)? Whatever happens I manage to tread on his sore toes of which he has an unseemly number, and I think it most extraordinarily disinterested of him to continue to champion my poems as I hear he has been doing.

Have to get to the P.O. now & then for a bicycle ride with Nik. Haven't ridden one since we were in the S. of France with the Creeleys, so I hope I don't fall off or anything ignominious. I well remember the long steep hill into Aix one evening—me all dressed up to go to the music festival—Mitch likewise—Bob at our house babysitting—and the brakes gave way—I sailed on down at breathless speed, overtaking cars, pigs & people, my finger on the bell certain my end was approaching—admiring the sunset as for the last time—& saved myself by dexterous use of my feet on the cobblestones as I swept into the amazed populace of the Place Centrale.

I've started on a children's book about a French shepherd boy which I hope Nell Blaine will illustrate—Nik is going to be the critic. As long as I keep it up & don't get bored I shd. finish it in a few weeks.

Love from
Denise

---

dear Denise:

Negotiations afoot to pool Poetry Center and my own subscription plans in one reading so that, as I wrote Ruth Witt, the Poetry Center may add to its prestige. But I will have particulars on this tomorrow and write to you on Monday again.

I wanted to send you some passages from my notebooks. The first one that came among notes preparatory to writing on Marianne Moore; and the other two notes preparatory to the review plannd of your work.

1 (sometime in August) Character is an adventure of the imagination. Life, the cosmic process, of suns and planets, plants and men, creates by, and then

towards, a coherence in diversity, propositions of character. The unfolding of its forms—as particularly we see man and our contemporaries the elephant, the wood-weasel, the porcupine: instances of evolving form—is inspired toward intricate resistant structure, specialized, to provide a lasting mobility. We die by the decay of the more susceptible parts. Arêté, in Homer (Werner Jaeger tells me) the idea of manliness where "the rival factor is *to kalon*, the Beautiful as a determinant ideal, is character: "backbone" as we call it, and the French word "arêté" is the skeleton of a fish, sharp-edged resistance.[1] Related perhaps not by etymology, but by the impulses of later experience. Invertebrate life is far from the lasting individuality, the unity in complexity, the particular Beauty of the manly. Moral force is, Freud tells us, an aesthetic; an effort embodied in civilization that barely holds its own against deeper instinctual discontents. Where we are discontents, we struggle for containment, for a concept in which the discontaind will become content. The "aesthetic" of the sublime that Edmund Burke in his *Philosophical Inquiry into the Origin of Our Ideas of the Sublime and the Beautiful* (1756) tells us is "a sort of delight full of horror, a sort of tranquility tinged with terror" is reflected in our day by the evaluations of depth psychology with its search for primal archetypes, breakthrus of demonic power; by the dark humorists, sophisticates of human nightmare, enurosis and pathology—among which some of our greatest poets—Joyce, Picasso, Breton, Ernst, Artaud. These have genius that battens upon demonic thrill; their art is protean, a richness that contains the repugnant, vertiginous.

These two qualities we demand now of Art—the beautiful and the sublime. As Marianne Moore demands of poetry "imaginary gardens with real toads in them," a passage quoted to triteness, but I hope I provide new context to account for its haunting. We cannot, as Charles Ives valiantly in the support of manliness does, "prefer Whittier to Baudelaire—a poet to a genius, or a healthy to a rotten apple"; we cannot conclude so certainly that "we like the Beautiful and don't like the ugly."

Glamors are gasses thrown off in decomposition; iridescence, richness, may combine sensual pleasure and that grue that comes when we recognize death. It is because life is real that we are deeply attracted to *to kalon*, to the Beautiful. Surely no instant can lie deeper, more ancient to us, than this striving for articulate, moving, lasting form which we can see thruout the Universe. It is because death is certain (tho unreal, in that we have no experience there) that we are deeply alienated—and then thrilld to face it— by the sublime.

2 (Nov 29) Of Denise Levertov's work: when I consider her work in regard to my feeling of the course, as it may be influenced or shaped, of poetic energies in history it seems minor: I do not have the sense of great alterations, because of concept, in the possibility of what a poem might be. But

when I consider her work in relation to my feeling of my own poetry, its course and possible achievements, her work is major: I have the certainty that both in her use of language toward the poem and in her poetry as it opens fresh routes and particular insights in experience she presents a challenge. Olson's *Maximus*, like Pound's *Cantos* substantially change and renew my vision of potentialities. Creeley and Denise Levertov, like Marianne Moore or William Carlos Williams in the preceding period, give a particular measure of what achievement must be. I am quite certain that, whatever my differences (and they are observable) I belong to a second category—or rather, that my work does not move into the realm of potentialities projected, but must be taken, like Denise Levertov's or Robert Creeley's, as limited in its imagination and energies to the immediate. I can imagine a larger scope, a "universe" being more included in the immediate. My criticism, my sense of the crisis in which we have either to enlarge our feeling or to become mannerd, is that the "achieved" must struggle (as much as the "potential") toward width and depth in intensity. The order of the achieved comes with the interplay of a total work. And Shakespeare has shown us how powerful, how every*where* moving an enclosed art may be. Mastery, within process, is possible, that is—even where one does not have the temper . . . well, the genius, that initiates process. In the other, in the world of Pound or Olson, I find mastery, disturbd by (that is, our sense of that mastery is disturbd by) the fact that it is unsettled in relation to the immediate poetry (in relation to the lifework) and projects its achievement out over energies and forms that include the works and achievements of others. Their largest vision thrives on incompletion. Even tho Olson is a contemporary I have always the sense of *inheriting* from his work: where with Creeley and Denise Levertov I have the sense of *approximating* to their work.

3 An important element in a poetics is the emergence and definition of a total concept large enuf to include form and content that can allow width in intellection and feeling and achieve at the same time an emotional unity thru-out. What's in question here is the poet's understanding of what is happening, so that the individual poem has reference to a context: it comes, fragmentary or complete in itself, to be a part of a larger context. But by "concept" here I mean not a rationalization (the inventive mind, mercurial, supplies answers readily enuf if the unity is posed as a problem of inter-relation) but a vision. What the creative mind waits patiently for or rages in impatience for is the unifying experience. The artist rightly rejects all solutions and works at the borders of necessity: it is the need where the advent may come. This unity—and I would propose that it be thot of as a congregation, wherein a unity of unities appears, each member being center of a wholeness—is a focus or pitch of perception or understanding. The poet comes first to be aware of, to hear, the unity of the poem. It is a

complex unity and the experience is that of apprehending what one has faild to do out of what one has done.

Achievement prepares the creative artist for new growth; where forms emerge we are given new intimations of form that slumber unrealized within the medium. So, first coming to hear the unity of a poem I think of as an eternal operation. We are, in hearing, hearers among generations of hearers of the unity of the poem. Then there is hearing the unity as it appears as Poetry. I am not sure that this is a progression—the "first" and "then" are misleading. But the coexistence as fact of the poem, Poetry, and beyond that, of something I would call the Life of the Language, and in another even larger universe of statement that we know as the Arts of Man, is the fact of one Being, not single but multifarious. The poet needs dream magnificently if he is to imagine how small and how vital his largest achievement here will be. History is the tale of individual genius sloughd off as the body sloughs off the individual cell; in the morphology of spirit our intensities of experience have their full meaning when they are seen as epiphanies, sympathies or opennesses in consciousness in which the shared is cosmic, the "Our" reaches toward the universe and stretches the active imagination. This is one experience, which we may have at many levels. The struggle which we call growth is felt as new understandings of this experience develop: the grasp of form in the poem; the grasp of form in Poetry, where the poem is seen as a member of a new body; the grasp of form in the Medium, where Poetry is seen as a member of a new body; the grasp of the Medium as one among mediums, members of a new body, Spirit.

This, only to share with you, what I seem to need as "background," to know finally what must be defined, and what concentrated in giving meaning to a critical feeling—in the last case it's the fact that altho you had the central proposition "Here and Now" for the first American book—and one that I find always a meaningful one now in reference to my own work (it's central to your sense of where I go off in things like the "Enamord Mage") at the same time you did not have the decision to form the book yourself, the necessity that would determine the poems in relation to each other as surely as parts of any one poem have their position contributing to the form. You would not have been able to let out this act to anyone else, if the meaning of the book had occupied you. I have the general feeling that all the poems in these two books belong to a very large book which has not appeard (to you, and thru you, to us). I am elated to have the poems between boards: but I have also the desire that eventually they will be all reprinted in each its *rightness*.

Love
Robert

dear Denise/

Vacillation in first letter went between my proposal of 3 readings (working to force a campus reading out of the Poetry Center, and toward a reading at Cal) and my phoning Ida {Hodes} to check and finding out that the universities wld all be in registration—so that campus readings were out. Which didn't affect the $100 minimum but made the $150 I hoped for seem more difficult.

Now [Dec. 10th] I have arranged the reading Sunday the 19th of January under the auspices of the Poetry Center who will hire the hall, send out publicity and contribute $25 to the fee. Which gives me a good starter on the subscription and I'm working for $150.

So it's only one reading—which hereabouts means an hour to an hour and a half . . . you can do as you want for a program. It's close on to the arrival date of the 18th but there would be time to go over yr. program with you if you have doubts. The audiences here are avid and toughend—they've survived top poetry read badly; ghastly poetry read ghastly; the mediocre read with theatrical flourish; poets in advanced stages of discomfort, ego-mania mumbling; grand style, relentless insistence, professional down-the-nosism, charm, calm, schizophrenic disorder, pious agony, auto-erotic hypnosis, bellowing, hatred, pity, snarl and snub. But the audience for your work will be in large particularly concernd to hear it: between Rexroth and me there's been some rumor of special interest. And more important—the younger poets are really concernd *pro* and *con* about you, Creeley and Olson. They've read your work, and will be wanting to hear you read what you will be reading. I mean, they aren't affected by gross misapprehensions that might be let loose by articles like Rexroth's last one in *Poetry* where you seem to be portrayd as an article of culture and civilization, a learned lady of some kind whose work will expose the fraud of half a dozen reputations.

63

Dec. 10, {11} 1957
{San Francisco}

---

I followd the path of monstrous thot and just beyond the passage I sent you from the notebook I came to . . . well, here is the continuation:

The "here" and "now" which appears as the title of Denise Levertov's first American book is a tentative proposition appropriate to the largest vision. Whitehead in his ripeness had such a proposition: "Every actual entity, in virtue of its novelty, transcends its universe, God included" and "The communion of saints is a great and inspiring assemblage, but it has only one possible hall of meeting, and that is, the present."

But in relegating the selection and ordering of poems included in *Here and Now* to another hand (in this case, Lawrence Ferlinghetti as publisher) she postponed the appearance of a book that might discover her intention beyond the individual poem.

The doctor in Valery's *Socrates and his Physician* says to Socrates: "I can say, with some—tho not absolute—assurance, the kind of person you will be, and in what humor, at your next awakening. But what you will do with that humor, and with all the beautiful surprises which it will bring to your mind and which will enchant us in the evenings . . . You are ignorant of yourself, Socrates, in so far as you are a mortal, for your mind in its purity is engaged inside time in separating off its own essence from every condition of perishability . . . "

The critic is physician who may say that a crisis has come: but how the man at his crisis will choose and the meaning in that choice lies in the man's own spirit: it is the event of his creativity.

The genuine in poetry is clear to us in so far as we sense in the restrictions and unfoldings of the poem a formal necessity that originates in its source. The poet at work toward the essential must discover and embrace his fate. Whatever his cheats or charms, his affections or sympathies, the secret of the genuine lies in the fact that a man's Fate is not heartless but is a great heart that draws into circulation all warmth and becomes the center of the red. Facing his bloody fate, the poet is cold, and his yearning for the genuine is a freezing, a crystallization toward characteristic form.

Which[1] image may exorcise at least one distracting demon and free me for work: it's having to go thru this, exhausting some polemical appetite, and an aptitude for the pompous; emptying out metaphysical bigness of head—that makes arriving at me natural feeling and thot such a struggle. Even about your work that I have experienced, coming as it has over the last two years, fresh from the pen: and before that my finding it for myself in *Origin* and excited there by some similarity of "realm": I must clear away detritus of over-feeling, grandiose literary shadows that I dislike more and more as they grow. [and they grow by Medusa-freezing the poor writer to their own face where there is no trace of the poems he had set out to explore. Well, Whitehead's ideas are large and lovely in his books; and Valery's dialogues are intimate with the fascination of the uniqueness he calls his "essential" . . . but in me they take on distortions of "authority"—{]}

My sense that the poems so far "belong" to a larger book; that your first *book* in this sense has not appeard remains and is sufficient.

I am rather enamord of the Poet's having dreams of a universe: but something of real beauty seems to be destroyd in the other idea of the poet becoming masker-seer of creation.

Dec. 11:

Not writing K.R. wld be wounding to his actual affection for you. The man is deranged, and no object of his affection now can be separated from the projection of his hatreds, envys, sense of pervading treason. His affect at a recent reading (which I did not attend) struck a disinterested spectator as *self-loathing*. He still makes threats against Bob; but his behavior in the last year to Marthe makes it painfully clear that she has been in a reign of terror and contempt. Well, all one can do is not to feed his fears. Write to him, because it is best that K.R. know from you that you are coming. At worst he will ((as he did after your writing sympathetically—(as I counseld when you askd me then) at the time of the Creeley episode)) see it all as an attack upon him, and prepare himself for your possible neglect of him by suspecting whatever treacheries. I do not think I have known a more furious man beset by wretched shadows.

But at best, if he is happy—a letter and visiting him while you are here may call up his good nature—he's a man who is ardent in his friendships. Not only his fears of losing all but his love of life has its center there.

So write to him, but be willing that his fiend may read it. It depends upon the freak of the wheel (his head full of wheels).

Last Friday I went, unhappily it proved, to K. Patchen's reading at the Poetry Center. After an hour of Patchenism, wounded attitudes flowing out into "I pity you" and beyond that into "I pity you, you stupid little man who works for a stupid living" and beyond that into "I pity you, you stupid little man who works for a stupid living because I am going to wipe you out!" The last growing into a fanatical roar (so empty that only its volume—aided by the microphone and full demagogy—remains): that hath nor rage nor right. After an hour of which I was reduced to writing messages to myself and other uncomfortable parties around me, out of spirit with the harang.

> O soft wet sorry voice
> O milky verb
> dont swat me with yr.
>      funny flap. . . .

or

> at the depth of the pool
> sediment
> pore sedimental frog croaking
> nice to softy stars
> donja know
> thay's gas your
> gazing at?

Don't pitty on my rug, Pat.

---

The aberrations of both Kenneths seem to be linkd to the "sons of bitches" who excluded them from publication. All actual emotion has died in Patchen and the deracinated sentiments of the revolutionary poet remain: he writes for his own Noah (in whom he no longer believes) and promises world destruction of those bastards (who do not believe in him). He has not the reality of Céline, to be destroyd at the root by taking on the burden of his real loathing. (In a recent interview Céline askd:—*Vous ne croyez plus a rein*? replied: "A ma haine et à ma mort qui n'est pas lointaine et au plaisir que ca fera à tous les coins de l'univers. Est-ce que ça vous suffit comme ça?){"}

Patchen wants at once to be *good* and to hate. Both the good and the hatred become gratuitous—

—Robert

(Jees. to mention love after that last thot!)

Jess has a show opening at GUMPS [swank imports, objects d'art and luxury emporium] in January. With wild hope of finding a new buyer or two, of fortune.

Next weekend a man is coming from another gallery—and there may be a prospect of a collage show?

I wish you and Mitch could see the work he's done this last year. If you'd been able to visit us in a place like this you'd have never left here.

## 64

Dec 11ᵗʰ {1957}
Crespo 19
{Oaxaca, Mex.}

Dear Robert,

The excerpts from your notebooks are most valuable to me—thank you very much for sharing them. Here's something from what I wrote to myself about it: " . . . another kind of poet (minor) in contradistinction, with our small completenesses perhaps, to the large—huge—incompleteness of poets like Pound & Olson who are of a major *kind*, whatever their actual achievement in separated instances, how it may vary. And I see it as a matter of scope & power of *intellect*—a masculine intellect, in a sense quite separate from personality & physiology. The masculine or major poet is able to "project its achievement out over energies & forms that include the works & achievements of others. Their largest vision thrives on incompletion" (R. D.) My sense of being unable to grasp large areas of *what is*, which I sometimes think of or used to think of as merely immaturity, is probably something more integral to what I am, is an actual limitation which confines my action in poetry to the immediate & is what makes it impossible for me even to attempt prose fiction. I simply don't know how things *are* for others or in other areas; even tho' in daily life I am not alienated, am a sympathetic listener, quite practical, am asked for & give advice, etc. But there it is personalized, made concrete—& just so I can write a prose piece about certain paintings or poems, & analyze what I find, but have not the intellectual energy (or, concretely, capacity, as a vessel has capacity, room for) to create a system of general ideas. In Bob's case, his prose seems to belong *potentially* to the other category, of *initiators of process.*"

I think a Pound or an Olson could never experience the dreadful dullness & emptiness I feel at times when I am not "in a state of writing." Because a masculine intelligence, as I conceive it, is a constant, & even when not in creative action continues to inform the consciousness, whereas the feminine intelligence ebbs & flows and when it has no especial occasion is in abeyance. The poet with a feminine intellect is more at the mercy of '*possession*,' of the necessity to '*wait upon the Muse*,' he has not the same control over his powers. The powers of the others are greater but even so he has them ordered because his strength of comprehension matches the strength of his demons.

I can see how because its forms are not initiatory of process you would think of your poetry as belonging to your second category but yr. mind seems to me to belong to the first as does the extent of yr. field within poems, that is, content—tho' of course I don't like & in fact in a good poem cannot, distinguish so form from content.

By the way do you know I have never seen a copy of *Medieval Scenes*? Is it possible still to buy one? I don't even know who published it.

Does that sense you have, of how the poems in *H & N* & *Overland to the Islands* shd. be together to be right, mean a chronological order?

The presence of a sense of total order of which you speak in the 3d note is of course much harder for the minor poet, or poet of feminine intellect, to have than for a major poet, in whom it exists as a matter of course. The minor poet is down in the grasses, seeing particulars, perhaps with beautiful clarity or with, if not clarity, a beautiful intensity of personal, subjective vision, but he is less likely to relate the parts to one another, or if he does it will be in an instinctual way that may not reach a conscious level. He may know but he doesn't know that he knows. The major poet I see as tall, eating the treetop leaves like giraffes and the prehistoric tall ones, able to see a long way, to see the path he made coming thru' the forest, how it turns, the pattern it makes & its direction, seeing & knowing that he sees.

Maybe I'm talking poppycock. Certainly none of all this seems to apply to, for instance, Creeley, & I daresay, thinking I was generalizing, I was really only expressing my own feeling about myself, connected with my being shortsighted, as I feel Eigner's "nervous line" as they say of drawings often, and his "broken" content, are connected with his physical condition. Here by the way is a quote from Henry James (*The Bostonians*) which I copied into a notebook in 1954 with the comment "Quality of Eigner's poems": " . . . and wandered to the windows at the back, where there was a view of the water; Miss Chancellor having the good fortune to dwell on that side of Charles St. toward which, in the rear, the afternoon sun slants redly, from an horizon indented at empty intervals with wooden spires, the masts of lonely boats, the chimneys of dirty 'works,' over a brackish expanse of anomalous character . . . "

No doubt, going back, it was, tho' not directly short sight, still a combination, a complex, of that & my sense of being of strictly limited capacities, that caused me indeed to fall off my bicycle on the afternoon I last wrote. After mailing the letter I had a most exhilarating ride with Nik, who was beautifully calm on *his* machine—but sure enough, 2 blocks from home, somewhat rattled by a dog that made some pretence to rush out & bark at my ankles, albeit half-heartedly, I ran straight into a guy playing ball in the street (not a kid, either), & thereafter reclined in an Etruscan position under my bike, berating him in English as "Idiot" and "Peahead!" Two businessmen picked me up & dusted me & checked the health of the wheels. I said indignantly, "And the oaf didn't even apologize!," to which Nik replied, "But Den, *you* knocked *him* over!" By that time I was so shaken with laughter that the charmed onlookers must have felt sure I'd drink taken. All this has an obscure relationship with my inability to tell a publisher, "I want this & that and so, & that's how it's going to be."

We're reading *Alice in Wonderland* again & I've never enjoyed it so much before. Looking forward to *Measure*, thank you very much.

Love from
Denise.

## 65

Dec. 14<sup>th</sup> {1957}
{Oaxaca, Mex.}

Dear Robert

Good god, KR's article sounds terrible. I am horribly embarrassed. Have still not seen it—Ferlinghetti has mailed it to me though—but what you say makes me wonder if I really can show my face there—what the hell! However, I'm going to—the date is fixed—Mitch actually eager to see SF— & everything. So . . .

As for looking the program over with you *if I have doubts*, I'll say I have! The audience sounds quite frightening & what if they ask me clever questions? I don't want to pretend to be dumber than I am but really that is a paralyzing thought. Also, will there be a microphone? Needless to say I have never been near one; but have heard what horrid crackles & hisses they can produce—maybe there'll be a chance to try that out beforehand. But at the same time I also have a sort of devilmaycare feeling which I expect will see me through—besides which I feel that, (in spite of KR's blowing up of me in his madness) since I know what I am, really—since I stand back of what I've done & think it is good, but also know damn well that I'm not "important" or "learned" or even clever—if I behave naturally and do my best I don't need to be embarrassed. And if the young generation think I'm square or something well I damn well can't help it.

Just so long as nobody thinks I knew of and approved what Kenneth has written about me

I've written him to say I was coming, hoped to see him if he wasn't personally annoyed with me any more & to thank him for going on liking my poems even when he was annoyed, or hurt. Which is true; I mean, that I'm thankful—I think it is very un-petty of him. Only I wish to God he wouldn't overdo it.

The rest of your letter I've not read properly yet—the notes.

You know, when this came up—about the reading—I didn't realize all this work for you—raising a subscription etc.—would be involved. I just thought the Poetry Center, as I suppose it is at the YMHA in NY, had regular readings—invited people to read at your or others' suggestion— and had someone backing it so that it could afford to pay something. All that sounded pretty simple. I wouldn't ever have started on it all if I'd realized the difficulties—please forgive me and please believe I will try to do well, and if I don't, please don't get mad at me if possible. Well—

About *Here & Now* I never thought of it as "a proposition appropriate to the largest vision," but had a more modest sense in mind—simply that I aimed at in my poems, & thought they had to some degree achieved, a quality of immediacy, of hereness & nowness. None were *set pieces*, none were "made-up," all did come directly out of my life, & only therefore did it seem appropriate, as to say, here they are, they are *alive* whatever defects may be found in them, etc. A claim rather for authenticity than for any transcendent weltanschauung etc. Or further intention.

That's as far as I've properly read, I must postpone the rest until I'm undistracted by Nik & the cats & Casimina who all keep interrupting.

With love from<br>Denise.

P. S.

All this, reread, sounds rather defensive. But it is the idea of Rexroth's article that has rattled me, not anything you've said.

dear Denise/

I am most dissatisfied with that direction I went in, or the particular Eliot-blinkers or blinders I had on that made the road that-a-ways look all between "major" and "minor": it isn't some giantism of mentality that makes a book—it's just the same *making* that makes the poems, or designs the

**66**

Dec. 17, 1957
{San Francisco}

pages. There's something about male and female, masculine and feminine, emotions and attitudes; but I do feel that in passion, in spirit we are all pre-Adamic. And that insistence of Pound's—the passion endures, the rest is dross is beautiful . . . the more so in that I believe there is a passion in which the dross, as such, endures. There are times when any writing at all seems to open doors of the imagination to some vitality—O just the fact that the moving hand however unhappily writ there.

That we shape our poems in honor specifically of the enduring?

Anyway, it warn't that some vast Bach's *Missa Solemnis* of a book hadn't been composed, but just that you let it go—that final touch, the gift of this poem seems right with these, this don't seem to go—etc. For almost all early books I was chronological [since I thot of the poems as having "happend"] and the choice still remaind of what seemd to fit [as one might or might not use all ones scraps in making a quilt. For *Poems 1948–49* quite a few didn't fit in. By *Letters* I no longer pay much attention to chronology but arranged [and this was just by feel or smell or something that—well, like arranging a dinner table for a festival etc.{]} In the book I did for Grove—which it looks like they ain't having—I went back to chronology—And for the *Field* I am back at the poems "happen" level—tho as I go about it I have the conviction that a book is happening. And for the first time, since the beginning (in London, January 1956) I have had a reference point and a title in one "The Field" and I find myself going back to certain themes (or their coming back to me).

But take another look at Pound's early books—or at *Personae* as a collection; or at Lawrence's books—*Look, We Have Come Thru* has that sense of these poems happend.[1] Certainly, I think of your New York poems and your Mexican poems; and then among them of another kind—that refer to the experience of the poem happening. It's a constant theme with you as it is with me. As marriage is a constant theme with Creeley, and the imp on his shoulder is constant.

It was hard in reading Thomas Hardy to sort out the relations of his poems: in order to maintain the idea that all were occasional "songs sung in the evening" he obscured chronology in arranging: but they are rooted in experience, so he could not forego dating them.

Whitman's *Leaves of Grass* seems to me the most beautiful largeness. And is his intellection there so *masculine*? I would aim at such a closeness to self in preference to a scheme like Herbert's *Temple*. I just finished re-reading *The Temple* and found again certain poems to be whole and full

"Sighs and Groans," "Jordan," "Hope," "Time," "The Flower," "A True Hymn," "The Answer," "The Odor," "Discipline," "Heaven"

(so that in my notebook I put the title and a large *star*: if they were to be had, they were to be had entire.

## THE FLOWER

How fresh, O Lord, how sweet and cleane
Are thy returns? even as the flowers in spring,
    To which, besides their owne demeane,
The late-past frosts tributes of pleasure bring.
                Griefe melts away
                Like snow in May,
    As if there were no such cold thing.

    Who would have thought my shriveld hart
Could have recoverd greennesse? it was gone
    Quite under ground: as Flowres depart
To see their mother-root, when they have blowne
                Where they together
                all the hard weather,
    Dead to the world, keepe house unknowne.

    These are thy wonders, Lord of Powre,
Killing, and quickning, bringing downe to hell,
    And up to heaven in an houre:
Making a chiming of a passing bell.
                Wee say amisse
                This or that is,
    Thy word is all, if we could spell.

    O that I once past changing were
Fast in they Paradise, where no Flowre can wither,
    Many a spring I shoot up faire,
Offring at Heaven, growing and groning thither:
                Nor doth my Flowre
                Want a spring-shower,
    My sins and I joining together.

    But while I grow in a strait line
Still upwards bent, as if heaven were mine owne,
    Thy anger comes, and I decline:
What frost to that? what Pole is not the zone,
                Where all things burne,
                When thou dost turne
    And the least frowne of thine is showne.

    And now in Age I bud againe.
After so many deaths I live and write,
    I once more smell the dew and raine,
And relish versing: O my onely light,

It cannot bee
That I am hee
On whom thy tempests fell all night.

These are thy wonders, Lord of Love,
To make us see we are but flowres, that glide.
Which when we once can find and prove,
Thou hast a Garden for us, where to bide.
Who would be more
Swelling through store
Forfett their Paradise by their Pride.

"groning" and "sin" that are so real, intensities of feeling, not theological idears, in Herbert are his peculiarities for me. Only in a poem like above do they appear without special indulgence. Then there is a larger group of poems where a passage or passages or even only a phrase seemd "right" to me. "Right" here in its most demanding sense, what removes poetry from the unevenness of versification (where he is often skilld without wholeness). As from "Dullness" I found these:

from DULLNESS

. . . . . .

Thou are my livelines, my life, my light
Beauty alone to mee.
Thy bloody death and undeserv'd, makes thee
Pure red and white.
. . . . . .

Where are my lines then, my approaches, views
Where are my window-songs.
Lovers are still pretending, & even wrongs
Sharpen their muse.
. . . . . .

. . . . . .

or sometimes in a poem only a single line or phrase:

from "Holy Baptism"
Childhood is health

But I did feel that in setting about to fill out the form of a pre-conceived book, a plan: he was reduced in a number, more than I would have imagined, to perfunctory verse. One of his most intense experiences is crying and groaning: but in poems about crying and groaning he is grotesque indeed. Like a man trying to cry and groan when the occasion calls for it.

---

Yet, unachieved, the *Temple* is haunted by its own intended form. Now that I am thru the reading, and the testing and mining of poem by poem is done, it is not a conglomerate of good and bad poems that remains: but the feeling of a designd devotion, a temple, which has epiphanies, beauties, falsities of feeling and even stretches of churchy morality and conscientious piety: and in that some vital wholeness in which none of it is isolated.

There *is* then something more important than the best, or the aesthetic. Tho the striving is for the beautiful "right" working.

———————

re: plans for your time here.

I agreed to a Poetry Center reading at the downtown hall. It saves me having to rent auditorium, put out a mailing, make posters: all of which the P.C. does now. Ruth Witt is an arm-twister to get her own advantage as cheaply as she can and I hate her for it. She offerd $25 from the Poetry Center toward the reading fee subscription and I took it. As a boost at least toward the hundred and fifty I am resolved upon. But Rexroth [who roars from the upper jungles that it is an insult to Poetry etc. that Marianne Moore made a thousand (he still, I understand attacks her on his radio program as a notorious racist and a feeble-minded fraud "quote") and Denise Levertov the authentic article should get a full fee] already rages against my selling you out. I am, I understand, your "manager" and ought to be arranging readings all across the country. Well, all this comes thru information from others. He spoke on his KPFA broadcast this week urging all to hear you in January and, however he does it—his belief in your work is genuine and shld. carry.

I'm writing to him today, to put aside at least my not corresponding with him at all, and to say that I am glad of whatever help he gives. And that I am not "managing" you. God wot! It's Ruth Witt's custom here to own the poet during their stay and decide where and what they shall do. Staying with friends who ain't managers, you'll be the first poet to actually visit the region in some time. As far as calendar goes:

The reading will be Sunday evening: January 19.

And Jess and I would like you and Mitch and Nik to go up to the Tyler's in the country with us for Monday, to come back Tuesday afternoon. It should give us a breather; and Healdsburg, in the wine country, has hills and forest and orchards and stars and no phones. And cats, chickens etc. Mary Tyler will come down for the reading and drive us to the farm. We can come back by bus (an hour and a half trip).

Then let's make a date for dinner and evening here some day in the week at least—but just keep it open when you are arranging other dates.

What about a Chicago reading? I have a friend there Jerry van der Wiele who is enthusiastic about your work and who knows Paul Carroll I gather (from Paul's relaying regards in a recent letter).[2] If you think it might be worth the stop-over there (let's say the place for you to stay could be satisfactorily worked out; and there were at least $50 for a reading) I could write to Jerry and know he would, starting at that minimum try for the optimum. Rago has been very friendly indeed in correspondence and I could enquire there: to see if the possibilities could combine.

love
Robert

Afternoon, Dec. 17

1.  Raising the Fee is not a chore. I get the total amount guaranteed (by somebody who can well afford to do it) and then raise it if I can by subscription where whatever I manage will be to the good and if I makes more hooray! The idea rather excites my animal propensities for collecting.

2.  Audiences here don't ask questions—and they just like hearing poetry. The last thing they will have on their minds is a judgment of what you'll read. They enjoy the stuff. Whatever guff from Rexroth may stir up interest: but it won't change the fact that they'll be there to hear poetry—and hope to add to each his private anthologies of poems that are rememberd. And I'm not going to be advertising you as the greatest living etcetera.

I *will* be doing the notes for the reading. And for the biographical notes I'd like such plain particulars as where, when born, countries lived in, books publishd, magazines, etc. Dancing?

I shall restrain as best I can my more charged identifications with your work and try to hint that just what the poems are might be the thing.

3.  Joe Dunn (working on a multilith machine) and Jess (doing the covers) and I (typing and sewing) have begun to turn out some publications *White Rabbit Press*. We did a longish poem by Jonas that may modify the bad taste (ugliness, tho p'raps truth) of his expressions in *MEASURE*; and just finishd Spicer's beautiful Lorca book.

Point is, Joe askd Sunday would I suggest to you that we could do a booklet of four or five or six recent poems—a sheaf of poems—for sale before your reading. *This operation costs us nothing* so all proceeds could go to you. Not a huge sum, cause we'd only charge a quarter, but it would be pleasant.

And Jess is excited about the possibility of doing a cover to honor.

———————

And at lunch—this pome came, as aftermath of the letter; or started to come, I feel it may have more to it:

Yes, as a look springs from its face
a life colors the meadow
that is green with grass or in harvest
        in stubble aroused
to grace the eye, these poems
        came up from a ground
to illustrate the ground—a book[3]

Dear Robert

That's wonderful, now I feel clearer about everything and less nervous also. We plan to come to SF a couple of days earlier (the 16th probably) as the reading is planned for the 19th. The idea of visiting those friends of yours with the farm is lovely. Thank you very much for that in addition to everything else.

About Chicago, Mitch says it would be Siberian in January—also I think after SF we ought to get straight to N.Y. for Nik's sake; he'll be starting in a new school in February—the old PS41 on Greenwich Ave. is opening in its new building on 11th St in Feb. & I'd like him to start when it opens, & he'll probably have to have a few quiet days first after all the travelling & excitement. Maybe some other time. I had some correspondence with Paul Carroll once.

We're in a Xmas flurry here—I always mean not to but a child has such expectations & then as we're leaving so soon after there's a special sense of climax. And then there are lots of things to take back to friends in N.Y. etc., and the packing up looming. I keep making lists—losing them—taking Equanil—etc. And there are so many fiestas, candlelight processions etc., to see, just now. Nik accidentally got to lead the procession of the Guadalupe! He was proud. I guess if they'd known he was 3 parts Jewish & religiously open-minded they'd have been surprised—but Mexicans don't really give a damn anyway.

Glad to find you love George Herbert, as I do. "The Collar" for one seems to me one of the greatest English poems.

The booklet (White Rabbit Press) is another lovely idea.[1] Please use any poems of mine you think right for it & will send you tomorrow T.S.S. of some recent ones you may not have. Did you like the "Girlhood of Jane Harrison"? If you do (I do) that wd. be a good one for it—and "Seems Like We Must Be Somewhere Else."

Must go to bed now before Mitch falls asleep so I wont wake him up. He has the blues (no publisher) and the sneezes (hayfever). I wish to *god* he'd find a publisher. It is too good to remain a typescript circulating the cautious businessmen publishers seem to be. The rest of yr letter (about the previous discussion, & Herbert etc.) I must read more before I say anything—too distracted yet.

Love—
Denise

Particulars for those notes:
Born Ilford, Essex, Eng., Oct. 1923
Grew up in England, later lived (briefly) in Holland & (longer) Paris, S. of France, Italy, Switzerland, U.S. & Mexico.

Studied ballet but only danced at small private performances as I quit just at the point when I shd. have joined a "company" (nerves and no push—besides I really needed another year's study) so that is really not worth mentioning.

Books published: *The Double Image*, Cresset Press London 1946
*Here & Now* City Lights SF 1957
forthcoming: *Overland to the Islands* Jargon 1958

The stuff K{enneth} R{exroth}had in the back of *New British Poets* was of course exaggerated.[2] But I was a nurse for several years.

---

**68**

22[d] Dec. {1957}
{Oaxaca, Mex.}

Dear Robert and Jess

Here is my suggestion for the little handmade book. Please do as you think about it tho'—i.e. there may be too many.

Thank you both, & please thank Joe Dunn, for wanting to do it. None of these are in the Jargon book (which I refuse to call "Otti" as Jonathan does!) nor published anywhere else.

Love from
Denise

---

**69**

January 5, 1958
{San Francisco}

dear Denise/

Counting the fee offerd by the Poetry Center ($25) I have raised $96 to date and that without making a "drive" to do it. I am keeping the stipulation that no one subscribe unless it will be *easy*; arguing wherever I have my doubts to make sure that subscriptions do not involve any sacrifice. At this point I feel confident of the $150 I hold as my minimun goal. To pay for the actual costs of putting out the booklet (paper and the plates necessary for reproduction) I will use $10 of the money raised so far: it means that charging 25¢ a copy for the booklet, when 100 copies have been sold the $10 will be returnd, and you will have another $15 clear. Meanwhile Kenneth R. has been keeping the topic of your reading on his weekly broadcasts; blasting the Poetry Center for not offering a fee equal to the fee for a Randall Jarrell ($100) or a Marianne Moore ($300)—which makes a principle, where it is just the cash that one wants. And I feel much happier about a subscription toward a fee which reflects unpressured response than I even do about administerd honorariums from an institution. Amen.

All this in the midst of so many activities that only a manic fit would undertake them. I have Dahlberg's book to review; along with handfolding copies of Spicer's first book and getting them down today to be stapled;[1] and being in the midst of a new poem (which I enclose) and of notes for your reading, see below:

Sometime in the Fall of 1952 with the appearance of *ORIGIN* 6 is the date of my "upon first reading Denise Levertov": the opening lines of the poem "The Shifting" came like a key turnd in a lock of fresh possibilities in poetry:[2]

> The shifting, the shaded
> change of pleasure
>
> soft warm ashes in place of fire
> —out, irremediably
>
> and a door blown open:
> > planes tilt, interact, objects
> > fuse, disperse,
> this chair further from that table—hold it!

Rexroth in his article on Denise Levertov's work which appeard in *Poetry* is right at least when he remarks the element of presentational immediacy. There is a strain of perception that holds within the poetic order a disorder of the scene at the moment of its entering the order by which it is known; there is an epiphany then, a showing forth, of reality, from which the poem springs. It is containd, we may return to it: an experience that bears witness to the unity between the inner feeling of the individual poet and the outer becoming of the universe.

In his notes to *New British Poets* Rexroth tells us that she studied Russian ballet from the age of twelve to sixteen. Measure in poetry is kinesthetic—in folk verse and barrack ballads a steady force of the foot; in verse as subtly balanced as Denise Levertov's there is increased articulation, the art springs from a body tone in which a variety of pulsations and movements are discriminated and interrelated. Dance then is significant; and especially the further sense that a dancer has among a group of dancers with a choreography, the sense of a unity that involves more than self. Complex movements in the scene— traffic, winds, shifting light, children's games, the sea—question and answer inner felt movement. Objects are not static but conceived as part of a moving world, verifications of emotion. Form then cannot be taken for granted, conventions of the 18th century that viewd the object as static will not serve. "Here" and "now" demands an open composition, an open eye and an open ear for a fine adjustment of the changing elements of the poem.

Above first draft—and/but it is moving at least in me, the store of actual knowledge from your work.[3]

---

I want to get this off in today's mail and must postpone 'till tomorrow typing out the poem.

love
Robert

**70**

{January 1958}
{Oaxaca, Mex.}
Friday

Dear Robert

We are on our way. Arrive in L.A. Monday & in S.F. on the 15th, a
Wednesday I think, si Dios quiere—

If anything urgent comes up address in L.A. (13th & 14th) will be
c/o Nusset, 693 Quail Drive, Highland Park, L.A.

O Mexico! Now, about to leave, how I love thee—thy kind people, thy
tortillas, black frijoles, & especially the small-town bands of musicos blithely,
seriously, exquisitely discordant—andandand—vale, land of melancholy joys
and joyous melancholy—adios—D.[1]

**71**

Jan. 31ˢᵗ {1958}
249 W. 15th St.
New York 11, N.Y.

Dear Robert and Jess,

So we flew into the eastern night at 3 in the afternoon—at 3:30 the stars
were glimmering around the plane—below, great snowfields & icefloes of
cloud, white lakes in them through which the Earth peered up, salted with
real snow—

New York is very dirty. More than ever. And there were bugs in Nik's bed
& we had to throw it out. And the first person I met in the A&P was
Virginia Admiral. One of my best friends is in a mental home. I knew she
was at this place but didn't realize what it was. Nik & Mitch are thrilled to
be back, each in his way, & I feel rather sorry for myself. But that is rather
silly I guess when I think of the other 9 million.

Thank you for everything. It was you who made everything really be
there.

Please don't forget to send the record. I read the poems on the train &
my god they are good. I didn't really get all the Psyche when you read it.
Will write more abt. this next letter.

All that richness in Jess's paintings, big & little, & in your apartment,
is something I want from life. Anyone who MAKES anything in New
York is a hero—anything one can make, any richness of living one can
accrue is a heroic act, a magic. I feel weak & deprived here. Yet what
I saw with you gives me zest—if I can only cut thru all the junk,
dirt, pressure of organizational low-level demands, to get at the magic
zest!

With love—
Denny

Mrs. W{itt}.D{iamant}. gave me the $25 with the hope we had not told
anyone about it! We were startled into a lying defensive denial, I'm sorry
to say.

dear Mitch and Denny/

I had a sad afternoon with Mrs. Salz a mouse visiting a cat to ask for a donation for a country mouse—and the cat politely overlookd the most direct question as to whether she would aid (cat having supplied a grand opening by saying "She understood I had arranged for Miss Levertov's coming here."{)} Now I've to write her the more than most direct demand and somehow over-ride my anger at the social ploy. The heart goes out of me, and I've got to charge thru my mood to try for the $57. Don't count on it. Relieve me of that desperation. And then let me do what I can, by whatever inspiration.

But the record will be off in this same mail tomorrow morning. Jess is decorating the jacket cover (since dinner time) with an elaborate collage.

Marianne Moore writing to Spicer of *After Lorca* added in a postscript: "Solitude is the only cure of loneliness."

A letter from Mr. Moe arrived informing me that it wld. now be in order for me to submit specimens of my work to the committee etc., copies of previous publications.[1] So I am over the first hurdles, whatever that means. And have been in the throws of preparing said mss./packing off what copies I had of previous publications.

Denny:      Your reading has won the praise of all whose praise means something to me, and praise elsewhere. It enlivens all to have that Sunday group referring again and again to those poems to take measure. And perseveringly as I have read your work, eagerly, these last years; the reading for me too brought the concerted thing—together! I had my actual seeing (hearing) of the book. And saw things about the poetry I had only felt before, as if elusive—relationships and developments (no, I don't mean progresses or improvements etc.—but developments woven thru and thru the poems. I am the more impatient to clear this desk of letters to be written, mss to be sent off, the Dahlberg still to be finished—and get to work on what I know is there—something clearer, juster, and more of a whole than the program notes.

Tonight my wind won't range. But I want to exclaim well, just how rich a visit we had with both you and Mitch—and were delighted with Nik.

As Mary Tyler wrote: "we all liked the Goodmans all. I wish we could have had a few really peaceful days here—if only they were going to settle near by so they could come again when we weren't all in a rush." And she quotes a Lawrence letter—"In a world where most of the human influence is now destructive to be with people whose presence is an enrichment in the veins is everything."

I could not imagine goodbyes. Writing to you is always so vivid for me, a solitude in which you are, that I do not lose all in your distance. Yet the

# 72

February 4, 1958
{San Francisco}

reality, the company of you *you* and Mitch gives the firmer ground of actual companionship. I could not want to lose the intense thing as it comes in correspondence (I have not yet come to write other than *business* letters within the city), but I wish we were within the distance of easy visits, of company.

love
Robert

**73**

Feb. 8, {19}58
{San Francisco}

dear Denny/

Just a short note to accompany this checks.

*Partisan Review* decided against doing prose-poems; the rejection came the same day as a letter from Laughlin saying he wasn't interested in *Faust Foutu* (sent to him when I was in Mallorca). It's been a week of discouragements.

Mike Rumaker is going to New York on the 15th and I must get this in the mail and go by to see him.

love
Robert

**74**

{February, 1958
New York}

At Mitch's cousin's.[1] ¡SNOWBOUND!
Mitch will be writing to you too.

Dear Robert and Jess

Marooned by snow & Nik who is sick with "flu" I want so much to write to thank you for the record—the marvellous color—& the lovely surprise of the drawing—but on notepaper with this ballpoint I can't do it properly— I don't feel myself to be quite present. That you mean to send a painting too is just too much—what it means to have friends like you is hard to convey—there's so much in our lives in New York that's gloomy and sordid— already, or again—just as I knew it wd be. To have things like that arrive on a day of problems that I wont inflict on you was like the sun coming out.

Thanks too for the letter & for the checks. The note with the checks was abt. *P.R.* & other discouragements & I wish I had something besides this anemic letter to send you at this moment. A poem. Or some snow. I don't like the cold but this afternoon as I shovelled snow off the driveway in the sun I enjoyed it (being dressed for the part in all sorts of borrowed plumage) I enjoyed the sparkle & crispness—didn't feel numb & miserable. Poor Nik who hasn't had a chance to get out with his 3 cousins into the snow said (the 1st day—we'd (he & I—Mitch is at home) come out for a weekend & he got sick almost right away)—"Den, could you bring me in some kind of little container of snow?" I did, in a baking tin.

Love to everyone including the dear Tylers & very much to you, both of you—

Denny

I'm having an exciting time with the Mina Loy.

Dear Robert

I have a few poems now to send you. We've all been sick with some virus but are beginning to feel better & Mitch mailed off the damn Provence article today so he'll be able to get to work I hope now. Things are strangely unchanged here in many ways—I mean, what is strange is to think that all these people have been going on & on doing exactly the same things these 2 years—like the crazy (tight mouthed, withdrawn, Gurdjieff-disciple) woman underneath who mechanically bangs out the same (or almost the same) Brahms intermezzo or whatever it is over & over again each night, the same mistakes patiently and perseveringly repeated—& the amiable flutist above twiddling his pleasant pastoral notes—& certain gross demonish rooming-house landladies or janitresses across the street having the same grim conversations by the garbage cans—etc etc etc.

Nik has started going to gym classes at Greenwich House which he seems to enjoy (extremely nice Italian guy is the instructor & the atmosphere is friendly—Nik told me "when someone gets hit by the ball, which means he's 'out,' they all say 'Good try'—& I've got some new buddies there too") & tho' he has a rather grouchy old teacher at school he seems to be making out pretty well & is making an effort (for the first time) to catch up in his weak subjects. He goes around on his own, even as far down as Barrow St (Green-wich Hse.) & tho' I sometimes have qualms abt. the traffic I'm very happy that he has so quickly gained confidence—he used to be really scared of many things that don't seem to worry him at all now; also doesn't wake with nightmares. It's all the Language! I think there's something very interesting there, of more universal meaning, but I'm too tired right now to think it thru'—but you'll see what I'm after. I think in fact there's the seed of a poem there. . . .

In all the confusion of dirt, cold, bedbugs, & flu (from all of which we are now emerging into some sort of order if not grace)—I don't know if I ever properly thanked Jess for the poems—I may only have spoken of the drawing & the record—but the poems are so completely & uniquely Jess & I'm so glad to have them, & in reading them I can hear the mocking & tender shades of his voice.

**75**

March 6th {1958}
249 W 15th St
N.Y. 11

Had such a nice letter from Maddie {Madeleine Gleason}, I do like her.

Have mailed copies of *Overland to the Islands* to you, Helen Adam, etc. Would send one to Ida Hodes who was so nice to us & gave me the blue coat, but it might then seem too pointed that I don't send one to Mrs Fiddle-Diamond,[1] & I'm damned if I'm going to send *her* one. Or ought I to? O, to hell with oughts. It is meaningless if one sends *against* one's impulse.

Jonathan tells me he's sent you what I wrote on Mina Loy.[2] I got a kick out of his being so pleased with it, not because I value his judgement much but because his pleasure was so unexpected, as it was the first thing of its kind I'd ever attempted & I wasn't at all sure it would make sense to anyone but myself. I sure did write it with zest tho'. Doing the Guggenheim thing for you was a similar opportunity but I'm afraid I didn't use it intelligently enough, being made nervous by its being about you whom I know & love. Knowing nothing of M. L. made me able to be more precise.

Have to go to bed, will continue tomorrow.

D.

*Monday*

The next day the landlord sent a plasterer to patch the walls—& the day after was spent cleaning from morning to night—really with some effect too thank god—& yesterday we had company—so I'm now going to break off & mail this & say the rest in another letter. Pkge. from you to Nik was just brought upstairs by the unusually nice mailman & lies mysteriously on Nik's chest of drawers for him to open when he returns from school this afternoon.

With much love from
Denny.

---

**76**

Tues.
{March} 18th {1958}
249 W. 15th St.
N.Y. 11

Dear Robert and Jess,

The beautiful painting came.[1] Thank you! Summery (late summer or even September) afternoon, warm, gently simmering & humming with bees, into which the pleased personage has wandered from a French window, not having known even that the landscape lay there.

And *Tik-Tok*. Nik & I are reading it together. He's home sick with a nasty cough & we're both glad to have extra reading time. The week before I had found 3 old Oz books for $1.50 each—*The Tin Woodman of Oz*, *Jack Pumpkinhead*, and *The Scarecrow of Oz*.

Am reading KR's very lovely Chinese & Japanese translations, also a collection called *America & Alfred Stieglitz*,[2] do you know it?—came out in the 30's & has some good stuff in it.

Midi Garth's dance recital at the Henry St. Playhouse on Saturday was terrific. She's a *great* artist, at her best—& the evening had much of her very best. Wish you cd. see her. It's terrible to think she has about 1 recital a year at most & *often* goes hungry etc. It's such an ephemeral art so that one can't but think of the wastage. But at least this time (unlike the last time I saw her) she had a full house & very enthusiastic too. Afterward there was a party at which just about everyone we know in N.Y. foregathered (at Nell Blaine's place)—I enjoyed it but Mitch didn't; as always. Wish he were able to enjoy such things, I always feel guilty and rather a fool for having had fun when he hasn't.

I've been receiving some remarkably silly letters & poems from Gregory Corso (in Venice) & visits that are boring from Pete Orlovsky whose "saintliness" I begin to see through—not that he has not a very good heart, but his intelligence does not match it. But I'm sorry for both of them as they genuinely appear to have had a lousy start in life & after all are just trying to make something of their lives like I am so can't give them the brushoff but I sure am tired of the whole circle & of the conversation among everyone one meets turning inevitably to Ginsberg & Kerouac; I got a kick out of *Howl* & *On the Road* but now the whole thing is such a goddamn bore.

Still haven't seen W. C. W. because of all these colds in the family, at least one of us has been sick ever since we got here.

Saw Don Allen again & liked him better than the first time. He seems to have sincere affection & admiration for you, Robert. He seems rather a gentle & essentially lonely person. Seems to me you shd. go along with his idea of a *Selected Poems* even tho' it is in opposition to your conception of a Book, because it will serve as an introduction to your work to many people who had never read you at all before. Since you have written many different kinds of poems this does seem quite important for a book that would be well-distributed. Not just a shoddy compromise. What do you think? I agree with you about a book being a whole in general, but isn't this maybe a special case? Or has he been persuading me?

Jonathan will be here at the end of the month. He has arranged some sort of reading, wants me to read too. Joel Oppenheimer, Zukofsky, Jonathan himself, & so on. I don't feel very keen on it—N.Y. atmosphere seems full of ambition, insincerity, & chic.

Al Kresch has been in St Vincent's hospital a week with suspected kidney stone but was sent home today. The first day I felt very upset by it, suddenly realizing what it would mean to us if he died (he wasn't that sick but one thinks of it just the same) and that some day I at least will experience just that, (for I feel I'll outlive most people I know). I hope you get to know him some day, you would both certainly love him.

Wednesday.

This isn't much of a letter. Please don't think I am any different, it is just that there are so many pressures on me at this point (even tho' this little room here which used to be the junk-room, off the kitchen, is really a pleasure & gets nicer every day) that I am only half here—for example today Nik is home with a cold, I want to get him some linseed tea for his cough & the only place I cd. get the linseed so far as I know is a little shop near China-town I once saw, can't remember exactly where it was, ought to have visited an old lady painter, Frances Eckstein, by now, ought to go over to Al's place on Bleecker St. & see how he is, have to pick up shoes from cobbler,—

Wow! This is a very small section of my stream of consciousness, not intended as a complaint (because things aren't really bad for us here now) but just as an explanation of why this letter sounds as if written by a poltergeist. In Mexico my head kept comparatively free from clutter.

When we finish unpacking the trunks & boxes we left here during the 2 years & sorting out all my mother's stuff (most of which can't be sent to her because of customs, expense of mailing, etc.) & throwing out papers that 2 years ago seemed worth keeping but the very existence of which we had by now forgotten—when that's all done (almost is) things will clear a bit & Ill get more of a hold. Forgive me for boring you and please write soon. We *love* the painting and feel very privileged to have it. I'm looking forward to Al seeing it. Mitch will be writing to you one day soon also.

Love—
Denise

P.S.

I haven't forgotten about the Hans Andersen with Robinson pictures I want to lend you, & some other things I want to send, but haven't unboxed them yet.

Had a nice letter from Mae Belle {Beim}, sounding calmer & reporting that she & Alan are dieting successfully & that she'd seen you. "Sure do like them!" she says. Did she tell you she may go to Japan on a freighter this summer? Wish I could go too!

Love—
D.

Dear Robert and Jess,

Thank you for *Tik-tok of Oz*, I like it very much. Mitch and I are going to make some shelves. I have been painting.

love from
Nik X

dear Denny,

We were driving just two weeks ago with Harry Jacobus[1]—well, it wasn't quite like that, for a friend had sent on a postcard a clipping from a paper advertising a beach cottage, so we went to Stinson Beach for the drive and ended up taking a house with a garden—fruit trees, flowering bushes and plants, strawberries and artichokes and all—and a great peppertree at the south of the house. There is a new address then: P.O. Box 14, Stinson Beach.

We moved out last Wednesday which proved to be our only day of respite from a cold continual drizzle. Poor Pumpkin caught pneumonia and Jess had to catch the early bus in today to take him to the S.P.C.A. There is only one bus on weekdays: into San Francisco at 6:30 AM and leaving San Francisco at 5:10 PM to arrive here at 6:30 PM. It's like Bañalbufar then; and we're up above the sea again which is all white and grey now. With a deluge of rain to break the drizzle. There was a clear spell early after the bus left when I gatherd driftwood and managed two loads before the rain started.

Now I was just up to stoke the fire, and it's cleard. There's the sun! and a wide blue rift in the sky with the sea green and purple in the grey. If it holds I'll make another trip to the shore for wood. And there is watercress in the creek we saw yesterday by the road.

I've had a review to do of the Dahlberg's *Sorrows of Priapus* that has become a burden of conscience and nothing else yet—it quarrels with the tune of things. To have to do anything, I suppose, in part.

love<br>Robert

P.O. Box 14, Stinson Beach, California

77

March 24, 1958
{Stinson Beach}

Dear Robert

It is lovely to think of you by the sea, a vision of which came to me so vividly as I read yr letter this morning—a sort of compensation for being ourselves dangerously alienated from natural solaces and reminders. Sent you 3 new poems, *Overland to the Islands*, & letter thanking you & Jess for Oz book & for Jess's terrific painting, also letter from Nik and another letter to thank Jess for the drawing—none of which you mention—cd. your removal have caused them to go astray? I hope not—tho' they were a lousy bunch of letters. But let me know if you got the snake poem.[1] Have just been reading (beginning to anyway) the Jane Harrison *Prolegomena*. Expect pkge with small housewarming gift. Will mail it tomorrow.

Love<br>Denny

78

March 26th {1958
New York}

## 79

Dearest Robert

I am seized with the feeling that my dull letters of late or perhaps my not thanking you sufficiently (from embarrassment) for all the work & bother with the checks, have hurt your feelings or in some way annoyed you or something—I love you & Jess & yr. friendship is very important to me, I want to deserve it, but at times of strain like this return to N.Y. I do get stupid & dull & awkward & can't write letters or if I do they are such that I don't even know what the hell I did say. Anyway please forgive anything I may have said or omitted to say. Hope Pumpkin is recovering. We are not going to get a cat till the fall, in order not to have to switch it around in the summer. Jonathan was here yesterday looking very Episcopalian, not to say Episcopal even, potentially.

Love,
Denny

## 80

We went across the road (Duerden, the Creeleys and I) to hear your reading on K.P.F.A. They'd done nothing to edit the tape—and they had only to take out a few coughs and shorten the interval between poems. Damn them! But your reading is beautiful. I love that courage of the aged, courage of the young poem.

dear Denny—

Your postcards came yesterday and O no it was not any disaffection but only my procrastination, and there's no wonder to that, for there's been the business of acknowledging the sea, and there's been ten days or more of stormy weather. And Mr. Pumpkin our darling died—well, I knew when I wrote you last that it must be he would—he was so sick—And we were here without means to get him to a hospital until it was too late. There are so many levels of understanding what happend. There was the fact, Pumpkin just isn't there, there is the thing, the word "dead"—at once unalterable and I'm numb to it; and ununderstandable, and I want a grey ghost of him that isn't here either. And, as always, as before and no better than when I was a child—an utter grief has its way of taking over. O I'll refer to them, and then face it that there's only Kit. And two days ago Kit suddenly went into a while of searching the house and talking, going back and forth from Jess and me—about something, and not going-out or being food time—about Pumpkin. Amen to that. Let it lie still.

As it does most of the time. There is so much to do—new tasks of everyday: weeding, gathering driftwood, sawing—Kit flourishes. There have been enough clearings in the rainy weather for him to have claimd the brand-new pleasures of a country garden in the sun.

Bob and his wife—Bobby, and infant Susan arrived Sunday. She is quite striking, a beauty in her way. There's something in her effortful participation in "talk," in her "making conversation" that reminds me of Ann. . . . I was going to say it doesn't intrude, but it does of course subtly. As all who make up conversation feel themselves unrelated—reserve judgment.

Bob had sent three poems, at the same time you sent the arrival in N.Y. poem, the mice and the snake ones.[1] And I'd felt both sets of poems to be transitional. But then I was in transition (of yours, it was the arrival one that seemd to have a new tempo, almost narrative, in a short poem)— Now Bob has read his aloud, and he had been unsure of them—so that today was the first time he read them. Shifting from the characteristic syncopation. Something new is going on. . . . Well, I include them for your eye. Yet now, perhaps because my own continuous feeling is taking root again, the sea with its glare and its horizon—a base!, and the death of a cat are joind into feeling again: just so there doesn't seem to be the break I'd felt in the two birds flying poem or in Bob's "Heroes," as if I had to study them in order to grasp something.[2] I get the pace of the "pleading mysteriously, half-hostile, was drawn" and don't have to yield something to follow it.

Yes, I received *Overland to the Islands* and it was beautiful, rightly— as *Here and Now* at last I see had not been as a physical object and that that counted: it was mixd up with my discontent about the poems being "selected": and both of us have, even in this flurry of moving, found our peace in it. When we returnd (the Creeleys and I) from San Francisco Sunday Jess was sitting at the table by the fire reading thru the book.

The poems being given their place, not run on, is right.

I can't separate always the . . . ¿but what is the separation there? the love of everything you write and that I love you. There's friendship and its courtesies—you're perhaps right that we've to deserve friendship. But love is nature to nature and your being is what sustains me there, not your deserving. Could I send you the storm that is coming up again, blowing in with columns of rain? Or the vine flourishing single-roses at the north wall of the house? What natural solace or reminder? But wherever you find again—and the blessing is how, even in the terrible you do—the visible nature that's yours, it is mine too. That's your continuing gift to me, or thru you the poem, the gift that comes to me. When you warn against a direction I have taken in a poem—as you did about that "Enamord Mage"—for me it is love that warns, that you cry out O no, not there! Not that way! Or even, at times—the O don't disappoint me. Dearest Denny, we've that appointment everywhere. I feel it with Bob— and said it in a poem:

out of loving you
who color
now my death as it is.

A letter from you is never dull, for your handwriting itself renewd, found in the post, quickens my day. Can't love share getting stupid and dull and awkward . . . not blind but I treasure the wholeness. Out of which, it's all the only stem of it, being. But the letters had not been stupid or dull or awkward. There had been—well, I went back, go back here to the letter itself: what was it that haunted you so that you thot you had been dull or awkward? Damn it. There's the dullness, the stupidity, the awkwardness of the City, the belabord Brahms intermezzo persisting from the apartment below, the dirt, the landladies those drabs! But there's the germ of life in Nik's taking hold, returning thru his (our) native language, our nature, of a poem. I'ld mail you my actual heart, Denny, but I know it wldn't have half the strength to last against or within the environs of New York that you have. I can only visit the New York thing (when I was living there I came near to despair, and tried to commit suicide and then got out, scared in part but mostly because I saw that the me the island furnishd was starving another me). When I do visit, there is the old mixture of excitement, even old flashes of a glory, the wealth of objects— a visit to the Met., or the Museum of Modern Art, and there is the old crushing sense of not having money, and of being so poorly geard for survival there.

We got Nik's thank-you note—and we read his handwriting and remember what a delightful boy he was on your visit. Mitch's and your stay here is still vivid. I wish Mitch wld undertake the adventure of trying to make a living here—yet, it is not easy . . . it is not easy anywhere. I am so helpless, so least of help here—not knowing the *ins* of where work as a writer can be found, reporting, etc. And the rumors of a depression fly now barely in advance of the evidence. If the desperate times do come again, there would be comfort in neighborhood, for whatever actual help depends there. Funny about "making a living"—I feel confident about my own household, but panic stricken if I think of hardship in any other.

love,
Robert

Wednesday—April 2: We are in the midst of a savage rainstorm—what a visit for the Creeleys! Under attack from the north driving under door sills, a solid blur of water at the windows thru which, a turmoil, white within white, breakers almost show that there is land and sea. They become a deceptive horizon. All above and below is dove white, downy. Trees are tossing shadows, washd of their green, of denser chalky grey

Weather is immediate here. What a splendor of that foaming powerful horizon—today all things are unsettled

dear Denny/

The Creeleys got off this morning by 11—to drive to Los Angeles . . . a little grimly because Perkoff (who was up here for a Poetry Reading at the Center last Sunday) and a friend of his had pressd him against his reticence and Bobby's visible misgivings to drive them to L.A.

Last night at Joe Dunn's Bob gave a reading that stands now with Charles's and yours to make a triumpherate of the beauty the discrete voice can give to the poem—I had feard he would mumble or obscure the voice of the poem (for all reports of his last reading here had been that it was poor indeed). But there came right off the clear, somewhat higher (clearing out the distracting resonances) voice that belongs to music. Careful choice points to the word "lovely," if bird song and bell are lovely. ¿is there always a tristesse . . . there is a delight too in that voice. A frail strength? that reverses the movement of the line, letting all depth, solidity be entrusted to the poem itself. Bob did say that he had in the last year found how to read. Pride can be happy; I've got a kind of proud proof, verification of what I have admired in poetry, in these readings. To have Bob win completely the hearts and minds of the younger poets, and of Spicer who resists (and was enraptured at Bob's work at last coming thru) as you won them.

And earlier this afternoon I wrote the first poem since the move here.[1] It starts with the surf-line that fascinated me when during the storm several days ago there was a spell of heavy whiteness, an obscurity of everything in which the known demarcations were gone, and the breaking waves became a pun on the horizon, begins there and goes straight to a cry out for Mr. Pumpkin so that when I tried to read it aloud to Jess I could not read that line "O dear grey cat . . . " and had at last the full paroxysm of pain I had held back as best I could. God! everything lost in life rehearses in a little grief. And this loss is in the midst of happiness. Do I really dread so that everything might be swept away? Sometimes, Denny, I also say to myself that {I} have been prepared by all that accompanies me and would rejoice to be its survivor in a new life. It all tips there, like a table balanced in the wind—on a point of the wind.

There was your letter, a paragraph about Al Kresch's illness; and the poem "Heroes" of Bob's which I sent you last letter.[2] Spicer had askd last night for a repeat reading of it. You know, that word "labors" in Bob's poem clearly to me, means a woman's labors in birth.

love,
Robert

dear Denny/

The beautiful *Goblin Market* arrived this morning, with meadowlark and clear weather at last, for the much gossipd storm passd far out at sea in a black sky with flashes of lightning and thunderous exclamations; sent us a squall or two and went on.[1] Now everything and us too we is relieved. Tho days of rain had things to teach us.

Over a full pot of coffee we sit, Jess read the *Goblin Market* aloud. She does have command of tempo and knows the grace of departures within a steady stress. And Lizzie standing "Like a lily in a flood,—like a rock of blue-veind stone . . . etc." "Like a fruit crownd orange-tree white with blossoms honey-sweet sore beset by wasp and bee" is a heroine of native virtues beset by angry tempters. It needs heroics at times to realize what's going on. There's the greater pleasure in the fact that Christina Rossetti is {ink blot: perhaps "not"?} at issue in the aesthetics of the time (as we like furnishings, lamps, objets d'art that exist outside the concerns of modern taste). One can whole-heartedly like her without distractions of "use."

As Eigner writes "From what u say, you can turn others' stuff to yr own good, for yr own purposes; I gather quite a few people can too." Sounds a little horrid . . . "for ones own purposes." I'd read "for the purposes of the poem." Yet it's instruction not use I have from work like Eigner's. His temperament is that different from mine that it instructs my excesses—and then, writing a poetry of perception—where the language is a use toward feeling doesn't he have the immediate sense that I use the language toward another end, and it is what I call form that can use everything:

Teaching—and being taught by the teaching—is on my mind. Reading Zimmer's *Philosophies of India* and I balk at the submissiveness of learning (just what it seems also necessary to yield so to the language—not to use but to be used).[2]

The most important thing for me in the decision about the Grove Press proposal of a *Selected Poems* is my obedience to the order of my work. I've not to find new readers, nor have I to gain a better position. Mayn't I die tomorrow? and what position then is best? But I have to see these books thru, to sense that inspiration that moved me when I imagined them, and to piece together the text complete in each phase. I do not believe in gems, or in a reader's digest volume of the best. Where I myself have not had the information to select I do not trust other hands. A selection by Robin, or Olson, or you, or Robert (Creeley) or Spicer would mean something: yes, I would trust that. But what understanding in the world gives Don Allen insight to select?

In making the decision to do *Caesar's Gate* I had to stand by a group of poems I felt ill at ease with. At first I wanted to discard them, disavow them. But it was a complete phase, a whole round of the process; and I set my teeth to it. Allowing myself only the diversion of the later pieces to provide a setting. The book I submitted to Grove follows *Caesar's Gate*, and I am convinced I've got to see it thru. Here *The Field* is all but finished; yet the *Resemblances* must find a printer first.

Let it be my superstition. *Overland to the Islands* if it is selection by chance, etc. is a joy; and has what I delight in in a book—the interaction in juxtaposition. As, *Here and Now* seemd to me meaninglessly compiled. But your reading was the book beyond *Overland to the Islands*. As now, mightn't Robert's work be gatherd together from *Le Fou* to *The Dress* and the new poems in one?

Let it be my faith too. That there is an order; {words blotted out} but "evolution," the magic whereby forms come {words blotted out} mean works of art as forms, but I mean also {words blotted out} that sense. The form of Hamlet or Lear or Desdemona {words blotted out} And you and I are forms. The art is the area of {words blotted out} being manifest. We're calld up to dance. And damn the New Critics and the professors of Literature, what has that to do with the poem in itself, or the Best of Pope selected by Dr. XX. O something, yes—for the New Critics and Dr. XX are dancers too. That's the adventure of it. There's selection. It's rightly for us what Darwin calld natural selection. And I'd call by kindred spirit. Whereto I go without hesitation. There'll be the wherefrom I turn without explanation too then.

———————————

You know Jess and I admire Art Nouveau, and a great deal of it is close to heart. Have you seen Tiffany's exhibit at the Museum of Contemporary Crafts, 29 West 53rd Street?[3] We saw a catalog that a friend brought back from N.Y. Could you get us a catalog and we'll send the price promptly? And I'd love to think of your having seen some of that work.

April 9, 1958

The notice came yesterday that the application for the Guggenheim was not granted. A relief in the least not to be existing on the possibility—and we've to set to another year of piecing together (at least, the rent is coverd each month) the light bill, food, installments on refrigerator etc.

I might try to break thru the "prose barrier" and see if I can do a group of short stories. The damnd money looms large. For all of us—

Meanwhile I've got one garden plot ready for planting (about six hours of monomanical weeding—but I find it a blissful occupation in my own garden. A concentration in learning the {words blotted out}. Before I turn to the garden today and {words blotted out} as I did yesterday) I'll get this in an envelope {words blotted out} off to you.

No news of *Letters* being resumed.

love<br>Robert

249 (Don't put 259 again, I almost lost those letters! W. 15ᵗʰ St. NY 11

Dear Robert and Jess,

*Thanks for lovely letters.*

Mitch saw Tiffany show by accident but I missed it—it had closed the day before—however I enjoyed the catalog which I'm mailing to you. (Please forget the price, it's on me.)

KR{exroth} was here & made a nasty scene accusing *me* of having *"played a large part in destroying his life"* by alleged letters encouraging Bob to abduct Marthe. The poor man is insane, but I can't feel as sorry for him as I should; because he insulted me & got (I believe) a kick out of pouring out hours of filthy stories beside which Jack Spicer's making his own feeling (that the female genitalia are ugly) into a dogmatic statement, is an innocent gaffe.[1]

He was also threatening in a cool manner to kill Bob because he believed he had been seeing Marthe again, but apparently has now spoken to Marthe on the phone & believes this is not so after all, & has stopped threatening.

About Grove & a selection. *Of course* if it were to be Don Allen who selected I absolutely agree with you. I had been thinking of the possibility of your making the selection yourself. But I think I do see now why you can't.

If you see Joe Dunn cd you ask him if there are some copies of my & Jess's *5 Poems* I cd still obtain?

We went to see Greek vases from the Hearst collection at the Metropolitan, twice.[2] And looked again at Vuillard's *Cezanne's Garden*, one of our favorite paintings & incidentally one that many of yours, Jess, seem close to in certain ways.

We have gone through a kind of upheaval or revolution in our private life & are feeling timidly very happy, new, and in accord with these gentle blithe spring days.

Spent 3½ v. pleasant days with M. C. Richards & David Tudor at Stony Point.

Love to Helen {Adam} & Madeline {Gleason} when you see them. I *will* write to each of them—eventually. Have unpacked the Hans Anderson I want to lend you & will mail it soon.

Love—

D.

P.S.

Had a nice note from Bob's wife saying, "It was such a pleasure to hear you read while we were in S.F. One more point of joy in a trip that was overall happy. It rained & rained but Duncan's house had a huge window overlooking the coast & in the room a fireplace that went almost constantly so the feeling was one of shelter, together with Jess & Robert's solicitousness". . .

Thanks v. much for photos. You don't look "grinny" I think—v. nice picture of you both—& the lamp—& what a lovely house it looks to be. Wow! And thanks for putting the arrow pointing to the sea.

---

Bob's poems—I'm unsure about them. The "oh"'s in "Going to Bed"—a slight Gravesian quality in "Heroes"—; and "Saturday Afternoon" (tho it also recalls, faintly, some Graves poems) I like best, but have no idea what it is about—can you write some more about them, what you get there? What the monster is? Etc.?[3]

Dear R and Jess

This letter, the one about the nasty commotion, interrupted & temporarily superseded another abt. Pumpkin (poor Pumpkin—I remember Pumpkin poems of before) & the sea poem (which I love) (but which seems to me to end before the end, the last parts being a separate poem) & to say how surprised & sorry I am that you did not get the Guggenheim—but that letter is lost somewhere. I had to move all my things, (in fact everything in the house) because of the men working here at putting in steam heat (a bonanza for the landlord) so instead of starting over again I'll wait & see if it turns up, especially since the sea poem is with it, & I therefore can't explain properly what I mean. It is a grand poem—I don't mean that colloquially (only) but truly it has grandeur, the sea really got into it. But the pendant quality of the ending stanzas raises the question again for me of—but wait, I must get this mailed & will go into that when I find the ½ written letter and can do it properly.

Love—<br>from Denny

Were you able to move the stained glass window successfully?

**84**

Thursday
{April} 24th {1958
New York}

dear Denny/

The damnation of that man! K. R. I mean. I'd dreaded when you were here that he might blow off. As Jess and I once saw Joanne McClure after answering the phone stand stunnd with a white outraged face, and learnd when finally she managed to break off the tirade that it was a Rexroth "earful"—it was too insane, she said, for her to even think of putting the receiver down. And under the guise of telling Joanne "what Creeley was saying all over town about Marthe." It mattering not even that Creeley was in Albuquerque at the time. What stores such filths in a man's mind? The malice seems not to be its being told to influence the listener to believe what is not true, it's too often something the listener patently

**85**

April 28, {29} 1958
{Stinson Beach}

knows is not true—but in the thing being told to outrage or torture the listener.

As, everyone knows that Dr. Williams loves Marianne Moore— "synonymous with much that I hold dearest to my heart" he wrote in one of his essays. And K. R. at the Institute of Personality Assessment during the social hour before dinner (watchd, of course, by psychiatrists avidly) pourd out his whole vilification of Marianne Moore (sexual and political invective and fabrications) all over the suffering good Williams.

The madness is that beyond the cruelty to the hearer—the hearer himself is always someone Kenneth has a particular regard for. A fiendish force that isolates him from all goods of friendship—from all goods in himself. It's the straight Dr. Jekyll and Mr. Hyde. And in the actuality how it corrupts the scene. There's jackal and kill and hide mixed up in it.

Tuesday, April 29:

In the morning at nine I walk the two blocks down our hill to "town" which is just Airey's store and the postoffice; and collect the mail. Sit over coffee with Jess, stare at the sea. Then, after writing letters to go on the immediate response to the letters received—there's the garden. Where Jess and I spent most of yesterday cultivating a plot for climbing peas and beans. Today I'll put more peas along a fence, if'n I can root up the briar and morninglory: both of which take over the countryside. I spent a lot of the digging up, ripping out weeds, and throwing out rocks yesterday trying to rip out the weedy preoccupation with K. R. aberrations. Today, it's our and your blithe spring days I'd share.

I hope you find what you wrote on the last poem. I can see . . . maybe a possible break of "O dear grey cat" that might be pendant. That I had to (or did) collage in the "what it would mean to us if he died" from your letter about Al Kresch; and use also Bob's close from a poem "death also etc." to close is I think evidence of something being off. Do you mean—I can see {word blotted out} adjusting—an end at the line "upon an answering obscurity"?

love<br>Robert

P. S. Sorry and surprised abt. Guggenheim.

## 86

May 3d {1958
New York}

Dear Robert,

I cant find my original beginning of the letter about "A Storm"—must have thrown it out by mistake. But yes, that is it, an end at "upon answering obscurity." To me it thus is a complete poem. The rest (especially the 1st stanza of the rest—"O dear grey cat"—but of course what follows follows from that so that the "especially" is irrelevant) is something else—perhaps basis for another poem?—not a complete one as it stands—But in any case not a true part of the preceding poem—which is, if cut off at that point, one of yr *best* poems I think, one with a tremendous emotional & visual impact—or one that *is* emotional and *seems* visual because it is *in* the words, the sounds—as it shd be—& most, in the movement & its silences, or pauses—the articulations is the word isn't it?

Louisa Mat{th}iasdottir's show at Tanager Gallery opened yesterday—Lee Bell's wife whose paintings in photos you didn't like at Mallorca; but looking at them last night I was wondering how they would strike you & Jess in reality and decided you probably would admire them even if probably they would never be among those specially dear to you.[1] (Forgive my not mailing the Tiffany Catalog by the way—will do so Monday—I lost the envelope which fitted it and keep forgetting to get another.) I feel I could live without them but their strength (nothing of K. Mansfield-type femininity, the attenuated kind, there) and integrity remain very moving to me nevertheless. We went to the Seurat show—that was interesting but rather sad.[2] As you probably know he died suddenly at 32. Almost all the paintings were from between 1882 & 1888. The 3 or 4 we liked best, excluding some of the studies for *La Grande Jatte*, were dated 1882. The studies were wonderful paintings, including the larger—(tho less than ½ as big as the finished painting)—"definitive study." And then the painting itself: static, flat— beautiful *in a way*—but a so much lesser way than the vibrating-with-life studies—! Comparatively dead. And the circus paintings, & *La Poudreuse*— unconvincing. *Integrity* isn't enough, I see. Or in his case, it became reduction. His revisions were polishings, not re-visions (your note, I'm recalling now, in "The Artist's Vision"—one I often re-read).

This brings me back to what I wanted to say before. I'm torn between a sense of affirmation of that idea—*not* to revise, (not unless it is a complete new seeing) not to polish, to stammer if one stammers, etc.,—and my sense of craftsmanship, for the complete (by which I don't mean the closed, the dead).* Maybe the conflict is one of those blissful uncertainties that is fruitful—certainly it's one I've had with me a long time—so I don't want to solve or resolve it—but it interests me to know how far you'd go, or whether your own attitude has changed? e.g. you seem to be willing to consider cutting that part of the poem even tho yr. feeling abt. Pumpkin gave impetus to the rest of the poem by influencing your seeing of the storm. I had wondered if you wdn't say, "No, that was how it was, it was not 'pendant' to me, and therefore must not me tampered with."

*Complete as a pot is complete, i. e. it is no good if it leaks, anyway.

The acceptance of accident—the letting-go of the top layer of mind & its prejudices and restraints—the entering of magic worlds one cannot direct, natural magic not contrived by oneself in a tall mooned-& starred hat—the religious sense of abandonment—all that is very attractive to me, not just as an idea but as something I have experienced. But I've as strong a love for care, concern, intelligence—all the craftsman qualities. (Please realize I'm no longer talking abt yr. poem, god knows you have all those qualities; no I'm thinking now of the implication of "no revision"—for other people.) It bothers me a lot to read Kerouac's "Spontaneous Prose" stuff. He really has something, I acknowledge it gladly in *On the Road* & in parts of *The Subterraneans*, & if that's how he does it that's O.K. for him, but it seems wrong to publish notes drawn from his own quite long practice & development where young writers, 19, 20 years old, Black M'n-type kids, are going to take it over & use it as if it were just as much *their* way. Besides—is a systematization of spontaneity not very much of a gimmick? Again, the paintings I so much dislike (the Farrens, Gustons, Klines, Pollocks etc.—wait, I know you've defended this school to me, but I'm not defending my dislike at this moment, only asking a question)—their use of dynamic accident—is it not also the undogmatic dogmatized (like Kerouac's System)?—That is, even in a presumably perfectly "sincere" painter—(I'm quite sure some of them are *not*—but I know some are).

Then—my feeling that since the world (of men) is certainly as Dada as Dada, there's no point in making more of the same—there was a time for artists to destroy—destroy some of the false-faces—now with the world hurtling about in a frenzy of self-destruction there seems no need to try to reflect it—one wont have to try, it is reflected in all we do anyway— rather it seems we shd. again be constructing (e.g. as Cezanne)—not other falsefaces, little bits of nonexistent classic peace—but at any rate constructing objects against the stream, defiances of the stream—A Kerouac *reflects*—Edward Marshall, Steve Jonas, *reflect* (for instances) that madness of the world—& I guess that is necessary too—but when it becomes a "movement," almost a campaign . . . ? I'm stuck, can't finish my sentence.

In *Measure* #I Dorn stands out among the young poets for having *made something*. The poems of Jonas & Marshall, in contrast, are an extension of the stream-of-consciousness idea—nothing new god knows. (Rumaker's poem tho' formally conceived lacks vitality so I don't count it.)

These notes are not properly consecutive, just ruminations on paper, forgive their disjointedness—I've not come to the end but had best end as it is time to make supper.

Love—

D.

A STORM OF WHITE,

                    neither
    sky nor earth, without horizon
         a
nother tossing, continually in-
         breaking

boundary of white
    foaming    in gull-white weather
luminous in dull white,    and trees
    ghosts of blackness or greens
that here are
    dark whites    in storm

white white white    like
    a boundary in death advancing
that is our life,    that's love,
    line upon line
breaking in radiance    so soft, so dim-
         ly glaring, dominating.

         The line of outliving

in this storm    bounding

obscurity from obscurity, the foaming
    —as if half the universe
(neither sky nor earth, without
    horizon)    were forever

breaking into being another half,

    obscurity flaring into a surf
upon an answering obscurity.

**87**

May 2, {8} 1958
{Stinson Beach}

Above, a try at pruning that poem. Jess points out that "breaking into being another half" once the pendant is gone asks for the pendant . . . or after it. Did I have "verdure" for "greens" in the typed copies?—I've only got ms. and I can't decide about that word. There was a cleavage-break in the thing—perhaps the "outliving" now is an obscure turn, but then it's a poem of obscure turns.[1]

This is a period—outside of gardening, and a panel discussion at Stanford where Brother Antoninus and I lit into reading to be literate etc. and open season on the English department—a period of no poems, postponing still the Dahlberg review, reading quantities of mystery novels: malaise. Of what, I don't know. A letter from Zukofsky set me briefly off to sketch a section of proposed *Poetics*—on the monosyllabic line; only to collapse, with a will, if it can be calld that, not to go thru with anything.

From Jonathan came (unwanted) K. Patchen's new book, and I was actually nauseated at the use of (unwarrented) a phrase from a letter, which I think I used re- a new "Maximus";[2] and I certainly did not use re- a new Patchen. Whose work just seems blah. So's shall I waste time and expression to write to Jonathan, as I have written over and over again, that I don't like, am not likely to like receiving a patchen buk? The design of which is a new Jargon low. Well, I'm angry, at having such arrive to spoil my day. And I've got to see that Fredericks who is printing *Letters* and not Jonathan carries thru on the design of the cover.

—Saturday—

To arrange the mirrors? to observe—but you say "only to see" the enactment of rites. I'm reading with some pleasure books on stars . . . well, and here is your poem on how to see out, thru.[3] One of these books, by Peter Lum published by Pantheon, like most Pantheon books stresses the mythos—where I find exciting reverberations of the "Crosses of Harmony & Disharmony" pome.[4] Good thing I didn't have any "research" there; the bases are loaded as it is.

## 88

May 8, 1958
{Stinson Beach}

dear Denny,

Yr letter arrived this morning, reminding me that the enclosed was unfinishd . . . I've been at learning the stars (it was for stars and garden I wanted to move, with the sea thrown in), and reading Raymond's *From Baudelaire to Surrealism*[1] straight thru (where I'd only skimmed it, inattentively, put off by M. Raymond's pedantry—but now both for the romance of French poets, and to bring my mind back from two weeks? perhaps even three, of slough ¿of despond? And your letter comes right on then to carry me, with so much to take up.

I revise (A) when there is an inaccuracy, then I must re-see, as re. in the "Pindar" poem—now that I found the reproduction we had some place of the Goya painting,[2] I find Cupid is not wingd: in the poem I saw wings. I've to summon up my attention and go at it. (B) when I see an adjustment,— it's not polishing for me, but a "correction" of tone, etc., as in same poem "hear the anvils of human misery clanging" in the Whitman section botherd me, it was at once the measure of the language and the content—Blake! not Whitman (with them *anvils*) and I wanted a long line pushd to the unwieldly with (Spicer and I had been talking about returning to Marx to find certain correctives—as, the ideas of *work*) marxist flicker of *commodities*. (C) and even upon what I'd call decorative impulse: I changd

"~~obey~~ follow to the letter
freakish instructions"

to gain the pleasurable transition of l—to l—r and ƒ to ƒr.

The idea in back of no revisions as doctrine was that I must force myself to abandon all fillers, to come to correct focus *in the original act*; in part there's the veracity of experience [as you're quite correct, I do ask *how* and *where* the "O dear grey cat" is inbound/essential to the experience: the poem "comes," as I write it; I seem—that is—to follow a dictate], but it's exactly in respect to that veracity that I don't find myself sufficient.

But I won't go along with the poem as "pot"—it's an old misleading. Not only that a pot has a function [as it must hold water], but more to the point it has a medium (spatial) and a method that completes it in the round. Picasso's pots that refer even humorously to this whole function; vs. the cera-mist's pot that achieves beauty with the minimum departure of imagination from convention. But one misunderstands both function and substance of the poem to act as if it were analogous to a pot [must hold water] or a bridge [must hold up under traffic]. All spatial things have to be complete—or they fall. A poem has to engage the memory, so that it is heard continuously. It makes a pattern in time. But if it fails—it has its own character of failing. Nobody is walking on it, or carrying something in it etc. when it gives way.[3]

I hate to discard the "pot," cause it is the potter who can't revise at all. He has to throw it right or throw it away.

I had nothing like the "I write as I please," certainly not carelessness but the extreme of care kept in the moment of passionate feeling. Kerouac writes like Miller and Saroyan before him, there's the euphoric I-did-it that one responds to. Montaigne said he learnd to write only when it was *easy*. That's prose—one needs natural ease to feel generously. The defect comes in defects of feeling—much of Kerouac, Miller and Saroyan is defense of a dis-ease about feeling.

And this poet, me, gets—but I lose my thread; perhaps I wanted to be involved where I wasn't. Take Ginsberg's "Howl" or the earlier "Xbalba" that appeard in *Evergreen*: with the proposition "No construction—let the mind fall down."[4] My sense that there could be a poem is whetted. But then there is no dis-construction in it—only lazy lines, loose talk that get looser and soon he's asking "what love in the cafes of God" which is both exalted and gassy.

There's an austerity and beauty to Dada—in Duchamps and Schwitters. Dada poetry? Williams' "Hermaphoroditic Telephones" have a touch of it. This only to indicate that it's not Dada or Pollock or Kline that we're talking about. Nor is it that the derangements of Marshall (which I believe to be genuine) or of Jonas (which I believe, like Ginsberg's and Kerouac's, to be indulged) aren't truthful, accurate symptoms, and have some value. But you're talking about another thing—and I'm with you there—"defiance of the stream." "I do not want to drift"—"The Venice Poem" went. It meant there—drifting with events. But there's drifting with one's vitality; there's the fact (as in Kerouac) that writing where there is vitality (like talk) will go anyways.

My "no revisions" was never divorced from a concept of the work. Concentration. Whatever "vitality," you've got just whatever you have there—but the poet makes a concentration, a focus. I've got to have the roots of words, the way the language works, at my fingertips, learnd in the nerves from whatever studies, in addition to the thing drawn from—the sea, a painting, the face of Marianne Moore—before there's even the beginning of discipline. And decide, on the instant, that's the excitement between the word that is surrounded by possible meanings, and the word that limits direction. I see or am a sculptor, cutting a resistant medium, straight on and can develop a stroke that will be at intricate play with all forms around it—or another stroke that will exclude those interconnections and hold the form to itself.

There's a law of the heart that the mind's to be temperd to. The mind's the careless organ—[how careful the heart must be, a steady, to keep blood feeding whatever impulses of the brain] and it's the obedience of the mind I admire—that brings itself to tune.

I don't mean "heart" here as metaphor alone—but start with it straight: actual heart, actual nervous organism, and brain—the concept of order— and your completeness of the poem must relate to that. Well, that the experience be complete, searched out; and must be orderd then.

The bass rhythm of the poem is the heart-beat, in counterpoint to which the breathing–speech rhythms are developd. Simple (as in Schubert's melodic line) or complex (as in Bach, or in moderns with Stravinsky and Webern). But isn't there also what we "know by heart," and aren't there sureties that contradict the stream of consciousness idea.

—I have to get this in an envelope and off to the mail—and as you closed praying forgiveness for disjointedness—I close with some such prayer. Some of these paths of thot are worn and look "too good."

love
Robert

**89**

May 19, {1958
Stinson Beach}

dear Denny,

There's still, from yr last letter, the questions about what I get in the last poems Bob sent. I'll take your word "unsure" (that you were "unsure about them"), because isn't it Bob's (Robert's) (Creeley's) psychic counter often to be the-one-of-whom-we-are-unsure. I've pictured that *persona* as an imp on the shoulder; or another time picturing a ten-year-old Bob (—the boy in puberty who, like the girl, excites poltergeists) that dances about the man. It's a lilt in the mature melody (; like the "impish" airs that spring up in Richard Strauss, a Til Eulenspeigel tweedle of reeds) of boyish sprite, puckism. And that Puck, I learn from folklorists, was often seen—well, as in "A Poem of Despondencies" I call his (Puck's) number—I couldn't get the saucer-big eyes in that poem, but the "coverd-with-hair, scares girls" gets the combination of impishness and monstrosity.[1] There's something about that age of puberty, the just before adolescent (it seems to me that my own psychic carry over is much from adolescence—and short on the resources of this impishness)—that's source of "fun" and "mischief"—and then mischief includes too the great mischief; as the cruelty of boys includes those terrible boy-men the *Monsters* of political tyranny: Hitler, or Nero. And "fun" includes doesn't it the true ripe gaiety, and Delight? There is something in even the baby that is strong to survive, demands his own immortality, in the man.

"Melody . . . is the intonation of the *melos*, which signifies a fragment, a part of a phrase. It is these parts that strike the ear in such a way as to mark certain accentuations . . . is thus the musical singing of a cadenced phrase— I use the word *cadenced* in its general sense, not in the special musical sense" from Stravinsky's *Poetics of Music*[2]—but now I've copied it out, it doesn't say right there what I get from it—there's another passage in which he talks about obeying "the eternal necessity of affirming the axis of our music and to recognize the existence of certain poles of attraction" and again:

"a succession of impulses that converge towards a definite point of repose" . . . "But nothing forces us to be looking constantly for satisfaction that resides only in repose."

"So our chief concern is not so much what is known as tonality as what one might term the polar attraction of sound, of an interval, or even of a complex of tones. The sounding tone constitutes in a way the essential axis of music" and "the drawing together and separation of poles of attraction in a way determine the respiration of music."

O.K. I had exactly your stoppage at the "ohs" of "Going to Bed"—yet the text gives the turn of the thing the "melody"; between "Oh!" and the unaccented "Oh wisdom to find fault with" where the whole line is a single stressd phrase. I was taken by surprise (over my up-to-then persisting misreading) by the grace of recovery (exchange) when Bob read the poem.

There's a melody of "content" in which the things and beings of a poem are the *melos*—form items of attraction that seek to be established in the tone of the poem. And back now to the picture I get of the possible psychic equilibrium where Creeley has to give voice to a certain increased manliness—it's a boldness of the imagination and a longing for even

"stately" being that gives a new tone to "Heroes." Not disrelated from to be still a man, and to be also a friend of one's being a "monster," a good humor, and more, the woman loves him, burns him { exorcises him
{ but the love to "burns.

"Heroes" I mean are a boy's dream of immortality: the strength of the poem comes thru the manliness of Creeley-Virgil to whom the Cumaean Sibyl speaks, who has then inner counsels.* And I take the "*hic opus, hic labor est,*" "all that industrious wisdom" "lives" and "the old labors" as just the dimension that permits (gives *tone* to) the inclusion of mountains, desert, and death. To a profundis.

* As new depths are given the woman when she is also Sibyl (is this the Gravesian note you feard?).

It's not what a poem is about that feeds me here; but the work (poetic) whereby fresh routes lie open to old necessities. A man longs for certain strengths—broad "backgrounds"? "depths"? a reality that permits a humanity to thrive in the personality and the self without disproportion. It's to fulfill a potential being. The immortal fame that romantics longd for is solid if it means a lasting just survival of all that has lived. Where the industrial strives to awaken seeds of wholeness that may have closed or been in their time poor: for the helpless babe to make the journey thru time from his first need to his last and keep the faith by which need can mature fruitfully—to see aright the "breast of the world." Labor is one of those true breasts of the world whose milk nourishes. I can feel it. But it's another triumph to render it *true* in the composition of a poem, to seek out its scale.

Isn't "Going to Bed" a labor of Hercules? and "Saturday Afternoon" like old Beardkin in Grimms that fascinated and fascinates me now—a *human* phase more than a personal? Childhood had the terror where the "Monster" was all fiend; and the romance where the soul finally loved the beast who proved to be manliness: a prince! Well, in Creeley's poems we see him as Virgil and as the Robert Creeley linkd—drawing upon two thousand years; and there was, third, the play where the Monster was pet or toy, "my friend." As "wooden-eyes" delight not fight. There's terror and love and friendship to hold in one scale, without injustice.

The poem arouses some such a potentiality. As its line [thinking now of "Heroes"] must be longer, *slower.* The playfulness remains as an element in the turns of phrasing. I can imagine anyway a full emergence of interplay of the "poles of attraction" I've been suggesting.

———————

My thots still dwelling, dissatisfied with the course so far above, on the "Heroes" poem during lunch. What I don't account for is that the poem does not dream of some potentiality, but establishes a potentiality already experienced. The mountains, desert—are certainly the realized landscape. Then another thing certainly experienced is this thing of *labor* and *waiting/* and Virgil, wherefrom *hic opus, hic labor est,* is a solid part of that labor. There's no mere literary association in this Creeley-Virgil tie: it is thru having to teach Latin—undertaken as a labor (and in the sense of expiation of "sins against labor"—in that Creeley conscience (consciousness) and a waiting then. He'd to work at Virgil to earn his "keep" ("to be still a man"); and only thru *hic opus, hic labor* does Creeley come to those *two thousand years,* where Virgil is *dead* and yet lasting (where one has one's labor), and there's establishd at last: "death also."

It's this element of its being established in the real (experienced) somewhere in actual life so that the life in the poem draws from and feeds—that distinguishes the fanciful from the engaged image. It don't add to the poetic of said pome to enlarge upon its *meaning,* but it do verify my simple initial certainty in unsureness: that the elements (*melos*) of the poem had authority (melody).

———————

Time to swim.—We got the Tiffany catalog—with great delight. Wish they'd had hundreds of color pictures.

love

Robert

Dearest Robert and Jess,

Just to explain my silence—these have been hellish weeks—not wasted tho' I think—but in their depression & up-&-downess & intervals of precarious happiness quite paralyzing to me as far as letters are concerned— tho' I do have 1 3-part poem, somehow, not out of it but somewhere alongside it—also in the last 2 weeks there's been the collecting of Nik's camp equipment & the sewing of nametapes—well . . .

We spent last weekend at Stony Point (2d time)—I love M. C. {Richards}, she really is a damn good person. Cage & Tudor we like too. Al {Kresch} came with us. It was good. Nik loves it there. But we wdn't want to live there. Aside from Karen Karnes the other people there don't seem like much. I want to write about the pot, what I meant, 'thingness' etc., but not in this note. Nik leaves June 28th and we will go away a few days later; I'll take some letters & things along & write properly from some field somewhere in Maine . . .

Met Robin Blaser a few weeks ago & we may visit him in Boston.

Made a recording for that Lee Anderson guy a few nights ago, at short notice, & am to read at the Y. next winter on one of their 3 together

## 90

{June, 1958
New York}

programs. No other news. Saw a Fr. bk. on Satie with beautiful cards & things he drew, made me think of you Jess.

Love—
Denny

P.S.

What has happened about the children's story—McClure/Jess?

**91**

July 9, 1958
{Stinson Beach}

dear Denny,

With a fire on the hearth, and a foggy day, and poor Kit with a humiliating patch where we just clippd his back bare in our war on his eczema; coffee done and cups washd; but Jess is swearing at the mess of the table in the studio where I left the workings in progress of scatterd moonstones, tweezers, broken and cut colord glass—the debris out of which we've been making plastic panels. I've finishd eight of twelve small panes for our bedroom window that faces on the road; and I'm working on a large bathroom window commissiond by Broughton that will be the first money I've earnd in a long time. It's been four months with few (only three) poems. In the last month these panels of plastic in which mosaics of translucent materials are suspended have provided a medium for my designing spirit to come to life in. Some imitation the soul can have of the ready burgeoning of geraniums and poppies. That we see all around us and even attend. Lettuce has a green translucence that rivals the rose. But how angry Jess's broom sweeps up! and, well, my punishment is that once the clean-up started [I'd just sat down to this letter] I'm not permitted the somewhat expiation of participating. In a dream last week I'd decided I was spiritually sick and tho we had no money to afford it *had* to have a doctor's care. After a series of encounters with stages previous to my case's being accepted, elaborations of the waiting room (reception)—all of which enacted the idea of indulgence and expense and even exclusiveness involved (making it clear that the retreat I sought was socially fashionable: one was declaring oneself too sensitive and profoundly unusual to survive without care) I found myself "sick," in a hospital bed. I had just witnessd four doctors and four nurses operating on James Broughton, probing beneath the epidermis, lifting up the skin to make pockets where the flesh was reachd—which was calld "talking with the Id." Jess sat by the (my) bedside and held my hand—my being "sick" and seeking help had been kept secret, until now; and worried too because the costs of my sickness were more than we could manage. Weeping (treacherously) I said when he askd what was the matter—"I'm so selfish it hurts" and felt, as if there were reason or vindication there, intimate pangs of a heart that had drawn up tight as a fist.

No wonder the few gifts—that in a colord window or a poem—my spirit can allow bring with their practice a sense of liberation. And Olson/Rimbaud's

what soul
isn't in default?

can you afford not to make
the magical study

which happiness is?

becomes a text rememberd. • "I'm not *angry*" dear Jess, "but *I* am, I'm angry
at myself" Oh, the damnd litterd desk *has* been a kind of "I'm so selfish it
hurts" statement.

Now we've, the two of us, made the bed, changed sheets and pillow cases,
and picked up shoes and clothes. My desk remains, a permitted debris of
unanswerd letters, unwritten Dahlberg review, of a crisis that needs only
clearing away. News that's no news of being eaten away by privilege.

• I'm not all a brood of *mea culpa* this morn. Tho Browning with his "the
snail's on the thorn" was no rose gardener, the snail's himself so elegant a
critter, in a sculptor's dimension as extravagant a beauty as bee or butterfly.
And there may be an economy yet that can share with snail. That here verge
upon pestilence, leaving lace of lettuce. . . .

————————

The Zukofskys are here—that is, in San Francisco, where Louis is poet-
in-residence/actually a full teaching job. We had thot they would be out
often, but the first week-end was marrd by the fact that Paul got car-sick.
The road's a blessing in that it keeps this little town separated from the
omnipresent suburbia, within twenty-five miles of the city. But one has to
take old-style mountain and coast roads to find the refuge.

With Ebbe Borregaard in his workshop evening session, Zuk's confronted
straight on by what he don't understand in poetry—the governance of *desire*.
Pound's "only the passion endures" is the strand of the *Cantos* that with its
mythos, aesthetic fervors rather than reason, that Zuk mistrusts. It robs a
long work like *A–1–12* of emotional proportion and hence of epiphany.

With the three poems since the "Sea of White," I'm sending on Borre-
gaard's "Each found himself" which Zuk I gather has attempted to curb.
"Tremendous" he objected too; well, I guessd that one. But the sentence
"Each found himself at the end of/a tremendous age" was a donné—a
sentence out of some book (exactly as Borregaard accounted for it—he cldn't
remember *what* book): part of the poem not (as it wld be for Marianne
Moore) for its precision; but the contrary—for its expansion. And cldn't
Zuk see that with the attack on the precise that follows a poetics is at work?

I feel sad anyway because I had imagined that there wld be a direct
exchange between Zukofsky (as *I* have found myself thru his work an area
of sympathetic contrary) and the small group of young poets here who
would need a contradiction to me own doctrines and Spicer's. But I think
Zuk sees Ebbe as *wrong*.

And a fond hope, soft-headed, cause it's only here and there that my own poetry ever comes into Zukofsky's sights [As from *The Field*—"The Song of the Old Order" and "The Question"] and I can still remember how hopeless was an effort to explain what good Coleridge was. I've taken a passage from "Songs of Degrees" 3 for an epigraph in *The Field*.

The sound in the Temple built after exile
Is never worth the sound
At the earth where no Temple stood
And on which no law of exile can fall.

Blood flows; not hateful good,
Not this measure is blood.
Crabbed and lovely both is root.
What is never imposes.

The tree's good of the field of Machpelah
As of Persia or of Mytilene.

But trying to explain what I saw there in relation to the *Field* when visiting Zuk was futile. Bound by his appreciation of my regard for his work, he is always puzzled by my allowance for dramatic rhetoric [I'll always be prone to "With tremulous cadence slow, and bring / The eternal note of sadness in." And even to

Wake! For the Sun who scatterd into flight
The Stars before him from the Field of Night,
Drives Night along with them from Heaven and Strikes
The Sultan's Turret with a shaft of light]

and the pursuit of the fantasmal, the l'oeuvre du Fantôme.
"trying to explain" *is* futility.
A philosophic restraint whatever ounce of prevention it is—if these are ills of poetics, don't do if they're forces that hold both ill and health in one potency.
"their life screwd-up into violent crowns"

love
Robert

---

**92**

August 4th {1958}
c/o Orne,
Pleasant Point,
Knox County, Maine.

Dear Robert & Jess

If I stop to explain why I've been so long about writing this time I'll never get to the letter itself. We are living in what was once a fish-house (for keeping bait & lobsters) then was lived in by an old lobsterman for many years. There are 2 rooms, 1 up 1 down—the downstairs is really a boathouse, with a sliding door opening directly onto the water at high tide

& onto rocks & seaweed at low tide—we launch'd the rowboat & have it moored so Mitch has plenty of room there for his tables & typewriter.

Upstairs we live: a wood-stove, elect. hot-plate, brass bedstead, lots of nails on the rafters to hang things from, a Morris chair, a good table & enough other chairs. Water comes from a spring in the woods abt. the length of a city block away. Seven or 8 small houses or 'camps' are round about—none so near the water as ours, which is built out on piles. It is salt water but we don't see the open sea—it is around a spur of land; this is what's called here a river, in the W. of England a creek—actually part of a network of tidal inlets, much islanded, flanked by spruce-woods & blueberry land. Nik, at camp, is about 30 miles off by road—much less by water—and will join us on the 23d when camp ends.

We visited him (after a couple of weeks moving thru' Vermont and N. Hampshire) just before moving in here—he's doing fine, has learnt to row & to ride and was a little shy of us at first, & very proud of all his new accomplishments.

We found this place through a very interesting man, Arthur MacFarland. He is a boatbuilder, native of Friendship harbor just across the water, & a violinist. He learned to play, somehow, as a 5-or-6-yr-old but has been going progressively deaf since childhood. He went to work on leaving high school, married early, had hard times, became a tremendously skilful cabinet-maker & boatbuilder, taught himself to make violins (wont sell them tho') makes only $1.50 an hour at his job (Maine is like that, which is good & bad, but I wont start on that) plays in a local orchestra, & in spite of difficulty in obtaining books is tremendously well-read; denies that he writes (but not very plausibly); is very much of a perfectionist & therefore tremendously modest & dissatisfied with himself, as deafness stymied his musical ability, lack of European training (he says) makes it impossible that he shd. ever make a violin that wd. satisfy him, & he doesn't seem to believe he is a poet—I don't know if he's right or not. Certainly he is a most perceptive & intelligent reader. Well, around the time *Origin* began Cid used to have a Boston radio program which Arthur picked up by chance one night, with the result that he entered into correspondence with Cid & became an *Origin* subscriber. Then Cid put him in touch with Larry Eigner & a tremendous correspondence and friendship developed between them, based not only on his feeling for Larry's work but on a sort of physical affinity—a deaf musician, and a so intensely life-savoring person confined to a wheel-chair. They met for the first time a week before we got here, Larry's family having driven him up here. Arthur, besides *Origin*, has read of *Origin* writers only what Larry has sent him—a couple of *B.M.R.*'s, *Caesar's Gate*, little else. But what he has read he knows much better than I do, & particularly admires *your* work. In the fall I'm going to send him all sorts of other material—god, the almost perfect *reader* we'd all like to have (I mean, aside from our close friends)—and all this while isolation & poverty have deprived him of poems! It's quite extraordinary *how* isolated he in fact is & yet picks up on things with so damned much intelligence. And his utter freedom from involvement in any fashions or side-taking, his ignorance really that such exists, make one feel bound to completer honesty & the highest standards in one's work, not to disappoint his innocent, sharp judgment.

Knowing only what of yr work was in *Origin*, & *Caesar's Gate*, he seems to have the clearest grasp of you I've seen. He's too diffident to write to you tho'—once was in Boston (has only been a few times in his life) & didn't finally feel he could inflict himself on Cid, for example. . . . But he's not the least bit obsequious or uncritical—put his finger on some home truths for me, for instance. I will enclose (if Mitch copies out) the one thing of his own he has shown us—he emphatically says it is not a poem—that he was reading about the Tarot pack & wanted to remember the layout, & this was simply his mnemonic. I think too as it stands it is not a poem, but it cd. well be a passage *from* a poem—and at one or 2 points does, within itself, heighten to poetry.

To go back to the *pot* image, you, because I no doubt put it badly & indeed hadn't thought it out, associated my pot with function, which I agree wd. end any parallel with poetry, but I thereupon (especially as that letter of yours came at the same time as one from England from a friend, En Potter, which used the expression "thingness" in the same connection) realized that I was thinking not at all of function or utility but of the non-attached non-associative aliveness of pots & indeed often of a small *shard* even. So that I guess what I really want is to write—or *make*—poems having an intense abstract or objective identity while not sacrificing, indeed, precisely *made out of*, the natural world, its connotations, connections, "ideas," sensuous attributes, etc. etc. Certainly not an original idea god knows but one I am only beginning to define & grasp for myself.

That dream of yours must have been shaking. I've had some lately that impressed me but in the utter confusion & depression & interim-feeling of the last weeks in N.Y. I failed to write them down & so have lost them. Strangely, or maybe not strangely at all, London, the topography of central London & the eastward presence of St. Paul's, seems often to be the scene. Once there was a good dream—in which to the northeast of St. Paul's I came to an unknown city-within-the-city—thru' narrow & narrower streets, across a great square where grass grew between the stones, up a very steep crumbly lane—to a plateau planted with all kinds of fruit-trees & flowers, & inhabited by idyllic gentle people who knew of London, or that bit of it nearest them, but didn't frequent it. At last one of them, an 11-yr old child, led me down angel-like to that forgotten square again & I caught an old double-decker, the open kind they don't have any more, & got back to Aldersgate or thereabouts.

Back to the pot, the poem—if a poem has sufficiently intense identity (by way of its synthesis of form & content, form & music, music as form, content as form) doesn't that identity act on the perceiving mind (tho' not to the eye) as "spatial quality"? Of course one can put one's hands round a pot & feel it—but that's not the *only* way of perceiving its roundness & its separateness from what it stands on or in front of—well with a good poem isn't the hearing-of-it-as-complete (not as closed but as thing-in-itself) equivalent to the seeing of a solid object?

The water is icy here, I was afraid I wouldn't have the courage to go in, at last forcing the plunge & feeling afterwards better about myself. We are not depressed here, that is, Mitch is still in a very delicate emotional state but is getting better & relaxing; sleeps a lot too, which he needs. It is so marvellously quiet & beautiful, & there's an island we row out to, with pinewoods & deep moss & hermit thrushes.

Mike Rumaker is living in our apt. while we are gone. McFarland's 16 yr old son took us sailing yesterday; it was so *lovely*.

Love from
Denny

P.S.

Thank you for notes on Bob's poems, which were very useful. With the quotations from Stravinsky, especially the axis & the poles. You ask what I meant about Graves but unfortunately I didn't bring Bob's poems along.

The Zukofskys bringing-up of their Paul struck me as monstrous. Pale unhappy priggish boy, his only hope seems to be to be a *tremendous* genius which I don't believe for a moment he is. Yet he's been ruined for any other sort of life. Imagine a 14-yr-old boy being escorted on the subway from B'klyn Heights to the Juilliard School! What excuse have they for that? I liked Louis' gentle scholarly presence & admire the purity & organization of his work—but how can such a fine intelligent man not see what is being done to that poor child? Celia I liked less each minute. Well.

Reading Ebbe Borregaard's "Wapiti" poem at last with proper attention{,} it seems to me that while having a great deal of *gift*, potential, etc., he is not honest. Or else simply doesn't know what he's doing; which, if he is otherwise intelligent, is the same thing. Or, he has pride but no sense of craftsmanship. He accepts his lucky accidents without humility: doesn't follow thru his thoughts, doesn't have the honesty that will throw out the most gorgeous line if he can't truly stand back of it. Or (& I begin here to get clearer what it is I do feel about his poem (maybe less about "Each Found Himself," I don't know yet)—i.e.)—he seems *to pretend to know more than he does.* Seems to me a poet's integrity lies in his trying to get into his poems neither more nor less than he can "prove upon his pulses"—& while it's hard *not* to get *less* in, it's so fatally easy to get *more* in, & forgive oneself for it. And it's *that* he seems to do. I don't think that is the same thing as what you call in regard to yourself (and quoting Fitzgerald) "dramatic rhetoric."

We're going to a "Church Food Sale" to try & buy an apple pie, which Maine housewives excel in. Never never have we eaten such pies.

Did I send "Under the Tree"?[1] Will enclose the little I've done since.

Love—<br>D.

*About yr. poems sent in last letter.*

I see that you've restored the last stanzas of "A Storm of White." I don't have here the original version but I do have the shorter one of May 2d which ended on "answering obscurity," & I still feel uncertain which I prefer. The part about Pumpkin & the quote from Bob still doesn't really seem to follow, & yet the shortened version (tho' all magnificent poetry) doesn't really seem complete. (I think it's a pity you changed *greens* to *verdure*.) Somehow, to make it compose or hold, it looks to me as if part of what's now the end, & at first seemed pendant, but now seems less pendant but yet imperfectly connected, should be right in the beginning of the poem—*then* the sea itself, then back to the cat & death at the end. It seems (if you won't think me impertinent) to resemble a problem I have sometimes had myself & have solved (I've considered) that way—I don't mean mechanically but as a revelation, of which an example is the enclosed poem "The Communion," where in the 1st version the frog didn't appear till the end of the poem, & therefore was so arbitrary as not to function.[2]

I thought I had things to say about the other poems sent also but I find I have not, except that I particularly like "Atlantis." There's a great deal I don't understand in the "Under Ground" poem but the sounds & rhythms of it interest me very much.[3] I feel I need a note on it tho' like the interpretive notes on Bob's poems—not paraphrase, which demeans the poem, but as Blyth says, "the aim of the explanation . . . is to make itself unneccessary. . . . the indispensible must be got rid of in order that the truth must emerge." (We obtained reduced (slightly damaged) copies of 3 of the 4 Haiku volumes in the Tuttle Oriental bookshop in Rutland Vermont on the way up—always seems such a curious place to find such things.)

Time to walk up to the mailbox with this.

Again—love from<br>Denny.

Will mail copies of poems tomorrow.

dear Denny,

**93**

August 8, 1958
{Stinson Beach}

>     In Pound's "Canto 85"
> fermentum et germina,
>     study with the mind of a grandson
>     and watch the time like a hawk
>                 taó tsi
> ½ research    and    ½ Τέχνη
> ½ observation        ½ Τέχνη
> ½ training           ½ Τέχνη

Which cld refer to potting as well as the word-Maker's craft [tho in English we can hardly refer to a craft without including some portion of the artisan's guile]. My not revising is linkd to one aspect of the potsherd: that once cast you can't recast it. The more haunting a reflection since I've found myself sweating over extensive rehaulings on the opening poem of *The Field* and right now am at the 12th poem of the book which I want to keep but have almost to reimagine in order to establish it . . . it's a job of eliminating what doesn't belong to the course of the book, and in the first poem of reshaping so that the course of the book is anticipated. I mistrust the rationalizing mind that comes to the fore, and must suffer thru—like I did when I was just beginning twenty years ago—draft after draft to exhaust the likely and reach the tone in myself where intuition begins to move. It comes sure enuf then, the hand's feel that "this" is what must be done. But I spent two days struggling with "Sometimes I Am Permitted . . . "[1] [with all the irony of the reference in the poem to the grace of writing at all]. It was yr "putting it badly" that made for my worrying the pot ↔ poem even to include the function. The rationalizer after all has the argument: "It won't hold water" and refers to the idealist or the innocent or the possessd as "crack-pot"; and it's to protect the virtue of the pot as *thing*, as embodying labor and function that you recalld the shard. A point where our references cross—for the shard was early a guide for my own ideas of beauty: that any and every fragment of work must be its lasting force.

What I was struggling against was I think the moral urgency. Wasn't it something about the special indulgence of inspiration in a poem like "Howl" that set us off to picture the responsibility [and did I bring in the labor theory of value? Spicer had raised the questions earlier this year: that labor ↔ care was of special import]? But your works, but especially you— the idea of you as poet, are in part *conscience* with me. Take this second poem I am working on [originally "A Poem Slow Beginning"].[2] There is conflict in the conception: how to keep and to allow full strength to that need for the sublime—it's a root of me; and to keep too even the mistrust of it. Now, in this particular need for the sublime I'm still in line with your what a poet "can prove upon his pulses" . . . and wasn't it your mistrust of a self-indulgence for careless and then grostesque pretending to know more than I do that reproved the "The Ballad of the Enamord Mage"? I'll be back to even this questionable indulgence below. In the specific case of Ebbe's "Wapitis" the fact is that he didn't know at all what he was doing or had done. And was angry at the poems, with the protest (when Jack Spicer and I seized upon them and told him they were the beginning point of his poetics) that they were no good. He's got the full mistrust you have of the "accidental"—but it's not accident, but *blind* working in his case. And then slow, stubborn and resisting learning out of that—that he can work by. The first of Pound's brief on poetry sent out circ 1948 in "The Cleaners Manifesto" was 1 "you must understand what is happening."[3] There is this given thing: that something is happening, a process begins in writing that demands an art. Most verse is something being made up to communicate a thing already present in the mind—or a lot of it is. And don't pay the attention it shld to what the poet don't know—and won't until the process speaks. Here's a passage I copied out of one of Eliot's last set of essays—I think it was the one in *Three Voices of Poetry*:[4]

> There is first . . . an inert embryo or "creative germ" and, on the other hand, the Language, the resources of the words at the poet's command. He has something germinating in him for which he must find words; he cannot identify this embryo until it has been transformd into an arrangement of the right words in the right order. When you have the words for it, the "thing" for which the words had to be found has disappeard replaced by the poem . . . it is—to adapt two lines of Beddoes to a different meaning—a
>
> > bodiless childful of life in the gloom
> > crying with frog voice, "What shall I be?"
>
> . . . the poet may be concernd solely with expressing in verse—using all his resources of words, with their history, their connotations, their music—this obscure impulse. He does not know what he has to say until he has said it . . . He is oppressd by a burden which he must bring to birth in order to obtain relief. Or . . . he is haunted by a demon, a demon against which he feels powerless because in its first manifestations it has no face, no name, nothing . . . unknown dark psychic material—we might say, the octopus or angel with which the poet struggles. In the poem . . . of the poet talking to himself, the psychic material tends to create its own form—the eventual form will be to a greater or less degree the form for that one poem and for no other . . . a simultaneous development of form and material; for the form affects the material at every stage; and perhaps all the material does is to repeat "not that! not

that!" . . . yet for his readers what he has written may come to be the expression both of their own secret feelings and of the exultation or despair of a generation . . . "

What Ebbe's got to do is to trust and to obey the voice of the "Wapitis." Where obedience means certainly your not to pretend to know more than he does. But the poem is not a pretention to *knowing*; it is not damn it, to be held back to our knowing, as if we could take credit for the poem as if it were a self-assertion. We have in order to obey the inspired voice to come to understand, to let the directives of the poem govern our life and to give our minds over entirely to know what is happening. But the whole thing a poem can do is to move us into such a{n} excitement of speech that something new and demanding might enter into the conscious world. It moves from below, from what them psychoanalysts call the Id—but the experience there is secreted in the language, where we instinctively, if we have faith in the communion, discover content (that then goes back, the dead speaking, roots into the embodied reality—O say in the word *cow* that's got not only what we *know* about cows, our individual experience, and the particular family meanings of cow from parents etc., but has also to be searchd out a collective history, Anglo-Saxon origins) (and the whole existence of *cow* in the testimony of poem, novel, treatise, mythos, painting and statue—with some bovine noises out of symphonies). How can we *know* all that is digested there in us? Anselm's "I believe and therefore I seek to know."—which don't slight the search for justifying [in the prime sense]—

I think there is a sheer pretending to know, and shld. being brought up under the indulgence of a family cult fascinated by the esoteric be acquainted with a degree of sham. But in *sham*, and this is where I wld. hold my ground, something is happening; the poet has only to bring it to test.

I'll take *honesty* as a particular criterion of a poet, but not as a test of a poem. It's the poet's integrity you worry about—well, I've still got it stuck in my head that the character of a man is a signature that he can't avoid much less evade. But a poem can be sly as a serpent and we'll still find it out. We're drawn pretty much to poetry that opens up life for us, "meaningful" we call it then. And rightly in terms of our living let go by even the great that does not belong to our way. But that's not the art we're thinking of then.

Let me make this a letter for your longish summer vacation day from one of mine—(tho mine here in August is fog and cold with the radio predicting rain and a fire on the hearth). And I'll take up your query about Under Ground with your questions about what the integrity is, the idea of pretend-ing to know more than one does.

1. The autobiographical (this is certainly not a necessary level for poetry to exist; but Dante is right that it's necessary for fullest dimension)
   A. In part grounded in knowledge of self—the only particular here is Jeff Rall (parallel to Pumpkin in the "Sea" poem[5] whom I loved and, since he was a companion and not a lover is as spirit a particular "hidden" souce; as I have a particular source in my love for Bob.[6]
   B. But most important in the poem is that it refers to feelings "unfelt"; tho I can remember some six months after my father's death when I was fifteen paroxysms of grief, I have no access to his spirit as person (where everywhere I am governd by spirit rooted in his, of architecture, of pre-Raphaelitism, of religion etc.)
   C. There's another autobiographical "fact" in the poem that prepares the fictional levels: that being adopted I refer to a hidden (to me) source.
   D. This, without going into the minutiae, section by section that I describe my own work. Because auto-biography is not primary there. See below.
2. The Poetic Fiction. Vaihinger's "*As If* Philosophy" argues that the fictive is falsified if we try to correct it,[7] to avoid contradiction or to make it likely. That it is of prime concern that man have a realm in which that, I'd say spirit, can display and demonstrate its movement and break down its boundaries.

   But even the largest flights of imagination make new boundaries, and we must take whatever route and are then bound by the route to free that.

In *The Opening of the Field* there was, and I've stuck to it, a basic fiction: the field that is: The poem as composed by field. (Feel?) See Olson's "Projective Verse"; the Field that Abraham bought for the cave of Machpelah "That I may bury my dead out of sight."[8] It's third, a field in the earliest dream I remember, a hilltop meadow with the grass in no wind bowing towards the east, and a circle of children dancing a ring around me as It, to be crownd initiating the fullness of fear and the destruction of the world by flood.

   Now, what do I *know* here? It's the pulse I go by—isn't it that the content of Abraham's field and cave can expand, flow into every meaning and eventually into the little I do know *appropriately*? The central absolute thing we all know is that there have been those that died, and that we will die: and *that* we know nothing of. Then, aren't there a series of longings for we know not what? Plato argues that we do *know* and from that his own concept of reincarnation. But I wld. argue that these are *honest* do-not-knows that we cannot deny, for we do know the longings involved in all of them

1. that individually we may die utterly, be "laid in rest"
2. that individually we may "make our mark," have immortal presence—in

a scribble on a cave wall, in generation, in a message, in a drama enacted
that becomes part of communal memory: this is *spirit*

3. that we may participate in the divine.

Can we settle for an integrity that does not allow the shapings of desire? of
desire that threatens exactly what we can stand by?

We moved out here in the midst of that storm, and Pumpkin died in it;
you wrote me about Kresch's illness, and Bob sent me the poem with that
line "death also / can still propose the old labors"—which came in turn as
signs during the period of work on *The Field* when the cave of Machpelah
was to appear as the place of the dead—tho the theme is everywhere in
the book.

There's a difference between my work here and Ebbe's. Twenty years of
involvement is part of it. My temperament for being consciously involved—
well, but I'd agree with what I think you are getting at about the "Wapitis"—
that the *poem* is an involvement at the level of awareness, and what I call
*consciousness* is central to awareness for me. But isn't *the pretending to know*
more dangerous here, as I write? Sometimes when I am most disconsolate
about what I am working at, and most uneasy about the particular
"exaltations" that may not be free outflowings of imagination and desire
but excited compulsions instead . . . I feel guilty before the ever*present*
substantial mode of your work.

The poem says once it asks where do the dead go? (and I meant my
dead—I was thinking of mothers and fathers but then the specific uncoverd
was Jeff Rall where too I had never felt the grief, it was *unknown*) among
other things that the *you* is double (as in writing to you, there's Denny and
then there's an everlasting you to whom Denny is appropriate), and the
grief survives in other grief (the paroxysm at Pumpkin's death, most recent);
that there's beyond anything we can *know* a Return (the Pole Star by which
Cheops' pyramid was built was not immovable but now is swung on the
great circle that will take 30,000 more years to return)—isn't that "out of
hand," but we apprehend it. To which the exaltation is a lyric gesture. There's
no more to Cheops' than a stone pyramid and the idea containd that
combines the contemplation of eternity with an overweening egotism
involving the suffering of a populace to make its statement. That's "beautiful"
by moonlight. A romantic place.

When it comes to "a life's disguise" I think that there's both a fantasy
and a confession. But I don't know what it is I feel is disguised—yet, ain't
the fact that I bridle at the accusation of the sham, of the "pretended" a
symptom too? Odysseus was a prototype of *the liar*; and I suffer particularly
at what is a truth or a lie. Embodied in my cross-eyes that never see "true."
That no sooner do I say, being tested, I see *two*, than I see *one* etc.

But this isn't *autobiography*; if I'm there, I'm a shape shifter. The poem is not an answer but a riddle in which pole star←→Cheops←→pyramid←→ Homer←→Oydsseus←→Charlesmagne←→(legendary one)←→tomb (legendary one, with those inscrutable bees, that appear later as the fleur de lys)←→mad Swift are an *I am what I am*, surely the most desperate integrity.

That the dead (grief for) are contain in the complex of feeling that exits in a poem (hidden therein)—

In the actual autobiography I have no parents, and will have no progeny ("looted of its emblematic bees"). . . . This poem is probably right when it seems to say that there is a tomb (womb), a hidden referent in my spirit, that I disguise (and may disguise in writing a poem to capture a grief I do not experience from one I do) and that like the course of the pole star my "sights" are adjusted to a course that I will not see realized. And *that*, even, "looted"—

Writing it I, of course, had to take what came to mind. Hippokleas, Ford Madox Ford, and Mr. W. H. are all *yous* who have been "immortalized"— and precede a fourth hidden object Jeff Rall. Perhaps what the poem does with that theme of preservation is interwoven with the other disclosure. I can't right now bring my mind to it further,

love
Robert

---

**94**

August 13ʰ {1958}
Pleasant Point
Knox County, Maine.

Dear Robert

That was a great letter. And the 2 versions of the "Often I am permitted" poem a perfect illustration of what you say about revision, work process etc. The original was beautiful but the 1958 version is the full flowering of what had seemed right before—& *was* right, as a bud is for its time, but here is come to maturity. One of the best things you've ever done.

This is not an answer, just a note to accompany poems.

Arthur McFarland's thing still isn't copied out, will send next time.

Love—
Denny.

---

**95**

Sept. 15, 1958
{Stinson Beach}[1]

dear Denny/

We've two new kittens—one white, male Merlin, and one black of the black, female Miranda [that sissy bell had made it impossible to name him Ferdinand, and she got named before we got him—or she might have been Viviane]; and the long dreary fog-bound over-cast summer is gone, swept away by clear predominance of blue and sun, with fly buzz in the room and busy chirrupings, trills—the buzz of a saw. The countryside is a city too. With the surf our highway-roar.

Jess has had a month (thru those now-passd fog-filterd daze) of painting, getting ready for a show. Mrs. Gechtoff of the East/West gallery in San Francisco had askd for one this fall, then she droppd dead before her summer show went up. Now there are enquiries from two galleries and Jess is busy framing.[2]

The new canvases are allegorical, arising sometimes from references to and then illustrating a literary counterpart [there are four paintings of scenes in Hawthorne: Beatrice in her poisonous garden; Georgiana rising from her bed, where in the middle ground [room] Aylmer boards, and in the far background Aminadaba rakes his furnace; the Snow Maiden led by kind Mr. Lindsey towards the stove-side, with Violet and Peony entreating him not to bring her in; and Faith and Goodman Brown standing before the Magister Diaboli, in the flame of a forest-fire].[3] The larger allegories spring from the ground of MacDonald and Charles Williams, with shifting images and perspectives, a metaphorical light. There are roses [as in the garden here, we attend nine rose bushes, and have in addition three rambling briar roses.] and threads (or beams) that have one reference to the thread that the Godmother discovers to Curdie.

The re-writings in *The Field* are finishd and the book put in order, showing 40 of 50 poems finishd. I include the last three which I am sure you don't have. I will send you a manuscript of the book in sections anyway. So that I can feel that it's on its way in the circles of true readers. I despair of publishers and delighted (among other discoveries thru a book by Gershom G. Scholem calld *Major Trends in Jewish Mysticism*) to find the Sefardic mystic Abulafia that his writings have been so revered that since the 13th century they have never been publishd, but were and are copied out by hand by the devout.

—O I must hope that you and Mitch and Nicky might visit us again some time; that it not be summer but spring or fall or even winter, when there is some happy proportion of days like today. I'd send it off to you with the copies of the poems, but I know you have most

Dear Robert,

Those poems—how can I say it so that you will know this is something special? They are so wonderful—but I don't know how to say it without sounding as if I were implying criticism of what has gone before—the point is that these are even more so, what in the ugly phrase is called "a new high." I respond to them with complete joy & wonder—a light shines from them

# 96

September 22d {1958}
249 W. 15th St
N.Y. 11

that is mellow like my favorite long-shadow time of day in autumn—they have virtue—they speak to me as if written especially for me—enough, I can't get at it in words that do my bidding—I'm tonguetied except in poems.

We had a very wonderful time in Maine—then spent 2 days in Boston on the way down, staying with Robin Blaser, who was a marvellously kind host, & who showed me an interesting long poem, "The Transparencies"—I liked very much his serious attempt to deal with a large field & not choose the easier aspects, not leave out what I call "Monday morning"—the groups of long lines growing out of this, a search & I think (on the whole) finding of *a way to do it*, and his use of periods which added speed (unexpectedly)— like the use of staccato marks in music. "The Preface" which he sent afterwards. I may be quibbling but for him to say "Belovéd Yeats" is like wearing your clothes ("Belovéd Frank Baum"). But more important, a form which grew organically out of the material of "Transparencies" can't be made so easily to fit a new poem, there's something a little mechanical about that— even if W. C. W. did the same. (Went to his 75th birthday reception last week by the way.)

Have some new poems from Ed Dorn which use a different kind of long line—haven't read them yet. I admire him very much.

Spent a day in Boston Museum of Fine Arts, a great museum. Also went out to see Larry Eigner. He is so lacking in the self pity he if anyone has a right to have, that it is as if he lacked a dimension. His imprisonment in his grotesque body & head is one of the most brutal things I've ever seen.

We've been having the apt. painted (the landlord [word illegible because of ink blot] it) and at last Jess's *Majorcan Pastorale* has a clean white wall back of it—& its season has changed (to me) from late to early summer— even spring—it looks so incredibly light and gay.

Mike Rumaker is having a breakdown & is going into the Psychiatric Institute on Thursday for 15 days—then maybe some months—who knows? But he doesn't *seem* in such bad shape. He's a nice boy to whom we feel rather parental (tho of course he's not really that young, or vice versa)— he watered my plants so faithfully all summer while he lived here. Hope he'll be OK.

Almost saw Olson at last but didn't. However he's supposed to be coming to N.Y. soon. But I distrust him, the idea of him, that is. He seems to impress people too much—I don't like the goggle-eyed effects. Awestruck etc. I don't feel his *work really* justifies it—it seems to be his personality that people are really excited about when they think it's the work itself. Sure, hes good. But— well, time for bed. Am reading Jacob Wassermann, do you know his work?[1] Am longing to get straight here & get back to work—my room looks good, a good place to work. Mitch just finished painting floor of front room.

Gael Turnbull arrives in N.Y. this week, we look forward to meeting him.

Wish we could see Jess's show. I got a big kick from Robin's collection esp. the big portrait.

Love—<br>Denny

Love to Helen A., Madeline Gleason, and the Tylers. Please tell them I *will* write.

P.S.

Cats sound delightful, kittens I mean. We at present are catless after a bad experience with a delinquent cat earlier in the summer. I was fond of him in a way—we all were—but he was an alley tom-cat & just unsuitable for apt. life—with impudent manners & a zest for mischief. He now lives in Brooklyn.

---

The poems remind me of my beloved rockface or cliff near Guadalajara.

---

Am also reading H.D.'s *Tribute to Freud.*

What about *Letters?* Is it at last ready? Jonathan is in New York but I haven't yet seen him.

---

Mitch spoke to Rexroth & Marthe on phone when they were here 2 days en route for Aix en Provence and we wd. have seen them (he was very apologetic it seems) for Marthe's sake anyway but a muddle occurred & we didn't in the end, to my relief. Wd have liked Nik to meet Mary again tho'.

dear Denny/

It was Eloise Mixon's saying when I had struggled with the first re-vision of "Yes, As a Look Springs to Its Face": "But it isn't the poem you wanted in the original"; and her disappointment—that it had constricted and been renderd by in-forming of content, etc. that set free the second "*Yes.*"[1] And in this— for when the poem was there, there was a release; there was a possibility of boldness (to get "fresh")—you were most present. Don't women have both a secretness (that can be desirous—I think how shyness and slyness intermingled in Mary Fabilli) and a candor that men don't have in themselves, have only in sharing thru love? There's always "a criticism of what has gone before"—anyway it's out of a crisis in the what has gone before that, ill or health, life must take its path. Well, I don't want to diagnose the feeling. Them am pomes writ for you, wasn't it you who askd me if I had read Buber's Hassidic masters books, and that three and a half years back. There are rumors of a natural joy and devotion there that fill in part of the picture.

## 97

Sept. 27, 1958
{Stinson Beach}

There sure are times when my right boldness is to go against your criticism ("The Enamord Mage" retaind in the design of *The Field* tho I pruned back, cutting eight poems, in shaping the work—but here it was Helen Adam's demand that establishd this too to shape), and I am wary of your moral persuasions. The more wary since I find them close enuf to the moral persuasions of life.

And then, there is a liveliness in the allowance.

•

I've got to get me to my composition table to work on a new window for James Broughton. I pourd the base layer of clear plastic and have now a couple of days of designing, cutting and colord lights and moonstones. The new *Paterson* on the table, I am still in the stage of excitement and wonderfull pleasure at the lightness and depth he gets; and beginning to be aware that how his interpolations, the breakings, seem special and not a necessary part of what one must take over. Tho it's a part of even our poetry—the way the correspondents come thru in our day. Is it because all other means of actual communications are stoppd, twisted, EDITED, postponed? Even a book—only the closest friends receive the book in its own time. It's taken over two years since the summer of '56 when I finishd the "Preface" for *Letters* and the publication of the book began. The printing is complete. I have the proofs, an unbound sheaf of the book. And only the binding remains. Amen.

You are right, I think, about the trouble with Robin's "Preface to Works to Come" (tho much of the writing precedes the "Transparencies"). The Transparency piece was spontaneous—so unlabord I take it, so un-"contemplated" that Robin did not trust it, did not send me a copy and luckily sent a copy to Spicer with an apology—etc. I mistrust the O'Hara casual line, I take it anyway that some of the style of "Preface" is that. It's a manner that mimics candor. And awkward too for the ecstatic. I've postponed reading closely the "Preface" tho.

love
Robert

---

**98**

October 7th {1958}
249 W. 15th
N.Y. 11

Dear Robert & Jess

It's at last that kind of NY. October weather, cool sunny & clear. But I don't get out into it much.

Was interested in what Gershom Scholem says abt. my ancestor Schneour Zalman. Have you still not read *Tales of the Hasidim* (2 vols—*The Early and The Late Masters*)—Martin Buber—? It is a world I enter, which nourishes me in a way I can only think of as atavistic or as "a heritage"—considering my ignorance and other factors. Anyway—do get & read them because I know you'd find things in them.

I went out to get a job—(cut my hair—not very short but still, cut—everyone likes it tho' & I'm glad of the change) but it has now been decided that my working wd. be too destructive to family life, (not to speak of to me as a poet, since even without a job I can't get enough useable time to myself). Unless I cd find a 1-day a week sort of job that paid well.

I long ago talked about sending you an illustrated Andersen on a long loan—I didn't forget but am just hopeless abt. organizing any sort of a pkge. However I have desperate intentions of doing something abt. it very soon, as I think you'd like the pictures.

We've just been making some rigorous rules abt. seeing fewer people and getting to bed early, so that we can make better use of the mornings. We almost never go out, but if someone calls up I have a sort of reflex action that makes me say "Oh, you must come over, we'd love to see you"—not out of hypocrisy because its usually quite true, but without thought that this means a late night & an unuseable next day. And often people take out so much more than they give, of vitality & stimulation. It wd be O.K., only one needs to be abt. 10 different people.

I enclose copies (wd. you return please?) of the first 2 poems by M C Richards that I really like. Others seemed in a curious way, that is in a way disagreeable to me, female poems, something menstrual or hysterical about them, not in their content but in the very language—something I couldn't possibly say to her because it was something no-one, I'm sure, could possibly smell about themselves. These 2—the "Giant" already a year or so old, the other new—seem freed from that. In fact the "Giant" (not typical of her work) seems quite complete and right & I like it *very* much. The other is more like the ones I disliked (or rather, about which I disliked a certain aura) but seems to me to have come out in the clear & to be very interesting in several ways. Please let me know how they strike you. I don't like the end of "Levity"—something wrong. I've heard strange rumors about her but to us she has been very very pleasant, forthright, friendly & we like her. Maybe she used to be different. She went to a psychologist for a while and she said it did change her, or rather shook her up & propelled her forward.

I feel so happy these days that I want to brim over & sing it out and yet I want to keep it unsaid and untouched. Out of some very bad times has come something so lovely, new, fresh—I cannot think we ever will relinquish it or be as if it had never been, again. It's not in the illusion that there are no more problems. But in a new conception and sensation of true marriage.

A girl we know who's a zoologist is going to bring a skink and a potto home with her soon, & we can visit them. She has some nice tortoises & a lizard right now, & let me hold the lizard, a black one with a wide body it can inflate like toads do. It eats dandelions.

I have it in mind to write at last to Helen, Madeline, & the Tylers. I often think of all these but have been too pressured most of the time to write, except in Maine where I just luxuriated in the absence of pressure. Did I tell you how we rigged up a dress on 2 oars & really sailed? (an oar over the stern as tiller)

Love from
Denny

## 99

Oct. 10 /{19}58
{Stinson Beach}

dear Denny/

Can't find my pen, and clearing my desk—a mound of pending papers—found an envelope with this letter (Sept 27) to you etc. What sloth and chaos! Aie! we too discuss how to reclaim [from the middle of the night] our morning hours.

I read the Later Masters volume, and have been waiting to find the first volume in at the library. Currently I am reading in Louis Ginsberg's *Legends of the Bible*.[1] It's that the hassidim live within the imagination [as reading Yeats or Synge's volumes on Irish fairy lore one is excited how the folk there live or let live this withinness of the world]. "Our" own civilization—but no it's no part of the ourness or we—but the folkway goes thru, lives upon, the precincts of fortune. Americans believe in money like the Irish believe in the faïrie or the hassidim believe in radiances of god. It's why Pound is right that the dragon is fed now upon and bred out of money-suffering, and money-lust. Well, I ain't no jew so it must be more than the blood that is aroused by these practices and poetries of those despised joyful rabbis. It's the spirit that leaps to them—and the heritage, the source for the spirit recognizes its own in African lore too. Strangeness seems nearness, the almost too closeness. There is everything I love in their transformd living, in keeping to the poetic image of life within the actual day.

But I'd shy from those hassidim I think too, as I'd not shy from the elemental lore. I could not keep genuine the pan-fraternity. They share more than I can think of myself sharing.

There's an interpretation in one of the tales of the Later Masters of the "thou shalt not make a graven image" where the Master says that the true song is not heard, the word not cut [withheld from the flowingness of speech and held to the rigor] but the whole to be rhapsodic. Well, in the period of *Heavenly City Earthly City* I tended towards it. Now there is some reference to what was once fire becoming stone.

love
Robert

Dear Robert,

As a matter of fact I now look on the "Enamourd Mage," & any other poems I ever was dubious about, in an entirely different way. I don't mean that I am absolutely non-critical in advance which wd. be stupid but simply that I now have a much better over-all view of your total work, which seems to me extraordinarily beautiful, important, and potent, (and also against-the-stream in a way that has a particular attraction for me now) into which everything you do fits, belongs, has a place & a meaning. To put as I've recently been doing the poems of your different books, and the ballads, and the Africa poems in *Origin*, and the ones from the last two years culminating (for the moment) in the last 2 you sent, up against each other is to see what range, integrity, & mastery you have. Of course there are some I like less than others but I can accept the "Mage" ungrudgingly in the light of its companions, by which its own light is illumined.

What's this I hear about your withdrawing from Don Allen's anthology?[1] Robin told me something about it but wasn't very clear & I didn't want to ask him too many questions; and when I saw Don a few weeks ago I didn't want to ask *him* because he's not a close friend.

Such an anthology doesn't make sense without you. And I feel you owe it to the innocent readers who will buy it, to *stay in*, so that they can see *what there is*. I don't see how seceding from it does any good.

No poems for 59 days. I paid for my hubris in telling you how happy I was in my last letter by being at the other extreme since then. But not now.

Jess's covers & illustrations for "Crow Castle" & "O'Ryan" are marvels. Am writing to Helen Adam—love the poem, & can just about hear her voice.[2]

Dreamed a piece of music which I cd. repeat for some time after waking—curious.

Do you know Berlioz's "Nuits d'Été," sung by Eleanor Steber or Stebel?

Love—
Denny

100

October 17th {1958}
249 W. 15th St.
N.Y. 11

dear Denny/

I was delighted to see in *Poetry* magazine your group of poems.[1] The damnd Dahlberg review that I've gone at time and again over the last ten! months has proved my nemesis—so that I always face it when I would otherwise be free to send off work to Rago. Rago's response to my work, even in rejecting, has always carried conviction. I suppose if I read the magazine—like Pound used to read it when Harriet Monroe was going—I'd go wild.

101

October 22, 1958
{Stinson Beach}

Well, that's part of the story with Don Allen, Evergreen etc. That there the directive, intention, is the thing. And with my book of resemblances [the poems from the *Origin* period], and Antoninus's book turnd down it was clearer that where our work will be used there, it will be not in our spirit.

Not getting that book thru, and the "Pindar Poem" and later "Structure of Rime" pieces not being taken by Evergreen, made it clear enuf that I couldn't *use* Evergreen. But Allen's correspondence in returning them burnd me up.

I had to send over twenty poems before Rago finally got the group he wanted for *Poetry*; and Bob always has to see as many as that before he gets one he can use for *Black Mountain Review*. Both of them—well, no, it was only Rago, like *Evergreen*, returnd the "Pindar" and the "Structure of Rime" pieces. But I trust the nature of their judgment. [As with Corman, who printed—except for the work I sent for the last issue of *Origin*—everything I sent, I was always put off by his correspondence: that whatever he meant to do condescended.]

So I'm trying to hold to certain criteria for this business of contributing to anthologies:

1. That it be edited by someone genuinely concernd with poetry, certainly at a minimum that the editor be an involved poet. I never replied when Rolfe Humphries askd for work for his first anthology—and I wouldn't now. I feel strongly that he's a poetaster, genteel fashion. Altho I had no choice in the case of Auden's anthology (by the time I was askd the book was already set up), I would view him as *involved.* Tho his work represents a phase of the great process in poetry that I can't [outside of the first book] read; even Marianne Moore seems unconvincing to me when she tries to show his virtues.

   Under this criterion, I am burnd up that Don Allen who is an entrepreneur cashing in on a good thing should be the editor of the first [or any] anthology to present the work with which I am most concernd. Altho it is clear he has directives from Charles, Robin etc. etc. as to what shld be in it; it remains that he is making himself a place where he has no place. You or I, Charles, Bob, Corman [uneasy as that would make me]— anyone who was and is actually involvd wld. have root that gives meaning to the critical activity involved.

   When Allen first proposed the anthology I wrote that I was eager to appear with those contemporaries who have given me directive and contrast, but that I had also a mistrust. And I finally blew up and wrote him that he was insincere and that was the crux.

2. and/or that there be adequate payment. And that I set at fifty cents a line. The Auden anthology paid me $15 a poem which came to that.[2]
   *Evergreen* offers as far as I can figure out at $2.50 for 44 lines about 17¢

a line. We have never been paid for the recording. And for the San Francisco issue which was a great success we were paid $3.50 (?) a page.

Where I note from the contract that Don Allen is adequately paid for his activities as an editor.

summation: I mistrust the purposes of Evergreen's presenting our work. In the extreme of my sense there is an evil afoot in their cult of "sick" litterachure. And I have found my own work badly used in the past there.

And I am determined that Don Allen shall not define my relation to contemporary poetics.

"I mean to show you as one of the four major poets of this period" he wrote to me. Wherein I smelld the brimstone of my own vanity and of a LIE. Nor did it help when upon enquiry those four proved to be: Olson, me, Ginsberg, O'Hara. A con-man's table!

I have not the equanimity to be one of four major poets. It makes large my own presumption and obscures the art. The truth is that my life is parasitic [*parasitos*, one who eats beside or at the table of another] upon a host of poetry.

The oak is a work that we mistake if we consent to the voice that sez: I am the oak, you are the oak.

cummings put part of it in:

> mr u will not be missed
> who as an anthologist
> sold the many on the few
> not excluding mr u

———

Keep fame bright
and the song in the light
obedient to the true sun
that fed the heart

love
Robert


dear Denny/

Plans for a writers theater seem to be going ahead—Broughton is advisor—it all started when an admirer of Broughton's plays got the idea of putting in money to prime the pump! etc. And I don't think there is much more idea afloat in it all. But the *MEDEA* is to go into rehearsal in December: Broughton asks if I could get the whole trilogy to be done in one nite: and so I've this month to see if I can. And the Workshop I'm directing (courtesy Poetry Center) has led me back into the meshes and knots of

**102**

October 31, 1958
{Stinson Beach}

sounds and measures. With this coming week the complexities of stress to contemplate. as the text on the breakfast table here shows:

| animal | ǽnĭmăl | terrific | tĭrífĭk |
|---|---|---|---|
| animate | ǽnĭmèyt | | |
| | | refugee | réfyŭjìy |
| | | effigy | éfĭjĭy |

The distinction between ˘ and ˜ not being, for said professors, of the same order as of *kind*
and the distinction between
       an òld máid
    and our ôld máid[1]
gives total of four orders of stress contrasting. [And knocks to hell the assumptions of conventional versifiers to their stressd and unstressd system: stress = loudness; unstressd = hiatus]

That some of this conscious study and effortful recognition might quicken inner connections, unconscious use . . .

And to send you two poems I found myself writing in a letter to Robin yesterday. The first in ¿is it a month? or more? The concern in them arises from an afternoon at my favorite Aunt's [who tho does tend to be ferociously sweet] where I met her "teacher," a Mrs. Swanson persuaded to the enlargements of life sense and higher truth known as Free Thot or New Thot, the more euphoric elements of Whitman and Carpenter. Whererin or where*at*, having a fondness for Carpenter and a predilection for Whitman, I liked the old dame in part but was on edge about the superior spirituality of it all.

It's not my sense that they were "fake" but that in some way they were mistaken. Talking about "the spiritual man" as if it meant a less troubled being. And I was aware too that I could only conceive of *my* spiritual self in some other way—all nerves and extremes. *A lofty benevolent wise me would be an unmitigated fraud.* [Like trying on a kindly smile for the camera?] To do her justice Mrs. Swanson warn't benevolent but a little puckish.

I love higher thot where it gives a certain quality to events [as i.e. orders in which there are angels give a certain mode; and as this I delight in the thot of a lofty benevolent mage—it frees me to be me; just as a sleeping emperor frees my pride from being entirely real?]; but dislike it where it asks self-improvement. I would like immortality to be an ever-present quality in the immediate; an immortality that is unique; and everlastingness of what actually disappears.

As in the poem—it must be immutable, written for eternity; and at the same time be thot of existing only in itself, a unique certain time then. And mistaken elsewhere.

M. C. {Richards} sent me a poem (recent?) and I did get a letter off to her with I think a sympathetic reading (tho in guessing what it is I am leery of by filling with how the poem is conceived I probably get false identifications . . . ) The crude objection is that she thinks of the poem as an emotional or atti- tudinal expression, whatever form accidental to saying whatever she feels. And not the poem as form in an art. So she has not reason to select; and the word "sincerity" means I feel this way: not the sincerity of the form feels this way. [No, I don't mean there's a choice; but M. C. doesn't demand the second foundation of *feeling* in the poem.{]}

She ends up trying to make what she feels *true* or *real* by overworking the words [and paying no attention to what the words are establishing as *tone*].
"the ocean's belly dance, its lover hovering horizonside"
Well, I guess that's the ocean from a ship's side. Sure ain't from shore-side.
There's a crudity of feeling-tone somehow just where I want a finer tone.
I don't get any idea that she establishes any poetics—that is, any signature (which takes making a form (so's the maker leaves his inevitable, rather than his whimsical, trace)) I just take it she writes 'em off.
What I respond to is that she has feeling and wants to relate it.
Tho God! how can she exclaim
Decant th' Imperial flame
and than carry on about
NATURE! her spittle etc.
all mixd up together in one pot.
I remember M. C. was tops at making a stew or a salad. With a relish and an appetite; and abundance.
Words as mixd greens?

love
Robert

Dear Robert

Thanks v. much for clear explanation. I think you are absolutely right— for yourself. Of course it makes nonsense of the anthology & that is sad. But an anthology giving equal prominence to you, Ginsberg, & O'Hara, is nonsensical anyway, obviously. I don't think it is a case of *insincerity* on Don's part, though, but of having no confidence in his own judgement— and/or, *having* no judgement. He is at the mercy of whoever has currently impressed him. Ginsberg & O'Hara are always shouting and whispering (respectively) into his ears, so he thinks they're great. But I can't bring myself to pick a quarrel with him because I'm sorry for him. He has been (disinterestedly, as far as I can see) really kind to Mike Rumaker, and I feel obliged to him for introducing me to Octavio Paz, whom I liked very much.

## 103

November 2d {1958}
249 W. 15th St.
{New York}

I expect to be a minor figure in the anthology, & if some of the company is undesirable, well, I'll just stay in my corner, so to speak, and[1]

As for the payment, it is of course ridiculously low. But I do think, to be fair, it shd. be pointed out that that loathsome Rosset[2] is responsible for the inadequate amount being put up in the first instance, and that Don Allen as Rosset's employee is paid pretty shoddily in general; for instance it seems that Rosset only just recently reluctantly supplied him with secretarial help (part-time). Of course a man with more self-respect wouldn't *be* Rosset's slave in the first place; but I see Don as a sad disappointed weak person rather than an ambitious go-getting one.

By the way I hope you know that if it had been a case of his *ignoring* your work I would not have thought for a moment of letting my poems be used.

I've been working, thank god. Dont feel very confident of what I've done but it may be alright. Will send as soon as I can copy (rather long). I have the last poems you sent me tacked up on my wall.

Have you seen *The Nation* Nov. 1st issue?—article with mention of you, me, Olson, etc.?[3] Has the best Blackburn poem I've ever seen—I had thought he'd stopped short long ago, but evidently not. And a little W. C. W. poem. Will send you a copy if you don't have it. Let me know.

I have a small present for you & Jess—something I think you'll like. W. C. W. has had another stroke—not severe, but he has been forbidden any more platform readings. It has affected his speech rather more. But I spoke to Floss on the phone a couple of days ago and she sounded pretty hopeful & cheerful.

Love—
Denny.

P.S.

Met a pet honeybear. Has the general friendliness of a dog with the suavity of a cat. Do look up in zoo or book if you are not familiar with their appearance. It comes from Central and S. America & isn't in the bear family really, but I can't think what its other name is. A long ribbon of pink tongue, golden brown fur, inquisitive pink snout, melting look—yet alert— and the most endearing confiding way of climbing into[4]

**104**

November 18h {1958
New York}

Dear Robert

Enclosed letter was written & not mailed, as inadequate. But meanwhile I was in the hospital so will mail anyway as being better than silence. Operation was for excision of a very small tumour that thank god was not malignant & I am perfectly OK except for still feeling sort of groggy. They kept me an extra day because I twice passed out in what I thought were fainting fits but what they consider resembled *grand mal* attacks so now apparently I am of the confraternity of Dostoyevsky etc., but only mildly. However I have to get a neurological exam now. I've "fainted" about 8 times in my life since age 7 so at that rate it's not much to worry about; but seems worth some sort of investigation I guess.

I've been entering the hassle on another front (really the same one) by declining to send poems to *Yugen* because its standards seem so low (poor poems even by good people) and so "beat," and by writing to A. Alvarez (see *Partisan Review* for November) to object to being called "one of the S.F. beat poets."[1] Since writing the earlier letter in answer to yours explaining abt. D.A.'s anthology etc. I've gotten much more disgusted by it all (including in my feelings Mike McClure's "Ode to Jackson Pollock" which, whatever intrinsic worth it may have, I just can't *see*, because its having been chosen *not* for intrinsic worth but for its chic appeal of catchy title gets in my way) and am resolved not to send Don any more stuff. However, the things he already has ("The 5-Day Rain" "A Communion," a trans. of Octavio Paz and that Toltec poem[2]) I shall leave with him—I don't want to begin a whole megillah but just quietly recede.

Will enclose a long several-part poem which as yet has no title except the provisional one of "From a Diary."[3] Does it seem to you as if there should be more of it, or has it a sense of having grown to whatever fullness it has? I didn't feel as if I could go beyond the end of it, but at some re-readings I wondered if the connections seemed strained, or rather as if there were not enough, of the earlier sections.

Arabel Porter of *New World Writing* asked me to submit a long poem— 20 pages—for their June issue. Of course I don't have anything even half as long. I gave her your name and address & suggested she ask you. Hope you don't mind.

Has Jess's show opened? Or not yet?

Oh, about M. C.—what you say expresses what I have felt about all her other poems and to some extent about the sunflower poem, but not about the atypical poem about the giant, which seems as if written by another hand & which she herself at first rejected because "it had written itself out of nowhere," & in which there seems to be none of that straining to express feelings and ideas without respect for the sounds & associations of words. She makes lovely pots—and, as you say, salads. And has a feeling for weedy thistly seedy wild plants that has made me see such things newly. We are waiting for her fluffy cat and/or her Siamese to have kittens so we can have a cat of character instead of an alley tabby this time. I'd still like a honeybear tho'.

Write soon—love—<br>
Denny.

dear Denny/

One level the last few weeks has been awake to the cold, the blue diamond of Sirius east tonight below the body of Orion flashing. Each night addressing those named stars that are entering my world . . . El Nath, Aldebaran, the Pleiades, the great chair swing thru the high heavens, Mars climbing thru the sign of the Bull this last month, beyond the Pleiades now, into the Ram.

And in the workshop this week studying pitches and stresses, as they are determined by and determine by junctures. That opens out such a suggestion of subtleties, if poets, we drew close to the graces and orders of actual speech. So various in the regular. There's a book by Trayer and Smith *An Outline of English Structure* put out by the American Council of Learned Societies, 1219 Sixteenth Street, N.W. Wash. D.C. that's opend up a lot for me[1]

How complex the possible materials are:
in regular American there are 9 vowels (with in addition diphthongs like ay (as in *light*), ey (as in *plate*), iy (as in *see*), ɔy (as in *boy*), ao (as in *loud*), etc.

24 consonants

4 stresses

4 pitch levels

and 4 junctures.

If I could only write out clearly how I begin to see what some of it means in what we are all trying to do in poetry!

And have been reading a book on Yeats by Wilson where I find quotes from Yeats' edition of Blake:[2]

"besides the Trinity, a fourth principle, a universal matrix. . . . To this emanation is applied constantly by Boehme the word *looking glass*. . . . God looking into this mirror ceases to be mere will, beholds himself as the Son . . . and enters on that eternal meditation about himself which is calld the Holy Spirit."

"The dead, as the passionate necessity wears out, come into a measure of freedom . . . they are moved by emotions, sweet for no imagined good but in themselves, like those of children dancing in a ring"—thus from *Per Amica Silentia Lunae.*

from the Blake notes: "that the mobility of heaven is distinguished from its eternity, that mobility is Christ, that it fell, or went out into the void which thus became nature, and that on returning it formd the joys of heaven with what it took from the energy or 'eternal hell' outside."

The finishd *Letters* has arrived. Fredericks has taken the same care in binding it that he did in printing and attending to my lengthy proof corrections and suggestions. Fredericks' aesthetic is contrary to mine, but his service to his art is devout; and there is I feel in the book a strength in the contest of my intention and his. What is left of my page has been just the notation, defined by Fredericks' battle for his typographical style that is in contradiction to the open-space-time-form concept of the poetic. What I like is that the poems are more solidly conceived once I have been forced to question everywhere whether my usage in the line is structural or "effect." And thruout correspondence with Fredericks was direct and rewarding. I had to ask at times for a complete resetting [the paragraphing in prose sections he always assumed was arbitrary and then wld. send proofs that completely obscured or discarded my meaning—well, that meant for a good little essay on what a paragraph meant].

But along with this came Jonathan Williams' announcement that he was obliged to raise the price of the trade edition to $8. And the thot of the reader, after both printer and writer had had such care in shaping the book, having to pay for the publisher's carelessness remains a permanent source of outrage. Enclosed my first draft of an open letter, which I sent to Williams two weeks ago—asking him to give me an accounting of why or how his new pricing was *just*. But now I find his whole view of the book ["I happened to want to present *Letters* like Bristol Creme instead of Virginia Dare," he writes, "which, god knows, is in keeping with the spirit of the work"] rotten, damnd rotten. And as I have written him I will no longer have anything at all to do with him. Neither write to nor accept letters from him.

Since he had no hand in the design of the book the pleasure may remain in the qualities of the thing. . . . And I will sell the copies of the trade edition which I am to receive as royalties (50 copies) at the price first announced of $4.

The decision to strike Williams out of my world entirely has been a relief; like the absolute exclusion of Ruth Witt-Diamant.

I think I see what I loathe, once I reflect upon publishers I came to loathe and publishers that did honor to my work.

Bern Porter, Jonathan Williams, and Don Allen all saw themselves as promoting my work. And as I came to observe working for the Poetry Center promotion and exploitation are one: the thing "promoted" and the "public" are terms of an exploitation to support the vanity of the promoter.

James Broughton in publishing *Medieval Scenes*, Creeley in publishing *Caesar's Gate* and Joe Dunn in publishing *Faust Foutu* just wanted to get the work into print.

Happier almost news, is that now, just last night N. O. Brown whose name is Nobby (from N. O. B., I am told)—a resident scholar at the Berkeley campus from Wesleyan College, who is doing work in German mysticism—has ventured to ask if I would be interested in having my new book the *Field* printed by Wesleyan. It's only at the stage now of Brown's suggesting to them that they shld do it—but he has considerable influence there. It would mean if it all comes about that I would no longer be a special item.

love
Robert

What Williams replied to the above was: "I propose all author's copies to be $12.50, signed or unsigned, decorated or undecorated."

I had anyway between the above letter and receiving his reply reflected that I questiond using my out-rage to coerce Williams' action. For a just action has meaning, ground in justice, only when it is voluntary.

So I wrote in my closing statement to Williams that I would prepare limited editions as I had promised in the announcement to the reader, etc.[3]

**106**

Nov. 26, 1958
{Stinson Beach}

dear Denny/

At third reading I begin to get a concrete quality [concentration] in the opening section of "Notes from A Diary."[1] Shldn't there be a clear referent for "afraid/it may reveal a dirty emptiness" that the opener is so afraid. In line with the first stanza the seed (unit) is afraid or the plant [and then the poet] is afraid the green, bitter, of no account. That meaning is truer hidden within ones mistrust of the *other*. But then I see you want to force the subjective here. It's a more direct, less figurative statement I want to gain truth and clear away sentiment. The presence of *I* and *other* within the real identification. As telling a hazelnut to know when ripeness has hardend you and sweetend you has some vital true necessity for the human right experience; (of hazelnut, that the man knew when and what the ripeness is).

But—there'll be the dry rot and the green sour pit—The "sentiment" or mistaken convention transfers to subjective fear of being "dirty emptiness" "green/bitter, of no account."

When in his works, the human is like a plant—and his will is what it is: be it empty, dry rot, bitter green, or full ripe. Isn't that the courage that's askd of us everywhere?

> "fall and rot
> enriching your rich brotherhood"

you have it; and puzzling, must include in that generosity of being—the failures, the sterilities.

This may be what's in my mind about the poem: that it is *you* who are afraid of the (poem) being empty, green bitter, unnourishing. The (poem) ain't so afraid. It is as it is conceivd. The nourishing is (?courage?) to be afraid. Ripeness may be a loyal inclusion of having faild.

"to dig shame up . . .
    and tie it to my breast"

As I get it at this point (and Jess had a similar reading) it's in the third
part that the speaking seems most contrived. There's *dreams* and then there
are near conceits: almost true statements that strain at a leash.

and "kindling my cold heart" is left abruptly without substance.

"eyes of my love for you flickering at the edge of you" has image; *is*.

Mightn't it be the . . . but I like the bold fairytale quality of "as I roasted
your pheasants by my night fire?"

And the *cold heart* belongs to such a fairy tale.

It may be the rhetorical questions the
    "Have they not nourished my life?"
instead of "They have nourished my life." The
    "Have I not poached among them, as now on your desk"
instead of:
    "I've been poaching among them.
    My cheeks have grown rosy, my hair curly
    as I roasted your pheasants by my night fire."

---

Now I see what I want to do to the poem, the argument I had as I read with
the diction. It's that the *you* in the poem is not a person of the poem; is not
the reader, but a particular person; and there's a confusion in the voices and
persons, inside and outside of the poem.

---

IV is beautiful. Links in my mind with Blake's thistle (or is it a dandylion)
father. But to keep the simple image of a rose Wldn't "wide open" be better
than "open as a daisy"? Picky, perhaps. I can certainly see said rose "open as
a daisy" a briar rose then.

---

I use this question [as "Have I not withheld the hearts of men from you?"]
but in this poem of yours you make me doubt the use at all. For I feel that
where in V the question "What holds us upright" . . . has full force of a
search [answerless as we may know it] . . . But the next one the "Were we
suspended . . . by a filament" is infolded with a (conceit?) "museum
butterflies . . . from a hidden nail?"

But damnd it, it's *I* who am off the circuit worrying this poem along like
this. It gives me a closer reading, and the poem's own world begins to insist,
and haunt my reading. Cause I've got this really impossible proposition of
being stuck butterfly-wise suspended from a hidden nail; and I've protested
that that *is made up*, like saying we're just puppets, etc.

Except that every reality gathers in and leaps from

"Has it broken when we begin to
fall, slowly, without desire?
(But we don't fall . . . "

And from the first reading of the poem "living room," "work room" at the close were, continue solid, (cut, placed) so that meaning is containd.

———————

When the worrying is done, I still have the sense that there is something to be got in section III, a clarification of (focus) image and quality that would clear thru the poem.

For other worryings [the *issues* that come up where the work, of the soul, which is evident in that thing the poem is treated as this society treats all things, as a commodity] I am glad when the swift decision has laid them away. With Jonathan Williams I took one swift look at what he has always actually been saying and doing [and because I *want* to be able to buy at any price and have at hand your work, Bob's, Olson's, Zukofsky's] that I've over-lookd or excused or dismissd before . . . but there was the language as he uses it, saying the things it says and means then, demeaning spirit to a use, to be a cultural commodity, to be "dug," to keep a cognescenti in the *know* . . .

I wrote it off the books; I have surely no more to do with the fate of Jargon than I have to do with the fate of Random House that made Williams' *Journey to Love* available.

It is part of the demonology of exploitation that a publisher "promotes" the writer. I'll not be promoted any more than I'll be initiated or saved: it would be bad for my character.

My own belief in my fame is so lovely [a dream] that what a public (of two, twenty, two hundred etc.) offers of fame seems ugly.

China lilies in our garden now are putting out first bursts of fame [we did not even know what they were, dying back there last March . . . some kind of lily]—a pungency that conquers the season—

love
Robert

## 107

{December, 1958}
249
{New York}

Dear Robert and Jess,

At last I have *Letters*. It is a work of great strength and richness and of a kind that will never wear thin but will last me a lifetime. You say strange things about your own place as a poet sometimes but to me this book shows forth your stature more than any of your other books yet, and in the world of imagination you have a hero's stature and stride about shining. What petty mind will presume to criticize this book? Ants only, who can't see up further than a man's ankle. As for the book's appearance, it's really beautiful and fitting.

About my poem, I think when I send you part VI it may seem more complete, and I will reply on a separate sheet to your doubts etc. (can't start on that now as I have to buy supper, the Bells are coming & I have an empty icebox.)

About Jonathan and the price of the book, it is of course not only wrong of him to double the price of the book but also stupid, because less than ½ of the people who might otherwise have bought it are going to be able to ~~afford $8 for it, so he'll end up worse off anyway. But I don't think you ought~~ to get so involved in protesting it, even though you are in the right. It makes me feel bad to see you whom I love and admire so much expending your energy on the affair. Poets more or less have to expect to get cheated—if they spend their time fighting that they are using time that rightfully belongs to their work, & so are cheating themselves too. You only inflate Jonathan's ego probably, by deigning to pit yourself in protest against his silly business ways. Moreover it's one of those things that could have been settled—& to your satisfaction—if only you & he had been able to talk about it, however angrily, in person, instead of by mail—which makes it sadder. He's a silly ass but I don't think he's vicious and I'm sure if you & he had been in the same room together when this thing came up he'd have backed right down.

A curious scene took place a few days ago when a sort of Xmas Folder was prepared at the apt. of old Bob Brown,[1] poets writing each a poem in handwriting on sensitized paper, accompanied by a drawing of sorts by Fielding Dawson (who can't draw) and then photographed by some process. Mitch & I arrived first since we didn't wish to go to the Cedar Bar which we avoid like a plague spot, and where the rest met—so we were witnesses of their arrival in a long procession of jutting beards. Odious Oppenheimer was among them and altogether they were a pretty poor crew & I wished I hadn't come. However some good people are included including Zukofsky so it may be of some interest. A strange little photographer (also bearded) was present, tripping over everyone's feet in this incredibly crowded room piled with books almost in canyons & avenues like those hermit brothers', and causing others to trip with the long wires of his lighting arrangements, but some of the photos really came out well (they were shown to me some days later)—if I can get a copy will send you one of the ones he took of me.

I had some poems from Madeline {Gleason}, the longest of which seems to me very very good.

And Helen Adam to whom I had sent a little old Welsh sampler sent me the most beautiful mirror {small drawing of oval mirror with handle} I ever saw.

I mailed you at last a small object I've considered to be yours for months & months. It was intended for a salt cellar & comes from Czarist Russia, around 1910. It is for you both and please do not consider it a Xmas present or the sort of gift that makes you feel you have to reciprocate, indeed as far as that's concerned it is I who am reciprocating & in a very miniscule way. It's just something that I felt belonged to you as soon as I looked at it again. (I remember it from my infancy, there are 2, Mitch has the other one now; they came to me with other things my mother saved & brought here when the house in England was sold, and which remained packed as they came while we were in Mexico, & which I at last unwrapped last June.) A very tiny silver spoon should go with it I guess but that I don't have.

Will finish this later—must get that shopping now.

*Sunday*

I see if I start on the poem questions now this will not reach you before Xmas so will put that off. I get very scattered at this time of year, undertake more than I can manage, etc. There was a reading at N.Y.U. Friday night, I read and Allen Ginsberg, & contrary to all expectation he really read some good things—I think you'd have thought so too. Also he is very mild & chastened & not bouncing all over the joint like Tigger in *The House at Pooh Corner*—which almost is sad somehow. Like with a child; at one stage one can't wait for them to grow up, & yet when they begin to one actually feels a twinge of regret for all the noise etc. they used to make . . . Of course I don't know how these poems wd read on paper, but at any rate they were not just more of the same howl and there were really moving, as well as funny, things in them—and I felt humbled, having thought contemptuously of him for a long time and discouraged his coming here, etc.

We went to see Cocteau's *Beauty and the Beast* for the first time, and loved it.[2] Lots of things have happened to us this year & one is that Mitch has come to love fairytales which for complex reasons he never used to read. I read him one in the evenings sometimes & never mailed you the Hans Andersen I wanted to lend you because of the wonderful illustrations because Mitch has captured it—but I will yet.

We at last have a record player & have played your recording—that too was a great pleasure and excitement. We also have Wallace Stevens, W. C. W., and Seobbhan (—Shevawn, it's pronounced) MacKenna reading Yeats—she is the only actress who can read poetry, except maybe for Sybil Thorndike. And we have our Mexican records which I'd love you to hear.

Had a good letter from Bob, and in a letter from Ed Dorn was a poem of his (Bob's) called "My Love" which I'll enclose a copy of.

Expected Joe Dunn before now but so far no sign of him. I wanted to invite him for Xmas Eve or Day. He sent me some books I asked for— {Harold} Dull, {Richard} Brautigan, {George} Stanley. So far have only skimmed, tho' they are short, but they look very good, especially the Albas of G. Stanley.

We're going to a crêche service at St. Luke's Hudson St tonight, it is like a play & all the children go in procession & sing carols.

Love—
Denise.

*My Love.*                    *By Robert Creeley.*

It falleth like a stick.
   It lieth like air.
It is wonderment and bewilderment,
   to test true.

It is no thing, but of two
    equal: as the mind turns to it,
it doubleth,
    as one alone.

Where it is, there is
    everywhere, separate,
yet few—as dew
    to night is.

dear Denny,

Just the shortest note!—to accompany new pages of *The Field*. Just one poem to go to fulfill the plan of fifty poems.

Did we write about receiving the salt cellar? Which is a jewel and sits a-glow on a velvet cloth of olive color. An article of the in-binding. What minute and careful working it takes to enrich so—

love
Robert

## 108

{December 1958,
January 1959
San Francisco}

Dearest Robert and Jess

What a delight and surprise! Your wonderful gifts, arriving on Xmas Eve, set the tone for a wonderful Xmas—the best we've ever had. I'm mounting the little painting (is that encaustic?) on a dark ground. The trees have their heads together for an exchange of wisdom by full-moon light. As we look at it in time we'll come to overhear them perhaps. Robert, your roses and new-year rose poem go up on my wall with "The Natural Doctrine," "Yes, as a look" (2 versions) and "The Question."

The book brings alleluiahs to our lips—and following so close on the *Letters* gives us a joyful pride in being the friends of such a poet. We couldn't

## 109

December 30th {1958}
249 W. 15th St.
N.Y. 11

possibly have had anything but a beautiful Xmas when it began with the lovely generosity & thoughtfulness of you two.

Xmas Eve we lit the tree (Nik & the kids next door decorated it in the morning) at dusk—we always have real candles, & "sparklers" from Mexico (no longer obtainable here, as a fire-hazard, but we're very careful)—and the eyes of the 6 children present were just shining—it was lovely to see. Then we had Mike R{umaker}, Al Kresch & Pat, & 2 unattached friends (at least, 1 is married but is waiting for his wife & child to come from L.A., having come here to look for work etc.) to dinner—with flaming Xmas pudding— afterwards to a friend's house for a sort of tree-decorating party; and then for the first time went to midnight mass at St. Luke's (on Hudson St., where Nik used to go to school), which was preceded by half an hour of well- played baroque music. For years we've felt embarrassed by Xmas—at least I have, having experienced as a child a believing Christian Xmas, & wishing to give Nik some kind of rich experience, not just an orgy of presents, but, not being Xtians, not knowing how to do it without hypocrisy. This year it solved itself because the universal, new-life, winter festival aspects of it at last appeared clear & strong to us, not rejecting but including the specifically Xtian in a way that seemed natural & acceptable. And Nik too added to it because he was so anxious to *give* presents not just to receive them, & spent all his saved pocket money with touching generosity.

This weekend just past we went to J Laughlin's at Norfolk Conn.—an odd experience. Here's this man who after all has known artists of various kinds all his life, & does write poems however slight & modest, but who evidently has *chosen* the most rigidly conventional kind of life for his own. His house, wife, baby, table, servants, and conversation are a Connecticut version of British "County"—the kind who ride to hounds & take a house in Town for the Season. We enjoyed the food, the books (a good library) the sun on the snow (Nik & I had our first (& perhaps last) skiing lesson) and of course they are genuinely well-intentioned & asked us out of kindness. But it is always instructive to be reminded of the rift that exists between the rich who patronize & ourselves who are makers.

Mitch & I gave each other records for Xmas & we have some wonderful ones now, including Berlioz's "Nuits d'Été" sung by Eleanor Steber, Hugues Cuenod singing French & Eng. 17th cent songs (Dowland etc.) & piano music of Satie.

I've been so busy with Nik being home all day for the holidays that I haven't yet written to Helen about the mirror, so I'm going to stop & do so now.

Nik (as well as some toys) received a good globe of the world, *The Red Fairy Book*[1] (with the good old illustrations not the nasty new ones) some Arthur Ransome books and a dart-board which he & friends enjoy v. much but which entails grown-up's supervision.[2] He is obliquely courting a red-head his age—bought a present for her little brother but is too shy to speak to *her*.

Love from
Denny, Mitch, and Nik

Dear Robert,

I wanted to tell you about the "Enamourd Mage." I've moved a long way from where I was when I first saw it for it now speaks to me & I see it as a great beauty.

January 12th {19}59
249 W. 15th St
N.Y. 11

The new ones came today—thank you—I had been going to write you about *The Seventh Seal* which we saw a week ago but now I need not.[1]

I still haven't written about my long poem but I have such awful arrears of correspondence—haven't even told my mother about our Xmas yet—so I'll have to put it off again.

Your cutting-off of people who offend (Don Allen, Jonathan) which at first seemed to me too extreme, as I think about I see is right & admirable. Sometimes it takes me a while to get around to seeing things clearly, as with the poem. I have at times a perhaps neurotic desire to please, and with it a genuine liking for rather diverse persons, and also a naive inability to believe someone is 2-faced as long as they're being nice to *me*—but if I let a little time go by & look at these people & situations without those obscuring sentiments intervening, I see there is no alternative (without hypocrisy) to your decisive action.

Jonathan's folder I told you about turned out to be quite ridiculous & I feel ashamed to have participated (tho Zukovsky & one or two others did too)—but it is ridiculous not only from the idiotic jumble of qualities but because the holograph poems are mostly quite illegible. And the drawings are just plain silly.[2] A poem by Ginsberg, which when he read it was moving, is nothing on the page, & I see its force was not of art at all but of confessional—like a newspaper report of victim's words at some catastrophe. Or: I put my hand on your shoulder & you feel it; but look at a photograph of hand on shoulder & you feel nothing. Yet a Giotto or a Rembrandt could paint that hand laid on that shoulder so that its original force was equalled or *increased*! His poem as he reads it (even tho' he didn't read very "well") is the original act—on paper, lacking form & care as it does, it is nothing but a dead photograph.

Madeline Gleason is one of those to whom I owe a letter, & I must do it soon or she will think I don't like her poems. I don't care for the "Willie" one but the long one she sent impressed me.

And I'm always meaning to write to the dear Tylers of whom we often think. It's a whole year (less ten days or so) since we were there. How lovely it was.

Will send some poems next time.

Love—
Denny.

---

dear Denny/

The "Selected" pomes for Ferling's Pocket Poet Series is decided on. It will be 72 pages and sell for $1 like the rest in the series: and tho a larger volume might have had more ease, when I was designing this minimum text I found I had a very definite sense of what is well done in that early work. After the inclusion of two poems from 1942 "African Elegy" and "King Haydn of Miami Beach" I found myself pruning with a zest. I cut "Festivals," "The Adoration of the Virgin," and "Huon of Bordeaux" from *Medieval Scenes.* And from "Domestic Scenes" I cut "Real Estate," "Mail Boxes," "Bath," "Lunch with Buns." "The Venice Poem" is there intact. I rescued "The Homecoming" from its lonely appearance in *The Pacific Spectator* and "The Temple of the Animals" from *Poetry.* Cut "Harlequin's Dinner Table" from the "Homage to Grimms" and substituted "Jerusalem," a short poem that has not been printed before.

The "I Speak of Love" and "Revival" from *Poems 1948–49* I like but did not include. The selection was already composing towards a display of the legendary, the l'oeuvre de fantôme, and that decided the canon.

From *Caesar's Gate* from the surrounding muddle of "Four Poems as a Night Song" I cleard out with the song beginning "Garcia Lorca Tasted" and re-titled "The Drinking Fountain." Plus "Processionals II" and "The Second Night in the Week"

So: I kept it *Early* Selected Poems. And off it goes, so Ferling tells me, next week to the printers!!!

By the way: cut from the "Seventh Seal" poem the passage "this one / who despairs of his cock . . . " etc. thru to end of stanza. These are, I think, false particulars, the more misleading since they are actually true but don't belong.

My sense of it when I came to look at that poem detachd was that: "there are no such particulars." I had supplied them, even in the excitement of the poem, for a moment dutifully "modern" and adding instances. . . .

I am again up to the point in applying for a *Guggenheim* where material is to be sent in: and have a stack of books to send off, plus the manuscript of *The Field.* The old letters of recommendation still hold. Parkinson and Norman Brown (who stirs up Marx, Freud and history; and has some reputation as a classics scholar) have both written on their own protesting my not getting a grant last year. ??? I am a disbeliever.

Art critics are just like poetry critics—the one local ass to date who wrote on the show Jess has at Gumps said: "dubious mysticism . . . lugubrious color." At least shows a family resemblance twixt poet and painter.

McClure relayd to me from Paul Carroll that there's a new magazine starting, deadline February 15. It is to be, I take it, centerd on the zen-dopsters axis and I haven't settled yet with my spirit whether I will be happier aloof, or if I have immunity and can send a contribution in good will. Last time I was in town I had my fill of the new spirit (its slavish ambition, fawning upon opportunity etc.) in the spectacle of Philip Lamantia performing for a reporter from the *N.Y. Post*.

love,
Robert

post script:

Just remembering that peformance of Lamantia's, simpering, oggling, an apish affair; and also my brief visit with McClure who is now obsessd with getting ahead and with the importance of dope [the doctrine being that the imagination is passé. The real news is being "high" on . . . whatever] Philip Lamantia saying to the reporter "All the mystics were on it. That's what it really means, man. You know . . . Dionysus was a hemp god . . . etc."]

It's such a loveless and then unlovely stupidity.

And I don't think whatever "good will" would turn out to be good there.

But it's sad, thinking of the young stupified.

No, I'll wait for a magazine that has a green stem.

dear Denny/

Here is the closing poem of *The Field*.[1] What remains is a page of epigraphs . . . that will set the reader off on a thematic search and then, I don't know at this point if I want a preface. That can wait [as did the "Preface" for *Letters*] until a publisher turns up. The poem came about oddly enuf. I had despaird of "receiving" just what I felt was needed for the book—which was a poem that would be both within and without the law. Last week during a storm Jess ventured to make up the bed with an electric blanket: we'd never used it for ourselves before but left it for guests. But what heaven! to be able to let even one's private furnace go to sleep, unimpeded. Well, I woke, satisfied with sleep, and I'd only been asleep three hours. One fire in the front room-hearth had started up again and crackled, flickering in the doorway. Jess got up to bring food. Then I saw or knew that there was a beneficent flame in every cell of the house. It seemd that Jess brought a branch of the house that was blossoming with that fire visible. The words

# 112

Jan. 27, 1959
{Stinson Beach}

"Food for fire, food for fire . . . " started in my mind and {I} turned on the light and wrote them down, following to "the good wood{.}"

There's a contrast, and there was no way to get it in the poem. That two nights previously both Jess and I had dreamt of the malevolent fire that burns down the house, charrd treasures, to rescue the cat. . . .

Ferling has the *Selected Poems* announced; and he sent the contracts, the terms seem excellent to me at this point. And thank god! to have them all in conscious agreement and not at the mercy of impulse and disappointment.

I have a reading for the Poetry Center the first part of March; and there are plans afoot for Brother Antoninus and me to read at the University of Washington. With another big public event in May when Antoninus, I, Ferlinghetti and Ginsberg are to read for a University of California culture in the West celebration, it's a busy spring. The U.C. also has plannd a program of Henry Miller, William Saroyan and Kerouac!!! ★

Zukofsky sent that 14 poets and one artist—but the one artist's "portraits" were so revolting that I couldn't rescue even the group of poems from that that I liked. The Ginsberg poem just seems dismal. It's all the *false* auto-biography. As so it *begs*. There's a sense in which we don't exist—and this demand, this "man or woman what do we care?" is the hollow man blues. The crux of it is that the "poem" neglects whatever beauty of song. The verse is used as blatantly as in "This is My Beloved." [Jess noted the undevelopd handwriting—over-aged school boy script.] When I overcome my initial distaste at those grotesque drawings, I'll have another go at the poems. That is, on first glance, I saw some unfamiliar qualities.

love
Robert

---

## 113

February 10th {1959}
249 W 15th
{New York}

Dear Robert—

In haste—to tell you Cecil Hemley of Noonday Press is very interested in your work and wd. like immediate permission to publish "Often I Am Permitted to Return to a Meadow" in the next *Noonday Review*—please write to him post haste if yes, at 80 E. 11th St. N.Y. 3.

He is the one with the brains who does the work; his partner has the money—not too much money either, it is rumored. However there is some possibility of his asking to publish *The Opening of the Field*—i.e. he wd like to, & if he doesn't it wd be from the financial shakiness of the Press. Don't mention to him yet tho. Will tell more in proper letter. He also particularly liked (of those I took the liberty of showing when he came to dinner) "The Question" and "Evocation." (He likes least the 1st of *Letters*, i.e. he likes least the most "modern." This is just to give some idea of his tendencies.)

Have been terribly busy becos of Mike Rumaker's attempted suicide—chance (more or less) has made me responsible for seeing doctors, placating his parents, etc etc. A number of other occurrences among friends have turned me into an amateur social worker for weeks. So please forgive silence—am delighted about the City Lights book to come, & thank you v. v. much for the remaining poems, and did you get Nik's p.c. of thanks for *Dr. Dolittle*?[1] I took it to mail & left it in the store I believe but since it was all stamped trust someone kindly mailed it.

Love to you & Jess

Denny

dear Denny/

## 114

Feb. 5, {11} 1959
{Stinson Beach}

Did I ask you to look around for Pound canto*s*? Robin Blaser sent me #99 [from *The Virginia Quarterly*] and I got the *Illustrazione Italiana* out of the library and typed a copy of Canto 98[1]—so, unless you just happend to find a copy of the Italian magazine (which has a colord picture of Pound on the cover) don't worry about it. There are flashes in these later Cantos : in 99

Food is the root.
    Feed the people

and again:

Manners are from earth and from water
They arise out of hills and streams
The spirit of air is of the country
    Men's manners cannot be one
        (same, identical)

but perhaps one has to be addicted to Pound, believe in the utter "charm" of his versification to get thru much of it. I like the digest where I am familiar with what it digests: as in the Byzantine-European 6th & 7th century Canto 96. But when I don't know references the stuff seems scatterd. In his face [see current *Yale Literary* mag] the character is screwd up to hold disparate forces at bay—the fasces, the binding of many (unruly) parts in one, is in the face: eyes drawn in a troubled axis {drawing of eyes and furrowed brow} with three pronounced lines of effort branding the brow. So we know that he in writing has some of the perplexity that we in reading have.

Where I know at all what he is doing I recognize the verse as superior [he does not need poetic "touches," where the lyric and melodic occurs it is inherent in the statement], and the account in "Canto 96" of what is going on in the 7th century is both a digest and has the quality of 7th century mind [it's the voice of somebody who lived in those days giving an account]. Where

I miss what he is doing I wonder if the faith in the line is superstitous . . . tho I must say he keeps what the line is so strickly fixd in those (frowning) brows of concentration that one knows (tho one don't know what metal it is) that the metal has been HAMMERD.

{drawing that looks like an initial J in an illuminated manuscript} Jess sold only one canvas at the Gump's show—and now we find out we have to wait a month to get the money for that one. And the Poetry Center had askd if I would read at the University of Washington, which I took when I accepted that I was going to; but now it turns out the University of Washington doesn't want me. Phantoms of vanity unfair. But there's just enuf of some me, starved for recognition?—but it can't be for my work, that is meant for the ideal reader; for my personality—to be cock-of-the-walk of the world of ours, and crow and get gifts and prizes and acclaim. *The Field* was never meant for the university of whatever or whichever, and its poor old author eats out his liver at times with the thot of fame and fortune, flatterers and fervid admirers.

And here and now is our most splendid season, days intensely clear, and birds a-chirrp and a-twit, trilling over their nestings—so kind that those little fat grey-browny ones hop about near my hands where I cut away the dead briars. The artichokes thrive and in a month or so we shld have crowns. It's in all ways the season that demands only our being here for its rewards, that don't need money. And by the end of the month, we'll be able to buy seeds and seedlings for planting.

Feb. 11, 1959

Marvelous storms, with such sudden changes and the vista of the sea broken up from all monotony into perspectives by sunlight far and storm clouds near, and north—with shafts of light and shafts of dark on the horizon and yesterday our first lightning during which I wrote the enclosed, that may be as little reasonable as lightning is—but comes the closest I have yet to why I think all members of the art are instances of the same order. Well, why it's as simple as either poetry or not for me. Given one's natural fanaticism. As some people seem almost blasphemous at the heart of poetry/ and others are clearly non-believers, versifiers. I find myself in search of a high-church and uncomfortable at subjective religion like Ginsberg who are popular rousers in the name of poetry.

Where a Donald Hall is just a business man and churchgoer who would think one *mad* to be moved by God.

I've at last got into that Paracelsus volume Bollingen put out and that I bought six or seven years ago and then let be—the pictures were interesting and I sort of hoped the text would be.[2]

But now the text brings flashes out of its accumulus of pontificating— well, the enclosed notes for my reading at the Poetry Center show bits of it.[3]

I've to get this off if it's not to sit around for another week!! The mail goes out soon.

Love,
Robert

Dear Denny/

Just the briefest note to accompany the enclosed letters for Rumaker.

I am most in betwixt and betweens these days—with *The Field* completed, but still subject to minute adjustments in new typescripts. We've just got enuf money for me to plan beginning on a new set. There have been notes for my reading at the Poetry Center a week from now. And I am working on a piece on prose and verse as mediums for poetry. There is now more movement toward defining (summing up past creation, and I hope making new necessary to throw overboard the laborious definitions).

O, yes—what about Mike? You write only "his attempted suicide," when I am left curious about particulars,

love
Robert

**115**

February 21, 1959
{Stinson Beach}

dear Denny/

We're in a spell of March weather, clear and radiant, a-swarm with birds and butterflies—and drinking it all in, in a lazy restlessness that would have liked to be just there *in the world*, filld with it past recognition. Got a poem:

*ROOTS AND BRANCHES*

> Sail Monarchs, rising and falling
> orange merchants in spring's flowery markets,
> messengers of March in warm currents of news floating,
> flitting into areas of aroma,
> tracing out of air unseen roots and branches of sense
> I share in thot—
> filaments woven and broken where the world may light
>
> casual certainties of me. There are echoes
> of what I am
> in what you perform this morning. How you perfect
> my spirit, almost restore
> an imaginary tree of the living in all
> its doctrines by

**116**

March 5, 1959
{Stinson Beach}

fluttering about—intent and easy as you are,
  the profusion of you
awakening transports of an inner imitation of things.

And send it off, as were you here I would have read it right off, at lunch—
an orange profiteer myself in those open markets.

love
Robert

---

**117**

*But will mail this separately. It is Geo. MacDonald's *Robert Falconer.*

Dear Robert & Jess,

I found this* a few weeks ago but did not have time to copy out the
different parts I found missing. It is on the whole better without them (tho'
I like Falconer's poem) but they must have been additions since yr. copy
here is certainly earlier than my paperback of 1907 which is a reprint. So I
felt you shd. have them with it. It's very much of a tract in a way but I love
large parts of it especially the boyhood part. And the London scenes that are
like Dostoievski's description of London too.—"The streets swarmed with
human faces gleaming past. It was a night of ghosts."

I couldn't resist marking in pencil a paragraph on p. 349 (when you come
to it) that I particularly like.

Yr poem (Robert) came as I was copying this morning and enlivened me.
Thank you. A lovely abundance. Will soon send you both what I have been
doing, & a picture taken in Jan. by a friend from England.

Saw Mike at Rockland last Wed., not bad. Gave him yr. letter.

Love from
Denny.

P.S.

How was the reading for which you wrote those introductory notes I so
much admired? Hope it went well.

What happened to Jess's children's book? I can't tell you how much I wish
I cd. have seen his show. Has he been writing any poems lately?

---

**118**

dear Denny/

*Robert Falconer* and your letter arrived—the first, yesterday morning,
pickd up at the post office as James, Jess and I started out for the City, and
the second, today, to add to the relief, relish, reasonableness, risk and reap
of returning home. I'd gone on to Berkeley to record for an "illlustrated"
lecture Tom Parkinson was doing on your work, mine and Spicer's, using

excerpts from our readings where he quoted poems. But he showd me his lecture and while there was an almost glimmer here and there of an other view of the work most of it was appreciation. He practices appreciation. He cultivates it. It's most important to his sense of values that we be valued. I tried to hint that "values" might not be the whole of it; but values are for him the whole of it, of life, . . . that poetry civilizes.

And, of course, he selects for examples so as to civilize us. By the time I had had drinks and dinner—the food so good (his wife has a real genius for casual cooking)—and the conversation mellow, and insights from the vintage year and . . . I was almost civilized myself. And was comfortably sunk into an expansive mood of imports, considerations, literary mouthings and sage maturities, grand old manisms, grand young manisms . . . all on the front of what might have been poetry.

Then, this morning (March 18) a "challenge" directed at me from Philip Lamantia, and inspired I am sorry to see by the itch to direct my concern toward him coupled with La Martinelli who must be an ugly spirit indeed.[1] "Robert Duncan YOU MUST STOP, STOP OR CHANGE" the missive goes, as ultimatum. Where one cannot exactly disobey—for life, not Philip Lamantia or La Martinelli, gives that alternative of stop or change. "Sodom is NOT!! IS NOT HOLY!" it goes on—and I can't say that I can sensibly disagree there.

Closing with a statement: "My generation *is* beatific" and calling my attention to "A Demand for Extinction of Laws Prohibiting Narcotic Drugs":[2] such sad evidences we have of the deficiencies of intelligence abroad. But there are nasty suggestions that go out from the composition—one knows, for sure, that back of "Sodom is Not Holy" is an exclusion of me, in so far as I am homosexual, from the holy body of Man-Kind. And there is a deeper or more hidden voice of the snake in it that would call up, thru retaliation if need be, an existence of me at their level—to incite correspondence.

Gratuitous in this case, for "A Demand for Extinction of Laws Prohibiting Narcotic Drugs" doesn't excite my concern. It seems vaguely sensible— Santayana has an argument for living with opium etc.—tho I am sure Lamantia wouldn't be interested in drugs except that there is an element of "underworld" in it. I disagree only with the statement that his generation is *beatific*: he takes the name of Joy in vain who claims it for his own ? no that's too glib. It sounds good—but I mean just that there is nothing joyous or of joyous news about the note.

Reading MacDonald again is for me a great liberator of the spirit—I am more keenly aware for a while at least of certain hardenings of the heart that are all mine, and that part of my yearning is to reinterpret injury or insult. You were most right that in relation to *Letters* I was more concernd to make it painful and almost impossible for Jonathan to do the right thing: I incited all that in him that would turn away from the fair.

Have you found the paperback book of Böhme selections *Six Theosophic Points*?[3] There's so much of the dark world disturbed and up-lifting in me. But you know, it *is* a joyous news I almost expect: to be able to read. The first alphabet, Böhme writes, is Nature. And there's the full lovely alphabet—the news of "The Natural Doctrine" is true and I must hurry there. The second is *Hebrew*, the third *Greek*, the fourth is Latin (which alphabet we all use now) and the fifth is God's spirit, the Holy Spirit—the by-which-we-read.

I've a letter written in my living that I cannot yet read that is, I am sure, a news of joy (tho often I have thot these words must be disappointment, jealousy, mean envy, insulted vanity, lecherousness, greed) and I must to school I know not where—to everywhere and every time—to learn to read a message of water, air and light, earth and stars.

love
Robert

## 119

**April 20, 1959**
**{Stinson Beach}**

dear Denny/

The title on the enclosed[1] is tentative. What I want is something that establishes the reference of music, and there—of *études* or *bagatelles*: but both those words are wrong in mood. And there should be, I think, a division between "scale of souls" and "where the poet can take hold etc."

Perhaps "Four movements"—there will be two more movements. I've been reading Boehme: started with *Six Theosophic Points* which Ann Arbor Paperbacks (University of Michigan) printed. And then Spicer got on long term loan from U.C. library *The Signature of All Things* and *Of The Incarnation of Jesus Christ*.[2] Boehme carries me further than the *Zohar*, the jewish thing— tho it's all there, the underlying acknowledgement of a wholeness in which all that we see and hear in Nature, the figures and sounds of heaven and hell are in-bound: that what we feel right now if we bare ourselves nervously and sympatheticly to evidences of human being—as if it were a river of the species and had in one current the cruelty and the kindness, the stupidity with malice and the wisdom etc.—to be felt with love must be fearful. And I find there the inseparability of hell, earth and heaven, bound by longing: as if Debs had recognized that not only was he not free as long as any one was imprisond,[3] but he was not just as long as any one was unjust: I don't want to leap to a statement here that is clearer than my feeling. Boehme throws my thought forward just beyond my reach, where it may someday gather my mind to itself. But you will see what a lodestone the *Theosophic Points* was with its flame and fire, its darkness and light, and a doctrine of Magic: "Magic is the mother from which Nature comes, and the understanding is the mother coming from Nature. Magic leads into a fierce fire, and the understanding leads its own mother, Magic, out of the fierce fire into its own fire."

And of language he says there are four alphabets [which turn out to be five in four]:

"One . . . in which is found the language of Nature . . . signd with the character of Mystery"

"The second . . . Hebrew"

"The third . . . Greek"

"The fourth . . . Latin"

"The fifth is God's Spirit, which is the revealer of all alphabets"

The good Boehme is close enough to my heart that I might have drawn directly on his text for *Letters* and *The Field*. Tho long ago I began drawing indirectly thru Emerson, and George MacDonald.

I'm at work on the fourth set of five copies of *The Field*—and I think when I finish I will send you a second copy—for you to replace your first one with. In several places I have been able to clarify the text—particularly, in this set for the first time I got what I wanted in #30 which started out in an abortive state.

*Partisan Review* returnd, with a discouraging note, "The Question" which Barbara Guest had accepted for publication a year ago. Are we, by policy, excluded from the Olympian reviews?

love
Robert

---

**120**

{April, 1959}
249 W. 15th St.
{New York}

Dear Robert and Jess

I am mailing you a package containing the Andersen fairytales I've long meant to lend you; please keep it as long as you like; also (to keep) a smaller edition of same which I found recently which has some, but not all, of the Robinson illustrations I thought you wd. like; also the Eilshemius catalogue (which is from Mitch) and some poems.[1]

Jess, it was so lovely to get your letter and poem. Yes, I have that Mac-Donald poem in his volume *Violin Songs* but it is not quite the same—I wonder which is earlier.

I hope to be able to write you a longer letter soon.

Love—
Denny.

---

**121**

April 27, 1959
{Stinson Beach}

dear Denise & Mitch/

Your packets arrived this morning (and the poems, Friday). We pourd over the Eilshemius catalog—*The Afternoon Wind*, *Christ Intervening the Dragon of War*, and one I remember that isn't in this group—of a wild bear chasing shipwreckd women—have a visionary quality; *Malaga Beach* reproduced in *Time* in color gives a key I take it to the tonality of landscapes.[1] And in *Dreaming of Temptation* there's a memorable (or rather it won't, I suspect, let itself be let go, once seen) showing forth of his obsession. That disturbs almost everywhere in his work. Women are drawn and shaped like drawings in men's rooms—a sexual urgency that has to by-pass a character-structure in which sensuality has been bound up and de-formd.

Take # 7, 9, 11, Apia, Samoa (1903), Samoa (1907) from his traveling in the South Seas (1901–1902) and compare with Gauguin's Tahitian canvasses from ten years before, or from the last years (1901–1903) and Eilshemius's color range begins to have a negative meaning (I mean it is not selectively restraind or restricted—but repressd: and finally, not expressive—Gauguin who has freed his sensual nature can paint in the expressive range of the repressd as seen in Skira Gauguin book his last painting of *Breton Village Under Snow* which is free to speak to us of what is felt.

The color reproduction on the catalog shows, given the repressd range, a permission for color pleasures and free spirit, but the women can't be seen freely and something dammd up uses their faces to make faces at us of glowering or simpering idiocy.

And there's some territory in these naked women paintings that Eilshemius shares with Jack Bilbo (who has, from my perusing of a volume of his works in a bookstore, no other sharing).[2]

All life of the spirit (like the words *soul* or *spirit*) is so subverted to business (in all its extending tentacles of meaning or rather demeaning as a word) that we are likely to want whatever outbreak of a soul in things. Like people in cities crave animal life and even have joy at the sight of a shabby caged up lion, and must have zoos because they provide some sop to a love of wild-life. So, our biggest error is I think to give any spiritual phenomenon an almost uncritical assent. To go mad or to be sick is we know a breaking out of the evil thing that is the dominating order of the time: but the very evil of this order is that it throws up sacrifices of the mad and the sick. And once we have the evidence of a Gauguin we can judge the failure and sickness of an Eilshemius; but Eilshemius can be compared closer at home with Eakins and Ryder. And "judged," "compared" only because *creative* has got to mean something other than or more than *genius* in itself.

I'd built up the idea that Ginsberg's trajectory was in search of any and whatever "genius," and even built up a criticism of such a purpose in a poet, a critical project toward undertaking the old struggle to give reality (realize) the good, beauty etc. But damn it, I went to Ginsberg's reading last Saturday and in the middle of the sixth poem suddenly saw that it was all a sell, and had no more to do with poetry than an evening of Randall Jarrell or Richard Wilbur. So I got up and walkd out. Into the bliss of not having to have any ideas about Ginsberg at all, but only my prejudices or rather, because I was prejudiced to believe I was going to hear something *really* wrong at worst and at best that I was going to hear something that must be of concern wherever the imagination and spirit are of concern, a reaction then based on impulse before all information was in etc. But, tho many told me they were "bored" etc., all took pleasure in sitting thru that reading in order to have an opinion about it. And, because of the epiphany of that suddenly realizing I did not have to listen to this (it was like first walking out on a lecture at school), I thot how often we sit and writhe when we should go free before we start feeding on our annoyance. I shall now make my honest profession to know no more of Ginsberg than I know of geology (a lecture series I all but flunked in college because the drone of it put me to sleep). But I have learnd that there's a real joy in escape! If only I had had the courage of inner urges and been able to walk out on Jarrell, Garrigue and Wilbur, Spender and many others who provided doldrums of attention.

Put all of this aside. Because in some way I've got to convey to you how "With Eyes at the Back of Our Heads" has set my attention leaping and returning, and I'm going to learn it so I can keep it with me—the page is too far away. How the rhyme *arms* (our arms) enters the arms that are in the garment. Well, that cannot stand for the crux because once the whole poem is there it is thru out. For the poem is so beautiful and change-fully built and then knit that almost (because in the poem I felt yes, it is just for this I have always been longing and I couldn't admit myself to what it was as this poem now admits me):

when the doors widen
when the sleeves admit us

it occupied everything and invited me into the world. So that only later that evening was I able to see "The Park" and "Relative Figures." These three now stand solid, with poems like "The Pepper-Trees," "Sharks," "The Spring-time," poems that quicken the center of me that finds its intelligible life only in and thru the imagination: so that Blake, Yeats—but it's Blake's "Crystal Cabinet" I was thinking of—and some remnant of the "professional" in me went on with naming Yeats.

Creeley once told me that Williams had written to him when "Mrs. Cob-web" appeard that the core of your future work, or something like that, was "announced" in that poem. Well, this area of your poetry now, which has given to the "here and now" a dream and vision under and over dimension certainly has its announcement in "Mrs. Cobweb."

You know how readily I will go with you as

"Already a ghost of fire
glides in the lake!"

it's when

  "only the boy, my son, at last
    ready, comes, and discovers"

that is the disclosure

of it I could not have shared had you not made it possible. No, not "you"—
but the poem makes it possible. For you too.

love
Robert

[the new manuscript on *The Field* will be sent when we can spare the
postage]

---

## 122

May 25, 1959
{Stinson Beach}

dear Denny,

    Last Saturday we had a group reading for *Measure*—where Ginsberg
read from his "Kaddish" for his mother—and for the first time I heard him
read "with emotion"; once you grasp that the poem—like "Howl" is designd
in order to wind up an hysterical pitch (at the close of the poem he was
shouting like Hitler or an evangelist, so that the audience having risen with
him on wave upon wave of momentous lines ROARD). As the seizure of
the poem increased, the content became disorderd, then idiotic and finally
disappeard. But no wonder it is impossible to attack his work as bad writing
—it is almost exactly calculated to be an agency for such a frenzy. And what
we see (hear) when it is not used to arrive at the seizure, is like the funny
expressions of a face separated from the terrifying fit it is going thru.

    I dislike *using* a poem, and that's the crux of the matter.

    Did I write last week that I am planning now definitely to make a trip
East in October of this year? N. O. Brown wants to get me a reading at
Wesleyan—and is sure he can. And I have the Poetry Center working
away to see if they can get me one in New York. Do you know of any routes
round? I'll write to M. C. {Richards} who might "have connections." It wld
just be for a month at the very most—but that will involve more money
than is in sight yet.

    *Poems in a Floating World* arrived in the mail today, sent by courtesy
of Rothenberg. Asking what I thot—which I wrote back as clearly as I
could. Both *The Fifties* and *Floating World* have a suggestion or reminder
somewhere about them of old Stalinist literary approaches: well, I askd
Rothenberg in essence to clear-up for me his intent. [Because of that Celan
poem: you know how us anarchists bridle at "Madrid and Vienna."] But I
did think the insistence on image a healthy one. Especially since my work
right now seems to be getting more and more didactive "opinionated" —

and I read with increased admiration the solid reality of a poem like "The Goddess" (which I hadn't seen before)—last night reading aloud "The Park," "Relative Figures" . . . and "With Eyes in Back of the Head"—[1]

I shall rejoice when my poetry comes again into those true places—

[Enclosed a recent one—-all but without images][2]

love
Robert

Dear Robert

I keep ploughing through duty letters of various kinds in the hope of emerging to where I can indulge the pleasure of writing to you about many things, but the more I write the more there seem to be, damn it. I haven't written abt. how pleased we were to see that tremendous poem of yours in *The Nation*,[1] nor about the one you sent in your last or last but one letter (a beauty) nor about *Dr. Zhivago* which at last we've read, & loved with humble joy, after fearing it wd. be just some rubbish that critics & cold-war-experts had blown up; what happiness to discover its dense reality!—Also I want to write about T. Parkinson's suggestion that I write abt. you; I want to explain my uncertainty to you—it is just that while I feel I can sometimes do a damn good job of pointing out defects & suggesting remedies (when people send me poems & ask for advice) when I deeply admire a poem I have nothing to say about it. Incoherent exclamations, the page snatched up & kissed or clasped to the heart—those are my reactions to poems like yours that with very rare exceptions I accept totally. Now I plan to reread all your work, from *Medieval Scenes* through to *The Opening of the Field* and see if I find myself analyzing either why I like what, and/or the development shown there over the years, & if I do I'll try to make a statement that wd. approximate to a short article; but if I find myself writing only what will be taken for gush I will have to decline. I hope you understand this.

When is the *Selected Poems* going to appear?

I am just about to go to the Gauguin show with Mitch (he was away so we didn't go before).[2] I agreed with most of what you said about Eilshemius, tho' there were genuine works of the imagination among the dross, too—the *Funeral*, a war scene, and a landscape I remember particularly. But in any case I am tired of the snobbish acceptance of insanity that is current—madness and disease politely ignored or even glorified. A talk by M. C. {Richards} at Living Theater on Artaud was a case in point—moving & inspiring tho' *some* of his work was. There was pride in her tone as she told of his last appearances & of how he hung on obstinately to his

**123**

May 25th {1959}
249 W. 15th St.
{New York}

madness, unless I misunderstood her. The whole *Evergreen* bit is a glorification of corruption. Well, I must get this mailed. By the end of this week I should be able to write a *real* letter. Meanwhile, love to you & Jess as always.

There has been some sparkling late spring weather here and the other day I had a real country walk as I missed Rockland bus on way to see Mike so took one to nearest village & walked—it was terrific—quiet, & the fragrances uprising, & the sense of abundance—I picked wild geraniums & blue-eyed grass.

Love—
Denny.

*Monday night*

What I wanted to say was just that I felt that poem ("In Perplexity") had a sort of hasty sound to it for one thing. "Pious female" for instance. And certain forms you have so beautifully used in other poems seemed used *habitually*, not of necessity. (Wondrous, I maintain this dame is most right, whereof, bringeth)—it is not that I any longer (not since way back) have any objection to them as such but somehow here they stick out & don't seem to belong. The tone is of anger or indignance & the poem doesn't seem fully alive in its own right, it is still so much attached to your immediate feelings on receiving someone's letter. So that tho the last stanza is so beautiful the rest of the poem puts me in mind of the long, indignant protesting or scornful letters I have often written in response to some criticism but next day have thrown out. Yet there's so much substance there—I would hate to see the poem rejected by you yet I don't feel it is a free thing as it stands.

God knows I may come to think myself wrong & foolish about it, as I did over the ballads & some of Bob's poems too.

The straw bottom has almost all fallen out of my chair, I am perched on the frame mostly & one leg is falling asleep so again

goodnight.
D.

Please let me have the Eigner piece back right away because I must send it to him.

P.S.

The friend who is going to live here while we are in Maine *may* sublet Barbara Bank's apartment in the fall—she is going to England for 2 years.[3] If so, since it is big (for one person) he might be able to put you up—. It's in this building, upstairs. However, he is someone we scarcely know as yet. A flutist. But it might work out.

Dear Robert,

It's wonderful that you may get here in October. Let me know if there's anything useful I can do. Café readings don't pay more than $10, but I suppose a couple wd. help—? Blackburn is the great arranger, it seems he enjoys it. What abt. the Y.? May I send a note to the person there, a Miss Kray (who is also Mrs. V. Ussachevsky)? I don't know how much power to arrange she actually has, but she shd. be told of yr. visit anyway. What about a place to stay? We now have no spare-room, but please count on lots of meals with us anyway, won't you. (We have a bed, but it is in Mitch's workroom which also doubles as the livingroom, and our bedroom is sort of joined onto it, so there is no privacy whatever.) Please let me know if there are any enquiries I can make, etc.

I wanted—very tentatively—to describe Robert Bly to you. He is a big noisy fellow who if you give him a cup of coffee always mislays the saucer. He is hasty, tactless, naive, and opinionated. But with all this, he has (I really believe) a heart of gold. And though he often can't recognize a good poem when he sees it, when he *does* he has a passionate love for it. He's without cynicism or venom—and when he himself comes up with a couple of good lines, like,

"Ah, occasionally,
Above watermelons, I have seen woven leaves
And the ground beneath alive with grasshoppers"

it is with deep feeling and conviction. He's made an awful ass of himself,* but I think he'll do better eventually. Well—I don't want to get embroiled. But I have a nagging desire to explain people to each other. If you would meet him you would see he wasn't grownup enough (not in age but in actual development) to bother getting too mad at. What I long for is for him to come under your influence—but I guess he has too much hayseed in his blood for that.

I was very happy that you liked "With Eyes at the Back of Our Heads" etc. I feel the long poem (about which I never did write you the long explaining letter I meant to—& which (slightly revised) will be in *Poetry* soon)[1] was in a way a necessary transition to those.

I just tore up a much longer letter to you because it was written with a ballpoint pen and looked so damned ugly I was ashamed of it.

I'm writing something about Eigner's poems. I hope doing so will "oil me up" to do the thing for T. Parkinson, but I remain doubtful about my ability for that.

I don't think you need to be unhappy about any lack of visual images in recent poems because there is so much music in them that the visual is

(*in more ways than one)

124

June 7th {1959
New York}

unnecessary, as in actual music. Only this one poem ("In Perplexity")
doesn't seem up to you perhaps—I think I can see why—no, I am too tired,
and perhaps you have already changed it—forgive me. If you want to know
what I was going to say I will say it in my next letter.* Meanwhile, much
love to you & Jess from

*Denise.*

---

* If I say it now I'll probably write 10 pages and then throw them out, so it
makes more sense to go to sleep.

## 125

May 28, {June 10,}
1959
{Stinson Beach}

dear Denny,

I tried to get across to Tom that you were "uncritical" of my work—but
he wouldn't understand. And he's a professor of literature, not a poet—the
appreciation and evaluation is the important thing. I am not enthusiastic
about the prospects of *Berkeley Review.* For Tom—you, me and Spicer are
*new* writing; and he has no idea of, much less interest in, the swarm of
young writers hereabouts. There, evaluation is an adventure. And damn
him, T. P. likes pomes of sensibility and civilized response!! Both Spicer and
I have refused to give him any poems, but he don't understand. What he's
got of mine is a "story" or legend about poetry before the brain took over.
Amen. Only that I don't enjoy the idea of your setting yourself the task of
rereading all my work: there's so little of the grace and nature that I'd like to
believe a reader has—to read on impulse, to be in the mood for. I'm wary
anyways as you rightly are because this task of reviewing was assignd—and
moreover, for reasons very different from yours.

And, so far at least—even with the H. D. where I so heartily respond to
her spirit—I find the task of critical prose all but impossible. I just can't go
at it naturally but have to discard false attempt after false attempt. You
know, I've long ago discarded, if I ever had it, the thot of whether some
reader would think whatever of a poem. I live directly in that medium—
and if there's any judgment then it's in the poem itself and not outside it
listening to it.

But in writing criticism so far I always have to fight off a swarm of straw
villains set up by myself that I find myself writing at. As if one could be
persuasive.

June 10, 1959

I thot I'd maild this, or some such communication, right off to you.
About not assigning yourself a "task" of reading my work. And here this
morning as I decided to spend the entire day if need be to "catch up" on

letters is this partly written letter above—inviting me to enjoy myself for the rest of the morning perhaps and write to you.

James Broughton brought out the Daisy Aldan anthology which lookd like a must.[1] We liked the *Yellow Book* reminder, and especially Nell Blaine's cover. When you see her would you convey that both Jess and I have the highest admiration for her work from the few reproductions we've been able to see. The Larry Rivers drawing I liked. Of course, we only had the evening's looking thru it—tho I have the impression that there's a settled conformity and expectedness (which I take to be a combination of taste triumphing over any creative urgency, of a supine imagination among painters at large) about most of the drawing. But the anthology does right in bringing painters and poetry together—and is so far better than other efforts along this line that I do have regrets that I couldn't have playd my part there. And, I note that Daisy Aldan had two poems therein and would have come under the permission of an anthology edited by a poet.

But there's some pleasure that my appreciation can have the more freedom. I've written to Rago to see if I might have it for review: as an occasion for describing what is going on—and what interrelations I find given the poems there as primary evidence, and my own experience as general background. If I can do it—there ought to result some definition worth the struggle.

Rothenberg sent me the first issue of his Lilliputian magazine[2]—which somehow set me off at first [it was the exaggerated estimate of Neruda, I think—plus the poem by Celan where I suspected the reference to Madrid as standing for Spain in the Civil War] or a prodding letter to him to see if there was any neo-Stalinism going on there. But I find that I liked the contents of the magazine, the "problem" or crux of it stays by me. The poem of Neruda's printed I thot quite good, and true to life. And the Breton poem, and its English translation by Antin, is tops.

I didnt write to him anything about your poem. For one thing, in a letter like this one was I am always concernd with finding out what I think (feel) about it; and the true context of your poems now, for me, is always your poetry. But thinking of how your "goddess" operates there, it seems to me you give directive [where Breton or Neruda give background or model]. You've gotten closer to the economy of the dream than I've managed—I'm struck anyway by the right force of poems like this one as something I wish I could break thru to. And would have to break thru just the "lore" and the symbolism (here I have in mind the inbound reference I have kept for over ten years now to the making of the poem) that I have myself deliverd my art over to.

And Bly and Rothenberg are right that there's something essential to be realized in the art, hints of which lie in the art of Surrealists. Do you know that volume of Eluard's *Dur Désir de Durer* that New Directions brought out?[3] It seemd to me that I had indeed been mistaken in "A Song of the Old Order" when I read Eluard's direct lyrics. Well, I've a ways to go before I will have completed the natural language for song (for hearing right words in melody). How fresh Eluard's line "Couple trempé dans son printemps."

love,
Robert

## 126

June 14th {1959
New York}

Dear Robert and Jess

The *Oz* book marked as *un*birthday gift came on the very day before Nik's tenth birthday! He jumped right into it with great delight. And will be writing to you. Did you like the illustrations in the Hans Andersen? They are so bound up with my childhood—but also now I find them very beautiful. One of the best is the bad Queen looking for simples, by night, with which to turn Elise's brothers into wild swans.

I'll be glad to tell Nellie you admire her work—I do too, very much, except that she is sometimes endangered by too much facility I think. Did you see the article about her in *Art News* for May?[1] It's a horrid magazine but sometimes has good reproductions. There was an article on Lee Bell (to whose house you came once, do you remember?[2] He & his wife & daughter are now in Iceland but will be back in the fall. I wd. like you to see Louisa's paintings, there are new ones I think you'd like tho I remember you didn't care for the photos of them that were sent to Majorca. But they don't reproduce well.) The article about Lee was in the issue of[3]

About *A New Folder*. I am somewhat annoyed with Daisy Aldan because if she was not going to pay anyone she could have at least (1) Sent proofs (2) Let one know what poems she was going to use, before going to press. In my case she did neither—as it happened it turned out alright but I don't like such highhandedness. Also in spite of some odd exceptions there seems to me to be far too much of the pretentiously avant-garde in the volume. Granted it's personal taste—still, I don't much like her taste. I'm so *tired* of the current acceptance of bad writing such as Jack Kerouac's piece and those by Emilie Glen and Elliot Stein (for instance). Or maybe it's not a question of "current acceptance" at all but just that I have come to notice, & be affronted by, such things, more often. Poem by poem, going through the book, I truly find very little that pleases me. Among the pictures I too like the Larry Rivers, also the Jane Freilicher and the de Niro and the Earl Kerkham.

Ginsberg's "Ignu" which seemed so funny and endearing read aloud seems stale and thought-up in print. Creeley and, *I* think, Eigner, stand out beyond all the others, just about. (I like my own things.) Olson's "John

Smith" of course—but not the other. Parts of the Frank O'Hara perhaps. (He strikes me as extremely talented or whatever one calls it but fatally smart.) Koch just picks up what he can from O'Hara and Ginsberg/Corso— and succeeds in being cute. Ashbery sometimes seems a true poet and then again only seems to be showing off for his friends. In all that school—or say, the interlocking schools—New York and Beat—there is a sense of the poets keeping their weather eye on the potential reader—not, as you say "living within the medium." I think Barbara Guest does it too—she has moments of real inspiration but lacking the intelligence to *construct* with her god-given raw material she pastes images together with bits of irrelevancies she thinks will go down well with her friends (who can't tell the difference anyway). At least that is what I have come to think must happen.

A clumsy poem by one Ruth Lansdorff York has a sort of conviction about it as if she had struggled to say it. Someone called Kenward Elmslie has a poem more or less Corso-ish but having some magic to it . . . ? Corso himself compulsively funny . . . And I forgive Edward Field (has anybody ever met him? Does he exist?) the flatness of his lines for the sake of his love for donkeys. Etc. etc. Your letter came the day after we got the book, so it was all fresh in my mind, hence so much space given it.

About your New York visit: I think Wesleyan is rather far to commute regularly but am not sure. You certainly ought to have a piedaterre in N.Y. itself. For one thing, it will be expensive going back & forth. You know, you can always spend odd nights here if you don't mind the close proximity of our bed to yours. Another possibility wd. be Blackburn—he has a room just down the block. I've never seen it, but I believe John Logan stayed there when in N.Y. a month or so ago, so he presumably has a bed. We know (slightly) someone at Wesleyan by the way—a very pleasant modest man called Willis Barnstone who has been translating Machado (& incidentally had the courage to refuse a bombastic and irrelevant preface by Kenneth Rexroth which his publisher, I think, had arranged for). He has a Greek wife & a beautiful little child about 2 yrs old; and is, we thought, badly vitiated by the academic world he lives in—but nice.

Good god, don't think it would be a "task" in any way but an enjoyable sense to reread all your poems I have. I had anyway been wanting to do that. Enclosed is what I've written as introduction for Eigner's poems,[4] if & when J. W. ever gets to them (he has now re-committed himself to do them in the fall). What I wd. do for Parkinson cd. only be along the same lines, i.e. a personal appreciation—but obviously your work is so much more diverse & complex that I doubt my ability to find words for what I feel about it. I still haven't heard a word from him (Parkinson) by the way.

Did I ever tell you how much we admired your Dahlberg review by the way?[5]

I'm so glad you don't feel personal animosity towards Bly and can see something in his poems.

I have never read much of Eluard at least not since I was first in Paris in 1947 when what I read was just a part of the excitement of Paris and aloneness. Maybe I'll take the N.D. Eluard book to Maine with me.

By the way, I have talked about Jess's Morgenstern to Laughlin several times, pointedly—he never commits himself but he did raise an interested eyebrow. Wd. Jess be interested in New Directions? Laughlin is talking about a new European translation series.

What about *The Opening of the Field*? Has it a publisher?

It is midnight. I think I must go to bed. We went to see *Modern Times*[6] as Nik's birthday treat. I have to finish putting name-tapes on all his things for camp this week—the trunk goes off on Friday. He goes on the 30th & we will probably leave N.Y. on July 2d or thereabouts. We'll go to Maine but don't yet know just where—somewhere near where we were last year. Were you ever there?

We have been putting our winter things away, late, as usual. I think I told you we were to have gone to Europe? But Mitch managed to get the money instead. I am a bit disappointed but very glad he got the money which will give him time to get started on a new book, which is a million times more important.

Oh, one last thing—a funny little Italian professor turned up here today (that mark was Hawthorn jumping onto my lap) sent by Marie Rexroth— he was so pleasant and entertaining and quite brightened a day that had been a bit glum. He said he had visited you—did you like him too? And he recited Edward Lear in Italian & told a funny story about Claire Booth Luce and the Pope. I must write to Marie to thank her for sending him—wd. you please let me have her address? By now Carlo Izzo is above the Atlantic on his way to Bologna. Nik was quite fascinated with him.

I think you will find Nik nice when you see him—he is less shy and rough.

Oh, I forgot to finish what I was going to say about that poem of yours in my last letter, damn it.

Well, tomorrow. Goodnight.

Love—
Denny.

Dear Robert and Jess,

I liked *The Road to Oz* a lot, especially the part about the Scoodlers. It was very nice of you to send it to me. It arrived the day before my birthday.

Love,
Nik

dear Denny,

I've come over to the view that Parkinson is the best possibility of a
magazine—and written that I will give him whatever he wants in the poetry.
Part of this is that Wiener's plans for *Measure* 3 have broken even my
superstition that "the young" must be right. He came out here to coerce
me into yielding on a refusal to send work for the new issue [I had been
outraged at his featuring a Ginsberg revelation that is absolute bosh, hokum
and flagrantly bad verse]—and took finally a poem ["What Do I Know of
the Old Lore"] at the declared cost of friendship. "O.K.," I finally said—
"You can make me give in, and give you a poem which it will offend me
personally to see you print. If you use the poem I will have nothing further
to do with you." But as Jess says Wieners wasn't listening, he just wanted the
public impression that "I was with him" and didn't give a damn for any
actual relationship.

Well, then, there was that: and Parkinson's proposals for what would be
in his first issue lookd solider and solider to me. What I've done is send him
"Structure of Rime" 8 thru 13. He's printing Creeley's "The Dress" [which
has the dream quality—the dream as immediate experience rather than
symbolic—that your "Relative Figures" has]. As I've written: this is for
me now the challenging thing. If I can't move without the network of
"reading" . . . that's it, that where I "read" you and Bob seem to me to be
"seeing" and the actual vision is the marvelous thing. Did I relay to you the
remark I found in Boehme that devils *know* all about heaven but they can't
see or feel it. "Reading" is that knowing, damnd knowing if it is isolated
from sight and feeling.

> At night
> wafts of primrose and honeysuckle
> Heaven is about us, and thru everything
> stench
> where the cats shit
> crumbles away as hell crumbles away
> into the ground

or some such. The "butterflies" poem[1] is what I want for the new book—
but that was really the difficulty not the ability to let myself go and ask the
world to come thru into everything.

Recently—when George Stanley and Ronald Primack were here—
re-reading thru your new work, that poem[2]

> "shells, husks, the wandering
> of autumn seeds"

127

July 5, 1959
{Stinson Beach}

came thru as a position—a positive part of what your work is. There are some of your poems that overtake me entirely, from the beginning. And they're the heart for me, the constancy that grows. Then—like this poem—there are others I worry from the beginning, and that must win their way, insist. The ones that I can't let go if I am to understand at all, and must, in search of the wholeness of the poetics, come to cope with. Then there are, as there should be, some that are casual: moments that belong to the wholeness and bring the naturalness of what is sketchd in passing, the fleeting possibility of a needed thing.

What I've got in mind is how it parallels the wholeness of someone we love—we don't "accept" every factor—we have come to love it, which is a different thing. And, even, at the most important crisis, must admit what we had tried to overlook; and yield some obstruction in our very selves that what we love flourish in its own character to "correct" us—

love
Robert

## 128

July 11, 1959
{Stinson Beach}

dear Denny/

The Browns (he is a professor in Classics at Wesleyan) have suggested that I make their house a place to stay—retreat, etc. I'm in a state of appalld disbelief when I reflect upon my committing myself to make the trip. New York seems formidable and futile [for I've got to see what I can do about the Morgenstern and the children's books; and I've got to approach the Roths to finance my making the trip. etc.] You know last time I was in N.Y. I stayed at Nik Cernovich's; which may be possible again. But isn't Wesleyan within commuting distance for most purposes? I haven't checked on it. Aie! However, I'd rememberd your apartment, and then over these last three years—well, for the New York of it, which is only this last year—I've had a solid picture of the discomforts and impossibilities you've had with visitations. I shall haunt your company—it's everything that sustains me in the thought of being "East," but I understand that you and Mitch have no room.

I'm writing straight off to you (your letter about Bly came this morning) because I've got the same sense you have that Bly's actual poetry has sincerity (not his *personal* sincerity, but I mean that the poems have a tap root, are real animals). And I got something of his personal sincerity in all that ineptness of commentary that clutters *The Fifties* and I guess in berating him I must have left him more with a feeling I was mad at him than with the fact that I was concernd. The Creeley article *was* irreparably stupid.[1] And I couldn't resist throwing that last line back in the editor's face for having countenanced it if he didn't write it:

Mr. Creeley is still very young, and his poems, even so far, are a contribution to American literature, but I think his work also shows that sheer honesty and the American literary tradition alone are not enough to make a rich *avant-garde.*

Wow! It's the university professor, not the hayseed, that I lashd out there. Amen.

Well, I'll have to write off to Bly and see if I can get across to him that. As for my influence, that's in the realm of volitions and likenesses.

Anyway I have gone at reading Bly's poems over and that means I'm somewhat under *his* influence.

Back at work on Shelley—finding nothing but disappointment in "Alastor," and out of the "Witch of Atlas" (these are admittedly poor hunting grounds) a few passages. The following I admired for the shifting stresses in rhyming, and at the same time (the passage refers to Pan) Shelley awakens for me here an awe of the daemon Pan:

> . . . through the adamant
> Of the deep mountains, through the trackless air,
>     And through those living spirits, like a want,
> He passed out of his everlasting lair
>     Where the quick heart of the world doth pant

and of what I can't remember—but it could be of dreams, visions, of souls or sleepers:

> . . . each like a flower
> Out of whose depth a fire-fly shakes his light
>     Under a cypress in a starless night.

The alive and beautiful thing in Shelley is this turning as reader to the world about him, to an alphabet of clouds, mountains, flowers and birds etc.[2]

love
Robert

Dear Robert and Jess,

This year we're in a little, emphatically wooden house perched on top of a miniature cliff at the base of which is the sea when the tide's in and a pebbly beach & then a mudflat when it's out. I like the mud (full of clams), and very much like the constant change. The road runs by but there's not much traffic, and between us & the next house (home of a boatbuilder & his wife & 7 children, with their boatyard alongside, in which a Friendship sloop is nearing completion now) is quite a thick spinney of firs & poplars & bushes. The sea isn't the open sea—this is a deep bay—so there are ripples,

## 129

13th/14th July {1959}
P. O. Box 1,
Friendship, Maine

not waves, & no sound of it except at high tide when it washes on the boulders below us—but from the little balcony or terrace one can see a horizon of open sea beyond some small islands and between the headlands. It's only a few miles from where we were last summer. It's very close to the house of Arthur McFarland, about whom I expect I wrote last summer—he's a Maine boatbuilder (employed—quite poor) who plays violin in a local orchestra & makes violins as a pleasure & who became thru' letters a close friend of Larry Eigner's. He is going deaf pretty steadily. A lonely, pessimistic, extremely kind man. Larry expects to be driven up here some time during the summer. I changed that nasty "wise-guy" expression in the "Note on L. E.",[1] but I don't have a corrected copy here so I don't remember exactly how—perhaps I used the word "knowledgeableness." You know, he is quite shockingly crippled (yes, spastic). His body is all contorted, & his speech grotesq. and spitting, and it seems almost incredible that he has managed with his one useable hand, twisted as it is, & with the frequent typical jerking movements his body makes, to type out all those poems & stories. Out of this miserable body look two clear, light, greenish-blue eyes of perfect innocence—so innocent and truthful there is a coldness about them, even to iciness, like mountain water.* (extra pages)[2] But I think it wd. offend him and also inevitably *seem* a special plea if I were to speak of it directly. Indeed, I simply can't. It must remain a slightly mysterious reference, as I've made it—and the reader who is interested will no doubt eventually hear of it; but he will first, by then, have read the poems purely as poems.

And the other change you suggest, while I quite see your point of view, I find myself on consideration unable to make for the following reason: I feel it is the only honest way to express my own approach to Eigner's work. I've been reading it for years, yet I confess that time & again my first reaction to a new group of poems (or to old ones read over after an interval) is to suspect that he doesn't know what he's doing & has no sense of coherent form. It is only when I give myself to the poems with greater attention & empathy than I probably give to anyone else's that they come alive for me— (or I for them). Since this book (if Jonathan does anything to distribute it, & if Paper Editions is to do it, it will get around a bit) should introduce him to some new readers, I feel it would be unfair to start on a note of full acceptance, which would seem to me like pretending never to have had any difficulty with the poems. Then the reader who may be puzzled at first would only feel discouraged or perhaps disgusted; whereas if I show, as I instinctively did, that I also was puzzled, and about many poems remain so, and yet came to greatly admire them, & to receive illumination from many, the reader may wish to follow me.

I'll be sending Parkinson some more poems since you feel it's going to be a solid kind of magazine. I wish they cd. pay—I used not to care, & still don't really, but I have undertaken to pay part of Nik's school-bill & some other expenses, so I am trying to place as many poems as possible in paying places. (So long as they are decent.) It is a great pleasure to me to be able to make a real contribution to our living expenses out of something I've done "all by myself" (tho that of course isn't true in a certain sense, I mean one can't bid the spirit of poetry).

A poem Don Allen took 2 years ago is finally to appear,[3] but that will be my last appearance in *Evergreen* unless they change editors & policy, which it is rumored may happen. The last issue was so repugnant to me that I had intended never to let them have anything more—but the poem in question, which I had thought forgotten (indeed had sent it somewhere else at one point) appeared yesterday in proof with an urgent note not from Don Allen but from someone called Jeanne Unger, Asst. Ed., so I let it go at that. They now pay $7.50 a page, incidentally. *S.F. Review* invited me, but the 2 issues they sent were so awful I couldn't stomach the idea of appearing there no matter what they paid. However I am inconsistent because *Chic. Review* & *Contact* also solicited & I sent without any idea of the type of magazine they respectively are. *Contact* wanted "6 Variations" but when they informed me they pay in "shares in the company" I withdrew it as I thought they ought to have told me that in the first place. However I let them keep the other poem anyway ("Under the Tree"). I haven't yet heard from *Chicago Review*. They wrote that they wanted my "vision & suggestions" for their special "experimental work" issue, so I took occasion to sound off, i.e., that every work of art, act of poetry, was of necessity experimental, but that I could not pretend an interest in the self-consciously experimental, an idea which suggested to me people lying awake at night trying to think up ways to be different. So I may have frightened the young man who wrote—it certainly is time they replied, I asked for a quick reply as I'd like to publish some of those poems before Laughlin gets the book out.

We had a wonderful time in Boston (2 days) on the way up here. (If you are writing to Robin Blaser please don't mention it as we did not look him up.) We spent almost all the time at the Fine Arts Museum which I loved so much last year. I think it is almost more to me than the Met. There are 2 Etruscan tombcovers that you must someday see, for any photo distorts them by making them appear upright. And the Ancient Near East & Greek things are great—not so numerous perhaps as in other collections but of quite marvellous quality. The Greek terracotta figurines made me long to see again the British Museum collection of them which I "discovered" as a child. Then we visited (all too hastily) the Isabella Gardner Museum, which I think you & Jess wd. love—some of it is sheer eccentric mish-mash—a huge Sargent scene of a Spanish gypsy cafe on the wall of an otherwise ecclesiastical-looking Spanish medieval gallery bordered by a cloister garden, for instance—which is comic and (sometimes) exhilarating, and then there are very handsome things well shown, & many really fine ones—a Rembrandt self-portrait, a Botticelli & an as-lovely "school of" Botticelli. And a small portrait by Masaccio. And the ghosts of Berenson & Henry James, etc., frequent it.

Also we walked by the river and heard some Mozart in the open air and saw a family of brown ducks heading resolutely for Cambridge against the stream. We didn't look up anyone at all because we were enjoying being alone and wanted to spend the time just looking, especially in the museum. But probably in September we will—Robin I suppose will be in Europe but Dick Stone and Ed what's his name whom we met thru him will be there, & Mitch when he was in Boston on his own a few months ago rediscovered some old college friends who are pleasant too.

I'm so glad you found something more in the beginning of "A Ring of Changes" than at first. Do you have this month's *Poetry?*[4] Because as printed there are 1 or 2 minor changes made after you wrote first about it. I never did get around to the long & probably tedious explanations I was then going to make & now don't remember what I would have said, except for the 1 note I then made, "I think I can as well suppose the fear of a cracking husk as the fear of my neighbour human on street or subway as I see it in his face.

The 1st stanza describes what is seen.

The 2d stanza describes what is seen with the inner eye, which surmises the fear that causes the hesitation noted in 1st stanza.

After a pause, the 3d stanza seems to exhort—but in fact it is only speaking of necessity, & does so in acceptance."

Now I'm going to make supper.

*Next Day (Tues.)*

I've been reading Vincent McHugh & somebody Kwock's Chinese translations with great pleasure[5]—they are I think the best I've ever seen—the spacing on the page & the phrasing so perfectly expressive, never done for show. I don't know McH.'s own work at all—if this is any indication it must be good—do you know him?

Also just finished (1) Mann's *Dr. Faustus* (begun months ago)—a breathtaking tour-de-force—and (2) Lawrence's *The Trespasser*,[6] in the preface to which Richard Aldington reveals himself once again as the spiteful boor he is, who evidently can't (or hasn't) even read what he prefaces. It has an awful first chapter but thereafter is a sustained intense poem, quite fantastically dense & rich. Did you ever read it? It was the only DHL novel I'd not read.

I think I'll stop here so that a friend can mail this in Rockland tomorrow.

Love from
Denny

P. S. (See p. 3)*

I meant to explain about knowledgeableness, or what I at first clumsily called "wiseguy logic." I mean that when a non-crippled person passes a house he can make a guess at what sort of interior it has based on past experience of similar exteriors. (And he will be superficially correct—but likely will miss what is unique & important.) But there are such limits to Larry's everyday experience. There are many many places they just can't get his wheelchair into, and other places where the excitement it wd. be to him forbids him going as it wd. be bad for him & a disturbance for others—for instance he has seen few stage presentations & even fewer movies (except on television) because the firelaws forbid wheelchairs in the aisle & if he were lifted into a regular seat he'd go into uncontrollable spasms. All sorts of things we—everybody—take completely for granted he has to make his guesses at. So he makes no assumptions and what he sees sees with incomparable freshness. I'm sure I'm repeating myself by now but I want to explain it to you. If I tamper further with what I wrote for his book I'll only make it worse not better as I don't feel I can now reënter the mood in which I wrote which was a more lucid one than, with all this unaccustomed fresh air, I'm in now.

Love—

D.

By the way, we got the most lovely letter from Nik's camp which I can't resist quoting:

> "We couldn't be more pleased with Nik. It seemed to us that he has just opened up & blossomed. We rarely see him but that he is smiling, he loves to talk with us, grownups as well as children, & just seems to have lost the tongue-tied suspicious air he had early last season, especially if we had to reprimand him for something. This year, so far as I know, there has been no need to reprimand him, & he has been just a joy to be with. He seems to be enjoying every activity we have to offer. Yesterday he worked hard helping gather wood & brush, & building the huge 4th of July bonfire . . . He spent a wonderful evening skipping rocks & playing with the other boys on the beach until it was dark enough to light the bonfire. We know you will be pleased to hear he has gotten off to such a fine start. We are confident that he will have a wonderful summer."

[Nik's voice on the phone, & his own letters, certainly bear all this out— and the man who wrote it, the director, is a man who really knows & loves kids (& they love him) so it made us very happy.]

**130**

July 17, {18,} 1959
{Stinson Beach}

dear Denny,

The artichokes have come into their purples crowns . . . the choke of the central stalk is calld the Mother. And now, after harvests for the table of the branching blooms—we have the final crowns in full flower, that will dry: green and gold with intense purple bloom.

{RD's large drawing of an artichoke} and the first crown pickd we have placed on an art nouveau candlestick (but it spreads more open than I have allowed in the drawing)

from Whitman's "Song of Myself":

"Do you guess I have some intricate purpose?
Well, I have, for the Fourth-month shivers have, and the mica
    on the side of the rock has."

    •

"To me the converging objects of the universe perpetually flow,
All are written to me, and I must get what the writing means."

    •

"I moisten the roots of all that has grown."

    •

"Something I cannot see puts upward libidinous prongs,
Seas of bright juice suffuse heaven."

    •

"I have instant conductors all over me whether I pass or stop,
They seize every object and lead it harmlessly through me."

    •

The 5th section seems to me now (with the exception of stanza four— the "brotherhood" theme of WhItman's that is foreign to my feeling) a magnificent poem. The measure of the last stanza, of :

"And mossy scabs of the worn fence, heaped stones, elder, mullein and
    poke-weed."

something to hope for.

    •

Section 28! and 30! following. Most wholly moving speech that releases disclosure. And he can break from my shyness of "brotherhood" when he evokes

"I believe the soggy clods shall become lovers and lamps"
" . . . until one and all shall delight us, and we them."

Perhaps I turnd to Whitman because the Christian doctrine of Boehme that reflected the marvelous of life had deformd itself (as the Christian thing does) around the encysted separation of Sin and Death from the goods of living. And perhaps too because after the initial almost delighted response to the Daisy Aldan anthology came the deeper questioning and disappointment in the psychic ingenuities of the day—masters of mythos and prestidigitators of the subsonscious and connoisseurs of the old mysteries that we are! • that so little in that collection moved from the center, had the urgency that gives sinew to the speech.

Thursday—18: Your letter arrived this morning with verification from your view of the suspicions above. I've only had a couple of chances to look thru the book—and only one that allowd for getting a good look at it (the other morning at James's in town). With diminishing returns as it went along. But how much I get taken in by the business of names and literary alignments! I felt that I should have submitted poems because so many friends were included. But I don't, when I'm responsible for it, confuse friendship (and the special view we have from it of why and what the poem is) with poetry.

More entrenchd than ever in my holding out on anthologies unless (a) they pay adequately or (b) they are edited by a poet with whom I share a concern.

Have you seen *The Holy Barbarians*?[1] It's a rotten part of the rotten "beat" bubble—I'd hope the full stink of it (the mediocrity), but there could be worse now that the existence of a pariah mentality has caught on.

(A) The photo of me included there was one that I rejected as a botch in the fifty or so that Redl took of me.[2]

(B) Redl had askd me two years ago what I thought of Lipton and I told him that I wanted nothing to do with Lipton who was a self-pusher or "scene" pusher and a bad poet. *Bad* here means just that conjunction of form and content to debase. (So that dope is rightly calld "junk").

So Redl never askd my permission (he knew I would say *No*) and sold the photo to Messner for the book.

I've put a restraint on any future editions that the photograph not be included, and via a lawyer instructions to Redl that he cannot sell more photos of me. With a suit in court for damages. Which ought to scare off future invasions.

Perhaps I will rewrite on ("In Perplexity"), your feeling about it is right I think. I'd been taken by the fact that I could start out in the sophisticated tone of "pious female" and shift tone; but life as well as you corrected me. The tone I thot of as "sophisticated" doesn't last true beside my own sense of the why and trouble (as well as the duplicity that made "pious female" almost right) out of which the letter was written me. Being offended by a letter could save us from being troubled by it; but the trouble, and not the offense, is the thing difficult enough for poetry. You and I are the only ones who have questioned the poem: I think just the facility, the less than demanding attitude of the verse, made it more popular than others. It brought me closer to the gratuitous protest of street poetry: that avoids roots and feeling, substituting attitudes and hysteria (I think the thinner tone of avoidance, what you call the "hasty" sound of it, is the boundary of hysteria).

――――――

Didn't we write how much we enjoyd the Andersen/Robinson brothers volume? I think I like the high style of Charles Robinson best. The "fairy" in whose service the storyteller and the illustrator workd was a sterner Master than Art—who seems to allow us all so many self-deceptions and vanities along the way.

Well, self-deceptions in fairy tales really *are* self-deceptions. And that world responds readily to reward cynics and the worldly-wise-guys with just what they'd been asking for.

――――――

The note on Eigner's *Poems* starts off too distantly I think: my impulse is to cut in something like this:

> Often in his poems Eigner is noting the disconnected passage of objects as seen from a moving car. He notes these caprices of the unintegrated world—a world unthinkingly modified by self-absorbed human activities—with the precision of an innocent but intelligent mirror. In a room, at a window—it is always, not what you see, or I, but a view narrower and wider—more aware of some humble details, more aware of greater spaces also. Anything may happen, since Eigner does not let preconceptions close in his horizons. In his best poems he shares with us this wide-open field of vision in which disparate objects activate themselves, move apart or closer to each other, or at great distances from each other reveal to us an essential connection of which they remain unconscious.
>
> Reading Eigner the reader etc.

anyway you've got that strawman reader haunting the first paragraph, and must put to rest his suspicion that Eigner is "careless," his disaffection from Eigner: whereas actually you are writing for me, for anyone who has already the recognition to want this volume by his side. Do you or I have "a certain wise-guy logic"—if we had it, we'd never get near reading Eigner. Certainly that acquired wise-guy logic does exist among writers and none of them are going to put it aside to read in the Spirit of your "Note" or in the spirit of Eigner's poetry.

Once you get going, forgetting that strawman who isn't going to be reading you or Eigner in good faith, and telling your own experience (god knows, *you've* no pride that is offended at the attention due a pebble!) the writing to my inspecting eye is straight forward. And concentrated with special new suggestions—the bit about how the seas appears is exciting.

[O, I notice—in the following paragraph, if you take my suggestion to start straight off without "preparing" the reader—"as I began saying" is not necessary. But don't you need—maybe at the beginning?—well, someplace where it won't seem a special plea—the abrupt and simple statement that is a reference thruout because it isn't said: that the special threshold Eigner has in registering what he sees and hears (he *has* an extra keenness in getting the movement of speech) cannot be separated from the fact that he is disabled by disease (a spastic cripple, is it?). The outward disability has heightend observation and "inward performance."] But once I think of it—it's as much a strawman as that possibly protesting reader is. There's nothing "special" about Eigner's threshold except its concentration in the particular. And once he's establishd it—his perspective seems to me less interfered with, remarkably like it *is*—than the mirrors the rest of us provide that have to give back the real in all the shadings of mixd purposes. Amen. Anyway, Eigner sets a model of what a poem can be: and without special proviso.

It's only that first paragraph that's awkward. The rest I like immensely.

———————

I hope I *do* get *A New Folder* to review for *Poetry*—it will give me the chance to clear the air a bit.

love,<br>Robert

The "Six Variations," I liked especially—and "Song for a Dark Voice," where I like the sensuality.[3]

I'm shy of "The Wife"—it risks "How do I love you let me count the ways."[4] Do we know enough about whatever is such a daily continuous experience? "Do I love you enough?" upsets something—well, and there's a false proposition in it. Is there any choice? It seems that you hurry on in the poem, away from some content in the first proposition:

> A frog under you,
> knees drawn up
> ready to leap out of time

"out of time" may be the wherefrom of "do I love you enough?"; "laugh for joy" comes to me reading as a hopeless approximation.

Everything in the household saturates us, the exchange too always intimate for us to know any summary about, everything appearing in the aura of what we are too. Heracleitus' "We are most estranged from what is familiar." And then in marriage isn't there rightly what cannot and is not to be said?

Jess says he likes the poem—but that it would come into shape as a haiku sequence—if each stanza kept its universe 1) one, frog 2) dog 3) I 4) it 5) you 6) swallow 7) I but that there's a vagueness, a self-identification to the I.

Well, to my sense—there'd be a terrific and very different poem if 2, 3, 4, 5, 6, (tho that may be up to the charge) and 7 met the demand of 1.

———————

Jess exclaimd with delight at the bits of old fence and field "wondering if the country won't still come back after all."

And I hadn't even registered it—how taking it for granted I read! too quick to want to arrive at an impression, or distracted by my dissatisfaction with the first paragraph.

If setting yourself to *Letters* would set you off like Eigner's work has, it would be worth it.

But I have, from latest (two weeks ago) impressions visiting the Parkinsons, the idea he is not decided about the review. And as I wrote you earlier I have doubts about his purpose, so I cannot urge him to go ahead.

Maybe you can use the extra copy to send around (I typed it so that I have a copy to keep).

What you say about the given in Eigner (the natural responsibility he has that each poem is indeed "a searchingly experienced area having the form of its limits") is most true. I feel when a poem of his doesn't register more that I have missd the poem than that the poem has missd me.

Apropos of which—doesn't my work demand your, my, anyone's suspicion? I feel at least that pretending and pretension, impulse and assertion are part of the art as I go—that I could always be brought to some more exacting responsibility without loss. Because of which I warn "We go whatever route to run un-/obstructed." I think the primary for me is that I love being in the dance of a poem—and then aren't there times when the love of dancing "carries us away," and only later do we realize it wasn't exactly true. The actual dance-hall, dancers, poorness intrudes—but I don't mean that, I don't think of old frat dances as being such dances . . . ? Well, you see what crops up when I thinks of suspecting myself always.

**131**

July 21, 1959
{Stinson Beach}

dear Mitch and Denny,

Is Friendship too far North to allow for year-round address there without a bitter struggle? I picture frozen mud-flats, rescued by a sea that in winter modifies the worst of the cold. But I would like to write from Friendship, Maine., not "the open sea" but "a deep bay"—"so there are ripples, not waves." • Bob and Bobbie Creeley have been here this week, with time divided between the city where they had Okamura's studio to themselves, and visits here, making tapes of records to take to Guatemala (Ballet Mechanque, Varese, Cage, Harrison, Stravinsky and Schönberg—with Jannequin song ("L'Oiseaux") and Berg) (Caedmon recordings of Williams and Marianne Moore).

Bob has had *Letters* to review for *Poetry* since it appeard; and he puts it he is having his difficulty "placing" the work. Which I took gradually to mean finding what in where the poetry is, relating it to the literature in part. Not a task I would envy. After all I am often fabricatiung boundary lines—out of the sheer wool. And staking out claims in nowhere. Or *as if* I were staking out claims in nowhere.

But I think the real difficulty for Bob is how to face straight on to make judgment when he knows I have often flared up at being judged. And then—I wouldn't want to have to locate myself.

For the Parkinson piece, Denny, couldn't you, as you do do with Eigner, give some account of what your beginning experience was with the poetry? of how and why as far as you can tell, for instance, you mistook "As An Amuse Meant"? Mightn't some critical area be there?—between my intent to be moved and do homage to that poem of yours ("The Shifting") and the actual impact of the poem.[1] That it could be mis-taken. You know I will be eager to see the work anew. I don't really want it liked or disliked (except as these are part of seeing at all) but seen into, through: and the description of the conditions of reading which Eigner's work creates. . . .

I wish there weren't thousands of miles across this continent, for on a day like this I would love to have you two visiting—and Nik too—for there is sunshine today, and the kittens after seven weeks are all daring and dancing and climbing curtains. I read your long summer-vacation letterin the afternoon to let myself expand in the idea of its being written in like time—and am really restless this afternoon to entertain the thot of you both.

O yes, those thousands of miles . . . N. O. Brown wrote from Wesleyan:

The (poisonous) faker who runs our Distinguished Visitors program had departed for Berlin by the time I arrived back. Since (1) he has to be *pinned* before he can be relied on, (2) he has to be persuaded that it has long been *his* idea to bring Robert Duncan to Wesleyan, I have nothing— neither yes nor no—until his return, in the middle of August they say. . . .

upshot of which is that Nobby is sure he could manage this Fall but the whole would be more propitious in the spring.

And certainly, more propitious for me! To postpone the somewhat dreaded effort of the trip. And maybe allow for preparations.

The Rothenbergs arrived in San Francisco the same time as Bob. We saw them in the city and liked them very much. They're to come out tomorrow to visit. And they askd me to stay with them when I *do* go to New York— the which apartment I take it provides enuf room for a guest.

---

But Denny, I didn't mean straight out that I feel Parkinson's magazine is going to be a solid kind. For one thing he has in mind presenting what he himself values, an adventure in personal appreciations.

Which is all contrary to solidity. Good wines and good poems.

In the first issue—the fact that Bob's "The Dress" and your "Relatives"[2] are promised did contribute to my wanting something solid there too. And now—the most promising thing of all is that Tom writes that I can print what I want when I want: and gladly goes ahead with publishing "The Structure of Rime" 8–13, which I wanted to see intact, and couldn't get anyone else to take. In *The Field* as you know the poems are not continuous in one block.

Must get this off for the mail—with love/

and typescript of a new poem I like,

Robert

## 132

{July 1959
Friendship, Me.}

Dear Robert

That is *such* a poem—the "Rodilla" poem.[1] It has such a grip—on two worlds. The kind of grip people seem to find in Olson (tho' I very rarely do), on the external or (in a wide sense) political world; and on the world of the image. It shd. surely allay your fears about having lost touch, lost the immediate.

I've been making some dim notes for that article but nothing has emerged yet. You see with the Eigner note it was so different because it was a question of recording sense-impressions, almost. There aren't really any ideas to mull over in Eigner, nothing to think about—one must feel it or nothing. With you there is the whole sensuous world—phanopoeia & melopoeia—*and then* a structure & interplay of ideas, or intellect, & that's what stops me; because anything written abt. your work that doesn't touch on all these wd. be "like *Hamlet* without the Ghost."

Enclosed are 2 new poems (written here).

Love from
Denny.

## 133

{July–August, 1959
Friendship, Me.}

I have a hat—something I've not had in many years—15 at least—which looks like the Ideal Reader's hat.[1] I think you and Jess wd. love it.

Dear Robert,

Have finally started something.

Cd. you tell me whose is/are the quoted line/s on p. 32 of *Poems 1948*—the "Imaginary Instructions" part of the "Venice Poem"?

And is the Ferlinghetti volume out?[2] Cd. you please let me have one, if so?

In looking thru' my lovely-big-fat folder of letters etc. from you I re-discovered the note on Eigner ("3 Poems, an open letter")[3] which I am glad I'd quite forgotten when I wrote mine. Glad becos' it wd. have made it harder to separate out my own feelings about him, I suppose. Haven't reread it yet tho.

I am having a great time now I've got going—but can't tell if I'll end up with anything useable. The process is of value to me, anyway.

Love from
Denny.

P.S.

I think I did not say anything abt. yr. probably not coming to N.Y. in the fall. I am disappointed—it had figured as something to look forward to when we had to go back to the city—and I was going to have the apartment all so swept and garnished for you—and I love October & was so glad it was to be in October . . . Well. Do make it in the spring, won't you.

No, Maine I think is not a place one wd want to live in year round. The winters are very long and rigorous. And the people tho' there are many very nice ones are rather blighted by various sectarian glooms—Adventism, Methodism, etc. You have to drive miles off to buy a bottle of beer as many towns are utterly dry; and one of the 2 stores here won't even sell cigarettes. This is nothing in itself but it indicates the rather stuffy atmosphere. But it is the climate above everything that would stop me.

## 134

{early August, 1959
Stinson Beach}

dear Denny,

From the March 1948 issue of *Four Pages*: "Manifest.

1. We must understand what is really happening.
2. If the verse-makers of our time are to improve on their immediate precursors, we must be vitally aware of the duration of syllables, of melodic coherence, and the tone leading of vowels.
3. The function of poetry is to debunk by lucidity.

We, the CLEANERS, D. Simpson, L. C. Flynn, Igon Tan."

It is my impression that this directive actually came from Ezra Pound; previous to its appearance in *Four Pages* (which under the editorship of Simpson (Flynn and Tan are pseudonyms of Simpson's) printed excerpts from letters to Ezra Pound and presented the "Pound" line) I had received the directive on a postcard from Washington, D.C. just at the point of composition of the poem where it became one of the "Instructions."[1]

The above is one of the notes on "Venice Poem." Excluded from the

Ferlinghetti volume because I had a limit which I managed to push to 80 pages and no more. I'm sending a copy of *Selected Poems* off to you, but not inscribed because I want to send a 2nd edition for your own library (and damn it, the second edition was out when I was in town two days ago but I put off getting copies until I could turn in the remainder of the first edition)—You'll see why . . . Villiers bound the first edition wrong.

So—a copy of the second edition will follow and you can give the first edition one to the friend of Eigner's who lives there in *Friendship*.

Now that you've "finally started something" I find the prospect exciting—like having a drawing done by an artist for the purposes of the art, that must then judge some thing of what the presence in the face is, and who also has an abiding concern, close to my own. At the same time I am shy of such descriptions—because if the critic sees the difficult thing, the crises between the person and the poet, the human difficulty of the poem—it's just that that one can't know oneself. The conflict I always face when I am reluctant to write (like the conflict between the medium of sand, air, and sun and the dash into the other medium of sea, the Pacific is so cold as to ask for a conversion in every immersion) is between what the use of words as poetic atmosphere offers—the whole concept of magic woven ground with {illegible} But there dammit, I go leaning over your shoulder and wondering if you couldn't make my eyes a little more honest, but with a suggestion of mystery and I always thought if they were portrayd right my lips could have a worldly sensuality so that there's be an interesting. . . .

Did I write that I've reachd the stage now with Macmillans of bargaining on the contract? They accepted the book, but offerd what only comes to 6% royalties. And I wrote back asking for something commensurate with my City Lights contract (which is 8% on the first five thousand). But if the deal goes thru—you, Creeley, Blackburn and I (and possibly Olson if Evergreen does bring out his *Selected Poems* in the spring) will all have volumes in one season.

Portland State College has askd me to take part in their Festival of Arts early in November—to give a talk which I've accepted and will talk on "The Meaning of Form in Poetry" said title giving me swinging room to make clear the difference between conventions in verse and creative form, between recipes in writing and disciplines of the art (that is also in part a science).[2]

Among current books you might skip, I just read Kenner's book on Eliot because the librarians at the subscription library in S.F. said I would be interested etc. and I complied.[3] I'm sure Eliot cannot be as dreary as Kenner appreciates his being. Altho Kenner may be correct insofar as he offers a believable *cause* for the little Eliot writes at all.

I wonder if I would ever want to refer to

"Superfetation of τò ἔν"

or try for the rare expression of

"Paint me the bold anfractious rocks"

tho there are Eliotisms in "Domestic Scenes": "vernacular peace-pipes" "tautology of coming attractions" and the *mis-en-scene.*

The "Coda" of "Venice Poem" was straight *Four Quartets*—or had its origins in the Eliot I still find moving or enchanting. *This* Eliot anyway Kenner either misses or deplores.

_____

The most interesting thing from the book is that all the suggestive openness of *The Waste Land* form came about because Eliot didn't know what he was doing, and so couldn't see how to render the total form; and was done then by Pound who gave it its aesthetic. Of a collage, synthetic cubism: using what Eliot had written as pieces to be collaged.

love,<br>
—Robert

T. S. E.'s "superfetation" and "anfractious rocks" are blood cousins of Keats' "most copious and rural harmony" and "plumdomphious manner."

dear Denny,

I think you can get an idea of Parkinson's limitations from the following quote from a letter where he is trying to prepare me for his not liking "The Venice Poem." I hope in his review he makes more of a try at locating his dislike (I am somewhat sympathetic with his problem, since in reviewing the Dahlberg my dislike of its spirit took over from whatever attentions I had for the shape, size and nature of the animal—as if in approaching the skunk from a zoological responsibility we were to argue pro or con concerning its protective discharge; or in discussing tigers write a short essay on the necessary evils of carnivorous behavior): but you'll see the real area of misreading. In his own poetry and in his life Parkinson is humanistic, concernd with values and rewards, appreciative and associative. Here and there gives vent to his disapproval of mysticism (reproving the symbolist) and ecstatic practices (reproving the saint) and throughout celebrates a concept of the good (approved) life. It struck me in reading his volume that he avowedly presents himself in the most favorable light he can—the "creative" being for him the ability to imagine what this most favorable light may be. Here is the passage on "The Venice Poem"— I don't mean to have you alienated, but to give you a perspective on his interpretation of our work, what it is and how it is that he admires there (which he does).

"Will I eat crow about "The Venice Poem"? I will not. I can see its necessity for you, but it has none for me. I find both the "Imaginary Instructions" and the "Coda" repellant, and you would have nothing but contempt for me if I pretended otherwise. You found it necessary at that point in your being to present yourself in a self-abasing and unfavorable light. In order to release your full power, you imagined yourself in poetry to be considerably less than you had hitherto allowed your poetry to show. This meant that you then had a feeling of complete freedom as poet, that any exaltation or idealisation you should from that point on find necessary was validated by your refusal of all pretense in "The Venice Poem." You had won your freedom. But it is yours, and you had it before you wrote the poem. The poem then becomes a self-assertion rather than a process of discovery in which your reader moves with you. You already before writing had finished the poem.

It actually will, in the totality of your work, have little of the desired effect. Its chief effect will be on younger writers who might be clarified along their way by it, but even there it will be a center of confusion. It will be like Ben [the professor at the University of California who sponsord Parkinson's career as a professor] telling students that they must have experience if they are to write, forgetting that experience is what happens to us because of what we know and are, and it fades like smoke when we follow it, seeking."

I think that Parkinson's present (and probably lasting) relation to our work is like his relation to any work of art, appreciative, inclusion places him in a favorable light as a professor and as a man of letters. In the first issue you will find a disparity between "The Dress," the "Relatives" and "Structure of Rime" on one side: and a body of poetry by Stafford, Nathan, etc. on the other that is literary in its focus, poetic attitudes. Tom thinks of "form" as being effective or not—as appearance, a strategy taken by the poet. Not as an architecture or a structure, a law in making. It is unimportant to him, compared with the "low" self-image that the poem might dictate in its laws—that under directives the perspective changes (the poet may have whatever attitudes or opinions concerning what is going on—his work is obedient to the medium of the poem). I am sometimes shockd myself by what a poem demands (or reveals). I don't approve of the opposition between upper and lower that the "Albigenses" explicates. When that poem emerged it came as a nightmare: the information that we are not emotionally as we would like. Not an information of sickness but an information of fact. As our longing for wholeness is a fact.

But I still cannot put it all together. You know, I have been admiring these dream poems of yours and I prayd for dream data to draw from; and there was first the dream given in dream data—and then the next night just one horrid fascinated looking at an ass-hole emitting a black turd. Hasn't the soul then to take that into its effort to reconstruct what is created? If it is left out, avoided—it belongs still then in Hell. Boehme writes in *The Incarnation of Christ*:

> Thus was even man's external eating. He ate the fruit with his mouth, and required no teeth to do that, for at this point appeared the separation of power. There were two centres of power in Adam's mouth, each of them took its due. What was earthly became transformed into heavenly quality, as we know that we shall in our body be changed, and be made a body of heavenly power. . . . But if he should have brought his eating into the intestines and had such a stench in the belly as we have now, I will ask Reason whether that can be Paradise, and whether God's Spirit can dwell in that. . . .

Jerome Rothenberg read us Whitman's poem "Compost":
"O how can it be that the ground itself does not sicken?"
and then his joyous "What chemistry!"

The bliss of reading Whitehead's *Process and Reality* was that one emerged into a world view tending not towards a dialectic of opposites tending toward a higher synthesis but towards conflicting factors held as contrasting elements in increasing totalities.[1] Well, I could almost feel like an infinitely graceful performer of reality, only to stumble over some intolerable detail and find that my own being was restricted by conditions insulting to what I knew: that parts of nature were still reacted to as morbid infestations.

I know I want to hold back for at least the year before I get swept up in the idea of a book again. I am idling and avoiding the main currents of the stream, so perhaps the metaphor is exact and I find myself in the stagnant side pools and fens of a delta after the river of *Letters—The Field* and have to give myself up to the sun to be drawn up into the source of torrents again.

This morning Parkinson sent a copy of his review and for all of his letter anticipating that I would be displeased—and I took it to mean that he had at least gone on record about what was repellent; in the review he hedges and surrounds with adjectives: the tone of *Selected Poems* is "meditative" and "laconic" . . . the only expression referring to the troublesome areas of "The Venice Poem" is that (in "The Venice Poem") is "the ignominy and incompetence to be accepted and transformd at the depths of self-defeat."

The thing is he still is not sure of his distaste—it is finally to be relative to a literary fortune. . . . Aie! These notes are sufficient to suggest how little we may expect to be created by *The Berkeley Review*—certainly that there will not be a challenge!

———————

Enclosed, a beginning on a sequence of verses that I think of as possibly finishing to send for H. D.'s birthday (Sept. 10th)—as "Gold"/"The Question" was writ for Pound's birthday two years ago.

Did I write that I'd accepted Macmillan's terms, low as they were (but Ferlinghetti tells me New Directions had offerd to him the same)?

love

Robert

The "Animal Presence" poem is of the best.[2] I've read it everywhere, as if it were mine. For the *l*s of "guileless," "llama," "mildly," "armadillo" and "palm," if there were nothing else! George Stanley and Harold Dull who are always worrying about what one ought to be doing in a poem, thot one oughtn't write a parallel second verse—where everything was expected, retrospected. But even trying on their wanting a poem all presence and no comment as if it were a sufficient principle I could not let the "What is this joy?" go—nor the "Those who were sacred have remaind so" I could worry the "bronze" of the close but mightn't that only belong (my worrying) with the sight that falterd.

The joy of animal presence after all will win us back—you've got our oldest longing with you: to see *them*. O to see the llama! Well, these days it's that I've not seen the koalas yet. . . .

Do you know Henry Vaughn's "Childhood"? I send two passages one the opening, and the other toward the close.

> I cannot reach it; and my striving eye
> Dazles at it, as at eternity.
>     Were now that Chronicle alive
> Those white designs which children drive,
> And the thoughts of each harmless hour,
> With their content too in my pow'r,
> Quickly would I make my path even,
> And by mere playing go to Heaven

---

>     Dear, harmless age! the short, swift span,
> Where weeping virtue parts with man;
> Where love without lust dwells, and bends
> What way we please, without self-ends.

> An age of mysteries! which he
> Must live twice, that would Gods face see;

I'd like to live now to something verging upon senility and title a book then *Second Childhood* thinking of the above.

Dear Robert,

Here's what I did. I hope what I say about the earlier poems will not offend or hurt you.[1] Reading all I have of your work from *Heavenly City, Earthly City*, through *The Field*, it struck me sharply what a development there was—and the *Selected Poems* being in fact a *Selected Early Poems* doesn't show it. I wish you had not confined it to those years, as the book will circulate among many people who don't know your work at all. Or that you had given it a title that included the word "early." However, with Macmillan bringing out *The Opening of the Field* that doesn't matter. I am so glad about that.

As for their rates, royalties & so forth, I can't remember what Laughlin is giving me but I think it was the same—I'll look at the contract when I get back. He gave me a $200 dollar advance. I had the 1st proofs a couple of weeks ago—they were all mashed up because the typeface was too big for the page—you can imagine the result!—but that is being set to rights. It shd. be out mid-November. When will yours be? I'm so happy about it. What about Jess's Morgenstern translations? Laughlin sounded interested when I told him about them and he is planning a European translations series of some sort.

*Next day* I was interrupted by a visit from Pat (Al's {Kresch} girlfriend) who has been reading you for some months now & has made a drawing to go with some lines she copied out, which she's going to give me to send you. She's a person you & Jess would love if you ever meet her—well, when you do get to N.Y. you will. Al & Pat are staying abt. 2–3 miles from here—we walk or row over to see each other every few days.

I had finished what I'd written abt. you before yr. letter wondering & surmising what I might do came—which is just as well.* So there is no mention of Eliot or anything. I am afraid you will find it all too vague & imprecise.

*Because I might never have had the courage to go ahead.

I'm sorry. But after a perfectly awful false start that, built on a chronological framework, read like what I imagine college freshmen's papers must be like, I let go into this, which at least is my kind of thing, and got the same pleasure & exhilaration from doing it, or rather in being the instrument of it, as when writing a poem. So—please excuse the limitations, and I hope you will like it anyway.

While I write this letter I am also trying to make some jam of blueberries and huckleberries. It's a lovely color but so far hasn't begun to jell.

In your letter of yesterday you use the phrase "ecstatic practices"— speaking of Parkinson's disapproval of mysticism etc. It's a phrase I question & which ties up with the use of dreams and with what you say of Harold

Dull and George Stanley's worries about comment etc in the poem. I mean, I don't approve of the conception of "practicing" (i.e. inducing) ecstasy—it surely has to *happen.* (Of itself, from a confluence of natural causes.) The same about dreams: of course sometimes one longs for a dream, for specific revelation or for any dream as token that one's deepest, creative self is not torpid; but sometimes one seems to do that very self a violence by a kind of insistence of such longing. And similarly if one tries too hard to wrest a poem from dream isn't one in danger of betraying the dream itself? I have something of this feeling—or maybe that's not it, maybe it is even *too* faithful for communication—about yr. Japanese dream.[2] It is frightening but doesn't quite seem (to me) to have become a poem. It's somewhere nowhere between dream & poem. I was afraid this was so with "Relative Figures Reappear," but from your reception of it I conclude it broke through—perhaps because of the close form in which it made itself.

(By the way "The Goddess" is not a dream poem but the condensation to image of last year's confrontation with truth in my personal life—ridiculous phrase, as if one had any life that was not personal.)[3]

Finally, what I mean abt. Dull & Stanley's feeling abt. "parallel 2d verses" etc while I quite see what they mean (reading Robert Frost here last wk., & so on) I disagree with its aspect as a theory, a preconception—how *can* one make such decisions, it seems as if one who did so must think of poetry as fabrication—god knows I love craft but there must (mustn't there) first be the *happening,* before which one is swept headlong, and if that happening is a question and answer then the poem must have the form of question and answer—there can't be blanket decisions not to write poems that reply to themselves.

Your other new poem ("I must wake up into that light world") seems to belong with the poems of *The Field.*[4] And thank you also for sending the lines from Vaughan, which I do know but haven't read in some time. As it happens I had wanted to bring in Vaughan, Traherne and perhaps Herbert into what I wrote about you but since I had none of them here I didn't in the end, except to recall the field of orient and immortal wheat. I love all 3 most especially.

I'm very happy that you like the "Animal" poem. It was curious for me to read "The Temple of the Animals" after that. I had either not read it before or else completely submerged it, until *Selected Poems* arrived. I like it very much. Did I tell you where I saw the llama? It was at a television studio! Blackburn, Galway Kinnell, Ed Marshall, Leroi Jones, & I all appeared on a "non-commercial" ($10 apiece) television program a few months ago. The 2d ½ of the program was about "Animal Talent Scouts" (you've probably seen ads of the bk. called *Kangaroos in the Kitchen*) so we had the opportunity of meeting the llama & one of the kangaroos in a sort of stage drawing-room—the people were awful but the animals were marvellous.

They aren't trained to do tricks, thank goodness. But they do live all in one house without fighting. It was interesting to see how much like a hare the kangaroo was really—the head & ears especially. We got close to a large almost bold hare here one day—it seemed to stop & almost invite one to follow, which I did till I lost it in the bracken raspberry tangle. Its ears were rimmed with black.

Love—

Denny

P.S.

"Bronze" in that poem is because I have a very strong feeling for almost any of the smallish bronze objects—bowls, pins, and of course especially figures—of the ancient world, whether Greek, Persian, Etruscan, Sumerian etc. They mean more to me than I can understand. I think I didn't send you my version of Gautier's "L'Art" (a very free one!)[5] where I speak of them. I will have to copy out. It's didactic in the extreme (of course) and I'm rather afraid to show it to you—I guess I was going to wait till it was irremediably in print—but I ought not to be so cowardly.

Had a card from the Rothenbergs saying that you & Jess alone had made it a good summer for them, aside from anything else. I once sent "This Compost" to W. C. W. who had never read it and he loved it in spite of his mostly not liking Whitman.

Robert Bly writes from Minnesota about his pet owl. He once rescued it and brought it there from some other place, south. It lives free in the woods but when he returns to the farm the owl returns & sits around near him. But it gets after the chickens & ducks which have to be locked in at night against it. Among other pets he seems to have a collection of stray dogs he's rescued from the dog pound.

This letter seems to be all about animals—before I stop I must ask if I told you abt. Hawthorn. He is the noble cat who shares his life between us & the Kresch's. He's really Al's but has stayed with us for a total of at least 2 years (when Al was in Europe & so on). He's spent most of his life shut into N.Y. apartments but this summer is running free up here (at Al's) and is having a most wonderful time. He pounces about in the long grass, eats blueberries, emerged victor from an encounter with a ginger tom, and takes long walks, sometimes walking down the road to meet Al & Pat when they return from somewhere.

D.

I had sent tape of S.F. reading to Bob Creeley a couple of months ago & before returning it he and Ed Dorn recorded some poems on the blank end of it—am dying to hear them—have to wait till Sept.

dear Denny,

I just (yesterday) finishd and maild off to you a copy of *The Book of Resemblances* typescript. It is a perplexing book—certainly "The Essay at War" poem, which had me out on a limb or up a one-way branch-track of the line for almost a year, is a problem: I kept stubbornly at working towards my own defeat in the poem, throwing up impossible positions and *straining*. An essay at recovery of position, I suppose. But it's also a gesture beyond the bounds of actual resource in feeling and so I'm alternately pleased with passages and dismayd with others. If I could have got "The Horns of Artemis" and "Africa Revisited" into the *Selected Poems* I might have begun a book with "Borderguard" and dropd the "Essay" as a botchd poem—which it is—The whole period 1950–53 is one of a scattering of focusses:[1] it's the period of over a year writing in imitation of Gertrude Stein to change my metabolism, it's the period too of first contact with *Origin* and coming from the feeling of being utterly alone (especially the Stein period isolated me in my workbook—tho there were a close group Jess and Lynne Brown who particularly liked the work). *Faust Foutu* goes along with this work.

What did I mean "cunning Isaac" (in the "Two Poems for the Jews")? The poems were done straight from *The Zohar*, and I guess that I must have reflected the doctrine there that Isaac came from the sinister side (*The Zohar* is worried by and tries to ad-just Jacob's cheating Isaac.) But in my own work Isaac, like Esau, is an innocent party, and if I meddled (as I sometimes do these days, but wouldn't here) with the verse I'd make it "cunning Rebekah." That "be ye cunning as serpents" command [and Moses and Aaron manipulating snakes] and the dialectic of deceptions of the Torah are the most fearful part for me of the Jewish heritage [and here the New Testament unless one follows a Greek gnostic tradition is wholly in the tradition—Judas *has* to perform his role in the crucifixion]—It gives full splendor to the doctrine of the great Adam [that we are *all* involved, so that whatever deceptions, cunning, sides, propitiations and riddances are twined, twinnd Esau/Jacob in one being]. Well, anyways, re-typing that poem I was puzzled by "cunning Isaac," for either obediently waiting beneath Abraham's knife or blindly waiting for Esau's presence to give his blessing Isaac has innocence for me.

*Evergreen Review* wrote, in the person of Jeanne Unger, asking if they could print the "Pindar" poem.[2] At first I thot absolutely not. The poem is appearing in *Foot* [which should be out within the week—there are only 100 copies and it will be an almost local event—I'll send a copy as soon as it appears], and then as far as a larger audience goes it will be there in *The Field* when that book appears. Then I thot of the money and replied, calling attention to the fact that the poem was appearing in *Foot*, that Miss Unger might find on file my statement of mistrust concerning *Evergreen*'s purposes (as it seems most evident to me that the "Pindar Poem" attracts because it gives voice again to the "disaffiliation" theme, however minor a thread in the composition, and changed in meaning) etc. and askd, if she were still interested in publishing the poem, her to tell me how much they were going to pay me for the poem before I made my decision, since it would be on that grounds I would decide.

But my position shifts in relation to this movement of the black humor— what goes on in *The Big Table, Evergreen Review* and *Yugen.* Paul Carroll wrote recently and I sent him a group of poems. There's a portion of pure waste (Kerouac's *Angel Midnight* is certainly in the excited nothing depart-ment), of bardic going on without art or rather without *the* art, rousing verse (Allen Ginsberg's *Howl* and *Kaddish*) that are as close to poetry as Kipling's "If"; and there's the real stuff of a nasty spirit like Burrough's *Naked Lunch*; and the real stuff of a bitter life-hating or rather body-hating mind like Dahlberg's . . . all of that is repellent. But there in conjunction are H. D., Olson, Creeley—Antoninus. There's an actual penumbra and a light source somewhere hidden that something {is} going-on, where outside, the other reviews are inert.

Yet having riskd the statement I realize I would wait for that editor to arise who belongs to the light, who brings me closer into the tuning not closer in thru the discord. The fact is that today we've got to give the *life* its due, even when it speaks as sickness. But damn it! there's a deal of deadly writing going on. Dahlberg's writing hinges on an attitude, and excludes the possibility of being informed by experience. He maintains his "self" in defense. Where Kerouac, Ginsberg and Burroughs spread themselves on the offensive—and in Burroughs case the "self" that is spreading is very offensive indeed.

But interesting as the conjunctions of *Poems of A Floating World* are, the vision is too literary to be moving. We liked the Rothenbergs by the way and from their talk I got a glimpse or two of the more official poetry-world of the hunting reserves of the big reviews. It's part of Parkinson's perspective and ambitions that he resisted all suggestions that Creeley might be invited to teach writing at U.C. and went ahead to persuade the University to bring out Louis Simpson.

---

We have a little break in the fog, a sunny day! and to bathe in it all I've to get to the garden and go after some corner of the everywhere neglect. Aie! it brings to mind Wieners of *Measure* saying when he was in the garden Williams wouldn't have weeded, he'd have let everything grow.

But I've a long way to go as a gardener before any lovely working shows. Our cares are sporadic.

love
Robert

Oh yes, I seem to have left out the last page of your manuscript of *Resemblances*. The closing poem, by the way, is quite out of order: it was written just before we left for Mallorca in 1955—someplace contemporary with "Brought to Love" and "To Vow" in *Letters*.

## 138

dear Denise/

I've got the same feeling about the lushness in the "Medieval Scenes"/ "Domestic Scenes"—the Christian church has a term for the vice *luxuria*, which is translatable into our concerns as poets as a vice. I still have to allow for it at times in order to get at a poem at all. Anyway, I'm not likely to be "Medieval Scening" The problem of the virtue of a poem doesn't get solved, it only increases.

And your distinction between creating a world and mirroring it seems to me right, or at least lifts some burden from my shoulders.[1] I've tried to make the responsibility be, via the word poein to *make*, "creative" but it's never exactly fitted. And then, haven't I had to exclaim in protest in poems (like a vain person wearing shoes too stylishly tight) that I can't put it all together. Your "nothing is alien to it" or my poetry is at least a redeeming hope. It lifts my trying to make nightmares operative—for I don't belong in a hell and am uncomfortable there, caught moving in the wrong circles.

I'm not sure about "startling truth from her nesting places" (I mean as startling truth from some nesting place in me). But whatever your notes will mean to whatever other readers, they were, this morning, a release for me of some knot. (By the way, I *do* think of there being a thread of a "deception to startle" in my workings, tho early I pictured it as a sleight-of-hand and I think the word used in later poems is "betrayal" not "deception"—where I like the activity of the word that suggests disclosure. The curve of her belly betrayd that she was pregnant.)

There's a point of correction where you say I pay homage to "The African Anthology of Cendrars,"[2] which I've never read, and at most have only heard of. I typed the manuscript for Radin's African Anthology[3]—but I think what he did in retelling the tales (in removing the telling from its native syntax, so that only the minimum translatable content is left) is a disappointment. However I do owe something to the fact that in typing from his sources I had access to and read literal translations before he simplified 'em.

I can't remember what I wrote you, Denny, about "ecstatic practices" but when it's put the other way round and is "practicing ecstasy" I'll question it along with you. "Inducing" is still another step toward the questionable (certainly leading further and further from the freedom of impression and feeling necessary to the writer) and I think your comments on these recent dreams might clear the air—I do know I've induced the trouble of them (and in some poem the Lady says "Do not trouble the water") Part of my conflict too, in relation to the current beat-sick thing (the Artaud cult etc.) where I have a regard I am not sure isn't sentimental, i.e. induced. In order to make a cause, to keep my hand in the negrito at times when I have no actual reference to it. As if I *ought to* feel pain, despair, deadly boredom.

Well, Jess likes these notes. And so with the specimen's approval and the pleasure of one other close fellow reader you have a good start to be reassured in your labors.

Did I write that I've been corresponding with H. D.? And today she writes that in addition to a sequence of seventy-four poems (*Vale Ave*) she is sending me the entirety of *Sagesse* (twenty-six poems) "I would be glad if you would 'house' these two sets of poems for me" she writes. Your note about Robert Bly's owl fitted almost into design. There was an owl several years ago for sale in San Francisco—but if it were in captivity it becomes beastly (they have to have live or freshly killd mice or small birds and while I would love an owl's company, I'd hate to have to take on part of an owl's rapacious nature) Bly's owl flew in most lively. There *is* a difference between the animals of "The Temple of" and the llamas that exist in a correspondence between the llamas of your dream of llamas and then the real pleasure of any actual llamas for us.[4] The rightness of "not disdains but mildly/disregards" that captures the llama's expression. It isn't until "Africa Revisited"'s giraffes that the feel of the animal, something more than the thought of the animal, occurs. "fleetingly"—

I must get this off—with the vague sense that perhaps I had something more to say today . . . but the mail truck leaves at 3:30 and. . . .

love
Robert

Dear Robert,[1]

*A Book of Resemblances* came and it is so *beautiful.* I must add a few words to that piece I wrote, to at least mention it. "Salvages"—"An Evening Piece"—well, only gestures, a dance indeed, wd. do to tell you how I feel about that.

Please write soon because I am anxious about what I said of the early poems. You know, the rest has more weight to the reader if it is not all eulogy—that's one reason I felt it had to be said. But I'm afraid you might be hurt at my saying it even so. This is not an answer to yr. good letter (which I'll do later)

Love
Den.

## 139

August 27th {1959}
P. O. Box 1
Friendship, Me.

## 140

Dear Robert and Jess,

Your letters about my notes came before I'd mailed the enclosed. I was relieved.

And, Jess, a letter from you is such a special lovely treat. I'll be so happy to get the Morgenstern MS., and anything else you think I might do in that way I wd. be glad to undertake. (I mean anything you think Laughlin might be interested in, or—well, anything . . . )

The children's book (with Nelly Blaine) is only a dim memory of something that never got finished. I wrote a few pages, got bogged down, and stopped. I guess it's just not my line. I get involved in too many details and boredom sets in. Maybe some day, tho'. I enjoy reading children's books so much that I always have a haunting yen to write one. But then I tend to feel the same way about painting & drawing & that always ends in sheer frustration.

What happened to the beautiful book you made with Mike McClure?[1]

I put in a slight change of sentence in the second paragraph on p.1 & sent it to Parkinson (to include mention of *A Bk of Resemblances*) also at the top of p. 2. Also I took out the mention of the *Anthologie Africaine*. I had thought the myths in *Origin*—#X was it? (I had it here but it was McFarland's copy & I gave it back)—were homage to that.

We are getting a great deal out of the book. It seems to me you are the only person who has made any *use* of what Gertrude Stein did.

Pat Kresch is reading *Letters* & *The Field* over & over, copying out bits. Things (good things) that have happened to Al & Pat's life this summer seem to be closely connected with her reading of these poems.

*Migrant* 2 with Bob's "The Awakening" came yesterday.[2] And with your letter and very beautiful poem. Wasn't it Marianne Moore said that? But to whom? I can't remember.

The same day the poem beginning: "I must wake up into that light world," arrived, I read this: "They asked the Rabbi of Lublin, 'Why is it that in the holy Book of Splendor, the turning to God which corresponds to the emanation "Understanding" is called "Mother"?' He explained: 'When a man confesses and repents, when his heart accepts Understanding and is converted to it, he becomes like a new-born child, and his own turning to God is his mother.'"

By the way, did you know the Russian pronunciation of Solovyev is "SolovYOV"?[3] It was a familiar name in my childhood for my father often spoke of him. I remember at one time when I was about Nik's age (10) how irritated I was, by a book of his which was read aloud a chapter at a time at breakfast. It wasn't only that it was above my head & therefore bored me, but that something of the same quality of morbid asceticism, or whatever—masochism?—repulsed me about it as is present (& has on me the same effect) in the Leon Bloy letter in *Migrant* 1 (which to my surprise Ed Dorn says he liked). But I know the story of his visions of *Sophia* and rejoice in them. Later he is supposed to have had one in the British Museum Reading Room, where my father too spent so many hours of his life.

By the way, Ferlinghetti turned down Dorn's Mss. which I sent him, with a "No indeed, I don't see this poetry at all."

We are getting rained out (See blots, above!) here this week, and just now at breakfast decided to leave a few days earlier. We're going to make some stopovers—maybe in New Hampshire, & pretty certainly in Mass. Will be back in N.Y. by the 15th. I have to start packing. Nik has been with us (from camp) since a week ago—he had a wonderful summer there.

Love from
Denny.

dear Denny,

The story of Solovyov's visions came from preface notes in a book of his calld *Godmanship* (Eloise Mixon had wanted to find out what he was like and askd me to get something of his from Mechanics Library).[1] The text was a great disappointment after the hope aroused by the thot of his visions. Solovyov is a Professor of Philosophy, that hints or sparks of a wonderful life can show up in such a ground is a miracle in itself. What if Christ's disciples had not been simple fishermen and a whore, and he the son of a carpenter, but the whole lot been the faculty of some college? A saintly pedant is a trying source—I couldn't get started at reading the text. The Eternal Woman vision spoke to me as an image of the indwelling of all parts of the created world, well the world being created, in all others (that he'd seen the blue that was everywhere), but it speaks too of how disembodied, narrowd to the field of blue, the intelligence, the image was. But "narrow" means nothing restricting when it is true and (I'm thinking of what responsibility we've to keep with the truth) becomes a key of the wholeness of experience. I shied at your reference to the truth of the poem in those Notes, and then there was something about my work I think that made for your having to deal with a bird startled by a deceiving hunter from her nest to uncover eggs of what will be new birds—where my own uneven relation to truth is reflected. An appetite with whatever aptitude sets us to the poem, dependent upon our feeling of what the form will be; and I accept that I've only to do my best. At the same time more and more aware that whether I ever achieve it or not— there is an optimum in which the artist is true to the object. Simplicity and straightforwardness render the truth of a metaphor free from all effect. The "furniture" of those early poems, all the lavishness—is lush because it is

## 141

Sept. 8, 1959
{Stinson Beach}

diffuse: an accommodating mode. I didn't see any better than that and had I been "sparse" would have missd the ground and seed. At least now I take more courage that I may come to greater strength and purpose in rendering the statement of a poem, when I also allow for the fact that we can none of us exceed our own nature.

We do want to "render it true" as a primary purpose in the art. And when I read I try to find out the truth—some things I do not doubt. Well, that such a sense of woman-blue-everywhere-wisdom is a true part of the beauty of the world, or that it rang true, that it had been seen: true to itself. Free.

What we feel as "morbidity" is what we are still bound-up by, haven't liberated our spirits from. But often we've to keep facing the morbidity, keep it as the "problem" until we recreate the world. Boehme is certainly morbid: sexuality, digestion, elimination—almost every internal function of the body is a Hell, morbidly present. The "torture-chamber" he calls the stomach. But it's the seventeenth-century and plagues of syphilis and bubonic plague sweep the cities—there's a real stink of shit everywhere that will only disappear with the flush toilet and the best drains. Sickness, filth, pain and stink are the physical conditions of life itself—and Böhme senses that they are not true (ie only and necessary conditions)—as death is true. So evil has some part in them. Death is part an evil and rightly where we sense the particular death is due only to our own minimal condition.

Well, as you know—the morbidity thing is catching. It's the contagion in reading Christian and Jewish religious sources where the individual is involved in the divine. For the Greeks that Prometheus was morbidly devoured by the vultures did not mean that the individual man was to be *Promethean*. It served as a warning, not a duty or command. But the essence of Judaic religions is that we are all involved and so even have our share in Prometheus. We sympathize and there is always a good deal of morbidity possible there (and morbidity's attendant sentimentality). I still identify in order to sympathize at all. Pain especially becomes "my own" so powerfully that I am very poor at being of help. But it's true isn't it that only when at last our fellow feeling is "true to the object," when we can know what the pain is, but also where it is and still be involved that we can be doctors. I've *not* anyway to be a doctor. Right now in reading and in my work I am struggling to render more clear what seems true in the Judaic-Christian experience. To keep them. Or to keep my share there. But it shall be tested against the reality of living.

Along with some passages from Boehme's *Incarnation of Christ* which I copied out, I'm sending a new piece of my own, written after a dream— "The Carpenter" had some reference to Christ and that is the first appearance of Him in my dreams I think. (I've many times had appearances of Satan or of Demeter and of God the Father . . . )

from Böhme:

There is no better test than by the likeness of God which we understand
to be desire, sense, and mind. These three things contain the center of
the spirit, from which is generated the strong will wherein lies the true
real likness and image of God in flesh and blood, which the outer man
knows not. For this image is not in this world, it has another principle in
the angelic world, and during this lifetime remains in the mystery, in
hiddenness. . . . The mind is the wheel of nature, desire is the centre
as the first thing for the realization of nature, and the senses are the
essences.

For the senses arise from the essences, they have their origin from the
sting of desire, from the sourness; they are the bitterness and run always
in the mind—the wheel of anguish, and seek rest, to see whether they
may attain the freedom of God. It is they who, in the anguish-wheel or
mind, kindle the fire, and in the kindling, in the terror, willingly give
themselves up to death, and thus sink down through the torment of
fire into freedom, into God's arms; they proceed into freedom as a life
which proceeds out of death. They are the roots of the new taste, which
penetrate into God's wisdom and wonders; they bring desire out of the
pangs of death; they fill their mother the mind, and give her power for
God's essence. . . .

Thus the mind (das Gemüth) is the wheel or true chamber of life . . .
and is the fire-life, for from the fire-life arises the mind, and the fire-life
dwells in the mind. The senses are the mind's servants and are the
subtlest messengers; they go into God, and again out of God into evils,
and wherever they become kindled . . . that do they bring back to the
mind. [I think of the mind-hive built by, infomd, and then served by the
instinctual-obedient-sense-bees]

(God) manifests himself in humanity as in the mind, senses and
desire, so that the mind feels him; otherwise he is in this world too subtle
for us to behold. But the senses behold him in spirit, understand in the
will's spirit, for the will sends the senses into God and God gives himself
up to the senses and becomes one being with them. Then the senses
bring the power of God to the will, which receives it with joy, but at the
same time with trembling; for it knows itself unworthy, because it comes
from a rude lodging, from the wavering mind; therefore it receives the
power in sinking down before God. Its triumph is changed into gentle
humility, which is and embraces God's true nature. It sinks into the mind
and dwells in the fire of the soul.

love
Robert[2]

Dear Robert,

This is just to explain my silence. A "trip" on the way back from Me. (a visit to a beautiful part of N.H. where a friend has a lovely old farmhouse, a short stop in Boston inc. a visit to the Fogg,[1] & another visit, in Williamstown Mass, where there are 33 Renoirs, a magnificent Turner, etc.) was the first reason becos I just can't write anything while travelling—not even p.c.s! And then followed one of those "readjusting to N.Y." periods, consisting of housecleaning & looking for things put away before leaving & calling friends & being called by other friends & scrubbing & soaking the Nik after more or less unwashed barefoot weeks and hastily answering incredible numbers of "business" type letters that seem to pile up at such times, unexplainably. And dental appointments & school health certificates etc etc. Well.

We had bad news a few days ago which will distress you too. Only a few days after getting a cheerful p.c. from her, & still fewer after writing her a long letter in wh. I told her of yr. & Jess's admiration, we heard that Nell Blaine had been stricken with polio in Mykonos—she was flown to Athens —is paralyzed from the chest down—is in an iron lung—may be sent to Germany or back here in some weeks when the fever has subsided. It is a shock. All our closest friends in N.Y. are her friends too and it is on all our minds constantly. It is apparently not the very worst kind of polio but pretty bad anyway & at least a year will go by before she can expect to recover. She had planned to leave Mykonos 2 wks or so before but stayed on because one of those Greek shipping millionaires had promised to return & buy a painting.

Enclosed is an unclassifiable prose bit I've sent to Gael {Turnbull}. I don't know whether it makes sense to anyone but myself? Perhaps it is too naive? Anyway, I had to write it & it seemed like what he might like so I sent it.

Your piece, the "Letter to the Carpenter," is very very moving & the modest simplicity of it is beautiful. Thank you for sending that.

Jerry Rothenberg is bringing Jess's projected cover—? or titlepage? I forget now what he said—but anyway he's bringing it over for us to enjoy one day this week.

A friend who's a zoologist & is going to a new job out of town is leaving her frogs (in a terrarium) with us.

Have had good letters from Bob & from Ed Dorn recently. Tho I find Dorn's Santa Fe / Olson piece confused, & so does Mitch.[2] (I think you have never met him? He's O.K. I hope one day he'll go to visit you, I know he'd like to.)

There were some things in recent *Combustion* by Michael Shayer that I liked. Also Gael's things.[3] The form is too easy; but the honesty and clarity are valuable. Hope to write again (with poems) at end of week.

Love—

D.

P.S.

Mitch thinks he once heard you mention having an old friend who was an editor at—Crown?—Vanguard?—If so cd. you let us know in[4]

dear Denny,

Re-read this morning your "Note on the Imagination"[1] as first, distrusting its discrimination (that just this is imagination and that—"the feared Hoffmanesque blank—the possible monster or stranger"—was Fancy), but wholly going along with the heart of the matter: the seed pearls of summer fog in Tess's hair, and the network of mist diamonds in your hair. But the actual distinction between the expected and the surprising real thing here (and taking as another term the factor of your "usual face-in-the-mirror") is the contrived (the work of Fancy), the rememberd (how you rightly "at no time is it hard to call up scenes to the mind's eye"—where I take it these are rememberd) and the presented. But you see, if the horrible, the ugly, the very feard commonplace of Hoffman and Poe had been the "presented thing" it would have been "of the imagination" as much as the delightful image. In the illustrations of Rackham and Dulac the hair of every child and princess is sprinkled by a routine that is not even "Fancy" with pearl seeds of fog, diamond mists of morning.[2]

Jess said an image he particularly remembers from *Tess* is stars reflected in puddles of water where cows have left hoof tracks—But, you know, I think I am so eager for "concept" that I lose these details. Or, more exactly—that my "concept" lacks details often. For, where you or Jess bring my attention back to the "little fog" intenser "amid the prevailing one," or the star in the cowtrackd puddle: the presence of Tess and Angel leaps up.

The evaluation of Fancy and Imagination gets mixd up with the description. All these terms of seeing: vision, insight, phantasm, epiphany, it "looks-like," image, perception, sight, second-sight, illusion, appearance, it "appears-to-be," mere show, showing forth . . . where trust and mistrust of our eyes varies. However we trust or mistrust the truth, necessity, intent etc. of what is seen (and what manifests itself out of the depths thru us): we can't make the choice between monster as fancy and the crown-of-dew as imagination.[3]

Jess suggests that it's not a matter of either/or (in which Fancy represented a lesser order and Imagination a higher order—like hot and cold), but of two operations or faculties. Shakespeare is rich both in imagination and fancy, at work in the same passages. Where Ezra Pound totally excludes or lacks fancy. But here "fancy is the capricious, the playful, "made-up" thing. What of fantasy? The fantastic is a constant in the *Cantos.*

## 143

October 6, {19}59
{Stinson Beach}

George MacDonald calld his poems and fantasies "Works of Fancy and the Imagination." But I think he means playful and serious. Sometimes we use the word "fancy" to mean the trivial; but that surely does injustice to Shelley's landscapes or Beddoes' skeleton's songs or the description of Cleopatra's barge that gives speech to Shakespeare's sensual fancy.

You know I took Joyce's *Finnegans Wake*, Blake's works, and *The Zohar* with me to Mallorca because I thot I might write something about the Imagination and how it takes over as master, compelling the poet into its own shape. That is: I thot of Blake as being obedient to his imagination, so that he lived in the actual world as a creature of the real world of his "imagination." Hardy seems to me a man obedient to his imagination: He saw and lived "enchanted" by the Schopenhauer-awakend vision.

Shakespeare is so completely a "writer" that we cannot locate him. The imagination is *all* there; and gives us no instructions; binds us to no particular way of seeing. There are as many eyes as created persons. And Lady Macbeth does not give voice to some view of Shakespeares.

Certainly Tolstoy has a "point of view" that remains his, and is never obedient to the imagination. I don't anyway open myself freely to Tolstoy but must confess that my antipathy to his essays on Art is such that I avoid the man. I do remember sermons interpolated in *Anna Karenina* that exemplified that the man had a higher opinion of his own "ideas" than of the secret natural thing in him. And I remember too, what boggd me down in *War & Peace*, tedious re-constructed verisimilitudes of scenes that lackd the economy of the imagination. I certainly do not mean here to deny the faculty to him—for there remain from *Anna* and from what I read of *War and Peace* vivid realities; and the deeper truth that Anna Karenina is a living member of the human communion.

Nor would I think of Tolstoy as other than one of "the greatest"—but my concept of the greatest is entirely social and historical here: I recognize the shaping force. So that Hardy, who is immediate and vital to me as Tolstoy is not, I do not think of as "one of the greatest": Schopenhauer is his master.

Tolstoy like Homer and Shakespeare has no master.

I don't think that the "great": Homer, Aeschylus, Plato, Aristotle, etc. mean much to me in that quality. Some—Cervantes, Tolstoy, Rabelais I have never read or am not atune to.

Shakespeare and Dante I return to again and again. But for me it's not the *perceived verity* (your seed pearls of summer fog from Tess; or Madeline Gleason years ago to demonstrate the genius of imagination chose a perceived verity from Dante where the eyes of the sodomites turn and:

e sì ver noi aguzzavan le ciglia,
come vecchio sartor fa nella cruna.

"towards us sharpend their vision, as an aged tailor does at the eye of his needle").

I am drawn by the conceptual imagination rather than the perceptual imagination. By the correspondences and counterpoints of several levels of composition. The *meaningful* image rather than the, or before the realistic image. We have been reading Yeats' *Mythologies* which are full of [[At which point I became so frustrated with this new misbehaving Parker pen that I hitchhiked into San Francisco to have it adjusted. And am sitting here at the Parker office to give the new adjustment its test.]] details that are ornamental and atmospheric not conceptual or perceptive: particularly I think now of a peacock screen in his *Rosa Alchemica* series that furnishes a luminosity or enriches the strangeness without being at all necessary. How, in a fairy tale or myth only the operative remains. Yet your mist of dewy diamonds is ornamentive not operational, the verification of *morning*? as Yeats' peacock curtain is verification of fin-de-siecle solitude or study: the distinction is only and importantly that the diamonds clearly appeard to you, confronted your will; where the peacock screen was contrived as setting by Yeats' will. [Where let us say the contrived furniture of *Medieval Scenes* is distinguished from Yeats' screen in being operative forces or figures of the whole.][4]

dear Denny & Mitch /

144

October 16, {19}59
{Stinson Beach}

My friend I spoke of in relation to Mitch's novel is Mrs. Robert Manley (Seon Givens); at the time we talkd I had not seen her for several years.[1] But this last summer the Manleys were in San Francisco (he is an electronics engineer) and they came out for a week-end. She is no longer with Vanguard; but she has her old close ties there. Now, she is a free-lance adviser on adolescent books. Aie! I'm writing her in this same mail to find out if she would get Mitch's book a hearing. The damnd thing in all this is that I *do* know the owning-editor at Vanguard, so that all I can remember from the old days is her first name and so that Seon in speaking or writing only refers to her as Evelyn . . . Evelyn what?!?! When I am in town next I'll get from City Lights the information—that last name I am wracking my brain for . . . and write directly to her. With all our hopes that it works all round.

I've not written for several weeks because I was waiting for the decision on my letter to Macmillan to be final. After seeing the format of their series I wrote them that unless I had the cover I wanted for my book the deal was off; well, I did write more than that, because I thought and still think that their format is ugly, the kind of ugliness that arises out of commercial art courses and I do hate it. It means they aren't going to go all the way with the poets they publish to realize however inexpensively some equivalent of the spirit of the book. So now, *The Field* is without publisher again: but I'll wait until Jess has done a cover design before I submit the manuscript to anyone . . . and then they'll know exactly *what* the project is—and so will I.

Did I write that about a month ago an anarchist in Chicago wrote me saying that one Jeff Rall had written the *Industrial Worker* (which had had some article on the new poets calld "disaffiliated") asking where I was? Now I have written to Jeff and heard from him:

> Your letter was forwarded to me from home, and eventually caught up with the boat I'm working on. . . . For a long time now I've realized that the only way I was ever likely to learn your whereabouts would be by reading your name in print, and I've plowed through a good many publications over the years with that thought in mind.
>
> I cant imagine where Harry Roskolenko got that idea about me expiring at Dunkirk. Needless to say, I survived the carnage, and my only cenotaph will be an imposing mound of empty Tokay wine bottles. But I like the lines of your poem—it suggested a sort of Rupert Brooks air, you know "some corner of a foreign field that will forever be LIFE cafeteria, etc"
>
> Anyway, I'm glad to learn that you are well, and have negociated the years since the war with no loss of faith or spirit. My own ideas have not changed either, to any great degree, although I suppose that I'm lacking the capacity for total commitment I had in my salad days. I'm still an anarchist, and belong to the small Libertarian League. I also write regularly for the *Industrial Worker*—I'm an associate editor at present, and although the IWW falls considerably short of being the kind of an anarch-syndicalist movement I am in favor of, it still is the closest thing to it presently in existence, and for that reason I want to be associated with the organization.
>
> *The Industrial Worker* was one of the last places I ever expected to read about you, but when your name was mentioned in Joffre Stewart's article, I wrote to him right away. I don't know him at all—apparently he is a friend of Chuck Doehrer, who used to edit the paper. He was very helpful, although he does sound just the least bit ODD, judging from his letters.
>
> Well, a time comes when a gypsy dies and a peasant is born. That is the case with me—I have been living here in British Columbia among a sour bunch of Scotchmen ever since 1946. For the past ten years I have made my home on a dim, foggy little island located in the Gulf of Georgia. This is North Pender Island, about 40 miles from Vancouver.
>
> There is no town here—Port Washington is composed of a weather beaten wharf, a general store and post office, school etc. A couple hundred

people live here, in scattered dwellings in clearings along the beach. I have a house and garden, and live with my wife and children—I have three girls and a little son. It's splendidly wild and remote; deer look into our windows at night, and the whole place has a wonderful, pine-scented spooky elegance—sort of a Charles Addams land among the conifers. I guess I'll be here until the great mushroom cloud appears.

I make my living as always by manual labor—I'm a seaman on a coastal tanker. I work seven days a week, and get my days off all at one time. This gives me six or seven weeks at home several times a year. I'm at work now, and expect to be home early in December, and will be off the job then until after New Years.

It is not too difficult to reach Port Washington. A small steamer leaves Vancouver four days a week and calls there. Also there is a daily ferry that leaves from a place called Swartz Bay, on Vancouver Island, near Victoria, B.C. . . . . . .

which I copy out—because this news restored to life some integral part of the world that was young, and has brought new confidence forward in me to revive the full force of what I desired to be as a writer when "anarchism" was an allegiance to a reality in daily life itself: "I make my living always by manual labor." And share it with you, Denny and Mitch, because the thot {of} you as friends keeps that reality going too, sweeps aside for a moment all the particular evaluations of poetry that a competitive society makes and brings my thot to the book well-workd that gives romance and grace to honest lives. Rupert Brooke, "faith and spirit," "a time comes when a gypsy dies and a peasant is born" "splendidly wild and remote" and "a wonderful, pine-scented spooky elegance" are all part of the heritage we have of transformations and intimations writers have made, sharpening the senses and desires in living for common things.

You know how involved I've been in the romance of poetry itself . . . and have the sense here that I need only to restore the ground of that involvement to its ground in some ever needed realization of common life—and the great breath of air then for me from my eternal wrangle with literature. For damned thing and damnation that it is I am so much turnd aside into the concerns of competitive letters, the evaluations of a market-place, the settings up and throwings down of what ought to succeed and what must fail.

This morning a savor of fresh life and the joy of news from an old friendship, most dear to me, comes anyway for me to share.

I am working on a presentation of an essay of mine "The Homosexual in Society" which appeard in *Politics 1944* and is to be reprinted now in an anthology edited by Seymour Krim: so my mind has been returnd on another level to social concerns, to defining, however clumsily, what I feel is the good. I'll send you a copy when I am done. How elaborate when it should have been simple that early effort of mine is, it *is* more a symptom than any information.

O yes, and another part of current freshness was meeting Wendell Berry. I was hitching in to the city and he pickd me up at Tamalpais junction. Introduced himself by name and when I gave mine said that he thought he had recognized me from the picture in *Evergreen.* (I am clean-shaved again!)—we had a day then, gathering up his wife and infant girl and coming back to Elfmere for tea.[2] I am oppressd as much by the atmosphere and concerns of "San Francisco poetry" where "I have always earnd my living by manual labor" has long given way to "driseling drinks and petty crime," and the splendidly wild and remote house and garden has been replaced by the hypodermic and the "cosmic turn-on," I'm oppressd as much by those associations as I am by anything in myself. It was a relief of some oppression of heart to have just the afternoon with an earnest young man whose perspective had vista. And your reading of his poem and sorting it out, redirected me to read another poem of Berry's that had been in an issue of *Poetry* I had work in.[3] I see why his poem didn't emerge from reading thru the issue—there wasn't the formative urgency that brings a poem to operate upon the imagination by insistence. Well, there wasn't the sheer clamoring that brings so much false or waste news to our ears,

love
Robert

Seon Manley's address is 43 Morton Street, New York 14, N.Y.

---

## 145

Nov. 3d {19}59
249 W. 15th
{New York}

Dear Robert and Jess

I took the Morgenstern book to Laughlin and as I had feared he does not want to do it himself because it is too expensive to produce. But he *was* impressed, and suggested showing it to Kurt Wolff of Pantheon books, who, he says, knows all about Morgenstern and wd. be in a better position to do something lavish. However, he lives in Switzerland so it is a question of writing to him first, describing it (i.e., J. L. said one shd. say it is folio size & that the drawings are worked into the layout). What I thought one might do is this: you write to him now, & at the same time give me the word & I'll send it off (in its wrappings as it came here, I saved them all) with a covering letter. (Of course he wont know who *I* am, but it wont hurt to sound my enthusiasm anyway, & at the same time make much of Laughlin's recommendation.) If you think, tho', that it shouldn't be sent until you hear from him, let me know. Or perhaps you'd prefer to have it mailed back to you? My feeling is that the actual sight of the book might convince him, whereas if you only describe it & ask if you *may* send it he may just be frightened by the idea of its size & so on.

Robert—how beautiful about the reappearance of Jeff Rall from the shades. And I'm so glad about Wendell Berry too—I had a nice letter from him also, about your meeting, which I'll enclose if I can find it (please return as I've not answered it yet.)

I'm also glad to hear from Don Allen (he called specially to tell me!) that you've consented to be in his anthology after all. He was tremendously relieved, I think. He knew very well the whole thing didn't make sense without you. And I really think that though he has included some people whose work isn't very good, it will be a really interesting book, affording useful comparisons for the serious reader.

If you have nothing else in mind, & can't come to an agreement with Macmillan, how about trying Laughlin with *The Field*? I know he turned down something of yours before but maybe he would feel differently about this. He's an ambiguous chap & I don't feel I have the slightest influence on him although I've had amicable relations all along over my own book. Sometimes he seems very simple & sincere but not very bright. Other times he seems crafty as hell. But anyway, if you would like me to show him my copy of *The Field* just tell me. (Actually I did, once, last spring, when he had dinner with us—but it was in too social a moment & he didn't bite—he was in any case too preoccupied with the Ford Intercultural stuff & so forth at that time.)

You'll be sorry to hear that Gunther Grass, who was to have arrived here this week on a Fellowship, was found to have T.B. so can't come. I guess it was lucky he had to have the medical as they found it before he knew he had it.

We went to see Nell Blaine on Friday night—she's in Mount Sinai. She's still in the iron lung, but every day they take her out of it for longer periods. She can move her left hand & arm. No one can yet say how much paralysis will be permanent. She *might* make a complete recovery. She is extraordinarily courageous—full of humor & spirit. Everything seems to depend on the next few months really—if the muscles don't revive in that period they usually atrophy. What a future to face. But I think she believes in her recovery— & she certainly has made good progress so far; little though it seems it apparently means a great deal that she can move the fingers of her right hand a little bit.

I have lots of errands to do now as I have been sick with a cold for some days & have let things go.

*Kurt Wolff*'s address:

Hotel Esplanade,
Locarno
Switzerland.

Love from
Denny.

P.S.

Please tell me, Jess, how you want the book mailed (if you do)—i.e., insured? or whatever. If it costs less than $2 to mail (I have *no* idea) please let me pay it—if it's more than I can afford I'll let you know—O.K.?—& you can refund me.

---

**146**

Nov. 5 {19}59
{Stinson Beach}

dear Denny,

Your letter with the sad news about Günther Grass not arriving, and the visit to Nell Blaine, came this morning.

Jess sent the Morgenstern book to Kurt Wolff last summer, and received a personal reply, appreciative, but saying that Pantheon didn't plan on any poetry on its list. So sending it again to him won't do the trick. . . . But it's encouraging that the book does get seen. Jonathan Williams wrote recently asking permission to list it on a publishing project submitted to foundations, and Jess consented. And then too we liked the idea of you & Mitch having the book itself to look at.

About sending *The Field* to Laughlin—I've two reservations: where Laughlin has taken the initiative in the past to ask for work he has never liked it; he dislikes particularly my derivation-as-method, and if he were to say *yes* to *The Field* I would not trust now the genuineness of his response.

But more seriously—I am thinking of my possible income from the book. If I publish it myself in the Spring, I think I can realize at least $400 net and even more depending on whether I try to keep the price down to a respectable $1 a volume or inflate it to $2. [Spicer realized $400 on *After Lorca*.] There would be the important added advantage that I would own all secondary rights; and if any of the poems were good enuf in the eyes of an anthologist I would have full rather than half income therefrom.

To make anything like $400 at the rate of royalty offerd now by publishers the book would have to sell 6,666 copies. Instead of the 600 copies that would net me that amount.

What I have in mind is that having my work published by an established publisher would be worth while then only if the publishing house were solidly behind my work; if it meant I would be able to bring out a book with them whenever one was ready. Otherwise let whatever rumor of the quality of that work grow as it will—the actual quality won't be increased by whatever critical attention might come with prestige publication. And, unless I come against new information in the forthcoming issue of *Faust Foutu* (comes out in three weeks, and will be a good test case), I believe these little typed, plain editions may solve my problem.

love<br>Robert

Thanks for sending Wendell's letter—

dear Denny & Mitch,

Enclosed is a piece I just finished editing, with an introduction, new notes and retrospect, for an anthology Seymour Krim is doing . . . built around the Beat Generation literature, I take it.[1] While I don't like the association, in this case I wanted the opportunity to consider that old essay again. Well, and I think I did find some lasting core of belief and concern between the urgencies of 1944 and these happier days (if *only one* thinks of the immediate world of concerns; tho other, the world I call "society" in the Essay has remaind the same—it lives on *its* fear and hope for total destruction). But what a phantasm "it" is!

Creeley sends a beautiful poem [middle of last month] which herewith in case you haven't seen it:

THE WOMEN

"What he holds to
    is a cross
and by just that much
    is his load increased."

"Yet the eyes
    cannot die in a face
whereof the hands
    are nailed in place."

"I wish I might grow
    tall like a tree
to be cut down
    to bear such beauty."

Did I write, Denny, that I have agreed to take part in Allen's anthology? His plan for the project, just the fact that there's work in back of it, and then that it takes the risk of young new poets, many problematic—won me. I've objected to your not being grouped with Creeley and Olson and me—

**147**

Nov. 5, 1959
{Stinson Beach}

& may have force in my objections, because it wasn't temperamental but critical—both that we all had our beginnings in the common territory of *Origin* and that not only I but a number of critics have made the observation that your work was preeminent there.

And I suggested that he might well make a section of *Origin* beginnings —which would bring Eigner and Blackburn into line with us—and transfer Jonathan Williams and Oppenheimer to the New Poets where they belong.

———————

Also—some of the poems I've been sending you come into focus I hope now that I've located them in the enclosed "suite."[2]

love
Robert

P.S.

Rothenberg writes that Charles Tomlinson is arriving. Would you convey to him that I greatly admire "Autumn" (*Poetry*, April 1959) and always meant to write to him? If he comes to the coast, would he come to see us?

## 148

Nov. 25th {1959}
249 W. 15th St
N.Y. 11

Dear Robert and Jess,

First, about the Morgenstern. After your letter saying K. Wolff had already seen it, someone else at Pantheon asked to see it (Laughlin having spoken of it) so I took it in; but in 2 days they called & said they had looked at it; so I called for it (not trusting their messenger) & now it is with me again. It seems whoever read it told J. L. "Morgenstern is untranslateable"—silly ass, of course everyone is untranslateable if it comes to that, but translations are for those *unable* to read the original, so the degree of approximation is the *least* important thing about them really (Tho from the little German I know these seem extraordinary feats of fidelity anyway.) . . . How can he (whoever) be so stupid as not to see that by way of Morgenstern's world Jess has created in the book a world of equal value? Well. So—tell me if I shd. send it back to you, or where.

Second—thank you so much, Robert, for the article which is lucid and moving and of great interest to us. I have been increasingly aware of my ignorance and confusion on this subject & this really helps—and also frees me to ask you several questions I wouldn't otherwise have asked—but not in this letter, damn it—I have to make supper now, then after supper plan my Toronto reading—Tomorrow some lonely friends have invited us for Thanksgiving (they are fairly new in N.Y. & we're almost the only people they know here)—Friday Mitch's parents are coming—Saturday I fly (paid by Canada Council) to Toronto, read that night, stay over till Monday afternoon—next week shd. be a bit clearer, except that there's an Art Fair at Nik's school in aid of the scholarship fund & we must help—.

I'm working on a long translation—a narrative poem by Machado—for Angel Flores' anthology—& have several new poems of my own to send you too.[1]

Saw Mike Rumaker yesterday—externally he is better (works around the hospital, has honor passes, even has written a little) but internally (I felt) he is worse, or at least no better. There was something almost venomous about him. It frightened me. Don't speak of it to anyone else—but I don't think he will ever get really better. He is like a plant the frost has bitten. And this happened to him long, long ago.

We have the cat from upstairs staying with us for a few days. He's a fierce mouser—& we've had mice lately, being catless since Hawthorn went back to Al {Kresch}. It's rather gruesome—I saw him catch one. I really have nothing against mice if only they weren't such dirty little creatures. But he's a nice cat.

Have you seen the Tylers lately? Please give them our love—I think of them often and am always meaning to write—by Xmas I *will*.

Love—<br>Denny

P.S.

Cecil Hemley (Noonday) said to me "Tell Duncan I will publish his book if he'll send it to me."

Two notes on the above:

(1) My impression of him is that he is a nice guy with real feelings.

(2) He had had a few drinks at the moment he said it.

You will be glad to know that Nell Blaine (who is now in Mount Sinai Hosp. here) is making some progress. She can now hold a pencil in her right hand—just—and has done drawing with her left. Back & legs still paralyzed, tho.'[2]

Dear Robert,

I just spent an hour writing you a letter of questions arising from your article—tore it up as it seemed stupid, i.e. I think most of the answers are in the article itself if I study it with more care. Chiefly I wanted to ask abt. homosexual society as it might influence a boy growing up in the Village— i.e., are there homosexuals who are so by mistake, not true inclination, because of chance influences at impressionable ages?

On Mitch's birthday (Sunday) we went to the new Guggenheim Museum.

## 149

Dec 15th {1959
New York}

It really is exciting & pleasurable—I can't see why so many people object to it. There are some *awful* paintings especially the new acquisitions—but some lovely ones too—the Brancusi sculptures, a wonderful Cezanne (*The Clockmaker*), a very early (Blaue Reiter period) Kandinsky (*Blue Mountain*) & some very late ones that are lovely (I thought I disliked Kandinsky—but not these), some Klee's and some Delaunay's that were a surprise; we hadn't realized how good *he* cd. be. Etc The building from the outside looks best at night, & of course is hampered by the surrounding apt. buildings, but it *is* an imaginative & essentially a *romantic* work & as such a great relief in N.Y.'s architectural swamp.

I wanted to get my book to you & Jess by Xmas and may yet do so—it's promised me for the 18th—. Won't be in the stores till some time in Jan. tho.

Are you really going to let Grove do *The Field*? D.{onald} A.{llen} had asked for the loan of our copy for anthology purposes—next thing I heard, he called up to say cd. he keep it a while longer as Grove was trying to contract with you. I'd beware of that slimy Rosset if I were you—but I guess you're well aware of that.

By the way, I stumbled on a wonderful novel they published this year but which hasn't been advertized or reviewed, at least we've not seen anything. It's Andrei Biely's {Belyi's} *St. Petersburg*, translated by John Cournos.[1] Not everyone's cup of tea I guess—it is a direct line from Gogol I'd say—much of it is pure poetry. Read it.

I am both delighted & annoyed to hear from Jerry that you're enjoying the Hasidic tales. Delighted because I love them & feel closely related to them (my father used to tell versions of them, and Schneour Zalman of Ladi {Lyady} was my ancestor) & annoyed because if I hadn't thought you knew them already *I'd* have liked to be the one that introduced them to you and Jess. I envy the Rothenbergs that pleasure.

By the way, did you see 2 poems by James Reaney in I think the Sept. issue of *Poetry*?[2] The first was reminiscent of Jess—and Morgenstern—a bit—and I liked the other too.

Wd. you send me the Tylers' address in time for me to send them a Xmas note please?

I'm in a muddle of untyped poems & unanswered letters & unironed clothes—have been overtired ever since someone in Toronto told me her life story all night—so at this point—arbitrarily—will stop.

But one thing—I think I never thanked you for Seon Givens' address— we met her & her husband—she was nice—now M.'s book is in her hands —wd. like to invite her to return the visit but it wd. be too awkward while she has the book. Haven't heard if she has begun it yet.

With love—
Denny.

dear Denny/

My tour North was successful enuf that we will have [have begun to have] a Christmas. Something of a feast is most important to us—to gather round old companions of Christmas, Ida {Hodes}, James {Broughton}, Harry Jacobus—and spread the board. In Vancouver I found a gorgeous edition of *The Reign of King Herla* for Jess with mint jacket, and on the boards brilliant color illustrations, an illustrious little book then furnishd forth by Robinson.[1]

And in the whole trip I found too new friends and renewd old friendships, more important than the success of it—that I have verification of my belief that there are kindred that a book might reach. Literary associations obscure what the soul seeks, fellow being.

But when I try now to call upon my feelings from the trip—they have not ripend, and I'd have to struggle to get at them. Well, I don't think I want to *use* them, but will let it grow.

Back to your question after that essay of mine on homosexualism. I have myself questions to ask of the essay. Tho my sense there was that we are all by nature bisexual (just as I have the prejudice often that there is one god, one god of the gods), I'm aware, no sooner do I call up the adamic nature in which man and woman in-dwell, of the individual creation each of us sets about with its hierarchies of intensity, and multi-phasic kindred feelings— what happens to Eros in the being we enter in friendship? and isn't there the *enchantment* or seduction of Eros that poets have sufferd under and call *false* or glamour, or faerie? Poets have always treasured their *belles dames sans merci*, their dark angels and "moons" and warnd against them. Thomas the Rhymer is poetic initiation and human seduction, peril of the soul, in one adventure.

Sometimes in "falling in love" we know we have been ensnared in our fantasic life and become prisoners as if "by mistake, not true inclination." And there are wandering indefinite "homosexuals" who belong with Dante's trimmers, whose sexual life is only an appearance: i.e having no real response, psychicly or physically at all. Freud's criterion is just that the body either is erect or limp in its response—but here it is the penis, I mean; for I think there are diffusions of sexuality that rob or distribute the genital focus—so that the whole body cannot come into the major chord or the scale. I mean that men and women who exhaust themselves in necking seem to have a different sexuality—and can also be more undifferentiated in response.

I always wonder about homosexuals who are impotent with men—but from what I gather of such men, their *story* can no more be solved by the simple view that they are homosexual by mistake than can the impotence of men with women be solved by changing the object. There are impotences with life itself, and impotences of speech etc.

150

Dec. 24, {25 19}59
{Stinson Beach}

For a boy growing up the surrounding tone would govern how he viewd his own sexual inclinations. If he were vague in his being, passive, and wanted others to give him his who he is and why he is—then he would seek seduction or instruction—he would seek impressions.

But thinking of my own boyhood I remember myself as possessd by images and romance that arose within as almost possessions as desire. At twelve or thirteen I thot the world was demonic, and it was. There was a lure in woods and river banks that never materialized tho I sought it, calld by it and drunk with it—not knowing *what* there would be. Was I seduced by myths and fairy tales? But they contain *all* things, and I discoverd my own maze in that garden. What was "true inclination" where there was so much ravening in me for experience?—I was intimate with panic and dwelt upon the very edge of Pan's courts.

But I do know too that many friends have had casual homosexual influences and chance impressions that remaind incidents—because sex in itself does not engage us—it is Eros that governs us, who becomes a god over us: and there mistake, chance and influence reappear as threads of a design the soul seeks. Men with women who eat out their being, men with men who violate their inner nature,—in the rituals of self abasement or self bondage sexual choice conforms to the meaning the object has.

But I take it the "boy growing up in the Village" is just that you think of course of Nik [as Virginia {Admiral} thinks of Bobby]. Parents have something to do, I think, with guarding and cultivating a child's sense of his "true inclination," just in his confidence that what he feels can be shared. But that's me in my mind sharing, because I could talk with my mother about it, the facts of falling in love—and it was mixd up with intensities of my relation with *her*. Jess never shared anything with his parents, grew up in an environment that gave no cultural preparation for homosexuality at all: well, but he is all but immune to those influences and impressions that I still can be taken over by.

---

Before I rush to get this in the mail/a word about the Grove proposition. My signing the contract is dependent (a) upon acceptance of Jess's cover design as part of the book and (b) inclusion of clauses giving me all secondary rights once the book is out of print—including a series of definitions of *out of print*. I get a considerably better royalty than Macmillan offerd [Macmillan offering 6% of retail, and Grove 7½%], with $100 on signing contract, and an additional $100 upon publication. I agree with you on the subject of Rosset, but crossing my fingers take advantage [I hope it will be advantage] of the offer.

love
Robert

P.S.

since I *didn't* get it in the mail—an added note now on Christmas day before guests arrive.

I am enclosing a first draft of autobiographical notes for Don Allen's anthology—the final draft is a job of adjusting and bringing into focus that improves this copy in several passages—but the gist is there.[2]

Jess had an added view to the question you ask about sexual influences upon a young man: his comment was that no sexual experience could harm providing it was volitional. what the parents have to protect against is sexual use under duress. There's duress of guilt—and this, I think, was on my mind when I thot of confidence between parents and child as a protection. I've known two girls who were used when they were eight or nine by friends of their parents under the duress of asserted permission from the parents in one case (where the girl had feared her parents) and under the duress of guilt in the other. The small son of our neighbor here in Stinson Beach was used by an older boy at knifepoint (this was some five years ago when the boy was five or six), but here the parents' (really the mother's) understanding made it possible for her son to tell her.

Seduction is only a more subtle duress, using our shame of not being in-the-know to force: but then it is mixd isn't it? And volition must always cooperate with seduction—here what parents might provide is just to cultivate the virtue that is in volition, to treasure desire. But maybe Emerson's

> When half-gods go,
> The gods arrive[3]

can only be known when half gods *have* gone, and gods arrived. At forty-one, I am still accompanied by half-gods.

PART TWO     1960–1963

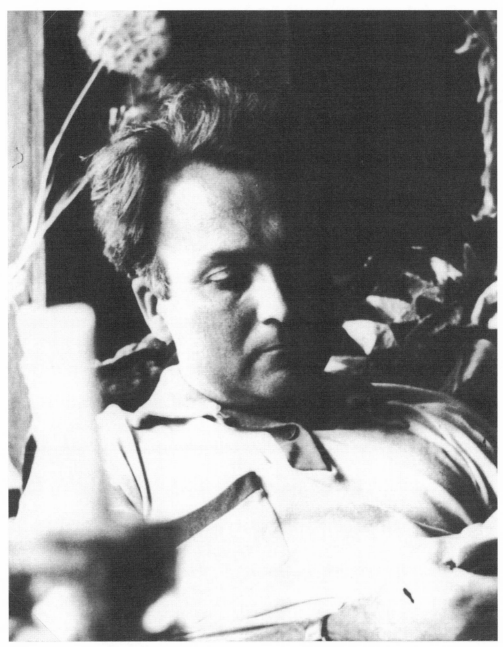

Robert Duncan at Stinson Beach, early 1960. Photographer unknown.

dear Denny,

Your book arrived yesterday and I crawld away into bed reading thru accumulated manuscripts and volumes old poems and some new—the "Dream," and "Note of a Scale" were new, and my heart laid claim to them.[1] This is my property—wilderness and cleard acres. I've inherited the homesteading spirit in reading, and, like China am very confused about boundaries. "Waiting to see them again."

I've lost my sense I had when *Here and Now* came out, that I wanted more of a "book"; for with three volumes there is a gathering fullness, and the whole is the more free that it hovers over the poems that have their independence. That very "Ring of Changes," that I remember worrying when you sent it to me, delights me more and more—so it's where you are free of what satisfies my prejudices in poetry that you lift me, "lift" must mean out of, out of something I would otherwise have been satisfied with, taken for granted.

There's one, "The Lost Black-and-White Cat" that I wish you would publish in its first version too—the second seems truncated—well, my sense is when I meet it [as in the White Rabbit, or in the new book] that something is missing, and then I remember and read again the earlier version. Going over manuscripts I find unprinted to date: "The Depths," "Takeoff," "The Innocent (II)," "Today's Saint," "Formal Reply," "The World Outside," "Six Variations," "Song for a Dark Voice," "Come Into Animal Presence."[2] Well, I can see that the first two may not be quite *there*—but the rest are of the essential. I am somewhat vague about exactly what is writing post the composition of the latest book—but "Innocent (II)," "Today's Saint" and "Formal Reply" I shall be advocate for—that you include them before all is done.

There are poems that possess me right away and grow there so that touring the garden I stop and admire: this is "The Springtime"; these are the "Scenes from the Life of the Peppertrees"; here is "With Eyes in the Back of Our Heads" and "The Park," where I remember all the earlier readings flooding in to fill my new reading. But there is another discovery now for me in reading, of poems I had *overlookd*, it's the recognizing the charm, the essential friend in someone I've known, well, met but not known over years. "Continuing" in *Overland* came thru this way for me. Perhaps at first

"repeats the head, the fantasist"

was too close to the flying head of "The Venice Poem" for me to accept response—but now there is a link to

"irregular
displaced at a breath: secrets . . . "

151

New Years Day 1960
{Stinson Beach}

Noticing a clump of blue-eyed grass for the first time, or four-foot tall evening primrose in yellow full bloom that had escaped the eye. Come to rest thereon. "I didn't know we had that!" Winds and cold strip leaves from the bougainvillea so that areas of mountain and sky appear at the window. On the youngest branches clusters of blossoms still.

---

News comes from Tom Parkinson today that the plans for his magazine have droppd out from under—his printer and would-be publisher going broke. I had divided feelings about the possibilities there: he promised on one hand a vehicle for whatever we (you, me, Creeley) might write, but Tom would not I think recognize or risk younger writers.

*Evergreen* grows more repulsive each issue—it is hard to believe the policy of "junk" "crap" "shit" (all terms of the new evacuation, terms of dope etc.) can take over so. For sixty-five dollars I sold my "Pindar Poem" to that coffin. May Pindar's ghost forgive me greed.

Where have we to go at all? There's *J* and *Foot*, Turnbull's *Migrant*; *Poetry* will consider poems, but outside of that I despair. Does Paul Carroll really want to print more?

---

Do you have that earlier version of the "Lost Cat"? I close with a copy, for I wld. be reading it aloud to you right now again to see if you might not by captured by it—

love
Robert

THE LOST CAT

Dead silence. The cat
four days lost. Only the child's deep
drifting-into-far-distant-sleep sigh,
and the perturbed crackle
of chairs devoured by deathwatch.
Already the crazy
backyard roosters are trying
to split it up—barely midnight!—and
crickets skillfully re-form it in
minims and quavers. The child turns,
bangs the bedboard, struggles
with dreams. Last night in dreams
he found the cat in the bathroom.
                    Come back,
cat. Interrupt with your
inflected voice, tie up the silence

in tangled string. Or if you're
dead, at least send
your black-&-white pouncing ghost.
Come back and thrash
the silence with your autonomous
feather tail. I see you were
the imagination made flesh and fur,
informing the dark with mystery
and making poems out of the whole
cloth of silence.

"Did she take Death out of that?" Jess askd. And, that he must have done his drawing to the above.


What is *The Reign of King Herla*?

Dear Robert and Jess,

First—thank you so much for letter about book. And "The Law." Now I feel book is baptized. Will answer questions abt. "Lost Cat" etc next time.

Second, Krim sent me (incomplete) copy of article.[1] How come he is not doing it after asking for it? I haven't yet had chance to compare with other draft. Thanks too for letter answering mine, especially for wise postscript (what Jess said).

Third. We spent an evening with this guy Hubert Crehan in order to reclaim Morgenstern book which his wife had come to get 3 days before and to show him other things of Jess's. (*Artist's View*, White Rabbit books).[2] (He also wants something from me) He turned out much nicer than we expected. I don't know what sort of painter he is but the magazine sounds like a really interesting prospect. It is not to be chiefly on painting, but general. What sounds like a very fascinating article by a woman and her anthropologist husband on "Natural Childbirth" ("A New Image of Birth"), articles fiercely pro and con the Bauhaus as it has influenced art teaching, an article by Olson (I forget on what now)—these are some of what he mentioned for the first issue. I don't think it is going to be another *Evergreen* by any means. And it sounds well backed so shd. pay reasonably.

I had heard he is a champion of "abstract expressionism"—which I have so little sympathy for, but he said nothing of that—in fact all he did say sounded to me rather attractive and as if it would be attractive to you too— and he seemed on the level. He has a pleasant modest young wife & an absolutely charming cat. Their place is a loft, not swanky at all. He himself is a rather strangely shaped pigeon- or barrel-chested un-handsome man who seems to get short of breath & makes long pauses between phrases as if he

## 152

Twelfth Night
{January 5–6, 1960}
249 W. 15th St
N.Y. 11

were making a speech. Mitch (like Jess) is inclined to be cautious about new people. However he also thought he seemed quite decent and on the level. His dislike of the Bauhaus (which I had always thought of as preaching the functioning of all parts in a whole, which is OK.) seems founded on the premise that they were rationalistic and opportunistic & so settled without protest for the industrial age & for working in it with the powers of the day, as against magic, personal integrity, romance, and nonconformity. My words (poorly chosen) but I think that's what he was saying. Which sounds OK to me. He says their philosophy dominates the art schools. Of course I said most of the artists didnt come out of the art schools anyway. He answered, no, but Madison Avenue poisons us all & *its* "artists" do, and "contemporary design" in all its low boring forms surrounds everybody. In any case, he seems to have sincere opinions which is better than nothing.

I may be completely wrong, but that's my impression, and Jerry Rothenberg who saw him last night called me and told me his impressions were similar.

Love—<br>Denny

P.S.

I saw Elizabeth Kray a few days ago. She said she felt badly at not having been able to "fit you/Robert in" at the Y—said they had to keep certain "open dates" for possible profitable readers like Isak Dinesen & so on. I think she wd. like to have you read there some time next year, if you wd. Robert Bly is writing to ask you if you wd read at N.Y.U. when you come to Conn. And I have sent a note to M. C. Richards asking who wd. be the person to tell at Living Theater that you wd. be in New York. Or have you done so?

Creeley sent a beautiful poem called "The Rose" in a recent letter. But I find it hard to write to him since I was shown a letter he had written to Leroi Jones in praise of *Yugen*, a magazine I put in the same category with recent *Evergreen*s except that Leroi is a nice fellow with terrible taste whereas *Evergreen* is definitely aimed, with pornography and sensationalism, at a special public, with the idea of making money. When one reads Creeley's letters to all & sundry one feels they are like form letters. Also he wrote to Ted Enslin, a nice guy with whom I've corresponded for years, whom Creeley used to speak of contemptuously, asking about teaching jobs on Cape Cod, much to Enslin's surprise.

Enslin (who lives in the country, and admires Bob's work very much) was astonished to get a letter from him and also astonished because Creeley praised Ginsberg's "Kaddish" very highly. Well, I think parts of that are moving—the 1st time one reads it anyway. But C.'s sense of craftsmanship— how does it accept so much that is slipshod?

And then—there are one or two other things that make our ancient affection for Bob seem a little attenuated at this point. It is sad. But he doesn't seem to have a *core*, somehow. But "The Rose" is *beautiful*. I suppose one must settle to love him for his work and draw a charitable curtain over other aspects of him.

P.P.S.

Is the Norman O. Brown of Wesleyan whose book we have seen reviewed in the *Observer* (London) & elsewhere, your friend there?[3] It sounded like an v. interesting book; I am putting in a request for it at the library.

I *hope* to get up to Wesleyan when you read there. Willis Barnstone (who is in the Romance Languages dept.) would put us up.

Yet another P.S!

(1) Would you be interested in Crehan's seeing article Krim is not using?

(2) Crehan said he wd. be interested in seeing poems of yours (Robert). If you send, & he uses, wd. you think the thing I wrote for Parkinson's magazine might be a possibility—changed a little perhaps? Or wd. it be better to revise & expand it & see if somewhere—*Poetry* perhaps?—would use it as a review when *The Field* is published? How long will that be?

dear Denny,

Bob had written several times brief references to your no longer corresponding. . . . Today with your letter again in a letter from him: "Also—what do you hear from Dennie, whom I've written to, some time back, yet feel must be in some sort of slough(?) since there is no answer. Ed Dorn wrote her new book is to be out shortly, and I want to see that, very much. . . . " If you could write him about *why* you haven't been writing, would that at least restore the communication? The only important thing for us is our correspondence—and that becomes empty if it {does} not carry disappointment, anger, outrage as well as our appointments and joy. "He's long tho," Jess says, "been in this pattern of ingratiating"; and Olson at Black Mountain when I had occasion to write to Bob that one of his form letters was just that and that I felt like I was writing to an answering service or some such, said "But that's just one of his bread-and-butter letters." And I realized that much of the time Creeley is in his own life like a man is in jail or the army: waiting to receive letters, reassurances from *outside*, that are needed because he is there/then incapable of restoring the bond himself.

In my notes for Creeley's last reading here I wrote:—but I can't find a copy of those notes—anyway I talkd about the "what the hell" surrender of

# 153

Jan. 7, {9, 19}60
{Stinson Beach}

continued presence in the poems (particularly in early poems), that it had some relation to the central form of the poems, the recovery of equilibrium thruout [each line askew by just one glass eye]—and in a letter, it will sometimes be writ by a glass eye.[1] "Damn it" "I damn well" "Wow"! etc. The eye gestures: where the responsibility of the poet would not let *hell* and *damn* go as if they were intensifiers and had not got circles of increased suffering and evil to account for.

*Yugen*—that is Leroi Jones has twice written asking for work from me and I have withheld; yet I've given "The Pindar Poem" to *Evergreen* with the thot of money and bad conscience. Bob has always printed everywhere and anyhow, gone everywhere, known disparate people. When he read here the reading lackd center, which he had to regain thruout by entering the poem itself—because he was conscious of those disparate actual personalities: Broughton, Ginsberg, Spicer, Helen Adam, Whalen or Duncan. And in this instance I was such an integer of such a sum, impossible to add. He wanted to ingratiate, and where we love a man his wanting us to like him is a painful experience.

But back to *Yugen*, to the new writing that you and I are both alienated from [I have come to the place where I cannot read McClure because the disorder of senses and the monstrosity of ego seem gratuitous, opportunistic], it is not a vice but a virtue that Creeley keeps trying to read and understand it. His own writing increasingly has shed its manner where it was not necessary and in the last years has gaind in nature. The poet Robert Creeley has deepend his share—well, I include a selection of poems—

But now I am concerned with my own bad conscience. I've to write off today to Seymour Krim against any possibility that that article might be published by *Evergreen*. You see, he was concernd about its finally being rejected by the publisher (and rightly, the publisher wanted an all "beat" anthology) and further concernd, as I was, that it be printed and read. And I suggested that *Evergreen* would be interested, not without being aware of exactly the ugly why.

Would you give the article to Crehan to read to see if he is interested?

---

But . . . still remains more about your "one must settle to love him for his work and draw a charitable curtain over other aspects of him"—I just don't believe such curtains are charitable. I'm going thru the torment of a love right now in reading Pound's *Thrones* and there *is* no charitable curtain one can draw "for his work" that wouldn't be a curtain against his work. Everything you know about Bob is there imprinted in the work you are to love him for—there are, after all, poems that are "Letters to Enslin" reveald. There are in the new book:[2] "Please" (for James Broughton), "A Wicker

Basket," or "A Folk Song"—where the distance from me renders the speech exotic; and there's "Heroes," "The Flower," "For the New Year," "The Hero," or "The Hill" which are so true to my heart I know not whether I read or write them.

—off we must go: the white cats Sybil and Tom Bombadill have to have shots, and this must get into today's mail. With some Creeley poems on reverso.

love,
Robert

Have written to Bob & had a letter back already. One of the issues was his enthusiasm for *Yugen* & I have written notes on *Yugen* 5 to explain exactly why I don't like it, poem by poem, as much for my clarification as to prove my point to him.

Dear Robert and Jess,

I sent that article over to Hubert Crehan with a covering letter.
Haven't heard from him yet.
However, in the meantime (I feel a fool but must confess it) I think I was wrong about him—heard him give a radio talk on the new BAI stations (just taken over by KPFA) which I afterwards found in print in the December *Art News*, which I think you'll agree is the most complete junk, & pompous into the bargain.[1] He had attached some introductory paragraphs, not in *Art News*, which were better than the rest, much better. Also I have learned some things about him personally which I dont like to put on paper because it seems like retailing gossip, but which are vouched for by someone who is not a gossip, & which are just the opposite of "on the level." We now have weekly Rexroth in N.Y. (on BAI) & so far have found him dreadfully self-important & boring.

But I suppose the magazine might be interesting anyway . . . ?

Jonathan came & took the Morgenstern, he said you had written to say he might borrow it—I hope this was right. I hadn't seen him except on the street for a long time—he's just the same. I've been cool to him ever since the *Letters* affair and because he delays so on Larry Eigner's book—but one can't really be mad at him when he's actually there, there's something so comical about him.

Saw Bischoff's show & thought it was terrific, but Mitch didn't.[2] I wanted Al {Kresch} to see it very much, but he had a cold & couldn't make it. M. said the first impression was good but after 20 minutes the paintings seemed tricky, crude, etc. We didn't go to it together. Please tell me exact dates of

**154**

Sunday
{January} 23d {1960}
249 W. 15th St.
N.Y. 11

April visit—I'm going to try to get up to Wesleyan for the reading—Willis Barnstone will put me up. I spoke to Jim Spicer at Living Theater & he said he wd. write & invite you to read there. A supercilious young man, I thought. But I thought you might like to read there. And he asked to see *Faust Foutu*, which I took him next day.

Love—
Denny

## 155

Aha! who is he?

Dear Denise,[1]

Thank you for sending the Duncan mms. I remember the first essay he did on the subject which was in *Politics*. I am writing to him asking that he do a final version of the two draft versions you sent me. Thank you very much for sending it to me and I will wait for your poems too. Yes, and please call us. We'd like to see you both again. (Also I am requesting something from Jess, although I have not done so yet.) I'm glad you heard the radio talk. Naturally I am against the Manichaean strain in Still's art and I believe if you could read the essay in *Art News*, Dec. '59 this will come thru much easier than in the talk.

Sincerely,
{signed} Hub
Hubert Crehan

Well, here I go. Maybe I mistook him again? I am at sea.

One thing is sure, he can't spell. And another, apparently he can't read (vide 2d sentence of his letter).

Mitch's mother had a stroke, is very very ill, we are spending most of our time at the hospital in Brooklyn.

Have had a second, good, letter from Bob, & am glad you impelled me into frankness. Here's a poem or two.

Your poem "The Law" broke slowly upon me but more impressively for that. It has no colored surface to immediately attract—one must get to know it in time, like a sober looking person of inner virtue & radiance.

Love—
Denny

The trip to the hospital takes 1½ hrs and riding back & forth these last three days I've read (after many years) *The Mayor of Casterbridge*. I have never asked you I think if you share my love for Hardy.

dear Denny,

"Naturally I am against the Manichaean strain in Still's art . . . " which remark of Crehan's I've to adjust to my sense before I go on. Still is ikono-klastic [which may have its origins in the Jewish and then Moslem war against the images.] It would seem a long shot to make him Manichaean—maybe the violent statements of black and white? But certainly one of the first knowledges from his painting is that he is personally hostile and paints against the history of painting (and more distressing, paints against previous beauties in the art). Yet I can bear witness from a canvas I saw in London that here too a man in his ardor or fury can achieve beauty—where the personal elements of the ikonoklasm are transmuted into a composed spiritual fact. As a man, Still seems to do everything to prevent one's arriving at this state of rapt satisfaction—of being "charmed," and from what Jess says of him I gather he would himself hate this state, this end as charm or composed contemplation. & wants his painting to be acts in themselves.

It was a show of Still's painting here in 1950 that lead me to stay in San Francisco instead of going to Europe, and to search out the new painters where I found Jess.[1] It was not to be until five years later that I ever saw a canvas of Still's as an instance of the beautiful [and these in painting are rare enuf], but what was clear then was that this was authentic, a *command* within the spiritual history of art that involved more than painting—as uncharming, as hideous in strength as revolt is; it had or I gave it authority. Not to be like it, but to take my place in a world where such painting must be a definition of the real.

Withal I no longer think of that iconoclastic expressionism as the crux of the matter these days. All we have left here are modish derivatives, and the betrayal of the original impetus is the more striking in that the direction had been angry and all but stultified in its opposition to mode. There might be an irony in the fact that striking against the Beautiful—an artist is in danger of securing the chic. Even where his art is beautiful, Still's work is grandiose, megalomaniac: he is incapable of the intimate. And the force of his egotism makes it impossible for me to think of him as heroic. Heroism for me has something to do with the engagement with and for the Beautiful.

It's why, too, you would have liked Kandinsky. Well, he never was an ikonoklast in the above sense: he turnd to a world of inner forms and pythagorean visions. Where the expressionists of action are style-bound, Kandinsky happily paints as he wants to [so that a painter like Paul Klee relates to an area within the total range of Kandinsky]—he could be sublime, but then in late canvases that I most love he could paint like Hugh Lofting's moon writing.[2]

Kandinsky is Platonic, serving the imagination of forms; where the directive in the new American painting was the sheer act (for all of dwawdling around about Zen etc.), to achieve an autonomy of "power"—a parallel to power politics, breaking out in act. [and isn't it this *push* that is the center of the Ginsberg, Corso, Kerouac team?]

———————

You seem to have a day to day battle of pros and cons. Well, when my mind turns to it I am in such a battle myself. How out of place "Kore" looks in *Big Table* / tho *Big Table* is not a new thing to happen in the avant garde— William Carlos Williams's *Contact* in the 30s was entirely given over to a programmatic sensationalism and predicted the necessity for violence in and of itself.

"The unchristian sweep of Shakespeare." W. C. W. writes—"the cantless, unsectarian bitterness of Dante against his time"

and cummings in the first issue sarcastic calld for "you know something genuine like a matik in a toilet."

W. C. W. said "Nothing is beyond poetry" but in the same note warns that: "every school which seeks to seclude itself and build up a glamour of scholarship or whatever it may be, a mist, that is. . . . "

But let these reports pass on like gusts. Today we are in the middle of a storm uneven in its impact—over days—there's no rain outdoors now, only a cloud into which the slopes of Mount Tamalpais disappear just above the town. And the wind still tosses the garden. Later there will be fierce driving rain again.

And I've cleard my mind by turning to your poems. That most lift my mood when I am sure you cannot do what you are doing—the old man and his dogs, the awkwardness promised by the word "dis-proportionate" that leads to "imploring" and "arcane," disturbances of the sensory image (what are these words doing? a reader with imagist doctrine in hand asks?) Nature leading to the "liturgical red" of the lights changing.[3]

➜ I've to write off to Seymour Krim and direct him to get the ms to Crehan. It would be a good bit of money, if the article made the first issue.

And I'm enclosing a poem that could stand on its own as a whole / but which I hope to loop out into a sequence on.[4] I just wrote it two days ago so I am still nervous about *what* it is, walking around its area with the vague feeling of what it calls for—

love
Robert

dear Denny,

A reading seems to be shaping up at the Living Theater. I've had no word from Ellie Dorfman at Grove Press, but then she took over only a couple of weeks ago. The official letter from Yale came. I'm sure to read there the evening of the 20th and I'll be staying with the Pearsons.

Rains have brought almost more immediate concerns—both the excitements that came at the beginning of this week with high seas and storm winds conjoining at a morning high tide to wreck houses along the shore and pour down the roads from the beach; and for us, the new excitement of mushroom hunting along the slopes of Tamalpais and then, a beautiful walk, more plentiful and various crops—in oak groves about a mile from where we live, where cow pastures run under oaks. The garden demands weeding and a sunny day like today accuses of a hundred chores to do.

Jess's new book is out, and we are sending off in this mail copies of *O!*, *Faust Foutu* and Jack Spicer's *Billy the Kid*.[1] I had a hectic day yesterday; the manuscript for *The Opening of the Field* arrived *here* from Macmillan which I had instructed them in December to forward to Grove Press. Aie! and with Jess's help I enterd all the proof corrections on the ms itself, and retyped pages that were too confusing.

That article "The Homosexual in Society" I learnd by telegram yesterday had been taken by *Evergreen*. I wrote Krim asking that if it could be done diplomatically the article be available for Crehan.

Jess asks me particularly to tell you he is writing to Jonathan Williams to return the Morgenstern to your keeping. I have the feeling that he is using the Morgenstern as an entré where he (Williams) hopes to get backing. And certainly that he is not likely to be trying to find another publisher for the book.

Did I write and ask you about any possibility of my making a Canadian reading while I am East? I have a Canadian postal-order to cash among other interests.

love,
Robert

157

February 13, 1960
{Stinson Beach}

Dear Robert & Jess

The books came this morning—thanks so much—Jerry had already given me a copy of *O* (it looks just fine) but Mitch's mother died last week & so with the sorrow & the funeral & Mitch's father staying with us for a few nights, & all sorts of relatives (many of whom neglected & failed to appreciate her in her lifetime because they had more money than she did)

158

Wed. 23d Feb. {19}60
249 W 15th
NY 11

calling up & even paying condolence visits, I had no time. And since the funeral Mitch has been sick with some virus—not seriously but enough to need to stay in bed—he was run down with all the subway rides & long hours at the hospital and the emotional strain too. Indeed I feel worn out too, especially when I think of the long prospect of loneliness for the old man which means many dreary visits to Brooklyn for us—a selfish reaction I know but I've been so nice to everyone for the last sad month & now I'm reacting. I can act well in crises but I lack the patience for long-run goodness, alas. I think it's one of my worst faults.

Did I tell you how much we liked "The Directive"?

I have a new poem called provisionally "The Muse" which I'll send as soon as I can copy it.

Did I ever send you the one called "A Map of the Western Part of the County of Essex in England"? It will be in the next *Poetry* I guess, I just got the proof.[1]

Jim Spicer at Living Theater has not called me or sent back the *Faust F.* copies I gave him. M. C. tells me you are sending him the *Medea* too? I hope something works out there.

Someone at BAI is starting a Poetry program & asked me for suggestions so I of course said, be sure & get Duncan when he comes. (I'm sure they dont pay, it is the same as KPFA, but as it is non-profit I presume you'd like to do it anyway?)

Had a letter from Pasternak, that was a big thing for me. Short but tremendously *present*, a speaking letter.

Had some v. v. good poems from Bob, & a couple of good letters.

Cecil Hemley's partner, one of those people to whom I must have been formally introduced at least 5 times & still don't know his name, informed me he was at Berkeley with you & the Tylers. (And spoke with enthusiasm of you & of them)

I've been invited to read at Princeton March 7th & will take the opportunity of suggesting they ask you in April—O.K.? They are paying me $75 & train-fare.

Enclosed ad. looks so much like Jess's work—isn't it lovely? I must find out who did it. Wanted to go, but couldn't of course.

Jonathan is returning the bk. to me this week. Jess, please forgive me if I did wrong in letting him have it—he gave me to understand you had definitely given permission.

I have to go out on an errand now. I feel so glad you (Robert) are coming here soon for I think my letters have been getting more & more rushed & unsatisfactory, & I wish Jess were coming too—so much; but I suppose that wont be possible?

Wish I cd offer to have you stay but the way things are here now makes it impossible—we managed with my father in law but it was uncomfortable & there's no privacy. Will you stay at the Rothenbergs?

Love from<br>Denny.

P.S.

Cd. I get *J* and *Foot*? Will send subs. if you'd let me know how much (if not too expensive). Have never seen either. Are they good?

dear Mitch and Denny,

# 159

February 24, 1960
{Stinson Beach}

Jerome wrote us in his last letter that Mitch's mother died. While we would share as concern of friends does in the event, we know nothing of what the event is or will be for Mitch (as, indeed, I do not know what will be involved for me in my mother's death for there is a violent area between the mother of childhood so ardently loved and the mother of adolescence who was desired with paroxysms of aversion, and hated: and they must be powers of the same ghost in feeling). I was taught reincarnation which I believe is the immortality the dead have in our hearts, that in our lives we re-member what we know of them [and those of us who live for the good, re-member what we love and come to believe that to be the wholeness, the real—what we would realize]. And I believe in the utter and material death of individuals, of *Robert Duncan* me: that gives us an utter and material *life*. In Jewish Kabbala and in Plato I find such a possibility as interpretation: that both immortality and mortality are true intuitions. As certainly heaven, purgatory and hell are everywhere about us.

For the rest, Mitch, we are glad that her death was not long pending.

Our own days are kept busy with unsettled and some unsettling negotiations. The book with Grove is up in the air. Last week I had my first word from them (and at Don Allen's suggestion I had submitted the book and its cover last December): no mention at all of the cover Jess did. Instead Richard Seaver askd my approval of a design by their designer and wrote further that contract and $200 awaited my approval which must be made within the week or the book would not be accepted in time for the Fall list! I wrote immediately that what was in question was not my acceptance of their cover design but their acceptance of the one Jess did. And that if they do not accept, would they return promptly manuscript and cover design.

The essay I have informed *Evergreen* was submitted to Crehan and accepted a full week before I heard anything of their wanting it, and two weeks before they actually requested it. Amen.

Today I had happier news from New York—The Living Theatre plans

a program of my reading + an act or two from *Faust Foutu* directed by
Cernovich. And will pay $100 fee. (May 2nd.) And *Chelsea* took five of
Jess's Morgenstern translations for their next issue.

love,
Robert

## 160

February 27/ 1960
{Stinson Beach}

dear Denny/

The cover Jess did for *The Opening of the Field* has become its shield
against misuse. After two months, Seaver at Grove sent me "a cover sketch
from our artist which we feel is indeed a delightful one, retaining the
elements and atmosphere of your suggested design. . . . " (February 15)
[February 19] I replied: "So let me be clear here. The cover design by Jess
Collins is an integral part of my intention, subject to such specific alterations
as information (price of book, publisher, etc.) require. If, reviewing that
cover, you cannot agree on it (and I take it, if you have had your own artist
make a substitute in "style," you have reached some such conclusion), would
you return to me the cover design and the manuscript of the book which
you must have by now? I am not so concernd with *when* the book appears as
with *how* it appears."

(February 23rd) I explicated further:

For you the cover of a book—even when it is as closely allied as the cover
of a paper book is (as distinguishd from the jacket on a hardback) to be
integral to the whole—is a question of attractive packaging of a commod-
ity. I have had occasion before and shall always have to attack at its roots
what art becomes when it becomes a commodity. Today, painting has all
but become slave to the designs of a market where Picassos DeKoonings or
The New York School are analogous as conspicuous expenditure to Jaguars,
and whatever fancy cars. Style must be like the signature on a check,
unique but dependably recognizable = cash value. Now, while in the late
forties and early fifties I had direct relation to what is rightly calld "action"
painting, it was not then the commodity action painting, but a living
movement. And, more importantly, since 1952 I have in (my) own work
developd affinities with a view of the world that is —to use Whitehead's
word—"illustrated" by what we see. The structure of correspondence and
melody is not only poorly but falsely allied with the come-on derived from
the action strokes of so-calld nature expressionists. If you think over what
as a poet I come in *The Opening of the Field* to show nature to be, you may
reflect that there is an incapatibility between the content and the dominant
taste in Madison Avenue art. I do not live in New York, I live in a little
town on the Pacific coast; my household is not modern; it thrives, as the
imagination thrives, upon images. So I had designd a cover in a mode

close to my own work, where words and scene, image and experience have something like the exchange I seek in my own medium.

But this is like those controversies where we always remember later what should have been said—for what I don't say and what is the issue is clear in Seaver's decisive letter (February 23): between a design that has an artist's responsibility (Jess's) and a design with the market-purpose in mind: i.e. to show the brand of the goods.

Seaver writes:

"It was our understanding that you would submit a *suggested* design which we would then work with, attempting to incorporate the spirit and at the same time not betray the type of cover design of the *Evergreen* line. I personally think our artist made a valiant effort."

. . . "I must say in all sincerity that the design you did submit, while it contains some nice elements, would not really enhance or do justice to your book."

In some sense the contents of the book could be "the type of the *Evergreen* line." The eye that sees is more immediate to what it likes (is like) than the eye that reads.

*The Opening of the Field may yet* have to be an Enkidu Surrogate. Tho the length of the book would make that a formidable task.

News also comes that The Living Theater will present a reading along with "a performance of one or two acts of your play" (*Faust?*) May 2nd

love,
Robert

[for which, two performances guarantees $100 fee{]}

dear Denny,

I've been dating letters the 27th for a week. In the "waiting" period already for the trip a month away. The Grove business kaputt, I will have the added hope again to find a publisher for *The Field*. There's a gnawing regret along with anger (for Grove adroitly waited until it was "too late" to negotiate at all) at the fact that the book will not be published this year: and at the state of publishing where the commodity, mass-produced and consumed, has so won over the work. Part of what the "public" poetry of Corso or Ferlinghetti, of Whalen and Ginsberg is that it is produced, not made: it must have currency. As in turn "action" painting must—in order to be a commodious style—exist on a level where it can be turnd out, as automobiles are turnd out. It must exclude "inspiration"—since that cannot be turned on like a machine; and must entirely exclude imagination, since here qualities or spirit show.

161

February 27/ 1960
{Stinson Beach}

re. Princeton, if you'd send me the name of whoever schedules readings there—I'll write myself—or if you write to them the point is I'll be available between April 15th and May 18th with the exception of, at this point: April 20th (Yale), April 24th (Wesleyan) [while I will be at Wesleyan the following week, the program in The College of Letters seems to be fluid enough for me to accept an outside reading that week following April 24] and May 2nd (Living Theater). Anyway, I go for $75 plus fare from New York.

Yes, Ill be staying with the Rothenbergs when I am in the city. They write they have an actual guest room and I am much relieved to have something that substantial—the prospect of a day-bed made up or an extra cot in the kitchen etc., the usual Manhattan possibility, begins to get grim.

*J* and *Foot* are being sent straight off under separate cover. I couldn't re-member if I had sent you *Foot* or the first copies of *J* etc. and about a month ago I acquired the last set of complete *J* in order to bring it with me when I come East in case you had never seen it. So . . . you'll have it ahead of time.

love
Robert

## 162

{February 1960
Stinson Beach}

Dear Denny,[1]

I'm under the obscure and lovely imperative once more—a musical composition, contrasted and interlinkd movements, with themes beginning to emerge; and so I must send off these sections as they come. As here I must read them to Jess, and then in the morning read thru again to feel the first section with the second. I got out from our town library two books of Frank Lloyd Wright but found nothing there as haunting as whatever this *house* is—glimpses maybe in the Unity Temple. But in the poem "temple" referrd to Pound's "The Temple is not for sale." And what I can't work in yet is the need heightend because threatend everywhere by the pious snigger of chambermaids, and the (envious?) (uncomprehending?) giggle of school boys. That the genius of Aristophanes is subverted by the appreciation of the insincere. Rootless titters. Eternal sophistications.

love,
Robert

## 163

March 8, 1960
{Stinson Beach}

dear Denny,

I'm sending the whole of "Apprehensions" to date (three movements out of five are done) because where I have reworkd the poems [as see elimination of the Friedländer reference—because, for one thing it wasn't a *source* book as I thought it was going to be; at adjustment of 2 part one at the end to admit verb *direct*.{]}}

While you have been snowd in, we've had a steady rain. And today all is clear, with the breath of plant life freshening the air. And I'm at the end of a cold—having spent the rainy days in bed with all three cats on top of me and the unilluminating life of James Joyce to absorb my attention. Ellmann's mind is consistently dreary, one follows his fascination which is also a distaste for the artist's life where he can only see what a pedant of modern letters can see.[1] There was one flash from Joyce when he defines a lyric as the "simple liberation of a rhythm." But Ellmann pays no attention, such trivia are incidental to the false biography which allows Ellmann to have his superior sense of the character of Joyce. So that when Pound and Harriet Weaver become convinced or rather recognize the virtues of Joyce's work, Ellmann writes:

> Discovered and coddled by Pound, mothered by Miss Weaver, he managed not only to finish *A Portrait of the Artist* but also to begin to write *Exiles* and *Ulysses*.

Well, I should perhaps have resisted the loan of the book, but I hoped to gather more threads of the weaving in *Finnegan* and then, "knowing all about Joyce" etc. had its appeal. Hence, I suppose, my superior sense of Ellmann's character when he feeds that appetite.

Put away my talk, left over from those indulgent days—and it's the poem I meant to send

love
Robert

dear Denny & Mitch/

A short note, to accompany the enclosed 4th movement of "Apprehensions," and another occasional poem. I've got my train tickets—I had been going to go by cheap flight but my Denver reading made that impossible—so I'm off by train. Leaving here March 31st—and the last lap from Chicago to New York April 9th to arrive the morning of the 10th at Penn Station I take it. Last Monday I got a letter from Grove, after return of manuscript and all, offering a compromise which I accepted. Jess's original cover drawing will be used as frontispiece; and on the paperback edition Grove can do as they want with the cover. At least Jess's drawing will be there intact—and as sent back with the manuscript to Grove the drawing is much improved for not carrying price etc.

We are having a week, and now it looks like more of weather in the 70s—blaring winter days that bring thousands of cars to our beach, but

## 164

March 19, 1960
{Stinson Beach}

they are garden days for us—and yesterday with Ebbe Borregaard, Joy Atkin and Helen Adam we climbd up the ridge to the forests above.

First roses and poppies, lilac and fuschia are in bloom. Gael Turnbull expected next weekend, and Tuesday we're to see Wendell and Tanya Berry— last minute (or weeks etc.) up-turn of business

love
Robert

---

**165**

March 24th {1960}
249 W 15th
{New York}

Dearest Robert

I am so happy at the thought of your soon being here. Just a short note now—thanks for *J.* and *Foot*—& for poem—your rabbit is in my mind, "large as the cows"—have not absorbed the relations of the parts (of "Apprehensions") to each other yet—but feel elated by the "cire perdue."

Good wishes for your journey & readings. I just had 2 rather heart-warming readings, at Princeton & N.Y.U.—I feel there really are a lot of people who do *care* for poetry. By the way I want to explain about NYU & you—Robert Bly wanted to ask you to read but long ago he had asked Roethke and Cummings & suddenly both accepted for this spring & since they have to be paid much more than the usual allotment he is now stuck. (These readings are paid for by the Adult Ed. Dept.—the English Dept apparently does absolutely *nothing.*)

I have to go to Cambridge a few days after you get here but will only be gone 4 days. Please let me know time of yr. arrival as I wd. like to come to the station. Do you remember meeting us at the Greyhound in SF, and the bottom fell out of the basket you took from my hands & the contents were strewn all over? And then M. lost the typewriter & found it again. . . .

Love—
Denny.

PS

Rago gave me *"A" 1–12* for review. I feel my temerity—. Am working on it.

---

**166**

March 27 {19}60
{Stinson Beach}

dear Denny,

At the last minute—I am fighting a cold. That has me awake staring at the room emerging in the morning light—where sounds, a rooster, cats up and about, the sea, Jess's deep breath of morning sleeping—are right at the threshold of the ear. As if later there was so much noise to being awake, one hears nothing. And how my pen scratching sounds thunderous. I began to think of writing you, about you not yet absorbing the relations of part to part in "Apprehensions" and about the poem. I've finished two out of three poems plannd to form the fifth movement: to make a close. Since the first movement there's been the probability [so that the impulse that shows in the Qumrân reference will be fulfilld in the sequence] of closing with a hymn of thanks or adoration (The hymn of the initiants in the Dead Sea Scrolls opens with an evocation and day, and then too in reading those actual fragments I am sending for a hymn that is not there.{)}

This morning I thought that the close—including it's being that hymn that is not there—will be as simple a thing as waking in the morning. So that the musical structure of contrasting movements can be reconstructed on the imitative level of falling asleep, dream, waking recollection, and waking.

But what I wanted to say about the relations of parts in sequence is that they spring into life along a line of my feeling of the right [mood model and weight], fitted by their changes and echoes. Not "unconscious" workings— I recognize as soon as they occur repeated structures (I'm thinking here of "O flames O reservoirs" that restates with a new aspect of meaning "cave of resemblances, cave of rimes" and appears again in "cards of coming, cards of going") and let them occur and even become a refrain. And the sequences of sections were plannd, with my memory of Boulez's setting of René Char's "Marteau sans Maître" as a model.[1] Ida Hodes gave me Shapiro's attack on Eliot to read—and it led I think to the Eliotean mode of the two poems of the 5th movement so far.[2]—Now Jess is up, the curtains pulld back at the western window where there are clusters of single roses. There is a light steady rain. I hadn't heard it, and can't now. The sea takes over.

Turnbull came up for the weekend. To find me with this cold—tho I got up yesterday. And now rain. It must have just started because there's the sound of it from the eaves that wasn't there before.

I was reading last night from Mead's collection of Hermetic fragments, Stobaeus "Of the Decans and the Stars": "And under [the Decans] is what is calld the Bear—just in the middle of the Circle of Animals, composed of seven stars, and with another corresponding [Bear] above its head"[3] and woke up just before dawn from a dream about polar bears (as now writing I am kept company by a polar-bear white cat) that [*the* polar bear] may have been fateful as a star but (faithful as a pet) he would go too far in play and tear open a vein or artery with his claws—(an artery, at the neck, because the blood spurted out) and I become too slippery with blood . . . so the dream explanation was that the polar bear dreaded this moment because he became blinded by the spirits of the man's blood.

The train I'm to arrive on leaves Chicago at 3:15pm April 9th train #48* and gets into Penn station the following morning. But I don't have the arrival time.

Love
Robert

*car # 3

---

**167**

Dear Jess,

Just a greeting—hoping you will not be feeling too lonesome in Robert's absence. I expect (& maybe Mitch & Nik too) to meet him at the station a week from today, & the Rothenbergs will be there too.

I wish you were coming also. The Monet show now at the Museum of Md. Art[1] is so breathtaking & you wd. be of all people perhaps the one to enjoy it the most—Is there a chance you may come for a part of Robert's stay?

I have a few poems I think I've not sent—will try to get them copied out soon.

Nik has been making a grand tournament picture while I read *Ivanhoe* aloud this wet Sunday afternoon.

Love from
Denny.

---

**168**

dear Denny,

A letter to you, and then I want to write another to Mitch about the novel—which *does* remain vivid in the mind, something that memory has to make use of—before I set myself down to the first part of my study toward the H. D. Book: a "review" of the *Madrigal* novel.[1] I found in the really quite wonderful three volume life of Lawrence,[2] the one Seon {Givens} referrd to that had been composed of testimony from his own letters and from the memoirs of his friends—of those who had known him, found an account of the charade that is one of the key scenes of the "novel." Lawrence's own poems from the war period, poems like "Two Wives" with its:

> "Take what you've got, your memory of words
>   Between you, but his touch you never knew."

and

> "Stand a way off, and if you like commune
>   with his wan spirit somewhere in the air
>       Like a lost tune."
> "But do not touch him, for he hated you
>   to touch him, and he said so, and you knew."

Tho in the poem, it is more important that the "two" wives are one. "She Said As Well To Me" "Don't touch me and appreciate me."—but that's surely to Frieda. But the thing here, and in the H. D. novel is keeping the lovely intuition—which for her is a *fever*, and for Lawrence is a corruption

"it is the scent of the fiery-cold dregs of corruption"

that must in part have been his actual disease—the tuberculosis fiery-cold that he bred in himself.—but it's not to puzzle out my sense of it here. Except, as always, that I "correspond" for a while of the morning with you. Send news—of a houseful of kittens, but they are asleep now in a ball of four—three white and one black black; of the work Jess had done in the garden lettuces, cucumbers, squash and artichokes laid out in orders; and marigolds and bachelors buttons. Or that it is blazing this week, not here so much for we've the sea and breezes, but it was 94° in San Francisco yesterday, the hottest ever the newspapers say.

Don Allen wrote asking for "Apprehensions" for *Evergreen*, which I will send as soon as I have a release from Rago at *Poetry*. And there was a warm letter from H. D. today, saying she had seen you again.

I'm enclosing a copy of the Blake Variations—I've sent to Rago with hopes he may use them in place of "The Directive."[3]

love<br>Robert

Dear Robert & Jess

It is quite primitive here—dirt road (dead end) river for washing, fishing, laundry, drinking, etc., 2 rooms 1 of which is kitchen & bedroom for Nik & his friend Michael, the other our bedroom & diningroom—there's an outhouse, lots of devils-paintbrushes & (unripe) strawberries & blackberries in blossom (so beloved by Machado) and quite thick woods all around (though 50 years ago it was all farmland).

Yes I saw H. D. again—she called & invited me to tea & I enjoyed it very much. And she sent me the novel (which she inscribed, under her name, with the words from my "Ring of Changes": "A room in a house in the city became . . . a Holy Apple Field." (I had given her my N.D. book.)[1] I read the novel all in one evening & part of the next day which was wet (the boys having gone to the village 4 miles away) and found it beautiful & an experience in which I became completely absorbed. I have not felt so *permeated* by a book since I read *Dr. Zhivago*. (By the way I never talked about Pasternak with you but I had a very strong feeling for him & sent him my book as a way of making contact, and in his reply he said, "I feel that we shall be friends," so that his death was to me a personal grief & is I suppose

## 169

June 19th 1960
Red Camp
Temple, Maine.

one of the reasons why I've been feeling so strained & nervous of late—tho'
of course I had been overtired for weeks somehow.)

That was a good letter you sent to Mitch, Robert—he'll be writing to
you. Ted Enslin who has this old abandoned farmhouse about ½ mile up a
turnoff just below here, met us when he got here but had to go down to the
Cape next day & hasn't got back yet, so Mitch has had the use of his house
all to himself to work, away from the noise the boys make.

I have not written anything (except some notes for an article I have to
do for something, will tell you more about it when it has crystallized a bit
more) since you left—I think the enclosed poem was written while you were
still in N.Y., maybe a few days after. You will recognize the animals I guess.

In 10 days Nik goes to camp & we go down to N.Y.—on the 5th July I
go to Mexico & Mitch will return here.

I had a most peculiar phone call from Zukofsky the day before we left—I
really do not like him at all, or respect him, as a man—even tho I admire
some of his work sincerely. It appears he *really* was piqued because my review
was not a eulogy—& instead of saying so plainly it took him half an hour of
some of the most invidious (is that the word? or do I mean insidious—or
both?—anyway, unpleasant & devious) carrying-on to more or less admit it.[2]
His pretext for calling was that in my note (which I sent him purely as a
courtesy—as I had previously sent the T.S. of the review—to tell him Rago
was not going to cut any of the quotations) I had said—also purely out of my
damned English politeness, since he had seemed to invite further discussion
(perhaps you remember his note)—something about maybe I cd. come to see
him in the fall, & have him explain some of the points (such as the relation
of the Whitman poem to his essay) so obvious to him & so unclear to me.
*His* point was that he thought I shd. have thoroughly discussed the book
with him before writing the review!—which to me wd. be a loathesomely
immoral thing to do. But he kept saying, "It's not that I want disciples sitting
at my feet, but. . . . " Wow! Evidently that is what he *does* want. It was a
horrid conversation, & I ended up saying, "Well, I'm sorry, I just don't have
time to talk any more" (which was true, I was surrounded by packing) &
putting the phone down. Well—I really have not thought of it since, but it
came back to me as I started to tell you.

I just read *The Legacy* by Sybille Bedford, a remarkably good novel—
tho probably not your cup of tea particularly—& am just reading *The
Magician of Lublin* by Isaac Bashevis Singer which if it keeps up as well as
the ¼ I've read is a masterpiece & which you *would* like.[3]

Am still working though the Maritain *Creative Intuition in Art & Poetry*
in which I find a great deal that interests me very much (as well as a good
deal that seems way off or wrong)—wd. like to know what you think of it.[4]

There are some of the most beautiful large green & small spotted frogs around here that we've ever seen.

Love from
Denny.

P.S.

S.F. was too far—so I couldn't get Helen Adam for those Y. readings, alas. Hope you didn't by chance mention it to her—if you did I will write & explain. I haven't heard yet about Ed in Santa Fe—I think they may stretch to that.

D.

Did Jess like the scarab?


dear Denny & Mitch,

I had worried about the letter to Mitch about the novel. For tho I dislike the whole tangle of identification with judgment of one's work that young writers often have—you know, so that criticism of a poem becomes tangled up with personal criticism—I know too that the only thing wrong in the beginning writer's taking that stance is his having so much to learn before anything of his inner spirit really is there. And in talking about Mitch's novel I felt as I do when brought to think about my own work, that something is askd of the inner spirit wherever something is wanted in the work. Had I said clearly enuf what it means to me that the shape of the work— its sequence and as a *rite de passage*, as an initiation of the soul into a knowledge of the world (and then, for me reading, a vicarious initiation— for the experience of the apocalyptic orchard of the second part, and the revelation of the last scene becomes part of what I know being some preparation/seed/for feeling)—that the *feel* of the novel remains, had its passional depth then? So much of what I had to say seemd in retrospect asking for more or other. Well, that part was right—for it takes or can take so many works to establish the full statement. No, I mean a statement full enuf to carry the burden of ones nature—*the* full statement seems to me most and rightly unknowable and unfeelable.

Working on the H. D. book—but I have no more than sketchy paragraphs —I am overwhelmd at what is involved in mastering prose—in managing anything natural and direct. I am so unprepared there that I become confused by the complex activities (the ones I am used to working with in writing a poem) of a single sentence. It's a matter of establishing a new rhythm—one that will carry thru and allow for more sweeping composition.[1]

## 170

June 22, 1960
{Stinson Beach}

## 171

Dear Robert and Jess,

I found my mother reading *Frederick the 2d* by Ernst Kantorowitz—what a fascinating book. Her garden is flourishing and it is agreeable to be back in Oaxaca & see the Abascal family again & Casimura who was my maid then & loves me dearly (& I her) and the hills where the wind is always blowing and miniscule wildflowers abound.

Jerry & Diane {Rothenberg} got here for a week yesterday—no, the day before—I am enjoying seeing them & playing Cicerone.

Jess, thank you so much for asking what *Dolittle* & *Oz* books Nik has—I can't answer until the fall as I don't remember offhand. I think he is having a good time on his island—it's a small camp & seemed ideal when we deposited him there on June 28th. Mitch after having to spend an unintended week in N.Y. (after seeing me off) for various tiresome reasons, was pretty frazzled when he got back to Temple & for the first few days was lonely but now seems to be enjoying the quiet & solitude as I had hoped he would. I will get back there by about the 4th of August.

Enclosed are a few poems. The Mexican ones are very slight. They came all in a rush in the first days—more out of the 12-hour bus ride from Mex. to Oax. than from Oaxaca itself. I hope I'll be able to do some more while I'm here but so far I haven't, since those.

Am reading Meredith (*The Ordeal of Richard Feverel*) for the 1st time.

Wd. love to hear from you before I leave here (July 30th) if it's possible.* Have you new poems? Or is the H.D. book taking up all your being at present?

Love—
Denny.

*Counting up, I see it is really—so soon—so write to Temple, Maine when you can.

"Cups, Wands, and Swords"

Love from
Denny.[1]

## 172

Dear Robert and Jess

It was wonderful to come back here. I enjoyed visiting my mother, and Mexico, very much. But I was longing to have a couple of weeks alone with Mitch in this beautiful place while Nik was still in camp. (We are going to get him tomorrow. He's had a v. good time. And he's going to like this house, I know.) We have moved out of Red Camp into a larger house (with views) which we would very much like to buy. Keep your fingers crossed, and hope, please, that some day you'll come to visit us here. We are trying to arrive at a possible price—I'll let you know at once if it works out. If it does, we would come to live here year round when Nik graduates from City & Country in 3 years.

Here are a few poems.[1]

While I was in Oaxaca I reread the "2 Dicta: Variations" many times, pausing especially on the wonderful lines:

> where we have lookt up
>     each from his being

which I think may lead to a poem of my own.[2]

Mitch is reading Flaubert's *Letters* aloud to me—we had never realized how steeped in Romanticism he was—I would have said just the opposite— He is still only 25 in the letters we've got to, and sounds like an old man. A very strange character. I know only *Mme. B.* & the *3 Contes*—of which "Un Coeur Simple" has everything to make it moving & yet doesn't, finally, move one—how tragic that such devotion should not have *quite* made it. (I read half of *Bouvart & Pecuchet* when I was still a child & really couldn't figure it out.)

Also we are reading Whitman's *Specimen Days*, and I'm reading Evelyn Underhill's *Practical Mysticism*—she shares a style with Jane Harrison, in a way—I've read only a few chapters though.[3]

Am putting in a few sprigs of catnip for your cats.

Stayed a night at Dick & Ed's on my way up here (spent only 3 abhorrent hours in N.Y. between the plane & the bus). Saw Jess's beautiful painting there.

With love from
Denny

Got a card announcing Seon's {Seon Givens} baby.

---

dear Denny & Mitch

I started a letter, that now is somewhere is a stack of papers, interrupted, and then I got wound up about my sense that the first part of the Pasternak poem was not rendered clear [the adjectives and adverbs, especially the latter, accumulate] that was all, but I tried to say more: the second part is beautiful, and the germinal incident of the first.[1] We liked the Mexican poems—and Jess said that the Rose was, for him, *the* Rose poem.

It's not exactly been the H. D. book, but rather the steeping, cooking or just waiting on the book. I've not had the stone of your "Jacob's Ladder,"[2] and you're right that airy sensations ascending or descending [light-headed],

# 173

August 22, 1960
{Stinson Beach}

whatever angelic concepts, make one (this one, me) need the solid resisting thing. So, I've been in my own kind of a funk too.

There's a part or maybe two, fragments of a problematic sequence referring to fairy tales—but I'd messd up the first part and have had to discard it completely. And there is, since then a poem I like ["The Risk"]— tho I'm still unsure about relating the song itself to the statement that I felt I was trying to make all the way thru.[3] And couldn't for some other thing that had to be said, say it out. As simple as: I wanted the Tiffany bowl—that gold ewer—that I saw in Chicago. But $50 was too real, too much; more than the curve and the gleam were. To risk.

But was it that I didn't want to risk something else, involved, to be so involved with having the pride of the bowl?

As it is now, I've perhaps to take the cue from Lawrence and return to the thing I was trying to say until I find it.

I was transported with admiration when I read Flaubert—*The Temptation of St. Anthony* [which is translated by Lafcadio Hearn], *St. Julian* and *Salambo* (for its movie-splendor). But Flaubert's cruelty in *Bovary* almost stoppd me at the point of the operation on the foot.

My first reading of H. D.'s new novel[4] was counter-current to the work. Testing? no, something more pusillanimous: haunted by the idea of some "critical reader," seeing it in the eyes of that particular world that sees nothing, that balks at the very idea of sensitivity, much less at an ardent and exposed spirit. Randall Jarrell had written of "The Walls Do Not Fall" "H. D. is silly in the head"—or something as crude and brutal in spirit as that, some *Partisan Review* sneer (that a whole generation of mind has bent itself to now—the *P.R.-Time* magazine cant).[5] I read the book with some sneering antagonist daring me to defend it, as if I were to be a defense attorney.

But once home the book didn't have to be what it wasn't—and my second and third readings have been a rapture—well, there was from my first defensive reading (be careful not to estimate it too highly, don't get swept away) the gathering sense of what the book really was, the submerged realization that rose to the surface, to be acknowledged. So that what the book was "dawnd" on me, seepd up into view as the light does, morgenrot—exposed by reading to the developing picture. I gatherd first impulsively that it was about an affair with Lawrence, and was it true or not, was it a confession one should or should not have made. . . . but then, actually reading, wasn't it about the loss of the child and the loss of her husband, about adultery? What a rash gatherer I am, and yet the time does come when I stop muddying the pool with my feet, and suddenly notice that there is a clear necessary real flow of the stream. And may come yet to consider the *gloire*.

It's led me back too to re-read Lawrence's poems. Where I came upon poems (in volume I of the Heinemann complete poems),[6] as they always are at Lawrence's hand for me, so fresh and revealing—and I long when I read to be able to speak in a language as he does that reflects birdsong or flower's perfume. The music of the "Isar" poems is in sound what the perfume of flowers at night is—it wafts upon the air, lightly exciting the ear as in a garden not only smell but breath is excited.

I wanted to re-read his work thru the war years, along with her poems. Anyway, thinking of the "charade" or masque of the Garden that they enact in the novel (the very masque is described by the way in the composite biography of Lawrence), I found these two poems of Lawrence's:

D. H. Lawrence, *Poems* vol I, p. 232

PARADISE RE-ENTERED

Through the strait gate of passion,
Between the bickering fire
Where flames of fierce love tremble
On the body of fierce desire:

To the intoxication,
The mind, fused down like a bead,
Flees in its agitation
The flames' stiff speed:

At last to calm incandescence,
Burned clean by remorseless hate,
Now, at the day's renascence
We approach the gate.

Now, from the darkened spaces
Of fear, and of frightened faces,
Death, in our awed embraces
Approached and passed by;

We near the flame-burnt porches
Where the brands of the angels, like torches,
Whirl,—in these perilous marches
Pausing to sigh;

We look back on the withering roses,
The stars, in their sun-dimmed closes,
Where twas given us to repose us
Sure on our sanctity;

Beautiful, candid lovers,
Burnt out of our earthly covers,
We might have nestled like plovers
In the fields of eternity.

There, sure in sinless being,
All-seen, and then all-seeing,
In us life unto death agreeing,
We might have lain.

But we storm the angel-guarded
Gates of the long-discarded
Garden, which God has hoarded
Against our pain.

The Lord of Hosts and the Devil
Are left on Eternity's level
Field, and as victors we travel
To Eden home/

Back beyond good and evil
Return we. Eve dishevel
Your hair for the bliss-drenched revel
On our primal loam.

Where my sense of the realized beautiful thing is not satisfied in the whole. There's such a deliberate art in the innocence of the simplistic rhymes in passages—I begin to hear a daring music in rime of "closes" and "repose us" that would be most unstable were there not such a sure sense surrounding it. But the final quatrains fail at present to my ear "primal loam"—I am unsure. The second poem tho is now one of the immortal poems for me— and I send it as if it were from my own heart:

D. H. Lawrence, *Poems*, vol I, p. 254

ELYSIUM

I have found a place of loneliness
Lonelier than Lyonesse,
Lovelier than Paradise;

Full of sweet stillness
That no noise can transgress,
Never a lamp distress.

The full moon sank in state.
I saw her stand and wait
For her watchers to shut the gate.

Then I found myself in a wonderland
All of shadow and of bland
Silence hard to understand.

I waited therefore; then I knew
The presence of the flowers that grew
Noiseless, their wonder noiseless blew.

And flashing kingfishers that flew
In sightless beauty, and the few
Shadows the passing wild-beast threw.

And Eve approaching over the ground
Unheard and subtle, never a sound
To let me know that I was found.

Invisible the hands of Eve
Upon me travelling to reeve
Me from the matrix, to relieve

Me from the rest! Ah, terribly
Between the body of life and me
Her hands slid in and set me free.

Ah, with a fearful, strange detection
She found the source of my subjection
To the All, and severed the connection.

Delivered helpless and amazed
From the womb of the All, I am waiting, dazed
For memory to be erased.

Then I shall know the Elysium
That lies outside the monstrous womb
Of time from out of which I come.

love
Robert

dear Denny & Mitch,

This morning for letters after weeks of inertia. I've got, I think, the first chapter on the study of H. D. I have at least the voice, my voice, for the thing: after two months of trying to turn myself to the purposes of what is usually calld a "study." Poems go on as usual . . . and so, I've got another to include.

Jess is in the thick of preparing for his Dilexi show—that's to be in November, I think.[1] We aren't sure. He has just completed a master-piece in collage —a four x six foot figure from *The Sun* in the Tarot, swarming with sun and coupled twinned forms, and counterpointed by fire and water themes.

I think we interchange directives. I do know that this work, extending over weeks as it has, makes me more aware of my own fitting and interlinkings. He gets a flow of images by reoccurrences of number, element, kind or shape (i.e. twos, or water or angel or the continuum of line)—I forget color. And I can see how far craft in the sense of cunning can be brought to serve beauty [Loki—tho in the wreckage of the Gods he ride with the great Evils—be part-builder, in that there is craft at all].

It looks like the Grove book won't be out until October at least. The last proofs didn't clear until a week ago. New York summer doldrums and vacations tying the thing up.

Your prospect of a house up-country sounds wonderful. Our little beach town has just made an historic protest against State plans to open up our section of the coast for development with a super highway. There are, however, powerful investments in the open lands around us, farms bought up by the Bank of America—I do not know how long our seclusion here will last.

---

A letter from Jerry just came this morning with "Notes on the Poetry of Images" by Robert Kelly, that looks like the best thing in a long time on the poem.[2] What I find that verifies immediately is his insistence on the in-formation of the poem (he calls it "the mutual relevance of every percept to every other percept") and then his stress analysis on page 4—shows he is aware of four stresses (brings him in line with an ear for the music). Well, you will have seen the document. The earnestness, the radical drive, in pressing these notes towards his ultimate sense of what poetry is, his complete responsibility to the poem and his complete lack of concern for the critical juggling of the day—wins me to him.

love,
Robert

---

## 175

September 20th {1960}
249 W 15th
NY 11

Dear Robert and Jess—

Robert—"4 Songs the Nightnurse Sang" is so beautiful & gives me such depth of pleasure.[1] Thank you for sending it. (I should think H. D. would like to see it—did you send it to her?)

Jess—that was Catnip, for the Cats! I should have said! Anyway, here is some more, plucked at the last minute just as I was leaving Temple with Nik (M. stayed behind but will return on Friday).

Will tell you more about house in Temple in next letter. Also we may move from 15th to downtown Greenwich St (*not* Ave.!) What happened in the end about your studio? And I hope Stinson Beach wins out against the "developers."

Mike Rumaker is "out." Living near his doctor in Nannet, N.Y.—don't know how; but he is coming in to pick up some stuff we've held for him since he lived here that summer 2 yrs ago, so will find out. He sounds pretty good.

Nik has had his 1st French lesson & first typesetting lesson too.

Poems etc. in next letter—I've been cleaning, ironing, etc. since we got back & now there's this possible move which will mean a lot of work. . . . Some readings coming up also. Want to reply about Pasternak poem but can't just now.

Love—
Denny.

Dear Robert and Jess

We have *moved*!—To a wonderful big place from which we can see the ships on the Hudson and at night the fruit being unloaded in the Washington Market (which alas will only be there another 3 yrs or so). Still unpacking—so can't write now—& I expect you are busy with Jess's show—but I just wanted to let you know about the new address—also that I had a letter from N H Pearson & will be reading at Yale in Feb.—also that Cid turned up much mellowed, no advice etc., really a nice visit—tho poor man he has gotten much worse to look at. I've hurt my thumb, can't hold the pen properly. Wish you'd come & see this marvellous place—it's old with generous windows, hardwood floors, & our only neighbors are the Newtons[1] whom we love. (Sausage making in lower part of building.)

—Love—
Denny.

**176**

{October, November 1960}
277 Greenwich St.
N.Y. 7, N. Y.

dear Denny—

With you and Bob recognized for your work too, I almost feel as if that prize from *Poetry* means something solid.[1] Add Tomlinson's group, and at least it would seem that Rago recognizes that Dr. Williams's metric is something more than a personal eccentricity. That there might even be a creative mode in free verse. I've been reading *The New Freewoman* and *The Egoist*, finding out the environs where Pound, H. D., Marianne Moore, Williams first appear. And there it is—the word we hardly hear today "free"—free thot, free verse and even will—particularly free love. Free women and men. A practiced and responsible scorn for the standards of the day; a responsibility to dress as an individual and not in "style," to reject commodities and comforts and seek beauty and individuality, individuality, individuality. That was the secret and life of having an organic line—

**177**

Nov. 17 {19}60
{Stinson Beach}

because it did not conform, because it was in itself individual—a cadence that was felt as opposed to a metric that was fitted.

Well, I'm sending along with this a hunk of typescript. Not because a new book is in sight, but because I wanted to take stock of where I am since *The Field*—and I do have, now, having typed straight thru, another view of what I'm "free" to do. Or what I've to do to be "free."

I've reworkd "Risk" and, after a middle stage of wrestling with that poem, trying to bring forward the simple factor that is in my not spending $50 on a gold Tiffany bowl in Chicago and even more in the not acting there staying stuck in my mind [where *it is a beauty* had come up against *it is a bargain*, falling apart into *is it*? a *beauty*? a *bargain*? ], so that at one point when I tried to type out a copy of "Risk" to send Creeley I got lost in trying to amend the thing; at last I've got it clear, and then for the first time saw some of the personal "message" of that poem that made it so hard to work with. That "I did not buy the vase" was all tied up with the falling in love in the "Two Dicta" thing—that I didnt "buy"; and the tree (I *had* spotted, because I always pay attention to puns, the yew = you) was just the lasting love, even "at hell gate." Well, I didn't see that until I'd got the poem clear of the false leads. [The yew tree or rather trees had been offerd us for the price of having them transplanted: and what a time I had trying to get "I did not buy the tree" to work in the poem. It refused to ring true.]

Do you have H. D.'s 1925 *Collected Poems*—the one Liveright put out? In addition to what Pearson got into *Selected Poems*, "Pygmalion" is a permanent realization.

And both "The God" and "Eurydice" as well as "Adonis," which Pearson saves, are clearly related to the context of her Madrigal *Bid Me to Live*.

But working closely, over and over again, poem by poem—with these poems that I have *known* in some sense for over twenty years some of them —I am the more aware of how *hidden* the real life of a poem is. Or can be. I'm sure the sense of Vachel Lindsay's "Chinese Nightingale" doesn't ask, need or become the clearer for being taken this way. But the H. D. poems *do* come into a new life, if one searches out what was an impression and looks further for the life in it that gave the impress. On the peripheries it is still obscure for me. "Prisoners," for instance, baffles me. She writes to me not to pay too much attention to those old things. "It was a way of life," she wrote. And seems now to her makeshift. "Oh, the times," in the novel.

————————

There's some news. Jess's collage show opens at Dilexi Gallery on the 11th of December (you'll get an announcement), and he has been working day and night matting and mounting collages as well as creating new ones— there will be over fifty in the show. Ebbe Borregaard has started a "Museum" that will be showing a retrospect of Jess's paintings at the same time as the Dilexi show.[2]

We've a huge Thanksgiving company for this year—Robin Blaser and his friend Jim Felts, Pat and Helen Adam, Ida {Hodes}, and the Burtons. A crowded next month coming—the crowding, as always, a sluice-gate of socialities that leave, even me, a little fierce about having "my own time"— but that is likely to be claimd by idleness or garden industries—as to give way to fits of industry on that prose book.

Lunch time now, and this must get into today's mail or it will linger on top of a table, lost in a shuffle of papers where starts of letters finally months later get cleard away into the waste.

Has it been so long since I've written you? I know writing now it seems like a long postponed pleasure—maybe "weeding" has been taking the place of writing letters. And my troubles in conceiving this book on H. D. take the form of avoidance. The poems, since they take hold of me before I have to take hold of them, can't be avoided. It's the "assignment" of the book I think that gets me. And I return to a school-boy mode of anxiety before a term-paper. Tho the work, when I am at it—the close reading—is bliss.

love
Robert

dear Denny,

To send a new poem, writ this morning, to add to your book in progress. It sprang up from the announcement of a new magazine *Set*:[1]

> "I hope that you will be in sympathy with its idea," the editor writes me: "and will contribute something appropriate. Its name plays with "set" in the places of (1) jazz, wch most readers will probably think the primary sense, (2) direction or course, (3) form, (4) series, (5) stance, but also, underlying these, Set(ekh), who was, by the Chenoboskion gnostics, identified with the Biblical Seth, as well as Shem, Melchizedek, and Christ, and is otherwise identified with Typhon, Antichrist, and the planet Mercury, and related, through the sacred ass for example, to Saturn, Capricorn, Dionysos, and the constellation Orion."

and later, it might be an intelligent reflection on the course of *Evergreen*: {five words typed in} "College humor will be excluded." I've been waiting for some non-literary magazine to appear, for a vehicle of thought and spirit. And the very Set (because also it is so central to H. D.'s later work) Osiris thing brings into action everything I love. That figure of the boat, and the realization that Set is the prow—I owe to a book published by Grove calld *Myths and Symbols of Ancient Egypt*.[2]

Denny, I've had two readings of you in two days—first those "Meditations" in *Chelsea 8*—that come thru as fine as I can desire.[3] I wish they'd

**178**

November 22, 1960
{Stinson Beach}

been elsewhere; as I wish my Bergmann poem had been. I haven't read the Dorn poem yet.

What burns me is not only that we got swept into that mound of refuse—but that there was a prize! Fittingly—for it's writ in the predominant aesthetic—given over to that piece of gratuitous liberal guilt (gilt) of Mr. Wright's.[4] Aie! and I'd thot he had the possible commitment of a poet!

The other piece of yours is the Zukofsky review which I sat down yesterday and read thru in *Poetry* with even excitement. You are beautifully clear in registering the impression.

Robert

## 179

November 29,1960
{Stinson Beach}

dear Denny,

That "Risk"! how hard it seems it was for me to come down to cases there. This time it is not the wording (tho I did alter "simple" to "domestic" in "turning the mind from domestic pleasure," but what necessitated my redoing the whole three pages was just the annoying fact that I had phrased certain lines wrong—against my ear. I never did read it "not luck but the way it falls choose I for her, lets" etc. which would mean either an odd stress on "for" or a stress I didn't mean on "her." I was reading it from the first "choose for her" with the stress of the phrase on "choose"; and that terminal pitch heightening "falls" in the line before. And again: what did I think I was hearing when I divided "I had not the means" / "to buy the vase" or whatever—was it, worse! "I had not the means to buy" / "the vase" etc? Anyway, here I was going on like any hack academic of the automatic line breaking school . . . not listening to the cadence of the thing.

My cadence, my care, is changing perhaps too—and I was notating this from old habits contrary to the actual music.

Have you seen the new edition of Emily Dickinson's poems, restoring her punctuation?[1] So that we see she was nearer akin than we might have suspected. The dashes (are spaces) articulate the line. And what a lovely measure, what an immediate thing comes out! I'll copy some on the back of this sheet—[2]

love,<br>Robert

## 180

December 6th: {1960
Stinson Beach}

dear Denny,

Like the poor heroine of fairy tales who is set to separate seeds or spin gold from straw, or the hero Hercules, I've been trying to get some order about my attic workroom—and came across this now year old and more letter to you. After thots on your Imagination piece—that seem to just stop mid-air. But reading the letter over I thot the first pages are talking to you; and so I send it on.

I've done a piece right off on Eigner's work, and as soon as I type it up I'll send you a carbon. It's among duties for today—so it may even get done and off to you.

We had a great wind all night last night that whippd rose vines and bougainvillea about, shaking the house, and leaving today swept clean to the horizon. Fishing boats off shore seem enlarged. Perhaps my mind too . . . ?

Did I write that we have from our last litter, or rather Sybil's last litter of kittens, a new member of our household who looks exactly like Lear's C is for Cat? Dubbd "Mary Butts."

Emily Dickinson still instructs me. And the new round at her poetry has sent me back to Whitman, and to Emily's letters. (Emily Dickinson's dashes had sent me back too to read the opening of the other Emily's *Wuthering Heights* with its exclamation points) E. D. did know Brontë: "gigantic Emily Brontë" she writes. But of Whitman: "You speak of Mr. Whitman. I never read his book, but was told that it was disgraceful."

love
Robert

---

Nik made this linocut (& the envelope too) Don't you love the disappearing reindeer?[1]

To both: A joyful Christmas.

Dear Jess,

I was going to send you a note of good wishes for the opening of your show but mistook the date & now it is much too late. I do hope it has been going well. I would love to have seen it and thanks for announcement and letter.

Dear Robert,

I have now at least 3 marvellous letters of yours to answer, and the poems, which it is very good to see together in their relationships. I have been having a harassed time and have been tired & therefore rather depressed; and not getting down to the pleasure of writing to you is one of the things that englooms me. I won't go into one of my boring catalogs of what has kept me busy but please forgive me for not getting onto paper yet the response I do feel to letters & poems. It is horrid to get no reply but you will SOON.

Love—
Denny

**181**

Dec. 18th {1960
New York}

## 182

2 Jan 1961
277 Greenwich St
N.Y. 7

Dear Robert,

Here at last (after a false start and many many delays I won't go into) I can begin what I've been longing to do, a letter to you, like some calf tied in a field & longing to get into the next one, over the hedge. Since I have several letters of yours to answer, I'll start with the 1st which was back on Nov. 17th.

Yes, the $100 from *Poetry* was a nice surprise & I bought myself a type-writer (Olympia portable) with some of it.

I dont have H. D.'s *Collected Poems* & haven't seen it around anywhere (I suppose it is hard to come by?) and have for the longest time intended to treat myself to a day at the Library with it because the poems of hers I do know seem better & better from year to year as I read them. As well as the novel.

Then you wrote on the 22d with the "Set" poem. (I'll come to the poems later on.) I was glad you liked "3 Meditations." It certainly was a horrid grab-bag, that *Chelsea*. Did you like Dorn's poem?[1] I do—in a way—but I've had in the last year (barely) certain revulsions of feeling about his work—it doesn't satisfy me because more and more I need a care for form in a poem for it to satisfy me—I need poems that have some sculptural quality—not that they should be static but that they should be solid bodies in movement, instead of (what so many modern poems are) fluid substances (in movement or at worst stagnant). The Kelly/Rothenberg/Schwerner/Economou group as in *Trobar* have more concern with craft, so much more, than the Beats for instance, and yet their poems do not satisfy me and even their premises (as set forth naively by Bly and subtly and interestingly by Kelly) seem to me very very shaky. There is no moral backbone, no sharpness of necessity, in these poems. I find the same thing in many of the W. Coast poets that were in Spicer's and Duerden's magazines. I will enclose copies of 2 short pieces I just wrote after reading *Trobar* #2 (I haven't seen #1 yet).[2] Did I send you the thing I wrote for *The Nation*.[3] If not I will—or it may be out soon. It's about the same thing as these, in a way.

I wasn't surprised about J. Wright. I heard him read a year or so ago & his Oxford Group–type confession of guilt & conversion in regard to the iambic pentameter & the poetry of the French & Spanish Surrealists, followed by a reading of his *old* poems (disavowed 5 minutes before) & subsequent publication of a volume of same struck me as a weak hypocrisy.[4] He didn't have the courage of his convictions because he didn't really have any convictions.

Ed Dorn's "Los Mineros" does have a certain grace of movement that is specially his but which in some poems of his is totally absent or suddenly gives way to an unbelievably clumsy inept carelessness. He's going to be here to read in Feb.—havent seen him for 6 or 7 years, and then not for long.

Oh, and I certainly am glad you liked the L. Z. review all right—he graciously sent a note when it appeared to say he thought better of it, or at least bore no rancor—and considering the kind of man he is I thought it really *was* gracious, & touching, because it was the nearest thing to an apology a stiff-necked man could make, I believe.[5]

On Nov. 29th you sent me the revised "Risk" and some Emily Dickinson poems. You know, actually those dashes bother me—it seems to give a monotony of tone. I can't quite explain it. But if they were actual spaces it would work better for me. I'd like to compare those poems with their versions as usually printed but I don't have an Emily D.—we used to read Barbara's {Guest} before she went to Europe—and now we've moved too so I guess will never share her books again (she lived upstairs at 15th St.).

I keep finding horrible lacunae in our library although we have rather a large number of books. But rather a haphazard collection it is.

There's something cold and perversely smug about E. D. that has always rebuffed my feeling for individual poems of hers extending itself to her work as a whole. She wrote some great things—saw strangely—makes one shudder with new truths—but ever and again one feels (or I do)—"Jesus, what a bitchy little spinster."

Which leads me to mention someone of a very different order as a poet but—well, I wont finish that sentence—what I'm thinking of is Edith Sitwell who has been publishing a series of personal reminiscences in *The Observer* (London Sunday paper)—in which she shows herself as so petty, so mean spirited, and cheaply vain, that though I know you value her poems, or used to anyway, more than I ever have, I believe you too would be revolted by them.[6] Even so I grant some things remain—some or all of *Facade*, her notes on certain poems, her gathering of certain quotations in her notebooks. But the later (wartime & after) poems in which I never did believe, yet doubted the rightness of my own disbelief, now seem basically fake to me. They are literature. Nada mas. With that letter you sent an old one (from October 1959) about my "Note on the Imagination."[7] What a good letter—I'm so glad you found & saved it & sent it.

You know, you say you "distrust its discrimination (that just this is Imagination and that—'the feared Hoffmanesque blank—the possible monster or stranger' is Fancy)"—now, I think the crux of the matter is necessity—if it is contrived it is not of necessity, & then it is Fancy, but if the unconscious *needed* to see a monster or a blank then it is not contrived, it happens, & it is not Fancy but Imagination, which is larger than ourselves and doesn't work by our contrivances. So that in the dream my fear already suggested the monster or the blank and that was enough, all I needed— if I had looked in the mirror & seen what I feared it would have been by contrivance, I myself would have supplied it, but as it was Imagination within the dream supplied—with beautiful fidelity—the unpremeditated Real image.

When this *kind* of imagination—the presence of felt-through absolutely convincing details—is manifested it excites and delights me—shakes and moves me to tears—more than any other single manifestation, I think. I'm sure I don't have as good a sense of the overall drama as you, or Mitch, for instance (you were speaking of Tess & Angel)—perhaps it is being a woman. But I have this love of certain kinds of verisimilitude so that even thinking of it in quite a generalized way is almost a sensuous, no, sensual, experience, sharp and exquisite. That quotation from Dante (the one M. Gleason gave) is a marvel. And that Stifter story "Brigitte" (which I cant find since, or before, we moved) was full for me of shocks of *psychic* recognition.[8]

You say "I am drawn by the conceptual imagination rather than the perceptual imagination." I guess that's what it is—and I think the conceptual imagination is of a higher order, in fact—or it is primal, & the perceptual can only follow & illuminate it. But when you go on to distinguish between the ornamentive & the operational, saying that my diamonds of dew were ornamentive, not operational, because the verification of morning, I don't follow you—"is not at all necessary" but "atmospheric." I look on that verification as operational because it convinced the spirit.

A few other things not related to your letters: I had a very good visit (3 days) to Muhlenberg—Kinter is a kind of saint I think—I don't know how "good" he is,[9] I don't mean that, but he has an innocent eye and a fervor that is almost Hasidic, and while his students are not particularly talented & (like him) not very well able to distinguish between one modern poem and another, he *has* expanded their lives, helped them to *turn towards* poetry and to have a sense of wonder and reverence for poetry wherever they can see it, find it, and I had a sense of reciprocation &—oh, something else—love, perhaps—quite different from any other audience I've had. They're *open* to experience, maybe that's it. And then I enjoyed a Syrian meal cooked by Charlie Hanna's mother—that was fun. I liked Kinter's relationship with the students—he is without pretensions. And I had a brief but quite wonderful experience—of *in-sight*—when he showed me some abstract "Stations of the Cross" in the student chapel. Then on the way back by bus, exhilarated by all that had happened in the 3 days, I *saw* the landscape with a wordless intensity that I've written about in a poem—a little—something really happened to me.

The week before or a little more I'd flown to Pittsburgh & that comprised some interesting scenes & feelings for me too. But not as intense as that New Jersey landscape.

I will send you a few poems—but separately. It has not been a very productive autumn—I have really *suffered* from a lack of leisure—I sound complaining but it's really been worse than ever before, I suppose mainly because I became physically over-tired early on—cleaning up before we left

Maine, then 15th St—then the tremendous job of the move (packing & unpacking the books & all the things—Mitch was busy painting this place so I did almost all the packing)—and never really regained my energy. I've been taking huge doses of vitamin and am beginning to perk up I think. (But it's not all physical—I know part of it is boredom with housekeeping because I can always summon energy to do what I really enjoy!) (Like writing to you—and of course once really engaged on a poem I can stay up all night without any trouble—until the next day at least.)

I was going to write about what you'd said of Kelly's "Notes on Deep Image" (which I'd not read) when you first spoke of it, & was somewhat disappointed in when I did read it because after a good beginning it seemed to become a rather too deliberate program. That was my first, rather mild, reaction. But the enclosed (the short one written first, the other written after and only because the short one left out too much, not because I felt it didn't say right what it did say) is my reaction to the conjunction of his piece with some of the poems in the magazine. (His own is quite beautiful I think—though not as strong as a whole as in its parts, somehow) And with the thought of poems of Jerry's {Rothenberg}which he admires.

I like the people concerned & am wondering about how to show them this without making enemies. I don't feel antagonism or anything—I'm fond of Jerry, & M & I both liked Kelly when we met him again the other night—and I think I like Schwerner too, even if he's a bit too much of a professional "scream"—he's the life & soul of the party, an' all—but he's OK—. So I hope one can disagree with them without causing ill-feelings. I'll know soon enough, I dare say.

Now I'm winding down and I may as well stop and go to bed. I'll leave a space for—oh yes, I know what it was I wanted to tell you—when in Pittsburgh I saw the Art Nouveau exhibition which had been in N.Y. while we were in Maine. My god, what a beautiful show.[10] It was so full of riches I can't begin to speak of one more than another. And the inclusion of paintings by people who weren't strictly speaking Art Nouveau at all but were influenced by the movement in individual ways was very instructive. All the objects—glassware, jewelry, furniture—ha, people think of it as a time of decadence but it wasn't that at all, it was full of fresh & robust inventiveness —of course it was romantic and romance is a fever—it was full of indoor feelings not of weather—but it was a vigorous movement not a weak faute-de-mieux one. I wonder if it came or will come to SF? I know it was to go to L.A. One of the very best things was Hector Guimard's own desk.[11]

Love—and to Jess—from<br>Denny.

(P.S. A separate letter for the poems.)

dear Denny,

What I do—in that letter regarding your essay on Imagination, or yesterday in response to your letter and the reply to Kelly's piece on the deep image—is to contend. And it obscures perhaps just the fact that I am contending my own agreements often.

With all that reacting I did not send news—for my mother died just before Christmas (on the 21st, the longest night): and left me the beneficiary of a trust fund that should bring me at least two hundred and fifty a month the rest of my life. It means I will not have to hang on to the generosity of others, as often I have done. And it means too that we can afford now a larger place—a place with a studio for Jess. He has been these three years painting and working in a space barely big enough to move around in. Crampd. I'll miss leaving the country and the sea, for it means too that we will return to the city. Jess had such trouble getting his collages in for the show this last month that he wants to move back. He doesn't like to hitch hike at all like I do. And, then, he misses making the rounds of the Goodwill and Salvation Army bins. When it comes, what we require, we too will be moving then.

The other re-shaping thing I've found in the series of lectures I've been, am, giving at Borregaard's Museum. At present I have between twenty sure and thirty (last time) at the most attending. At a dollar a lecture (one-third going to the Museum, but that is voluntary), both those attending and I am held to a certain "investment" or exchange.

Well, the thing I've found is how my own judgment has shifted. Tho I aim at keeping my consciousness open (my ideal would be an expanding awareness), my appreciations narrow. I am impatient and disheartened by stage effects (this was *The Waste Land*) (but it's also the primary question, I think, re. Sitwell's poetics: whether we can take richly what is manner and charade). . . . And Rilke's *Duino Elegies* which once seemd *all*, show up patches now of make-shift. But I did too get into his Orphic sonnets and found there "fountains" (remembering this lovely last poem you sent me)[1]. I don't mean that there is some poem or ought to be without "lapse" or "patching" or "make-shift." For, here is part of what I am getting at—I took these three (*Waste Land*, and Rilke's *Duino's* (the ones from 1922) and his *Orphic* sonnets because it fascinated me that in 1922 these two poets should both set about poems that were deliberate rituals of Orpheus, interpreted in each case as vegetation rites; and that in the 1922 *Duinos* we find figures out of Eliot's *Waste Land* (in the Saltimbanques) as if they were haunted by a common dream.

Then there was Williams's *Spring and All*—the same "time"; and it too, filled with the vegetative myth of the dead and the flowering of the earth.

Well, back to my shifting judgment: the opening of the Williams, those first three poems have ground. But it is necessary (for there to be the whole poem) then to bring in the unnecessary. It's your word "necessary"; and my sense of "making-do" that's on my mind. Williams's "hermaphroditic telephones" is no more sound than Eliot's "bats with baby's wings" (can I be remembering that straight?), and in the *Duinos* I could not take the appearance of a modiste as Fate, a Norn doing up hats—as anything but the intrusion of the writer's own doing hats.

Then, to release the pending thot, we too if we are to realize some wide and generous risk, to let a poem go out that far to include (you say the whole man)—well some substitute—ersatz, stand-in for we knew not otherwise how to do.

Then in Keats' letters I found:

> I mean *Negative Capability*, that is, when a man is capable of being in uncertaintys, mysteries, doubts, without any irritable reaching after fact and reason—Coleridge, for instance, would let go by a fine isolated verisimilitude caught from the Penetralium of mystery, from being incapable of remaining content with half-knowledge. . . .

again. It was a passage Olson insisted on at Black Mountain until it must have been memorized. But weren't just these "doubtful" "uncertain" parts, means etc. in Rilke and Williams what showed their negative capability? A verisimilitude is a counterfeiting, a making do, an impulsive likelihood where there "should" have been sound truth. "A fine isolated something-like-it"! There's brio in that for me today, for I can often begin or undertake nothing for my mind does not find its necessary or radical responsibility in things. The thought is that we find grace too in risking the thing, in fancy then. Aie! tho I shall never be without and must work from those "irritable reachings after fact and reason" that must have haunted Keats too—

love,
Robert

dear Denny,

I had hoped from the early issues of Rothenberg's *Floating World*—and still do, for there is a recognition of life, of spirited life, there—that the Buber-hassidic spring would flow forth again. As Kelly too has the instinct to search out a reality in his catholic "past" or heritage. The "deep image" is then a moving element—both Kelly and Rothenberg are so young they baffle me. But that they long for their deep image (it *is* depth, in some way, that is a meeting ground where spirit or soul is no longer "catholic" or "hassidic," where traditions reappear as one communion).

To search it out! But their first impulse is to produce some *effect* of it, and

## 184

January 12, 1961
{Stinson Beach}

that's the futile mocking quickly-evaporating stuff that appears in their poems. "Effective" contrived figures that are to stand for the strange, unusual, grotesque thing they think the numinous must be.

I've just come from reading *Spring and All* and then exploring it (in a series of lectures I'm giving on Modern Poetry). Williams too, in 1922, was caught up with being "dada," with contrived "interesting" displays. Well, in him, they are very much "being the life of the poetry." They are arabesques, skips and jumps about the room with a lamp on one's head—for a crown. The thing is that *Spring and All* is *moving*, moves along a depth that is feeling and whose images are: what? Certainly nothing contrived or even imagined. We do not believe that Williams imagined the road to the contagious hospital or the flowers or the farmer—in the sense that he made them up—but he followed a melody in which those first three poems set into movement his form. And the imagination was what he saw the trees, the stagnant pools, the flowers, the farmer contemplating—with greed, towards a harvest (maybe even those marketable interesting effects, those hermaphroditic telephones)—what he saw all this to be. His intuition of reality, of the truth or a truth of the matter.

But you know Denny, I always have,—when confronted with the contrivances that are made-do for poetic feeling, the trying for effect, in Rothenberg's verse—the fact of my own first six years of verse—and more than that before there was form enough to my own being to appear as meaningful form—for a poem to appear. That's it! It's the hidden currents of life, the revelation that takes us over, that comes to speak at last in a poem. There is no way, when we are all so many things of youth—if that is our organic pattern—to "find" the meaningful, except the meaningful appear.

I don't mean there isn't every possibility of losing the art—there always is in attitudes and effects. The important thing for me in Jerry's work or Kelly's thought is that they are searching for their depths; the mistrusted thing is that they have identified "depth" with strangeness. Or, closer to what I mean—the art has to do with what life must be; the waste has to do with what literature must be.

We are not searching out "real poetry," but by our art for a real life. Whitman in that beautiful preface to the 1855 edition says "to show the path between reality and their souls"; and I had the hope in first writing to Jerry and then in responding to Kelly—the hope that sprang, not from their thought thruout, but from a sense I gathered from hints of a life they would come into that it was that art that is a way of life they moved towards.

Pound in giving up the "idealism" of the Whitman who could turn poetry directly to be a song of life, did so with the right feeling poets had at the beginning of this century that "Life," "Truth," "Beauty" had been betrayd, mouthed. But the evil of mouthing, of virtues that are spoken, is that words first become corrupted, and men out of decency turn from the words—and turn dangerously to despise the words when it is the betrayal of the word that was ill.

We need courage and care for the truth of what we feel and the truth of what we do to take up Whitman's challenge.

Well, I *do* feel some rousing theatrical gesture (as if I were pursuasively thumping the table and widely flinging my arm—to impress!) and must return to the table where I am sitting (the sea now washes in and looking up into the glare of the winter sunlight, reflected painfully from the mirror of the sea, catch the flicker of monarch butterflies again. The battle for truth, banners flying and heart roused, settles down to allow for Sybil's white furry face looking about the room. Alert, drinking in sounds perhaps—for she does not want to go out. And the faint punctuations of the fire.

The literary editor of *The Nation* writes asking will I contribute to a special issue which they plan for April on "Form-Smashers"—"vandalism or iconoclasm" and will I perhaps write on *Poetry*.[1] Well, I will write on *Form*, for I most do not believe the editorial proposition: "from time to time the continuance of a vital culture requires demolition—form and image smashing—as the only way by which the imagination can be freed to do the next important task."

I am so angry at the consciousness—the allegiance betrayd in the liberal-progressive mind to "vital culture," "demolition," "form and image smashing," "important task" as terms—and aren't they exactly the terms of atom-smashing? It is time to re-iterate what to be radical means, what roots are, what form and image, and service means. That creation is neither conservative nor liberal, but radical. But my mind in recoil goes into a knotted tangle.

A rambling immediate reply to your own rambling letter. I'll not give at all on your sense of Emily Dickinson—it *is* oddly enough one expressd by Edith Sitwell in an early volume on poetry. But her work comes thru to me without any interfering bother about her personality, and in poems like the one I sent comes thru as a pure voice. I'll give on the Edith Sitwell question—not give up my appreciations of the later poetry, as I appreciate exaggerated manner; and while I don't know these late memoirs I have relishd the grotesque snobbism of her attentions to critics like Alvarez—but ally my self with your view in this: and that is the mistake of attitude in itself, of devoting energies and attentions to putting things in their place.[2] Making grandeur an affair of rank and costume produces hauteur, and misses then what one would honestly call grand. She emerges as a character in some poet's play, the poet having been devoured by what was no more than a passing lion—all roar. That there have been no poems for—is it ten years? No, since Monras's death. . . .

Tho, you know, Denny, any man or woman's personality is something very different from their vitality. "petty, mean spirited, and cheaply vain" have a lot to do with attitudes towards other people and resentments at critics that are not entirely mis-taken; and since I, too, often smart and would bite and hiss at being overlookd (as if I wanted my work to be valued rather than understood), I am not unsympathetic with the outcropping of certain mean, petty and vain streaks in a character. Well, the difference is that Edith Sitwell has positively cultivated them, to revenge herself upon an English social system that has stuck her from the beginning with her class.

But:

And seeing all glory hidden in small forms,
The planetary system in the atom, the great suns
Hid in a speck of dust.
                    So, for his sake,
More proudly will that Sisyphus, the heart of Man,
Roll the Sun up the steep of heaven, and in the street
Two old blind men seem Homer and Galileo, blind
Old men that tap their way through worlds of dust
To find Man's path near the Sun.

is theatrically grandoise, cloak and grande dame clouds of "great thought"; lacks the concrete engagement of a life in which glory is not all; but is not personal, excludes the possibility of the pettyness, meanness, vanity.

I always felt that Edith Sitwell's animosity towards Lady Wortley Montague in the book on Pope was an animosity towards her own character that was so like Lady Wortley's:[3] she saw her own cruelty, her own gratuitous swipes of claw and fang at what appeard vulnerable.

But isn't our agreement just that same purpose to seek not manner but form, to attend the actualities and consequence of life itself—you call it "the necessary," I'm sure that what Whitman meant by reality what Williams meant by

so much depends
upon
the red wheel
barrow

in which sight there is no "glory in small forms"; we too have to come past whatever sense of glory to the wheelbarrow—not to deny the glory we have to come past, but to seek out what is. Amen. Enuf of it.

Your letter is full of revulsions from other people's work (Dorn's as well as L. Z.'s, Dickinson's as well as Sitwell's, Rothenberg's as well as "many of the poets in Spicer's and Duerden's magazines"), and then in another response of yours to your audience (but they are here "friends") in Muhlenberg: "I had a sense of reciprocation &—oh, something else—love, perhaps": all the course of your thought is a sentence of our, any of us's, yearning for response: for the responding thing we will see in some other face or poem or painting, for whatever room that can be given for our spirit to go—it's that that I feel must, and by nature, seem most repulsive in Emily Dickinson's shutting herself up in her house, or Edith Sitwell's crushing repudiations of people she has disliked: we too are rejected, turnd out, alone; or might too be rejecting, leaving, solitary. Mirror images.

And I've been fighting about in some paperbag in this letter, Denny, of dangers or walls I contend against in the conflicts you present.

Dearest Jess, who sees clear (where I try to struggle) says: The major sin is making the arts citadels to be defended or attacked, then our thought becomes military.

To have to be "right" in living is to attack the liveliness, the variety of it itself. It is one thing to know in one's heart one does not *want* to be like Edith Sitwell; it is another to cultivate not liking what one does not want to be like. No one, outside of Sitwell, *is* like her—want to or know. And what I struggle against is the reproof of the living that seems to be necessary.

I remember once at an Anarchist meeting when under the rigors of Anarchist righteousness I was impelld to speak for my own living. That I had fled my family because they disapproved of what I was and felt and how I lived— silly or weak as it might seem. And when at last I sought *the* group that spoke for individual freedom, I found there too that I was to be free only if I were generous and not mean, imaginative and not fanciful, humane and not cruel, beautiful and not ugly, intelligent and not stupid . . . but given these virtues Fascism would itself be an ideal and also a practical government.

What now seems to me my purpose is that I write as I do and live as I do not because these are "right" but because I want this kind of living and writing to come into existence, to be realized. To imagine what the good is and to imagine what evil is, what goods there are and what evils: this is releasing to our powers, it helps us prepare for actual works—and we're often mistaken in our imaginations. We cannot imagine the evil workd by a man who means good (as Moses in leading his people out of Egypt led them into Jewry instead of humanity); we cannot imagine the evil worked by a man who means evil (as the evil actually workd in the souls and bodies imprisond in Buchenwald—as Bettleheim described them, I remember— was *unimaginable*). But good and evil are what Jess calls military tactics.[4]

As *The Nation*'s "form and image-smashing" is military tactics.

And we've to create our own reverence as part of what is—let me close with a passage from Hopkins I came upon yesterday—-from his "Henry Purcell": from the prose preface.

. . . he has, beyond that, uttered in notes the very make and species of man as created both in him and in all men generally.

and isn't another part of what is "the very make and *variety* of men as created in the most individual" in which we might admire (as I feel Elizabethans did) even monstrous vitalities or mediocre vitalities, become biologists not moralists, fascinated finally by facts and forms of how life goes on, beyond judgments?

love
Robert

**185**

Jan. 25, 1961
{Stinson Beach}

dear Denny,

*The National Review*, with my poor mis-used poem set in the midst of all that wishful-fascism, arrived over a week ago and set me brooding, outraged by the insult thruout to any truth (like the article on Vanzetti where the mind behind it—the editor's—is evil). What does "Nel Mezzo del Cammin" mean in that context?[1] Where church and state, in their most repressive-oppressive authority, are given the blank check without principle (principal)?

*The Nation* is planning an issue on what they call "form-smashing" or "wrecking" of faiths etc. and askd me to contribute on Poetry. Where I might, as best I can, make clear against whatever opinions and impressions might be gathered from the above ill-advised association, where my allegiances are. I proposed anyway to attempt some distinction between "convention" (or anti-convention) and form—and try to get across that the imagination of what is (or of the good of what is) is a form.

Well, when I get the essay under-weigh I'll send it on to you.

Last week our community (of consciousness not geography) took an immediate shock, when a crazed divinity student, inspired by God, walkd into Tom Parkinson's office with a sawed-off shotgun and shot at Tom, first tearing away the side of his jaw, and second blasting the stomach of Tom's teaching assistant who had jumped up. "Because Parkinson was a communist or a communist fellow-traveler."

After initial reports that pictured Tom as critically injured, it turns out that, tho repair of his face will be a long process, his speech, hearing have not been critically affected. But the event is fearful, even at this remove, and there must always be, however forward-looking one's resolve might be, the irreparable association in which another man is the victim, before one's eyes, of an attack in some part springing from and towards one's own acts. (The murderer had some seven years ago been a student of Tom's and moved from old convictions.) "One might *shout* at Tom, but why shoot?" Mary Tyler wrote. There was, somewhere in the circumstance, the fact that

Parkinson *had* made any of us, his friends, mad enough to shout at his wrong headedness.

Yet, dangerously, warnd as we are by life at any point we might reflect, I too am not likely to remedy the satisfaction I often take in pursuing what ever idiocy I think to find in the opinions of others . . . (not a moral reflection—but it's a good thing I'm not a public teacher{)}.

With it all, I realized too the curious affection I have for Tom. Perhaps in part a friendliness towards my own arrogations. More markd, since Jess has no affections for him at all and registers as boorishness what I take for granted as eccentricity or color of a personality. He is a character in the fiction of my life (as he is for the Tylers or for Jack Spicer) and has in that the affection of "belonging" that endears impossible characters in Dickens' novels—as members of cherishd occasions.

But back of that is my sense that Tom is earnestly a champion of the good, he strives to find the good life. He's dense, and to have a champion of the good who misses the subtle complexion . . . I have always to hint and try to adjust whose sights to the mixture I am of malices and allegiances of good will. It takes the inspiration and responsibility of a poem for something fair and benevolent—

I have the opening fragment perhaps of a poem following my mother's death[2] . . . but I have no idea of whether or when the source will return with its stream of feeling and its coordinates in given things. In the opening part people getting on and off a city-bus, leaving, "passing-on" into swirls of others—and young girls, particularly a young Hindoo girl who was in a sense performing to catch my interest keyed in to the old and new feelings of separation from my mother (of her being a "girl," of her existence other than mine)—but there, it's a statement partial even to what's needed for a poem among other poems.

love
Robert

Dear Robert,

A beautiful letter—the second one I mean especially—& a stitch-in-time it was too, because I am foolish to get into controversy—there's too much talk as it is. Some I need—to excite my energies sometimes—but when it leads to a tone of irritability & a whole train of such animadversions as you so gently (& rightly) reprove me for, it is something that works against poetry and against all I love.

I do in courtesy have to reply to Kelly's reply—but I won't let it go further than that and from a talk with Jerry I did clarify for myself what it

## 186

Jan. 25th {29} 1961
277 Greenwich St.
N.Y. 7

is I demand or desire in a poem (i.e., the interplay of objective & subjective, which is what makes it interesting to me, as against the isolation of either which doesn't move me) so that I should be able to answer without a long drawn out argument. Jerry gave me copies of his letters to Bob, with Bob's cogent replies—and it all seems such a goddamn lot of *talk*.

Mitch and I reread most of *The Opening of the Field* together, and then the new poems. When I don't like something I can find plenty to say but when I do I am happy & speechless. *The Field* is I believe a major work, one of the living real rare precious things of our time. And the poems that have followed don't in any way decline from it—the next book will take its place beside it surely. Some poems I respond to more than others, some may have impact on me that is partial, as, through sound but not to my understanding, but the sense of their relationship to each other is strong. I have come to understand what you mean by *a book*. And from *Letters, The Field*, and these I begin too to get a sense of something I can't put a name to yet, some overall quality, like a pervasive color or a space-sense like one has about a great building, a Saint Sophia let's say, whose inside & outside & all the aspects & details thereof one can't possibly see at once & yet whose character, or tone, what is it, is present to one as a quantity.

Your mother's death—you know we've experienced my father's & Mitch's mother's deaths so I know you must have suffered; but I am *very very* glad you will have that money. Though a little sad it means moving away from Stinson Beach so that I'll never now see your garden & house and view.

---

NEWS: Mitch has a publisher. Horizon Press. He signed the contract today, got a $500 advance, and the book is to come out in October.[1] We are very happy—especially as they seem like very decent people who see the book as a work of art, not just a commodity. Raeburn the owner/partner was the friend & publisher of F. Ll. Wright. A paper-back deal is in the offing. They'd had the book a long time but were investigating the paperback possibilities, as they don't have much money & have a "quality" list. Yesterday they called him & today he signed the contract. Viva! You will know what a very important thing this is in our lives. Mitch needed that assurance so *badly*.

---

I also have a thing in that *Nation* issue—I wrote it last summer so it is uninfluenced by all this recent argument.[2] Hatch asked me to suggest people & I said "Duncan" so I may be at least partially to blame, I hope you don't mind. Also that you won't find my piece too silly. I got rather a kick out of writing it but I know it's not my forte and it probably reads like a sophomore's paper. One advantage of the college education is that such things are gotten out of one's system early, whereas the request galvanized me into action, somehow. It is now late & I am tired & have some sort of virus that's around. So I'll stop & continue tomorrow.

*Saturday night.*

Here it is 4 days later. That's what happens. Mike Rumaker was here tonight. Did I tell you how good we feel about him now? He's better than I've ever seen him—I mean even before he became really ill. Very witty, warm, spontaneous—just a lovely person & with somehow quite a clear sense of himself—and he is seeing a lot of a girl, whom we haven't yet met but whom he may bring over next weekend. It's not a resurrection so much as a coming-to-life.

Your letter with that horrible news about Tom Parkinson has come meanwhile—I'm writing to him & his wife, if I can't find his address will send c/o you.

That awful Nims is a complete idiot & one will just have to wait till Rago comes back.[3] I don't know where to send my new poem—I just can't *afford* to send it somewhere where they dont pay, as it is quite long—about 95 lines I guess—& besides I'd like it to be somewhere with more than 10 readers because I like it. (Will send when typed.) I saw a letter Nims wrote to my Korean friend about his translations which was literal-minded to the point of absurdity. I have half a mind to eat my words & send it to *Evergreen.* Kenner has 2 or 3 poems of mine & I'm distressed to find out what kind of mag. it is.[4] Still haven't seen it. Still, I don't think poems are as much affected by their prose surroundings as by other, bad, poems, do you? There were many things in your letters I responded to in reading & wanted to speak about but I think I'd better stop here.

Much love from
Denny

dear Denny,

I'm so glad about Mitch's novel having found a publisher at last. Seon {Givens} had been provoked at the Vanguard editor backing down on her initial response, and said it was just the usual aesthetic cowardice of the editing species. As Donald Allen was most provokingly stupid about the book, arching mockingly in resistance to my affirmation of my own response. But I agree with Seon that one of the virtues of the book is the excitement that builds up once the battlefield scenes open—I mean that I think the publisher has a book that appeals to one's sense of adventure as well as the level that most moved me: the way the war becomes a scene of revelation.

I try not to think of Allen's stupidities—it's not only re. Mitch's novel but also Eloise Mixon's which I found exciting. It's such a tricky business,

## 187

February 1, 1961
{Stinson Beach}

because it makes me doubt, as so often I have, the substance of his response to poetry.

Then too, what a release it must be for Mitch to have the book "delivered," the worries and doubts about whether it would find print dispelled. It takes so much work for a novelist to establish his world—I think of Melville.

I guess about Kenner and that *National Review* thing we had better let it go as it did and note in the margin that we are out of place. You will see what I mean. God knows I am in all kinds of disagreement with the mentality that produces and consumes *The Nation* and *The New Republic*; but my radical disagreement there is that they *use* our vital interest in the welfare of man at the level the journalist promotes—of crises and causes. Where it is our daily action and principles that need clarification.

But not searching out the roots of the good and instead feeding all the liberal good causes is one thing; and what I feel is back of a thing like *The National Review* is another. I mean "unprincipled good" is what I dislike *The Nation* for, or rather, why I don't read it. But I positively bless it, when I come across the unprincipled evil of what is called conservatism.

I hope I will find my way toward the right possible thing re. this *Nation* issue. Could you send me what you wrote? It might take care of part of what I would say . . . but then I think I'd better set about the work without such a reference.

I read last night three stories by Ludwig Tieck translated by Carlyle: "The Fair-Haired Eckbert," "The Trusty Eckhart" and "The Runnenberg." I've known since childhood "The Elves" which William Canton included in his *King Herla*. But coming after Wagner's *Ring* (which I read several weeks go) and the new Ernst Jünger novel *The Glass Bees*—these evoke how ancient the German experience of wrath and sin is.[1] "The horrors of the Thirty Years War, followed by the conquests and conflagrations of Louis the Fourteenth, had desolated the country," Carlyle sees it. But Tieck, Wagner and Junger make us aware of men who are their own desolations, of compulsive self-violations.

One thing that brings the feverish mind of the hero in "The Runnenberg," or of all in Wagner's *Ring* close to home is the gold, guilt that is the root: the alternative Wagner has of either power or love. And the ordeal of the soul—Brünhilde in Wotan's disowning of love. I note only that my poor Germanic mind is fascinated with the fortune of my inheritance (that is and will be for another six months "unsettled").

Thereupon he loosed his sack, and shook it empty: it was full of gravel, among which were to be seen large bits of chuck-stone, and other pebbles. "These jewels," he continued, "are not ground and polished yet, so they want the glance and the eye; the outward fire, with its glitter, is too deeply buried in them, in their inmost heart; yet you have but to strike it out and frighten them, and show that no deceit will serve, and then you see what sort of stuff they are."

My sense of those who in the forest went warriors and warblers of the word has gatherd some disturbing images.

How could the Nazis have taken up Wagner as if exactly those works did not most move the heart against power and empire? For Wotan is the source and worker of the deep evil in the play. And Wagner sees it so.

Well, so Germanic things are on my mind. And disturbing thoughts too of the congress there must be to bring forth from the sins and evils of nations and peoples the hope of a unity in mankind.

You write about my idea of the book, but right now I am disturbed at just that level, unable to envision the whole without letting go certain threads that are grievous threads: if I can work them, they will be there.

————————

Let the above wandering be—I don't quite see what seems so real in the conjunction here of Germanic nightmare and whatever I know. So, in the letter I'm trying to keep at it, as I might talking to you.

————————

I leave Saturday for the North (to read at the University of British Columbia on the 7th) and then another small reading on my way back in Portland.

Jess has a kind of retrospective of oils opening this coming Monday at *Borregaard's Museum.*

love
Robert

Dear Robert & Jess

Virginia Admiral wants me to tell you she wd. like to do a little (White Rabbit–style) bk of Helen Adam's poems with drawings by Jess if you & Helen are agreeable. She would like to have some of H. A.'s poems to choose from first (i.e, she definitely wants it to be her own choice because she says it is boring for her otherwise) & then if Jess wd. provide drawings for those. She loves the drawings you did for my 5 poems. So wd. you or Helen write & let her know? I had a good time at N{orman} H{olmes} P{earson}'s at Yale & reading went well. Ed Dorn etc. read here last week— good. We have an azalea.

Love from
Denny.

## 188

{February 27, 1961
New York}

dear Denny,

My sense of outrage has been mounting thru successive reviews of Allen's anthology. That the established mediocracies seem to be setting you, me, Creeley up as "best" or "good"—as having then the likeliness of belonging to the same world of "poetry" as Louis Simpson, Richard Wilbur, Merwin or Snodgrass, for instance—is one outrage.

At the University of British Columbia I heard Snodgrass read, and for the first and last time was confronted with his verse—as stupid and ugly a bid for a place in the sub-urban conscience as I've heard. I loathe these personal problems that have no deep root but are all social currency—case history of a social worker. Wld. as soon attend divorce court.

But one's thrown back to that level because the verse itself is so miserably contrived.

James Wright's review with its summary dismissal of Charles, or {Cecil} Hemley's, where taste must do where intelligence and understanding is required—*do* make me immediately aware that here, just here, and now: one must practice a severe art and keep me muzzle out of the honey-pot (as Charles calls rime and heady rhythms.[1] There is, anyway, some deep rancor in my heart that these would-be advocates of our work against the extremes of Olson's "Projective Verse" or of the "beats" demonstrations or of the City poetry of O'Hara—but Olson's work is not an extreme; for me it as ever is a discipline, exemplary to hold me to responsibilities of the actual art—

to the syllable and the sound

in each part; and to the demand for contrast and articulation in movement.

The piece I've done for *The Nation* is an opening—in which I plough into the Rationalist-Conventionalist idea of form—and wants now, in sequence—some essay on expressive form, and then on musical? form—On process.

In the series of lectures I've been giving here, I've arrived (this week) at Charles's work (next week, the close—yours and Creeley's; with, now I see, some attention to Ashbery's poem in *Big Table* (the collage of changes) and to Spicer's new work, after Lewis Carroll and Lear.[2]—The key there is the dream, vision, in-sight in poetry where we see a reawakening of what is in Dante's work, or Bunyan's of the imagination of the real—I wish you were here for these lectures—O, especially for the earlier ones, for I found in Carlyle and Whitman, Keats and Browning 19th century keys, and I wonder if I'll ever want now, the discovery having been unfolded in those talks (for I'd keep from exploring my recognitions in these passages until the night of the lecture), to do essays along these lines. Some of it must enter whatever work on poetics I do, but the tradition now seems intricate to trace out. It's "ours"—and from the beginning in the revival after that awful age of reason—there has been the directive that a melody in our daily speech is the human echo of a melody we experience in the real, the deep heart of things, Carlyle says. And then, doesn't all this dreadful trying to put things in their places or thru their paces, imposing a beat upon the (or to counteract) revelation, show up for what it is?

And there is then an alliance between free verse and free thought and our free associations that means the imagination (the great imagination that goes towards revelation and spirit in the world about us, towards "so much depends" the red wheelbarrow).

It's the meanness of the conventional idea of what is, the worm's eye view in which reasonable men concur as to the nature of the real that offends my spirit. Snodgrass and Simpson are miserable or inadequate as versifiers, but in Robert Lowell there's an admirable mastery of the art, there's a love then of the feel of language at some level: but the soul of the man inhabits the restricted area of a *Partisan Review* or *Hudson Review* mind. His *Life Studies* are conceived in that perspective of the real. Even the demonic glimmer disappears; an urbane limbo takes the place of Hell.

These are after-thoughts, Denny, from my *Nation* essay, which I'll hope to get to you in copy as soon as I get a new set typed.[3] Particularly, of course, if Hatch doesn't take it (the study is long; and not journalistic).

My poor mind is a churn these days, nearing the equinox as we are with changing weather, fearful that butter will not come.

love
Robert

Dear Robert,

Did I tell you I'm going to be working as poetry editor of *The Nation* for 3 months? It means about a day's work a week & $50 a month. I want of course to use something of yours—not too long because then it will take ages to get used—also, tho' I think I'll have a fairly free hand, it will have to be something they wouldn't really buck at, I guess. May I choose something from among the post–*Opening of the Field* poems that I have, or from the many marvellous unpublished things in *A Book of Resemblances* (checking with you first, of course)? Or do you want to send others? By the way, rereading *A Bk of Resemblances* made me think, have you any prospects of Grove doing it? They wd be crazy not to and it really *ought* to appear.

I saw a really terrible poem (in T.S.) by Snodgrass when I went into *The Nation* offices last week to see Merwin (who has preceded me there) & find out how things are done. However I must in honor state that his poems have sometimes seemed very moving to me—the concerns real (obsessed, yes, but *really* obsessed, & with real things) & the effort to make poems from them a genuine & sometimes successful effort.

## 190

April 2d {19}61
277 Greenwich St
N.Y. 7
Easter Day '61

Laughlin wanted another book from me & I was unhappy about it thinking I was not ready & shouldn't do it, but when I put together the poems I have I found they did make a book after all.[1] I hope you'll think so too. Mitch is finishing up articles already commissioned & then will stop (in May) altogether. With the article money & his advances (from Horizon Press & from Signet who have bought the reprint rights) plus what I can earn with readings & odd jobs such as *The Nation* one & revision of Korean translations (for which I'll be paid $250 by Unesco) we will be able to live for a year, maybe more, before he has to do any more hack work. I just got $300—absolutely unexpectedly—from The Longview Foundation, which helps too.[2]

Something I read recently which you might like is *Till We Have Faces* by C.S. Lewis.[3] Do you know it? I had been prejudiced against him before, I don't know just why—even tho I knew he loved MacDonald. Nik is reading some of his children's books now.

Nik suddenly started writing poems. He always made a terrific job out of writing anything, even a letter, before; & then one evening he sat down & wrote 7 rhymed poems—all nautical—in one go & since has written several more. Will send when I have time to make copies. The kids at his school mostly write unrhymed, unstructured, rather Sandburgesque things which can be very nice but I thought it was good that he demanded of himself rhymes & an aural shape, especially since he is apt not to demand of himself all that he's capable of.

One night we went to Nell Blaine's and John Button was there—he spoke of his delight in the times he'd spent with you—of how much he admired Jess's paintings—of how exciting he'd found your lectures at Borregaard's Museum. I dont know him well but have always liked him. Al Kresch had sent him to us for information before his trip to Mexico a couple of summers ago, & he went to Oaxaca & became quite friendly with my mother—she & Elvira were really fond of him & he took some walks on the mountain with Mother. I was amused & yet sad about it because I guess if she'd realized that he was a homosexual she wouldn't have liked him but fortunately her naivete caused her not to realize that & so she was able to respond to him affectionately without prejudice, just as a human being.

Did you ever get my card about Virginia Admiral being anxious to do a Helen Adam/Jess Collins book? She really means it (as far as I can judge), so do write & let her know.

There's a story by Mike R{umaker} in the new *Evergreen* which is a lovely thing, especially in relation to his earlier work, which I admire but which is pretty heartless, and to all{.}[4] Do read it.

Also I just read the whole of *Kaddish* for the first time & am impressed with it. I don't think anything of the rest of the book, but "Kaddish" itself like "Howl" one *is* moved by (more than by "Howl" really) & the experiences revealed are so horrible (& he is able to make some sort of structure of them however naked) that one can only marvel that he's in as good shape as he is. I had a sort of rapprochement with him the night of Ed Dorn's reading, a long story which I'll tell you some day. I keep in mind what you said about rhetoric—you said for me what I had felt—but I realize now that when I read it I *used* your words to back myself up in a small-minded, selfrighteous literary prejudice, which is deathly & was not, I know, what you intended.

I wish *so much* I could have heard those lectures. And I wish you *would* write them; you say you feel having just finished the talks that you wont want to—but I hope that was only an immediate reaction.

It's ages I think since I sent you any poems. Will soon have a whole bunch of carbons to send—usually when I've got copies I send them to you before anyone else but it happened that I lent someone here all the carbons I made when I typed up the poems for the new book (which by the way I'll call *Come Into Animal Presence* I think).

Nik is now listening to Gerald Durrell on "The Abominable Snowman" and I can't keep my mind on what I'm writing.

> Love to Jess and to you
> from Denny.

Are you going to move soon? Won't you miss having the summer there at the beach—more than if you moved in the fall?

I had a letter from N H P{earson} & he said he'd not heard from you since sending you Pound / H. D. correspondence—or, H. D.'s account of her relationship to Pound,[5] was it? But I expect you've written to him since then.

Did I tell you how marvellous it was to turn on the radio & unexpectedly hear the "Poem Beginning With a Line by Pindar"? It was Rexroth & he quite turned off his pompous and mumbling voices & just *read* it. When he really means something, really cares about something, he can be so that one feels like forgiving him a good deal. And while the best is to hear a poem in the poet's own voice, it can consolidate one's sense of it, certify its validity, to hear someone else read it.

dear Denny,

Your letter arrived this morning. It's my second day of being somewhat recoverd from the flu—tho I still have it—and Jess is in the midst of it. A way to celebrate Spring—but the shifts from a March storm, cold with heavy rains, into clear sunny spring days—in the 70s earlier this week— did it. It's been a sort of limbo, with two cats sick with their own almost

## 191

April 5, 1961
{San Francisco}

pneumonia earlier, when it *was* cold; and then, just when I got started on the H. D. study again I smashd my little finger—which made for wobbly (not I.W.W. but the other kind) writing, and couldn't type up anything. So, today, too, the nail finally came off. And—with only the gruesome task still to do of income tax—the worst of the year should be over.

We've not had a cent yet of insurance money or the trust fund. It's worse than not having money because we keep living as if we were going to start living some different way tomorrow morning, on promises, I mean. Just now when everything is in bloom—we've a mass of Belle of Portugal roses framing the sea view, and the one I call the "Chaucer" rose—(it's really a pre-Raphaelite single rose) at the bedroom window, the one I most love, is a mass of bloom. It's the weather, the time, the place for the mind to drift or soak up leaves and light, yellows, rose, orange, crimsons . . . yet still will return, dog that the mind is, to chew over how many bones might be, could have been, are, aren't in, on, over, under account. The blessed thing my mother did was to leave me as much as she could where I would not have to think about it. For, all on my own I can worry money and look over some ancient envy, some more or less, whenever I loose hold of garden or sea.

But actually, having sketchd such a picture, we've been doing well—for the readings and little C.B.S. lectures I had in February, and Jess's sales (two from the collage show; and then four paintings from the show at Borregaard's) have us still above water.

There are at least two good sections in the new "H. D." work I've done. Her notes, revelations, on Pound set me off. To return to short paragraphs as best I could, to try to keep my thought from snow-balling, I mean rolling along gathering in everything as it tends to do—and also I could get something immediate and revealing. Which I am enclosing herewith; for I've made an extra carbon for you as I went along this time, typing up the new material for Norman. Well, no I won't "enclose" it—since it's a manuscript— I'll send it today regular mail.

Trying to work with the mind I've got for prose at this point (at forty-two with my prose all a bog, where there are only a few rivulets of clear water, only a scattering of islands that are sound for the foot.) I am aware, remember, all the testy points in the course of realizing a poetry; and worse can see how the bog I get into with prose *is* there, but barely accounted for as best I could, in the poetry.

Why do we, I—but you too (more than Bob or Olson, I think) go on, at it, settling literary values? It's the most disheartening thing I find myself doing in this H. D. study, trying to win her her just literary place—and what I find (when I reflect on it) is that I lose heart (I mean I get that sinking feeling in my heart and lungs, I guess it is, as if I had played it false) I know I can't just avoid this playing it false—you know, direct sentences like sound bridges from good solid island to good solid island; and contrive thought lines like pipe lines to conduct those few clear streams—because the bog is the bog and I really want to discover it on its own terms, which must be the naturalist's terms.

There is something of us that looks all wrong when we think of investing in it (that damnd bog would have to be drained and filld in to be worth a thing), but is a paradise for the happy frog-lover, or swamp grass enthusiast —and in its most rank and treacherous backwaters a teeming world of life for the biologist with his microscope. I did feel, anyway, as you do about that aspect, that revelation of what life has been that is in "Howl" and is also in "Kaddish." And I respond, too, to the troubled love for his mother Ginsberg gets across in those opening sections. But as strongly *react* against that "caw caw caw" thing at the close; which is the ugly hysteria, the shout in our ears, that tells only, by demonstration, that where the father is concernd he can tell us nothing, he is unmannd, reduced or increased to shouting.

The wealth of particulars, the full current of his mother's being that the earlier sections of "Kaddish" provide remain thrilling. Ginsberg gives us in his mother, in recreating her troubled, angry, fearful, starved nature, some beautiful human thing that he cannot give us in himself in his poetry—his own account of *his* life or experience goes bad on him. Well, but I've in mind all the "way out, man" stuff. For I still like the shorter poems of the *Howl* volume.

And if he has this shouting idiocy, I've come into the thick of my snow-balling idiocy. The H. D. section I'm sending you starts valiantly with a picture of a poetry as a network of meanings, weaving a dense reality—and has workd in me now a sense of how oppressive that wanting to make everything good can be.

Which does remind me now of that poem of mine Turnbull used about letting things go—reminds me of your questions about could you use anything for *The Nation* and about *Book of Resemblances*.[1] Of course you can. Do you think you could find a section of that "Essay at War" that would work? I have another piece of a long poem (written just after the "Venice Poem") that I've long treasured, that's short and might do.[2]

But wouldn't the real opportunity of your being poetry editor there for a while be to get some poets into print who are not likely to be printed somewhere?

For the first time—in Cid's new *Origin* Enslin's work came thru to me.[3] The four poems on 36–37 I found most beautiful. And called to my attention how this snow-balling thing is built in to my syntax—I've made it a possibility of moving in the poems. But what a lovely thing for me the direct attentive measures of these lyrics! I've yet to write him, and, in keeping, shld. be a postcard—so that my appreciations don't pile-up; but in homage go free—lovely poems—

*The Book of Resemblances* is planned by Grove. Don Allen tried to get it on the fall schedule, but they don't want it until 1962. Spring I hope. The long-range plan is to bring everything back into print. The book I am at work on now (poems) to be done in 1963—then *Letters* to be reprinted, and a *Collected* early poems 1940–1950 (where I shall select only so far as rescuing from manuscript only what seems demands it; but will include all of the first books thru *Caesar's Gate*).

About Virginia Admiral's plans—Jess wrote her right off; and now things are waiting on Helen's sending the copy to Virginia. But we are all most enthusiastic.

I've got to stop someplace (to get back to the task of getting typed up what I have done so far on the H. D.)—but about C. S. Lewis. The *Till We Have Faces* is his best, I think. And very exciting as you begin to see that he's, it's, going to go deeper than was obvious. The thing that rightly makes for distrust is that Lewis has a mind closed by his religious views. George MacDonald's mind is never closed; he writes from the truth of a heart that has found a way in Christian terms.

love
Robert

## 192

April 19, 1961
{San Francisco}

dear Denny,

Did I sent you a copy of the enclosed version of "Arethusa?"[1] Jess had done a painting of Arethusa's fountains and turnd to the Shelley to find a passage that fitted.[2] Then we tried to read the Shelley aloud, but its on-rushing regular stresses and rimes rang ludicrous in our ears, as if they did monkey imitations of themselves, having lost some secret of conformity—yet something in the poem haunted too and askd to be renderd. It was a bet too, over coffee, and I set myself to keep the current, the stream-form of the original, and wherever I could to keep the original intact: the basic thing was to get a shifting pace and pattern to it—to have pools, eddies, and fast and slow on rushes etc.

I did like Shelley's "pearléd thrones" in the opening of the 4th stanza; but it triggerd, stronger than the sound of it, a Walt Disney or fish-bowl grotto kitsch image. Well, once it was done—I saw that the bet could now be a dare in the book—for to work at the poem at all was so purely at first glance a labor in love of form; subject to attack as critics have attackd Stravinsky for using Tchaikowsky thus—by partisans of the original. And a dare too of your criterion of something real-life in a work. Tho here, it is true, I've known study and fascination in how water moves, waterfalls, pools and rushing streams are mothers, real enuf, of movement; and then the other current of the poem the two phases or lives of the lovers actually serves some meaning I found myself searching out.

The second new poem (writ yesterday) after reading a new sequence of H. D.'s[3]—a troubling piece (poetically troubling then) where she disturbs the poem's (the poet's) voice with her own. But this *own* or ownd voice plays us false, or plays something false in us: uses a poem in its course to ask the reader to sympathize{.} Yet the sequence is called "Hermetic Definitions" and the formal disturbance is around what is hidden and where it is defined.

I've to type out for you some new translations from Morgenstern Jess has completed that occurrd to me might interest you for *The Nation*.

Helen told me you had taken some of her unrhymed poetry as she calls it. I had liked the tear-raindrop poem which she sent me. But I think Helen is not sure of my response in these areas (as, I felt, the tear-raindrop poem was personally involved at a conscious level; she is shy where the poem is in the first person); for she seldom shows me such work—

love
Robert

Have you finished your H D book? N H P wrote that you had written "wonderfully."

Dear Robert

I'd certainly like to use "Fire Dying" (from "Essay at War")—however I don't want to hand it in right now because it would be tactless on account of its length (I saw what trouble they had getting in my poem "The Path" which Rosenthal had accepted a whole year ago).[1] So if I may I'll wait until towards the end of my spell there (in June) before doing so; and meanwhile, may I have "Salvages: Lassitude" from *A Bk of Resemblances*? "Of the Character" I don't truthfully care for as much as for most of yr. poems— I cd. tell you why—but I have several other things to say & I wont take the time—I will next time if you want me to.

Thanks for sending the Morgensterns,[2] and I'd like to keep "The Balls," please.

My idea at *The Nation* is simply to use only poems I really like; but not to make difficulties by trying to force in things they might feel are too far out, or which are simply too long for that kind of magazine. I am only there for 3 months & I need the money. I've turned down poems by famous bores. And I've got an H. D. & a William Carlos Williams & some other nice things. If they like what I do they may ask me to come back in the fall. In that case I

**193**

May 4th 1961
277 Greenwich St
NY 7

would feel more secure. But in fact tho I don't now feel so secure, nothing controversial has come up. I'm not asking Olson or Zukofsky for poems, simply because there's so much of their work I don't really like and it would only lead to hurt & offense if I didn't like the ones they might send.

On the other hand I'm trying hard to avoid accepting things by friends just because they're friends. I've not asked Jerry R or Kelly because I find their poems so weak (Jerry's a *fine* translator I think but his own work seems to be only just begun). I'm turning down some Blackburn poems.

Did you see the Spring Book / "Form-Smashing" issue? It wasn't what Hatch had intended & he says he will use my piece later. I was glad as I want to re-do it anyway. What happened to yours though? There was an idiotic piece by Bly—I now find it hard to remember liking him. Ug. But the article on painting I liked very much indeed, especially the paragraph where he speaks about Rembrandt.[3]

A poem came from Wilbur & without even looking at it I took it home to write a tactful rejection as it had been more or less solicited by Merwin before I started there; & to my astonishment found that it was a really marvellous poem, not a bit Wilburish—it has an Anglo-Saxon form (that caesura, alliteration etc.) and is a lovely strong poem. I wrote to him saying I was keeping it because it had convinced me in spite of my general dislike for his work & he wrote back saying he "guessed we were at war" but was glad there could be truces & saying he liked my "Well" poem & its sequel.[4] By the way, please note that all that's in current issues is still Merwin's choice (tho some I wd certainly have taken also, such as Barbara Guest's "Brown Study," did you see that? The best poem she's ever written, I think). Wd. like Robin Blaser's address, please.

We had a very pleasant weekend at Bard, with Ted Weiss & his wife. We picked violets & enjoyed the Hudson.

Have you seen *The World of Apu*?[5] It's one of the best films I've ever seen. My other absolute favorite is *Les Regles du Jeu*.[6]

Some of Helen Adam's "other" poems weren't so good but there were several I liked very much and what's curious is that they're so clear and bare—winter trees—so different from the *texture* of the ballads.

I'm writing some poems about the Eichmann trial, around some of the evidence, things he said, etc. One is done—the others only just hovering.[7]

I have a reading next week for which I need the typescripts I have & after that I'll send you a bunch of poems—at last.

Creeley'll be here before long—I hope his visit isn't too disruptive as we'll be in the middle of packing for Maine. (I'll be doing *The Nation* stuff by mail in June—they don't know it yet. But I think it will work out.)

Love—
Denny.

Dear Robert

The "Arethusa" is most marvellous. I have been comparing it with
Shelley's. If I were trying to show someone who didn't know another
language what an inspired translation could be, one that didn't try to copy
the original slavishly but to give it new life by imitating the spirit of it this
wd. be the shining illustration. I suppose Shelley's rhythms struck the ear
differently in his day. Indeed looking at my 1826 edition I seemed to catch
for a minute something of *his* freshness & newness. But you've made
something not only right for our ears now but of itself richer, and carried
further. (In reading his by the way I find it sounds better read [inappro-
priately] slow, with a pause, almost a caesura, in each 3d line—

Shepherding
                        her bright fountains
.    .    .    .    .    .    .    .    .    .    .
Which slopes
                    to the western gleams
.    .    .    .    .    .    .    .    .    .    .
The bars
                of the springs below
Weave
            a network of coloured light
.    .    .    .    .    .    .    .    .    .    .
And the meadows
                        of Asphodel
etc etc.

Almost like a rallentando in a waltz.

And in the other (after reading H. D.) poem I love the movement through
it of the thought of bees, and the way "lunch" can come into it just as much
as Isis.

Then there's your article which I haven't taken in properly but which is
full of interest & which I'll take to Maine to reread at leisure. It's true it's
not very suitable for a weekly like *The Nation*; but surely you will publish it
somewhere?

I am hoping to get them to do a page of prose poems (you, Turnbull,
Russell Edson, Robert Nichols, a purposely mixed bunch, with an intro-
ductory note I've written[1]—what I have of yours is the other "Salvages:
An Evening Piece" (which I've typed)—is that O.K.? The poem "Salvages
(Lassitude)" will be held back for a little while as they are deciding on a
new, bolder typeface for poems that will mean a delay in getting proofs out
for a few weeks. (Also the Jess/Morgenstern poem)

I'm sending you mine, I mean my article, hoping you wont think it is too
sophomoric—I'd never written an article before & am glad he didn't use it

**194**

May 29th {31 1961}
277 Greenwich
NY 7

so I have a chance to rework it some time. Let me have it back please, as I don't have a readable copy.

I am really longing to send you some poems—there are quite a number you've not seen. But I've just not had time to type them. We are trying to get ready to leave for Temple, Maine by the 7th and are swathed in Mitch's proofs (which look great—nice Jansen type). At least I've just about finished Nik's camp stuff (nametapes) because I misread the notice & thought it had to be expressed by the 1st—really it was the 10th—so I'm a bit ahead. But I am so tired I am almost sick—you can see it in my handwriting—I must try to arrange my life differently, this is not the way it should be I know.

Creeley is here & I just spoke to him on the phone—he & Bobbie are coming over tomorrow morning. We'll miss his reading at Living Theater tonight because we only heard of it yesterday & have an engagement involving other people that we really can't put off.

In July while Nik's at camp we *may* get to Europe (Italy & Greece)—I hope it works out. 6 weeks. I want to send you & Jess something for your new dwelling but haven't seen the right thing yet—perhaps I'll come upon something during the summer. I regret not having seen Stinson Beach.

I thought Ted Enslin's "Landscape with Figures" the best thing he's ever done, & very good, but in general I am despondent about his work which strikes me as very weak & actually lacking some vital part, I'm not sure what.

> Much love always—
> Denny.

May 31st

What's the explanation of a pkge. of *Here & Now* I received? A mystery. Thanks very much anyway—but let me know what, how, etc.

A black kitten has come to us. She is to be called Marimba as we were playing a marimba record at the time. She's no more than 6 weeks old. Lucia will keep her for us till the autumn.

Bob & Bobbie were here yesterday. Glad to see them.

> Love—
> Denny

## 195

June 19th {19}61
Temple, Maine

Dear Robert,

Wd you consider reviewing H. D.'s *Helen in Egypt* for *The Nation*? I'm asking you well in advance in the hope that, if you can do it, you could begin on it before the review copy comes in, as you will no doubt have had the poem directly from her anyway. If for some reason you don't want to undertake it, would you do me a favor & suggest someone else? I feel it as a great responsibility, to find the right reviewer for it. Can't do it myself because a) I feel—honestly—too ignorant, just not up to it. And b), I don't like to thrust myself in while I'm poetry editor (they have asked me to continue there in the fall for another 3 months) If it is not you, it has obviously to be someone who properly appreciates H D, & preferably someone eminent.

Saw the loveliest fat woodchuck, & a doe, & lots of birds, & lovely moths on the window at night—such big-eyed personages *they* are.

We are leaving to go to Italy & Greece for 6 weeks at the end of June—free (fare)!—did I tell you? Then back here.

That article Hatch returned is a really terrific piece. I gather his trouble was he'd never heard of Elisabeth Thing so he thought it was an attack out of the blue.[1] I do believe that if you'd put a note giving the name of her book, publisher, etc., he would have reacted differently. Though I suppose it would be too long even so—and I can't really see where it could be cut. Wd you want me to talk to him about it? He actually admires you very much in his way—"He's a magician," says he—to which I fervently assented. This was before I heard what he'd desired you to cut, & I then had no further opportunity to talk to him about it.

One other thing: He is interested in doing that prose-poem thing I got together, but it looks as if there'll be a space problem. He suggested cutting the 2d ½ of the "Salvages: An Evening Piece"—i.e., "Notes on Use & Values." I hate to be asking you to cut *anything*, & I wd. be sorry to lose that last paragraph ("Beautiful litter! . . . "). But I *do* ask, in case you wd. be willing, & hoping you will not be annoyed. The other things I have (Russell Edson, Bob Nichols, & Gael Turnbull) are none of them as long as even the 1st part alone. Please let me know soon about this if you can because I want to hand it all in completed on June 29th if poss. (the day we will be in NY before leaving for Rome.)

Our kitten Marimba seems to be having a good time with the Newtons & Lucia writes that she rides on Jeff's shoulder (he is 3 yrs old & about 2 feet high!)

Mitch has an abcess in his nose, his cheek is swollen & he's had to stay in bed for the last 2 days & take pills. I think it's getting better. Otherwise all is well here, I wish you & Jess cd see it. Some day you will, DV.[2]

By the way it seems as if I might have a chance to come to Berkeley to read—I can't stand Louis Simpson, who asked Paterson Soc. to arrange it,[3] but I'd be so glad to visit SF again that for the sake of seeing you & Jess there again I'd put up with him as gracefully as poss.

Love—
Denny

P.S.

Did you see the article on Perse which I obtained for *The Nation* from Octavio Paz?[4]

I think I may say that if you do the H D review it could be the same length & I will get him to use it in the same way as a "lead article" because he will agree that it is a literary event—he was quite excited when I got a poem from H. D., & plans to print it with special prominence.

P.P.S.

W. C. W. has had another stroke. All I know is that, & that he was in Paterson Gen. Hospital when we left on the 8th. My god, we've not seen a paper, he could have died for all I know. I have poor hopes for his making a good recovery this time, alas.

Hope to have news from Floss or Laughlin soon.

## 196

June 22, 1961
{San Francisco}

dear Denny,

I airmaild off the first 86 pages of the "Day Book" yesterday, and now with this—another installment. Hoping it will arrive, surely it will, before the 28th—

1. Yes, I would want to review *Helen in Egypt*. The only part I have seen is the "Winter's Love," the close, I take it. But I'm sure Norman Pearson will be able to arrange for me to have the rest of the text to prepare me. This "Day Book" is the center section of the whole H. D. study; the opening section—Did I send any to you earlier? being the early memories of reading poetry. ["In the Beginning"]

Then I want some summing-up essay at the close. And, if the shaping of the book permits, some scatterd analyses of poems and scatterd notes.

I'll try on the *Helen in Egypt* review to keep it of a reasonable shape and size. I won't have, anyway, the feeling that I've to say everything about H. D. there—for the book takes care of so much.

2. I *was* disgusted when I glanced over Bly's account that took the place of the piece I wrote. But there was nothing in Hatch's correspondence with me that wasn't cordial and even solicitous.

What I had was the occasion to tackle writing the essay. I just don't know yet—and may never succeed there—how to get my mind and feeling of a thing moving in a form that is appropriate for a weekly. If someone along the line wants it, O.K. but don't make any issue of it.

3. Since the complete poem will be available, all going well, next spring or summer when *A Book of Resemblances* is brought out by Grove—I think it would be O.K. to use only the opening, if you need it{.}

We are elated by the prospect of your coming here again! But did I write that, after all my resolutions about not reading again in the East until the new book is finishd—the poems, and that wouldn't have been until 1963, an invitation came two weeks ago from the Institute of Contemporary Arts in Washington asking would I either in the Fall of 1961 or the Spring of '62, and I wrote immediately saying I would, in April or May of next year.

Now I am elated and dreading too that we might not have schedules that work out. When does Berkeley plan for you to read? And will the Paterson Society get in touch with the Poetry Center here?

I've not yet heard from the ICA about actual dates set—

love,
Robert

H. D. too has had a stroke—and, it's been a week, Norman writes that tho she can move a bit and tries to talk "she has not really recovered any very measurable consciousness." He left for Munich on the 16th and will be seeing her this week.

[herein pages 161–174; the others are being sent separately]

dear Denny,

Clearing things preparatory to fly north tonight for three weeks—during which I've got the Perse article and the H. D. review in mind to do. Pearson had evidently long ago asked Grove to send me page proofs for they arrived just after I wrote this earlier letter to you. Since I wrote another item has been added re- the prospects of coming East in the Spring: Over all my very bad temper and deliberated flare-up in correspondence with Betty Kray two years ago [I had wanted to make sure I wouldn't ever be tempted to read for the YMHA], she followed up the I.C.A. invitation, writing and asking if I would read. Which I all but shouted YES to, and did have some rudiments of grace to thank her for over-riding my frame-of-mind.

Now you've got a great part of what I've done to date on the H. D. And I do want to anticipate queries you may have.

1) The "anger" at critics and the dominant school of poetry (or dominant taste) all needs to be rendered, focussed, and developed. As you will see in the later part of this section, the parts on Ransom begin to yield something.

2) This whole "Day Book"—will be organized in the final revision in larger sections

    I -   The Weaving

    II -  Disturbance

    III - The Work

    part 4 of III   The Child

But it would be a real aid if you would take this thing to task; I find new things open for me sometimes if I set about "making things more clear"

197

July 14/ 1961
{San Francisco}

(rendering) or trying to face up to the distortions (focussing). And this is a book of learning how to write a book for me.

H. D. has recovered consciousness, the course of life, but with all the agony of the speech-centers in the brain being injured. "Yet she does have fiercely the desire to communicate," Norman writes—"and strikes her breast in passionate frustration when there is no word at her tongue's tip. Sometimes whole sentences will come; sometimes, everything but the key word. So it is "I want . . . " but one can never tell what it is she wants. One simply does not know how this will come out. It will be six months, maybe a year. Meanwhile she says, "When? When?"

love
Robert

## 198

Aug 18th {19}61
{Temple, Me.}

Dearest Robert

We left a day or so early so only heard from you on arriving back here yesterday. I am so distressed about H. D. Do let me know what else you've since heard. I'm writing to Norman & to her right away also. I wrote to her from Greece—the only letter I sent anyone except Nik & my mother & Mitch's father the whole time I was away. The 6 weeks was wonderful. Will write to you properly about it in a day or 2. I've not even looked at yr MS yet as we got here very tired last night and I have to get a few letters off before anything else.

Nik had a good camp season & Mitch's book is coming along nicely & will be in the stores Sept. 1st—we shd have an advance copy by Monday. You'll get one very soon.

Weeds have grown up madly all around house including nasty prickly burdock but otherwise it is a very heaven-haven. I have enormous quantities of work to tackle but I feel like it after the journeys.

Love to Jess & to you
from Denny.

Took yr rejected *Nation* article to Europe & dug into it—it is a marvellous thing & if you haven't sent it somewhere else I intend to try to persuade Hatch to use it when I go back in Sept.

## 199

Wednesday 23rd
{August 23, 1961}
Temple {Me.}

Dear Robert,

I'm starting on the H. D. now. Had to work my way thru' accumulated *Nation* stuff first to get it out of the way. Just piles of it. Also things like laundry. Will make notes as I go if I think of anything, & hope they wont come too late to be of any use.

Haven't found a house present for your no-longer-new apartment but yesterday in an old furniture shop in Farmington found 2 little books which I'm sending with the thought that Jess might find collage bits in them. Sending separately.

Abt. Berkely, don't know till Ellie D.{orfman} lets me know—maybe it won't even materialize.

What news of H. D.?

Love to Jess & to you—
Denny

dear Denny,

Your note, upon return, came today, so I've the sense of your getting this letter right off; and hasten to check up on a few points.

1) did I write about my accepting The Poetry Center in New York (for April 8th, it looks like it will be) next Spring? The date for reading at the I.C.A. has not been set, but the commitment there has been made. Robin is in correspondence with Sweeney at Harvard who is putting the possibility of my reading there before committee. As it is, I have enough from the YMHA and the ICA to make it possible for Jess to come East with me; and Harvard would begin to finance our actual expenses beyond transportation.

2) Re. the H. D. book—what you should have on hand now is the ms of the central portion of the book, provisionally titled "Little Day Book" and numbered pages 1 thru 174. But I've ended up, I think, with an extra of pages 127–160—do you have these O.K.?

Did I ever send you any of the first section? The readings of "Heat" and "I hear an Army—"?

3) "Ideas of the Meaning of Form" should have some kind of subtitle— "Part One" would be best. For, when I am at last able, I most want to do another essay on *Organic Form* of the nineteenth-century, evolution of melodies or melody as the evolution. The essay written for *The Nation* tho has had good reception in Vancouver where Warren Tallman has had the piece mimeographed for his classes. I'll write him and have him send you a copy, for I don't think the manuscript you have on hand is the corrected manuscript as prepared when I submitted it for publication.

• Did you know, when you suggested O'Gorman ask me for a piece on Perse,[1] that Perse was central in one of H. D.'s unpublished works?[2] or that, long ago, when I was in Woodstock I set out to translate Perse's *Éleges* which had been the first book I had to read in French, there being then (1940) no translation? The last month has been spent in an intensive reading of *Anabase, Amers* and *Chroniques*; and since I came back from Vancouver, of *Exil.* How hastily and vaguely I seem to read poetry! If it *is* poetry, it's built up of resistances to generality, of meanings crucial in each part to the whole. What's happened in reading Perse is a moving realization of what his meanings are; and that they not only are not conceivably Catholic, but they are not Christian, tho they include Christianity as one among religions. There is no deep understanding of life or the real, for Perse, outside of poetry. There is no way fairly to present that to the Catholic understanding without making clear that we are concerned in this poetry with a communion not in Christ but in the human spirit.

I found a beautiful passage in Plotinus *Against the Gnostics*: "To those who assert that creation is the work of the Soul after the failing of its wings, we answer that no such disgrace could overtake the Soul of All. . . . We assert its creative act to be a proof not of decline but rather of its steadfast hold. . . . What fire could be a nobler reflection of the fire there than the fire we know here?

"Still more unreasonably: There are men, bound to human bodies and subject to desire, grief, anger, who think so generously of their own faculty that they declare themselves in contact with the Intelligible World, but deny that the sun possesses a similar faculty. . . . Their own soul, the soul of the least of mankind, they declare deathless, divine; but the entire heavens and the stars within the heavens have had no communion with the Immortal Principle."

In *Amers*, Perse evokes beyond the more explicit human communion (as in his Nobel address)—a "life" communion, an alliance with the Sea—it is the Sea that dreams in us; that women in labour imitate; it is the Sea that is the Language that changes its dialects at all ports of call. "la face inachevée du dieu" It is the full crowd of humanity:

> "Toujorns il y ent, derrière la foule riveraine, ce pur grief d'un autre songe [page 50 of *Seamarks*]—ce plus grand songe d'un autre art, ce plus grand songe d'une autre oeuvre, et cette montée toujours du plus grand masque à l'horizon des hommes, ô Mer vivante du plus grand texte! . . . Tu nous parlais d'un autre vin des hommes, et sur nos textes avilis il y eut soudain cette bouderie de lèvres qu'engendre toute satiété,
>
> Et nous savons maintenant ce qui nous arrêtait de vivre, au milieu de nos strophes."

• The article on Perse, whether appropriate to publication or not, is to be done by the end of this week. Then, with the *Helen in Egypt* essay I will return to the H. D. Book (currently now, on Thursdays the group that was meeting to hear the H. D. book is attending my reading of the Helen text)—but I will be so glad, relieved! when at last these duties to "Poetry" are done, and I might collapse into or relax into an empty or yearning mind waiting for the invasion of words and lines.

Friday,

Just that I almost tore this up, Denny—as if I could somehow start any fresher. My mind is overloaded for the few circuits that can carry thru the information. Damn it! I wish I could let go having to bear down on any critical object so. That's what I think caught me in the Plotinus passage— once I went back to copy it for you, it didn't seem so beautiful in itself. There's the high thot of a god who is in the sun as well as in the man that most moves me. But this morning, after more Perse, where such a mise-en-scène gathers that there never seems to be place for the so much that depends on wheelbarrow—so many thresholds that actual immediate door sill is dissolved in the glamor of greater orders.

Then, without laboring it further—the actual immediate poem of Perse, the just-what-I-am-reading, is lost in over- and under-meanings. I've been following for some time now a criterion of *meaning* for the poem (versus ornament or grammatical effect)—but the fabric of Perse, swarming with meanings as it does, throwing up a net of suggestions (he is really adept at what I only try in the "Structure of Rime" things) does not lead me on further now but awakens a keener sense of how right we are (as in this Williams most was) to insist upon the saving grace not of the common place object but of keeping the presence of things actual in the poem, insisting on evidence of the sensory correspondence—as the condition and ultimate verification of the thing.

The "une même vague par le monde, une même vague par le Ville" thrills me, as waves, after all, do overwhelm one, and Perse's verse that in *Anabase* fascinated in *Amers* sweeps on. But then I begin to realize that the feeling of a sweeping vision leaves no residue of seeing for the specific fact. I've got to have particulars and individual realizations to give me a concrete beauty— it's the very material world that Perse seems (especially in his Nobel Award speech) to cast aside as unin-formed by Poetry that offers some presence to resist my understanding. The spiritual (breath) world is all already there in words, all its secrets are secrets of language as a medium, intoxications of logos. It isn't that there's no challenge in the language in itself—but I think now that there is an order of ideas that must come into counterplay (I used to consider that any *idea* was verbal—but then there was the key in Plato's pointing out that an *idea* was a thing seen: now I think "ideas" can come to interplay not only with the medium of words, but with working in stone, or sounds as music, or actions as history or drama. What we "know" ultimately is a realization or capability of the real)—

and there is an order of things, of actual happening that must come into counterplay towards fullness: thru our recognitions and striving after the quality of experience, withholding the use of things to feed our emotions, in order to gain their own presence.

The Perse is so beautiful (I'm thinking here of the *Amers* which has been the overwhelming experience for me, and left me fighting against its undertows). I think that I learned more about melodies of image and phoneme from my early adoration of *Anabase* than from Pound or Williams or H. D. from whose texts I began later to gather patterns of our American poetic speech. He leads by sound alone as I do, to trust and celebrate the line of feeling as part of the real. Well, the sound is as actual a sensory evidence of what is as the sight is—the difference is that each sound thing perishes with much less duration. The chair endures when the sound of "the chair" is lost as a particular sensation and lasts only in its memory, and memory is more likely to rise as a current of feeling. It takes an effort of memory to establish an immediate particular.

Well, it's only to write to you, I realize, how much I agree with your response on Kelly's "Deep Image," where you get at what I've been trying to get at about ideas and words and things so much more fully—it is, I see now, the quest for wholeness (the whole self and the whole world lie in the same event—we find ourselves only as we find the world)

It's a piece, Denny, that I find "speaks to me" and gains new assent every time I go to it.

love
Robert

## 201

Have read all today & all yesterday & the evening before. Do you need this copy back? I hope not.

Dearest Robert

It is a treasure-mine. It will be a book I shall live with. That's why my notes are all so pernicketty—all minor points, for what small use they may have. There's no major point in such a rewarding complexity for me to query.

A large beautiful green grasshopper who must have come in by daylight is on my wall—will have to rescue him for he'll starve indoors. But he'll be hard to catch. P.S. *I did.*

If you see *The Nation*, look for the next issue because that poem by Wilbur I told you about will be in it I think.[1] Hope you like it. The two being run by it were chosen by Bill Merwin before I started, but luckily I like them. Hope after this to have only my own choices used as long as I am there.

How was your visit North?

Look forward to seeing HD review. When is publication date of *Helen in Egypt*?

Is there another opening section of "The Day Book" then?—"In the Beginning"? What I have begins March 10, Friday—Naming the stars—

If you will be East in May perhaps you could come up here with us for a few days in June before going back? It's not a *comfortable* house to stay in, exactly—I mean, washing is at a minimum, the outhouse tilts to one side & so forth—but I think you'd like to see it. Will Jess come too?

Love—

Denny.

Notes on "The Little Day Book." [See final comment, p. 8 here, first.}

*p. 1*  To me the reference to *O'Ryan* is irrelevant despite its obvious relevance to opening paragraphs, because the Olson poem is not a meaningful one to me.[2] I wonder if, then, the reference will have any *function* for other readers, save for those who already admire O.? I think bringing this in here is perhaps a bit self indulgent.

*p. 3*  Paragraph on Cocteau—Meaning, I take it, that this book is a Poésie Critique? Yes. But maybe the paragraph itself is set too much alone, needs to join onto before & after sentences?

*p. 4*  I like very much the passage ending "no longer *her* art but *The* Art."

*p. 4*  I don't feel sure if this is the right place for what amounts to a bibliography—it shd be in a place of its own, at beginning or end, so that one can turn to it easily for reference.

*p. 6*  From whom is the quote, "the valiant yet totally . . . "?

*pp. 7 & 8 & 9 etc*  on Pound & WCW very fine. The relating of the movement of their lives & work (& hers) to the movement of history.

*pp. 10/11*  Might not the *O'Ryan* passage I objected to come in here, at the end (or near it) of this? Echoing back to the prologue of p.1, and forward to the "Stars, spirits, the dead" passage that follows here?

*p. 12*  I don't really like the "resumé"-like part on Bryher taken from WCW. Much as I feel towards him I don't trust him on H. D., trust the whole *Autobiog.* little, written as it was when he was deeply disturbed, *half-cracked* one cd. truly say. So that I think you shdn't use it as direct source. And in any case I really hate this style of quotation which is journalistic & not worthy of you. That you call it "rancor" on *p. 13* doesn't really undo it, either.

*p. 18*  "& even Wallace Stevens" is ambiguous—no indication given of why "even." Could be taken for a sneer.

*p. 17, p. 26, other places*  I think you overuse the DHL—or DHL-period—expression "the this *thing*"—"the that *thing*"—OK in its use on p 17, at the end of that section, ironic use. But in "What I had meant to" etc. on p. 21 (& some other places I think) it begins to look like a mannerism taken over.

*p. 49*  I find lines from: "For, as in Bosch's vision," up to: "troubled eras" unclear. In what way do "realists & cynics of troubled eras" live in "a kingdom not of this world"? And aren't artists, poets, etc. more truly "of the world" essentially, than anyone else? And can one equate (as you seem to here) these classes of people with members of any "little cult"—of Beauty or whatever? I don't believe you do, but that's the way it reads to me.

*p. 58*  Should not "We have introduced . . . " follow directly after "onto account.," without space and star*?

*p. 62*  "Williams writes" etc. shd come after "or whatever it may be" not after "inheritance," which breaks up his sentence wrongly in emphasis.

*p. 63*  How marvellously you say ("The secret of the poetic art," etc.) just what I was trying to say in that piece I wrote for *The Nation*—[& which I just discovered you retyped for me—thank you!—so that even tho' you don't say anything about it in a letter I suppose you didn't *dislike* it, or you couldn't have borne to type thru' it!]

*p. 71*  Here your use of the word "cult" comes into the focus it does not have on p. 49
Passage beginning "In *Narthex*" is very illuminating.

*p. 82*  Why do you lump Rexroth in with Ransom, Bogan, Tate, & Winters? I am curious. Whatever Kenneth is, that seems unfair. Can you really justify it? Shdnt you qualify it with an "*even* Rexroth"?

*p. 83*  My copy ends "as my own book of" and *p. 84* begins "To be aroused." Please let me have missing page—83a, perhaps? Or is it that (what I have at top of p. 85) "women" is the next word. Oh, I have it straightened out now, all those page numbers were wrong.

*p. 88*  I disagree with Jack Spicer because, just because such a work as this is beyond being an academic textbook, it is a soul-work, it is a process for you, & through you for the reader, of understanding, of penetration, so that all possible "trying" you (or whoever engages in such a work) can do is—what shall I say?—honorable, fair (in both senses) and indeed necessary. Even in poems it's the same really, I've come to think, i.e. the argument against revision is not a moral one but simply the practical one, that, so much being *given* by the Muse, one is only liable to botch what one has if one fusses about after the Muse has left, or if one tries to induce her to stay . . . In prose (I think) less is given in the first instance so that one has more latitude, in changing, for improvement—or perhaps that shd be the other way round, more possibility for improvement when one revises. And wherever the possibility exists one has an obligation to follow it. That's what I think.

*p. 90*  "whose name I did not recognize." I don't remember—tho I too looked it up. Wasn't it "Peter Warlock"/Philip Heseltine and isn't it he who has the house in Cornwall in *Bid Me to Live*?[3]

*p. 106*  ends "inscribed above their bed:"/but p. 107 begins "Lilith

Outcome." The phrase was "God is a Woman," correct? But there may be a whole page missing?

From here on, (up to *p 127* & then the section *161–174*) I've found no comments to make.

---

N.B. Some of the first of these notes (all written as I read along) were biased by an ignorance of the form (nature) of the book. e.g., note on Cocteau passage.

dear Denny,

Just arrived—your generous letter and reading of the "Day Book": you will have gotten now a letter from me asking if your ms. was complete. It sounds as if the section I have left over here 128 thur 160 *does* belong to your copy, and so I send it directly on.

Thank god, your notes "are all so pernicketty" it must (I must) be brought to full responsibility—against self-indulgences. Robin Blaser noted a whole series of points; Don Allen caught other doubtful areas—your page by page directions bring a fresh demand. It's not that I want the book "fool proof," but that there be only the real in it. And these notes will help me immensely in the task before me of the realized draft. (re: your note on prose revisions: what I took from Spicer's advice was to write straight ahead and *then* work the whole in typing the text.)

I feel I render the text. The notebooks are most unsatisfactory in many places. (As I still feel the whole introduction paragraphs of the worrisome academic poets theme must be rendered true, which it just isn't yet)—

But damn it! I've *got*[1] to get the Perse thing done and off. I can't let my thought get caught up here, Denny—for now, just how much help it is to have you query the text, and, of course, how rewarded I am that you find passages that communicate.

The pages 127 thru 160 are enclosed. I'll be sending the first section of the book as soon as I can find copy or type new copy—

love
Robert

**202**

August 28, 1961
{San Francisco}

Are any of Robert Fitzgerald's own poems good? I don't know them. He seems to me a very fine translator.[1] Paz who is too vague himself did not get hold of that vagueness that used to make me unreceptive to Perse. But he did give me a keen sense of Perse's virtues & sent me to reread him which I did with new appreciation.

**203**

August 31st {1961}
Temple {Me.}

Dear Robert,

I think I gave you the page numbers of the H. D. MS. I have. But, no, you never sent me a section on "I hear an Army" etc. Look forward to getting all I miss now.

If *The Nation* article is to be subtitled "part I" it should really wait, I think, until you have written a part II, so that if poss. they could go into adjoining issues. I long to see what you'll do on Organic Form. This has been a year for me of preoccupation to some extent with the formulation of (or organization of) theory & I am continually finding that you've said is just what I was trying to get at. Actually I know there is great danger for me in all this for it can keep one from writing poems. Yet perhaps there are times in one's life when one *must* define to oneself & to others what one is after. A periodic (seasonal) clearing of the ground. I've been asked to give 8 lectures at School of Visual Arts—turned it down as 8 is more than I cd do without padding, I felt. Now they say 4 wd. be O.K. But fee is very low & after discussion with M.{itch} I decided not to do it unless they offer more, because of the time and energy involved.

But it is an attractive proposition in a way as the students wd. "be 3d yr (graduating) averaging 21 yrs of age, & about as heterogeneous as you can get, both in terms of potential & background. Few have read Joyce, not many more have heard of him. They are not likely to know Eliot, or Pound; they dont know Hopkins & if they by chance encountered him, they still wouldn't know a sprung rhythm if it bit them. But they *are* extremely sympathetic, & what is important, they *do* want to know. The class may run as high as 60 students."

I would not presume to do this sort of thing with an already knowledge-able audience such as yr group in SF, god knows, but I feel I could do something useful with people like these. Yr. liking my Deep Image thing encourages me to feel I *can* say what I mean in prose. In fact I'm almost sorry I didn't just accept without dickering. But when I think of the price such an involvement may make me pay in fatigue, housework inefficiency, danger of irritability with Nik, etc., I guess I was right to hold out for more money which wd mean more household help (I did have a weekly cleaner & ironer come in last spring & it helped).

I must tell you a vain thing concerning Perse which gave me a lot of pleasure. When *Chroniques* came into *The Nation* I had an inspiration in suggesting Octavio Paz (whom I'd seen a good deal of during his N.Y. visit, & who'd just returned to Paris) to do the review. He did a beautiful one in Spanish, Jerry Rothenberg translated it, I revised the translation, and it appeared. Then, it appears, George Kirstein the owner/publisher/chief editor (behind McWilliams) was in Washington & Perse invited him to dinner specially to tell him thank you for the review. Not only that but it turned out that he knew & liked *my* poems; which was a great surprise & pleasure to me because somehow I'd never imagined him reading his younger contemporaries, he sounds so lofty & remote & besides isn't American. If you didn't see Paz's essay will send it to you in Sept.

Ned O'Gorman at *Jubilee* whose poems I reviewed rather critically last spring when I did Ignatow & that odious Yale Younger Poet Alan something {Dugan}, is a dear sweet chap, curiously naive tho' having various *connections*, social & literary—a cradle Catholic of fervor, with a bad stammer & a heart of gold.[2]

Did I ever tell you of my meeting with Muriel Rukeyser? We both read for Grad. Eng. Society at Columbia, bunch of deadheads, in company with Anthony Hecht who is all manner & mockery, so our meeting was like a thunderclap, we practically rushed into each others' arms. I thought her a quite wonderful Giantess, a kind of Great Mother terrible & encompassing, with her hem coming unsewn & hanging down & a vast Pentacle on her pinky (a silver ring). A shy engineer asked, "It must seem a foolish question, but what shd. I bring to poetry to get the most out of it?" & she answered after a moment's silence, both vehemently & modestly, "One *must* 'make a fool of oneself' and ask these questions. And I answer, you must bring to poetry neither more nor less than one must bring to life itself (or, to anything in life that one truly *lives*)—that is, *all* of yourself." That's not quite exact, but almost. It was a beautiful spontaneous thing. I expect to see her in the fall. You know, it was a quote in her review of yr. early book in *Poetry*, read in Florence U.S.I.S. Library in 1948,[3] that was the first I ever knew of you. "There is an innocence in women that asks me, asks me . . . " and, "Among my friends love is a great burden"—I misquote I'm sure, burden's not the word, but that line anyway. Then when I first came to NY I found & pounced upon the book on Cornelia St.[4]

How much I'd like to read the unpublished H. D. in which Perse figures. Is there much unpublished work? I suppose there must be.

I received a kind letter from Bryher which I'll enclose (please return). I expect you have this news but thought you might like to see it anyway. The poem ("A Small Grain of Worship") she let me have for *The Nation* is to be run very soon—it will be mentioned on the front cover and run on the 1st page of back section. I hope seeing it will be a small pleasure for her, knowing her feeling of neglect here. Will see you get a copy. No doubt you already know the poem.

Hope the little pkge to you & Jess comes safely—Nik was supposed to have it weighed & add postage if necessary but he forgot. Nik just read *Tale of 2 Cities* & seemed to get a lot out of it. Is now starting *Red Badge of Courage*.

Love—

Denny

P.S.

Yes, am delighted about yr. Y reading. It seems Charles has not accepted as yr partner tho—a pity. Betty {Elizabeth Kray} wrote that she thought of Ashbery—I immediately wrote to discourage this idea as it seemed to me a bad one. Personally I can't see his work. But not only that, I knew you would not want a predominantly N.Y. homosexual audience which is what he wd. draw. Did I do right? She wants me to "introduce" which since I'm probably introducing Creeley & Blackburn in October I'm not keen on as it makes me look like a professional M. C. But I may if she can't find anyone who'd do it better. Who wd. *you* suggest as a possible partner? (If poss someone already in the East) I seem to have gotten involved. I wish she'd ask me to be yr partner! Or do I? I'm not sure. Wd sooner just be audience.

Love—

D

P.P.S.

Let me know if you like the Wilbur poem, "Junk," which I took. It's in current *Nation* (Sept. 2d) together with 2 poems chosen by Merwin.

## 204

September 6th {1961
Temple, Me.}

P.S.

School of Visual Arts doubled their offer and I'm going to do that. I have 3 or 4 new poems which I'll be sending you, I hope, soon.

Dear Robert & Jess,

I'll be seeing you somewhere between Oct 21–Nov 11th, it seems! Ellie D.{orfman} has dates for me at Berkeley & S.F. Poetry Center. Whew!

This means also that I cant "introduce" Creeley & Blackburn at Y on Oct 22 and that I *will* be doing the introduction for you & Gil Sorrentino (probably—well, pretty certainly).

Hope by the way you feel OK about Sorrentino. Moi, I feel an increasing respect for him. I liked his letter on Burroughs in *Floating Bear*,[1] review of Whalen in, I think, *Kulchur*, and many of his recent poems.[2] Betty Kray wd have liked to have someone of yr own stature but as you know Olson didn't accept. (Why, I wonder?) And it seems Sorrentino was very pleased to be asked.

Received latest batch of pages. Will make notes. Wonderful things here.

Love—

D.

Letter from N. H. P. this morning much less optimistic about H. D. than the Bryher letter, alas.

dearest Denny,

When your letter arrived this morning, with your readings here at last an actual fact I set about arranging the library-study so that now in an afternoon, lacking only the moving in of a studio couch, we have a guest room! I had been postponing shifting my desk and work tables into a more convenient grouping for months. Tables had been added, awkwardly, as papers seemed to flood out to take up more surface space. Here now I am with the surface organized into a beautiful consolidated block and the desk turned around at last the right way for the light—with the result that there's lots of space for a bed and moving around too. Well, it was a big room to begin with.

Will you be our first guest then? This room is quite separate from the living room and kitchen where we do most of our daily living room—I'm more likely (except for typing) to write in the kitchen at the dining table. There are several points gathered in New York and elsewhere—a guest room is best if it's away from the living room (at Klina's in Boston I had a room opening off of the living room;[1] and at the Rothenbergs slept in the living room itself you remember. It makes one a victim of late hours)—And here, when Ruth Witt would have captive poets to lionize I remember another bother, the difficulty of visiting or having them visit without including the hostess.

So I would urge you ahead of time to think of your staying with us for our having you here—and where people here really want to see *you*, we will try, where we anticipate that is the case, to help matters.

I am so pleased with the way I've fixed up the study I sit looking at the whole thing smugly in between lines.

The books arrived—the language-picture book is some kind of epitome in itself—And *Little Thistledown* has joined Jess's treasure-trove.[2]

love
Robert

Dear Robert & Jess

How lovely. Of course I would *love* to stay with you, and I thank you fervently for offering me that pleasure.

Ellie with typical vagueness has still not told me the dates but I gather it wd. be in the last week of the 3, i.e., the week ending Nov. 11th.

I'll let you know as soon as I know myself. Have lent H. D. M.S. to Ted Enslin for a few days—will reread and annotate that section as soon as I get it back. Forgive me, but Jess's Morgenstern poem has gotten mislaid—can

you send me another copy? It is the one in which Korf makes paper balls &
the night is nightcrawly.

Love—
Denny

I had kept it by until vacations were over just so that it wd. not get lost in
*Nation* office!

---

dear Denny,

I'm not sure about how late you are to stay in Temple, and I'm taking the
chance you are still there, and/or that the letter will be forwarded to New
York if you have left. Sorrentino had written me early in August about my
possibly contributing to an issue of *Kultur* he is to edit. What I have replied
is that I will send something—if I can get an essay done especially for this
issue, by the 25th of September—I will: but if not, I suggested he might
get from you the piece on conventional form I did for *The Nation*. I think
*Kultur* will be freer to take the essay (Hatch after all, though he liked it,
*did* reject it; and when I think of that empty talk by Bly that took its place
I am not particularly convinced about Hatch's expressions of finding my
essay "worth while").

The opening section of the H. D. book which I promised to send on
will be delayd now, for I have started work on the final draft of the book,
shaping from the beginning. And it has involved some agonies over sections
of discussion or exposition that prepare the body of the book. The establishd
passages in this first section are life story. It would be so beautiful if my
consciousness were wholly given over into life story, but it isn't. And I've to
follow as best I can my way into literary matters, efforts at definition. With
more and more distrust where there are so many possibilities of rationalizing
poetry as a  cultural product, and selling H. D., Pound, Williams and then
my own view. Readers so far have been more indulgent of the text than I
would be—and with all the hope and help of notes of question, I've still to
bring the more severe testing and rendering myself. Not towards perfection
or writing somehow better than I actually do. That is the essence of the
indulgence and vanity—but, now that the matter or material is projected, to
shape the whole in that light and to find the content wherever I seem to have
lost it in the first draft. I know the passages that seem to me to miss fire.

But the task goes slowly—for I am writing the first draft of the section on
*Helen in Egypt*, keeping up with the weekly meetings of my little group of
auditors or hearers, my hearings—where I present chapter by chapter the
book. I've completed a first chapter of the section, "Magic" and am in the
midst of the second, "Dreams"—what you will have for *The Nation* will be a
gist after these expositions, a sort of summing-up.

Yes, I heard, as you did, from Norman how sad indeed H. D.'s state is. For if she has lost words in waking life, she will have lost them in dreams too—and while I can imagine living entirely in the language of what is seen and felt and heard as sound—what an utmost agony it is not to find the word for it! Our feeling is so strong that "In the beginning was the Word," that the actual presence of a mountain (as a painter can see it) can seem insubstantial if we cannot find its word.

And all thru H. D.'s writing this evocation of things, this finding the word has been the urgent thing in writing. *The Hedgehog* is the story of locating the word "hérisson"—And in "Murex" of *Palimpsest* H. D. conveys how acute the insistence of words can be. A rhythm trying to find its words.

I'm sending back the Bryher (I'm not sure if I have or not—but I mean here I will search and if I find it include it—

love
Robert

Dear Robert

We found H. D.'s obituary in the *Times* this morning.
Have written to Norman & to Bryher, briefly.
The poem enclosed,[1] which I was going to send to you anyway, I now dedicate to her memory.
I am sad.

Love—
Denny

**208**

{late September 1961
Temple, Me.}

Dear Robert

Will you be able to let me have the H. D. review soon? I hope so because I want to try to get it in as soon as possible after publication date, & as I hear from Norman that she saw an advance copy 3 days before her death I suppose that will be soon. While poetry space is always difficult there is actually a shortage of reviews sometimes, isn't it absurd? They shd give the space to more poems. But then there are lots of *Nation* readers who don't really want that I suppose. Marimba the kitten is all over me as I write, jogging the pen.

Gave the MS to Gil Sorrentino, I suppose you have heard from him.

Just completed a review of Sorrentino, LeRoi Jones, Paul Blackburn, and Robert Lax.[1] Will send you a copy, hope it makes sense.

Changed copy of Jess' Morgenstern poem as he directed.

On rereading "Fire Dying" couldn't bear to cut & I think I can get it in, complete, before long.

**209**

October 3d {1961}
277 Greenwich St
N.Y. 7

Hope to go to one of O'Gorman's lectures on Friday, he is a good person & I am glad to hear he has gotten into correspondence with you.

Thanks for the City Lights review.[2] Besides your own piece I like the one by Kay Johnson where the rhythms of the sentences are one with their content. There are days when I feel that way; & other days of noli me tangere when what she says turns me up; but I like her for saying it & saying it the *way* she does.

Love—

D.

## 210

October 4/{19}61
{San Francisco}

dear Denny and Mitch—

Your novel arrived, Mitch, and I hope soon to get to one of those right times for reading it again. It's a handsome job of book making, which is something these days. A proud member to take its place with *Kaputt* and *The Skin*,[1] the only other testimonys of the real war on my shelf.

Then your H. D. poem, Denise—I had written a sequence "Doves," thinking of what the aphasia might mean. . . . There must be some intense wordless reality that could be human, but it is hard to think of it. For, if those connections are lost between words and references—then the interior connections would be lost too—words in dreams are the same as words in actual life. . . .

But your poem came as a breakthru for me, you speak so close to my heart. May I include the poem as an opening for the last essay in my H. D. book? What I want to do is to take up, as directly as you do, the allegiance we few have to "the old ones"; the themes of "alone on the road" and "the light of their presence,

> moving away over a hill
off to one side . . . "

Last night, trying to read the poem to Robin, brought a wave of grief, so that at last that intense dumb sense of loss, aloneness . . . could come into actual feeling. The inner valiant resolve you have reference to thruout has ultimate pathos for me.

I think too of Norman Pearson, who has lived in her service for years. How long he stood by her when book after book her major work was snubbed and cast into critical oblivion by the ruling editors and literary dictators in America. (So that when Shapiro and Wilbur take over the editorship of Untermeyer's anthology H. D. is entirely eliminated).[2]

love,

Robert

Dearest Robert

I am tremendously affected by your wanting to use that poem of mine dedicated to H. D. To become thereby directly involved in your wonderful book is a privilege. I mean this deeply. Thank you.

I am just starting to reread the part of the MSS. I have & when I come to the pages I missed out (because they were sent later) in annotating it I'll send you any comments that occur.

Look, I have a practical problem: I hate to bother you with it but I think I'll have to: Ellie finally has sent me the facts & figures, at least some of them, I've been asking her for for ages, & it turns out that tho the Mid-Western part of the tour can be financially worthwhile in spite of her 30% (which seems awfully high) the Californian part hardly pays for itself because of the great distance involved, *unless* I can get other readings in & around San Francisco. Gael {Turnbull} and also Jack Hirschman are trying to come up with readings in L.A, in which case I wd go to L.A. from Minnesota & *then* to S.F., but these are still uncertain. And Paul Blackburn tells me he read at Mills College for $50, which if I could arrange on my own (not thru' Ellie) wd help too. But why I'm asking you is in case you know of other places in or near SF I could quickly write to. Paul also suggested Reed (Kenneth O. Hanson) where he got $180, but I wouldn't have *time* to go to both L.A. & Oregon (can't leave M. & N. more than the 3 weeks) so I can't really write there until I hear from Gael and Hirschman. If they can come across I might find it more profitable to go to L.A. than to Oregon anyway. But if I don't get *any* other W. Coast readings I may have to cancel the ones I have (SF Poetry Center, $200, and Berkeley, $100). I am looking forward so much to seeing you & Jess—and California—again, so I do hope I won't have to. But if you consider taking the Minn./Cal & return fare, plus 30% to Ellie, out of $300, plus the fact of leaving my family for a third week, you will see how it wd be. Do you think whoever is now in charge of the Poetry Center would have suggestions? The dates involved are Nov 4th–11th. I read in Minnesota on the 3d. The SF dates are, Poetry Center 8th, and Berkeley 10th (if Ellie has them straight—god, she is inefficient). I am supposed to go home on the 11th but could stretch it to the 12th I guess. So that *if* I can read in L.A. it wd be the 4th, 5th, or 6th, I guess, leaving open the 7th, 9th, & 11th. I don't like the idea of reading every day like that but it wd be worth it as an alternative to giving up the visit to California altogether.

$100 is the usual minimum but for anything not arranged through Ellie I would read for $75 or even $50 especially if it were really close by.

Forgive me for involving you—you did so much the *other* time—I don't

## 211

October 10th {1961}
277 Greenwich St
NY. 7

mean you yourself shd try to arrange anything, please don't give time to that, just that you send me a list of names & addresses.

Love—
Denny

P.S.

I had thought of sending the (Sept. 61) poem[1] to *Poetry* or somewhere. Would this get in your way at all? Let me know & if so I wont send it out at all.

## 212

October 14th {1961}
277 Greenwich St
NY 7

Dear Robert & Jess

Another W. Coast reading has come through, thank god (U. of Southern Cal., $100) so there's no question of having to cancel the visit. Will arrive (maybe with Gael, by car) on the 7th Nov. & stay through till the 12th (i.e., leave on the 12th). If any other readings in SF, wd have to be the 9th or 11th.

Have you heard from Bob the terrible news of Leslie's death?[1] Though we'd never seen her it was a shock to us. She must have been a lovely child. We have a picture of all of them together from which she looks out with quite a special steady gaze. I hope to see Bob briefly before I leave on the 21st tho' I won't be able to hear him read.

The poems you sent are beautiful. Especially (for me) "Strains of Sight" and "Doves."[2]

With love—
Denny.

## 213

Oct. 16/{19}61
{San Francisco}

dear Denny,

Just a word. I think we can move faster here than you can in writing and waiting for answers yourself. It turnd out that both of my "contacts": Linenthal at the Poetry Center (I'm afraid that my practiced contempt for Schevill makes it difficult to confer with him on my part) and Parkinson are out of town. But I'll get Tom tonight and see him again on Wednesday, to see if he can swing a reading at Mills, St. Mary's or Davis and/or as many of these as possible. Wednesday Linenthal will be back and I can get the Poetry Center moving if it has not acted already. I phoned them as soon as I got your letter, but got a "secretary." Will one hundred dollars more make the trip possible? Let me guarantee that whatever comes. Then if readings come up we can let them pay the hundred. Damn it, I *knew* that Ellie was a roadblock. It is unfair to what ought to be our organized labor. Certain the "Paterson Society" didn't do much for their cut. The Poetry Center–University of California combination is automatic here at the level you were invited. And if you didn't get expense money—what in the hell did the Paterson Society have to do?

But what I really am provoked by is myself. For after the fiasco of disorganization when Paul was here, I shld. have anticipated the need.

Love
Robert

dear Denny,

**214**

October 20, 1961
{San Francisco}

I hope this gets to you in time. Thomas Parkinson got Mills College on the phone and arranged for a reading there Thursday afternoon at 4 I think it is (can't find my record of it right now, but I'm fairly sure). This means you will have $50 there in addition to the U.S.C. reading fee. And I won't load you with more.

A letter from Mae Bell Beim this morning.[1] Shall I organize your time and portion it out? It would work fine if she could visit with you Thursday and then drive you out to Mills for the reading.

Thinking of the almost grim array of those who will want to see you in the four days you will be here, I think it might be solved by a reception sort of thing here—just for those who have some personal claim, a real concern —anyway I leave the suggestion to you before I decide. The Poetry Center will surely have some kind of a reception and it may be pointless then for me to worry about those who like Rexroth will expect to be invited and whom we are not on familiar terms with. But here's an idea, and you might remember others:

| | |
|---|---|
| Cid Corman | Richard and Joan Duerden |
| Robin Blaser & Jim Felts | Ida Hodes |
| Helen Adam | Marthe Rexroth |
| Madeline Gleason | Donald Allen |
| James Broughton | |
| Philip Whalen | |

—This might be on the evening of the 9th. I won't do anything about it until I hear from you anyway.

Against the idea, is that the reading on the 8th for the Poetry Center would take care of seeing "everyone."

Schedule to date:

Tuesday evening:   you arrive.

Wednesday Nov. 8th:   Poetry Center mid-day and evening reading (Reception?)

Thursday Nov. 9th:   Mae Belle Beim drives you out to Mills for afternoon reading.

Friday Nov. 10th-    U.C. reading (evening) dinner with Parkinsons*
[if you wanted to, for $25, you could read to or talk to an English class
the afternoon of the 10th.}
Sat. Nov. 11th-
Ida has plans to have you and Marthe and us to dinner*—it would give
an easy last evening.

*and Gael{Turnbull}, if he comes as I hope he can

love<br>
Robert

But Jess says—and I think he's right—I exaggerate all this. Nothing as formal
as a "reception" need be held at all; you so patently have so little time here.
And you can arrange to see whom you like. The Mills thing tho I think would
work out perfectly for Mae Belle and I'll suggest it in replying to her note.

## 215

October 21st {1961}
277 Greenwich St
NY 7

Dear Robert,

I feel terrible about my cri de coeur because meanwhile several midwest
readings have come up & actually I wish I had a few days clear with no
readings—so hold your horses and let whatever is not *conclusively* arranged
just drop—of course I'll be glad to fulfill any actual commitments, I
wouldn't back out of them, but *dont* make any more—cd you tell Parkinson
also?—I'm all set to leave in the morning & should have mailed this earlier
but Tom Parkinson's letter only came by a late mail. Forgive me for causing
commotion—and THANKS, you are a brick—

Love—<br>
Denny

P.S. If you want to reach me midway you cd write to me at:
c/o Paul Engle
State U. of Iowa
Iowa City
Iowa
where I'll be reading on the 30th In L.A. you can reach me at Gael's.

D.

## 216

{October 28, 1961
Chicago}

Thanks very very much. About People: I would of course like to see the
ones you mention but as far as some kind of a gathering is concerned why
don't you follow your own inclination?—ie, if you are in sociable mood &
*feel* like asking them all over that's fine with me—but if it is a time when
you don't really feel in the mood for it well then let's count on most of them

coming to one or other of the readings & my seeing them there, or some-
thing quite impromptu developing. I myself can get terribly bugged
by arranging to do something hospitable & then not really enjoying the
doing of it & I don't want you to get into that position. The only people
you didn't mention I think were Mary & Ham Tyler but I guess it's too far
from them maybe—but if there were a chance I'd love to see them again; I
guess Ham doesn't often come into SF tho'—but maybe Mary would? That
sounds a good idea about Mae Belle & Mills College. Yes, I *would* like to go
to the English class the 10th & get $25—will write T.{homas} P.{arkinson}
but just in case, you might tell him also, if you speak to him (don't go out
of your way). Thanks for everything, and love, from Denny

I find I like Chicago—unexpectedly.

dear Denny,

The past two weeks have been taken up with a masque for a Halloween
party—that will be over tonight, and somehow I managed to do it. It's
the first Halloween masque since 1948—tho I did do a satire at Black
Mountain when I was there.[1] The advantage of the satyr play is that everyone
understands it has been thrown together or stirrd up to resemble a play, a
nd that the gestures are going to be make-shift. This one is a horse play.
With no subtleties—writ mostly in Elizabethan rhetoric. With the "hero"
referring to Bottom in *Midsummers Night Dream.*

• 

Then I want to have the *Helen in Egypt* piece ready for you when you
arrive. My difficulty may be in part that I am still working on the Helen
section of the book, and my sense of the work becomes more and more
complicated by a surrounding of associations I have found or drawn. Then,
as always, until I find my voice, I am distracted by polemics. In the case of
H. D. the contemptuous reviews Louise Bogan and Randall Jarrell wrote in
the middle forties when the War Trilogy began to appear;[2] and finally
Shapiro and Wilbur eliminating her work entirely from the Untermeyer
anthology of American and British poetry.

• 

What I'm going to do about an "evening" is to ask Cid and Don Allen
for Thursday evening (after your Mills afternoon—Mae Belle could either
have dinner out with you or come back to have dinner with us here)—and
then have it open for whomever else impromptu you want. I mean, we want
the opening for those who want to see you. And at the same time to avoid
"officially" inviting.

Then, if there is a Poetry Center reception after the reading (I haven't
heard of any), the Thursday can be as intimate as we want.

**217**

October 31/{19}61
{San Francisco}

•

Robin has planned to have dinner at his place on the evening of The Poetry Center reading, with Helen and Pat Adam—and you, Turnbull (tho I haven't heard yet if he can come), Jess and me. And (but I think I must have written all this already) Ida on Saturday evening will have us to dinner with Marthe and Mary and Katharine {Rexroth}.

Does it begin to sound frantic?

love<br>Robert

postcript:
our telephone number is Atwater 2-9783 it's not listed, but you or Gael may want to phone us.

---

**218**

{November 6, 1961
Santa Monica,
California}[1]

ROBERT DUNCAN
3735 20 ST SFRAN=

ARRIVING TRAILWAYS BUS 655PM THE 7TH MEET ME IF POSSIBLE=

DENNY=

655 PM 7.

---

**219**

Airline Terminal—
Wed. am
{Chicago
November, 1961}

Dear Robert & Jess

Here's the key of your kingdom . . .
Sorry I forgot it.
Thanks again for a lovely time.

Much love—<br>Denny.

---

**220**

{November 13, 1961,
written airborne and
mailed in New York}

Dearest Robert

As soon as San Francisco could no longer be seen I took out "Strains of Sight" and "Doves" to reread, for themselves & to feel myself still near you. I realize I didn't speak about them while I was there. They are beautiful. But I can't say what I feel about your poems, usually, any more than I can say what I feel about you as a presence, except to say I love you. Perhaps some of it can someday be a poem for you.

Now I'm reading the Perse essay. I've come to where you speak of "not to make that mystery less but to make that mystery more," and broke off to wonder if my Ibsen quote ("The task of the poet is to make clear to

HIMSELF, & thereby to others, the temporal & eternal questions") were in contradiction to what you're saying—but I think the contradiction is only superficial, because in the Ibsen the key is not "clear" but "to HIMSELF," and moreover I take "clear" to mean, not clearer than the intrinsic nature of a thing is, but, to see true, to see in light what is light in its nature and to see in dark what is dark—to *recognize* mystery, not to attempt to undo it. And besides he says, to make clear the questions, not the answers. So I think the two sentences, yours & his, can accord.

I've written to Rago about Gertrude Levy.

Thank you for all you gave me, and have always given.—Enough—

love from<br>Denny.

Now I'll write to Jess. Then I'll go back to the Perse.

East of Chicago—West of the Moon

Dear, dear Jess,

I feel you & Robert could just as well have come along—to see the Rockies & the cloud-fields—for the seats beside me (& many more) are empty. Surely TWA could have let you ride!

The Rockies were vast & splendid; and now the clouds with whales and castles and, back over my shoulder, the sun getting low, close to them, left behind—My watch is still telling San Francisco time as my heart is.

Jess, I want you to know how much I appreciate the *time* you (& Robert) gave me, as well as everything else. And to live for a few days among your paintings was to be doubly with you. Bless you—not for a sneeze but for being Jess.

A rainbow! Not a whole bow but a shaft of colors! Not a bow but a shaft—a rain-arrow! And now we're in deep cloud and the sun's gone— we're arriving already—

Love—<br>Denny

**221**

{November 13, 1961, written airborne and mailed in New York}

Dear Robert

Finally turned up Don Hall's letter: "Sep. 12th. . . . I thank you for your help—I found myself able to print Duncan's whole 'A Poem Beginning with a Line from Pindar' & a large selection of [short] Creeley poems."[1]

What he had asked me was what poems I thought might best represent you to English readers coming to you for the first time—I gave a mile-long

**222**

Nov 19th {1961 New York}

list but emphasized the Pindar poem as essential especially if he did not have space for many, i.e. that I felt sure you'd not want any "excerpts" so better to concentrate on one longish poem if that was the available space. Of course I took it for granted he'd then write directly to you.

He's having quite a correspondence with Bob, it seems.

Enclosed will be a letter about Bryher which I'll address to Robin as well as to you & Jess as I felt he'd want to hear it too.

Also a list of people to whom I've written suggesting they write to you about Spring readings.

There's also a possibility that Ted Weiss may set up something at M.I.T. tho he himself will be in Europe by that time.

Nik & Mitch were glowing & sparkling & looking alike when they met me & it was a happy homecoming.

I'm too busy but hope to get clear by end of Jan.

Will be writing & sending new book to Robin, Helen, Ida, etc.—yours will be mailed with this in separate envelope.[2]

Love from
Denny.

**223**

Dear Robert, Jess, and Robin,

You might like to have my personal impressions of Bryher, just for the record. She called me & I went to see her at 6 pm Saturday at Hotel Beekman Towers. I was unprejudiced—didn't even *remember* what WCW had said exactly, & expected to like her, as H. D.'s friend and (as Robert had written) Patroness of a wing of a *Triptych*, & more.[1]

She met me in the lobby—a little, quick-striding, very English-looking woman in English country walking-shoes & dowdy tweed coat, a beret on her cropped gray hair, & we went up to her small hotel room, 20th floor, the U.N. etc glittering outside. (The Scott Fitzgerald hour when everyone is going somewhere—for pleasure—& N.Y. is full of *promise*) Her face close up is older than her only middle-aged general appearance—weatherbeaten & much wrinkled. We spoke first of Cornwall & Wales, & that was pleasant, & she promised to "see that I got" Gwyn or Glyn Jones' book on the Welsh mystics.[2] Then (as if this were a duty & the chief reason why she had sent for me) she told me all the circumstances of H. D.'s illness & death—that the sudden forced move from the Küsnacht home had (she felt) been too great a shock (all the other 6 or 7 old ladies who'd lived there too have had something happen to them—one threw herself under a car, one went off her head & had to go to a mental hospital, one got jaundice & died or is dying, etc. A terrible story). Then at the hotel Sonnenberg (Aurorastrasse) Bryher, visiting (which she did about once a month) came in to find HD sitting on the bed holding the telephone. "What's the matter, Hilda, can't you get the number?" No answer. Bryher goes across room, does something or other, again asks question. No answer. Suddenly realizes H. D. cannot speak. She had felt ill, got Dr. on phone, & that was really the last time she spoke. Dr. arrived a few minutes later. H. D. gotten into hospital that evening. Then seemed (with many anti-coagulant injections etc.) to be doing (physically) pretty well. Bryher (in July) asks Dr., "This is the time of year I always charter a boat & go on my holiday [to the Scilly Isles]. Can I go?" The Dr. says yes. When Bryher returns in August HD has a virus & is "much changed." She died in her sleep.

Now all this was told very matter-of-factly & I began to feel a great coldness in Bryher. She had said "Of course, I think she was lonely at the hotel." Why then didn't Bryher with all her $$$ see that she was somewhere where she *wasn't* lonely? Why did she have to take her holiday? All her life she (I believe) had bossed HD but she didn't have the warmth & humanity to stick around at that most difficult time. And hardly a word from her about what Norman spoke of as "the psychic agony" H. D. underwent in being both stricken dumb *and* unable to hold a pencil.

However the cold air I felt blow over me was something I scarcely noted for the moment. But then we went on to talk of the quality of Eng. poetry at present which she agreed was pretty dull, but this led (through her saying that English writers' ignorance of American poetry was all due, not to national pride etc. (as I think) but to Marxist propaganda!! And from there on she led off into the most illogical & melodramatic type of Anti-Communist fanaticism, with side shots at Negroes & the Yellow Peril, AND a complete (illogical) system of belief in benefits of shelters, use of bombs (in preference to being "overrun"), belief that an atomic war *can* be "won," etc. etc. And much talk of how she'd rather die than lose her liberty. "Isn't liberty really something inside oneself anyway?" I asked (it was all very polite, you understand—perfect manners à l'Anglaise on both sides). She replied she would die rather than lose her physical freedom. But what she is talking about is her freedom to have her own way—to dominate, if need be to bully. Also the kind of freedom riches brought her.

I came away with the feeling that this Patroness had in fact been a bully to H. D. & perhaps even, in ways I can't tell, something of an evil genius. One can imagine her doing many "kind deeds" for those who would do as she wished. Also she was much less *intelligent* that I thought she wd. be. I am god knows no debater & am only too easy to convince sometimes, or rather I often *feel* I am right about something but cant see what is cockeyed about someone else's arguments nor give intellectual backing to my own— yet I was amazed at the reasons she gave for her opinions on various political and moral topics.

I guess that's all I have to say. A dangerous woman because of her[3]

224

Nov. 21/1961

{San Francisco}

dear Denny,

Your account of Bryher is in line with McAlmon's account of her character in *Being Geniuses Together*:[1]

"Wealth, the war, and the phobias, manias, dementias, prejudices and terrors that come from both, were the dominant factors. Bryher's life had been unfree throughout her childhood years. She had never been allowed proper pets or friendships. One could not do this or that, know so and so, one was being used, such and such a person was trying to know one simply because of the wealth in the offing."

"Bryher, with her fervour for education, had taken on the up-bringing of Hilda Doolittle's infant. It had black hair and eyes, an utterly blithe disregarding disposition and at the time looked a Japanese Empress in miniature. Hilda, an American. . . . "

"Bryher was on the train with Hilda Doolittle and the infant. Bryher, having educational theories, managed the "Lump's" upbringing, and already the child, not five, could name all of the countries, continents and main cities of the world, so Bryher claimed. The child also had a firm grasp on history, but she refused to show off for me. She stared solidly when Bryher told her to do her piece, and finally blurted out, "You're a liar. I'm not your experiment. I'm a wild Indian. I'll skin you alive."

As it was one of Bryher's cherished ideas that "the horde" is dumb and should be lied to, she was delighted, but said fiercely "Hippo, hippo, if the Lump is naughty." She meant she would use an oft-threatened hippopotamus whip on the child, but the infant's eyes flicked amusement and she re-asserted "you're a liar."

"Whenever (Bryher) was particularly approving of Hilda or myself she would assert that we were her twin or her brother monkey. Her idea of a loving relationship was somewhat the same as her father's. The beloved was to be reduced to a state of shrieking, trembling, hysteria, and then she would be conciliatory and say, "There, there, calm, calm. It's a nice kitten," or in her father's case, "Mother, darling," in tones calculated to bring apoplexy upon the already infuriated lady, who was far too emotional and natural a human for all this involved tosh." "When Bryher started her tactics on me and I felt helpless fury, I slipped away to the nearest pub. Bryher then would call on Hilda and realizing that the solid 'Lump' was too much her own emotional age to be made hysterical, she tackled Hilda, and always produced results. By merely mentioning experiences of the war years or an unhappy episode in Hilda's past, and dwelling upon it long enough she soon had the highstrung Hilda acting much like a candidate for a straight-jacket. She did this, she said, because of her own thwarted childhood."

"He (Bryher's father Sir John Ellermann) persisted and persisted in whatever idea he had. She (Lady Ellermann) might escape going for a run one day, but the next and the next for all the weeks and months and years he would be back insisting. Bryher had the same monomaniacal capacity to be rebuffed, screamed at, wept at, but to persist, long after one had forgotten the idea upon which she was insisting. I managed to slip away, but she got at the Lump and through her at H. D. She got at me too, but I knew some day I'd go away for good.

One night during a cheerful dinner some man's name was mentioned and a bright expression flashed over Sir John's face and in his eyes. He turned to Bryher. "'Dolly, that man once did something against me. I waited fifteen years, but he had to leave England. Now I will let him return."

Bryher's face beamed also with pride. That type of emotion, the vengeful, she understood, and she understood the possessive instinct: for money and for people. The mania for management and directing she also understood, but her education had paralyzed her abilities in that direction. The old biblical Father Abraham guarding his flocks and ready to sacrifice his son because of his own megalomaniac immortal-soul and property-desiring will had left them his heritage."

Etc. etc. McAlmon writes his memoirs to pay off old scores and never can be done with his seeing people at their meanest and most appalling. But he lacks the even rudimentary imagination to transform: his grievances are never fanciful but grounded in fact.

Look again at the willful faces of those donors and patrons of the Medieval and Renaissance works. Should I make it less ambiguous that when I note how the painting *and* the Madonna or Nativity belong to the donor and are only by the painter, I have in mind that these great patrons of the arts are tyrants or wills that appear as factors of the art itself?

•

But one impression or after thought you had must be corrected. In 1959, Norman explained to me (as H. D.'s analyst Erich Heidt had the year before in Stinson Beach) that H. D. had absolutely no economic limitations:[2] it was because she was afraid to travel any longer, to leave Küsnacht that she stayd there. Every provision was made three years ago for her to return to America, but she couldn't face it. And one of the aims of her analyst was to help her to find the freedom to go where she wanted.

The other injustice I feel in your judgment of Bryher is the one about her coldness (yes, from all accounts she was "cold," as willful people are. Dear Helen Adam, for instance, is often cold—as I was shocked that she would have nothing to do with Ida when she was sick for fear of catching her illness which was not contagious) about Bryher's going on her holiday to the Scilly Islands and not being loyal to stay by H. D. in her loneliness. The truth of the matter here, if we picture a Bryher as McAlmon draws her, and as she appears in H. D.'s memoir of Pound where she launches upon H. D.'s reveries of her love for Pound all the fury of a tirade on that dreadful man and his anti-semitism, or as you sensed her dominating and unfeeling guardianship, the truth of the matter is that her staying could hardly have *helped*. The forthrightness of doing as she wishd has the virtue of honesty. There is nothing more dreadful in this world than the code of loyalties and right behavior that would take the place of what we actually love (as if it ever helped to attend when we do not love) or the truth of things. I would think it would be more shocking had Bryher stayd with H. D. when she didn't really have other feeling for her than a patron has. A patron can sponsor a life and the arts—but one can't patronize a death.

What seems in question for me is that the response actually be there: cold or warm. And not take on some conventional look

---

As for Bryher's historical perspectives, they give information again how little she and H. D. shared in world-view. I think I told you H. D. had confided in me that "they" (and I took it to mean her daughter and Bryher) did not like her mysticism. Bryher's anti-communism is, like her anti-Nazism, in part the pro-war vitality of a dominating person (she was a leader early against the Nazi threat to the West—uninterested in rescuing Germany from Hitler—she calld for a war against Hitler as early as 1936) and in part the survival of the fittest ethos of the wealthy.

It is absurd that at Bryher's age "she would rather die"—does she have the choice—

Robert

---

**225**

Nov. 24th {19}61
{New York}

Dear Robert,

I agree of course that for Bryher (or anyone else) to "stay" when not led to do so by real feeling is worse than useless. But I had supposed she loved H. D. Or if I'd given it further thought (instead of taking for granted) I might have thought she hated her also. But at any rate I assumed strong feeling, & what I encountered appeared to be coolness, & that itself was what shocked me.

In yr. book I had thought you quoted the few words from McAlmon with antagonism to McAlmon, not as if they were to be taken as true—[somewhat as (eventually) I saw the WCW quotes as light on W. C. W., not on those he wrote of ]. This longer one from his book is startlingly horrible.

When Bryher said (lightly) she supposed H. D. was lonely at the hotel, she wasn't referring to Küsnacht but to the Hotel Sonnenberg on Aurora-strasse, Zurich.

About coldness as such: coldness as honesty is O.K. But then there's an ugly coldness too. Helen not visiting Ida when Ida was sick is neurotic but not ugly—what would have been ugly wd have been a resentful hypocritical visit. You being (as I see it, forgive me if I am mistaken) cold to me in this letter is not ugly, because it is a natural response to *my* having, especially in my airmail letter written on the plane to N.Y., been over-warm. (Not more than I felt but more than I had a right to impose on you.) But a coldness arising from a person's whole Being being centered in Will, in having her-own-way-&-be-damned-to-anyone-else, is different from coldness as honesty, coldness as the refusal to pretend what you don't feel—in fact Bryher *was* putting on a pious act for me, "poor dear Hilda" sort of thing—& I do think it was ugly, & that it is important to make these distinctions.

Something that worries me is that in writing those 2 separate letters to you & Jess on the plane I appeared to be (perhaps) putting Jess in a sort of second place in a way that could well be offensive to you & hurtful to him. In fact Jess is one of my favorite people in the world & I can honestly say I have just as much feeling for him as for you—but it is of a different kind, of a different pace & tone. Hence the 2 letters instead of 1. It was done clumsily, I have felt in retrospect. Maybe it didn't strike you & Jess that way though—if so, ignore this page please. But if it did, please, accept my apologies.

Is the question "Should I make it less ambiguous that when I note how the painting of the Madonna or Nativity belong to the donor & are only by the painter, I have in mind that these great patrons of the arts are tyrants or wills that appear as factors of the art itself" an actual question? I will take it it is:

I think, yes, it *is* too ambiguous perhaps. At least, I think it does not come very clear to me, & though I am not subtle, I know, there are going to be other readers no more subtle & perhaps less so, yet not to be discounted, because they *will* be people who really want to know; but for whom such a book will be a new mode.

When you said (on p. 24 of the copy I have) that McA.{Robert McAlmon}, with his limited imagination, was incapable of seeing how Bryher, "taking over," was "an angel of the hour," a true "God-mother," *I* got the impression that you were saying Bryher "took over" out of love, however domineering, & that this was to the benefit of H. D.'s life in poetry. Now I'm not quite sure *what* you meant.

Of course, I have only portions of the book, it's true.

Thanks very much for mailing the books. Something I forgot (over &

over) to ask you was, what was the story of those *Here & Now*'s you mailed me some months ago?

Nik spent Thanksgiving Day reading *Ayesha*.[1] He'll be writing to you about the *Oz* books.

Love—<br>Denny.

P.S.

Yes, my confusion is about the nature of a Patron's feeling: you say "I would think it would be more shocking had Bryher stayd with H. D. when she didn't really have other feeling for her than a patron has." Right. But despite those grim patron-faces in the paintings, altarpieces, I've been mistaking, evidently, what it is a patron *might* feel; & I still don't know; nor how they, except as the artist lets them, do become factors in the art— in paintings, there they are, fitted in, made part of the whole;—in poetry how have they actually entered? "It took wealth," you wrote (p. 29 of my copy). . . . "For Karnak to be present in London." That brings one—if that's it—to one of those maddening "if's"—how wd. H. D. have written without the aid of Bryher's money? Surely she would have been as much a poet? Or was she *so* finely poised as to have been unable to stand the strain of having less wealth?

---

## 226

November 28/{19}61
{San Francisco}

dearest Denny/

Your eyes must help mine in seeing Bryher, and I *do* begin to put the picture together anew (for all of my immediate *if*s and *but*s) with McAlmon's drawing, and a photograph of Bryher I have seen that promised little warmth (as if so much heat went into *will*, only incidental willful bits of human warmth might escape): and these, in turn, with those other donors as painters have borne witness to their faces. We can't see the faces of those Tudor donors, addressd by Shakespeare—but I'm thinking now of Spenser for whom Elizabeth *was* the Fairy Queen.

I don't want ambiguity in the figure for the book, not any way in the sense of the author's and then the reader's not being to be sure which or what. But I *do* want the double play of things. And drawing Bryher more exactly (helped by my being more sure of McAlmon's picture now) I will be able to get what I want there: the will, the identification in place of sympathy, the taking-over as helping—without—it's my hope—judging what Bryher is in herself (it's a picture of the force in H. D.'s life, I want) but with making that figure of the patron more true. And then—that's where I am most happy about all this—I can give a better relation of the "angel" and "godmother." That needn't entirely wait until I get to work out the portion of the book in question. For I have in mind what you will find in the chapter of *At the Back of the North Wind* called "Diamond and Ruby": Jess and I have thot of the love that appears as a burden (the way parents can "love" without the least understanding, as a matter of fact all the time grieved by what one has turnd out to be) as angelic. Tho our most immediate angel was Kit, the black cat who died last year of cancer. His secret name was "Pride," and we had made a pet of our pride.

————————

But let this picture of Bryher wait now until in the light of the book I can draw it more fairly and then render it clearer. And get the larger drawing of patron-angel-godmother into focus.

I want most to write that you weren't wrong in writing as you did to us on the plane. It was for both of us continuous with all the joy of your being here with us. Yet you are right about that letter of mine that was cold somehow springing up in reaction to your "I love you"—it was from the same love for you, Denny, in my own heart that I cannot say somehow and can at best refer to. I know I had to write—wasn't it, under everything, "Say I was to prove as dreadful as we now see Bryher can be, then will you, Denny, not be loyal but see me in truth, yet somehow love me?"

You see you have three presences for me, Denny, that touch the deepest life feeling. One is the Denise I have been able openly to speak of, the companion in art—where in certain poems of yours, by grace of your "poet," I am brought into that heart of life that poetry opens: then this poet you are I love because you are most true. No . . . it seems more that through loving this you so I come to love what is most true. And then, sometimes you are a poetic conscience for me. Not that my truth will be like yours— but that just where I fail my own *poet*, I betray this love.

Then there is, related, another presence: an idea of you or something you mean to me—yet it also seems to be really *you* and to reach the heart. I am troubled here, Denise, to make it clear, but just as my poet has existed in the light of your poet, my self does. And the "to thine own self be true" has existed, for always now it seems, as if that meant being true in your eyes. So I am always just that shy of, just that troubled in thinking of your love or mine because so often I seem to fail so miserably to "be myself." Maybe, I wanted to say "Be loyal to my *self*" but also "love me as I am not my self."

The third is just your real actual presence, where I have never felt these ghosts of conscience. When I've been with you, Denny, you are at last just you and I could not possibly not be just me as I am. That's what I did want to write most—how real all the rest is—but the pure joy, all the ever-lasting delight of these times in my life when I am actually with you.

love,
Robert

O, yes—your question about *Here and Now* copies. I came across them at Stinson. And I think they were left over from that reading you gave here years ago. Ferlinghetti contributed them or charged them against your royalties—I don't know which: the idea was that proceeds from the sale were to go towards your fees etc. during that visit. They belong to you, anyway.

---

**227**

Nov. 29th {19}61
277 Greenwich St
N.Y. 7

Dear Robert,

Could you please send me correct addresses for
Ida
Helen
Robin
Marthe
Madeline Gleason
James Broughton
        please?
I started sending all the books c/o you & Jess—then realized it was going to clutter up your box & be a bother.

Love—
Denny.

---

**228**

Dec. 3d {19}61
277 Greenwich St
NY 7

Dearest Robert

I keep all yr letters but that letter I'll keep apart from the others especially.

Here are 3 new poems, the first since coming back. They seem to be of a new kind. "The Elves" is for Robin really but I crossed out the dedication until I hear whether he likes the poem. He may feel I'm bracketting him, which was not what I meant—only to celebrate a beauty of which he's a part, or in which, rather, he has a part. His own poems which he sent me recently set me off writing again.

I send also a copy of that poem "The Message"—about or around another "setting off." The Bard in the dream seemed to be, not you but Eberhart, who is not even a friend—but every so often a poem of his speaks to me. A day before he had sent me a poem in which he spoke of *The Hermit of Cape Rosier* (Maine) and the name of his house (Eberhart's) was *Undercliff.*

An Israeli writer (aged maybe 60) called Itzak (or Yitzach) Norman has become acquainted with us. He is also an admirer or your work & wd. like to meet you when he goes to SF soon. He's a chatterbox but an interesting man, knew Blok & Biély & Pasternak, Akmatova, etc. etc. & many U.S. writers too. And knows the *Zohar* etc. He seems like a man who has really *read* what he's read. May I give him yr address? (Not your phone number of course.) He also knows & loves I. B. Singer's work. He's a bit full of himself but I think he's pretty solid behind that. He values H. D. Finds Gershom Scholem a bit too rationalizing.

Anyway, I think you might find him interesting to meet. One of the things he told me was that *Eyes at the Back of Our Heads* is a Kabbalistic idea—in *Zohar* angels have them & see over the mountains. Now I wasn't conscious of knowing that at all. Yet when he said it, it was as though I did know it. And since as a small child I heard without listening a great deal of my father's talk of such things I may well have unconsciously known it all along.

Love to Jess
and you—
Denny

dear Denny,

In this latest issue of *The Nation* I found Merwin's "Hermit" poem— which seemd to come wholly out of the real world.[1] Where the poet is so pure an agency of the universe, that he disappears and a world appears. The other side—and it isn't a question of the academic but of the humanistic— is the poem where we admire or dislike the character of the poet himself, not as agency of the real, but as a person as if he were. In any other sense than his role he has to perform. My dislike of the Wilbur sort of thing is a dramatization of putting away, as best I can, in myself, the Wilbur idea of the poem in which the poem performs the abilities and human qualities of the person Wilbur; or my dislike of the Eberhart thing is of his using the poem to have transcendental "ideas." As I must hold myself from using the poems to display *my*[2] ideas, and set myself to be empty so that only what comes to me will enter, or so that what comes to me can enter at all.

This is all in the midst of pre-Christmas things: but, just when so many businesses seem to be going on, the world grows oracular again. I will soon be back at work on the H. D.; tho *The Nation* essay is the thing that has to move first.

How to get at the importance to us all of the message or story any soul has to tell. I'm trying to move out from Browning's preface or dedication to *Sordello*: his "my stress lay on the incidents in the development of a soul: little else is worth study." But the soul tells its story, tries to get across, to whom? To find what, when men are careful of these things, they call the spirit. The earnest struggle we make to tell the truth, is to come into tune with our very spirit which only exists in the truth.

And we have only what we actually experience within which to find the

**229**

Dec. 18/1961
{San Francisco}

way: what comes to us, or "dawns" on us, or lights up in daily events, in dreams, in the course of writing when we have put away trying to be something and suddenly, there, where our self might have been is the Hermit, and we do then tell what he knows and says.

Yet just here—the poem "The Message" which, as you wrote, has to do with the Eberhart thing (as his work speaks to you) is most real. And may have stirrd up in me with its:

here on my own land, recalld
to my nature?
                    O great Spirit!

my own nature and spirit. In a poem like this, the "I" is not only yours but so pure an inner truth of us all, it most belongs to the heart we share. So, just this man, Richard Eberhart, that I might have put away—"comes a letter in a dream: a Bard"—bids me in this poem (that now being poetry, true, is a command to this *me* too) "remember my nature."

The poem is a blessing, calling forth as it does (letting myself be filld with it now) in the thing you saw at work, the "centaur-sea horse-salt carnation" or sea-pink—the "*flower of work and transition.*" and there (I had forgotten the poem, and then trying to tell you how Merwin's poem of the hermit had come thru to me, I suddenly went and got your little sheaf of poems, as if some clue was there): I find "out of sea fog, from a hermitage."

The poems I rememberd, the two of being inside the Sow-Leviathan-Wifeness of Ishtar, being "in its belly"—weren't what was secretly at work.[3] I couldn't, not without going and reading it again as I did, have accounted at all for "The Message." It was hidden from me, and now I find it was hidden in my thought.

The letter then is a necessary turning to your thought, Denny. I thought I had something to tell me, and as I began to tell you I found you had "the Message" for me.

love
Robert

## 230

January 2d {1962}
277 Greenwich St
N.Y. 7 N.Y.

Dearest Robert

I hate to bug you, but is the *Helen in Egypt* review almost done? Blackburn starts at *The Nation* on the 15th—A notice of my departure & his arrival there will be printed as soon as the last of the poems I gathered is printed. I would like to have the pleasure of your H. D. review being published under my aegis, not his—I hope that doesn't seem petty to you, but I really would.

I was very happy that "The Message" was a message to you too.

By the way, the Bresdin print (which you should receive around the same time as this letter if not before) has nothing to do with the current show at the Museum of Modern Art which I haven't even seen yet (there are big queues because of the Chagall windows)—I have one like it in the house at Temple though, & thought you & Jess might like it, tho' it is rather enormous so you may not want to put it up.[1]

I've done the H. D. appreciation for *Poetry* & sent the copy to Norman {Pearson} but will make another to send you once I've started to get my damned Korean stuff under way.[2] Also I must send you a letter of Norman's about Bryher.

Before I came to SF I had bought a bulb & put it away & by the time I came back & began to water it I'd forgotten what it was supposed to be. It grew with marvellous speed & the day after Xmas the first flower appeared & since then every day a new blossom. It is some kind of narcissus; very sweet scented, with many six-petalled small white flowers growing out of each of the two sheaths. Just the stamens are light orange—all the rest white. I've never grown bulbs before & it is a miraculous experience. {a pen drawing of three narcissus blossoms on a stem with the following notation} At the base of each leaf-stem is a little striped jacket like a scallion.

With love and wishes for a New Year of peace and of many poems & paintings—and we loved *The Willow Fairy*—and Nik his book—thank you[3]—

to you & Jess from
Denny & Mitch

P.S.

Race Newton has given us a book of photographs called *Designs in Nature* by Tet Borsig. If you see it anywhere do take a look at it—both you & Jess would like it.[4] It is closeup studies of leaves, seeds, cones, grasses & seed-pods & buds. No tricky effects, just the marvellous forms against black backgrounds.

---

dear Denny,

I just haven't been able to get the right start on the H. D. piece. It's the not hearing the voice of the writing—and without that I get contentious or sententious in the first sentences. I took the *Helen* with me when I left for the Southwest the day after Christmas; got several pages started and then gave them up. My poor mind is still getting off on defending her literary repute against old insults from Fitts or Jarrell, or acclaiming her work in terms of "major," "great"—bringing in formidable counterparts like Malraux in his *Psychology of Art* or Mann in his *Joseph* or *Dr. Faustus.* But what I know any essay must be is clear of that, to get at the qualities of the

**231**

January 18, 1962
{San Francisco}

work itself. Damn it! it's my own unnecessary grievances and outrages that take on a cause in approaching her work. What I mean about the voice thing is that in writing I've got to follow a lead of a kind in myself—so the voice leads off into thickets of argument, then I've got to wait on it, kept at starts until the thought and feeling has reachd the voice level. I know what I want to "say"—how from those first things, image and persona, cadenced phrase and organic rime, the later complex organization came with its levels of meaning and thematic rimes (how not only sounds but images and persons can return in the changes of the poem).

Your letter, anyway, didn't "bug" me. Could I have found my way, I'd have joyfully gotten the H. D. review to you by the time you came here to read, by Christmas . . . it was identified in my mind too with your brief period of editorship.

•

We've had a sad turn since Christmas. Helen Adam in a complex of events—losing her job, having her play produced but drastically redone by James Broughton and Kermit Sheets, then her cat Kilty being "put away" by the S.P.C.A. (it's not clear now but what Helen taking Kilty down to the S.P.C.A. might not have been over-ready in her distraction to have him killd)—has had a period of serious despair and obsessive self-blame. She had herself committed at Langley-Porter psychiatric clinic the day before New Year's. Last week they began a series of six to eight electric shock treatments, and now we hear from Ida that Helen has begun to recover interests outside her obsession (of being worthless, a burden—and having to commit suicide). Jess saw her just after she enterd the hospital, but she did not want him to come again, to "see me as a nightmare woman" as she wrote. She wants to see noone outside of Pat and Ida.

In Santa Fe the news of Helen's going to the hospital came to take its place in alternate highs and lows, lights of the authentic (pueblo dances, nature photographs by Eliot Porter, the opening section of Creeley's novel) and drabs of the meretricious (my being "lionized" at a dreadful gathering of poetry lovers in Taos where I was, *mea maxima culpa*, thoroughly enmeshd in the toils of arguing over T. S. Eliot's not being the sole and greatest living poet etc.; and again, in Albuquerque (where I read at the University of New Mexico) in the same meshes of vanity arguing over Pound's not being worthless and vicious). These drabs of the meretricious being my *own*. The authentic stirs responses in me that enlighten; but just so, as if I were a stew of whatever is astir, stupidity can arouse responses in me to stupefy.

•

So, with my brief visit with Bob (the day before and the day of my reading) with all the zest I have in his company,[1] there were turns of his special seriousness—his concern with respect, I think it is—that would play me false. That his effort was in part to picture me as a member of his literary respectability—along with the actual common concerns. This "respectability" is not to be separated from his very real and necessary involvement in earning his living, keeping his "position" at the university and his feeling about the handicap of having (being) one-eye missing. He told a story that made this clear: when he went to get the report on his lung condition, at the point where he was to be told whether or not it was cancer, the specialist took the first minutes of his time asking Bob why he didn't wear a glass-eye, and when Bob managed to say that he had got his job at the University and the respect of the faculty there as he was, the doctor said "Don't you think it might have been *pity*, not respect?"

But he's too immediate a person, both in my fondness and in my reading, for me ever to "respect." I only "respect" poems that no longer move me; a recognition of excellence that does not touch my living concern.

I did get a tape (I had taken my recorder with me) of the poems that have appeard in *Poetry*,[2] and a recent poem "The Sea" or "Water"—I am not sure of the title.

love
Robert

Dear Robert & Jess

I feel terrible because I came across a note to myself from way back in Nov. saying "Give Robert names of possible reading dates for his spring trip" & I realize I never did. What sort of a friend must you think me! It is all of a piece with what's making me right now be in a sort of crisis, i.e. the pattern of the last year or so for me really has been increasingly an involvement to the point of exhaustion with inessentials (critical jobs, answering 10000 letters from semi-strangers, the Korean Unesco revision nightmare, & such) & a neglect of essentials (real friends, notebooks, reading, even, to some extent, poems even). I'm attempting a drastic change of direction but it took neuritis in my left arm & an almost complete absence of dreams to make me admit what was happening to me. It's a case of hubris because I thought I could do all those things I'd taken on (to pull my weight financially, principally) *and* be myself & not let my work suffer. I *have* written some poems all along but fewer & fewer. Not sending you that list—just making a note & letting it get buried on my desk—was part of it. Forgive me.

I'd spoken to Mac Hammond about Helen on the way to California & am glad he's written to her.

I guess it is late now to be of any use but I will in any case append a list of places & people just in case.

Had a very good letter from Helen, I was amazed & glad that she was out of the hospital. How does she seem? Is she really herself? Eve Triem as well

## 232

Feb. 11th {19}62
277 Greenwich St
N.Y. 7 N.Y.

as you, Robert, had written anxiously about her.—Helen before going into the hospital had written her a letter of farewell it seems, & sent her some cherished possessions as if she did not expect to return to life.

About the H. D. review, again it has been a part of my wrong direction to have *fussed* so about it. When it's ready it'll be ready & why should I be so goddamn vain as to care that it appeared while I was poetry editor.

I've had no response to the ad I put on the bulletin board at Nik's school. Very hard to find a sublet for 1 month like that, especially in spring. Have you any prospects yet? One friend (Midi Garth) who is moving out of her dance studio into a nice apartment as she got a $3000 award (after being near starvation for years) did say she might move back into her studio for that month but it is very vague. Shd. I put an ad in *The Village Voice* & *The Villager*? Let me know.

We will be away for part of your stay here, alas. It's like this: Nik has his Easter vac. (10 days) & he & Mitch are very eager to get up to Maine. I am too, except that you will be here. But I can't not go as it would not be enjoyable for them without me. However I thought of 2 things, (1) if you have not got a good place, you could have this place while we are gone (April 13th–22d) and/or (2) if you could afford to get up to Maine & didn't mind primitive conditions & probably a lot of mud, you could come & spend a few days with us at Temple. If you wd be going to Boston/Gloucester around then, it is not too much further. Let us know when you know.

Love—
Denny

P.S.

Nik chose *Ayesha* for a book report for school (did I send you this before?) & wrote as follows: "*Ayesha* is about 2 Englishmen who have a desire to see again a beautiful Spirit whom they had seen before (in the book *She*) in the form of a beautiful woman ruling a people in Africa. As in *She* they only reach her after long & terrible travels & adventures; some part of her guiding them to her human part. There is a great deal of talk & proof of the theory of REINCARNATION in it, which is fascinating! They find her, but the younger one whom she loves is killed by her kiss and the author goes sadly home & throws his manuscript on the fire, in a fit of desperation."

Then he quoted: "Ayesha let fall her rein. She tossed her arms, waving the torn white veil as though it were a signal cast to heaven.

"Instantly from the churning jaws of the unholy night above belched a blaze of answering flame, that also wavered like a rent & shaken veil in the grasp of a black hand of cloud. Then did Ayesha roll the thunder. . . . "

I liked the way he emphasized not the "adventures" but the mythic element. Also his choice of quotation.

| | |
|---|---|
| Mr. Mac Hammond<br>  Eng. Dept.,<br>  Western Reserve University,<br>  Cleveland Heights, Ohio. | (Have written.) |
| Mr. Z. S. Fink,<br>  Eng. Dept.,<br>  Northwestern University,<br>  Evanston, Illinois. | (Have written) |
| Sister Mary Jeremy,<br>  Eng. Dept.,<br>  Rosary College<br>  River Forest, Illinois | (Will write if you're interested.<br>Nice people. Suburb of Chi.<br>A $50 "extra" if in Chi.) |

over—>

| | |
|---|---|
| Mr Howard Levant<br>  Morningside College<br>  Sioux City,<br>  Iowa | (Will write if you feel<br>it is not too far<br>out of the way<br>Let me know.) |

In Minneapolis if you want to go up there write to James Wright—but probably you won't want to go up there. If you were going to Minn. I wd. contact 2 Catholic schools there about you also.

Ask Betty Kray if she has any suggestions too. U. of Pittsburgh gave me 250 when I went there last year (Student Union sponsored) thru' her but have lost the man's name—also he may have left. Will be writing to 2 others—at U. of Conn & at Syracuse (where Im going Dec. 12th for 3 days) but dont have the names on hand.

Then as I said there's Ted Weiss who is currently (till Feb.) "visiting poet" at M.I.T. You might write & follow up my nudge to him. (He was here this weekend.)

OVER—>

Love—

Denny.

Oh, and Paul Engle at Iowa U. if you think you can stand it. But be forewarned, it wd surely exasperate you.

dear Denny,

This is one of those days when it almost seems as if I try to find my pen I'll not get a note off to you. Foremost, that Helen is home from the hospital and—tho she's got getting a job and the sorry mess the Playhouse have

## 233

February 12, 1962
{San Francisco}

presented as her play still to face—she *does* seem her old self. Hammond at Northwestern had written her, thanks to you in part, I take it, about the possibility of a reading—and yesterday she did a tape recording for me that came out splendidly: to go off tomorrow with an accompanying note from me. I want him to forward the tape to you in New York when he has made use of it to persuade his colleagues to give a go ahead on it. The reading of "At the Window" is a wonder—she had never read it aloud before, she said— and tried it just once before our taking the tape. I think we got that rare conjunction of the poem and its living aura in the poet's own emotions, the beautiful immediacy that lasts just as long as the poet is not used to the poem.

Second news is that this morning very disappointing word came from the Bank—we'd already heard that it might be another six months before the trust would be realized in full, and that meantime my income was to be only $125 a month. But I had had expectations that this would be retroactive and now I learn it won't be. It means that Jess won't be coming East with me. We'd plannd on that only because we had been sure that we would have the extra money to make the trip, at ease—as a sort of present to ourselves. That will have to wait now until later. We don't want to go thru the business of just getting by. And now what I can make on this trip will count as it is for home expenses as it did before.

Denny, I will still want to take a room for myself in New York beginning the evening of April 7th thru to the morning of the 14th—a week. I go to Ithaca to stay with the Bensons at Cornell—where I will be reading on the 16th.[1] Then I'll be back in New York but en route to Boston and Gloucester to see Charles—try to get in visits to N. O. Brown and to Norman Pearson in New Haven. Well I'm just trying to picture it here but it does make it all seem *rushd*. And I don't want to do it that way. The point is, as above—I do want a room in a hotel or, if you know somebody downtown Village area who wld rent one. The Rothenbergs offerd quarters again. But I think I will prosper if I can have some corner quite of my own that first week.

Would you, Denny, find whatever is most reasonable? I know "reasonable" will not be very cheap, but if you could find something around $25 for the week it would be fine.

Don't despair on the H. D. and I won't—

love,
Robert

---

**234**

Feb. 14/1962
{San Francisco}

dear Denny,

You *did* send me a list of names of places to read, etc. and most wrote in replying that you had written them too. It's just that I've been disheartend about building up a concentrated tour of readings. Don't think that the finances of the trip (our original plans for Jess to go along) depended on the readings. I thot I was going to get retroactive payments on the trust that would make the trip possible, with some ease and pleasure. Instead, there is still a delay, with only enuf coming in now to meet the rent.

Don't make a task of my asking about your reserving a room for me at some hotel for a week April 7th thru the 13th: it's just that I don't have any idea what hotels wld be expensive and what reasonable.

But this morning, with your letter, one from Robert and Joan Benson arrived. Cornell—for a lecture the 16th and a reading the afternoon of the 17th will pay $150 *plus* travel expenses (round-trip plane fare from New York)—and I'm writing to see if that can be made fare from New York to Ithaca and then *to* Boston. Then I'll take your suggestion and add myself to mud and whatever at Temple for two days, as a northern extension of seeing Charles in Gloucester and Ed Klinà in Boston, heading back for New York.

Norman's letter and the Marianne Moore piece on H. D. enclosed.[1] His devotion to H. D.—where love so wholly enters in and can see too that tho Bryher "wavers between moments of selfishness and moments of complete generosity and self-effacement," "that was like Hilda herself," and that we are included in it, in our own devotion, remains moving, a major moving thing at times for me.

I got a book of poems in the mail yesterday *The Lover and Other Poems* by Mimi Goldberg that I've been delighting in.[2] The language and feeling is so close to its origins in Williams that it's hard to place why it is so beautifully a new poet—and so much the person—that I've been delighting in Mimi Goldberg too.

This in the run of two other books arriving that would have made me angry if I had taken it to heart that attitudes and posed questions still do duty for, in place of, imagination or feeling—

love
Robert

---

Relieved to hear I did send you those names. Card from Mac Hammond says "Nice letter from Helen Adam, hope to be able to invite her."

Dear Robert & Jess

We're *so* sorry Jess isn't coming. I'd wanted, for one thing, to show him this part of N.Y.—or rather, for Mitch to show it him who has such a keen sense of it. It is full of things you'd like to see, I think. Will of course see about the room. Will soon let you know.

The poem about Helen struck home for me too, you will see how from my last letter.

## 235

Feb. 20th {19}62
{New York}

It suddenly struck me I didn't know if you ever got that Bresdin print* or a book of Arthur Hughes pictures (*Speaking Likenesses*).[1] It's not that I want a thank you! but if lost maybe I could set a P.O. enquiry on foot. Though I have little faith in such. Nik's been having the flu. Now I think Mitch may be getting it. I hope not. Al & Pat (Kresch) are going to France in 2 weeks, for a year or 2. We shall miss them.

Love<br>Denny

*which was in a long cardboard cylinder

---

## 236

Feb. 26/{19}62
{San Francisco}

dear Denny,

We received the Bresdin and are still discovering new creatures in its foliage. How could I have not written to express our delight—not because I hold by the duty of thank-you notes; but because the print (on the wall by the toilet) has become so much a part of our life. We bring back news every day of some changing view of the world there.

And now, happily, Jess's transportation will be paid, as far as Washington D.C. and return—by Bill Roth as a commission for Jess to do an assembly "A political machine" from objects found in Washington. Whether he will come to New York for the week with me still depends on him—at this point he wants to come back here on April 7th. But we will see the Redon-Moreau-Bresdin show in Chicago en route.[1]

I've hopes yet that all going well Jess's mood may extend to coming on to New York. His own work is part of his not wanting to be gone more than two weeks. These last three days he has been bringing into itself a large collage of the tarot "Chariot"—working eight to ten hours a day on it, cutting and pinning, following along the maze of continuing and corresponding forms that evoke the final image.[2]

And, by contagion perhaps—tho by the happening of it too—I am back at work on the H. D. Corman, after reading the "Day Book"—made extensive selections from it for further consideration for *Origin*.[3] Where my feeling of my writing and its possible appearance there co-operate (as I can never feel my purposes are appropriate to *The Nation*, but become some kind of strategy I dread to undertake), so that the work again moves for me. I have been bringing these sections Cid askd for into their final form, and more than I thought could be realized—all that I wanted—has been opening up in parts that needed clarification. Not re-writing or re-working, but I like the term *rendering*: bringing out what had been but dimly perceived.

Yet what time it seems to take—two and a half hours last night, to emerge with three paragraphs that may, I hope, illuminate ideas of the true and false.

I've been, I realize, DEAD—however it lookd to others, SULLEN—in these last months when it seemd impossible to work on the book. But "dead" or "sullen" or "unwilling" was also an impatience to be at work, in a period when now I see the process was in an incubation stage—and I was overloading my system with more material from biology, physics, zoology—trying to get an in-formd image of animal and cosmic orders. Finding other "keys" in Corbin's book on *Avicenna* which Robin gave me.[4]

At last, the work in prose begins to be as satisfying of/for my restless spirit as I had thought only verse might be. Being back in that work a blessing that begins to extend what writing can be. The exhilaration of following my leads and correspondences in a maze of materials (that I may have learnd from the maze of Bresdin, or from Jess's own paste-ups working towards an emerging image)

• 

→ But the Arthur Hughes did not arrive, Denny—and since you didn't mention it before we didn't expect it. I hope a tracer can find what happend.

• 

My own plans now shift—I don't think I shall attempt the trip to Temple. I want to stay East after the Cornell reading on the 16th to finish the H. D. book and place it with a publisher before I come home. My hope is that I might stay at N. O. Brown's; and have some time along the line with H. D. manuscripts in New Haven.

love
Robert

---

Have you any arrangement to read at Harvard? Does Mr. Sweeney know you are coming?[1] In case not I'm sending him a p.c.—don't know too much about him but he was very pleasant & courteous to me when I met him a couple of years ago. I suppose Robin knows him well.

Love—from D.[2]

**237**

{March 1962
New York}

Am reading galleys of Geo.Oppen/Charles Reznikoff—Good.

Dearest Robert & Jess

Before your last letter in which was the good news that Jess *may* come to N.Y. too, (What a glorious fantastic quest—elements for a Political Machine!!) I had booked a single room at the Hotel Earle, on Washington Sq. & McDougall (cater-cornered from the 8th St Bkshop; it is where Jimmy Broughton stayed when he was in N.Y. I remember). The room is $28 for the week—you had said $25 so I thought you cd. go to 28 but if it doesn't sound right I'll try elsewhere. I thought it has a nice location & the room I looked at (sworn to be typical) has a desk, goodsized (3/4) bed, & bathroom; & all rooms at $28 (the least) are quieter than the more expensive ($35 & up) rooms with view of the square.

Now, should I get it changed to a double? Or look for cheaper ones? Let me know. I tried to think of someone with a suitably private room they might have available but Race {Newton} (downstairs here) comes & goes at odd (jazz musician) hours—his sleep wd be disturbed and your privacy not assured; and Barbara Bank who has a b-room apt. in the building where we used to live has a friend from Eng. staying thru' April; so on reflection I didn't even ask them. And I can't think of any others. There are 2 other hotels in the Village area which might be possibilities but I imagine the cost is about the same—I wish *we* had a guest room but in spite of considerable cubic space this apt. is not workable that way. We do put people up in the livingroom sometimes but it is exactly the kind of situation you would be most uncomfortable in, even alone, & imposs. if you both come.

Nik & Mitch have both had the flu. I've been in the doldrums; no poems since those 3 in December, but today I think I started something.

I'm anxious for you to read A. R. Ammons' poems. He gave one of your books a bad review once, Robert, but it was the result of a temporary blindness like my mistaking your "Letter" years ago, remember.[3] And he has since been reading you with true feeling. His poems are becoming illuminations to me & I will try to copy out a few this week, & send them.

Too bad about *Speaking Likenesses* getting lost. I should have registered it but since most things arrive I didn't think of it. It's the 3d thing lost in the mail I've had in the last 2–3 months—my faith in the US P-O. is shattered. I don't think tracers really go anywhere but into a huge wastebasket.

A young poet, Sandra Hochman, whom I met through Galway {Kinnell}, & like, has been reading you intensively Robert & asks me to tell you she is in a new world.

I would be sorrier you decided not to come to Temple if we were more decided on going there ourselves. Ted Enslin tells us it can still be terribly wintry there in mid-April & we may go to Narragansett to visit Mitch's brother & his wife instead, for those few days. Perhaps we will be in Boston about the same time anyway.

## 238

dear Denny,

Monday Mike (McClure) came over at lunch, and talking about Shelley, then reading aloud his "Hymn to Mercury" I got started on "A Set of Hymns," I call'd it first—then "Romantic" hymns because it let me go that free.[1] Following two haunting scenes: the Indian dancers I saw in January at

Santo Domingo (No, it was December 26th, the second Xmas day I saw) and conjoind: the dancing files of genes in the chromosomes.

It's been so long since I've had a moving sequence to work in—I mean surrounded by music as I was, and it *does* come thru. . . .

This morning, it didn't just come but had to be workd, listening and leading, going over and over what started to strike the changes of it. The *Faustus* echo (?) kept insisting, and I could not see how or what it wanted to do. It's not there in the poem but I think the Christ-Sun may be one of the centrioles and the other pole be a Divine Woman (just as there is some human play between me and the *other* figure of a woman).

The dancers are generations.

So soon now I will be seeing you!

love,
Robert

dear Denny & Mitch—

I doubt that I wrote thanking you for the hotel reservation, Denny— Anyways here's the O.K. on the single room April 8th to 14th at the Hotel Earle. It will make a real difference for me, having "a room of ones own": for all the excitements of New York, I have the p'raps vain hope to get some work done. Norman has written that he "will plan how best to implement it (the H. D. study)" when I come to Yale—If the possibility's there, I want to make copies of her poems that I do not have (and of the prose works, the Moravian/William Morris/Mithra trilogy she told me about{)}.

In all events, I am determined to stay East until the Book is in the hands of a publisher (or, granted that things might go awry at the publisher stage—*ready* for publisher)—But that won't be New York; I'd thot to work at N. O. Brown's at Middletown. Yet for all my invitation to visit there, I've still to write to Nobby and Beth and ask if I might make *use* of the invitation.

These days are, as you can imagine, crowded—Jess and I managed to prepare and deposit with *Auerhahn Press* the first volume of two for *A Book of Resemblances*

[with a break to clear the dishes from last night's dinner and breakfast . . . and wash-up. Letting my mind wander about]—

Jess's beautiful illustrations for the book—to revive some richness.

Then getting the sections of the H. D. study done for Cid—at least 26 pages to copy before he left for Japan two days ago. He'd taken sections that involved new writing—especially the Christos sections (where I am[1]

**239**

March 16/1962
{San Francisco}

**240**

Thurs. 29th
{March 29, 1962}
277 Greenwich St
N.Y. 7

Dear Robert & Jess,

Welcome to the East.

Let me know if you (Jess) are coming on to N.Y. after all. I hope so. If so I will rearrange about room. (Another single? A double? Interconnecting singles wd. give you most working space—what they call grandly a "suite." All our travels have made me a hotel expert—of sorts.) I'll in any case reconfirm yr. reservation & try to get to see the room the day before to make sure it is as decent as they come.

You both of course have an open invitation to dinner any night of the week but especially for the 7th (if you arrive early enough—or even if you don't I can always provide a meal{)}—and the 8th itself when I thought we would have a very earlier dinner—5:30—& I would ask Gil Sorrentino also, & we cd. all go up to the Y together.

I haven't made any plans this time for a party or asking anyone over to meet you here. I don't feel equal to a party & besides during the week it would get in the way of Nik's homework; but if there's anyone you want to see in domestic sort of surroundings instead of at the hotel or outside, please let me know &/or just bring them over.

I should have made all these remarks earlier; but, well, that's the way I am, I don't seem to think ahead.

Mitch is hoping you got his letter before you left; he should really have addressed it to Washington.

I'm going out to see Bill & Floss on Sat. afternoon but will be back by 6–6:30 & will have prepared supper earlier in the day, in case you can come. Please call us when you arrive from Washington (RE2-3197)—also, let me know when & where you arrive & perhaps I can meet you. It's too bad I have to go to Rutherford just that day but owing to various complications it was the only possible day I could go.

By the way, Gael {Turnbull} is supposed to be coming (from Toronto, en route back to Cal.) on the 13th & will sleep here the 13th & 14th (departs the 15th) so it would also be very nice if you would have supper with us on the 13th. We leave for that vacation on the 14th. We're not going to Temple after all but will visit Mitch's brother at Narragansett, Rhode Island, where he's just settled in a house near the ocean. We'll also be in Boston for a few days, returning on Easter day or the Saturday.

Love from
Denny.

dear Denny & Mitch/

Jess and I have been glutting ourselves with seeing. And then we are most fond of Jim and Anne Truitt as well as the clan of little Truitts, so this week is a happy one all round.[1] But Jess will have had too much of being away by the end of this week, for all of the fact that things have gone so well in Denver, Chicago and here. He'll be heading back for San Francisco from here on the eighth or ninth.

I shld be in New York at least by seven or so on the 7th (Jess and I are going to a Pre-Raphaelite museum in Wilmington in the morning)—I'll telephone you as soon as I get in;[2] or of course, if my plans get more definite, I'll send a card. I will want to see you right away. The plans for the evening of the reading sound the best! How odd it will be reading a half-program. But I did it with Whalen in Sausalito last year and know it can come thru—

love,<br>Robert

**241**

April 2nd/{19}62
{Washington, D.C.}

dear Denny & Mitch/

I won't be getting to New York Saturday until 8:15 (on the Pennsylvania line). Jess will be going as far as Philadelphia with me, to see the Arensberg collection again and the Rodin museum.[1] We'll have an early dinner there and Jess will return to Washington. So—don't worry about my being at dinner . . . and I'll go to the Hotel Earle from the station and then phone and find out about seeing you. Tho it won't be so late I guess—Let's say I'll just come on over after I get my luggage deposited. Around about 9:30.

Love<br>Robert

**242**

April 5/{19}62
{Washington, D.C.}

Dear Robert,

Jonathan Greene called to say that if you wished to go directly from Ithaca to Bard you could go (presumably by train) to Poughkeepsie & be picked up from there. Kelly's # at Bard is: PL8-9731. (That's a Red Hook number.) If however you wish to go to Bard from N.Y., Jonathan Greene will be in the city at his mother's that week (of the 24th) and will drive you. (I should tell you that when we drove up with him a bird flew in front of the lights & he almost went into the woods.) 277 University Ave. is his home address.

All this is the same message I gave Margery but I thought it wd. be a good idea to write it also.

**243**

April 14 {1962}
Boston

Ted Enslin will be at our place while we're away so if you want to spend a night you might send him a p.c. We'll be back the night of Sunday 22d.

Love—
Denny

---

**244**

May 10/{19}62
{Washington, D.C.}

dear Denny & Mitch/

I'm sending the ninety-five pages I got done of the final draft on the book (tho the last couple of pages may not be final) with 3 sections of Part I left to do. It will have to wait till I get home—as also the "Day Book" part II and the Part III on *Helen in Egypt*. But here anyway is something to read.

I'll be in New York Saturday and I'll phone you as soon as I get in in the morning. The rest of my plans are unclear but I'll be headed home by the end of this week.

love
Robert

---

**245**

May 21st {1962}
277 Greenwich
{New York}

Dear Robert & Jess,

I wrote this poem for or around John Button. Please tell me if it works as a poem. Visually it is a shapeless thing—but I don't take much account of visual effects in that sense anyway. Aloud, as I read it to Mitch, uncertain of what I had done, it astonished me by seeming to have a forceful presence— but how much was in my voice, in the emphasis I gave, & how much is there to the reader on the page? Mitch was very moved by it, but you know, I can't go by that—because he's too close, too partial, & doesn't anyway make certain demands of poetry that I make. I've never before felt such a need to have it told to me whether a poem were *there* or not—I usually have some pride in feeling able to know it from within.

If it does—work, or is there,—I wish Button could see it but how can one send a young man a poem about his dying. Or can one. Well, I can think of some people to whom one could; but I don't know Button that well & if he has not the belief that he will die soon it would be a vulgar cruelty of self-indulgence to send him the poem. Yet there's that in it would make him glad, if I've said what I think I've said. Will you advise me? I feel you will know what I should do—you, Robert, because you've seen him and you, Jess, because you are a wise man. Of course if you think poorly of the poem there would be no question of sending it to Button anyway.

By the way, I received from him a typed sheet headed "Some recent pictures by John Button can be seen in the following exhibitions" and ending with "Last Show: Tanager Gallery May 25–June 14"—now, does that "Last Show" actually mean that he presumes this will be his last show? Or what? It might conceivably mean "last" show this season?

It was wonderful to have you here Robert & I wish Jess had been here too & that both of you could have seen Temple. We'll be going up there about June 8th D.V.

Love—
Denny

Will send copies of other poems soon.

If John Button is to die soon[1]
how is it that my future
spreads out with only
the general shadow on it?

He who (I think, loves Duncan as I do—from afar;
He who paints clouds, roofs, walls, bodies
    as I in dreams would or try to reach
in words
        "the clouds as I see them—
rising
urgently, roseate in the
mounting of somber power"
(and his name got left out of the poem
because a You got in who was not he)
who walked on Mexican mountains with my mother
            . . .
I tell you I said the clouds were "surging
in evening haste over hermetic grim walls—"
I had nothing to tell me the haste was in him.
I saw the hasting clouds as through my own
dusty late-afternoon windows. No thought that
death was whitely pursuing
    "in pomp advancing, pursuing the falling sun."
Duncan had not yet told me that Button had had cancer
and that (he may live in the shadow of that thought)
he heard it had reoccurred. He does not know
(if this is true)—
            The future,
intricate valley of hillocks and boldly spangled shadows!
Where I'm to be and he is not?

John Button, if that's the truth, yet
you've found love,

a calm in the midst of
the dark brickwork, the sun
always swinging, sweeping
the spun-out beautiful shadows
in its wake

(and I have so far to go).

Don't feel (if this is true)
I pity you. You've made
that luminous and defined
presence, multiplied,
you were born to make.    And I?

The kids that play ball weekends in the parking lot—
my crumbling father-in-law trying or pretending to
    try to remember when he was last here and what
    day of the week it is, weeping
false tears of remembrance at a picture of me as
    a small, fat, eager child in a cane chair
    in my garden of brick walls
—I've made nothing of these and so much else,

nothing to say: (if this is true)
this was life for me in 1962, with a new desk
    (not replacing my old one but added space, an
    other desk—oak, Pennsylvania carving, circa 1901),
a son my own size, a husband
moving erratically towards. . . .

                    . . .

—nothing, yet,
of the oppression and charm of letters,
coldness of wonder, tedium of female cycles, intricate
waterfall of dream and breathing and daily
death and rebirth—going to bed in tears,
waking grumpy or full of decision or simply
reborn, nothing yet.

The clouds are on your side, Button,
the bricks
have glowed for you, you've spoken
for the roofs and he old grim walls of warehouses.
From hermetic silence your silent
song has gone forth.

dear Denny,

Robin told me when I askd him (as I couldn't ask John) once I got home—that John Button had been assured by his doctors that the cancer was cured. Yet my apprehension of how drawn he lookd *had* seemd real, not entirely a sentiment of the thought of the cancer. So your poem is (as the "if" of the poem *does* establish) awkwardly pitchd.

And wouldn't he be shy of (shy away from) "loves Duncan"? The poem too must make conditions "If John Button is to die soon . . . " "(if this is true)" but also "(I think)" and "I tell you"/"I had nothing to tell me."

"From afar" the poem is colored by an emotion seeking thru participation to find itself. As if certain added particulars (but we weren't sure of them, even tho I had what I thought of as a definite report—I mean we weren't sure of taking the report) might add some *fact* of death to

> Last night
> as if death had lit a pale light
> in your flesh, your flesh
> was cold to my touch

That's the real knowledge of what we know of the death of a moment, ourselves, those we love, to us—Besides which

> "No thought
> cancer was whitely
> pursuing him through his
> bloodstream. . . . "

*has* to be too much. These are not things wrong in the poem, but, mining them, or holding them up to the light, we *do* see how much you had said it in "Clouds," and may in this poem have sought to revisit what had been felt. The second poem becomes a most human note of your relationship to the poem "Clouds." The passage in which your father-in-law appears concentrates in his image

> "trying or pretending to try to remember when he was last here and what
> day of the week it is, weeping false tears of remembrance at a picture of
> me as a small, fat, eager child in a cane chair in my garden of brick walls"

"false," yet we must often borrow a picture in order to weep. Your "I've made nothing of these and so much else" must borrow something out of place to express a real (felt) thing.

That old man fumbling for tears is the nexus in experience around which the poem has tried to organize, as in "Clouds" the organizational experience is in the actual moment of cold, fading, and fear. These, most real.

But your unsureness about whether this second "John Button" poem isn't shapeless is not mistaken. In some sense we write in order to feel, or, writing *is* feeling: but the *virtú* in it is that we can render it most true. There's one thing that comes out of this morning for me—that's how splendid, how condensed a thing "Clouds" is.

It does the greater honor in taking John Button's clouds as most real— One of the things that plays false in the second one is you telling Button what he's done in painting, your "Don't feel you've lost out" Whatever his spirit is, it isn't anything of losing out. The paintings have no such regret. And it calls up soon—your

> "Don't feel (if this is true)
> you've lost out."

the other "I've made nothing of these and so much else" that plays all the very real makings your poems false in another effort at regret.

In the midst of the stuff of this second poem is the realized image of the old man trying or pretending to try to remember—and then unrealized the articulation of some regret or of how important and urgent regret is. In itself, I mean.

———————

I've got to get to my H. D. book—the coffee has been pourd and drunk and Jess has vanishd into his studio.

Dave Haselwood and the Hoyems (of Aurehahn) were over last night to talk about the projected volume I of *A Book of Resemblances*. The plates for Jess's drawings will come to around $800 before they can begin. We will be sending out a prospectus for a limited edition in a few weeks. Do you have any ideas about libraries or wealthy individuals you've come across who might be interested in a $30 edition (which will have an original drawing by Jess and a poem in holograph by me in addition to the contents of the regular edition)?

love
Robert

## 247

May 24th {1962}
277 Greenwich St
{New York}

Dear Robert & Jess

Thank you very much for answering fast, & as you did. Your reaction confirms what I'd begun to realize since sending you the poem. I'm relieved in a way to know that I have enough instinct to *be* doubtful when a poem's weak. Knowing that I can better trust the feeling of sureness about the good ones. This poem was written at a pitch of excitement not quite natural to me in working; and it was based (I can see with your help) on a muddle which never resolved itself in the process: the thoughts A) If John Button has no future how come I do? and B) if he has & I don't, it must be that he has completed himself, his work in life as an artist, and I obviously haven't because look at all the things I fail to speak of ever—these are basically sentimental thoughts in the sense that they are passing, ephemeral, not beliefs on which I'd take a stand, not things I *go on* feeling/thinking— belonging to the realm of fancy & not of imagination, in a word. From this muddle (of course) followed structural muddle—addressing first myself, then the world in general, then Button himself. Etc. I can still see beautiful things in the poem, the last part & the thing about spangled shadows, but these, and the thing about the old man (M.'s father) might grow into another poem perhaps, I hope.[1] But the poem itself—why, it's not there at all, there is no poem, it's a conglomeration of undeveloped and insufficiently rooted impulses.

I must explain about "loves Duncan." After Button had been to SF I met him at Nell Blaine's one night & he started to tell me about having attended those lectures you gave, Robert, and with a kind of wholehearted enthusiasm that delighted me—I hadn't even known he knew you and I felt he had a sense of you akin to my own and I liked him for it. I can see it would sound like something else, maybe again something sentimental which is not what I meant but which—the wrong impression given—rose out of the false premises on which the whole poem was based. How fascinating and instructive it is to see the falseness of one impulse infect all the parts of an action. I am not sorry it happened for I feel I've learned several things from it. Not least that when I feel unsure I can take it pretty much for granted it's with good reason. Part of what happened in this case was that I was reacting to the academic world as experienced in Michigan with its over- emphasis on the "right" the "well-done" the polished and balanced and clear—overreacting so that I wanted to let myself trust boldly in the wrong, the badly done, the clumsy, ill-balanced & murky—while I know very well, thank god, as a rule, without having to think about it, that one is *not* faced with these as alternatives at all, really, but goes a third way. I even (I must admit) was not quite sober when I wrote; now, I don't drink or feel the slightest impulse to drink (not a tea-totaller but just don't care about it and certainly don't look for ways into my own feelings by means of liquor) but on this occasion I had 2 drinks because my father-in-law was hovering about—& he makes me very tense & I had thought how nice it would be to be able to sit & write with everything going on around one the way Robert does. Afterwards (in my uncertainty) I thought, O lord, how horrible if this *is* a good poem, some new way—I who've always been so intolerant of anyone artificially stimulating themselves to work, am I going to find I do better when I've had a shot of whiskey? But apparently the Muse does not demand I get drunk in her honor; how nice.

What I've not-said a word about is that it seems Button is going to get better. It's wonderful news and I'm so glad I hadn't written to Al about his being ill, he would have been so distressed and for nothing. I met Hyde Solomon on the street the other day, do you know him?[2]—and he'd had an operation for detached retina, but is O.K.—For a painter to almost lose the sight of an eye (& having then to put so much strain on the other!)—This had happened 8 wks ago and he had been in the dark for several weeks—the day I met him he was so happy, the Dr had just told him he could take off the special blacked glasses with little holes in the middle & wear his own glasses & paint for a couple of hours a day now.

About that special edition of *A Book of Resemblances* I can think of (so far) one good prospect: Robert Wilson who has bought the Phoenix Bookshop Cornelia St, N.Y. 14 from {Larry} Walrich is a collector on his own account—he seems to really read poetry & I should think would be sure to want to subscribe for himself, & no doubt would know others.[3] If I think of anyone else I'll let you know. Oh yes, Jens Nyholm the Librarian at Northwestern U. Evanston, Ill., is trying to build up a good poetry collection and spends his evenings translating into Danish. He's done my "Peppertrees" & other poems & is a very simpatico man.[4]

So glad you like the English fairytales Jess. Did Robert tell you what a pleasure it was to me to take another look at your Morgenstern book? Especially, among the poems, that chair again—ah . . .

Well, I do most seriously believe you are what I mean by wise.

I've been rereading William Barnes of Dorset—aloud as well as in silence—thinking of Finlay, & Chaucer in the right pronunciation, & Barnes, it seems appalling how smooth plain Eng. or standard American has become, it would be nice to have a dialect natural to one, but we have to do the best we can with what we've got.

—love—
Denny

## 248

May 31, 1962
{San Francisco}

dear Denny,

We'd pursued your doubt, but some last note is due on the side of the casual intense, that in a possible poetry sentiment, the ephemeral, misplaced thing can have its voice. The responsibility must remain, it's the principle of the art, that the poet find out the truth of what the poem feels; in the "casual" he might wander and wonder more to find. After all, the youngest son in the fairytale who is always responsible as a poet must be to his guest often goes astray, almost as the form of the thing must do wrong things to come out right. There is a special virtue in your "If John Button" for those of us who live close to your poetry, for the verse, here previous to a poetry, gives us a share in moods and impulsive feelings that a renderd poem might only rarely convey. It's not *murky*, you know, nor clumsy (tho there are passages where line-feel seems arbitrary)—it's *confused*: and as the record of such a confusion it is straight—i.e. we trust its elements as being actual but afloat. Now, in this letter, you supply more of the conditions: perhaps if the actual drinking and the "to sit and write with everything going on around me" had been there, the "*If* John Button is to die soon," "clouds" and "walls"—might it also have been your father who "walked with your mother"?—"late-afternoon windows"; "the sun/always swinging": would have found their scale, the notes their tone?

However it goes, you're not a "drunk with words" poet. It's of the very nature of your calling in the art that a clear-eyed "in back of your head" care is the key. Tho, unless those were water tumblers of whiskey those probably weren't late-afternoon windows of intoxicated sight yet.

The only poem I remember drink-writing was that "Imaginary War Elegy" where I drank a fifth of Cutty Sark while I wrote, listening to the golden color, taste?, tone? of the whiskey.

I'm reading *La Kabbale Pratique*—the book of angel and demon lore that H. D. drew upon in "Sagesse" and her later work.[1] The word "art" there does seem to stand for the word "art" at large—so that not only for the Kabbalist's art but for the poet's too: "Le but de l'Art est donc, *pratiquement*, de mettre l'Adepte en liaison psychique avec les Plans Supérieurs et les Intelligentes qui y résident. En outre, d'agir altruistement et occultement sur ses semblables, au mieux des intérêts supérieurs de la Collectivité humaine."

Just here that listening for the forms of things around, there is an archeform one discovers or *feels* and follows towards the poem. And the form of things is a collective intuition.

That must go along with Breton's "*Je ne suis pas pour les adeptes*"— the opening lines of "Pleine Marge" which I'm working on. It was that counter-principle that drew me to attempt the poem, given the Bollingen commission-at-large.

As, counter-statement to Ambelain's "liaison psychique avec les Plans Supérieurs," I'd hold to an idea I found stated in Teilhard de Chardin's *Phenomena of Man* that form exists only in the totality.[2] Our alliance with an imitation of "Form" then must always be *psychic* or intuitive.

Jess, anyway, added the observation this morning that you hadn't let the poem go on into the elegiac mode where the archetype of the young son-Sun soon-to-die would have appeared. Mightn't "He who paints clouds, roofs, walls,/bodies" be, beyond the thought of Johnny Button, an older figure. Certainly we would have recognized him in Stevenson's *Child's Garden* as the sun. Not only then "a son my own size" but "a sun my own size." Going to bed and waking. "And his name / got left out of the poem—" There's some double play between the Sun we see cast out the shadows each night and "die" long before we do, the great creator, casting light upon (creating things out of light) what we SEE; and the Sun we know "always swinging" does not "die"—lasts beyond us as we are. As too, some mixed feeling apprehends that a son may live on "beyond."

I love the line "The clouds are on your side, Button"

•

Might a longer freer line movement have made for a greater *condensare*? Keeping the two themes (I'll risk that there are two and maybe find more)

> If John Button is to die soon     [the life and death
> how is it that my future          of the Sun along with the
> spreads out with only             ever living Sun, beyond our
> the general shadow on it.        lives.]
> He who (I think) loves Duncan as I do from afar.
>                                [Sun here still; but also
>                                the "If" into "I think" a
>                                second theme of uncertainty]
> He who paints clouds, roofs, walls, bodies as I in dreams would or try
>      to reach

going at it that way "in belovéd words" is the first uneasy point now.

>        "In words" ?
>        "as I see them—
> rising. . . . "

etc. quote directly and the "try to reach" rings out towards the full second theme: how we try and reach, will use anything and everything towards a poem, tears, feeling

> (and his name got left out of the poem
> because a You got in that was not he—)
> Who walked on Mexican mountains with my mother

then "as with a Welsh aunt" seems out of key, is there an actual phrase from a letter from him, a quote again that (from your mother's letters or Button's) gives this Welsh aunt more locality? It's a particular that if you return to whose source may tell more.

> I tell you I said the clouds were "surging
> in evening haste over hermetic grim walls—"
> I had nothing to tell me the haste was in him.
> I saw them
> as through my own dusty
> late-afternoon windows.

[The whole "No thought/cancer was whitely/pursuing him through his/bloodstream,"/we realize now must be conditiond to come true. Can you get in the movement of the poem here

1. That clouds and then words change their shapes and then meanings.
2. So that, when Duncan had heard there was a reoccurrence of cancer, the clouds are shapes of death "in pomp advancing . . ."
3. The thought of death advancing (towards the pomp of the poem)

The future, intricate valley of hillocks and boldly spangled shadows!

["And it's for me and/not for him?"—is another statement I balk at in the poem. The future, well, is it "for" whomever?]

"Where I'm to be and he is not" [?]
John Button, if that's the truth,
you've found                                [I cut "and you found love new joy"
(a calm in the midst of                   because it seems diverse, and to be
the dark brickwork, the sun            contain'd (love and art in the "calm"
always swinging, sweeping              in the midst" in its wake)]
the spun-out beautiful shadows

(The measure of these lines ending "in its wake" is beautiful in the original, with the moving rime of "sun" to "spun-out")

cut thru to "and I have so far to go." (outside parentheses)

I have abrupt troubles with the next nine lines. That they are broken by "(if this is true)" is an important requirement of the poem. And

"You've made
that luminous and defined
presence, multiplied,
you were born to make."

is again beautifully measured and right—keying in both on the level with the particular paintings of Button's and with the Sun's)

But, dammit, there *is* something off about "Don't feel/you've lost out." You volunteer the suggestion from some "you" that's *not* Button. A person doesn't paint that way and feel he's lost out. (As above I cut that about paintings ripening so fast etc.,) And ouch! even the words in themselves won't move in "(And I believe we each were born to make something worth making)" will

Don't feel (it this is true)
I pity you. I think
(if this is true) *yet* you've made
                        ^
[etc. *to*]
         ^

you were born to make. We each
were born to make something worth making
and I?
[new stanza]
The kids that play ball weekends in the parking lot,
my crumbling father-in-law trying or pretending to
    try to remember, when he was last here and what          continuous
    day of the week it is, weeping                            long lines
false tears of remembrance at a picture of me as
    a small, fat eager child in a cane chair in
    my garden of brick walls—I've made

(if this is true) nothing of these
Nothing to say: this was
life for me in 1962, with a new desk
    (not replacing my old one but added space, an
    other desk—oak, Pennsylvania carving, circa 1901)
a son my own size, a husband

[here again I depart from the sense of the text as is. Don't we want here,
some prediction of Mitch's course, but as with the son and the desk, the
Mitch that is "life for me in 1962"]

    —nothing, yet,

[Okey—thru to, and here it's line measure I've the impulse to let move out]

    the bricks
    have glowed for you, you've spoken
    for the roofs and the old grim walls of warehouses;
    from hermetic silence your silent song has gone forth.

[What I get here as a residue of the close is that in speaking for the *walls* of
warehouses, where *bricks* glowed for him—he is heard by the small fat eager
child in her "garden" of *brick walls.*] [There and *not* there] I've heard it.

The poem itself—the problematic element about your hearing from me
that John Button had had cancer and that I feard he had had a reoccurrence
—so that the mind tried to find the sense of the idea of his death (like a
tongue searching out a cavity in a tooth, or a finger searching out a wound)—
all that could be set in a prose argument or explication as in Dante's *Vita
Nova*—increasing the condensation in both prose and poem proper.

For example: the fact that John Button visited your mother and walkd on
Mexican mountains is one thing in the prose explication and *another* as a
fact of the poem.

To heighten the operation of things as we once knew them and as they
are known thru (as of) poetry.

"Where angels fear to tread!" I'm not sure, Denny, that I *could* or would take suggestions about a poem this way. That I could *doubt*, and it's been your query that has led me to see it this way. What I mistrust in my imagining a right composition of the whole is that where your measure compels me I cannot imagine it changed; and wherever I am not compelled I suspect I convert the measure to something of my own.

The truth of the poem is something only you have clues to (tho in our "false" clues we may stir something anew). Well, I *do* have an urge to have those lines move out into long lines with phrases moving in their own grace.

love
Robert

Jess remarks "I liked her lines"—so my wanting those long lines was to mar it; against the spirit of the poem. I am convinced that I was also marring the feeling over into a foreign poem. But Jess felt as I did that there were {illegible}

dear Denny,

I *did* belabor that poem, and then throw back to you a taxidermist's job, flaying the life out of it and sewing up the animal in some stuffd Duncan-semblance of an improved example of the good beast. As if our job as poets, involving as it does what the mathematician calls the most elegant solution, meant some art of posing speech in some artistic reminder of its native habitat. Now, it is your living poem's voice that haunts me. I'd stampd your voice out of it. But the record, the best of the poem is that all its versions remain and the living actual happening reminds me what my rearrangements are.

It did tho serve to arouse me to my own voice—and so here are some poems to send to you. These and my getting all wound up, once you had doubled the realization of a form in the Johnny Button thing, redoing your material, are related to my finding when I returnd here that "Night Scenes" in *The Floating Bear* had caused a scandal at my ineptitude in North Beach poetry circles.[1] Robin was distressd and could not account for the poem's possibly being other than a botchd job. And on two occasions, by George Stanley and again by a Lewis Ellingham the poem had been read in ridicule, as evidence of my infatuation with my own habits and of my decline.

Had the poem been recent, so that I was immediately involved in the question of it, I think I would have succumbd to the attack. But back in 1959 when it was written I had gone thru the full sense that it was questionable and had resolved to stand by it, to admit it to the book. But to be read as the butt of a joke, exposed as a contemptible parody of what it was!

## 249

June 13, 1962
{San Francisco}

Well, I do remember reading Saltus or Aleister Crowley's purple-verse for laughs.[2] It was a healthy response to their wallowing in what they thought the evil of sex-sins. As, Lamantia and Ginsberg too can verge upon the ludicrous excess, times when the gesture is so mannerd and showy that the emotion seems affected. This North Beach attack was not that, but a mistaken advantage, a goad back of which was the sad fact that the poetry had come not to matter but to be only a proposition in their alienation from its spirit.

------------

First thing working on this review of Bob's *For Love* I realized that a great many poems have been eliminated.[3] Which goes along with his sense that the poem is also some trust, "the misdirected intention come right," so that, tho they belongd to their book at the time, poems later may not fit (as too, I get it, the instances of love and being loved, may be "right" in their time but not "right" in the decade). Rectitude is of the essence for him, and the poem arises as a fitting try at the right way of it. He searches for a charged and natural decorum: as a one-eyed man must adjust his sights.

Where with you Denny it's not intention but sympathy that must be incorporated and thru imagination come to its fullness in vision. It's to enter the arms of the knitted garment.

—But what I'm doing in the review itself is to note the reference that reoccurs to Dante and to Guido Cavalcanti—and their discourse of love. How the Lady and Virgil belong in Creeley's world.

With all my usual struggle in the writing of it to keep in tone.

love
Robert

You must be north in Maine by now, I'll send you this tho to the New York address. I'm not sure.

## 250

June 25th {19}62
Temple, Maine

Dear Robert,

Your second letter about the Button poem was full of things I can learn from, so please don't feel apologetic about it. I welcomed it deeply. Thank you for the beautiful poems. Here are a few, I think you've not seen several of them & 1 or 2 are quite new. I think you may not like "A Secret"—it is dry, isn't it—but perhaps it has some virtue.

I've been occupied (when not simply trying to relax, unwind, up here) writing a long letter to my sister and in a day—no, 2—I'll be off for Mexico for a little over 2 weeks (back here July 18th) Will write when I get back, I mean, a proper letter. It's been good here, green & quiet, but I am still tired & not at my most alive. The visit to Mexico & then the weeks while Nik's in camp (up to Aug. 27th) I'm hoping will do me good.

I hope to use some of the components of the Button poem—you see I feel the most basic error was that I was packing into a single poem elements that were really meant to go into several.

Love to Jess—love to you—
from Denny

Dearest Robert,

I find I left myself no copy of that poem called "To the Muse" (the MSS lacks corrections I made in typing)—cd. you let me have it back when you've read it. I don't have any *Floating Bears* here in Temple & can't remember which poem "Night Thoughts" is. If it is what I am thinking of I think everyone is crazy but I often mix up titles so I am not sure I saw it. Will look as I pass through N.Y. Sat. on my way to Mexico. We leave here (Nik & I) tomorrow. Back here July 18

Love—
D.

**251**

Thurs.
June 28th {1962
Temple, Me.}

dear Denny & Mitch

I managed to finish the 9th chapter, with some rewriting necessary in sections you already have. Meanwhile the "Lammas masque" idea has grown into a play[1] and I postpone the H. D. ms. again for a while. There are some new poems and I'll send them in next letter. This is a load as it is—

This summer seems to be a visiting season or rather visitor's season—the Tallmans are down from Vancouver. Johnny Button is expected next month. And we had an evening with the M. L. Rosenthals, and all liked them both. I had thot he was here for a whole summer session from the Poetry Center announcements—but it turnd out he was only here for two weeks: and I almost missd seeing him. Jess begins to make references to the social whirl and going out or having in every night of the week.

But it does leave me a bit distracted—not in some sense having this morning in which to write a letter because I am going off to Berkeley this afternoon. Yet here is the actual easy time!

There's something tho I did say I would write you about—you may have gotten a presumptuous letter from a girl here who is obsessed with Robin and has, over the last few months, made life miserable for him with it. (Sending letters that he *has* to see her, that "they" must work it out—when there is only her delusion and no *thing* at all). She works where Robin works and, for instance, when I visited the Library about a month ago cornerd me—it's like that hell-possessd little secretary in Charles Williams's *All*

**252**

July 16/{19}62
{San Francisco}

*Hallow's Eve.* But the immediate reason to write you any of this is that she has told Robin she's written to you, Denny. I think she wants to punish everyone who seems at all related to Robin; and she'd seen that "Elves" poem of yours. Robin would like to see the letter, to know what she is doing. That you've to decide if he asks (well, he askd me to ask about it, and while I said right away that I would, now that I write to you I'm not sure but what Pandora's box oughtn't to be sent back to Pandora unopend)— but I can't remember her name. We met her once at Robin's house several months ago, when she wanted to buy a painting of Jess's (like the ones Robin had)—and Robin saved us from her learning where we lived. But we both disliked her (this was all in advance of this recent outbreak) and have avoided any social contact, so, I guess, it is I can't remember her name.

Robin dreads, I think, that she may go so far as to seek out her (as his) employer, the head of the library, to tell her "troubles" to and incidentally to confide that he rejects her because he is queer (which she doesn't know but presumes). God knows, whom it is she is persecuting in Robin, but what an ugly haunting it all is. [It had originally started with her telling Robin she admired his poetry and wanted to give him $2000 to go to Paris to write— etc. and as Robin began to see how unbalanced she was he rejected the offer, persuading her to donate the money to the Auerhahn fund to help in publication of new books].

———————

Jess back from the market, and lunch time already! I had wanted to say for you to brush your mind clear of whatever might be in that letter from Robin's succubus (or is it incubus?) and then I've gone on to unload my own mind. It is not the afternoon ahead in Berkeley that was distracting me but the thought again of that thwarted hate-full woman.

I suppose Robin really must see what it is she is writing if she has written you—for his own peace of mind.

love
Robert

---

## 253

July 21st {19}62
Temple, Maine

Dear Robert,

I have written Robin immediately with all I can remember of the letters from that woman (2 or 3) (last winter)—what she said & what I said. She had written to ask (utterly misunderstanding "The Elves," to my embarrass-ment) whether I didn't think persevering love on her part mightn't ultimately meet a response in Robin and whether it might not be a good thing for his poetry & his general happiness! I felt sorry for her (picturing a lonely middleaged virgin) and tried to disillusion her firmly but kindly & point out that this idea was arrogant, immoral (since even if not wildly unlikely it would involve breaking what I regarded as an existing marriage) and also that she could bring herself nothing but misery by fostering unrequited feelings— if she couldn't get over it I suggested she went away to another city.

Later she wrote again saying my advice was well taken & she *did* feel she had gotten over it. I replied saying I was glad to hear it & must now end the exchange of letters since I didn't like having to discuss my friends behind their backs. I wrote all this in more detail to Robin—perhaps he will show you my letter. The one thing that worries me is that I may inadvertently have given her fuel to burn him with in assuming (as I did) that she knew he was a homosexual. I took it as a matter of course that she did know, and as I say, tried gently but plainly to say she ought to have as much respect for his relationship with Jim as if he were living in marriage with a woman— especially since she painted herself as so damn full of Christian charity. Perhaps I ought to have ignored her letters completely but really & truly I did feel sorry for her.

It is the 2d instance of possibly misguided kindness (or what I thought was kindness) on my part in a week: a young woman called Carol Bergé who has written some good poems, I think, & whom I've tried to help in various ways, turned on me viciously because I had kept things impersonal between us & rigorously excluded her from my private life—she wanted to be an "intimate friend" and now accuses me of hauteur, patronizing insincerity, etc. etc., in long typewritten letters. The fact is, as a person she bores the shit out of me if you'll excuse my language—I'm so exasperated I have to say it—Somehow, tho' one knows one's motives were good, one feels disgusted with oneself for ever having gotten involved with such people.

Perhaps the answer is that it is *wrong* to make (as in Carol's case) a separation—"being objective" one calls it—between the person & their work—if one doesn't love the *person* perhaps one's admiration of their *work* is a false thing? And in this Berkeley woman's case, perhaps it's the vain response to being asked for advice that is operating, not a genuine kindness. But *at the time* in both instances I felt I was doing right—I felt, or thought I felt, a dis-interested desire to help Carol get published and to advise her not to try to write too *much*, or to *care* too much whether she was published or not, & so forth—along with keeping her firmly at bay as far as visits, phone calls, and social exchanges were concerned. Of course, I *was* patronizing her in a sense —but god knows she seemed to be asking for it & lapping it up. And the Berkeley woman—I felt pity for her; but perhaps pity that isn't accompanied by love is a vice. Or maybe right now I'm indulging what Catholics call the sin of scrupulosity, (I think) in questioning my own impulses this way. ?

When I looked up "Night Scenes" I found it was a poem I'd thought, & think, beautiful. What was everybody upset about? I don't understand.

Thanks for retyping that poem of mine. I'm not sure if you like any of these recent poems (aside from what you saw & did like in N.Y.)—I am conscious they are a mixed bunch & am at a point of uncertainty in my work anyway—I think something will come through for me in the next 2 months though—.

Did you see the H. D. piece I did in *Poetry* last month?[1] Did you like it?

I have been to Mexico & back since I last wrote. Poverty and misery were what struck me this time, not the ancient bloody grace I have known there before. Something is daily being drained away into the past, and the present is joyless and full of fear.

Temple & the country roundabout is good to come back to.

Love—
Denny

P.S.

In typing them out I notice "A Figure of Time" seems related to that dream (tenuously) and "Shalom" to Jacob's musing on the well ("the well of stairs") but both were written beforehand.[2] All these were written between August 1st and 10th. That is a lot for me.

## 254

July 24, 1962
{San Francisco}

dear Denny,

I read the H. D. essay just before your letter arrived that you were going to Mexico, and so I did not write off my immediate response. The morning I pickd up *Poetry* at the library and found it there, I read it twice over, trembling. For fifteen years, since *The War Trilogy* so fully took its place as a source and a measure for me, I'd been waiting to read what you had written (and what I've been unable to write). Marthe had discoverd (it's odd, I suppose, but none of us here seem to follow *Poetry*, but have the feeling of looking up each issue to "discover" what's in it) the essay and made a library photostat of it. And then Robin, when I told him, made copies again.

It was having that dreadful woman (for such ruthless invasion of other lives by means of compulsion, accusation—the claim the possessd person makes *is* a thing of dread) on my mind that crowded out what I was to have written—the joy we've had in the H. D. essay and the new poems. It's of the essence of the evil such people command that they demand we turn from what we are concernd with—our lives, loves, writing, natural pursuits— and be concernd with *them*.

The poem you thought I might find too—dry was it?—"The Secret" delighted me. I too always have that hope that others will find their own secrets in my work (so that it will come to be their own) and lose where it all was to find another where in the poem.

"Another Spring" and "To the Muse" are among your foundation stones. Reading them over and over only increases the feel of levels and depth.[1] But I do worry the expression "(since when?)" in

"Noticing you are not there (since when?)" that's so hard to turn away from the slang meaning (like that word "joint" in my "Mabinogion" poem).[2] But don't you mean (when did you leave?) or (how long since you were?)

Well, when I try to work with it, I do see that it's awkward to say right; and "(since when?)" turnd in tune does say what you mean. The music of the rimes "cries" to "writes" and "faithless" to "failed" is strong in this passage so that measures can be most varied without losing organization.

*Tish* 11 came in the same mail with your letter and your definitions there get said clearly what is needed to make *Testimony* mean what I'd have it mean. (As the Lionel Kearns letter does too).[3] Testimony depends upon truth, must be true; and "true" here is the same "true" that is in any craft (a "true" angle, or a "true" shot). Our realization of a form is the only way we know to realize an experience: MAKE IT REAL. To experience at all is a formal imperative. The other way living without experience is letting it go.

•

But I do know what set Davey off with that word *testimony*—and that was some risky talk of mine trying to get across that poems do not exist "in themselves" but are parts of a life-work or testimony. Carelessly taken (and I may have been careless to in presenting it) it might tend to obscuring the crucial fact that it is always in the thing we are doing right now that our "life" exists and is created. That's why only intuition, the life feeling or our inner nature, can apprehend the formal necessity. And where we are "formalists," we are consciously obedient to, responsible to that inner nature. The beautiful thing in the work is that this obedience to a form we recognize as a law in the thing we are doing opens up the freedom of our nature; and that we find it opens up our communal selves.

I wanted to get across to them in Vancouver (last summer in the seminars I gave) that the craft is itself not a matter of performance or professionalism but a science or care in life. Now I find in Creeley's Preface to George Bowering's poems:[4]

But in the care with words, a world occurs, made
possible by that care.

———————

There are three "Sonnets"—*sonnets* because I mean to find in writing them the possibility that the Renaissance sonnet had and that is a real "form" but isn't supplied now by the old formula; these are, like Stein's "Sonnets," felt sonnet-forms.

And the scenes so far from a play or masque I am working on—with Helen, Ida and Robin in the group working with me along with five others.

I had the idea of doing a masque for Lammas but when we began (about the 8th of this month) we all began to see we couldn't do it for Lammas. The "actors" wanted to memorize their parts (they had read them for the Halloween masque I did last year), and I wanted time and room to let the play develop. These beginnings of a play then to entertain I hope as vacation reading. (I wish I could whisk away to Maine and read them to you). Written in a language that belongs only to the stage it's on.

---

With chapter X of The H. D. Book still brewing in my mind (tho a draft of most of it has been written), and the play pressing (I have to turn out scenes twice a week for it) and the feeling the essay on Bob's poetry must be reconceived (it's got to live up to what you do in the H. D.—I mean here the directness and direction of your voice; disposing of all that detritus of "evaluative" criticism and literary shop-talk): I've tied myself up in knots of things that must be done. "Just let me get out of this tangle," I find myself promising, "and I'll never bind myself up with tasks again"—and knowing I am sure to make only a more impossible heap of straw to spin into gold tomorrow.

Meanwhile I took on an actual job, working with Warren Tallman to design a correspondence course in Poetry (as literature) with the impossible decisions of ten "lessons"—assignments and particular poems, with associated readings. But that led this last week to rereading Spenser's *Faerie Queen* (the selections given in the Auden-Pearson anthology);[5] we'll use "Waring" for Robert Browning as one of ten; and Whitman's "Passage to India." But the breakthru for me was in Wordsworth—where any sense of a task dissolved in a readiness I had, and came upon the "Prelude" and the "Immortality Ode" or the "Moods of My Own Mind" with what a joy

Love<br>
Robert

---

**255**

Wed. 15{, 17th}
August {19}62
Temple {Me.}

Dear Robert

I am just reading *Joseph & His Brothers* for the first time and I came just now (on p.56 of *The Tales of Jacob* in the 1 volume edition) upon this which seems so completely H. D. that I thought I'd copy it out for you right away —for probably it's a long time since you read it yourself: [It speaks first of Jacob "*musing*," and describes his presence]

> ". . . Men of feeling are expressive, for expression comes from the need bringing to proof the feelings that well up unsilenced and unrestrained; it springs from a lofty and sensitive nature, in which shyness and austerity, high-mindedness and sensuality, straightforwardness and pose all appear

on the stage in one single dignified rôle; producing in the beholder a sense of respect together with a slight inclination to smile. Jacob was very expressive —to Joseph's great joy, for he loved his father's high-pitched emotional key and took pride in it; but it troubled and agitated others who had daily business with him. . . .

" . . . Jacob's power of expression, the vibration in his voice, the elevation of his language, the solemnity of his nature in general, were linked with a disposition and tendency which was likewise the reason why one so often saw him powerfully and picturesquely musing. He so inclined to association of thought that it characterized and controlled his whole inner life, and in such thoughts his whole nature almost literally exhausted itself. Wherever he went, his soul was played upon by chords and correspondences, diverted and led away into far-reaching considerations which mingled past and to come in the present moment, and made his gaze blurred and broken as in deep introspection.

" . . . it might almost be said that in Jacob's world intellectual value and significance—the words taken in their most actual sense—depended upon the copious flow of mythical association of ideas and their power to permeate the moment."

What follows has a connection with H.D. also:

"But why had it sounded so strange, so strained and charged with meaning when the old man in his broken sentence had given voice to his fear that Joseph might fall into the well? Because Jacob could not think of those depths without connecting them in his thought, to their enrichment and consecration; with the idea of the lower world and the kingdom of the dead—that idea which played an important part, not indeed in his religious convictions, but probably in the depths of his soul and in the power of his imagination: that primitive mythical inheritance of all peoples, the conception of the underworld, the realm of Osiris the dismembered one, where he ruled, the place of Namtar, the god of plagues, the kingdom of terrors, whence came all evil spirits and pestilences. It was the world whereinto the constellations descended at their setting, to rise again at the appointed hour, whereas no mortal who trod the path to this abode ever found the way back again. It was the place of filth and excrement, but also of gold and riches; the womb in which one buried the seed corn, out of which it sprouted again as nourishing grain; the land of the black moon, of winter and the parching summer, whither Tammuz the shepherd in his spring sank down and would sink each year, when the boar killed him, and all creation ceased and the weeping world lay sere, until Ishtar, goddess and mother, made pilgrimage to hell to seek him, broke the dust-covered bolts of his prison, and mid laughter and rejoicing, brought forth the beautiful and beloved out of the pit and the grave, to reign over the new season and the fresh-flowering fields.

"Why then should Jacob's voice not shake with emotion and his question wake strange, significant echoes, since to him—not with his mind but with his feeling—the mouth of the well was an entrance to the lower world, so that the mere word called up all this and yet more within him? A man of dull & untrained sense, void of imagination, could utter it and have only the most immediate & practical reaction. As for Jacob, it imparted dignity and solemn spirituality to his whole being, made it expressive to the point of painfulness. . . . "

Friday 17th

Yesterday I was reading your description of your Atlantean dream & recalling my own recurrent dream in childhood (which I learned to induce at will for a time): A great barn, filled with sweet hay-smell & candle-glow, & around the walls all kinds of animals sitting (in an almost human pose, or as dogs sit {DL's drawing of a dog, sitting}) and I with them, and all in an atmosphere of mutual love and joyful peace. And then suddenly all blackens to a crinkling, crinkled blackness, corrugated like iron & blackly twisting like burning paper.

I felt fearful, thinking, is it true then that we are of a generation that is to see an end in holocaust? Last night I dreamed that while Mitch and I were alone, picking flowers or weeding, or both, on the slope before the house, the front door opened and a figure appeared on the steps which was all white, white like paper, flesh, clothes, everything. I was so startled both by the appearance of anyone from within our house and by its glaring whiteness that my heart jumped and I woke; & lying there affrighted I thought, Was it Death? And I found myself calling inwardly, O Lord, I am not ready.

But talking of these things today with Mitch I began to see they could be taken not as warnings of unique events but as reminders of everpresent death-in-life without which no resurrection.

I had marked in Thoreau's notebooks lately: "June 13, 1851: We do not commonly live our life out & full; we do not fill all our pores with our blood; we do not inspire & expire fully & entirely enough, so that the wave, the comber, of each inspiration shall break upon our extremest shores, rolling till it meets the sand which bounds us, and the sound of the surf come back to us. . . . "

Those 3 "sonnets" of yours are wonders; the 2d one especially.[1]

I'm going to type some new poems now, and one that Archie Ammons sent me.

Is Robin still having trouble with that woman?

Love to Jess & to you—

Denny.

dear Denny,

A gleaning from Palmer:[1] "Let not the painter say 'I have done many pictures, and therefore should be able to do this less carefully'; for each time invention is a new species, though of the same genus. . . . If the painter performed each new work with that thirsting of mind and humility of purpose with which he did his first, how intense would be the result," which, as I read, took on echoes of the passage from Thoreau that you sent—of "our extremist shores" and "the sound of the sky come back to us."

Where your "Claritas"—it's a bird-song—comes to illustrate that our extremest shore may be the shadow of a difference.[2] This morning I sit over coffee and a cigarette. A crew of young men is tearing up the street to install new sewage pipes, so the light-song of your All-Day Bird comes thru the drill . . . but there! There's an other persistent chirrup! Reading these poems over when they arrived, I must have prepared this hour when they burst thru a period overcast—I've been at odds with myself—Your letter came in a delivery with a letter from Bob and another from Cid, recalling me from the glooms of trying to find a job—(but I think even this trying to find a job has been, is, a disposition to dwell upon whatever difficulties) to possibilities of freedom. And the poems take on or enter in to speak for my own inner need, to break a way thru. "Shalom" would always have been close to me, evoking as it does the ancient pulse, the Jerusalem I would see reborn in the hearts of all men. But today "the dark they can't help" speaks too of the dark I've let the least unsureness about money be (with a flood of anger that there should be such days at all of not being able to afford whatever)—yet just this unsureness has often been and seems to me in the fondness of this morning most free. This too is "the bush we call/alder"

There *is* a birdsong at the root of poetry—for, needing these poems as I have, new things sparkle in their aftermath and I can feel an answering urgency for song, it presses upward and outward—sets me swinging on the morning as if it were a full branch to be translated into music.

"Answering"

A burst
of confidence. Confiding

what treasured thing

kept in-
side—as if it were a burden

—worrying about money—
or mere pride

and ambition struggling—

256

August 22/ {19}62
{San Francisco}

sings out:
it was a song I did not sing.

2

The men are working in the street.
The sound
of pick & pneumatic drill,

punctuates
the chirrup a bird makes, a natural will
who works the tossing dandylion heads

a sheaf of poems
—they are employd
at making up a joyous possibility.
They are making a living
where I take my life.

3

with no more earnest skill
than this working song

sings
—as if the heart's full

responsibility
were in the rise of words

as momentarily
that bird's notes he concentrates

above the swaying bough,
the fluttering wings.

4

For joy
breaks thru

as if insensible to our human want,
were we birds too

upon some blowing crown of seeds
it would be so—

we'd sing as we do.
The song's a work of the natural will.
The song's a work of the natural will.[3]

5

I could not sleep, for money weighd upon my mind.
I was like a tree with broken limbs.

I had no confidence to meet my need,
I earnd no living to ease the importunity I was in.

In my work most out of work I lay awake
thinking with dread of being a typist-clerk

where millions of my fellows daily go
in thought sought my place in the impatient mill
in the works, where

There's no heart in this kind of thing (5)—I would let the "Answering" song end with evoking the natural will. (5) cultivates, even if protestingly, its own wrong—and the lingering complaint begins to be untrue somehow. (If I knew *how* and could render it true in tone . . . )

love
Robert

What I am untrue to here is that, while I am angry at having to go to work (and "having" here is just relative to securing, making sure, our living), I also *hope* to find a job, as if there is to be some happiness in it too.

Here's the poem given more exacting line. It seems to clumsy to *explain* as part of the song that it answers your "Claritas." "Our" reader will discover that for his/her self, or maybe but hear the relation without laboring it in consciousness.[4]

"Answering"

A burst
of confidence. Confiding

a treasured thing

kept in-
side, as if it were a burden

—worrying about money—
or were pride

and ambition struggling—

sings out.

It was a song I did not sing.

\*

The men are working in the street.
The sound

of pick and pneumatic drill

punctuates
the chirrup a bird makes

a natural will
who works the tossing dandelion head

—a sheaf of poems.

They are employd
at making up a joyous

possibility.

They are making a living
Where I take my life.

                    *

With no more earnest skill
than this working song

sings
—as if the heart's full

responsibility
were in the rise of words

as momentarily
that bird's notes he concentrates

above the swaying bough,
the fluttering wings.

*

For joy
breaks thru

insensible to our human want.
Were we birds too

upon some blowing crown of seeds
it would be so,

we'd sing as we do.

The song's a work of the natural will.
The son's a work of the natural will.

post script:

But now, in typing up a copy for myself I've added the subtitle "(after 'Claritas' by Denise Levertov)" which seems right. Singing after your song as it was.

---

"Answering" has released in a form that rings true a content that, unwilling to release, I had bound myself in. In the immediate crisis (just that at the beginning of the month again we didn't know where or how we would be able to meet the cost of daily living—we go from week to week, with that trust fund providing rent and gas and lights with ten dollars to spare) "job" and "work" were pitted one against the other. Yet I see I would be happy with a job if it were also meaningful work—in some activity like public health or education or manufacture that is for the communal good. What I dreaded was the slavery of useless typing that can go on (like making commodities that have no purposive good). In the poem "making a living" sings out there for me with its full meaning restored, and restores in my heart some of its natural will. (Is "natural will" a term of Wordsworth? I've been reading him again in these last months with a sympathy that is an excitement too, as if he might wake me from habit. Here's a bit in the "Prelude" that rang out:

> Not seldom from the uproar I retired
> into a silent bay, or sportively
> glanced sideway, leaving the tumultuous thing,
> to cut across the image of a star
> that gleam'd upon the ice:. . . .

Dear Robert,

Lovely to get your "Answering" still hot from the fire as it were.

I'm distressed you are having to look for a job. I'd no idea there was so little left over when rent & utilities were paid. Not that I'd thought there was a heap, but still, more than that.

Instead of a job, couldn't you do some more W. Coast readings? With so many colleges I shd. think you could pick up enough of them to make a difference, & yet not have to be away from home more than 2 or 3 days at a time? But I suppose you've thought of this & there are reasons why not.

I do think you should consider reapplying for a Guggenheim tho'—I do have the feeling their policies must be changing a little, otherwise they wouldn't have given one to me. If you didn't want the bother of starting the application all over again you can simply ask for your earlier application to be brought forward, and add to it whatever data you care to, plus any

**257**

August 29th {19}62
Temple {Me.}

extra references. (Maybe as they've "recognized" me I could now help as a reference.) One must say for them that tho they are arbitrary in giving Fellowships, and the application is complicated, they do *not* attach strings or bother one or ask for reports once they give one; they just mail the checks in quarterly installments & all they ask is that you let them know of changes of address so that you get the $ alright.

I'm beginning to work on a thing about organic form[1]—it is based partly on the School of Visual Arts lectures I gave last winter and partly on notebooks and partly on a letter to Archie Ammons which a letter of his started off. I've wanted to coordinate some of these ideas for some time as they keep buzzing around in my head as I read & write, and in December I have to go to Wabash Coll., Indiana where I'm supposed to talk as well as read, so I thought I'd talk about this. When I've typed up what I'm doing I'll send it to see if it makes sense to you—tho' of course to you it will seem pretty rudimentary, so much of what I understand having come to me through you.

But it may turn out to have a usefulness & will answer a lot of the questions people mostly ask me.

We went down to Portland to meet Nik. He looks wonderful and has had a good experience. The camp was not well-run and there was even a brief strike (of counsellors—because their paychecks bounced!) but he made some real friends, & tho the "workshops" (auto-mechanics, ham radio, "pioneering" & so forth) which he'd looked forward to—and learning tennis—turned out to be practically non-existent he did learn lots about unexpected things— just living, that is, & how to get along without tears or fights, & all sorts of things. He's much more grown up. He's seen lots of problems in those 2 months. There was one real tragedy, an eleven year old girl who died. Her parents came up to walk around the camp & see where she spent her last days, afterwards. Quite a few of the kids were Negroes from Harlem with quite tough backgrounds. We were talking of a boy whom they called a "spaz" (teenage word, the opposite seems to be a "boss"—spaz seems to mean dunderhead or a dope) & I said I hoped they (Nik included) hadn't made the kid miserable by teasing him; & Nik said—"Oh no—you know, it's funny, a lot of these guys who really are hoods with each other can really be nice when something like that comes up—they stop one another really hurting anyone sort of helpless, or hurting someone's feelings."

We often feel we've let Nik be somewhat overprotected so we're really glad he's seen a slice of life and apparently gained a lot of confidence in the process.

Moreover he cleared the breakfast table without being asked, this morning.

I'm enclosing a poem of Ammons' I thought you might like.

While in Portland waiting for Nik's bus to arrive we found a v. good old- &-rare bookshop in which I found a book I've wanted for 13 or 14 years &

never found—since losing the copy I had once, one of the 1st Penguins I think, which weren't printed in such vast numbers & went o.o.p {out of print}.—*The Story of My Heart* by Richard Jefferies.[2] Do you know it? The first 2 chapters have lived with me always, since I read them when I was about 15—. They must surely have influenced D. H. L.—some of the rhythms of *The Trespasser*, and of the much later essay about the Dandelion seeds, and much else of Lawrence, seem surely directly descended from Jefferies. I hardly like to trust it to the mails after what I've experienced with book losses in the past 12 months but if you don't have it maybe I'll send it, *registered*, after I've re-read it & M. has read it. I can't really remember how it goes on beyond those first 2 chapters. They are so marvellous one can't but fear a falling-off but it is a treasure just for them in any case.

I had read those Wordsworth lines to Mitch, the ones you quote, just a week or so before your letter came. I've always adored that section. The orange sky. And "the leafless trees & every icy crag tinkled like iron." And the way he sits back on his heels to stop skimming & listen.

While looking up the lines (I don't have a whole Wordsworth here, but that section & some other W. are in an anthology we do have) I found these lines:

"Air listens, like the sleeping water, still,
   To catch the spiritual music of the hill"

where the 2 unexpected extra syllables are a great felicity to my ear.

Reading an autobiographical book by William Plomer I was glad to be reminded of the late Lilian Bowes-Lyon, an English poet whose work I used to like but had completely forgotten, or written off, anyway.[3] What he quotes seems to me very good (written some time in the 30's or late 20's) and I mean to look up more when I get back to New York:

. . . Sigh & they are gone,
Like snowbees following sweetness,
The ghostly are blown,
Are chosen away to brightness.

Something from another long-ago love of which I later became ashamed for a long while—A. E. Housman—has been haunting me all summer, & again, I think it's not just memorable but very good:

Tell me no more, it needs not saying,
   What tune the Enchantress plays
In aftermaths of soft September
   Or under blanching Mays;
For she and I are long acquainted
   And I know all her ways.

When I was 12 I knew more of it but only that first stanza has remained with me.

I'm so glad you liked "Claritas," I think it's the best of this summer's work. I'd long wanted to write something about this bird whose song I first heard 5 summers ago in New Hampshire and finally identified this year. The All-Day Bird is its local name.

Nik's just come in from the barn where he's been reading most of the morning (*The Enchanted Island of Yew*, by Frank Baum, which I found at an auction) (he still loves fairytales, as I hope he always will, tho' he reads a lot of "grown up" things too) and I must make some lunch.

Love to Jess & to you from
Denny

## 258

Oct. 3/1962
{San Francisco}

dear Denny,

By the margin of a week, I managed to complete Act One of the play I had started last July—for presentation Oct. 1: the project looks like two more scenes in a second Act. *Adam's Way*. And now that the drive to get the presentation in order is over, I am beginning to come to. As soon as I have clean copy on the play (there are retouches needed to render the whole thing right), I'll send it on. These last two days, I've managed to do a version of three stories from Ovid that Jess askd me to try.[1] In *Adam's Way* I let myself go in a free rhetoric, outside the bounds of modern taste, and now these "Songs" from Ovid seem to me very much in the spirit of the rhapsodic mode I thought I had done with in *Heavenly City Earthly City*— tho the language is more free of ornament. These rhythms, anyway, are not articulated but continuous. And I have to read what I am doing over aloud to get the movement: i.e. there is no local control, but the verse moves in an accumulating stress, changing by something felt, not by craft.

The first two I think are adjusted—but the third still is unsure in parts. Reading this mode aloud I either recognize what to do—where the stresses lie—or (and this is what I mean about "adjusting") can't find the stress for certain. There does seem to be a set then in which the form lies—irregular (for only in certain passages can regularity of stress occur without marring the movement—and even here I feel such a regularity as a risk of the form), but depending not only upon the phrase but upon the sequence of syllables in the phrase.

I've always been struck by the tearful voice in poets—I think of Creeley's remorseful tones, but of H. D.'s too; not only of the power poetry takes on towards the lament but of the contain ghost in other passages. And working on this Ovid it came to me that all arts (whose Patron is Apollo)—music, painting (as Apollo signs his flower) and bardic poetry have an eros of their own. That Ovid in telling of these youths may be telling of a power that moves men in song. The satirists, my translator adds in a note to Hyacinth, even in the classical period found this excessive strain ridiculous: "The lamentations of Apollo on the death of Hyacinthus formed the subject of bitter, and, indeed, deserved raillery." [As here in San Francisco the more knowing and critical poets made fun of "Night Scenes" when it appeard in *Floating Bear*—the fervor of the measures has something to do with rushing on beyond this possibility of ridicule]. Of the fear and knowledge we knew as children that we were not only charming but also ridiculous in adult eyes. How the society shames by ridicule even powerful emotions until we too deny them reality in ourselves and "would to be caught dead" crying but, having no bravery in it, out of cowardice "take things like a man." Well, emoting carries us beyond what we mean and the whole art for me is in finding the meaningful, for there is meaning beyond what we mean.

———————

Jess reminds me to ask you if you would intercede with Virginia Admiral to return the drawings and script of Helen Adam's ballads. It's been two years, and in this last six months both Helen and Jess have written, with no reply. When I was in New York, she told me she would have them photostatted and return them. What I feard was that—she is so risky—they might be lost or destroyd. Perhaps if you urge, she would get them off.

Do you have a tape recorder yet? I want to make a tape for you (including the H. D. tape that Norman sent me) but if you had a 4 track, I could include so much more.

love
Robert

dear Denny,

I came down Friday with a cold—I had not only retrograded to rhetoric in the play, but also to old habits of smoking my way thru line by line (drawing on a cigarette supplanting the immediate locus in the line)—and for the last three days I've had such a miserable sore throat and coughing that last night I by a pun spent hours it seemd in a dream of designing the lid of a coffin or a grave marker—with the motif of a man standing above a circle (which I thot of {in} the dream as being the sun) I could not be certain whether it should be wingd—and in the lowest third (a) wavey lines for water (b) plant forms.

The groggy rounds of being in bed for days—and reading Joseph Campbell's *Oriental Mythology* when not dropping off to sleep.[1]

# 259

Oct. 7/{19}62
{San Francisco}

Bob arrives a week from tomorrow for five days—with a reading for U.C. at Berkeley and Poetry Center readings. Parkinson's circuit plan of last Fall seems to have evaporated.

love
Robert

## 260

Dear Robert

I woke one morning with a feeling of anxiety about you which remained with me through just those days when you, it turns out, were sick in bed. I only didn't write to say,—Are you all right? Is something wrong?—out of, I suppose, just that cowardly shyness before one's feelings of which you speak in the letter (when writing about people's embarrassment before the rhythms of "Night Scenes" etc.). Actually I guess another factor was just New York inertia or whatever it is that happens to one here. We came back feeling so cheerful & strong after the Temple summer but one has to fight to keep one's head above water & retain whatever wisdom one seemed to have gained in the country. We plan to spend much more time in Temple & less in the city as soon as it becomes possible, i.e. if Nik goes to boarding school next year. The school, Putney, sounds right for him & he is anxious to go. But it depends on how big a tuition reduction they can offer. We're going up to see it this weekend—I'm looking forward to seeing the fall colors & breathing fresh air again.

Did I tell you how the last days at Temple were so special? The light, the first changes of color in the leaves, the grapes ripening. And the last day but one—which was actually to have been the very last—a double rainbow and then later the same day *another* double rainbow. I had so strong a sense of rapport with the place—I think we all did—& though I like this apartment Temple is now more home to me & indeed I feel homesick for it now.

The Cypress poem is most beautiful.[1] I read it aloud. It truly re-animates the story. I don't feel quite the same conviction in the other two, I'm not sure why—but there's less of yourself, of inner impulse, manifest in them somehow. One word in "Cyparissus" I don't feel is quite right & that is "various" "various flowers"—because of its current careless use which makes it seem not precise enough here. (I mean, you know how people say "there were various forms & stuff to fill out so it took me longer than I'd thought" etc. It doesn't actually call up *diversity* as it should but only *quantity*.)

When you say the lines here are not articulated it makes me wonder if I am sure what you mean by articulated. Would you please explain this, I am very anxious to get it clear. I've taken articulated to mean that the line moved flexibly in the rhythms of feeling/perception, which is true here too, of course. Do you mean that you're using the word as a sort of opposite to enjambment or running-on, merely? So that here the end-of-a-line infinitesimal pause is yet smaller? I am mixed up about it. All the lines of the Cypress poem seem to be the most natural entities but so do your lines always & I don't understand the differentiation. Of course I hear the *flowing* movement where some poems might be, are, much fuller of stops, of hesitations, having a more difficult *passage*—but I don't see that as "craft" v. "the felt"—surely both are craft allowing manifestation of the felt?

Please tell Jess I'll try to see Virginia right away. I've not seen her since— oh, March I think it was, when I was getting that Korean stuff typed by one of the people she farms things out to. I'll try to make her actually give the things to me & mail them myself.

The John Simon Guggenheim Memorial Washing Machine has been installed & the dryer will be here by next week.

Did you get a thing from something called *Poetry in the Round*, listing your name & mine as contributors when *I* certainly never had heard of it? I wrote & complained.[2]

Am looking forward to the Vancouver festival if it comes off. I'll come alone, as when we really thought about it we realized it wd. be madness to try to all come, with highschool fees looming before us. (Tell Bob, if he's there now, I'll be writing soon about this.)

Al's wife Pat is very ill, mentally I mean, much like Helen was but perhaps worse. She shd. go into a hospital I think but so far Al is carrying the whole thing alone. We wandered around with them for 6 nightmare hours last Friday. He seemed to me an Orpheus struck dumb following Eurydice deeper into the darkness not drawing her into the light. He has incredible patience & fortitude but it is not enough. She poor thing had not slept or eaten for 4 days & looked like a wraith.

Thanks to Mr Guggenheim we've subscribed to *A Book of Resemblances*— what a pleasure to look forward to.

I've not written a thing since getting back to N.Y. I think I really am better off in the country, seem to feel so *assailed* in the city; instead of giving me more to write about I can't focus on anything. We *drove* down from Maine this time however, the car seeming after all fit for the long trip, so we hope to get up there this winter, and out of town some weekends during the fall too. We have it parked in Staten Island for the moment.

I loved the Finlay poems in *Origin* and wrote to *Kulchur* to say so as I had mentioned his booklet not very enthusiastically there before.[3]

I must put another load in the machine.

Love—<br>Denny

We don't have a taperecorder yet but I think we will get one. Wd. so much like to have tapes of you, Jess, H. D., etc.

**261**

Oct.12/{19}62
{San Francisco}

dear Denny,

I had and have the same feeling you have about the second and third pieces in relation to the "Cyparissus"—the Cypress thing calld up a fullness of response when I set about it. Whereas, I didn't have any real feeling for the Ganymede ideas—raping or being raped didn't strike any right depth in experience (and then, in Ovid too that story is very briefly told), and with the Hyacinth I had to contend with a lot of manner in the Ovid beyond the matter. I think I may prune the Hyacinth back from its present near conformity to the Ovid—but whatever there might be done, the fact is that the Cypress is mixd thru with an awakend response in my own essential feelings.

I think I meant some distinction between "consciously," inventively articulated and the regular articulation where one is not really aware of the actual count of each phrase and line, but does by the feel of it. The craft in a poem like "Apprehensions" is a directing force—where changes of pace, duration etc. are paramount in the poem. In a rhetoric—the elements are subordinate to the flow of the thing. Well, it doesn't seem to get much clearer than that trying to explain my feeling further.

The discovery of new formal possibilities by Stein and then by Pound and Williams had to do with a greater awareness of articulation. When each part is recognized as an entity in itself in a dance or co-operation with each other part then it is fully articulate. And a syllable can be articulate so (because a change of pitch or stress in a syllable of a word can mean a change in emotional tone) Yes, then, I do mean the stops and hesitations (and another strong feeling I have in articulation is the hovering of parts in the whole, allowing for even contradictory parts to co-exist). Your "A Stir in the Air" I think of now: it's

your response to the poem will
and then "waver" comma "maybe"

The "that fine" anyway is a design (*intent* in the work)—where in "Cyparissus" the craft subserves the narrative voice going on.

———————

No, I've never heard of "Poetry in the Round": it sounds awful. Do they mean on records? Maybe you shld send me the notice and I'll protest too. I hate the presumption that my work is to be made use of regardless. (*The Outsider*, for instance, writes with almost threat because I've not replied to their request—no enquiry that!—for contribution).

Jess is marking time now against the flu—forwarnd and taking all precautions—I hope it will mean he doesn't get further on than he has. Except for some residue still in my chest, I am recoverd. Ida Hodes came for dinner last night and we went to an early showing (she and I) of *David Copperfield* —which swept me back to all the boyhood excitement of the movie when one really did *adore* W. C. Fields and Edna Mae Oliver. Now today it seems particularly unreal, as if I'd had two hours of 1935 in the midst of 1962. And this morning at breakfast Jess and I started talking about our fathers. I see now, for me, it was related to the movie too. As we talkd, I relived too fragments from thirty years ago.

I'm at work now again on typing ditto sheets of the play *Adam's Way.* Marthe Rexroth will run them off and when they are done, you'll get a copy right away.

Barbara Guest sent a card with her new address—and a reproduction of Burne-Jones *King Cophetua and the Beggar Maid.* She askd if I'd seen her book. I had got the book from the library because I liked her so much and wanted to, hoped to make some kind of break thru to her writing. Well, in Washington, reading aloud a poem she wrote for the Motherwell Spanish canvas, I did have a whole pleasure in it. But nothing in the poetry was alive for me in reading as the memory of Barbara herself *is* alive for me. I hate having the reserve. But if a poem doesn't seize me completely, it's very hard for me to respond adequately.

Bob will be here Tuesday (the 16th) and stay, we have the hope, at least until Saturday and maybe Sunday. You know, thinking of Vancouver next summer, won't it be the first time any three of us will have been together in the same place at the same time?

love,
Robert

I hope that the thing with Al's wife is only temporary—if it's melancholia, it may be passing (if treated).

Dear Robert

A quick note to ask you if you'd mind telling me how much Cornell/ Ithaca paid you to read there. I've had a rather odd request to come for only $50 & that they'll increase it to $100 if they can. I don't want to undercut myself but I don't want to be ungenerous either. Knowing what you were paid will help me decide what to answer.

Hope Jess fought off the flu?

Love to you both,
Denny

## 262

October 21st {1962}
277 Greenwich St
N.Y. 7

I haven't been able to get hold of Virginia yet—we were away from Fri till Tues. night & her line has been busy when I've called but I'll go by there tomorrow. Saw John Wieners Fri. looking very well.

P.S.    Monday am.

Just spoke to Virginia. All apologies, & says she has every intention of actually starting on the printing or whatever next week. I was sceptical, but am to see her at 4 tomorrow when she promised to explain more fully what has been going on. She says "she doesn't blame Jess if he's very angry." I guess one might wait 2 weeks more & then if nothing has happened I'll insist on her giving me the MSS & will mail it back—Or don't you want to wait at all? I think one might just give her this last chance?

Love—

D.

---

**263**

Oct. 25/{19}62
{San Francisco}

dear Denny,

Cornell paid me $75 for the reading and another $75 for a lecture, plus the expenses of the trip from New York, around $44 by a rickety little plane, with an almost intimate view of upper New York State. (In the beginning, there had been offerd only $50 each for talk and reading but with Benson working at it, they managed to round up the additional). I'd say hold out for $75—it's not as if Cornell were a poor man's college.

The countryside environs Ithaca is beautiful, with waterfalls everywhere and the long "finger" lake. The faculty was friendly, and a little grim. What made the trip for me or saved it at least was staying with the Bensons (he was a visiting professor in medieval history) who were old friends.

And on the matter of Helen's book with Virginia: of course, give Virginia the leaway she proposed. If nothing is begun in two weeks she promised herself, then it will have proved only another delay—and we will be the more sure that the book should be returnd to Helen (or to us, to return to Helen).

love,
Robert

---

**264**

Nov. 14, {19}62
{New York}

Dearest Robert,

The play arrived just now.[1] Even a quick glance into it thrills me. Thank you

I couldn't get to see Virginia last week to inspect because I went up to Boston to read, but saw her yesterday, & tho she's still stalling I think something *may* be about to happen—give her 2 more days—Friday I'll report again & that will be it, if she doesn't produce by Thurs. I'll mail the stuff back to you—incidentally she has it in a locked safe, I have seen it.

Love—
Denny

Dear Robert & Jess

Virginia did make (has made) a beginning on the book—I've seen the first sheets. However she is now stalling again. I *will* say her office *is* very busy & half the time she's in debt, to boot, & so forth—but as she says, that's all excuses. I go in just about every Tuesday to prod her but it's harder now she's begun than when I could threaten to remove the whole MSS unless she *did* begin. What a character. Well, I shall persevere anyway.

Love—
Denny

The play (Adam) is marvellous. I adore Mrs. Maybe. Why did Auerhahn give up?

**265**

{November 30, 1962
New York}

Dear Jess,

Virginia has decided to stick to your lettering after all—for which I am thankful. The typeface she'd used for trial sheets looked incongruous. She asks me to ask you therefore to please write out "Kiltory" (same size letters as rest of book) & mail it to her. She is slippery as an eel because when she has trouble making up her mind just how to handle something—size of page, for instance—she invents 1000 excuses for procrastinating. But basically her intentions are good & I think things *are* materializing tho slowly.

Much love from
Denny.

**266**

{December, 1962
New York}

dear Denny,

What a hassle I got you into over Helen and Jess's little book. We had despaird of its being done and were alarmd at not hearing—for we began to dread the loss of all that work. And poor Helen who treasures those drawings of Jess's, and had stripped her walls to send off the illustrations to be done.

I've been away fifteen days, reading at the Ruth Stephan Poetry Center in Tucson: and on the way visiting Gael, and reading at San Fernando State College. Now it seems months since I've written to you. Did I answer your enquiry about what Cornell paid? It was $75 each for reading and lecture plus round trip fare. That was because I wanted to see the Bensons, old friends who were there. For I do think it is a good idea to hold to a hundred dollar minimum fee.

Tucson provided another glimpse into the Indian world: a true folk. No matter how one twists ones sights on it, the fact remains that all remnants of the folk are obliterated in our big cities. Indians have their native beauty,

**267**

Dec. 16/17 {1962
San Francisco}

their animal (living or breathing or soul) grace. And it is that same animal grace we sometimes know in ourselves in love, in the work of the poem.

I'm back at work on the H. D. material for *Origin*, which now is due, and I've to clear that in the next two days. After a hectic evening or two doing my share on the Christmas cards Jess had devised: we did manage bravely to get out some sixty cards.

Of poems? I'm getting more and more from Finlay (reading wise, not writing wise)—and now most of the *Dancers* book has come thru for me.[1] The poem "End of a Holiday" in *Origin 6* I love. And "Dunira."

Your "Another Spring" stays by me. And writing to Cid about the *Poetry* Anniversary issue, I caught on how

"I am speaking of living,
of moving from one moment into
the next . . . "

speaks in one of both form (moving from one line into the next) and content (life). And "Shalom" for me is "my" poem. As if it had come for me thru you. And the more loved for your voice there. "It's all right"—"alright." . . .

I've lived in some part of this last summer of yours in Maine. As, reading your "Claritas," I heard here, another bird outside in or thru the poem. Answering.

Tonight Robin and Jim were here for dinner, and he (Robin) hadn't got the Finlay poems, so I've been reading aloud. Keyd up then. And then, pouring over old drawings to find one I did years ago of Princess (for Ida). But I'm not sure. The cat looks too fat to be Princess. And now, there seems to be (at midnight) the right time to have all the time in the world to be writing to you.

O yes, about the Auerhahn book. We began to realize we weren't going to be able to work with Andrew Hoyem, and Jess was going to have to if we went ahead to realize the book as we *did* want it. Someday, the publisher will come along who will want to do the illustrations the right way—and the poems will have to wait for that. We are relieved anyway that we didn't go on with it as things so obviously stood.

I don't remember if I did or didn't give you a copy of our book plate that I designd last year. Anyway, here's one to accompany this letter. And a couple of photographs taken at Tucson.

Jess will be writing you; and Virginia—to send the needed title. Well, I still can hardly believe the book may be realized. It will mean a lot to Helen I know. She and I are reading at U.C.L.A. in an extension division program in May ($125 each, plus expenses), and she is quite excited about the prospects.

love
Robert

About Virginia. I'll keep on it but in any case we love to see the job done.

Dear Robert & Jess,

268

Jan./8th {1963}
277 Greenwich St
NY 7

   How many things to thank you for—letters from each of you, the card, the book for Nik, the copy of *Letters* from your mother's library. And the Raggedy people, & friends, who sealed the gifts! You gave all 3 of us a great deal of joy. And the photo & copy of bookplate also . . . Will send you some photos at long last, soon.

   Here's a dialog between me & Nik as he undid the *Irish Fairy Tales*:[1]

N. Maybe it's an *Oz* book?

D. No, it's the wrong shape. Besides, I think I told them how you read such grown-up books now, so I don't suppose they'll send any more *Oz* books.

[Pause for unwrapping. N. pulls out the Stephens & holds it aloft.]

N. Great! They haven't given up on me yet! Look, it's fairy-tales!

---

   I'm going to be sending you an after-Christmas present soon because I just came into possession, at last, of the intended "special edition" of *Overland* which was never finished as the lithographic stone Al Kresch had prepared was destroyed, & then Jonathan had them in hock to an unpaid printer . . . Now I have my copies, and to my surprise found them more bound than I'd supposed, i.e. they are sewn into plain white covers, over which the special cover was to have gone. So I am going to decorate one for you myself.

   We ended the year with a disaster—the heat went off just as the cold spell hit N.Y. and all our beloved plants froze to death—almost all, at least. The *offshoots* of the great philodendron were saved, & the plant Ida gave me of which you have a piece too. But the philodendron major, that went all around the window, & the bronze begonia 3 feet high & 2 wide which Jay Laughlin gave me, & the Jerusalem cherry, & my characterful avocado, & 2 or 3 others, all are gone. Water in vases froze solid. We had gone to Pennsylvania for 2 days, & when we left it was mild damp weather. After we got to Pennsylvania we were more or less snowed in & there was no radio so we didn't know it had gotten so cold in N.Y., or we would have called & asked Galway Kinnell (who's living downstairs while Race is away) to go in & light the gas.[2] Marimba (cat) was downstairs with him & he had a key but didn't think of the gas heater till it was too late. Well, it was a dramatic ending to the year, but we began the new one by getting the floor scraped & treated with something that will be easy to keep clean (Fabulon) (a transparent coating) & looks lovely. And we've bought some new plants, an ivy & 2 kinds of philodendron. So we're recovering—but the big plant, the one in "A Ring of Changes" had been started in 15th St & was an important presence for us for over 5 years.

What are the dates you will be in Vancouver? (Will you both go?) From a communication received today I realized we may not be there at the same time—i.e. I don't think I can stay longer than 10 days—will we overlap? I so much hope so—in fact if not 'twill take the shine off the breakfast as my mother's uncle used to say by mistake for "take the gilt off the gingerbread."

I have other poems to send & other things to say but what with Christmas festivities (involving rather a lot of company & cooking this year) and the trip to Pennsylvania and then moving all the furniture & books to get the floor done, & cleaning up the rest of the apartment to match a bit, there are lots of things piled up to do so I'll stop here.

By the way, Robert, I've sent in your Guggenheim report which it gave me great pleasure to do. I didn't make a carbon because it would embarrass you anyway but you can rest assured that it wasn't only enthusiastic but also clear and calculated to stir them into action: I hear that Mack Rosenthal (which I'd never have supposed) is a power there & his recent *Reporter* review[3] plus his recommendation (I presume you do have him? If not, do—there's still time!) should help a lot. I think you'll get one. I just feel it in my bones. I really think attitudes there have changed.

> Much much love
> from Denny.

---

**269**

{early February 1963}[1]
277 Greenwich St
N.Y. 7

Dear Robert & Jess,

I just did the cover of #1 of the author's edition of *Overland to the Islands* for you. It may not get mailed till Monday tho as I'm going up to Cornell & Buffalo tomorrow till Sunday.

On Saturday I'm going to see Niagara. I'm very excited about it—in the middle of the city winter to see a great force of nature for the first time.

Do you know Paul Goodman's story about Niagara—the sound & smell of it from afar & the 4-yr-old saying *It keeps on coming*? I am very fond of the "American Stories" in that collection, some of them seem to me really great.[2]

Mary de Rachewiltz Pound was here, she is very nice, I liked her a lot—a very honest person, unsentimental, modest. We met her at the house of H. D.'s Perdita first,[3] & then she spent a good deal of time here yesterday & we went over the poems of mine she's translated. Perdita was tall, with H. D.'s voice, but though happy in her 4 children there was some sense of blight there. There were some beautiful photos of H. D. as a girl—my god she was lovely. Do you know the photo on the back of a dull-looking book called *The Classical World of H. D.*[4]

J. Laughlin told me (he was here with Mary & brought us plants from the country) he finally has begun to realize you, Robert. "I'm always slow," says he, "but I pick up eventually."

Had the saddest visit of my life with W. C. W. last week. Every other time over the last 9 years (I think it's 9) I've left 9 Ridge Rd. in a state of exhilaration but not this time. He just *can't say* what he feels or thinks any more & the sad way he gives up in the midst of a stammering sentence now—"O well"—& the slow shake of his head—it's a slow ending to a life so quick & quickening.

Brother Antoninus was here & I went to hear him yesterday expecting something good but it was terrible. He tried—even before reading a single poem—to *force* a show of response from the audience—so that whatever there was in the *poems* got lost anyway, because it was put on a basis of personality. First I was embarrassed, & guilty at *not* responding—by the end I was bored, hungry (it was in the afternoon & I'd forgotten to eat lunch) and *resentful*—because he was trying to do me & everyone else a violence.

What a contrast to John Wieners' modest & deeply moving reading a month ago, in which the *poems* spoke, were let to stand & speak & *did* speak—whereas Antoninus in arrogant humility was really trying to get an audience to emote because he was a religious with a tortured (or sour?) face. He did say 1 or 2 good things but they got lost in all that hamminess.

I don't want to discuss Jack Gilbert but I have to say I wish a desire not to be churlish had not made me join in that "Celebration" in *Genesis*.[5] Or at least that I'd made much more clear that I *only* like the 3 poems I mentioned. The interview with him turned me up, & so do his more recent poems. I ought not to go around being so *nice*, I mean it, it's neurotic and I've only just begun to realize it. I mention this only because various people now look on me as a champion of Gilbert—I have half a mind to ask Gordon Lish to print a public disclaimer, except maybe that wd be making too much of it.[6] I don't even like those 3 poems as much any more.

I'm lending John Wieners the H. D. book—yours, I mean—we've become quite close friends in the last few weeks.

I've not looked into Virginia's activities since I last wrote about that— she promised to keep me informed but I said, "well if you don't I'll start coming in & checking up on you again"—& I will next week. She *likes* to be prodded & scolded I think. I *do* hope it's going on alright & that she's not stumped again.

I have the beginnings of a prose book going but won't tell you about it this time, in fact I'd better do a bit more of it before I talk of it at all I think.

John Button has a show next week.[7]

Love—
Denny.

## 270

dear Denny,

I've got ahead on the "H. D." book again, and will be getting an install-ment off to you Monday, of rewrite pages and about half of Chapter 10 on the First Part. Why it seems such an involved matter to get at an idea of image and person, I don't know. Except that when I really go at it, there is no element of the poem that's not enmeshed in a life that's a dense weave for me. Or I crave density, depth in lives beyond my own. I wish she could have seen the Blavatsky chapter. When I work on the book, she does not seem dead but to be still the recipient of it. I'm working now on the thing about one's Mother. I keep thinking of a quote I read once from Kerouac—that the world was his "Mother"—it had been quoted in derision as usual. Yet I don't know of another as clear statement of the soul's wanting to belong to everything as a child. To be understood! It means for me being understood by a woman

Your impressions of Antoninus agree with accounts of recent readings here. I can't bear the thot of investigating. I got his *Hazards of Holiness* out of the library, choked with outrage at his dismissal in his preface of the art: he wasn't interested he said in mere craft or techniques of the poem—he was driven by really sincere feelings and wrote from the heart. I paraphrase, but he did deliberately pose "sincerity" as a substitute or superior to "art." Bad art is bad feeling, miserable work is miserable emotion: and the poems are grotesque with bathos. If only they were "false"—but the truth glares at us of a self-obsessed ego. Jess said the book must have been a religious one because I kept exclaiming—O God! O God no!, O God, not that!

Against which the devotion of the artist shaping his art for the eyes—the love *and* the demand—of God. I don't believe in gushy angels. "Here," the soul of Antoninus must have to say at the end: "I have brought you as a gift, World-Father, my soul which I have reshaped into an abject, sincerely unlovely thing that only you can love"—

As if one falsified feeling and emotion by testing, clarifying and rendering resistant! Our sense of what the art demands is a sense of what feeling and emotion demand. The thing involved with the "personal appeal" is that we are askd not to respond to the actual poem but to the special claim of the man, as if in his person he were *sincere* or more real than in his attention and making in the poem. That's what you got caught up in with the case of Gilbert—you were asked, after all, to write in celebration of *him*, it would have been apparent had you been asked to write about the poetry that there was not enough there to have very much to say. *He* may be a John Keats type, as his critics sense him in his work: but the thing I sense in John Keats' poems is *not* John Keats but a world; not an attitude or romantic personality but a revelation.

Anyway, how can one be "churlish" to poems? Either you do have something to say about them, something pressing to be made clear, or else you don't. Yet now, after somewhat heated letters to *Genesis* editors, first to make clear why I did not want to write on Gilbert (that was easy because I had absolutely no interest in his work, and had had him in my workshop in 1957 etc. so I knew I didn't); then, more difficult to explain why I didn't want to send poems (it was the matter of context and relatedness which is still very important to me); and finally, at Tucson I'd been pressed to agree to introduce George Bowering's work and *agreed*! being "agreeable"! As soon as I got back home, I wrote off to Childs who had askd me and retracted.[1] I have no real feeling or understanding of what Bowering is doing. Vaguely, I had approved because he was working in the mode of Williams. But the whole virtue of such a mode of directness should be the virtue of direct presence everywhere of the needful charge of the poem. Otherwise it is just a style.

I found a poem of Tomlinson's by the way of looking thru *The Poet's Choice* anthology that rang out for me.[2] But I find more *wonderful* the art that's *contained*, not exhibited, in those lovely works of Wieners' in *Locus Solus* V.[3] I've read them over and over again since they appeard.

Love,
Robert

dear Denny,

This is not the whole of chapter 10—there will be about a third again to go. But I've done passages of chapter 11 (12 is postponed until after my reading at U.C.L.A. in May when I will see again Robert Haas for the first time since 1938 or 39. And the theme of 12 moves from Robert Haas and Louise Antoinette Kraus, his wife, instructing me in "the moderns"—will be an essay on taste and then form.[1] (11 is on adultery, mixing, fears of the universal, suffering in the process of loosing boundaries).[2]

I'm in the midst of a writing stretch and (with the Bollingen commission to complete at the same time) feel the pressure of "no time at all."

Once a week I read to a new group in Berkeley (beginning with chapter 1 —and now running right up with the writing I am doing. After chapter 11, I will start on the final writing of part II—The Day Book which I think now of calling "The Mixing Ground."

I've had to make outlines and start indexing in order to keep track of the parts.

We've got beautiful spring weather—after dreary months (our "cold" not even dramatically cold, after all)

love
Robert

## 271

Feb. 22/{19}63
{San Francisco}

dear Denny,

New replacements for pages in the H. D. book. I've revised the chapter divisions (to fit the actual reading divisions I've found in reading aloud to groups), and in retyping the pages concernd it's meant too some rewriting, even some happy rewriting.

And to add to the accumulating poems since 1960 the "Cyparissus" (I agree with you . . . {(}and Jess, and others) that the other two "translations" don't strike fire) and then a sequence composed from abortive bits in notebooks written between November 27th last year and Feb. 16th—but the real writing of the Sequence is in the composition last night—almost too close for any perspective—but I read it aloud to Jess and felt I had done what I wanted to do. To express some impending mistrust, that crowded out, has crowded out, all other impulses of the poem. In a sense I didn't want to but had to work with it. To define the figure undistorted by grievance (which I did unworthily feel, and that prevented any depth of feeling).

Grievance, like pity, confuses and then alters the deep—grief or compassion or hatred or fear. As kindness can confuse the issue of love. The things in the notebooks were more frightful than any feard thing could be—I'd let myself go, in order to write at all, and the "I have been deserted by the words spoken in the rapture of being deserted" in those sorry verses was also the "indulgence of being deserted."[1]

The effort is just to make real what was happening in the charged rejection of my work in "North Beach." Of the *Adam's Way*—that was the crisis, and it involved even Robin. But then I found it had involved Robin for some time, for Robin and Spicer and others had since the publication of *The Field* posed their poetry as a poetry of attack, against the poetry of celebration which was mostly my work. And mine became then "just the poetry of celebration" some indulgence in itself.[2]

The whole issue is a false one, a strategy on Spicer's part to keep a gang partisan to his own poetic (which can achieve beauty only by surmounting or exorcising something very ugly in Spicer's psyche), and in Robin's poetry there is the derived cultivation of the ugly (as in my own work I learned disgust from Spicer's work; I think I would not have admitted it in myself otherwise.)

But the estrangement has been the estrangement with Robin, for I have for years (he was the only fellow poet here who was at all sympathetic to "The Venice Poem" . . . well, no, there was Donald Bliss, Hilda Burton's first husband, who committed suicide). I have for years had a confidence in Robin's sympathy (more important than critical judgment for me, after all I've got to have my own judgment as part of writing—but sympathy is necessary for the communication of the finishd work) and this last year gradually I've come to understand that not only Jack but Robin too thinks my work inferior now to what a poem ought to be.

We never get the newspaper and so it was just last night that I heard of Williams's death on KPFA. That did not come as a harsh blow—for your letter about seeing him had prepared me—but yet came as a loss, another emptiness *within* as well as in the world. For the life I've drawn from his work and from the fact that he was working. Now only Pound remains of our "great ones," and from that little group that were gatherd in the *Egoist* (as we in turn were gathered in *Origin*) only the two others remain—too cautious to be great—Eliot and Marianne Moore.

> He hes reft Merseir his endite
> That did in luf so lifly write,
> so schort, so quik, of sentence hye

Is Dunbar right that the emptiness we feel is some *timor mortis*?[3]

Rainy today, and I too may be overcast . . . It's time to get back to my typewriter, for today I've to begin the final draft of the "day book" which I think I will call "Nights and days" [as if, "Dreams and days" echoing Hesiod's *Works and Days* but also Heraklitus.]

love
Robert

dear Denny,

Here are the concluding pages of chapter (once was 10, now) 6. On world-consciousness. Charles in *Maximus* may be the last of 'em concernd with the world-poem where the here-there axis of field and locality is paramount. The type that first appears with *The Cantos*: Certainly you or Creeley or I—or Charles in his poems apart from the framework of *Maximus* (i.e. such as the "Maximus at Dogtown" that can be considered apart as well as within)—are concerned with something different, tho springing from the ones who are our masters. We no longer live within a possible history, I think. As Charles is the only one of us who had a life— "before the War." Born in 1910 he had just his childhood within the formative years (here I'm thinking of the total organism of the human society at large) of the creative era that was giving birth to (a) the war, and (b) the world-mind—

Where our seed is planted in the distinctive soil of 1919–1929—the post-War, pre-world Depression period.

## 273

March 9/1963
{San Francisco}

1919–1929.

| Charles Olson | 9 to 19 |
| Me | 1 to 10 |
| You | 1 to 6 |
| Creeley | 1 to 3 |

Bob would be the youngest possible bird out of this world-egg. (I'm thinking now of a tone; a distinctive scale of the prevailing economy)— Charles would be the oldest you could be to still have been a "child" during this period.

    —But there goes Jess to take the mail to the post office.

Love
Robert

**274**

March 11th {1963
New York}

Dearest Robert

    I am distressed to think of Robin's alienation. My own friendship with him, genuine but tenuous, is based, I realized, in part on his being a friend of yours, & if he lets the kind of criticism that grows out of envy, (I'm afraid),—the envy of those who are gifted but not *strong* in their gifts somehow, for someone with mastery and abundance—alienate him from you then I am alienated from him. But what the devil is the matter with people, "N. Beach" or wherever, anyway, not to see, not to hear?

    The new poem is beautiful & there's not the note of "grievance" in it.

    I'll be sending you what I wrote for W. C. W. for *The Nation*.[1]

    And will copy out a notebook page about his funeral.

    When I opened the last pkge. of pages the first thing I saw was the name Eros & the word herm. These words come in 2 poems of this winter that I've not sent you yet so I enclose them—tho' they have only the most remote relation to what you were saying.[2] They were written at the end of Dec. or very early in January.

    I have an idea for a prose book on the basis of which I applied for a Gugg. extension, not very expectantly tho'. Will tell you more about it before long.

    Please let me know if you hear from the Gugg., i.e. if they ask you how much $ you'd need. If you get that sort of letter, you're in. I desperately want you to get one. I'd like to have shown you what I wrote about you but you might have been embarrassed.

    Muriel Rukeyser called up last night to say she wants to recommend me for one of those Ford things where you hang around a theater. Very damn nice of her. What a great walloping splendid creature she is. I only wish most of her poetry weren't so flowing & soft. Too much of her goes into her *personality* I guess. But her translation of Octavio Paz's "Sun Stone" is a miracle of sympathetic, I mean empathetic, virtuosity—wow, what a sentence![3]

We've had Mitch's father living with us for several weeks now, until he goes into an old age home (a nice one thank god) & it is rather trying, also we've had terrible colds, & I've been in the usual state of clutter this time of year sees me in. But there've been a few poems, & a Volpe concert we enjoyed, and *Shoot the Piano Player*,[4] & a few other such pleasures. And it's beginning to feel like spring. Did I ever tell you my impressions of Perdita & Mary de Rachewiltz? Let me know.

Mitch's book is out in paperback at last—a pedestrian cover but it cd. have been worse.

With remaining Gugg. money we bought a *dish*washer!

Nik has been accepted at Putney, with a big scholarship. He still hasn't thanked you for the *Irish Fairy Tales*—but he loves them. He's no letterwriter. He *feels* thankful.

*Will* we overlap at Vancouver? My dates there are Aug. 5th –10th.

Love to Jess & to you from
Denny.

P.S.

Have only skimmed the new pages as I've lent the rest to John Wieners & want to put them together first. But what I've read looks terrific.

March 7th

Yesterday the funeral. The old men, perhaps boyhood friends. The foolish music. The poem coming over the loudspeaker suddenly [it was that Prologue to an unwritten play—don't have the Coll. *Early Poems* on hand but it's in there]—what a relief! The general ignoring of "Tract." The pouring rain on the way out there with Jay & Ann & Bob McGregor[2]— over the wastelands (we took a wrong turning or rather didn't get off the freeway in time)—then upon emerging from the [windowless] funeral parlor the incredible bright sunshine & blue sky & the wind blowing in the trees—

"Whee—clacka tacka tacka
    tacka"—

a March day such as he loved—& up to the windy cemetery on the ridge, with the City standing clear to the northeast, beyond the swamps, beyond the unseen River—

**275**[1]

{March 1963
New York}

"A dream
a little false
toward which
　　now
we stand
　　and stare
transfixed—
All at once
　　in the east
rising!
　　　All white!

　　small
as a flower—

a locust cluster
a shad bush
　　　blossoming" . . .

---

**276**

March 13th {1963}
277 Greenwich St
NY 7

Dear Robert & Jess

Enclosed are a few rather recent poems by Archie Ammons, the man who didn't "get" *Selected Poems* but has since come to be a reader of *The Opening of the Field* & to regret that. You may not like them . . . ? but I want you to read them anyway in case you do—at his best they feel very good to me, that is, when the *thinking* rises into a music.

I'm also sending one of Nik's latest essays into poetry. No need to return that, I've another copy, but wd. you mind sending the Ammons poems back soon? I'm putting in postage for this because if you don't like them it's exasperating (I know) to have to fuss with them.

Was it *Adam's Way* the North Beach objectors most objected to? They have eyes & see not, ears & hear not.

Is it true James Broughton got married?

I forgot to tell you in writing of Williams' funeral that Flossie was looking quite wonderful & went thru the whole thing poised as usual but afterwards at the house there were 2 moments when she showed her feeling—one was when she said, "No, I'm not mourning now, I've been mourning for the last 10 years" (years when she's seen him go slowly down, in spirit & body both). And the other was when, clutching a bundle of telegrams, she extracted the one from Ezra Pound & said (to me & to Mack Rosenthal) "This is the one that means the most to me," & read it out with a crack in her voice, shedding one or two small tears—"He put up a great fight for you & he bore with me for 60 years. I shall never have another poet friend like him." It also said "sympathy to you & the boys."

Today I had a letter from Mary Pound {de Rachewiltz} saying she'd enjoyed meeting us and "seeing a bit of America. Lord, have I lived in prejudice!—& now I feel head downward, probing *this* country (& my home) with my brain—a funny feeling, my business—hope the quicksilver will soon stabilize in the center again."

Just heard that Creeley did not win N.B. Award. William Stafford did.[1] It's a promotion gimmick anyway, but it wd. be nice to see the dough go to a friend. Oh well.

Love—<br>D

dear Denny,

The thing is that Robin's alienation is ambiguous. I don't think it's a thing he is convinced in. But he has let go our invitations and made none himself. And I don't want to have it be a realized break either. I do see how fond I was, am of him in the claim I want to make, in the rejection felt.

But today, this morning I'm in a fine mood and the phase of trying this being rejected feeling—that hung over me for so long—seems gone. Changed in the writing of the part sequence.[1] In the last few days I've done three new sections of "Structures of Rime,"[2] and beginning the final type-script of the "Diary" of the H. D. book, which now I call not a Daybook but "Nights and Days," I'm exhilarated. For all of the fact that I found I had tampered wrongly with the movement of the diary, in the work I did yester-day, as if it were to be made good, when the whole essence is that it does suggest and not conclude. Thank god I've got this little group in Berkeley to whom I read each week the work I complete, for once I was reading it aloud I saw clearly what I had done. There will need a few alternations to fit now with certain parts of "Beginnings." And some of the rewriting I did do this last week was actually clarification of the immediate area (i.e. not explanation but rendering) which does improve in the spirit of the original.

That chapter 6 must surely be the extreme of composing all but entirely with other writing than my own. Bending Stein, Roheim, *Zohar* to my own weaving, like a chair maker bending the wicker-work.[3] I pause for a second along the way to hope that I am not to be permanently infected with references. This sunny morning at my desk I am quite willing to declare that I've not only allowed myself derivation but made the too much of the good thing; or will have made the too much if I don't let go a bit.

277

March 15/{19}63
{San Francisco}

The permission liberates, but then how the newly freed possibility can insidiously take over and tyrannize over our alternatives. I think when I began the book I really believed in the idea of a totalitarian work, this universal comprehension idea that I find myself coming back to all the time. Well, even before the H. D. book began, the *Field* proposed something like that. I knew it wasn't true, but the master-minded work of art excited me, and there was some hidden persuasion that this was the real challenge.

Maybe I'll get to it in the book itself—the forced equilibrating recognition —that the making a thing in which feeling somehow exists and shows its face is the full wonder. Big face, little face, baby face or that old man of more days than we can count hairs in his beard.

Your poems and letter arrived yesterday, and the day before there arrived from George Herms[4] (whose *Poet* is shown in that Museum of Modern Art *The Art of Assemblage* catalogue) in Los Angeles a little household altar, enshrining two photos of Garbo as enigma, beauty and woman; but the as-semblage is also a homunculus, with the woman in two phases enshrined in his heart. The curving brace from some table rises as a lyrical penis. A rusted metal top as a hat or head. And then, what triumphs in the work is the tri-umph we knew in childhood—that it's a curved piece of wood that's a penis, or a top, or a head, or the whole an altar or a little man is not the wonder. But the aliveness of the work. How George Herms is entirely with us in it.

All that to tell about how last night (Thurs.) writing the third of these structures of rime (the other two were Monday, I think) I went along with the herm. The herm that was in my previous text (but I don't remember where), the George Herms Herm, and the herm that "In Abeyance" is talking of in

"and no house has its herm"

yet our house does have its herm I realize!

•

Your two poems are part of my lift this morning.

Love
Robert

dear Denny,

Just a short note with the enclosed final revision of "Structure of Rime XX"—correction on previous copy: insert "light" between "flight" and "like" (typing error in previous sheet) and "Structure XXI":

actual changes in text. "solitude" for "loneliness" (both for the "made" to "wood" sequence, and also because the meaning is right now).

And "A depresst key" for "a touchd string"—a depresst key is what it actually is (when the sympathetic sound rings) and also because both "depresst" and "key" refer to the substrata of the poem.

"steps of wood" = notes of the scale on a xylophone

"watery" removed as (see in XX "watery eaves") to be postponed to possible opening in XXII

Watery ladders, watery eaves!

I want to get how "watery" is a sound, but also is a wavering image somehow different from the sound.

Robert

dear Denny,

The enclosed came back today—I had addressed it to "San Francisco" instead of New York—and I'll add this quick note before Jess remails it. I'm (at this point) 39 pages out on the final version on the second part (page 20 of the original text). The new material is mostly actual reference and weaving in of poems—a little exegesis of H. D.'s "Iphigeneia" translation, for instance. And I'm getting the Bryher picture right, I think. Most of that is just ahead of where I am. But a lot came clear in reading H. D.'s *Narthex* (in the *Second American Caravan*)[1] and with that her "Let Zeus Record" from *Red Roses for Bronze* which is a proprietary tribute paid to Bryher.

I'm not using at all Bryher's own *Heart to Artemis*, which I found more chilling then any one else's portrait of her.

But what I want in the book is not "Bryher" but H. D.'s trial. As soon as I have finishd this first "day"—the March 11, 1960 section—I'll send it on to you. I think the change is important and makes the whole a new thing.

love<br>Robert

**279**

March 21/{19}63
{San Francisco}

dear Denny,

I just got the enquiry from the Guggenheim about "expenses" and "needs"—and I'll wait until I hear from you to send the information back to them. What is the usual procedure? I mean, how much does one ask for? I'd like the full $300 a month—but would that seem too much (given my already having $145 a month income?)

With that possibility in sight, I'm going to include a trip East this fall to stay in New Haven and finish off the H. D. book (the ms. I anticipate to have completed; the "finish" wld be the notes and indexing{)}.

**280**

March 26/1963
{San Francisco}

But, I need advice—or did you find out anything about the ropes? (I remember you too were wondering what you could ask for.)

It's times like this that not being able to include Jess in accounting for my expenses is inconvenient.

But what a prospect. To have a year with the damnd business of making-do lifted! Those months when "Where is it going to come from?" is on one's waking mind.

---

re. Ammons' poems. "Catalyst" (reminding of Whitman's sense in the poem on manure), and "Rising" come thru for me. "The Strait," you'd think, would be preferred with its gain of a stanza form that allows definite variations; but the concept didn't vary but seemd to be carried out.[1]

Where I do have disaffection it's with the descriptive adjectives—such bog me down even in prose. No, I don't mean

duck-neck purple of hairy abdomen

this Marianne Moore-like exact particular—but as in "Salience" "the narrow white path"

Yet that's a minor disaffection. It's a blessing to read poems where you know why the poem exists—I'm more responsive reading "Saliences" over again to find the adjective thing, and do get something of Ammons' spirit.

By the way, "Saliences" begins with p.3 part II in the copy you sent me.

Thanks for sending them on. My not being wholly aroused by these doesn't mean I wasn't interested and engaged. You did right to send them for me to see. It's one of the hazards for any poet that we readers have got to get *used* to work so often before we begin to see with understanding.

He wrote and askd me for a poem for *The Nation* and if I write one, or can find a free one, I certainly will, anyway. I've still to reply and (right now I have a typing job I'm doing for Nancy de Angulo)[2] I'll send him something to read in exchange anyway.

I must get this off and get back to work.

love
Robert

---

**281**

March 28th {1963}
277 Greenwich
{New York}

Dear Robert,

Hurrah! I'm *so* glad & relieved. They don't ask you financial questions unless they have definite good intentions.

Galway, who—aside *perhaps* from contributing to the support of his mother—has no dependents, got $4000. And I got $4500. Certainly you shd ask for that much. When it comes to breaking it down I suggest (a) trip

(Europe or Mexico) for part of year (you don't really have to go, they don't know or care) (b) equipment—tape recorder, typewriter ("present one needs replacing") (c) maintenance (or improvement for the year) of present standard of living comprising such & such expenses paid for normally by work you will not undertake during year of Fellowship.

M. says, ask for $4000. He thinks the $500 more (than Galway) that I got was accounted for by my including Nik's summer camp among my expenses. I was probably much more specific in what I listed than Galway, & it's probably not really necessary. Certainly tho', $4000 is considered by them a reasonable sum. If you put together regular expenses, travel abroad, equipment, books you wd. like to buy (related to yr writing indirectly), payment of a cleaning-woman maybe (to give you more time & less annoyance) & it doesn't amount to $4000 for 12 months, then fill it out with a section called "sundries." Don't forget that normal expenses, which have to be covered by the Fellowship, might include horrendous dental bills for instance. They don't ask for proof or otherwise conduct a means test. In fact I dare say you cd. specify a lot less & still get about the same amount, but I'd be as specific as *poss.* just to be on the safe side.

> In haste, with love,
> Denny.

P.S.

So glad you like some of Ammons' poems.

P.S.

I *think* the only single people (& women supported by husbands) who get as much as Parkinson said, $7000 or so, are people with costly scholarly or scientific projects—stuff where equipment or long journeys to obscure places etc were necessary. I.e., the larger amount is figured towards that while basic living remains about the same. Or a sculptor whose materials etc. were expensive. Writers, how can we think up more expenses?? Ha!

*The Sullen Art*, from Dave Ossman's program,[1] is out & has a few interesting sentences anyway.

dear Denny,

Bolsterd by Parkinson's saying single people usually got from $4500 to $7000, I askd for $4500.

Meanwhile I'm in a mess trying to make out my last year's income tax. I find I'm missing train fares—I just go "off the record" at some stage in traveling.

## 282

April 3/{19}63

{San Francisco}

But would you phone and get for me the following fares?

1. Washington D.C. to New York one way
2. New York to Annandale-on-Hudson one way
3. New York to Middletown, Connecticut (by bus)
4. fares from N.Y. to airport

{The fares are listed in Levertov's hand next to the items: $10.65, $4.21, $3.75, and $1.75, for a total below of $20.36.}

Every year I go thru this April crisis I so rebel against thinking thru the facts of income and taxes—in the first place that one's taxed when one isn't making it or barely making it, and then that one's taxed for the whole evil show—the top-dogging it over the rest of the world and the insane war "hope-chest" to back up the general coercion.

Amen to which, but the struggle to account remains to mess up the next week or so. Those fares will help immensely!

love
Robert

## 283

{April 1963

New York}

Dear Robert,

| | |
|---|---|
| Washington DC - N.Y. 1 way: | $10.65 |
| N.Y. - Rhinecliff N.Y. (Bard): | 4.21 |
| N.Y. - Middletown Conn. (bus): | 3.75 |
| (return fare: $6.75) | |
| Airport bus to Idlewild: | 1.75 |

You seem to be the only one of the people I know who've applied who's received that enquiry. I did not get an extension (but I didn't really expect, hope, to). Mitch got rejected again, also Bob Nichols, also, alas, Midi Garth (dancer) who really *shd.* have had one but they are funny about dance anyway. Katy Litz also applied & it may be she got it—they only give one dance Fellowship a year it seems.

We are having dinner at John Button's tonight. His show was gorgeous.

Love—
Denny.

## 284

April 17th/{19}63

{San Francisco}

dear Denny,

A spring poem.[1] That I'd started with the thought that I would write a diary poem, but the themes took over and it turned out to be not a series of poems but a sequence in one form. And this is the beginning of a new book now, for I had closed" Windings"[2] with the "Structure of Rime" pieces. Last week I wrote off to Mack Rosenthal and also to {Donald} Hutter at Scribners (Bob wrote me he was interested in the possibility of publishing me) to see how far they might go with keeping me in print (the *Roots and Branches* still not definitely on Grove's Fall lists, and this new book ready with the H. D. coming up—Grove is hopelessly behind the possibility of keeping up).

We went out yesterday, in betwixt spring showers, and then a patch of storm with hail (north of the mountain—Tamalpais) to catch the last of the mushrooms. A great day in the hills back of Stinson, over fields and in oak woods. With a supper of chanterelles, Blewits, inky caps, and the prize— two fist-large puff balls. I've been sitting at the typewriter so many days— this outing was splendid. And now today, the clouds are gone—knock on wood—and the sun is here again. Jess's at work on his Xalba soccer players,[3] shifting tones in the painting that needs clear light. And I'll be off, once I get this note to you, and a copy of "Continents" to send to Rago to see if he's interested for *Poetry*—on errands and walking again.[4] "Out."

love
Robert

dear Denny,

What I was granted was $4000, so your advice was well taken in referring to Galway Kinnell. Begins the first of May (if they go along with my answer to their questions about when I wanted it to start).

Meanwhile I have 100 pages of part two (mid-page 39 of the original day book). I've kept the movement of the original (tho, for instance, I've redivided or revised the divisions of the days often according to the new feel). What more than doubles the text is the development of the picture of H. D.'s work, new tracings growing out of the old impulses. All my reading seems to be falling into place or coming alive in a new way; and the picture of her life too emerges much more vividly. It's as if I am just catching on. And with the catching on have come new dreams—the dream visit from H. D. herself two weeks ago that came just at the end of my work on section I of the second day, and last night after my working yesterday on the tapestry section with its animals and stars there was another dream of the House of the Poetess ("Muriel Rukeyser" in the dream but it was never actually Muriel) and the revelation of all the stars visible and invisible.

April 26/63

I put together the ms I've been keeping to send you of part II—but I couldn't find the first 42 or so pages. Did I send them? I have no memory of it; and still hope to find them somewhere on table or desk, in drawer or box. My idea is still to start up the query in the reader's mind whenever I can, so

# 285

April 24, {26}/{19}63
{San Francisco}

that many passages of my work will happen there and not in the book. So far I feel my filling out the form has not interfered with that intent. How much one can explore without robbing the would-be reader of his own discoveries.

Right now—my finding that "I fear Poverty" passage of H.D.'s has brought Claribel ("Good Frend"), the Poor Clares, and Lady Poverty to the wings, waiting for the cue. Today was a windy magnificent day, and I took *By Avon River* in hand, walking up over hills and along by-streets reading almost or maybe really aloud. In this work I've got to read hiding from myself what and how I will use what I am beginning to be familiar with. Scraps of melody run in my mind, and I wake up in the morning preoccupied with rehearsals of passages, composing. (A symphony of Beethoven's on the evening program now seems to parallel my feeling). Here an announcement "the inner light" will come—and there there will be a development that we'll almost recognize but experience as some need for a passage to come. "Poverty" will bring out the Depression/depression thing. (As stars and light lead into and thru the motion picture camera. Do I have to spell out the fact that H. D.'s "Tributes" (to Freud, to the Angels) are a form derived from her essentially feudal relation with Bryher? Payments for a debt.

In the book I think I won't go further into the business about groups—I'm not sure. If not, I'll want to do a note to publish somewhere for I think there are distinctions here that really clear things up.

1. The fellowship we have with those who are working in the same spirit we are—that's one very real "we" (the Imagists, the Surrealists—or the group of us who begin to find our correspondence in the pages of *Origin*, in our concern for the integrity and movement of the line (after W. C. W.), and for the immediate presence of the form in every locality of the poem{)}. It's here that a mode can be defined in all the various expression.

2. Very different the in-group of say *Kenyon Review* or *Partisan Review* that had its origin in academic (university) associations or being members of a political group.

3. Then distinct from this is something like the Bloomsbury group, an exclusive self-protective literate social group. (like my association with Spicer and Robin over years).

4. The in-group of a Master personality—Stein or Joyce or Sitwell—in my own life Patchen or now Spicer surrounded by his acolytes.

Well, outlining it, I find it's not so very interesting. The fellowship of the work is the only company of spirit. #4 makes for an ingrown art. #3 for a highly civilized atmosphere of letters, and #2 is a deadly proposition.

No wonder I knew to leave only the suggestion in the book for scholars to go into!

Did I tell you that Ted Weiss took everything I sent him, for a feature in the next issue of *Quarterly Review*? I think it included the two "messages" or "presentations" piece,[1] "Doves," "Returning to the Earlier Mode," "A New Poem."

I wish I had something appropriate for Ammons for *The Nation*—I've been hoping a shorter poem would happen. But they are rare with me (thirty lines or under I think he wanted).

The other thing pending is that something may come of Scribners towards publishing. Right now the decision awaits the return of an editor from Europe on the 29th of this month—so Hutter writes me. He'd put out a feeler via Bob as to whether I would consider publishing with Scribners. And I wrote that I would like to know if they would consider a plan to get all of my work into print (*Windings, A Book of Resemblances*; then 1964–5 reprint of *Letters* and the H. D. book, and *The Cat and Blackbird* children's book—1966 *Faust Foutu* and a collected volume 1942–1952, with another book of new poems and a book of essays).

At the same time, Lockwood at Wesleyan has askd for the Morgenstern book and Jess sent it—it will be decided this next month!![2] No wonder the windy day seemed magnificent—with everything in the wind—

Love<br>Robert

Let me know how these poems seem.

Dearest Robert,

I'm so glad about the $4000. Use it in good health. Muriel Rukeyser called me to rejoice. And the new pages came today. Some I do have but John Wieners has them & I can't correlate the page numbers. I'm anxious to get them back & reread everything, with the new parts, as a whole. I dipped (forgive me!) into the last of the new ones & came upon the dreams, H. D., and Muriel. There's not a page of this book that has been in any way a let-down, it's a true marvel.

I'm reading *News from Nowhere*,[1] it's lovely how instead of a tract it is really a romance. I've read only a few pages.

A few weeks ago I wrote something about Paul Goodman's poems[2] & George Oppen who is an honest man of strong feeling, contentious mind, and a sort of nervous subtlety that makes me aware of what's blunt & almost simple-minded in myself, was deeply troubled at my praising (tho' not without qualifications) a poetry he does not think valuable, & doing so as *he* thought because I agreed with P. Goodman's work in General Strike for Peace, etc.[3] What I'd *meant* of course was not that—I *do* admire him for many things (he's not a friend, barely an acquaintance, but I know from

## 286

{early May 1963<br>New York}

Gene Smithberg, an old friend, of his work on the W. Side school board, & I've seen him trudging with a sign at peace demonstrations, etc.—i.e. I don't know much of what he's like person to person—a bastard, they say—but I honor him for unpretentiously trying to *do* what in his polemical writing he says *should* be done). However I would never ever praise his *poetry* for that reason!—god knows!—and I did so because I *do* like about 50% of his poems that I've seen, very much. I imagine you don't, somehow—but while his whole way of writing is very different from most of what you or I love, it just seems to me a *different beauty*; not the *kind* of thing I like—(e.g. some dreadful imitations of it by M. C. Richards in *Locus Solus*,[4] unconscious parodies, would I think have revolted me even if I hadn't read what it was she was (as she thought, I suppose) "paying tribute" to;)—but facts, actual poems whose unique selves I respond to—to pauses in them, to a consistent *voice* in them. Maybe I'm crazy—maybe they really are terrible poems. . . . But there it is, they spoke to me and I said so. I'm telling you all this because you may see or have seen the piece I wrote and feel as George did, and doubt me— & while I can take it from George & argue back & profit by it (I *have* convinced him I really believed in the poems & wasn't condoning them for the sake of Goodman's *opinions*) I couldn't bear to have you be angry with me. Don't seek it out if you've not seen it—all this is just prevention.

Mitch is in Paris—or maybe somewhere else by now, Brittany perhaps. He was again in his Sargasso Sea, the novel a host of clamoring or sullen fragments, & at last brought himself to take the ticket he had been given by an airline quite a while ago, and leave. Only for 3 weeks, though, as Nik graduates early in June & there are lots of things to be seen to, before we leave for Temple. No sooner had he gone than my own cloud lifted, energy renewed in me, I began to write again & also to get through my domestic tasks with resolution. It's shown me, this past week, how close he & I are underneath, for I'd not even realized my own almost unbearable fatigue was related to his anxiety and difficulties, I thought I was (emotionally) ignoring them in fact. But also, I see more clearly how neither of us is alone enough. His room has a door but much of the time he leaves it open when he's working; and when he's working—(or rather trying to work—it's different at those good times when the work really moves for him) he's restless & I'm always meeting him in the corridor or the kitchen; but these meetings aren't real *meetings*, they are vague purposeless semi-accidental interruptions. What we need is a far more clear-cut way of living so that each is alone *completely* more of the time, and then together with full clear attention when we *are* together.

At first, the first 2 days, I felt ashamed that I felt so much better with him away—seeing only the other aspect, that it's so hard for me to be a poet *and* a woman, & hard for me anyway to give my attention to more than one person at a time (& almost all the time I'm called on to give it to *two*, Mitch & Nik)—but thinking about it—& reading in an old notebook of my first impressions of Paris, before I met him—"the lonely, poignant, exhilarating freedom"—& (with his permission) many notes, old & new, of his, I've come to see it differently, it's nothing to be guilty about but something we can live out *towards* each other. I've always known, & loved, Rilke's words about marriage as a "mutual guarding, bordering, and saluting of two solitudes" (I perhaps misquote, the book's in the living room where Nik's having a small party, his first teenage party, & I don't want to butt in—I'm in Mitch's work room)—but how hard it is to live that & not simply invade one another!

That would be great, if Scribner's would properly publish all of your books. Jay Laughlin said something some months ago about how he'd come to "see" your work anew but I don't think you'd be happy with New Directions as he *is* a skinflint, I guess—tho' I like him and indeed am very fond of him in spite of that—and have no complaint myself, as I think he treats *me* fairly—but others say they have trouble. And production is slow. Scribner's is big enough to be faster, I presume.

I have a few suggestions to make about "The Continent," there are a few places that don't sound quite right to me, at least, at present they don't—I remember before now having come around to complete acceptance of poems of yours that I'd not responded to at first—"The Ballad of the Enamourd Mage" for instance. In this case though I *feel* the poem as a part of the whole work of you, but there are details that seem—hasty, perhaps.

(1) and sees the theme is *much too big* to cover all *o'er*—"much too big" sounds somehow banal, or a wrong note or wrong rhythm. And "o'er"—this abbreviation, the archaism, doesn't seem to function. (Unless a reference to "loading every rift with ore"?)

(2) "In Iowa" up through next stanza—these 4 lines don't quite seem to say it, the Buddhist temple comes in arbitrarily to me; I mean, again, it doesn't function—& in fact I don't really understand how the 3 phrases or instances, "In Iowa they do not dig / the swarming locale," "this port of recall," "there's no Buddhist / temple in the midwest town" really relate to each other & to the theme—I mean, they do, but in a sketchy way somehow.

(3) In the last stanza of the 1st part I'm not clear who the "they" of "They do not remember" are, nor quite what the meaning of "*against*" is.

In Section II

the sound echoes of mother in line 3 again seem non-functionally arbitrary, that is on examination they seem not to work in their context, for how can Gaia—No, I now see & read this differently. It comes to me now as death-into-life, that "murther" there, decomposition of the leaf to enrich the ground. O.K. This is a marvellous part of the poem. Yet—once more reading it through—it seems whole without those first 3 lines which, I have the sense, perhaps really belong elsewhere; in the 1st section perhaps?

Section IV

line 3—I don't see why there's that "to" there—"*to* the great wheel of sooty shear-waters."

Section V   I am dubious about the words "Love's hero." It's too bad it should be so, for in their naked selves the words mean what you intend them to mean, but *in our time*, in conjunction & in that context, they don't quite escape a weightlessness, an almost glossy surface as of imitation leather, they are almost "cheap" to the ear, that is they produce the wrong associations especially since in stanza 6 you have taken the risk of speaking of the soul, anima, as Sleeping Beauty & as Snow White. One or the other risk—Love's hero *or* stanza 6—can be brought off but not I think the two so close together.

Nothing in stanzas IV or VI that distracts me in this way.

Yesterday (I started this Friday night, now it's Sunday afternoon) I saw 3 pairs of migrating birds in City Hall Park, each of different species* & each lovely & colorful. How lucky to have passed there on perhaps the one day they stopped there.

With love, and love to Jess,
from Denny

*My bird book's in Temple so I can't find out what they were until June.

P.S.

Could you let me know if you ever received a package containing a decorated copy of *Overland to the Islands*? I at last got hold of what was to have been the deluxe edition; lacking their covers but bound in an under-cover of plain paper. I numbered one #1 and drew some leaves in gold on it & inscribed it to you & Jess & registered it on Feb. 18th—I have the slip. If it is lost I will make another try.

Also—should I try to get at Virginia again? I feel terrible that it all seems to have done no good. Has Helen—or Jess—heard from her? What news from Wesleyan on Morgenstern?

---

## 287

May 7th {8th}/{19}63
{San Francisco}

dear Denny,

Yes, we got the limited edition of *Overland*—and I wrote off to you in the exhilaration of reading as if new, finding some poems that were as if I had never seen them before, and recognizing how deeply others had incised themselves so that it was almost a surprise to find they were on pages and not something that had happend to me. Well, then there was a letter from here that did not arrive to you, but not the other way round. The illuminations are beautiful, Denny, and there's a mixture of pride and delight in having the volume. And in it all, satisfaction at last, for that grass-paper jacket Jonathan had used had always botherd me.

To reassure you, I think you're right about the Paul Goodman book. I went and read your piece in *The Nation*, and admired what you'd done— you are clear, direct and without any "yes . . . but" formula locate your sense of limits in what you feel.[1] George Oppen (whose book I read, and whom I heard read—I wanted to hear Reznikoff whom I do like) may have strong feeling and nervous subtlety but damn it he has a tin ear and slow foot. I suspect he has with the above a narrow mind.

Your review of Goodman set Donald Allen to reading and favorably Goodman's poems. And now having read the review, I see how your quotes do open one's eyes past prejudices. (As, for an other instance, Paul Blackburn's quotes from Kelly made me see in a new focus.)

I'm not at all tempted to read Goodman tho, for he seems so upsettingly civilized, urbane, citizen-hearted. That's my personal intolerance. Inversions as manner mean something different in urbane verse—they can be a gesture of skill, not ignorance. Yet what you quote, and what Don pointed out for me to read, was something we should be for:—I think you in that review refer to his being out-spoken is it, or explicit—And what is important: in this mode he is an *artist*; what he does in structure is rooted in his engagement with experience.

The only thing that has sort of thrown me so far in your responses, Denny, was the encomium for Gilbert—and there it seemd to me apparent you were exercising sympathy and generosity past the point of reference. But thruout the Goodman piece you are clearly in focus.

on your exceptions to the "Continent"—

1. "much too big" and "coverd all o'er" sounds somehow banal as my own ear wanted to strike the note. And you are right about "ore" being in the conception a pun. But I wanted you {to} see something like the page I saw as I was writing, elaborate, leafy margined—but "pretty." And then the "much too big" refer{s} to my own tendencies in theme, and the "coverd all o'er" to the seemingly decorative—"conceits," the *Yale Review* calls 'em.

2. Here, even in the writing, I have the same queries you have. I've sent the poem to *Poetry* and if they take it I'd like to have it publishd at least once in this form. But I think I mean *Hindoo* not Buddhist. That this is sketchy is what I feel it ought to be. I had Bly, Wright,—and the Iowa Poetry Center on mind—their sneering at Ginsberg's Buddhism??

But that was someone else. Leroi Jones wrote when I objected to his calling Damballah a "forgotten" god (for after reading Maya Deren's *Divine*

*Horseman*,[2] I have not "forgotten" Damballah one of the great good gods of man—anyway, Leroi wrote back that Damballah was a "shamed" god. As even Christ is "shamed"; and the shaming of gods was on my mind about the Protestant righteous middle-west. i.e. that only in the miscegenation of the ports, coastal cities—(where also times mix "ports of recall then"{)}—is there the real earth ferment.

Later "our West's the Orient" echoes that Buddhist temple.

"They" in "They do not remember" refers to the people of the mid-west (now, the middle class, the middle-mind): and I had a definite image of Iowa feet braced against the downward tide-pull, current of the rivers toward the underworld sea—Gulf of Mexico.

Section IV   "to" means that the imagined image of birds leads "to" (or we turn from that figure "to" the actual wheel of sooty shear-waters; anyway that was what was going on in the poem—The word "to" cause just there I was conscious of the eye shift from image to the image.

Section-V   I sure don't mean anything glossy or slick in "love's hero" (as above I *did* mean the banality you got in "much too big")—but damn it, the mistake is yours and our time's, not mine. I do want (as in the Sleeping Beauty passage) the romance-fairy-tale. And I'll have to take (unless something I don't see to do now comes to me) the potential "weakness" of them both.

I think this is an "opening poem"—some of these points may come into focus as meanings accumulate. Anyway, I think like the opening poem of *The Field*—this might have later drafting. I know and also see in the poem what I meant about "Iowa," but even at the time I wonderd—yes, but why "Iowa" at all?

Wed. morning, May 8th—

Your testing the poem *does* keep decision alive. My affections still surround "The Continent" which came as my spring pome, and it's a good thing to take a look just when I'm nursing the song. *But what we as poets must often face when challenged is how wrong we must go (I think now of course of Williams challenged by H. D. about his hey-ding-ding touch, and later by Marianne Moore about the Lesbian section in* Paterson*)—back of such instances, that we do have to dig, set impulse into motion in the poem to find out deeper currents—and seem just there most arbitrary. And by "impulse" I mean, not some thought, but necessity strong enuf that one sees and feels—as I'd think it shld. be Hindoo temple (for the swarming "shamed" gods I wanted) but I saw our San Francisco Buddhist temple (built by its congregation—a good portion being Westerners), or as in that other word "against" it was "feet braced against" I saw as an ideogram —a buckboard? Just as when in a dream I know I've lost something of it then I also go in faith that the content will return, so here it's not risk but trust that I engage.*

And then maybe too I'm haunted by the thought of Bob's discarding a really beautiful poem on the death of their daughter—"on"?—working a series of equilibriums with the fact and the idea of death—was it because the poem was not "right"? or was too explicit? *He did fear the explicit*—which his New England temper sees as indiscrete where feelings are involved. But too, now that all of us are being more read and even discussd—there's the very real danger I see in your "*in our* time" consciousness of the reader who will play our words false. (I don't mean here to contend against your sense of the facility in "love's hero"—but putting that aside, to go after the part bring off the poem, performing, plays.) Just here and now we've to close off the more appreciations and depreciations of the current readers. I know my reader will finally depend, can only depend, upon what is most *real* in my own feeling as I write—and where I do see the greater truth of what is felt—"realize" anew what is going on in the poem, I'm ready to rework. But *not* when I see the advantage, how much better it would look or sound. I've got in writing to hold against how it will look or sound to the most perceptive eyes and ears, in order to follow the inner lead of image and melody. The musical feel— here it must go lax, quick, here *banal*—here *grave.*

But also now—how to break the illusions of mastery of the poem? In truth, we've only masterd certain possibilities of the line—and when just such possibilities of line appear again I wish the illusion to go. (Bob is an extreme here, where he has so masterd the quatrain, song-wise—I suggested to him when he was here he shld break his fear of the unconquerable measure—go beyond his controls in the line)—

I've got to go off to Berkeley now, mid rambles—with a last bit. I think the form we realize is a boundary, and writing, we've to traffic with what's outside that boundary as the core of feeling—

love
Robert

P. S.

I enclose also another poem, and also a letter from George Oppen in which what he says of "The Jacob's Ladder" relates to what *you* say of it on p. II 72. (I am glad to be woven into your tapestry there.)

[I think to use some of this at Vancouver so if you happen to like it I wd. be obliged if you'd nevertheless *not* pass it on to anyone who might possibly be there, as then it will seem too boring. I mean to expand the main paragraph on p. 8 to deal with what I have come to see I left out—i.e. the poem that arises *chiefly from* the formal sense, the longing to write, say, *a short songlike* poem, or a poem that will have some certain quality such as, say, abruptness, "shagginess" or "butteredness" or whatever. This isn't really a

**288**

{early May 1963
New York}

contradiction of my emphasis on the donnée, but is surely itself another *kind* of donnée.]

Dear Robert,

Reading tonight pp. II 60–II 78 {?} I suddenly decided to send you this,[1] which I've been shy to do before as there will be little or nothing new in it for you & anyway was written for delivery so that at times the style drops to a gross banality I'm afraid. But there *are* parts I do like and even though I know unceasingly how much anything good in it I owe to you, it gives me a thrill of pleasure to see how close, here and there, what I was doing, not having read those pages at that time, & what you were doing, came together.

Love—

D.

## 289

May 10, 1963
{San Francisco}

dear Denny,

I'm glad you sent the letter from Oppen, for in principle I find myself (but then any of us wld agree) in agreement about a poem having its verity in showing the truth of what is felt and thought—and, just there, must ward of what we think we ought to feel or think. Ezra Pound in "The Serious Artist" has it: "to bear witness and define for us the inner nature and conditions of man." I'm as leery of approved social, political, religious sentiments as ever Oppen might be; but what if just such a sentiment actually is what one has to bear witness to? Then the definition and condition is the more difficult to win thru to.

Looking back at the "Eichmann" sequence—yes, it's an area of feeling, of even feeling for a feeling in the content, that is not realized, that we can't trust.[1] Are we to be restricted to the stone? Will the unhappy soul never be able to go its way, where sometimes it must loose all *touch*? When we're at it, we've to render it as clear as we can. Miss, in earnest. But I think now—what goes off is given the Eichmann trial—the three images of the figure Eichmann himself—"as man"; the ogre of the garden figure (garden, tree, ogre-devil-god, and the boy-trespasser), and the piercing scream/it demands the utmost containment (as, for instance—the sentence "that Eichmann killed him in a tool shed, not beneath the tree" is all there, and beside it the poem is a vehicle not of the image but of an *undefined* emotion that uses the image).

But say we decline, sadly—the responsibility of the record remains. In my own time I've lost (a) the impetuous rhapsodic intoxication that I had in "African Elegy"; (b) the propositional invention of *Letters*: what if the real stone staircase were "lost"? there would be then the conditions there were.

I take it, as I have that same faith in myself, that the Eichmann is testimony to conditions where the stone staircase wasn't—but there it is on record, and we know how much the stone staircase verity must mean because of this other.

---

The lecture is admirable. Take that delineation of the data of experience —*sight, sound, feeling, memory*—that would clear up what happens when we begin coloring in indulgent to some emotional vagary: for we cease to construct that pathway between reality and our souls, no longer searching for the peachtree and the murder in the tool-shed *where* and *when* we've known it (and then we'd have the dream or phantasy or memory or immediacy tone right), but use the poem to react.

But we'd never be able to touch upon war or tyranny, or courage etc. any area of disturbed, unlocated feeling if we had to not fail. I think what I don't like about Oppen's work and calld his lack of imagination and ear is that he occupies a stultified and stultifying area of the reasonably real.

The Jacob's Ladder is after all a stone stair *in the sky*.

Some exceptions: Free verse is *not* organic form that fails. In organic composition every element is conceived of as belonging to every other element, as parts of a body, systems within a body, are: rime and meter, theme and departure, breathing and even throwing off of "waste" in sweats and excrements—are *functions* of "the poem." But in free verse parts are free of each other, gestures in language as if "form" were a bondage—back to the underlying philosophy:

| | |
|---|---|
| the conventional poet = | the universe and life are chaotic; the poet (the civilized or moral man) is given an order to keep against chaos. Every freedom is a breakdown of form. |
| the free-verse poet = | the universe and man are free only in nature which has been lost in civilized forms. The poet must express his feelings without the trammel of forms. Every formal element is a restraint of true natural feeling. O wild wild wind etc. |
| the organic poet = | the universe and man are members of a form. Our freedom lies in our apprehension of this underlying form, towards which poetic invention and free thought in sciences alike work. |

We've also to keep in mind that these are only three views and there are more and more views in which poetries take form.[2]

## 290

dear Denny,

Your lecture was a great pleasure and did have finds for me—There was
the new in your seeing "Ask the fact for the form" in a passage that I must
have read over many times (certainly I did if it's in Emerson's essay on "The
Poet") with my eyes always looking elsewhere. And, tho I've tried to draw the
map over and over—there was a new lead you make thru Hopkins inscape
to "sensory . . . intellectual, emotional, psychic" that freshend these terms
I have to use so over and over in the H. D. trying to find their edge. And
"recognition of what we perceive"—I'm going page by page over the lecture
now and I do have a few remarks about the trouble you get into with
"fabricated" "contrived" "induced" "faked"—for it seems to me that
recognizing as we work how we not only perceive and feel but also fabricate
etc. and even "fake" is a further consciousness—a requirement of the poet.
Let's take Pound's passage in "The Serious Artist" (page 43 of New Direc-
tions *Selected Essays*) "This brings us to the immorality of bad art. Bad art
is inaccurate art. It is art that makes false reports" which hinges upon the
responsibility as Pound sees it that the artist's good is, his task is, his record
of the inner condition of Man in his own experience. And in "How to
Read": "It does not matter whether the author desires the good of the race
or acts merely from personal vanity. The thing is mechanical in action. In
proportion as his work is exact, i.e. true to human consciousness and to the
nature of man, as it is exact in formulation of desire. . . . " and then below:
"In depicting the motions of the 'human heart' the durability of the writing
depends upon the exactitude."

What's on my mind is that we might well be engaged in the poem with
our human experience in our contrivances, fakes etc. And how exactly we
made clear what is going on in a contrivance or a fake (our writing to make
clear) is the criterion. I think the issue of what you caution against as a
"contrived" experience is whether anything *is* an experience at all until we
(and then any reader, for the writing achieves this experience here) see, feel,
articulate what is going.

The word "contrive" or "fake" (in the *Yale Literary Mag.* along this line,
missing as far as he hits, a young critic Aronson speaks of my "stretched
conceit" and "explosive, bizarre adjectives")[1] is felt when we believe some-
thing has been substituted for experience in the poem. Now I am misjudged
where the reader takes some element as a conceit; yet there is a territory
where I would accept being close to the "conceits" of Donne or Vaughan
for I think they had intuitions of the inner relations of things that inform
compass and rose.

Back to your paragraph—this troubled area of "real" "unreal" "fake"
"genuine" "true" "false" is not clear and one (you/me) has got a task to
distinguish between the prejudicial cast of the words and the actual meaning.

The "induced" seems to me an entirely different question—and here, I'd say we can not at the same time "induce" and "focus" where *induce* has the meaning of *overspread*: Had you in the second part of the Eichmann poem in what you envisiond got thru to where and how you saw it (how the Tree in the Garden is for sure the one forbidden Tree—then who is "the Devil?"—and who the boy?) there would not have been the confusion there is—This issue here is not faking but confusing and even in "confusing" it's that you are not deliberate and careful in the fusing (is it Eden-story + Eichmann story + ??? what? we don't know). In the first part you do locate (eyes) (the human face) the fact. But then you had *seen* in foto or T.V. him "isolate in a bulletproof / witness-stand of glass." And we do not know, you do not find, the vision and source of "The Peachtree." Feeling then seems induced because it is floating.

We do do a service where we bring emotion to its stations.

I'm glad you sent Oppen's letter, for, tho I've not to amend my sense of his limitations, his earnestness counts more here. My own conviction is over years different from his—for I've seen you always clear—a challenge to my own conscience in writing—where you know how to do it. And I feel that there is more danger to the life of the poet in not undertaking tasks he may not be able to perform than in being cautious. You've got to tackle this area of feeling again and again (I mean the "Eichmann" one where there's a mixture of sympathies and identifications that makes feeling unclear) for the life of you. And the poem will be achieved that will illuminate the trouble. To exorcize here is to render complete.

But on to the clarity that you do render in this lecture. You make another find for me in word *contemplate*. "his faithful attention to the experience from the first moment of crystallization." Well, you know how much this can ring in my own feeling of it.

The second exception or query I take is when you come to "free verse"— which I don't think is *failed organic poetry*, but itself an idea of what poetry and form and freedom is different from both "convention" and "organism" (As I would venture that "linguistic" poetry—and I think of my own as linguistic—is different from "organic"). Let me close with an outline{.}

| convention as "form" = | goes along with the natural is formless; man puts the world in order // *or*$^2$ with God formed the world as a paradigm in the beginning and disorder enterd thru man's sin. Only by conventicle, good behaviour, does man return to the lost order. A poem (subject always to man's sinfulness) attempts to atone by obedience to prescription. Here freedom = (a) disorder or (b) sin. |
| --- | --- |

organism as "form" =

all experience is formal—We feel things at all only in so far as we awake to the form. Here the form of the poem *is* the feeling (and where form fails, feeling fails). "Inner" and" outer" are, if we could grasp the terms of cosmic form, in tune. We have only to discover the scale (so here I am organic as well as linguistic)

"linguistic" form—

the artist uses language to make forms, and in this he {is} in a creature/creator relation to a god who is also creature/creator of the whole. Where "organic" poetry refers to personal emotions and impressions—the concourse between organism and his world; the linguistic follows emotions and images that appear in the language itself as a third "world"; true to what is happening in the syntax as another man might be true to what he sees or feels.

free verse =

the poem does not find or make but expresses, and the poem has its virtue in the ecstatic state or emotional state aroused by rhythms and rime even, where the poet can pour forth what he feels// *and/or* God speaks thru the poet once his voice is free. Here form = restriction I'm thinking of a Hassidic interpretation of the law against making a graven image meaning that speech should not be made in that sense but speak from the heart. Free verse just doesn't believe in the struggle of rendering in which not only the soul but the world must enter into the conception of the poem. Experience is an engagement and responsibility to outer as well as inner.

Two forms of free verse would be Amy Lowell's impressionism and Ginsberg's "Howl."

love
Robert

SONNET IV

He's given me his *thee* to keep,
secret, alone, in Love's name
for what sake I have only in faith.

Where it is? how it is near?
I would recognize him by the way he walks.
But it is so long ago and I was never sure

except in his regard and then
sure as the rose scattering its petals to prepare is sure
for ripeness near to the perfection of the rose.

I would know the red *thee* of the enclosure
where thought too curls about, opens out
from what's hid

until it falls away, all the profuse allusion let go,
the rose-hip persistence of the truth hid therein from me
enduring.

dear Denny,

I'd written this fourth sonnet but then I so mistrust the burden of the
sonnet-form-thoughtful proposition and answer thing, and the simple figure
it gives rise to; and the hubris just possible always in speaking of love close
to home as I mean to do in this sequence—that I closed the notebook on
it and, returning from Los Angeles today decided, yes, it was sound. I'm
happy too because it gives me something short to send to Ammons at
*The Nation.* I'd wanted to respond to his enquiry for work, to show I was
*with* him, but you know how seldom I manage anything in a short form.

love
Robert

**291**

May 23, 1963
{San Francisco}

Dearest Jess,

I am trying to get the stuff from Virginia but she says it is at the place
where plates are made & is being worked on. She has promised to get me
at least some of the material back before we leave for Temple Wed. am. but
you know what her promises are worth. Well, will know by tomorrow night.
I ought to have gone to get it as soon as yr letter came but have been so busy
that I delayed, thinking the stuff was anyway safe in her locked safe which is
where it was when I last saw it. I planned to pick it up and mail it this
afternoon. She's so bold-faced, what a strange one.

Much love,
~~Denise~~ Denny.

**292**

Monday a.m.
{June 1963}
New York

**293**

June 11/1963
{San Francisco}

Dear Denny,

You must be in Temple by now?? Anyway, cleaning up my desk I found these pages of a letter to you; I think I put them aside because I was trying thruout to write about things where I have no clear sense of them i.e. the whole matter of that controversial Eichmann poem sequence of yours. This morning the letter doesn't seem as awful as it must have seemd to me when I wrote it. I might have a stronger feeling that the question of convention vs organic vs free is to be answerd by convention plus organic plus free; where another trio might be the communal language and art plus the life experience plus the will to individual being. Each in each.

And best of all wld be to throw the terms out, and go ahead to make clear what is happening in mine, in patterns and statements that have a force of their own to stand out from rime and pattern like rock ledges standing out from forested land—

A long and encouraging letter came yesterday from Pearson. It had been several months? and tho I did understand that he was loaded under and over with end of the semester duties, still I had a growing dread that he might find the picture of Bryher disaffecting.

Now it seems that he won't be back in New Haven until Spring 1964, and I plan now to go East then. Wenning (the book dealer who has been buying stock from me) has invited me to stay with him and his wife, with the added encouragement that they have lots of room.[1]

Looking forward, I'll write now to Betty Kray about possible readings. And would you know whom I shld write about maybe having a lecture series at the New School of Social Research that summer? I'd have plenty of material as you know—and could send a course plan now.

Our thoughts are all and often on seeing you soon. Ellen Tallman has found an apartment for the Burtons and Jess and me, so easily we can stay for the duration of the season.

love
Robert

**294**

June 11th {63
New York}

Dearest Robert

This is one of my non-letters. Since your last one, Mitch's return & Nik's graduation & various seasonal loose ends intervened & I've not had a chance to write though I've lots to write about & have had you much in my thoughts. We are leaving for Temple on Saturday & I'll be settling down, DV, to write a real letter soon after we get into the house again.

Love to you & to Jess
from Denny.

At Academy Typing

Dear Jess

I am going to take dictation from Virginia who has trouble writing:
She is giving me the following:
A) Text of "The Stepmother"
B) Couple of drawings wh. wd. not be used.
C) Cover of "Queen of Crow Castle"
D) All material of which she already has negatives.
All the rest of the material is at the plate-maker.

"Jess, I am very, very sorry there have been so many delays. And all I can say is that I think you will be pleased with the layout of the book. By Monday the platemaker shd. send me the rest of the negatives back. At which time I will send you all the stuff by registered mail. I am enclosing dummy wh. I am hoping you can return to me at yr earliest convenience. I wish that Robert if he thinks it's a good idea wd. write a 1-page intro. which wd. help the distribution. You will notice that p. 31 is blank; due to the way you have laid out 'Kiltory' it has to be even if we juggled things around. Cd. there here be a design as subsidiary title page for 'Queen of C.C.'? I am making all of full-page illustrations bleeds on all sides, wh. looks v. good. Please return dummy as soon as poss & PLEASE try to forgive me for all this, and I just hope that Helen Adam will too . . .

Love<br>Virginia."

"P.S. I wd prefer to put copyright in name of Acadia Press but if you &/or Helen object let me know."

"P.S. If you & H. A. want sep. number of copies to number and sign?"

A guy here has promised to try to see the stuff *is* mailed to you (registered) as soon as it come back, and to send me a p.c. at that time.

Love—<br>Denise.

295

Wed. 26th
June {26}, {19}63
{New York}

dear Denny,

The short story in *Harper*'s is beautiful work.[2] I read it last week at the library with too much excitement at the idea of a short story by you to read the full impact. That must be another reading, yet, as it was, where I was able to go slowly enuf to take care of the immediate sense the writing was careful of the immediate. It's one of your best things, worthy of the recall of Lawrencian spirit that is there (I mean *his* spirit of what a story is)—a revelation of what happens in life.

296

June 29/{19}63
{San Francisco}[1]

This morning, dishes washed and the sun decorating the kitchen table, I've sat myself down to some notes on the great batch of poems you sent a month ago. On one ["A form upon the quilted/overcast . . ."[3]] you askd: "Do you think there shd be question marks instead of dashes after 2nd and 3rd stanzas? I'm not sure if this is all of it . . . etc"

As it stands the dashes (standing off from their lines "desire—") have the effect of the • that Williams began to use, which I take as a suspended point in the structure. The question has this element of suspension, and it has seemd to me at times that the "?" removes the valuable uncertainty of a question—making it obviously a question. The suspension of statement is richer in suggestion.

The three dashes are structural in the poem—and make possible a unity between the questioning tone of the opening stanza that isn't in the definite syntax of a question—and at the same time give statement to the following stanzas in question-syntax.

In "Into the Interior" the ? is right for its being an out and out question.

re: "Puñal." Do you mean "come" in the poem to mean (as it does by pun once the stress is heightend by the line division) semen? The thing is that the "hand . . . squeezing crow's blood," "idiot," "bog" "dragging to a/cold end" "congealed" "pleased fingers" all cooperate to force a special tendency.

A change of line to

"having come in shoes that hurt"

would shift the movement so that the simple masturbation content (which given the conglomeration of images must be a given unconscious content) is containd and does not, as it is likely to in the present form, take over.

For isn't the poem actually meant to convey the primitive fantasy life, a folk homage? If you used the word "arrived" rather than "come," the primary intent of the poem would be renderd free without falsifying the unconscious content.

The rimes of "squeezing," thru "real" and "congealing" to "pleased fingers" still charges the poem with the content of masturbation so that "pleased" *shocks.*

"Into the Interior," "The Ground Mist" and "Novices" stand strong in my rereading. What does the easy-going pace and purpose of "The Novices" go toward? You also in writing surrender strain and weight on the great chain. Something, like the wood-demon, portends in the poem and then fades from view. "The Willows" and the "Who is at My Window" satisfy— the craving one always has for your touch afresh in things.

The morning has evaporated and here it is noon. What was my mind wondering about? "Purpose" and Dante's "intent," the conscious engage- ment in the poem . . .

Certainly an interview with Brother Antoninus read recently in the *Harvard Advocate* in which he put down Williams and then Olson as "mental" or lacking in unconscious power, and posing himself and Ginsberg as having unconsciousness,[4] was in my mind as I was considering how the unconscious content of "Puñal" (I'm sure you were unconscious of the organization of the poem, so that things you did not mean took over) upsets the composition.

Antoninus in his "Preface" to *Hazards of Holiness* posed sincerity vs. art, and it's along the same line that now he poses the unconscious vs. intelligence. When the real thing in question is the difference between an intelligence and a stupidity of conscious operations.

But we do as poets concernd with being aware of what is going on as we write have to be most wary of unconscious repressed content taking over (like the idiot subliminal voices in a medium) to use the poem in order to insist upon having a hearing. . . . Recognized, the repressed has, after all, come to consciousness and can be fairly "heard"—but if the poet remains unconscious of what is going on . . . The point I seem to be laboring beyond need here is that the attention of the poet must involve his most keen recognition of what the poem involves as it happens.[5]

Dear Robert

I must write once anyway before I see you in Vancouver.

Has the letter & material from Virginia that I mailed here arrived safely? Has the rest, which she was to mail 5 days after my departure from N.Y.? It was unfortunate that everything but what I did send was at the plate-maker, as it completely blocked me. Let me know please.

I had a couple of letters from you in May just before Mitch got home that were "important" letters which I had the desire to answer right away but M.'s sudden return intervened & then I got caught up in Nik's graduation & various other things & now the time seems past. But I want anyway to say that what you wrote about free verse, organic, & poetry of linguistic impetus, did get to me—my subsequent silence might make you think I hadn't been listening. The word linguistic was particularly meaningful to me as it suddenly showed me what it was I'd dimly felt I'd left out of that lecture (I mean, I'm sure there's much else out too but this was something I'd been half-conscious of—) & especially in reference to much that in your work didn't really fit into the scheme of things I'd posited there, even though it was a loved, fascinating part of your work—i.e. my description of poetic activity really doesn't leave much place if any for puns & multiple meanings, does it. Now I'm trying to get something of this realization onto paper to use in

**297**

July 10th {19}63
Temple, Maine

Vancouver. Like an ass I left almost all my notes in N.Y. where I can't get at them till I'm passing through on my way to V., so I'll have to put together what I write here & what I'd written there (including parts of that lecture) on the plane.

I'm coming by way of Seattle so am stopping over a night with Eve Triem. I really don't know her, you know—met her that evening of 1st arrival in S.F. at Ruth W-D.'s {Witt-Diamant's} reception to wh. you didn't come, & that's all—but she writes to me, & tho' her gushing embarrasses me some, yet I've enjoyed her crazy letters & some of her poems, & feel fond of her—I hope actually meeting her won't be a terrible disillusionment! And I wonder what her ancient husband is like.

A lot has happened inside me since May, mid-May. Realizations, re-clarifications I'd experienced in M.'s absence had been counterparted in him. So it was a good homecoming. Then there was one of those falls into an abyss which turns out to be a tunnel from which one emerges into a new landscape, a new time of day, maybe another season. The trip up here (proceeded by the packing, which always seems to be a major upheaval) in the heat, the car breaking down twice, the 3 of us together night & day for 3 days therefore, was tough, & blurred what had happened a bit, but only superficially. Nik was remarkably pleasant throughout that rather trying experience.

And I have quite a lot of new poems.

I'm sorting out all the letters I've ever had from you. I've let them get all jumbled up, & all spring was planning this as an enjoyable summer task. I've only just begun. Rereading as I go.

Yes, I much regret the Jack Gilbert thing.[1] I made myself sound like a regular champion of his, whereas I actually *only* like the 3 poems I mentioned in the piece I wrote. His opinions (in the interview they published with him) or rather opinionatedness & his Guggenheim statement (he had the nerve to give my name without asking me, but I declined to recommend him) which was dreadfully conceited, really set me against him.[2] But at the time when I was asked to write the few paragraphs, it was like this: I'd heard him read (in double program with me at the Paraclete Bookstore) & been impressed (& told him so, & did a poem in *The Nation*), even enthused (he was com-pletely out of the blue to me). And then, the poem dedicated to you gave me the idea he was a friend of yours & I must confess that prejudiced me in his favor. Later I heard you speak slightingly of him, & of that poem. Then when *Genesis* asked for the "celebration" piece, I felt that even tho I'd by then read his book & some other poems and not cared for the bulk of his work, I *ought* to stand by my enthusiasm for the 3 poems I continued to admire because . . . well, partly anyway because it would be dishonorable & ungenerous not to; & also because having been originally predisposed in his favor because I thought him a friend of yours, I would feel like a reed in the wind if I "switched" upon finding this was not so. It's childish & I'm ashamed of the whole thing. Mitch at the time thought such a "celebration" ridiculous & that I should say no, but I thought that wd. be mean. And I thought I could, by carefully mentioning only what I genuinely admired, do it without any loss of integrity. But when it turned out to be the longest statement of anyone's, the context changed the sense.

Enough. Or too much.

The cats, Hawthorn & Marimba, are enjoying the country in their different ways. Marimba who never purred has started to do so.

It's so good to be here again.

I'm very worried about John Wieners. He was in hospital with hepatitis, & during that time I had 2 letters from him; but he was discharged May 30th & since then I haven't heard a word. I had sent him something to help his convalescence so I wrote again but still no word. Then 2 days ago Ted Enslin (who's up here at his farm) told me Jackson MacLow had told him John was back on drugs. Also that he was in Atlantic City. I do so hope it's not true. He had certainly seemed perfectly OK all the time we've known him during this past winter & spring. He lost his job at the 8th St Bkshop & was worried about money, but was hoping to get a Centro de Escritores grant I'd told him about (Mexico City) & also to get a job for a few weeks that wd. give him enough to go to Vancouver for the 3 weeks. Of course getting hepatitis killed *that* plan. He shd. hear this month about Mexico— but now if he's hooked—? If you have any news of him please tell me.

We were reading Jung's autobiography *Memories, Dreams, & Reflections* during the last month or so;[3] it was quite a tremendous experience. I wish you'd read it. I guess some of the earlier chapters if translated into Freudian terms would make you laugh; that's O.K., never mind, it doesn't matter whether or not you agree with him, read it as a record of a man's bold & poetic confrontation of inner experience. The dreams, the period of letting himself down into the unconscious almost to the point of being drowned there, the carving of stones and building of Bollingen (the house itself, I mean) are moving experiences beyond any question of ideology. And the somber openness of the last chapters belongs with something in Whitehead, & Einstein, & things you have written about the deathliness of closed systems.

I'll stop here. Did I write how much I like (like! sometimes I so debase the language—forgive me)—how very beautiful I think the 4th sonnet? Which reminds me, I'd been invited, & accepted, to be poetry ed. at *The Nation* again for an unspecified period starting in Sept., but now it's all off because Lincoln Kirstein has bought *The Nation* from George and has his own ideas about poetry.[4] I suspect he wants to install a boyfriend there—I gather he belongs to that Auden / V{irgil}. Thompson set that sounds coldly calculating & sort of glittery. I'm relieved in one way—I know I'll feel freer & write more poems. On the other hand I am much put out at the way it was done (& Mitch is furious) which was shabby. And I'm disappointed at not being able to publish people like Wieners & a few young poets—Jim Mosley among them, the boy from Delaware—whose poems I've seen & felt excited about. And it means having to write to several such to whom I'd committed myself, explaining & apologizing—really a pain.

Gael {Turnbull} visited us on his way to Britain, and wrote a wonderful letter about Finlay on his way back—I'll bring that with me. Also I've had a note from Jessie & Finlay, & they've put me on the mailing list for *Poor, Old, Tired, Horse.*

Now I must stop & wash some of M.'s wool socks.

Love from<br>Denny.

---

## 298

July 13/{19}63
{San Francisco}

dear Denny,

Along with your long letter, Bob's novel arrived this morning. A bonus mail delivery. And I've started reading the novel (*The Island*)—it's like reading your story was—so good that the excitement makes almost too much to read. The way seeing treasured friends is over charged for the first day or two. . . . At breakfast I could read passages aloud to Jess. Well, you'll see. He has done it, written a novel that takes its place for me with the best: Lawrence, Joyce, Ford, Dorothy Richardson, Virginia Woolf. The identity of words and feeling and thought . . . but it's the *presence* of the book that is a miracle. Presence or voice, and then, in that, reality. I feel some mystery of "authority" in it. How could he have realized this that I am reading? And a painful nearness, that just the way his sentences move, dance or enjamb, seems now as I read so much more than I would have imagined. How did he ever have stored such veridities of Palma? or of himself?

"He so loved the confidence of anyone, to be trusted, regarded. Like a dog, almost, the wagging smile. She told him his smile was lovely, it changed his whole face. But in the arguments he frightened her, she despaired of him, she shook, shook, shook, caught, broken crying, over and over, shaking. The children stood in the doorway, watching."

Saturday morning—

The packet you mailed from Temple arrived this morning in good condition, but I wish we could have withdrawn that book entirely from Virginia. From the beginning Jess has demanded a contract on the book (and he typed out a contract agreement and sent it August last year). She has never responded, but gone ahead with the book, tho he wrote *she was not to.* Now I just don't trust her "I wd prefer to put copyright in name of Acadia Press but if you &/or Helen object let me know." As it stands Helen has absolutely no guarantee of any income on this publication, no guarantee of advance copies even, etc. and if Virginia went ahead and copyrighted in her own Press name I am sure she would collect the royalties from any reprints. Justifying herself by referring to her own expenses in publishing.

Jess anyway will not consent to her going ahead with the book without a contract agreement covering questions of royalty, copyright, etc.

What a mess tacit agreements are! And I swear I will not get into another one—that was one of the troubles in the Auerhahn deal—they didn't like contracts they said because they felt agreements should be friendly . . . but "friendly" meant constant arbitration on every point. They had sent out that flyer and gotten a full subscription when they calld me in and said—{"}You seem to have a misunderstanding about royalties, it isn't our custom to pay them. We aren't printing for business or profit but to help the poet get printed. If we sacrifice our profit, the poet should make some sacrifice too—his royalty" etc. I gave in on the royalty, but then the matter of the quality of printing came up and I saw this "misunderstanding" more seriously.

The thing is Virginia has good intentions, and with that, refuses to face what good practice would demand.

Sunday

We went to see Helen yesterday. Getting her to focus on the subject of copyright and royalties was impossible. It was too, too kind of Virginia Admiral to consider at all publishing her, etc. etc. And then Helen was at her most distracted for she didn't want to admit the thought of her mother who now at 86 is dying. Radiant, bearded, emaciated—for she's not taken food for over a week . . . Mother Adam is one of the dearest spirits we've ever known, and yesterday may surely be the last time we will have her blessing—the lighting up of her eyes and smile and the kiss of her is a blessing. "O don't wake me," she said to Pat. "You know Mother is never angry," Pat told us, "but she was angry this morning" "Don't wake me, I was a little girl again."

These last two years Helen has refused the idea of her mother, almost with fury at times, and that was part of Helen's breakdown I think. It was strange in that house, with Helen entertaining in the back parlor, frantically—and Pat crying at the door to her mother's room and Jess and me on that tremulous edge of saying goodbye to a most dear old woman for it may be the last time.

---

Just one last note—what wld. be most valuable in the lecture wld. be to consider how the different ideas of form appear in your own work. . . . We have after all one thing any of us has to tell that someone else can learn or hear only from us, and that is the experience in the writing of the poem.

What we knew about the poem as we were writing, what we discovered in the writing / and then in reading the poem later. It seems to me important in this business of the "unconscious" that on one hand we deal with very conscious "unconscious archetypes," we know the echoes of our own experience in the caverns of Man's experience—but on the other we deal with what we do not know and there are certain patterns of sound, images, utterances that "come to us." Not to put a premium on these but to awaken a young poet to how various and deep a resource there is in the language, and to reassure him about how much *faith* means in work . . . beyond knowing or gnosis—And I remember too how important for all of us is the discovery of the pathway or company that goes with us. I'm thinking now of my reading Buber's Hassidic collections always associated with you and Mitch reading them.

There can be no misleading if you keep to the testimony of what is happening in your work and how you came to recognize what is happening. How you have felt what in your work to be "conventional," "organic" "linguistic" . . . and what puzzles you in your work too. . . . Some if not many in this "course" will be fellow poets; and those who aren't will understand what *work*[1] means. Well, anyway, they will have heard from me what works and work means; for that is the subject I am going to lecture on. A sort of "Serious Artist" 1963. Credo.

love<br>Robert

Dearest Denny—

Thank you ever & ever for your good offices & I know how painful awful it is to go around to pry out Virginia's strongheld advantage over the Helen Adam stuff. I've not been able even to get clear replies from her, let alone be informd of her shifting policies on format since first
I sent to her. I really meant to relieve you at New Year's of this business, which you've had to suffer too much of already, and hope you'll not blame me too much for reniggling on my letter of then.

I look forward eagerly to Vancouver whitherwards we wend next weekend. It'll be wonderful to see you again, I hope you'll be able to come down to visit in SF after the session there.

Love—<br>Jess

---

**299**

July 15/{19}63
{San Francisco}

dear Denny,

Cleaning up my desk I found the enclosed. It often happens with letters— Perhaps I felt that I had belabourd the Freudian warnings re. "Puñal". . . . Or it could have been too some dissatisfaction about starting off on the "unconscious" when I am in the midst of worrying that word, and don't have much of a feeling that the light has broken thru yet. I suspect to use the word decently (in a critical sense) we'd have to have a series of meanings, some of them unrelatable to others.

Oh yes, it is true I'm most likely to bridle at "Jung." But, while there is an argumentative cast always in Jung that I find exasperating and dislike finally (the having the answer to things in a schema), there is always much and often so much else that I find revelatory. I look forward with the usual mixture of prejudice and expectation to reading the *Autobiography*.

We're in the first paroxysms of getting ready to depart for the North. We found kitty-sitters at last, so Jess is going for sure. And I think he is happy to be going. He and the Burtons will be going on to the north again to Prince Rupert, and then driving back . . . a real tour of British Columbia.

love,
Robert

Dear Robert

I'm changing "come" to "having set out" in "Puñal," in case anyone else (quite naturally, I see) misinterprets it as you did. I think it *is* a *mis*interpretation for the following reasons: (1) You forget that as an allusion to masturbation (if that's what (however unconscious) it were) it wd. be a masculine one, which wouldn't be too likely a part of a female's unconscious! (Even tho I did recently have the enclosed dream—in which however it was a question of stroking not "squeezing") (2) The image is based (unfairly?— but I've justified it by supposing that tho' the origin was unknown it gave rise to a communicable image) on an ink drawing in that Hans Anderson I once lent to you & Jess (by one of the Brothers Robinson). It actually shows Hans Clodhopper holding up a *muddy* crow, & he was not an evil personage; but as a child I interpreted his grin as very evil and supposed the mud that was dripping through his fingers was the dead or dying crow's black blood. So that the first stanza is saying,—*So it's as if that indeed were so, & were, besides, a picture of a "real" event.*

And the next stanza (with perhaps unconscious or semi-conscious reference to 2 other Hans Anderson stories, "The Red Shoes" and "The Girl Who Trod on a Loaf" (she was taking it home, a fine white loaf, to her impoverished parents, but coming to a boggy place used it as a stepping stone in order not to dirty her pretty shoes)) is saying,—*And having taken risks, they did not work out.*

And the third,—*And the day that started badly didn't get any better as it went on.*

# 300

July 24–26 {19}63
{Temple, Me.}

And the last,—*Yes, the black blood remains & in congealing grows even more real, solid, undeniable; & evil & idiocy are pleased that it is so.*

It's called "Puñal" because there's a poem of that name (means "Dagger" or "Knife") by Garcia Lorca which says, "No! Don't stick me with it! No!"— I forget the rest, it's a short poem about the worst happening. Before I called it "Puñal" I thought of calling it "Childe Roland to the Dark Tower Came" except that I've never been sure if I've really understood what does happen in that poem, & if what it means to me is at all what Browning meant or what it means to others.

Anyway—I'm very glad you told me, especially as I have an aversion to the word "come" in that sense, having never heard it until I read Peter Orlovsky who gives me the creeps, & I associate it closely with him. Too bad. The thing is he seems to put it on a level with picking his nose, which he wrote about too.

Your letter about possibilities for the lecture gave me many ideas. I'd already written most of what I planned, which wd. quote from the lecture I sent you but is mostly new; but I'll try to incorporate some of your suggestions and then at the reading I can do some more, especially if, as I hope, the lecture comes first & the reading after—I've no clear idea of the sequence of events.

I do wish I would be hearing you speak about *Work*—I hope there'll be anyway some kind of transcript of it. Mitch too now wishes we'd arranged after all to all 3 come for the whole 3 weeks. But that had seemed so very extravagant. Then tho' Nik seems to half-secretly mean to be a writer he's not yet old enough to have enjoyed that much writing-talk. Mitch might have arranged free transportation he thinks, as a travel writer. But by the time that came up I was against the whole idea as I thought it wd. be inhibiting for me to have M & N around at such a time. So often M is ignored by poets who are interested in me but haven't read his book & that is very embarrassing for me & not good for him. Or for Nik if he sees it. Well, anyway, it's too late now & I'll hope anyway to bring home for Mitch transcripts and whatever notes I can make of what I do hear.

Dear Jess, thank you for being so forebearing about Virginia or rather, I mean, about my part in it. I feel at fault—not in this last episode, in which there was absolutely nothing else I could do beyond forcing her to dictate that letter & give me at least what you do now have back—but in not being much harder and disbelieving way back, when I could perhaps have wrested the whole thing away from her. At that time she soft-soaped me and I seem to recollect pleading her case to you. She seems so impervious, one can be so rude to her without her taking offence, & then it ends in one's feeling she must be O.K. But really she is not respectable & there's nothing so good-natured in her acceptance of abuse. Thanks—I'd love to have come to SF after Vanc., but have to come right back.

There's a young woman called Linda Wagner who wrote a thesis on W C W, & visited him (Bill & Flossie liked her) & who now has a contract to write something about me for some series published by Twayne;[1] & she's enrolled for the whole course at Vancouver. I hope she's nice. You'll no doubt have come across her by the time I arrive. She wants to ask me a lot of questions so I guess I'll have dinner with her some night.

I'm terribly pleased you liked my story. I was timid about it, feeling that perhaps in wanting to keep it austerely simple I had made it weakly thin. To begin with I envisioned something only a paragraph long—an anecdote. But I found that falsified by omission. I have a feeling it might be several years before I write another, tho' I'd like to.

We are dying to see Bob's book.[2] Mitch has written for a copy.

Had a letter from Don Allen about his magazine—it sounds as if it cd. be good.

Love—

D.

Robert, about the New School I suggest you write to Leroi Jones, his address now is 27 Cooper Square N.Y.C. Or else Frank O'Hara but I don't know his address.

Dream referred to on p.1 of letter.

Dream    (July 13)

In this dream I am now man, now woman, mostly a young man though. I am the leader of a group of people with some common cause—not exactly an outlaw or guerrilla group but one involving some risk though at peace. Yet I'm not fully, or not autocratically, in control as a leader, for it is on the advice of others that Ive come to the place I'm in. It is a strange kind of room and this is the first time I've been in it. It's a sort of loft perched at an angle among an agglomeration of great ancient barns. One climbs into it by a ladder. In the front wall is the large unglazed window-space or loft opening (for hay) through which I can see a great landscape, hill behind hill and mountains back of the hills. It is very beautiful, full of light and shade and colored hazily, softly, not brilliantly. I am alone in the room and alone at the whole farm, having sent all my associates off on various errands which will take them hours. Only my old father is there, and came to the foot of the ladder at one point, with his newspaper and pipe, to tell me he would keep watch at the farmhouse itself. But I feel apprehensive, and that I was foolish to leave myself so alone here—even tho my friends said it wd be alright. The old man wd. be no support. I see how beautiful everything is—the great landscape, the motes of golden dust in the sunlight—and so quiet—but I see too that the wood of the step from which one reaches the ladder down is half worn away—and the floor-boards are uneven—I dont feel as if the whole perched room were quite safe, so high above ground. But of course, it's all solid *enough*, I tell myself—and as for anything happening, who in the world would come, what's there to fear? But I don't dispel my unease. I have arranged for my brother Edward to join me here, travelling from some place in those hills I can see—I look forward to his arrival and to his support, yet realizing that it will be dark before he can get here (on foot)—for it's already late afternoon, almost—I worry about that too, imagine him twisting an ankle in the heather somewhere, unable to send a message—

As I worry I catch sight of a toy metal animal on a heap of quilts lying on a low bed near the hatch or ladderway—a giraffe or something between a giraffe and a deer, but thought of as a giraffe—. I am nervously half-masturbating —as a man, that is,—as I stand worrying, and absently looking at this toy: when as I look it becomes, though just as tiny, *alive*: I see it raise its head and twitch its ears, and browse the leaves of a tree overhanging it from a bank that just a moment before had been only a fold of old quilt. It is extraordinarily beautiful. I don't dare to change my position an inch, to move or to stop moving my hand mechanically or to look at it other than aslant, for fear that if I change anything it will notice and the vision of it will fade. I see its tiny muscles ripple even—I see the minute individual hairs of its close fur. And I realize—even though *still* I'm half-afraid—that this is a magic place, even if the floor of it is not quite sound, and even if it's strange that I can't see the sea, come to think of it, which surely should be visible straight ahead from the loft-window—a magic place where I am going to see marvels and should be glad to be—and at least part of me, entranced by what I'm witnessing, *is* glad.

---

## 301

Sept 4th {19}63
Temple Maine

Dear Robert & Jess

I am longing for a word from you. I did hear from Warren {Tallman} the good news about Charles' having the biopsy & its proving non-malignant. Where is he now, do you know? I'd like to write & tell him how glad I am.

What was the last wk. in Vancouver like? Bob's candlelight reading, Charles's readings? I am awfully anxious to get the tapes, & plan to get the machine very soon.

The few summer-people, seen only at auctions & in Farmington buying groceries, are all gone, there's the special after-Labor-Day feeling. The grass as Mitch says is sere, the grapes are ripening (from green to rust) mornings are cold, the days sunny but windy & quite cool.

That Dilexi gallery announcement is up on my wall, "pasteups & assemblies," & I have it tacked in such a way that the fold will open or close.

I'm working at trying to put the Edson book together,[1] it is harder than I thought because since I can't multiply I have to count every word & even then there are problems about how much can go on a page without looking crowded. But luckily David Ford at N{ew} D{irections} will come to my rescue if I can't do it right. I've agreed to be on the board of the Wesleyan Poetry series for a year. It may be totally frustrating as the other 3 members are none other than J M Brinnin, Wilbur, and Nemerov! But I thought I'd try it anyway, in case I *can* exert some leverage on behalf of people like Wieners and Turnbull, if they care to submit books while I'm there. And I can use the $250 they'll pay me. But if it gets too bad I can always resign. I take Donald Hall's place, but he will be back the next year & then (he says) we might both be on it & there wd perhaps be more chance of doing some good things—tho he's a terrific fence-sitter. What it involves is 3 or 4 meetings a year, & reading & reporting on the MSS that come in. Each member takes a turn as "first reader," who eliminates what he considers not worth further thought. One wonders what may have been eliminated by some of those readers! But I suppose there *is* plenty of real rubbish, judging by what used to come in to *The Nation*.

We had a week on the coast, Deer Isle. It is like another country. We enjoyed it very much, rocks & gulls & lobster boats. But for some obscure reason Temple & the country round it seem appropriate for us as the coast never would.

I have only 1 new poem since Vancouver. The one I began there hasn't emerged. And I'm struggling with another one that perhaps also will never come to anything. It may be that after Nik starts school (Sept 14th) & we are alone here, so that I will be completely alone for some hours each day, I'll be able to work better. Nik's impending departure is an anxiety to me— not the going away itself but wondering if he will be happy there. Then there's the immediate preoccupation of nametapes & marking-ink & checking off a list, etc.

I was given a copy of a poem by Barbara Moraff which I want to send you,[2] but can't find. I don't know her & scarcely know her work—but this poem is a marvel. (Just found it—will copy)

I'd like to have the Burton's address when you write.

I told Betty Kray we all 3 wd like to accept her invitation,[3] & also nudged her about other readings for you. And I told her I didn't want to be "editor" of the event, that if anyone it shd be you, Robert, for you were the one who'd immediately had ideas for it; & if you didn't want to be, then it cd simply be a cooperative effort.

Paul Triem sent me his bread recipe, but I've not yet acquired a suitable pan for the dough.

Half of me is still in the Northwest.

I can hardly bear to ask if there's been anything further from Virginia. If she's still stalling when I return to N.Y. at the end of October I'll make every effort this time to get all the material back from her. So let me know.

I had a short but good letter from Margaret Avison. And we heard from Bob—but I now see one has to get through, under, over, anyway around his letterwriting for the letters rarely have the real thing in them. His book came,[4] & was no disappointment, at least not to me. Mitch while acknowledging it very good felt he wished it had been less factual, had transformed what happened; but with my passion for seeing—again—*inscape*, I felt satisfied with the book as it is.

At Deer Isle I had some kind of dream, unfortunately not remembered, about bears, & it made me want to re-read "Snow-White & Rose-Red" which I'd always loved—& lo, I found 2 fairytale books in the shelves (at the Fussiners' rented house) which both included it. But as so often I seemed to have remembered it wrong, or else to have put into it more than the words said. I had thought Rose Red fell in love with the bear. There was nothing of that in the story as told in these books. And at the end when he is revealed as a Prince it is Snow White (or Rosewhite, as I thought her) who marries him, while Rose Red marries his brother who wasn't even a bear.

We're still reading *Njal's Saga* in the evenings.[5]

When we went to Deer Isle we didn't get a cat-sitter but took Hawthorn along, he is an excellent traveller & had a good time.

> With love from
> Denny

P.S.

Did I send you that photo of our house?

Wd. you like the one of you (R.) sitting on the steps of the Vancouver house? I've taken Nik with his machete for Stevie Burton but light may have gotten into the camera, I don't know yet.

The poplar that leans across[6] is half-uprooted but fully alive. It's caught in the branches of a silver maple which supports it. It's been that way a long time—since before we first saw it over 3 yrs ago at least.

## 302

Thursday
{early September 1963}
Temple, Maine

Dear Robert & Jess

The poem I was working on has seemed to emerge after all. I think. . . . Here it is.

Also enclosed, a letter from Archie Ammons with quote from Kenner I thought you might like to see. It's a critic's prose, but I liked that "gingerly efficiency" (self-descriptive, of Kenner himself, maybe?) tho it made me see among the flowerpots (not jamjars!) a *ginger* cat instead of what has always been a tabby with white bib.

I guess I have that *Nation* job back after all, Lincoln Kirstein having backed out for reasons of health & George now asking me to return on my own terms in a manner hard to refuse. I think I'll try it—the term is indefinite so I can resign if I find it is bugging me. I think they'll let me have more space this time—so I hope to do better than before. Keep me in mind, please. I guess I'll begin in November. I'll see if I can get some more poems from Helen, also. Can you get me an address for Ch. O., please?

We had a frost last night. Even by day I find I need slacks & sweaters, though at noon by a sheltered bank the sun's quite hot. Asters & goldenrod. Squirrels & chipmunks busy, tho the butternuts don't seem ripe.

Love,
Denny

dear Denny,

I've been in a Sargasso Sea, with a mind both weedy and humid, settling back into old home ways. The first two weeks were not entirely "back," for the Tallmans were down here and there were exchange visits and aftermaths of Vancouver. I had three splendid days dubbing tapes, rehearing your reading, that part of Bob's that got recorded, and the amazing bonus of it all the two readings in which Charles read thru the remaining Maximus, and then requests (that last reading was three and a half hours, halted only by the University janitors{)}.

The night of Bob's reading (your flight home) you will remember there was a thunderstorm brewing. As he started to read "A Form of Women" the electrical circuits on campus began to suffer. Lights dimmd and threatend clearly to go out before the current from which the tape recorder was running faild. What we experienced at the time was spooky enuf, for as he came to the lines "to have seen things / looking in at me thru the open door" we all began to fear for the light. So that someone got a candle; and it was lit even as Bob continued to read. "If it is dark / when this is given to you," was synchronized exactly with the final dimming and going out of the lights.

But there was something even more haunted, uncanny, in the recording. The current there begins to fail in the next verse which goes as follows:

| | |
|---|---|
| my face is my own | |
| my hands are my own | [all in Bob's regular voice] |
| my mouth is my own | |
| but I am not | [in an entirely (almost) other voice a pitch higher, a woman's voice] |

and the poem ends in a demented Donald-Duck voice (both higher and speeded-up) "But-I love-you-Do-you-love-me—."

303

Sept. 10/{19}63
{San Francisco}

Margaret Avison's reading was not well recorded—I didn't get a dub of it. But I did of my lecture and so heard myself for the first time in this kind of thing. One thing I did discover from that tape comes from the recording of me writing on the blackboard ie. that my chalk (pen) writing beats a definite little dance punctuated with crossings and dottings which delighted me in the hearing.

---

Charles's address is 28 Fort Square, Gloucester, Mass.

re. your bear dream. In *East of the Sun & West of the Moon*[1] there is a mixture of *Beauty and the Beast* and *Cupid & Psyche* in which the youngest daughter lives with an Eros–White Bear, another variation is in *The Lilac Fairy Book*—"The Brown Bear of Norway."[2]

I always think of another story in Grimms, "Bearskin," where the hero really grows into a bear-like creature.

Did Warren tell you that I have prospects of returning to Vancouver next summer (same summer session) to do a play? It will be the first chance I've had since Black Mountain 1956 to work with a theater. Those taking the course will be the cast and "witnesses" or "attendants" while I project from the first scratch the play. Given the possibility, I find I have a crowd of ideas—and, better than ideas, a dim impulsive company that would like to have their lives, already haunting me as I go.

Whilest I've been reading and dozing, Jess has turnd out illustrations for Helen's *San Francisco's Burning*. Did you get the flyer for it in Vancouver? Or was that after you left? Well, anyway, I'll include another. I'm afraid that when you go back to the city in October you may have the Virginia Admiral affair still unsettled. She's not written a word nor sent a drawing since the letter you wrote "at her dictation" and the drawings you rescued. Amen. But then, since I am going to be in New York it looks like next April-May— maybe we can face it down then. What an unpleasant business! Jess just groans when he thinks of it at all.

Thanks a lot for the Ammons letter quoting Kenner. And the copy of the marriage bed poem by Barbara Moraff.

Somehow, in between these paragraphs I got the morning dishes done up, and now here Jess has lunch on the table and it's time to close.

love
Robert

Dear Denise—

I cant seem to sit up to a sustained letter yet but want especially to add here my love and say how wonderful it was to be with you in Vancouver this summer. I'm just recoverd sort of from flu. And horrid V. A. hasnt written even a receipt of the final contract attempt I sent in July! She shld at least send back the autographs Helen & I had witnessd on the forms. Well, well!

Jess

dear Denny,

Perhaps to[1] celebrate your second appointment as *Nation* Poetry editor, last nite—at last! For it has been in the works for a month—I got this 5th Sonnet right.

Right now, having seen the day's paper with the news of the Sunday school bombing in the South I am too shaken with rage or the grief of it to recover myself.[2]

If you want to use the Sonnet, it's yours of course.

love
Robert

304

Sept. 16, 1963
{San Francisco}

Jess, I will return to the attack on Virginia early in November. Don't worry about it, I mean not about its being a nuisance me. It is, but I feel fully involved and I *want* to do it.

Dear Robert,

The 5th sonnet is beautiful & I am honored to have it for *The Nation*. Thank you.

We took Nik to school[1]—it was a lovely crisp autumn day, sunny, & we left him in a cheerful mood riding his bike from the (small, 4-boy) dormitory back to the main buildings with his "student advisor," a very nice boy, a senior. But that was a week ago & I'm on edge wondering how he's liking it—the new people, early rising, hard work, etc. etc. It's quiet here—we look at each other with a sober smile, conscious of being cut off from our child.

Tell me if you liked "Earth Psalm."

I hope Jess is really better from the flu. Mitch had a sort of faint, that is he jumped up suddenly in the middle of the night, perhaps from a dream, tense anyway, & fell his full length, on his back—& he's had a stiff neck ever since having strained some muscles as he fell.

Please send me the Burton's address.

Finished the Edson job last night.

Farmington Fair is on, we have gone several times—we like to see the ox-pulling, & the animals in their barns (oxen, cows, calves, sheep, drafthorses)—& the great Grange displays of the fruits of the earth—

305

September 20th {1963}
Temple Maine

wonderful squash of all kinds especially. Today we may go in to the sulky racing for a while.

Had a good letter from Bob.

Love—

Denny

Will be getting tape recorder early in November. How do I get those tapes—from you or from Fred Wah? If from you, let me know cost. I did send you that $5 didn't I? And the photo of our hse.?

---

## 306

October 16th {19}63
Temple {Me.}

Dear Robert & Jess,

So glad to get your letters. The Peacock show must indeed have been wonderful—even the peacock's feather of the announcement is.[1] The announcement was a bit of a mystery as I could not decipher a little message & signature on the back—until M. said "It says *Robin.*" What is Robin's part in it? Could it be that he has started a gallery? Just read an awfully good George MacDonald Scotch novel, *Alec Forbes of Howglen.*

And what good news about Virginia. Well now at least you have a legal contract, & I think if anything will get Virginia moving that's it; after all she does run a business, & quite successfully, so she is not totally invertebrate, obviously. But I'd like her a lot better if she were wriggly-floppy in her business & vertebrate with her friends, instead of the other way round . . .

How can I get a copy of *San Francisco's Burning*? (Wd. like to *buy* it (or several{)}, if not expensive). Who is Jim Alexander?

The preface to Helen's book is magnificent.[2] And so *useful,* so apposite to all one's thinking about poetry, that it puts me in a sort of delirium, an enthusiastic seizure where I get up, twirl on one toe, snatch up and embrace & replace the sleeping cat (who immediately returns to his sleep)—sneeze—and sitting down but slightly sobered, clasp my hands and take again my vows to the art. (That says ART, not ANT.)

The prospect of the New School lectures is a wonderful one too—even though, alas, I would miss the May lectures as we have long since given each other a solemn compact to come up here in the first week of May, for various good reasons I won't trouble you with. But it would anyway mean that we'd see you, all during April, and hear the first 4, & get tapes of the second 4. And it would work in so well with the April 16th date Betty Kray wants to arrange for us, wouldn't it. Let me know as soon as you hear, wont you. As soon as that's fixed we can perhaps begin to give some further thought to the form of that occasion?

Have had 2 marvellous new poems from Bob—"For Leslie" and "The Messengers";[3] & Charles has given permission for me to use that blue monster (but I'm waiting now for him to send a title). As well as some other miscellaneous poets. So I think I'll get off to a good start.

We plan definitely to buy a 4-track like yours, probably a Sony. Let me know the cost of the tapes. And can I get any of those morning sessions I wonder. From Wah? I'll write to him c/o Bob . . . There must have been good things said, along with all that hot air. And I'd especially like to hear the different readings of W C W, the last Monday morning, before I left. What I want *most* is your lecture though. My notes went round & round (a spiral) both sides of a tiny scrap of paper (as I was afraid of crackling & annoying my neighbors—tho' Philip Whalen was one neighbor I'd have been glad to annoy at that point—but any way I didn't want him & Allen looking at what I was writing{)}. So when I came to write them up in my notebook I found a good deal had disappeared. . . .

We went to see Nik for the Columbus Day weekend. He is happy, thank god. We caught a glimpse of him laughing with another kid before he saw us. And talking with him we got a clear sense of his appreciating the place & making himself, week by week, more at home there. Of course he has a few worries, like finding time to get all the reading done, & he finds the *Review* he got himself onto the staff of is not a lit. mag., which he wanted, but a newspaper, & wants to switch, either to the Magazine or to an "introduction to architecture" which is another "evening activity." But these are details. The place is in fabulous country & as his chosen sport is bicycling he already knows quite a few of the back roads & their farms & orchards & old burying-grounds. A stirring performance of *Noah's Fludde* was part of the Harvest Festival. Hated to part from him—but not because I felt worried about him, just because he's so nice.

I wrote a poem called "October" which I don't think I've sent you—& now with most of the leaves gone I find it shd by rights be called "1st wk of October," the colors & form of the landscape so changed. The weather mild & beautiful, *clement* is the word I think. The woods loud with leaves underfoot, & otherwise so hushed.

Love—
Denny

Dear Robert

I feel terrible about not hearing from you for so long. Quite out of touch. Tonight M. & I were talking & I got out my notes on your lecture & we were reading them, sketchy tho' they are; & M. said why don't you write to him, so I am, though I had thought to just wait.

One night recently I dreamed about Jess; it was a coming-into-focus, an encounter, very good in feeling. We had seen not long before *Winter Light*,[1] which certainly confirmed for me all that you & Jess had said on behalf, as it were, of Ingmar Bergman & made me all the more eager to see again the films I had misread and to see those I've missed altogether.

We have a wonderful new cat or kitten (4 months, male)—Muzio Clementi, a ginger Persian. He made me make all these smudges.

I've 2 new poems you've not seen, "Seedtime" and "A Psalm Praising the Hair of Man's Body."[2] And one in the works, I think.

I imagine you're hung up on the Olson introduction; but please send a note soon, a postcard even.

> Love from
> Denny.

P.S.

I've been pretty busy since we got back, reading 100000000 MSS, for *Nation*, Wesleyan, etc. So far I have been borne up by my unquenchable curiosity & the thought that it is paying for Nik at Putney but it may be I'll feel after some months as if I were being smothered. However it hasn't made me unable to write, & live my thoughts & feelings, so far.

I have a beautiful new winter coat. It's red & has a cape (like your Spanish highwayman's coat, but detatchable). It only cost $50 and looks like a Paris model. I've not even taken the price tag off yet. Love—D.

P.S.

What news of New School? Leroi said to me N. Sch. Deans for their part wanted you. I'd like v. much to have confirmation of April 16th date for Guggenheim reading as I have possibility of $300 reading + (3 day visit) at Drew U. in N. Jersey around that time & can't decide anything till I know. Betty Kray says she has not had definite confirmation from you, is waiting to hear from you.

## 308

Nov. 19, 1963
{San Francisco}

Dear Denny,

First some news notes, then I want to make a start at recalling phases in my reading your work, towards our April reading.

Scribner's has (last week) said yes to publishing *Windings*, with their suggestion that the Halloween masque not be included (to which I assented:[1] it *does* seem to me that it will be more properly presented in a private edition). Their second query was that they wanted a book at least as large as Bob's—could I do a selection? Since then, Donald Allen when he was in New York negotiated for me the shifting of *Roots and Branches* from

Grove to Scribner's, to combine the two into one volume.[2] All round (since *Windings* is uneven compared to *Roots*) an improvement for me. I'll keep the title *Roots and Branches* and close the volume with "The Continent."

Still in possibility is that Scribner's might want to do a decade volume: *Letters, The Opening of the Field* and the new work.

No word at all from the New School, I am proceeding with the chance that the lecture series may yet come thru. Shifting reading engagements to late March and early April, so [read straight thru and then reverse] that I could make them en route. Nothing from Betty Kray so far about other readings.

On my own I've rounded up (or in the case of Bard, been rounded up by) Bard and the State University at Buffalo (thru Mac Hammond) for sure; and had word from Bernard Waldrop that he is hopeful for Wayne University in Detroit and Ann Arbor.[3]

---

It's with "The Shifting" in the same issue that my work first appeard in *Origin* (summer 1952) that I start.[4] I had been studying Mallarmé, looking for a form that might be like clouds or fumes, having strands, the inconclusive active in it. This poem of yours was what I had been wanting. I don't know if my "Salvages" pieces precede, were written at the same time, or follow. I think I remember feeling your voice present in the one calld "Lassitude" and am almost certain that "and a door blown open" and the imperative of your "Turn, turn!" haunted the "Sweep. Sweep. O for a great mind/to beat the impatient air!" of that piece. (For instance: this "Turn, turn!" seems an entirely different utterance from the "Turn. Turn. Turn" of "The Venice Poem."{)} This poem still thrills me as if it were initial. It's that close. "Loyalty betrays," "change of pleasure" and "of golden cold sea" seem my own.

Yet I am sure it is here that I began to get the feel of the shift in lines, the movement of

> the shaded
> change of pleasure

which I had heard in William Carlos Williams but not felt as a way opening for me in form. Is that entirely true? Certainly in just those years I was fighting the battle for *Paterson*, where I knew at least here in the way this poem moved was the ardent cause. I never did forgive Madeline Gleason her dismissal of Williams (but it was also a dismissal of me in my adherence)— "I know you are excited by this poem, Robert, but do you really think anyone will be reading him ten years from now"—The break-thru of Charles' *In Cold Hell In Thicket* follows in 1953.

Hadn't Williams' poetry since 1948 been preparing the way, converting what I wanted of the poem? I sent *Medieval Scenes* to him when it was written in 1948, and then at his rebukes wrote "Domestic Scenes". . . . The thing is I had just that stubborn unawakend certainty that here I must learn my craft. Could I read "The Well Disciplined Bargeman" and "The Mind Hesitant" from *The Clouds* . . . ?

"The Fate Tales" and "Grace" had already brought Creeley into view— but my reading of them was in passing.[5] For there I have a date: it was late in 1954 when Jonathan Williams arrived that, reading "Grace" aloud, and reading thru "The Gold Diggers" I had any full sense of his voice. (Having Jonathan read Creeley's verse aloud came near destroying it there—but then I remember I must have had some sense of what the true voice was for I cringed at the readings—as with Jonathan's readings of Zukofsky—? but how confused years become. The readings I am thinking of where I cringed were in 1957 after the publication of *Some Time*. In 1954 I think Jonathan did give a distorted swing to Creeley's line.{)}

"Le Fou" is a primary poem of Creeley's for me (the movement away from itself at the end)—but when? I don't recall, did it come thru. There it is in *Origin* II. "The Crow" would be a second in order of appearance. But it is "The Crisis" (in such a misreading that I thought it was about not having a clean towel in the house or dirty towels) that for a long time was my phantom "Creeley" poem.

But back to recapture my sense of following your work in those years. "The Hands" summer 1953 relates to that first poem "Merritt Parkway" (but *when* did that appear?)*—with a new excitement in "Merritt Parkway" of traffic . . . By *Origin* XIV Autumn of 1954, we must have been in full correspondence. "In Obedience" recalls my asking who/where Mr. Despondency's daughter was and finding that there was more of Pilgrim's way than I had read.

* Black Mountain Review, 1954)

Reading thru these years now I especially like (tho I do not remember its impact then) "Xmas Trees on the Bank's Facade."

With *Origin* XVII Fall-Winter 1955–56 (I do recall how undependable these dates were . . . waiting in those years for *Origin* to appear—I bought it at the magazine stand) "An Innocent" I, II, and III opend a new phase in your work.[6] (I realize that in this period I must have been getting poems in typed copy from you, and not been entirely dependent upon publication)— These three all operate on a two-fold sight: where the cat and the scavenger are also the artist. The earlier poems had advanced ideas of the poem; now ideas of the poet emerge clearly. Was it Rilke? I wonderd. The poem "A Night" suggested that, but so did the scavenger II and III recall *The Notebooks of Malte Laurids Brigge*.

Now following thru my own poems, where I hear echoes of you or recall thinking of your work as I wrote. It's not in "For A Muse Meant" or not as wholly there as certainly it is in "Upon Taking Hold," where also I hear many recalls of Williams; "moves over the keys" must move in part from your poem "The Hands." The poem was "for Charles," but writing the last stanzas, from "This is the bunch of ranunculus" on I was eager with the sense of how you would respond, and "The joys of the household are fates that command us" had you as a member of its "us" (for your poetry like mine had taken a root in household things. (It strikes me now how much Bob's does too—but not the joys) "traffics" etc. in the Adam,[7] but not the conception of the poem itself, is your "Merritt Parkway" or perhaps also Williams, somewhere. "Source" I remember as particularly being a speaking to you. When was "Something to Wear" written? It reaches forward to the knitter in "With Eyes At The Back of Our Heads." It was "Mrs. Cobweb"—W. C. W. had pointed to it—that establishd the Imagination proper. "Scenes from the Life of the Peppertrees" is the great one for me in this order, and" The Rabbits."[8]

And then, close to these come fulfillments of the earlier poems—"A Stir in the Air" (where "The Shifting" and "Hands" ripen), and "The Sharks," "Lonely Man."

With these "Illustrious Ancestors" pointing to or preluding (as it happens in *Overland to the Islands*) "Broken Glass."

When I come to these poems I enter a reading of your work that is still contemporary. This whole time in Mexico is crowded with poems that retain their life entire and deepen for me. What do you especially remember? I askd Jess just now—the dog one. What dog one?—it was "Overland to the Islands."[9] And "The Pepper Trees," of course. The knitting the sleeves one[10] and the Moon. No, the one about taking the Moon along!—That would be "The Departure."

"With Eyes at the Back of Our Heads" and "The Departure" I relate to a further phase for me as reader. It was poems like "With Eyes at the Back of Our Heads," "The Dead," "A Ring of Changes," "The Goddess," "Relative Figures Reappear," "The Park" and reading on here I see that "Notes of A Scale" tells much of what was (is) going on—you remember I thot you were being initiated in dreams or into dreaming (and at the same time there were poems of Bob's that seemd to be dreams or initiation poems)—what I had longd to experience in my own work was appearing in both of yours— "A Form of Women," "They Say," "The Three Ladies," "The Hero."[11]

---

The mail just arrived—with your letter, and into the envelope with a hairy male stamp[12] goes the above to bring word to you after so long. No news from the New School. I sent off a confirmation to Betty Kray for the April 16 reading/

Love
Robert

## 309

Dec. 31st {1963}
277 Greenwich St
N.Y. 7 N.Y.

For the New Year I wish you and Jess Peace, Health, Joy, Poems, Paintings, Leisure, Quiet, Laughter, Love, & Dreams.

Dear Robert

It's ages since I got your good letter so soon after wistfully longing for one. I've been overworking, am rather tired, & anxious too because my sister in England is very ill. I may go over there, by myself, for 10 days or so. It depends, partly on whether Mitch can arrange a plane ticket, partly on what we next hear from Harry.[1] Olga had a very severe cancer operation back in the summer; this is a complication, not a recurrence, or so they say. She is 49.

You know, you had never before told me that "Sources"[2] was, in a way, for me, which makes it all the more important to me that, without your having said it, just that, just what "Sources" is saying, is the very core of what I've learned, or been given, from you. Before yr. last letter came I'd been writing some notes for myself for/towards the April reading: . . . [3]

hard to name individual poems because the influence so pervasive. The emphasis on incorporating all the ramifications of a process in the "final" work, not arriving at a "finished product" by a refining-out based on "good taste."

"*Words not counters but powers.*"

The re-entry into my life of the magic, the "romantic," which (under En's {Potter} Bauhaus influence & then W. C. W.'s "the poem is a machine" etc., & Creeley/Pound emphasis on a kind of economy—all of which were necessary for me too, in learning to get beyond the vagueness of my early (English) poems) had been submerged.

. . . R. D. as exemplifying Olson's idea of "composition by field" (much more than Creeley, tho Bob had known Olson longer & perhaps better).

The kind of charity shown in the notes on poems by Harold Dull & Joanne Someone Robert showed me at Vancouver. So far from the charity that's a wooly liking everything & caring really for nothing. A charity based on the ability to discern, distinguish, many kinds of excellence & beauty.

The love of a river, of its flow, its energy, the truth of it, the *currents of language*. To allow, allow for, the "activity of the unconscious."

How much I needed that, to counteract the "Japanese General" in me (I'll explain that illusion—someday—it's a story I must write.)

I have to stop. Thank you for the offprint of *The Mabinogion* etc.[4] And the card. I'm so glad about Scribners. On the radio a 1917 piano work by Prokoviev is being played; it is very lovely; like Satie but Russian.

I enclose some poems—some you may have seen "October," "Seedtime," the "Hair" psalm?—others I know you haven't for they were written this month—the Agony poem most recently, Xmas Eve.[5] Not that I was feeling agonized on Xmas Eve, the poem just got written or at least finished then. Also something found among Mitch's forest-floor of scattered papers. With love to Jess. What news of Helen Adam *Ballads*?

With love from
Denny

Did you get the *Wonder Book*?[6]

P.S.

My book is going to the printers early in '64. It will be called *O Taste and See* and includes the story, "Say the Word" but "Face to Face," "Grief, have I denied thee?" & "Like Dogs in Mexico" would begin a new book, if in time they seem to stand up. I had to leave out one poem you said in Vancouver should stay in, "The Willows of Massachusetts," because *Old Sturbridge* (N. H. P.'s the adviser for which) paid me $50 for it but can't print it until later. It wasn't essential to the book so I don't care.

I have been reading *Dombey & Son* as my bed-time & insomnia book & enjoyed it so much. It is such *good* Dickens that I wonder it is so little read. What else? Oh, that exasperating T. E. Hulme essay on "Classicism."

We had a horrible encounter with John Berryman, he is an evil man. Yet some of his *Dream Songs* are real (black) poems. The twisting, wrenching, of grammar does seem to function there as a new music, doesn't it? Like for instance IV & V of those in the recent *Poetry* double issue?

He invited himself here—we received him—he came drunk, 2 hrs late, with young bug-eyed wife & old *P.*{artisan}*R.*{eview} (female) friend—came to mock, to insult—as it turned out—In the end I yelled at him & more or less threw him out—but at the door he grabs my hand, kisses it, tells me all is O.K.—as if *that* were all it took! It was an ugly scene but instructive. I guess.

Love,
Denny.

# PART THREE     1964–1968

Photograph of Denise Levertov by Rollie McKenna.

dear Denny,

Yes, the wonderful *Wonder Book* arrived in fine shape and has its proud place beside Walter Crane's *The Baby's Opera*, which must have been a book-to-look-at-while-mother-turns-the-pages because it has survived from my childhood in shape.[1]

I've never had the sense that I wld want to read T. E. Hulme. The poems Pound preserved showed definitely that the "image" chez Hulme was an illustrative device at the level of fancy—the sun as a red farmer's face O.K., but the way of it seemd to promise that Mr. Hulme wld. begin the creative imagination, any sense that the image was an intuition of the real. So . . . anyway, I've not read nor am going to read his essay on whatever. People who bring up Hulme in discussion of poetry have always been arguers.

And may I never have to face-to-face undergo Berryman. I have the same sense you have of the virtue of these black poems, they are twisted against themselves (it's the way consonant clusters become menacing), and *demented*{.} I underline the word because I think it is a mentality voiding itself. What is exhilarating is that the music is not contrived, not a manner or pose, but an actual seizure of "bile," evil. As Jess commented, there is so little spirit that we find ourselves celebrating evil spirit for the sake of the spiritual.* In poetry terms, so little music . . . etc. But now I go too far, for I did find the songs admirable, and that they express a twisted psyche but do not at all infect with twisted psyche. Berryman is known as an acute alcoholic, and the sickness itself is one of bile.

*the "spiritual" wld now be the spirited.

I'm in the midst of a commission for the *Voice of America* series—a half hour talk "on my poetry" which I hope to use to get across (in a half-hour?) the concept of the poem as a lasting event contributing to the human reality we call language—but I want to use a term that does not refer finally to the tongue alone.[2] Could I render *communication* free from its bourgeoise uses, as if it were an affair of the market place, and bring it back into its company with *commune, communion, to commune with, communicant, community* (and the hidden, unnamed term then "communism," etc. it's true sense of the common good) I would go on then, I *will* go on then to relate the first known communion in the lasting event of the cave paintings so that "language" (and then writing as a language) is seen as one among other poetries or makings—to make "real"—as those herds and animal persons have been brought into that "magic," made magic and having a magic not anticipated, of so lasting to speak thousands of years later.

Since the day after Christmas I have been at my notebook, sporadically at first, and then with the feeling of the Sun's return into the new year, since Wednesday each day. I do have a lone poem (Bromige says it is a "sonnet"

310

January 3/{19}64
{San Francisco}

again) from a month ago or so that I don't think I sent you. A poem of Bob's that he sent a week after I'd written it did verify for me the concern; I think I toucht upon a spring of my not "speaking" in this last half year. And how everything will conform to such a refusal! Or the pattern of things will shift and delays, waitings, disappointments come into the significant foreground. Thought of as a crisis of "conscience" and that in relation to poetry: I *am* apprehensive of my idolatry of the poem (as this morning waking I thought of my evocation of the poem as an intense ritual event comparable to the cave drawings—and thought then also of how interior withdrawn the sanctuary of the cave was. . . . This idolatry is what I think the Hassidic masters meant when they taught that one should not make, "carve" a poem [graven image]{)}.

Jess reading your new poems remembered a poem of Emily Dickinson's that he had memorized in adolescence. (#1243 in *The Complete Poems*)

Safe Despair it is that raves—
Agony is frugal.
Puts itself severe away
For its own perusal.

Garrisoned no Soul can be
In the Front of Trouble—
Love is one, not aggregate—
Nor is Dying double—

One of the mortal sins of Edith Sitwell is her contempt for Emily Dickinson. It casts a cold shadow of doubt in any reading of her serious poems.

About the title of that agony dog poem what about Agonía (both that the Mexican keys in and that the recall of Lorca's "agonía" fits) The unfitting of the reference to something happening is that agony has a deeper root than is indicated by whatever reawakens it in us. Your poem is not anyway about what happened but the agony itself.

Both of these poems "Grief Dismissed" and "Agonía"[3] are moving by their nature; grief for the loss of things and agony in deformity must underlie our urgency to raise a memorial in language and even to resurrect feeling. But in the lyric, though in my first readngs only the figure of the crippled dog and the begging agony took over, this morning I find, asking everything of the poem, that "to have eyes of kindness" leaves me unsure of what *kindness* means in the context. Is it friendly eyes the dog has? But I bring this up only on the chance that there may linger in your sight of friend dog Agony some just word here.

Have you noticed in the Grief poem, "Face to Face," and the "Psalm Praising Hair" the—is it Stuart?—mode? The refrain of the "Psalm," and then the echo refrains of have I denied thee? Denied thee.

and:

> of stone and velvet goes down,
> goes down.

As in the Grief poem, the attire of Sorrow and Summer evoke Tudor-Stuart masques and the french phrases too "Juno de sept ans"—the cloistral shadow, so that the "blue curtains at trailer windows framing/the cinder walks" flashes out vividly. In contrast is "Grief in the morning, washed/in coffee, crumbled to a dozen errands between busy fingers"

blurred? The blurring is a mode very characteristic of your work. (Where one washes "grief" in coffee, crumbles "grief" into errands and just beyond, morning coffee washing dishes crumbling toast between busy fingers fingers busy at? And errands (in order to be busy?) are all mulled, hurried into one, almost elided)

This is different from the reflection of one image in another—as in "trailer windows" the other meaning of trail reflects the swept shreds of clouds.

As in "Face to Face" "river of longing" or the above questioned "eyes of kindness," blur— Isn't it that *longing* or *kindness*, are affect and want either to be the core of the poem or mood but not merely asserted? Say "Face to Face" went:

> A nervous smile as gaze meets
> gaze over deep
> river—
> what place

The other possessives "air's curtain" and water's black glass (where things get into a mise en scène of windows and mirrors that brings Cocteau to mind: rideaux de l'air, les eaux et leur vitre noire. . . . ) the mixing of air, water, curtain, glass (and the suggestion of "window") illustrate the confusion of the plunge, but some actual curtain, glass and window seem lost in the process. And, just beyond, not clarified in the poem, that the longing for embrace, for each other is also longing to smash thru a window. (To let in air, to break thru the even transparent obstruction?) To be in touch, not only to see.

I think it's the preposition "of" and the possessive case that is one of the points at which to be wary. Pound's warning is apt here (in "A Retrospect"):

> Don't use such an expression as 'dim lands *of peace.*' It dulls the image. It mixes an abstraction with the concrete. It comes from the writer's not realizing that the natural object is always the *adequate* symbol.

The coffee, the crumbs, the washing (it comes to me now that "washed in coffee" might be simply dunked or soaked in coffee, as toast?) the errands, the busy fingers would gain in containing grief in the morning had they been as concrete, specific, as the costumes of Sorrow and Summer, the etched figures, the windy skies etc. Grief washed in coffee is nothing compared to "grief in the morning, the toast washed in coffee, crumbled between busy fingers, a dozen errands to do."[4]

or across cloistral shadow, insistent etc.

I don't know in what sense Eliot used the term, but what is involved here is an objective correlative. Wherever an image appears or reference to an image (as in "river of longing") the directive is to remember the object, the river itself,—for here the key or lock of the experience is. As in the dream, Freud's insistence that we remember the thing germinal to whatever abstraction. Williams' "No ideas but in things" and Plato's insistence that an idea is something *seen* insist upon the same directive. The articulate thing is not that toast confused with grief is washed in coffee but that toast washed in coffee becomes a ritual of grief. Just here, here and here, we realize in the poem Grief was enacting itself. (As grievous denial was enacting itself)—

Well, as you realize, these are imperatives for myself, morning incentives to "kindle the fire wood" as I find looking up the word: [L. *incentivus*, fr. *incinere*, to strike up or set the tune, fr. *in* + *canere*, to sing] got mixed with L. *incendere* to burn and once meant kindling.

Love,
Robert

## SUCH IS THE SICKNESS OF MANY A GOOD THING

Was he then Adam of the Burning Way?
hid away in the heat like wrath
    conceald in Love's face
or the seed, Eris in Eros,
    key and lock
of what I was? I could not speak
    the releasing
word. For into a dark
    matter he came
and askt me to say what
    I could not say. "I—"

All the flame in me stopt
    against my tongue.
My heart was a stone, a dumb
    unmanageable thing in me,
a darkness that stood athwart
    his need

for the enlightening, the
    "I love you" that has
only this one quick in time,
    this one start
when its moment is true.

Such is the sickness of many a good thing
that now into my life from long ago this
refusing to say I love you has bound
the weeping, the yielding, the
    yearning to be taken again,
into a knot, a waiting, a string

so taut it taunts the song,
it resists the touch. It grows dark
to draw down the lover's hand from its lightness
    to the underground.

(I thought that this referrd to my not being able to say "I love you" in scenes
with Ned, my first lover—but now typing it I see behind, before that scene
my refusing to cry at my father's death)


dear Denny & Mitch,

The rains that have brought floods north of us, here have brought a long
dreary period, colored glower that coincided with Christmas holidays this
year haunted by its being the time of my mother's death, not grief but an
oppression of mortality, of turning away from mortality and then an inertia
before it. In which the review of John's book (which has only gaind in my
heart in the time I've been with it) chokes all writing: every approach to
the review seems wrong. All the aspects of my own personal ambitions
crowd in and so far I've not been able to get straight on with the concern
for what the *Ace* is in the poetry I believe in.[1] The H. D. is now two months
off schedule, and until I get the Wieners done there seems no way out of
the bind.

Meanwhile I read, making my way in Boehme again, and recently a
pamphlet-book in the Library of Liberal Arts series of Novalis *Hymns to the
Night* and a Fairy Tale. Frye's study of Blake,[2] but that's a disappointment
for there's nothing in Frye that can rise above the level of the academic to
strike—!!! well, I will let Mr. Orlando's wet feet leave their mark,[3] for if I
begin all over again I will never get this off to you—

To tell you, at least, that we are all in good shape as far as health etc.
goes. Jess has just started work again after the Christmas holidays (and for
him the darkening of these rainy days is a direct hamper). He has been

## 311

January 6, 1964
{San Francisco}

selected by the Museum of Modern Art for a show of 14 American Collagists this coming summer.[4] So he had to get work off to them before the 1st of the year. Yesterday, at last, he had a couple of hours in the studio beginning on the new group of paintings in that long project of eighteen.

It's been a year withdrawn to the local scene—most of my work (outside of "The Fire") went to *Open Space* that has no distribution at all outside of the city. *Open Space* also publisht a beautiful sequence of sonnets by Ebbe Borregaard and an Odysseus-Penelope sequence by Joanne Kyger that were major events for me. Just at Christmas, Robin's *Moth Poems* came out.— We've just ten minutes more now before taking off for Marin County, we hope in between squalls of this storm that is expected to go on for the rest of the week.

There's one new poem dedicated to Kenneth Anger, an "Illustration" of a collage Jess did for his Christmas card—I'll send on soon.

love,
Robert

---

## 312

Jan. 6th {19}64
277 Greenwich St
N.Y. 7 N.Y.

Dear Robert

Thank you very much for your useful criticism. In "Face to Face" I will take up yr. suggestion & drop "of longing"—you might make the change on yr. copy if you will.

In the dog poem: Agonía is a good title & I'm ½ thinking of it; thank you; but on the whole I think I'll depart from my usual practice & call it by the first line, "Like Dogs in Mexico"—which is how I think of it. "Eyes of kindness" is "kindly/kind eyes" or "eyes showing a spirit of kindness" (not quite the same as "*friendly* eyes") but I don't like the sound of the 2 i's so close to each other (the "f" of "of" separates them more than the "ly" of "kindly"{)} & besides in "eyes of kindness" there's a sort of associative reference to the H Jamesian "eyes of a kindness"; meaning, of what a rare kindness . . . So in this case I am determined to stick to my "of" which is not of the "dim lands of peace" variety. [Also, it seems to me to be saying by implication, or as "understood," "*the*[1] eyes of kindness," i.e. the eyes a personified spirit of kindness wd. have.]

In the *grief* poem[2] what I mean is that grief, the sense of grief, the feeling, is washed away in the drinking of coffee, crumbled away [like toast] between the fingers (always busy with this & that, anything not to admit the presence of sorrow—& errands of the day are planned at the breakfast table . . . for the same reason, errands of distraction because this poem is about my pollyannaism, my stiff upper lip). What I may do to make it clearer is to say something like this:

> Grief in the morning, the
>     lump in the throat
> washed in coffee

—but no, that leaves one with the busy fingers and tho I could extend that to refer to grief as what on waking had been clenched in the hand (convulsively) that seems to me to give to this passage a too-involved portentousness. Perhaps then what I could do is simply add the word "away,"

> Always denial. Grief in the morning, washed
> away in coffee, crumbled to a dozen errands between
> busy fingers.

[Or perhaps "away" will go into line 1 of these 3—I have to listen over to it until I know{.}]

I am always somewhat bothered by the disturbance to the total sound-structure revisions make; but I guess this is absorbable.

There is just one thing in your letter that distresses me, & that is where you say that "blurring is a mode *very characteristic* of your work" (my underlining) but I daresay it is true so I must swallow it. Though maybe you don't mean it the way I'm taking it, after all there are many good paintings in which outlines are blurred, I've certainly never gone along with Blake's idea that everything must have a sort of knife-edge outline. But in the context of your admonishment (which I accept) to recall precision/no ideas but in things/keeping one's eye on the apple, the sense in which you use blurring doesn't seem *that* one, (the reflection of the actual atmospheric blurring in nature ((& not only *visible* nature but all nature including one's thoughts)){)} but the sense in which one uses it to say that something which *ought* to be clear *isn't*.

Of course, going back to EP's "the natural object is always the *adequate* symbol," in speaking of an abstraction like Grief I'm evidently doing some-thing he wd, or wd have at that time (any time, perhaps?) disapproved of. But that I cant help, or rather I don't care, because I'm not interested in adhering to anybody's rules at this point—for instance there've been several poems in which I've used thee & thine & otherwise departed from Bill {Williams}'s American Idiom—because I must. So in this poem, that has been a long time a-brewing, I *had* to use Grief, although I *could* have used natural-object objective-correlatives, i.e. alluded to Grief (or called up Grief) solely through speaking of the symptoms or manifestations. But my sense was of a presence *almost* personified, actually indwelling in the attributes. Thinking of it, the Isaiah/N. Testament phrase, "A man of sorrow, acquainted with grief, despised & rejected of men," comes to my mind; for so is Grief itself, often enough—which shd. be an acknowledged part of our lives like our shadows, like night—despised & rejected. Well, this reference is not in the poem & shd. not really have entered here. It suggests—far-off—another poem.

Do you think, though, that the additional word "away" there makes it work?

I hope so.

---

How amazing to think of the Voice of America inviting you. Weren't you startled? Something must have happened to them. I thought Frost & Sandburg (the hillbilly minstrel Sandburg laced with bits of Lincoln scholarship) were about their cup of tea. It's a funny thought—you know the image of the listener they have projected is of collective-farm personnel gathered in startled longing around their ancient radio set. The idea of this mechanized hayseed audience (if it exists) tuning into *you* is comical. I hope you'll send me a copy of the script, please.

Yes, you've got Berryman described just right, I believe.

---

There's just one thing in "Such is the Sickness of Many a Good Thing" that bothers me & it is such a silly one that I hesitate to mention it except that I think many English or ex-English readers might be similarly bothered. It's the word *underground*. Now, when this word is not thrown into isolated prominence it doesn't carry for me that London Transport association (you know, in London one speaks of "taking the Underground" as often as "taking the Tube"). If for instance one speaks of the underground kingdom of the gnomes, I don't think of the Tube at all. But here—because it is a noun and isolated—it's dreadful, but I do. I immediately pushed the thought away, but it had been there. Forgive me, there is nothing more painful than having something absurd pointed out in reference to something most serious; but what if others should have the same association? My suggestion is that you might switch it around thus:

> It grows dark
> to draw down to underground
> the lover's hand from its lightness

Or, I see now it is the "the" that does it; would it be possible to say, simply,

> "to draw down the lover's hand from its lightness to underground"?

I think it is true this is another "sonnet," it has the same basic form, something having to do not with the inner details of its structure metrically, but with a form I feel would need the terms of logic (syllogism) or algebra, of which I'm ignorant, to express; or which I *could* express in dance-gesture, I think.

I've done what I so rarely do & should do always or often, that is, indulge myself by sitting down right away to answer. Not an indulgence at all actually but a recognition of need. I'm still among the coffee-cups.

John Wieners was down from Milton for a few days. He & Joel Oppenheimer gave a reading. John's reading was beautiful. I've never liked Joel or his poems but on this occasion there was something clumsy but genuine that I did like.

I had a good letter from Ellen Tallman.

Thanks to Jess for drawing my attention to the Emily Dickinson poem. Mitch gave me the complete E. D. for Christmas. A few years ago you sent me some E D with the original punctuation & I didn't really like / understand it—the dashes, that is—but now I infinitely prefer the varied measures the dashes reveal, to the simply-comma'd versions punctuated by strangers.

Today we have to give our Persian Muzio Clementi a shampoo. He is so overeager that he gets things spilt on his head, & is such a careless grubby small-boy kitten that he doesnt bother to wash them off.

Wish you & Jess could see him while he's still a kitten.

Love from
Denny.

P.S.

I've made, thanks to your questioning, a more extensive revision of "Face to Face," which now reads:

> A nervous smile as gaze meets
> gaze across
> deep
> river.

space→)        ←(space)

> What place
> for a smile here;

>       it edges away

> leaves us each at ravine's edge
> alone with our bodies.

> We plunge—
> O dark river!
> towards each other

> into that element

a deep fall
the eyes closing as if forever,
the air ripping, the waters
cleaving & closing upon us.

Heavy we are, our flesh
of stone and velvet goes down,
goes down.

I think what you speak of as Stuart or Tudor is what I think of as a response that arises in me in rhythm & diction to a desire for some richness always loved, needed, & present embryonically (or rather, in inept youthful form) in my early poems (in *The Double Image*, see for example "Enter with riches" a sort of brocade poem about Death & his Bride, a girl I was very fond of who was threatened with T.B. at that time) (& in many later poems—e.g. "Song for a Dark Voice," etc)—or rather, not just needed but *felt* as a reality in life, but sort of kept out or under, as I came so strongly under Williams' influence for so long. I guess it's in "Earth Psalm" too, which you never mentioned, perhaps because you didn't like it, but which I think of as one of my best poems. It is a great danger, I know, to be too ornate or romantic, it can end in being just mushy, as I was at 19, 20, 21, *The Double Image* poems—but somehow I feel I'm old & experienced enough today to take that risk. The "Earth Psalm," for better or worse, was an absolutely necessary poem for me to write & I wd. be a hypocrite if I didn't let that side of me out of its captivity tho it be a Caliban.

**313**

Dear Denny,

What a beautiful job you did with "Face to Face," sharpening, so that there's a lovely pivot (that exact) in the verb "edges" I hadn't recognized in the earlier version. It's exhilarating to get these articulations that ring so right (I'm thinking of an experienced worker's hand going over the joints, fit to fit, of a cabinet). Even elaboration of detail when it's been workd with a testing hand and eye can emerge as necessary form—the *condensare* that Pound evokes in "How to Read."

I do see now the value "eyes of kindness" has in personification (without actually advancing the personification), and it suggests that someday that dog Kindness will have his (her) own poem. In the Grief poems "away" not only clarifies, but it rimes too—with a modulation from "betraying" thru "always," shifting stresses.

You are right about "Earth Psalm." If I did not write of the poem it was that I was shy of it (it still seems to come close in, and at the close the "dream-hill grass" toucht upon my dream of the hill of grass, walkd-over-my-grave feeling). Bringing it out this morning, rereading your letter with Jess and then finding out "To Death"—what a beautiful poem! I begin to conjure the Tudor, no Stuart (something between King James's Bible and Bunyan) dimension (a fourth dimensional of you) with figures from a masque. And the dog Kindness can dance on his hindlegs. Haven't we, where we have found a source, or some expression of what we love in human kind, to give it a place to live today, in our own gesture (which may then speak of nobility or ardour)—Well, if Orpheus can come forward, so by the work of the poem Death and His Bride in brocade—

How many correspondences there are between your *Double Image* (1946) and my *Medieval Scenes* written in 1947. In this poem "To Death"—"brocade of fantasy": in "The Banners" where the "bright, jerkins of a rich brocade" is part of the fabric of the spell; or in "The Conquerors" compare "The Kingdom of Jerusalem. . . . "

Was I unclear in my intent in speaking of this Stuart dimension? What I felt was the presence and potency of a real virtú: and now reading *The Double Image* these early poems I see how fitting it is.

> We've our business to attend Day's
>     duties, bend back the bow in dreams as we may,
> til the end rimes in the taut string
> with the sending.
>     Reveries are rivers and flow
> where the cold light gleams reflecting the
>     window upon the surface of the table;
> the pressd-glass creamer, the pewter sugar bowl,
>     the litter of coffee cups and saucers
> carnations painted growing upon whose
>     surfaces; the whole
>
> composition of surfaces leads into the other
>     current disturbing
> what I would take hold of. I'd
>
> been in the course of a letter, I am
> in the course of a letter to a friend
> who comes close in to my thought so that
> the day is hers, my hand writing
> in thought shakes in the currents, of air?
> of an inner anticipation of? ghostly
>     exhilarations in the thought of her
> at the extremity of this
>     design

"There is a connexion working in both directions, as in
    the bow and the lyre," only
in that swift fulfillment of the wish
    sleep
can illustrate my hand
    sweeps the string.
You stand behind the where-I-am.
The deep tones and shadows I will call a woman.
The quick high notes . . . you are a girl there too,
and I would play Orpheus for you again

recall the arrow or song
to the trembling daylight
from which its sprang.[1]

I'm a little shaky with this having happend here. You know I've thought
again and again in imagining my sonnet sequence of certain sonnets in
which I could speak of what loving you means. The poem doesn't say
"touch" but it has toucht me—maybe my admitting my being "shy"—
shying away as I do—left me unarmd—well, with love still shaking a bit,

Robert

## 314

Feb. 4th {19}64
277 Greenwich St
N.Y. 7 N.Y.

Dear Robert

That's a beautiful poem.

Thanks, for it & for the letter.

I'm going to send you a strange ballad[1] my sister (who almost died, but
is a little better now it seems, so that I'm not after all going to England at
present to see her) wrote. But I've mislaid it, so will send separately unless
it turns up this morning.

The Reznikoff/Zukofsky reading at the Guggenheim, introduced by
Kelly, was really great. Zukofsky was in amiable mood afterwards—
positively genial, indeed. "The Man in the Moon" & "The Shadow Song"
were especially beautiful—Even the Catullus bit was good, & in general I
really cannot take the Catullus because it sets my teeth on edge, *literally.*

I have a new poem which I'll type & put in with my sister's poem.

Betty Kray is truly trying very hard to work something out for you; she
has a good idea she's working on. Unfortunately she has no power on the
"Circuits" although she got them going in the first place. Her position
makes her look like a politician but in fact she's a most remarkable and
lovable person with no axe to grind.

When are you coming to N.Y., and are you giving those lectures at the
New School, and where do you plan to stay? Would you like to spend some

nights here? I don't think you would be happy & comfortable here for many days & nights at a stretch, & as you know, houseguests make Mitch nervous, but I hope you know too that we both will be very happy to have you for any odd nights—you did speak of staying in Long Island I think? & you may want not to go all the way out there some nights, & so on. I hope you don't think this is an inhospitable way to put it—it's just that, even aside from Mitch's peculiarities, I have to acknowledge that I'm not a good house-keeper & therefore not a good hostess! I do best on the most spontaneous occasions. . . . (As a matter of fact, I don't think anyone in N.Y., or the E. generally, is as good at making people comfortable & happy as most people on the W. Coast, but especially you & Jess & friends.) (It has a good deal to do with the more leisurely pace of life in the W., which I'm always very conscious of.)

Monday night I read at the 5-Spot with Diane di Prima—she was very good. We went to her house afterwards, it is an amazing place, with all sorts of people doing all sorts of esoteric things all over it—I mean, rehearsing a play in one room & mimeographing strange poems in another, etc. Also, babies everywhere—Diane's (one of whom is Leroi {Jones}'s) and Nik Cernovitch's (who has a beautiful dark-eyed wife), etc. She's a sort of 1-man (woman) avant-garde, or the hub of it anyway—& looks like a 16-year old schoolgirl, with pigtails.

I liked her.

I have to stop now. Oh, Dartmouth invited me to read with Charles on the 20th—I hope he has accepted—*I* have, despite lowish fee, as it should be a nice wild occasion.

Love to Jess.
Love to you.
Denny.

Dear Robert

Your lovely present came. What a beautiful thing to do, to prepare the H. D. poem like that. The sort of thing I wd like to do but never get around to. Thank you. And I'm writing to Jess to thank him for the "Brothers." I presume he is not coming on this long trip?

I don't even know when you're getting here—please let me know, & how long you'll be in/around N.Y. Bob will sleep here the night of the reading, would you like to also? One cd. sleep in Nik's room, one on couch in front room.

Enclosed is a list of poems (obviously too many, alas) *I'd* like you to read. When I discussed it with Bob it seemed to work out best like this: We'll sit round a table. I'll make a short introductory introduction. Bob will read

## 315

Last of March {19}64
277 Greenwich
RE-2-3197
{New York}

first. Then me. Then you. We shd each figure on ½ hr's reading—no intermission—that is, no big intermission with people wandering out of the room. Since your poems are in general longer than mine or Bob's, your reading last will give you scope to read longer than ½ hr if you feel the audience has stamina. Each of us can talk as long as he likes during his section, (remembering though that if there's *very* much talking there won't be many poems read). And if we can get warmed up enough there may be spontaneous questions we'll want to ask each other, too. But in case we *don't* get warmed up, I think the form I've suggested gives us a way to do the reading in any case.

*Choice of poems*:

We thought if we each gave each other a list like these we could use them as a basis. I'd say that where each 2 lists (for you: mine & Bob's, that is) overlap, you might try to definitely include the poems we *both* ask for, as a start. Then, each poet, besides the poems that the other 2 want him to read, may have poems he (she) knows were influenced or specially connected with one of them, & so wd wish to include. (Though I think it wd be more those "technically" connected than "emotionally," the latter connections are too private for such an occasion maybe—at least, I think I wd not read "Homage" maybe—though I suppose I could, too . . . But that's not important.) Plus very new poems. You already mentioned some of mine & I know which they are but if you have time, you might make me a regular list. I've gone & left all this to the last moment but maybe it's just as well. I think since I *live* in N.Y. I'll make my reading shorter, 20 minutes say, to give you & Bob more time—OK?

Hope your readings will go very well & that you wont be too tired when you get to N.Y. I tried (a while ago) to get Vassar and St. Louis (Geo. Wash. & St. L.U.) readings for you but dates don't work out—sorry.

Nik just returned to Putney after 2-week vacation. We are to visit him (a parents' weekend) around the 20th. If you're going to be in N.Y. at that time you might like to have this apt., to yourself, for the 3 days we'll be gone.

With love—
Denny

Poems I'd like Robert to read at Gugg. reading:

Any of *The Berkeley Poems*
    The Cavalcanti variations ("I Tell of Love")
    There wouldn't be time to read the whole "Venice poem" & it wd seem
        mutilated if read in part?
    "Revival"
    "The Construction" (from *Caesar's Gate*)

*A Book of Resemblances*:
   "Eluard's Death"
   "Africa Revisited"
   Sections from "En Essay at War"
   "This Is The Poem They Are Praising As Loaded"
   "A Dream of the End of the World"
   "Conversion"
   "Salvages: An Evening Piece"
   "Love Poem" ("Because I have been in the service of love")
   "Salvages: Lassitude"
   "The Fear that Precedes Changes of Heaven"

*Letters*:
   "An A Muse Meant"
   "Upon Taking Hold"
   "Light Song"
   "True to Life"
   "Words Open Out Upon Grief"
   "The Human Communion, Traces"
   "Brought to Love"
   "Correspondences"
   "Source"

From *The Opening of the Field*:
   "Often I Am Permitted"
   "The Dancer"
   "A Poem Slow Beginning"
   "Structure of Rhyme" III, VI, VII
   "The Ballad of the Enamourd Mage"
   "The Propositions"
   "Crosses of Harmony & Disharmony"
   "A Poem of Despondencies"
   "Poetry, A Natural Thing"
   "Keeping the Rhyme"
   "The Question"
   "Yes, As A Look Springs to Its Face" (I & II)
   (No time for "Pindar" poem perhaps—which is more often read than
      some others)
   "A Storm of White"
   "The Natural Doctrine"
   "Structure of Rhyme" XII and XIII
   "After Reading Barely & Widely"
   "Food for Fire, Food for Thought"

"Roots & Branches" ("Sail, Monarchs")
"What Do I Know of the Old Love"
"Nel Mezzo Del Cammine di Nostra Vita . . . "
"A Dancing Concerning A Form of Women"
"2 Dicta of Wm. Blake"
"Come, Let Me Free Myself"
"4 Songs the Night Nurse Sang"
"Shelley's 'Arethusa' Set to New Measures"
"A Set of Romantic Hymns"
"The Sonnets"
"Such is the Sickness of Many a Good Thing"
"Bending the Bow"

(It seems to me that there are typescripts I can't find that wd be from after the "Arethusa" & before the "Sonnets"—?)

---

**316**

April 9/{19}64
{Ann Arbor, Mich.}

dear Denny,

I'm planning on arriving in New York the 14th and as soon (that would be tomorrow, when I have the money from the reading here in Ann Arbor) as I book flight I will send you when for sure. And will be staying at Diane and Alan Marlowe's—at least that was the invitation.

The night of the reading I certainly wld like to stay at your place. That would make a full celebration of it.

And about possibly having your apartment for the weekend you and Mitch will be at Putney that would be great. As I think I wrote, I've got an open invitation to stay at the Wenning's in New Haven, and I'll be going there as soon as I can (with that weekend of the 20th coming up right after the 16th—I guess it will be following that. . . . And Seon {Givens} Manley has reiterated their invitation to Bellport (where she is "lying-in" a pregnancy, and writing a book on literary movements of our times). I sort of hope to get another section done on the H. D. Book.

You will have heard by now that Betty Olson was killd in a car wreck at the beginning of last week.[1] Charles seems to bear up remarkably—I will be back in Buffalo Sunday and have another day to see him before I come on to New York.

Now Bernard Waldrop has arrived to take me to a Hopwood tea and then dinner. If the note is groggy twas writ during nap hours. Perchance to dream etc. With love. And we *will* have a good reading.

Robert

Dear Denny/

Here is the manuscript of Duerden's book—the copy of which I lost en route to New York. Poems from the "Spring Light" section were among the first I heard when I returned to San Francisco in 1956. They seemd so much a music that I did not imagine them being printed, but as Rick sounded them: the "wish," "thing," "listen" of "Music 1" lighting upon the air in phrases that his thought—of wishing to slow down the passage of time, of longing after the fast moving-on-kept. As "Poem: completely naked" incorporates the body's movement and the being toucht in moving (as in your poem "A Stir in the Air," walking around the reader creates a wavering in his attention, in the room and in the poem then). The changes of Duerden's first poems here are fine, as in "Bee: Flowers,"

> . . . hinged
> so delicate they are
> the light comes thru them

What he's done is to find the shape of his book, of his poetry; and that's given him the twin sections of the first period—"Spring Light" and "Lit By the Moon." The "in warning" of the latter going back (1955) of the "music" (1956) with which he begins.

If he has addresst the book to me ("Man, & Poet" he puts it; and in an earlier version had included also "Mentor & Friend"), he has so cared in his work to awaken the life he cares for, the edge of feeling, he gives me measure in this book as he has made it—"Man, & Poet" challenges in its recognition, for what he recognizes is my responsibility.

Look at the two versions of "Right Now," for his demonstration of what form does and means in doing; his movement—line and phrase within the line—demanding and rewarding attention.

It's in "Poems 1958–1961" that, given the music, given the moon's warning in the blood, the light of the song (light as consciousness (con-science) in light of which the poet sees his work. What he calls "event" poems appear now—"In Spite of It All," "The Sonata," or "All In A Day's Work." His humor ("Mr. Boswell & Dr. Johnson") enters in. More and more elements of the man are allowd to play their part in the poet. In the decade that this book covers, from 1955 to 1964, Duerden has shaped a poetry in its maturity. The earliest poem "3 AM Black" is a ripend poem— it may be the first showing of what was mature, but he began there—and what happens in the book is that that mature poetic awareness expands, deepens, grows. Best of all, it is bold and joyous to take over new areas of experience, risky areas of experience, in its maturity.

Which in turn establish new entities of the poem. His "event" poems arise from this make it new where before we had dramatic monologues. As he renewd the Lawrencian poem of the man's mysteries where the man and the woman are married. The mysteries the man and the woman have together in the poet's imagination. And declared his will to love there, his celebration and obedience in love, his solitude and his humor and play in love. Day and night are enlivened thereby.

Duerden is a man wedded to his life, to life itself, to the world and the woman—having that creative will that we recognize in marriage—a marriage that is joyous, as song is; that must contain its warning in the ring one gives and receives; that needs conscience, needs the break of humor then; needs the sense of the sacred; needs recall of moon and of sun:

> me moving in its field,
> the homage exacted out of doors:
> sweat beads running down my sides—

needs . . . but Duerden says it best, most concisely: "They are, all of them, responses."

This letter turnd into a kind of "Preface" to a book that so clearly does not need a preface, and certainly not for your reading . . . but it did make a way for my reading the book again intensively, and raising some picture of it again in my mind. This book of Duerden's—and the also ten-year postponed book of Robin's—like Stevens' *Harmonium* start with a matured art: and ought to have the entry of an establishd publisher. Tho one despairs of Lamont prizes—they do stand above most first volumes, (I think of my own—where so much is unrealized).

As you can imagine, many letters to catch up with but I wanted to get this ms off post haste to you, with Norton in mind. . . .

love
Robert

---

## 318

June 14th {19}64
Temple, Maine

Dearest Robert

It was a pleasure that the 1st communication from you was that generous & beautiful letter about Duerden's poems. On the other hand I came to read them when they arrived (over a week later) with mixed feelings—of anxiety lest I *shouldn't* find myself liking what you so believed in; & of resistance, almost resentment, because I felt I was being pressured, pushed, put on a spot. . . .

Now I've read (once, quickly) through the MSS all that is gone—it *is* a beautiful book and I do think I would have responded even if I'd come to it cold—I couldn't not have. There are 1 or 2 poems that seem not up to the rest, perhaps, & some lines unclear to me, & such details, about which I'll be writing him when I've gone through the MS again carefully; but as a whole I'll certainly back it with conviction, joyfully. Amen. You can (please) show him this letter because I'm not ready to write him yet.

I also got Barbara Guest's MS which is *not* a pleasure—I like a few poems of hers but I have never felt confident in her work as a whole. She has a direct line to her unconscious a lot of the time, which means she gets a welling-up of beautiful (or striking) images, but she has no driving force of deep feeling so they aren't really coming from a deep level, and she has no intelligence to coordinate, interpret, apperceive. I haven't written to her yet as I've not really read her MSS but I know her work & am sure I will not want to keep it. *Don't* sic anyone else onto me now, for god's sake!—3 or 4 books a year is what Norton will do,[1] my contract with them is for a trial year, & I have at least 4 years' books lined up in mind as it is—so if you have any ideas, propose them *to me* but *don't* encourage people to send me books. Thanks.

Listen, what's the status of Jess's Morgenstern at present? Norton does also want to do translations (not poetry particularly) etc (I have proposed a reasonably priced Golding's Ovid, & Stifter's novellas—though this line is out of my province as contracted) & it is *possible* I cd interest them in that. Jacobsohn is German which cd. be good or bad—i.e., people who know the original from their youth are *never* satisfied with any translation, you know how it is—I mean, those who know & *feel* the original language better than they'll ever know & feel English. But I can try, anyway, if it is still floating around—it *MUST* be published! Especially now that those terrible other versions have appeared. . . .

It's paradise here; Nik came home yesterday; Mitch has built a little house up the field well away from the house, to work in; & I now have a really good room for my work room—the one he has vacated. I have some new poems which I hope to type up & send you *soon*. We have had lilac, lilies of the valley, violets; now have irises, yellow lilies, lupins, snowball-bush, columbines of many shades.

Love to Jess & to you from
Denny.

P.S.

The Loewinso{h}ns were here for 2 days & are now heading back to SF. They'll be able to describe the place to you.

dear Denny,

I'm glad the Duerden book survived my getting carried away with my second reading thru. I shld have withheld the letter after writing it, but it's turnd out O.K. I think I see Barbara Guest pretty much the same way you

## 319

June 18/{19}64
{San Francisco}

do. I *did* make it clear to her that you were doing only four books at the most a year and that I had the impression you probably had yr first year in mind ahead. . . . Your instructions re any future ms have been taken to heart.

The page proofs of *Roots and Branches* got off to Scribner's Tuesday this week (174 pages), and the book has been announced, I understand, for September. Second great news it that Scribner's took an option on the H. D. book (after reading the six chapters of Part I) and I have agreed on February 1965 for the delivery time of the finisht book. So I am back at work, and slow going (I'd stopt because I had reacht a snarld stretch of that Day Book). The way I envision it now does involve rewriting of sections involving argument and definition. So that in sections there will be overlay, a geological stratification: and allowance for new impulses that may arise.

From the unpublishd works of H. D.'s, I did gather a perspective on the extent of problems that I had felt present in the publisht works. Both the *persona* and the *image* involve reality: H. D. in breakdown periods sufferd from splits in personality (so that she lost the truth of what was felt within; the inner *being* passd like a single eye among Grey Sisters) and from hallucinations (so that she lost the trust of what was presented.{)} Plagued by questions of was it really there? did I really see it? Did it really happen.

In one work, where she is giving an account of a serious period of illness, she had written in after reading the typescript where she had been trying to give an account of the injury she had sufferd from Aldington's desertion *"But this never happened. Surely this was fantasy."* . . .

•

The concept of writing passages has opend a way for new poems / as enclosed. There shld be, needs be—to free the concept, prose passages.

At Wenning's I got a copy of *Spring and All*, and from Phoenix *Exile 4* which has "Descent To Winter" in their proper forms. Encouraging too, in their witness that some days Williams had only a sentence, as in "The Descent of Winter" (to correct that title from above) "$^{10}/_{13}$ a beard . . . not of stone but particular hairs purpleblack . . . lies upon his stale breast"

Jess is in the long process of the fifth canvas towards his show-to-be. Often working ten hours a day, he has been on the canvas since April.[1] With challenges of painting water and fire, and elaborate chemical apparatus.

love
Robert


**320**

June 20th {19}64
Temple, Maine

Dearest Robert and Jess,

I was amazed this morning to receive the enclosed from Wesleyan.[1] I had supposed Scribners would do all your books. Please tell me in a hurry if Wesleyan is what you really want for this one, i.e. (1) the meeting is on July

8th, (2) wd. you not sooner I tried Norton? Mitch says, "But Norton will not want to be in competition with Scribners, i.e. they will say, *This is the old stuff, & his new poems he gives to Scribners.* He may be right. Shall I do this: push it as hard as poss. at Wesleyan & if they say no, then try it at Norton? The trouble is, I have so many ideas for Norton so that if I wait until finding out if Wesleyan wd. do it the "places" for the next 2 yrs wd. be filled at Norton, unless I kept everything (everybody else) hanging until then. It is a predicament. If I had only known, I'd have suggested trying Norton first, & *then* Wesleyan. Why on earth didn't you ask me, since I'm involved anyway? Surely you know I would always be happy to have the opportunity to do anything at all for you! Anyway please let me know whether you think Mitch's prediction is probably right about Norton's reaction to a book of that date if they aren't to get recent & future work too; and whether, if you think it shd. be tried at Norton's anyway, you want (on some pretext) to withdraw the MS from Wesleyan & have me present it at Norton first. The pretext would have to be one (like "for rearrangement, revision" or something) which wd permit of its being sent back then (to W. U.) later if necessary.

Barbara Guest's poems turn out to be a lot better than I expected, on the whole. Much less chic & flip, much more felt-through. That's a predicament too. I'm going to have to tell her (probably) "yes, if she's prepared for a long wait." These plots are beginning to thicken altogether too much—however, so far I'm still breathing—if you like my new poems, "the Olga poems,"[2] I'll feel like I can manage—no, I won't make it sound dependent like that, the fact is I *don't* feel my life as a poet is threatened, *even though* I *worry* so about these publishing-type things I've gotten mixed up in. God knows I didn't seek them out, they came *at* me. I could have said no, it's true: but I have a compulsion to meet challenges, I suppose. *For every such thing I've turned down, in the last 2 years, 2 others have sprung up—like dragon's teeth.* So that I feel it must be a part of my life, fate, not to be evaded. Or are they temptations sent by the devil? At the same time I feel, here & now, creative & alive, not drained by extraneous[3]

dear Denny,

Right off: about the book sent to {Willard A.} Lockwood at Wesleyan. This is the first book of *Book of Resemblances* (as plannd for Auerhahn); the whole special project being to get it done, as we want it, with Jess's illustrations. And we did have the lead that Lockwood was interested in doing an illustrated book. This will be under very special conditions: as discusst with Willard, we will forgo certain royalties in order for me to retain secondary rights (this is because I want to be able to reject anthologys); the

## 321

June 23/{19}64
{San Francisco}

main thing is that I've got to get *Book of Resemblances* publisht before I will be clear for a *Collected Poems 1942–1952* volume with Scribner's (say, in 1966). The contents (as you will see) goes thru the "Essay at War."

So: it wld not do *at all* for Norton. Did I write that Scribner's has taken an option on the H. D. book? {Donald} Hutter there is most certainly backing my work now, and I consider myself a Scribner's author.

Mitch is certainly right in relation to Norton; where, as I see it, the important thing will be to build up a solid core (as Creeley and I would want another core at Scribner's) of "Norton" authors. I've taken it for granted that Scribner's would not be interested in *Book of Resemblances* with illustrations. But if it fell thru at Wesleyan, I will try to do it ourselves perhaps. The whole thing at Wesleyan is that if Lockwood can get clearance (and here I think the decision of the press board is what will count, for it won't be in the poetry series) Lockwood does have a feel for Jess's work (as Auerhahn did not).

And I had some hope that now the Poetry Board might not turn down my work (as they turnd down *The Opening of the Field*; and as the German department board turnd down Jess's translations on the Morgenstern that Lockwood had wanted to do{)}}.

Good news that Barbara Guest's book had more body in feeling than you (and I too) had thought likely.

I am very excited about the possibility at Norton, if you really can get done there what you want, for a solid list (and having only four a year wld make for such care in decision).

Wonderful news came from Gael {Turnbull}. Rago has taken "20 words 20 days," entire, for *Poetry*. Gael read it thru when he was here, and the vistas of the poem grow in my mind, and heart too. As a fulfillment of a promise, that that rare spirit I so feel him as, would come into its flowering season.

Before summer is out, there will be a little book by me from the new White Rabbit series;[1] and it does look like *Roots and Branches* may be in yr hands before September. More "Passages," but I've still to type copies—

love

Robert

---

## 322

Dear Robert & Jess,

On the good side, what wonderful news about Helen getting that $4000![1]

And: after almost falling through, the Zukovsky/Norton contract has been signed—with option clause on all his other books.

But on the bad side: at the Wesleyan meeting *A Book of Resemblances* was shown to me & to J. M. Brinnin (Wilbur being absent) & I made an impassioned plea for it (Brinnin being non-committal) *but*,[2] I *don't* think they're going to do it. Neither Lockwood nor Bueno like the pictures. Bueno is a nice, modest, decent man but he just isn't responsive to this kind of design—I mean, he doesn't like Art Nouveau or Beardsley etc either & to him it is "pastiche of something he doesn't like anyway." As to Lockwood he is strictly a businessman (& a cold-hearted person in my opinion) & he is thinking of the financial aspect: (1) the bk wd be expensive (i.e. they cd. do 2 ordinary books for the price) (2) they don't get the rest of your (Robert's) work—(he feels you shd make Scribner's take this one with the rest, anyway) (3) he thinks very few people would go for the pictures, so they wd. not get their money back—etc etc. Also (4) he feels the pictures are not appropriate to the poems. I retorted, (1) "But think of it as a prestige item," (2) I guess I didn't have a retort ready for this one, & (3) well I said there were lots of people who wd be crazy about the look of the book, & lots of others who wd. buy it for their Duncan collection even if they *didn't* like the pictures. And to (4), that surely you were the best judge of that.

But I don't think I swayed him in the least—his mind was made up before I started. Brinnin (who whatever his past sins does not seem an obnoxious person I must say) remained pretty silent in order not to take sides against me, but he didn't speak *for* the pictures either.

Gael's book is pending, while people read the long poem. But it seems less, not more, likely to be taken than before. I'll try it with Norton if W.U. {Weslyan University}turns it down.

And (this is the last of the bad news) when I went carefully through Duerden's MS. I was disappointed & felt I had made an awful mistake in writing so affirmatively before. My reasons are given in detail in my letter to him which I've asked him to show you. *I am very sorry about this.* However, the things I do like in his MS. I like a lot and hope that later. . . . Well, anyway, you will no doubt see my letter to him. After what you wrote it seems almost like an insult to you, but you know, Robert, I think sometimes when it is someone one knows, & one knows what they *intend*, & also one hears them read aloud, one reads more into poems than is starkly there on the page for the stranger far away. But it is that stranger who is going to be reading a published book.

*July 24th*

At this point I was interrupted as Adrienne {Rich} arrived for a 3-day visit. Your new poems had come meanwhile—before that—. I have not properly absorbed them yet & put the ones I've already seen into relation with the new ones, but they seem to me like some of your *best*. I hope to live with them now & write more, in response, in a week or so. I am not sure how to read (aloud) the sections of columns.[3] Across or down? Thank you. I feel there is too much missing from my Olga poems still & so have not sent them, hoping for 1 or 2 more (there are 5, or 7 really as one is subdivided into 3).

Much love to you both,<br>Denny

P.S.

I read James Dickey's new MS. and was very impressed. There are some long poems which are clearly Duncan-influenced in the movement of the long lines. He must have been reading you with care. I found much that was moving & beautiful—much more than in the last book.

P.P.S.

Your "Fire" especially seems to me poetry of tremendous power.
Received copies of Helen & Jess's book.
On my way to Middletown who shd I meet—in Boston airport—but dear John Wieners! We had 40 m. en l'air. He was going to Buffalo to read.

---

## 323

July 27/{19}64
{San Francisco}

dear Denny,

Disappointing news on the *Book of Resemblances*, but I was taking a long shot on it, mistaken in not (and how wld I?) anticipating their not liking Jess's illustrations, but I had anticipated that expense would be an issue. *Merci* for yr. going into the fray, however hopeless the prospect.

Zuk wrote about the book going thru at Norton. It's a beautiful beginning—one of those books I have long waited to see, wanted to see. And don't worry about my reaction to your decision on Duerden's ms. There's just the margin of my personal interest in the book and in the maturity Duerden does show in many ways in it (and with that, some margin of doubt, I realize, for would I have found it necessary to explain what I found, wouldn't I have taken it for granted you would have found it in your own reading, if I hadn't had a shadow). I did not tell Duerden of your letter to me in which you were thinking of the possibility of publishing the book. I wanted for one thing not to anticipate a decision where there were things you were dissatisfied with. And then I've been back at work on the H. D. book (there will be some new pages to send, as soon as I finish the chapter I am on), driving ahead to meet that February delivery date.

And with many things that could spill over into a letter, or that would have arisen in talk. It's a struggle to try to get clear the "image," that has levels and shades in levels of meaning. No wonder the controversy about "deep image" felt like wrestling a tar baby or swimming upstream in molasses.

Saturday, *Writing Writing* arrived from the Wahs, and last night and this

morning I got fifteen of the twenty-five drawings done for the limited
edition: colord in crayon and then scraped with a knife (which makes for
a beautifully luminous surface without flakes that would come off on the
opposite page). The book is just as I wanted it, neatly mimeographt, with
an interesting squarish sans serif type face, and in blue heavy paper covers
(I'd said I wanted it to look like a school notebook or "bluebook").

And Saturday too Mackintosh brought the proofs for *Testimony* (you
remember the "Door" essay I gave you to read in Vancouver?) which is
coming out as a White Rabbit, I hope some time next month. I got the
proofs read and back to him the next day anyway.

And Rago was enthusiastic about publishing "The Fire" in the April issue
of *Poetry* on Works in Progress and long poems etc. O, about the ideograms
—I read the words (each, a unit, a block or a piece of a jigsaw puzzle scene—
I workt from recall of playing at ships and harbors by the bank of a stream,
with shadows and lights in the water) across, but they can be read down the
columns. It *is* important to me that the last word in the poem is *jump*. (To
make the ideogram at the close I read up the columns right to left).

In "Chords"—The whole comes from readings in WKC Guthrie,
*Orpheus and the Greek Religion.*[1] "A dazzling light . . . *aither* . . . Eros . . .
Night" is all that is remotely legible of a mutilated fragment of Euripedes.

There are a few changes. In "The Fire" after

"faces of Princes, Popes, etc.
 of whatever Clubs, Nations Legions meet
     to conspire, to coerce, to cut-down,
 of Gang-Leaders."

---

Enclosed a new one (following "Chords").[2] I want to set up not contrast
so much as a widest range for the play of the poem. But now the "poem" is
the book. And in my feeling the second act of *Adam's Way* might follow: the
whole to date thought of as an opening. (As the title of *Open Space* the very
local journal is suggestive{.})

We are eager to see your new Olga Poems—

love,
Robert

Chèr Robèrt, as I sometimes rhyme in addressing you, in mind,
   A few notes as I sit here, Sunday sunny morning, reading aloud
"Passages" to myself:
   "Tribal Memories" and "At the Loom"—how marvellously the sounds
enter the mind as meaning once the voice takes over from the dreadful

## 324

{July 29, 30, 1964}
Temple, Maine

insect-like silence of eye-reading! It all works, the little ship travels back &
forth & the clack & whirr sing to me and the pictures grow into being.
There is one demur, from me: at the end of "At the Loom," the section
beginning "but the battle I saw" is a pendant; it does not seem to grow out
of what precedes it but to be irrelevant to it. The musical energy that
informed *that* is gone, or is not gone into this, which is of another order.
Actually I am objecting on 2 counts: (1), that it seems to be tacked on, so
that however right it were within itself it shd. stand as a separate thing I
think; and (2), that I'm not sure that even as a separate section it rings quite
right, i.e. it is too explanatory. Anyway—I'm sure it needs to be separated
from the loom poem.

"What I saw" One thing troubles or at least puzzles me here, the syntax,
perhaps—does it mean might have been Xrist or [might have been] the
feathered robe of Osiris, OR, is it calling Christ the robe of Osiris? (i.e. an
incarnation of Osiris)

"Where it Appears" This is obscure to me—I'd have to pore over it.

"The Moon" This one is beautiful, uncannily the counterpart in sound of
vision of moon shine and shadow.

Now I must stop & do something else.

---

July 30th

"The Collage" connects in its visual quality with "Spelling" (which came in
yesterday's mail). A fascinating other exercise for the mind, the imagination
grasps hold by other means, that is. "The dance of the intellect among the
words." But what puzzles me is what you would do if you were reading the
series aloud, when you come to {drawing of the Greek letter "gamma" on a
tablet} or in *spellings* to new/old spellings!

I am sad this morning at having received from Richard Duerden an
angry, hurt letter in which he says he is not angry or hurt but (!) that he
cries "Shame!" to me—for not responding with enthusiasm to his book.
I wish people would *admit* they were angry & hurt when they are. *I* feel
angry & hurt now because what he is doing is denying me my right to my
own view of things; and because he ignores the fact that I wrote *kindly* &
took 2 whole summer days when I might have been picking blueberries &
swimming & things like that to go over his poems line by line with every
care. I didn't even reject the book outright, only deferred it with the
suggestion that if he could relinquish some early poems & add new ones
as they came along we might yet work something out next year or so.
Naturally I knew he would be disappointed, & I expected him to argue
back about some of the points—god knows I was prepared to listen &
ponder his arguments.

Sometimes one wonders whether it is worth taking so much trouble to explain why one is turning something down—I feel such explanations are owed to serious poets—but it would be a damn sight easier not to bother. When he objects to my saying that something is "incomplete" he seems to think I mean that it is not neatly tied up in bows and polished smooth. Here in "Structure of Rime XXIII" I come to "Only passages of a poetry. No more." I think (from what I've heard you say as well as from the poems) I understand this: you are disclaiming autonomous objets d'art because too often such "finished" works pretend too much for themselves—you want to emphasize that all the poems are but parts of one poem or poetry, "instance," as you say somewhere—and this because you feel it is all that can *honestly* be done, that the life-work is that carpet you spoke of, & the individual poems are knots in it. And that to "finish" may be not only to deaden but—even if not—a denial of the interdependance of poem and poem. Something like that? But "incompletion" as I mean it, in regard to some of Duerden's poems for instance, is something else. Each knot, surely, must be tied properly (fitly) or the whole carpet may suffer. One must (I believe) bring each possibility to *fullfillment* as well as one can. Not to an abstract of "completion" but to *its own individual completion.*

If the possibilities are slight, or spare, there's nevertheless a completeness of slightness or spareness. To explore to the limits the unique potential of a given poem—that seems to me to be what matters. I call "incomplete," those poems in which the potential appears to be stunted, unrealized, or realized only up to a rudimentary point.

I am indignant at having "For Shame!!" cried at me simply because I will not call sloppiness a virtue. Duerden's schoolboy use, over & over again, without precision, without taking thought of what the word *means*, of "weird" is an example of sloppiness. Well, I shd not be writing this to you but to him but it is obviously no use writing to him & I feel better now I've got it off my chest.

In "As in the old days" what does the quotation come from, "they *want to have little beds, & tables/& everything else?*" I must have written earlier about "The Architecture"? I love it. And the beautiful quiet-voiced solemn marriage poem.[1]

Who is the He of the two quoted lines at the close?

There's one thing I query—not as writing but as a statement—in "Shadows": "for poetry/is a contagion." I have known, know, feelings pleasures & pains that cast glamour & are a contagion, & are too, a part of poetry; but poetry itself I cannot see so named. Poetry is a possibility without which humans are incomplete. This is health not sickness. "I am come that ye might have life & have it more abundantly" is what poetry means to me, how can I look on it as a sickness then?[2]

## 325

{July 1964
San Francisco}

XORDS

dear Denny & Mitch,

"Passages" now opend out into the book title. And I've dropt the numeration. Giving the poems that much individuality, of a title. In the "Collage" I hope I have now brought out more of the meaning I saw in the ellipsis of the first part. Here[1] I've tried spelling *Christ* and *Chronos* with X for the Greek chi or X but when I tried it on "chords" as above it was so patently grotesque (leaving the reading puzzled over what to do with the "X") I have decided to drop this pursuit. "Cords," "chords" are the same word. Johnson, curse him, pontificated the correction to *ch*ords (the play of "cords" meant sweeping the strings or cords of the instrument).

I mean to take a poem in the series for breakdown and reordering of my own spelling. A demonstration. And directory. And then "Spellings" is a great title.

We're off to week's shopping etc., so I close to get this in the mail. With love and all. . . .

Robert

## 326

August 10 {19}64
{San Francisco}

Dear Denny,

There is a felt or recognized-in-taking-it lead from "a flood-gate" to "but the battle I saw" if it must be rationalized; open the door and the battle is what one sees. In writing there was the imperative that that *was* what I saw and in the course of "Passages" the plain, the battle will return. But the whole effort too was to undo the "weaving" in the course of weaving (the "holey shawl" patcht with whatever, belonging only in the new conjunction itself). I want to open my work up to material that lies just beyond my recognition of use as I work. But this scene of the weavers and the "battle I saw" is one that I have already reflected on in the H. D. book, that the scenes of Troy were sung not to warriors but to women weaving, who were weaving what they saw into their work.

I've come across more and more passages about the *real* war, the theme just has not returnd to my poetic consciousness. Whitman's "As I Ponder'd In Silence" is one:

I too, haughty Shade, also sing war, and
    a longer and greater one than any,
Waged in my book with varying fortune, with
    flight, advance and retreat, victory
    deferrd and wavering
(Yet me thinks certain, or as good as certain,

at the last,) the field the world,
For life and death, for the Body and for the eternal Soul,
Lo, I too am come, chanting the chant of battles,
I above all promote brave soldiers.

But to get back to your wanting to separate what "does not seem to grow out of what precedes it but to be irrelevant to it . . . the musical energy that informed it . . . gone etc." This holds O.K. if the poem is thought of as an organic form ie growing out of itself like tree, man etc.

But what I have in mind (for all of the fact that mostly I still proceed here to produce a tissue or woven "body"{)} is to be free of that "forge, loom, lyre" and work in the air. Words having just that physical reality of the temperd air, upon which I had meant to go free of my composing the matter, acknowledging (as psychoanalysis begins to be aware) that beyond *making* meaning we can also proceed by trusting meaning and work to recognize the meaning of what we are saying, not to say something we already mean.

If, indeed, "The battle I saw" needs to be separated from the "At the Loom," the fact remains that *it was not separated*: once the flood-gate opend, there it was. And my job was, as I saw it, to get that sequence right, even if I did not see how it fit. What I know is that in the large mosaic of the work I will come to see what that configuration of Kirke, Worm, "hid in its showing forth," the light bounding then from Tom's fur that bounded from a shield and the allegiance theme (think of which in relation to "The Fire") that puzzles me more than the battle scene by far.

How can I explain that "What I saw" is a triple image? The light bounding from the fur/from the shield/from the sword. I kept refusing the sword-flash, for it seemd too much, and I knew something was just beyond. Then I rememberd I had seen (as if enclosed in the flash or opening in the flash) the white peacock.

The white featherd robe of Osiris *is* the Christos (the garment of light without a seam, that I already knew from working on the H. D. book) but I'm sure that behind this "What I Saw" is looking at an eclipse of the sun (the fumed-glass slide here was the clue) and that the always active Son = Sun sign is present here.

No, I don't think of Christ as being an incarnation of Osiris, but if you can discard the argument that if A = (is)B and C = (is)B, A = (is)C which I don't think true, (for one thing equals(?) aint *is*), both Christ and Osiris are the Sun, are the Robe without Flaw, the Sun-glare. Beyond White.

On the other hand the white peacock was just that too, as the fumed-glass slide and the cat's eye opening were. . . .

"Where It Appears" is not "obscure to you" but just states as a purpose what you wouldn't accept—that the poem, woven in the air, is to be cut loose from its warp . . . and that I propose "momentous inconclusions"—so far, evidently only that embattled battle has provided the sense of being "up in the air." Well, it does seem to me that I've far from gotten into what I had wanted, to *disconnect*, to unweave—towards a much more fugitive, *inconclusive* relation.

Why is it so hard to make clear? I've got such a feeling, Denise, that ποιείν [*poiein*] the process of Making is Creation itself, our individual awakening up to creation we are involved in. And that's beyond what we know how to do for sure. There was a point (circa 1953) when I suddenly realized a poem did not have to be engineerd a bridge, (I think I saw it first clearly not about poems but about paintings, the absolute confusion of painters balancing and working out stresses when working on a canvas with oils where balances and stresses were self-projections and not recognitions of actual happenings, expressive intentions of fears that were unreal—as if a painting would "fall down" or "buckle"—where for a bridge artist, where trucks etc. have to pass over balance and stress had *real* meanings).

Well a poem then: that what it had to do was to tell the truth (and here skill came to get the shifts of tone right) of what happend in the orders of words (thus meant thought, speech, and song).

---

re—your query re "poetry/is a contagion," I would have the same strong bias for affirming *health* (as I would balk consciously at the Augustinian attitude or absolute declarations they seem in the "Imaginary Instructions" section, but they came as a revelation, the voice of the poem speaking to me. I do not always feel comfortable at declarations in the course of the poem. But in "Shadows" I think what goes on is aching, feverd, shadow voice (in which, that surely is the pathos I get in the close, the grail passes) . . .

It surely is quite clear that the voice that takes over with "Was it fore-warning of disease? some/painful core of the body's aging"—will see poetry too as a disease. "The while • They had brought forth/certain wonders he did not remember what"—

However, I may at a deeper level (from some unconscious assent) or at a higher level (from my thought and study in which I have found many men who believe all of creation is a dis-ease: the turmoil of Māyā for the Buddhists, the *turba* of Boehme—but also Schrödinger's concept of life as disequilibrium) I may subsume Poetry under disease.

However, I don't say, the voice doesn't say, that poetry is a *disease*, the context says that but what is actually said is "poetry/is a contagion," even laughter and joy are contagions.

"Wine" is built up of passages from "Du Vin" by Baudeliare, part II, the last three paragraphs, with parts translated from my reading, and as the guitar takes over, the poem takes over. I was lead to read this essay by a book on *The Orphic Vision* (not certain of this title) by Caroline Bays (not sure

here again)—an excellent book, but wait! I *do* have the title in my notebook: how provoking I seem not to have taken any notes! I find "Wine" but no bits leading to or from. Anyway, it lead me to Baudelaire, and either the line was quoted in *The Orphic Vision* (which contrasting to Sewell's book actually did have to do with the Orphic religion in French poetry) or I found it in going back to Rimbaud—the last lines of the poem are Rimbaud.[1]
. . . . . .

Oh yes, one last footnote—the passage in "As in the Old Days" "In the stream of the wound{"} etc.—comes from Zinzendorf[2] notes I had taken three years ago in H. D. notebooks—as in turn does the "There is really no circumstance of human life . . . " which refers to Christ{.}

love
Robert

dear Denny,

It's awkward moving in on the first two sections of the Olga poems (the first two *poems*, is it?) shying away from very personal opportunity . . . but then the third takes over right away (and this is my third reading, a reading when I have the time here to be focusst on the poem, and familiar enuf not to be struggling for it)—Could the "black one, white one" theme be brought forward? but then it comes forward . . . "quarrelled like sisters in you—" tells something that may belong to that theme. Five opens out splendidly. There is some exhilarating music for me in which in 6 the word "ennui" rings, I think it comes by rime from "brown eyes" obscure as it may seem the wī, n, and ī are in the "w" and "n" of brown and the ī is in aī of eye . . . "rainy"? Anyway it is a resonant passage and bursts into the recall of Beethoven sonatas.

Did I tell you that FINALLY!!! the Ballads of Helen's are out?[1] At the point of a gun! Jess is sending you today a copy of the special limited edition we had done (to include a cover and two drawings that Virginia Admiral had cut out of the publist version).

And in a week or so (awaiting now only the printing of an errata slip) the Wah's Sumbooks edition will be out of *Writing Writing*—I've done eighteen of the twenty-five colord drawings now for that limited edition. With seven still to go, and Robin askt if I would do a set of crayon "tiles" for his fireplace (paper to be coverd with fireproof plastic)—so I have a set of drawing and coloring sessions assignd.

Reading aloud. In "The Collage" you just say "and this. is gamma" the voice assuming the tone of "and this—is grandma," where [E] {capital *E* in

**327**

August 11/{19}64
{San Francisco}

hand drawn 3-D cube} is read "e" like "this red block," in "Spellings." In the first reference X is read "ex" *chi*, "ex," not "kay" (kappa) and Xristos is given some aspirate sound but not spelt out. "*X*" is read *chi* "hw" is sounded "*w-h-*" is read "double-u-atche" /k/ are examples of sounds k—

A-K-E is now spelld out and at [poet's drawing] pronounced. As connection slip shows I have included now an interpolation about what happend 1700—which has been in and out of the text three times—but the play of the poem allows for this bit of informative tone; the shift adds to the variety in reading aloud—

love
Robert

---

## 328

September 5th {1964}
Temple, Maine

Looking forward to *Writing Writing* which I ordered from the Wahs.

Dear Robert & Jess,

We have been away at the coast (& before that, in Quebec). It was good, a real holiday, but it is so good to be back. Many of my flowers which failed to blossom in August, & which I'd given up on, have begun to blossom— "Marvel of Penn" (also called "4 o'clocks") and nasturtiums & morning glories. And the grapes are beginning to turn color, from green to their indescribable ripe shade, somewhere between sherry & rosé.

*Thank you*, for Helen's book (I had received copies of plain edition) and for the H. D. pages (not yet read because of being away). And for the "Falconess" poem which is marvellous & strange & completely convincing. There's a whole vein of balladry in among the other kinds of yr poems, Robert, that (tho at first I mis-took it as wilful archaism or something, stupidly, remember?—when at first I deplored "The Enamourd Mage"?)— that I've come to feel is one of the deepest veins in the whole mountain. Read Hoffman's superb story "The Mines at Falun" aloud to Nik the other day, speaking of veins & mountains. Do you know it? It's in the Angel Flores, Anchor Books, collection *German Romantic Short Stories* in which is also my much loved "Brigitte" by Stifter.[1]

James Dickey sent me the limited edition of his 2 long poems "The Fire-bombing" & "Reincarnation" which I think are tremendous poems.[2] I had not shared too much of yr interest in his work back in the spring, tho I did like those you pointed out, but read his new MSS (which includes "2 Poems of the Air") for Wesleyan a few weeks ago, & was very much moved & excited & wrote him to say so. He has obviously been reading Duncan & has really learned something, is not just imitating, but making his own poetry new. "Reincarnation"—about a man reborn as an albatross

—gave me, reading it aloud to myself sotto voce, an extraordinary sense, *in its line movement*, of what it must be like to *be* a great bird floating through vast antarctic skies, & yet to have fragments of human consciousness still. An amazing poem. The book, physically—in calligraphy by a Reed student, based on 8th cent. Carolingian script—is one of the most beautiful I have ever seen.

Nik has been writing extraordinary poems & prose. So far there are just 2 copies, his own & ours, but I am going to retype them & show you. When he was a rip-roaring little boy preoccupied with cars & trucks I used sometimes to suppose him *prosaic*! Wow! Do you know, I feel a pang at heart, this instant, realizing that you both have forgone this experience, of witnessing the child of one's body reveal himself, in a poem or a painting. It is such a miraculous thing, one seems to shudder, to feel it in the marrow of one's bones—a veil lifts, and there's a glimpse into a world of Imagination back of those dark bright eyes. Perhaps it's not quite the same even to a father, tho—maybe it is the thought of having carried this same creature inside one 9 months that makes it so extraordinary. I have never felt it quite so strongly ever before as I do this morning.

Will send some more poems soon. Don Allen's pamphlets with beautiful Jess pictures came.[3] Tho' sorry the mag. folded I must say I like the format he has hit upon.

One idea in the "Olga" poems was to approach the focal point from different distances & in different moods etc. So that tho' it is a sequence it is I hope more importantly a wheel of sorts. {a drawing of spokes of different lengths radiating out from a central point} This accounts for some poems speaking of "her" & some of "you"; & in some, switching from one to the other. One section, "In a garden grene," is an unconscious homage to your sonnets—that is, I did not realize that until it was written. Rago is going to print it in the next double issue.

I have a new "psalm" but am not sure if it is ready yet.

Recent *Sum* or *Matter*, the Kelly thing, had sections of long poem by Ted Enslin I really liked—better than anything I'd ever seen of his.[4]

Have "discovered" a young poet, Jim Harrison, I think is really good. Will show you some of his, and Joel Sloman's poems before long.

Mitch is really getting on with his novel, has written some pages I think are terrific. Quite different from the other book, multifaceted where that was single, or almost single.

Thank you too for the explication of those passages of "Spelling" etc I'd asked about.

How is Barbara Joseph? I have not heard from her at all, since she was in N.Y.

Is Helen Adam still planning to come to N.Y.? I feel afraid she'll not like it & it will drain away all her Merrill money. What do you think?

We will stay here until about October 20th, as M didn't get a teaching job.

Just as well since he is working so well on his book now. We take Nik back to school on the 11th. Then I have to go down to Cambridge for a few days around the 21st—& have a week of readings in early October. But otherwise we will happily be in Temple.

Am reading with great pleasure the 4 books that comprise *The Master of Hestviken* by Sigrid Undset, about 13th cent Norway but not "historical novels," real novels.[5]

Love from
Denny.

Please forgive illegibility of this letter, it's just one of those days when my handwriting goes completely sloppy.

<table>
<tr><td>

**329**

Sept. 7/{19}64
{San Francisco}

</td><td>

dear Denny & Mitch/

Another section of the H. D. book goes off to you today (tomorrow, the 8th) and the first of the bumper crop of publications expected this week— *As Testimony* issued by White Rabbit.

When you get back to New York would you package up what H. D. typescript you have and ship it back to me regular mail (or ms. educational rate)—time is not a factor. But I want to assemble it in order and with the book coming up I'll want an extra copy. As it is, I have no copy I can lend out to be read; and once my copy goes off to the publishers I'll have no home copy. (I'm referring to this final draft. Part I "Beginnings" and Part II "Nights and Days")—don't worry about the earlier drafts of the book.

I got chapter 5 of Part I—the chapter on Occultism, Blavatsky, Yeats and grandmother, typed up for a magazine Chuck Stein is planning, to be called *Aion*, and centerd on the occult tradition, not on literary matters. Which meant in the final writing of Chapter 5 I've gone into a paragraph on Aleister Crowley, Black Magic and Black Poetry to indicate my view in brief.

The Summer has raced away and I've written few letters. Now I don't know if I did or did not send you my last poem—"My Mother Would be a Falconress" one. I've a new "Passages" in process. But it is in suspended animation right now I guess, I've got to wait past wanting to work on it, for the thing to come clear on its own again.

And am working a tough new section on the H. D. ms., an interpolation about schizophrenic aspects of the authority the art has over the artist. What

</td></tr>
</table>

set me off was an article by Bettelheim on a machine-boy in an old *Scientific American.*[1]

John Wieners' book came Friday and it's beautiful.[2] Twelve of the poems (one of these a sequence of five "days") are first rate which is a high proportion. I have already started notes, and copied sections; I'd like to quote the poem "Cocaine" entire in the review, 19 lines in 5 stanzas. It's as good as the best of Verlaine for me. Would you write and tell me whether to send the review of the book to you in Maine or directly to *The Nation*?

John makes one feel the pathos of the individual "right" to his own life, the desperate unhappiness of being unfulfilld in that life, and feeling the disapproval of the world about him for his homosexuality and his drug addiction.

"we fixed in the night and
   sank into a stinging flash . . . "

convinces me of some real experience (where the usual junky line of Ginsberg etc. seems to me gesturing for effect and rebellion).

And in "Let the heart's pain slack off/to that secret place we go to in time" there is a passage of rare poignancy:

"No book I turn to but I hear
   An inner voice so dear say
   Pass over the commands today; forget
   What is allowed and what is not. . . . "

In "The Acts of Youth" the line:

"If
   I could just get out of the country. Some place
   where one can eat the lotus in peace."

He so beautifully does not attack or sneer at us who do not "eat the lotus," and at the same time he so desparately needs that freedom. . . . The poems assert the validity of a great unhappiness and have such authenticity I am ashamed to come back with any criticism that he ought to live a different life.

Then I find a pleasure in rimes rung out loud when there's a song to it and it dances.

---

Coffee on the table and prepared for breakfast, a few minutes before Jess gets up. Dawn has crept up to 6:30. And these last four days or so being overcast, Jess is overcast—he had only two or three painting hours yesterday.

Here now . . . (breakfast) And off to work.

Love
Robert

## 330

September 15th {19}64
Temple Maine

Dear Robert,

I too am reading John Wieners' book & feel just as you do about it. But I want to warn you about something—because I don't think you can know that John is (or claims to be) off all drugs (for some time now) & leading a different kind of life, & that he hesitated about publishing some of the poems because of their being part of a past he shudders about. As he is so very vulnerable a person I think one must be very careful not to identify him, in a review, with drug addiction at a time in his life when he seems to have renounced it, as it would hurt him—I mean *pain* him, I'm not talking about other people, for he himself god knows has never *hidden* anything, but pain him if he thinks his friends cannot separate him from the thought of drugs. It may even be that he does not wish to be identified as a homosexual at this point, I am not sure of that at all, but at any rate I think it would be best not to put emphasis upon it. I do hope you understand that it is only about John, whom I love dearly & want to protect, that I would ever make such strictures (if that's the word)—once a poem is printed it's in the public domain, and god knows *he's* not hiding anything, it's not that, it's just that he's special. I may even be wrong about his reaction, but in his case I do think one has to think about his reaction. I'm hoping to do a short review, too, for *Poetry*, so I had been thinking about how to do it on my own account, even before your letter came.

We took Nik back to Putney, the drive was beautiful & his new room-mates looked agreeable (new students entering in the 10th grade) & Nik seemed at home there. So we didn't feel badly, or not too much so—though it does seem so *still* back here without him.

We are using the hearth tonight—it doesn't give as much heat as the Franklin stove, but it is a live creature in the room anyway.

Reading Sigrid Undset, *The Master of Hestviken*—I love it.

We just spent an hour ordering some concert tickets for the winter (including Paul Zukovsky's Metropolitan Museum concert in the Young Artists series) and—even more exciting—a whole lot of plants from a nursery (Things that you plant now—shrubs & certain trees not native to the Maine woods).

I have the H. D. typescript here, so will send you the sections you want soon. I hope I'll be able to have it back before *too* long though—I mean, as soon as you don't need it. I'll try to get it mailed this week.

I liked Joanne Kyger's poems in *Writing*, especially the 1st 2—about her father, and the Uccello. The 3d one I didn't like as much.[1]

Will enclose a recent poem, the best of what I've done since the "Olga Poems" I think, the others being rather slight. Oh, there's also that "City Psalm" which I've sent to Robert Hawley for a broadsheet.[2]

Love to Jess. Love to you.
Denny.

Here's that poem I forgot to put in.[1] Do you know Wordsworth's poem from which I took the title?

Dear Robert,

God, I mailed off that letter about John Wieners which I wrote rather late last night, & now I feel sure I must have put it all the wrong way—I wish I didn't get into these things. I am left not remembering just what I said but feeling sure it was not exactly what I meant to say. If I seemed to imply that I felt John was ashamed of being anything he is then that was not what I meant. What I did mean was that since he seems to be off drugs it would make him sad to feel identified (by friends) with drug addiction even though lots of the poems are about it. I also think he would feel the dislike of "homosexual" as a de-individualizing *label* that you wrote about in that essay some years ago—but I didn't need to tell you that and it was just oafish of me if I sounded as if I *were* telling you that. If so, forgive me. Sometimes I am a prize oaf, or oafess.

Reading a great garden catalog, dreaming of wondrous lilies and exotics with strange names—then we have to remember the climate here. But there are many flowers that do excellently here—what is lacking is gardening experience—but we do have lovely golden-glow, morning glories, and marigolds right now. We have ordered some bulbs & some flowering shrubs & things like that.

Love—<br>Denny.

dear Denny,

Just to send on a new poem, a "version" of Verlaine's "Parsifal," after our seeing *Parsifal* last Friday; and the weekend before, borrowing the recordings from San Francisco State via Robin, listening thru with libretto. We are in a spell of hot days, into the 90s in the city, with fires in the countryside (not far from where the Tylers live). Weather like this excites a dim substratum of thirty years ago in Bakersfield, and I rehearse adolescent moods. In a current "Passage" since August 9th, I've been accumulating bits of longing for coolness, water, . . . ? depth? And reading or writing takes on revenants of school work beginning again.

*

No great point in belaboring your being off key in your first impulse about wanting to hush up the homosexuality and the drug addiction references in Wieners' work; you did reflect quickly enuf that something was aksew.

The poet who wrote in 1959

> I took love home with me,
> we fixed in the night and
> sank into a stinging flash.

In 1964, five years later, after his terrible incarceration (and the terrors in which he was incarcerated) and the will to life in which he has made his ascent surely is not the same; but he would not (as you would have) denied the authenticity of his experience in himself in the interest of a more respectable personality. (As Rumaker certainly did in the *Butterfly*,[1] a book which, with the recent review of Scott Fitzgerald's *Letters* in *Writing*, has convinced me that he has been brain-washt to the norm of the *Ladies Home Journal* and the men in cigarette ads).

In the review of *City of Night* Wieners does disown his experience—but that is not a poem—and as prose it does not have poetic justice (a sense of what it is doing)[2] Wieners anyway can throw out "How can anyone straight read your book?"—he does have the idea of "straight" (as when I wrote him to write straight, meaning straight out, he took it to mean "heterosexual") and he (the poet who wrote "Tuesday 7:00 PM" or "Dream") can rant like a hypocrite (attacking in Rechy what he projects from his own person): "it's morally corrupting. I don't mean in a moral sense, but in the sense that your senses are impaired by coming into contact with that sort of artificial, hysterical neon-lit cheap glamour." And then: "that has no mystery to it, only the drabness of daylight at dawn. Like the dawn, it has no impulse to it at all."

"And I didn't like your look, because I just wanted to go to bed, and pretend that your world didn't exist, and that I would not have bad dreams because of it."

I would grant your point then that Wieners has times when he would disown "Recky's" (his own) world and also he has put away his addictions. But this speaking from a moral advantage I mistrust; it's too much like my own "moralizing," that makes writing critically such a chore, for I must vomit up my strong puritanical attacking drive. (In its extreme, this attacking in others what one fears to attack in oneself appears in bloody wars against error, the lynchings of lustful black men in the South etc.) But I don't think this hypocritical mode, moral projection, enters in in the poems. I've analyzed the images of love, then the cultural references (to Munch, for instance, Apollinaire, Klee, Marlene Dietrich, Mistinguett) and the *mise en scène*; now I am in the process of tracing thru the references to the Woman; I've still to get an ideogram of his concept of fate; then God—and I think that identification (admiring, for instance) contrasts with longing. In "For Marion" there is an authentic longing for a woman found "snow white in my head" to be realized "just for one glance of her sweet eyes." In "For Jan" there is authentic identification, leading to "*our* due"—The Man must also so divide into Self image and Other.

Thurs. 24th: The analysis I must go thru—in order to find my materials. But I do not have in mind raising poetic issues or to diagnose the crisis in Wieners' work. For one thing the poems that come thru are not incidental but central, and they are so beautiful, to my reading them aloud, so ardent—and finally it is ardor that burns away dross of feeling—that I would not criticize the fever. It's Wieners' nature not his disease. But I do have to understand what is going on and write from some depth of under-standing as well as from the lasting impression of his virtues (poems). The above and my notes along the way are questions re. our poetry at large, questions I entertain that I am not at all sure are pertinent to Wieners' value. He seems lacking in any imagination of form, but he only the more clearly demonstrates that *formal feeling not formal consciousness is the seed of the art.*

Love<br>Robert

Dear Robert,

I'm sure both my letters were badly written & unclear so I am not sur-prised that you did not quite understand what I meant, tho' I'm chagrined at myself for not saying it better.

I do *not* feel John is suppressing anything about himself. I *do* think that he looks on these poems as belonging to a part of his life that has gone by. I also think he is a painfully sensitive person. Therefore I think that when his friends who know these facts undertake to review him they should take pains to avoid identifying John, as if for ever, with the period in which he wrote the poems, as if one didn't know or care or *believe* in change for him. It wasn't homosexuality, it was the drug addiction, I had chiefly in mind. As for homosexuality, I only meant "also, not to *seem* to identify him as 'a homosexual' first and a human being afterwards"—now, obviously I didn't need to tell *you* that; but what I meant was, "John being so oversensitive is liable to take it that way *even from you* if you don't choose your words very carefully."

I *don't* think (as you seem to think I do) that John is interested in "respectability."

But I don't think *either* that Mike Rumaker has sold out to respectability & *The Ladies' Home Journal.* The last 3d or so of *The Butterfly* was terrible—mawkish, feeble, inept etc. But the first chapters are to me a deeply moving recreation of a human being's beginning anew; and the chapter about the Japanese girl's falling back into her darkness is equally moving. What courage Mike had to write these chapters so transparently; what courage it took to allow himself his own tenderness instead of simply repeating/ imitating his own successes with stories of obscure violence!

## 333

September 30th {19}64
Temple, Maine

As for the Scott Fitzgerald review, I guess you mean you don't think Fitzgerald worth writing about. Well, I do. I really care about *The Great Gatsby* & *Tender is the Night* & the unfinished one.

I didn't see John's review of *City of Night*—where was it? However, the point seems to me to be that John is not (I'm sure) "disowning his experience" but deploring Rechy's way of writing about it, which is usually cheap & plays right into the hands of the *Evergreen-Review*-type public that gets lascivious satisfaction out of reading about all sorts of sexual "deviations," or *any* sort of vicarious experience they can get—the more freakish the better. Rechy is essentially a commercial writer as he was a commercial lover. He could never have written a poem like John's "Sonnet" (p. 64)—I mean, even if he were writing poems he would not *feel* like that. John's exclamation, which you quote, "How can anyone straight read your book" surely means— something like: "You make homosexual love merely a freakish special category, you divorce it from *human love*, you divorce it from *love*, & make it only a vice—how can yr book be of interest then except to the specialist?"

Of course I'm guessing, not having read the whole review. But I bet I'm right. Or, isn't it just possible he didn't mean "straight = hetero-sexual" but "straight = not of twisted soul, whether heterosexual or homosexual"? I see nothing "like a hypocrite" about it either way. John never gave glamour to addiction or homosexuality, in his poems, in order to titillate his readers, the way Rechy would. His poems are filled with glamour but it is a glamour he felt, suffered, lived in. One just can't lump Rechy & Wieners together, just because they have had experiences in common.

All else you write of his work, that is the description of what you anticipate writing in the review, is only of the greatest interest to me—I'm sure it will be a beautiful piece. And thank you for the poems.[1] They're beautiful. I've never read Verlaine's poems of that phase—only the "Il pleure dans mon coeur/Comme il pleut sur la ville" etc. ones, poems about Pierrot, etc. I must read these as soon as I get back to N.Y.

You know there was a poem you sent earlier this summer ("Where It Appears") which I said was obscure to me, & you replied that it wasn't that it was obscure but that it was a poem I would simply "disapprove" or disagree with in its basic assumptions or substance. This *may be* true but I can't assume it is, & you shouldn't, while it remains genuinely baffling to me. How to convince you I just don't understand it? Do you mean, "You only don't understand it because you are constitutionally *against* it"? Or "on principle against it"? That could be: but really, I am *aware* only of not understanding what it's "about," what it *is*.

We've planted 3 silver maples, 3 weeping willows, 3 catalpas, a rowan, a red-flowering crab, 3 tamarix, 2 Norway spruce, 4 Rose of Sharon (and a partridge in a pear tree). Wish them well.

Back to John Wieners for a minute—I hope you won't be too irritated with me over this. I daresay it was unnecessary for me to embark on the controversy in the first place—but you know, he brings out the Mother Hen in me, I can't help that. My clucking won't help him but it's practically a reflex. Try to forgive me the annoyance.

Yours ever,
Denny.

P.S.

*Disregard all that about "Where It Appears."* I just reread it, &, along with what you then wrote about it & the surrounding "Passages," it suddenly came perfectly clear to me. I think I begin to understand the *non-organic* concept of poems better.

D.

Our next to last day here this year.

Dearest Robert

**334**

October 21st 1964
Temple {Me.}

I've mailed (registered) all the typescript of the H. D. book that I have, in 2 envelopes. Let me know it arrives safely. And may I please also have it back when you don't need it? I treasure it. Thank you. And sorry I didn't mail it sooner but I was away for a week & we have had problems here too—we bought nursery stock & planted a lot of trees not native to Maine & some flowering shrubs & then have had a terrible drought here so that we had to water them extensively—& as our well was low that meant lugging water up from the stream (a distance of a city block). Each one needed about a bucket a day—there were about 30 plantings—so you can imagine how much time & effort we put into it. Now it has both rained & (last night) snowed. And we must leave on Friday.

Your book came![1] I was astonished as for some reason I didn't realize it would be out yet. Hayden was here & asked if he cd. review it. I told him, only if you feel the same way I do about it. He said, "lend it me for a week & I'll give you a draft; if you don't like it you don't have to use it & no offence taken." He also said (which he'd told me before) that he had admired your work a long time & fully expected to care for this book; & that he wanted to give it the kind of close attention he felt your work deserved. So we'll see. I had planned to ask you if you had a suggestion. Ted Weiss, maybe? Or Pauline Wah? (Except that it shd. really be someone better known.) Anyway — when Carruth sends me his draft I'll let you see it before coming to a decision.

When the book arrived I sat down outdoors with it and plunged in. The water buoyed me, I swept downstream. How glorious it was! I drifted into bays where the lilies grew—I was pulled through dark echoing underwater tunnels & out into the light again. All was familiar & yet strange and new. *Thank you.* I will get it back in under a week I trust—had to part with it so soon.

Don't let any disagreements (? if that's the right word)—arising from the letters about John Wieners, Mike Rumaker, Scott Fitzgerald etc., seem of any lasting importance. Robert: I love you, I love your work, & at the same time in my very slow growth (41, in 2 days!) have *just* come to the point where I can dare to "disagree" with someone I so much admire.

Love to Jess & you
from Denny

## 335

dear Denny,

The mss for H. D. book arrived today—just now—and as soon as I collate them, checking on pages I may have neglected to send you etc., I will return them. With the idea, that where I might want the book read by someone in New York it might be borrowd from you.

Meanwhile, in the same mail there was the little mag *Things*, with your "Admonition" beautifully—*clearly*—done. For me, an Affirmation—"It is that *presentness* that is the 'direct statement' I *do* believe in; not the banishment of Acteon."[1] Your "form is the total interactive functioning of content and language, including every contributing element" gets it said better than I've managed anywhere. Affirmation? Acclamation? anyway your use of those passages from poems lift me to walk on air somewhat off the ground for a while. Well, no, I find no matter how I feel "lifted" the ground meets my feet as ever.

However their propositions may wander, (and the doctrinaire approach does want blasting) it's good to have a magazine taking its ground in Williams, if they open their eyes and ears and minds to what he is actually doing their limited and limiting sense will not long survive.

But it was poems (in *Coyote's Journal*) by Ronald Johnson, not any of the poems in *Things*,[2] that gave such striking perception—the emotion immediate to the world about—As in "Still Life" the poem articulates the poet's "attentions." His books open directly to "squash blossom & calabash," and in "When Men Will Lie Down As Gracefully & As Ripe" oak leaves floating downstream and the ebony spleenwort rime as things of the poem where

> "How can I say the 'tangled actual,'
> but that, as we sit here on the banks of the Potomac,
> above wind in the leaves

I still hear the cars on a distant bridge—
as Thoreau had heard trains
at Walden."

stirs me to the edge of something of my own, as if "listen" awoke me to hear too a distant bridge and cars (now water running in the taps, and traffic on the Portrero freeway)—[3]

Dear Robert,

I didn't send you Hayden Carruth's review, because it was so good & they wanted it in a hurry.[1] I'm sure you'll like it. The book (I've got it back now) is such a wonder—a mine—an ocean—

Your silence confirms my sense that you have taken offence. I'm grieved — what else can I say. Only that I hope this misunderstanding won't last long.

Love—& to Jess—
Denny

Mailed you a magazine called *Things* to show you a short prose piece I wrote last fall. Over—>

Am off to Baltimore—Chicago—Cambridge—for 10 days, now.

**336**

Nov. 8th {1964}
277 Greenwich St
N.Y. 7

dearest Denny,

If I get this right off in the mail, I hope it will arrive in time for you in Chicago. The enclosed letter from Oct. 26th will make it somewhat clear that I haven't taken offense. I've always and will always have whatever misunderstandings with you out loud, argued out in letters. But times when I'm behind the 8 ball in writing, like right now with the Wieners review and Zukofsky review still pending and the H. D. book some ten days off schedule, when my spirit can't or won't get on with it (right now I have begun on the H. D. book and in eight hours battled thru four pages—it's a matter of getting maybe a phrase but one that shld. tell wrong) SILENCE is liable to close in. Even letters seem stolen from the writing I am not doing.

So don't grieve. I can't imagine not loving you, and love can find no offense in misunderstandings. Nor in disagreements, which we've often had. But I do know what you can fear, for there are times when I've not heard from you when I think "O now she has turnd away. I've lost my place in her heart."

Larry Eigner's "The Reception" arrived in the same mail today from Duende which I look forward to reading again.[1] And a card from Helen who with Pat is on her way to New York where they will be for the rest of the year.

**337**

Nov. 10/{19}64
{San Francisco}

Scribner's forwarded to me a copy of the proofs on Carruth's review and I was very pleased that the book seems clearly to have won a reader in him (especially since I had been struck by his full response to Creeley's *For Love*). He goes beyond me to see that the scales are also "scales that cover our eyes" and to note that this may occasion the poet's "grief"—I still have no certainty of *cause* of grief—but I do know that the music and the marvelous seem often to blind me and I feel a deficiency in sight: I'm sure that the world immediate to the senses is the most real book.

Anyway, it is a terrific review to get—I am amazed by how much of the book he could glean right off, and pleased again that he pays attention to metrics. Never thinking in terms of iambs, I am taken back at the idea that "the ear detects the *ostinato* of the standard English iambic. . . . "

There are some new "Passages" (16 & 17) since the version of "Parsifal" out of Verlaine. Right now I don't have them typed up satisfactorily in copy, but when I do I'll send them out.

love<br>Robert

## 338

November 16th {19}64
Cambridge {Mass.}

Dear Robert,

Your letter *did* reach me in Chicago, & made me, as you may imagine, very happy. I spent the afternoon of that day in the Egyptian rooms at the Oriental Institute. The gods there were present, even in their glass cases.

I hope Helen & Pat will be alright in N.Y., it doesn't seem the best place for them but maybe I'm wrong. Where can I get in touch with them? I will be back in N.Y. next Sunday.

Henry Rago said to me that your work was the most important to him of any of his contemporaries.

I am here at the Radcliffe Institute for a few days, doing a little cloistered pondering.[1]

Love from<br>Denny

## 339

Nov. 30, {19}64
{San Francisco}

dear Denny,

Here are "Passages" 16, 17, 18 and 19—the last two coming in the last two days (today as I typed the final copy, having just finisht "The Earth," I got the hieroglyph of the body section). The "So thou wouldst smile" passage is from Marlowe's *Edward II* and later I want to use the passage in Gaveston's speech in which he imagines pageants of the Greek god world he would present to the King. The Teutonic and Celtic wandering tribes have appeard again; and from the Egypt the image of Heaven theme, I hope to get a passage on the Image of San Francisco.

I wonder if Stevens in "Chocorua to its Neighbor" had any memory of, had ever read the *Poimandies* from which I take my "Being more than vast."[1]

Robin {Blaser}tells me that James Dickey's book of criticism is dreadful.[2] What I've seen and what correspondence I've had would persuade me it could be the case. It doesn't embarrass my interest in certain poems of his, for I don't think that the feel of the language and thru the language of a world which is what a poet must have, be it song or didactics is the same faculty as a critical intelligence. But what is alarming is that I've never found (tho I have not lookd past my occasionally coming across reviews of Dickey's) any passage in the reviews that shows the poet's feeling. It's all corrupted by taste and the attitudes of the schools. He seems to feel it's improper of Lowell to be sick of soul. (Tho I've got a note of that attitude towards Lowell as I remember in my notes to his Poetry Center reading—a caution at least against indulgence in sickness, recalling Virgil's cautioning of Dante against his hatred of the lawyers in the Inferno). Against being carried way.

As, how, for the outrage of it, could one handle the murderous madness of negro hating White Southerners? For it would raise a murderous madness. The tangle of wrongs is very old indeed.

Did I tell you Paul Carroll took the "At Lammas" to submit to *Harper's*? I haven't heard from him yet as to how it went. But isn't it strange to have things shift this way? Like the prize list on *Poetry* magazine, which lookt like a landslide election . . . [3]

Are you missing any "Passages" to date? I hope one of these days a short one will happen, fitting to send you for *The Nation*.

love
Robert

---

The new "Passages" came—thank you. A sense of great space, amplitude—like knowing one is on a *continent* not an island.

Dear Robert & Jess,

I wish this came in color, it is *so beautiful*; you would love it.[1] I'll see next time I'm there if I can't get a slide. Helen Adam called while I was still away & left her address & number but Mitch lost the piece of paper he wrote it on. Please send it to me if you have it! Not only do I want to see her, but Jerry Benjamin is terribly anxious to ask her if he cd. try to produce *SF's Burning* here.

Love—
Denny.

**340**

{early December 1964
Cambridge, Mass.}

**341**

Dec. 8, 1964

{San Francisco}

dear Denny,

Helen's address is [Robin Gay] 324 W 84th Apt. 82, N.Y.C. (and you shld be able to find the telephone under that name). Pat has been ill. The composer Helen had hoped would be interested in doing *S.F. Burning* sd. not unless there was going to be a production etc.

I am fearful from her letter (which arrived yesterday) that the Merrill money is running out (they had heavy debts) and Helen speaks of trying to find jobs coming up. . . .

I'll write more fully later; we are just now (when your card came) on our way up to visit the Tylers—and we will give them remembrances from you and Mitch.

Love,
Robert

**342**

January 13, 1965

{San Francisco}

dear Denise,

January 8th I woke with the certainty on my mind that I must return to my first sense of Wieners' book, to the interpretation of its message that has been so impossible to unfold as long as I have struggled to keep your admonition not to talk of drugs. I saw clearly that I must free myself from that regulation and I would be free to write from the heart. It will be after all your decision and Wieners' as to whether the "review" shld be publisht. I know that whatever your decision, discretion, there, you both will read this essay aware that I have realized what I wanted to say. I do not know that the truth of what I feel is appropriate for *The Nation* or even for publication. I could not, struggle as I would, shape anything as long as I had the possible necessities of "reviewing" in mind. Before the spectre of merely acclaiming, if it not touch upon what was so meaningful to me in John's poetry, every creative source stopd.

Poor John! I have been so guilty about not getting this review done, I have not written to him at all; and I can imagine spectres of my disapproval troubling him. Now, at last, what I have written will make clear to him the "awe and love" I have for these poems.

I must get this in the mail before dinner; I send it to you directly—so that you can decide about *The Nation* question; and in sending it to John I will ask him to decide whether he wants it publisht.

But Denny, if John decides he does not want it publisht, don't think of a cut version. Let this statement stand in its full, and find someone else to do a review that will do.

What a release this has been for me! In the last two months I've been in a funk. Now, I've less than a month before the H. D. is due; I've askd for an extension. But I might even make it on time. I feel like them fountains of Weiners' "Ode" let loose.

love
Robert

Dearest Robert,

The review is just beautiful.[1] I got to Cambridge yesterday & called John today—he had not received a copy but says whatever you say is OK with him. He is leaving for Buffalo tomorrow to be a Teaching Fellow!—I'm going to see him off & so he'll get a glimpse of the review anyway before he leaves & I mail it off to Grandin,[2] the very nice new young literary editor (was asst.—Eliz. Sutherland left to be head of SNCC[3] & he's been promoted)—I don't anticipate any trouble there.

Have seen Helen & Pat several times.

Thank you *very* much for doing this, I know how much it cost you. My review of John's book will be in *Poetry* soon.[4]

343

{January 1965}
The Radcliffe Institute,
78 Mt. Auburn St.,
Cambridge 38 MASS

Dearest Robert,

I haven't written you for so long, because I've been, oh, almost sick I guess. I won't go into it—but just say that writing any kind of a letter recently has been like grinding pepper, or coffee, in an old stiff grinder. Now I've had a week's solitude in Cambridge, and have taken several steps, namely resigned from the Wesleyan Poetry board, completed my 12-session teaching at the Poetry Center (that was a happiness though, I loved my students & after we warmed up it went well) turned down several job-type things, cancelled some readings, & am preparing (by not accepting any more poems, & using up "inventory" as soon as I can) to turn the *Nation* job over to Hayden Carruth; so I feel somewhat better. Mitch is now teaching twice a week at Hofstra & likes it; pay is terrible (because he's part-time) but may be better next year and with that & my once-a-week teaching job at Drew (just contracted for) & some readings—plus possibly a renewal of the Radcliffe grant (a big difference if so!—$3000!) we'll do OK next year without my spreading myself all over the lot, in spite of Nik's school-fee just having gone up from 875 to 1250.

I really have been doing too many things & if I were prone to breakdowns would, I guess, have been having one. All this is just an unnecessarily complicated way of explaining why I've not been communicating with you.

That Mitch has started teaching is a very good thing in our lives. He had for too long been too isolated from people. Some other good things in

344

Feb. 21st {19}65
New York

recent months have been the showing of the Norbert Schimmel Collection of ancient art at the Fogg—I was going to buy a catalog to send you (good photos of almost everything) but alas they have sold out. I will try & get one at the—not the Wheye (?)—that other gallery/bookstore in N.Y. which someone said might have them, though. If not I'll lend ours to you eventually.[1] This was one of the great art-experiences of my life.

Then, Muriel {Rukeyser}'s extraordinary recovery from her stroke-like complicated illness just around Xmas (referred to in "Joy," enclosed) & her ensuing new clarity of presence & a poem "The Outer Banks" which seems to me the best thing she's ever written—not blurred & gushy like so much of her work. And the reading & meditation I've been able to do during those brief but condensed spells at Cambridge—seeing deep connections between the apparently arbitrary entries in my green notebook (of quotations). And talks with Adrienne {Rich} there. And some of Ted Weiss's Shakespeare lectures, sending me back to Shakespeare with a sense of receptiveness & excitement I've never felt so strongly before, especially about apparently unimportant plays like *Love's Labor's Lost.* And re-reading Rilke, Keats, Traherne. And my mother writing the letter quoted in "Joy{.}" And walking about in the snow in Cambridge & not feeling cold. And having a stack-card at Widener. Such things.

Nik seems to be doing better at school this term. He has a 17 yr old girlfriend (he's 15) with whom he's deeply involved, & she with him, & that's a problem in some ways, one of which is that of course she's a senior & will graduate & leave him behind—but at any rate he's *living* his life & really he is such a terrific *person.* Next year he won't have to take math. So that will help him, it is his sword of Damocles, (Demi-cockles, as someone in Dickens says). He's painting, & I think doing some writing.

The "Castle Psalm" (enclosed) takes off from a "Pottery Watchtower" about 2 feet high, Han Dynasty, in the Fogg permanent collection, which affected me very much.[2]

We see Helen & Pat fairly often & I'm trying (without mentioning it to her, for the moment) to get her some readings. Their apartment doesn't seem as bad as she says it is, by the way—tho' of course much too expensive. Perhaps they will be able to move in *here* for the summer if they've not found a better one by then. Our cat Muzio Clementi (whom you saw as a lumpy-furred runny-nosed kitten, but who has become a most beautiful & endearing creature) stayed with them while we went to see Nik at Putney & for a few days beyond that (as I was away) & he & they seem to have enjoyed it. All those art-noveau statuettes & lamps that they crated across the continent, & all the beautiful & interesting paintings & photographs, make their place quite wonderful & magic-cave-like—I'd never seen a place where Helen lived before.

Betty Kray broke her leg badly & had a heavy cast for weeks but is going about successfully with a crutch now.

How is the H. D. going now? Have you had galleys of the Wieners review? I have been out of touch with *The Nation* for almost 3 weeks now because of going to Cambridge—will be checking on it on Tues. though. Conover said it was fine—hope there's been no problem of any kind? It's a marvellous piece & I do thank you again for getting it done.

Ted Enslin has good long-poem section in *Corno Emplumado*—have you seen it?[3]

I enjoyed *Aion* & thought I might send them the "Castle Psalm" as it is a sort of mandala-poem I suppose—but I don't think I will really, I guess Chuck Stein's intention in *Aion* though very interesting to me (liked Kelly's piece esp., did you?—& glad to see the H D chapter) is too "specialized" for me to really join in, I guess, I mean I'm in a way not really with it.

I found a book by Hope Mirlees, the "spiritual daughter" of Jane Harrison —a very faulty novel yet full of the spirit of the early 20's & just before in a very appealing way.[4] And I believe it gave Virginia Woolf the seed idea for *Between the Acts*. It's called *The Counterplot*.

Love to Jess. Love to you.
Denny.

dear Denny,

It is no wonder before the specter now of Johnson making like a ham Lincoln and his vice-president grinning and laughing—behind which moves all the evil that one saw openly in Goldwater's presentations—that our minds choke in outrage and can barely move—to write a letter or a poem or a passage of the H. D. book means each time clearing away the thought of the do-nothing policy in regard to the plight of the Negro and the bomb them policy in regard to the opposition of the Vietnamese to American occupation. Blake and Boehme with their revelation of what a time of wrath means may give a key as to the vision one must have. For these men—the Johnsons and Stevensons and Humphries—are creatures of the malevolence that moves liberal and progressive men to enslave a people in the name of their freedom; I am working at a translation of a poem "Pleine Mer" from Victor Hugo's *Légende des Siècles*, an evocation of the raging sea of the psychic world and time in which man has made his spirit-ship—And as I work, in the stage painfully because I most prevent/postpone the vision that struggles to take over until I have done the task of word by word getting the Victor Hugo—the history in which our spirits now all but despair appears to me as a raging of the waters

## 345

Feb. 26/{19}65
{San Francisco}

in which my mind flounders and has no sure course in navigating but must ride it out.

The Hugo text is the only sanity I can turn to, for here at least I know I must navigate and focus. Today the poem that is to grow in the translation is most insistent. As I was walking to the cleaner's to pick up a load of sweaters and trousers—the headlines speaking of U.S. Refusal to Negotiate mingled with the thought that "Passages" 22 (which I have for some time thought of as drawing upon the Hugo poem) might be "to be read in the Yeatsian mode"—at that slow and incantatory pace we hear in Yeats's recordings; then that the Hugo poem might be in its final rendition in that signature—with "Passages" 22 related to it but not identical with it. (In the composition of this book I have already the versions of "Saint Graal" and "Parsival" from Verlaine; and I can feel the fitting and the potentiality in the Hugo poem coming after "Passages" 22, the two being conceived in one complex; followd by "Passages" 23 which I have done—did I sent it? Well, anyway I'll include with this "The Multiversity" (21) and "Arrival" (23). I wonder if I could work, as Yeats does with end rimes (as Hugo does in *La Légende des Sièdes*) and the ritualistic stresses. I love reading Yeats in his own mode. The poetry really becomes something entirely other than rhetoric in that voice.

What has stopt me for the last three months—with my mind coming to life again early this month—what drove my will back was that I did not want to be embroild and balked at writing in the . . . "La rafale qu'on voit aller, venir, passer," Victor Hugo writes—"Squall; strong qust, blast" my dictionary tells me and I see an iron-black sea, a desolation driven into the air by winds that squall now an angry and miserable baby. "(b) Burst, storm," the dictionary continues: "of gun-fire" *rafal-ment*—want, distress; *rafaler* to bring to ruin. The flood furiously ruffled.

> The abyss; one does not know what terrible thing that groans;
> the wind, the obscurity vaste as the world;
> everywhere the floods; wherever the eye can penetrate
> the squalling waves that one sees go, come, pass on.

—but a squall is a blast of wind—for all of the resonance of waves after "penetrate"—How many times I've been over these opening lines, beginning as I used to years ago when I would return when I lost the voice of a poem to sound the lines in my ears until the din carried me on; maybe in the end I will not have the rank disorder of that sea enclosed, as Hugo and Yeats would enclose, in the amber measures but fragments of the Hugo tossd up, broken timbers that survive my reading. I undertook the Hugo because Gwendolyn Bays' *The Orphic Vision* revived my sense I had had from the work of Denis Saurat of Hugo's depth and beauty—the grandeur of his mind.[1] I've never read his novels, but he must be all but unique—for his poetry—his verse—is actually poetry, having a music that rouses visions—

I'm caught up in a turmoil of tunes, as if here too there was the confusion of a storm—with "Arrival" opening upon a clearing that has not arrived yet; ahead of where I am—still working on the passages of darkness and depression two months ago that must be lifted up into sight and hearing, into the formative power of the book, no longer chronological, going in one direction but "qu' on voit aller, venir, passer"—

---

There is news. I've accepted a Graduate course in Poetry writing at San Francisco State for the first six months of the year (but actually, it is just the Spring semester—teaching four of the six that I am paid for)—which clears up our household finances for that time). I am oppresst by how much beginning in poetry—they know not what they do; and that only in experience does one come to see that each act in writing sets into motion desire and fate striving to become real. Such specters crowd in on my mind when I mean to keep these would-be poets directed to the immediate tasks of gaining a craft; and they, not yet awake to the feel of the language, much less to the depths that words are filld with, are impatient of hearing the vowels and consonants, at taking soundings—I find myself already raising my own specters in their minds, as if it were their part to know how the power of a word can overwhelm the spirit, that they must at once work with the greatest discretion, knowing the finest and most exact measures in the materials at hand—the exacting of the sounds and timings, the concern for localities, melodies and resonances of meaning—and at the same time tremble, and contain the trembling in the steadiness work demands, at the energy (content) of the material with which they work.

I'll have to go on with the Hugo translation this morning, it wants to take over as I write to you now—my eye straying to the open page of "Pleine Mer" on the table and seeing/hearing "Le abîme," "Le vent," "Les flots"— his nouns tolling bells over the wastes of sea—

When I've cleard the last ringing of the din he sets up, the morning sun will be here again, the translucent green of the potted avocado tree will have its day and, writing to you, I will not be overtaken, taken over, by this brooding scene that right now won't let go, let me let go—

Love
Robert

dear Denny,

You did a beautiful job in the Wieners review. Especially getting clearly the "believing abandon" and later that here "pity and terror and joy" are "beauty in the poems themselves"—And, against the grain of your own usage, that "the peculiarities of language in these poems are, I have come to

346

March 15, {20, 31} 1965
{San Francisco}

see, often the very crises of poignant truth, the pivots of the poem." "Change them and you change a note of a chord."

No word from *The Nation* about my review. Much less proofs. What's happend? Shld I write *The Nation* directly now that you are no longer acting as poetry editor? If they don't want it, I will want to send it some place else.

A passage from the Commentaries of Proclus on Plato's *Timaeus* (translated by Thomas Taylor):[1]

> The festival [the Panathenia] is an imitation of the eternal hilarity in the world: for if it is filled with gods, it celebrates a perpetual festival. But the *contests of rhapsody*, are analogous to the contests which souls sustain, weaving their own life together with the universe. And *the rhapsody itself*, resembles the above-mentioned woven life of the universe. For this has an imitation of intellectual forms, in the same manner as the contests of rhapsody have of heroic actions and manners, possessing together with an harmonious conjunction, a connected series. The many poems of many poets, adumbrate the many natures, and many circum-mundane productive powers and, in short, the division of physical imitations. But *the new poems*, are images of forms which are perpetually flourishing, always perfect and prolific, and able to operate efficaciously on other things. . . .

March 20th, a rollicking Haydn cantata from *The Seasons* on the radio to celebrate the first day of spring, and warblers outside to verify the morning. With a fine sunny day to make it seem "first." Did I write that I'd taken a workshop at S.F. State?

March 31—your *Protest* forms at least mean this letter gets off today. With the job at State College we have enough to help on something like this. We feel as we know you and Mitch must feel—a helpless outrage at the lies upon which the American policy is run, and at the death and suffering "our" armaments, troops and bombers have inflicted upon Viet Nam.

Count on us for all protests and write if the protest needs more money. We will tell you if we can't make it; but we want to do whatever we can.

love<br>Robert

---

## 347

{April 8, 1965}
277 Greenwich St
N.Y. 7

Dearest Robert & Jess,

Very touched & glad at yr. support. You'll be glad to know we can (MAYBE) see a way to improve the statement without re-canvassing the 2000 people we sent it to—by insertion of "shamed" after "grieved" (which surely no one will argue about) and by a postscript speaking for those who wanted a stronger statement, without involving the more . . . conservative signatories. Robt., yr review has been delayed only because Conover wanted to give it a "lead" place & has not had the space up to now. He is writing to you tho' about 1 or 2 small (not substantive) queries—he showed me briefly what these were & I don't think you will object to them—he does feel enthusiastic abt. the review—these are suggestions for minor clarifications.

Much love,
Denny

dear Denny,

I've been having such a hard time pushing myself, hours, moods, and worst of all times of despair at being able at all (and the damned actions of the United States in Viet Nam and in Santo Domingo a confrontation for despair), to the bringing into completion of the H. D. book. Correspondence has vanisht; my weekly class and dealing with those fifteen young poets rescues me within it. But today the Work In Progress issue of *Poetry* arrived, and your "Olga Poems"—if it be only for now—make so much seem possible. The

> "Black one, black one
>   there was a white
>   candle in your heart"

is so beautifully measured, exactilly felt I feel it as verifying the human good of the care and attention to feeling that a poem demands. And then *"Everything flows"*—the movement of those lines following—I'd seen those when I was in New York, but they have a marvelous immediacy here, as if just happening. And 5i is most lovely. I got so keyed up I am too impatient to listen to the last two parts ii and iii and I want to write right off before I've come around to the time when I will be able to read all the way thru. It is a beautiful beautiful work, Denny. The hardest of all to do or hear (that too is part of how hard to hear reading all the way thru at first)—but I am sure (reading and not reading those last parts, getting just how the time and pace fits the total poem) you've workt a miracle here of the immediate and the flowing in one mode.

Now I've got back at reading iii. How I love those long lines that in the Map of Essex poem you spoke with. They make possible inner phrasings. . . . I've not to point such things out but I'm still in the stage where I want to shout and exhaust the excitement of coming across this and this and this and lay some claim to the beauty of it—See, *I* see it too! etc.

You've, you *have*, brought a whole experience of your sister's living and being over into my experience, my human experience, translated out of whatever might have been personal into a communal "you." I've got for a

while to shout "*I* see it"; but I really want to tell you somehow that every-
thing you have worked in this poem lifts me up with—O just the way a line
can carry such a direct current of its meaning and music as it goes. This is
one of those poems that opens up in me a new determination.

I have completed 367 pages of part II of the H. D. which brings me within
25 pages of my original draft-end [i.e. to page 151 of 174 pages in the
previous draft]. Scribner's is getting a bit on edge about the size of the work
and so am I. I've altered my concept to see part III as a concentrated essay
[paralleling the chapter on the history of Eros] of circa 50 pages in place of
an exegesis of the *Helen*. But I'd promised the book for the end of this month
as of last February, and now that is not in sight. I can't push it, I have to let
the whole thing rest in my mind and feeling for sometimes a month in
between before I have exhausted my sense of conscious opportunities and am
ready again to work from hidden resources—(so that new material springs
from the work itself to reveal as I work). I *have* kept that and at the same
time worked and worked to get the range I need for what I feel.

No poems since the "Benefice" which I think I sent you, the sun *rising*
in the West and the Shinto gate—but reading the Olga poems has got
something going in me, a great feeling that much can be cleard away. I've
had in the last months a sense that the whole idea of the poet I have so long
dwelt with can be let have been and shed, even with a sense of relief, to
write as you do here (so I've been thinking and dreaming and knowing the
time was ripe for it), without that project having to be going on in the poem
too. Well, you understand there may not be any great sign of "change" but
the admission has been in my heart and my mind recognizes a freedom in
surrendering the poet and turning my cares and imaginations over more
wholly to the poem itself . . . the poet seems an obsession; and I know this
person of the poem is not necessary to poetry itself—Away for a time from
*creation* towards singing and speech.

U.C. Extension has a Berkeley Poetry Conference launcht for this summer.
I was an adviser along with Donald Allen (who in the mind of the U.C.
programmer is an authority above me in what's what in poetry)—I wanted
Clayton Eshelman and Jackson MacLow and got neither. At the time we were
framing the four lecturers I was for LeRoi—but after his public appearance
here in March, was it?—I have grave questions indeed. He read entirely hate
the whites and worse than that hate the white-loving negroes which came off
at about the level of Governor Wallace on hate the nigger-loving whites—But
poetry often has to include the dementia of the poet, the thing was that what
he read was blatantly demagogic. Written for its effect on the audience and I
suspect swept up in the sense of its opportunity. *Insincere* in the only meaning
of that word that seems important to me. There have been poems of LeRoi's
in the past where the hate was most really communicated—but now the hate

is being put across or put over—it does not take long in that direction for the writer himself to be taken in by his own opportunity. LeRoi will support the conference financially (along with Allen) but—but what? He has forfeited the goods of the intellect in becoming a voice of racism. And I mean in the sense that he would have forfeited the goods of the intellect in whatever loss of the complexity of inner feeling. It's sad, because he has written some fine poems; and he has turned against that humanity in himself. [Even Burroughs does not write as if his obsessional cruelty were *righteous*]—

Jess is doing some wonderful paintings; I want to write some wonderful poems to send to you with love for the Olga poems—

Robert

W Poems 1965
"Travels"—"Abel's Bride"
"The Wings"—[1]

Dearest Robert

How much it means to me that you like the "Olga Poems." It means more that it is now, later, you do respond to them, after not having done so when I first sent them, or anyway not fully. When I was writing them last summer, & especially when I'd just finished them, I had a sense of their being for me a "big" work, something that had not only been a sustained experience but also had materialized as solid & forceful; but then when neither you nor Bob seemed to think well of it, not really well, I began to wonder if I was kidding myself. Other friends, like Adrienne & Hayden, spoke well of it—but much though I love & respect them (& Bob) in the end it is only what *you* think of a poem that really, *really* counts for me. I know that a poem you didn't care for might be well-made or have all sorts of decent virtues—but something at the core of it would be wrong, false, or just lacking. Well, that's a rationalization; I don't think you're infallible, nor do I care about *every* poem by other people that you approve. So I guess what it really is, is that since I love you I can't feel good about a poem of mine you don't care for, even if I objectively think it's O.K.

It is a relief to be here, though I haven't yet unwound, don't yet feel quite *in* it. It is almost too green. The eye seeks the lilac & what tulips the deer have not eaten for dessert, in special pleasure at their non-greenness.

Did you see Barbara Moraff's poem called "Cunt Poem One" in *Sum*?[2] I thought it quite wonderful. In fact all last 4 issues of *Sum* seemed full of good things, I am sorry it is ending.

Gael has sent me his new long poem, it looks good. I've brought many such things along to read properly in the quiet. No *Nation* or Wesleyan MSS

**349**

June 6th {19}65
Temple, Maine

to read this summer, thank the lord! The summer will be interrupted by our visit to Mexico in July to see my mother, but otherwise I have no commitments, beyond preparing for my Drew U. classes in the fall. (I'm also to give some Seminars at C.C.N.Y., but they don't require much preparation as they will be for a group of "advanced" students & I'm going to read to them & just talk about my current preoccupations & see what *they* come up with.) I hope to just read & write & ponder, & grow some flowers.

Harvey Swados & some others who helped get that protest ad. out in April wrote to enlist my aid in deterring Lowell from going to the White House, so I wrote to 2 people who know him well asking them to try to stop him—but lo & behold, he had already made the decision himself, & made a really decent, honest sort of statement. I wonder if W. Coast papers carried the story? I suppose so. I have come to dislike Lowell personally—(not violently) as I dislike his verse for the most part. But this made me respect him more, anyway.[3]

I was given $2500 by the Institute of Arts & Letters (out of the blue) & therefore was present when Lewis Mumford made a very fine speech there, enraging some of the stuffier people.[4] He is a noble man. I obtained the text from him, hoping to get *The Nation* to print it, but tho' I persuaded them to agree to do so it turned out it was being printed elsewhere, as—being a speech—it was not copyright; so they're not going to after all. Would you want to see it? Let me know, I can send it to you. Its being given in that place on that occasion with the entire lit. establishment, just about, present in serried ranks like Satan's cohorts in *Paradise Lost* (with a few unfallen angels amongst them) made it a dramatic & memorable event.

Adrienne, whom I had introduced to Jane Harrison's work, sent me J. H.'s *Reminiscences of a Student's Life*—a delightful little book with wonderful photos—do you have it? I can lend it you if you don't.

At Helen & Pat's we met (or re-met, for he had once come to see us in N.Y.) Lew Ellingham. Mitch enjoyed talking to him, & I sort of liked him (altho' he is rather repulsive to look at) for being in some way, as it seems, genuine—is that it?—& for having so many intense thoughts & feelings about poetry, really being *involved* in it. But he does turn out to be awfully Dostoyevskian—he quizzed me about Robin's poetry & then went & repeated everything I'd said in a letter to Robin, & then confessed to me that he had done so & that Robin was hurt & I'd better write to him right away! I liked him for confessing it, but I feel as if I'd put my hand into a wasp's nest. The silly thing is, I said *nothing* to Ellingham I hadn't already said to Robin himself, so there was nothing for anyone to get excited over. I did write to Robin, & I think it is all straightened out.

The thing I feel about Robin's poetry is that you have to have special knowledge (I mean be one of his *circle*, I guess) to understand much of it,

even though it does often sound beautiful; & that he won't or can't admit
this fact. Does this seem so to you? Of course, it is not easy for you to say
since you *do* know him well. It's hard to get into focus—I mean, I believe
that the *particular* is the universal, & that that is what Williams meant by
the local, & that it becomes felt as universal (by the "receiver") by means of
the intensity with which it is (in the first place) felt and written; yet I find
Robin's poems, for instance, often remain *private* particulars, unshareable,
not *universal particulars*. Well, I guess what it points to is a lack of precision,
a lack of intensity, a diffuseness—so that it may be pleasurable the way a
song half-audible, sung in the next room behind closed doors, may be
pleasurable, but not in the degree the same song may be when the singer
comes right into your room (or you into his) & you can hear if it is a good
song, each word distinctly. It may be the listener ought to take the initiative
& go on into the singer's room, not wait for the singer to come to him?

But even so, the *great* works of art seem always to present a large *accessible*
area, accessible without special knowledge, however much of special riches
they may yield to seekers & initiates. If this is true of the great, one must as
an artist demand it of the small, mustn't one?—not easiness, not smoothness
of surface, but a foothold; & I don't mean a "rational" one!—no, when I
think further I realize that if Robin's poetry had more powerful[5]

from the black frosts. And you are struggling with the H. D. book. And
someday when people are reading it, they will not (most of them) know of
the struggle that went to create it, the life, the heart beats.

The sense you have of work, of the knots in the rug, of the constant
functioning through its seasons of the artist's life, is sustaining to me when
my spirits flag (& I have alas the idea that just as my 30's were a time of
great zest & optimism even though Mitch & I had such a bad time between
1956 & '58 or '9, so my 40's are likely to be a time of struggle to make
something out of, in spite of, a lack of zest & hope—I don't mean all the
time, but a lot of the time). (How could it not be so when we live in such a
political period! No, that's not it either—it is when a[6]

dear Denny,

If you have a copy of the Mumford speech for the Institute of Arts and
Letters, I *would* like to read it. Or maybe it wld be just as easy if you told
me where it was printed and I can get it at the Library.

The issues raised about Robin's poetry get tangled. I feel guilty because I
have not read them in earnest as you have, asking what I want of a poem of
them. I find them curious, evasive, distinctive as something in itself, select.
Jess says he thinks Robin aims at the poem as an object in itself, and to isolate
this objectness removes the work from the communicative (your "universal").

# 350

June 12, 1965
{San Francisco}

I may be superstitious in my regard for such art values in poetry; for my own concern, like yours, is for meanings, for the universal reborn in its particular. (At the same time, I do have my reverence for "She teaches all and she hides the key"). But just now, talking with Jess about this and reading aloud the passage from your letter, he says we are both off the track. That Robin's approach is like the Hopi design (and also the song line, as Jaime {de Angulo} told me) that must never resemble the hidden paradigm but stands for it. And I do see that one should not arrogate in the name of "great poetry" over the variety of what poetry can be. We get mixd up in explaining why a poetry is not clear to us in the unclearness of our own reading. And Robin when he objects to being found "obscure" and tells us that he intends to be transparent confounds the issue further. He could very well (but he doesn't say this) believe there are or want there to be only particulars. [Here again he would be like many "primitive" folk who do not live in universals, in *this* time, *this* sun, *this* particular curve of the hand—as a thing in itself.]

I think there is a strong case to be made that he often is concerned with private properties (and *privacy* is the quality here, not the *élite*: I, at least, know no more about Robin's privacies than his poems make available. Once there is a book, a larger book than the *Moth* sequence, another dimension I expect will emerge. But that is for Robin to do yet.

But don't feel you have to explain your difficulty in finding meaning to Robin. The burden at this point surely remains with the writer to create his own readers. In any event I am sure you do not have to have a special knowledge (take these poems as *roman à clef* ) to understand what is going on; I think he means the reader to accept an immediate presentation, a feeling—not necessarily intense, because not intending—but a feeling in itself, for itself.

Well, going back now to read *The Moth Poems* it does not seem so obscure. But it is a little book of *ephemerae* and one wld take it ephemeral realities. "almost a tune," "unease," wings brushing the interior of a piano, *fantômes de sentiments*, and especially in "The Medium," that it "is essentially reluctance" and trying, "tried me" in this poem as in the previous poem the moth tries the way into corners. And in the poem "My Dear" that the poet means to write as language "some center where one is helpless / even to oneself"— "considered as paint full of secrets."

There is a simple witch-craft in the poem of living in the apparitions of moths, in the "damp" of the first poem which reappears in the "red water" of "The Borrower," "juices" and then comes to a full statement in "Invisible Pencil."

> watery source
> as if the hometown river flowed
> into the room and out of the heart

and in "Atlantis" I and II is surely the interior sea in which "smokers of poetry bathe" and also a particular "spilled glass of water"—here he has a particular that is also a universal. And in the poem built of quotations ("some body else's idea" the previous poem ends) these two are the fluids of the body.

And it is clear that another level of statement unfolds in the relations of the two wings of the moth and the moth body "because the way had never been taken without / at least two friends, one on each side"—"The Medium" has it.

In "Salut" "the mind / nearly destroyed by the presences" suggests his may be a magic to keep certain presences.

*Don't*[1] in any event get tangled up in Lew Ellingham's meshes. He lives, as far as I can surmise (we have kept as absolute a distance as we cld., given that we knew so many people in common)—he lives in a phantasy-psycho-drama. Only this last week I received a card—would I write a Preface to his works? I don't even answer. He sent a message via Robin that you were very hurt that I had not proposed you for the Berkeley Poetry Conference. Taking the risk of his not really knowing anything about what went on and why in the programming of The Poetry Conference, and the greater risk of his having no conception of the confidence between you and me, if he would cause some havoc. He means to try us out to see if he can get us involved in something he will be party to.

There are other things in your letter I wanted to write about—but now (after an hour reading thru Robin's book and doing it a little better justice than my mere appreciations) it is time for me to get to the market. Henry Wenning and his daughter are coming for dinner and I'm to prepare; for Jess in this weather paints thru the light hours.

Yes, I will see to getting the Vancouver tapes copied for you right away.

love
Robert

Dearest Robert & Jess

We're off to Mexico in the morning. Saw a scarlet tanager (singing) today, & a baby raccoon in a tree.

Your *Medea* came recently from Bob Hawley[1]—I know it from the type-script but it is so lovely to have it in this form. I was able to sing out the song tune remembered from your record.

Godwilling we will be back in the first week of August. Give my love to the Creeleys please & say we will write soon. We wished they'd been able to come here in June but they decided to have Kirsten fly back.

Much love—
Denny.

# 351

{July 13, 1965}
Temple, Maine

P.S.

Dave Bromige sent me his book, I really like it.[2] If you see Ron Loewin-sohn please give him & Joan our love, he too sent us a good book & I haven't written as I lost his address. Had ecstatic p.c. from John Wieners from Rome.

Love—
Den

I guess you know someone telegraphed to invite me to Berkeley? It was impossible though.

## 352

July 17th {19}65
Temple, Maine

Dear Robert,

Thanks very much for careful discussion of Robin's "Moth Poem." I am about to go over it with your letter in hand.

What a crazy bastard that Lew Ellingham is! Somehow I don't feel angry at him (tho' if he had *succeeded* in making mischief between you & me I'd have felt like killing him)—because he is so screwed up I guess he can't control these things. But I do feel very wary of any future contact with him. He seems so lonely that one's impulse is to try & be warm & friendly to him, but I wonder now if it is possible.

Just to make sure you don't feel I *may* have felt hurt at all, let me assure you that I absolutely did not. When I first heard rumors about the existence of the summer school I wondered vaguely if I *would* be asked & actually hoped I would *not*, because a chance of coming to S.F. & seeing you would be a temptation but I most firmly did not want to go *anywhere* this summer, just be here quietly (except for the necessary trip to Mexico in July, & some coast-of-Maine visits). When I learned that you were one of the choosers of who wd. be invited, I took it for granted that a) you knew this, & realized I'd been doing far too much running around as it was, and b) that there were undoubtedly some good other reasons for *not* asking me, such as, getting some younger people in, not a familiar line-up.

I think what happened at Helen's that night was, Lew said, "You'll be going to the SF poetry summer school, won't you?" and when I said no, he said (in tone of astonishment) "Why?" & I must have laughed & said "I wasn't asked!" Of course if I'd known what he was like I'd never have said anything so liable to misinterpretation. Actually I'm not plumb sure I even *did*—I'm not sure if I really am remembering or just trying to make some rational supposition. Well.

Reading Mann's essays on Goethe I find many things that remind me of you. For example: "[Goethe's] *productivity* is closely bound up with his *capacity*, his positive genius for admiration. . . . This admiration is one of the main supports of his power of artistic creation. . . . He admits that he could not read without feeling such compulsion [to emulation]; & he brings home to all artists the fact that it is necessary for them to keep in constant touch with masterpieces, so that the creative spirit may be maintained at its height & prevented from backsliding. The word expresses a sense of peril with which even he, the greatest, is familiar. It displays the modesty, the constant striving, learning, adaptation, imitation even, which does not dread losing its particular identity but proceeds on its way with blithe confidence." And after quoting Goethe (at 44) saying, "We can do nothing but what we do. Applause is a gift of the gods," Mann writes: "Such is the fatalism of a man who lives his life & knows he has to stand what the world makes of it. At bottom it is modesty that determines his attitude towards his work—I mean now each single work, each stage & creative phase of his life. 'For who produces nothing but masterpieces?' he asks. . . . And (Goethe:) 'In a progressive activity & productivity the point is hardly what particular work is worthy of praise or blame, is of importance; but rather what direction has been taken as a whole & what has resulted therefrom. . . .'"

Nik was 16 last week. He brought lots of paintings home from school, & other art work—all completely lacking in "expertise" but almost all having a freshness & some kind of forcefulness that seems pretty remarkable to us. He also has 2 poems in the school mag.—one from last summer & a new one which I'll copy & send.

I don't know where Mumford's piece is being printed so am sending this copy. It may strike you less favorably, with its old-fashioned rhetoric, than it did us actually hearing it delivered—but the act of getting up & *making* such a speech before an audience half composed of the stuffiest stonyfaced or booing stuffed shirts in the country, not out of any kind of exhibitionist motives, obviously, but in the most sober conviction, was beautiful. And usefully so, for I know there were people present who really were influenced, people who had felt vague about the issue before.

I'll send it separately. If you think it wd. be useful to get it mimeo'd (for distribution how, & to whom, tho?) could you ask Dave Hazelton if he could do it?[1] I would put up say $25 for the purpose—I have *no* idea what that wd. cover, tho'. Just a rather random idea, this . . . Maybe it would not be a good idea?

I'm reading Gaston Bachelard, *The Poetics of Space*, which[2]

dear Denny,

Afterthots and aftermaths of the conference are as crowded as the conference was. Poetry ranged from the deadly extreme of egotist-sincere honest and unpardonably insensitive—which was Ken Irby to the lively

**353**

August 9/{19}65[1]

{San Francisco}

extreme of performer entertaining personable and glib—which was Lew
Welch; both raising questions as to whether poetry really does range so.
But at least entertainment is not a gross misuse of the audience. A program
of Leonore Kandel, Ted Berrigan and Ed Sanders was a delight—Lenore
coming up in the Coffee House circuits a true popular poet, sweet sentiments
of sex and homilies of Buddhistic-brotherhood.[2] A young man during inter-
mission running down toward the stage called out to a friend—"I've but to
touch that girl!" Returning to read "To Fuck With Love," I see it is a script
for a performer (as much of Ferlinghetti is){.}

8/12   This putting the poem over (or as with Allen Ginsberg who read
with much bathos, trying to put it over with feeling) doesn't have the
beauty of reading towards the feeling of the poem—here both John and Bob
were memorable in their readings. It's taking some time to get copies of the
tapes but I certainly will get these two readings for you; both reading so for
the tempering of the verse itself, and the emotion of the poet returning to its
form there, not using the poem as an occasion for the emotion's display.

If I belabor this distinction again and my abhorrence of the "personality"
occasion, it's because not only Allen but Charles made such use of their
readings. In Allen's case the reading began well, with a full voice being given
to some of the same diary passages that I disliked in Vancouver, but soon
Allen was drinking from a flask and bellowing off into a personal confessional
to out-right ham whining and pleading [don't we have more than enuf of this
from the monstrous emoting of Johnson?]—to be expected. But then two
nights later we got the same treatment and more so from Charles, who
arrived drunk and drinking, Barbara Joseph in some stupid sympathy having
given him two dexamils to lift him out of his actual depresst pre-reading
temper. After forty-five minutes or so of Charles emoting and throwing up
chunks of what he does not like about himself, I calld an intermission from
the floor, shouting out "Charles. Give us a break to go pee." But it was a
break too to leave without making a scene of it; as it certainly wld have been
had I expresst my disgust. He had begun reading very badly (too drunk to
get thru) his "Ode On Nativity," then he announced he was going to talk,
and (belligerently) that "talk was poetry"; O.K., but nothing was moving
anywhere but up and at 'em in the first part. After the break when I left, he
talkt on "out of his head" until first the janitors and then the campus police
arrived at midnight to remove him and the remaining audience from the
building. At dinner last night, Paul Sawyer a Unitarian minister who stayd for
the whole thing and went then to the party afterwards recalld an interesting
episode. During the second section Bob calld out for Charles to read some
poems. Olson stopt in tracks and tried, reading with distaste an opening
stanza, and then came over to Bob's side of the platform and said: "This is
the last time you are going to correct me Robert Creeley!" At the party Bob

confronted Charles and askt him what he had meant, but Charles could not remember saying that and denied it of course.

The thing is that there was some diabolus playing in the performance—the very opposite of talk seeking out its own inner form and content, spinning out webs of thought; for in this talk of Charles's one got right off the purposive drive.

It had a beneficial severance for me of my adherence to the power of the personality. In some sense I have more respect for his poems than he had that night (well, except there was a respect after the fact of being drunk at the service[3]

where I would take Kung's "no ought" for my way (which don't mean I'm not as ridden by "oughts" as you could be, but only that I don't vote for them as a directive). And, often, I will take a directive from some possibility in poetry that has been prohibited. As, perhaps in life *Poetry* itself was prohibited as a vocation in my family's view. I do know that the "no ought" came as a great relief from the false law of the super ego—which can take over against the order of the whole nature. Freud observes of the Id that it knows no ought (has not eaten of the Tree of the Knowledge of thou shalt and though shalt not).

Only to say, nor would I make an "ought" out of the by-now belabord "Winter Song." To be responsible to it, is not to be subservient or beholding to it.

———————

We dont know yet how it will turn out, but after Jess's sell-out show in Los Angeles he received only a $200 check—and that (with no explanation) in reply to four letters asking what had come of the some $5000 due Jess after the show.[4] All this, just when I was away (I went up to Vancouver January 3rd) and poor Jess had the brunt of the whole thing, tho I wrote as often as I could manage. Three years work! The dark presentiment is that when Jess wrote to Lyn Foulkes,[5] who also is with Rolf Nelson, he wrote back that Rolf owed him $4000 from his last show—over a year ago . . . It doesn't mean that we will be deprived, but that we will not be able, if the money has been embezzled, to make the down payment on a house: more years for Jess without a proper studio and work space. And, of course, the shock and betrayal, when you have been misused in a friendly relation.

———————

We've come home to a crowded week or two of things to clear up. Taxes to face. And news came this morning that Ida Hodes is in the hospital with something wrong with her back, we are off in another hour to see her. And, more happy,—indeed, joyous—Joanne Kyger and Jack Boyce (a very good painter—a "real" painter, that is) are to be married tomorrow in a big (seventy-five guests) wedding at the Swedenborgian church. . . .

I am at work on composing a *Selected Poems* for Stuart Montgomery's *Fulcrum Press* in England. Given up to 120 pages at 45 lines a page, it will be much more than the *City Lights* book. And I will use the run-on format of *The Opening of the Field* and *Roots and Branches* for maximum contents. Including a good number of poems that have not previously been included in books, like "The Ballad of the Green Lady" or "The Revenant"—

O yes! I seem to have received from Norton a copy of Raymond Roseliep's book but no *All*, Zukofsky.? As soon as I have the right poetry-reading time I will venture out in the Roseliep volume.[6] Did I write you how struck I was by Dorn's two poems that appeard in *Paris Review* 35?[7] I had dismisst his long poems as aftermaths of *Maximus* and worse of Charles's dogmatic directives—and saw clearly, these two poems had such a power and directive of their own—I was off the beat. I feel better prepared, anyway, to read the Dorn volume *Geography* which Montgomery sent me from England— including the poems I spoke of above "The Problem of the Poem for my Daughter, Left Unsolved" and "The Sense Comes Over Me, And the Waning Light of Man By the 1st National Bank": they're magnificent poems

> "No woman is Helena
> unless the culture has provided for the passage of pain
> and no people can construct the delicacies of culture
> until they imagine Helena. . . . "

but the above high ringing passage is most beautiful in its full context of personal prejudice, crankiness, delighted use of vernacular and vulgar—and thruout a following out of the dance of consonants and song of vowels a real poetic intelligence—

At the Vancouver festival,[8] Robin read the entirety of *The Holy Forest* (*Cups, The Park, The Faerie Queen, The Moth Poems, Les Chimères*, and the four or so poems since then) which came as a great delight—I was struck with the poetics of the whole as a ritual of magical objects (including the individual poem itself as a magical object), to cast a wonder or spell, in and of itself, such as a fairy-persona maintains itself by, a privacy in that sense, in which the actual soul appears. In the context the chimeras are most true, not to Nerval in the original, but to the Nerval who is resurrected in the spelling of the poetic world of Robin's own things. "It all coheres" can be taken over from the claritas of Pound (the force-field of his work) and in *Les Chimères* is evocative of the miasma of drifts and moth-lights, lightning-bugs, in which the projection of Blaser's fairy-field exists. The critical problem (his work *is* problematic) arises from the fact that he takes the spell as an ultimate and essential reality (so that he thinks the appearance of Nerval to be more really "Nerval" than the original)—and by extension I would guess he takes the world he presents to be more real than the actual life he derives from. Here I would take exception. I love the interplay of worlds. Not whatever world asserted against another. William James, again, here with his pluralism comes closest to my sense of the real. Robin presents a kind of poetic positivism, as if one distilld the essentially poetic from an insulting world.

But since that distillate is all gloriously the works of a poetry and a very crafty and craftsmanly works within its own order it works very well indeed.

love
Robert

Dearest Robert

*Thank* you for the tape. It is a treasure.

If you don't tell me the cost of it I'll anyway be able to find out when back in N.Y., how much tapes do cost. Also will make one, of the "Olga Poems" & some new ones, for you & Jess.

Look—send me the poem you sent to *The Nation*, which you will no doubt have gotten back with an offset notice saying (euphemistically) that I am on vacation. If it does not present vast typographical problems *I think* I can get it in there—i.e. George Kirstein wrote me a formal letter upon my resignation saying that if I ever have a poem of mine or another's that I specially want urgent publication of I shd regard *The Nation* as home base, etc. etc.—so I'll see if he means it. Actually it is rumored the whole thing is changing hands in the new year. If you'll let me have it (by return, if possible, please) I will rush it to him (or bypass him & send it to Grandin Conover) with a special letter. There is a poem by Wm. Burford on the same theme which I am hoping to get in similarly.

We had a good visit to Mexico on the whole—M. feels it broke up the summer for him too much, but doesn't utterly regret having accompanied us anyway. My mother was very well (at 80) & very nice, & Nik enjoyed it all so much that we left him down there for an extra week & he had the advantage of travelling back alone. Only thing is, we all managed to get sick—Dr. here is still taking cultures of intestinal bugs.

Also, I have an allergy—something (not yet located) has made me photo-sensitive, caused a rash (beginning before Mexico), & I have to stay indoors a whole week, at least—& possibly (tho I hope not, because it is such tricky stuff) I'll have to have cortisone. Damn drugs & products of all kinds are full of poisons, i.e. there are apparently dozens of ordinary things on the market which have this photosensitizing effect on certain skins. It may have been soap, hairspray, perfume, insect spray, etc etc.

The Western wildflowers Eve Treim sent me have come up & are lovely. Luckily they are near my window so I can see them tho' I can't go outdoors.

The 15-month-old baby of our friends the Fussiners is being operated on tomorrow at Ann Arbor—open-heart surgery. I keep thinking of them, today especially. They have been told it is, well, a 50/50 chance.

Your letter about the SF Poetry Conf. says some important things very clearly for me. Bro. Antoninus' reading in N.Y. a couple of years ago was the worst thing of *that* kind I've witnessed. But even aside from "live perform-ance," the little mags seem to me currently full of *printed* "performances," uses of language & ostensible poetry to "express themselves" in the crude sense in which excess/unwanted milk is "expressed" from a woman's breast (or a cow's udder)—a sort of excretory function. I hope there won't be any more poetry-fests for a few years. Don't you think that what most young people who attend take away from them is just that memory of performance, of personalities?

Charles saying "Talk is poetry" (even if drunk when he said it) is revealing —because, to me, tho' I am susceptible to the grandeur of what I think is his best work, much of his published work is *not* poetry, *only* talk. Talk can be poetry but not all talk is poetry. Much of Olson's talk, in prose & in poetry, has always seemed pompous, inflated, overextended (I can't judge of his conversational talk, since Vancouver was my sole experience of it). That he shd. make such a remark seems to me to be tied up with something in him that obstructs him from being more of the time the marvellous poet he is in the best poems; & who is there in the world that he wd. listen to, & thereby perhaps come to admit & overcome that obstruction? (Not a rhetorical question. You? Creeley? Is there anyone? Is there anyone he respects & does not need to dominate? His age, his size, his influence on so many (who hero-worship him), all combine to isolate him, insulate him from constructive, caring criticism, it seems to me. Am I wrong?) Prime recent example of what I mean by overextension & windbaggery is the introduction to Ed Sanders' *Peace Eye*.[1] You probably disagree I guess—but to me it is a disservice to Sanders to have produced such an introduction.

All summer I've been trying to work towards a "Hymn to Eros" & I've finally done it but it is much much shorter—2 stanzas, 11 & 12 lines respectively—than I had thought it wd be. Altogether, what I've been able to do this summer seems slight—I'd hoped to be given some large work to do, as last summer with the "Olga Poems"—but so far it has not been so, & we have only until Sept. 8th or so this year.

We hope John (Wieners) will turn up here before the month is out— though we also hope some other possible visitors won't come. We have some now—Jake Leed ("Jacob Lititz" of *B.M.R.* #1 or 2) & his wife & 2 kids— old friends, (at least, he is,) but curiously passive people, shut-off really, she especially, for whom one has to make a continuous social and emotional effort—or else, as we've done now, send them all off to swim without us. . . .[2]

Alas, the fact is one's human concern for any individual ebbs & flows but social structures (such as summer visits) take no heed of that. Fatigue, & longing to come to grips with one's own work & (in a marriage) to explore one's most intimate relations more deeply & fruitfully causes the ebb of one's concern, one's *interest* in, friends who are not one's closest friends. They come seeking—vitality, refreshment? warmth—& one can only squeeze out little drops for them . . . unable to give or to take, to maintain the sense of I-Thou. Here they come, & I must go & suggest hot-dogs to them.

Love—
Denny.

and again I can't really tell you how much it means to me to have that record (tape). M & N listened avidly likewise. Nik is absolutely gorgeous these days, I feel extraordinarily lucky to have such a son.

dear Denny,

"The Up Rising" enclosed. At the present point Grandin Conover writes that decision on the poem will be held over until after Labor Day when a new literary editor will be going in on *The Nation*. In the version I sent to Conover I had added to the first draft the Lawrence eagle and the burning figure of Blake which I still take as a development that fits—but also I had added particulars that now seem to me out of place here. The poem needs to be a blast. Anyway, the copy I send is a later version than the one at *The Nation* at present, and I think more what it shld be.

On top of Charles' inflated/depression, bringing questions and new judgments for me, on the first of August Jack Spicer was taken to the County Hospital in a coma with a combination of alcoholism, pneumonia, internal bleeding (from his falling on the street) and some unlocated infection that following the pneumonia sent his temperature to 106. Tuesday the 17th at 3 AM he died. There was only one day, Saturday the 7th, when he seems to have been conscious enough to recognize and talk with those who visited him. I went the following Monday and found him in the low of a terrible relapse. The poets who had been in his Magic Workshop—Ebbe Borregaard, George Stanley, Harold Dull, and Joanne Kyger who came to San Francisco in 1958—had come free of his dictatorship of the poem; but for younger poets his death will surely be disorienting. It is for all—such was the force of his own poetics and challenge—the end of an era.

For me, his opposition to my poetics had been so fanatical, his death did not mean the loss of a friend. But even in this short time since his death, which I have accepted as certain since that Monday two weeks ago, I've been able to read his work freed of its person, the programmatic content is no

**355**

August 23/{19}65
{San Francisco}

longer significant of quarrels I must have with Jack, and I find much more of meaning and feeling released. With all, there too, such a terrible obstruction thrown up against any fullness of life.

I must get back to my typewriter, but I want to get this off in the mail first. Along with "UpRising" I'm sending some photographs Jess took of the cartoon stage of some of the paintings he has done for the coming show (November) in Los Angeles.

O yes, about "cost" of tapes, I get them for $1.50 a tape and it costs me nothing to have the reproduction made at the Tape Center. Please, let it be a present. I hope soon to have the copies of the things from the Conference to send you (Richard Baker has been on vacation since the Conference).[1] We look forward to a tape of your work. Jess heard a beautiful reading of the "Olga Poems" on KPFA from their New York affiliated station. That I missed.

love
Robert

---

**356**

{August 23, 1965
San Francisco}

proof reading the typescript on UP RISING

stanza 3, line 8 read "below in the jungles"
    for "below in jungles"
page 2, stanza 1 for "exploitations" read
    "exploitation"

o, yes. page 1, stanza 3, line 5 for "Blakes"
    read "Blake"

RD

---

**357**

Sept. 1st {1965}
Temple {Me.}

*Thanks* for the photos of Jess's cartoons (wish that word were reserved for its original meaning) I *love* them.

Dearest Robert

"Up Rising" is going into this week's (next wk's) *Nation*.[1] This means you will almost certainly not have received proofs in time to correct them—but please don't worry, I have been on the phone going thru' it word by word & I think (am sure) all will be correct. One thing—we are probably leaving out the notation "Passages 25" for this reason: the poem takes up so much space that it's going on 2 pages, & Con {Grandin Conover} fears that the subtitle, or rather—well, whatever one calls that—might confuse some readers, making them think it is 2 poems. Hope you don't mind.

The rush is not only because "the sooner the better" but because it is

Con's last week at *The Nation* & it's a conspiracy between him & me to make damn sure the poem doesn't get killed by someone.

We're probably leaving for N.Y. on Tues. 7th, then will go up to Putney from there on the 10th.

The poem seems to me to relate to certain French poetry—i.e. what a magnificent flexibility such work as your Breton translations has helped to give you.

In haste—love—<br>Denny

dear Denny,

I finally got the tape of my U.C. reading and lecture off to you, after one session of making copies in which I had forgotten to account for the fact that with the introduction by Parkinson and my own opening remarks the tape was too long for 1800 feet. Luckily, the tape center machine for reproducing tapes is freely available for me and there was no expense involved. This time, as you will notice, the opening of the reading itself cut off part of "from Julian, Hymn to the Mother of the Gods" and I erased that phrase and dubbd it in here, not too well I fear, but from there on you are in the performance.

Jess registers that reading in the context of a group of friends in a room does more justice to "Passages." Well . . . I think this may be true in relation to "Fire" (where on this reading the opening ideogram lacks pulse) but for "The Torso," for instance, the impersonality of a public reading seemd to me to give just the distance to register shifts of tone exactly.

I've got myself out on a "Passage" opening with

"They take their souls in war
     as we take soul in the poem. . . . "[1]

which has stirrd up such a tangle of my own feelings of categorical opposition to war, when at the same time I feel this obscures the fact that men fight *false* wars—"for an eidolon of Helen, who was never there, never abducted" that's part of it; but now that men who are not soldiers, who do not "take their souls in war" must fight, against their soul's volition; and not to protect what they love (for their cities, their wives, their companions and children are destroyed behind their lives); nor against evil men (for they bomb and burn from a distance, having absolutely no knowledge of the nature of what they destroy).

There is too much, too many opportunities at this point in my stored-up reactions to "they" and "war" that obscures and chokes up in me the inspiration of the poem that would blaze a way, a figure out of all confusion. (I hear, for instance, whenever I turn to the poem, Roland's horn—as in *Medieval Scenes*

**358**

October 7, {19}65
{San Francisco}

—but in every judgment my mind has at this point the Chant—*Chanson de Roland* seems a figment of a nationalism I mistrust. "For clear as are the different racial or national traits throughout the medieval period, they constantly appear in conjunction with other elements," I find in Taylor's *Medieval Mind*: "They are discerned working beneath, possibly reacting against, and always affected by, the genius of the mutual interaction of the whole"[2]

Hesiod, as I remember, stands as a farmer in disapproval even contempt of war. There are two kinds of strife he argues in *Works and Days*—"For one fosters evil war and battle, being cruel: her no man loves" but then he goes on to praise the strife of men's competition in work, tho even here at most he says "strive" thru works. "War" and "work"—//but I am sure when the matter of this comes clear (the inner process of selection and concentration done) that pendant of "Passages" II, in which men fought upon a plain (connected in my mind with a nomadic people fighting the expansion of empire—here, of the Mongol Empire in the Danube), the battle will reappear.

And then Whitman's "I too haughty shade also sing war" will come into place.

I've accepted an honorary office as advisor to the Poetry Collection in the Rare Books Room at U.C., which brings an honorarium of only $250 a year—where in these first months I am having to spend a full day each week getting a picture of what the Library has to start with; but I receive also full Library privileges, which I have long wanted (extended borrowing, for instance), and I will have direct effect in getting a solid collection in the stacks for open circulation, as well as a free hand in building a non-circulating collection (all local publications, and all significant publications outside that field)—it would be a great help if you would send me lists of poetry (books, magazines—including special articles in particular issues) that you find curious, amusing, interesting, important, significant—in an ascending order of impression. I want to assure "key" works from a variety of grounds (for instance, from Jackson MacLow's or from Clayton Eshleman's view). All this is exhilarating, in the collection (deposited with the Library by Tram Combs) I've already found out eddies and backwaters of the mainstream I had passed by or never known of. Where the form and content muddy-up in confused minds and confusing spirits. Perhaps my library job may encourage the tolerance necessary to come to some view of the poetry of our time as an ecology. There is some interest in what happens to Pound's poetics in its swamps and deltas (Martinelli's *Anagogic and Paideumic Review*); or in the overflow (let's say salt-crater invading the land) of Beat poetics (*Beatitude* series).[3]

A current magazine I had never seen before (*Residu*) provides an extreme symptom of the sickness and cultivated debility of the self-poisoners (meth-head literature).[4] "Noxious," if that could mean hurt, rather than hurting, damaged rather than damaging, would be the word for the product. (This area, then, must relate both to the aspect of Ginsberg's "Howl" as a poetry of the injured, and of the "sick" school following Robert Lowell's lead). Spicer's poetry in its drive towards alienation as the greater reality belongs in this movement. "Poetry has ruined my life," he wrote me a year before his death; and I think the *intent* of his poetry was to prove life wretched. (So that my poetry always seemd false to him, because I am sure that we but fail to live, that wherever we even come alive we are aroused with the magnificence of it).

Out of all this emerges a reconsideration of the terms "rational" and "irrational" which in their most common meaning both describe aspects of man's good nature: i.e. that it has certain ratios and in these is comely; and that it has not only what goes by the numbers but in its variety the disresembling, the unfactorable / and in both these has the beauty of an open field in which stones, grass, insects, bits of waste paper, a path, a beer-can, rabbit-holes and snails trails conjoin beyond ratio in a larger reality.

And differing from the sense of irrational, any meaning of madness, unreasonableness (we must think of the beer-can here and the waste-paper as having been recognized and permitted—human intrusions as they are— as parts of the composition of the field; we might remove them in reason of our love of the ground they were in contempt of)—what's on my mind is that the unreasonable so little can be identified with the absurd or the surreal. The basic concept of reason and ration, of what is larger than ratios can account for, and of what intends to demean or destroy any ground of reason, needs to be distingisht.

Greatness, Dante in his *Convivio* (which I have been reading, towards a Dante lecture later this month)[5] values, "because it is the light which brings out with clearness the good in a person and its opposite. And how much wisdom and how much virtuous disposition remains concealed by not having this light, and how great madness and how great vices are exposed to view by having this light." He means greatness here, I think, as the power of action great personalities take. But I would relate the passage to the vividness which writing can have to bring both good and evil to light. Burroughs and Lamantia in their ruin of nature we are not vacillating or weak, nor do they falsify their experience; they are resolute in their dismay.

The mass of writing in such a collection of what is current seems to be in limbo, whatever experience there being characterless. Writers who present some homogenized personality to the world made after the world's models, having no heart or urgency. This way and that way madness. Or this way and that way goodness (As I find Robert Kelly's intentions of love and blessing without the force of necessity.) This way and that way badness (the limbo of popular anti-social poetry).

I don't think in such judgments we define the object (say in this case the nature of Kelly's work)—that the artist himself does, but we do delineate perspectives of our own objectification, we give a key to anyone else who has read Kelly, *how* we see it in comparison with how another has seen it. I am the more reacting to Kelly at the present time because he sent me his "115 Weeks" at Christmas time, a monumental ms, as a present and homage. Where I was saddend by the lack of force and how much muddling around and cud-chewing of whatever emotion there was. Deep or shallow, the image, that may burn its way into the reader's consciousness or haunt his unconscious or decorate his fancy, has its art in its being vividly realized.

Amen. We are so much of one mind on much of this, Denny, that I begin to feel redundant. (Its being so long since I've written, has me wanting to spend the whole day once I have started.)

love
Robert

## 359

dear Denny,

Your "Notes on Organic Form" clears a good deal of way for me.[1] The opening statement seems to be more succinct than any I've tried to make of this fundamental formalism (perhaps because I get wound up in extenuating circumstances). "a method of recognizing what we perceive"—that paragraph is close to home. The whole account of the process of the poem—of your own way in it—is lovely. And when you get to "whether an experience is a linear sequence or a constellation raying out from and into a central focus or axis . . . discoverable only in the work, not before it" I feel like I'm sailing. (Tho my most excited feeling of constellation comes not from centrality but from a complex of origins of force that set all matters into a need for a particular equilibration—not a mandala or wheel but a mobile) The next paragraph on rime and returns in the poem is beautiful. [so much of this essay reading it now comes as if it were new, as if you were just now (I just now reading for the first time) writing it.] "distinct units of awareness" flashes out—mint; and right.

I would say here about the "free verse" and organic poetry question that the organic as you define it "of recognizing what we perceive," and further as a working consciousness of the field of experience is different from that organic form which seeks to imitate the growth forms of shell, tree, or human body for in your concept of organic form the poem itself is an organism growing (living) into its own life as a form.[2] (Here Henry James novels arising as they do from a germ or seed and growing are *organic*.)

The thing is that not only do we feel that some poems having that creative intent are organic but we feel everything is so in its inner vital nature; and so the imitative or conventional modes appear as organisms under constraint of outer conformities.

"Free verse" anyway most notably sought the discharge of feeling, the poem conceived not as an experience having its own process and organism-life, but as a by-product of a person's sensibility or passion, a fragrance or sweat of the poet. Where we are never confronted with what is going on in the poem but with what the poet thinks or feels about whatever. "Free" verse is anyway primarily "free" of just the awareness of what is going on, of form/process, that is crucial to the organic.

I have been reading and at the same time studying Dante's *Convivio.* Because the work is out of print in English translation, I copy out as I go where I find passages I will want to return to. In his discussion there of his four-fold reading of the poetic real, he insists upon the "literal" as fundamental, not to be lost in the higher levels of allegorical (which he calls truth "hidden in a fiction"), the moral and the eternal or anagogical. The exact passage is The Second Treatise, Chapter I: "And in this expounding, the literal sense should always come first as the one in the meaning whereof the others are included, and without which it were impossible and irrational to attend to the others." There follows "It is impossible to come at the inside save we first come at the outside" and "Inasmuch as the literal meaning is always the subject and material of the others, it is impossible to come at the knowledge of the others before coming at the knowledge of it."

The "literal" here is Williams' "things" in his "no ideas but in things"; as Dante would have it "no fictions but in the literal"—our actual life being the literal life we live and the poetic life having its origin there (as we ourselves have our origin there; the poem and the poet twins of the same life).

It seems to me that the allegorical "truth hidden in a fiction" refers to the actual life experience seen now as *creative*, a fiction in which a truth is to be uncovered. This would be our sense of the story in the actual (at its most simple) or of the romance; for Dante it was a sense of the creative intent, the divine sentence moving towards its message, the literal now words as a nexus of our own experience moving towards communication and of all happenings as God's expression moving towards communion.

In the Frederick Will notes on my work in this same issue, he is misled (as most contemporary criticism is) to try only for a sense of the author and to disregard so the terms of a world the poem opens out upon.[3] The "mountebank" with its direct accusation of the fraudulent is the sign of how much distaste the critic suffered in reading; but in just this area that he finds "wrong"—that is, elusiveness and pretension he is on the track of my way, for I had, after all, to address directly the question in myself of permission for the complex of pretend-pretense-pretension that I saw as a threshold I must pass towards the eternal. (The bank I had to mount)—(The critic in the *N.Y. Review of Books*, the one who approached the work by way of philosophy at least got something of the attitude towards truth by hypotheses that I feel.)[4]

[Where I feel taken all wrong by this recent critic in *Poetry* is in his taking fun in the reading. "It has been fun," "to hear him air . . . ," "coy," "archness," "tricks"—all these seem unfair to me, they are so far from an appropriate approach.]

But back to the matter of the "fiction in which truth is hidden"; Dante does not mean, and certainly I never do mean, that the poet hides truth in a fiction; but that (to refer to *Paterson* again) sensing truth at work he will—like Madam Curie with the pitchblend—work in the fiction. Where the analogy doesn't work is that this "fiction" is necessary for the truth to emerge. We can't render the truth free from its fairy tale.

But I like to play in the excitement of this realm of fictions.

Dante in The Second Treatise of *The Convivio* explicating a line of his Ode—"for I may not tell it to any other, so strange it seemeth to me" relates this to his "loving" wisdom (so that wisdom appears as the fiction hiding the truth of the lady) which he knows men will not understand, and so he addresses the angelic powers of Love itself (the planet Venus) as his hearers. Wicksteed, as editor of the *Convivio* notes after "Chapter XIV" of this allegory:[5] "This chapter is full of curious and interesting matter, but it would be vain to attempt to find any real penetration or wisdom in its fantastic analogies. . . . " (But I am off the track here, the passage I was searching for provides a much more apt sequence. Dante in Chapter xiii, writes: "Wherefore, feeling myself raised from the thought of that first love even to the virtue of this, as tho in amazement I opened my mouth in the utterance of the ode before us, expressing my state under the figure of other things . . . [then] nor were the hearers so well prepared as to have easily apprehended straightforward words; nor would they have given credence to the true meaning, as they did to the fictitious; and, accordingly, folk did, in fact, altogether believe that I had been disposed to this love, which they did not believe of the other." To which Wicksteed comments: "His readers did understand him to have been moved by love of a mortal woman. But as he has never till now made the experiment of telling them anything else the passage seems singularly inconclusive."

The clock has raced around to time over since I should have been on my way, to get to Berkeley for some of the Viet Nam Day scene. I've to get a bit of lunch and go.

Love
Robert

Dear Robert

Although it's so long since I've written to you I feel very close to you, both because of your letters and because I've been—as I always do, but more—rereading your poems.

Reasons for not writing are of the usual kind—the transition from Temple to N.Y.; adjustment to new jobs (teaching once a week at Drew, also once a week for 1 semester at C.C.N.Y); a 3-week visit from Elvira, our Mexican friend, involving much sightseeing since this was her 1st & very likely only visit to N.Y.; the pile-up of work of various kinds that occurred while I was devoting myself to taking her around. Plus the fact that tho' I've been (despite all the political horrors) feeling very buoyant & happy this fall, I have *not* been writing, at all, since August—until a few days ago—and that, in some obscure way, made me reluctant to write to you. I don't know whether out of a sort of shame, or because I felt obscurely I might let something that might have gone towards a poem go into a "real" letter, or what. None of the reasons I can think of really rings a bell.

Now I at last feel again that I've got something going, am again a working poet. Dare not yet send what I've done, am too unsure of it.

Your two recent letters were specially good ones. The comments on my prose piece in *Poetry* give me a glimmer of an idea of where I can take up the theme & go further. The quotations from Dante's *Convivio* send me to it: I'll read it in Widener when I'm up in Cambridge next week, my 1st visit this year. *Thank you* for the tape. We haven't played it yet as we wanted to wait till Elvira had left. I plan to play it tonight. Haven't made you that tape of the "Olga" poems and new ones, yet, because (mainly) of my timidity with the mechanics of it—but Nik gave me detailed instructions and I think I'll manage it.

I enjoy my trips to Drew—take the Hoboken Ferry, then a little Erie-Lackawanna train which, after it gets past the N.J. industrial mess, runs through oldfashioned backyards, wooded lots, & eventually real woods. The campus of Drew is green & it has beautiful big trees & some nice Victorian brick buildings. I love my students, both there & at City College. With the latter I'm preparing to read some of you & some of Bob.

I've been reading in French a strange &, I thought, beautiful novel by Henri Bosco called *Malicroix*.[1] I think you & Jess might enjoy it. Also, for its eerie parts Helen would, but I don't think she reads French so will not mention it to her & frustrate her. We see her & Pat sometimes. They see a good deal of Lew Ellingham & I remain leery of him, his excessive twisty-ness makes me feel positively simple minded.

Diane di Prima & Alan Marlowe & kids are planning to emigrate (with a printing press) to a small town in Nova Scotia. For some reason they put on

360

Sat./Sun.
October 30/31st {19}65
277 Greenwich St
N.Y. 7 N.Y.

a big "square" act for me—it wd. be perfectly convincing if I didn't know, from Helen for instance, about their other side. I don't like their passing bad checks & boasting about it but I've always admired Diane's ability to lead a "free" life however painful, I have felt she had a courage I might not have had if life had called upon me for it, & it makes me uneasy that she should somehow think it necessary to assume a special persona before me. I wonder if she knows she's doing it. But anyway, they do sound genuinely enthused about going off to Nova Scotia & leading a different kind of life, I do hope it works out for them. Mitch has been joking about it, saying they must have found a magnificent supply of LSD or something there. One thing seems sure, their experience of the physical reality of the printing machine is v. important to them, in contrast to posing for photos, especially to Alan.

We've been seeing Galway Kinnell quite often. He has new poems which seem far in advance of what he's done before—I have an idea you would like them, tho' I know you've not thought much of his work before. Can't get copies (yet) as he's one of those poets who keep revising, are never really through with a poem. We're concerned about him, he injured his liver drinking heavily after having had hepatitis, & was actually told he has cirrhosis & might not have long to live, but he's on the wagon at the moment & looks well & perhaps he'll be OK—but he gets very tense & it is a struggle of will for him to stay off it—not that he's a real soak, but he is a tense person who used to feel more at ease with a few drinks, & quite *often* drank a lot also. Now it has become a battle between love of life & the death wish. The new life in his poems has all the poignancy of his having come close to death— yet maybe it—certainly only it—will keep him living.

Mitch has been reading Blake, Keats, Wordsworth, Coleridge, in connection with his classes. This is a period he hasn't read deeply or widely in before & his discoveries are stimulating. I feel a love & intimacy for some of the writers of that period, whom I used to read so much when I was very young & with whom I've always felt I would be at home if I could get back into the past. Crabby fiery Hazlitt & desperate noble spirited Haydon as well as the poets themselves. Often when I read about Coleridge I think I am reading about you, till I come to some regret that he wrote so few poems & then I am so relieved that it is he not you, & that though the range & power of your mind & conversation are so like his you are constantly fulfilling your possibilities, writing the poems, while Coleridge stopped short as a poet when he was younger than we are now, much younger if I'm not mistaken, turned from the poem to those dull tracts . . .

Three of the students I had at the Y last year, Emmett Jarrett, Dick Lourie, & Jason Miller, are writing a lot & well & come to see us sometimes. Jason especially is a solitary who lives in & for poetry & I think will really ripen. He wanders—& if he shd. go to S.F. sometime, could I send him to you? He's a gentle person I think you & Jess would like. If you were doing a workshop he would be a devoted student. Some day he may turn up there. He's not a kid—about 28 I think.

I've been rereading a good deal of Stevens & Pound. We have those Caedmon records of E. P., the second of which has Canto 99 on one side. I keep finding short poems of Stevens I've forgotten, or feel I've never read at all.

*The Nation* job has been given, quite at random & ignoring my recommendations, to a young guy called Michael Goldman whom I suspect is a lemon. Did they ever send you the issues containing readers' letters praising "Uprising"? If not I'll copy & send. Kirstein almost flipped his lid over Conover's conspiring with me to print it but McWilliams stood up for it and Kirstein backed down. I was of course still in Maine, & K. couldn't fire Conover as Con was leaving the following week anyway.

Oh, you asked me about magazines in connection with your advisory work at Berkeley: (how intelligent of them to get you, I am amazed!)—but the thing is, I feel very much out of touch, I don't think I know of any you don't know. If something "local" turns up I'll certainly let you know. I suppose you've seen the one Ellingham has started? I haven't even been to Bob Wilson's since the spring,[2] and I don't go to Metro & Hardware readings because I shrink from seeing all those people, I like them but that's just it, I begin to feel like Keats & the sparrow, I feel as if I am being crowded out of myself by a host of identities. Therefore I don't have full access probably to what is going on in new little mag.s, pamphlet poetry books, etc. But I will certainly tell you if I see anything I think interesting which you might not see. Do read Jim Harrison's *Plain Song* (Norton)— ignore silly blurb ("D. L. says" etc.). Do you receive *Secant*?[3]

When we were returning from visiting Nik earlier in October we stopped at the Clark Institute in Williamstown. Had seen it some years back when it had first opened—now there are more paintings on view including a magnificent Piero della Francesca. Among them is a tiny Monticelli landscape I think Jess wd. love & I'm going to try & get a transparency of it to send you. Were you ever there?

We took part in the 5th Ave march (25000) Oct. 16th—rather heart-ening to see all those people soberly & yet in good fellowship gathering, passing the strung-out morons with rotten eggs etc., really stupid-looking people. But then yesterday they got together a march *for* the war—which I didn't see—using Boy Scouts etc. When I say I've been feeling happy I mean that in the face of constant disgust & tension the joie de vivre that has nothing to do with the Reason mounts in me & brims over—never has the fall weather enveloping brown city trees & pigeons & dusty windows & river clouds looked more wonderful to me, even tho' the last 2 falls we've been in the country.

People's faces in the street, the tug boats on the Hudson.

On my birthday Mitch & I took a walk in Central Park at dusk—the lights were coming on in the huge cliffs of 5th Ave & CPW,[4] the bears in the otherwise closed zoo—& the sealions—were lively—I can't articulate it, it was wild & strange, beautiful, brought back my childhood, the sense at that hour of being on the edge of another world.

Love—

~~Denise~~ Denny.

---

**361**

Dec. 3/{19} 1965
{San Francisco}

dear Denny,

Back from Los Angeles just last night, I've crawld into bed for the day, reading bits from books found there—where we were for Jess's show Sunday Nov. 28 or 29? Then Jess came back with the Burton's who had driven us down with the paintings in a trailer. The show was beautiful and twelve of the paintings (out of fourteen) had sold by the opening day of the show (the 1st of Dec.) after a Preview, champagne and all, on Sunday. The Burtons bought the portrait of me, and Barbara Joseph the Homage to Sir Edward one of the Babe on a white cat.[1] He has gone far ahead in these paintings in exploring color tones and sets (what in poetry would be vowel progressions), and, reflecting upon what he has achieved, I can see what correlating the intuitive organization of vowels with the designing organization of numbers—so that in composing vowels might appear by progressions of three and of four, giving another more obscure source of measure in the poem, particularly as the deeper imagination begins to awake to the numbers as meanings—I can see some such development of trinities and quarternities in the patterning of the poem as opening out archetypal feelings such as Jung is fascinated by, and also organic-cosmic feelings of mathematic and algebraic relations—of music.

Did you see the *Trinity's Trine* when it was at Macy's?[2] It is built of triads of color as well as of image and pictorially of the elements air, fire and water active within the environment of the fourth—earth. [This canvas and two others were bought by Fraser's in London for a show which is to open there in January of new California artists.]

I don't mean, of course, that one must calculate such triads. Calculation I find closes me off from resources rather than opening the way. But I mean that now I am excited that I am prepared to recognize such elements of number when they appear and so participate consciously and cooperatively in their action. I would like to work with counts (perhaps listening to records of Dante's *Commedia* with its tercet rime moving $\nabla$ (or was it $\Delta$) two rimes in one tercet and the third (angle or point of the triangle) in the following, giving an interlocking graceful pattern) perhaps listening to the *Purgatorio* while I was preparing for my Dante lecture last month excited this idea. Not to make the sets regular, but to set such counts into motion.

I'm still having trouble with "Passages 26—The Soldiers"—things surge up in me almost to the point and then feel wrong or not ready—or I will be some time or where where I cannot start working on it. And every conscious attitude is baffled. It's not to be an anti-war passage, but another vision: of those who have only the war to take their lives in. The vision appalls me but impels me, and I do not want to see it perhaps. See = say. Yet I feel that when the poem comes thru clear again it will move passionately. Months of being on the edge of it.

*Poetry* has taken the sequence of "Passages" 22-23-24. For some time in the Spring I take it.

In reaction to Robin's version of *Les Chimères* of Nerval, which he claimed was not a version but a translation, I set about and did as near a literal translation as I could to restore particularly the personal and communal keys, in the light of scholarly exegeses of the poem. The set of twelve will follow perhaps "Passages" 27 in the plan of the book (27 is to be "The Dancers").[3]

I have still to complete my task I set myself of translating Hugh's "Pleine Mer" (which goes after "Passages" 24).

A tract of lectures by Steiner on *The Four Seasons and the Archangels* which I found in Los Angeles talks about withdrawing from the cosmos and returning into the "bosom" of ones self (as the elementals of plants return into the earth, leaves falling into mould, life drawing back into the root), life secreting itself) in the winter rhythm.[4]

Dec 19/65

Whatever I thot I had to go on to say before I sent the above is gone now. And the Steiner tract led to the Christmas poem I have already sent you. Enclosed a typescript of the "Earth Song" as it is now after having been some twelve times copied out by hand. You will find I've eliminated effects and moved towards a more common level ("blind Earth" for all its usualness). And writing it over and over, which meant hearing it thru over and over I found myself making shifts to render its music more open.

Also a set of translations I made of the "Chimeras" of Nerval after realizing how far Robin's "translation" was from a literary translation. Especially here with Nerval the literal is essential. (Looking back I see I have already above spoken of these).

Now from Vancouver an official commission has finally come thru to do a play there (it will be *Adam's Way*, with the second "act" being written there during the month of rehearsals) around the 10th of February. So I'll be going up the first week in January. Staying with Warren and Ellen {Tallman} and writing a little madly perhaps—for I have not only the play to do but a preface for a University Books Inc. edition of Vaughan's alchemical and magical works, which gives me the opportunity for an essay on the meaning of the esoteric tradition and of magic in the work of the creative artist. Had to revisit the Vaughans . . . And in turn the Vaughan (which I have read twice before) will feed back into the Second Act of *Adam's Way* which in its sequence of Gardens will move into Nature's garden and Hermes' garden. If the University resources can come up with it, I would like to costume the second play in Tudor or Stuart period—a Jonson masque.

Jess is working steadily towards the completion of the full *Book of Resemblances* which will then go off to Henry Wenning who will publish it this coming year, and we are determined to let it go thru as best it can be without worrying the question of exactitudes. It means that this next year I will be getting all my early work substantially into print. I am preparing a manuscript of *First Poems* from 1940 thru to include all of *Heavenly City, Earthly City* to submit to Oyez for next year, along with a smaller book of the program notes from the *Poetry Center* 1955–56 series.

*Open Space–White Rabbit* have already in process the Dante lecture (due, Stan {Persky} tells me, by the 28th) and *Cat and Blackbird*. Next year they plan to do a volume *A Looking Glass* which is to include the work between *First Poems* and *Poems 1948–49* [this latter book + *Caesar's Gate* I intend to combine for publication the following year]. And *Open Space* plan also in 1966 a new edition of *Letters*.

Jonathan Greene has *Fragments of a Disorderd Devotion* which he hopes to have out early in the year in his Gnomon series. I drew new plates for it. [This is a reduplication; because the text is in *Book of Resemblances*, but it will make something like the original available with my drawings etc.]

love<br>Robert

ps.

O yes, could you arrange, Denny, for a copy of Zuk's *All* to be sent to me? He wrote me I wld be getting a copy, and then one never came from the publishers.

---

## 362

1/10 book from Norton arrives: poems by Raymond Roseliep. Maybe not the *All* of this note.[1]

Dear Robert and Jess,

Many thanks for Christmas poem[2] and for yr letter (Jess) with the good news about your show. I didn't see the painting that was at Macy's, alas—

Helen told us of it but I went too late. I've finally made a tape, with Nik's engineering help, to send you, & will mail it as soon as I've played it over to see if it is alright. We erased the first reading of the "Olga" poems as it wasn't good. For the New Year, there is only the one main thing to wish—PEACE in Viet Nam & everywhere else.

Mitch is busy with a Veterans for Peace group.

Did Norton send *All*?

> With love always ever,
> Denny

Dearest Robert

I've been absolutely paralyzed by unwritten poems. But have at last come out of it, with one absolutely direct anti-war poem (finished this very day, though "brewed" & begun with false starts back in, oh, October I guess) and a completely *dis*engaged poem about angels,[1] and a short story. All of which I intend to type up for you to read this very week, so help me.

I'm very unsure if the "political" one is a good poem but it is even so a tremendous relief to have at least opened my mouth.

Your Xmas poem[2] was one about which I have felt & still feel considerable reservations. As you know I've come round in the past to particularly caring for poems of yours that I've not appreciated to begin with, so this may be a similar case. But I'll tell you what I feel anyway to *keep the weirs open.*

(1) The tender passage with which it opens is too smooth, too easy, bland. I think I know & share the response you are writing about, the beloved beauty of those young people *demonstrating* (literally) their concern for life & for each other. But the language somehow is slacker than the facts of what you are saying, I think.

(2) The part about Humphrey's head emerging from LBJ's asshole doesn't convince me the way similar things in Dante do. Dante *saw* such things with so much graphic detail (even tho economically, not needlessly elaborated) that one sees with him. This, rather than making me see it by hell's gloomy light makes me see a newspaper cartoon. And perhaps the reason is the same kind of reason you pointed out to me concerning that poem I scrapped about John Button; i. e., hyperbole/sentimentality—the reduction, to a willed 2-dimensional state, of a living person. Aside from the fact of Dante's graphic vision, he was writing about persons already dead. Humphrey, (though I have felt much *more* bitter about him than about Johnson because he seemed when I first heard of him, back at the Election, a man who might conceivably do some good, & who surely must know right from wrong, whereas LBJ is an ignorant Texan)—but Humphrey in any case is not yet dead like the people in Dante and surely

363

Jan. 25th {19}66
277 Greenwich St
N.Y. 7 N.Y.

if one is for peace, positively, one has to believe in the possibility of an inner turning in *any* other human being, according to his capacity, no?— so that however strongly one may condemn and be revulsed by their present actions one cannot assign them to hell while they live—one cannot deny without intimate personal knowledge that they are not at least *suffering*, from guilt, confusion, or whatever. I'm afraid I sound priggish?—but it is exactly of a kind of self-righteousness that an artist is guilty when he condemns any other human being to the hell of caricature. Or not *self-righteousness*, exactly—but I mean if one *judges*, one is setting oneself up as capable of judging, whereas the more fitting attitude is to *grieve, deplore, agonize*, without judging, because anguish doesn't separate itself from compassion. Or, compassion is indivisible, & if one is to learn to really feel compassion for the victim one must learn to feel it for the—what's the pair word?—victimizer?—too. It's so *easy* to think one is feeling for a burned child but so hard to remember the human soul, capable of change, of the murderer. And whether I'm right or not in this, it seems pragmatically true that for the artist some force of truth leaks out of the work *unless*, in such a case, his compassion can somehow manage to stretch as far as the criminal—even just to touch him with the tip of the outstretched fingers. . . .

(3) Then again the return to love, the tender vision of the Crèche, seems inadequately (not *freshly*) seen—too easily taken for granted.

Well, I may very well be quite wrong but you would not want me to withhold what I think, I know. And also, exactly what I am saying about "Earth's Winter Song" may be true of "Life at War," the poem I just finished. It is still too new for me to have much view of it.

Mitch's father died last week. He was "The Old Adam" of that poem, but as I stood at his grave I began to understand I had done him an injustice when I questioned his love because it was so incurious, so unknowing. I was *judging* him (again) for his lack of intellectual understanding & calling his love a "shadow of love," because of that lack, when it was something he was *incapable* of having. His love was blind as a baby's, an animal's, or an idiot's—no, that's exaggeration too; but it was totally nonverbal, not merely in expression but within him: simply because he *had* no words in which to register what he felt. That doesn't mean he didn't feel. I have to write something else to say so, some day, if I can.

Nik loved him, was always so patient & kind with him even after he had become senile.

I haven't got Robin's de Nerval back from Adrienne {Rich} yet (put off my visit to Cambridge this month so that Mitch & I could talk about the things Dad's death brought to mind). I'm anxious to compare your versions & his, & the originals. Robin's seemed very beautiful to me (of course yours do too) (but I wasn't checking against the French) & the framework of the preexisting de Nerval poems seemed to give him the clarity & coherence I've always felt insufficient in his own poems—I was hoping it would (this task undertaken & printed) lead him into a more open (less cagey) way of writing his own poems. Now your sense of them makes me wonder.

Current *Minnesota Review* has interviews with Bob & with me (mine 2 or more years old)—table of contents is buried in middle of issue so you might miss it in library.[3]

*Kayak* 5 has prose piece, "How the Poem Speaks" that looks worth reading (came today) by Louis Z Hammer.[4]

Did you get the Zukofsky all right?[5] Will have them send you paperback of Golding's *Ovid.* Print is small, but at least it is *there.*

I must go & get dressed now to meet Mitch & have supper in an Italian restaurant. He has the use of Tram Comb's pied à terre on Spring St., the old Italian part. It is much better for him than working in the house—& better for me too.

We saw *Marat/de Sade*[6]—I was disappointed because I'd expected it to be moving & it wasn't, tho' a very ingenious & original piece of theater. One remained too conscious throughout of how ingenious it was.

> With love
> from Denny

Dearest Robert,

I wrote the enclosed then felt afraid to send it. I've made "criticisms" of poems of yours before, & you of mine, & it's always been a part of everything else, in a context of the deepest friendship. So why should I feel afraid to send what is, after all, only a rather mild reservation? Well, it's because I've written so seldom of late, so that though the context is there for me always, of love for you, of the presence of you in my thoughts & feelings always, a hundred ways, yet a letter that expresses being bothered by certain things in a certain poem might be seen by you out of focus. In fact, for instance, something of which *I didn't* write was of much more importance to me: the reading (& writing up on the blackboard, the sheer physicality of that act, a re-living in the instant of the actual word by word sequence of the poem) by a young man, a painter, called Willard Boepple,[1] of "The Fear that Precedes Changes of Heaven" & his speaking about it in a way that drew everyone in the class (at CCNY) into some new awareness, of poetry, of living, esp. one hitherto inarticulate boy for whom it was surely a crucial moment in his life. What I say in the letter is only "true" if taken along with at least one such instance of the positive. It's so partial, so easy to see as

## 364

Jan. 28th {1966
New York}

more important than it is. But I'm sending it anyway because not to wd. make an unnatural silence, a gap. Please write soon though.

With love—<br>Denny.

## 365

Feb. 8th {1966}<br>277 Greenwich St<br>NY 7

Dearest Robert

I am distressed at not hearing from you.

Don't think I think there is anything to be said for Humphrey. On the contrary. But even so your picture of him doesn't seem to work, to ring true, for me anyway—it is more of a frustrated gesture, like stamping one's foot. Oh dear—well, everything I say probably makes it worse. Maybe anyway it is not that but that I thought the contrasting, praise, sections of the poems weren't strong, that has hurt you. Or maybe you aren't hurt, nor angry with me, but just thinking about it before answering. I hope so.

We'll be seeing Bob this week at a conference we've all 3 been invited to.

Went to demonstrate at Washington this past weekend, & then to the Phillips Gallery for the 1st time. Al & Pat (Kresch) came along.

Love—<br>Denny

## 366

March 9th {1966}<br>Cambridge {Mass.}

Dear Robert & Jess

I've been away 10 days—am on my way home today. Saw this in a window & thought you'd like it.[1]

I was very glad to get yr last letter[2]—had flu & didn't respond.

Am deep in Tolkien. Reading also CR Leslie's *Memoirs of the Life of John Constable*.[3]

The Vict. & Albert loan exhibition in Baltimore of small Constable oils—each so noble & vast tho' measuring only a few inches—was one of the *good* things of the last months.[4] Now I'm longing to see the Turners at the Museum of Mod. Art—from the Tate.[5] So many years since I saw them.

Love from<br>Denny.

## 367

Tues. 19th April {19}66<br>277 Greenwich St<br>N.Y. 7

Dearest Robert

Yesterday I drank 3 whiskeys and wrote you a poem-letter. It is not a good poem (alas)—but I send it anyway. I send the MS. and a typescript with some changes but haven't made a copy to keep as I know it is more a letter than a poem. Later decided to make a copy anyway in case there's something to salvage as poem. In a way it is a shabby thing to send you a poem I know is not a good one, but you will forgive that if you keep in mind it's a *letter*.

Love to Jess. And you.
Denny

PS.

I have a few real poems to send too but can't type them today & want to get this off.

To Robert: a letter

Dark these days are
when we are silent to one another.
The time is taken up.
We are in mid-life,
in 'Middle Earth' (another Age of it).
Read-Ins, gatherings devised
by men of good will
for the giving of testimony
claim one part of the giving mind.
The many voices
that claim answer from those who,
like you and like me,
utter ourselves,

are loud at the doors.
Some desire in innocence
that which dwells in the poet.
Some (unknowing)
tempt with their seductive
questions, some
(almost knowing it?)
desire our downfall (that the muse
leave us).
The first claim,
the claim of
being *in the world*,
is the strongest.
                    It wakes me
with daylight;
as if I were a Hobbit
(not a Ring-Bearer, but a Companion)
I seem to move bidden by fate,
yet with consent. Not in hope,

yet in constant longing
to give my word, to be
alive.
      My master, my Orpheus,
who should live as it were in Lorien,

you are called to the same need,
called with a louder voice than I.
In the twenty-fourth Passage, I read it.
(You didn't know that
twenty-four is my number, the one that's
not only my birthday but has been
always the number of joy and meaning for me.)
As a child in England (Hobbit-land?)
I seldom used the word *corridor*:
the way from the kitchen to the living-room
where I wrote and drew pictures and heard music
and back again (past the deep cupboard where my playthings lived,
               beloved dolls and animals)
was a *passage*.       In *A Child's Garden*
*of Verses* (with its black Robinson pictures)
'Northwest Passage' meant many things to me:
among them the upstairs corridor,
the fearful passage to my own room's haven,
that cabin of dream-substance.
      So I know
deeply your word:
          Passages.

Passing into this darkness,
this time of our mid-lives rocked
in war of black waves,
we struggle with the spars,
you
struggle to speak, and speak
loud in the wind
I struggle
      and am almost
silent
almost quenched—.

I send you therefore
as if on a seagull's wing

one word—

what word shall it be?—

'Love'?—I love you but
I love
        another, as you do.
Love I send, but I send it
in another word.
                Longing?
                        Poetry.

                                From Denny


dear Denise,

Keep the poem-letter in its own tempering. It means so much to me
personally, and more than meaning it touches as a poem must some part of
me that needs the courage—we need tears and trembling. In response to the
tenderness of friendship: the radiant side of the other dark terror that would
also move us to tears and trembling.

It's a lovely poem. Surely it is true to itself thruout. It relates for me to the
way H. D. let her poetic creative self move into intimate unpublic feelings.

And the poem projects this period in history the way I most feel it "The
time is taken up" seems to ring with meaning on many levels.

the claim of
being *in the world,*

and then:

                Not in hope,
yet in constant longing
to give my word, to be
alive.

You speak so close to feelings of my own, and this "letter" comes magically
at a time when "Passages" is stiring again in my womb-thoughts. The
Soldiers! The Soldiers! I've dared to write to *Audit* that I feel that "Passages
26" will at last be there within this week or ten days.[1]

For that issue I started with the text of the "Play with Masks," and now I
have in the last week got off to them two groups of previously unpublisht
poems from the 1950s, my translation of Nerval's *Les Chimères* and just
Tuesday of this week I at last got into form a long essay or account of my
disagreement with Robin's "translation"—I still am not easy about being
called so to attack where I could not but be aware how weak his position

368

April 22/1966
{San Francisco}

was, untenable—but I was outraged by what he had done, and by the poetic assumptions involved. And then hereabouts the work was riding on Robin's authority, no one was questioning, and most did not have the French or the concern for what Nerval might actually be to question. In the tangle of controversy, however, I did get some steps sketched out along the way, suggesting the need for if no more some definitions of mysticism in relation to the poet, and fantasy. I think these parts of the essay will lead towards something more enduring.

Did you get the *Open Space* issue of my Dante lecture that I sent?[2] The Tylers got theirs, but I've heard from no one in the East. I never did receive Zuk's *All*, tho I got a volume of Raymond Roseliep.

With the *Audit* issue finisht, I've got now to get the Preface for *Book of Resemblances* into shape from my first draft in my notebook. Did I write that a volume of First Poems with a rambling kind of a Preface is already on its way with Oyez? for August they hope. I've gone as far back as two poems from 1939. . . .

―――――――

Going back to your "To Robert: a letter"—the reality you recognize in the mid-life, Middle Earth sequence related to Hobbit-land and Lorien to Tolkien's world as a vision of how we somehow know the world of our adventure to be, related in turn for me to your "September 1961" poem— "Shalom" kept knocking at the door, and now searching it out again I find

"it's alright—there are many
avenues, many corridors of the soul
that are dark also"

I'd meant to get to the feeling I had that what makes fantasy "poetry" is when it is alive with the underlying desire—it *is* longing "to give my word, to be/ alive," and as in the close of the poem "in another word / Longing? / Poetry" There is longing that gives Tolkien poetic truth, and returns us to life itself.

―――――――

Before I get off to the morning's work, I'll type a copy of a letter from Bob written after I wrote him troubled by his acceptance of a State Department job this coming summer in Pakistan, in which I argued that the only possible non-political response would be to plead off on grounds of over-work etc. That to accept on any grounds would be political in significance. It did seem to me that one should *not*[3] make a political opposition to the government unless one faced the gravity of what might be the consequences and had the courage of convictions and an unambiguous feeling. But, as you will see, Bob made a political decision. . . .

love
Robert

Dearest Robert,

I was so glad you liked my letter poem. Thank you.

Please forgive me for not writing before to thank you for the *beautiful* Dante lecture. I will reread it many times. I plan also to read a portion of the *Commedia* in Eng. prose, Italian, & the Binyon version, every day during the summer in Maine.

And the lovely little book from Hamady came too.[1] Did he send you my broadsheet?[2] If not I will. Let me know. And did the books (Zuk. etc.) from Norton come at last? They told me the warehouse had sent them out *twice*—I can't understand what goes on.

News: Mitch will teach in John Hawkes{'} "Voice Project" (a freshman Eng. experiment) for 10 weeks at Stanford in spring of '67. I will join him for the last 2 weeks. (My Vassar job will keep me from a longer stay unfortunately.) I might be able to come out on a short visit in the middle of the 10 weeks if I can get a reading or so on the W. Coast, to pay my way. In any case, it does mean I'll get to see you in S.F. a little under a year from now.

More immediately: Mitch is (suddenly) flying to Stanford in this connection for a 2-day conference this coming week. He has to rush back on Thurs. (because we have to be at Nik's school Friday afternoon—last day of school and the 11th is his birthday (17!)). But the conference is supposed to end about 6 on Wed. and he hopes to get into S.F. &—if you're free—see you & Jess Wed. evening. Could you put him up for the night? His plane leaves around 10 Thurs. am. Of course at such short notice this might be completely inconvenient, we realize. But he'd love to see you if you *are* free, & feel like it. Since you have no phone, could you get in touch with him? c/o Albert Guerard, Eng. Dept., Stanford. (415) 321-2300.

Much love—
Denny.

dear Denny,

I am trusting that you will be at Temple (especially, after reading of New York's sweltering heat). It's two weeks ago or so now that "Passages 26 The Soldiers" finally came into shape or came to hand (it is the feel of the poem before the sight, or that brings it to sight). I woke one morning with the key somewhere so that I was ready to work with the sense of how each part fit. "From the body remains of the bull Hadhayans" leaping to mind, and later, "containing without deception / what so deceives us" coming in there, . . . . Except for the Xmas verse, which did not spring from such an active inspiration but from attitudes, and for the prose narrations for *Adam's Way* done at Vancouver, the Nerval Translations, and a version of Parmenides Prolog

**369**

{late April, May 1966}
277 Greenwich St.
N.Y. 7 N.Y.

**370**

July 13/{19}66
{San Francisco}

which I have not yet typed from my notebook—the first poem in a year. And a poem that has been hanging over me for a year. Waiting for the content of "Up Rising" to undergo its sea change or alchemical phase towards rendering up its purely poetic identity, where the figures do not *refer* to contemporary history only but are happenings of the poem itself. [Why I always wanted "Up Rising" especially to be labelld "Passages 25" so that even the incidental reader should have some consideration that it belongs in a larger context. Now—"The Soldiers" delivers up its images of my own actual mounting blood pressure:

> tho we fight underground
> from the heart's volition, the body's inward sun
>     the blood's natural
>   up rising. . . .

that over the last year has had me under a lid imposed by reserpine orderd by the doctor to keep my blood pressure within range. But it has also kept *me* subdued, "lowerd." The day before or I guess it was two days before writing on "The Soldiers" I decided not to take the daily reserpine and to go as long as I could, returning to the reserpine only when the symptoms of pressure became troublesome (which happend four days later). The first day going back on my own temper I got started at last on my preface to Vaughan's Alchemical works—and did most of the section of theurgy and spiritualistic alchemy, embryos and prophetical heads or skulls.[1] The second day, "Soldiers" was ready and written almost as fast as I could type, working from the sections in my notebooks; and I had the start on another poem [This was July 1], a kind of interlude, a return to a rhapsody in stress meters that, perhaps after the suggestion of "Prime Evil" in "The Soldiers," takes up from the beat of "This is the forest primeval, the murmuring pines and the hemlocks" or however it goes. I am not sure how far (how deep) this sense of the primeval as the first evil goes beyond the immediate punning activity. I do know the Boehme's concept that Wrath is the Father and Love the Son, rage and—"an astringent, harsh, raw and bitter essence and spirit" Boehme calls it, "the fire-flagrat."

from *Mysterium Magnum*, "Of the Two Principles":

16. . . . First, a hellish thirsty wrathful source, being as another property; in which the great fire's might and will in the anger of God, or the wrath of God, ariseth. Which Lucifer desired to be, and to rule therein; and therefore he is a devil, that is, one spewed out of the love-fire into the dark fire. Fourthly, there proceedeth forth also from the wrathful property, through the devoration in the fire . . . a watery property; but it is much rather a poisonful source, in which the life of darkness consisteth

something of this concept working in an other poetic concept I think to be going on in "Passages" now. The outrage of "Up Rising" to be reveald in other lights in the course of other poems. In this same potent chapter Boehme concludes:

19. Understand it aright: There proceedeth forth out of the fiery property in the spiration the vital source; which according to the free lubet is holy and joyful, and according to the darkness is painful and wrathful. The wrathfulness and painful source is the root of joy, and the joy is the root of the enmity of the dark wrathfulness: So that there is a contrarium, whereby the good is made manifest and known that it is good.

"lubet" seems to be a word all of Boehme's own.

The war in Viet Nam and the lies and compulsive decisions of the war party in Washington becomes a *mantra* for our thought, our inner struggle to retain and/or throw up our being American, and to hold all men within the image of Man or to split into devils and men. . . . Lama Govinda in a book Richard Baker has urged upon me, and gave me last Christmas, furnishes this passage on the image as *mantra*:[2]

quoted from Heinrich Zimmer, *Ewiges Indien*: "The forms of divine life in the universe and in nature break forth from the seer as vision, from the singer as sound, and are there in the spell of vision and sound, pure and undisguised. Their existence is the characteristic of the priestly power of the seer-poet (of the *kavi*, who is *drashtar*). What sounds from his mouth, is not the ordinary word, the *shabda*, of which speech is composed. It is *mantra*, the compulsion to create a mental image, power over that which IS, to be as it really is in its pure essence. This it is knowledge. It is the truth of being, beyond right and wrong; it is real *being* beyond thinking and reflecting. It is "knowledge" pure and simple, knowledge of the Essential, *Veda* (Greek "oida," German "wissen," to know). It is the direct simultaneous wareness of the knower and the known. Just as it was a kind of spiritual compulsion with which the seer-poet was overpowered by vision and word, thus, for all times, wherever there are men to know how to use mantra-words, they will possess the magic power to conjure up immediate reality—be it in form of gods or in the play of forces.

In the word *mantra* the root man = *to think* (in Greek "menos", Latin "mens") is combined with the element "tra" which forms tool-words. Thus mantra is a "tool for thinking," a "thing which crates a mental picture." With its sound it calls forth its content into a state of immediate reality. *Mantra* is power, not merely speech which the mind can contradict or evade. What the mantra expresses by its sound, exists, comes to pass.

Here, if anywhere, words are deeds, acting immediately. It is the
peculiarity of the true poet that his word creates actuality, calls forth
and unveils something real. His word does not talk—it acts!'"

So the image and drama of Viet Nam is aroused in our minds, hearts (in my
mind baffling, in my heart a trial so that my blood pounds and my heart
labors) as a creative field of emotions and entities: the people of Viet Nam,
the tyrants over them, the war parties, the "hawks" at home, the invisible
"people of America" and the "public" the instruments of a lie reenacting the
old myth of Ahriman as the Lie and the Lord of War. . . . And were there
not some content here to be reveald, renderd clear, we would not be
haunted, fascinated.

The war makes Kenneth Anger *ashamed* he writes from England,
"ashamed to be American"; it makes me wrathful with outrage; in your
"What Were They Like?" there—is it pity? or remorseful sadness? that is
"bitter." The "Sir, laughter is bitter to the burned mouth" [As it is my own
mouth burns with out rage] echoes not only the "laughter" in "Life At War"
but its line from Rilke: "My heart could I say of it, it overflows with
bitterness" and its demure: "but no."

We are not reacting to the war, but mining images here the war arouses
in us. The "all-American boy in the cockpit" has back of him the poet James
Dickey's actual war experience that I found affecting (infecting) in reviewing
*Two Poems of the Air* (as I wonder now, the Lammas Dream poem of the
poet as a gerfalcon may well have been stirrd up by Dickey's other poem of
the air.[3] Both poems left me stirrd and yet dissatisfied. And in time the
centralizing images they had aroused "as if kissed in the brain" ripend into
active elements of my own poetic.

Now I see the ghost of that boy in his play of total demolition, his
decoration Boehme could call it, striving thru Dickey and then thru me
(the boy-me in my own fantasy play of burning houses and people) to reach
the redemption of the real, to be "containd" . . .

what is going on in your
still turns without surprise, with mere regret
to the scheduled breaking open of breasts whose milk
runs out over the entrails of still-alive babies
transformation of witnessing eyes to pulp-fragments,
implosion of skinned penises in carcass-gulleys

The words in their lines are the clotted mass of some operation . . . having
what root in you I wonder? Striving to find place in a story beyond the
immediate.

It's this in poetry that quickens me, that its elements arouse elements to
work in my own being—I may be sailing with the poem or contending

against it even (dissatisfied, even, as I was with *The Two Poems of the Air*: but deeply involved, working on that review for months)—and invisible (as invisible the presentations of our actual life reappear as entities creative of a dream life or as workers in the poem). . . .

The morning has all but flown, and Orlando is right now stretching his paw persistently over this page so that I have to write around him (moving his paw and then going on). Did I write that Tom Bombadil died of cancer—that was two months ago I guess? It has left Orlando trying to make us take over Tom's role and place and times. Tho Orlando's times of querulous searching and meowing are infrequent now.

"A Vision" is one of your miraculously beautiful and realized poems. More beautiful in more readings. Your verse has a pace I most love and otherwise would envy in poems like this, a freedom in movement that is at the same time obedient to a compelling music (so that the poem everywhere has definition [intaglio] in its ease). And I like to see in the *intellectual love* of the two great angels "both in immortal danger of dwindling" the kind of intellectual love I experience myself from the poet in me when confronted in admiration by the recognized perfection (fitness everywhere) of your poem, showing the perfection of the poet at work. "A Vision" comes anyway not only as the poem it is but as a personal message from you I must have wanted or wonted. [January, I just notice it was you wrote it.]

Well, I've got to get to my typewriter if I would get "The Soldiers" copied and this all off to you today.

Love,
Robert

---

That quote from Zimmer's book on India is a marvellous one. Perhaps it shd. be inserted as a note in your *Day Book* at the point where you speak about words looked on as *counters* or as *powers*?

Dearest Robert,

The poem, the "Soldiers Passage," has the depth & grandeur & complexity it needs to have. I think you must know it?—It is not the kind of poem the poet could have doubts of. And the movement, the wholeness, of the "Passages" has come clearer & clearer to me—I felt it when I heard the tape but now even more so. (Did I tell you how I played the tape (at Greenwich St.) to my C.C.N.Y. class of 10 who had not yet been reading you (with a few exceptions) & who were in some ways quite unsophisticated—& how nevertheless at the end they were quite still & silent, & then at last spontaneously burst out clapping?)

I'm sorry the # got left out of *The Nation* printing of "Uprising"—the

**371**

July 18th {19}66
Temple, Maine

whole thing was done in phone calls & telegrams as I was in Maine & it had to be rushed in before Conover left—& at the time the sequence number seemed unnecessary to a magazine presentation of it.

But I (and Mitch too—who also joins in my response to the poem) am anxious about you—the high blood pressure—the medicine that keeps it down but keeps *you* down too—the need you've felt to leave off taking it for the work's sake—I am fearful—could you not perhaps try some other medicine or treatment, that would be more livable?

Thank you for your good letter. I've been thinking about a parenthetical question you ask there—You quote the lines in which I wrote of physical horrors and say they are "the clotted mass of some operation . . . having what root in you I wonder?"[1] Consciously the history of the poem is this: looking at the fragile beauty of human bodies I was struck afresh by the extreme *strangeness* of men actually *planning* violence upon each other—I mean, it is so *bizarre* when one stops to think about it, isn't it. That we can ever take it for granted. Especially when those who do take it for granted are in a majority and *not* some minority of (in other respects) wildly barbarous or brutalized persons.

Then, I wanted (& want) to keep my participation in the Peace Movement (minimal though it is) in a *real* relation to my feelings—this seems to me terribly important—& part of that, I feel, is a matter of trying to grasp with the imagination what does happen in war—so that even if one hasn't been there, in the flesh, one doesn't let the horror of war just be an *empty* word—all our words have to be filled with, backed up by, imaginative experience. (Along with this, I think peace has to be a daily experience, or at least as daily as one can make it—something *realized*, not a future ideal because those unexperienced ideals soon become mechanical & ugly, the emptiness fills up with some other substance. . . . ) (I'm not *telling* you this, I know you know it—just trying to straighten out my own sense of it on paper). So that *consciously* the poem envisions that horror, of meat-people chopping other meat-people, *on schedule*, without even being angry at the time; & contrasts it with man's tender & wonderful capacities. Obviously. But yr question seems to mean, what affinity in you (in me) makes you capable of imagining those words? That reminds me that where in the poem it says "we" it said "they" in the 1st draft—then I realized that since the whole point of what I was saying was the common humanity of slayer & slain it *must* be *"we."* So *that* far I had already acknowledged the sharing in the possibility of such hideousness. But yr question makes me requestion myself & ask in what way the horror *at* violence (that makes one need to make oneself face it by writing it down in images one makes oneself see,) is related to, first, my own violent temper which in the last few years seems to have been converted into other energies, & second my anxieties, my "imagination of disaster," which so often presents the most horrid possibilities to me in graphic terms? I'm not sure where (except as further warnings against hypocrisy—& fear of being insincere can itself be a scrupulosity that is paralyzing, so that to counteract it I have to remind myself of Thomas Mann's, & your, sense of the essential *play* of art)—I'm not sure where such questions lead. But I have the feeling it is well to ask them.

---

I've been shocked & grieved this week by the suicide of a young man (21, I guess—a senior) from my class at Drew. One of the most promising in every way. I've written a letter to send out to the other students who were in the class, since we are now scattered and shall never meet all together again (some were seniors). I'm getting it xeroxed as I can't make that many copies (16). The horrible thing is that he did call for a doctor—who didn't arrive in time. I have the idea it was a mood, not a settled conviction of despair. He was a very gifted painter—poetry was probably just an overflow, a secondary activity for him, but he had begun to do some things I really liked, too. I can't believe it.

I've put a book together called *The Sorrow Dance*, of which the "Olga Poems" will be the core. I think it coheres. I haven't followed chronological order this time, but have grouped the poems in sections I felt were more organically related* & wd. play back & forth upon each other better than the chronological order of composition. I hope you will like the arrangement. Shall I send you a xerox copy or would you sooner wait till it is printed? It won't actually be published till next March.

*i.e. some poems separated from each other by intervening ones seem closely related to each other.

Am reading *The Roots of the Mountains*.[2] Occasionally the language gets out of hand with too many washens, holpens, etc. but on the whole I *relish* it; & love the tale. Have been rereading & annotating Yeats' autobiographical prose, thinking about Pound's place as (among other things) the connecting link between Yeats & Williams, who otherwise (superficially) seem to exist in utterly different worlds—& about what Pound must have learned from Yeats, who learned *some* of it from his father (the Beauty/Unity of Being image, of the instrument so tuned that when one string is touched all the others vibrate, for instance, is so close to the Poundian concept of goodness which he reinforced in his Confucian studies, & Yeats had it long before Pound met him)—but I don't know the dates well enough yet to tell if Pound had himself formed such concepts before he knew Yeats. Do you? Then, I was thinking how Yeats very early had a clear sense of the relations between language & a people's moral state—long before either Pound or Williams were old enough to have thought about it. Yeats, as an Irishman, a member of a small nation with a real peasantry and at a time of crucial change, had a field where art & action could for a while at least (in the founding of the Irish Theater) be one, could see certain specific results from his work in "purifying the language of the tribe" whereas Pound & Wms. with an equally strong sense of that relation were baffled, as Americans (in their different ways) by the sheer unwieldy size of the country & its population. Of course that very bafflement became a power in Wms. work. I don't feel I understand *The Cantos* well enough by any means to have any measure of its effect on Pound—yet, suppose Pound had been bard & sage of a small principality . . . ?

I can't think of Wms. ever mentioning Yeats, & Yeats certainly can have taken no interest in *him*. And most readers, I think—including myself heretofore—tend, even if they care for the poetry of both, to exclude one from the mind in thinking of the other. So it will be interesting to try to consider them (I'm thinking of the course I'm to teach at Vassar) as contemporaries, even sharing friendship with at least a few (E. P. & Ford)— at least to keep remembering their having lived for most of the same years. How Williams must have hated, (feared) if he ever read, Yeats' occultism! It wd have brought out all his most exasperating rationalist regular-guy side, I think. Yet the old lady, Wms.' mother, would have been quite at home with Yeats' ghosts. Maybe that's why.

---

I'm sending you some poems (typed from a transcript of his own ("rough," he said)) translations as read at a meeting at a private house, by Thich Nhat Hanh, the Buddhist monk who was in N.Y. in May. Maybe you met him in SF? I think he went there. I'd never seen a Vietnamese before.

Also I will send a prose piece written by Emmett Jarrett, one of a little group of friends made through that Poetry Center workshop the winter before last. (He once wrote to you to apologise for printing in his little mag. (*things*) a silly poem by Gerard Malanga that mentioned you & Jess & at which I took offense.) Emmett, Dick Lourie, Jason Miller (who may go to SF soon—may I send him to see you? I think you & Jess wd. like him) & the youngest, Gordon Bishop, & to a lesser degree (because she's a housewife in N.J. & can't get out much) Phyllis Schub are the ones from that class who've remained in close & fruitful touch with each other & with me. I like them all very much, & the fact that they don't write like each other (or like me). In the fall I plan to have them meet the 10 CCNY students who have decided to stick together & meet at my place once a month (besides meeting elsewhere without me) to read poems & play tapes etc. The 10 are younger & much less developed—few will probably really go on in poetry—but they are really passionately interested & I think it will be stimulating for them to meet these older young poets. A few of the ones from Drew may be able to come too. But mostly it should remain something small & intimate—the

CCNY ones really got to know & like each other & that atmosphere of trust was what made it such a good class, while the 1st group I had there was mostly a mess.

Nik spent 3 weeks at Haystack (where M. C. {Richards} & also Howard Fussiner used to teach—not this yr. tho') & learned how to do lithographs. Maybe I will send you one. He & his girlfriend Liebe (whom we like very much) then spent a week here & turned out the barn (like cleaning the Augean stables, almost) & painted the living/dining room, including floor & ceiling. They've now left on a Youth Hostelling & bicycling trip.

Did you finally get the Zukofsky & other books from Norton???

I wish I could understand Yeats' *Vision* better. It is not the ideas but the mathematical aspect of the system which is hard for me to get hold of; reference to the chart & so forth. I have the same difficulty (but more so) with the *I Ching*. I can *literally* barely count—cannot do simple subtraction & multiplication. Never got as far as fractions. Anything to do with figures makes me go blank, a sort of panic. Except that when I'm pumping water (with hand pump at sink) I can guess with absolute accuracy how many pumpings will make the bucket fill up to a certain mark even though flow is variable. But I guess that's more like whatever used to make me know what horse would win a race when I was a kid (never made a cent tho', as I didn't know how to place a bet!). However, what I *do* understand of Yeats' ideas of that kind helps me, I think, to understand some of the propositions in "Passages 26" & in your letter, as for instance the concepts of *mantra*, of Prime Evil, of Ahriman. That's to say, the Yeats reading I've just been doing has, though not a necessary preliminary for it, in some way chanced to prepare me for the poem. I suppose because many of your absorbed sources are the same as his. (And in certain ways, therefore, I hope that absorbing some Yeats will prove a good preparation ((for my Vassar students)) for reading you. I'm not going to be very chronological but plan to move back & forth between the old great ones & today.)

What books does he refer to when he speaks of "the Christian Cabbala"? (Not that I intend at this point in my life—maybe later—reading them; I don't feel that is what I need just now. But I'd like to know what he means, whether a definite roster or a looser embracing of various late medieval & later—up thru' the 18th cent.?—books{})}.

I'll send you, with the Nhat Hanh poems, some things of mine— including a story—that were in the *Chicago Review*.[3]

The "What Were They Like?" poem came rather directly out of meeting him, when he struck me as so delicate, fineboned—and for the first time I heard the Vietnamese language which is most musical, melodious, the most caressive language-sounds I've heard except for Zapotec (which sounds like hummingbird feathers look, or how down feels against the cheek). I have since revised it so that question 3 now says "quiet" instead of "rippling" laughter, because rippling sounded forced (insistently assumptive)—yet laughter had to be qualified; and answer 6 just says

"There is an echo yet
of their speech" etc.

In this poem I imagined a time future in which the *questioner*, though quite without malice, a sort of innocent & quite eager researcher, has no conception of the outrage he is skirting; & in which (though he would have to be impossibly old to actually be a lone survivor,) yet the *answerer* is very old, very weary, & is the last sad bearer of certain memories; perhaps actually a survivor, but more likely one who was the son of a survivor & in extreme old age no longer knows, himself, whether he or his ancestors experienced the extermination. [For it is such a small nation that, as Thich Nhat Hanh pointed out, extermination is quite possible (i.e. even without use of atomic bombs).] So that, (the questioner being ignorant, the answerer one of the vanquished) the tone is not "pity" nor "remorseful sadness," as you suggested, questioning, but rather a sadness almost more weary than bitter. I don't know if it comes through without explanation. Of course if it doesn't it is not good enough.

By the way, in writing of the Rilke quotation, you speak of the "but no" etc—as "demure"—did you mean to write "demurrer"?—You must have! That "but no" has to me the tone of choked nausea.

I too have found, & continue to find, *Two Poems of the Air* moving & puzzling poems which I value; but some further acquaintance with Dickey certainly proves him to be—oh, what shall I say? Well, I think he is *possessed*—a literal schizophrenic, of whom one half is in the shadow or toils of *Ahriman* and *liked* being a bomber pilot & advertizing man & if called on to do so wd. go out there & throw napalm any day *and believe he was doing it to save democracy* etc (& who *actually says* "War's a pity of course but if a commie attacks your wife & children" etc., the most idiot jargon coming out of him—(& I have little doubt would lynch a negro with equal selfrighteousness)—and the other half *is* a poet and experiences the imagination of reincarnation & many other visions. Almost I would suppose he had no soul—no center—just these 2 split halves with nothing but his body holding them together. The *uncanniest* man I have ever met. There is really no *person* there to talk to. I wd. prefer not to run into him again—but did so unexpectedly in Wisconsin last March and I daresay will do so again somewhere, sometime.*

*Because I defended his work when I was on the Wesleyan board he asked me to be his literary executor!—& not knowing him then I agreed, though unhappily. After I had met him in Wisconsin (not the 1st time, but

the 1st time he was sober & alone) & challenged him on the War, I wrote to say I could not possibly continue even tho' I valued his poems. So that is no longer burdening me, thank god. Such a false position to be put in. A weird request on his part, wasn't it?

Yet there are parts of that albatross poem (the one you were less interested in of the 2) that seem great to me in the absolute conjunction of sweep of long line with visioned sweep of long wing.

Yet in some way he seems to me a manifestation of whatever is inimical to poetry. And some people think him a jolly fellow, a banjo player, a companionable drinking man.

He is not to be trusted in anything, I think.

Do you know Hindemith's Octet? I like it very much.

Have received (I don't know who sent them) several magazines put out by admirers of Bukowski, lately.[4] They are so sick & ugly, they make Lew Ellingham look wholesome. Do you see them? Poems, or verses rather, that seem like eruptions. It seems rather frightening for there is evidently quite a large group involved. I suppose it is the least one can expect in such desperate times, though. Perhaps writing these ugly poems is those poor people's way of not going completely off their rockers?

Dear Robert, do you think we are coming to the end of the world? Mitch generally thinks not, speaks of all the goodness & striving & hope there is in the world too (& which god knows I experience over & over again)—but sometimes I am very fearful. Of the end of all things. But then, people have always, all through history, had that fear & had to live with it. It is a devil-whisper that makes one have that fear, in any case, because meanwhile, what-ever happens, one should live & do one's work; & the fear can paralyze one.

Mitch *very much* appreciated seeing you & Jess, & sends his love.

> Love from
> Denny.

dear Denny,

The poems by Nhat Hanh are beautiful with a strength and directness that comes across in our language. "Our" language! not English or American, but the words we love for the treasure of our humanity we have found in them: "pray for," "darkness," "little stars"—that infallibly conveys its affectionate regard for the greatest lords of the cosmos. "In innumerable existences they are inseparable friends."

It reassures me too in my own wanting to come to a common language, one cleard of personality, having its meanings in the community of meanings. Yet I am not without having some pleasure as a reader in the

**372**

July 22/{19}66
{San Francisco}

intensely personal, not entirely cut off from responding to the peculiar "language" Spicer cultivated. Well, that word "cultivated" suggests too deepening and maturing a process. He insisted and restricted rather than cultivating to get there. Even, like a man using weed-killer to prove a field truly barren and all the lovely lushness of the earth in its rich areas to be a whorish taunt and deceit.

I have the page proofs of Jack's *Magazine Verse* on hand for the possibility of writing an essay on his work, if I find a fruitful approach. Not that I mean to search for it: if it *occurs* to me. And it may: I must over the years—even in my opposition (and more often in Spicer's opposition to what he saw me as) have some kernel of understanding that now might open up. If it doesn't, it doesn't. A gesture towards seeing Spicer as part of a human language he had sought to withdraw his language from—to have a poetry all his own (to have a self of his own "authentic": to be an author) or, if not that, even more refusing his humanity to have a dictation from any inhuman entity—ghosts from outer space).

[I pace about the house. Do not find the sheets of Jack's book. Change the record, putting on Satie's *Parade*, and see then the issue of *Vienna Today* featuring Vienna 1900, with that proliferation of the fantasmic blossoming and leafing of vine and branching tree, the music lush and excited (later the pomegranate will be sweet and astringent).

Phantasy and "Jugendstil"—the style of the magazine *Jugend*.] We had in the years when the questions of technique and form were paramount a "style"—"The Black Mountain" style, finally: because Cid in *Origin* lackt and then was careless of and even turnd against what was happening. It was an open style. And with Creeley's editorship had a vehicle proper to it. It's most there in the first years of *Origin*. A sort of pruning of the tree, in which, in some there will not be a nature strong enough to take over and grow after the shaping artifice and we see still the awkward "style" of the line endings and the composition by immediate localities rather than currents.

Spicer's "style" isn't a "tree" of language—for he was even vehement in his scorn for anything like my feeling that the language itself is alive and communicates. Words and constructs were "mere" instruments, and could not communicate. Well, I would agree that words cannot communicate feelings or ideas that are not common properties: I go back here to Sapir's exposition in *Language* (11–12)[1]

> . . . the single experience lodges in an individual consciousness and is, strictly speaking, incommunicable. To be communicated it needs to be referred to a class which is tacitly accepted by the community as an identity . . . the speech element "house" is the symbol, first and foremost, not of a single perception, nor even of the notion of particular object, but

of a "concept, . . . " of a convenient capsule of thought that embraces thousands of distinct experiences and that is ready to take in thousands more. . . .

Jack became a fanatical partisan of the single experience against even the mutuality of love-language. (Tho ironically, there *was* a group language, a cultic-"community" or *church* of poets and poetry followers around Jack. Today, after Jack's death, what had been under his leadership a kind of fundamentalist puritanical cant of the poem; has become, with Robin Blaser as leader, a kind of aesthetic snobbism: puritanical poetry giving way to pure poetry)

Antagonistic any way to anything "embracing thousands of distinct experiences and ready to take in thousands more." . . . The antagonism (in both Jack and Robin) is grotesque and wrong-headed. For the single individual experience and the communality of thousands of experiences (what the Kaballa calls the "Treasury") are reciprocalities of one thing: language.

---

Your question about the "Christian" Cabala: The *Zohar*, the homeground of Hebrew Caballa, arises in a book of the meanings of the Torah—and likewise with Boehme, particularly here his *Mysterium Magnum*, a Christian Caballa arises with a mystical reading of Genesis etc., in which "Christian" meanings (revelations) are sought out. Boehme, in that terrible time when Protestants and Catholics exterminated each other in a blind religious rage, and in turn the fires were set to burn pagan witch cultists, came to the beautiful belief that the Father (the Jehovah of wrath and vengeance, the jealous god of the Old Testament) must have projected creatively, out of his torment and yearning for a love he did not have, a Son: and a world of darkness (not plunged into darkness, but stirring out of its own darkness) labored towards a world of light. Love would never give rise to War; then War must be striving, out of its incapability, to find Love. I do violence to the sense Boehme has of how much is involved and not so summarily realized. But this idea of the Father (we know as the Old Testament knows him as tyrannical, jealous, raging, yet would-be loving) having in us to bring forth the Son who (as Dante too sees in the *Comedy*) gives "Freedom," a Permission, an inner Permission, and the end of all Jealousy and Rage. Which we know in anguish, we ourselves the Earth that labors to bring forth. This idea speaks so eloquently for our world experience. The wrath of the Father and his jealousy is fearful or arouses in us wrath (so that the Jehovah arises in me to put down the little would-be Jehovah Johnson), and we search the life of Christ, the poetic image of the Son as Love, to deliver up our fear and rage into bringing forth "the Child" who in His Nativity reveals "fear" to be "awe" (the shepherds were fearful) and "rage" to be the

Last Days and Judgment, the end of judgment, with the promise "thou shalt be with me in paradise" *in Love.*

As, I think, the isolate particular experience labors to bring forth itself as the eternal communal experience: i.e. as language (of picture or words or music and dance). A mystery of creation in participation. We labor to make the War *real,* to make it really happen so that it will speak to us. As we labor to realize life. If we did not so labor we would not, I suppose, experience fear or wrath, our reactions as its reality grows. And I have—more than "hope"—the faith but it is also the artist's sense of his work (that he is making sense) that your fear "of the end of all things" or my outrage at "the lie" will lead on towards what they strive to be in us.

> love
> Robert

---

## 373

July 25th {19}66
Temple {Me.}

Los dictadores estan dentro de nosotros, la Bomba H esta en nuestro interior, de alli ha salido. Todo lo malo que ha hecho el hombre lo llevamos dentro, los regimenes politicos no son sino objectivaciones de lo que somos.

> Ernesto Cardenal

The dictators are inside of us, the h Bomb is in ourselves, it is from out of us that it burst.* All the evil done by man we carry in us, political regimes are only objectivizations of what we are. (*or more literally, "from there it emerged")

Dear Robert,

I copied this out a couple of years ago. Cardenal is a monk in one of the Latin American countries, I forget which. Nicaragua? I think he translated a poem of yours along with others from Don Allen's anthology so you probably know of him. It is not a particularly original thought but I was struck by the way it was put—and now find it pertinent to what we are talking about.

However, typing it out just now I wondered how much the guilt strain in Catholicism caused him to leave out any consideration of the good. If each microcosmic man carries all of man's evil in him doesnt he also carry the good? Of course, Cardenal may have said so, too—this quote, from a letter or essay, was printed as an epigraph in *Plumed Horn* so I have never seen its context—what I copied was all that was given.

Yr letter came this morning and I have not properly taken it in yet so will not make this an answer, except to thank you. Glad you like the Nhat Hanh poems.

Here's the piece by Emmett Jarrett I mentioned. I squirmed at his use of the term "waste product" until I saw how he qualified it by pointing out that oxygen is a "waste product" in a sense.

Something (on a different train of thought) I noticed recently and thought you wd like is Yeats saying:—ach, I cont find it now. Bother. The gist of it is, the power of a god is increased when he is confined (concentrated) in a statue.

Love,
Denny

dear Denny,

I wonder if Cardenal would extend his concept of the political regimes of tyranny and war mongering being "in ourselves" to mean that in over-throwing such regimes, in fighting against them we fight to overthrow the dictatorships and H bomb in ourselves. There certainly is a difference between being guilty for inner feelings and seeking to end the regime of inner feeling. "The revolutionists are in us, the refusal to make or use the H. bomb is in ourselves." It's not whether we carry *evil* within us, it's whether we back the evil. Anyway, as writers we've to make clear what the word means, or rather, what we mean by the word. Cardenal says "malo" which is not our word "evil" but "bad," denoting not compulsion but what spoils, corrupts and destroys.

I don't feel that Johnson is inside me, bursting out from my wishes and secret dreams, any more than I feel that the Reverend King (who seems to be "good") bursts out from my secret dreams, or that I carry in me "all the evil done by man" or "all the good done by man." The idea is preposterous. I carry in me just that generation of a history I barely bring into existence, and it is in terms of works of art, drawings and poems (which neither Johnson nor the Reverend King carry within them).

The neo-Platonists calld only those gods who were "good in their very essence," but then they got tied up in the idea of all events being "good" in essence. It is our own creative will that acclaims certain goods and disdains certain evils; we "name" them so. It is a creative act in history to name this War and its ends *evil*; as it is a creative act to name the individual volition that does not seek to coerce other individual volition good.

Jess in reading Wordsworth (in connection with a painting he is working on, referring to a passage in the "Intimations of Immortality Ode") found his letter to the Bishop of Llandaff and set me to reading passages.[1] There are some splendid things—one I wld relay: "There must be a strange vice in that legislation from which can proceed laws in whose execution a man

**374**

July 28/{19}66
{San Francisco}

cannot be instrumental without forfeiting his self-esteem and incurring the contempt of his fellow-citizens"

Which rings nobly when we feel, as the Romantics did, that "self-esteem" comes from a libertarian spirit and that "contempt" is directed towards all that is servant to the constriction of freedom.

But what is on my mind here is how exhilarating the effort to redefine ideas of liberty, the people, and good is, to revive the old challenge.

That God's intent in Purgatory is to liberate the individual volition is a lasting concept of the good on Dante's part. Vanzetti's *voluntarism* ultimately the nature of political good lies in our imagination of how to extend this volition in a wider and deeper range of the communal good: i.e. the concord of individual volitions.[2]

And whatever would curb or coerce that volition is evil; whatever would corrupt or destroy that concord is bad or *malo*.

But I'm not sure that all aspects of what determines our sense of evils and goods can be reasond out and explaind. Some are life-intuitions, inner recognitions of what is appropriate to our nature, and may be obscure in its intent. But even these must be *creative* intuitions, for I would follow here Darwin's insight that evolution has within it no "plan." The concord of volitions is then an environment in which individual volitions so fit that they survive; which must always be reimagined, for from every paradise the terms of its not being free for new volition to thrive will become clear.

(As in creating a Poetry as well as making poems, we seek to create an environment in which our own creative spirit *fits*. And in these current "Passages" I feel this dance of coming to fit, the most exciting part of the form). Projecting its own lawfulness.

love
Robert

---

## 375

Aug. 17/1966
{San Francisco}

dear Denny,

As a letter, some scatterd notes as I go from place to place today. A performance of *The Beard*, a play of McClure's (that when it was published last year I dismissed as a dramatization of a hang-up and had absolutely no concept then of what was going on), jolted me out of all previous assumptions and has sent me eagerly re-reading McClure's *Meat Science Essays*.[1] With a great liberation and exhilaration then, in some part Mike has set my spirit free from much it had bound itself about with, as if to make a dogged outline and be done with it. The play is one a reader can make nothing of unless he recognizes the spiritual vision—and here it is very much the vision of poetry I most love—of Blake, of Milton's "Areopagitica":

it's after all the tradition I hoped to awaken McClure to, and then closed my fearful mind and heart to when it was manifest. In fairness to myself, Mike's own personality in its transformations made that difficult [I should surely have balkt at contact with the actual Rimbaud! and been blind to his splendors]. But *Meat Science Essays* shows so clearly and splendidly the knowledgability of McClure's experience; in this it is a different matter from Rimbaud, and akin rather to Blake. What is most striking is that is considered and informed by an experience that is moreover armed with the study and deep reflection upon the science of life (as the essay "Revolt" so shows), an empirical fantasy.

And the second recent joy was not a conversion to a new view but a striking up again of an old view. Seeing Zukofsky on the N.E.T. series program, and realizing once more how I delight in the lively inventions of a word-maker and musicker.[2] It sent me back to reread and then with Jess read aloud from the collected volume, from *Some Time, A*, and exchanging bits of *Bottom* Jess had relisht. A little night's music. I've had saved up the title "A Salutary Act" for a review of or essay on Zuk.

Yes, (I'm thinking now of your enquiry in the last letter) Norton did send the Zuk volume and the series. I've been embarrassed I guess by the fact that outside of Zuk's book none of the others belong even to the world of what I seek in poetry. They all seem to be what's called "good," in good taste and "A" work in any poetry workshop. It's like trying to read Hayden Carruth because he had been responsive to my work on some terms and to find to my dismay that nothing opend up for me in his work.

I think I understand what appeals to you in these poets, it's a world of genteel sensibilities in which or before which I feel the more acutely how unfitting the violence of any inspiration must seem. It's the difference between the kind of good soul for whom the policies of the United States ruling party seem deplorable and the—it must seem extremist—outrage I feel of my spirit flaring up before the fact of an evil power manifesting itself.

But I'm off the wave-length here, for the question of poetry is *not* whether one feels outrage at the war or feels whatever—other than the imperative of the poem. It's the force of word-work (I mean in the sense I always use the word "work," the recognition of the process of language as a spiritual process) that I miss.

God, Denny, I think of Jackson MacLow, Gael Turnbull, Ian Hamilton Finlay, . . . well, it isn't that you didn't happen to publish some poet I already am keen on, but that you didn't come up with one. And I don't hold that against you, Denny. It's an area of your response as a reader of poetry where I don't agree, and I would not close off from myself that opening possibility that it may come to me that Adrienne Rich or Jim Harrison have all the time belonged to that heroic company I call *poet*.

That having been said, and forgiven in the saying—for it is no more than a statement of *my* not responding—I want to return, with joy, to speak of the little collection—the short story, notebook pages and poems you sent (from the *Chicago Review* I think it was). It's a lovely intuitive composition it gives. "In the Night" like "The Tree" is so truly a prose extension of your inner experience—belonging to the same created world as the poetry. And the terms of prose, and of this short story form, do extend. As in another dimension the "bells" of "Remembering" and "the angels bringing attributes" do extend. I begin to hear more resonances that waken poetic apprehensions in the content of the Viet-nam question and answer poem, and "The Postcards" relates beautifully to the poem of the angels passing each other in ascending-descending presence. The lines are so sure, or I am so sure in reading them, given a grace and then gracing the reading. An *"incarnation"* you quote out of Wordsworth; but I am thinking in terms not only of incarnation but of a spiritual process or the very process of spirit (breath in words upon which concepts, feelings, ideas, visions of what is evolve)—not the crystallization [which directs our attention to the beautiful arrangement left after the growth of an element has taken place]. When you see crystals in formation, in micro-moving pictures, you see a mineral *life* besides which the beauty of the final crystal. The product of the inner formative nature and the outer conditions of its growth, is static.

Where is Stendhal's passage on the word *crystallization*? But certainly, I do not mean to dismiss this view that life crystallizes its forms. I would, as I do anyway in the H. D. book, refer on to Schrödinger's sense that life consists in how long a movement can be in the process of formation without reaching crystallization or the terminus of its form.[3] Once a cell is not an end in itself but a member of a larger body, even its death is not the end of its formative process but it has a kind of evolution in the extension of its *self* in the larger evolving body. So we as *Man* have no terminus or formal crystallization except in the totality of forms participating in the species Man; and we have a larger immortality in our union with Life which in many species does not exhaust the process of its formal reality. [So, I wld. take poems as cells of my poetry—but even this body is unreal besides the great process of human language itself in the arts: so that in "The Postcards" rightly you are living under the signs of the Minoan Snake Goddess, the Chardin still-life and the Mohammedan angels. And *poetry* meaning the world of created meanings, *made* things, is the only term that really does hold for the drawings on cave walls, the first circlings of dancers, the makings of cosmogonies. . . . "Language" only means "tongues," what we talk with, and can go on as jabber with no thought of creation.

The "Notebook Pages," anyway, as you must know, are close to my heart.

It's after all (like my H. D. Book) a kind of world I think of as being "ours." They've made the word "Dialogue" such a slogan I balk at using it; and anyway I have in mind a ground of ideas like in the *Zohar* where one brings in theme and counter theme, ideas called up by the conversation. ["Meditation," I find in my work on a Preface for Vaughan, had the meaning in Renaissance alchemy of a conversation with one's self or with angels or other spirits.{]}

I would bring in, after your note to a student ["You must get the material *into the poem*"], that the material of a poem is not brought into it but native to it. Any material gives rise to a poem when you start "making" in the material, seeking its inherent creative form. If you aint got a formative feeling of the material, leave it alone.

Denny, don't take my disappointment in the Norton Series to heart. I don't. And I may have overstated my reaction.

Right now I've stirred up new things in my talking about those pieces of yours and I want to reread and ride the wave of it.

love
Robert

Dearest Robert,

First—that "Interlude" is one of the most beautiful things you've ever written, I believe.[1] And "Passages 27" is a continuation worthy of the whole series. Much harder to understand than the "Interlude" though—for instance the first line even. 27 offers some surface, but not much—most of it is to be *mined* out by those capable of it, & willing. It is that kind of poem. The "Interlude" is there for everyone who would approach it at all . . . like a brook in the woods. This comparison of the 2 kinds of poem is not a "value judgement."

Second—the accompanying letter (and even more the one just before it, of July 28th) was one of the most essential & gratefully received (by Mitch as well as by me). You liberate me by helping me distinguish the undifferentiated potential for evil (Man can commit crimes—I am a man—therefore I can commit crimes) from the differentiated facts. "It's not whether we carry evil within us, it's whether we back the evil" you wrote. (You are wrong however about "malo": there is no word in Spanish that actually makes a distinction between "bad" & "evil" as we do. There's *depravado*, depraved, *pernicioso*, pernicious, *dañoso*, hurtful or injurious or damaging, *malicia*, malice—but if you want to translate "evil" into Spanish the plain word wd. be "malo," & so I think it perfectly justifiable & indeed necessary to reverse the process. One has to judge by the context, & as a

**376**

Sat/Sunday
19th–20th Aug. {19}66
Temple {Me.}

Catholic monk I feel sure "evil" is the sense of "malo" Cardenal is likely to have had in mind.)

Actually the line between not selfrighteously saying "they" are evil while not acknowledging that it is due not to our virtues but to our blessings that we are not doing similar acts (& indeed who hasn't on his conscience "minor" acts of cruelty, coldness, hostility, neglect, malice, etc. from *some* period of their lives?)—between avoiding that selfrighteousness (that insists its hands are clean) & the *masochistic insistence* on sharing responsibility for what we *have not* done & from which our whole being does revolt. It's a thin line but a real one & I feel a good deal clearer about it now.

About the new letter, which came this morning: there is one thing I feel I must mention, & that is, that in repeating, here & elsewhere, that you feel *outraged* by the war you seem perhaps, just a little, to assume that others— Mitch & I for example?—*don't*, but only "deplore" etc. Maybe I am wrong but that is the way you, in several allusions or rather in these allusions taken together, seem to me to make it sound & if it is true it is something I cannot let pass. In reference to me it is probably (if the attitude does exist) based on 2 things—(1), *that I criticized your words about Humphrey in the Xmas poem.* Now, as the war drags on & more people are slaughtered & lives wrecked of those who survive, I feel more keenly than even a few months ago that, on one level, nothing is too vile a term to use of such a man, but I didn't make myself clear if you thought that at any time I was defending him! No—but I felt the words used in the poem weren't grave enough, weighty enough—they sounded like screams of a temper tantrum —or, to put it another way, they weren't artistically strong enough. (2) *That my own poems that object to the war are elegiac in tone, and don't express outrage.* That is true, & I can only say humbly that it is not because I, and just about all my friends, don't *feel* it just as you do. You are singularly fortunate in being such a mature and powerful poet, Robert, that almost alone of all the poets I know (& far more completely than any other) you have been able to *word* your outrage, in poems like (well I don't have all the "Passages" here, but "Uprising" & the ones before & after it tho' perhaps not the Xmas poem). We were talking tonight to Grammy Barker, an old village lady who has never been out of Maine but once—she's 88—& she is just as *outraged* as anybody could be—for instance. And Johnson was booed in N.H. & Vt. yesterday. A lot of people can't *express* their outrage, & most people are politically & morally *confused*—but it doesn't mean they have no feelings.

About the Norton poets—no, I'm not upset about it. I had thought there were some you would like—the whatever-it-is I find so stimulating in Joel Sloman, the music of Helen Wolfert, the sharp authentic lyric impulse I find in Jim Harrison, for instance. But I don't like all of Roseliep myself &

knew you'd be put off there—though there are poems of his like one I have here, for instance—I forget if it is in the book or not but will copy & enclose—that make me willing to respect what I *don't* care for—this kind of poem of his makes me feel what I feel when in a rock in the river I find grains of something that shines like gold, little clefts filled with shining granules—Try rereading (or reading) Adrienne's "Spring Thunder" or "The Knot."[2]

Well, & that is what it comes down to, I stand fast by what has caused me to *feel.* And the range of response in you & in me overlaps—& that is a large area—but beyond the area of overlap extends in quite different directions. Years ago that shamed & embarrassed me—but now not. You are more the Master, a Master poet in my world, not less, just because I feel that the only emulation of such a master is to be *more oneself.* (As I wrote in a little piece written at Bob Hawley's suggestion recently, which I hope you will like.[3]) One doesn't try to *be* a mountain; one feels living in the presence of a mountain that one is a free being who must stand straight & breathe deep, which in human terms means that one must have the courage of one's own responses even if someone one so much admires is appalled at them.

If I had the various books here I would maybe quote examples of what I care for in each case but it is as well I don't for it wd. probably seem only argument. As long as you do remain open to the possibility that some day you may discover things you value in some of them, it's enough. And you will be glad to know that Ronald Johnson & Gael Turnbull (with a much stronger book than the one I tried to get Wesleyan to do 3 years ago) are among the future books to be done by Norton.

I cannot believe that you really meant that the reason I liked these poets was because they were "genteel"—you may think they are "genteel," but you don't really believe that that's *why* I like them & yet in the same breath speak of my own work with love. Or if you do, it requires a redefinition of the word genteel.

I enclose a few recent poems I think you haven't seen.

By the way I wonder if Margaret Avison's book was included with the other Norton poems?[4] I marvel if you cannot care for *that*!

Love—
Denny

dear Denny,

Oyez sent me your lovely piece on the poet as mountain, "master" of a landscape that comes so true for me to speak of that other—the otherness of poetry itself—the poet in his poem is to the man writing and reading, that

**377**

Aug. 29 {30}/1966
{San Francisco}

can seem more himself than he is. And that poetry that is clearly and truly poetry for me opens up as a mountain that is like the Self Jung talkd about, man's self in which we dwell. For, after all, like you, I have to be "more oneself" to emulate ("to strive to equal or rival" my O.E.D. gives; but how strange! in the presiding spirit of your writing the word so clearly means and says "to enter into a company with, to commune with") [but now I look back to your opening words "a powerful presence acknowledged"]—in that sense, that I too like you, like the few, acknowledge that as poets we are in the presence of this Poet, as in a landscape; and I too in your "On Reading the Earlier Poems of R. D."[1] can accompany you to experience those poems not only as evidences of my own talents and liabilities as a writer but as the approaches of a world that so desired to become real and had only those talents and liabilities to do so.

Jess loved your noting "bitter fungi full of worms." How much I had disliked what went on in these early poems, wincing at tangles and morasses of old ways of feeling—our writing so immediately betrays the conditions of its going on! And only as I set about this manuscript last year, did I find that I no longer saw it with the pain of self-exposure but saw it as you so readily do (love is all here) as truly the beginnings of the world of the poem in which I would dwell in my work now; and in those sometimes grievous moods and passions and the stances and posings of feeling taken I understand lasting elements of my inner being and of a life would not be out of tune with its benefices.

The two poems started in 1965 ("The Heart" and "The Curve") have resonances [between the two: "an old caboose" and "an old / china plate" and the work the world as artist works in us to weather the tint and crack the glaze]. There is a resonance of the question in "The Curve" "Shall we / ever reach it?" and in "The Heart" "What / is under the cracked glaze?" That last question I wanted to eliminate from the poem; it seemd "lame" to me: but the structure would indicate it is required. Somewhere that "What is under the glaze" will return in full.

I'm just listening as I write to a radio interview Creeley made in Los Angeles this Spring—he's talking beautifully about what it is like to write a poem (clearing away the stupidities of the interviewer who cannot understand writing apart from rendering ideas already "on your mind") Now he's talking about his reading tour and I'm back talking with you.

Did I write that some poems of Galway Kinnell's have begun to come across for me? One was "The Library," I think it was calld, in *Poetry* which I found moving;[2] tho since, when someone questiond immediate areas of the poem [reference to Weldon Kees' suicide, etc.] I was not sure of how solidly they were realized. It was a matter of a "poetic" pose missing a content that needed a direct statement. . . .

Aug. 30, 1966

My thot goes on from yesterday's content, and after breakfast talk with Jess, thinking particularly of the role of numbers in the science of the universe, in the science of spirit and of "creation" in the work of art. Jess is reading Mead's *Thrice Greatest Hermes*, having read last month Jonas's *The Gnostic Religion* and I guess Klibansky, Saxl and Panofsky's *Saturn and Melancholy* enters in here, for he has studied that book (which I orderd for him from Basic Books) closely indeed storing up in-formation towards the long-plannd future rentering of Dürer's *Melancolia I* . . . anyway in our conversation both of our readings in gnostic, hermetic and Pythagorean myth and speculation was being brought into consideration with the hypotheses and theories of chemistry and physics. We had just got a new book of Gamov's*—new to us, I mean: the book was published in 1958— and I had added a book by Read *Through Alchemy to Chemistry* to my alchemical studies.[3]

\* *Matter, Earth, and Sky*

Out of all of which we came to talk of numbers. Let me first type out here a passage I found in Read:

> To the student of alchemy it [the electronic constitution of the atom] brings echoes of the ancient doctrine of the Two Contraries, and of the later sophic Sulphur and sophic Mercury, now represented by the positive proton and the negative electron; of the Hermetic Androgyne, now figuring as the neutron; of Aristotle's idea of a primordial matter, linked with the alchemical belief in the unity of all things; of the undying faith of generations of alchemists in the possibility of metallic transmutation; and of Plato's view, conceived more than two thousand years ago, that Nature rests upon a mathematical plan, and that the ultimate realities must be sought in mathematics.
>
> *Through Alchemy to Chemistry*, p. 164

Juxtapose to this the Pythagorean concept that the ultimate realities at once of the spiritual and the physical were contain in the operations of the numbers one to five, the roles of positive and negative matter and numbers (where zero has its meaning) in extending our understanding of spirit as well as physics.

What I want to get to here is what was on our mind thru it all—the scientia of art as creation. How intuitions of relationships are strengthend and focusst—made more keen and lively—by our conscious development of the structure, why rightly it is *form* that must be our primary exploration towards new invention. In Jess's new paintings content and form has advanced to a conscious involvement with chords and relations of threes moving then potentially towards four. I am still in the articulation of the form of the poem at the stage of threes, barely working with elements of four. "Passages" at the stanza level, for instance, for some time has been working with articulations of

1— line to line: represented by single space on the typewriter forming stanza groups

> but light-years away    a diamond spark in the host of stars
>         sparkling net    bejewelld wave of dark    over us
> distant corruscations
>                         "play of light or of intellectual brilliancy"

2— "stanzas" to "stanzas": represented by space and a half on the typewriter forming groups of stanzas and [b] lines free from stanza, derived from Larry Eigner's versification—first appearing as a principle in my work with "Where it Appears, Passages 4" "momentous"/"inconclusions" in that poem refers to the Eigner articulation. His specific development has not only to do with a meaning developed from the space between lines but with a meaning developed in the establishment to individual (i.e. "momentous," "liberated," "active") margins

>         invisible
>             so that it seems no man    but a world speaks
> for my thoughts are servants of the stars, and my words
>         (all parentheses opening into
> come from a mouth that is the Universe    *la bouche d'ombre*

Where in syntax I pick up on Charles's open parenthesis which I first ceased to take for granted I remember because you questiond his usage in a letter to me and I then had to find out at a meaningful level and read, really read, for the first time his "La Préface" where the meaning was first given (1950, in the beginning of things)

Draw it thus: (    )1910(
It is not obscure. We are the new born, and there are no flowers.
Document means there are no flowers
                            and no parenthesis.

It is radical, the root, he and I, two bodies
We put our hands to these dead.

The closed parenthesis reads: the dead bury the dead

                    . . . .

Open, the figure stands at the door, horror his
and gone, possessed, o new Osiris, Odysseus ship.

This element makes it possible for me by use of a closed [ ] bracket to present John Dee removed from the poem. (One thing I had not thought of was that the listener or reader would take Doctor Dee not as the venerable Dee, but as D for Duncan; tho admittedly, clearly in the poem the alchemist conversing with his invisibles is a counterpart of the poet)

But back to the business of numbers.

3—sections of a poem: represented by double space on the typewriter or earlier and under the movements of a long poem or the items of a serial poem.

What interests me is that tho I entertain ideas and feelings of fourth articulations in this dimension I have no "mastery" (i.e. consciousness of intuition in articulating). I can immediately recognize three syllables, but four is liable to be three + one, and in any question of whether a word is four or five syllables I have to count on my fingers. What is dreadful about learnd meters, let's take particularly here the pentameter, as contrasted with invented meters is that habit (a rehearsed stereotype) takes the place of active intuitions, so that a poet can write by rote in five stresses, when he would be at a loss if he had to work consciously in fives. For instance, I could *memorize* that gradually had four syllables or I could count out the syllables to fit a prescription: but neither of these would be my having a language of four syllables. At any rate, a language in which I am participating consciously—and it *is* the awareness that concerns me.

It must seem a long ways back to my thought yesterday about "The Curve" and "The Heart"—the "what / is under the cracked glaze" was more markt because the one line contrasts with the sets of two. The image set of two [heart and crackt plate] begins to set in the poem into an equation so that touch and fissure begin to be systematicly translated. The *life* of the poem is real enuf, heart and the crackt-glaze plate are living associations, and touch and new fissure, and the

> if on the bloody muscle its namesake
> patiently pumping in the thoracic cavity
> each flick of fate incised itself

and the progression from "flick" to "live" to "gift" and of "thoracic" to "habit" to "absolute" is so certain, that the poem has already aroused its "form" in the reader's imagination. Why? is on my mind—have to carry out an idea about or a conclusion to what is already there: *except that it is felt as pending in the structure* and the artist (like the scientist or the mathematician) must supply a—well, not "must" but "does" or feels the lack of a—development to stand for the needed development.

[The trouble with using the poem here is that I do not want to worry your poem but to explore the movement thru the poem. There are plenty of places where I seem involved in my work with questionable utterances—and I am searching for how to contain them (towards a larger structure then) and not how to eliminate them or straighten them out. In terms of content, I wld take my tack from the Freudian idea of content—that it is not *wrong* when it does not seem to be meaningful, but *incomplete*: we work for a context in which each part is recognized, the configuration in which "impulse" is justified. As evil needs the recognition, definition and atonement before it is felt to be justified: our sense of injustice is identical with our sense of composition. One way, men seek to eliminate evil in order to be composed, to be insensitive to it (self-satisfied) or to erase it (kill off or destroy the offender): the other, men seek to understand the nature of the evil (to redeem the criminal, not punish him; to get to the truth of what is going on). Our difficulties with the War is that our reactions make it difficult to come to what the War is doing (we want so to have it end that we neglect the reality that it is happening). It struck me this morning that what has been im- pending in "Passages" and I don't know when or how it will emerge at the level of the poem's content is—that the Vietnam war is a stripping away of pretense and hypocrisy from the social order in which we live and a showing forth of the true face. [As, in the Bible the joy in the catastrophic rings true because a wish is made evident] We see truly that our decision is allied with those people fighting in the jungles, dug into caves and tunnels, holding to a way to life against surrender, and have emerged into something larger and truer than "nation"—our world share of humanity in justice means shedding what's falsely calld our American "wealth." We have no "advantages" to bring other peoples up to. We or the "we" of a future time will come more vividly to find ourselves in that same War the Viet Cong now wage: but we are in it—how easily I forget it—tho we may live with our homes and our personal lives not immediately under attack. . . .

The greed and fear that drive Johnson on, even now as the economic structures of the establishment groan and crack, and the impending catastrophe of the costs of the War rise like a sea that is about to flood us [and there our homes and lives will first rock and our servitude bind], are deep motivations in our total society and yet, as we make our vow to serve truth, and keep our allegiance to the common good of humanity this American society can be "ours" only in so far as it serves those ends—

The End of the War will not be realized in whatever peace might be arranged except as the nation is made subject to the good of humanity at large—[*We* want peace because we are agonized to realize how much we are involved with and subject to the will of murderous and conceited men; but the Vietnamese who are fighting for the truth do not want *peace* at the sacrifice of their vision of the good—we, not they, are the ones who need immediate surrender of the war for the good of our human souls.

---

Turning to close here, I reread "The altar in the street"[4] and all my outpourings are containd as I would want them in

"The hale and the maimed together
 hurry to construct for the Buddha
 a dwelling at each intersection. . . . "

Among whom we too are. What a lovely poem. To stand along side
Whitman's "As I Ponder'd in Silence" which has always presided over the
"War" in writing "Passages."

love
Robert

dear Denny,

**378**

Sept. 12, 1966

[San Francisco}

One morning, when Barbara Joseph was here, we had a radiant session
with the tape you sent of the "Olga" poem and the selection of poems that
seem to stream out from that center. What a moving and awesome reading
that is! So intimately *you*, the voice is such a lovely gift, and comes, I feel, in
this intimacy at its fullest. The "Olga" poem, as when I first *found* it for
myself in *Poetry*, is the fulfillment of a deep wish for such a poem to be.
What a caution that I listend with such deaf ears at first hearing!

Do you have a copy of this tape? In a few weeks I am going to be spending
several days making copies of certain tapes, and I will make one to send you.
It *is* an outstanding reading you did.

That was only a little over a week ago. . . . And I meant to write right
off. Then, maybe inspired in the rapture of hearing those poems again (and,
in some way, giving myself up to the listening, going deep into the voice of
the poem), and set off too by the publication of the *Passages of the War*
(which I send on with this letter) [the limited edition will take a bit longer
to be done],[1] I got two new "Passages." Number 28, swiftly, coming even as
I was walking to the streetcar stop, so that I walkd along resisting anything
so obviously so Hopkins as "down-falling doom's darling"—an echo or
ghost if not an actual passage of him; and then, taking it on, willing to
accept that lead and writing it down once I arrived at the car-stop; then
the poem going on in rushes on the streetcar and on the Berkeley bus, me
muttering ecstatically. All there by the time I reacht Berkeley.

The other (29) has been brewing from several sources [only the other
day I followed a lead from a French *Encyclopedia of Divination* to a meaning
of "sorcery" derived from "source" and from "sorts":[2] drawing the "source"
as in the dream of Olson as the Doctor in the H. D. book, and drawing
the "sorts," as often I do in "Passages"]—a book on *La Crise Mystique de
Victor Hugo* with a moving chapter on his vision of the Angel Liberty,[3] born
from a feather of Lucifer's wing, transfixt in the light of a loving intent than
shone for a glance from God's eye (the artist's momentary full love for his

creation, even in its fall) And who then becomes the agency of Satan's redemption.

I've been reading this book on Hugo for several weeks, and then, searching out the Caodaïst movement (one of the largest groups in the Viet-Cong), I found a book by a French convert Gabriel Gobron, written in 1939, before the Second World War, and the vision of a Universalist Viet-Namese religious commune, worshipping Laotse, Buddha, Confucius, Christ, and the Genii as five Masters or five Ways.[4] [So that, I see a world-view, non-nationalistic, and a vision of the community of Man, has its heart in Viet-Nam]—In another pre-War book on the Cao-Daï there are photographs of the devout praying for the soul of Gandhi, or communing with the soul of Gandhi . . . ?

So . . . along with the new book, I send two new "Passages" . . .

Love<br>Robert

## 379

Oct. 21st {19}66
Temple, Maine

We're here for a few days. (Leaving Sunday)

Dear Robert

Your last letter, with beautiful poems, was dated Sept. 12th—since then, the packing, returning of Nik to Putney & ourselves to N.Y., a week of flu, the getting used to new jobs, & various household reorganizations (we are finally getting the apt. painted, floors scraped & refinished etc.) plus a visit to Nik the weekend of the 8th & helping him with his college applications. Actually, I guess we had left here by Sept. 7th or 8th & I got that letter of yours in N.Y. It certainly seems longer even than that because the time has been so packed & busy. I find I like teaching at Vassar very much. I had feared to find the girls tame & bland after my dear wild CCNY ones— but they really are not, at all; they're varied in personality & economic background & every other way; (though I think I do prefer *co-ed* classes). I have a very nice office & the general atmosphere is good, & the grounds with their glorious big trees are a great pleasure; also the train ride up the Hudson. Staying over & being there 2 days helps to make it a different & less sketchy experience than last year's 1 day a week each at CCNY & Drew—I feel more a part of the life of the place & I like that.

I'm terribly glad you liked the tape I sent a year or so ago, you had never said anything about it so I never knew if you had played it or not & liked it or not. I gather now (tho' it's not quite clear) that you'd played it before but not liked it; so I'm all the happier you did so this time with Barbara Joseph. I've often as you know come to care very much for poems of yours I had been deaf to at first, and that experience of coming late to love a poem often seems to intensify one's relation to it, somehow—like surviving troubles with a person.

The "Passages" you sent (28 & 29) are most wonderful—28 full of some golden darkness I know in no poems but yours, or elsewhere but a line at a time & rarely. I would like to know if Anteros is pronounced Antéros?—I hope so—and who is Crysaor? The Cao-Dai poem seems a very important one in the series, having for it some of the coordinating effect of the syncretist faith itself.

Thanks for the pamphlet of war poems—it is useful to have printed them thus.

Next wk. I'm going to read at several colleges in Ohio (Wed–Sat.) & a man who says he's a "very close friend" of yours & Jess's has kindly written to say he wd. like to meet me. I hope he really is a close friend, for then I'm sure I will enjoy meeting him—I feel slightly skeptical as he is Director of American Humanist Association, which seems a somewhat unlikely connection? (aren't they aggressive, militant "rationalists," or do I have the wrong party?) and because though claiming fond familiarity with my work he spells my name (3 times) "Levertove"! His name is Tolbert H. McCarroll. Well, *on verra*. There won't be time for me to have heard from you about him beforehand: Mitch will deliver me straight to Vassar on Monday morning, & I'll get to N.Y. Tues. evening & take off for Ohio first thing Wed. morning.

We have Muzio with us here and he is so happy to be back in the country. He came for quite a long walk with us this morning. It's beautiful to watch a cat in a field—that stop & go gait—rippling & bounding along, long fur streaming back, one minute, a slow swaying stroll the next—stopping to wash—prowling among the bracken (he's almost the same shade as dead ferns)—leaping over some brush.

We got here on Wed. & it started to rain, & rained all through Thurs. It wasn't disagreeable as one could feel very relaxed & indoor-y by the wood stove reading Thackeray, & taking naps. (I haven't been sleeping well lately, & needed just such a quiet day.) Then the wind came up & the leaves flew & it began to snow—a wild scene. We bundled up & walked down the road, & the brook was all cascades. Today it's all changed, warm sunshine & the special blue of New England fall skies, which I love. Many trees are bare but there's still a lot of color & I found my pansies were still blooming. I'll try to remember to put one in this letter for you to see.

I wrote a "street ballad" in rhymed couplets (a "come all ye") about the Fort Hood 3—not a good poem but something the Greenwich Village Peace Center may be able to use as a leaflet I hope. And another, a better poem, which I'll send you if I can find a copy among the stuff I brought along, which evolved as a rather bitter response to a laughable request for a poem on "Love in America" for the *Saturday Evening Post*!

Of course it is unlikely to say the least that they will use it (it refers to the children beaten up in Grenada, to the steel breasts of the Great Society, & to napalm).

Otherwise I don't have any new poems since "The Seeing" and "The Altars in the Street" which I think I sent you.[1] I've been reading 1st galleys of *The Sorrow Dance* tho' it won't be out till March, & on the Hindu poems which should be out soon.[2] (Will send.)

Nik's 1st choices for college are Rhode Island School of Design and New College (Sarasota)—I hope he gets into one of them. RISD wd probably be the best for him. But he's applying to 4 or 5 others also.

Mitch has been rather politically active—e.g. speaking to 2 groups of Rotarians (!) up here, telling them things about the history & conduct of the war & what napalm is, etc., to which they listened attentively & about which they were *really* shocked—decent local tradesmen, not one's stereotype of a rotarian; telling (as Sunday evening speaker when we were visiting Nik) the Putney kids what the possibilities for C.O. application were & so on; leafleting & engaging in conversation with soldiers (returning to Fort Dix N.J.) at the Port Authority Bus Terminal in N.Y. on Sunday evenings; & so on. He's teaching at Drew once a week, the same class I did last year except that his is for prose.

Now I must stop as we are going to get some old manure from under the barn & mulch the flowerbeds with it.

A big eagle has been seen near here lately. And a white robin.

> Love to Jess. Love to you.
> Denny.

Bob (Creeley) & John Wieners are reading in N.Y. on Monday—I'll miss it, but Mitch will go.

---

**380**

Oct. 28/1966
{San Francisco}

dear Denny & Mitch,

As soon as our checking acct. can cover it for sure—an honorarium from the University for my work with the poetry collections there is pending—Jess and I will send something for the defense funds for those soldiers who have protested service in Viet-nam. It is a matter of at most a week, and may come in the mail today before I mail this letter. The cause has been on my mind, Mitch, since you sent the note, but in all such things I've still got to weigh the timing against any pressures for payment on our own living budget.

I've decided definitely I will be coming East on tour next Spring—Bob this last summer urged my coming to Buffalo for a reading and now I've got to start a correspondence to get enuf to finance the trip. There has been a feeler from Bennington about my going there, that is—from Claude

Fredericks, preliminary, I take it, to pressing the suggestion. I would be interested in one quarter and possibly the summer session, but not a permanent move. . . .

All this is tentative and playd against a background of the more than possibility (I have been told "we want to give you a grant" by Carolyn Kizer) that I am to receive a National Foundation of Arts and Humanities award. Given even that event, I am not sure what it involves. If it involves in any way the Administration so that one would seem to receive it *from* something other than the Foundation, it will be good-bye to the $10,000, but hello to a great opportunity for a protest that would be heard. It would not only be me, I am sure. Robert Peterson with whom I have talkt is most concernd,[1] and Hayden Carruth I take it would be too. All of which is very exciting, but has not happend yet.

My horoscope must be set up for delays (no "hurryscope" I wrote poor Henry[2] who is beside himself with the postponements of the *Book of Resemblances*)—for not only is that book delayd, but my volume of "First Poems" still has not been begun after galley proofs three months ago, page proofs a month ago . . . and the limited edition on those *War Passages* is still not done. I filld out the application blanks that Carolyn Kizer sent me in August and have not heard from them since (it was Peterson who told me *she* told *him*, etc. . . . )

•

About the hearing of the tape of the "Olga Poems," Denny, if I was unclear about previous hearings it was because I was troubled to admit that I had not listend to the tape. It had arrived at a time when I was not "with it." I've learnd not to *try* to respond over a felt inertia. Tho often awakening out of these periods will come with suddenly reading or suddenly hearing. Then the tape waited, postponed . . . and that morning when Barbara was here was suddenly a time that was all its own. I cannot believe I could ever not have recognized the beauty of that tape, Denise. It is a radiant and immediate reading. Your poems particularly come fully to life in the radius of an intimate company. No, I would tho have felt the more keenly the muffled nature of my own response. Like having only the wrong day on which to see a painting one has longd to see. As it was, it was my first hearing that came also with the full thrill of hearing.

It was not, in any sense, the other experience we all must have with each other, for we have it with ourselves, the unsureness of the poem itself (I still, for instance, am not easy about the "Interlude"—it was greatly reassuring to have you write you liked it, but my own sense of writing it remaind a different question than how the poem would be in the reading)—And especially with you, I have made free to worry poems when there would arise some feeling of a possible form wanted as I read. Sometimes, as your questioning the pendant of "Passages 2," such queries are most pertinent to the actual intent of the poem. And I think that even seemingly pointless dissents from the realized poem arise because along the line of reading a formal apprehension, vague but demanding, has arisen that differs from the author's form. In a mistaken reading, this will arise because I want to use the matter of the poem to write my own "Denise Levertov" poem. Crucially astray.

•

Didn't I write that "The Altars in the Street" is mounted above my desk to speak, as it does so beautifully, for my own sense of what our work in the art means.[3] It needed the extremity of this war (that is everywhere) to show so clearly the verity we have always known we stood by, the "dwelling at each intersection" constructed. Let my poems always be such a child's altar. I think of Jaime {de Angulo} dying of cancer, waiting for the intersections in the internal pain to build again a sentence, an affirmation: that he himself thot of as being for itself. "If I can learn calculus before I die" . . .

The protest is only true when it is such an altar, an expressive act. When it is directed towards a *means-ends*, it is either futile or, succeeding, belongs to a complex of political meanings that can have no "truth in itself." This is of the nature of all acts in so far as they are *means*, i.e. not identical with their own intent. Like lines or images of a poem that are not felt as immediacies of "form" but as means toward an end of the poem.

Peace, I am more and more convinced is not an absence of war or in opposition to war (all the drama of the confrontation of opposites is polemic) but, like good, a means that is its own ends.

But this is beside the point, for the war itself is "an altar in the inter-section" if it be true; it is the utter falsehood and evil of this war that has quickend in my heart (that still wld not give up the immediacy of the work) an adventure—our beloved Walt Whitman has given words to in that answer to the Muse's demand to sing of war. . . . How can times of inertia come when such challenges ring? At such times I over-read, as others over-eat, gorging myself on texts of history, philosophy, magic or myth, or reading with horrid fascination the scandals of the war, (as recently the murders in the bloody aftermath of Kennedy's assassination, the growing evidence that more than a few are sure Johnson himself was a mover in that so convenient murder, as he was certainly a most interested and principal "beneficiary," stepping into the control of the Kennedy War.

---

Re, your questions on Anteros and Crysaor, Denny: The English pronun-ciation *Anteros* would be disastrous in the poem. I had in mind (and always have so pronounced the name) an accent on the penult as in the Greek Ἀντέρως. Rose (whose *Handbook of Greek Mythology* I use all the time) refers to legends or romances from Pausanias, and Ovid, principally and betrays some distaste for the same: "It is rather a libel to call such rubbish mythology" (The word "rubbish" is beside the point here; where the point is that legend or romance are not myth).[4] There was an altar to Anteros near the Athenian Akropolis, who was "counter-love" or "love returnd"—as distinguisht from Eros who was the god of falling in love (which was not a reciprocal experience).

Chrysáor is more obscure or unexplaind. When the Medusa is slain by Perseus, from her trunk springs the wingd horse Pegasos and Chrysaor "he of the golden sword"—

from Hesiod's THEOGONY

"And when Perseus cut off her head, there sprang forth great Chrysaor and the horse Pegasus who is so called because he was born near the springs (*pegae*) of Ocean; and that other, because he held a golden blade (*aor*) in his hands. Now Pegasus flew away and left the earth, the mother of flocks, and came to the deathless gods: and he dwells in the house of Zeus and brings to wise Zeus the thunder and lightning. But Chrysaor was joined in love to Callirrhoë, the daughter of glorious Ocean, and begot three-headed Geryones."

Cook in the second volume of his Zeus, I find, discusses Chrysaor as the lightning itself:[5] and right now I am at a loss for a story as to where Pegasus became the thunder and lightning bearing flight of the poet's trip, but Chrysaor then would be the bolt from the blue inspired word or image that strikes the poet.

love
Robert

Dear Robert & Jess,

We are here for Thanksgiving & it is snowing hard. A few chick-dees—one or 2 other winter species, very silent—& the bluejays. New shapes of tree revealed. Our house, so secret-seeming in summer when the trees hide it from the road, now strangely naked—the way most people here must think of it ordinarily. Ted Enslin looking, as he is, most at home. The good smell of our woodstoves. Deer tracks everywhere in the woods & right near the house—being covered now by the new snow. A few squirrels still up & about—looking as if they'd only jumped out of bed for a moment though, to get something to eat & run right back.

When I last wrote we were just about to listen to that Berkeley tape. We did, & it was wonderful. Thank you.

**381**

{late November 1966
Temple, Me.}

William Burford[1] has been reading Duncan lately & writes: "About Duncan—he's done really an extraordinary body of remarkable work, & has wonderfully surpassed himself. . . . there is in many of the poems a profound working in the depths, brought up toward the light." And (in another letter a week later): ". . . reading Duncan again, & I find so many lines I like I have kept a record of them that now fills pages of my notebook . . . even in their abstraction there is a tingling physical presence. In such a line as this, for instance: '. . . this peril/in which as towards a secret trust/life springs.' There, I think, is the secret of his powerful art. In the midst of this poem "A Set of Romantic Hymns" an arm pit is evoked but in connection with *sound*; & the poet has gifted himself in a extraordinary way with a metaphor that probably Aristotle could not have imagined as a possible metaphor when he speaks of the first gift of the poet."

These date from mid-November—while back in October he had first written, before getting *into* the poems, with reservation, along the lines of "something wonderful but marred there"—I can't find that one now.

For 2 days I was haunted by a rhythm without words—Campion? Wyatt?—We were driving, to Putney & then here, so I couldn't search. Suddenly it came to me, Raleigh—but I still couldn't remember any words—After we got here I looked it up, of course, it was Raleigh's "Walsingham" poem. I can't remember remembering a rhythm without its words quite so strongly ever before.

I spent part of an evening with Robert Lowell at someone's house in Cambridge recently & discovered that he's aurally *stupid*, simply blunted, dull, stupid.[2] Imagine, it had *never occurred* to him to think of Emily Dickinson's dashes as aural notations, rests or rallentandos. He had supposed them to be merely a sort of scribbles, meaning nothing, presumably intended by E. D. to be *filled in* with "proper" punctuation later. At first in a prideful immodest way he vigorously denied they could be anything more. Eventually tho', he evidently decided to mull over this "new idea." Of course, that accounts for much in his own poetry—yet I wouldn't have supposed him to have been that unthinking, it is after all years now since the dashes were publicly restored, so it is not a question of the first surprise. But I suppose it is characteristic not only of him & his followers but of the whole school of critics from whom he learned—they never have been accustomed to *listen*.

Found a couple of good things recently, this from Klee: "The work of art . . . is experienced first of all as a *process of creation* rather than as its passive product. The creative impulse suddenly springs to life, like a flame, passes through the hand onto the canvas, where it spreads further until, like the spark that closes an electric circuit, it returns to its source: the eye of the mind."[3]

And Buber: "To produce is to draw forth, to invent is to find, to shape is to discover. In bodying forth, I disclose. I lead the form across—into the world of It."[4]

This was quoted without book-source where I saw it & I must enquire concerning its context. The Klee was quoted in that big (Gombrich? Abrams Co.) book about him & was from a lecture.[5]

P.S.

During the summer someone brought us some sea lavender from the coast and though faded it is still itself a cloud of mauve mer-hair it seems.

The flakes of snow are now in the form of very small sticks, about this [rectangle about ½ inch high drawn with a narrow stick-like rectangle in the middle] size.

Nik is reading the Book of Job.

Advent 1966

Because in Viet Nam the vision of a Burning Babe
is multiplied, multiplied,
                         the flesh on fire
not Christ's, as Southwell saw it, prefiguring
the Passion upon the Eve of Christmas,

but wholly human and repeated, repeated,
infant after infant, their names forgotten,
their sex unknown in the ashes,
set alight, flaming but not vanishing,
not vanishing as his vision but lingering

cinders upon the earth or living on
moaning and stinking in hospitals three abed,

because of this my strong sight,
my clear caressive sight, my poet's sight I was given
that it might stir me to song
is blurred.
              There is a cataract filming-over
my inner eyes. Or else a monstrous insect
has entered my head, and looks out
~~at~~ from my sockets with multiple vision,

seeing not the unique Holy Infant
burning sublimely, an imagination of redemption,
furnace in which our souls are wrought into new life,
but, as off a belt-line, more, more, more senseless figures aflame.

**382**

{December 1966
New York}

And this insect (who is not there—
it is my own eyes do my seeing, the insect
is not there, what I see is there)
will not permit me to look elsewhere,
or if I look, to see except dulled and unfocussed
the delicate, firm, whole flesh of the still unburned.

Denise
Dec. 1966

Dear Robert,

Could you possibly send me another copy (or tell me how to get one) of your Dante lecture? During the painting of the apt. I have mislaid it and want a lovely student who cares very much for your work & who is relating her reading of Dante in an Italian course to various poets she is reading in my course, to have a chance to read it as soon as poss. Thanks. Have been trying to get you a Vassar reading in the Spring but they seem to have spent their budget. May still be *possible* however.

Love (& to Jess)
Denny

Mitch is working with Peter Schumann (Bread & Puppet Theater—a great artist) in preparation of some war protest, peace events.[1]

## 383

Dec. 16, 1966
{San Francisco}

dear Denny and Mitch,

Along with Christmas greetings—at least the felicitations of friendship—the copy of the Dante lecture to replace the one you lost, Denny. This was a limited edition—only 500 copies, so this "first edition" is rare right now. But a second edition will be coming out with Oyez early this coming year. And I hope to have a copy of the "First Poems" volume by the first of the year—an advance paper-bound copy that is. Your "real" copy will be one of the bound edition, but that will be later, subject to the binder's schedule.[1]

I have been reading Bultmann's *Theology of the New Testament* and in St. Paul's presentation of the creative will found verification and coordination for ideas I have had concerning the difference between organic and creative form,[2] and between them and conventional and in turn ideal form. And flashing out in the midst of these considerations of the nature of our ideas of form—flames that pass quickly from the torch of Christians in the first and second centuries to our own torches: v. I, p. 256: "Then the eerie fact is that the «Kosmos», the world of men, constituted by that which the individual does and upon which he bestows his care, itself gains the upper hand over the individual." p. 257: "In modern terms, the «spirit of the world» is the atmosphere to whose compelling influence every man contributes but to which he is also always subject." v. II, p. 69: "he [John] sees the meaning of the synoptic message of Jesus to be that ultimately it is the shattering and negating of the «world's» understanding of itself"

Denny, the last poem[3] brings with it an agonizing sense of how the monstrosity of this nation's War is taking over your life, and I wish that I could advance some—not consolation, there is none—wisdom of how we are to at once bear constant (faithful and ever present) testimony to our grief for those suffering in the War and our knowledge that the government of the United States is so immediately the agency of death and destruction of human and natural goods, and at the same time continue as constantly in our work (which must face and contain somehow this appalling and would-be spiritually destroying evidence of what human kind will do—for it has to do with the imagination of what is going on in Man) now, more than ever, to keep alive the immediacy of the ideal and of the eternal. Jess and I have decided that we will wear black armbands (as the Spanish do when some member of their immediate family has died) *always* and keep a period of mourning until certainly the last American soldier or "consultant" is gone from Viet-Nam—but may it not be for the rest of our lives? until "we" are no longer immediately active in bringing grief to members of the family of man. I started to wear a Peace button for the first time during the Poetry festival in Houston, and I found that it brought me to bear witness at surprising times—a waitress, a San Salvador millionaire, a Texas school teacher askt me what it meant. And I rejoiced in being calld to my responsibility. Just at times when I was most "forgetting myself" and living it up.

Even "Up Rising" is not this kind of witness; for ultimately it belongs to the reality of that poem and a vision of Man. And I do not answer for myself in my work but for Poetry. Tho things in "Passages" *do* haunt me, and I would fly as a banner the declaration I took up from the Gāthās, the Hymns of Zarathustra "To unite ourselves with you we have renounced all creatures of prey: False gods and men"—

We have these the more to wear in that our personal lives are filld with so many good things, both in works given us to do, and in the expansion of possibilities. Jess has just finisht three beautiful new canvasses and almost finisht the self-portrait at the age of three, Wordsworthian vision, that will be ours.

And we have found a house! at last! Barbara Joseph is advancing $22,000 in mortgage and our savings make up the rest of the amount. It will be—it *is* a world in itself. So that for the rest of our lives we will have this new dimension in which to create. There will be too guest rooms. When Mitch comes West next Spring and when you come, there will be a place in San Francisco where you will have a bit of your own apartment. It's a three story house, with—after two huge rooms are joind to form Jess's studio—still eleven rooms!

Still no word about the N.E.A.H. grant, and Carolyn Kizer told me it would be announced Dec. 15th!, and more importantly, that I would receive my first allotment then. Aie! Luckily this house business does not hinge on this money.

After our mound of Xmas cards have been sent, I'll write more of some of my current ideas on the matter of forms—

love
Robert

---

## 384

January 2, {7} 1967
{San Francisco}

dear Denny & Mitch,

This morning I seem at last to have found just the time for a cup of coffee and the east morning light I most love for writing you, the particular formula for your almost being sitting about the table in presence as I concentrate upon the reflecting surface I write on. We had been sitting earlier going over wiring plans for the house that Jess drew up. David Koven, one of the old anarchist group from the mid-forties in New York, who is an electrician, is coming later to go over the scheme and advise us on how to go about having the work done. And in another month and a half I must be about laying a kitchen floor in mosaic. (Day dreaming of growing mosaic designs). The bathroom is smaller; if I can do that satisfactorily, then I will have the confidence of the kitchen.

Blanche Cooney, from longer ago, from the beginning of things, writes that just in these most terrible and agonizing times, she and James seem to be in the fullness of their personal world.[1] And we too, keeping most aware of the enormity of the State now so much in the control of evil men and men stupefied by ambition and opportunity, [Olson's "They weren't here two weeks before they began cashing in on the continent"—an instruction from the Gloucester colony to us who, living in the language, would cash in on our talents]. We too have come into a time that is *ripe*, a pressing inner fruition. So, I have had Jess sew black bands of mourning on all our suit coats, that even in moments of joy we will bear witness (our eyes reminding our hearts) to our concern, our volition of mourning, for the lives of those conscripted to kill and to lay waste the good works of men and the country-side, and for the suffering and loss of those maimd and bereft. It is this war that has awakend me, but I am convinced that that black band was always to be worn. "To which our grief refers." Just as more and more we strive to awaken to the realities of sex, to redeem a language for sex and speak out what we can; so too we've to strive, given the fact enuf that much of grief is our hidden "unconscious" share, to acknowledge to ourselves and others the share we know.

«talent», looking the word up for the spelling I found [Gr. *talanton* a balance, thing weighd: a gift, then, weighed or a gift in the balance of what weighs]. That once meant, I find: ["Disposition, esp. to do someone harm"]. (Not my O.E.D. but my little Webster's Collegiate old-style.)

———————

Thinking now of Jim Harrison's "War Suite" and the war as the matter of the poem.[2] The way, for one thing, the outrage of the war is the war's own way of taking over our minds. It has released (relieved a bondage) something for me to have compassion overtake outrage, to move from "Up Rising" to the "Eye of God"; and last night, reading Boehme, I wrote in my notebook: "And that we pray that compassion will grow in our hearts where outrage now burns."

It cannot be death that is the evil of war, nor the suffering itself; but the will of men and the acquiescence of most men to dominate, to "win," to cash in. [The Viet Cong by "losing," collapsing, surrendering at this point—like France in the Second World War—could leave the U.S. and its henchmen floundering in a morass of a hostile surrenderd populace?]— I can imagine the war, the bloodiest aspects of the war, the deadly cold-blooded raids on textile-mill towns and the bombing of flood-dykes, not as a sadism (I am sure the sadist needs the immediate sexual key of the masochist's excitement) but as the ruthless determination to win one's own way. Whatever.

Jan. 7, The letter seemd to get out-of-hand, or off-the-top of the head. I can get tired of that extent of my thought and feeling about the lies and dreams of this war state that is set into place, not alive, but a fixt response. Maybe *that* is what I had in mind (not specifically about Harrison's poem, but the war and the poem) how to keep the immediate area of response *alive*. One thing about Harrison's poem is that from its initial proposition of a "we," meaning it seems we-Americans and larger we-mankind, after the initial four lines, he gets into the effort or essay to feel the war, feel instances of death enuf, to make it real but then, I sense too, to try to make instances he has no inner instance of immediate. Well, I flounderd around in that "Essay At War" and came to feel I could not really feel what the war ("over there") was.[3] Then it would flood back on me. And I saw I wanted to surrender: the poem. Give over trying to win thru the poem.

Thinking now of the poem as a suite in music. I see he does want a moving structure. The articulations markt—three for part I, three for part II and five, including a coda, for part III—stands for a formal feeling I don't find in the actuality of the work—no such structure of images, nor of lines and stanzas comes across in my reading. Nothing picks me up and moves me beyond my prejudices for the poem into its own insistence. (As, for instance, among younger poets Eshleman, Diane Wakoski, Spellman, Gail Dusenbury, Ted Berrigan to name those not immediate to my own style— have swept me up into their own "voice." Particularly I think here of Diane Wakoski who moved me off of my prejudice that she was a self-indulgent "poetess," doomd by cleverness and preciosity [I recall Bob's letter to Olson back in 1952 or so picturing me as precious]; but then I had to see it all differently with "The Ice Eagle." I am still not converted to the extent of searching out her book.

But keep with me on the poetry series, Denny; I do not throw the books away that I don't "get." And, as now with Harrison, when the need comes up I can return to the book for another reading. And I am looking forward, of course, to Gael's book—as always: and the 20 days 20 words poem is a major work for me, as was your "Olga" poem.

Jess is off to get painting materials, and I must get back to my Fulcrum typescript for the *Selected* Volume II—Our love and we are looking forward to your coming West, Mitch.

love,
Robert

## 385

Dear Robert & Jess,

I haven't even congratulated you on the grant and the *house*!!¹ Wonderful news. Nor did I thank you for Dante—it was *much* appreciated. I know I haven't lost, only mislaid, other copy, so will keep this one only until I find it, then, if you'd like it back (as it is rare) will return it to you. OK?

I was as near a sort of crack up as I have ever been at the beginning of Jan.—but we went to Puerto Rico for 10 days & I pulled myself together. It was beautiful. Since then have been busy with Angry Arts which went *very well*. It has given impetus to the participants to think up more such. Crowds were turned away from the "Act of Respect."² You must see the Bread & Puppet Theater when you come east. Will you both come or will you Jess be busy with the house?

Bob read "Uprising" at the Wed. reading. Jackson was esp. moving but almost all, inc. unknown young poets, were very good—hardly anyone in any of the events *used* the occasion for *themselves*, as has happened sometimes. People who before were not friendly to each other cooperated with real positive peaceful feelings.

Will soon have copy of *The Sorrow Dance* for you.

*When* do you come east? Mitch goes west about April 3d.

We have gotten to know the Wennings at last. How nice they are and how beautiful the book is![3]

Love—<br>Denny

P.S.

Two of my former students, Dick Lourie and Gordon Bishop, were among those arrested in St. Patrick's recently, the Spellman protest. I feel[4]

dear Denny,

I have thought often how, if the outrage and grief of this war preoccupy my mind and heart as it does, the full burden of it must come upon you and Mitch with Nik so immediately involved.[1] And I was fearful in January that you were having a bad time. Compounded with that other constant claim upon one's life the whole literary structure would make, and where you have a greater exposure in New York.

From a review somewhere of a{n} autobiography of Rumer Godden[2] I pickt up her observation that one must remember that the center for the writer is his writing and his own center of feeling and that in that writing, that in the beginning, if he not be ambitious, that center is given in the quiet of only those most a-tune having to do at all with his work, but the cost of "recognition," much less of "establishment," is that the world in recognizing lays claim to the very center as *its* own.

I shld have noted down the actual passage quoted, and I see now I shall have to read the book itself, for however the original went it formd or struck a seed already formd and has grown: that it is of vital need to keep and strengthen the living inner consciousness, the authenticity of the heart-tongue immediacy—against whatever claim or opportunity social recognition (attack or praise) makes.

Rundle Clark in that *Myth and Symbol in Ancient Egypt* of his quotes this passage of "Ptah, the very great [or ancient] one, who is the heart and tongue of the Divine Company":[3]

> In the form of Atum there came into being heart and there came into being tongue. But the supreme god is Ptah, who has endowed all the gods and their *Ka's* through that heart of (his) which appeared in the form of Horus and through that tongue (of his) which appeared in the form of Thoth, both of which were forms of Ptah.

The heart was, for the Egyptians, the very center of intelligence. And, indeed, it is, when we reflect that it is the flow of life-blood that feeds the

386

Feb. 15, 1967<br>
{San Francisco}

brain that we now call *mind*; and reflect also how little of the full living intelligence is represented by such a mentality.

So, I think also of how much war groups and organizations would lay claim, as if the vital force of one's testimony against the war did not arise from and belong to deep inner intuitions and will towards being, from the very authentic "hidden" heart. In public I would bear witness from my own heat (heart). And I find that the witness I would bear and speak for in the arm-band of mourning must need many times of revival for me to get it into a saying. Certainly, all the ready formulae of anti-war thought and feeling as they are so ready for social use—the lighter-mechanisms that serves for pacifist groups—not only to so serve but mis-use the tongue. (as if the *heart* were not the very organ of the living body but could be posited in the program in order to give life to a faction) . . . What we *ought* to feel (the approval or disapproval of imagined good people for our actions and attitudes) put in the place of the writer's testimony that must be the truth of what *is* felt in the poem.

But back to that armband. Miss Keough,[4] along with the beginnings of the excitement of what poetry could be and the release of feelings that could come in writing, left with me (a redeeming recognition, given how it might cure the mystery-mongering opportunity ever present in my heritage of a theosophical religion) a lasting sense of the moral mystery in Hawthorne. Even in the first thought of our armbands, along with the picture of arm-bands worn in Spain in the period of mourning [and it is my conception to wear these armbands for the rest of my life that the grief of this war not be forgotten, not be "over"] came the picture or was the picture of "The Minister's Black Veil." I remember Miss Keough askt us one question on a test—either what did the minister's black veil mean? or why did the minister wear the black veil? Today it seems to me that he wore it in order to find out what having to wear it meant . . . in order to *tell* what it meant.

I've written out sentences of what the black band is for. I had the idea too of having letter paper printed with the black band and the inscription: "in mourning for those conscripted to kill and to lay waste the country side and for those bereft and maimd in the War." And I have thought too that it should be "for the souls of those conscripted" for I have in mind the *violation* of souls which the state strives to achieve and so often can succeed in. But it seems to me too that whatever is not volunteerd from the heart, even goodness and demonstration against the war, when it is conscripted is grievous. I certainly do not mean ones not participating in any organized activities; but I mean one must participate authentically. [Again, here, it is Vanzetti's volitionism that strikes closest home: and the earlier communist-socialist "from each according to his abilities" [now, seen also as "from each according to his volition (free will)" "to each according to his needs."]

In the group of books that arrived yesterday from Norton [for which, again, my thanks—and not only for the Ronald Johnson, but I find the Peters book, where I have sampled it, very real and moving: tho in "Theme II" I object to his turning up with the old grave's worm for all of the actuality that worms or maggots do not attack bodies that are well buried but only meat exposed to the air] came Wheeler on *The Design of Poetry* where of course—but you too must likewise—I take umbrage at his restriction of the word *meter* to conventions of regularity.[5] "Verse" does not refer at all to the measure but to the projection by lines returning to a margin or margins [returning to a moving initiation of the poem]. Anyway, it is to be expected and so I find, in the chapter on "Meter" this guy writes: "As everyone knows, meter is not a design of meaning: it is the arrangement of words into regular patterns of sound, and is addressed primarily to the ear. It has no poetic qualities itself, nor is it necessary to poetry."

His block-headedness strikes off the more clearly one's immediate sense that any given convention or regularity of stress, rime, syllable is *telling*. Sometimes it can be inappropriate to and falsify the content of the poem. We rightly can find the heroic couplet *meaningful* in Pope and empty of meaning in much of empty-headed 18th century verse. As too in the variable meters of Williams or the free meters [when they are most meaningful, having to do with that same volition of reality that Vanzetti means in his voluntarism] we strive for, we strive for meaning in the very beat. Is the author of *The Design of Poetry* ignorant of or contemptuous of the Imagists' "A new cadence means a new idea"?

I'm not sure where I have gone in writing on to you here. Time now to return to 3735 for lunch, and my mind is moving on along this line once started. I'll let it rest in the matter, and maybe the thought will move on to clearer associations.

love
Robert

Dear Robert,

I wrote you a long letter the day that your most recent one arrived, but so much of it was devoted to my indignation at {Donald} Hutter's trying to get you to leave out the war poems that on reading through it I thought it would bore you and didn't send it.

This is an urgent note to ask if you would be willing to read at Vassar for $300 plus expenses and if so to let me know by return the inclusive dates of your trip east and all the dates that are *impossible* for you. Actually it doesnt have to be by return come to think of it because I will be away in Kansas

**387**

{February 1967
New York}

from Tues. till Sunday. Or yes, in fact the best thing wd be if you *could* send it right away (special delivery airmail) and address it to me at Vassar (as Levertov, not Goodman) (V College, Poughkeepsie, NY) so that it would get there by Tues. a.m. before I leave for Kansas. Or if that seems, even special delivery, impossible, send the information to Miss Elizabeth Dore, Main Building, Vassar College, one of my students. This wd be a student sponsored reading. It is possible the NY Council on the Arts might add to the sum—I will enquire. The $300 wd come from the Senior Class funds. It wd be held at Alumnae House in a not very large but quite beautiful room with a fireplace and a ceiling with painted beams. My class has not yet been studying your work but a lot of them have been reading you ahead of time and by then we will be reading you in class and they are very eager to have you visit. Of course that is just a tiny class and so is my other, workshop, class who are sophomores and a few juniors, so I don't know how much more general interest there would be but I know there would be an *appreciative* audience anyway. Albeit a little timid, a little ladylike, maybe. The big problem wd be working out a date which did not conflict with Senior Seminars, other events, and my absences, which will be Sat April 15, April 19–23 inclusive, then Wed 23 I myself have a reading at Vassar, and the 28 and 29th there is an Arts Weekend which already has 3 poets— young ones—coming to it, so that it wd be too much for them to take in even if time allowed, then I will be away to attend a friend's concert in Cambridge and visit from May 2–6th or 7th, whew! (But if nec. might return sooner)—By the time we have eliminated *your* engagements it doesn't seem to leave much time, does it. Classes end around mid-May and then there is a study period. I shall leave before exams to join Mitch in California. If you are free, I would think the Wed (10) before your Guggenheim Museum reading (11th) or the 12th, the day after it, wd be excellent if that turns out to be OK with the Vassar calendar.

Anyway—let me and Liz Dore know just as soon as you possibly can, unless of course you already have all the dates you can cope with and don't want this one, which god knows wd be understandable.

Love
Denny

## 388

Feb. 28, 1967
{San Francisco}

dear Denny,

It looks like I will get East again this coming Fall, for I have accepted an invitation to participate with two other poets (as yet not announced) and three historians of early Christianity in a conference on myth in poetry and in religion to be in Washington, D.C., October 13–15, 1967: "Each participant is to prepare a paper and to engage in discussion."[1] It's a great opportunity for me, both the occasion for an essay comparable to the Dante lecture and to advance my own ideas of mutho-poeic mind and its truth. [For years, I have been trying, always unsurely, to pronounce poeic poe-ay-ik and checking on spelling the word when I was writing to accept I faced the fact that there is no dictionary alternative to *pee-ik*, for English pronunciation. Greek wld be *poe-ay-ik*. I'm going to have to get settled what I am going to do with the *ei* in Ameinias. In Greek it is ay-ee, a sequence of two distinct vowels—but I can't find what to do if that combination is Anglicized. . . . ]

In every way this conference of the church society sounds exciting. They clearly [or at least the Mr. Stoneburner who is organizing it] have read and know my work and why it is they have me in mind.[2] [Including the sections of the H. D. book in *Origin* which he mentions in his letter.] And looking forward to that time, I shld be able to line up a few readings around the date. More to the point, I will love being in the East for the late Fall.

We are, after over a month of moving in fits and starts, completely in the new house—that we love more and more. And already have the dining room set up, like a stage set with a kitchen still minus a sink, crowded with cabinets that have not yet been assembled and a new refrigerator in position and a new stove that has yet to have its final installation flush to the wall, and on the other side a living room still—but I look and see that while I was downtown earlier this morning Jess has "installd" the living room. I had walkt right thru it, blind, and sat at this table. . . .

Orlando roams around the house all nite meauo-meeow—how do you spell cat meeows? And hides during the day from the possibility of more troops of friends loudly moving in furnitures or laborers—the roofers are still to come.

Next week I go to Portland and will be gone until the following Monday. And the middle of April when I start on my way East is just around the corner. The Vassar reading is most welcome, Denny. And I like the prospect of reading in a room with fireplace and a relaxed propriety. Poems must always be at least a little ill at ease in having to be projected from a public platform.

I will miss so much not being here when you visit our house this first time. By the late part of May, things will have begun to come into their own. And the third-floor guest room is so beautifully light, with views of hills and roofs and backyard . . . I would have wanted to attend your arrival.

—————

With my tour of Oregon colleges just five days off now, things begin to press. But I want too to send the enclosed enquiry about some Norton books, and also a copy of my "Epilogue" to date.

Love,
Robert

## AN OLD MAN SPEAKING BEFORE THE CURTAIN

I have grown from a wrathful bough of the tree.
When I say *Love* the word comes out of me
like a moan—life-sap. From broken wood.
Yet I would not have it come easily.
The word, the truth, and the light of it,
are one I have not won in myself.
Yes, how many times have I broken word
with you, generously, broken my word,
with you generously understanding me
I cannot understand. It's all but words
and men have said that too many times it seems.
I do not know in what I am myself, true,
untrue, to that speaking with these *things*,
sounds and compounds of sounds men define
and pronounce differently riming. How is one
to speak, making speech with such uttering?
Sometimes I think all that I call my life
is a placing, a place in the wood of that tree
the universe would face, force to come green,
make a way, and I am—what a man is—
is no more than a blind—but it's pent up—
forcing out of us a statement, a bud of a leaf
where creation that's a tree
must speak as it can to make
figures of man-kind, word-speakers,
in what it cannot see.[3]

This is the beginning of a curtain speech I see now as the closing poem for *Bending the Bow*. O yes, I forgot or wasn't even thinking of it in writing to you just now. But Scribner's has raised the question again of cutting poems from the contents on *Bending the Bow*; here's the passage from {Donald} Hutter's letter:

> On the whole, everyone is agreed that *Bending the Bow* is a very strong and rich collection, in respects better even than *Roots and Branches*. There was one reservation generally felt, however, and it concerns certain poems dealing with the war and political scene. This is not on the basis of the political sentiments expressed—which if anything are shared by the people here—but rather simply that these poems did not seem up to the rest of the work. They seemed rather didactic and shrill, without the complexity or, broadly speaking, the fine quality of the other poems. The ones in question are: "The Fire, Passages 13," "The Multiversity,

Passages 21,"* "Up Rising, Passages 25" "The Soldiers, Passages 26."
Could these be omitted from the collection?

This being the only question of content, I would think a contract
would then be in order. Burroughs Mitchell will be taking over on your
books. . . .

* This one has all along been a stumbling block, as, for many, has "Up
Rising." And both posed real problems of equilibration for me in the
projection of the form as reconsidered in each poem as a proposition of
that form. "The Multiversity," "Up Rising" and "Soldiers" were completely
rejected by Blaser and the Spicerean circles as examples of bad verse and
the public corruption of my talents.

But there were others, you among them, and Rago (who wrote personally
in the case of "The Fire" and "The Soldiers" in appreciation), Bob, Laughlin,
and I remember Hayden Carruth's letter in *The Nation* concerning "Up
Rising." And Bowering now in a review of 22–27. . . [4]

> {March 1967
> San Francisco}

There will be more in this section and then a finale. But it makes a
beautiful close for *Bending the Bow* (the bow and the harp announcing the
emblematic closing figures of tree, cup, river, star, bird . . . )

Dear Robert,

Maybe by this same mail you will hear from Liz Dore about the Vassar
date—May tenth, which I hope and pray is still OK with you. Quite a story
lies behind it all: my students were terribly eager to have you come, and as
the Eng Dep was apathetic they decided to arrange it themselves. I had said
you must get $300 (which is what I ask and get—I didn't have time to
enquire from you before they began their campaign) and they felt Senior
Class funds would cover it. But then the head of the Senior class, one of
those political science majors who take on that sort of job, objected because
*she* had never heard of you—so there was a meeting and it was decided to
put it to the vote. To succeed, this meant that 2/3ds of the class would have
to vote yes; and these girls from my class set up a voting table outside the
senior diningroom, made phone calls, ran around to all their friends, and
made sure they all voted. It was quite exciting and I thought you would be
touched to know about it.

Next day we can go down to NY on the train together (unless someone
offers us a ride) and unless you have other plans you can rest here before the
Guggenheim reading on that evening. I am not going to be living here while

## 389

{March 1967
New York}

Mitch is in Calif., but will stay up at Vassar, but a friend will stay here looking after the cat, and the apartment will be available for me to stay overnight when I want to—and if you would like to use it that can be arranged too I think.

I just got back from Detroit and as it was a trip disrupted by storms— plane landed in Cleveland and I had to bus to Detroit, and on the way back plane was circling 2 hours before landing and finally landed without radar, etc—I am very tired, so will not write more now, except to say we met {Basil} Bunting last night and he was charming.

Love—<br>Denny

Freud books (the ones they have) will arrive from Norton—let me know that they safely do so.[1]

## 390

April 12, 1967
{San Francisco}

dear Denny,

Altho I have yet to receive a statement of refusal from Scribner's, since the 10th has past and I gave them notice that I would consider it to mean their refusal, if I did not hear by that date, *Bending the Bow* will go to Oyez. It will delay by a year the second volume of my collected works (tho there is the possibility that another small press will be interested, I very much want the series of collected works to be with the same publisher).

It is a happy turn of events tho, for Oyez is solidly in back of me (a thing that was never true of Scribner's—I remember they wanted "Night Scenes" out from *Roots and Branches*; and they were not interested in "reprinting" as they put it earlier work when the question of bringing the works into current publication came up). For I will have the added advantage of being able to work out problems of typesetting notation that I would have had to give up on entirely with Scribner's.

We have not heard from Mitch. Ron Loewinsohn phoned yesterday and said they were expecting he would be West around the 6th, but I imagine getting settled with the work at Stanford will be demanding. And I heard you will be at U.C. while you are here. You could commute from here easily—it's a matter of an hour and often less to the campus. Well, we can discuss all this when we get together.

Oh yes, could you get me a round-trip ticket from New York to Pough-keepsie and a train schedule: to send ahead to me care of Bob in Buffalo? I am to arrive in New York airport (LaGuardia) at 1.27 PM on the 9th. Should I come up to Vassar that afternoon? If that is possible I would prefer having that ease of not arriving the day of the reading. And I will be anxious to see you too. It seems to me I might make helicopter connexions to

Grand Central Station area from the airport. I could, hopefully, make a reservation from Buffalo where I will be as early as May 1.

love,
Robert

Dear Robert

Here are time tables. Was waiting to get new ones.

Mohawk flies from Buffalo to Poughkeepsie.

The dinner for my class (prime movers in your invitation here) is at 6 Tues.—hope you can make it. Nancy Lindbloom, young poet who is teaching here, very nice, & her husband who ran as a peace candidate here (Poughkeepsie) this winter, will also be there but no other faculty except

yours truly—
Denny—with love.

Love to Bob & Bobbie & to John

**391**

Fri. {May} 5th {1967}
Vassar College
{Poughkeepsie, N.Y.}

Robert! Welcome!

The students who meet you will have explained that I have my last class this morning (last official one—I'll be giving an extra one next week) so could not meet you myself.

The class ends at 12.20, & *if you feel like it* you might come down & meet us there. *But if you're tired, stay at the Alum.House & I will come up there by 12.30* & we'll have lunch there.

Love from
Denny.

Class is held in one of the parlors in Main—your escorters are supposed to know that.

**392**

Tues. 9.30 am
{May 9. 1967}
Alumnae House
Poughkeepsie, New York

Dearest Robert,

Concerning delay of the enclosed, I can only refer you to R. C.'s "The Dishonest Mailman" etc.[1] I hope it was not too important.

I have some lovely things to send you, by students, as a result of your visit. (Will show them to Jess, and either mail them or save them there in S.F. as he advises.)

The poem I was stirring while (or rather, just before) you were here has been baked & is done. I will send it before long. (Not yet typed.) But it

**393**

May 20th {1967}
Vassar
{Poughkeepsie, N.Y.}

seems half-strange to me for it is sad and ever since I saw you I have been happy. You, and the blossoming here—every day more of it in trees and in people.

The sense I've been given of great mercies, blessings, profound beauties in the midst of the world, the war—Well that's a different poem.

Tomorrow to California. I'm going to stay at the Leites' tonight.[2]

Love—
Denise

---

**394**

June 14, 1967
{San Francisco}

Dear Denny,

I did not reflect when I urged you to accept the conference on myth proposition that for all of how appropriate it would be—both for your own potentialities in reflecting upon the part myth plays in your poetic process and in your life experience—and also for the happy conjunction of the two of us, where sympathies and differences shld give rise to a dialectic—for all of that opportunity (which I viewd so much from my own sense of opportunity), the proposition involved (involves) a task accepted and just— the thot has been dogging me—when your happiest act may well be to let the ground fallow for gathering out of your nature.

Well, tho it has occurrd to me that you might thoughtfully have come to decline that invitation, it still is helpful to let letters to you give me a time to do some preliminary exploration. Right off: the very domain of the *mythic*— the word centers around the act of telling, to tell a story, a reality spun out of the whole wool of its being told (and we, in English, would have the added connotation of a story's being *telling* "it was a telling story to tell")—this very domain of the what is told *happend* stands almost opposite to your *Here and Now*, and your *O Taste and See*. I mean here the imperatives in these titles as declarations in themselves. Yet, right off, in this last book—"Song for Ishtar" "The Elves" (given that the lore of folk is "mythic"), the "leviathan" and "ark" of "The Ache of Marriage," and I think the "you" of "Love Song": the *mythic* (the properties of a story, of a thing being told) is present in the immediate experience.

One of the preparations we might make is to list first what myths we think ourselves most involved with. Mine would be more obvious for me, because I am so consciously starting out from myth as objective source: Apollo and Hyakinthos, Orpheus, Sphynx and Medusa, or from the *Zohar* Adam, the Tree, the Fall, the Garden, and from the New Testament the Annunciation, the Birth of the Child, the Kingdom of the Child (Christ's command that we be like children), the miracle of the loaves and fishes, the water into wine, the Passion of the Crucifixion . . . or from the Epic of the Djerma the Lute of Gassire, these all were tales that were telling, and as here and now, as immediate to my consciousness (revelations of my life experience, my own "story") as light, leaves, answering eyes, whatever factors of the actual. "Telling" and also "stirring"—here then there is the sense of arousing the content of unconscious alliances in the context of the objects of consciousness. But "stirring" can mean too the stirring up of consciousness which can be sluggish and inert and spring into life when toucht. A key may unlock a notion of what we are aware of but neglect in feeling.

I am trying now to remember what myths outside of the Graeco-Roman, the Judaeo-Christian and the African enter in. Certainly I work in relation to and towards world-myth (as in writing to LeRoi Jones I urged him to see Damballah as a World god) and the imagination of Man. Yet I do not design to draw upon all the communities of myth—it is by belonging not by my effort to be eclectic, that the Lute of Gassire enterd in. In fact, Gassire enterd in from the ground of poetry itself (the

4 times was the city rebuilded, Hooo Fasa
Gassir, Hooo Fasa    dell' Italia tradita
now in the mind indestructible, Gassir Hooo Fasa

of the opening Pisan Canto): and back of that, Pound's references to Frobenius had sent me to read Fox-Frobenius, *African Genesis*—[1]

O yes, Set, Osiris, Isis and Horus have "made up my mind." But I have shied from the Vedas and the Upanishads. (Just venturing out upon the latter.)

It makes this step of preparations more confusing for me I take it than it will be for you. My thot is so often turnd to myth lore that a crowd wants to break thru into this foreground of the creative consciousness. Archetypes might organize the dramatis personae into fewer entities: but I very much apprehend Apollo as Apollo, Zeus as Zeus, the Father as the Father. Mary Mother of God is not for me the same as Aphrodite or the Great Mother (tho in "The Venice Poem" they are confounded, as I recall; but in a magical operation the transformation (different from revelation) comes thru a confounding of elements—it is a poem of adultery, mixings-up).

---

I have in mind now to work from the title "The Mytho-poeic Ground" for my essay, and if I can keep to it, to try to make clear what I see involved in the conjunction of *mythos* "the telling of the real, the unreal and (it's Redon's great word) the irreal" and *poieo* "to create": both to make a thing and to make happen = to bring into existence. And third what I mean by "ground."[2]

Well, time is overdue to go on to pressing duties. I have 115 drawings to do for *Epilogos* which John Martin is issuing in a limited edition, and have done 32 to date: what I am doing proves to take 8 hours for that many, drawing from images (in Cook's *Zeus* and in another book Glueck's *Deities and Dolphins*) of a leafy daimon Cook identifies with Dianus or Virbius, consort of the Moon—a very image of the old man born of the wrathful bough of the Tree.[3] I find looking over my accumulation of faces so far, and thinking of them as projections of my own face in the full perplexity of doing all those drawings (an ordeal I volunteerd for!!): perplexity, vexation, glowering menace, grief, querulous acquiescence, quarrelous acquittance ( I found that in the dictionary following acquiescence) and guar—garrulous reflexion. The difficulties of spelling increasing as my own difficulties of drawing do. Perhaps at the last he will wear faces of exhaustion and ineptitude. . . .

love
Robert

---

**395**

July 3, 1967
Temple, Maine 04984

Dear Robert

I am editing the 1968 War Resisters' League Engagement Calendar.[1] This calendar, with which you are perhaps familiar, is purchased each year by a wide range of people and is an important fund-raiser for the WRL.

Will you please help me by sending a poem of yours for possible inclusion?

I shall make my final selection with a view to the harmonious and meaningful effect of the whole (52 poems, one for each week in the year). I hope to achieve a balance between poems on war and on peace, poems of protest and poems of hope. Therefore I trust that if, even though I am soliciting a poem from you, I do not include it, you will not be offended.

To ensure publication in time for pre-Christmas sales, I must get the entire manuscript to the printer early in August, so this is a rush job: please mail me your poem (or poems) before July 15th—the sooner the better.

Poems can be up to 40 lines long, but it may be hard to accommodate typographically any poems with extremely long lines.

There will be no payment—just the pleasure of contributing to an excellent cause. There will be an introduction by a distinguished writer and the calendar will be dedicated to the late A. J. Muste, who loved poetry throughout his long, active life.

I am hoping to use mainly unpublished poems, but if what you consider your most suitable poem has already appeared in a magazine or book, or will have done so before the year is out, please specify name and date of issue (if a magazine) and publisher (if a book) so that we can obtain permissions and transference of copyright.

Please send me with your poem(s) a *short* biographical/bibliographical note (date of birth may be all we'll use).

I shall notify you of inclusion or non-inclusion by an early date in August.

Thanks for your cooperation.

Sincerely,
Denise
Denise Levertov

Robert—I know your feeling about anthologies but maybe you'll feel differently about this. Hope that, if you do, you have something short enough? Will write soon—much love to you and Jess—Denny

Dearest Robert & Jess,

We've only really now settled down here. After Nik's graduation we were here for a couple of weeks, then went down to N.Y. to see him off for his summer in England (or wherever he gets to—England to start with)—then on some visits to Poughkeepsie (Leites' gone for summer, but we stayed in their house & got my things) Norfolk, Conn., East Dorset, Vt., where we used to stay years ago, then to visit Galway {Kinnell} & Inez at Sheffield & see their baby, Maud, with a side trip to Adrienne & her family who have bought a farm not far from them (but with whom I don't feel much rapport these days)—& now finally back here for what shd be a good uninterrupted stay.

Don't please feel troubled, Robert, by my WRL calendar form-letter. I know how you feel about anthologies & respect it. This, for me, is a job I'm glad to do for the sake of the WRL & in memory of A. J. {Muste}—I'm not accepting any fee. I'd certainly love to have a poem or even maybe just a fragment, like a quotation, if feasible, but I don't want to put you on the spot and will not feel hurt, reproachful or anything of the kind if you are unable to send.

I've made some notes for the mythology thing & as soon as I have a bit more will transcribe them or make a resumé for you, with references to your letter.

Jess, the children's books I was telling about, *The Box of Delights* and *The Griffin*,[1] I mailed to you & Robert from N.Y.—no, from here—please let me know if they arrived safely—they're a loan, because they're as much Nik's as mine, but you can keep them till we come to S.F. next!

Tom P{arkinson} is working on that, & Jo Miles too I guess—so the plan may materialize—we hope so.

Next day

Nik has not written yet, it is as if he had vanished into thin air. But I remember doing the same thing to my parents a number of times, without *meaning* to make them worried—just that in a completely new place time passes so fast.

We have a lot of roses here this year—old fashioned kinds with lots of

---

**396**

July 11th 1967 (12th?)
Temple, Maine

thorns, & that don't much like to be picked (I'd sooner see them growing, anyway). Seeding grasses make parts of the field coppery-mauve this time of year—it looks like a Jess painting.

Love
D.

## 397

dear Denny,

I'm sending the enclosed "God Spell" which I hope will do. Both the editor and the intent of the anthology is, after all, something I am much in tune with. It has the advantage that I hold the copyright on it (amend: it is previously unpublisht, and *Bending the Bow* probably won't be out until Spring '68; so it will come under your calendar's copyright. *If there is to be a picture with it, will you try to have it be a drawing by Jess or by me?*

There! I meant to be writing to you every morning on myth; and months have gone by. Not so *mythy*, either. I have completed 100 drawings for the regular limited edition of *Epilogos*. Since I get 21 out of this lot, and John Martin is picking them from some 30 I designated as ones I myself most liked, you will be getting one of these as soon as they are done. I got some beautiful drawings from a photo of Ezra Pound in the series.

And, at last! We got typed and proof-read the final typescript for *Bending the Bow*. And Oyez and Jay Laughlin have been working out things evidently. So, that task is lacking now only a Preface and a publications list (not a bibliography). Enquiry has come from England indicating that "Jonathan Cape are considering publishing [*Roots and Branches*] and they have said that they would like to publish, providing they may have the option of seeing *The War*, which I believe you are currently working on."

love
Robert

This hastily writ, Denny, before taking off for Berkeley. But in order to be sure to get the answers off.

## 398

dear Denny,

I am sending on John Martin's letter: he is so in awe of you he dreaded he would be unworthy in writing and wanted me to read the letter to see if it was all right. I hope you may have something for this series—both because I'm there too, and because John works towards a beautiful job and he is a true *amateur*: i.e. one who has the care that comes from love of what he works in or studies. For Martin it is both the enthusiasm of the bibliophile—

and the devotion of a reader who has, as he told me, been "saved" by discovering himself in certain writers work.

———————

Yes, *The Griffin* and *The Box of Delights* (which is indeed a box of delites, a real adventure book for a wintery San Francisco–style July sit up in bed late reading session—and carry along on street-cars riding *inside the story*) did arrive. And we will hold in our care until we see you again. I can, remember, bring them East when I come in October. In any event, both Jess and I enjoyd them immensely.

It is all but settled now that New Directions will work with Oyez to publish *Bending the Bow* under both labels. Jay Laughlin in a four page letter to Hawley clearly is going all out for the book, and offers to undertake so much of the burden that it is a kind of gift to Oyez. With the great advantage still, if it is set by Graham {Mackintosh}, that I can preside over the setting itself in the shop. This week-end I have then to get the Preface done which I want for it, and terminal notes both to acknowledge and to send the reader off to certain sources.

And I have been working on the transcript of an interview with Larry Dembo at Wisconsin to shape up new notes on "The New Poetics."[1] And have got a page or two in notebooks towards the myth. All of which work as I type it up I will send on to you. *Tri-Quarterly* is printing both Chapters 3 and 4 in their winter issue this year. And I've got off an installment of Chapter 6 to Clayton Eshleman for his new journal *Caterpillar.*[2] No pomes. I'm still leery of the opening section sitting there in my *Notebook* that seemd related to what was going on (a kind of dramatic monolog) in *Epilogos*. And a passage or two out of John Adams on *Myth* that seemd to be—may yet be—a "Passages 31" beginning.

Well, I guess I had better get off to the typewriter and get typed up what I have in the notebook—then it can go along herewith and I can see the shape of things I am working with.

love
Robert

Oh yes . . . can you next time you write send on Galway's address? He askt for a copy of "Processionals II" which now is a long over-due promise. And he wanted to see the text for *Bending the Bow* and I do have an extra copy I could send now.

And . . . in that issue of the magazine David Posner edited for poetry— the Greek word ἄτρεμής was left out of the line[3]

having an unwobbling pivot, an unmoved heart—ἄτρεμής
is the Greek word: an untrembling center.

love
Robert

399

July 16, 1967
{San Francisco}

dear Denny,

That added note I wrote to you, going on about the difference I felt between the craftsmanship of Williams, Pound, Olson and Zukofsky; and Bob, you and me, is at best a bridge towards thought I have come to puzzling over why and how I felt such a difference.

Certainly, first, I did not mean a comparison of worths: here each poet's work has limitations as well as powers as terms of its unique being. And it's that unique being, the life in poems of the poet, that I respond to. The *kindred* life or the *attractive* life (thinking of how very different from me fascinating poets can be).

Craftsmanship is paramount, I think, when the poet, like Williams, thinks of himself and his responsibility as a writer first of all as a word-worker. Think of Williams's insistence that the paint is the thing in painting and, after Flaubert, Cézanne, Mallarmé, Stein: "It is the making of that step, to come over into the tactile qualities, the words themselves beyond the mere thought expressed that distinguishes the modern."

Olson is certainly a borderline; but Williams, Pound and Zukofsky are artists, keeping words at play. The rest of us are that close, that we work from the feel of words and line: but we tend to reverse the very directive of the change from feeling "the taking of that step over from feeling to the imaginative object" that Williams' generation sought. (As, for instance, in our own household I can see that my response to paintings, sculptures, books, rugs, mementoes—is associational, not objective.) Even Williams, Stein, Brancusi or Duchamps are charged for me with the *romance* of the modern. And, against their avowals of intent (here I would provide that Brancusi does not aim at the stone but conceives of it charged with romance), I see them as conveying soul and spirit. . . .

It does seem clear, Denny, that you are more an expressive poet than a formalist: the poem so often bears the burden of conveying the feel of something or the emotion aroused by something or a thought—giving rise to the poem instead of the poem giving rise to its own objects. Often as I raise the specter of this latter kind of poem I am also raising a model, even it can seem an imperative. But rightly I would recognize that "poetry" in its particular meaning of *making* is an aspect of a much greater and creative thing, that includes all the varieties of man's conventions, expressions of feeling and thought, presentations of vision, formulae (as H. D. sought in her later work) of emotion or power, epic narrative . . . we've only to start to be quite aware that the poetry of process is a very special phase of the ever various propositions man makes of poetry. Just as the Objectivism of the modern movement was very special.

And in Williams and Brancusi the imagination is deeper and larger than any limitation of "modern" can circumscribe. There are poems where we can see Williams has indeed succeeded in "taking of that step over from feeling to the imaginative object" and is a precursor here of Rosenquist, Lichtenstein, or Rauschenberg:[1] but mostly there is no such step over from. Expression of feeling moves him towards the poem, the poem gives rise to new feeling; and Williams will have in this very expression all the paramount concern with the feel of the words that his objective formalism, the poem as a machine of words demands.

"The Modern" is a style, and tho we derive from it, we aint "modern."

It's time and more than that that I shld. get back to the Dembo interview and work a while. It seems likely that this stage of expansion from the original will finally be mid-way to an effort to clarify and direct the original statements without expansion and new exploration. Right now I have very much in mind Olson's "it's not *either . . . or,* but *not only but also . . . and also*"

While I'm going, I seem to be filling notebooks in this period. And perhaps the store of thought on myth and poetry will be loosening up along the way.

love,
Robert

Dear Robert,

I'm so glad you & Jess enjoyed the books. I must try & find *The Midnight Folk* for you—it precedes *The Box of Delights*—i.e., Kay & Maria are younger.[1] I cared for it less, perhaps because I came to know it later—but it's good too. Of course *The Griffin* is not of the same caliber—but as a child, as I was telling Jess, it had *mana* for me—every element of romance in it was intensified—Lal was not just a little girl in short socks but a romantically delicate princess whose near loss in the bog was a serious, dramatic event close to tragedy; fat Fulke's sensitive serious nature in a somewhat comic exterior had a pathos of similar intensity; Ralph was a dazzlingly attractive hero, & as for the heraldic beasts and the secret panel the heraldic stained-glass light shines on at only a certain hour, that really sent me. I invested even the less magic-y scenes with the atmosphere later rediscovered in *The Grand Meaulnes* (which I suppose you know?).[2]

Many thanks for the wonderful letters of the last few days. Reading them over with Mitch we were especially grateful for the passage where you say, (of Williams) "Expression of feeling moves him towards the poem, the poem gives rise to new feeling"; etc. It further defines something that boy Bernard Kramer whose letters I read you (& poems I showed you) said, if you remember: "almost inspired as much by the form I saw take shape as by the feelings that engendered it I was able to write the last few lines."

**400**

July 20th {19}67
Temple {Me.}

(By the way, did I leave Bernard's poems at your house? I can't find that "Shabbus" one. But don't *look* for them!—just if you happen to turn them up.)

This understanding of how, once one starts to work with the material words—{(}tho' I long ago with painting & Mitch recently with pottery have experienced the same thing in other mediums too) the original impulse is augmented—is something we have both known in practice but sometimes (in an excessive, or at least over-simplified, insistence at times on something like "sincerity") forgotten or overlooked—as if "sincerity" was not as much involved in the succeeding waves of impulse as in the first!

I'm reminded here of 2 things—one the beautiful description of how one forgets & remembers such things, by Francis Ponge, which I'll enclose, & the other the quotation from Rabbi Elimelech of Lijensk which I included in a poem called "Notes of a Scale" in *With Eyes*—"overwhelmed with the wonder which rises out of his doing."[3]

It's of course when I am in a state of forgetting this that my poetry is weakest, and that gap between feeling & language, feeling & craft, occurs, & leads me into sentimentalities or stridencies. When instead of riding the wave of feeling from a non-verbal point of origin through first verbalization on to succeeding waves of verbally-, formally-inspired revelations, I insist on sticking with the *1st* wave even after it has subsided, as it were. . . . Something like that. A non-acceptance of the unpredictable. And in my best work, the exact opposite happens, (has been let to happen).

By the way, it's this experience of the transformation of the first feeling into the second (& succeeding) feeling(s), as dynamic impulses, by the coming into being of form in process, that non-artist readers (& critics!) almost never understand even if they are good, appreciative (receptive) readers. (And maybe ((unless they do set up as critics & teachers)) they don't have to—maybe it's unnecessary or even harmful to try to convey a sense of it to them, any more than a sword-smith had to teach a knight just how he had wrought a blade.)

My "myth" notes are becoming a rather monstrous exercise in introspection & egotism—I'm half-embarrassed by them, yet so much enjoying the task that I don't care. I've started from 2 premises:

(1) That the mere mention of mythological persons in a poem doesn't necessarily give it a mythological character—i.e., a character of being energized by myth. (This is put better in that "Admonition" for *things* #1, which you have somewhere I expect—if you don't, I'll send, but I remember you liked it at the time so you probably do have it.) (2) That—whether or not there are overt & conscious mythological allusions in it, the whole opus of any serious writer will be found to reveal a dominant theme which can be defined as myth. (Tho' perhaps all (or most) in the end are found to be

forms of the one longing, for salvation, regeneration, rebirth?) (No, that is an excessive statement.)

(I fancy I see the Promethean in Williams seeking to animate man ("unwilling or unable") with the fire of language ("the language is missing them / —they die also / incommunicado") and in Pound—don't laugh, it's not intended as a comprehensive definition, just something that popped into my head just this minute—something of Cadmus, the seeker for Europa, the founder of a city (as in E. P. can be found stones everywhere of the Civitas Dei) and inventor of an alphabet (as E. P. in the *ABC* etc gives a critical apparatus).[4] (I don't want to pursue this fancy down to analogies for the sowing of dragon's teeth. I just looked him up in *Tooke's Pantheon* (33d edition, London, 1810) (1st ed. was 1713) & it says the 5 survivors "peopled the country afterward" and (which I'd forgotten) that Cadmus & his wife were themselves eventually turned into serpents ((of wisdom?)).)

Anyway—to get back—I proceeded to look through my own poems chronologically (from the very beginning) searching firstly for this constant, or ever-recurring, dominant: which emerged as the sense of life as pilgrimage, quite plainly from an early age & with much more consistency than I'd ever been aware of. (Not a rare theme at all, & tying in with any number of myths of course in all cultures and including the Bildungs-Roman.) I've found myself following this trail through poem after poem, with excursions into childhood reading influencing this predisposition or partiality. Alongside of this main search have been the poems I've come across along the way in which other, but usually also recurrent, mythic themes occur, which I've been trying to sort out according to the principle of my other premise. Some, while not a matter of mere dragged-in unfelt allusion (i.e. not merely "descriptive" in the sense defined by Creeley) seem to me metaphor, not myth, & I'm trying to clarify what I mean by this distinction (which I think has to do with *static* & *active*).

Writing along chronologically is leading me into something much too long, and besides, not well-organized for an audience without a hell of a lot of interest in me (i.e., whose interest is in myth & poetry in general, & not in my poems in particular), and to make it suitable for its occasion I shall have to cut out the irrelevant or at least redundant examples & move according to theme not chronology.

One other main strand not related (as far as I can see) to *pilgrimage* is that of the innocent man, the Abel of "Abel's Bride," also present in "Scenes from the Life of the Peppertrees" (III), "Lonely Man," "Sleeping Figure," & I think elsewhere; but I haven't tried to think about that yet.

It somewhat frightens me to become so self-conscious. But maybe it's what I need. I've not been writing much, & as you noticed all my recent poems seem to be questions—questioning the ground I stand on. Maybe this will help me move on to something new. And there's at any rate the pleasure of finding I have lots to say, when I'd feared not to have *anything* to say.

Many many thanks for sending the poem for the WRL. (It is just right.) I feel its being a calendar, & no poem facing another poem, each facing only its week in the year, will keep it from seeming to you just another anthologistic grab-bag—(though what the WRL wants is not an expression of my "taste" but something fairly varied so that there'll be something of interest to the different kinds of people who buy it each year, & I'm acting in a sense as their ((voluntary)) "servant.") I'm going include a number of poems only rather obliquely or subtly "relevant"—but am going to have to leave out some beautiful ones of no relevance at all—which kills me, but I have to remember I'm not making a collection for my own pleasure. This makes the task harder than I'd bargained for; but on the whole I'm enjoying it—each day's mail has brought a fresh crop and though my room is now uncomfortably full of MSS it *is* exciting to open the envelopes, and fortunately I have a bigger room here than in N.Y. where it wd be chaos by now.

We often see deer around the place but for the 6–7 years we've been coming here now I've always hoped to look up from the kitchen sink & see one in the part of the hill-field one looks out on from it—and today I did. A beautiful young (yearling) deer, amber-gold, browsing & looking up & flicking his white tail & browsing again. We walked up towards him but of course he heard us & bounded away—but Mitch caught another glimpse of him in among the woods.

Also saw a beautiful toad today with snake-like markings. And just now a nice fat woodchuck person who's taken up residence in the bank only a few yards below my window.

I'm reading *Henry Esmond* for the 1st time since my mother read it aloud when I was 10 or 11. The strange relationship of the hero with the 2 women is quite dreamlike. Since they are almost mother & sister to him it has strong undertones of incest & from a Freudian point of view wd reveal odd things about Thackeray, obviously; & also in Jungian terms they are each in different ways classic "anima-projections." But the book's complex enough not to be reducible to boring diagrams; even though Thackeray lacks *visionary power*.

Mitch has just finished *Ishi in 2 Worlds*[5] which I expect you know (if you don't, please read it—it will interest you v. much), & I shall begin it when I've finished *Henry Esmond*.

With love from<br>Denny

P.S.

(1) Nik seems to be having a marvellous time in England & wishes he could stay there. (If it weren't for the draft* I suppose he could, & go to an

English art school or college instead of R.I.S.D.[6] But I think he will enjoy R.I.S.D., as long as he doesn't undercut himself by pining for England.) Anyway, it's a great experience for him to have this summer—and my dear faithful Hampstead friends whom I haven't seen for so many years seem to have taken him to their hearts. Gael has also invited him.

*He'll have student deferment, presumably, under the unfair, but to us advantageous (aagh!) draft laws. (Is registering as a C.O.)

(2) Helen Adam sent me a wonderfully typical, yet fitting, poem for the W.R.L.

dear Denny,

**401**

July 24, 1967
[San Francisco}

I've got to go shopping now—when both Jess and I are working, meals become a kind of crisis. And today I face right now that nobody has "gone out" for food. Aie! However, I got thru the enclosed pages of that interview. I took Dembo very much on his word for me to "feel free to add, delete, introduce, or modify anything you want," keeping only the areas of the original, enlarging everywhere

Your letter arrived today and I hope now to postpone work on this interview[1] and have some work on the myth to send in a few days. *Bending the Bow* is going ahead rapidly, it seems towards the contract stage. Now Oyez has suggested (in a letter I received a carbon of this morning) that New Directions go ahead as sole publisher, with Hawley helping in the production here gratis.

I've still to write the Preface I want for that book. . . .

But—as I started out—now I DO HAVE TO rush out and get something for us to devour at dinner time

Love,
Robert

This is only question and answer #1; and while I don't think even most answers will be so transformed, the interview is proving to be a gold-mine for me to get across my present views. When above, by the way, I say Olson, Zukofsky and Pound for that *feel* of words I do not exempt myself from my consideration—my sense of how craftsmanly their work is derives mainly from my own feel of my work in comparison. Often I envy you and Bob certain things in your own craftsmanship, you have each precisions (well, too, each precision is a unique event in a particular work, which you meet with artistry) but the three of us seem to me definitely apprentices. Bob inhabits his capabilities and does not go afield where his feel of words would be tested. The message can take over from the work at times for you. And not only have I had even mildly to make do (like shaping *Faust Foutu*) in absence of a sure craft, but to my own sense the feel of the poem is intoxicated often in "lighting effects". . . .

Perhaps happily, we will not and mean not to be masters.

---

## 402

August 16, 1967

{San Francisco}

dear Denny,

I have been launching out into Nietzsche's *Birth of Tragedy* for the first time; and from gleanings where he strikes close to the heart of the creative process, setting up an opposition and conjunction of picture and music, my own thought quickens around what he is most blind to Eros which he wants to see as a weakness when the Xtian Love appears: as he frames his attack, my consciousness of the power coming to be of redemption not *of* our Nature but within our Nature. Right now anyway I find Nietzsche marvellous: "For now in every exuberant joy there is heard an undertone of terror, or else a wistful lament over an irrecoverable loss. . . . " It's my hope too that the confrontation with Nietzsche may strike the key note I need for starting the myth paper which still pends. Pends to the painful point. Struck dumb.

This morning from Robert Bly's crunk-headed *Sixties* in Minnesota came the new issue with his essay on your work.[1] Where he can follow you (ie. what he would define as "the best poems") he is eloquent in his own terms:

> Despite the criticisms I have made, Denise Levertov is an absolutely genuine artist, in whose best poems words come alive by mysterious, almost occult, means. She does not think her way through the darkness of a difficult subject, she feels her way through the tunnel with her hair and the tips of her fingers that seem to give off light. When she comes back up into the day-light with the water she has found, it burns on the plate like pure alcohol, leaping up into the cold places.

And writing of "Life at War":

> All her strength, her depth of feeling, sound cut out like a granite, her feminine compassion, the rhythm able to carry grief, the images that rise from far down in the mind, all come forward. The clear resonant words are set one next to the other like stones in a stream. In the war poems she is not a poetess among her subjects, winning easy victories over words; she is rather a human being facing her enemy, the Pentagon, who is stronger than she is. The result of this confrontation is not propaganda, but private poems whose movement is at times magnificent. The public work overturns our clichés about engaged work, being more private than her personalist poems. . . .

But in his alternate vein, the dominant Crunkish humor, he belabors your poems as having "no real *ideas* in them, as there are ideas in Rilke's work or

Marx's. As a substitute for ideas, there are liberal *attitudes*, mostly taken
from Williams Carlos Williams": which only continues to exhibit his own
utter incomprehension of the world itself as *idea*. Here his attack is
ultimately on Williams (and comes in the department of Louis Simpson's
concluding paragraph in his article in *The Nation* on the anthologies)—
"Williams was essentially a poet of pleasures—" sharply sets off Bly's
crippled, critically crippled, sight of the poetry.[2] So "the weakest poems are
those in which she becomes objective. . . . " Back of that Bly's contempt for
all ideas of the universe as revelation (I take it the whole school of the deep
image views revelation as being from the subconscious alone; and atheistic
and mechanistic, refuses any hint that spiritual reality is shown forth all
about us). Praising "Sharks" he writes: "She goes downward in the mind, as
Williams was rarely interested in doing." . . . ! and of the poem "With Eyes
At the Back of Our Heads"'s last six lines: "The sound of these lines cannot
be overpraised." But then: "They out do any six lines of Williams in their
decisiveness, and far out do anything of Marianne Moore's."

Rejecting the vision of your poetry (he scoffs at "From the Roof,"
rejecting as contemptible sentimentality the question "who can say / the
crippled broom-vendor yesterday, who passed / just as we needed a new
broom, was not / one of the Hidden ones?" back of which is a rejection and
contempt for the broom vendor, *any* broom-vendor. At points like this, as
Bly launches out on a lecture on what *real* saints are: "They didn't see the
muse in every butterfly. They took harsh steps, believed bitter things . . . ,"
thinking of Saint Francis as well as of George MacDonald, just beyond your
own vision, Denny, I choke with outrage at the presumption from ignorance
and stupidity in Bly's. Actually he has utter contempt for the "seraphic" and
"demonic"—which he attacks as "sentimental" in your work, and clearly
would, if he dared, find sentimental in any other source. "A Victorian mist"
later he calls the whole area of the poetry (no wonder he can find no
ideas . . . ). And launches an all out attack on the appearance of Apollo,
Ishtar, and the Muse "from dustjackets of mythological text books":

> It is probably Robert Duncan's influence that has brought in these pagan
> gods, but Robert Duncan has jabbing intuitions about what may have
> been going on with these gods and their ceremonies which Miss Levertov
> does not have. Because she has no ideas of her own about the gods, their
> names lie in her poems like stones, utterly inert.

I think of great living movements when poems of yours opend my eyes
and heart to fresh awareness of "the gods." First of all is their presence, the

> So look: that almost painful
> movement restores the pull, incites
>         the head with the heart: . . .

of "The Hands," or the "Turning"'s

> pleasure
> sound and sequence
> lift
> of golden cold sea

(This *sea*, the immediate presentation in its apprehension of one of the divine powers). What an idle exercise "these pagan gods" are, if they are but the occasion of "jabbing intuitions"—here Bly sees me as a Crunk *seeing thru the gods and showing them and their carryings-on up. . . .*

But now my outrage is dissolved in returning to the poems (the poems, and "life" returning to me in them), and how your experience has in-formed mine. "Not history, but our own histories, / a brutal dream drenched with our lives." The vision of the tree of life, the tree of lives, in "A Ring of Changes" stirs me. "Jabbing intuitions" comes to mean in which context something new and beautiful, for the poem opens up the vine's jabbing intuitions, not ours, but

"Buds are knots in our flesh, nodules of pain"

It's this immediacy of a power (a power in every world, a power in the poem having such resonance) that I see we must insist on. Where the actual presence of Apollo, Ishtar, the Muse is denied, what can it meant that we tell and must return to tell their *myth* or true story? If the primordial is a matter of ancient history, we are antiquarians. But the primordial pattern is *Here and Now* as you titled your first book after the poems of girlhood.

I must begin the Myth essay with the reality of the spiritual world and its powers (the poet's spirit prays to—your "Hymn to Eros" is one of the poems Bly would dismiss out of hand), with poems as prayers and evocations, awakenings of being in us; yearnings for awakenings of being; and poems as testimony of the spiritual world—Well, to get about the work that's pending! I've to dare to write much of what most troubles us in restoring us, human spirits we too of the spiritual world reverberate, and *myths* are melodic stories that come to us (here that Overture to *le Crue et le cuit* comes to mind) in notes that are trembling in the full risk of solemnity and play. . . .

Strange that the attack of a critic incapable in his scorn of all that smacks of seraph or daemon throws the mind in *reaction* to come afresh upon the point of its life-source. Bly—an agency of the divine, messenger out of whose noise my own daemon breaks whatever shell of "Bly"-mind I too have.

"Cracking husk . . ."

And then to tell something of the interchange in me thru your poetry, your dreams speaking to me—

love,
Robert

Lunch. And read the "Ring of Changes" to Jess aloud, filld with it. And, exploring, how *Terror* reappears in "A Ring." At the back of "With Eyes . . . " I had tucked in the section from *The Chicago Review* was it? That included the "Notebook Pages" on inscape and melody.[3] The myth of being lies hidden in it, too: both inscape and melody; and comes to us. Describing the incubation of thought and feeling previous to the Word, you seem to speak exactly for the painful pending I feel before I can write the Myth paper: "The awareness of them remains vague—perhaps oppressive—perhaps *very* oppressive—yet the poet does not give way to "irritable searchings" but waits in passionate passivity. . . . " For the words to arrive. Let me in closing type out one slim passage that did arrive for me in the course of searchings:

> April 14. (Beginning to read Nietzsche's *Birth of Tragedy*) The theosophist asks "What does the union of god and goat, expressed in the figure of the satyr, really mean?"; the psychologist asks "What was it that prompted the Greeks to embody the Dionysiac reveler—primary man—in a shape like that?" But the mytho-poeic maker gives us what he looks like, his story and what he says as the satyr comes to him. Yes, it is true, he may really be Time, Time may really be a satyr: this is the informing of one person by another. Time in myth, it occurs to me, may climb his mountain and enter his own mouth that in turn names twelve, bringing them forth, among whom is the Destroyer of Time. But the meanings of myth are not antecedent to myth; they come into being thru myth. Man does not explain Nature by myth but discovers Her in his stories of Her.

---

Also I enclose Bernard Kramer's poems—were these four the lot?

Robert

Dearest Robert

I'm so glad Robert Bly wrote as he did, for it brought me your letter which made me feel like a million dollars.

I had just finished my draft of the talk for the myth symposium when it came, & that turns out to be "about" lots of the things he complains of— didn't see his article till a couple of days ago though. He is so sophomoric & *ignorant*, gets so many simple *facts* wrong—like saying Mitch was Bob's room-mate!—that one can't take him seriously.

Am sending you this messy copy—hope it doesn't strike you as embarrassingly egotistic—it *is*, & it was a strange experience writing it, but I don't see how else to do it.

Nobby Brown & his wife visited us for a couple of days. We enjoyed it. Nik returns tonight from his 2 months in Europe! He had a wonderful

## 403

Aug. 31st {19}67
Temple, Maine 04984

time & to my surprise & pleasure went to lots of museums to look at
paintings, went to other places to look at scenery, etc. I say "to my surprise"
because when a kid is younger he doesn't voluntarily do those things, you
know, & an anxious person like me wonders if having parents who do those
things ruins it for the child—& then to find he likes the same things after
all is always a kind of surprise & relief. . . . We're driving to Lewiston, 50
miles away, to meet his bus at 10 tonight.

On Tues we'll set off for the Montreal Poetry Conference to which Ezra
Pound is supposed to come. Jay {Laughlin} is anxious about him, thinks
Olga Rudge lets him in for more than, at his age, he ought to do, & is afraid
some of the 30 poets may be hostile to him. Many are Latin American,
several from Eastern Europe—it's a strange line-up, as more or less left-wing
poets seem to preponderate, with E. P., Allen Tate (ugh) and me representing
America. It was arranged by the *Maison des Poètes* in Brussels mainly I think.
Big deal, with Mayor of Montreal giving receptions etc. We all get to hear
the Vienna Opera in *Figaro*, nice bonus. Margaret Avison will be there as
an "observer," whatever that means. Hospitality extends to Mitch & Nik.
Guillevec, French poet whose poems I like, will be there—also Neruda, I
think Ungaretti, & I forget who else having lost the list. We'll be there
though Sunday 10th.

Nik starts college the 18th.

The "conscientious resistance" thing we're planning fits with visit to
Washington for myth . . . If you feel able to join it, maybe you cd. come
back to Temple with us afterwards (if we are not arrested). I plan to stay on
in Washington for the days which intervene between the myth symposium
and the 20th—possibly participating in some of the other Resistance
events which will take place that week, & certainly visiting the Nat. Gallery
& the Corcoran, neither of which I've ever seen. What are your plans? If
you can't take part in the action but wd. be free after it's over maybe you
could come up here anyway then, I mean even if you don't drive with us.
Actually I don't know if Mitch (who'll probably not arrive in Wash. till
the 19th) means to drive or to fly down. But anyway—keep the dates
in mind.

Paul Goodman's 20 year old son of whom he was so proud & who was
one of the students who started the "We Won't Go" movement (at Cornell)
was killed while climbing a mountain in New Hampshire where they have
a summer home. I feel so appalled, & can't decide whether to write to Paul
& Sally or not. Not a bad death for the boy, but so bitter for the parents.

I don't think I said how glad I am things have worked out satisfactorily
between you & Oyez & N.D. I think that shd. be good all around.

Have sent John Martin a rather strange poem to do as a little book[1]—will
send you a copy soon, it came out of writing that paper & I think I like it

but am uncertain if it comes off or not. I mean, whether a gradation in tone from rather colloquial to rather . . . lofty, I guess—works.

Helen writes she was giving ballad performances on the Cape—glad she got out of hot New York for a spell.

I have learnt quite a bit about mushrooms this summer—it has rained so much that I've been able to find & identify many species. It's been almost my own relaxation as I've worked hard on the WRL calendar.

A very nice and efficient carpenter, our neighbor Dick Blodgett, has been putting in a window & shelves & doors & proper walls (before, it was just slats) in the upstairs, where up to now only the guestroom was "finished." It is very simple but looks just great to us, a miraculous transformation. Inspired by whats happening upstairs, I spent this morning moving all the furniture around in our downstairs bedroom. I love to move furniture. I read in a book on Yoga that one shd sleep with one's head to the north & started the changes last night by moving the bed around & am convinced we slept better. "In this way," it says, "yr body gets the benefit of the earth's magnetic currents flowing harmoniously through it in the proper direction." I believe it. But what if one lived in Australia?

Much love—& to Jess—
Denny

Dear Robert,

Many thanks for your cooperation in sending me your work for the WRL 1968 Calendar.

I am happy to include "God-Spell" among the poems chosen.

It will probably not be possible to send the proofs out to the contributors; but I and the printer will take all possible care to ensure that there are no errors.

You will of course receive a copy of the calendar when it appears.

Yours sincerely,
Denise
Denise Levertov

**404**

August 1967[1]
Temple, Maine 04984

dear Denny,

The pages off at last (last Monday) to New Directions; and one would hope with two of us at reading and rereading and rerereading and even a third hired for a section of the galleys (during that week I was East in October that this book might come thru better than *Roots and Branches* did as far as errors go. I did manage an "Introduction" which I had much wanted

**405**

Nov. 26 {28} 1967
{San Francisco}

to do; it had to wait for that myth paper to be done before it wld come. But now I have shots of making up. I had written a "Passages" 31 (before "Epilogos"), but shown or read it to no one. I felt guilty about letting myself go on the grandeur of the stars and letting Boehme come in—and in reaction had put away how much Duncan had come into that making too. . . . Last week I dared admit the poem and reading it aloud to Jess as he was painting with a "I wrote this last February and I think it is what I thot it was then." Well, I'll type it up for you, and also the opening of 32 which I've had for some time and am very excited about now. Especially, I think "Passages" will be tackling its own questionable grandeur etc. straight on. Reading Viatte's *Les sources occultes du Romantisme 1770–1820*,[1] I've begun to gather some definitions of what my own concern is with that pitch blende (tar baby that it usually is for Brer Rabbit poets).[2] And I begin to feel what is needed in the concluding pieces of the H. D. book.

Last week I had a solid week of meetings with students at Berkeley, where I found myself particularly concernd with suggesting what the life cycles for the poet might be; and relating the larger life cycle (between the germinal cell and the individual body) to a picture of organism. Why the *feel* of the poem is the crucial thing; and from that, the *feel* of what to do. And returning to me in that an idea long present (why we so readily imagine the tree or the flower even we are, or the "totem" animal), that life unfolding its forms, we, having our source in *life* ultimately—are informd by an intention that dreamt of trees as well as us. We do, rightly, I am sure "blossom forth" in poems; and have not to bear all year round. And can see the hot house variety of the poets who force production. But show that man is a tree who can also tend to his affairs, an agri (I started to write *angri*) culturist.

And from Parkinson I have news that plans are going ahead for you and Mitch to be at U.C. next year. In May I will be going to London, having finally got enlisted on one of those charter flights.

Nov. 28/

I had the second half of the "Rites of Participation" Chapter of the H. D. book to get off to Clayton Eshleman for *Caterpillar* 2 yesterday. Did you see the first number? Paul Blackburn has a beautiful poem, a name-casting, that opens the issue.[3] It brings my list towards the ten poems (for the National Foundation magazine awards) to eight. Your "Vision" is very much there. I am happy that such a number are not just of the year but proudly of the most permanent recognition. There's a circle range in length—between Aram Saroyan's "Light" and Zuk's "A-18." I was torn between three of Saroyan's poems that appeard in *Chicago Review*—they make a powerful impress.[4] But "lighght" came thru in a dream information. To capture so in terms at once of the sounding of the word—*li-ite* and of the silent letters of the word *igh ght* the after life of light itself is a stroke of genius.

I had reserves when you were explaining at the Conference in Washington about your sense that the Concrete poem was wrong—even morally wrong. Of course, I do differ with you in my conviction that Confucius is right—one's morality must begin with the rule *no ought*,[5] which I read as leading towards a purely volitional good. i.e. the man creating his way as a good.

But in the case of Concrete poetry it is not only my argument that men can always enlarge or shift the meaning of what poetry is by their poems; and, in turn, our idea of what Poetry is must account for what men have written as poems (or else we are applying prejudgments to What Is and get caught like the zoologists of the nineteenth-century who argued that there couldn't be an *okapi* as reports of same began to come in).

Once the poem is written down and the poet becomes a writer, the area of the poem extends all the way from those remnants of oral poetry (i.e. memorized pre literate forms to letterd poetry. And rightly the poet as letterd works in the full gestalt of man's experience as a reader{.} Saroyan's concrete poems are in a range that includes sound—but Ian Hamilton Finlay's extend into silent sound—the apprehension of sound, and here too I wld recognize the poem. Mallarmé (and Saint-John Perse in sequence) felt that the poem shd not be read aloud at all, because the voice distorted the finer apprehensions of sound in the poem: a hint at least, long before the fact of pure notations, of visual sounds and inner hearings.

As, I find it most important to get across to would-be poets that the inner ear (I mean the actual inner ear) is the organ of equilibriums, weights and measures. That, for instance, a tone beyond the sensation of sound will still be sensed as a weight and will cause the visual field to readjust its horizon balances. In the physical actuality the sound waves are deeply felt as governing the vision. (Hence, music can readily *read*, up (visual) means up (auditory)).

All concrete poetry is not aware—much is shallow enuf. But there is clearly a body, and are clearly a variety of real poets at work in it—I'm not likely to get very far into the purely letterist (and {any?} more than I am likely to get into that other area of the "concrete" pure sound or phonetic poem); I am definitely in a range that has a boundary in one direction where notation (tho I can conceive of wanting that boundary to extend into the notation of silent sound) borders on typography of the word. Yet, even here, since I find capitalization more and more important (a silent stress?) I get into visual signs. (And, of course, I have extended into diagrams as part of the poem)—

And have a strong temptation to try the sound poem, but an equally strong fear of the consuming lure of it. While I love Schwitter's *Urlauten Sonate*, I have not dared try to do it aloud myself.[6]

There does seem to be a distinction between something like Emmett

Williams, where (as in "mirror field inside random field") the poem presents an extention of the lettering of language as such; and Mary Ellen Solt who uses the letters of a word to make a picture. (first cousin to portraits of Lincoln done on the typewriter—a scale of word making would go from:[7]

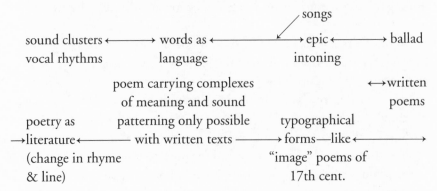

Certainly Celtic books come to mind, the illuminated title pages and fugal developments of word that lead. And the mouse-tail poem of *Alice-In-Wonderland* or is it *Thru the Lookinglass*?

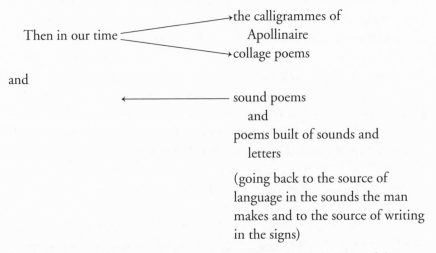

As, potentially, the happening as poem returns to the vital origin of the dithyrambic poem proposed by Nietzsche (and still again by Jane Harrison) in the movement and outcries of a "chorus" in which the god is born.

———————

    I got off on what shld someday be an essay on the range of the word in poetry—and it's the first time I've had the occasion to try to get across a growing sense I have over the last three years or so following the Concrete poem (tho earlier I had been interested in Mon's Lettrist Movement in France,[8] and in Schwritters and the collage poem). I certainly don't— Denise, mean that you should agree with my view. It is important to keep to ones nature in ones own art in these things. But you shld be reserved about deciding that some expression in an art is "wrong" when there is evidence everywhere of creative activity in said direction.

Wonderful news from Bob in a letter today—they are returning to New Mexico at the end of the Spring semester. N.M.U. has offerd a solid salary—and both Bob and Bobbie have been wanting to go "home" as Bob writes.

Love<br>Robert

To: RESIST

From: Denise Levertov

**406**

December 1967
{New York}

Lecture and poetry-reading engagements provide an excellent opportunity for war-resisters to tell potential sympathizers what is going on, to activate the apathetic, to encourage isolated activists, and to alleviate their isolation by helping to put them in touch with one another. As I have just returned from a two-week tour during which I tried to use my opportunities in these ways, Florence Howe has asked me to report on my experiences.

My invitations were all to colleges and were all for the purpose of reading my poetry and, in some cases, conducting seminars in poetry and in conferring with student writers. My first stop was Tucson, where I was to spend three days at the Ruth Stephan Poetry Center at the University of Arizona. Beforehand I obtained the name of a local representative of the Resistance, Mrs. Doris Stanislawski. She was not feeling well, but passed my letter—in which I asked what I could do to help with Stop the Draft Week in Tucson—on to another local peace activist, Patricia Ackert, so that on my arrival I found waiting for me a full typewritten account of the peace movement in Tucson, and within a few hours had met several of the key people. Tucson has a Peace Center (P.O. Box 50031, Tucson, Arizona 85703) which sponsors speakers, tries to disseminate information, and currently is distributing copies of the Medical Report of Vietnam prepared by Physicians for Social Responsibility to every medical doctor in the area. Associated groups run a weekly Vigil and (as the Tucson Committee to End the War in Vietnam) organize demonstrations. Three hundred people walked to the rally on October 21st—twice as many people as ever before. In a very conservative, Goldwater-supporting city, this is not bad, especially considering that these are local organizations built up without help or advice from larger centers.

After several years of apathy and poor organization, I learned, the student peace movement at the University of Arizona has become very active this year, and had planned several events for Stop the Draft Week. On Monday, December 4th (the first day of my visit) they demonstrated at the Induction

Center in downtown Tucson, several students burning their draft cards. They attempted to block the entrances and to prevent a bus load of inductees from leaving for boot camp. Some were hurt as induction staff stepped over and on them. Two were arrested. I intended to be present but the action took place earlier than I had been told it would and I arrived too late. However, the reason for my lateness was a newspaper interview scheduled by the Poetry Center; and though this took place because I was a Visiting Poet, I utilized it to make some public statements about the war and in support of draft resistance. An account of the interview appeared next day in the Tucson *Daily Citizen* under a photo of a student demonstrator being arrested, and with the headline, "Poet Backs Draft Card Burners." (A comic sequel was a crank phone call in which the caller said I was "a Benedict Arnold.")

On the evening of the 4th an informal meeting was arranged at the home of Byrd Schweitzer who works both with the Peace Center and with some of Tucson's oppressed and poor Indian population. Members of the community peace groups and the Student Peace Association were there. Those who had been at the Induction Center in the afternoon described what had happened and discussed possible strategy for future actions. I was able to tell them about the Justice Department action of October 20th; about the history and intentions of *Resist* and *The Resistance*; and about the Pentagon action (concerning which they had heard conflicting reports). People in New York, San Francisco, or Boston have little idea, I came to realize, of the degree of isolation in which their brothers and sisters in places like Arizona exist and try to work. Rather than criticizing them for not doing more, I think we who live mainly in larger centers of action should respect them for doing as much as they do in places where there is so much ignorance, inertia, and hostility. The Tucson "peace people"—both adults and students—are touchingly modest and apologetic about their relatively small numbers, and often wonder if what they are doing is of use. I was able to encourage them simply by telling them that they were not alone. What they most need is to be *kept informed* of what is happening elsewhere. A newsletter could be of prime importance for such groups. They would like also to have a list of signers of the Resist and Conscientious Resistance Statements (with professional fields and status of signers included) with which to urge on still-timid faculty and other professionals.

Next day I had another newspaper interview (for Tucson's other daily) and various conferences with students and faculty poets. In all these I was able to refer to the war and the draft quite naturally in the course of conversation. I also addressed several English classes, and in these I was able to read some of my own anti-war poems and to mention the phenomenon of the large amount of anti-war poems being written now by other American poets.

That evening (Dec. 5th) the Student Peace Association had sponsored a lecture—very well attended, in a large auditorium—by Dr. Neiland of Berkeley, a scientist who attended the War Crimes Tribunals at Stockholm and Tokyo (the latter as Bertrand Russell's personal representative) and who was a member of the investigating commission sent by the War Crimes Tribunal to North Vietnam. He was a most excellent speaker and there was a lively discussion period afterwards in which I was able to participate. After he and the main part of the audience left, there followed a meeting of the S.P.A. for which I was invited to stay; and again I was able to contribute information on activities elsewhere.

On the third and last day I spoke at a noon open-air forum on campus. I was originally intended only to read some poems from the WRL 1968 Peace Calendar, but ended up making a speech about draft resistance and—as well as I could!—countering hecklers. (This was my first experience of quite this kind, and also the first time I have ever had an egg thrown at me . . . ) There are a sizable number of student hawks at the U. of Arizona. I asked why these war-supporters didn't enlist but got no answer. U. of Arizona has compulsory R.O.T.C. but this is being fought, with the support of the Student Senate. One of the Student Peace Association speakers is a returned Vietnam veteran.

Last of my Tucson experiences was my public reading on the night of the 6th, which was also well attended in the same auditorium in which Dr. Neiland had spoken the night before. I dedicated the reading to the students who had demonstrated a week or so earlier against CIA recruiters there and to those who had blocked the Induction Center on the 4th; and I included in the program, along with some of my other anti-war poems, the litany which I wrote in collaboration with some Vassar students for the last May's interfaith Peace Service at Vassar, and which seems to be an effective conscience stirrer.

The Tucson peace workers feel isolated and indeed are in great need of communication with other parts of the country; but Tucson is a peacenik's paradise in comparison with my next stop, Union College, Barbourville, in East Kentucky: a small school that does not have any student or faculty peace activity at all, and where few students ever even read a newspaper, it seems. In such a place I think a visiting writer (or other lecturer) has to begin with the basic moral issues. For instance, in informal meetings I tried to tell people a little about napalm. They need to know about the history of the war, the definition of war crimes, the nature and history of dissent. I did find a small number of interested and sympathetic English majors one of whom had worked in Lexington during the summer on circulation of *Negotiate Now* petition. To her I suggested obtaining from the WRL and from AFSC a large selection of informative pamphlets and setting up a table in the Student Union. A foundation of basic anti-war feeling and protest must be laid before any kind of *resistance* can be built—and that seemed like a first step that even one or two individuals might usefully take.

From Barbourville I went—with a brief visit to Thomas Merton at Gethsemane to perk me up in between—to the University of Kentucky, at Lexington. Here I was scheduled only to read, not to hold any classes or conferences, so my opportunities were more limited. But through my good friend Wendell Berry who teaches there I met the student activists, a small group as yet, operating in a fairly hostile environment and with very little faculty support, I gathered, but numbering among them a very fine, mature, impressive young man, John Lewis, who is also doing some work among the Appalachian poor. With Dave Elkinton he has started a newsletter and is organizing a Conference on the Draft. I was able to give him the addresses of the various Resistance groups listed on the back of the Palo Alto Resistance Newsletter and to put him on the *Resist* mailing list immediately. He, incidentally, is in need of financial aid to further his efforts. Steering committee please note!

Wendell Berry arranged for him and about five or six other young men to attend an after-the-reading party at someone's house the night of the 11th. About an equal number of other guests were there and a good discussion developed concerning the nature and value of civil disobedience. I think the anti-war people gave the more neutral or apathetic ones something to think about.

On the 12th I flew to Chicago where I had arranged to give a benefit reading for the Chicago Cadre. This is something else people might think about doing when on such a tour, if they are writers, actors, musicians, etc. Often there is a free evening or afternoon that can be used in this way; instead of just relaxing in such free time, one can put it to work as a part of one's contribution to the peace effort.

This particular reading had not been too well publicized, so it was not a big success as a fund-raising item, but it did gather a finely attentive audience. Donna Holabird, an actress with the National Repertory Co. in Chicago, read from "Where is Vietnam?" (Walter Lowenfels' anthology); Florence Levinsohn, poet and activist, read her own work; folk guitarist was to have played but was prevented by illness: and I read from the WRL Peace Calendar and from my own work, as well as speaking about *Resist*. Chicago has just started a "chapter" of *Resist* and some of the audience were potential members. Copies of the Peace Calendar were sold at the door. Dennis Riordan, of Cadre, whose trial—from which he expects to go straight to jail—was to take place two days later, acted as master of ceremonies, and spoke of local needs and plans.

Next day I arranged to go to the studios of WFTM (FMT?) with Dennis Riordan and Chuck Matthei, who are two of the most articulate,

unshakeable, and deeply humane young men of the Resistance, to tape an
interview with Studs Terkel (author of *Division St. USA*, a signer of the
Conscientious Resistance statement, and a great guy). This long tape will
be, thanks to Studs and to the beautiful statements made by Dennis and
Chuck, an important document of the movement, I believe. (It was due
to be broadcast in Chicago on Tuesday the 19th of December, and by
WRVR in New York probably sometime in January). This suggests another
possibility. Wherever one goes one could try to locate a sympathetic radio
or television interviewer and get them to do a program in which one can
try to introduce the subject of draft resistance and if possible bring a local
resister to be included in the program. Of course, many stations will simply
not handle such material; but it is worth trying.

My last stop of the trip was St. Teresa's College, Winona, Minnesota.
Here the student body (all girls) ranges from hawks with boy-friends in
the marines, through the indifferent (a majority) to a few deeply anti-war
people of whom the most active and influential is Jennie Orvino, a senior
who is the fiancee of Bob Gilhaim, a Catholic Worker draft refuser now in
the Sandstone Federal Penitentiary. Faculty of St. Teresa's has not been very
active but does include some definitely sympathetic people including Sister
Immanuel, Sister Bernetta Quinn (the well-known critic, now on leave of
absence), the poet William Goodreau, and the head of the art department
and his wife, whose son at 17 is a convinced pacifist.

Among the Winona townspeople I met, was a highschool teacher who
has participated in much local protest and is now intent on committing
civil disobedience. He has six children and is going to need help from the
Resistance Defense Fund if he should be sent to jail. I was especially moved
by this sincere and very serious man. A newsletter, and in general a better
communication system, are—again—much needed by people like him.

I gave two official readings—one a convocation—at St. Teresa's,
dedicating the convocation to Dennis Riordan whose trial was, if on time,
taking place in Chicago at that same hour. (The dedication gave me a
chance to say who he was and why he was going to jail.)

My presence on campus was made the occasion for a showing by Jennie
Orvino of a film made by Grenada, the British independent television
company, about a) the Hiroshima Day demonstration in New York when
demonstrators in death's head masks made by Peter Schumann of Bread and
Puppet Theater tried to board a visiting destroyer in the harbor, and b) the
decision of Bob Gilhain to refuse induction and go to jail. It showed Bob at
home with family and friends, included several excellent statements by him,
and ended as he thanked a supporting picket (including several nuns and a
Catholic bishop) outside the courthouse as he entered to be sentenced.

A group of about twenty Poor Clares (contemplative sisters) who are at

St. Teresa's for a study period, were permitted to come to the movie and were deeply moved. I afterwards spoke informally to the audience of nuns and students, emphasizing that what they had witnessed was representative of thousands of other young men moved by conscience. Sister Gretchen, who is in charge of the education of young women who are still college students, asked me to get her a copy of the interview with Studs Terkel etc. to play to them, as a follow-up. Many of the sisters who will hear it will later go out into the schools as teachers; so this is important.

Conversations while travelling can also be fruitful. A peace button can start a dialogue that may be used to teach or to give encouragement. I met one airline hostess who is a "peacenik" with a C.O. husband (a doctor) but who did not know about *Resist.*

To sum up, there are many of us professional people who have opportunities to influence others which we do not use as fully as we could. There is not really a conflict between one's responsibility to the people who invite one to read or speak about poetry or whatever, and one's responsibility to the peace effort. I know I can say truly that I honorably fulfilled all my official commitments in each place I went. And I did not, for instance, read only war poems, by any means. But the fact is, if one's life is a whole, and not compartmentalized, one cannot speak of one's art without speaking of one's moral convictions. In the case of some fields of endeavor—say music, or some branches of science—it would, I can see, be harder to introduce a "political" note into one's talks. But for the people in such fields there remain the "free time," the informal talks with students (and faculty) and the possibility of contacting local peace groups and speaking for them.

I received no criticism or disapproval from the faculty anywhere for using part of my visits in this way. Even at Union College, the least sympathetic in general atmosphere, it was never suggested that I was misusing their invitation and in fact wherever I went I was thanked by faculty for "stirring things up." At the U. of Arizona, the head of the English department offered me a job after witnessing the open-air forum session and hearing my anti-war pitch at my poetry reading. This should encourage those who fear they might seem to be abusing their position. A concerted and determined utilization of such opportunities seems to me one of the most fruitful things we in RESIST can do.

Denise Levertov

Appendix:

A few tips:

1) Contact peace people beforehand so that they can make the best use of you when you come.

2) Try to find out local conditions so that your remarks will be on the most useful and appropriate level.

3) Wear a peace button of some kind while travelling.

4) Perform whatever you are being paid to do with extra zeal—it will give more weight to your peace activities.

5) If you can arrange to give a benefit performance of some kind, try to have them use "local talent" too. It gives more feeling of solidarity—and at the same time takes a bit of strain off you.

Note: Further copies may be obtained by writing to

RESIST
Room 4
763 Massachusetts Avenue
Cambridge, Mass. 02138

or

Florence Howe
Goucher College
Towson, Maryland 01204

This manuscript is the property of Miss Levertov and should not be reproduced without her permission.

(till the 15th of March—then c/o Jarrett at 277 Greenwich St.)

Dear Robert and Jess,

Forgive my long silence.

Dec. I was travelling (a reading trip, I mean) and then came back to rather distracting circumstances in NY—living in various borrowed apartments etc., because we had not intended to be in NY, you know, and had sublet the Greenwich St place—Nik was home for the vacation of course, and Mitch was awfully busy, and then had the flu—then Jan 5th came the indictment and the phone never stopped ringing from then on—plus newsmen, TV crews etc.[1] Rather exhilarating really, especially as there was so much support and practically no hostility—even from the newsmen many of whom are quite sympathetic to the anti war point of view—it is at higher editorial levels that the news gets blocked. Well, then there were trips to Washington (I made a draft-resistance speech at the women's rally) and Boston (for the arraignment) and various rallies and support meetings where Mitch spoke etc etc—And we were beginning to "fail up" as they say in Maine, from exhaustion, the sheer pace and externalization of it all, getting so far from one's own work and not getting enough sleep and everything. So

**407**

Feb. 25th {19}68
Box 59
Rincon, Puerto Rico

once the Town Hall defense-fund-and-further-complicity meeting, which Mitch had worked so hard on, was over, we managed to get away here. At first the lawyer was afraid we might not be allowed to leave the continental US but it was OK and we have been here unwinding for 2 weeks now and hope to stay till March 15th. It is a kind of paradise, even though minor annoyances like chickens and dogs that tend to crow and bark all night do exist, to keep one from total levitation. I have been working on a new longish poem which tells all about it,[2] and about waiting for the trial, etc etc, much better than I can rise to in a letter and as soon as I can I will send it to you. I'll also be sending you the little book John Martin is doing, as soon as that comes. I hope you'll like it. I also have a sort of story, or at least a piece of prose that includes a story, and am in the middle of a lecture for the Hopwood thing in Ann Arbor in April. As soon as we got here, almost, I started to work again thank god. We have a housekeeping cottage just yards from the beach and I enjoy doing the simple cooking which is all we need, and a delightful criada comes in to clean up every day—not that there is much to clean, but she keeps changing the sheets and towels and picking up grains of sand. There are plenty of lizards around to delight my reptophilia; and the sea—oh the sea. And pelicans (the small dark kind, frigate birds, not the big white ones). And coquis—a little fluting treefrog.

I have often the sense of world's end you express in your last letter but then again I think there are so many things beginning, little shoots of feeling and love and realization and of courageous trying-things-a-new-way, that it cannot be so. The 2 days I spent with Dennis Riordon in Chicago— he's a 21 year old draft resister—just a few days before his trial (he's in jail now for 3 years) were very moving to me. He's half my age but I feel he has influenced all of my life from now on. I shall not give up as long as he does not, whatever else happens.

I guess the nicest thing that happened to us, just about ever, was when Swedish TV was filming us at Peter Feibleman's where we stayed in the last weeks in NY, as we were eating Sunday breakfast, and Nik was home for the weekend so they asked him suddenly what he thought of all this, the indictment and all, and without a moment's hesitation he answered, "Well, it seems perfectly natural. My parents have been getting gradually more and more involved in the peace movement for 2 or 3 years now. And—I'm one of the very few people my age I know who feels they can respect their parents." Wow.

No, no, you mistook me, I never said people shouldn't be writing "concrete" poetry—I only said people shouldn't regard it as evolutionary in the sense of its being a progressive development, a *substitute* for the full aural oral use of language. I believe it's a branch, not the main limb of the tree. I even like some of it.

I think your admiration of Aram Saroyan is excessive. It is based on clues to something in your own caverns of treasure which that poem of his chanced to reveal to you, not on the intrinsic worth of his work in itself. I think something of that kind—an identification of suggested possibilities with what suggests them—accounts for many enthusiasms on the part of artists, e.g. Cezanne's for Ary Scheffer.[3] (Including no doubt some of my own enthusiasms, god knows!)

Yes indeed, we know you would have been a first-signer of the "complicity statement." I don't know who was responsible for the choice of names, but I do know it was prepared in a big hurry. We hope better communication between E and W coasts will soon be established. Mitch has been writing to Don Kalish about it.

When are you going to England, Robert? Wish I were. This was the year when I was going to at last, but of course until the trial is over I can't even think of it and anyway can't afford it. I put off Mexico too—at least until things get a little clearer—fortunately my old mother is full of indignation about the war and sounds more revolutionary with every letter, so there's no problem with hurt feelings at least, which is a great blessing because I wd be so miserable if she didn't understand.

When will New Directions have your book ready?[4] I meant to ask Jay when I talked to him the day before we left but always get so flustered on the phone and forget everything.

Walter Hamady is doing a little book of Mitch's poems which we'll be sending to you.[5] Nik was thinking of transferring to Wisconsin, partly to study with Hamady, but missed the deadline for scholarship applications.

I expect you know from Tom Parkinson that we expect to come to Berkeley for the 2 terms from Jan 69 on—we still don't know when the trial will be and it may not be till the fall. But even if it is in the spring we will not come till then as we shall badly need the fall in Temple to make up for all the loss of time to just write and meditate that this year was planned to give us and has so notably failed to give us till this little lovely respite here; besides which there will be the period of appeals up to the supreme court and so on (unless the trail is won by a jury verdict which of course is not too probable, though the lawyers say it is not impossible). If it should turn out that Mitch has to go to jail I am not sure what I wd do. I wd want to be near enough to visit him. Also not too far from Nik—but of course we don't know for sure where Nik will be at that time. On the other hand I will have to earn money. All this is too speculative and too far away to cause me any anxiety at this point though. Don't discuss the above with Tom, please. He was just as nice about adjusting the schedule to the 2 terms instead of 3 as anyone could be, but I don't want that question as to what I would do if Mitch is jailed to come up with him until it becomes necessary—and so much may happen between now and then that it may never *be* necessary. In fact Mitch just told me that the whole appeal process will take so long that our Berkeley thing will be over before he wd have to go to jail anyway, even if that *is* how it turns out.

Do you get the *Resist* newsletter regularly? Just checking.

Have been working on my Guillevic translations which Jay will bring out in a bilingual paperback.[6] The work is a great pleasure to me and indeed provided me with the way back to my own work after those weeks of rushing around. I managed to do some of them in the midst of the New York frenzy.

We saw Muriel {Rukeyser} just before we left, and before she left for California. She was at her most wonderful. Maybe you've seen her by now too.

> Much love to you both from
> Denise

**408**

Feb. 26, 1968
{San Francisco}

dear Denny,

I hope you are back from the islands, for I am to be in New York just for next Saturday and Sunday. With the prospect of a reading in Buffalo in their March festival week I decided to go first thru to the City, to see you and Helen, and to have a museum gallery day. With fingers crosst against its being stormy weather! Here we are in a warm spell between rains. Great mushroom weather, I have a feast of bluets for lunch today.

Since I wrote you last the Gallerie Odyssia has taken Jess on beginning in May (i.e., after he finishes the two current canvasses which had already been sold) at $800 a month, with the assurance that his income will increase.[1] It means that when he finishes the sequence he is working on—thru to the *Narkissos*—they will be showing the whole series to date (i.e. all the paintings now in private collections plus the remaining ones to be painted) in New York and then in Rome.

This is being written in installments in between shifts of dish washing and pan washing; with the kitchen floor still to be cleand. Right now it is a grim reminder that I have neglected it too long. But a cheerful day for such duties.

Last night friends were over (hence that *lot* of dishes to do this morning) and I had out the *Tree, Telling* and Creeley's *Finger*.[2] With a growing sense of the music of your poem this time, savouring the measures and the slow movement. I love the way the rimes give rise to the poem in falling into place or pace. My first impression of the poem had been that it was more casual. But now, the narrative pace remains but my sense is no longer of anything casual but of exact measures. Learning the phrasings of the sonata.

Has it struck you that the poem predicts from your actual experience of the sequence of states in poetic inspiration another sequence of events in your being called to uproot yourself, aroused by "stirring events," the world crisis we are all *in*, and anticipates life in the after-world of those events, vegetative growth and awareness in a new place "with its ancient grove that was bare grass then"

The silence-sickness-boredom-coldness in the midst of burning comes as a revelation.

Love
Robert

Dear Denny & Mitch,

We saw the PBL report on the Rankin Brigade Washington protest and the sudden apparition of Denny in full ardor.[1] The person that the *demos*, the *citoyen*-mass of an aroused party, awakes is so different from the individual person; recognizable—something of you, Denny that calls up the fondness of intimate continuities of feeling was very much there—and thrilling—it's the fieriness that all demotic personae have once they are aroused. As special an increase of commitment or earnestness over the fullness of commitment or earnestness [as always in the demotic urgency, the arousal of the group against an enemy—here the enemy clearly being the whole state structure against our *humanity*—commitments must be withdrawn from the wholeness of the individual life to be focusst, driven into the confinement of a single-minded purpose] as the erotic zeroing of a heightend and specialized power of the person. So that it is very agonizing to coordinate sexual excitement or "political" (but it is not only political— the polis or city—thing, it is societal)—*societal*, then, excitement with the freedom and fulfillment of the individual life; certainly at first, agonizing in the conflict between the sacrifice of all other functions that Eros or Eris (that strife Heraklites has in mind, a striving for a higher order of things that casts existing orders into the aspect of disorder) demand and the process of the fulfillment of human potentialities in the individual life. In the PBL view of you, Denny, you are splendid but it is a force that, coming on *strong*, sweeps away all the vital weaknesses of the living identity; the *soul* is sacrificed to the demotic persona that fires itself from spirit. All the searching, atoning, undergoing, failing, vitally querulous, sympathetic and self betraying, humorous, sensitive, greedy,—but I am not sure (or I am *sure* that they are not) that negative characters don't belong here: "failing" is a positive realization—all the fine delineations—I am thinking now of the lines of a face, not the strong usurping lines of a great face but the other delicate

409

March 30, 1968
{San Francisco}

wrinkling of transitory experience kept alive in the heart—blotted out in the spirited arousal.

Writing to you now, this question of where one's allegiance lies, of something wrong to my sense of life in urging the conscience to take up arms against the war (I have in mind here to urge young men to go to prison or to rebel) *as against* the conscience to stand by the individual life, to go underground, evade or escape the conscription. As in South Vietnam, it is not the Liberationists that I identify with but the people of the land who are not fighting to seize political power but are fighting to remain in their daily human lives. It is the villagers in their fight for their village life, the farmer and his ox in their labor that are counterparts of the writer in his labor (to reveal the truth of his vision of things and to work to free from its boundaries that truth).

This, not against those who have been calld to the adventure of the revolutionary, or those upon whom a categorical imperative has descended or in whom ascended, not against inspiration—but against the persuasion that youth must be calld from its tables of study to die and from its beds of love whether that call to arms comes from the power of government or the power of a new politics.

To bear witness to the outrage and grief or even to the moral indignity one truly feels in knowledge of the lies and dreams of men in power is an essential act of that revelation of the truth of things; and another, for me, is to bear witness too to the exile and underground survival of life—standing by ones life-work in the face of catastrophic times. Joyce's

> "I will not serve that in which I no longer believe, whether it call itself my home, my fatherland or my church: and I will try to express myself in some mode of life or art as freely as I can and as wholly as I can, using for my defence the only arms I allow myself to use, silence, exile and cunning"[2]

(with all the paradox that here *silence* speaks its cause and commits its conscience for all to see and hear) haunts my thought. And recently (in *Liberation*,[3] Paul Goodman's opening paragraph "We assume that the Americans do not *really* will the Vietnam War but are morally asleep and brainwashed . . . " an assumption that I do not make, in the face of half a century of living in America, of having American parents—I see the Vietnamese War (as I saw the Second World War) as a revelation of the truth of the potential evil of "America"—Blake, Hawthorne, Melville, Lawrence—Whitman in his "Eighteenth Presidency" (or just think of {what} novelists like Faulkner or Sinclair Lewis or Hemingway reveal about the nature of American folk) the Vietnamese War as a revelation of the truth of American Karma, what Commager calld the consequences of the unacknowledged, unrepresented crimes.[4] There are those, even among those who feel Vietnam is a revelation of the evil, who think the carnage of Berlin, Dresden, Hamburg, Tokyo, Hiroshima "was in a good cause."

"If in fact (Americans) are so complacent, arrogant or callous that they will do it or don't care about it, we have to talk not about resistance but exile, going underground or civil war."

Well, I *don't* believe in the change of the government but in the Robin Hood or guerrilla existence. Not for the future. But from the beginning of life. The essential is not how to win but how to keep alive, once known and acknowledged, the seed of life "to express [the Self] in some mode of life or art as freely as one can and as wholly as one can." The seed is and remains the individual volition, the unsacrificed inner volition. *If it die*, the Bible argues: but the plant does not grow by the seeds dying but by its firmness, even devour, to keep and use every circumstance towards its vegetative life. It is the devotion of the priests ringing the *son* in the thunder of the attack (that one province Tay Ninh the subject now for years of the war of American attack), obedient to the requirements of an art.

I've not got easy thoughts here. And perhaps in my paper on "Language and World Order" more of a context may come clear.[5] Dante sees the fountain of true government (the intent of creation) in a form in which the meaning of all beings and things thruout time is reveald, a civilization of all civilizations: where there is disorder not only the war but the civil war escalates and as Dellinger defines in the current *Liberation* seeks a larger enemy and a more violent solution in every cycle of frustration.[6] The two suicidal possibilities envisiond by the *Scientific American*: 1) atomic war, and 2) biological overpopulation of the species (i.e. loss of relation between the individual organism and its ecological field{)} have counterparts in contemporary politics in the alternations of 1) the rivalry of national establisht governments and 2) the overthrow of all existing orders in the return of power to the populations (the very ones that are biologically deranged).[7]

Civil war, where the numbers of people are not related to the functions of the earth but living in massive exploitation of those functions, is not "civil" but the same world holocaust first seen in the international war.

And I find it again in studies of cancer growing in societies of cells: they are calld to grow in power where they have no sense of functions and needs of the total body. Men deranged from productive life, seek the products and despise the productivity—but even here think how far diseased the populace of "products" is. I think immediately of my being a voracious consumer of music where I cannot *make* or produce more than wandering notes on the piano.

Canst thou carry Schubert from the
    burning town,
or resurrect when all is gone
the husbandry of sheep or grain,
    bring story or song
containing the growing seed of Man
    and the dream that certain
singers sang that Paradise
    is the hidden Tree therein?

And do you labor to render clear
    the shoot green force
free in the field of its true form,
    cut abiding images from stone,
or work in the steaming phantasies
    fever and the body's disease raise up
those chemistries wherein Amor
    and the Holy Spirit first appeard?

And can you wander lonely as a cloud
    and like the lily neither
weave nor spin? begin again
here where men's rage and miseries crowd in
    the communion in which
the soul from its binding cocoon
    takes wing?
                    To work! To work!
O wanderer, work the ancient ways
    and open the idle hours the Sun
in all of Nature's greeny house conveys.
Old gardener tend your vines, your grapes
that store      ripening dreams of wine to come,[8]

---

## 410

June 19, 1968
{San Francisco}

dear Denise and Mitch,

I hope you will be at Stony Brook this coming weekend, but, if you are at
Temple, this will find you. So long overdue. And should have come, if only
it could have whole heartedly, with some comfort in this time that, though
you have long anticipated it, must be an ordeal. It is hard, indeed, to write,
for you both stand now so definitely at the Front of—not the still small
inner voice of conscience that cautions us in our convictions but the *other*
conscience that draws us to give our lives over to our convictions, the
righteous Conscience—what Freudians call The Super Ego, that does not
caution but sweeps aside all reservations. I realize (but it has always been

clear enuf whenever I have considerd the nature of Law) that I draw back
from commanding conscience, as I wld avoid whatever tyranny of the will;
being so convinced seems deeply involved with conviction for me. And
where there is conviction I would be neither convicted nor convicting, but
undo the very conviction itself. This, only to begin here with what you must
know already, how troubled I am by the very commitment, by the very
courage of your convictions with which now you stand, by the very con-
science for which you have made a front and hold it at a great personal cost.
And, just here you battle for the freedom that most concerns me, for the
other inner voice of conscience, our inner knowing what we have to do
(*not* what we must do, not a moral imperative; but our sense of the given,
when we "have" to do, a creative permission), for the individual nature,
against all (including conscience) that would draft us, coerce us, use us for
intents not ours.

No, I very much do not subscribe to the Old Testament idea of a
covenant or a commitment as a morality. The righteousness, the revival of
the Judaic-Puritanic covenanter's Salvation Army against the Evil of War in
RESIST repells me. The "Thou shalt not . . . " written in stone or written
in the heart is the absolute authority standing in the place of the truth of
things, the old dragon again; and "*Thou shalt not kill . . .* " is the very evil
of a resolution in the place of free immediate individual experience of
choice. This element does not trouble me; I actively seek to keep alive all
volitions.

But I am troubled still by the New Testament thing that comes into it
too, the Christ-will that so loves mankind he gives his life up as a sacrifice
for "our" sins. And the accusation that this hero of the inner conscience,
writing in the place of "Thou shalt not kill" his "Thou shalt Love," lays
upon us, that we are unwilling to forgo the pleasures of our lives in order to
redeem "our" sins. There it is deeply written that no man is free, until *all* be
free; no man has life until *all* have life. Well, in the immediacy with which
the RESIST conscience (I mean here my own share of that Conscience)
brings that demand, the Christ demand that no man have a right to life
except it be given to redeem life for all—the Debs "So long as any man is
in prison, I am not free"—I am but the more aware that this is the very
imprisoning message itself. I wld evade the inner command, even as I would
evade the draft of the social command.

As in my work I would undo the commands even in obedience. This is
not a lawlessness, but a working with ideas of law. No, I do not mean to
*evade* conscience but to confront it, to know it out, appalled by it; neither to
go with it nor oppose it but to be concernd with its nature.

It is the sacrifice of your human individual lives that you make in your
convictions that so appalls me. It is like the carnage and destruction of lives
in Viet Nam—the breaking up of ways of life. I see it that way, but I realize

too that you have not given up a life that was a "way"; you have volunteerd another *way.*

I certainly do not think that poetry is a way; I would strangle poetry in the bud if it presumed to take command of life. But more and more I puzzle over Blake's idea of the Man of *Art,* of the Art of Life. Where Poetry is not thought of as an Art, it begins to be concernd with Discipline and Uses. (As my concern with "Up Rising" remains how it *fits,* with its operation in the art of the poem).

"The reason Milton wrote in fetters when he wrote of Angels & God, and at liberty when of Devils & Hell. . . . "

As it is I so resist any sympathy with Johnson or Humphrey, touching upon what I sympathetically feel at work in the war imagination as I do in "Up Rising" seems so much grander than their mean faces reveal them to be, I am not "at liberty."

---

Well, I've wanted—as often in writing you—to unburden myself of whatever reservations. And hardest of all, just here where we might be thought to be in agreement, to drive thru to the doubts I have in the area of agreement, the resistance to Resistance. And driving thru I find I go with a free morality, I do not assent to whatever social covenant nor do I assent to the inner command as *authority*; but seek a complex obedience to "What is Happening." The answer that the Pythian priestess gives *Ion* in H. D.'s "translation" of that play haunts me here:

Ion:     to strike at Evil, is pure:
Pythia:  you must know why you strike

(In Willetts translation in Euripides edited by Green and Lattimore, these lines have no such impact . . . indeed little impact immediately:

Ion:     All men are pure who kill their enemies
Pythia: No more of that—Hear what I have to say.

In place of H. D.'s Freudian persuasion "why you strike" I remember it as "what is happening," or "what you do."

And here Christ's "They know not what they do" comes to mind.

Yes, I seek a morality of knowing *what you do* (or coming to know) as I seek an art of coming to know what I do.

---

What you do remains. What the six of you, Mitch, do as active statement that the drafting of men against their conscience has made *conscience* the issue of life, and any life outside that confrontation intolerable must in its sacrifice of personal life to its cause encourage those opposed to the war and bring others to question.

Meanwhile it is not moral but actual issues that force the government to the negotiation tables—the loss of monetary credit and the loss of planes in relation to the possible aims of the War. "The United States now wants to negotiate," the Indian woman presiding over the Conference on Language and World Order this Spring declared: "not because of feeling against the War at home and abroad, but because they are losing."

And we are far indeed from establishing the right to a *human* life in place of a heroic one.

love
Robert

Dearest Robert

I hope the telegram reached you in time, & that you weren't inconvenienced by not hearing from us sooner.

Mitch had to see publishers about an anthology he's doing (civil disobedience, etc.)[1] & we didn't leave N.Y. till Wed. a.m., even tho' we didn't go to the airport to see Nik off on Tues. Then we didn't leave Cambridge (where we spent the night) till fairly late Thurs. Here, it was so wet & cold, you would not have enjoyed it, plus the fact that we're so tired that all we want at this moment is to be alone & not even say more than "pass the salt" to each other.

How about the weekend of Fri 12th July? We have to be in Boston the 10th for the sentencing, & if I could persuade Mitch to stay over till the Friday we could meet you there and drive up to Temple together. Meanwhile we will find out about connecting flights from Boston→ Lewiston, & the Blue Line bus from Lewiston→ Farmington.

I have decided to put off once more (this has been going on since last summer) my visit to Mexico to see my mother. She firmly says not to come but to stay with Mitch, bless her, & tho' I feel a bit badly about it (she's 83 today, June 29th) I'm going to take her at her word because though I'd like to see her the thought of yet another journey appals me. I've been, since Dec., in Ky., Arizona, 3 times in Illinois, in Iowa, Minnesota (twice), Michigan, New Mexico, Seattle, Ohio, Puerto Rico, Washington D.C. (twice), New York, Boston—and all the time with people (except Puerto Rico) and not doing any writing. I need desperately to just stay put for a while—as you know. So actually any weekend you want to come, from that one on (I know you are planning to go to N.Y. *next* weekend, no?) we expect to be here.

You couldn't possibly juggle classes a bit & come to Boston Thurs the 11th, could you? Mitch is if anything even more eager to get back to some sort of normal life here than I am, & if you *could* do that it wd. be marvellous, as we wd. not have to spend an extra day in Boston.

**411**

June 29th {1968}
Temple, Maine 04984

But it may turn out there's a reasonable connection anyway. . . . Will write again in a couple of days with that information. If only I knew how to drive it wd be no problem. But we'll solve it anyway.

I am mailing the copy of *The Box of Delights* I found for you & Jess, to Jess, to cheer him in your absence.[2] It may be one of the books I lent you at one point, I forget. But anyway—it's an old favorite of mine & Nik's & I think you'll like it.

It's very good to be here in spite of the cold, (which is really incredible for the time of year).

Don't forget to send me the other letter you said you'd half-written. I need it.

We have Mitch's poems (hors commerce) from Walter Hamady—he'll send that to Jess too, & you'll see it, them, when you come to Temple.

> With love
> Denise

---

## 412

July 6th {19}68
Temple, Maine 04984

Dearest Robert,

Just to confirm that we can meet you at the Boston airport on Friday 12th if that is when you can come—I hope so—and we can drive from there straight to Maine—much the best way to do it. Of course if you can get off on Thursday, tant mieux, but only because it wd give you a longer weekend, not because Mitch minds staying over till Friday—in fact it turns out we might need that time for something anyway. Please call us in Cambridge where we will be going on the 9th—we will be at Wassily Leontief's at 14 Ash St., Cambridge, Mass—617-547-1822. If we are not there please leave a message with plane time, flight number, and if poss a Buffalo number where we can call you back if there is any problem. If no answer, you could call our friends across the street, John and Barbara Hammond, and leave a message with them instead—they are at 19 Ash and the phone is 617-354-7520. Lots of kids there so make sure message is written down.

> With love—
> Denise

Had beautiful note from Jess.

---

## 413

July 9/ 1968
{Buffalo}

dear Denny & Mitch,

Before I start work with students' workbooks, some of them really challenging for me—it's a joy at this point—; I want to get off this note re. making the trip to Temple. I can, by foreshortening my morning class,

make an 11:30 AM flight to Boston, then the only Boston-Lewiston flight
wld be 7:35 that evening. This wld mean probably I wld have to take the
bus to Farmington the next morning? The time in Boston wld fit in with my
wanting to see Joe Dunn and Larry Eigner. . . .

But in any case it won't be this coming weekend, because it is a weekend
here of campus activities in which I am involved. It would best be the
following: July 19th-20th-21st weekend. If that will work out for you, I will
go ahead and plan for it. But *you are the ones who will know how that will fit
or not with the time you need now.* No matter how we plan it, it will mean
some interruption of your time if only for picking me up at Farmington and
returning me Sunday morning for the bus. . . .

Scribner's has officially (by letter) notified me that the rights to *Roots and
Branches* are now reverted to me. So I will be sending Jay a Xerox of that
letter, and, all things going according to his propositions, the book will be in
print again in the ND paperback series this Fall.

Well, I've to meet John Wieners for lunch in a few minutes; and then
back to this desk to work with the students' papers.

And a little stack of letters to take care off begins to pile up here.
Eshleman wants a book blurb quote; Jim Harrison reminds me the section
of the H. D. book is due;[1] that letter to Laughlin must get off. I too, Denny,
hired someone to help with my mail at home.

Somewhere those clearings must come along for writing you or Jess, the
correspondence one's gathering speech is waiting for.

Love
Robert

Dearest Robert,

Mitch will write the actual travel information. I just want to say that
much though we would love to see you & have you see this beloved place as
we've always wished, we are worried that you will knock yourself out coming
so far for such a short time.

I don't want you to feel we might feel hurt if you *don't* come.

If you could possibly arrange to shift a Fri. or Mon. class so that you cd
have a longer weekend it wd. make a lot of sense. Or if you cd. bear to come
at the end of your stay in Buffalo—I know you will be longing to get back
to Jess then but if you cd avoid going all the way back to Buffalo after being
here . . . ? Well, anyway, I'll leave the rest to Mitch & only send

love—
Denise

## 414

Sat. 13th July {19}68
Temple, Maine 04984

## 415

dear Denny & Mitch,

Your letter, Denny, postmarkt July 6 airmail and with "Urgent" written on the envelope arrived here late Friday afternoon, in the last delivery. Well, I hope this makes it the other way round. If you get it Thursday you might call me around 9 o'clock at my room number 831-4179. After getting a picture of air schedules and bus schedules, the trip begins to look like an awfully long one for the little more than a day we would have. There is no regular flight from Lewiston to Boston on Sunday, and the American Airlines office is still trying to find out about an air taxi.

Meanwhile, thinking of my work here especially with my eight o'clock on Monday, I've decided not to try it. Sadly, for the thought of being even that brief time with you in Temple at this time was a happy one. But not when so crowded with difficulties of travel and timing.

So, my being with you must be all the more by writing. This note must get off in the mails immediately. Then I will, as I promised, return to thoughts of my earlier letter as I remember them to go on.

Love
Robert

## 416

dear Denny & Mitch,

I have bought my ticket, to leave here at 8:55 AM Friday, August 2nd for Boston and then take the 1:50 PM flight from Boston to Lewiston. Where, all going well I will be meeting you.

Return to Boston on the 10:30 AM flight Sunday Aug. 4th from Lewiston. And there is a 5:45 flight direct to San Francisco.

•

In a letter sent this last Sunday, Jess writes of a dream in which I sang to him:

Those years are gone and that body is wasted. These tears they are flowing but these joys they are lasting and now at the well of our lives is it glowing: I have raised my cup and, toward a sky that is blinding, gaze thru it, sing thru it, move thru it, for the world does not dim (and?) (though?) (where?) long the sun has descended.

•

Tonight there is a program for the Resistance group here where I will be reading.

After which, I went out for a brief evening (even this extending until near eleven) with John Wieners and Bob de Niro who is teaching in the third session here, overlapping the second by three weeks.

John, who was in very bad form in San Francisco, seems here to be much better. Tho I'm always aware of how precarious his state is. He has only his parents or family as a resource I think. I insisted upon his having something to eat, and I am sure he had not eaten before that day. At the same time I set myself against any involvement here, for it is a psyche drama he would draw whomsoever into.

Time for breakfast and then my eight o'clock class!

love<br>Robert

Dear Mitch,

Your letter, of course, made it clear that the Lewiston airport was closed, but then the Travel Bureau where I bought my ticket persuaded me etc. etc.

Now—thanks to the reservations you made for me I am straightend out. I will be arriving as per your reservations:

August 2nd, Friday
at Augusta airport
on flight 906y
2:35 pm.

This last week is a seven round circus. Quasha arrived Thursday from Stony Brook to pump me for his thesis. There have been rounds and rounds of good-bye dinners. And one of my students is—I learn from her workbooks—in a serious crisis, what looks like a real breakdown—and all of a sudden I have to get thru to her to get her to psychiatric aid. In betweens I am trying to get a ms. in shape for a book coming up! And hopefully I will also be packt by Friday morning.

It will be good to have the quiet of Temple as a threshold for home. And to see you at last at the airport in Augusta—Green thots in a green shade.

love<br>Robert

**417**

July 29, 1968
{Buffalo}

dear Denny & Mitch,

The piece on Myth in Poetry and Religion, with the final subscript "An Essay in Essential Autobiography," took still some rewriting (of strangled sentences) and then in proof-reading an exacting attention—I employd a friend Betty Berenson who is a professional proof reader (for McGraw Hill and for the U.C. Press) to go over my own proofreading. Well, the book is

**418**

October 8, 1968
{San Francisco}

due now in a few weeks. And *Names of People*, the Stein imitations from 1952 with Jess's illustrations, is due in another week. So, there will be these in the mail soon.

Then for more than a month I have been working to derive from my extemporaneous talk (which Central Washington State College sent me in transcript from tape) into a reading matter. At first I was utterly dismayd. Surely that talk was as elliptical as ever Charles Olson's talk at the University of California conference—ominous and unfinisht sentences, hopeless shifts. I was faced straight on with having to deal with my own manic talk compulsion and to work out of it meaning and content. When I say that I've been working on it for more than a month (but it has been for two whole months and I am still on the concluding pages—since the first week in August!), a good deal of that work was brooding, self-despairing brooding in the chagrin of being more and more aware of the worst of what I had done. Then bits would begin to move in my head; I'd wake up with sentences beginning, and elations of the possibility of working, only to find that the drive disappeard by the time breakfast was done and I would undertake clearing up the accumulated litter of unwasht dishes and pans. Then would come a breakthru that would have me writing (the first session awaking at two in the morning and writing until Jess awoke; the second writing thru the night). Then brooding over the notebook version, dreading and postponing typing each session. But it has workt, the thing would labor of its own *underground*. And the essay has brought forth the fullness of feeling in which the chatter of the talk can be redeemed.

This is the talk for the conference on *Language and World Order* last Spring. The essay has the title I proposed at that time for the talk "Man's Fulfillment in Order and Strife," but it may come to another title. What emerges is how deeply I am persuaded to a vitalism—it is life that is primary and our humanity but one of the evolving modes of life. The fronts of war and, within, the same war (burning of cities, destruction of forests and resources, slaughter of resisting forces), do not seem to me *morally* wrong but true faces of what the society disowns within itself. The periods of brooding are not only brooding in the sense of incubating ["to nurse (wrath, etc." I find in the Shorter Oxford], but in the sense of a mind being in a dark cloud of trouble. The waters the Elohim brood upon were appalling.

In the last bout of typing I have got into clear draft a section in which I am thinking of our "democratic" state, and even as I workt (a line comes: "Art Thou brooding over Thy Works, Old Man?"—but this is thinking of Pound now; go away old line and come back when I am ready for you) my mind returnd to the change of our consciousness in relation to the War from "Protest" to "Resistance" to "Confrontation," as a parallel of how the individual psyche deals with unpleasant realities. We too in coming in contact with a truth protest against its existence, resist the truth, confront the truth. And deeper in this series I see that we can "admit" the truth, no longer morally superior to it, but all our being now including it, involved in it, as a condition of what is. This is what I meant Denny when I argued that the true pacifist would not oppose the war, but would go deep into the heart of it, to the reality of the front where the burning and blasting is taking place (in Jungian alchemical terms, into the nigrido) to stir up among the armies acknowledgment of what was going on. Not to make them "protest" but to awaken them to what they are doing. And in the depths of what they are doing to begin to be concernd with what is happening.

In this I am profoundly *not* Protestant. In my studies of protestant texts I admit the reality of the protest. Helen Adam is, for instance, so outraged at the injustice of Hell and the tyranny of the Judgment, that she cannot imagine Hell in other light. That it might be real, or the creative truth of our human state demand it, is an impossible consideration for her.

Certainly an example of this protesting set is shown in the difference between arguments against the war and the concern to know what is going on in the war. Rudolf Steiner in a very Blakean lecture "Luciferic and Ahrimanic Powers Wrestling for Man" portrays the Ahrimanic process as seeking to enslave the spirit of Man from his realm of consciousness in experience into an Ahrimanic realm of purely sensual-physical reality;[1] and the Luciferic spirits work to enslave Man in a realm of moral reality, where the knowledge of good and evil prevents all other realms of knowledge.

What is on my mind here is searching again for the thing at work, the creative potentiality. . . . Your confrontation, Mitch is not *against* the War but within it; bringing into the ground of What is Happening a war within the war, a multiplicity of potentialities. The individual *conscience* (not what we tend to call conscience which is a moral obsession but "conscience" in the French sense, awareness of self) takes root in the ground of war as a creative challenge.

But then I see immediately, thinking at all of the reality of that confrontation, it is not within the war but within the law that our *conscience* takes root. The dominion of the state is the realm in which your challenge is raised. We are none of us within the war, as we are within the state. So, it is not at all doctrines of pacifism that have come to us, but doctrines of civil disobedience. Freud's *Civilization and Its Discontents* and his rejoinder to Einstein *Why War?* are more relevant than—but I realize I know of no pacifist text that rings true.[2] "Peace" in any living context means only that nothing is happening—or, more, that nothing "bad" is happening.

What I object to in {Senator Eugene} McCarthy is that he posed and poses a reasonable good—as if reasonableness were in itself *good* and the passionate or emotional = bad. This is in itself an *evil*[3] doctrine; in which reason, no longer an element of our nature, could "control" the passions. So, too, Nixon poses a reasonable evil. And Humphrey is just dishonest.* Not until a passionate good seizes a man will there be a contestant to the passionate evil: and the agon of contraries move into the creative realm. Do we want or dare passionate reality? To suffer the reality of what we are? It is some hovering suspicion of what the passionate reality of Man may be, some hovering suspicion *in* me of what I have always recognized as true in the testimony of others, that darkens my brooding.

*Like Nixon he poses a reasonable evil, a "rationalized" evil. McCarthy's rationalized good is more appalling, for what does his mistrust of the passionate conceal?

•

This letter goes off into an essay yet to be, as my thought does, if it start at all. Working ahead toward the Whitman lecture I have to have written by the end of this month as well as from the World Order essay. I think I will work in the Whitman lecture along the lines of the contrary selfs at work in his poetry—the man as a personality, his "own" projected self, and the self; and both as contrasting and concerting participants in the poet.

Jess works daily; and in long runs of full light that means seven out of seven days; and it goes very slowly, as slowly as intensively. He is reading {Gertude Stein's} *The Making of Americans* with much the same delight as I had some four years ago when I finally got the unabridged version.

And our new garden is another area of preoccupation for me. In between paragraphs and in longer stretches of that brooding, I am not to be found glowering upon the deep, but vacantly weeding or digging in the earth. Our rainy season will come only too soon and take over my tasks of evening watering.

love<br>Robert

---

**419**

Oct. 10th {1968}
Temple, Maine 04984

Dearest Robert,

I haven't written since your (totally pleasurable, to us) visit here. Why? Nothing to do with you. Reasons obscure within me, which perhaps I'll try to talk about when we get to Berkeley, end of December.

I have written a lot more poems, and have thought sporadically of what you said about the poem about Nik being one which seemed to imply or demand others, a further context.[1]

The one you advised cutting I have cut, but it will appear uncut in *The Outsider* because he had set it up before I could tell him to cut it.[2] It doesn't matter—I'm glad in a way to have the *process* go on record that way (for in my next book the *short* version will of course be).

Am rather deep in David Jones, who does seem to me *very great*, having to my sense of it, and ear, all that Zukofsky has plus the warmth & humanity & humility Z so often lacks. Plus more. Why comparisons? Simply that "generation" & possible sources, "influences" etc seem in some ways parallel. Of course Z is an *American source*, himself. But for hybrid me, D. J. has a very special value in awakening, or reawakening, my own Welshness . . . a connection not to be denied or undercut but deeply welcomed. Where Z has too for me the Jewish possibility in that sense, but alienates me from it because he is of the divergence towards the rational my own ancestors rejected, seeking the new, the poetry of Hasidism, perhaps . . . (Hasidism as romance . . . for some it must have *been* that, tho' I know one can't *categorically* say it *was* that.{)}

After a quiet (externally) "productive" summer (I put it in quotes only because it is such a damn mechanical word) I'm just about to rejoin the fray—a draft-resistance conference in Pittsburgh Sat. (to which a lot of kids who worked for McCarthy & now wonder what to do next, have been invited) & readings at CCNY, Princeton, & Pace College in NY next week. Then Nov 14th I'll be at draft turn-in in NY (M. will be in Philadelphia where they expect a big action)—then a week at Stony Brook. However, this time around I hope very much to strike a better balance between "private life" and that conscience-necessary involvement than I did in the spring. It's true that after the self- neglect & externalization of the winter & spring I had a summer of almost unparalleled (for me, I mean) activity in poetry; but I don't think I can *stand* that kind of pendulum existence, it would break me, age me, faster than I can bear.

Only one of the poems I've written (besides the passage you advised cutting from that other poem) is overtly "engaged" by the way—it's about Biafra.[3]

I'm reading a good deal—some for Berkeley. We will be there by or before Jan. 1st, & Tom, Jo Miles, Al Young, & possibly others are looking out for a place for us to live. I didn't even ask you, as it must be in B'kley not in SF. But in case you have ideas, let Tom know, as he, I feel, is coordinating these efforts bless his heart.

We didn't go to Chicago—M because this book took precedence (deadline now passed—but it will be *good*)[4] and I because I couldn't cut short my visit to my mother (which incidentally was pure pleasure, I'm proud of her, she's come out from under the (unconscious, benevolent, but tyrannical) domina- tion of my father & blossomed forth (by 83) as a quite marvellous person{)}. If I live that long (which I hope I don't, however) may I have as much guts & as much humanity.

Nik has his girlfriend living with him this fall & seems happy. He's majoring in sculpture (mainly because he loathed the way painting was being taught), has a drawing teacher he *likes*, for a change (very good thing as he does need to learn to draw as he wants), & a course in Mythology he really digs. Viva.

We also didn't go to Baltimore this week to support the Berrigans etc., for much the same reasons (I was sick with a virus & M is deep in book).

Jim Harrison was to have visited right after I get back from N.Y. but now may not make it, which we regret. I expect to see Muriel, & Jay, and George Quasha in N.Y., maybe Helen too, & maybe go to a movie (ah, but *which*??) & see the frescos at the Met. (special exhibition) and buy some new clothes since I have shrunk a size, 2 sizes just about, during the summer, god be praised.[5]

*How are*[6] *you*?

With love—
Denny.

---

**420**

Thursday
10th Oct. {19}68
Temple Maine

Dearest Jess,

I can't tell you how marvellous it was to get those copies of the collage, & how pleased the recipients were. The other letter is really to you as much as to Robert but a note of thanks is very long overdue, hence this separate one.

Many owls this fall. And quite a few mushrooms too.

One of things I most look forward to is seeing you & the paintings you're working on. To the new year, then, that holds ("if we live") that pleasure.

Our well went dry but we found (& now use) a marvellous spring in the woods.

Nik did a poster for Biafran relief (no words—just the word Biafra & an almost abstract design of rows of huts & a rifle that is also a spear—black on white, silkscreen) that is really fine & strong. No signature—that's the way he is. Around 10 or 15 of them went up around Providence—we have 1 copy—the rest will probably be lost or destroyed.

I have this perennial poem with copies of poems but will bring stacks with me, end of December. Did Robert bring Mitch's poems home safely, and did you enjoy them? I hope so.

Much love—
Denny.

---

**421**

Dec. 2nd {19}68
Temple {Me.}

Dearest Robert

Rereading some old letters of yours which I'm going to let George (Quasha) look at (& then put in hands-off safekeeping—no one else is to see them unless with special permission) I realize how much I've lost of you, through my own silence, this last year or so. Out of touch as never before (tho' our brief meetings, here & at Stony Brook for a couple of hours & at the airport then, were good). First because of my being caught up, from this time last year, till June, in the maelstrom, a necessity I don't regret but dread to repeat & indeed cannot; & since June in a maelstrom of another kind, interior, of which I've not been able to write to you. It's in the many poems I've written just before & since I last saw you but I still can't get it into a letter. But I don't want to come to Berkeley without having at least written this much, to say I'm still here, still love you tho' all my letters this summer have been written to someone else. And that I'm down, way down; but still eating, drinking, cooking, laughing, & writing; and that I hope by New Year's when we get to Berkeley I'll be back in communion with you.

Mitch is beautiful & has been a staff to lean on—but I dread to lean too hard. Nik is well & happy with a quiet intelligent appreciative girlfriend (I think you saw her) & they have their own apartment now.

I have a new long poem of which part I is written but I have only disconnected fragments of what might be part II.[1]

We leave here Dec 13th (M.'s birthday) for Cambridge, Providence, N.Y., Tucson (where we'll spend Xmas in that little house I hear you didn't like; but I did, & shall be glad to be back there & show it to M for a couple of days sandwiched between the E and six months' different life in the W). We'll get to Berkeley (unless something necessitates our cutting out Tucson) in the last days of the year. I don't know if we'll be in time to spend New Year's Eve with you & Jess (do you have a party?) but we hope to celebrate yr birthday with you in any case.

Various people, of whom the most active seems to be Gail Dusenbery, whom I've never met, are trying to find us a place to live. I guess someone (Tom, principally) should have arranged a sublet with some faculty couple who're to be away this semester, way back, but no one did & we're getting a bit worried. I've not asked you, as for convenience we must be in Berkeley not in SF itself. I want to feel free to walk back & forth, talk to students at odd hours etc. However if you hear of anything please call us collect at 207-778-4031. Rent up to $200 a month if necessary (we *hope* not more!) —a "garden cottage" wd be ideal. Quiet, flea-free, & room for M to work even if I have to work in office or something. But *don't*[2] take this on as a search, please! It was to avoid embroiling you I didn't mention it before. Just if through a friend you happen to think of something. After the 12th (till the 21st) you cd reach me thru New Directions—call collect or get charges & I'll refund.

I'll show you & read you new poems when I get there.

Longing to see Jess's paintings from this year.

Well, I am in pain and sometimes don't know where to turn, as if all salt had lost its savor, but perhaps indeed my life has deepened as it has darkened.

I want to say Pray for me, but to whom.

I don't know which god has afflicted me. Is it Eros? I thought so but now I'm not even sure.

> Love—
> Denny.

---

**422**

Dec. 4, 1968
{San Francisco}

dear Denny,

It is a moment long overdue, to write to you, and your letter this morning gives me the appointment. Swiftly, however that can be—(your letter came swiftly)—to reassure you that my thoughts are with you. And a prayer (as your address "dearest" toucht me and I shied, but now a prayer for your spirit in my answering *dearest*) not to something I know, yet "to," but *from* something I know very well—the deep resources I have had in our friendship, the so much we have shared and share in what we hold good and dear for human life, and the service we would dedicate our art to. My own thought has been dark this year and in some part of it I have been apprehensive of how much more vulnerable and involved you are: I mean here about the crises of the war and then the coming-home-to-roost of the American furies. That we begin to see are the ravening furies of Western civilization. And it corresponds with our own creative generation's arriving at the phase when the furies of our own art come-home-to-roost. Denny, just as I have been carried in my work to a deeper, grander sense of the ground, I have begun to be aware of gaps and emptinesses—in my being? in the ground?—and I have now to turn next to work again on the H. D. book where I had begun to dread having to do with the inner conflicts I sensed at work there. The World Order essay, as I wrote, was written in phases of inertia, dread and break-thrus.

Does it help at all to consider that in part your affliction is the artist's? The personal pain is compounded in it.

Well, I couldn't finally speed this off. My sense that I was doing no more than identifying a brooding center in my own feeling with your inner pain halted me in my tracks. Only, this morning to find that my thought as I woke turning to you still revolved around or turnd to the concept of a phase of inner trials belonging to the destiny of the creative artist, which we as poets and artists come to, as surely as the fairy tale hero or heroine comes to some imprisonment or isolation—to dwell in the reality of how the loved thing is to be despaird of. I am thinking of the story of the forgotten bride or groom dwelling close to her or his beloved in despised form.

Only, in this fumbling, to try to say that your dread, pain, and being at a loss—personal as it must be, is also the share of each of us who seeks to deeper feeling. Not an affliction in and of itself but belonging to the pyschic metamorphosis—we cannot direct it, or, it is directed by inner orders that our crude and unwilling conscious self dreads. Eros, the primal Eros and his Other, Thanatos, work there.

Last week (November 15th!—which shows how my timing goes now) I finally got a poem which had first started June 11th—with only the opening four lines, coming into my mind as I was on the way to Berkeley one day. The poem at its inception was addressed to Jack Spicer, as often my thought returns to how I turned away from him, from the difficulties and pain of being his friend, at the time some four years before his death when he pleaded for my staying by him:

> If I had kin
> then you were one.
> I banisht you to the dark.
> You shone out like a sun.
>
> And in the hardness of my heart
> set against where otherwise
> the thot of you had grown
> I meet
> the hurt and softening of your eyes.
>
> Old fantasies?
> I think I know,
> I think I knew then
> it was from love I withheld my hand,
> not you but I
> retreated. Old
> realities.
>
> And wounded brotherhood
> survived, some good
> I could not bear or would not
> haunts my care.

Meanwhile I have at last got the start on my Whitman lecture—it will be on his vision of the meaning of America, the meaning at work in America.[1] There is a true intuition on his insistence upon the "nation," as with "soul," that can shine forth from the doubtful shadows and certain mistake of his nationalistic arrogance. Intensive reading for some months now increases if that were possible my sense of the knowledgeable perspectives of Whitman's message—he knew both the content of the inheritance of Poetry and the content of the works of his contemporaries; and clearly saw *Leaves of Grass* as the part needed by the whole. He did not come to supplant but to cooperate.

How hastily Lawrence must have read to make out the Walt Whitman he does! To miss how much Whitman's self-knowledge acknowledges and faces up to what Lawrence after the fact throws up to him.

———————

I was not sure what the address for you and Mitch would be; and I've had *Names of People* on hold for you since it came out a month ago, I guess it is. Now, in all events, I will wait until you arrive (and by that time the little Myth book will be here too). No word from Stuart Montgomery in England! Those two volumes are now a half a year delayd from May when I proofread page proofs on the first volume and galleys on the second. *The Opening of the Field* is due, Cape writes, next season.

How good it will be to have you both here in the Spring. I will ask everywhere about an apartment, cottage or house in Berkeley. Tho my "everywhere" is not on the scene, it may strike a lead.

David Bromige is applying to be your reader or teaching assistant.

A note this morning from Wendell Berry who is at Stanford again it seems—until March 15th. So, I guess I will be seeing them tomorrow.

love
Robert

---

**423**

Dec. 12th {19}68
Temple, Maine 04984

(I've often addressed letters to you as "Dearest Robert, " so I am not sure why it even for a moment bothered you, but maybe this is better?—Well, I guess I see why it did, but anyway you know what I mean.)

Very dear Robert,

Forgive me for having picked such a low point to have written to you. I'm feeling better tho' god knows I know I'll feel worse again, but *asi es la vida*.[1] And your letter is one of the reasons I *do* feel better. *Thank you*.[2]

This is to tell you Gail Dusenbery found us a place to live—it sounds O.K., & there's no lease so if we dislike it & find something better we could move after the 1st month. Tom P. put the money down on it. It's an apt., not a house—2726B, Stuart. Will arrive with suitcase full of poems, etc.

Gail was marvellous, taking it upon herself to search & find.

We leave tomorrow (M's birthday) for Cambridge, Providence etc. Will let you know as soon as we arrive. Do you have a phone this year? Well, it will be hard to let me know, as we will be in transit now—tho' if you have a moment maybe you'd send it to me at 17 Montgomery Circle, New Rochelle N.Y. c/o Bishop—we'll be there Dec 22nd

Love to Jess & to you—
Denny

# PART FOUR     1969–1988

Robert Duncan, San Francisco, 1964. Photographer unknown.

Dear Denny,

Let's just take the assumption that the true war would be a *we* as the forces of life versus a *they* (the cops, the army) as forces of death; it's one of the propositions of your title "Revolution or Death," and when you utter the word "Death" it is with the full affect of loathing. The proposition owes something to the slogan "Better Red than dead"—that meant, and very sensibly, I thought—better surrender to the enemy than die. But would any Red read the slogan to mean that? It would translate, better a police state than be dead. And assume that "life" can take hold in any political ground. As in Franco's Spain, we found the people of Bañalbafur continuing in their thousand year old continuities of life: they were relieved that Franco had refused to participate in the Second World War—their young men had been able to go on living (i.e. participating in the community's life, fishing and working in the fields, dancing and carrying on the family circles). This way of life though *had* been seriously disrupted (at its roots) by modern medical sciences{'} victories over killing diseases: the human symbiosis with the micro-organisms had been broken, and now more members of the community survived than could *belong* to the ecology of the commune. This meant the migration of young men to the cities—to Palma, but mostly to the New World, to Venezuela.

Well, surely, it is not this kind of *death* that you have in mind. Or is it? In the cosmologies of good versus evil, light versus darkness, life versus death (that Mitch calld upon in his identification of *The Movement* as life-centerd as opposed to death) disease is the prime enemy; and great evils are great *diseases*. But the imagination must have an inkling that micro-organisms of disease are life; even as man the predator must appear as evil to his meat? Are cannibals *evil* in their eating their "victims"? It might be that killing more than we eat is more understandably "evil," for in this we destroy even what we understand is our life-sphere.

Nationalism has often and still can appear to me a monstrous evil: but then I have in mind Viet Nam nationalists North and South as well as American, Israelis as well as Arabs—those who would use the actual suffering of a people in order to transform them into a Nation. When it appears a great evil that young men are driven from their tables of study and beds of love by the National conscription—I have much in mind that in *their own lives* is where they ought to be. And to be conscripted into a *Movement* is as horrible.

"Revolution" is a Nation and has its own conscriptions, its own enemies who will be tried and punished or killed, its own contempt for the presumption of the individual life, its own insistence that now is not the time for good to done but for evil to be undone.

An answer that was not "revolution" was Vanzetti's voluntary state.

424

March 25, {1969}
{San Francisco}

Volition cannot commit itself to a future agreement or covenant any more than it can bind itself to the past covenants; for it must spring afresh from the message of the here and now. When I first heard the Trotskyite slogan of "Perpetual revolution" I thought it meant this volition ever ready to spring afresh, to strike out for freedom even from the parties that carried the name on their banners.

And in the poem, tho I am given to certain themes, I am not committed to them. Where I ever feel a cause binding me, let me strike out even blindly to release what felt inbound. O.K., but this is only to say that in both ideas of State and of Poetry I would be vigilant against building a pyramid, let genius be obedient to the sunlight at the window, to the sound of the words in which what might have been a sentence is a melody, to the light in eyes (Rago quotes in his often beautiful paper printed in the current *Poetry* which arrived this morning)[1]

Who did the whole worlds soule contract, and drove
  Into the glasses of your eyes
  So made such mirrors, and such spies

—a passage, I presume from Donne, I cannot find)

I am as sure that those truly called to "Revolution" spring afresh to it. And do not subscribe to tomorrow but are in love with it today. But in history we see them settling down—the Lenins and Castros, heroes of a people's desperation, to become magistrates and managers of the lives of others. To build CUBA has its glory, a project that must force all individualities into its own (his, Castro's, own) purposes: a political construct that must postpone all immediacies to meet its quotas of sugar cane and industrial growth.

What then *is* "Life?"

Old battles against Stalinists, or earlier against my parents{'} ideas of civil obedience and duties, and against doctrines that would ask for loyalties where love would not go, flare up again in me when I hear the battle cry for our being committed to a future: the new movement in this is identical with the Establishment—"there are dark days ahead and we must all pitch in and give up on selfish interests to the common cause." "Communism" for "the Establishment" is what "the Establishment" is for "Communism"; and what the individual sees is that their claims are destitute before the heart's desires.

What I really have on my mind is that the rallying speeches that interspersed the Readings for the Presidio prisoners charged with Mutiny, tho they proclaimd themselves on the side of life, were very unlively.

March 26,

After our talk yesterday, and then rereading this letter, I realized that I had not got at at all what was the serious misuse of that Reading for the Defense of the Presidio 27. We poets were reading for that group—we had certainly not understood or consented to be reading for "The Movement," in whose program are included not only things I do not agree or consent to but that I know to be lies—that I feel in my heart to be lies. The Black racism and the class struggle I believe to be lies in the face of our common humanity.

March 31

A weekend in the country, *the* weekend that the prune orchards are in bloom, a flowery cloud over the valley, and then today *Agenda* arriving with Stuart Montgomery's beautiful translations of Odysseus Elytis:[2]

> Those things which I alone took pains to find so that I could remain my true self in the face of contempt, they will come—from the strength in the acid of the encalyptus to the rustle of a woman—to be saved in the austerity of my ark.

> From the furthest most reflected stream the only bird to come was the sparrow, and from the shabby vocabulary of bitterness a bare 2 or 3 words . . . bread . . . yearning . . . love. . . .

Mustn't we, just here where we are askt to act in terms that use the lives and freedom of the people to write their sentence and that (since these terms conscript our own volitions) confuse and trouble mind and heart, mustn't we just here refuse to act in confusion and conflict? "The Movement" abuses the lives of its members, wherever it lays claim to absolute authority and shows contempt for or "tolerance" of the individual life. We've certainly to ask with Elytis "What are those things . . . so that *I could remain my true self* ". . . .

love
Robert

Dearest Robert

Still no opportunity to answer your letter about "the movement" life or and "life and death" etc. Not lack of care to, but just literally no time. But while you're in Kansas, I'll *make* time. Meanwhile, here's the "Alphabet" poem & one other.[1] Show the "Alphabet" to George {Quasha} if you like it now that it seems to be done, but not if you don't. Show him the other anyway—Melanie is his dog.

I received a wedding announcement written out in Trinidad's hand. I have been unable to imagine whether she sent this out of stupidity or spite (or both). I cannot believe George was aware she sent it.

I was at Colorado Springs yesterday & the day before & Brother Antoninus was also there. I was happy to get to know him a little. I told him how upset I'd been at his NYC reading a few years back & he very

## 425

April 26th {19}69
{Berkeley, Calif.}

genially defended his aggressive approach to the audience. I was not convinced but liked him anyway.

It feels strange to be here with you gone so far away—though I've been able to spend so much less time with you here, nevertheless you've been a presiding presence. I hope you're having, so far, a good trip. Are you, I wonder, staying in that terrible motel where I was so lonely & unhappy? I hope Stony Brook is making better use of your presence than they did of mine. Quite aside from my personal troubles while I was there, I've never been anywhere where my visit was so mismanaged & where I was treated with such coldness & neglect, it was really incredible. If it hadn't been for a grad student, Michael Lopes, & his wife I would have actually been left hungry & without transportation several times.

I found a wonderful essay on Chardin by Proust with which I'm going to introduce WCW to my 108 class—for it is precisely that Chardinesque quality of *illumination of the ordinary* that was my own first introduction to Williams.[2]

The day you left SF I went down to Pomona & had dinner with John Martin & his wife. They were awfully nice.

On my return flight yesterday from Colorado I had wonderful views of the mountains.

Love from
Denny.

---

**426**

May 1, 1969
{San Francisco}

Dear Denny,

Before I get into the "Alphabet," but having glanced at the dedication after the passage from Zimmer, and taken joy in being "R. who read me" (R. for "reader" too!), I want to write this morning, just to write. Don't press yourself to *make* time to answer my letter about the Movement—so much of my writing then must present confusion. For my life-center is so very different: the Movement, the War, the little and dwindling company sworn to non-violent action, the soldiers and citizens not wanting to know the truth of what they are doing, and the enthusiasts of panic—for us as poets—must be read deep into. Mostly I do not advance beyond the confines of my outrage at the War; I have yet to study out and raise an adequate picture in my mind of what has gone on in Vietnam. The origins of the Cao-Daï I did seek out; but I don't want to *know* what I am sure is mostly likely that there are further complicities there. As now I come across reminders that out of the administrations of Adams and Jefferson came orders to "Extirpate the Indian". . . . And this not to wander into that "selva oscura," but only to indicate that wherever my thought approaches the political actualities it as in a dark wood. And my spirit leaps up at Whitman's each man his own law; which is also

Vanzetti's: the volitional politic is NOT a movement, not, I am sure, in this light, a commitment but a freedom. Blake, whose annotations to Lavater's aphorisms I am reading as a bed side book here,[1]

dear Denise and Mitch,

A long overdue note—and it had better be today or it will have to wait for ten days. I am thinking you will be in Temple for sure, and it is good to think of that release from the unremitting engagements of your period here (and, I imagine, wherever you are *publicly*).

Well, in the light of that conflagration (or, more it seems a smouldering, before its conflagration), my own spirit turns to the watry way of Lao-tse.

Jess has finisht the figure of the Operation—which is clearly also an alchemical operation; and in his emblematic associations it is the torso of the Egyptian Nut, the sky. And he is at work concurrently on the Creation *Fiat Lux* figure from Fludd, and on the mushroom forest illustration from *Etidarpha*—a psychedelic trip scene.[1]

In a swift sequence of days, starting with an X-ray to determine whether I had some arthritis of the spine, and including—while they were at it—a check-up X-ray of the chest to see how the heart is doing, the radiologists found a spot on my left lung; four days of consultations and some thirty more X-rays of the left lung calibrated the spot and this afternoon I enter Mt. Zion hospital to have my chest opened for a biopsy. If it is, as it seems likely to all accounts to be, cancer, they will remove the lower half of my left lung. The whole thing started with a spraind right arm, an irregularity in reflexes (which called for looking at the spine)—a very lucky sprain, indeed, if it proves to be cancer in the lung. For the area, at this point, is no larger than 0 and not beyond the one spot.

The unhappy aspect is that the biopsy calls for the same drastic operation (opening the rib-cage) as the lung removal. Dr. Burstein projects a matter of ten days in the hospital. Luckily, the provisions of my mother's will in setting up the Trust Fund provide for just such emergencies. Or Jess and I would be in straits to cover the some $2500 estimated at this point for the whole thing.

As soon as I come to enough to write, I will.

This last week I have spent much time working in the garden, and reading in the garden house—the sunny afternoon hours, the almost smoky heat (which by yesterday had closed down with fog again in the morning) bring back earlier gardens—and an intense sense of what an empty bag of psychological, social, political drama we waste over years of divorce from Earth in. But even then, from the beginning, the demands of family, old battlefields and marriages of minds, contended with "being with it."

**427**

July 2, 1969
{San Francisco}

It is not a phenomenon of our time but of our species.

––––––––––

That was a lovely session, Denise, here with you reading the "Alphabet" poem (it was the letters of the Alphabet I had in mind in *Letters*)—still haunting. My mind returns to wonder over the "hut" you have yet to go back to, the poem says. Isn't that poem a central statement of the life-myth you speak of in your essay on "Myth and Poetry"? You are very much on a journey, a life-way. As perhaps, I am in a life-scene or place. The contrast *does* seem too ready. It must be no more than a passing impression or hint; yet to be grounded.

I got the Whitman essay done finally—that was two weeks ago, I guess—or some ten days. It needed redoing five pages even at the last. But to begin at all on the essay needed a massive attack on the transcript of my "talk."

After which I feel more and more I shld return to the by-the-paragraph construct I use in the second Part of the H. D. (and also, in that piece in the *Journal for the Protection of All Beings*).[2] I have now to begin preparing notes for the three weeks' session at Central Washington this Fall. Maybe there I will be able to test along the line of the composite of sections development.

Lunch time already! and then we've to go to the hospital by 3. I stay over there tonight before the operation tomorrow.

love
Robert

## 428

Dearest Robert

Your letter came this morning. You are a brave man. I love you very much. Your words are serene and strong. I am terrified—but by now the doctor must know if it's cancer or not & I pray it is not. But if it is, thank god for the strange accident that revealed the spot in time.

Jess must be—or have been—or must *still* be even if only the biopsy had to be done—terribly anxious. I'm writing to him too.

I felt strange about leaving California without more of a farewell than a perfunctory one at the party that night, but the 3 days that followed were full of students—classes on the Mon., conferences solidly from noon till 7 pm Tues., & packing on Wed. (with some kids helping deliver borrowed objects back to their owners)—& besides I didn't like to say goodbye. (*Especially* on the telephone!) Even though, with my busyness & your absence in the E., I didn't see you as much as I'd hoped—& Jess even fewer times—3 in all!— still, the time spent with you was very special & happy & I felt it *contained* more than the same amount of time spent with you in N.Y. or somewhere where you don't feel at home.

We liked Berkeley (& Calif. in general) so much that we definitely plan to return if we can in a couple of years. In fact if it were not for Temple we would probably try to move to the W. Coast.

We've been in transit ever since leaving & only arrived here on the 1st (so your letter—& your going into the hosp.—occurred on the 1st whole day we spent here.) The house & country are looking beautiful & it was a deep pleasure to rediscover it.

I will think about the "hut" to revisit, that you recall is in the "Alphabet" poem. Thank you for speaking of it.

My infatuation or enchantment with G.{eorge} Q.{uasha} is *really* over, & you know what?—It lasted, I realized yesterday, a year & a day, just as in the fairytales.

You will really like our new dwelling in E. Boston I think—it's 3 floors of an old bayfronted brick house & the landlords are artists & friends & there are 2 lovely cats, Kittycat and Blue. I hope you *and* Jess will visit us there. I won't write more now, even this much is probably more than you can take at the moment. But will write again soon & we'll call the hospital to see if we can get a report of your condition.

> Love always,
> ~~Denise~~ Denny and Mitch

Dearest Jess

(Robert took exception to my using . . . "est" once but I know why & how I'm doing it: you are both *dear to us* and *unique*.) You must be distracted by anxiety—*I hope*, though, they may have had good news from the biopsy?—and if not it is certainly very lucky to have found the spot so soon. . . .

One line, when you have 5 minutes, will give us some relief from the uncertainty. Meanwhile, know that Mitch & I are both thinking of you & Robert very much. If Robert is able to read it here's a letter for him—maybe you cd read it to him.

In haste to catch mail.

> *Love*[1]
> Denny

**429**

{July 1969}
Temple, Maine 04984

dear Denny & Mitch

Yesterday was not bad but this is the first day I have written anything, and this as I go is that anything. The growth was not malignant and it was a very small area of lung so all I am recovering from is that smallest of losses of tissue from the lung, and, unfortunately, the incision which took some six

**430**

July Mon.
{7–8, 1969
San Francisco}

inches of rib and made a boundary of pain I have been living at since they operated Thursday morning. Not a set boundary but one that day by day amazingly progresses from pain that exceeded whatever boundary and flooded into me, to a second day pain that waited at a weak and unsure boundary to invade wherever I touched the line.

Those two days flow together. Days of intravenous feeding, and another tube from the incision in my back (the cut running under my left arm to just under the left nipple) to clear the chest cavity of blood. But Friday they must have taken the tubes out. Thursday (the day of the operation) and Friday flow together because the pain that was there those days belongs to an age of its own.

Saturday and yesterday were days of beginning to moving, to walk—I have to keep my torso erect and straight. Any twist brings a prohibitive stab, but it is no longer the primeval pain at the boundary. This new one is the pain of a broken bone or a bruise or sprain. And my recovery seems to be very rapid. Today I've spent this morning episodically—washing, walking the round of the hospital floor, sitting, reading (Mann's *Confessions of Felix Krull*, a happy choice for hospital reading—I have just finisht the beautiful section of Kuckuck's dissertation on Nothingness, Being, Life, and Man where the charm of form belongs to the episodic—what begins and ends. As—true to today's episodic composition there was an end and a beginning just before the name Kuckuck at the bottom of the last page. For Dr. Burstein arrived for his daily check. It seems quite possible I may go home Wednesday morning!

Well, I was not, after all, ill; so that I had every readiness of a body in good order to meet the operation.

Tues. 8th

I am immensely better today. My thoughts are, as the jargon of the new generation aptly puts it, very much with it—tho I tire. Now Jess has arrived for an early afternoon visit and brought your letter. I want to write more about what I have experienced here, sharing a room with Angelo who is not only in pain but sick, and my mind searching over all I have ever known of sickness to wonder what it is that is going on. Experience returns this week with the special vividness of "recovery."

Well, Denny, I look forward to your letter. And I know you will be happy to hear here from me how very well it has been going since last Wednesday.

love
Robert

P.S. (at P.O. down the street): Tomorrow Robert will be home by 10 of the morning—Dr. Calliner the surgeon came in just as I was leaving & checkt his state—of the very best considering. Thanks so much for yr. loving extra letter for me—Robert must have spoken in passing jest, for he and I know we are all of us together & apart Dearest to one another, dearest Denny & Mitch. I so misst having easy days with you this past hectic season, but that will come in its good time. The garden here is blooming with one of the noble artichokes spreading its crown—I feel almost cannibal toward the others in tow. It is good news to hope toward your return to the coast in a year or two. I doubt that I shall find it in me to travel until the big "Narkissos" painting reaches completion (& that's not started yet)—the final 4 paintings of the Translation group are in the midst now.

Keep well & happy, with love

Jess

Most dear Robert,

**431**

July 8th {19}69
Temple, Maine

    I'm waiting suspended between fear & the faith that you are all right. My *feeling* is not of dread—that, the anxiety, is almost intellectual. But I can't *trust* my feeling that, though ill, you're not *desperately* ill, until I've had some news. We'll try calling Barbara Joseph tonight.

    What you wrote—"You are very much on a journey, a life-way. As perhaps, I am in a life-scene or place. The contrast *does* seem too ready. It must be no more than a passing impression or hint; yet to be grounded."— reminded me of your:

> I am on the road, by the road,
> hitch-hiking. And how, from one side,
> how glad I am no one has come along.
> For I am at a station. I am at home
> in the sun. Not waiting, but standing here.
> And, on the other, I am waiting,
> to be on the way, that it be *my* way.
> I am impatient.[1]
>
>    . . .

I love that poem, which inherits from Whitman & from Lawrence & makes that inheritance so much your own.

    The Carruths were here for the weekend & got a bad case of food poisoning which of course was attributed—by the doctor anyway!—to mushrooms. However, I too had eaten them & had no symptoms whatsoever; & they were a boletus of the safest most identifiable variety. . . . But since there was nothing at all that *only* they had eaten it remains a mystery—& I don't suppose they will venture a boletus again!

    Prospects for repairing "their" house—the one whose roof caved in from the winter's exceptional snows—look better than we had supposed.

By the way, did you see the review of *Bending the Bow* (a fine one, I thought) which Hayden wrote in *Hudson R.* last year?[2] When you are better will you let me have a copy of the Whitman essay?

What do you mean exactly by "the composite of sections development" you say you'll test out at Central Washington? It follows your speaking of writing "by-the-paragraph" in the 2nd part of H.D. bk. So I presume you mean something like letting each paragraph give rise to the next as the lines of a poem do to one another; but I wondered what you meant to do at Central Washington, what "testing" you mean? And also, did the Whitman essay then have a much more predetermined structure?

I realize it may be weeks before you feel up to answering such questions. . . .

Sent my Mss (60 poems, I found there were—*after* weeding!) to Jay, who so far has read ½ & sounds enthusiastic. I also sent a xerox to Al Gelpi for an independent opinion as I wondered if it was unbalanced as a book & thought a non-poet who hadn't read most of the poems before wd. have a useful response. And he felt it was OK too—in fact he raved. So I feel reassured. I always have conniptions about new books. So far I've not decided on a title—*Relearning the Alphabet, Red Snow,* & *Earth Dust* are 3 I'm considering, what do you & Jess think?[3]

A small plump woodchuck just bustled down the path, evidently bent on {illegible}

Love—<br>D.

---

dear Denny & Mitch,

The "Spock" decision was discusst on "Newsroom," so we realize a new appeal must be under way. I hope that can go on without interrupting the Temple time of year. It was delightful, Denny, to have bits of your country in the last letter.

I still have discomforts enuf to remind me I am convalescent, but aspirins have replaced codeines, and itches and ouches have replaced knife-stabs and moans.

July 15—How our few songbirds here in the midst of the city rescue the morning. What was not so long ago an ordeal of washing and then at a later time shaving goes straight thru now almost happily. And Jess has washt my back and I am writing in the sleepy aftermath with my knees drawn up. Yesterday I arranged the mirrors in the bathroom and saw for the first time that the incision does not stop at my waist but goes diagonally across to a mid-point between my shoulder blades. Well, I wonder how I did think they got at the lung as it is—thru a kind of letter-slot running under my arm? It's at the back they could get to the lung clearly, and these days (it's that that made for my trying to see what was going on, the incision below the breast and the left arm has grown tame enuf that the back begins to claim its major attentions. Late this afternoon I go to have the stitches removed.

The periods are longer for thought and reading. I am reading—it must be for "the tenth time," as my mother used to say "I've told you for the tenth time"—Porphyry's *On the Cave of the Nymphs*—and, at last, partly because I read it between bouts of weariness but much because it reads now close indeed to my underlying phantasies of my body's reweaving, and I find myself conversant most with the drama of this incorporation, enblooding, enfleshing, enboning—it comes to me as a first reading, an i at last! I can read experience.[1]

———

Years ago, back in 1939 or 1940 when I was first gathering mushrooms, I remember in a New York State pamphlet (really a book sized publication) there was considerable caution about the edible Boletus, with some mycologists advancing the theory that individuals of the species are poisonous. Yet my *Field Book of Common Mushrooms* says quite clearly that "Any boletus which does not turn blue when cut or broken, has not orange-colored or red tube-mouths and is mild to taste (they are thinking here of the fact that some boletus are bitter) may be safely eaten."[2] I've never been able to find since that New York State bulletin the dark suspicions of the boletus that I rememberd there. But a couple of years ago up near Ham and Mary's {Tyler} in Healdsburg a man and his wife, experienced mushroom hunters, became violently ill after boletus. And there is the possibility that some people are allergic to mushrooms.

Jess will mail this on his way out to shop.

Love
Robert

Dear Robert and Jess

Some sign of our joy & relief is long overdue. But having un-wound at last I'm slack, floppy, & negligent & just didn't get around to writing down how GLAD we are. Incredible sense of relief. *Thanks*[1] for letters.

All's well here—even possibility of Mitch's having to face being retried all over again doesn't disturb us, & somehow (speaking for myself) I'm managing to be happy and—for the moment—lazy, without feeling guilty about it.

Will write soon.

Love—
Den

## 433

{late July, early
August 1969
Temple, Me.}

Am reading Valery Larbaud's *Diary of A. O. Barnabooth* (he's the guy in Pere Sebastian Râsles section of *In the American Grain*—also he wrote lots of poems about trains). Also read *The Golden Apples* by Eudora Welty,[2] a discovery to me—a real writer—she speaks of night in one passage— a particular summer night—as "a beast in gossamer." I'm cooking deliciously, lots of vitamins, resting, recharging. Please give my love to Barbara Joseph.

---

**434**

Aug. 19th {19}69
{Temple, Me.}

Dear Robert & Jess

How are you? Isak wrote that he met you (R) at Bolinas which was reassuring.[1] Saw Bob & Bobby in Cambridge a week ago—such a good meeting! Very happy occasion. I found *Pieces* full of gists, openings, stimuli.[2]
The tiger lilies are pouncing & purring today.

Love—
Denny

---

**435**

August 29th 69
Temple, Maine

Love to Jess.

Dear Robert,

Are you all right?
I haven't felt like writing letters myself lately, so I well understand if you haven't either. But feel a bit worried in case there's been some other trouble in the aftermath of yr hospital experience. Send a p.c.

Love—
D.

---

**436**

Sept. 3, 1969
{San Francisco}

Dear Denny,

I'm back in full swing. With all my resolve not to get caught in commitments, I find myself with a Preface to do for a book of Charles's lectures on history from Black Mountain 1956;[1] and another for a collection of my own Poetry Center Notes. And my three weeks course to run at Central Washington State College (beginning Sept. 27th), so that I am assigned to a preparatory run of the texts gathering notes and anticipations of content. In the midst of all which working in the garden again is blissful. And some monitory dreams have begun (tho the second, with episodes of joy coming after great anxiety and fear)—climbing a tree whose topmost precarious branches prove to be rooted in the sky and to lead *down* into a world above of green fields, not my destination but a way station, with high mountain passes beyond—

Yes, *Pieces* came, for me too, at a time when its range and freedom in composition had (has) [will have yet more] impact. Bob told me it was the first book he has felt as a book. For me, the most liberating force of it is that incorporating great poems like "Numbers" and "The Finger" it as fully incorporates writing writing. Not as scraps and notes, but as in total the environment of the poetry.

One of those intensive full days of house cleaning interrupted this letter; yesterday's being a foggy overcast morning, Jess started vacuuming. And I set about oven scrubbing and (alternating) loads of laundry. We almost look up-to-the-city-sanitation-requirements at this point. Ending in a massive assault on stacks of mail unsorted and accumulating books.

A passage from an Italian art historian might suggest an extension of notes on organic form: ". . . though Art Nouveau did move towards a certain essentiality and synthesis of forms, they were not sought for as values in themselves; this was to be the preoccupation of the early 20th century. In the *fin-de-siècle* period, functional sobriety resulted from a striving for harmony with 'nature' or some other vaguely defined entity which was held to constitute part of human experience. . . . " The tone of "vaguely defined" and "held to constitute" betrays that the author's modernist functional bias is deeper than his tolerance allows—he sounds like W. C. Williams on the subject of Whitman. But the principle of the contrast—the utilitarian and functionally aimed art [as Williams proposes for poetry in the Preface to *The Wedge*]—as contrasted with the biological or cosmological art—does extend further than the art historian realizes.[2] "Whereas the early 20th century conceived of man as an autonomous being able to plan rationally in order to avoid injury by elements outside his control, Art Nouveau artists believed in a humanity convinced of its heteronomy, of the necessity to enter into a mystical harmony with what was other than oneself."

For us what the art historian sees as "a striving for harmony" or "to enter into a mystical harmony" is *process*, and a process not mechanical but creative and formal. H. D. used to talk about getting the *formula* for something.

It's part of it that along with the revival of the flower and tendril forms of Art Nouveau came Flower Power and the Flower children.

Maine too will be having Indian Summer I presume. The garden is wonderful now. Flourishing new growth on the artichoke plants. And a smokey dreamy warmth. And I have happily caught up with weeding. Three weeks away this Fall shld not throw me much off course.

Nothing at this point committed for next year. Maybe it will be a writing year. The gods and muse willing.

Love
Robert

**437**

{October 29, 1969
Boston. Mass.}

Dear Robert & Jess,

When's that show of Jess's in N.Y.? Are you (1, both) coming E.? When? Cd. probably arrange an MIT reading, Robert, but wd. have to have at least a full month's notice & wd not have any funds to bring you from Calif.— just if you were in the E. anyway. Let me know. All's well here, except that M. is feeling pretty tired & rundown somehow & Nik is up for trial on a political charge. Our place here is great. And I like my new job.[1] We're going to Maine for weekend.

Much love—
Denny

**438**

Nov. 10, 1969
{San Francisco}

dear Denny,

If I did not get a reply off to you after your last postcard, let me answer straight off now your questions. Jess's show has been postponed until Spring. Quadrani will be here this week and I guess the actual date will be set then. But Jess is still firm about not coming East. The time-schedule on his projected paintings is a full-time schedule.

Out of the blue an invitation came last week to participate in a Poetry Festival at Austin, Texas the weekend of the 20th–22nd this month. Not a giant one. But it will be the greater oppportunity to meet Octavio Paz and Borges.[1]

Right now, as I write, I am monitoring a tape of my reading of my own work at Central Washington. To my hearing my reading goes too far towards the dramatic and shld benefit from shedding that surcharge. Pound's Spoleto record is a beautiful model of *delivering the meaning direct, not directed.*[2] And at this particular reading, by the time I came to the third week I was reading to an audience that I was *with* and that was *with me.* Even at that ease I am still there between the poem and its audience (as if they were *my* audience and not the poem's—but that, of course, is what we tend to hear: the poet rather than the poetry).

Ronald Bayes wrote me over a month ago to ask if I would consider reading a Southern circuit, and I have replied at last to see if it could be workt out with a minimum fee of $300 and expenses.[3] If that shld work out for the Spring, I'll know I would guess in the next month and maybe we can work out an extension to get to Boston. I would, of course, very much want to have it coincide with the possibility of getting to New York for Jess's show.

You must be in the very midst of the fray again with M.I.T. up in arms—and how important it will be if that most culpable sector—the "scientists"—can come to be *con*scientists. Bob wrote me news of it when

Nik was arrested —it was amidst my work with my class at Ellensberg. And I found myself praying that nothing would happen to any of them during that Moratorium three days. Nothing did, of course. But I had seen how much I dreaded an immediate knowledge of the outrage sufferd by so many of their generation.

> And from the coercion of a generation,
>   from the now more than thirty thousands
>     of American youths
>   fed into the maws of that Minotaur
>     who howls in the depths of the Pentagon
>   from the isolation chambers and torture rooms
>     of Federal prisons
>   from the immediate contempt for the people daily
>   I take my esthetic distance.

Well, not "esthetic"—it's the same distance I wld declare (as in "An Animadversion") from the agony. And can't manage.[4]

What is the toll of Vietnamese lives?

Writing at the kitchen table has its hazards. As above. Next time, Denny, send yr. Boston address.

Love
Robert

dear Denny & Mitch,

This is one of the first draft copies I did on the Christmas card. After making about eight, every time wondering "how come *zählen* means hear?" I came to the point where that couldn't be and lookt it up—"to count"— but my working draft had "count" too. . . . Then, along the line of copying and feeling thru the poem some twenty-five times so far, I have made the following adjustments:[1]

line 1: for "will" read "control"; I have in mind that the "willkürlich" of
    Rilke's "Unwillkürlich" means "despotic"
line 2–3:
        at times there stands forth existing
        the full Face from the Profile,
      [the best I can manage with his
                          das runde
        seinde Gesicht]
    "seinde" is the existentialist participle, Heidegger's home ground, along
    with *Dasein*

line 4: an alternative to "all there" (which I liked in its recall of "all clear")
   now is "complete," which gives me a rime with "beat" (below)
line 5:
   which starts up the beat and strikes to a close.
   "starts up the beat" I tried in order to suggest Rilke's word "anhebt"
   which can mean to "strike up (a song)" and which seemd nearer his
   meaning than to "prime a pump" or "jack up a car"
line 6: for "hear" read "count"
line 7: "they do not mark": not in this case to avoid "mark not" but in
   order to enforce the ū of "dour" along the line of the "do"
line 8:
   "gloomy with earning a living, with the living dour
line 12: strike out the word "own"

When I went to write in the date on Rilke's poem, I noted it was Lammas,
so very much my "turn of the Year"

---

Our very best, our love and wishes for the very best for both of you, and
for Nik. Do send news once the busyness of the holidays has cleard. As soon
as I decorate its title page in colors, I have a letterd copy of *Achilles Song* for
you. Diane di Prima pirated a little book of mine in her poet's series, after
we had come to quits on the proposition: but now, I have done the book as
I wanted to with Julia Newman at Tenth Muse and that too may be on its
way before the first of the year.

Jess has finisht the mushroom forest painting and the *Fiat Lux*—and
started on the Icarus, which he hopes to have in a state to show in April or
May.[2] I seem to be in a long unripe, if not dry, period. But currently I am
keeping a dream journal, a *task*, but it's *there* that I know I have to get my
roots going, and where I hope "the other tree" will grow. The translation of
"The Child" grows out of another assignment I have made myself, to read
(and that means translate) thru the *Neue Gedichte*. I've done the first six, and
a first reading of the seventh. German, so long dormant, since my studies in
1949–50, is beginning to come back. And these particular poems of Rilke
so adverse to my idea of the poem, this ingrown poetry, growing into its
confines against its own natural form—like crystals growing within a
geode—sets me to work without infecting my own work. I am not likely
to pick up this kind of Rilke. Whereas the Duinos would swamp me out at
this time.

How long it's been since I've written you—these times eat us up. And
there seems so much to write.

love
Robert

Dear Robert & Jess

   The longer it gets the harder it is to write because I feel as if I owe explanations of why I *haven't* written & that paralyzes me. I'll try to make them brief.

   We moved to Boston in Sept & I began teaching at MIT &, just as at Berkeley, immediately became very much involved with my students and with various political actions. Under these circumstances I find the only way to not get exhausted & despondent (from fatigue) is to deal with each day's people & events as they come up & more or less ignore letter writing. I manage to get an enormous amount of work done this way, i.e. I do not neglect my own work, even including some lectures & other prose com-mitments. I also manage to keep cooking pretty imaginative meals (good Italian groceries here) & to give my students all the attention they deserve (which is plenty) but at the price of neglecting my distant friends. It's not an ideal solution but it's the only one I've been able to work out for myself. I do write some letters—answers to people who really need (or are asking for) answers to specific questions, & letters to people in jail, & to my mother. But that's about it, except for "business" letters & I'm not too efficient about that.

   However, there's an additional reason why I haven't written to you lately & that is that since the last *Stony Brook* came out with your (Robert) attack on Hayden Carruth I've felt I had to write about it & haven't until now mustered time & energy to do so.[1] Since you know how much I love & admire you (& *for how long*), dear Robert, I hope I can speak to you about this without incurring your wrath. I feel it was an attack not only factually unjustified and quite disproportionately contentious, but humanly a very thoughtless & cruel act. If you listened more attentively than you sometimes do (you *can* listen wonderfully, but often you don't) you wd. have recalled, I think, things that I had told you about Hayden—that he had had a long illness—some of it spent in a mental hospital & most in a room alone in his parents' house from which he was only able to emerge at night occasionally for a solitary walk—that then he came slowly back into the world, Jay L{aughlin}. providing a sort of ½-way house for him, where he met Rose Marie (who was working as nursemaid to Ann Laughlin's sisters' kids) & they married & went to live in Vermont. He has never since his breakdown been able to face groups of people (for instance when I read at Middlebury in Jan. & they drove over, he had to leave the auditorium almost at once) but he manages to make a living one way & another, sometimes by manual labor & sometimes by writing— scientific ghost-writing, reviews, etc. Rose Marie used to work in the diner. Now that little David is in school R-M is going to school so that she can eventually teach handicapped children. All this has little to do with your attack, you'll say—but what I'm trying to do is remind you of things I know I have mentioned before, so you know *who* it is you were attacking instead of Hayden being an abstraction to you. It was the Carruths who were to have moved to Temple to the house up the road to be our neighbors, except that the damage to the house & then some other circumstances squashed that plan. Hayden was also the guy who wrote a really beautiful piece about your work in *The Hudson Review* a couple of years back.[2] Now, if I read what seemed to me to be a put-down or something of William Carlos Williams or E P by someone I knew to be a dear & trusted friend of *yours*, & whom I knew to be someone who had had a severe breakdown & who therefore might be more sensitive to angry criticism than average, I believe I would at least take the trouble to document that person's critical record in regard to Williams etc., ask you "What gives with this guy?" and write to him personally to begin with—not just launch out into a public attack on him without warning. In fact as J. can tell you (with ample evidence) Hayden has always cared deeply for Wms & Pound & knows a lot more than average about their work. I don't have *Stony Brook* here (I lent it out) so I can't remember what exactly it was that you picked on but when I read it I was convinced that it was almost certainly a misunderstanding, misinterpretation on your part and in any case was the kind of thing one writes personally about, to argue, not makes a strident public issue out of (as one cd. very justifiably do—with some unequivocally sneering, ignorant comment). I don't mind yr picking on Adrienne Rich because she's a tough woman & perhaps actually deserves it anyway—my point is that if you'd paid any heed when I spoke (many times) about Hayden, you'd have guessd how much it might hurt him, & wd have refrained. Moreover, I think to pretend you don't know who he is & refer to him as "Mr. Carruth" (or something like that) in a sort of "whoever this upstart chap may be" tone, when you knew perfectly well he was a close friend of ours & that he had reviewed your books so warmly, was just silly. I *don't* mean I think the right hand shd wash the left & that you (or any of us) shd refrain from adverse criticism of our favorable critics! What I *do* mean is that the whole thing was unnecessary and insensitive. I'll enclose Hayden's response. He is a courageous man who wages a continual battle with depression & insomnia—he has humor & vigor & persistence, & most of the time he wins—but it is hard, he lives more than most of us on a knife edge.

Now Robert, I am risking a great deal in writing you this letter. You know you are a major person in my life & I cannot endure the thought of your being angry with me—but I cannot *not* write it & keep my self-respect, and I must trust that your friendship, our friendship, can admit this reproach. I was about to write to you when I heard of Olson's illness (when you called me) & of course I could not speak of it at a time of such sorrow for you.

Jess, this letter is so largely addressed to Robert but I think you'll want to discuss with him what I am saying. I think there are 2 parts to the issue: (1) if a public attack is to be made, its justification shd be more carefully considered & documented, a private letter considered as alternative, & its *tone* be commensurate with the supposed evil being attacked.

(2) If the person whose statement is being attacked is someone you have reason to believe is vulnerable beyond the ordinary, & is a good friend of a friend, the whole project (I believe) shd be discussed first with that friend so that you make sure you're not doing him (the attacked one) a real injury. These seem to me to be principles or guidelines not in this case only but in similar situations. Surely one has to ask oneself, am I doing more personal harm than pedagogic good by making such an attack? Is it necessary and is it humane?

In a separate envelope I'm sending you *Relearning the Alphabet*—advance copies just arrived. With my love, as ever.

I have quite a few more poems too & will try to xerox & send.

Oh—alas, I think a reading at M.I.T. is definitely *not possible* now. I held out funds as long as I could but am not really officially in charge of readings, & other faculty have their own ideas, e.g. Mark Strand (ugh!)—everybody & his uncle. So, I'm really sorry, but it is too late now, all the $ is allocated. When is yr NY show going to be, Jess? If I possibly can I'll go down to see it. And Robert, please write as soon as you can and don't be angry but come to East Boston if possible if you come E. for the show.

I know you must miss Charles.[3]

Love
always—Denise

dear Denny,

Your reproach re. my "Critical Difference of View" is quite justified. In any account I could give of from what my high handed polemic sprang the fact remains that it was "disproportionately contentious"—what must be saddest to relate is that I raised the question with myself as to whether I ought to rewrite the whole eliminating all reference to Carruth or Adrienne Rich (beyond quoting the two passages that had enraged me)—I did not have in mind Hayden Carruth's sensitivities and vulnerabilities (for one thing his tone in the review of Tomlinson set the high-handed tone which I took up with a sledge-hammer) tho I certainly did know and was aware that you and Mitch were fond of him, and I have never had the sense that that friendship did not have very real grounds. It doesn't mitigate my offense here that I was not attacking Hayden in his personal life where I should have had a sense of his vulnerability (for you had told me of his alchoholism

## 441

Feb. 26, {19}70
{March 17–18, 1970
San Francisco}

and his courage in making a new life for himself ) but I was attacking him in his criticism where he, charged by a hostility towards Tomlinson, expanded his charge to say of Dr. Williams's tercets that the form was "his alone, one hastens to say": well, at that red flag the bull in me faces all over again the fight against those who would allow that Williams had an idiosyncratic style that was O.K. for him; and who would then go on to insist: "I tried, without success, to think of a single self-respecting American poet who had *dared* to copy this form, at least for more than a poem or two." Them was fighting words, and they still rankled so that my rancor in my reply read five years later was still invidiously backd up by my still ready dislike of the concentrated impression of the passage.

I had never read any of Carruth's critical work, except in passing—and certainly I had written him that his review in *Hudson* was most encouraging; my piece reveals my utter ignorance of his other writing on Williams. But even if he had written nothing on Williams, that one not only high-handed but out-of-hand sentence of mine " . . . that neither Mr. Carruth nor Miss Rich had or have any great concern for the poetry of Pound or of Williams" is indefensible and by that time my scoring points and rescoring points in an imaginary debate has led me to the full wretchedness of the unscrupulous debater's closing remarks.

I can't undo the grievous human situation. That passage of his still gets underneath my skin. The "his alone, one hastens to say" hits on my own fanatical sore-spot about them tercets as a viable form not an individual style; and the following remarks about Williams tending towards the pentameter hits on old wars about the measure—where these come up I am intolerant; and that means not only ungracious but also to some degree deaf and in the refusal to imagine the terms of what is opposed—stupid.

But I can and owe it to the truth of the situation {to} criticize myself, calling attention to the distortions and projections that enter along the lines of the polemic address in which one fabricates the enemy and launches the attack. Elements of this certainly enter in to passages I have written on Elizabeth Drew (whom I saw as a particularly prejudiced school-marm), and on Robin in the Nerval essay where I had to imply and project much of his intent.[1]

I'll send on the critique on my polemic as soon as I get it done. Hayden's letter certainly gives me a vivid sense of how hurt he is and when he feels it all in an attack of self-loathing it is terrible and pitiable.

Don't forgive me, Denny, for what I have done in this—that anyway I know is not what you are writing about. Jess says it was my high blood pressure—. . . . well, that may account for the writing of the piece in 1964, but what is at issue in my mind is that in 1969 I decided on sending it to Stony Brook. And the underlying streak of going out for the kill in critical attack has been detected at other times. Evidently I view the arena of criticism as open season.

March 17/

The writing of this letter was so vividly present—and that I wanted to return with a perspective after a few days—that I had no idea almost three weeks had passt! This morning at last, other work having cleard (a Preface for Grossinger's *Ecological Sections*, which meant an intensive week of reading all of Grossinger's published work again—except for the poetry;[2] and two readings to present "Passages" to date, with prefaces discussing the form and performance of the poem) I have a morning to write a piece "Reflections on the Mode of Literary Polemics" (or "Beating the Dog"){.} Dahlberg in *The Leafless American* devotes a chapter, "The Malice of Witlings," to the venom of apprentices, hacks, those who cannot write, poeticals, olympian dwarves, who decimate in reviews . . . in which he refers to a sycophant "San Francisco versifier" who attackt him in "several thousand words, shrieking like a mandrake that has just been plucked" "divulging countless gargantuan defects of mine."[3] Well, the Dahlberg review was not an insult but a reflection upon rereading his work and taking thought upon the persistent rancor and the disclaimers of any such rancor. . . .

Hayden Carruth's opening statement that "these poems imitatively shaped" "arouse an immediate hostility" was the challenge that aroused in me the polemic mode. If there is an announced hostility, then I am there fighting mad in the cause of poems "imitatively shaped"—I've had to fight my way clear of the demand of school teachers, literary critics etc. for originality, and to insist on the derivative art as I have had to be willing to pretend and be pretentious . . . but the major cause was, of course, not the right of a poet to imitatively shape but the question as to whether Dr. Williams's "staggered tercets" were a personal property—"His alone, one hastens to say"—Carruth's "to think of a single self-respecting American poet who had *dared* to copy this form" makes me boiling mad all over again when I read it. That he has read Williams earnestly and extensively, only makes his view the more reprehensible.

It's there that I got caught; for picking up on Carruth's opening declarations of hostility towards poems in staggered tercets after the model of Williams (in back of which lay his attack on "that fake Tomlinson"), I came on with all hostilities flying. And succeeded only in losing all the discussion of *shape* versus *form*, of what is going on potentially in those "tercets," of whether or not a true form can be "his alone," a private property and not a communal resource, of metrics in Williams line . . . for the sake of a series of gratuitous insults. That you can remember nothing of what I was contending with and only the contentious air itself is proof enuf of this.

March 18

Meantimes *Relearning the Alphabet* and, from Hawley, *Summer Poems*
have arrived.[4] The "Alphabet" reads richer and stronger with the full mixture
of magic and moralizing, exclamation and expression—the letters and
sounds of letters giving a subtle shadow-warp on which to weave. And the
title "From a Notebook" gives perspective to the Revolution or Death
sequence.[5] (Did you separate the word "night" from its first relation to
"Mayor Daley"? anyway, as I read it now no pun appears active in "Daley").
There is a haunting sense of one-ness in the composition of the book,
poems like "An Interim" that seem to me to have a loose center are realized
to be the gathering nexus for persons of the book; Miss de Courcy Squire is
solidly there when she stands among the saints of the Revolution:

> And the great saints of outrage—
> who have no lawyers,
> who have no interim
> in which to come and go . . .

rings out as a passage. And is itself a feeling, rather than a claim to feeling.
It's part of the declared range you make in *Relearning the Alphabet* that
there will be "Hammering the word against my breast" and, in occasional
poems like "At David's Grave" or "For Paul and Sally Goodman" the
responsibility is assumed to be to the appropriate commiseration rather
than to the course of the poem. What comes to my mind is how right you
were about my "Earth's Winter Song" to question, I take it, the initial claim
to taking feeling in the courage of the young. Tho now, returning to that
poem I am not sure that that was what raised questions of sincerity in your
mind reading. What does seem clear to me is that the center had better be
what is happening in the poem and not what we are feeling about what
is happening. The "feeling" of the poem might be MacBeths or Lady
MacBeths, in that imagined world that "I" is such a person—not a model
but a raw origin of feeling. . . . well, but no sooner said than I realize that a
cultivated sensibility (not only MacBeths but Prosperos and Hermiones) is
also a raw origin of feeling.

But I belabor this disturbance of the poem's feeling and reality center.
Remembering a poem from *Summer Poems*, these are troublings of the
moonlight reflecting surface. It's in the projected realm of the poem we've
to find the Self the poet comes into being to speak for. "Bullfrogs to Fireflies
to Moths" concentrates some realization

> They inhabit their heritage,
> pluck the twilight
> > pleasurably

whose *dump* deepens with the accumulated debris of world and compassions
that thickens the section of "Elegies," out of which flashes of unbearable
reality flash.[6] "Moaning and stinking in hospitals three abed" is not colord
by special caressive sight. Is—the confusion of persuasions and actualities—
that dump our "heritage," . . . And "pleasurably" focusses one's memory to
attention to seek out:

> I stretch in luxury; knowledge of the superb badness
> of my memory gives me a sense of having thick fur,
> a tail, and buried somewhere
> a sweet bone, rotten, enticing
> . . .
> the black taste of life . . .

[the stink of burning meat that in "Passages" goes up from Viet Nam, from
the Texas barbeque,* then from the Roman Church with the burning of the
Albigensian martyrs, in the enclosed "Passage" mounts from a roast lamb]

———————

I assure you, Denny, I will watch that I do not repeat the grave error of
the mode of the attack on Carruth's views—

Love<br>
Robert

*Last night, reading Sauer on New World edible plants and cooking I found
this is an Indian (South American) word *barbacoa*.[7]

## AN ADDENDUM

Re "A Critical Difference of View") *Stony Brook*, 3/4), it seems that
there were readers for whom my contentious mode was more vivid than my
contentions. Indeed, some read the piece as a personal attack on Hayden
Carruth (all the more puzzling since he had written an understanding and
admiring article on *Bending the Bow*) and Adrienne Rich, savoring or
suffering the injuries inflicted and taking the content as fuel to the fire. It
does not help the matter that my attack was impersonal (inspired by a
Hayden Carruth and an Adrienne Rich imagined in their authorship of
the particular passages at which I had taken offense)—malice is malice. I
wanted, along with my attack on their views, to make those views so painful
to them that they would be disheartened from voicing them abroad again.
There are times when my own views regarding the nature and meaning of
poetic form flash forth with an intolerance that betokens remnants of the
Puritan bigot in me, whipping the poor would-be heretic anthologist or
critic publicly in the stocks or driving him forth from the covenant of the
righteous into the wilderness.

For those for whom the address "Mr." Carruth and "Miss" Rich already carries the smart of contemptuous courtesy, cross out "Mr." (Mr. Carruth, Mr. Tomlinson), "Dr." (Dr. Williams), and "Miss" and replace with their proper names.

I am often likely, as in this "Critical Difference," to take the stance of the debater in for the kill at the rebuttal before the summing up, needling his opponent until all issues are lost in the sense of personal injury—a leftover from high school debating zeal that might well have been let go by the time I was fifty.

In all cases, with a marking pencil so that the full disgrace for me of the excised passage will remain visible for reference, cross out the following: "What is most probably at issue is that neither Mr. Carruth nor Miss Rich had or have any great concern for the poetry of Pound or of Williams" thru to the end of that sentence. The above comes in the category of gratuitous injury, and, moreover, is injurious to my own concerns in the article as well as to my intelligence in the reader's eyes: it should be clear that a critical difference of view does not warrant the assumption that the opponent view does not have back of it "any great concern." Likewise, strike from the copy the sentence "I am unacquainted with their work so I cannot say," which is not only added insult (for I had meant to make them smart with the sense that once they had voiced the views they had, I would not read further), but also, it must be noted, seriously disqualifies the preceding assumption.

[I am trying out in my writing book a section on acting scourge or punishing power which has carried me on from the Puritan zealot to the terrible genius of Siva "Life, which can exist only in destroying life," and in which I want to analyze the configuration of the original attack for its content. For one thing, not only do I have a special identification with Zukofsky, whom I see as superior and as having discretion where I lack it, as well as a most subtle music—but I had, I remember, a special recognition that Tomlinson was the only other poet who was openly derivative as an homage to a line of inspiration I too drew on—(it was a poem in honor of Schönberg, I remember). Both Zukofsky and Tomlinson ran risks I saw myself as running (it is not incidental that Hayden's sense that Tomlinson is "that fake" has an echo in many a critic's outrage at my charlatanism—and in my own sense of "craft entering the art" or, very early, of a sleight-of-soul going on).

Can it be incidental that Hayden and Adrienne Rich, when we view them as figures in the configuration, stand as male and female—a syzygy of critical adversaries? And, you will remember both had been poets in the series you edited at Norton—I would not have come to read their volumes otherwise; a misfortune, for I have much less tolerance of poetry which does not suit me than most reviewers and critics. I'm not going to revisit their poetries—I have long ago ridded the library of the volumes—; my rereading the offending reviews only churnd up my ire again.

But the fact, as fact, of this literary intolerance, that it can be as extreme as it is with me (even with Jim Harrison, whom I am fond of and who almost wins me over in passages) ought to be laid out on the table. [Hayden in his attack on Tomlinson (in which he does not touch upon the important fact that he thinks Tomlinson a fake) knows that he means to stir up important controversy:

> Likely these considerations appear as unhappily abstruse. But they lie at the heart of the current dissatisfactions and disagreements in the "world" of poetry.]

Once the analysis is made, I can derive a section to be publisht which will make principles clear without bringing up again the principals of the action.

Love,
Robert

Dear Robert,

I'm sure you must know how *glad* your letter made me feel. You're beautiful. I'd begun to think you weren't going to write to me. . . .

No time to answer properly yet, but I will. And will send new poems. Thanks for yours.

Much, much love from
Denny.

**442**

April 4th 1970
177 Webster St
East Boston,
Mass. 02128

Dear Robert & Jess

The hectic year has come to one of its closes, we leave tomorrow for 2 weeks in Boulder Col., then July 8th I am leaving for Europe (mostly England, at last—20 years!) till end of August. I feel terribly out of touch with you & fear you may be hurt at my silence but I just can't help it & can't even get myself together to write a longer letter—hope that the poems will help bridge the gap & that you will somehow have faith that my love for you is still there even though so long unexpressed.

These are all from this (academic) year except for "Novella" which I wrote last summer & completely forgot having written till I came across it in a notebook a few weeks ago. Also "A Defeat in the Green Mtns" which got lost in 1955.[1]

Saw Allen {Ginsberg}, Bob {Creeley}, & John W{ieners}, & Muriel {Rukeyser} last week (a reading for the strike).

**443**

June 20, 1970
177 Webster Street
East Boston,
Mass. 02128

Nik was 21 last week.
Mitch has finished his *Movement* book.

Love—
Denny

One other I forgot to include (left my typewriter in Me.)[2]

---

*At the Justice Dept, Nov. 15th 1969*

Brown gas-fog, white
beneath the streetlamps.
Cut off on 3 sides, all space filled
with our bodies.
     Bodies that stumble
in brown airlessness, whitened
in light, a mildew glare,
      that stumble
hand-in-hand, blinded, retching.
Wanting it, wanting
to be here, the body believing it's
dying in its nausea, my head
clear in its despair, a kind of joy,
knowing this is by no means death,
is trivial, an incident, a
fragile instant. Wanting it, wanting
   with all my hunger this anguish,
    this knowing in the body
the grim odds we're
up against, wanting it real.
Up that bank where gas
curled in the ivy, dragging each other
up, strangers, brothers
and sisters. Nothing
will do but
to taste the bitter
taste. No life
other, apart from.

DL

(Untitled. June 1970)
(Plants since transplanted to Maine)[3]

Honeydew seeds: on impulse
strewn in a pot of earth. Now,

(the green vines) wandering
down over the pot's edges:

certainly no room here to lay
the egg of a big, pale,
green-fleshed melon.
                            Wondering
where the hell to go.

PS

Richard's book is probably not your cup of tea[4]—the next one (*Seller of Apples*) may appeal to you more—but thought you might like to have a copy anyway.


I'd like Dave Bromige to see this but don't have another copy at the moment—cd. you show him this one when possible please? Stuff about England is something he & I share.

Dearest Robert & Jess

Found Morgenstern[1] & the drawing book on my return from 3 weeks in Chapel Hill N.C. (& quick trip to New Orleans where I read with Allen G. who was fine). Such lovely treasure surprise packages. Thank you. In same mail wedding photos from Dave Bromige with cheerful Robert in them. Good.

Enclosed poem tells essentials of my visit to England (& Yugoslavia)—tho' not of my visit to Mary de Rachewiltz's castle where I sat in Yeats' chair (inherited by EP in Rapallo long ago) & saw many wonderful Gaudier Brzeska's—among other things. This poem is part III of that "Notebook" poem which is in *Relearning the Alphabet*. Between the end of part II (People's Park) & this comes another "Entr'acte" of short poems, which were among those I sent you in June.

You'll see from poem that Eng. did help me get myself together tho' I fell apart for 48 hrs upon touching U.S. soil again. . . . However, have been pretty much OK since, tho' overworking again as I vowed *not* to. (In Chapel Hill I taught 3 or 4 classes a day.)

Mitch's *Movement* book is done, we have an advance copy & as soon as we get more I'll send one. Nik is back at RISD {Rhode Island School of Design} doing sculpture (wood) & graphics (lithography) & is in good spirits.

Much love to you both—
Denny

## 445

Oct. 30, 1970
{Sebastopol, Calif.}

Dearest Denise,

I'm at Sherryl's and David's {Bromige}. After a reading last night when David and Ed Kissam (two real poets in one small pond . . . college!) opend a series for the Rimer's Club (Rimers' Club),[1] and again what an enthusiastic lovely community of young followers of the poem there are here in the Cobati scene.[2] Where after one leaves the highway and turns into back roads suddenly—only the matter of a half-mile off the main road you're in the real beauty of the land, the houses no longer commercial but homesteads, the farms real enuf that they illustrate fulfillments of the land.

And to wake in the morning with the stir and speech of birds in the air. Deer on the hill—they're not there, I just put them there as they have come up even close for a look to the house.

But I arrived minus your new part of the "Notebook" poem, having put it out on the table to take, I had but separated it from the mass of papers in my briefcase which I did take. Well, praise Xerox! It will be in the mail later today for David. And (enclosed) I've a long poem in progress, a kind of return of "Propositions" as a form from *The Field* that takes the form of Propositions of Santa Cruz, arising in the course of History of Consciousness sessions there.[3] But not those alone—for in my under-graduate course I am reading *Paterson* with a group of freshmen, sopho-mores, juniors, seniors—the fifteen represents all four stages of college life in its distribution. And, since they are keeping "Daybooks" to get involved with the modes of *Paterson*, and, beautifully (tho for them, unsure of whether there is anything really there: I told them to begin at the "I had oatmeal for breakfast" level if need be but keep it with *things*) they come across, where I am very aware now of the differences, not only of person, but of first year just beginning in that place, second year taking hold, third and fourth year, variously "belonging" to it. It—is a very beautiful country, grounds for the university—but still grounds of its own. I want to keep them to take root from the reification of their daily lives, to begin to let things of a room, trees, birds, weather, each other at once persons and the people of a world speak for them (and so, now, the oatmeal without the false link of "I had"—Brother hand and spoon, Brother table and Brothers mouth and belly, as Saint Francis suggested, are more vivid, more of life than that even holy ghost of an "I," tho he be redeemd by the homonym of the "eye")—

So I am back in reading *Paterson* too, which I had chosen as the sole pursuit of my work with the group because there was so much discovery (release) of a world for me in the first reading as the poem appeard in the late forties. And from the rush of the first book, the Coming to the Brink of the Falls, the Propositions take up their own flooding of feeling but the Sea not a River—as the sea is everywhere—is the *horizon* of Santa Cruz, and, as you will see, in the second section of the poem—just finisht!—lines of "Age One" Year and of the "Judy Collins" poem—the "There comes a time when only Anger / is Love" come into the text, even as you come to mind to deliver the image, Kalī dancing.

It's great to be in the throes of a poem that has the sweep I often feel in "Passages" but that is not "Passages" (tho it continues in that mode beyond the personal properties of the individual poet of a communal property in poetry, as the daily newspapers and your poems carry—and Plato too!— the "leading" voice). Rilke's beautiful passages on the One Poet, One Poem we poets and poetries ultimately belong to—and wherever I "turn on" immediately *are* have been almost thematic; and in the course-seminar "On the Nature of Poetry" I have returnd to it (as to his passage on "Laral Worth" to evoke a giving up of personality into the higher communality— the higher identity (more intense, more full, more imaginative of *Man*) in the communality.

The students everywhere at Santa Cruz are reading *Relearning the Alphabet*, talking about the poems, talking with the poems, finding what they really mean in the poem. In part, it may be that Nobby {Brown} in a big lecture course is giving wonderful readings of the poems. I heard only one lecture, coming in just as he had begun and was exploring his theme of Daphne and the maiden who is a tree, that lead into a reading of "A Tree Telling of Orpheus" that so spoke for itself and for him that he could make only that simple statement after the reading was thru. I think he has a tape and will be sending one to you.

But outside that course, the Moon-Lover poems (that so far Nobby seems to have avoided or not to have *caught on* to), the Alphabet poem and the Tree Telling are heard or overheard at lunch, coming up in talks with students. What a young world!

And it's in this same period, a little longer—the last two months—that I've finally got with reading that group you sent me last summer. As the new poem evidences, from my first reading—no closer it seemd to me than "reading them over"—they seem to have slept in me so that in reading new intensely they come *from* some "me"—As / . . . .

We went out to gather little red red tart apples for the Treat bags on Hallowe'en, and last night more children came than ever, until we ran out of hand-outs. That night was beautiful weather sandwiched between storms, one coming up now—so, out to get this packet in the mail. It was good to hear from you Denny; keep that resolve not to take on special burdens.

Love
Robert

**446**

January 9 {19}71
As from
177 Webster Street
E Boston, Mass 02128

Dearest Robert,

The typescripts of poems you sent, including the marvelous sea-surf-passage, & the Santa Cruz murders, & the Kali part, have vanished. It's just possible a friend picked them up by mistake with his own things one day recently and I've written to him—but in case that's a false clue wd. it be possible for you to send me another set of xeroxes? Sorry. I am furious about losing them. The surfer part is a most marvellous example of mimetic rhythm.

In what I'm now working on (part IV of "Notebook" poem) I talk about how in fact I'm *not* Kali at all—cannot (even if I wd.) sustain that anger—but this is not an *objection* to being mythologized, only a personal disclaimer. Will send it to you soon.

Much love—& to Jess—
Denny

**447**

Feb 9th {19}71
177 Webster Street
East Boston,
Mass. 02128

In March will be going to Mexico for 10 days or so to see my mother—she's 86. I rather dread it—Mex. has few charms for me anymore, & the parting is always hard because always maybe the last.

Dear Robert & Jess

Here's a new section of long poem. Plus revised last pp. of the European section.[1] The change was made after letter from Bet corrected my recollection,[2] & I was so glad because I'd known vaguely how weak that was, about the days just *going away*.

Am hoping to get from you the sections of your (Robert) work in progress, from surfers thru' Kali, which have so strangely vanished. Also enclosed a poem by English friend Geoffrey Summerfield who's been over here working on early childhood ed. projects in various places during the last couple of years. I have a xerox so if you enjoy it keep this one.

I was up at Clinton for 3 weeks' hard work for 3 weeks of Jan.[3] Now go up on every Tues. & return Thurs., which means 2 6-hr bus trips as Mohawk airlines is on strike & it is too complicated & expensive flying to Syracuse. In Boston we are (by we I mean lots of people) trying to organize various things re. Laos invasion & also in behalf of the "Hoover Conspiracy"[4] & for local collective that was busted. My convict friend on McNeil Island suddenly got 15 years knocked off his sentence, so may be out on parole as soon as next year, & I have to start helping to plan some "half way house" style of life for him to come out into if he comes E. as he hopes. And at Kirkland I'm trying to get some anti-war action started, also a lettuce boycott. So life is too damned busy as usual, but don't, very dear friends, cut me off & condemn me to Kali category, please—I am just as human as I ever was & am looking forward very much to a quiet summer in England & a year off.

Did you get Mitch's book?

Please give my love to Nobby Brown & Beth when you see them at Santa Cruz.

Dave Bromige's new book arrived a couple of days ago.[5] It looks fine.

I have a student doing indep. study on "B. Mtn. School"—listened with her to tapes of Bob & Robert interviewing each other—really good.

Have some new short poems—will send later. Nik had some prints in a show.

Love from<br>Denny.

P.S.

The "entr'acte" between Part III & Part IV is "Let Us Sing Unto the Lord a New Song," which I believe I sent you earlier. Let me know if I didn't.

Between the sections printed in *Relearning the Alphabet* & the European section the entr'acte will include "Looking for the Devil Poems," "At the Justice Dept," "I Thirst," "Ghandi's Gun & Brecht's Vow," "The Year One," "Today," & "Casa Felice I & II" but not in that order.

---

Dear Robert and Jess,

Some of the *Cantos* were first typed on this antique Remington which E P left behind here at Brunnenburg where I have been spending a week with Mary.[1]

I don't know how you feel, but I feel it is time we got back in touch.

I have been in England all summer recovering from a horrendous winter and 3 years of overwork. Mitch was with me till late August when he went home, and I will be returning around Oct. 10th. I feel better but am going to try to take it easy back home for a while, my stamina is just not what it was.

We have moved (in May that was) to a communal arrangement with 2 other couples so there is much less domestic work to do. I love it. We each have a workroom, plus our bedroom. The address is 19, Brook St., Brookline, Mass. 02146.

Nik is free of the Draft & has finished RISD and is living at Greenwich St. with Day and looking for work.

Mitch is returned to his long-shelved novel, with new heart and interest.

I have a new book which you will be sent.[2]

Also lots of unpublished new short poems.

**448**

Sept. 22 1971
Brunnenburg
As from
31 Downside Crescent
London, N.W. 3

I did not send you a check for *ground work* I think.[3] Sorry. I meant to but it was a time of crazy complications, much travel to lousy job, impending move, etc etc. When I get home I will do—right now don't know if any $$$ in account. Is it going well?

Please send me a word. To London if soon, to Boston or Maine if not that soon.

Oh, and I so much regret not having seen Jess's show in NYC—did not even get a notice of it, but saw catalog at Jonathan's {Williams} in Yorkshire in July.[4]

Love—
Denny

---

**449**

October 4, 1971
{San Francisco}

Dear Denise/

Jonathan had written that you and Mitch had been visiting and sent your regards. And there were rumors that you wld been staying in England. It's good to know that you are coming back to the scene of the crime. And, if I can get myself to answer an enquiry from Stanford, we might be reading around the same time there this coming Spring—tho I will also be on tour East in April. The YMHA has me scheduled for that time. And I will have to be getting a group of readings to make the trip worth the while.

Don't worry about sending money for *Ground Work*. In the first place, I received ample funds for quite a bit more of that; and then, secondly, I havent gotten any out since (tho I have six pages multi-lithed toward the next mailing). I've been typing the first volume of the H. D. book for publication, having decided to issue it at this stage in typescript edition. I have come to dread printed publications—I've had such bad luck with proof-reading and with faulty printers. And now I have it to issue all first editions from my typewriter straight off. Where any errors will be my own. Coercion has always seemed to me the only true evil; and it's a form of coercion to rage against what somebody else does to one's copy when right at hand is the means to do said copy for oneself.

It *has* been long indeed since we have corresponded. I have some two letters at least that I started and got bogged down in what seemed to me as I went only reactions and not responses to your "Revolution or Death" theme. Well, I hope to get some of that straight in seeing if I can't write something on the new book where you had designed to bring that theme together into a central position. The question is the poetry and not the revolution—the book clearly isn't "revolutionary" in the sense of the poem—and the theme may be *anguish*. I feel that revolution, politics, making history, is one of the great falsehoods—is Orc in his burning madness—this is not to disapprove of the fire's raging. But Art has only one place in which to be and that is in our own lives right now. That's how I read Blake's insistence on the loss of the creative. It would take Art, anyway, to get this matter of revolution into the dimension of the revealed, to create the idea, something more than and toward which one's longing goes.

Perhaps something of what I am questioning is in the People's Park— was it no more than a protest against the University? If there was in it any creative drive to have a People's Park, why is it that when it was no longer an affront to the University, no further interest flourished to have a park? The only thing kept going and alive was the protest. And the only meaning kept in the poetry alive is the killing of Rector and the blinding of Blanchard. Was this the creative issue of the "Park"???[1] Now it is the City of Berkeley that has {been} planting the trees and widened the avenues to include miniparks. The idea of the massacre is alive among students but not any idea of a park or even of keeping beautiful the grounds that are already there. Do we believe in unilateral peace? Then surely it is *we* who must create it where we are. But the revolution, like Nixon, believes in inflicting peace on their own terms. I do not ask for a program of Peace; but I do protest the war waged under the banner of Peace, no matter who wages it. It is false to the word. Men at war against the State are one thing—and that can at least be true to itself = even if it not be successful; but men at war against war are hypocrites if they argue that there can be no peaceful ways in a time of war. THERE HAS BEEN NO TIME IN HUMAN HISTORY THAT WAS NOT A TIME OF WAR. And any peaceful ways and deeds of peace have had to be created in the face of the need for war—for war against oppression, for war against injustice, etc.

It's the "Altars in the Street" I am for,[2] the acts of care in making and attendance in the midst of the apocalypse, that present most vividly, the test of Art. Revolutions have all been profoundly opposed to the artist, for revolutions have had their power only by the rule that power not be *defined*. And, as workers in words, it *is* our business to keep alive in the language definitions as well as forces, to create crises in meaning, yes—but this is to create meanings in which we are the more aware of the crisis involved, of what is at issue. In posing "revolution or death" you seem to feel that evolution—which as far as we know is the way in which life actually meets its test and creates its self—does not come into the picture. As if, i.e., Man got to "overthrow" reptiles.

And so forth: all this "issue" seems to stand between me and thee. I feel guilty or tired of my disappointment in what is clearly so important to you. And project on you some opposition to the issue of art. The art of the poem—which has fallen into disrepair—the art of long persisting and careful work. I am not talking about prisoners, blacks, children, and angry women in revolt—I am talking about those with work to do deserting their work. And our work is surely to get the words *right*, and, as Bet in your long "Entr'acte" says "Get down into your well, / it's your well / go deep into it / into your own depth as into a poem." Taken at face value, is the "Revolution" that well? "her face / painted, clownishly, whorishly. Suffering" is that the depth of it? Does "suffering" guarantee the image?[3]

This is only to say, by my distraction, that I am distracted when I start to write you. Our own immediate directions seem so at odds. Let's hope I arrive at something more articulate than this circular ("revolutionary") argument in attempting an essay. Without that I won't publish.

Love,
Robert

## 450

{October, 1971}
As from
19 Brook St.
Brookline,
Mass. 02146

Dear Robert

It was good to have a letter from you but before I can reply to it I have to try & find out what you don't make clear: whether you are objecting to *To Stay Alive* for (1) "not being revolutionary as poetry," i.e. for not being innovative formally, & therefore in your opinion not being decently consonant with its theme (in which case I'd say, "but then you have misunderstood the theme"); or (2) that you feel the quality of my work has fallen off, possibly because of the time & energy I've spent in political involvements (in which case I would of course feel *very sad* to have lost your approval—but I would not be *crushed* by it as I once would because in my slow (lifelong! retarded?) growing up (nearly 48!!) I no longer feel that kind of dependency, thank god—& I'm sure you will be as glad as I am that this is so, for not believing in coercion it must sometimes pain you when you find yourself by the sheer force of your being having a coercive effect—(do you understand?) —or (3) whether your argument is all ideological. If it is the 3d then I will write a response to your letter that will try to present my point of view & show you where I think you are setting me up as an adversary without due reason. Because you *do* have that habit of projection, of setting people up in rôles—of mythologizing, as you did for instance when you identified me with Kali. There are in all of us flickering moments when we are representative of this or that archetypal role—but it is wrong I am certain to *fix* on those moments, to assume that they are more than moments, to build a system out of them. That leads to the deadly abstract, the inhuman, the false. But anyway—if you could write to me quite simply & briefly whether it's (1), (2), or (3) (or if a mixture, which dominates) then I will do my best to answer.

Love from
Denny

dear Denny,

451

Oct. 16/{19}71
{San Francisco}

About contention, I came across this in Yeats's *Autobiographies* (while working on the final copy for chapter Five of "Beginnings," H. D. Book I.): "All creation is from conflict, whether with our own mind or with that of others, and the historian who dreams of bloodless victory wrongs the wounded veterans." And reflecting upon the problems of *To Stay Alive* in relation to the nature of the "Revolution or Death" proposition (or threat? or vow? or ultimatum?), has brought me at last to read Camus, in whose *The Rebel* I find the chapter "Rebellion and Art" begins: "Art is the activity that exalts and denies simultaneously" and "art should give us a final perspective on the content of rebellion."

Well, I have, I think, more than a *habit* of projection. I seek in any way to go beyond the passive projection toward active [i.e. creative, one that makes something up] projection. In that (as in the concept of *field*) I remain a follower of Projective Verse. In the "Santa Cruz Propositions" I am projecting, not a picture of you but (seeing again the moment photographed and sound-trackt when you were exhorting the assemblage of a women's march for Peace in Washington, D.C., when you were possessed by the demonic spirit of the mass, seeking to awaken that power in the assemblage, to awaken them as a *people* or mass power) a latent up-rising out-raging spirit in the mass. Of course *you* are not Kalī: one of the troubles you have as a poet is that even the flickering moments in which the grand vision of apocalypse might arise and some outpouring of the *content* of world-anger come, you cannot give it free imaginative expression, cannot "identify" with the anger, but must moralize and humanize. Camus can find in Lautreaumont and Rimbaud the content of rebellion at the poetic level—and in Nietzsche. Back of the argument: "the sense of who the guardians of life, of integrity, are, is extended to include not only those who 'disdain to kill' but all who struggle, violently if need be, to pull down this obscene system before it destroys all life on earth"* is a Nietzschean Kaliyuga idea of destruction, bereft of the insight Nietzsche had of how through and through that obscene system goes. "The whole system of insane greed, of racism and imperialism, of which war is only the inevitable experssion" if it were rooted out would mean, indeed, Kalī's great trampling out of the whole species. All the history of Asia, Africa, Europe and the "New World" is written in insane greed, racism and empires and exploitations. Back of "racism" where white enslaved black, was tribalism where black enslaved black, where Semite swore undying hatred of Semite, where Celt devourd (literally) Celt, and Rome burns Carthage to the ground and salts the earth.

*If we were to read the *content* of the statement at the same level as we do in dream analysis, the American general's "In order to save the village it was necessary to destroy it" is identical.[1]

The American general's "In order to save the village it was necessary to destroy it" *is* a primitive verity that comes with the authority of a voice in a dream or a poem—it brings to the surface the underlying *content*. The wish for *reprisal* is the Kalī wish, and not only the rebels—all up-risings, Nazi as well as Communist, anarchist as well as totalitarian—demand "reprisal" for wrongs—is epitomized and not obscured by excuse or justification. Well, this failure to project anywhere the force of Revolution, or of Rebellion, or of Protestant Fury is only a poetic "failure" if one subscribes to your sentiments of being in opposition to the whole system, etc. Actually, I would take it that while you entertain this sentiment, at the level of the poetic charge what you actually *feel* is anguish.

———

My thot will—

"How can you rehabilitate someone and punish him at the same time?" a prisoner says just now in a radio interview. "How can you rehabilitate a society and punish it at the same time?"

—come to more as I read Camus, I think. And as I analyze and discuss with you passages of *To Stay Alive*. As a book it has the difficulty that in relating the collection to "themes" of the "Notebook" poem [which, by the way, is very much like *Paterson* with the theme of "Revolution" in the place of Williams's theme of "Divorce"], the poems have been removed from the field they belong to poetically.

love
Robert

---

**452**

Oct. 19 {Nov 3}, 1971
{San Francisco}

dear Denny,

I've been Schumannizing for the past week, listening at various levels—while writing listening-with-the-other-ear, overhearing, or moving about in the medium of the Romantic, even my bones savoring his melancholy richness, until the profusion of attentions embodied in the objects and furnitures as sentiments and interests of the room about me seem to belong to a like melancholy in me. And last night in a dream, in the dream referring among other things to the anguish that has struck me, "got *to* me," in your poems, I found myself saying momentously, seeing it in the dream even as I said it as a monstrously selfish weariness, an accusation only incidentally about the war and the mis government of the state, but about the inadequacy of all that so visibly supports and enlivens me: "At fifty-three [leaping ahead in the dream to the beginning of the year 1972] I do not seek it, but I more than don't care, I will welcome the end of this life"—not a sense of the dreadfulness, but of the endurance. Your title *To Stay Alive* and the middle-aging sense of the opening of the preface: "As one goes on living and working" have also passed youthful exuberance.

Once I have begun writing you again, Denny, and I had no place to begin but with—be it projection, be it reaction to some actual content—the disaffection entering into the sympathies and admirations for what is going on in your work. But whatever love means, it must mean the whole confidence that so begins again in me when I address you. It's that that lifts whatever conscience of co-ercion, for once I am writing once more to you—[and that must be some projection, some abiding projection—and reciprocal, for, as always, you are so immediate in your response]. The "you" who would have been crushed by my crushing disapproval in the past was never the writing-you, or if that you was sometimes writing, there was always the sense that you were co-equal, if dependent only so as I was. Tho, I do remember, I questiond your letting Ferlinghetti and then Jonathan do selections—and that you had a strong feeling, backed up by Jungian concepts of anima and animus in relation to what was true to a woman in creation. I have, of course, the same question of your being shown by Mitch and Hayden "that other, earlier poems . . . had a relation to it that seemed to demand their reissue in juxtaposition." It's not only what others can point out to us as opportunities in composition [I think of Margie raging at {Hans} Hofmann's showing her what to do in her painting[1]] but our own opportunism that has got to be resisted, if the shaping is to come, as it must, from the formal urge and apprehension that is deeper than our opinions of form. It's not that, as writers, we should not be immodest, but that we must go into the depths of immodesty; not that we shld not be narcissistic, but that we should go into the depths of Narcissus. The *impulse* that informs (and makes *necessary* the artist's craft), the hidden and life-creative and destructive ID-entity underlying and overriding the conveniences of personal identity is what makes the difference between mere craft [the triviality of workmanship in and of itself] and significant craft; is why many a good craftsman is even an enemy of Art, and why men without craft can come thru in all their crudity to deliver up the form that moves us.

When you say that the public occasions come into the poems "not as a deliberate repetition but because the events were of importance to me, other such occasions were spoken of in other poems"—we are at the crux of this matter. For these occasions, sentiments, strong feelings etc., do not "come into the poems" but are "spoken of . . . because they are important to me."[2] Which I would contrast with the severity in which the artist must act upon his sense that, even if he cannot see what it means to him, the matter belongs to the poem.

As my sense in "Uprising" was not that the war was or was not important to me, but how come it was of import to the poem. Nor was I concernd to attack the war in the poem, but to follow thru the vision of the war and the terrific and terrifying identification with the fire-bomber which I had pickt up from James Dickey's fantasies let loose in his poem.

It's the deep-going and moving conjunctions in history—the seeing the poetic image—that the poet alone can precipitate (tho dreamers come close to it; and those monsters of history, the men in revolt against civilization—as the French Revolution, or Hitler in our own time—who write their nightmares in the actual instead of the fictional mode), the wanting everything flooded or swept by fire—that is the urgency that demands the poet to reveal what is back of the political slogans and persuasions.

I'll be getting into that, into what happens with a poem that begins like "Life at War":

> The disasters numb within us
> caught in the chest, . . .

or like "Tenebrae"

> Heavy, heavy, heavy, hand and heart.
> We are at war,
> bitterly, bitterly at war

where the opening voice of the poem proposes a *tremendum* in which all the empty-headed and heartless meaningless campaigns of Viet Nam even may be seen as "war," and speak for a being at war that is significant at the level of the individual soul life. We are prepared for the utterance of this pain in being at war at a level that might equal Williams's great feeling of *divorce* underlying the nation, the land, and the language, even as it was ever present between him and Floss the (personal), between the man and the woman (individual).

But no, in "Tenebrae" it is moralizing that sets in, to deny any ground to the heaviness and the bitterness might have verity in. And we get in its place the displaced bigotry in which women who are concernd about their gowns of gold sequins, wedding-partners who have not the verity of desire, food-storers, TV watchers are accused of "not listening."

If we were to read this protest of "*they* are not listening" with the possibility that the message of the poem does have content as a dream has content—then we would read that following the opening lines, it is the *poem* itself that is not listening, that has turned to the vanity that all moralizing is in order to evade the imminent content of the announced theme. Its the lines of the poem itself that are held in full solemnity of a political etiquette, or approved moral stand. I think the poems like "Life at

War," "What Were They Like," "Tenebrae," and "Enquiry" are not to be
read properly in relation to Viet Nam [they certainly do not come out, can
not come out, from an experience of Viet Nam] but in relation to the deep
underlying consciousness of the woman as a victim in war with the Man.
Then we understand why the adjective "delicate" in

>              that humankind,
>     delicate Man, whose flesh
>     responds to a caress

portraying the Man in his role as passive object of sexual sensualities as
most gentle, "turns" "without surprise" if he be active to be experienced as
"breaking open of breasts" etc. an explosion or "implosion" of the poet's
sadistic imaginings to illustrate a text for women's liberation.

And because it is so urgent in the poem, and so little permitted in your
conscious personality, in the etiquette of being a woman [or being a child or
being a black], it carries the truth of the unconscious. We realize that the
poetic truth of Viet Nam has to do with the deep well of your own life—
as the fire in *Paterson*, we realize has to do with the well of Williams's life.

But as a poet you won't go with the poem, "bitterly, bitterly at war" turns
from being the beginning of a revelation into being no more than a
moralizing reproof.

[installment No. 2; I'll be back in a few days with continuation from
here. I've got to let this gestate. But just writing here has given me a lead as
to what is happening when the Olga of "Olga Poems" nails and breasts /
round, round, and / dark-nippled" to "bones and tatters of flesh" the "black
one, black one," she who "muttered into [your] childhood" "dread . . . in
her," "pressing lives to disaster" "waiting / to rearrange all mysteries in a new
light"; and III

>          Black one, incubus—
>     riding anguish as Tartars ride mares
>     over the stubble of bad years.

This demonic person in the poem given the poignancy of her humanity you
also knew—it is one of your everlastingly moving and revealing poems,
Denise—when this Olga is claimd "as a worker for human rights"? What
language but the language of dreams with its displacement and reversal of
values can be at work?

It is as if women would give their assurance that altho they are filled with
rage, they will be good helpmates in the politics of the revolution. "In the
etiquette of the revolution, I have no desire that isn't at your service."

>                                             Love
>                                             Robert

Oct. 19/1971

(installment 3) Following the exposition of my reading on the Olga, and Preludes. I begin to see somethings in my outpourings here to share with you the preliminary critical questionings and readings—that will be of interest in the context of a review for readers in general.

I want, Denny, to respond to your questions about the nature of my objecting.

Well, no it certainly is not to object that your verse form is conservative and not revolutionary—your verse form *is* conservative; and, as I think, you would grant even a hostile critic, my forms are just as conservative. We both relate directly to traditions—we seek, after all, a long lasting community in time, and do feel the truest community with like spirits distant from our own "age"—I would be, if anything, the more conservative, for I find akin structures that are widely assumed today no longer to be relevant.

But our initial breakthru was not to be concernd with form as conservative or as revolutionary, but with form as the direct vehicle and medium of content. Which means and still means for me that we do not say something by means of the poem but the poem is itself the immediacy of saying—it has its own meaning. And in that is as immediate as the dream. We may go with the force of it, and read the poem as deeply as we can as we write [this "is" the ultimate craft or cunning of the poem] or we may not be able to read it or able to countenance what it is saying—then we will get the kind of cover-up of the content in the protestation of a moral attitude, a neurosis, etc.

The poem is whether or not we ourselves in writing it can countenance it so, always consonant with its theme. In "Tenebrae" whatever that *other* expectancy in which I as reader was disappointed—the poem that might have begun had the announcing chords of "bitterly, bitterly at war" been heard out in all their imaginable resonances [and I am finally convincd that when all evidences are followed in their resonances the themes of this volume will be reveald anew. One will understand WHY you are instructed "Get down into your well"—one thinks at first it means the well of one's own self—but in the context it means the well of the language not as *yours* but as poetry. "into your own depth as into a poem" the instructress says: but in the formulation, we would observe that you don't go into a poem, because you don't want to go into your own depth.

And you can't go down into it, poem or depth, as long as the line remains in the propriety of the measured statement—it needs long sweeps that exceed the guard.

There is a passage tho that comes to mind that, with the very word "exhilaration," rings out in memory.

> By afternoon, slogging
> through falling snow,
> yellow snowlight, traffic slowed to
> carthouse pace,
>         exhilaration, East Boston
> doubling for London.
>         I'm frivolous.
>         I'm alone.
>         I'm Miriam
> (in *Pilgrimage*) fierce with joy
>         in a furnished room near Euston
> I'm the Tailor of Gloucester's cat.
>         I live in one day
> . . .

and then the intrusion of the obvious "a manic-depressive's year." Even in the account of a case history that "manic-depressive" diagnosis is a let-down from any illuminating reality. My god! it's as if Goethe had come to the brilliant discovery that Werther was a portrait of a manic-depressive. Or as if Hesiod cinched the pack in his Ode to Aphrodite by noting that she was an archetype or a penis-substitute.

———————

What I find myself getting at is that your verse form has become habituated to commenting and personalizing just where the poem itself begins to open out beyond the personal into your imagination of a "you," a "world" or a history beyond your idea of yourself or your personal history. You remember that *your* husband is Mitch just to derail the imagination of a husband it would have needed a poem for us to know about. You remember that you are committed to "opposition to the whole system of insane greed, or racism and imperialism"—a political stance: but we are the more aware that it comes to forestall any imagination of what that system is, any creation of such a system of greed, racism and imperialism. These, Denny, are empty and vain slogans because those who use them are destitute of any imagination of or feeling of what such greed, racism or imperialism is like. The poet's role is not to oppose evil, but to imagine it: what if Shakespeare had opposed Iago, or Dostroyevsky opposed Raskalnikov—the vital thing is that they *created* Iago and Raskalnikov. And we begin to see betrayal and murder and theft in a new light.

Is it a disease of our generation that we offer symptoms and diagnoses of what we are in the place of imaginations and creations of what we are.

November 3
Wednesday

These pages above have waited now two weeks and returning I am still
involved in tracing out and unwinding lines of thought and reaction until
a structure of response appears. Sharing with you the working out of a
contention—not to change your cause but to bring into that course, into
your reading of the poem, the consciousness of an other reading, or other
readings. The idea of the multiphasic character of *language* and of the poem
as a vehicle of the multiplicity of phases is more and more central to my
thought. The most important rimes are the resonances in which we sound
these phases in their variety of depths [in Charles's *Maximus* this appears as
taking soundings of the ocean bottom, and knowing the patterns of the
fishing grounds]—the resonances that depend upon our acknowledgement in
our work of what we know of the range of meanings in the language so that
we remain, beyond our intent, aware of our actions in the realm of words—
for that we keep alive the historical levels of meaning, the sexual content so
active everywhere in human discourse, the existential propositions of syntax,
the changing concepts of the real [I'm thinking right now of recently follow-
ing a lecture on a Buddhist sutra and remarking that an analogy to not
knowing where a flame goes when it goes out has been seriously alterd in
a modern consciousness where fire is not thought of as an element but as a
state of elements; and more seriously alterd again when these elements are
not truly "atomic"—i.e. primary facts of the universe, but themselves in their
identity appearances far from bottom soundings—the bottom soundings
suggesting now a world or whirrld of unique sub-atomic events.{]} The
Buddhist imagination is wonderfully resonant with our present scientific
imagination of reality: but the old metaphors no longer go deep into the
well of knowledge to sound our not-knowing.

What does criticism ideally do for us poets? If it expresses only liking or
not liking, it is useless—unless we design to please or displease some specific
audience. But if it make clear some crisis in reading, if it read meanings
or misread meanings in some way that had not occurred to us, criticism
enlarges our sense of how language works.

Well, "liking" and "disliking" *is* a realm of meaning and can also be
brought into the design [that is working *with* the affect not *for* it—it is a
not to design to be liked or disliked].

———————

Our partisan feelings and resolutions act as censors of the imagination
that must go deep into the well we would call ours—not into a redundancy
of how we would like to think of ourselves, but into some imagination of
what that depth would be if it weren't "ours."

Writing the "Olga Poems," she appeard in the pathos of "the hatreds / that

had followd you, a / comet's tail, burned out / as your disasters bred of love":
and touchd, for me, upon a minor acknowledgment that in the deep-well
sense I knew in my own life such a comet's tail. What beside that then is the
assertion: "the personal response that moves from the identification of my
lost sister, as a worker for human rights. . . . "

There are those who (my mother was among them) mouth Polonius's "To
thine own self be true and it follows as the night the day" with no sense of
the sinister order of "the night the day"—and as if it were a benevolent
instruction existing apart from the shaking contemplation of what happens
in the truth of self that we come to know in Hamlet. In truth Polonius's
counsels are terrible; and there is no avoiding it—he prepares Ophelia for
despair. For me all history of human life makes terrible our resolves. What
else is our experience of valor but our sense of what in ourselves we dare?

This morning I follow thru now among your themes, the ones that seem
to me Polonius pieties of those who do not want to question their unmixed
good will.

> "committed to a solidarity of hope and struggle with the revolutionary
> young"

> "The sense of community, of fellowship,"

> "some of my heroes—that is, those who stand for integrity, honesty,
> love of life"

———————

> human kind,

> delicate Man, whose flesh
> responds to a caress, whose eyes
> are flowers that perceive the stars,

> whose music excels the music of birds,
> whose laughter matches the laughter of dogs,
> (1) { whose understanding manifests designs
> fairer than the spider's most intricate web

(1) there is of course an immediate sinister extension of meaning here—
for where designs are fair as a spider's web, they remind us of the cruel
machinations of Louis XI, who in the poetry of his subjects' speech became
"the spider King" as flies have a grim sense of the fairness of spider webs.
And as poets we be spiders who must keep alive the imagination of the flies'
relation to the web.

———————

> "whose language imagines *mercy*,
> *loving kindness*; we have believed one another
> mirrord forms of a God we felt as good—"

[think of the throng, Shakespeare, Lawrence, Hardy, Ibsen, etc etc. who must indeed be excluded from such a "*we*"].

"Language, coral island
 accrued from human comprehensions,
 human dreams"

—The whole sense of language here, separated as it is from our knowledge of the growth and nature of language is already eroded.

———————

"The first [revolution] that laughter and pleasure aren't shot down in"

[Yet in "Tenebrae" there would seem clearly to be certain cases in which you do not approve of laughter and pleasure.] But outside of this proposition that I see as manifestly untrue (and unnecessary) the Part I (October '68–May '69) faces the difficulties of consciousness involved. Tho here I would remark on the negative piety of: "the obscene sell out, the coprophiliac spasm / that smears the White House walls with its desensitized thanks" which comes in as if it did not raise questions of from where and why this image of a baby smearing the walls with shit comes into it to illustrate your distaste for the President I take it. Since I know of no story of Johnson's being a copro-philiac, I can only imagine that your projection alone supplies this as an image of evil. And why thumbs are "desensitized" must be hidden in the unexplored well of personal associations.

When I come to yr. account of the People's Park I am dumb-founded. I cannot believe that along with the sense you give of the building of the Park, there was not equally present the sense of the whole as a confrontation and protest before the power of the University in its taking over the land. "The clubs, the gas / bayonets, bullets. The War / comes home to us . . . " *After the Park?*[3] horseshit. Anyone saw the clubs, the guns, the gas for sure from the Free Speech crisis on. What kind of double-think can propose that there was no expectation at all of what would follow the Park?

Now let me make my position absolutely clear here, Denise. I find the People's Park, when I imagine it as, in full awareness, in ruthless determina-tion, making a Park that in its very virtue is a confrontation and will reveal the nature of the Power of the University as a murderous tyranny, admirable. And I am certain that there were those heroically inspired who in the planting of the Park are fully aware and creatively determined that all will be exposed—and that Rector will be shot and Blanchard blinded (i.e. that it will prove that the administrative tyranny is willing to kill and to blind).

And I know very well that there were many who did not want to believe anything like that [for all of the evidence of the contrary]—but these are deluded, self-deluded; hypocrites of the revolution. Those who thought they had *merely* "made for each other / a green place" and couldn't see that the green place was staked out upon a battleground for sure. This kind of thinking outrages me.

The "L-O-O-O-V-E" the Judy Collins bleats out cannot be more vacuous than the claim that would underlie the *"Thursday, May 15th"* view of "the people"—

There's doctrine I don't go along with, Denny; but that is never critical. "Keiner/oder Alle, Alles/oder Nichts" is no choice I would ever pay any attention to. But it is powerful in Brecht, and could be, if you were as brutally realistic and thorough as Brecht, a virtue and not a vice.

What I question is the debilitating stuff you take and ask us to take at face value.

The true poetic message of *The Peoples Park* and the message was true before the actual event [if, for instance, the picture as I saw it in "The Multiversity" was true] is, was, and will be, that to build a Park on, in, State land is to build a bomb, a battleground. And call up again the war in the streets. Where idiot by-standers (i.e. those too innocent to observe the perils of "watching" a war) get killed.

But to get at the deep well reading. After your recognition of

> Wanting it, wanting
> with all my hunger this anguish,
> this knowing in the body
> the grim odds we're
> up against, wanting it real.

The reader comes, if he read with the dramatist's sense of resonances, with Shakespeare's sense, to see that the death of Rector, the blindness of Blanshard, satisfy and verify your requirements of the Park, provide a joy's proving to be ultimately an anguish. The truth one suspects proves to be true.

Looking this statement over, I find that I am outraged not only by the hypocrites and self-deluded, but by the innocent. Those who think they can *merely* make a green place as a claim on University property. Well, yes. Their ignorance *is* outrageous. It requires so much willing refusal of facts.

Well, painfully, and sometimes with some fury I've got at sample points of what my disappointment was. The questions are not ideological but have to do with where I feel you do not get to the truth of your ideology. It's the truth of Lear Shakespeare gets us to and that we admire. Not in any other sense, his example. Brecht's *"Alles oder Nichts"* is, like your *"Revolution or Death"* and the American general's *"It became necessary to destroy the town to save it"* are poetically exemplary as embodying with great concentration the very principle of the world view they belong to. Ideologically, they are totalitarian and do not dissemble, sentimentalize, or delude us. But I would refuse such an ideology myself. I am and remain a pluralist. Within the plurality of forces the Heraclitean opposites have the drama and pathos of a heightened figure upon a ground in which a multitude of figures appear.

Well, how much more pleasantly, I can address myself to going into the poems [like all of the "Olga Poems" sequence; and many passages in the others that have come thru and continue to come thru as splendid{]}. Then I may have got myself readied to write at large about the volume.

love
Robert

**453**

Oct. 25th–
Nov. 2nd 1971
Temple, Maine

Dear Robert,

I've been making at odd moments some notes towards a reply to your 2 letters which I received on the same day (because Suzy brought them up from Brookline to Temple where we are staying for a few weeks).

Two things must preface this letter:

One is that I cant write a point by point response because it would take me at least a week's full working time and energy. I haven't been really well this year—too much travelling, often in lousy weather, last school-year, and an expenditure of energy with little return because the place I was teaching (Kirkland, in upstate NY) was such a sick place, really knocked me out and even during my long good summer in England I had one bad cold after another; so my stamina is low and if I sit at my desk too long I get just too tired. I'm starting to feel better but not better enough to do a really thorough job on this, for instance. So you'll have to excuse me.

The other thing is that your second longer letter has passages of warmth and affection that give me a basis for response the other letters didn't provide: the old connection seems to be there all right underneath. But it has weakened and it has a lot of stuff lying on top of it as it were which I'm going to attempt to clear away a bit. The sense that there *is* a connection makes it possible for me to hope that I can speak freely and critically—as freely and critically of you as you of me—without alienating you, or not for long. I hope I'm right. Anyway I can only try it and see. I have not forgotten the generous honesty of your response to my letter about your attack on Hayden in *Stony Brook*.

Because of point one above, I'm not going to approach your letter sequentially but just draw on my notes in the random order in which I jotted them down.

*Misapprehensions*: Your letters are full of them. "Wilful misapprehensions" is perhaps a cliché but it is apt: wilful because the mispprehensions are based on prejudices, opinionated preconceptions, a need to make things fit with your projections. Misapprehensions: = getting hold of things by the wrong end, upsidedown, sideways—demonstrating a disregard for their nature and function.

*Coercion*:  You say you object to coercion yet you relate to people in a coercive way. I have thought this for a long time but I had too much dependence on your approval to rebel against it.

*Taste*:  You object to the word, the concept; yet you (to a degree you must surely be unaware of ) set yourself up as an Arbiter of Taste. When do you ever ask, "What do you think? Do you like . . . ? What do you feel about . . . ?" or say, "It seems to me that . . . "? These forms of address are alien to you because you have so long set yourself up as The Authority, stating your opinions as unquestionable dogmas, de haut en bas. (I retract the implied "never" here, in rhetorical answer to the questions; in one of these very letters I do find one "I think that"; the word, then, should be "seldom").

Yes, you have indeed "played Orpheus for me," and then I'm exalted. And you have played Virgil for me, and then I'm enlightened. I have learned so much from you!

But there are other times when you pontificate. I can see it must be hard not to, because you are full of insight and knowledge about so many things and your friends and followers naturally drink all that in, often awestruck, so that it must get hard to distinguish, for you yourself, when you get way off course. Another thing that happens is that your special ability to realize puns and to give words the quick etymological X-Ray sometimes leads you into a twisty picky-ness (so that one feels one is walking on eggs in speaking/writing to you because you are waiting to trip one up (there goes a mixed metaphor!) instead of being the illuminating faculty it is at its/your best).

*People's Park*  What happened to the PP and Berkeley generally since the spring I was there has nothing to do with my poem. The experience of community I lived through there is inviolable, and in no way invalidated by whatever may have happened later. (In any case, if the city is now making more parks that's a victory not a defeat—and if they aren't the kind of parks people want then the people will have to make them so. But that's another story.) You were not a participant in the PP struggle, so what makes you think you know more about it than I do? It is damned arrogant of you.

*Olga*  Yes, she *was* a "worker for human rights." (This passage of your letter is less than clear but you seem to say, how can I, after seeing how manipulative of human lives she fatally was, claim her as some kind of heroine.) (It didn't seem to bother you back in 1966 by the way—but that may just have been an oversight.) Olga was an exceedingly complex person. Her basic mistake was certainly that she always thought she knew best for individuals and consequently tried to rearrange their lives without regard for their peculiarities and their *pace* of development and their organic growth processes. (She also was a liar and that was because she was afraid of my father.) BUT "compassion's candle alight in her" and the "vision of festive goodness" *were true* in her and were her equally basic *virtues*. And she gave years of her life trying to combat racism and war. This is history, for which there is plenty of documentation in England, where many people vividly remember her and not for her manipulativeness and lies and bossiness etc but for her courage, energy, eloquence, and *kindness*—not least Harry Green, her husband in the last few (¾) years of her life, whom I have corresponded with since shortly before her death and got to know this summer and last in London, a pure soul if there ever was one, gentle and innocent and with whom she too at last was gentle and innocent. No, I don't think you should presume to tell me what virtues I can claim for Olga. The "Olga Poems" don't claim to be a full picture of her but such as they are they do contain some sense of the tangle of good and bad she exemplified, with which her being "a worker for human rights" is in no way incompatible.

*Camus* I have a good quote for you from Camus but don't have the book here so it will have to wait. But your quoting him "at" me as it were just because I've quoted him in a poem is typical of something you do which involves both the highhandedness and the misapprehensions: you too easily assume that *because one cites one remark, one buys wholesale*. I like a lot of what I've read of Camus but not everything and I think probably wd find myself strongly disagreeing with many aspects of his thought if I read it all. But with you one has to be careful whom one mentions because if it is someone you disapprove/*dislike*, one may find oneself put in a defensive position on his behalf even if one doesnt happen to particularly like him either (excuse me, I can't remember the evidence for this so maybe I am not being quite fair) OR, due to the assumption above, even if it is someone you *accept* one is confronted by other things he said or stood for and is expected to be responsible for them, or to them: but in fact one may simply have found *one thing* that person said that one liked or found apt.

Stopped to get ribbon changed.

*Hayden and Mitch.* Long ago you showed me that just throwing a random bunch of poems at Ferlingh. and Jonathan was not good enough. (I let F have 1st choice because he asked me for a book first—taking over the book Weldon Kees had asked me for before his death—while Jonathan got 2nd choice because he asked me a few months later.) You showed me that a book could be something far more integrated than that. You revealed to me that poems have a relation to each other. Similarly, Hayden and Mitch, one evening at Crow's Mark, revealed to me what I immediately recognized *as* a relationship between certain of my poems that was more intense than the relationship between, say, the "Olga Poems" and some of the other '64–66

work originally published with them in *The Sorrow Dance.* That (chrono-
logical) relationship was not thereby invalidated; but I was excited at the
realization that there would be a new understanding made possible by picking
out and reassembling the poems I felt had this special *kind* of connection to
each other. In doing so I was in fact following through precisely what I had
originally learned from *you!* If the realization had occurred through something
you, not H and M, had said to me, and I'd put "RD showed me that . . . etc"
instead, wd you honestly have been just as critical?

In fact one can anyway only be shown something one knows already,
needs already. *Showing* anyone anything really amounts to removing the last
thin film that prevents their seeing what they are looking at. "You can take a
horse to water but you can't make him drink." The reprinted poems have
*not* been "removed from the field they belong to poetically" but revealed to
be closely related, a line of succession such as one might find in a family,
where, while all were related, "of the same blood," yet a grandmother,
an uncle, and 2 out of 5 siblings might have—or "carry"—certain
characteristics and have special affinity for each other.

*That film*: You seem to have forgotten all I told you about the circum-
stances and to be determined to evaluate what you saw as if it were a work
of art (which *is what it is* and must stand or fall on its merits, circumstance
and intention being only contributing factors). But in fact it was not (my
performance, that is) a work of art, and my air of fury or whatever (I never
saw the film) was not a result of my ideology or polit. stance or calculated
rabble rousing or whatever but of there being 2 factions organizing the thing,
and 1 (the more radical) wanted me to speak and the other faction wanted to
prevent me, as they were afraid of alienating the mass of middle-of-the-road
midwestern women who were there for the 1st time; so that after a nerve-
wracking wait (I'm very nervous about speaking at rallies anyway) I was
rushed on stage and told—You've got exactly 3 minutes—make the most of
it! And what was my message? You got so het up over the manner of delivery
you never seem to have taken in that what I said was

> "Mothers, don't let your sons learn to kill and be killed.
> Teachers    "    "    "students "    "    "    "    "    "
> Wives and sweethearts " " lovers " "    "    "    "    "
> Aid, abet, and counsel young men to resist the draft!"

You say you believe in war against the state but what is that but an attempt
to incite people to (nonviolent) war against the state?

(I was there not as a "famous poet" but as a private citizen who had done
what I was urging others to do and as the wife of a man at that time under
indictment for doing likewise. I remind you of *these* facts because I think
there is some confusion (amid other confusions) in you concerning the

relation of that incident to the development of my poetry. It wd fit in with your general argument better if I had "used" poetry and my position as a poet, on that occasion, in ways you felt were unbecoming (and one shouldn't USE poetry anyway, I couldn't agree more)—but in fact I was not doing that, I was there as Mrs Mitch Goodman, which is inconvenient for your argument in some way I can't quite get hold of. {(}This is parenthetical anyway, I think . . . Though maybe I'm onto something there. But I'm at least as confused as you are as to what it is so will not try to pursue it now.)

*Tenebrae.* The tone of this poem is one of lament—solemn, rather than wild, lament; note its slow pace. It's like a funeral march. "*We* are at war" changes to "*They* are not listening" because, though in "Life at War" I identify throughout with the crazy human taking-for-granted of horror, and our complicity-by-passivity in what we do not literally perpetrate on one another, stepping outside that identification only far enough to realize, express, horrified amazement at it, yet in this poem it wd have been hypocrisy to so identify myself with those who were "not listening" to the sound of the war-waves. The sequin gowns and white weddings are out of the newspaper pages right next to the war news. The families are the innocent/ignorant millions of families who do keep the kids quiet with the promise of TV or candy bars or hotdogs, and who make business or other plans regardless of whatever doom threatens and has become indeed part of the very fabric of their lives, economically and in all sorts of other ways. The consumers. Certainly I feel all this with anguish. Moralizing? Rather I am keening over them. That does not make it *moralizing* in any way *I* find aesthetically unacceptable! It is not in the words and sounds of the poem you find the preachment but in that projection of me as "preacher" (Screecher?) begun by that film, confirmed by the "Judy Collins" poem,[1] which alarms you and for which you are apparently determined to find further evidence in other poems.

*Woman at War with Man.* You say my poems which talk about Viet Nam aren't at bottom about Viet Nam at all but about the sex war. That is unmitigated bullshit, Robert. First of all, you again *assume* that I am active in the Women's Liberation Mvt apparently. Well, I've certainly come slowly to a lot of sympathy for women's problems I never realized existed (the ones I escaped through certain circumstances of education and environment) and more consciousness of the ones that affect *all* women in our society; and to a good experience of the possibility and reality of "sisterhood." But I am not and never have been (so far) a member of a WL [Women's Liberation] group and I am not at war with men. To say my V*N poems are not about the experience of V*N is self-evident if you mean I have not been to V*N even as an observer/visitor or whatever; but it is insulting if you mean they are not really about the war as it affects our lives, our whole lives. "We are members one of another." I've always believed that even if it was St. Paul, whom I dislike on many counts, who said it. I would not insult *you* by saying your "Multiversity" and "Uprising" passages are not really about— "ought not to be read properly in relation to" are your words—Clark Kerr,[2] LBJ, Vietnam etc but rather in relation to "the deep underlying consciousness of the [man] as victim in war with the [woman]." I call that kind of criticism doubletalk and evasion. Goya wasnt painting the disasters of Goya but the disasters of war. Of course, if we are indeed members one of another, and know it, we know also that we as individuals are full of conflicts, contradictions, weaknesses, and that our energy is in itself a neutral that can be manifested in cruelty and hate or in understanding and love. I.e., we are each microcosms. But that does not mean that we can reduce every piece of artistic work to something dealing with inner conflicts *under the guise of* the overt subject whatever it may be. See back of p. 5.

---

Note additional to p. 7

As far as not letting my rage go to its full limit but always getting into something "moralizing" or "humanitarian," hell, you have me wrong. In the 1st place I don't *have* as much rage as you think, & in the 2nd what you regard as a weakness (in my poetry) is precisely what most people regard as a strength.* If I did this in a hypocritical & dishonest way you'd be right but as I think I make clear in *To Stay Alive* I err rather on the side of expressing at moments a rage I can't sustain.

*In any case to reproach me for it is exactly like reproaching me for having brown eyes instead of blue.

Don't attribute your own complexities of mind & of intention to others—or not to me anyway. I mean really—do stop it. It's just silly.

---

" . . . *My sense of 'Uprising' was not*" you write "*that the war in it was or was not important to me, but how come it was of import to the poem.*" And you object to my saying "*the events were of importance to me*" etc. Well, I don't share your attitude on that point. It is expressed elsewhere as "poets have used our troubles with God, or religion, or social matters, as a *lure* to involve us with the poetic" (quoted in a friend's letter who says it is from something you wrote about Nobby Brown). I have always had a strong preference for works of art in which the artist was driven by a need to speak (in whatever medium) of what deeply stirred him—whether in blame or praise. I'd sooner read *Dubliners* than *Finnegans Wake*. Beckett bores me. Most of Gertrude Stein bores me—she's nice for tea but I wouldn't want her for my dinner. I love George Eliot. I prefer Rouault to Juan Gris or Mondrian. *Of course* all of the above *negatives* were "deeply stirred" by the problems and solutions of their aesthetic and their medium, obviously; so I should qualify the "deep stirring" I mean: I prefer, then, works where need to speak (in whatever medium was theirs) arose from experiences not of a technical nature but of a kind which people unconnected with that medium also shared (potentially anyway). I.e., a sculpture inspired by the potential of the piece of wood it is carved out of might move me by its beauty of proportion, texture, decorative qualities etc. but *usually not as much* as one behind which one can feel some other human experience, to which the artist-craftsman's feeling for the wood contributes, so that the emerging inscape (the revealed inscape) is of the conjoining of some other life experience with the present experience of the wood, the material. Each grasped, revealed, by way of the other.

I do not at all have a sense of luring anyone into the poetic by catching hold of them through my subject matter. The idea appals me in fact. Some events—whether a tree in a certain light, a mexican family looking at the movie stills outside the cinema, a dream, my own condition of being in or out of love, of some epiphany relating to husband, child, friend, cat or dog, street or painting, cloud or stone, a book read, a story heard, a life thought about, a demonstration lived through, a situation, historical and/or topical, (that's to say known in the moment of its passing into history)—it doesnt matter, the list is endless, but some events (selected by some interior mysterious process out of all the other minutes and hours of my life) begin to form themselves in my understanding as phrases, images, rhythms of language, demand to be further formed, demand midwifery is one way to put it. Not all that one feels most strongly makes this verbal demand, even if one is a poet—by poet here I mean prose writer too—(for some non-poets *no* experience makes that demand, and for some nonpoets very occasionally there is such a demand, those are the people who write one or 2 good poems in a lifetime, and for graphic/plastic-oriented people a similar demand is made but it is not for verbalization) but whatever experiences do demand it are always strongly felt ones. That is my testimony. I understand that for some people something like problemsolving is in itself a stimulus— e.g. the challenge of how to tell a story as a poem, not prose, without sounding archaic or stilted, might stimulate someone to make up a story to see if it cd be done. But I myself wd never be interested unless I first had a story to tell.

Damn this ribbon.

For me that is what the phrases

—ASKING THE FACT FOR THE FORM

—A METERMAKING ARGUMENT (Emerson)

and—Form is never more than the REVELATION (not extension) of content[3]

↘MEAN.

This does NOT mean that I believe in *manipulating*[4] the poem. On the contrary, if the poem's to be the real thing it's got to grow out of a most humble *un*manipulative listening. I've written enough about that for me not to have to re-explain what I mean to you, I shd. suppose.

*Violence & nonviolence*—to take up what I take to be the subject you're skirting when you equate. " . . . violently, if need be, to pull down" etc. with the US officer's "destroy the town in order to save it": No one has really solved this ancient problem & I don't pretend to, nor to say there's no paradox involved in what I say—but the equation you propose (a familiar one) is oversimplified for it abstracts from context & makes absolutes where there are none. The North Vietnamese are not to be equated with the U.S. forces just because they are using military force. The pacifist line is too easily used as an excuse for inaction. What the end of our movement towards what we call revolution (a *changed society*) (in which the components—individual lives—change not only the institutions) will ultimately be (if we indeed survive at all) I don't pretend to know, but I do know I really like my comrades in that movement, I like being with them better than I like being with most of the people I know who aren't in it, & I know that many of them accept (regretfully) the prospect that armed struggle may be on the cards. Some of them—those included—may very well be wiser than I am, not to speak of braver, but even if they are not, I wd sooner struggle, in any case, at their sides than go down—or even survive—desperately keeping my moral hands clean. I have some friends who are Weather-people, underground, & when I last saw them I was deeply impressed by their freedom & life-quality, good like good bread. I'm not optimistic about the ecological scene & I've long had the feeling a lot of the time that this ol' world's winding down. If so, I'd sooner spend my last days with the people who have courage & vision & are living their lives vividly right now, & not in a selfish way but always in relation to their sense of a need for a better life for others, even though they make lots of mistakes & are ignorant & often fall flat on their faces. Like I do. And if we manage just in time to stop pollution of resources enough to feel there's a future then that doesn't change my feeling that I want to be with the people who struggle. I'm in retreat right now for physical reasons only.

Yes, this is a naive, romantic, emotional point of view.

I know.

I'd sooner take the chance that my ideological understandings will become more sophisticated as I go along than wait inactively until I was perfectly sure all I did & all my friends did was morally, intellectually, etc., correct & justified. Because I cd. wait for ever. Meanwhile I have to live with myself, & I'm an impatient person.

"Revolution or death" is neither "threat" nor "vow" nor "ultimatum" but just a statement of the problem I felt (& still feel, tho' my feeling about *when* & *how* is subject to many changes) I/we had to face: the one chance, that is, of the world/(earth) I love being saved from annihilation lay in the forces for radical political/societal change. Either throw in my lot with them—I who belong temperamentally & culturally in considerable degree to a conservative past, who don't tend to like change but tend (in little things) to be a bit compulsive & to like things done in traditional ways, domestic things for instance, & am not even really an American (my Britishness has been reasserting itself more & more powerfully in some ways)—OR find myself on the side of . . . well at that moment Mayor Daley was the obvious symbol, & this was a notebook, diary, kind of poem. I don't see the sidelines, or Neutral Ground, as an alternative. My bones might creak as I "threw in my lot" & I may not always know just where we're heading but I sure do know the company is congenial.

This is a movement that can only learn by doing. (And by & large it does.) And that's true for me too. Maybe if you could walk around the autumn field in back of our house, & then come in to a dish of the good fuschia-pink apple sauce I made yesterday from our unsprayed apples you'd feel good & we wouldn't have to write long explanatory letters.

Love—
Denise
And love to Jess.

Notes on Installment 3

"  . . . *form as the direct vehicle & medium of content.*"

To me it *does* mean that "one says something by means of the poem"— but not in the sense of "using" (exploiting) the poem: rather that the writer only fully experiences his "content" (that which he is impelled to say by means of the poem) through the process of writing it, writing it with the utmost accuracy, honesty, trying always to get the tone of what he feels. Which is to say that the poem reveals the content, which is apprehended only dimly (in varying degrees) till that revelation takes place. If it (the poem) "has its own meaning" it is only that the revelation is not only the realization, concretization, clarification, affirmation, of what one knows one knows but also of what one didn't know one knew. I do not believe, as you seem to, in the *contradictory* (& autonomous) "meaning" of a poem and I think your insistence on that leads you wildly astray often, in that aspect of your criticism which insists people are saying what they do not mean. To interpret art as a series of Freudian slips (which is essentially what you do when that perversity takes you) is as tiresome and compulsive and reductive as, for instance, "the method of St. Beuve" which Proust railed against.

*The well*—"one thinks at first it is the well of one's own self but in the

context it means the well of language not as *yours* but as poetry." In fact what
Bet meant was the well of my unscattered, deepest, strongest, serenest self
in contrast to the part of myself that is frantically compunctious and tries
to do too much and actively share myself out between too many people &
activities. She has known me since I was 14, closely. Because the context is a
poem and because I have been a poet all my life *of course* it is also language
that's being spoken of, in a way, i.e. that deepest self is what is involved in
my relation to language. But this is "as well as" not "instead" and your
*substitution* of one meaning for another is typical of your arrogance.

"*Manic depressive.*" To you it is obvious or banal; to me the realization
that I was living through tremendous ups and downs in a single day (often)
was honestly formulated in that phrase, and I was laughing at myself too,
genuinely. In the whole poem I attempted to range in language from the
traditional literate that is my heritage to the flippest colloquial that is also
part of me and that I use just as much. A long diary kind of poem gave me
the opportunity to swing between extremes in diction (just as in my life at
that point I was swinging between extremes of gloom and cheerfulness etc
etc) which short lyrics don't give. My vocabulary and diction generally is
unusually variable, between 19 cent. English and 20th c. American, and I
want in honesty to use it *all* if I can, not just some of it.

"*. . . these, Denny, are empty and vain slogans because those who use them
are destitute of any imagination or feeling of what such greed, racism or
imperialism is like.*" THAT HAS NOT BEEN MY EXPERIENCE AND
I THINK IT IS BULLSHIT, WHAT YOU SAY, AND I WOULD SAY
IT IS DISGUSTINGLY ELITIST IF I DID NOT KNOW YOU
WOULD IMMEDIATELY DISMISS THAT AS ANOTHER EMPTY
SLOGAN. BUT I'M SAYING IT ANYWAY. And I find your tone here
offensively patronizing into the bargain—sounds like Uncle Cid {Corman}
at his worst.

*(Criticism)* "*if it expresses only liking or not liking, it is useless.*" But those are
not the only alternatives: liking, for instance, can be analyzed; and if it turns
out that what the reader has "liked" has been that his or her life has been
made richer by the poem, given that keener sense of being alive Stevens
speaks of as one of the things a poem must do, *then* the writer knows he or
she is on the right track, has been a worthy vehicle, and can rejoice. I am
of course not talking about "happiness" but about intensity of aliveness, in
grief or joy. If an unknown reader, a self-described "ordinary person," writes
to me that "You make me feel and remember. You speak to me"—that is not
mere "I like" criticism, and only an attitude of contempt of other people cd
dismiss it. To me it is a great treasure and makes me feel awed and humble.
Or if a poet friend with an intellect far subtler than mine writes, "Your
poetry keeps so much your self, and the way you feel the trouble the War is

makes a poetry that keeps the trouble everpresent as actionable in potentia in me—as in others I know" I feel again that I have spoken and been audible, and that is much, very much, to me; one does not want to have lived in vain. (Though the way I look at things, I need actions (deeds) of various kinds as well as writings in my life, to feel satisfaction: but this is not a prescription, just a passing note on my own personal needs. And don't tell me writings are also actions, I know that but am using the word *actions* in the most ordinary manner so don't quibble.) OF COURSE "it is a not to design to be liked or disliked." How many more glimpses into the obvious?

"*Whose understanding manifests designs fairer than the spider's most intricate web.*"[5] "*Sinister*" etc etc. Your criticism is based on careless reading. It does not say mankind's understanding manifests designs *as fair as* the spider's web, but *fairer than*—so that, to pursue your own method, the implication is of designs having the beauty of the spider's web but not having the purpose that flaws that beauty and makes it sort of creepy. A great gothic cathedral with its traceries and rose windows is a bit like the beauty of a perfect web with the dew on it on a fall morning; but (unless one wants to get into a whole anticlerical kick or something) is a gratuitous human act of praise, gratuitous in the way David Jones means in *Epoch and Artist* and other writings.

"*We have believed one another mirrored forms of a god we felt as good.*"[6]

You ask where that leaves Shakespeare, DHL, Hardy, Ibsen etc. I was not talking about writers but about people in general (including plenty of writers). People in general *have* shared this belief, basically, in many times and places. A faith in man's potential, his capacity for goodness. Certainly in all Christian times at least. The concept of the Incarnation is the concept of Man's redeemability, however fallen into corruption, for man was made in God's image. Even sceptics and atheists cannot help being culturally affected by that concept.

"*Language, coral island*" etc.[7]

That is, language as the inevitable result of mankind's understandings and dreams, which necessitated a form in which to get hold of them, realize them, concretize, apperceive. This relates to my note on "form and content" on p 1. I do not see this as an eroded way of looking at language. And along with it, by the way, goes "Language, mother of thought." I.e. it seems to me that while there were intuitive comprehensions before language developed, actual *thinking* could not be done until there were words to do it in. "Namers and language-makers" as Emerson calls the Ur-poets had to see and feel the thing in order to name it. But they cd not *cogitate* upon it or absorb it into consciousness until they had invented language. And this was surely a long process of accretion, each adding his little bit, out of his very life—just like coral.

*"the first (revolution) that laughter and pleasure aren't shot down in."*

You complain that I "do not approve" (however) "of laughter and pleasure in 'Tenebrae.'" Robert, really! This is unworthy of you. It shd be obvious to any reader not looking for evidence (desperately) of a perverse thesis, that the grownups (the children falling asleep and not listening to the sea still reverberating or whispering in their ears are only innocent analogies) in "Tenebrae" are not "disapproved of" for laughing (who says they are laughing anyway!) but that grief is being expressed about their resolute, deliberate halfconscious *refusal* to recognize the *disaster* occurring at the very same time and *in which they are implicated* by their tacit agreement to it at the very least. When people who have the responsibility of political consciousness nevertheless laugh and have a good time they do so in the knowledge that you can't make a revolution worth a damn by being grim and solemn all the time. The kind of obviously (stationwagon-owning, promising the kids TV to shut them up, having "big" weddings, buying selling, filling up freezers) middleclass people afflicted by consumeritis and "deaf" from the terror of losing their possessions as much as from any other reason, of whom I wrote in "Tenebrae," are tragically, guiltily, irresponsible. They *could* understand the score if they wanted to. They are not innocent. How can you be so dense as to equate the two and to try to fault me on that?

*"Coprophiliac thumbs"*[8]—not a baby at all, but Lyndon B Johnson (and now Richard M Nixon). Their actions and their lies have smeared shit all over the White House walls (not that they were ever clean before—but this has been a new thick layer). Babies playing with shit are not coprophiliacs, they wd be just as happy with dough or mud or applesauce. They are interested in *all* the textures and smells to be explored. Coprophiliacs are people with a yen for shit in particular. Why "thumbs" rather than fingers? Because clumsier— and sort of gross, like the gesture of Little Jack Horner—and because its thick monosyllable was what I wanted for sound there. Since you know damn well that one uses the word shit non-literally in various connections and that this connection (White House context) is obviously that of lies and evil deeds how perverse it is to quibble and say "I know of no story of Johnson's being a coprophiliac" etc. "Personal associations" indeed! Come off it. It is as if I should start to fault you because somewhere in this letter (#3) you say Horseshit. "Are you projecting your personal associations with police horses onto the People's Park demonstrations? I know of no story in which the National Guard or the Alameda Co Sheriffs used cavalry." . . . etc etc.

*People's Park:*[9]

A lot of us believed we could get away with it. Some people learned from their mistake. Even the sceptical (of getting away with it) thought there was a chance we might. Remember, the great majority involved had not been around at the Free Speech period. I myself was certainly among the naive—

even tho I'd been in the 3d World Strike the quarter before and seen some brutal police action. I myself only became a participant in *making* the park in the last few days before the battle. Once the battle began we all cd see what the score was, *but we stayed together and wd not be driven away by intimidation, and we did experience love and community.* The poem (that section of the poem) does not have pretensions to speaking of, and for, anything but that fact. It was a radicalizing experience for lots of people, tho discouraging to others. It began to show us some of our weaknesses (i.e. the lack of political astuteness you point out—with all the superiority of a nonparticipant) and some of our strengths (humor, courage, inventiveness). To say that we who were naive were self-deluded hypocrites is unjust and insulting. If some of the astute, sophisticated people on the sidelines wd get into the action a bit oftener we might all be better off. Maybe. Or maybe not.

This society is killing people off, and blinding them, all the time. The death & blinding of *Rector and Blanchard* were simply among those few whom a lot of people *noticed*—and which did some good in so far as some of those people were brought one step further along the road of radicaliza-tion, of raised political consciousness and conscience. In the same way, getting nausea-gassed at the JD is not *gratifying*! in itself but one wants to experience everything that can help to make one more aware, make it harder for one to ignore and escape the realities of our time and place, so that one is more activated to change them.[10] That is what "*wanting it, wanting it*" etc is about: NOT wanting the perverse gratification (as you seem to think) of things being bad so one can wallow in their badness, (á la the confessional-type poet who has to go to the bin because it is his stock in trade, nothing to write about otherwise—as one sometimes feels about some of them, though maybe that is malicious and I half-retract it) But wanting to get through one's thick white middleclass skin what is really going on, even if through small analogies.

You speak at the end of Installment #3 of getting "pleasantly" into poems or parts of poems that "have come thru and continue to come thru as splendid"—but Robert, how can I trust your praise where your blame is such a hodge-podge of mis-takings?

Denny

I've made a carbon of this & xeroxed the other parts so I can see what I said.

dear Denny,

I cannot imagine that my attack on your propositions in *To Stay Alive* has been easy for you so far. I had only the guarantee of your own determination —as you say whatever the coercive action of my pressing my own readings and misreadings, you {have} your own strong ideas of what you have to do. And against that "guarantee," I have—it had bound me so that I was not free to write to you when I had such contentions on my mind—the pervading sense of your inner conflicts and the refrain of anguish. " . . . almost unbearably, painfully, straddled across *time*"—yes—and between England and America, yes, and between your intense devotion to your household world and your intense commitment to the demand of the revolution that must be total. And that painful conflict appears again in the realm of the poem between the idea of the poem as revelation, as primary knowledge of the truth of things—and of the poem as a vehicle for personal, social, political or religious convictions. *Keiner oder Alle.* In this volume you propose that the justification is esthetic, and also "of some historical value, a record of one person's inner/outer experience."[1]

It seems to me, Denny, that both the protestation of an esthetic and of an historical justification are mistaken. Your decisions are so clearly not esthetic in character but—as I once as I remember in writing to you realized mine own were—sentimental. We both need to intensify and keep alive as a challenge the challenge of the esthetic. If that word refer to what is pleasing to the senses as the beautiful and not have its ground in a heightend sense [kinesthetic and proprioceptive] of formal elements—the formal elements of the language we build with—then I have no use for esthetics anyway. You've got to force that word to mean something before it fits at all as a term in poetry.

No. I am certain "language charged with meaning to the utmost possible degree" is our responsibility if we be language workers.[2] And that charge is not something we put into language but just the degree of our awareness of the charge of meaning in what we do. Let's take that word *Revolution* I reminded you referrd to the figure of time and space, the universe and man's lot as a wheel turning. The Wheel of Fortune. The card in the Tarot shows the wheel turning *to the right* with Anubis "the underdog" rising. "The genius of good," Papus calls the dog.[3] And the idea of revolutions belongs to the old Ptolemaic universe picture with its revolving concentric spheres. And far back of that to the cycles of "Ages" to which the idea of present time as the Kali Yuga belongs "the Age of Conflicts." The Kali Yuga started, Danielou relates, at the conclusion of the war depicted in the Mahābhārata circa 3000–1500 B.C. Charles's 1500 B.C. is the "Fall" or the beginnng of the Aryan migrations or the Kali Yuga.[4] And in his account of duration, Danielou gives the four Yugas—the Kali Yuga, "ours," lasts 432,000 years.[5] In that historical perspective, no wonder the Hindu civilization exhibits inertia to our Western eyes that live in cycles of the Sun. In the superstitions of that speech (ours) the Sun still rises and sets. We still plan to "overthrow" "establishments" in "revolution" in which the genius of good, the under dog,

has his day in the Sun. Yet some three hundred and fifty years ago the news
was in that the Sun does not go around the Earth. When we write "the Sun
rises" we write in the charge of a ghost world—and in the full charge of
language shld. keep alive the confrontation between the sense that haunts
us and the sense that we have of the actual earth rotating on its axis and
circling the sun. That solar universe in turn, we visualize as actually
peripheral to its galaxy.

At every point our language carries the old, the "dead," configurations—
and, not simply dead, not inert, but having the charge of a spectral reality.
As poets we must call to its full charge, in the fullness of its *myth*, this
ghost—in the full charge of our awareness of the reality it confronts. We've
just the one task: to find the word. We have no guarantee of success in that.
"Revolution" and "Death" are the words you have to deal with. That's a
fearful responsibility and a whole adventure in itself. The poet might well
admit only to convey a sketch, appropriate to "his" sense of it. . . . But what
is indicated in your

> "The wrong word.
> We use the wrong word. A new life
> isn't the old life in reverse, negative of the same photo.
> But it is the only
> word we have. . . ."[6]

? Do you really, a poet, take the charge of *words* as of so little account that
the "wrong" word can be "the only word we have"?

We have the word "rebellion"—to start the war once more, that belongs
to your "Alle oder Nichts" proposition. The old war between good and evil,
to the end. The apocalyptic crisis is something other than the Wheel, the
endless revolutions of eternal orders. *Rebellion* is the word for your resolve
"to pull down this obscene system before it destroys all life on earth."[7] The
hatred that backs that word "obscene" is apocalyptic; and apocalyptic fervor
charges the righteousness that accuses [brings to its sentence in the end
of things] "weddings /. . . / not of desire but etiquette": and true to the
rebellious resolve, to start war again, is the threat of that war in:

> And at their ears the sound
> of the war. They are
> not listening, not listening.

I share with you this rebellious intent, that in truth "We are at war"—it
is a strong imprint this curse of the Old Testament against Egypt, against
Babylon and Rome. That I am homosexual and have at least that counter
sense of being among the cursed [for the old Jewish hatred goes thru and
thru not only against Rome but against Sodom]—as well as the cursers. I
cannot overlook the contradiction in feeling.

But, when "rebellion" is certainly one word, why do you insist that "revolution" is {"}the only word we have"—is it because you will not face to face the apocalyptic content in the poem, the relentless judgment you call upon?

There may be an elusive word, one we don't have, involved. I think of H. D.'s analyst's (Freud's?) request:[8]

it gives off—fragrance?

I do not know what it gives,
a vibration that we can not name

for there is no name for it;
my patron said, 'name it';

I said, I can not name it,
there is no name;

he said,
'invent it.'

There is the name "Revolution" which you subscribe to tho it be "the wrong word" Kali belongs to the Wheel of Inexorable Revolution. Her wrath destroys good and evil alike, consumes us in an age of conflicts.

"Rebellion" the word you do not want to think of, that, indeed, you deny we have—is the name of the apocalyptic to end it all—"Alle oder Nichts"— wholly committed to righteousness no longer in conflict but *at war*.

Yet there is hidden a third name—a third vision of "a new life"—Christ's New Dispensation, profoundly different from the Christ of the Judgment, for it relieves the Law; Dante's *Vita Nuova*.

Can we poets propose the phrase "a new life" as if the creative force of the idea of the New Dispensation, of baptism, did not rush in; and the definition Dante gave to the *Vita Nuova* rush in to whatever presumptions we make, if we not powerfully create our own meaning to stand with the spectral meanings already present in the thought.

The very word *Life* if we be serious about our business of being workers with words *does* involve our being responsible to what science pictures life as. Or else the word is "no more than a word" or even "the wrong word."

•

Certainly, I don't believe "Revolution" is the *wrong* word. And "Rebellion" is also *the* word. And "a new life"—these are three contradictory structures. The eternal cycling. The hatred of the other side of the wheel in which all things are brought to an end in judgment. And the new dispensation in which the bindings of the law are dissolved and *all*[9] things are redeemed [in the fullness of this idea of a new life the enemy is redeemed].

•

There's still an other world present, a well come—the immediacy of *here and now*—that is very different from cyclic return, retribution, or a new life. The presence of Olga in the "Olga Poems" has this life, the life of immediate being that does not need to be redeemed or judged, to be "new," but toward which, beyond morality, an admiration streams. All of part VI vibrates with it.

> Your eyes were the brown gold of pebbles under water,
> I never crossed the bridge over the Roding, dividing
> the open field of the present from the mysteries,
> the wraiths and shifts of time-sense Wanstead Park held suspended,
> without remembering your eyes. . . .

There is no stay of possibility or impossibility to the life here. It is all there in the words, without the weariness, the inertia, of Fortune; or the accusation of the war against evil; or the necessity that life be new, or else. The old poetic religia of Mnemosyne.

Yet none of these worlds accounts for what must be another system—the one that has to do with the anguish, the straddling. The co-existence of your absolute commitment [commitment to the side of the good genius in the war against evil] and your conflict, your "straddling," your anguish, seems to me to point to a fifth, unresolvable, picture. Is it the guilt a poet would rightly feel in saying "we have no other word" when in her heart she knew there was another word, and that finding the word in its fitness was the only true responsibility of her art? But "rebellion" was not the *only* other word. *Alle oder nichts* would at least be a fix that would eliminate the anguish of a divided soul. There is the dreadful threat against life itself that unless it prove to be what you want you will refuse it. I am more struck by the condition of "hope" that you would wake to define "the life that wants to live."

*A new life* is not then here and now, as it is in Christian revelation and then in Dante a new life in this life, this world. "A new life" that demands not new sight of the world but the re-form of the world is the demand for a life not this life—a refusal of present living. Cassirer in his *The Question of Jean-Jacques Rousseau* sees in Rousseau something like this. In the individuation of conscience, Rousseau saw that where before the model of faith lay in the Word of the Bible or in the social conventions now it must and could only lie in his own conscience: society, in so far as *he* found it intolerable, demanded total change.[10] In his ideal, the total society must be changed, the conscience of the totality comes to agree with his individual conscience. Along one line the Rousseau-ian contribution leads towards ideas of a totalitarian democracy—for no true individual conscience can be at variance with the volonté générale. Cassirer makes it clear that the problem of Rousseau is not to be made simple, it cannot be disposed of.

It is a philosophy of conflict. A man who so hated the very society that admired him that he demanded a totally new "society," and was so miserable in his alienation that he demanded a totally new "self"—in which self and society would be indentical. No *other* or contrasting volition was tolerable.

There is some block here for my imagination. I so *react* to the Rousseau proposition as a presumption I can't get close enuf to allow for the world it envisions as true.

   •

One world-view I don't find in your thought, Denny, is the idea of evolution as it appears in Lyell's geology and in Darwin's biology; and it is the one that seems to be most true. Certainly, it is central to my thought. Well, this tremendous change in our view of what is actually happening— from Darwin to the D.N.A. is barely one hundred years old. But when you speak of a new life, of a vital change, the instantaneous awakening to life—the moment in time that reinforces all time has a counterpart [sets a counterpoint in the music] in the instant of mutation: but I see that instant, as Darwin sees the Yuga—slow and long durations of evolutionary change as without moral justification. The creation moves not toward perfection or goodness but toward variations upon the content of a theme. In which goodness and perfection, the tribal criteria of likeness and kindness [what belongs to the kin] are no more than variations—the imagination, any human imagination does, and where imagination has genius but the more, goes on to populate a world as various as the actual human community.

What—once the imagination addresses life, with some concern for what *life* is—does it mean to have an "own" life a man could "take"? Perhaps it is the only form of a strike for those whose only true production is their lives. As the workers shut down the power plants, rebels without factories shut down their factories of *self*.

dear Denny,

    A cover letter, for I would not have you launch out into another twelve pages of my inquisition to take the place of a correspondence. I send my continued "say," for not wanting to engage here has meant a retraction of confidence. Yet I remain engaged—my sense of something *wrong* cannot be laid over there like O.K. you are wrong. The "wrong" is—as everything has at times been—a commonality, it is between us. I cannot find a place to stand to say "How interesting Denise's conflicts are"; I am driven to pursue them.

    But today I've been back beginning in *O Taste and See* to find out the whole complex of ache, pain, suffer, constriction, hurt, cramp, locked in,

## 455

Nov. 9, 1971
{San Francisco}

pent up—and relatedly of "not kind" and of cruel, of weight and heavy, of blinding, burning, choking. The key poem (it's the one too in which the political theme appears as an extension) is "The Novel."

But how radiant the reading has been. The story "Say the Word" is so beautifully directly *there*, true in its telling.[1] And the songs of restoration in marriage—where most I questiond in reading, to see if there was some sense of making a claim, or of special sensual piety—stand with a full confidence. The most difficult and essential of all—to establish where there is so much transformational magic and passional ache in life—the woman's and the man's bodies as wife's and husband's. You speak for the return of fresh feeling that makes living together over years so special.

You bring me over and over again into events of your life as events of a Mystery And as recently as "Relearning the Alphabet" there is a major statement of that mystery. The theme of "anguish" (as a transformation of the elements of pain, hurt, ache etc. I am immersed in analysing now) is the term in that Mystery of a Passion (as in *Paterson*, "divorce" is: something that you realize must be deeply known, kept alive, working as an agent in the faith of a hidden process{)}. The politics of anguish rushes up to illustrate the theme (as the initiate—"pilgrim" your naming of it so far)—seeks to find, to verify, the presence of his Mystery in the actual world—where else is worth it? * Anyway, it is one resolve we do share in inheritance (by our own undertaking that inheritance) from the work of the *War Trilogy*, the *Pisan Cantos*, and *Paterson* that have in common the determination that what happens in the actual world has meaning and resounds, i.e. is a metaphor or an illustration of something going on [as in Freud's *Psychopathology of Daily Life* everthing is language, a waking dream].[2]

* The mail arrived and just here I interrupted writing to read hastily your letters, which do greatly relieve an oppressive sense I had of how unlikeable much of this unburdening of my contentions must be.

I will be writing soon to say more about the content of actual life as it becomes felt as belonging to the creative work in writing coming to bear all the implications the reader expects to be there.

love
Robert

**456**

Nov 9 {19}71
Temple, Maine

Dear Robert,

It is a beautiful sunny morning, cold, fresh after yesterday's snowflurries (I thought the little snowflakes whirling past in the pale sunshine were seeds till I went out to see what kind of seed they were and they melted on my sleeves). We are packing up to go down to Boston—probably not to return till Thanksgiving.

We have said some harsh things to each other. For my part I'm not sorry to have spoken to you about your arrogance etc because I have felt these things for years and assiduously suppressed them—and one must either truly *convert* such feelings or express them—otherwise surely they fester at last. You have been more critical (openly) of me than I of you always, though not in the degree you are now; so I don't know if you feel a similar relief at getting something off your chest, or not. But in any case, what I'm now writing for is to say, let us call a halt, and not go on with this whole thing until it becomes more rancorous and destroys our long and deep regard for one another: Let's try to just be friends again in a new way. I think it would be wise if you gave up your whole idea of writing something about my book, because you know from experience how tied up in knots you get when you get involved in this kind of critical argument, I am thinking of a letter you wrote me regretting how caught up in argument over HD's detractors you had become. I wish you would put the whole thing aside and not give me that kind of attention. But if you are feeling unfriendly you may think I am simply afraid of what you may say. Well, I can't stop you: but as I say, I am sure it wd be wiser, you will only exacerbate your already irritated nerves doing it, and it will be all the harder for our friendship to recover and since I think so much of your criticism is based on false premises anyway, I cannot see that history or posterity or anybody at all will benefit—but of course I cannot expect you to see *that* at this point, tho I have hopes that in time you will—and if so you will be glad you stopped.

At the least let me suggest the following: that from the day you receive this letter, you put aside my book and your notes thereon for a year and a day; and then if you want to look at it all anew at that time, do what you must, and I shall say nothing. And in the meantime let us write to each other of our daily lives, that is to say of that part of them concerned with things seen and done, oh, and maybe read too, but not with each other's work or character. Call a truce, in all courtesy and good faith. Do you agree? I would be so happy if you will.

> Love from
> Denise
> Denny

dear Denny,

I don't have what I wrote you to refer to, and a good thing at this point, for I don't want to defend my feelings but to find them out, and I am grateful you have had the faith to go along with me and to shout back *"Bullshit!"* if need be, to keep things going in the open and make it clear where you utterly reject what I have to say. But bear with me as I go on for a

## 457

Nov. 11, 1971
{San Francisco}

while to do some straightening out, without feeling there is a need for your "answering." The letters of the past years have borne increasing witness to the burden of correspondence you carry (as the poems bear witness to the growing company of those who have come into the painful responsibilities of your personal feeling). What I need is some working-out of long-held-back observations and interpretations (which from anything I knew of you personally I knew would be unacceptable to you{)}. I am not in the position of a psychoanalyst who wants you to assent to the way of reading I see—but I no sooner write that than I realize I am in that position, for how I read is how I write, and poet to poet I do want to win assent to my concept of the poem. But as a friend I need only for you to be in the full confidence of any view I have of your work. To unburden my heart is to unburden a good deal of arrogance, disagreement in fundamental things, relentless pursuit of life and literature driven by a sense of undercover meanings, as well as sympathies—and beneath it all the inconvenience of confronting views at variance concerning the truth of things.

There are things in my hasty first reading of your letter (gingerly, might be a better word, since I was so aware what an attack had been stored up, and how rightly you would challenge that in itself) that release certain snags in my thought. My mind still won't go all the way over there to say: O.K. Denny is at last making it clear that she rejects the duplicity and complicity of truth (the duplicity and complicity of God), and settles for we the people of the good and light verses they the dead (both St. Paul and Lawrence use that term) of the darkness and evil. I see it that way often enuf, but I know only too well my own duplicity and complicity. What makes me arrogant is that I cannot imagine that for some their words do not betray sinister meanings. Which reading of a spider's web is *careless*, the one that remembers what an actual spider's web is and is designed for and so sees the word "fairer than" charged with more than one level of meaning? or the one that argues against any further thought about spider webs past the visual delight? I likewise cannot imagine a gothic cathedral without reading the sinister figures of its gargoyles and, along with the grandeur of that architecture, the public costs of those edifices of competitive civic pride as well as of religious exaltation. We like to think of the communal Fervor with which men labord and of the embodiment of a common faith. But for the Albigenses those richly-jeweld Rose windows and flying buttresses were an image of the spiritual arrogance of a Church which laid waste all of Provence. The lovely Sainte-Chapelle is the jewel-box of a King and a Queen admittedly. And the peasants who destroyd the Cistercian abbeys were striking against visible tyranny. A great gothic cathedral with its traceries and rose windows *is*[1] a bit like the beauty of the perfect web with dew on it on a fall morning. To have a sense of that beauty is not sentimentality; but to have a sense of that beauty which does not care to go into the actual nature of the beauty is.

Henry Adams in the exaltation of his *Mont-Saint-Michel and Chartres* does not exclude knowledge of the nature of the spider:

> The equilibrium is visibly delicate beyond the line of safety; danger lurks in every stone. The peril of the heavy tower, of the restless vault, of the vagrant buttress; the uncertainty of logic; the inequalities of the syllogism, the irregularities of the mental mirror—all these haunting nightmares of the Church are expressed as strongly by the Gothic Cathedral as though it had been the cry of human suffering, and as no emotion had ever been expressed before or is likely to find expression again. The delight of its aspirations is flung up to the sky. The pathos of its self-distrust and anguish of doubt is buried in the earth as its last secret. You can read out of it whatever else pleases your youth and confidence; to me, this is all.[2]

I don't think I am arrogant or coercive to demand a fullness of what a spider-web is if there is a spider web in a poem, for I believe (and so do you) that images in poems like images in dreams are not incidental or mere devices of speech, chance references, but go deep into our experience. And who in this world has not watched with fascination the activities murderous and cannibalistic of a spider in its web? What child does not know the spider's invitation to the fly?

I'm sure it is perfectly possible to exclaim how lovely! upon seeing a spider-web dew bejeweld in the sun or moonlight. And I care not if it seem creepy. What is demanded by poetry is that we see (as Adams sees his beloved Gothic) the web in its full truth and loveliness.

Is it really without significance that the image "designs" [which has a widely used sense of *sinister plots*, as in "What designs does he have in mind?] / fairer than "the spider's most intricate web" is followed by images of murder and cannibalism [well known characteristics of the spider in its sexual life]. To read with every resource of Freudian interpretation a passage which projects sexual mutilations is surely not wilful misapprehension.

In "Up Rising" the image of the child in his phantasies of burning mothers, fathers, sisters, everybody up is out of my own childhood experience; verifying a common ground with James Dickey's "Firebombing" [which in turn had the actual experience of his own firebombing to verify the poem], and beyond a projection of the psychic significance of napalming.

| personal experience ] | phantasies of destroying the world by fire actually known in childhood art both of painting and story-telling by the poet. |

| | |
|---|---|
| actual experience in the war] | James Dickey's testimony, and back of that Count Cianos. |
| projective level] | the deep lying inner need to destroy the world by fire. |
| myth] | Jehovah's destruction of cities by fire. The destruction of the Egyptians by fire and disease still celebrated in the Seder. |

The Hydra as a person of a multipersonal God.

---

My complaint about the passage about the coprophiliac spasm that smears the White House walls with its desensitized thumbs *is* that unless there is some actuality to the President or someone smearing the White Hall walls with shit then this can be nothing but projection.

The idea of coprophilia as having to do with desensitized thumbs and with murderous phantasies (and hence with war) does have to do with Freudian ideas of a phase all babies go thru, "Not a baby at all" you reprove me. But only the Freudian doctrine that all babies go thru an anal-sadistic phase gives you the right to presume that you have in your personal experience a common ground here with Johnson and Nixon.

My difficulty is that I only believe that I have this baby experience of coprophilia. And in my disturbed feelings about shit I find some verification of that experience. Well, certainly the idea of a mad coprophiliac smearing them walls with desensitized thumbs is vivid enuf to be sure I was just such a one.

But I've got great doubts that Johnson and Nixon is/are a real grown-up coprophiliac. At this point I wanted to know whether this was phantastic (projected) or actual [as Dickey we know actually did have the phantasies and carry out the missions of fire-bombing].

If Babies playing with shit are not coprophiliacs; why in the world would grown-ups be coprophiliacs? Is it really quibbling to ask for some reality here? If horseshit appeared in a poem of mine, you would be remiss not to read it as being meant at every level. Do you think that I not hold myself responsible thru and thru for what the Hydra is (as it appears in "Up-rising"). This means not only researching myth and theosophy. But, since I see the dragon biting Strong's bowels (his actual bile attack which sent him to the hospital in the middle of "attack" on the students): I am certain the Hydra has a physiological entity.

If I believed at all that that passage (or any passage) in your poetry was just a colorful way of saying that "their actions and their lies have smeared shit all over the White House walls" I would have no trouble. But no images are *mere*. If the passage have no roots in personal associations, it is just name-calling. But no name-calling is without its projection from the personal experience of the repulsive.

It isn't incidental that "Mother fucker" where it is a fighting word, comes with the full charge of an Oedipal repression. "Shit!" as a derogation comes from repression of babyhood's shit-play, magic, money and "aggressions."

What is unfair in my laying it on in regard to the spider-web sequence and in regard to the coprophiliac sequence is that I know very well you feel it as my faulting you, my saying you are to blame for thinking what you find unthinkable. And then I am hammering away at you blaming you for not thinking the unthinkable.

But all that can be cleard away in writing publicly about these passages, for there it becomes a question of what is going on in the passage. The sequence from (good) male passivity to (bad) male aggressivity really is there in the sequence. And the commonly known story of the spider-web and the female's relation to the male, the reading one is sure is one the poet was unconsciously constructing.

It takes someone whose conscious mind knows nothing of hostility between the sexes [a hostility observable between female and female, male and male, as well as between male and female] to come up with such a sequence, meanwhile protesting the willful and perverse mis-apprehension of the reader who allows any consequence and significance to the transition. Are words only when we like it "little boxes" hiding meanings?

While you tell us that "they" are not listening, not hearing the war, I am listening and hearing more than you consider it legitimate to hear.

For a long time the gap between what you have clearly meant to say and what that saying meant to me has left me more and more guilty of an unfriendly thinking what you would not have me think. But mostly, I am left isolated in my concern for sinister meanings, undecided, underside? undeside, upside down and sideways twists.

By what quantity or quality do those who believe God is good get to be "people in general" [Plato and Plotinus wld be solidly among this company] and those heretics [myself among them] who believe God at times even to be evil—? Certainly Old Testament tyranny is evil, I won't yield there and only in a mystery "good"—I read the story of God the Father only as a jealous wrathful and evil (over-powering and tyrannical) creativity sick with itself and in its creation striving to imagine love and good. To think that the evil of this world proceeds from any true goodness is intolerable to me. But I can think that evil, sick of itself, imagines love and good. From what information do you assert "Certainly all Christian times at least—there was a belief in man's potential, his capacity for goodness?"

What do you mean when you dismiss Shakespeare, DHL, Hardy, Ibsen as writers and not people? David Jones is a Roman Catholic and it is prescribed dogma to feel god is good. A church that burnd men for thinking otherwise.

But clearly as I argued on (and as I argue on here Denise{)} I but add making you fruitlessly angry to your already being tired and needing rest.

I think I've had my say, enuf that when I write on my reflections on *To Stay Alive* they will be more directed to the text itself and ways of reading it; and I will have a strong sense of where you find my readings intolerable. And you do show that I need to discuss the questions of arrogating the meaning of the text. And the task and significance of misreading "mis-apprehensions—getting hold of things by the wrong end, upside down, sideways—demonstrating a disregard for their nature and function" provides a working definition. I am a reader of things into things by my own nature.

At least I shall start my would-be reader off with a wariness, titling the essay misreadings and darker reflections after *To Stay Alive*.

But I *have* exhausted my eagerness to hold you responsible for what *I* see as going on there. That is, I take it, all my own world. And I'll make it clear that that is what it is as I go.

Love
Robert

---

## 458

Nov. 12, 1971
{San Francisco}

dear Denny,

The heart is more than willing, and the actual concern in analysis cannot but gain in having a rest. Yes, a year and a day. And another season I will allow myself—for the dark of the year is always the coldest and darkest, the unforgiving time of my mind.

So . . . put the letter I maild this morning away too for a year and a day—

love
Robert

---

## 459

{late December 1971
or early January 1972
Moscow}

Love & New Year Greetings from Denise in Moscow! (Will be home before you get this.)

Dear Robert & Jess

460

{January 1972
Boston}

I spent Xmas in Russia!! In fact, I spent Xmas Day at Yasnaya Polyana[1] & saw the very table, & pens on & with which *War & Peace* & *A.K.* & *Resurrection* etc were written—& much else. Chekhov's, Mayakovsky's, & Dostoyevsky's apartments, *The Seagull* done at the Moscow Art Theater. A *perfect* ballet (*Cinderella*, great ballerina Maximova). And the Hermitage: Incredible Impressionist & post-Imp. collection, etc etc.

Love, & all good wishes for 1972<br>—Denise

Maybe I sent you a card from Moscow, I'm not sure.

dearest Denny,

461

Jan. 25, 1972
{San Francisco}

Your abounding will to hold firm in your affection for me wins thru— and what is most important for my confidence is not condescending to "forgiveness," but I take it, as I would take it, extends in the acknowledgement of the confrontation. But must be shakey. Mine is. Shakey, and yet [in my current studies in *Romeo and Juliet* where the whole alchemy of the play is the coming to grief before the "peace" of the community can be released—the opposing parties dissolved in tears] refinding itself.[1]

I have begun to see, along with my other considerations, my contention with you as contention with my own *anima*—as Jung proposes such an archetype of a woman and I would read it to be an idea of womanly virtues or powers created in the matrix of collective imagination [the cultural self] and of personal imagination [the individualization]. For much of what I suspect you of, or accuse you of, I suspect as some womanish possibility in myself. And thinking of Juliet as an anima projection so that for her father when she is in accord with his will she is "the hopeful Lady of my earth" and he is resolved "My will to her consent, is but a part, And shee agree, within her scope of choice, Lyes my consent, and fairie according voice."

And when Juliet does not "consent" but dissents and keeps her *own* counsels, he breaks into a fury of attack:

> How now?
> How now? Chopt Logicke? What is this?
> Proud, and I thanke you: and I thanke you not.
> Thanke me no thankings, nor proud me no prouds,
> But fettle your fine joints 'gainst Thursday next
> . . .

Or I will thee, on a Hurdle thither.
Out you greene sicknesse carrion, out you baggage,
you tallow face . . . etc. etc.

It would not but remind me to the temper of my long festering wound in my communal conscience. Well, in some right sense, I knew I had—to restore a broken correspondence, to restore the flow of feeling—to begin there, my even arrogance had to be (has to be) my primary ground. There is a sweetness I needed that is so ready to revive in you—and it's the answering sweetness in me that, shaken, beaten back, is toucht by your remembrances (and it was a kind of *wonder* to have the Russian cards and *stamp*).

The enclosed *Ground Work* Supplement 1 is a suite of poems, starting with poems written in the margins of a copy of *Moly* I was reading on route from New Haven to Portland in April of last year;[2] and then [the Preface and the Second Take] in October, after reading the poems to Thom and talking about how they had gone back to the experience of adolescent "crushes" we had both known—what adolescent had not known?—which gave rise to the Preface.

There will follow, as soon as I have got the two remaining parts, the "Metaphysical" suite that the Christmas retake on Southey's "Burning Babe" after your Advent 1966 poem, belongs to.[3] I think this sequence will lead into, *does* lead into, the emerging "Juliet" theme that my conversion to the anima concept belongs to.

Winter already unbinds. And we have, after months, it seems, of overcast or, even when clear, refusal to admit Winter—now, rain. The garden and I are releaved (relieved?)—

Love<br>Robert

The enclosed installment on *Ground Work* (1971) pp. 13–18 carries me half way thru the notes on Jess's painting—where I was deraild by my decision to prepare a typescript edition of the H. D. still in the works.

---

**462**

March 26/1972[1]
{Williamsville, NY}

dear Denny,

I've got verified my reading at Tufts during a weekend of Poetry April 29/30, where Bob also will be. I'm scheduled for Saturday evening the 29th. When I was working out my three weeks round originally the Tufts invitation was out of the question because the tour began with a date early in the first week for a reading at Storrs. But most fortunately, the Storrs reading has been maneuvered so that I am to give the Wallace Stevens memorial reading there on the 25th. And that has made getting to the Boston area entirely possible.

Will you be there that weekend? I am troubled, of course, about seeing you, after my trampling our friendship in my unburdening of my pent-up even cruel criticism—if "criticism" it can be calld where so much of its crisis is phantasmal.

And, dear Denny, I still need much of your forbearance to see much thru to next spring's truce-end. Tho I think my pouring out as fully as I could and even wildly what was then on my mind has eased the picture to make possible some better focus. I find from the publishing of an interview I did with George Bowering and Robert Hogg in Montreal[2] that then, three years ago, I was—in the midst mostly of talking about the crucial incompatibilities between Olson's poetics and view of myth and cosmos and my own—I was attempting to define your not believing in the primary meaning of the art of the poem itself, but more and more thinking of the poem as communication of meanings whose primacy was posited outside the art, in "Life" or social realities, causes that had clear and urgent priorities.

Well, it was because I was subscribing in some part to such arguments that I had to discuss them.

What I do realize is that I have myself to the particular responsibility in the Art I have so projected as being the responsibilities of other poets. I have been trying in the recent work I am enclosing (from 1971) to locate, as sets of relationships—personal, historical (projecting perspectives and compounds of images in the *Moly* upon earlier stages both in my personal history and in Man's—and in the "Metaphysical Suite"[3] incorporating elements of the Religious crisis of the 17th century in my own).

Sections 4 and 5 are drawn from your "Advent 1966" poem—tho not from your poem (as, for instance, I take Thom's actual poems as model in the *Moly* "replies") but from your reference points: (a) Southwell's poem and (b) photographs of napalm victims. And 6 and 7 still have much to do with the root the actual body is in the poem over against the phantasmal and fictional realms. It's in 8 that, in the close, the matter of my controversy with you comes forward as present in the content of "the end of an old friendship"—tho the "her" is you only in passing and soon is "very like" my mother. It is, I believe what Jung would call my *anima* and, perhaps, *the* Anima. (This suite, still short by two sections of its completion, is at the close of 8 in something like the same place as the "Santa Cruz Propositions" found themselves at the end of part 2 confronting the Imago of Kalī, via again some idea of you.)

I think, Denny, what the end of an old friendship means is the beginning of a new one; as it seems to me the body of my sixth decade—the significance of my 50s is the end of an old body and the beginning of a new phase, a new Age of being old—but actually this period of the seventh decade is not yet "old" that lies yet further ahead. But I do feel it as an other body entirely.

As both sequences announce so strongly some crisis in relation to a Kalī-Anima-Injured Girl—"Grief."

But this is not purely an individual personal confrontation, it is more and more the confrontation all men have in their machismo sex-class in relation to women. It is a social confrontation that not only whites have, but blacks (I am thinking of Cleaver's[4] writing) project powerful and disturbed pictures of such a "Woman"—

————————

Let me put aside this matter of what I feel going on in my work—my thought is carried away in the stream of that if I but touch upon it.

Back to the three and perhaps four (if I get up to Boston Friday) days I will be in Boston Environs. I want to see you and Mitch—to have some time that, however awkwardly, can be ours to exorcize in the actuality of our company the spectral imaginations I have so unfortunately raised. But I want too to see Octavio Paz, and a visit with Elizabeth Bishop (who was during her period of San Francisco residence a most welcome acquaintance). I hold myself as involved outside of my reading on Saturday evening, only with one possible workshop session or discussion; and I will want to hear Bob's reading. He is in a period of work that is most exciting for me.

If there is a possibility of our getting together on Friday April 28th, I will determine to come up to Boston then—to announce my presence only as of Saturday afternoon. Which would give us time as ours, previous to the involvement of the larger "scene"—

Write me before April 13,
    c/o Marvin Feldman
    33 Brookside
    Williamsville, New York 14221

                        love,
                        Robert

## 463

{March, April 1972}
19 Brook Street
Brookline,
Massachusetts 02146

Did you see (recognize) Nik? Probably not—he has a beard at the moment! It was a surprise to be introduced (& so nicely) by G.{eorge}Q.{uasha} but I cd not feel inclined to chat with him after.

Dear Robert

I'm not going to Seattle on the 27th/28th BUT I will only get back the night of the 27th & MAY have to spend the 28th at the Resist office (or some other similar convenient place) helping to organize a special photo-leaflet about what the current air-raids are doing. The enclosed xerox will explain the project which is getting good response so far, tho' not enough to make it sure we will go ahead & do it. It may even have been done *before* the 28th, if at all, but the thing is I simply cannot commit myself to spending the 28th with you the way things are. I shall be away 24th–27th and *just* got back from Ohio last night. It was a very busy week & I didn't feel able to properly read your new poems & think about it all. *But just hope the sense that where real mutual love once exists, it is phases[1] of friendship that end and begin anew, is what we both really feel. Surely.* Will try to get to Tufts in any case & hope you will call me at 739-1016 whenever you get in. If you decide to arrive the 28th anyway it is possible I may be free after all—I just don't want to tie you up.

There was an amazing night while at Denison when I was meeting with a student-initiated class on "Individual Writers & the End of Man" (take that how you will!) who wanted to discuss Baudelaire & Rilke, which we did, in a co-op living house, & every hour or so I was on the phone to Seattle where my convict friend had a sharp attack of paranoia after "speeding" for 2 weeks & he had a *gun* (loaded) & I was alternately talking to him & to Ken Osborne (a mutual friend, very good guy, Catholic radical who was in jail for draft-resistance for a while & is into Gay Lib. now) who kept me informed from phone booths whether Tommy had still got the gun. And meanwhile (in Granville Ohio) there was a wild rainstorm with thunder & lightning & kids running out shirtless to enjoy it & running back in to the Baudelaire/Rilke discussion, dripping & joyful, & *meanwhile* a girl had rescued a tiny baby rabbit (fully furred, thank god!) from the mouth of a Siamese cat (on her way to this meeting—the girl, not the cat) & I had it on my lap & eventually it unfroze from its fear & I was feeding it warm milk off a teaspoon . . . Life!

Maybe a poem will gather itself together out of *that* particular conjunction of experiences . . . Anyway—I'll try to get transportation to Tufts the 29th, in fact Suzy says she can take me. (Mitch is in Minnesota for 2 months & transportation (public) can be a big problem around here.)

Excuse scrawly letter but my eyes are bothering me. An allergy complicated by not enough sleep.

> Live & love & be well
> —I'm the same Denise as ever.

And thanks for coming to the reading, I was so glad of your presence there.

> {spring, summer 1972}[2]
> 19 Brook Street
> Brookline, Massachusetts 02146

Dear Poet (and some novelists and playwrights too),

Some of you have participated in group benefit readings for Resist, and some of you have contributed money, perhaps, if you are on the Resist mailing list. Others of you may never have been contacted, but would wish to contribute once you learn what Resist is and what purposes your help would serve.

Here is a proposal, based on my own experience, for an easy way you can give us valuable assistance:

In the past I have on numerous occasions spent considerable time and effort arranging benefit readings for various causes—readings given by myself alone or by a whole array of well-known poets. And I have come to the conclusion that, with rare exceptions (e. g., a huge hall—which usually has to be paid for—and a folk-hero/popular star attraction) the game is not worth the candle. Instead, what I have been doing for the past year or so is simply devoting the funds from a proportion of my ordinary dates at colleges and poetry centers to the support of movement enterprises with which I am connected. I have not even felt it a pinch, because I have simply accepted a few more readings than I would have otherwise done. For my own financial need, in other words, I would tend to keep down the number of invitations I accept when it rose above the number required for as much of my livelihood as comes from that source. In accepting extra engagements therefore, I am merely adding to my workload and the amount of time spent away from home, not cutting down my normal income. Some people —and I myself at certain periods of my life—may prefer not to take on extra engagements but to pledge a tithe of what they would be undertaking anyway. The basic idea remains the same: that those of us who are in the habit of giving a certain number of poetry readings each year have a readymade source of aid to an organization such as Resist, for which no special advertising has to be done and for which the money is guaranteed whether or not an audience of any size shows up! Of course, any of us who has the desire and the opportunity to utilize such an occasion to also make a special appeal for Resist might help even more; i. e., one might announce that one is contributing one's fee, or part of it, to this organization; describe its nature; and pass the hat, or ask the audience to try and match the amount . . . But there are occasions on which it does not seem appropriate to do that, and it is of course entirely optional.

I think we should keep in mind that, however welcome an addition to our incomes lecture and reading engagements are, the majority of American poets do not actually depend on them for a livelihood; most of us have teaching and other jobs, and the readings are "gravy." Therefore, if we care about ending the war and changing the society—and the record of American poets *has* been that we do care—we have a moral obligation to share some of our luck in having such a source of extra money with some of the people who are spending all of their time and energy trying to bring about some of those changes: the kind of people Resist helps. I hope you will join with me in this project. If you plan to, write to RESIST (763 Mass. Av., Cambridge, Mass. 02139) to tell them. Fees vary much according to age and fame and the type of group or institution which has invited you, I know. But it would help if you could tell us approximately how much you can pledge. If you are young or little known, your opportunities will be fewer and the amount lesser, but our appreciation would be just as great.

Thanks for your attention,
Sincerely,
Denise Levertov

Dear Robert,

**464**

Aug 16th {19}72
Temple {Me.}

I just cannot accept any more readings this fall and have had to tell that chap from Kent[1] it is impossible. I had been tentative anyway as I wished to reserve October for Temple, Maine. Now a thing involving a Russian poet (Vinokurov) I met and liked in Moscow who is coming to Kansas briefly in early Nov has come up, involving doing some translations from selected literals and going out to Lawrence, Ka. to read with him, and I have other work lined up that is all I can handle without getting frazzled. I wanted to tell you, as by now I have turned down several joint dates with you, it seems to me, and you will maybe think I am avoiding you. Actually I may be, in a way, as I feel there is so much to say that one of these heated hectic ego-fulfilled (I mean, filled with many other people's egos not just ours!!!) poetry gatherings is the last place I wd wish to meet you. But in fact there have been other practical reasons too, which wd have caused me to say no in any case.

I've been spending most of the summer down in Brookline and Mitch has been mostly up here but at the moment we are both here and Al Kresch is here with us, whom we have been rather out of touch with for the last few years for the sad reason that his wife Pat is (not metaphorically but very plainly) schizophrenic and paranoid and makes it impossible for him to see old friends much. But this summer she is staying at her mother's in Buffalo and Al is free to visit us. He is just as dear as ever and it is a treat. He goes out into the neighboring countryside to paint en plein air every day just like Pisarro or Courbet or Cezanne. . . .

I have a new book coming out soon from ND and another later in the fall from a small "Movement" press,[2] both of which I'll be sending you. I had expected advance copies of the ND one by now in fact.

The garden here is a tangle—not that I was ever a great gardener but my 2 summers in England and my hardly being here this year either do show. But the tigerlilies are just about to bloom and the grass is full of Bouncing Bet without any assistance.

Nik is in NY (at the old Greenwich St place, which he "inherited") and has his own graphic press and seems very well. He is coming up here for a visit next week. When is our "year and a day" up? I have the card that wd date it, but not here. It must be in November some time? Hope you and Jess are having a productive summer, and are well. I've been writing quite a bit and also working on the AFSC {American Friends Service Committee} coordinated "Indochina Summer" as well as putting out leaflets for national distribution and doing some fundraising for Resist and learning to play frisbee and going to movies and having coffee hot evenings at the Pamplona and doing my share of communal cooking and housekeeping. Etc. etc. Oh yes, still inching up to putting my prose book together too.[3] I wish I enjoyed writing letters instead of finding it a chore: then you wd not have such a painful sense of my having just *dropped* our old and intense friendship. I realize it must look like that. Whereas what has actually happened is only that I no longer have the emotional dependency on you, on your approval, I had for so long and which was not really a good thing. I'm a slow grower in many ways and it took me a long time to outgrow it—but I can no more help the fact that I have than I could help growing out of my clothes when I was 12. This seems to me a time, not only in my life but in many others, when reassessments of many relationships have become (more than usually, for reasons I cant wholly grasp) necessary and unavoidable and the way through into new ones (between the same people who previously were differently related to each other, I mean) lies only through those often painful reassessments. But neither letters nor the artificiality of meeting while "on tour" are a good medium of communication for me, so there are special difficulties in the way of our doing that. Your letters when controversial demand lengthy replies it tires me out to write in the midst of my very full-of-incident style of daily life. And in those artificial circumstances of meeting, you, I know from other occasions, are apt to get caught in one of your talking jags when you dont listen to anyone else and it becomes exhausting to listen to you. A quiet walk in the Berkeley hills, such as we took one day—well, more than once but I specially remember one lovely peaceful walk—would do more to set things right between us than anything —but I have no expectations of a California visit in the coming year so we will have to do our best with letters when the right time comes. This is just to send you my love, sincerely, for you know dependence is not the same as love and it is only my dependence that has gone, not to be transferred to anyone else either, just gone. Oh, not utterly: that is, I need love and friendship just as much as ever, and I wouldn't want to be a person who didnt.

But there is a difference, of degree, and in the lessening of insecure leaning on a particular source or two: more sense of being based or "centered" as quakers and potters say.

If you had been living in the same town it wd all have happened without misunderstandings probably, even if there wd nevertheless be the political/ideological/philosophical/aesthetic differences we doubtless do really have.

Rereading *Daniel Deronda*. And (more briefly) reading a story by Tieck, called "Runenberg." Somewhat reminiscent of Novalis.

Love to Jess
and to you
from Denise
Denny[4]

dear Denny,

The year-and-a-day, as I remember, was from last turn of the year, in the bad days (for me) of the Christmas, New Years, birthday syndrome. Always a time when I am at my worst. So I proposed a year and on into the spring. . . . But that, I take it, is for any taking up a critical reading again. And it doesn't seem to me that a critical reading was or is helpful. I'll agree with you, for my sense too was of a dislocated crisis in my reading—it was more contentious than truly critical.

It is good to think of you at Temple with Al Kresch proving to be as ever. I will always have that closeness to you that the thought of your resource in the place at Temple with its fields and woods life and old stone wall does me good.

And I concur, Denny, that the professional platform the universities make for us as poets even in readings, but certainly in forums or "discussions" is not a happy or appropriate place to find again some sense of common ground. Where we still have a community in poetry, it is best we be free to find it now as it comes. I do not feel happy about my so often belaboring you for views and responses I did not share. Yet I am often aware of how many directions in art that mean much to me are not agreeable to you. It's not a question of my adventuresome mind for new things; it's a question of old things coming due.

It's hard, when Blake is ranting against Titian, or Pound ranting against Milton, to maintain any sympathy that might lead to understanding what they are talking about. I'm sure much of what I wrote to you must have been rant, the kind of frantic talk jag that goes on when one loses sense of communication. In their easy sophistication *Vanity Fair* used to pose "Impossible Interviews." Well, we've come to the place over the years where interviews are more and more impossible.

Yet there must be points of a sure common ground. The mute shock of Paul Goodman's death, coming for me the day after reading the poem in the

## 465

Aug. 24, 1972
{San Francisco}

*New York Review of Books*—the poem, without the death, was profoundly moving that first reading, the admission of his broken health (but I thought of it as a last letting *youth* go) so direct and simple.[1]

I've had some days this week clearing the garden up, out of season sawing the lower limbs and the inner cross branches from the ornamental plum, taking out bushes of geranium.* I've got innocent starter slips rooting. It's lovely to have the open space. I garden like I write or talk, into densities. Overgrown mind.

*that were infested with bud-worm

"We shouldn't use a word like 'execration,'" the line comes in the episode of the Forsythe series on T.V. "when we know they ought to be shot!"

And I have been wrapping up a new edition of *Caesar's Gate*—literally "wrapping up," for I've just finished a 1972 Preface of 42 pages and a Postscript of another 13.[2] There will be, following the Postscript a 1972 POEM. The prose will annoy I guess—it tries me—and thinking of how trying my relentless going after the involutions of a subject has proved to be for you in the past, the Preface is almost over-doing that in writing. Pursuing my way unreasonably.

Yet there will be other parts, even passages, I may hope will please. I'll accompany the book when it is finally out with an index for more readable parts.

I hope it won't be ten years of going into devious ways in writing.

Jess's work is going beautifully. He paints seven days out of seven, with a half hour or so off for lunch. Tho now—with our summer fogs in—he spends time working at paste-ups.

Yes, keep October for Temple. And don't fear that I will interpret your not writing beyond what I do know—even I feel the shift and focus to immediate things—

Love
Robert

---

**466**

Nov 27th {19}72
{Brookline, Mass.}

Dear Robert, and Dear Jess,

I went to Hanoi for a week. I don't want to leave you unknowing of such a momentous event in my life—but of necessity I have to do too much description of it publicly to manage a proper letter about it, so hope this poem will in fact do better than a letter.

Much love—
Denise

P.S.

Muriel, & Jane Hart, a senator's wife,[1] were with me.

In Thai Bihn (Peace) Province

I've used up all my film on bombed hospitals,
bombed village schools, the scattered
lemon-yellow cocoons at the bombed silk-factory,

and for the moment all my tears too
are used up, having seen today
yet another child with its feet blown off,
            a girl, this one, eleven years old,
patient and bewildered in her home, a fragile
small house of mud bricks among rice fields.

So I'll use my dry burning eyes
to photograph within me
dark sails of the river boats,
warm slant of afternoon light
apricot on the brown, swift, wide river,
village towers—church and pagoda—on the far shore,
and a boy and small bird both
perched, relaxed, on a quietly-grazing
buffalo.      Peace within the
           long war.

It is that life, unhurried, sure, persistent,
I must bring home when I try to bring
the war home.
          Child, river, light.

Here the future, fabled bird
that has migrated away from America,
nests, and breeds, and sings,

common as any sparrow.
               November 1972
               North Vietnam

      Denise Levertov[2]

                        Love from Denny
                           to Robert & Jess

---

Did I send *Footprints*? Let me know. I've lots of other new poems & will try
to make copies & send.

## 467

April 2, 1973

{San Francisco}

Dear Denny,

It's spring, a year later. One of those bright mornings anyway, when my better spirits seem summond forth, with floods of sun and burgeoning tree leafing excited in the air, exuberant. And before I tackle this desk again, making my way hopefully thru a mess of due and undue correspondence that for so long hopelessly has been piled up here—after this note to you I will go at sorting again; and here and there answering, apologizing, disposing. At this point I've decided to make a tour East next Fall—and there's that to begin to shape up. And at my workshop desk there are still pending the little Dante-Giotto fascicle for the Curriculum of the Soul series, a kind of homage to Charles Olson's project;[1] and there also the selected Vaughan for Penguin. I've mislaid, at least, and maybe lost, the little notebook in which I was working. And have had to start all over again on the Vaughan. I'd typed up I–IX of some twenty Dante "Etudes," poem sketches done from Dante's prose works on language and government and while there is a loss there; there is the promise the more of working again [a break for sorting out a stack of miscellaneous]

April 4. That's the way it goes, and it must with you happen the more, the murrain of borderline mail, your undertaking, as you do, such extensions of conscience in this regard.

Meanwhile the time is ripening, I think, for my returning to review questions, new leads, that is, regarding culture (which I would take as a ground cultivated, i.e. disturbed, sewn, and fertilized in which Poetry can grow and cross breed), coercion (where a poetry is forced towards specific ends)—entailing a poetic righteousness or (as in the "New York" school) tribal code of behavior where narrowmindedness intensifies the local area) reenactment (as in Aristotle's theories of representation and imitation) and enactment (where the poem is its own event, and form is immediate)—

There's a "Festival" in June at Thomas Jefferson College where I have proposed to lecture on conventional form (to bring that earlier essay up to date) and to tackle a lecture on Organic form (a term that appears so far to be covering various incoherent ideas, some imitative, that the poem imitates a growing plant, a living animal; some original, that the poem has its origin in an organic impulse and shld be true to the originating organism —the poet, or the man, or the animal; to the society, or to species, or to life, or to the universe—the search for the prime mover in which the principle or origination or organism arises keeps enlarging as our imagination of what is involved enlarges; like the current anxiety about organic and inorganic substances (a kind of anti-Paracelsian reversion) the proposition of the organic seems to me to propose an opposition to the artificial, as if[2]

Dear Denny,

I read thruout these poems, as in "The Museum" and in the second part of "Santa Cruz Propositions" how much you have been fused in my projection of an inner disturbance with what the Jungians call the *Anima*. After my taking that *She* to be so specifically you in Passages 36, in the following section the persona proliferates and shows flashes of offended womanly powers.

But at this point, after so long a silence, and that following my adverse readings of your recent work, I would plead that you might have my trust that eventually (meaning: once the sequence of events has at last been realized) I will rearrive at what I feel to be a just reading, a reading in which all the work of these years must prove good—be made good. I see the good of it but it is not full in me.

Love,
Robert

**468**

Dec. 13, 1973
{San Francisco}

Dear Robert & Jess—

For "Auld Land Syne"—rereading loving letters from you (both) from the '50's & '60's while I try to get together a piece for that book of essays on you (Robert).[1] I'm at Yaddo for a brief 2nd visit, so am looking out into a vista of snow, mighty pines, & afternoon sun on copper-pink pine trunks, little patches of pale blue sky in between the horizontals of pinebranches.

Mitch & I are divorced; have been definitively apart over a year now. He lives at Temple year round now; his companion is called Sandy & Nik (who is on excellent terms with us both) says she's nice. (She's younger than Nik, by the way!) M & I parted at last with a minimum of hostility/rancor —as these things go. Grief, yes. But relief, too. We write to each other now & then.

Nik is wonderful. He is 26! Lives in N.Y. but will be in Providence for some months this spring.

I was all set to write to you, Robert, a year or so? ago, when lo, that book by James Mersmann arrived with its long quote from an interview with you in which you once more accused me most unjustly & unfoundedly of taking sadistic pleasure in the horrors I'd forced myself to depict in "Life At War."[2] I realized it must have been taped, this interview, at the height of that aberration on→whatever for which you had apologized on anyway→which you'd retracted back in '72, & thinking its publication by Mersmann might be as much of a shock to you (in a way) as to me I hoped you'd write and apologize and perhaps print a retraction some place, but there was never any word from you & so I felt our friendship twice broken, deeply betrayed.

**469**

Dec. 23rd {19}75
{4 Glover Circle
W. Somerville, Mass.}

But now I find again so much love and co-respondence, in the early letters especially, that I feel moved to write at least this note. And of course there never *was* any rupture with Jess, that I knew of at least. So—my true wishes for a good year for you both, and that includes blessings on your January birthday, Robert (I don't know month of yours, Jess)—

Denise

## 470

June 4, 1976
{San Francisco}

Dear Denise,

This Spring I've been reading and rereading your work from *The Double Image* on an analytical search, towards an essay that surely is due (ripe), as your "Relearning the Alphabet" comes around to begin at Childhood's End again. I'm confident of coming up with a grammar of things strung to speak (to, thru) you, in which you in turn would speak what they speak. Or (as in "Advent" turn away from what they speak) speak against. It means working out themes, modes or realms—childhood's end, fears and desires (the "in fear from unimaginable sound . . . music's green charmed" of that same poem you talked about at the myth conference), miraculous hours, and difficult ascents—eventually to read or project in reading the war and resistance as it comes into the language of your poem as a hieroglyphic sign. As I finish with my work sheets, as sections of the essay are done, I'll forward them to you.

But today as I started work again, going over what I'd have thought long familiar grounds, finding it all charged anew, I began catching poetry and a little suite of poems has begun that are dedicated to you.

Did I write you, by the way, that in the new volume "Bullfrogs to Fire-flies to Moths" continues to haunt me?[1] Like certain fairy tales and animal tales, the poem tells more than a moral about life, the tale. Tells facts of what is. (As the earth woman, waterwoman and Mrs. Cobweb, tho they were portraits of actual people for you, are for the reader persons of your poetry, your own creative realm. Members of the dramatis personae or cast, tho we do not see more of their drama. I think it is a matter of a "world" and not a drama.[2]

## 471

Monday
August 23 {1976}
1 Douglass St.
San Francisco 94114

Dear Robert . . .

Just after I talked to you, unexpected houseguests arrived, and I've been on a treadmill ever since—until just now . . . I'm not complaining. Among other things, was treated to a Shiatsu massage at Kabuki Hot Springs this afternoon, and a lovely Greek dinner after.

Well, to get down to the business at hand—Australia:[1]

In Sydney, I would refer you to

Betty and Bryan Kelley
24 Macdonald
Paddington, Sydney
telephone—31-9873.

In October, 1973, when I was there, Betty was managing an art gallery—
Hogarth Gallery, also in Paddington—telephone: 31-6839. Bryan at that
time was selling pharmaceutical (sp?) as well as playing drums with jazz
groups. They subsequently visited me early in 1974—and 'cause we're all
busy people and lousy correspondents havent kept in touch but do hear of
them through our Brisbane friends.

Paddington is an interesting part of Sydney—has the old "terrace"
houses—and many of the art galleries and antique shops are located there.

Also in Sydney is Warren Rigney (also known as Rhonda). His phone is
439-4491. Rather hard to reach, but keep trying. He is a very dear friend of
my dear friends in Brisbane—and I met him in Sydney and he was most
gracious and hospitable—drives a lovely Mercedes 280 SL.

If you're interested in jazz at all, the Kellys know where it's happening.

If by any chance you should happen to get to Brisbane, get in touch
with my very dear friends, Don and Dickie (Dacharina) Ross, 54 Quay
(pronounced key) Street, Brisbane 4000. Both are artists and musicians—
although Don also spends some time dentisting. They are fun, energetic,
and crazy. And they'll put you in touch with Eric and Ernest, and John
Woodward and Wally Fernance—all great fun people.

Eric and Ernest have a restaurant in Brisbane—name of Arts &
Battledress, at 216 Petrie Terrace, telephone: 36-2406.

John and Wally live at 51 Birdwood Terrace, Auchenflower, Brisbane
4066 telephone—37-8368.

This is Friday—and as you see . . . Am off to a morning wedding and
champagne lunch—and will drop this off on the way . . . have a fantastic
voyage, and if you see any of my friends give them many hugs for me.

Much affection—
Denise

dear Denny,

How much in your *Life in the Forest* has enabled me at last to break the
bonds I had wound around my feeling for you, terrible conditions, and
(as you will see the word where it came forward in a poem it seems long
ago*) "re-weave" . . . but when it comes it is not a re-weaving, as the poem
pictured, but a letting go of a position taken, guarded and I have been too
long suffering, not I ever thought the loss of your love, for I knew that you
have your own adherence there, but the retraction of my own and the inner

**472**

Sat. 11 Nov. 1978
{San Francisco}

pain of the break in vital circulations—in just so long not allowing myself
this writing to you as I have ever needed it for the release of an earnestness
in feeling itself, that whatever intelligence, whatever stupidity, whatever
contest come just from there.[1]

\* Probably November or December 1975

Of course, there are in this volume the poems that belong to the central
concourse of the human stream we have always been united in—in my work
too there will always be evidence of it. But I am moved from my soul, from
the life of me—for I'll take the soul to be the feel we have of the actual life
we live in of us, just what we have lived, are living, will surely live—by how
at one entirely your saying of being is with your actual line writing now. Your
only art being the care; and all the other properties we thought to be those of
art you sound direct. And yes, care, caring, that I so care as I read, illumines
the art I think to see now is care at the threshold of what we care.

That you have so gaind a life I have no gossip of, I have the intimacy a
reader has where no distraction of personality chatters, for I am as ever ready
to chatter of personal associations, reactions, bridle and claim, in reading—
but what I found, how I read you—the gift I would not desert—in "The
Shifting": not the proposition of a new poetry now but the coming with a
voice in myself, of myself.

O, it's not that I do not feel the most personal pangs of recognition.
Mustn't your "Writing to Aaron" touch, it can't but touch, upon

"And that's the way we lost touch for so long"

and I face how punishing I made that reaching out for you. Not that I am not
and always it may be will in all earnest have to it seems drive herd thru such
a field of egg-shell alarms. And I know I have not just to let go, to write my
palinode; I have still to find for myself what I so sense is there the nature of
the disturbance I had, not for the mere cure, but for the full admission. What
I do know equally, Denny, for since almost two weeks ago, in the midst of a
Whitman conference (where returning to my heart's alliance with Whitman,
it was so much "ours," the number of us corresponding, resolving in ourselfs
his courage of being "equal" to experience) and then of a week's conference on
Olson, I have been, the first day in New York racing eagerly through your
book, and then drawing breath in rereadings—

What I do know is that I treasure the voice you advance here and I know
its stubborn resolve to include the range of sentiments it does was won in
just those "War poems" I took even rancorous exception to.

The "Metamorphic Journal" is a miracle. But I could count the amber
beads of this necklace that is resonant thruout and in the mind forms not a
chronology, one bead after another, but coinherent realms of a life field?

love
Robert

By using energy wisely, and utilizing the sun, wind, and other "soft" energy sources, we can fulfill our energy needs in a safe, clean and efficient manner.

Nuclear energy, while making a powerful and wealthy few even wealthier, creates the risk of catastrophic accident, and exposes us all to deadly radio-active poisons which will be around for generations to come.

Join us in our struggle to stop the nuclear industry, and replace it with a safe and sane energy plan.

*NO NUKES*![1]

Dear Robert,

I was glad to get your letter (and to know you liked *Life in the Forest*). I'll try to respond to it in the New Year.*

Very best wishes to you & Jess for a happy & healthy year—

Denny

*I've still got final papers to read, & guests coming for Xmas, & have simply not had the time.

Dear Robert,

I'm sorry I've not been able to write before. And I'm even sorrier at what I feel I must say: That is, the saddest thing about all that has happened, or failed to happen, between us in these last few years is your assumption that come what may my love for you was too deep to fail. Well, I don't think that love was merely shallow; but it was not so deep that it had not a statute of limitation. You waited too long; and so, although I would have *liked* to feel, when you finally wrote, the relief and joy & deep satisfaction that I might once have felt, the fact is that I *did* not, and do not.

And perhaps, even if you had written this letter in, say, 1974, I would not have felt *deep satisfaction*, because although I can see—objectively—the pain & struggle involved in its writing, you *still* don't address yourself to the specific issue of having failed to apologize for the remark to James Mersmann & quoted by him, about my having derived some sort of sadistic pleasure from the composition of "Life at War." You will recall that when his book appeared with that quotation from you, I wrote (after I'd been re-reading your letters) to say that though you might not have remembered saying it & though you could not be held fully responsible for its appearance in print, yet once it had so appeared you owed me an apology. I had been on the point of writing you a "let's get back to our friendship" kind of letter when this quotation turned up (as I wrote to you) and an apology then would have cleared the way to a real reconciliation, for I was so moved by the accumulated letters of the 50's & 60's I'd been re-reading I spelled it out for you; and you

**473**

{December 22, 1978
W. Somerville, Mass.}

**474**

February 1, 1979
W. Somerville, Mass.[1]

did not respond. In the intervening years I'd occasionally get casual "Duncan says hi" sort of messages from people who'd just been in California—just as if nothing had happened, no wounding insult been given & never retracted.

Gradually my love for you dwindled, until I cannot honestly say I feel it any more. I wish I could. I *don't* mean I feel some other, negative emotion in its place. I don't even feel angry. How could I, so long after?

Not do I feel it would be impossible in the future to redevelop friendship between us; but it be of a different kind & never again of the same intensity. I think probably what would have happened if there had not been these wounds inflicted is that *anyway* our friendship would have changed in these years, for there was an element of dependence in it (my dependence ((and possibly your liking that dependence)) on your approval) and in the last few years I have belatedly grown out of a need for that kind of approval from any individual. Of course I still like, as we all do, to be loved, praised, appreciated; that's a basic human need. But the way I had you set up as *the touchstone* represented a need in me I have, as I say, finally outgrown.

I wish I didn't have to tell you I cannot respond to your letter with strong feeling, and that your words in it about your never doubting my love for you through it all are alas expressions of a false expectation. Perhaps I *ought* to have that degree of generosity and warmth. But I cannot pretend to it, & I feel that it was your silence that did it in. (My own belated growing-up would not have killed it, only changed it.) There doesn't seem any honest alternative to this brutal statement. Silence? There has been enough of that, and you see the damage it did.

About the poem: I get from it a sense of the stress, the conflict, the pain you have felt.[2] It ought to move me more—but most of it is so obscure to me that it misses its mark.

Maybe when it happens, that we meet face to face (which will happen sooner or later I suppose) *feeling* will come rushing back. I don't know.

I'm sorry to have hurt you but I have thought about it for weeks & I don't see how to avoid it. I must ask you to believe that I feel no *enmity*, nothing resembling the *opposite* of all I used to feel. I *was glad* to have your response to *Life in the Forest* and I *was moved* by your letter (I saw it must have been really difficult to write—the syntax even reflects that)—but in a remote, un-intense way that made clear to me how self-deluding your expectations of me, of unfailing love, were. I suppose one has to learn that one's friends are not Penelopes and that even very authentic emotions are subject to a statute of limitation. Any kind of relationship can die of undernourishing and abuse.

Enough.

Perhaps there will be eventually be a way through, to a new kind of friendship between us.

Denny

Dear Robert

I'm just about to leave on a long trip out of the U.S. (S. Pacific) & want to write before I do so.

The sad thing is that your letter came *at least* 2 years too late. I don't find it in me to respond with the warmth & gladness you expected. There can be a statute of limitations on emotional commitments, though one might like to think in terms of eternal loyalties—& that's what seems to have happened. I wish it were otherwise, but I can't pretend—it would of course be the worst hypocrisy to do so.

Who knows, perhaps a meeting some day, or some other exchange, whether of letters or poems, will awaken a new warmth in me towards you. There is always the recollection of auld lang syne, but you know as well as I do that that's not enough.

Be well—Jess too—& don't imagine I have *ill* will to you, emphatically I do not—just that I am changed too much to resume an old pattern, & the years of no apology for the remarks quoted in Mersmann's book made me numb in respect to new friendship-beginnings with you. I am truly sorry it is so.

Denny.

**475**

Feb 19th {19}79
4 Glover Circle
West Somerville,
Massachusetts, 02144

---

Dear Robert,

I was sorry to hear (from Carolyn K{izer}.) of your illness.

And felicitations on the ½ a Shelley prize—I expect they told you I am getting the other ½![1]

With all best wishes to you & Jess from

Denise

**476**

March 29 {19}84
{Stanford, Calif.}

---

Dear Denny,

A note to let you know that I've made considerable progress since the ten hospital days. Your note meant a lot to me.

"Heart failure," as it was diagnosed in Baton Rouge, meant in my case that my heart and lungs were swampt with retaind water, so that to climb stairs and even to walk had become a heavy labor. I got back home on Saturday March 12 and by 11 o'clock Sunday I was in St. Mary's hospital, where a crew of doctors and technicians in the following days saw me thru blood and urine analyses, the diagnosis of kidney failure as the underlying condition of the crisis, then the operation to prepare my arm for hemodialysis, blood transfusions, a biopsy of my kidney and a bone-marrow tap. In the period

**477**

April 20, 1984
{San Francisco}[1]

since I started dialysis, twenty-five pounds of water have been extracted (my dry weight has been set at one hundred forty-eight) and the body chemicals have been brought into line, my hemoglobin is normal and blood pressure lowerd. Three times a week I go to a dialysis center; but in May I go back into the hospital to have the operation preparatory to peritoneal-dialysis which I will do at home then four times a day every day.

So the filtering system of the kidneys has been externalized, and my conscious mind becomes an attendant in the process. My doctors tell me I will be fully recoverd by September, that is back to some two years ago, which is when they think the kidney condition began.

Jess is well. His care as always has seen me thru. It's knockt a month out of his work

Mind and psyche call upon April as the sun passes the equinox. The garden is splendid with masses of bright yellow oxalis and smaller-flowerd pale lavender to white, magenta mesembri anthemum and rose impatiens. I mean to spend more time with the plant world.

My love to you,
Robert

## 478

{September 3, 1985
W. Somerville, Mass.}
August 27, {19}85[1]

Dear Denise—

I have to share with you my delight in having belatedly "discovered" Robert Duncan. Somehow I've always had a blind spot as far as he was concerned in spite of your frequent praise. I've kept *Roots & Branches* around for several years and could never quite find my way around in it. Suddenly about a month ago some angel jostled me and said "Time to try again." So I did and now I cannot lay the book down. I read each poem over and over and wonder how I could have been so dull. I feel as though I'd come under some marvelous enchantment. And that I have to tell you, for if I had not followed *your* trail I never would have found my way to this marvelous poet. I feel as though my eyes had come suddenly open like a blind kittens. And that's quite an experience for an almost 82 year old.

With love and gratitude
Peggy Church

Thought you'd enjoy this!

Denise

Dear Jess,

I hesitate to write to you because you perhaps will be angry at my doing so, since Robert and I never reconstituted our friendship while he lived, & that automatically made you & me no longer friends either (though without the slightest "personal" reason for that being so, as far as I'm concerned anyway—"personal"'s in quotes because I can't think of a more accurate way to say it). But I am writing anyway, partly to say that I have thought of you with concern in your bereavement, & partly because I want you to have this poem.[1] The dream was intensely vivid & *really felt* like a reconciliation—the traditional belief in many cultures that the souls of the dead hover around for a little while, especially when there is "unfinished business," seemed substantiated. It was deep and clear.

I don't want to publish the poem till I know you have seen it, because of living readers you are the one who has the primary right to know this happened.

With love & fond memories—
Denise

P. S.

In the dream it was the "West Aisle"—of course that's not where the aisle wd be, but West is the setting sun, isn't it, so I stretch the dream-logic.

## 479

April 17, 1988
4, Glover Circle
W. Somerville,
Ma. 02144

March 31st '55

Dear Robert

I've wanted to write ever since you left but I wished to write such a special kind of letter — something befitting the effect on me of your visit — that I put it off, to save for a special day. But now I want to send you some poems so I'll write anyway.

If I were to really write to you it wd. be a real crazy letter — something like a loveletter, tho'not that — dominated by some image of the moon, a full moon, for some reason — I suppose because of that poem of yours, the moon at the window — no indeed, I just realized that what I've been wanting to write wasn't a letter at

Denise Levertov to Robert Duncan, March 31, 1955, first page.

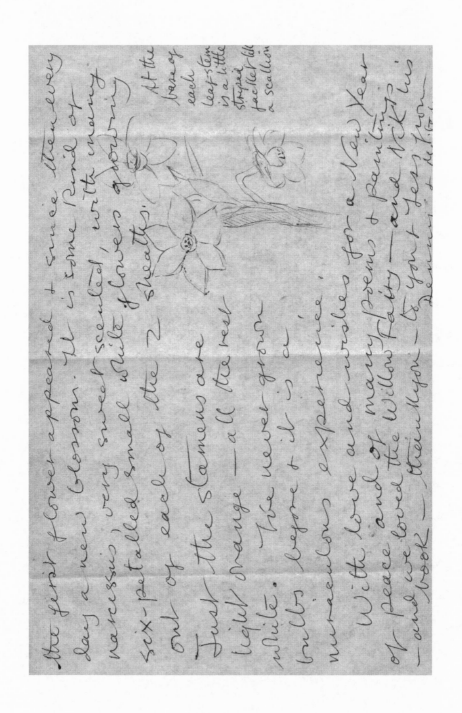

Denise Levertov to Robert Duncan, January 2, 1962, third page.

Temple ], Maine          July 18. 66.

Dearest Robert,

The poem, the <u>Soldiers Passage</u>,
has the depth & grandeur & ~~massive~~
~~complexities~~ complexity it needs to have. I
think you must know it? — It is not the
kind of poem the poet could have doubts
of. And the movement, the wholeness,
of the Passages has come clearer & clearer
to me — I felt it when I heard the
tape but now ever more so. Did I tell
you how I played the tape (at Greenwich
St.) to my c.c.n.y. class of 10 who had not
yet been reading you (with a few exceptions)
& who were in some ways quite unsophisticated
— & how nevertheless at the end they
were quite still & silent, & then at
last spontaneously burst out clapping?
I'm sorry the # got left out of the Nation printing of Uprising — the whole thing
was done in phone calls & telegrams as I was in Maine & it had to be rushed in before Conover
left — & at the time the sequence number seemed unnecessary to a magazine presentation of it.
But I (and Mitch too — who also joins
in my response to the poem) am anxious about
you — the high blood pressure — the

Denise Levertov to Robert Duncan, July 18, 1966, first page.

Feb. 5, 1959

dear Denny,
Did I ask you to look around for Pound cantos? Robin Blaser sent me #99 [from _The Virginia Quarterly_] and I got the _Illustrazione Italiana_ out of the library and typed a copy of Canto 98 — so, unless you just happened to find a copy of the Italian magazine (which has a color picture of Pound on the cover) don't worry about it. There are flashes in these later Cantos: in 99

> Food is the root.
>> Feed the people.

and again:
> Manners are from earth and from water
> They arise out of hills and streams
> The spirit of air is of the country
>> Men's manners cannot be one
>>> (same, identical)

but perhaps one has to be addicted to Pound, believe in the utter "charm" of his versification to get thru much of it. I like the digest where I am familiar with what it digests: as in the Byzantine - European 6th & 7th century canto 96. But when I don't know references the stuff seems scattered. In his face [see current Yale Literary mag] the character is screwed up to hold disparate forces at bay — the fasces, the binding of many (unruly) parts in one, is in the face: eyes drawn in a troubled axis with three pronounced lines of effort branding the brow. So we know that he in writing has some of the perplexity that we in reading have.
Where I know at all what he is doing I recognize the verse as superior [he does not need poetic "touches", where the lyric

Robert Duncan to Denise Levertov, February 5, 1959, first page.

dear Denny,

The artichokes have come into their purple crowns ...
the choke of the central stalk is called the Mother.
And now, after harvests for the table of the branching
blooms — we have the final crowns in full flower, that
will dry: green and gold with the intense purple
bloom

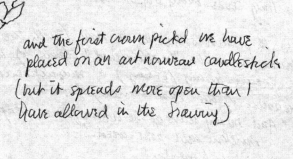

and the first crown pickd we have
placed on an art nouveau candlesticks
(but it spreads more open than I
have allowed in the drawing)

Robert Duncan to Denise Levertov, July 17, 1959, first page.

March 18/63

dear Denny,

    Just a short note with the enclosed final
version of STRUCTURE of RIME XX — correction
on previous copy: insert "light" between "flight"
and "like" (typing error in previous sheet).
and STRUCTURE XXI:
    actual changes in text. "solitude" for "loneliness"
(both for the "made" to "wood" sequence, and also
because the meaning is right now)
and "A depresst key" for "a touchd string"
— a depresst key is what it actually is (when
the sympathetic sound rings) and also
because both "depresst" and "key" refer to
the substrata of the poem.
"steps of wood" = notes of the scale on a
xylophone
"watery" removed as (see in XX "watery eaves")
to be postponed to possible opening in XXII

    Watery ladders, watery eaves!

I want to get how "watery" is a sound, but
also is a watering image somehow different
from the sound.
                                    Robert

Robert Duncan to Denise Levertov, March 18, 1963.

# APPENDIX

This appendix contains a number of the texts, prose and poetry, that most directly relate to and come under discussion between Robert Duncan and Denise Levertov in the contention that began in the late sixties and finally ruptured their friendship. "A Storm of White" comes under extended discussion earlier and is included here in its first version.

## Contents

| | | |
|---|---|---|
| Duncan: | "A Storm of White" | 728 |
| Duncan: | "A Critical Difference of View" | 729 |
| Duncan: | "Earth's Winter Song" | 734 |
| Levertov: | "Life at War" | 735 |
| Levertov: | "Tenebrae" | 737 |
| Duncan: | "Up Rising: Passages 25" | 738 |
| Duncan: | *from* "Santa Cruz Propositions" | 740 |
| Levertov: | "Author's Preface," *To Stay Alive* | 742 |
| Levertov: | *from* "Staying Alive" | 743 |
| Duncan: | *from* James Mersmann's *Out of the Vietnam Vortex* | 749 |
| Duncan: | *from* "Robert Southwell's 'The Burning Babe'" | 749 |
| Duncan: | "The Torn Cloth" | 752 |
| Levertov: | "To R. D., March 4th, 1988" | 754 |

ROBERT DUNCAN: A STORM OF WHITE
(version sent with Letter 81)

*A STORM OF WHITE,*     neither
    sky nor earth,   without horizon,   it's
       a-
nother tossing, continually in-
       breaking
boundary of white
       foaming     in gull-white weather
luminous in dull white,   and trees
       ghosts of blackness or greens
that here are
     dark whites     in storm—

white   white   white   like
    a boundary in death advancing
       that's
our life,  that's love,
      line upon line
breaking in radiance,  so   soft,  so   dim-
    ly glaring,    dominating.

"What it would mean to us if
    he died,"   a friend writes,
and that she feels she'll
       out live . . .     The line of outliving

    in this storm   bounding
obscurity from obscurity.   The foaming
    —as if half the universe
(neither sky nor earth,   without
    horizon)   were forever
breaking into being another half,
    obscurity   flaring into a surf
upon answering obscurity.

    O dear gray cat that died in this cold.
    You were born on my chest
       six years ago.

The sea of ghosts dances.   It does not
    send your little shadow to us.
    I do not comprehend   this
empty place.

Another friend writes in a poem:    "death also
can still propose the old labors."

R. D.

## ROBERT DUNCAN: "A CRITICAL DIFFERENCE OF VIEW"

TEXTS: "In particular, one notices the large number of poems in staggered
tercets, Dr. Williams's form. His alone, one hastens to say; and these poems
imitatively shaped, in Tomlinson's book, arouse an immediate hostility. At any
rate they did in me, and I tried, without success, to think of a single self-
respecting American poet who had *dared* to copy this form, at least for more
than a poem or two.

"I think Paul Goodman was the first to point out that Dr. Williams's ter-
cets incline toward the pentameter. Tomlinson's incline toward the alexan-
drine. A world, or at least half a world, of difference lies between the two, per-
haps even lengthened by the similarity of typography." Hayden Carruth
reviewing *A Peopled Landscape*, by Charles Tomlinson (*Poetry*, July 1964).

" . . . committed to an enormous, self-conscious struggle with language
and tradition . . . Zukofsky brings to the battle some inherited stratagems of
Pound (heavy use of allusion and quotation) and Williams (a short, breath-
phrased line, too often here a one-word line). One wonders if nature—in-
stinctual wisdom—might not have led him to drop the greaves and breast-
plate of those great old warriors and to step, finally, light and self-exposing,
into the fray." Adrienne Rich reviewing *Found Objects*, by Louis Zukofsky
(*Poetry*, November 1964).

If *shape* be taken to mean the appearance of a work as distinguished from *form*
taken to mean the significant structure, Mr. Carruth seems to mean by "imita-
tively shaped" that Tomlinson has taken over the appearance (as if Williams's
"tercet" were a matter of mere typography like a wing or pyramid poem) as dis-
tinguished, one would expect Mr. Carruth to continue, from the form
(Williams's "tercet" being a matter of notation to indicate the actual progression
of the line in three phrases or beats and the return to the next line (the *versus*)
with the fourth as first of another progression). But by the time he suggests that
Williams's verse inclines towards the pentameter, it is clear that it has not oc-
curred to him that Williams's phrasings are of formal significance. By the time
the word pentameter describes the measure of blank verse and also of Dr.
Williams's "inclination," much less his intention, in his later poetry, the word
has been divorced from our concern with the rhythmic structure of the poem.

Mr. Carruth considers William Carlos Williams's articulation of the line in poetry to be a device of an idiosyncratic style or signature—a matter then of private property or copyright—and he questions the propriety of other poets taking over this mannerism—but now he calls it "this form." As later, he confuses typography (appearance) with notation (form) and we do not know whether Mr. Tomlinson has copied only the appearance of a line articulated into three phrases (in which case he cannot be said to have imitated Dr. Williams's *form*) or whether Mr. Tomlinson has taken Dr. Williams's notation to develop a similar music given the different character of British voice, that seems to measure to Mr. Carruth's exacting ear as having six iambics with a caesura after the third or even more roughly as having six beats or whatever Mr. Carruth means by the alexandrine, as the Williams line tended in Paul Goodman's determination (*verse* here meaning the return to the margin in conventional *verse* usually identical with the line) provided a more subtle alternative to single movement of the verse or the traditional phrasing of the line into two parts; he had brought a new variety where the numbers might enter my feet.

What may be at issue is that I have not Mr. Carruth's sense of propriety or property when it comes to technical developments in the art, nor indeed do I consider virtues of character, of spirit, or of body, to be private but to be communal resources, cues for our own creation of self. So I have followed what Miss Rich (perhaps to be pictured as a most human Sancho Panza to my fantastic and deluded Quixote) takes to be Pound's "heavy use of allusion and quotation," "greaves and breastplate," for I took them to be the voices of many men and of souls stained with recent tears come into the poem and I desired also that there be the recall of other times and the words of other men brought into the music of my own.

And then to take from Shelley where he, forgetting self-respect and self-exposure, takes up from "The Homeric Hymn to Mercury":

And from the portion which my father gave
To Phoebus, I will snatch my share away;

Hermes, patron of thieves and of poets, abounded not in self-respect nor in self-exposure but in craft (both know-how and cunning) and in concealment. "And, as regards honor," Hermes says, "I too will enter upon the rite that Apollo has. If my father will not give it me, I will seek—and I am able—to be a prince of robbers."

But it is clear that William Carlos Williams meant every development in his art and particularly the music of his later poetry to furnish the "rite" or mode of a new poetics. "By its *music* shall the best of modern verse be known and the *resources* of the music," he writes (*Selected Letters*, no. 211, pp. 326–27). And, demonstrating the count of his tercets, he continues:

(1) Mother of God! Our Lady!

    (2)        the heart

                (3) is an unruly master:

(4) Forgive us our sins

    (5)        as we

                (6) forgive

(7) those who have sinned against

Count a single beat to each numeral. You may not agree with my ear, but that is the way I count the line. Over the whole poem it gives a pattern to the meter that can be felt as a new measure. It gives resources to the ear which result in a language which we hear spoken about us every day.

Mr. Carruth's "his alone" does not honor but outrages the spirit of Williams who meant his poetry, as Pound meant his, to increase the resource in language for poets to come. Reading carefully, we may see that it is the very use of Williams as if he were a resource that aroused Mr. Carruth's immediate hostility.

Williams's sense of a single beat to even a phrase like "Mother of God! Our Lady!," which contains an exclamatory juncture, may be related to the common low of our American speech that every utterance has at least one and only one major stress in relation to which subsidiary stresses are organized: "God" given the major stress, the first syllable of *Mother* and the first syllable of *Lady* I would give secondary stress; "our" tertiary stress; "of" somewhat less (my hearing at this point becomes impressionistic); and the final syllable of *Mother* and *Lady* falls definitely in a fourth order. "Heart" in the second phrase I would take to be the pivotal stress of the verse; and here the pivotal stress may accent the beat of the line. The beat in Williams giving tempo and the stress pattern an inner even syncopated pattern. In the poem the poetic voice retains the speech-structure of a central stress in each element in relation to which the stress systems are moving ("which we hear spoken about us every day"). The Williams line would have in its most exacting subtlety of reading such a major stress governing the movement of the three parts; it might come in any one of the three as determined in the rhythmic organization of each subsidiary system in which there would again be a stress center. In electing to discard the system that distinguishes only two degrees of stress (by which Mr. Goodman or Mr. Carruth count their pentameters and alexandrines in whatever verse they wish), Pound suggesting the musical phrase and Williams later the variable foot opened the way for a recognition of a more complicated stress pattern that renders the Alexandrian system (*iambics* and all) favored by pedagogues as inadequate an analysis for American as it had been in its time for classical Greek poetry.

I would note that the poet's primary base in language is musical not linguistic; in reading the various hypotheses of antiquated, preposterous, methodical, intuitive, scientific (empirically established) analyses of language and speech, I am, as I read Williams to be, concerned not with a correct view of language but with the apprehension of creative possibilities. Here, an even fanciful theory can *send* the creative mind.

In a beginner's manual of Linguistics (*Introduction to the English Language*, 1942) I find Professor Marckwardt asking his students: "What differences in total meaning would be suggested by (a) heavy stress on the word *John*; (b) heavy stress on the word *reading*; (c) heavy stress on the word *letter*? What differences in interpretation would result from pronouncing the word *letter* with high and low pitch respectively?" Asking such rudimentary questions of language might illuminate the Imagists' observation that "a new cadence means a new idea" and Dr. Williams's feeling that "the refinement of the poem, its subtlety, is to be known by the resources of the *music*."

Searching the work of other poets whose work relates to the work of Williams (Louis Zukofsky, Charles Olson, Denise Levertov, Robert Creeley, Larry Eigner, Paul Blackburn, Cid Corman), I begin to fear that only Mr. Tomlinson and I come in the category of those who have used the tercet Mr. Carruth so much deplores. But there is another "shape" or "stratagem" that all of us "copied" as if it were not a matter of personal style but, as Williams believed, a resource towards the delineation of meaning: this is the juncture that could raise the pitch on a proposition or an article at the end of a line and increase the stress on a noun at the return to give something like the shifts in meaning and tone that one heard in common speech. Not only linguistics but psychoanalysis, as well as the "new" poetry (to belabor the point), had observed that there was a significant difference, a hesitation that was meaningful, between "of the land," where one took the order of things for granted, and "of the/ land" or "of/the land," where shifts in stress and pitch were necessary to register exactly the shift in decision. Yet originally the possibility of this telling juncture may have been recognized in what had been otherwise accidental effects arising from Williams's measuring lines by syllable count. In the verse of Kenneth Rexroth, for instance, where the line conveys only the steady predominance of seven syllables, as in *The Dragon and the Unicorn*, and where the stress system is not linearly organized, though lines may end with "the" or "about" or "an" the actual movement of the poem goes on unphased.

It is no wonder when the contribution Williams made to our understanding of how the language may be more finely rendered is thought to be a matter of

idiosyncrasy or copyright, or when, as in Miss Rich's reprimand of Louis Zu-
kofsky's practice, not only Zukofsky but his kin before him, Pound and Wil-
liams, are portrayed as if she revered them ("great old warriors") even as she
pitied them (loaded down with the armor and greaves of "heavy" "allusion and
quotation" and short-breathed at that) from the advantage of one armed only
in "instinctual wisdom" (which we take to be a kind of naked innocence or na-
ture cult, poetic nudism, "light and self-exposing")—no wonder that Mr. Car-
ruth or Miss Rich might have difficulties in trying to cope with later develop-
ments of the line, such as Larry Eigner's poetry in which there is no verse (i.e.
no return to the margin) and each line must be particularly related to the mea-
sure of the whole as an immediate happening. Certainly they would have grave
difficulties in even approaching the poetry of Charles Olson or that break-
through in the theory of the poem made in the "Projective Verse" of 1950.

I mean to make no reflection upon Mr. Carruth's appreciation of the work
of Charles Tomlinson; I am sure he is accurate in telling us he felt an imme-
diate hostility and that is information of a kind. And I would not want to go
on record against Miss Rich's wish for "the coming honestly and uniquely by
the 'torsion' of grace and ungainliness, casualness and splendor" in a poem—
it sounds terrific; but I do have a certain understanding that my own task in
poetry is something other and less than what Miss Rich is so sure is "clearly
the task of all today" etc. What I question is the possible information of their
criticism as far as poetics goes: their confusions and impressions far outweigh
their recognitions of what is involved. What is most probably at issue is that
neither Mr. Carruth nor Miss Rich had or have any great concern for the po-
etry of Pound or of Williams and what is certainly at issue is that they would
reprove those of us who have had and do have such a concern. Are they en-
tirely original poets beholden to the work of no poets before them? I am un-
acquainted with their work so I cannot say. But given that Miss Rich does in-
deed speak in the language of nature and write in the high "torsion" that
proceeds from no communal forms but from "instinctual wisdom" even as in
Eden before the Fall, I do not grant that her natural grace has given her any
understanding of what should be the task of Louis Zukofsky or should have
been the task of Williams or is to be the task of me. An inadequate, much less
a prejudiced, reading of Pound or Williams will not lead to or support an im-
pression of what is going on where Tomlinson or Zukofsky has been influ-
enced by, copied, imitated, used, or inherited from, Pound or Williams.

*Stony Brook* 3/4 (Fall 1969): 360–63

## ROBERT DUNCAN: "EARTH'S WINTER SONG"

*1*

The beautiful young men and women!
Standing against the war their courage
has made a green place in my heart.

In the dark and utter destitution of winter
the face of the girl is a fresh moon
radiant with the Truth she loves,
the Annunciation, the promise
faith keeps in life.

Seed in the blind Earth, strikn by cold,
the spirits of the new Sun seek you out!

The face of Mary is a Star raying out.
And at the breast of her breth
"the Sun-element, the Child,
"forming Itself out of the clouds which have
"the Sun-rays in the atmosphere

"pouring thru them."

*2*

In the great storm of feer and rage
the heds of evil appear and disappeer,
heds of state, lords of the cold war,
the old dragon whose scales are corpses of men
and whose breth blasts crops and burns villages
demands again his hecatomb,
our lives and outrage going up into his powr
over us.        Wearing the unctuous mask of Johnson,
from his ass-hole emerging the hed of Humphrey,
he bellows and begins over Asia and America
the slaughter of the innocents and the reign of wrath.

But our lives are drivn downwards too, within, deep down.
The spirits of the living stars return where the Sun
underground works his light magic
stirring the deepest roots. We have been drivn
deep into the heart of our yearning, into the store
from which youth will rise, new shoots
of the spring-tide. O the green spring-tide

of individual volition for the communal good,
the Christ-promise of brotherhood, the lover's
promise of the self's fulfillment!
"The body of inner Earth is alive in mid-Winter"

In the Under Ground:
the sublime Crèche—the lamp's faint glow,
the enormous shadows—the few
frightend shepherds—the three
magi or magicians seeing in the Child
the child of their lore—Joseph
whose faith is father, and the girl
whose virginity engenders—and the new.
lord of the true life, of Love •

we remember, was always born,
as now, in a time of despair,
having no place there at the Inn,
hunted down by Herod's law,
fleeing by night, secreted in Egypt.

Love in His young innocence
radiant in His depth of time and night
has waited and now—this is
the message of Christmas—returns once more,
bearing the light of the Sun
fair in His face.

DENISE LEVERTOV: "LIFE AT WAR"

The disasters numb within us
caught in the chest, rolling
in the brain like pebbles. The feeling
resembles lumps of raw dough

weighing down a child's stomach on baking day.
Or Rilke said it, 'My heart . . .
Could I say of it, it overflows
with bitterness . . . but no, as though

its contents were simply balled into
formless lumps, thus
do I carry it about.'
The same war

continues.
We have breathed the grits of it in, all our lives,
our lungs are pocked with it,
the mucous membrane of our dreams
coated with it, the imagination
filmed over with the gray filth of it:

the knowledge that humankind,

delicate Man, whose flesh
responds to a caress, whose eyes
are flowers that perceive the stars,

whose music excels the music of birds,
whose laughter matches the laughter of dogs,
whose understanding manifests designs
fairer than the spider's most intricate web,

still turns without surprise, with mere regret
to the scheduled breaking open of breasts whose milk
runs out over the entrails of still-alive babies,
transformation of witnessing eyes to pulp-fragments,
implosion of skinned penises into carcass-gulleys.

We are the humans, men who can make;
whose language imagines *mercy*,
*lovingkindness*; we have believed one another
mirrored forms of a God we felt as good—

who do these acts, who convince ourselves
it is necessary; these acts are done
to our own flesh; burned human flesh
is smelling in Vietnam as I write.

Yes, this is the knowledge that jostles for space
in our bodies along with all we
go on knowing of joy, of love;

our nerve filaments twitch with its presence
day and night,
nothing we say has not the husky phlegm of it in the saying,
nothing we do has the quickness, the sureness,
the deep intelligence living at peace would have.

DENISE LEVERTOV: "TENEBRAE"
*(Fall of 1967)*

Heavy, heavy, heavy, hand and heart.
We are at war,
bitterly, bitterly at war.

And the buying and selling
buzzes at our heads, a swarm
of busy flies, a kind of innocence.

Gowns of gold sequins are fitted,
sharp-glinting. What harsh rustlings
of silver moiré there are,
to remind me of shrapnel splinters.

And weddings are held in full solemnity
not of desire but of etiquette,
the nuptial pomp of starched lace;
a grim innocence.

And picnic parties return from the beaches
burning with stored sun in the dusk;
children promised a TV show when they get home
fall asleep in the backs of a million station wagons,
sand in their hair, the sound of waves
quietly persistent at their ears.
They are not listening.

Their parents at night
dream and forget their dreams.
They wake in the dark
and make plans. Their sequin plans
glitter into tomorrow.
They buy, they sell.

They fill freezers with food.
Neon signs flash their intentions
into the years ahead.

And at their ears the sound
of the war. They are
not listening, not listening.

## ROBERT DUNCAN: "UP RISING: PASSAGES 25"

Now Johnson would go up to join the great simulacra of men,
    Hitler and Stalin, to work his fame
    with planes roaring out from Guam over Asia,
all America become a sea of toiling men
    stirrd at his will, which would be a bloated thing,
    drawing from the underbelly of the nation
    such blood and dreams as swell the idiot psyche
    out of its courses into an elemental thing
    until his name stinks with burning meat and heapt honors

And men wake to see that they are used like things
    spent in a great potlatch, this Texas barbecue
        of Asia, Africa, and all the Americas,
And the professional military behind him, thinking
    to use him as they thought to use Hitler
    without losing control of their business of war,

But the mania, the ravening eagle of America
    as Lawrence saw him "bird of men that are masters,
    lifting the rabbit-blood of the myriads up into . . . "
    into something terrible, gone beyond bounds, or
As Blake saw America in figures of fire and blood raging,
    . . . in what image? the ominous roar in the air,
the omnipotent wings, the all-American boy in the cockpit
    loosing his flow of napalm, below in the jungles
    "any life at all or sign of life" his target, drawing now
        not with crayons in his secret room
the burning of homes and the torture of mothers and fathers and
    children,
    their hair a-flame, screaming in agony, but
in the line of duty, for the might and enduring fame
    of Johnson, for the victory of American will over its victims,
    releasing his store of destruction over the enemy,
in terror and hatred of all communal things, of communion,
    of communism •

has raised from the private rooms of small-town bosses and businessmen,
from the council chambers of the gangs that run the great cities,
    swollen with the votes of millions,

from the fearful hearts of good people in the suburbs turning the
    savory meat over the charcoal burners and heaping their barbecue
    plates with more than they can eat,
from the closed meeting-rooms of regents of universities and sessions of
    profiteers

—back of the scene: the atomic stockpile; the vials of synthesized
    diseases eager biologists have developt over half a century dreaming
    of the bodies of mothers and fathers and children and hated rivals
    swollen with new plagues, measles grown enormous, influenzas
    perfected; and the gasses of despair, confusion of the senses, mania,
    inducing terror of the universe, coma, existential wounds, that
    chemists we have met at cocktail parties, passt daily and with a
    happy "Good Day" on the way to classes or work, have workt to
    make war too terrible for men to wage—

raised this secret entity of America's hatred of Europe, of Africa, of
    Asia,
the deep hatred for the old world that had driven generations of
    America out of itself,
and for the alien world, the new world about him, that might have
    been Paradise
but was before his eyes already cleard back in a holocaust of burning
    Indians, trees and grasslands,
reduced to his real estate, his projects of exploitation and profitable
    wastes,

this specter that in the beginning Adams and Jefferson feard and knew
would corrupt the very body of the nation
    and all our sense of our common humanity,
this black bile of old evils arisen anew,
takes over the vanity of Johnson;
and the very glint of Satan's eyes from the pit of the hell of
    America's unacknowledged, unrepented crimes that I saw in
    Goldwater's eyes
now shines from the eyes of the President
    in the swollen head of the nation.

ROBERT DUNCAN: *from* "SANTA CRUZ PROPOSITIONS"

*III*

[7:30 AM, 28 October]

But it is Denise I am thinking of—

> *"I feel terribly out of touch with you and fear*
> *you may be hurt at my silence but I just can't*
> *help it."*

           In the depths of the woman

in love,      into friendship,   the old injuries

         out of Love,


oo

out of the depths of the Woman's love,

*SHE* appears, Kālī dancing,   whirling her necklace of skulls,
trampling the despoiling armies and the exploiters of natural resources
under her feet.   Revolution or Death!
Wine!   The wine of men's blood in the vat
of the Woman's anger,   whirling,
the crackling—   is it of bones?   castanets?
tommyguns?   fire raging in the ghettos?   What
is the wrath of Jehovah to this   almost blissful Mother-Righteousness
aroused by the crimes of Presidents?

> *"And I know such violent revolution has ached my marrow-bones,*
>        *my soul changing its cells"*

—so immediately the lines of her poem come into mine.

           She changes.

Violently.     It is her time.     I never saw that dress before.

I never saw that face before.

["When she is in the depths of her black silence,"   he told me,
"Phone right away. Don't think you know what to do to help her.
She is dangerous."]

Madame Outrage of the Central Committee
forms a storm cloud around her where she is brooding.   This Night
opens into depth   without end in my life to come.

   The Four Winds come into the Womb of Her Grievance.

         Every woman      an Other      I fear for her.

She has put on her dress of murderous red.
She has put on her mini-skirt   and the trampling begins.
She has put on her make-up of the Mother of Hell,
   the blue lips of Kore,   the glowering
   pale of the flower that is black to us.
She has put on her fashion of burning.

Her tenderness grows tender,   enflames,

and, from the painful swelling of that history to come,
*"My cracked heart tolling such songs of unknown morning-star ecstatic
   anguish*
*. . . unquenched desire's radiant decibels"*

         I too know in her telling    and

   At the storm center
   her flashing eyes,   a shouting
   in the street rises and    against

the doctrine of Love as Need that Plato's Socrates tells us Diotima laid on
   him,
that untrustworthy Mind's father turning the Mother's words to suit his
   purpose,
against the pleading croon of the folk-rock singer
   to put down the rage of revolt with *Love, Sweet Love,* she cries

   from the center of terror
   that is the still eye of the storm in her:

*"There comes a time when only Anger is Love."*

## DENISE LEVERTOV: "AUTHOR'S PREFACE," *TO STAY ALIVE*

As one goes on living and working, themes recur, transposed into another key perhaps. Single poems that seemed isolated perceptions when one wrote them prove to have struck the first note of a scale or a melody. I have heard professors of literature snicker with embarrassment because a poet quoted himself: they thought it immodest, narcissistic. Their attitude, a common one, reveals a failure to understand that though *the artist as craftsman* is engaged in making discrete and autonomous works—each of which, like a chair or a table, will have, as Ezra Pound said, the requisite number of legs and not wobble— yet at the same time, more unconsciously, as these attempts accumulate over the years, *the artist as explorer in language of the experiences of his or her life* is, willy-nilly, weaving a fabric, building a whole in which each discrete work is a part that functions in some way in relation to all the others. It happens at times that the poet becomes aware of the relationships that exist between poem and poem; is conscious, after the act, of one poem, one line or stanza, having been the precursor of another. It may be years later; and then, to get the design clear—'for himself and *thereby* for others,' Ibsen put it—he must in honesty pick up that thread, bring the cross reference into its rightful place in the inscape, the Gestalt of his life (his work) / his work (his life).

In *Relearning the Alphabet* I published some sections of a poem then called, as a working title, 'From a Notebook,' which I was aware was 'unfinished,' open-ended. In pursuing it further I came to realize that the long poem 'An Interim,' published in a different section of the same volume, was really a prelude or introduction to the Notebook poem. And Mitch Goodman and Hayden Carruth, on reading new parts of the Notebook, showed me that other, earlier poems—such as those I had written about my sister Olga after her death in 1964, and included in *The Sorrow Dance*—had a relation to it that seemed to demand their reissue in juxtaposition. It was Hayden who, years ago, pointed out to me how, in writing about my childhood in England, my diction became English—and this fact becomes itself one of the themes of the Notebook poem; for the sense my individual history gives me of being straddled between *places* extends to the more universal sense any writer my age—rooted in a cultural past barely shared by younger readers, yet committed to a solidarity of hope and struggle with the revolutionary young—must have of being almost unbearably, painfully, straddled across *time*.

In the pendant to 'Olga Poems'—'A Note to Olga, 1966,' two years after her death—occurs the first mention in my work of one of those public occasions, demonstrations, that have become for many of us such familiar parts of our lives. Later, not as a deliberate repetition but because the events were of importance to me, other such occasions were spoken of in other poems. The sense of community, of fellowship, experienced in the People's Park in Berkeley in 1969, deepened and intensified under the vicious police attack that, for middle-class whites especially, was so instructive. The personal response that moves from the identification of my lost sister, as a worker for human rights, with the pacifists 'going limp' as they are dragged to the paddywagon in Times Square in 1966, to the understanding by 1970 that 'there comes a time when only anger / is love,' is one shared by many of us who have come bit by bit to the knowledge that opposition to war, whose foul air we have breathed so long that by now we are almost choked forever by it, cannot be separated from opposition to the whole system of insane greed, of racism and imperialism, of which war is only the inevitable expression. In 'Prologue: An Interim' some of my heroes—that is, those who stand for integrity, honesty, love of life—are draft resisters who go to jail in testimony of their refusal to take part in carnage. In the same poem I invoked the self-immolators—Vietnamese and American—not as models but as flares to keep us moving in the dark. I spoke with love—a love I still feel—of those who 'disdain to kill.' But later I found that Gandhi himself had said it was better to 'cultivate the art of killing and being killed rather than in a cowardly manner to flee from danger.' In the later sections of the Notebook the sense of who the guardians of life, of integrity, are, is extended to include not only those who 'disdain to kill' but all who struggle, violently if need be, to pull down this obscene system before it destroys all life on earth.

The justification, then, of including in a new volume poems which are available in other collections, is esthetic—it assembles separated parts of a whole. And I am given courage to do so by the hope of that whole being seen as having some value not as mere 'confessional' autobiography, but as a document of some historical value, a record of one person's inner/outer experience in America during the '60's and the beginning of the '70's, an experience which is shared by so many and transcends the peculiar details of each life, though it can only be expressed in and through such details.

DENISE LEVERTOV: *from* "STAYING ALIVE"

*from* PART I (*October '68–May '69*)

*i*

Revolution or death. Revolution or death.
Wheels would sing it
                     but railroads are obsolete,
we are among the clouds, gliding, the roar
a toneless constant.

*Which side are you on?*
Revolution, of course. Death is Mayor Daley.
This revolution has no blueprints, and
        ('What makes this night different
        from all other nights?')
is the first that laughter and pleasure aren't shot down in.

*Life that*
      *wants to live.*
                  *(Unlived life*
          *of which one can die.)*
        I want the world to go on
      unfolding. The brain
not gray except in death, the photo I saw
of prismatic radiance pulsing from live tissue.
      I see Dennis Riordon and de Courcy Squire,
      gentle David Worstell, intransigent Chuck Matthei
      blowing angel horns at the imagined corners.
      Jennie Orvino singing
      beatitudes in the cold wind
              outside a Milwaukee courthouse.
I want their world—in which they already live,
they're not waiting for demolition and reconstruction.
                       'Begin here.'
Of course I choose
revolution.

*ii*
And yet, yes, there's the death
that's not the obscene sellout, the coprophiliac spasm
that smears the White House walls with its desensitized
                              thumbs.

      Death lovely,
      whispering,
      *a drowsy numbness . . .*
               *'tis not*
      *from envy of thy happy lot*
              *lightwinge'd dryad . . .*
*Even the longest river . . .*

Revolution or death. Love
aches me.       . . . *river*
*winds somewhere to the sea.*

*from* PART II

What is the revolution I'm driven
to name, to live in?—that now roars,
a toneless constant, now
sings itself?

      It's in the air: no air
           to breathe without
     scent of it,
          pervasive,
     odor of snow,
             freshwater,
                    stink of dank
           vegetation recomposing.

. . .

Robert reminds me *revolution*
implies the circular: an exchange
of position, the high
brought low, the low
ascending, a revolving,
an endless rolling of the wheel. The wrong word.
We use the wrong word. A new life
isn't the old life in reverse, negative of the same photo.
But it's the only
word we have . . .

. . .

*May 14ᵗʰ*, 1969—Berkeley
Went with some of my students to work in the People's Park. There
seemed to be plenty of digging and gardening help so we decided, as Jeff
had his truck available, to shovel up the garbage that had been thrown
into the west part of the lot and take it out to the city dump.
     O happiness
     in the sun! Is it
     that simple, then,
     to live?
     —crazy rhythm of
     scooping up barehanded
     (all the shovels already in use)
     careless of filth and broken glass
     —scooping up garbage together
     poets and dreamers studying
     joy together, clearing
     refuse off the neglected, newly recognized,

humbly waiting ground, place, locus, of what could be our
New World even now, our revolution, one and one and
one and one together, black children swinging, green
guitars, that energy, that music, no one
    telling anyone what to do,
     everyone doing,
  each leaf of
  the new grass near us
  a new testament . . .


*from* "ENTR'ACTE" *between* PARTS II & III

 *'I Thirst'*
Beyond the scaffolding set up for
TV cameras, a long way
from where I sit among 100,000 reddening
white faces,
   is a big wooden cross:

and strapped upon it, turning
his head from side to side in pain
in the 90-degree shadeless Washington midafternoon
May 9, 1970,
   a young black man.

'We must *not* be angry, we must
L-O-O-O-V-E' Judy Collins
Bleats loud and long into the P.A. system,

but hardly anyone claps, and no one
shouts *Right On.*
    That silence cheers me.
Judy, understand:
there comes a time when only anger
is love.


*from* PART III

(Europe after 10 years; England after 20 years; summer of 1970)

 *ix*
But on a hill in Dorset

while the bells of Netherbury
pealed beyond the grove of
great beeches,
                    and Herefords,
white starred on tawny ample brows,
grazed, slow, below us,
                              only days ago,
Bet said:
There was a dream I dreamed always
over and over,

a tunnel
and I in it, distraught

and great dogs blocking
each end of it

and I thought I must
always go on
dreaming that dream,
trapped there,

but Mrs. Simon listened
and said

why don't you sit down
in the middle of the tunnel
quietly:

imagine yourself
quiet and intent sitting there,
not running from blocked
exit to blocked exit.

Make a place for yourself
in the darkness
and wait there . . . *Be* there.

The dogs
will not go away.
They must be transformed.

Dream it that way.
Imagine.

Your being, a fiery stillness,
is needed to TRANSFORM
the dogs.

And Bet said to me:
Get down into your well,

it's your well

go deep into it

into your own depth as into a poem.


*from* PART IV

And I? 'Will struggle without hope
        be enough?' I was asking
on a sunny island in summer.
                        Now in midwinter
not doing much to struggle, or striving mainly
to get down into my well in hope
that force may gather in me
            from being still in the grim
            middle of the tunnel . . .
(And meanwhile Richard and Neil in their collectives
get down to it: get into work: food co-ops, rent strikes;
and 'Jacob and Lily' create
an active freedom in 'open hiding';
and Mitch has finished his book, 'a tool
for the long revolution.')
                        (And meanwhile Robert
                        sees me as Kali! No,
        I am not Kali, I can't sustain for a day
that anger.
            'There comes
                    a time
                        when only anger
                                is love.'—
I wrote it, but know such love
only in flashes.
            And the love that streams
towards me daily, letters and poems, husband and child,
sings . . . )

ROBERT DUNCAN: *from* James Mersmann's
*OUT OF THE VIETNAM VORTEX*

Duncan's appraisal is actually even more stringent than this. He says, "There's another field of feeling that frequently comes up when she means to write a protest feeling, and that is her own sadism, and masochism, and so the war becomes like, becomes a not gloating but almost as fierce an expression as the fantasies of Dickey. She'll be writing about the war and suddenly—in one of the earlier poems that's most shocking—you get a flayed penis, and . . . when she reads it you get an effect and tone of disgusted sensuality. And when you look at her poetry it tells more to look at that flayed penis and realize that her earlier poems are talking about stripped stalks of grass! She's got one that loves peeling [perhaps the "Pleasures" poem quoted above]. Suddenly you see a charged, bloody, sexual image that's haunting the whole thing, and the war then acts as a magnet, and the poem is not a protest though she thinks she's protesting" (personal interview, 9 May 1969). Duncan's analysis will appeal to Freudians. There is indeed even in the few poems quoted in this study a great deal of peeling and digging and probing into, but I believe these are best seen as aesthetic and epistemological concerns (a desire to get at the "center," the "kernel") rather than sexual ones. (But if Freud is right, our aesthetics and epistemology may be sublimated sexuality anyway.)

James F. Mersmann, *Out of the Vietnam Vortex: A Study of Poets and Poetry against the War* (Lawrence: University of Kansas Press, 1974), 94.

ROBERT DUNACAN: *from* ROBERT SOUTHWELL'S
"THE BURNING BABE"

> The vision of a burning babe    I see
> doubled in my sight.    The one
> alight in that fire of passion that tries the soul
> is such a Child as Southwell saw his Christ to be:
>
> This is not a baby on fire but a babe of fire,
> flesh burning with its own flame,    not toward death
>     but alive with flame,    suffering its *self*
> the heat of the heart the rose was hearth of;
>
>     so there *was* a rose,    there was a flame,
>     consubstantial with the heart,
>
> long burning me through and through,
>     long time ago I knew    and came

to a knowledge of the bitter core of me,
the clinker soul, the stubborn residue
that needed the fire and refused to burn.

Envy of the living was its name,    black jealousy
    of what I loved it was,    and
the pain was not living,    it was ashes of the wood;
the burning was not living,    it was
    without Truth's heat,
a cold of utter Winter that refused the Sun,
an adversary in the body against its youth.

In this I am self possesst of such a hoarie Winter's night
    as Southwell stood in shivering—
a shivering runs me through and through.

O Infant Joy that in Desire burns bright!
Bright Promise that I might in Him burn free!
His faultless breast the furnace,
my inner refusal the thorny fuel!

All the doors of Life's wounds I have long closed in me
break open from His body and pour forth
therefrom fire that is His blood
    relentlessly

*"Who scorcht with excessive heat, such*
    *floods of tears did shed"*

—it is no more than an image in Poetry—as though

*"his floods should quench his flames,*
    *which with his tears were bred"*    until

tears breeding flames, flames breeding tears,
I am undone from what I am,    and in Imagination's alchemy
    the watery Moon and fiery Sun    are wed.

    The burning Babe,    the Rose,
    the Wedding of the Moon and Sun,
    wherever in the World I read
    such Mysteries come to haunt the Mind,
    the Language of What Is    and I

oo

        are one.

"*A pretty Babe*"—that burning Babe
   the poet Southwell saw—
a scorching,   a crying,   that made his cold heart glow,
   a fuel of passion in which
the thought of wounds delites the soul.
   He's Art's epiphany of Art new born,
a Christ of Poetry,   the burning spirit's show;
He leaves no shadow,   where he dances in the air,
   of misery below.

Another Christ,   if he be, as we are,
Man,   cries out in utter misery;
and every Holy Martyr must have cried
   forsaken in some moment
that from Christ's "Why hast Thou forsaken me?"
   has enterd our Eternity
or else is not true to itself.   But now

   I am looking upon burnd faces
that have known catastrophe incommensurate
   with meaning,   beyond hate or loss or
Christian martyrdom, unredeemd.   My heart
   caves into a space it seems
to have long feard.

I cannot imagine,   gazing upon photographs
   of these young girls,   the mind
transcending what's been done to them.

   From the broild flesh of these heretics,
by napalm monstrously   baptised
   in a new name, every delicate and
sensitive curve of lip and eyelid
   blasted away,   surviving . . .
   eyes? Can this horror be calld their
*fate*? *Our* fate grows a mirroring face
in the accusation beyond accusation
   of such eyes,

a kind of hurt that drives into the root
of understanding,   their very lives
   burnd into us   we live by.

Victor and victim know not what they do
   —the deed exceeding what we would *know*;

the knowledge in the sight of those eyes
   goes deep into the heart's fatalities.
And in our nation's store of crimes   long
   unacknowledged,   unrepented,
the sum of abject suffering,   of dumb incalculable
   injury increases
the sore of conscience we long avoid.

What can I feel of it?   All hurt
rushes in to illustrate that glare
and fails.   What can I feel of what was done?
All hatred cringes from the sight of it
and would contract into self-loathing
to ease the knowledge of what no man
can compensate.   I think I could bear it.

I cannot think I could bear it.


## ROBERT DUNCAN: "THE TORN CLOTH"

We   reaving

—"re-weaving"   I had meant
     to write,
  in twain
     did   I want her
to be   entirely   unutterably
   that raging Woman of every "Uprising" ?
     for the Glory   Wrath
   promises in us?
From Outrage
   not denied,   the Denial
       not denied   but kept,
as ever I spin out of kept feeling
   to let loose from my keeping,

from the Snarl
   the frayd edges of the inner Reft,
     the torn heart of our
     "Friendship,"   in the rift

   to work now   to draw
     the threads   everywhere tried,

they are like the blisterd
   all but severd   root-nerves
   of my sciatic   trunk-line.

   In pain   where I workt pain

      now I must spin

oo

the twirl of the needle stabbing
   my spindle,

the thread of a contention,
   the only thread my reparation
      may come from.

I may call up a mountain in me
   to sing most like a lark
or wrap myself in the Romance
   of a Dark Lover,

but for this mere
   re-weaving,

for this consent that this wedding-cloth
   of friendship

I had ript apart in what I thought
   righteous

I must draw out of my heart again,
   but without bliss,

   with blisterd and blistering fingers
draw the strands of no magic,

no wool or flax the storehouse of my
   fictions can release easily

      against my being in the right
      against my resolve
      against my undying judgment

I must weave   the reaving
   into the heart of my

wedding clothes;

for I will not let go
　　from the years of our rapport

oo

　　the momentary
War and the Scars upon the Land
　　　I saw as
the overflow of our human creativity
　　ever meaning
more than we want to know,　　the debris
　　goods and evils
are left, surviving, or to die in starvation,
　　lives smoking and stinking

come ever into the reweaving.
The very thread is bitter　　in its radiance

　　draw it out　　glistening
into the fabric of intentions
another body my body is

　　commands.


DENISE LEVERTOV: "TO R. D., MARCH 4th, 1988"

You were my mentor. Without knowing it,
I outgrew the need for a mentor.
Without knowing it, you resented that,
and attacked me. I bitterly resented
the attack, and without knowing it
freed myself to move forward
without a mentor. Love and long friendship
corroded, shrank, and vanished from sight
into some underlayer of being.
The years rose and fell, rose and fell,
and the news of your death after years of illness
was a fact without resonance for me,
I had lost you long before, and mourned you,
and put you away like a folded cloth
put away in a drawer. But today I woke
while it was dark, from a dream
that brought you live into my life:
I was in a church, near the Lady Chapel

at the head of the west aisle. Hearing a step
I turned: you were about to enter
the row behind me, but our eyes met
and you smiled at me, your unfocussed eyes
focussing in that smile to renew
all the reality our foolish pride extinguished.
You moved past me then, and as you sat down
beside me, I put a welcoming hand
over yours, and your hand was warm.
I had no need
for a mentor, nor you to be one;
but I was once more
your chosen sister, and you
my chosen brother.
We heard strong harmonies rise and begin to fill
the arching stone,
sounds that had risen here through centuries.

# GLOSSARY OF NAMES

ADAM, HELEN (1909–1993), was a Scottish-born poet (described as a "mystic balladeer") and collagist. Adam migrated to the United States with her mother and sister Pat (1922–1988) in 1939; after living in various places around the country, the three settled in the San Francisco Bay area. Helen established close relationships with RD and other poets and artists. Her reading of Blake's poetry in RD's class at the Poetry Center in 1954 focused him on the Romantic ballad tradition in poetry. After the death of their mother, the sisters moved to New York in 1964 and renewed their friendship with DL. Adam's collections of ballads of love, death, and transfiguration draw on the tradition of fairy tale and fantasy. Some of her publications are: *San Francisco's Burning* (Berkeley, CA: Oannes, 1963), a musical play written with Pat Adam and illustrated by Jess; *Ballads*, preface by RD and illustrated by Jess (New York: Acadia Press, 1964); *Selected Poems and Ballads* (New York: Helikon Press, 1974); *Songs with Music* (San Francisco: Aleph Press, 1982); and *Stone Cold Gothic* (New York: Kulchur Foundation, 1984).

ADMIRAL, VIRGINIA (1917–2000), was a painter (a student of Hans Hofmann) who was part of RD's circle in Berkeley in 1937–38 and in New York in the 1940s. She was the co-editor with RD of the little magazine *Epitaph* (1938). She married the painter Robert de Niro and was the mother of the actor Robert de Niro. She printed a book of Helen Adam's *Ballads* at her Acadia Press, with calligraphy and illustration by Jess and a preface by RD, in 1964.

AKHMATOVA, ANNA (1889–1966), was a Russian poet and co-founder of Acmeism, a movement that valued lucidity over the opacity of the Russian sym-

bolist style of the early 1900s. Many consider her to be Russia's greatest female poet. See *Complete Poems*, 2 vols., trans. Judith Hemschemeyer, ed. and introd. Roberta Reeder (Somerville, MA: Zephyr Press, 1990).

ALDINGTON, RICHARD (1892–1962), was a British poet, novelist, and critic. Aldington was one of the original Imagist poets, along with Ezra Pound and Hilda Doolittle (H. D.), whom he married in 1913 and divorced in 1938. He was widely published as a poet, man of letters, and translator. His poetry collections include *Images of War* (London: Allen and Unwin, 1919) and *Collected Poems 1915–1923* (London: Allen and Unwin, 1933). His fiction includes: *Death of a Hero* (London: Chatto and Windus, 1929), *Roads to Glory* (London: Chatto and Windus, 1930), and *Rejected Guest* (London: Allen and Unwin, 1939).

ALLEN, DONALD M. (1912– ), was an editor and publisher with *Evergreen Review*, Grove Press, Four Seasons Foundation, and Grey Fox Press, Allen edited: the anthology *The New American Poetry* (New York: Grove Press, 1960), which became the manifesto and showcase for postwar open-form experimentation; *New American Story*, with Robert Creeley (New York: Grove Press, 1965); *The Collected Poems of Frank O'Hara* (New York: Alfred A. Knopf, 1971); *The Poetics of the New American Poetry*, with Warren Tallman (New York: Grove Press, 1974); and Charles Olson's *Collected Prose*, with Benjamin Friedlander (Berkeley: University of California Press, 1997).

ALTOON, JOHN (1924–1967), was a Los Angeles painter who knew Robert Creeley on Majorca in the early 1950s.

AMMONS, A(RCHIBALD). R(ANDOLPH). (1926–2001), was a North Carolina–born poet and a professor at Cornell and at Wake Forest universities. His poems, many of which are self-aware meditations on natural process, include: *Tape for the Turn of the Year* (Ithaca, NY: Cornell University Press, 1965), *The Snow Poems* (New York: W. W. Norton and Co., 1977), *Sphere: The Form of Motion* (New York: W. W. Norton and Co., 1974), *A Coast of Trees* (New York: W. W. Norton and Co., 1981), *Selected Poems, Expanded Edition* (New York: W. W. Norton and Co., 1986), *Selected Longer Poems* (New York: W. W. Norton and Co., 1980), and *Garbage* (New York: W. W. Norton and Co., 1993).

ANGER, KENNETH (1911–1982), was an American filmmaker and commentator on film. His film *Scorpio Rising* (1963) was much praised for its intense spiritual power and experimental techniques; his book *Hollywood Babylon* (San Francisco: Straight Arrow Books, 1975) exposed the lush and perverse habits of the Hollywood world. He was a friend of RD and Jess; RD dedicated "Structure of Rime XXVI (Passages 20)" to him.

ANTONINUS, BROTHER (WILLIAM EVERSON) (1912–1994), was a California poet and hand-press printer, a close friend of Kenneth Rexroth and RD, and a central figure in the San Francisco Renaissance. He was noted for the emotional and spiritual intensity of his readings. He was converted to the poetic vocation and pantheism by reading Robinson Jeffers in the mid-1930s and then in 1948 converted to Catholicism. In 1951 he became a Dominican lay brother and remained one for almost twenty years. His many volumes of poetry are collected into *The Residual Years 1934–1948* (Santa Rosa, CA: Black Sparrow Press, 1997), *The Veritable Years 1949–1966*, introd. Albert Gelpi (Santa Rosa, CA: Black Sparrow Press, 1998), and *The Integral Years 1966–1994* (Santa Rosa, CA: Black Sparrow Press, 2000).

ART NEWS is an established journal of news of the national and international art worlds. During the 1950s and 1960s it was edited by Alfred Frankfurter and Thomas B. Hess. Poets such as James Schuyler and John Ashbery wrote for the journal, which established a link between the New York School poets and painters.

ASHBERY, JOHN (1927– ), is a poet and art critic associated with the New York School of poets (including Frank O'Hara, Kenneth Koch, James Schuyler, and Barbara Guest) and painters (including Jackson Pollock, Willem de Kooning, Jasper Johns, and Robert Rauschenberg). His low-keyed, ironic, conversational poems, tracing out the convolutions of alienated consciousness in a relativistic world, help to express postmodern sensibility. His many collections of poetry include: *Some Trees*, foreword W. H. Auden (New Haven: Yale University Press, 1956); *The Tennis Court Oath* (Middletown, CT: Wesleyan University Press, 1962); *Rivers and Mountains* (New York: Holt, Rinehardt and Winston, 1966); *Three Poems* (New York: Viking Press, 1972); *Self-Portrait in a Convex Mirror* (New York: Viking Press, 1975); *A Wave* (New York: Viking Press, 1984); *Selected Poems* (New York: Viking Press, 1986); and *Flow Chart* (New York: Alfred A. Knopf, 1991).

AUDEN, W. H. (1907–1973), was a poet, playwright, opera librettist, and essayist. The most acclaimed and influential British poet of the 1930s generation, he emigrated to the United States in 1939 and became a poetic and intellectual presence in New York. His poems, always extraordinary in their formal invention and virtuosity, abandoned his Marxist and Freudian concerns of the 1930s and became by turns satiric, meditative, and religious in their fusion of Christian existentialism and Horatian classicism. Some of his many publications are: *The English Auden: Poems, Essays, and Dramatic Writings*, ed. Edward Mendelson (London: Faber and Faber, 1977); *Collected Poems*, ed. Edward Mendelson (New York: Vintage Books, 1991); and *The Dyer's Hand and Other Essays* (New York: Random House, 1962). With Norman Holmes Pearson, Auden edited the anthology *Poets of the English Language 1907–1973* (New York: Viking Press, 1950).

AVISON, MARGARET (1918– ), is a widely published and distinguished Canadian poet. With the Vancouver Poetry Conference of 1963 she became a strong presence in Canadian writing. Some of her books are: *The Dumbfounding* (New York: W. W. Norton and Co., 1966), chosen for publication by DL; *Selected Poems* (Toronto: Oxford University

Press, 1991); and *Not Yet But Still* (Hartsport, NS: Lancelot Press, 1997).

BAUM, L(YMAN). FRANK (1856–1919), was a Kansas-born writer of children's fiction, especially known for a series of books about the charmed land of Oz, among them: *The Wonderful World of Oz* (Chicago: Reilly and Lee, 1908), *The Enchanted Island of Yew* (Indianapolis, IN: Bobbs-Merrill, 1903), *The Road to Oz* (Chicago: Reilly and Britton Co., 1909), *The Emerald City of Oz* (Chicago: Reilly and Britton Co., 1910), *Tik-Tok of Oz* (Chicago: Reilly and Britton Co., 1913), *Jack Pumpkinhead* (Chicago: Reilly and Britton Co., 1913), *The Scarecrow of Oz* (Chicago: Reilly and Britton Co., 1915), and *The Tin Woodsman of Oz* (Chicago: Reilly and Lee, 1918).

BEDFORD, SYBILLE (1911– ), is a British writer of travel books, biography, and fiction, including *The Legacy* (London: Collins, 1956).

BELL, LELAND (1922–1991), was a New York painter, married in 1943 to Louisa Matthiasdottir, also a painter. Both were friends of DL during her New York years. His paintings turned from his abstractions of the 1940s to a representational style in the 1960s.

BERENSON, BERNARD (1865–1959), was an art critic and expert on Italian Renaissance painting who advised wealthy Americans of the Gilded Age about acquisitions and lived most of his life outside Florence, where his villa, I Tatti, housed his personal collection. He wrote: *The Venetian Painters of the Renaissance* (New York: G. P. Putnam's Sons, 1894), *The Florentine Painters of the Renaissance* (New York: G. P. Putnam's Sons, 1902), *Italian Painters of the Renaissance* (Oxford: Oxford University Press, 1930), and *Aesthetics and History in the Visual Arts* (New York: Pantheon Press, 1948).

BERGÉ, CAROL (1928– ), is an American writer of novels, short stories, and poems. LeRoi Jones, as an editor, included her in *Four Young Lady Poets* (New York: Totem Press/Corinth Books, 1962). A larger collection of her poems appeared as *From a Soft Angle: Poems about Women* (Indianapolis, IN: Bobbs-Merrill, 1971). She attended the Vancouver

Poetry Conference in 1963 and published *The Vancouver Report* (New York: Fuck You Press, 1964).

BERRIGAN, DANIEL (1921– ), is a New York poet, Jesuit priest, and peace activist, whom DL came to know through antiwar resistance. He was jailed a number of times for his nonviolent resistance to the Vietnam War, most famously after he, along with his brother Philip and others, destroyed military draft records in Catonsville, Maryland. His books include: *Time without Number* (New York: Macmillan Co., 1957), *The World for Wedding Ring* (New York: Macmillan Co., 1962), *Trial Poems* (Boston: Beacon Press, 1970), and *Prison Poems* (Greensboro, NC: Unicorn Press, 1974). He wrote a play, *The Trial of the Catonsville Nine* (Boston: Beacon Press, 1970), and books of prose: *Night Flight to Hanoi* (New York: Macmillan Co., 1968), *The Dark Night of Resistance* (Garden City, NY: Doubleday, 1971), and *To Dwell in Peace: An Autobiography* (San Francisco: Harper and Row, 1987).

BERRIGAN, PHILIP (1923– ), is a pacifist and was for many years a Josephite priest. He was jailed many times for his radical, nonviolent opposition to war and militarism. Along with his brother Daniel, one of the Catonsville Nine, he was convicted for destroying military draft records in 1968. Some of his publications are: *No More Strangers*, introd. Thomas Merton (New York: Macmillan Co., 1965), and *Prison Journals of a Priest Revolutionary*, ed. Vincent McGee, introd. Daniel Berrigan (New York: Holt, Rinehardt and Winston, 1970).

BERRIGAN, TED (1934–1983), was a New York poet and friend of Robert Creeley. See: *Living with Chris* (New York: Buke Press, 1965), *The Sonnets* (New York: Lorenz and Ellen Gude, 1964), and *Selected Poems*, ed. Aram Saroyan, introd. Alice Notley (New York: Penguin Books, 1994).

BERRY, WENDELL (1934– ), is a Kentucky poet, novelist, farmer, and essayist whose work explores personal and social responsibility for the sacredness of life and for a human community within the ecological wholeness of nature. Some of his publications are: *Farming: A Handbook* (New York: Harcourt Brace Jovanovich, 1970), *Clearing* (New York: Harcourt Brace Jovanovich, 1977), *Collected Poems:*

*1957–1982* (San Francisco: North Point Press, 1985), and *A Timbered Choir: Sabbath Poems 1979–1997* (Washington, DC: Counterpoint, 1998). His fiction includes: *A Place on Earth* (Boston: Houghton Mifflin, 1967), *Remembering* (San Francisco: North Point Press, 1988), *Fidelity: Five Stories* (New York: Pantheon Press, 1992). His nonfiction includes: *A Continuous Harmony: Essays Cultural and Agricultural* (New York: Harcourt Brace Jovanovich, 1972), *The Unsettling of America* (San Francisco: Sierra Club Books, 1977), and *Standing by Words* (San Francisco: North Point Press, 1983).

BERRYMAN, JOHN (1914–1972), was one of the chief "confessional" poets, who explored his anxieties and psychological problems as a moral and spiritual expression of modern secular angst. Berryman published: *Homage to Mistress Bradstreet* (New York: Farrar, Straus Cudahy, 1956); *The Dream Songs* (New York: Farrar, Straus and Giroux, 1969), a sequence of episodes and reflections about his persona Henry struggling to affirm life and faith against death and madness; and *Collected Poems* (New York: Farrar, Straus and Giroux, 1988). *The Freedom of the Poet* (New York: Farrar, Straus and Giroux, 1976) is a book of essays.

BISCHOFF, ELMER (1916–1991), was a painter central to the emergence of California painting in the 1950s and 1960s and was known for his figures in landscapes and within interior spaces. He taught at the California School of Fine Arts for two periods, from 1945 to 1952 and from 1955 to 1963, where he was one of Jess's teachers. From 1963 to 1985 he taught at the University of California, Berkeley.

BLACKBURN, PAUL (1926–1971), was a New York poet, translator, and contributing editor to the *Black Mountain Review*. His translations of Provençal poetry were published as *Proensa* (Palma de Mallorca, Spain: Divers Press, 1953); by Robert Creeley. Some other books are: *The Dissolving Fabric* (Palma de Mallorca: Divers Press, 1955); *Brooklyn-Manhattan Transit: A Bouquet for Flatbush* (New York: Totem Press, 1960); *The Journals*, ed. Robert Kelly (Los Angeles: Black Sparrow Press, 1972); *Against the Silences*, preface by Robert Creeley (New York: Permanent Press, 1980); and *Collected Poems*, ed. Edith Jarolim (New York: Persea Books, 1985).

BLAINE, NELL (1922–1996), was a New York painter and printmaker who studied with Hans Hofmann and whose paintings changed from her abstractions of the 1950s to Matisse-inspired landscapes, still lifes, and portraits, vividly colored and boldly brushed. DL and Blaine were friends in New York City.

BLACK MOUNTAIN REVIEW, edited by Robert Creeley, published seven issues from Spring 1954 to Autumn 1957. With *Origin*, the *Review* was central to the emergence of the new American poetry, especially the branch inspired by the poetry and poetics of Charles Olson. Both RD and DL published in the review: RD's "Letters for Denise Levertov: For a Muse Meant" first appeared in the third issue, Fall 1954.

BLASER, ROBIN (1925– ), is an Idaho-born poet who was closely associated with RD and Jack Spicer and with the San Francisco Renaissance in the early 1960s and who became a Canadian citizen after beginning a long teaching career at Simon Frazer University in Vancouver. His early books include: *The Moth Poem* (San Francisco: Open Space, 1964), *Les Chimères* (San Francisco: Open Space, 1965; translations from Nerval), *Cups* (San Francisco: Four Seasons Foundation, 1968), *Syntax* (Vancouver, BC: Talon Books, 1982). *The Holy Forest* (Toronto: Coach House Press, 1993) is a volume of his collected poems, with a foreword by Robert Creeley. Blaser edited *The Collected Books of Jack Spicer* (Los Angeles: Black Sparrow Press, 1975).

BLOK, ALEKSANDR (1880–1921), was a Russian Symbolist poet whose idealism and patriotism, as expressed in *The Twelve* (1918), led him to support the Bolshevik Revolution in its early years. His works in English translation include: *The Twelve and Other Poems*, trans. Anselm Hollo (Lexington, KY: Gnomen Press, 1971); and *Selected Poems*, trans. Jon Stallworthy (Manchester: Carcanet Press, 2000).

BLOY, LEON (1846–1917), was a French journalist and fiction writer whose vehemently combative Catholicism informed his mystical, autobiographical writings, among them in English translation: *The Woman Who Was Poor: A Contemporary Novel of the French*, trans. I. J. Collins (New York: Sheed and

Ward, 1939), and *Pilgrim of the Absolute: A Selection of His Writings*, trans. John Coleman and Harry Lorin Binsse, ed. Raissa Maritain, introd. Jacques Maritain (London: Eyre and Spottiswoode, 1947).

BLY, ROBERT (1926– ), is a Minnesota poet, editor, and translator of European and Latin American poets. He edited the influential journals *The Fifties* and *The Sixties*. Given the influence of Surrealism and of Spanish poets such as Garcia Lorca and Cesar Vallejo, his early poems became associated with notions of the Deep Image, which connects the psyche with natural processes. He became, like DL, a vocal opponent of the Vietnam War. His later poems became more explicitly Jungian and archetypal. Some of his many publications are: *Silence in the Snowy Fields* (Middleton, CT: Wesleyan University Press, 1962), *The Light Around the Body* (New York: Harper and Row, 1967), *The Teeth Mother Naked at Last* (San Francisco: City Lights Books, 1971), *The Morning Glory: Prose Poems* (New York: Harper and Row, 1975), *Eating the Honey of Words: New and Selected Poems* (New York: Harper Flamingo, 1999), and *Iron John* (Reading, MA: Addison-Wesley, 1990).

BOGAN, LOUISE (1897–1970), was a poet known for her formal elegance and for the intellectual, ironic treatment of the stresses in her emotional life. For thirty-eight years she was poetry reviewer for *The New Yorker*. Her several volumes were collected in *The Blue Estuaries: Poems 1923–1968* (New York: Farrar, Straus and Giroux, 1968).

BORREGAARD, EBBE (1933– ), was born in New York, but moved to California in 1955. He was one of the poets attending classes at the Poetry Center and was part of the Spicer circle in San Francisco. See *The Wapitis* (San Francisco: White Rabbit Press, 1958).

BOWES-LYON, LILIAN (1895–1949), was an English poet, first cousin to Elizabeth, the Queen Mother, whose elegantly reserved and formal poems derive from the Northumberland landscape of her childhood. See *Collected Poems* (London: Jonathan Cape, 1948).

BRAUTIGAN, RICHARD (1935–1984), was a West Coast fiction writer of the counterculture whose work bridged from the Beats of the 1950s to the hipsters of the 1960s. Some of his books are: *Trout Fishing in America* (New York: Dell Publishing Co., 1967); *In Watermelon Sugar* (New York: Dell Publishing Co., 1968); *Please Plant This Book* (San Francisco: Graham MacKintosh, 1968), being eight poems printed on seed packets.

BRINNIN, JOHN MALCOLM (1916–1998), was a Canadian-born poet and critic who directed the Poetry Center at the YMHA in New York from 1949 to 1956. He taught at Boston University in the 1960s and 1970s, and wrote closed-form poems, controlled in their language play. He published *Selected Poems* (Boston: Little, Brown, 1963) and *Skin Diving in the Virgins* (New York: Delacorte Press, 1970).

BROMIGE, DAVID (1933– ), is a British-born poet who moved from Vancouver to California in the 1960s. He was a part of RD's circle of poets; he and DL became friends during her teaching stint in Berkeley in 1969. His poems were influenced early by the Black Mountain aesthetic and later became associated with Language Poetry in the 1970s. He wrote: *The Ends of the Earth* (Los Angeles: Black Sparrow Press, 1968), *They Are Eyes* (San Francisco: Panjandrum Press, 1972), *My Poetry* (Berkeley: The Figures, 1980), *Peace* (Berkeley: Tuumba Press, 1981), and *From the First Century (of Vulnerable Bundles)* (Elmwood, CT: Potes and Poets Press, 1995).

BROUGHTON, JAMES (1913–1999), was a San Francisco Bay area poet, playwright, and filmmaker. He and RD were friends in Berkeley in 1947, and in 1957 he was one of the poets in RD's "Maidens" group. His Zen-based poetry is ecstatic, visionary, and erotic. See: *True and False Unicorn* (New York: Grove Press, 1957), *Ecstasies Poems 1975–1983* (Mill Valley, CA: Syzygy Press, 1983), *A Long Undressing: Collected Poems 1949–1959* (Highlands, NC: The Jargon Society, 1971), and *Packing Up for Paradise: Selected Poems 1946–1996* (Santa Rosa, CA: Black Sparrow Press, 1997). *Seeing the Light* (San Francisco: City Lights Books, 1977) is a filmography, and *The Androgyne Journal* (Oakland, CA: Scrimshaw Press, 1977) is autobiographical prose.

BROWN, NORMAN O(LIVER). (1913– ), is a classicist and philosopher whose writings are deeply engaged with Freudian psychology and myth. Known as Nobby to his friends, he taught at Wesleyan University in the 1960s and then began a long teaching career at the University of California, Santa Cruz, in the 1970s. His influential books are: *Life against Death: The Psychoanalytic Meaning of History* (Middleton, CT: Wesleyan University Press, 1959), *Love's Body* (New York: Random House, 1966), and *Hermes the Thief: The Evolution of a Myth* (New York: Vintage Books, 1969).

BRYHER, pseudonym of ANNIE WINNIFRED ELLERMAN (1894–1983), was an English novelist who lived in Europe most of her life and was a close friend and companion of H. D. She co-edited, with Kenneth MacPherson, the avant-garde film journal *Close-Up* in the late 1920s and early 1930s. She wrote historical fiction: *The Roman Wall* (New York: Pantheon Books, 1954), *Gate to the Sea* (New York: Pantheon Books, 1958), *The Coin of Carthage* (New York: Harcourt, Brace and World, 1963); and two books of autobiography, *The Heart to Artemis* (New York: Harcourt, Brace and World, 1962), and *The Days of Mars: A Memoir* (London: Calder and Boyars, 1972).

BUBER, MARTIN (1878–1965), was an Austrian-born Jewish philosopher. His book *I and Thou*, trans. Ronald Gregory Smith (New York: Charles Scribners, 1958), was read widely by believers of many faiths. His many books include: *Hasidism*, trans. Greta Hort (New York: Philosophical Library, 1948); and *Jewish Mysticism and the Legends of Baalshem* (London: M. Dent and Sons, Inc., 1931).

BUNTING, BASIL (1900–1985), was a Northumberland poet who responded to Modernist experimentation, became a friend and follower of Ezra Pound in the 1930s, and wrote poems noted for their musical structure and effects. See *Redimiculum Matellarum* (Milan: La Grafica Moderna, 1930), *Briggflatts* (London: Fulcrum Press, 1966), and *Collected Poems* (London: Fulcrum Press, 1968).

BURFORD, WILLIAM (1927– ), is a Texas-based poet who wrote: *Man Now* (Dallas: Southern Methodist University Press, 1954), *A Beginning: Poems* (W. W. Norton and Co., 1966, selected by DL),

and *Gymnos* (Olympia, WA: Four Mountains Press, 1973).

BURROUGHS, WILLIAM (1914–1997), was a Beat fiction writer who became a close friend of Allen Ginsberg and Jack Kerouac in New York. See *Junkie* (New York: Ace Books, 1953), *Naked Lunch* (Paris: Olympia Press, 1956), and *The Ticket That Exploded* (Paris: Olympia Press, 1962)

BURTON, HILDA AND DAVID, were close friends and supporters of RD and Jess. David, a Berkeley architect, drew up the plans for the additions to RD and Jess's house at 3267 20th Street in San Francisco. Hilda met Jess before RD did and began collecting his paintings. Stephen Burton is their son.

BUTTON, JOHN (1929– ), is a California poet and painter who was a student at the California School of Fine Arts in 1949–50. His landscape paintings were shown widely in New York as well as in California.

CAGE, JOHN (1912–1992), was an avant-garde musician and writer who taught at Black Mountain College in 1950–52, invented the prepared piano, and experimented with the function of noise and silence in music, the use of chance in composition and performance, and electronic music. See *John Cage: An Anthology*, ed. Richard Kostelanetz (New York: Da Capo Press, 1991), and *Music Age: Cage Muses on Words, Art, and Music*, ed. Joan Retalack (Hanover, NH / Middleton, CT: University Press of New England Press, 1996).

CARDENAL, ERNESTO (1925– ), is a Nicaraguan priest, poet, and revolutionary who served as minister of culture in the Marxist Sandinista government of Nicaragua during the 1970s. His books in English include: *Psalms of Struggle and Liberation*, trans. Emile G. McAnany (New York: Herder and Herder, 1972); *From Nicaragua with Love: Poems*, trans. and introd. Jonathan Cohen (San Francisco: City Lights Books, 1986); and *Cosmic Canticle*, trans. Jonathan Lyons (Willimantic, CT: Curbstone Press, 1993).

CARROLL, PAUL (1927– ), is a Chicago-born poet associated with the Beats and the editor of the journal *Big Table* (1959–60). See *Odes* (Chicago: Big Table Publishing Co., 1969), *The Luke Poems* (Chicago: Big Table Publishing Co., 1971), *New and Selected Poems* (Chicago: Yellow Press, 1978), and the prose commentary *The Poem in Its Skin* (Chicago: Follett Publishing Co., 1968).

CARRUTH, HAYDEN (1921– ), is a poet and critic whose verse, written in a variety of forms, open and closed, ruminates on the violence and fragility of psychological and social existence in contrast to the beauty and balance of nature. He became a close friend of DL and of Adrienne Rich in the 1960s. His writing now appears in collected editions: *Collected Shorter Poems, 1946–1991* (Port Townsend, WA: Copper Canyon Press, 1992), *Collected Longer Poems* (Port Townsend, WA: Copper Canyon Press, 1993), and *Working Papers: Selected Essays and Reviews* (Athens: University of Georgia Press, 1982).

CATERPILLAR. Clayton Eschelman edited the twenty issues of *Caterpillar*, October 1967 through 1973. The magazine was a focus for a generation of poets deriving from Charles Olson and from Robert Kelly. RD and DL both published poems in the magazine; RD published sections of his "H. D. Book" there.

CENDRARS, BLAISE, pseudonym of FREDERIC SAUSER-HALL (1887–1961), was a Swiss-born French poet and novelist. Works in English include: *The African Saga*, trans. Margery Bianco, introd. Arthur B. Spingarn (New York: Payson and Clark, 1927) (a translation of *L'Anthologie négre*) and *Complete Poems*, trans. Ron Padgett, introd. Jay Bochner (Berkeley: University of California Press, 1992).

CERNOVICH, NICOLA (1929– ), was a student at Black Mountain College and printed both Charles Olson's *This* (Black Mountain, NC: Black Mountain College, 1951) and RD's *The Song of the Border-guard* (Black Mountain, NC: Black Mountain College, 1953). In May 1960 he directed RD's play *Faust Foutu* at the Living Theatre in New York.

CHICAGO REVIEW, a journal dedicated to presenting the best of contemporary writing, had many editors from the early 1950s through the 1960s. RD was included in a special section entitled "Ten San Francisco Poets," which appeared in the Spring 1958 issue.

CHURCH, PEGGY POND (1903–1986), was a Santa Fe writer of prose and verse about the human connection with the land. See *This Dancing Ground of Sky: Selected Poetry*, introd. Shelley Armitage (Santa Fe, NM: Red Crane Books, 1993).

COLLINS, BURGESS (1923– ), who uses the first name Jess, and not the last name Collins, is a California painter and collagist who became RD's life partner in 1951. His work—at once representational and surreal—shares RD's literary, cosmological, and occult interests. They collaborated on several of RD's books, including *A Book of Resemblances* (New Haven, CT: Henry Wenning, 1966) and a number of Jess's catalogues, including *Translations* (Los Angeles: Black Sparrow Press, 1971). *Jess: A Grand Collage 1951–1993* (Buffalo, NY: Albright-Knox Art Gallery, 1993) presents a retrospective of Jess's work.

COMBUSTION was a Canadian publication produced in Toronto. As editor for the fifteen issues between 1957 and 1960, Raymond H. Souster tried to attract the new American poets and the best of the young Canadian poets who were writing experimental poetry.

CONTACT, edited by William Carlos Williams, published five issues from December 1920 through June 1923. Williams attracted contributions by Kenneth Burke, Marsden Hartley, John Rodker, W. Bryher, and Ezra Pound. *Contact* helped to formulate the principles of Modernism.

CORMAN, CID (SIDNEY) (1924– ), is a Boston-born poet who was influenced by Ezra Pound and William Carlos Williams and the Objectivists of the 1930s. His ground-breaking journal *Origin* (first series 1950–57) featured the Black Mountain group. He has lived in Kyoto, Japan, since the 1960s. See: *Sun Rock Man* (Kyoto: Origin Press, 1962), *Livingdying* (New York: New Directions, 1970), *In Particular: Poems New and Selected* (Dunvegan, Ont.: Cormorant Press, 1986), *The Gist of Origin: An Anthology* (New York: Grossman Publishers, 1975), and *Of*, 2 vols. (Venice, CA: Lapis Press, 1990).

EL CORNO EMPLUMADO, edited in Mexico by Margaret Randall for thirty-one issues from January 1962 through July 1969, introduced the new American poetry to a Spanish-speaking audience and the new Spanish writing to American poets.

CORSO, GREGORY (1930–2001), was a New York poet of long free-verse lines, associated with Allen Ginsberg and Jack Kerouac in the Beat movement. His many books include: *Gasoline* (San Francisco: City Lights Books, 1958), *Happy Birthday of Death* (New York: New Directions, 1960), *Elegiac Feelings American* (New York: New Directions, 1970), and *Mindfield*, foreword by William S. Burroughs and Allen Ginsberg (New York: Thunder Mouth Press, 1989).

CRAIG, EDWARD HENRY GORDON (1872–1966), was an English actor, director, designer, and critic.

CREELEY, ROBERT (1926– ), is a poet and fiction writer, born in a Boston suburb, who became a close friend of DL in 1949 and of Charles Olson and RD in the 1950s. He established the Divers Press (1950–54), taught at Black Mountain College (1954–55), edited *The Black Mountain Review* (1954–57), and has taught at the University of Buffalo, State University of New York, since 1965. He and his first wife, Ann McKinnon, were neighbors of the Mitchell Goodmans (DL and her husband) in southern France in the early 1950s and also lived on Majorca, the setting for his novel *The Island* (New York: Charles Scribner's Sons, 1963). His intimate and domestic poems—at once tense and terse—charge ordinary language with anxious energy in their short, heavily enjambed lines. The poems examine the hesitant efforts of acute self-consciousness to break its alienation and engage the other, often embodied in the beloved. His many books include: *Le Fou* (Columbus, OH: Golden Goose Press, 1952), *If You* (San Francisco: The Porpoise Bookshop, 1956), *A Form of Women* (New York/Highlands, NC: Corinth/Jargon Books, 1959), *For Love: Poems 1950–1960* (New York: Charles Scribner's Sons, 1962), *Words* (New York: Charles Scribner's Sons, 1967), *The Finger* (Los Angeles: Black Sparrow Press, 1968), *Pieces* (New York: Charles Scribner's Sons, 1969), *Collected Poems* (Berkeley: University of California Press, 1982), *Memory Gardens* (New York: New Directions, 1986), *Life and Death* (New York: New Directions, 1998), *Collected Prose* (Berkeley: University of California Press, 1988), and *Collected Essays* (Berkeley: University of California Press, 1989).

CREHEN, HUBERT, was the editor of the magazine *Proof.* He was also an art critic who wrote about Clyfford Still for *Art News* and the *San Francisco Chronicle.*

DAHLBERG, EDWARD (1900–1977), wrote autobiographical novels—*Bottom Dogs*, introd. D. H. Lawrence (New York: Simon and Schuster, 1930), and *From Flushing to Calvary* (London: G. P. Putnam's Sons, 1933)—that marked him as a proletarian novelist of the Depression era. *Do These Bones Live* (New York: Harcourt, Brace and Co., 1941) is an excoriating survey of American literature. See also: *Because I Was Flesh: An Autobiography* (Norfolk, CT: New Directions, 1964); *The Edward Dahlberg Reader*, ed. Paul Carroll (New York: New Directions, 1967); and *The Leafless American*, ed. and introd. Harold Billings (Sausalito, CA: R. Beachman, 1967). RD reviewed his *Sorrows of Priapus* (Norfolk, CT: New Directions, 1958).

DAWSON, FIELDING (1930–2002), was a fiction writer and artist who attended Black Mountain College in the 1950s and wrote memoirs of his mentors there: *An Emotional Memoir of Franz Kline* (New York: Pantheon Books, 1967) and *The Black Mountain Book I* (New York: Croton Press, 1970), centered on Charles Olson. He has published numerous collections of short stories, including *Krazy Kat and 76 More: Collected Stories 1950–1976* (Santa Barbara, CA: Black Sparrow Press, 1982).

DE ANGULO, JAIME (1887–1950), was an anthropologist, linguist, and historian of the American West and of American Indian history and a close associate of RD in Berkeley during the late 1940s. See: *Indian Tales* (New York: Hill and Wang, 1953); *Coyote Bones: Selected Poetry and Prose*, ed. Bob Callahan (San Francisco: Turtle Island Foundation, 1974); *A Jaime de Angulo Reader*, ed. and introd. Bob Callahan (Berkeley, CA: Turtle Island Foundation, 1979). See Bob Callahan's interview with RD: "The World of Jaime de Angulo," *The Netzahualcoyotl News* 1.1 (Summer 1979): [1], 5, 14–16.

DE KOONING, WILLEM (1904–1998), was a Dutch-born painter who came to America in 1926. After years of working as a house painter, he emerged as a leader of Abstract Expressionism in New York noted for his gestural use of color and specifically for the series of "Woman Paintings."

DE NIRO, ROBERT (1922–1993), was a painter who worked in New York and San Francisco, studied abstraction under Hans Hofmann, and changed to a more representational style in the 1950s. He was married to the painter Virginia Admiral and is father of the actor of the same name.

DE RACHEWILTZ, MARY (1925– ), is Ezra Pound's daughter by the American expatriate musician Olga Rudge and the author of the memoir about her father entitled *Discretions* (Boston: Little Brown, 1971).

DICKEY, JAMES (1923–1997), was a Georgia-born poet and novelist associated with the University of South Carolina from 1969 to 1997. His highly emotive language, turning on the conflict between primitive instinct and civilized constraint, won him public acclaim in the 1960s. See: *Two Poems of the Air* (Portland, OR: Centicore Press, 1964), *Buckdancer's Choice* (Middletown, CT: Wesleyan University Press, 1965), the novel *Deliverance* (Boston: Houghton Mifflin, 1970), and *The Whole Motion: Collected Poems* (Middletown, CT: Wesleyan University Press, 1992).

DINESEN, ISAK, pseudonym of KAREN BLIXEN (1885–1962), was a Danish writer who composed her finely worked, intensely imagined, often exotic narratives in English. Her many volumes include: *Seven Gothic Tales* (New York: Modern Library, 1934), *Out of Africa* (New York: Random House, 1938), and *Last Tales* (New York: Random House, 1957).

DI PRIMA, DIANE (1934– ), is a New York–born poet who was associated with the Beats, co-edited with LeRoi Jones the journal *Floating Bear* (1961–69), and moved to the San Francisco Bay Area in 1968. Her books include: *Earthsong: Poems 1957–1959* (New York: Poets Press, 1968), *Revolutionary Poems* (San Francisco: City Lights Books, 1971), *Selected*

*Poems* (Plainfield, VT: North Atlantic Books, 1977), *Loba: Parts I–VIII* (Berkeley, CA: Wingbow Press, 1978), *Memoirs of a Beatnik* (New York: Olympia Press, 1969), and *Recollections of My Life as a Woman: The New York Years* (New York: Viking Press, 2001).

DORFMAN, ELSA (1937– ), is a photographer and a friend to poets in Boston and New York. See *Elsa's Housebook: A Woman's Photojournal* (Boston: David Godine, 1974) and *En Famille* (New York: Granary Books, 1999), a book of photos and poems by Robert Creeley.

DORN, EDWARD (1929–1999), grew up in Illinois but found poetic direction when he studied under Charles Olson at Black Mountain College in the 1950s. He was married to Helene when he wrote the novel *Rites of Passage* (1965). He later married Jennifer Dunbar. His poems use colloquial diction and popular culture to present a spirited, biting, satiric critique of American society and its values. Some of his many publications are: *Hands Up!* (New York: Totem Books, 1964), *Geography* (London: Fulcrum Books, 1965), the novel *Rites of Passage* (1965), *Slinger* (Berkeley, CA: Wingbow Press, 1975), *Collected Poems 1956–1974* (Bolinas, CA: Four Seasons Foundation, 1975), and *Abhorrences* (Santa Rosa, CA: Black Sparrow Press, 1990).

DUERDEN, RICHARD (1905–1979), attended classes at the Poetry Center, San Francisco State University, edited the little magazine *Foot*, and wrote *The Fork* (San Francisco: Open Space, 1965).

DUGAN, ALAN (1923– ), is a Brooklyn-born poet whose first book, *Poems* (New Haven: Yale University Press, 1961), was selected for the Yale Younger Poets series. He also wrote *Collected Poems* (New Haven: Yale University Press, 1969) and *Poems 4* (Boston: Little, Brown, 1974).

DULL, HAROLD (1934– ), is a California poet associated with RD and was a member of Jack Spicer's Magic Workshop at San Francisco State University. Some of his books are: *Bad Poems* (San Francisco: White Rabbit Press, 1958), *The Star Year* (San Francisco: White Rabbit Press, 1967), and *The Wood Climb Down Out Of* (San Francisco: White Rabbit Press, 1963).

DUNN, JOE, was a poet in the San Francisco scene who took a course to learn how to operate office equipment and then established the White Rabbit Press as a publishing house for the Spicer circle, using the equipment at the Greyhound Bus terminal in San Francisco.

DURRELL, GERALD (1925–1995), was a British naturalist and brother to the novelist Lawrence Durrell. His books and television films concern his experiences with animals around the world.

DUSENBERY, GAIL (1939– ), is a poet born in Albany who came to Berkeley in the 1960s, studied under RD, and became active in the resistance to the Vietnam War. See *The Mark* (Berkeley, CA: Oyez Press, 1967).

EBERHART, RICHARD (1904– ), is a poet and a longtime professor at Dartmouth College. His sonorous lyric verse seeks visionary intensity. See *Collected Poems 1930–1986* (New York: Oxford University Press, 1988).

ECONOMOU, GEORGE (1934– ), is a medieval scholar and poet who has taught at Long Island University (1961–83) and then at the University of Oklahoma. He edited the journals *The Chelsea Review* (1958–60) and *Trobar* (1960–64). His books include: *The Georgics* (Los Angeles: Black Sparrow Press, 1968), *Landed Natures* (Los Angeles: Black Sparrow Press, 1969), *Poems for Self Therapy* (Mt. Horeb, WI: Perishable Press, 1972), and *Harmonies and Fits* (Norman, OK: Point Rider Press, 1987).

EDSON, RUSSELL (1935– ), is a Surrealist poet and playwright. See *The Very Thing That Happens*, introd. Denise Levertov (New York: W. W. Norton and Co., 1964); *What a Man Can See* (Penland, NC: Jargon Society, 1969); *The Children of an Equestrian* (New York: Harper and Row, 1973); and *The Tunnel: Selected Poems* (Oberlin, OH: Oberlin College, 1994).

EIGNER, LARRY (1927–1996), was a poet from Swampscott, Massachusetts, who was published in *Origin* and in *The Black Mountain Review* and was reviewed admiringly by both DL and RD. Because he suffered from cerebral palsy, his poems are brief notations of immediate perceptions and observations, the phrases organized spatially on the typewriter. He spent his last decades in Berkeley. His collections include: *From the Sustaining Air* (Palma de Mallorca: Divers Press, 1953); *On My Eyes*, foreword by Denise Levertov (Highlands, NC: Jonathan Williams, 1960); *Selected Poems*, ed. Samuel Charters and Andrea Wyatt (Berkeley, CA: Oyez, 1972); *Waters, Places, a Time*, ed. Robert Grenier (Santa Barbara, CA: Black Sparrow Press, 1983); and *Windows/Walls/Yard/Ways*, ed. Robert Grenier (Santa Rosa, CA: Black Sparrow Press, 1994).

ELLINGHAM, LEWIS (1933– ), is a San Francisco poet and novelist who was part of the Jack Spicer circle and who went to great lengths to interview poets and friends of Spicer. He wrote: *The Jefferson Airplane* (San Francisco: s.n., 1971) and with Kevin Killian *Poet Be Like God: Jack Spicer and the San Francisco Renaissance* (Hanover, NH: University Press of New England, 1998).

ELMSLIE, KENWARD (1929– ), is a songwriter, playwright, librettist, and poet associated with the New York School. See: *Pavilions: Poems* (New York: Tibor de Nagy Editions, 1961); *Power Plant Poems*, ed. Ted Berrigan (Calais, VT: C Press, 1967); *Circus Nerves* (Los Angeles: Black Sparrow Press, 1971); and *Routine Disruptions: Selected Poems and Lyrics*, ed. W. C. Bamberger (Minneapolis: Coffee House Press, 1998).

ÉLUARD, PAUL, pseudonym of EUGENE GRINDEL (1895–1952), was a French Surrealist poet. See *Oeuvres complètes*, ed. Marcelle Dumas and Lucian Scheler, preface by Lucian Scheler (Paris: Gallimard, 1968); in English, *Selected Poems*, trans. Lloyd Alexander (New York: New Directions, 1988).

ENGLE, PAUL (1908–1991), was a poet and founding director of the Writers' Workshop of the University of Iowa. As Iowa's Director of the International Writing Program from 1966 to 1977, he was responsible for bringing hundreds of poets from foreign countries to America. His poetry collections include: *Corn: A Book of Poems* (New York: Doubleday and Co., Doran, 1939), *Poems in Praise* (New York: Random House, 1959), *A Woman Unashamed* (New York: Random House, 1965), and *Embrace:*

*Selected Love Poems* (New York: Random House, 1969). With Joseph Langland, he edited the anthology *Poets' Choice* (New York: Dial Press, 1962).

ENSLIN, THEODORE (1925– ), is a poet and musician living in Maine and a close friend of DL and Mitchell Goodman. His poems are informed by intricate musical structures and a profound sense of direct perceptions. His books include: *The Work Proposed* (Ashfield, MA: Origin Press, 1958); *Forms*, 5 vols. (New Rochelle, NY: Elizabeth Press, 1970–73); *Ranger* (Richmond, CA: North Atlantic Books, 1980); and *Then and Now: Selected Poems 1943–1993*, ed. Mark Nowak (Orono, ME: National Poetry Foundation, 1999).

ESHLEMAN, CLAYTON (1935– ), was associated with the New York poets around Robert Kelly and Hawk's Well Press. His early books, *North and Mexico* (New York: Trobar Books, 1962) and *Indiana: Poems* (Los Angeles: Black Sparrow Press, 1969), demonstrated his interest in psychology and wide cultural contexts. Other collections include: *Altars* (Los Angeles: Black Sparrow Press, 1971), *Coils* (Los Angeles: Black Sparrow Press, 1973), *Gull Wall* (Los Angeles: Black Sparrow Press, 1975), and *Under World Arrest* (Santa Rosa, CA: Black Sparrow Press, 1994). He edited the important journals *Caterpillar* and *Sulfur*. He also translated South American and European poets: *Aimé Césaire: The Collected Poems*, with Annette Smith (Berkeley: University of California Press, 1983); *Cesar Vallejo: The Complete Posthumous Poetry*, with Jose Rubia (Berkeley: University of California Press, 1978); and *Antonin Artaud: Four Texts*, with Norman Glass (Los Angeles: Panjandrum Press, 1982).

EVERGREEN REVIEW was edited by Donald Allen and Barnet Rosset during its influential first eight issues, beginning in 1957. Rosset remained the editor till the ninety-seventh issue of the review in 1973. The editors published the emerging European writers Albert Camus, Samuel Beckett, and Eugene Ionesco, along with new open-form American poets. RD appeared in a section of the second issue on the "San Francisco Scene."

EVERSON, WILLIAM. See ANTONINUS, BROTHER.

FABILLI, MARY (1914– ), and her sister Lillian became friends of RD in Berkeley in the late 1930s. Mary is a poet, short story writer, and artist who appeared in RD's *Berkeley Miscellany* publications and early in her career was praised by William Carlos Williams. She wrote under the name Aurora Bligh and during the late 1940s was married to William Everson. Her early writing is collected in *Aurora Bligh and Early Poems* (Berkeley: Oyez, 1968); later books include *The Animal Kingdom: Poems 1964–1967* (Berkeley: Oyez, 1975) and *The Old Ones* (Berkeley: Oyez, 1966).

FERLINGHETTI, LAWRENCE (1919– ), is a San Francisco poet associated with the Beats and with the San Francisco Renaissance of the 1960s and is the publisher of City Lights Books, including DL's first American book, *Here and Now* and RD's *Selected Poems*. His free-verse poems are informed by visionary mysticism and a political and satirical critique of bourgeois culture. His publications include: *Pictures of the Gone World* (New York: New Directions, 1955), *A Coney Island of the Mind* (New York: New Directions, 1958), *Starting from San Francisco* (New York: New Directions, 1961), *The Secret Meaning of Things* (New York: New Directions, 1969), *Endless Life: Selected Poems* (New York: New Directions, 1981), and *A Far Rockaway of the Heart* (New York: New Directions, 1997).

FIELD, EDWARD (1924– ), is a New York poet whose work recounts episodes of urban angst, sometimes with ironic humor, in images of popular culture: *Stand Up, Friend, with Me* (New York: Grove Press, 1963), *Variety Photoplays* (New York: Grove Press, 1967), and *Counting Myself Lucky: Selected Poems 1963–1992* (Santa Rosa, CA: Black Sparrow Press, 1992).

FINLAY, IAN HAMILTON (1925– ), is a Scots concrete and visual poet whose Wild Hawthorne Press published many experiments in new forms of writing and thinking. He has published: *The Dancers Inherit the Party* (London: Fulcrum Press, 1969), *Poems to Hear and See* (New York: Macmillan Co., 1971), and *Honey by the Water* (Los Angeles: Black Sparrow Press, 1972).

FITTS, DUDLEY (1903–1968), was a reviewer and translator closely associated with the Yale University Press poetry series in its early years. His translations include: *The Oedipus Cycle: An English Version*, with Robert Fitzgerald (New York: Harcourt Brace Jovanovich, 1977), and *Poems from the Greek Anthology, in English Paraphrase* (New York: New Directions, 1956).

FITZGERALD, EDWARD (1809–1883), was an English poet and translator best known for his rhymed version of the Persian poem *The Rubaiyat of Omar Khayyam*.

THE FLOATING BEAR: A NEWSLETTER began in New York City in 1961 with Diane Di Prima and LeRoi Jones as editors and ended thirty-eight issues later in 1971. The newsletter published a variety of poets from New York and San Francisco. Its distinguishing feature was that poems were published almost as soon as they were accepted, so that it was possible to get the latest work very quickly.

FOOT was a journal that began publishing in San Francisco in 1961 with Richard Duerden as editor. Leslie Scalapino helped with the editing of the sixth issue in 1978, and Lawrence Kearney with the seventh and final issue in 1979. RD made the drawing of a foot for the first issue. The magazine published poets from San Francisco.

FREDERICKS, CLAUDE (1910–1976), was a typesetter and printer for the Banyan Press before he took on the job of typesetting, designing, printing and binding RD's book *Letters*, published by Jonathan Williams's Jargon Society. From his home in Pawlet, Vermont, he gained the reputation of being one of the finest printers of his generation.

FREILICHER, JANE (1924– ), is a New York painter of cityscapes associated with Hans Hofmann.

GARTH, MIDI (1920– ), is a native New Yorker who emerged in the 1950s as one of the most original dancers of her generation. Her performances shifted choreography from the literal to the conceptual plane, and while she is known for her passionate, personal performances, her techniques are built on a movement or the qualities of a movement. *Prelude to Flight* (1951), *Anonymous* (1954), and *This Day's Madness* (1961) are three of her many successful programs.

GAUDIER-BRZESKA, HENRI (1891–1915), was a French-born sculptor in London who experimented with abstraction and participated in the Vorticist movement with Wyndham Lewis and Ezra Pound. Pound wrote *Gaudier-Brzeska: A Memoir* (London: John Lane, 1916) after the sculptor's battlefield death during World War I.

GENESIS WEST, edited by Gordon Lish in Burlington, California, published seven issues between Fall 1962 and Winter 1965. The magazine published poets from the San Francisco Renaissance as well as poets from Southern California.

GILBERT, JACK (1925– ), is a Pittsburgh-born poet about whom DL wrote a brief essay. See his *Views of Jeopardy* (New Haven: Yale University Press, 1962), *Monolithos Poems 1962 and 1982* (New York: Alfred A. Knopf, 1982), and *The Great Fires: Poems* (New York: Alfred A. Knopf, 1994).

GINSBERG, ALLEN (1926–1997), was the central poet of the Beat movement in New York and San Francisco, whose autobiographical poems in long Whitmanian free verse combine anxiety and exaltation, radical politics, and the drive toward sexual and visionary ecstasy. His books include: *Howl* (San Francisco: City Lights Books, 1956); *Kaddish* (San Francisco: City Lights Books, 1961); *The Fall of America* (San Francisco: City Lights Books, 1972); *Collected Poems 1947–1980* (New York: Harper and Row, 1984); *White Shroud* (New York: Harper and Row, 1985); *Death and Fame*, ed. Bob Rosenthal, Peter Haler, and Bill Morgan, foreword by Robert Creeley, afterword by Bob Rosenthal (New York: Harper Flamingo, 1999); and *Deliberate Prose: Selected Essays 1952–1995*, ed. Bill Morgan (New York: Harper Collins, 2000).

GLEASON, MADELINE (1903–1979), was a San Francisco poet and painter born in North Dakota. She started poetry readings in San Francisco, formed a group of poets in the 1940s, and thus built a foundation for the poetry renaissance of the 1950s. She was a friend and associate of RD. Her poems delineate an intense psychological and religious journey. See: *The Metaphysical Needle* (San Francisco: Centaur Press, 1949), *Concerto for Bell and Telephone* (San Francisco: Unicorn Press, 1966), *Here Come Everybody: New and Selected Poems* (San Francisco: Panjandrum Press, 1975), and *Collected Poems: 1919–1979*, ed. Christopher Wagstaff (Jersey City: Talisman House Publishers, 1999).

GOODMAN, MITCHELL (1923–1997), was a Brooklyn-born writer who met DL in Europe in 1947. They were married in December 1947, came to live in New York in 1948, had a son Nikolai in 1949, lived in southern France in 1950–51 (with the Robert Creeleys as neighbors), lived in Mexico from 1957 to 1958, and became increasingly active in resistance to the Vietnam War during the 1960s. In 1968 he, along with Dr. Benjamin Spock and three others, was indicted and convicted of conspiring against the military draft law, but the conviction was overturned on appeal the next year. The Goodmans were divorced in 1975. He published: an acclaimed novel about World War II, *The End of It* (New York: Horizon Press, 1961); a chapbook of poems, *More Light: Selected Poems* (Brunswick, ME: Dog Ear Press, 1967); and an anthology documenting the New Left and antiwar movements of the 1960s, *The Movement toward a New America* (Philadelphia: Pilgrim Press, 1970).

GOODMAN, PAUL (1911–1972), was a New York poet, novelist, and social critic with anarchist views who taught at Black Mountain College in the 1950s and became a radical spokesman for the counterculture of the 1960s. His poetry includes *The Lordly Hudson: Collected Poems* (New York: Random House, 1962). His social commentary includes *Growing Up Absurd: Problems of Youth in an Organized System* (New York: Random House, 1960) and *Utopian Essays and Practical Proposals* (New York: Random House, 1962).

GREENE, JONATHAN (1943– ), is a poet from New York City associated with Robert Kelly. *The Reckoning* was published by Kelly as one of his Matter Books (1966). Greene founded the Gnomon Press in Lexington, Kentucky, which published some of his books, including *Inventions of Necessity:*

*The Selected Poems* (Lexington, KY: Gnomon Press, 1998). With Island Press in Toronto, Gnomon Press published the second edition of RD's *Fragments of a Disorderd Devotion* (1966).

GRESSER, SEYMOUR (1926– ), is a sculptor and poet. See *Poems from Mexico* (Lanham, MD: Goosetree Press, 1964) and *Voyages* (Madison, WI: Quixote Press, 1969).

GUEST, BARBARA (1920– ), is a poet who moved from California to New York in the 1950s, worked at *Art News*, and became a figure in the New York School of poets and Abstract Expressionist painters, along with John Ashbery, Frank O'Hara, and others. Like DL, she was for a time poetry editor of *The Nation*. Since the 1980s her work has been linked with the Language Poets of the following generation. Some of her publications are: *The Location of Things* (New York: Tibor de Nagy Gallery, 1960), *Poems: The Location of Things; Archaics; The Open Skies* (Garden City, NY: Doubleday, 1962), *The Blue Stairs* (New York: Corinth Books, 1968), *Biography* (Providence, RI: Burning Deck, 1981), and *Selected Poems* (Los Angeles: Sun and Moon Press, 1995).

GURDJIEFF, G(EORGE). I(VANOVICH). (1877–1949), was an Armenian expatriate to Paris who established the Institute for the Harmonious Development of Man in 1922 and whose practices, adapted from Buddhist and Sufi sources, sought to shock the individual out of constricting habits and assumptions into a recognition of his or her true essence. See *All and Everything* (New York: Harcourt Brace, 1950).

GUSTON, PHILIP (1913–1980), was a Canadian-born painter whose early murals were influenced by the WPA Artists Project. In his middle period he was an Abstract Expressionist in New York during the 1950s, though in the 1970s he changed to provocative, comic book–like figuration.

HALL, DONALD (1928– ), is a poet, educated at Harvard and Oxford, who taught at Michigan from 1957 to 1975 before moving to his family farm in New Hampshire. His personal lyrics in a variety of forms deal with family, home, and history. See:

*Exiles and Marriages* (New York: Viking Press, 1955), *A Roof of Tiger Lilies* (New York: Viking Press, 1964), and *Old and New Poems* (New York: Viking Press, 1990). With Robert Pack and Louis Simpson, he edited the influential anthology, *The New Poets of England and America* (Cleveland: World Publishing Co., 1957); its conservative and traditional norms provoked Donald M. Allen's counter-anthology of experimental poetry, *The New American Poetry* (New York: Grove 1960).

HAMMOND, MAC (1926–1997), was a poet and a teacher at Case Western Reserve in Cleveland and then at the State University of New York at Buffalo. He published many small editions and then *Mappamundi: New and Selected Poems* (Binghamton, NY: Bellevue Press, 1989). He was the editor of *Audit/Poetry* 4 (1967), which featured RD's work.

HANSON, KENNETH O. (1922– ), taught at Reed College in Portland, Oregon, and appeared in *Five Poets of the Pacific Northwest*, ed. Robin Skelton (Seattle: University of Washington Press, 1964). Later books include: *The Distance Anywhere* (Seattle: University of Washington Press, 1967) and *Lighting the Night Sky* (Portland, OR: Breitenbush Books, 1983).

HARRISON, JANE (1850–1928), was a pioneering classical scholar and anthropologist of classical culture. Her major publications changed the nature of classical studies: *Prolegomena to the Study of Greek Religion* (Cambridge: Cambridge University Press, 1903), *Themis: A Study of the Social Origins of Greek Religion* (Cambridge: Cambridge University Press, 1912), *Epilegomena to the Study of Greek Religion* (1921), *Reminiscences of a Student's Life* (Cambridge: Cambridge University Press, 1925). Her books were read with enthusiasm by RD and DL as well as by Charles Olson.

HARRISON, JIM (1937– ), is a Michigan poet and novelist and co-editor of the journal *Sumac*. His first book, *Plain Song* (New York: W. W. Norton and Co., 1965), was selected for publication by DL. Later books include: *The Shape of the Journey: New and Collected Poems* (Port Townsend, WA: Copper Canyon Press, 1998) and, among his novels, *Wolf: A False Memoir* (New York: Simon and Schuster,

1971) and *Legends of the Fall* (New York: Delacorte Press, 1979).

HASELWOOD, DAVE (1931– ), began the Auerhahn Press in 1958 in San Francisco with John Wieners's *Hotel Wently Poems* (1958). After Andrew Hoyem, a poet, joined the press, they printed books by Jack Spicer, Michael McClure, and Philip Lamantia. The press contracted with Jess and RD to print *A Book of Resemblances* in two volumes but could not master the complications of the printing job. The publishing record of the press appears in Haselwood's *A Bibliography of the Auerhahn Press and Its Successor Dave Haselwood Books* (Berkeley: Poltroon Press, 1976).

HAWKES, JOHN (1925–1998), was an avant-garde fiction writer who began teaching at Brown in 1958, and whose fiction violates conventions of plot and narrative to explore the nightmare reality of modern angst. See: *The Cannibal* (New York: New Directions, 1949), *The Lime Twig* (Norfolk, CT: New Directions, 1961), *Second Skin* (New York: New Directions, 1964), and *The Blood Oranges* (New York: New Directions, 1971).

HAWLEY, ROBERT (1929– ), was a student at Black Mountain College who moved to the San Francisco Bay area after the college closed in 1956, founded the Oyez Press in Berkeley, and became an integral part of the poetic community of the area in the 1960s and 1970s. Oyez published DL's *Summer Poems* (1969) and RD's *The Years as Catches* (1966).

HECHT, ANTHONY (1923– ), is a New York poet who was influenced by Wallace Stevens and W. H. Auden and is noted for his formal finesse and technical virtuosity. See: *The Hard Hours: Poems* (London: Oxford University Press, 1967), *The Venetian Vespers* (New York: Atheneum, 1979), and *The Transparent Man* (New York: Alfred A. Knopf, 1990).

HERRMANN, JOHN (1900–1959), was an American expatriate fiction writer in Paris in the 1920s and later in Mexico, where DL met him. His novels *What Happens* (Paris: Contact Editions, 1925) and *The Salesman* (New York: Simon and Schuster, 1939) reflect his leftist-proletarian politics.

HIRSCHMAN, JACK (1933– ), is a San Francisco poet whose highly emotive language voices his left-ist politics and working-class identification. See: *Yod* (London: Trigram Press, 1966), *Lyripol* (San Francisco: City Lights Books, 1976), *The Arcanes of Le Comte de St. Germain*, preface by Alexander Kohav (San Francisco: Amerus, 1977), and *The Bottom Line* (Willimantic, CT: Curbstone Press, 1988).

HOCHMAN, SANDRA (1936– ), is a New York actress and poet of personal crises. See: *Manhattan Pastures* (New Haven: Yale University Press, 1963), *Love Letters from Asia: Poems* (New York: Viking Press, 1968), *Futures* (New York: Viking Press, 1974), and *Earthworks: Poems 1960–1970* (New York: Viking Press, 1970).

HODES, IDA (1914– ), was a figure in the San Francisico poetry scene from the early 1950s onward. She was assistant director of the Poetry Center at San Francisco State University after RD and a close friend of RD and Jess.

HOFMANN, HANS (1880–1966), was a German-born painter who came to New York City in 1930 and established a school for artists in New York and at Provincetown, Massachusetts. His painting is prized for its use of vibrant colors in blocks defining spatial relationships. RD knew him in Provincetown.

THE HUDSON REVIEW was edited in the 1950s by William Arrowsmith and Joseph Bennett; Frederick Morgan took over as editor-in-chief in the 1960s. This influential literary/intellectual journal tended to publish poets more formally conservative than DL and RD.

HULME, T(HOMAS). E(RNEST). (1883–1917), was a British critic, aesthetician, and poet, a precursor to Imagism, a member of the Vorticist movement in London in 1914, and a translator of Henri Bergson's philosophy. His criticism, articulating the Modernist critique of Romanticism, was collected after his death in World War I. See: *Speculations* (London: K. Paul, Trench, Trubner and Co., 1924) and *Further Speculations*, ed. Sam Hynes (Minneapolis: University of Minnesota Press, 1955).

IGNATOW, DAVID (1914–1997), was a New York poet influenced by William Carlos Williams and noted for authentic and direct registration of immediate daily living. See: *Say Pardon* (Middletown, CT: Wesleyan University Press, 1961), *Figures of the Human* (Middletown, CT: Wesleyan University Press, 1964), *Rescue the Dead* (Middletown, CT: Wesleyan University Press, 1968), and *Against the Evidence: Selected Poems 1934–1993* (Middletown, CT: Wesleyan University Press, 1993).

IZZO, CARLO (1901– ), was an Italian historian of American writing and culture. See, for example, *Civiltà Americana* (Rome: Edizioni di Storia e Letteratura, 1967).

J was a literary magazine edited by Jack Spicer, with eight issues of about 150 copies running from August/September 1959 to March 1960. Spicer, Robin Blaser, RD, George Stanley, Mary Murphy, and other members of the Spicer circle appeared in the magazine.

JARGON SOCIETY was a run of publications initiated by Jonathan Williams in 1951. In the following years, he put out books by Charles Olson, Robert Creeley, RD, DL, and others in the Williams-Olson line. DL's *Overland to the Islands* and RD's *Letters* both appeared from Jargon in 1958.

JARRELL, RANDALL (1914–1965), was a poet, novelist, and essayist associated with the writers of the Southern Agrarian Movement. He published in *The Sewanee Review* and *The Kenyon Review*. Among his books are: *Poetry and the Age* (New York: Alfred A. Knopf, 1953), a book of essays; *Pictures from an Institution* (New York: Alfred A. Knopf, 1954), a novel; and *The Complete Poems* (New York: Farrar, Straus and Giroux, 1969).

JEFFERIES, RICHARD (1848–1887), wrote about rustic and rural England. See: *Wild Life in a Southern County*, introd. Frederick Brereton, illus. Marjorie Anderson (London: Collins Clear-type Press, 1910); *Nature near London* (London: Chatto and Windus, 1913); and *The Story of My Heart: My Autobiography* (London: Longman, 1922).

JESS. See COLLINS, BURGESS.

JOHNSON, RONALD (1945–1998), was a poet who moved from Kansas to San Francisco and became engaged with the poetics of field composition. DL selected *The Book of the Green Man* (New York: W. W. Norton and Co., 1967) and *Valley of the Many-Colored Grasses* (New York: W. W. Norton and Co., 1969) for publication. Jonathan Williams published *Eyes and Objects* (Highlands, NC: Jargon Society, 1976). Other books include the long, open-form poem *Ark* (Albuquerque, NM: Living Batch Press, 1996) and *To Do as Adam Did: Selected Poems*, ed. Peter O'Leary (Jersey City, NJ: Talisman House, 2000). His cookbooks include *The American Table* (New York: William Morrow, 1984) and *Southwestern Cooking* (Albuquerque, NM: University of New Mexico Press, 1985).

JONAS, STEPHEN (1920?–1970), was an African American poet born in Georgia who settled in Boston in the late 1940s. His open-form poems were influenced by the Beat and the Black Mountain aesthetic. See: *Exercises for Ear: Being a Primer for the Beginner in the American Idiom* (London: Ferry Press, 1968), *Morphogenesis: Being a Conventionalization of "Morphemes" of Jack Spicer* (Cambridge, MA: Restau Press, 1970), *Two for Jack Spicer* (South San Francisco: ManRoot Books, 1974), and *Selected Poems*, ed. Joseph Torra (Jersey City, NJ: Talisman House, 1994).

JONES, DAVID (1895–1974), was a Welsh poet, fiction writer, artist, engraver, and calligrapher. His intense and poetic narratives are densely charged with religious, mythic, and historical overtones. See *In Parenthesis* (London: Faber and Faber, 1937), about his experiences in the trenches of World War I, and *The Anathemata: Fragments of an Attempted Writing* (London: Faber and Faber, 1952), centering all human experience in his Catholic mystical faith.

JONES, LEROI, later AMIRI BARAKA (1934– ), is a New Jersey poet and playwright who was associated with the Beats and with the Black Mountain poets in the 1950s and 1960s. He founded the journal *Yugen* (1958–62) and the Totem Press and co-edited (with Diane Di Prima) *Floating Bear* (1961–69). He was converted to the Muslim faith and the Black nationalist movement in the 1960s, changed his name to Amiri Baraka, and switched from expression of personal angst to a militant and polemical attack on white culture in the name of Black liberation. His many books include: *Preface to a Twenty Volume Suicide Note* (New York: Totem Press, 1961), *The Dead Lecturer* (New York: Grove Press, 1964), *Dutchman and the Slave: Two Plays* (New York: William Morrow, 1964), *Black Magic: Sabotage, Target Study, Black Art Collected Poetry 1961–1971* (Indianapolis, IN: Bobbs-Merrill, 1969), and *Autobiography of LeRoi Jones/Amiri Baraka* (New York: Freundlich Books, 1984).

KALISH, DONALD (1919– ), is a philosopher who taught for many years at University of California, Los Angeles, and is the author of *Logic: Techniques of Formal Reasoning* (New York: Harcourt, Brace and World, 1964).

KANTOROWICZ, ERNST (1985–1963), was a German-born professor of medieval and Renaissance history at the University of California, Berkeley, who became an inspiring mentor to RD and Robin Blaser in the late 1940s and lost his academic position when he refused to sign a loyalty oath during the McCarthy anticommunist witch-hunt of the 1950s. His books are: *Frederick the Second 1194–1250*, trans. E. O. Lorimer (London: Constable and Co., 1957); and *The King's Two Bodies: A Study in Mediaeval Political Theology* (Princeton, NJ: Princeton University Press, 1957).

KAYAK, edited by George Hitchcock, began in San Francisco in autumn 1964 and ended with the sixty-fourth issue in Santa Cruz in 1984. It published a wide range of poets from across the country, but RD and DL did not publish in this magazine.

KEES, WELDON (1914–1955), grew up in Nebraska, moved to New York, where he had an aspiring career as a painter, and then moved to San Francisco, where he concentrated on writing poetry and playing jazz piano. He committed suicide by jumping from the Golden Gate Bridge. See: *Collected Poems*, ed. Donald Justice (Iowa City, IA: The Stonewall Press, 1960); *The Ceremony and Other Stories*, ed. and introd. Dana Gioia (Port Townsend, WA: Graywolf Press, 1984); and *Reviews and Essays*, ed. James Reidel, introd. Howard Nemerov (Ann Arbor: University of Michigan Press, 1988).

KELLY, ROBERT (1935– ), is a New York poet and novelist who co-founded, with George Economou, the journals *The Chelsea Review* (1957) and *Trobar* (1960). His poems sought to present a "deep image" of the process of discovery and to charge minimalist language with resonance. His poems and stories include: *Her Body against Time* (Mexico: Ediciones El Cornu Emplumado, 1963), *Finding the Measure* (Los Angeles: Black Sparrow Press, 1968), *The Loom* (Los Angeles: Black Sparrow Press, 1975), *Spiritual Exercises* (Santa Barbara, CA: Black Sparrow Press, 1981), and *Red Actions: Selected Poems 1960–1993* (Santa Rosa, CA: Black Sparrow Press, 1995).

KENNER, HUGH (1923– ), is a Canadian-born critic of Modernism who has taught at the University of California, Santa Barbara, and at Johns Hopkins. His books include: *The Poetry of Ezra Pound* (London: Faber and Faber, 1951), *The Invisible Poet: T. S. Eliot* (New York: McDowell, Obolensky, 1959), *Joyce's Dublin* (London: Chatto and Windus, 1961), *The Pound Era* (Berkeley: University of California Press, 1973), and *A Homemade World* (New York: Alfred A. Knopf, 1974).

KERKAM, EARL (1891–1965), was a New York painter.

KINNELL, GALWAY (1927– ), is a poet whose late-Romantic poems turn frequently on the encounter with and acceptance of natural wonder, primitive violence, and death. He was a friend and neighbor of DL in New York. His books include: *What a Kingdom It Was* (Boston: Houghton Mifflin, 1960), *Flower Herding on Mount Monadnock* (Boston: Houghton Mifflin, 1964), *Body Rags* (Boston: Houghton Mifflin, 1968), *The Book of Nightmares* (Boston: Houghton Mifflin, 1971), and *New Selected Poems* (Boston: Houghton Mifflin, 2000).

KIRSTEIN, GEORGE (1909–1986), was the chief executive for the liberal weekly journal *The Nation* (1955–65), for which DL was poetry editor from 1961 to 1962 and 1963 to 1965.

KIRSTEIN, LINCOLN (1907–1996), was the publisher of *The Nation*, the co-founder, with George Balanchine, of the New York City Ballet in 1948, and a poet. See *Rhymes of a Pfc and More Rhymes* (New York: New Directions, 1963).

KIZER, CAROLYN (1925– ), is a poet who studied under Theodore Roethke at the University of Washington from 1953 to 1954, edited the journal *Poetry Northwest* from 1959 to 1965, and is noted for formal virtuosity and wry wit in her treatment of experience as a woman and poet. Her books include: *Knock upon Silence: Poems* (Seattle: University of Washington Press, 1965), *Midnight Was My Cry: Selected Poems* (Garden City, NY: Doubleday, 1971), *Yin New Poems* (Brockport, NY: Boa Editions, 1984), and *Cool, Calm and Collected: Poems 1960–2000* (Port Townsend, WA: Copper Canyon Press, 2000).

KLINE, FRANZ (1910–1962), was a painter who taught at Black Mountain College and was associated with the poets and writers of his period, including Paul Goodman, Joel Oppenheimer, and Fielding Dawson. His large, black-on-white abstractions won him a prominent place among the Abstract Expressionist painters in New York City.

KOCH, KENNETH (1925–2002), was associated with John Ashbery and Frank O'Hara in the New York School of poets and painters and was noted for the breezy tone, surreal wit, and satirical edge of his work. His books include: *Thank You and Other Poems* (New York: Grove Press, 1962), *The Pleasures of Peace and Other Poems* (New York: Grove Press, 1969), *The Art of Love* (New York: Random House, 1975), and *Selected Poems* (New York: Vintage, 1991).

KRAY, ELIZABETH (1916–1987), worked for the YMHA in New York City, where she arranged readings for poets in New York and in other cities. By 1969 she was the CEO at the American Academy of Poets.

KRESCH, ALBERT (1923– ), is a New York figurative painter who was a close friend of DL and Mitchell Goodman and did an abstract frontispiece for DL's *Overland to the Islands* (1958).

KULCHUR, edited by Marc D. Schleifer, began in New York City with the spring issue of 1960. Lita Hornick was the editor for the final issue (1965–66) but there were also guest editors, including Joel Oppenheimer and Gilbert Sorrentino. The magazine published poets from New York, but also some from California, including RD.

KYGER, JOANNE (1934– ), is a Midwestern poet who moved to California, attended poetry sessions at San Francisco State, was associated with RD and the San Francisco Renaissance, and was married for a time to Gary Snyder. Her work draws on American Indian and Buddhist myths but has a distinctive, elegant movement. She has published: *The Tapestry and the Web* (San Francisco: Four Seasons Foundation, 1965); *Place to Go* (Los Angeles: Black Sparrow Press, 1970); *Going On: Selected Poems 1958–1980*, selected by Robert Creeley (New York: Dutton, 1983); *Just Space: Poems 1979–1989* (Santa Rosa, CA: Black Sparrow Press, 1991); and *Again: Poems 1989–2000* (Albuquerque, NM: La Alamada Press, 2001).

LAGHERLOF (LAGERLÖF, LAGERLOEF), SELMA (1858–1940), was a Swedish poet and fiction writer who was inspired by Carlyle and was a figure in the Swedish Romantic revival. Her fiction told Icelandic sagas in highly wrought prose, including: *Christ Legends*, trans. Velma Swanston Howard (New York: Henry Holt, 1908); *The Emperor of Portugallia* (Garden City, NY: Doubleday, Page and Co., 1916); *Gösta Beling's Saga*, trans. Lillie Tudeer (London: Jonathan Cape, 1918); and *Wonderful Adventures of Nils*, trans. Velma Swanston (New York: Pantheon, 1947). She was awarded the Nobel Prize for Literature, 1909.

LAMANTIA, PHILIP (1927– ), was called a natural Surrealistic poet. In 1944 he became an assistant editor of Charles Henri Ford's magazine *View*, and in that capacity he knew RD in New York City. In the 1950s he was one of the first poets to experiment with mind-altering drugs, and he became a central figure in the San Francisco Renaissance. After spending most of the 1960s in Europe, he returned to live and write in San Francisco. His books include: *Erotic Poems* (Berkeley: Bern Porter Books, 1946), *Touch of the Marvelous* (Berkeley:

Oyez, 1966), and *Meadowlark West* (San Francisco: City Lights Books, 1986).

LARBAUD, VALERY (1881–1957), was a French poet and fiction writer who translated and championed experimental English and American writers and explored stream of consciousness in his own fiction. He wrote frequently through the persona of A. O. Barnabooth, a South American millionaire: *Poems of a Multimillionaire*, trans. William Jay Smith (New York: Bonacio and Saul, 1955) and *The Diary of A. O. Barnabooth: A Novel*, trans. Gilbert Cannan, introd. Robert Kelly (Kingston, NY: McPherson and Co., 1990), a fictionalized autobiography.

LAUGHLIN, JAMES (1914–1997), left Harvard in the 1930s to study under Ezra Pound in Italy; at Pound's suggestion, Laughlin founded New Directions as a publishing house in 1936. It quickly established itself as the most important publisher of experimental writing in this country and perhaps anywhere by making available avant-garde work in prose and poetry by English-language and foreign writers (including Pound, William Carlos Williams, Kenneth Rexroth, DL, RD, and Robert Creeley). Laughlin began publishing the annual *New Directions in Poetry and Prose* in 1936. His own verse— compact and often wryly ironic—is gathered in *Collected Poems* (Wakefield, RI: Moyer Bell, 1994) and *The Man in the Wall: Poems* (New York: New Directions, 1993).

LAX, ROBERT (1915–2000), was an American poet who was at one point an editor at *The New Yorker* and at *Jubilee*. Associated with Abstract Expressionism, he wrote abstract, spiritual poems as well as concrete, visual poems: *The Circus of the Sun* (New York: Journeyman Books, 1959) and *Love Had a Compass: Journals and Poetry* (New York: Grove Press, 1996). DL published an article "On Robert Lax's The Circus of the Sun" in *Voyages 2. 1/2* (Winter–Spring 1968): 93–94.

LINENTHAL, MARK (1921– ), was a teacher at San Francisco State University who edited an anthology of commentary on poetry entitled *Aspects of Poetry* (Boston: Little Brown, 1963) and published pamphlets of poems, including *Growing Light* (Oakland, CA: Black Thumb Press, 1979).

LEONTIEF, WASSILY (1905–1999), was a Russian-born economist at Harvard and later at New York University whose pioneering work on input-output economics won him the Nobel Prize in 1973. He and his wife Estelle became close friends of DL in the mid-1960s during her fellowship at the Radcliffe Institute. His books include *Input-Output Economics* (New York: Oxford University Press, 1966) and *The Future of the World Economy: A United Nations Study* (New York: Oxford University Press, 1977).

LEVY, G(ERTRUDE). RACHEL (1883–1966), was a British archaeologist and artist, born in South Africa. Her books include: *The Gate of Horn: A Study of the Religious Conceptions of the Stone Age, and Their Influence upon European Thought* (London: Faber and Faber, 1948), *Plato in Sicily* (London: Faber and Faber, 1948–1956), and *The Phoenix Nest: A Study in Religious Transformations* (London: Rider, 1961).

LEWIS, C(LIVE). S(TAPLES). (1898–1963), was a lecturer in philosophy and literature at Oxford (1925–54) and Cambridge (1954–63), whose Christian faith informs his fiction, fantasy tales, literary criticism, and theological reflections. His books include: *The Screwtape Letters* (New York: Macmillan Co., 1952), *Out of the Silent Planet* (London: John Lane, 1946), *The Allegory of Love: A Study in a Medieval Tradition* (Oxford: Oxford University Press, 1936), *The Problem of Pain* (New York: Macmillan Co., 1940), and *The Four Loves* (London: G. Bles, 1960). He edited *George MacDonald: An Anthology* (London: G. Bles, 1946).

LITZ, KATY (1912–1978), was a dancer whose work "The Glyph" was created and performed at Black Mountain College in 1951.

LOCUS SOLUS was a defining publication for the New York School of poets; John Ashbery, Kenneth Koch, Harry Mathews, and James Schuyler were editors. The magazine ran for five issues from 1961 to 1962.

LOEWINSOHN, RON (1937– ), is a San Francisco Bay Area poet (influenced by William Carlos Williams and Robert Creeley), novelist, and professor at the University of California, Berkeley. Some of his publications are: *Meat Air: Poems 1959–1969* (New York: Harcourt, Brace and World, 1970), *Goat Dances* (Santa Barbara, CA: Black Sparrow Press, 1976), *Magnetic Field(s)* (New York: Alfred A. Knopf, 1983), and *Where All the Ladders Start: A Novel* (New York: Atlantic Monthly Press, 1987).

LOGAN, JOHN (1923–1987), was a poet whose lyrics are informed by his Catholic sensibility. He founded and edited the journal *Choice* and was a professor at State University of New York, Buffalo, from 1966 to 1987. His books include: *A Cycle for Mother Cabrini* (New York: Grove Press, 1955), *Spring of the Thief: Poems* (New York: Alfred A. Knopf, 1963), *The Zig Zag Walk: Poems 1963–1968* (New York: Dutton, 1969), and *Collected Poems* (Brockport, NY: Boa Editions, 1989).

LOWELL, ROBERT (1917–1977), was a New England poet and one of the most important writers of his generation. He left Harvard to study under John Crowe Ransom at Kenyon College and became associated with Allen Tate, as well. He was a conscientious objector during World War II and a vocal opponent of American policy in Vietnam. Locating his own history within the doom of region and nation, his poems moved from the formal intricacy and Catholic apocalyptic vision of *Lord Weary's Castle* (New York: Harcourt, Brace and Co., 1946) to the free verse, confessional mode of *Life Studies* (New York: Farrar Straus and Giroux, 1959) and *For the Union Dead* (New York: Farrar Straus and Giroux, 1964) to the late unrhymed sonnets that muse tragically on history and the traumas of his own life in *Notebook* (New York: Farrar Straus and Giroux, 1969). See also *Selected Poems* (New York: Farrar Straus and Giroux, 1976) and *Collected Prose*, introd. Robert Giroux (New York: Farrar Straus and Giroux, 1987).

LOY, MINA (1882–1966), was a British-born avant-garde poet and painter in London, Paris, and New York, whose work, daring in its formal experimentation and feminist perspective, was rediscovered in the 1960s. Her poems are collected in *The Last Lunar Baedeker*, ed. Roger Conover (Highlands, NC: Jargon Society, 1982); a selection is *The Lost Lunar Baedeker*, ed. Roger Conover (New York: Farrar

Straus, and Giroux, 1996). DL published an essay on her work in *Mina Loy's Lunar Baedecker & Time−Tables* (Highlands, NC: Jargon 23, 1958).

MACDONALD, GEORGE (1824–1905), was a Scottish preacher, poet, and novelist, best known for his romance and fantasy fiction, which includes: *Robert Falconer* (London: Hurst and Blackett, 1868), *Malcolm* (London: Henry S. King, 1875), *At the Back of the North Wind* (London: Strahan and Co., 1871), *The Princess and the Goblin* (London: Strahan and Co., 1872), *The Princess and Curdie* (London: Strahan and Co., 1882), *The Light Princess and Other Fairy Tales* (London: Blackie and Sons, 1890), *Lilith* (London: Chatto and Windus, 1895), and *Violin Songs* (London: Daldy, Isbister, 1874). He was a best-seller in Victorian England, avidly admired by C. S. Lewis and G. K. Chesterton, as well as by DL, RD, Jess, and Helen Adam.

MACHADO, ANTONIO (1875–1939), was a Spanish poet (from Seville) and a partisan of the republic against Franco in the Civil War of 1936–39. DL translated a number of his poems. See *Poesias Completas*, introd. Manuel Alvar (Madrid: Espasa-Calpe, 1975); in English: *Selected Poems*, trans. and introd. Alan S. Trueblood (Cambridge: Harvard University Press, 1982).

MACKINTOSH, GRAHAM (1935– ), is an illustrator and printer in Berkeley and San Francisco. He revived Joe Dunn's White Rabbit Press in Berkeley in 1962, and, after refining his printing skills, began printing for Oyez Press; he later did the typesetting for John Martin's Black Sparrow Press. He left out a page of poems in RD's *Bending the Bow*, and renumbered the pages (or had the pages renumbered) to cover the mistake.

MACLOW, JACKSON (1922– ), is an experimental poet who since the 1970s has been associated with Language poetry. He met RD in New York City in the early 1940s. His books include: *August Light Poems* (New York: Caterpillar Press, 1967), *22 Light Poems* (Los Angeles: Black Sparrow Press, 1968), *Words and Ends from Ez* (Bolinas, CA: Avenue B, 1989), *Barnesbook: Four Poems Derived from Sentences by Djuna Barnes* (Los Angeles: Sun and Moon Press, 1996).

MALANGA, GERARD (1943– ), is a poet, photographer, and filmmaker who worked as Andy Warhol's assistant in the 1960s, played in a couple of Warhol's films, and edited with Warhol the journal *Interview* as well as *Screen Tests/A Diary* (New York: Kulchur Press, 1967). His books include: *Ten Years After* (Santa Barbara, CA: Black Sparrow Press, 1977) and *Mythologies of the Heart* (Santa Rosa, CA: Black Sparrow Press, 1996).

MANSFIELD, KATHERINE (1888–1923), was a New Zealand–born novelist who lived mostly in London and wrote skillfully wrought fiction about complex psychological and sexual relationships. See *The Short Stories of Katherine Mansfield*, introd. J. Middleton Murry (New York: Alfred A. Knopf, 1984).

MARSHALL, EDWARD (1932– ), is a poet associated with the Black Mountain and Beat groups; he published in *The Black Mountain Review*. His long poem "Leave the Word Alone" was included in Donald M. Allen's *The New American Poetry* (1960) and was a source for Allen Ginsberg's *Kaddish*. His books include *Hellan, Hellan* (San Francisco: Auerhahn Press, 1960), and *Transit Glory* (New York: Carp and Whitefish, 1967).

MARTIN, FRANCES (1906– ), is a writer of juvenile fiction, including *Nine Tales of Raven* (New York: Harper and Brothers, 1951).

MARTIN, JOHN, was the owner and operator of Black Sparrow Press, which published DL, RD, Jess, Robert Creeley, and many other poets.

MATTER, edited by Robert Kelly, ran for four issues from 1964 to 1968 and has published mainly poets from New York City.

MATTHIASDOTTIR, LOUISA (1917–2000), was a painter who was born in Iceland, moved to New York in 1941, married the painter Leland Bell in 1943, and was a close friend of DL during her years in Manhattan. Her quiet landscapes and empty cityscapes, reminiscent of Iceland, were composed with simplicity and economy of means. See *Louisa Matthiasdottir*, ed. Jed Perl (Reykjavik, Iceland: Nesútgáfen Publishing, 1999).

MCALMON, ROBERT (1896–1956), was an American poet, writer, and editor who spent many years as an expatriate in Europe, co-edited the journal *Contact* with William Carlos Williams, and published avant-garde writing in his "Contact Editions" from Paris, financed by Bryher, H. D.'s friend and companion (with whom McAlmon had a marriage of convenience in the 1920s). His books include: *Distinguished Air: Grimm Fairy Tales* (Paris: Contact Editions, 1925), *The Portrait of a Generation, Including the Revolving Mirror* (Paris: Contact Editions, 1926), and *Being Geniuses Together: 1920–1930*, rev. ed. with supplementary chapters by Kay Boyle (Garden City, NY: Doubleday, 1968).

MCCLURE, MICHAEL (1932– ), was born in Kansas, went to San Francisco to study painting, but, after coming into contact with RD and the poetry classes at San Francisco State University, focused on being a poet. He was influenced by Charles Olson and Robert Creeley, became a figure in the Beat movement and the San Francisco Poetry Renaissance, and participated in the reading at Six Gallery with Allen Ginsberg, Kenneth Rexroth, Gary Snyder, and others. His poems are Dionysian and erotic celebrations of bodily and biological existence and natural process: *Hymns to St. Geryon and Other Poems* (San Francisco: Auerhahn Press, 1959), *The New Book/A Book of Torture* (New York: Grove Press, 1961), *Ghost Tantras* (San Francisco: City Lights Books, 1964), *September Strawberries* (New York: New Directions, 1974), *Selected Poems* (New York: New Directions, 1986), and *Rain Mirror: New Poems* (New York: New Directions, 1999). His prose includes *Meat Science Essays* (San Francisco: City Lights Books, 1966) and *Scratching the Beat Surface* (San Francisco: North Point Press, 1982).

MEASURE, edited by John Wieners, published three issues between Summer 1957 and Summer 1962. The magazine was supported by Charles Olson and RD and published poets associated with Black Mountain and San Francisco.

MERWIN, W(ILLIAM). S(TANLEY). (1927– ), is a prolific writer of plays, essays, reviews, and translations as well as poems. He was poetry editor of *The Nation* in 1962. His books include: *Green with Beasts* (London: Hart-Davis, 1956), *The Moving Target* (New York: Atheneum, 1963), *The Lice* (New York: Atheneum, 1967), and *New Selected Poems* (Port Townsend, WA: Copper Canyon Press, 1988). More recent poems, such as those in *The River Sound: Poems* (New York: Alfred A. Knopf, 1999), show an increasing ecological concern.

MIGRANT, edited by Gael Turnbull from Worcester, England, and Ventura, California, published eight issues from July 1959 to September 1960, including poems by Ed Dorn, Robert Creeley, DL, RD, and Larry Eigner.

MILES, JOSEPHINE (1911–1985), was a poet and professor at the University of California, Berkeley. Her books include: *Prefabrications* (Bloomington: Indiana University Press, 1955), *Fields of Learning* (Berkeley: Oyez, 1968), *Collected Poems* (Urbana: University of Illinois Press, 1983), and the prose commentary *The Ways of a Poem* (Englewood Cliffs, NJ: Prentice-Hall, 1961).

MINNESOTA REVIEW began publication in 1960 with Sarah Foster and Neil Myers as editors; it published its last issue in 1973.

MONTGOMERY, STUART (1940– ), is a British poet and publisher. His books of poems include: *Circe* (London: Fulcrum Press, 1969), *Shabby Sunshine* (London: Fulcrum Press, 1973), and *From Calypso* (Newcastle-upon-Tyne, England: Pig Press, 1976). He was the owner and publisher of the Fulcrum Press in London, which published many contemporary American and British poets, including RD's *The First Decade* and *Derivations* in 1969.

MORGENSTERN, CHRISTIAN (1871–1914), was a German mystical poet of the fin de siècle whose *Galgenlieder* (Berlin: Verlag von Bruno Cassirer, 1920) were translated by Jess and published as *Gallowsongs* (Los Angeles: Black Sparrow Press, 1970).

MUMFORD, LEWIS (1895–1990), was an influential critic of American culture, architecture, and urban planning. His books include: *The Golden Day: A Study of American Experience and Culture* (New

York: Boni and Liveright, 1926), *The Brown Decades: A Study of the Arts in America 1865–1895* (New York: Harcourt, Brace and Co., 1931), *The City in History: Its Origins, Its Transformations and Its Prospects* (New York: Harcourt, Brace and Co., 1961), and *The Urban Prospect* (New York: Harcourt, Brace and Co., 1968). He publicly questioned U.S. military policy in Vietnam.

MUSTE, A(BRAHAM). J(OHN). (1885–1967), was a Dutch-born American social activist, trade unionist, and pacifist, who spent his last years in vocal opposition to the American involvement in Vietnam. His books include: *Why a Labor Party* (New York: Conference for Progressive Labor Action, 1927); *The World Task of Pacifism* (Wallingford, PA: Pendle Hill, 1941); *War Is the Enemy* (New York: Fellowship of Reconciliation, 1942); *Essays*, ed. Nat Hentoff (New York: Bobbs-Merrill, 1967); and *Non-Violence in an Aggressive World* (New York: J. S. Ozer, 1972).

THE NATION was a well-established weekly magazine of liberal political views that also chronicled the artistic and literary events and movements centered in New York City. It published poetry regularly. M. L. Rosenthal, DL, W. S. Merwin, and Michael Goldman were poetry editors for the journal.

NEMEROV, HOWARD (1920–1991), was a poet associated by DL with the academic poetry fostered by the New Criticism in the midcentury. He taught at Brandeis University (1966–69) and Washington University (1969–76), and was consultant in Poetry, Library of Congress (1963–64). His many books include: *Mirrors and Windows* (Chicago: University of Chicago Press, 1958), *The Blue Swallows* (Chicago: University of Chicago Press, 1967), *Trying Conclusions: New and Selected Poems 1961– 1991* (Chicago: University of Chicago Press, 1991), and *Reflections on Poetry and Poetics* (New Brunswick, NJ: Rutgers University Press, 1972).

NERUDA, PABLO (1904–1973), was a Chilean Marxist poet whose work mingled love and politics, landscape and history. He won the Nobel Prize for Literature in 1971. Some of his books are: *Obras Completas*, ed. Herman Loyola with Saul Yurkievich,

introd. Saul Yurkievich, prologue by Enrico Mario Santi, 4 vols. (Barcelona: Galaxia Gutenberg, Circula de Lectures, 1999); and *Selected Poems*, ed. Nathaniel Tarn, trans. Anthony Kerrigan, W. S. Merwin, Alastair Reid, and Nathaniel Tarn (London: Jonathan Cape, 1972).

NEW WORLD WRITING (no. 1, 1952–no. 22, 1964) was the title of an annual anthology of new writing from Europe and America, published in New York City.

NICHOLS, ROBERT (1919– ), is a poet, writer, and landscape architect, husband of the fiction writer and poet Grace Paley. He has published *Slow Newsreel of Man Riding Train* (San Francisco: City Lights Books, 1962) and *Daily Lives in Nghsi-Aetai*, 4 vols. (New York: New Directions, 1977–79).

NOONDAY, an annual of stories, articles, and poetry, published three issues between 1958 and 1960 in New York. Cecil Hemley edited the first volume and, with Dwight W. Webb, the second and the third. RD's poem "Often I Am Permitted to Return to a Meadow" appeared under the title "The Meadow" in the second issue.

NOVALIS, pen name of FREDERICK VON HARDENBERG (1772–1801), was a German Romantic poet, novelist, mystic, and student of philosophy. See *Novalis Werke*, ed. Gerhard Schulz (Munich: Beck, 1969); in English, *Hymns to the Night*, trans. Dick Higgins (New York: Treacle Press, 1978).

O'GORMAN, NED (1929– ), is an American poet. See: *The Night of the Hammer* (New York: Harcourt Brace, 1959), *Adam before His Mirror* (New York: Harcourt Brace, 1961), and *The Harvester's Vase* (New York: Harcourt Brace and World, 1968). He also edited the journal *Jubilee* (1962–65) and *Prophetic Voices: Ideas and Words on Revolution* (New York: Random House, 1969).

O'HARA, FRANK (1926–1966), was a defining figure in the New York School, along with John Ashbery, Barbara Guest, and Kenneth Koch; he also associated with Allen Ginsberg and the Beats. His art criticism helped to define the new school of Abstract Expressionists, and he served as an associate curator at the Museum of Modern Art. His conversational, open-form poems about "what is happening to me"—*Second Avenue* (New York: Totem Press, 1960) and *Lunch Poems* (San Francisco: City Lights Books, 1964)—were gathered after his accidental death into *Collected Poems*, ed. Donald M. Allen, introd. John Ashbery (New York: Alfred A. Knopf, 1971). His prose includes *Standing Still and Walking in New York* (Bolinas, CA: Grey Fox Press, 1975) and *Art Chronicles, 1954–1966* (New York: George Braziller, 1975).

OKAMURA, ARTHUR (1932– ), is a native Californian artist who trained at the Art Institute of Chicago and at Yale and has exhibited his vivid and at times abstract landscapes in Los Angeles and the major galleries on the West Coast. He lived for a time in Bolinas, where he became friends with the local poets, among them Joanne Kyger and Robert Creeley. He illustrated Kyger's book *I Am Now in Canada* (Grindstone City, MI: Alternative Press, 1982) and Creeley's book *1. 2. 3.4.5.6.7.8.9.0.* (Berkeley: Shambala, 1971), as well as Robert Bly's *Point Reyes Poems* (Half Moon Bay: Mudra, 1974).

OLSON, CHARLES (1910–1970), was immensely influential as a poet, critic, and teacher. His 1950 essay "Projective Verse," proposing "composition by field" as a development of Ezra Pound's and William Carlos Williams's experiments, became the manifesto of the Black Mountain poets. He made Black Mountain College, where he was rector during the 1950s, a center of artistic revolution. *The Black Mountain Review*, edited by Robert Creeley in the mid-1950s, became a showcase for the new writing. He was a close friend of RD and Creeley and a mentor for younger poets such as Ed Dorn and Jonathan Williams. His books include: *Y and X* (Washington, DC: Black Sun Press, 1948); *In Cold Hell, in Thicket* (Ashfield, MA: Origin Press, 1967); *The Distances* (New York: Grove Press, 1960); *The Maximus Poems*, ed. George Butterick (Berkeley: University of California Press, 1983); *The Collected Poems of Charles Olson, excluding the Maximus Poems*, ed. George Butterick (Berkeley: University of California Press, 1987); and *Collected Prose*, ed. Donald M. Allen and Benjamin Friedlander, introd. Robert Creeley (Berkeley: University of California Press, 1997).

OPPEN, GEORGE (1908–1984), was a New York poet in the Objectivist group, along with Louis Zukofsky and Charles Reznikoff. They sought to extend the Imagism of Ezra Pound and William Carlos Williams. Oppen published avant-garde writing in France under the imprint of "To Publishers" and, after abandoning poetry for a period of leftist political activity, resumed writing in the late 1950s in San Francisco. His books include: *Discrete Series* (New York: Objectivist Press, 1934); *Of Being Numerous* (New York: New Directions, 1968); *Selected Letters*, ed. Rachel Blau Du Plessis (Durham, NC: Duke University Press, 1990); and *Collected Poems*, ed. Michael Davidson (New York: New Directions, 2002).

OPPENHEIMER, JOEL (1930–1988), was a poet and journalist who studied under Charles Olson at Black Mountain College from 1950 to 1953 and became a figure in the New York poetry scene with Allen Ginsberg and Frank O'Hara. His short, uncapitalized, heavily enjambed lines also show the influence of W. C. Williams and Robert Creeley. His books include: *The Dutiful Son* (Highlands, NC: Jonathan Williams, 1956), *The Love Bit and Other Poems* (New York: Totem Press, 1962), *In Time: Poems 1962–1968* (Indianapolis: Bobbs-Merrill, 1969), *Names and Local Habitations (Selected Earlier Poems 1951–1972)* (Highlands, NC: Jargon Society, 1988), and *Collected Later Poems*, ed. Robert J. Bertholf (Buffalo, NY: The Poetry/Rare Books Collection, 1997).

ORIGIN, edited by Cid Corman, has published five series from Spring 1951 to the present. *Origin* and *Black Mountain Review* were the two most important journals for the emerging poets of the new American poetry. RD and DL both appeared there. RD wrote to DL for the first time after reading her poems in the issue of *Origin* for Spring 1953.

OUTSIDER, edited by John Edgar Webb and Louise "Gypsy Lou" Webb, published five issues between Fall 1961 and Winter 1968/1969.

PARKINSON, THOMAS (1920–1992), was a poet, critic, and professor at the University of California, Berkeley. He met RD in the late 1940s in Berkeley and became an active participant in the San

Francisco Renaissance. He was a scholar of Yeats and a friend to many poets. His poetry includes: *Thanatos: Poems for the Earth* (Berkeley: Oyez, 1965), *Homage to Jack Spicer* (Berkeley: Ark Press, 1970), and *Poems: New and Selected* (Orono, ME: National Poetry Foundation, 1988); his criticism includes *A Casebook on the Beat* (New York: Crowell, 1961) and *Hart Crane and Yvor Winters: Their Literary Correspondence* (Berkeley: University of California Press, 1978).

PARTISAN REVIEW was born out of the left-leaning politics and literature of New York City in the 1930s. From the mid-1950s through the 1970s William Phillips and Philip Rahv were editors (and then William Phillips alone). Irving Howe, Leslie Fielder, and Saul Bellow were frequent contributors, along with a somewhat conservative line of poets, including Richard Wilbur, John Berryman, John Hollander, and Daryl Hine.

PAZ, OCTAVIO (1914–1998), was an internationally recognized Mexican poet, social critic, and diplomat, who was awarded the Nobel Prize in 1990. See *Collected Poems*, trans. Eliot Weinberger and Elizabeth Bishop (New York: New Directions, 1991).

PEARSON, NORMAN HOLMES (1909–1975), was a professor of American Studies at Wesleyan University and later at Yale. During World War II he was stationed in England, where he befriended and assisted the poet H. D. He persuaded RD to write a tribute to H. D. in 1960, which led to the extended study "The H. D. Book." With W. H. Auden, he edited *Poets of the English Language* (New York: Viking Press, 1950).

PERSE, SAINT-JOHN, pseudonym of ALEXIS LEGER (1887–1975), was a French diplomat and poet, important to H. D. and RD; he was awarded the Nobel Prize in 1960 for his subtly evocative poems about the harmony and totality of the cosmos. See *Collected Poems*, trans. W. H. Auden (Princeton, NJ: Princeton University Press, 1983).

PETERS, ROBERT (1924– ), is a poet and scholar. His books of poetry include *Songs for a Son* (New York: W. W. Norton and Co., 1967) and *Poems:*

*Selected and New 1967–1991* (Santa Maria, CA: Asylum Press, 1992.

PLOMER, WILLIAM (1903–1973), was a British poet and novelist, born in South Africa, who lived in Greece for a number of years before returning to England in 1932. His many books include *Double Lives: An Autobiography* (London: Jonathan Cape, 1956) and *Collected Poems* (London: Jonathan Cape, 1973).

POETRY, founded by Harriet Monroe in 1912 in Chicago with Ezra Pound as foreign editor, became the central magazine for publishing and reviewing British and American poetry. Later editors include Karl Shapiro, Henry Rago, and Daryl Hine. Both DL and RD published there, with RD publishing more poems there than in any other magazine.

POLLOCK, JACKSON (1912–1956), was an American Abstract Expressionist painter known for his spontaneous and Dionysian method of painting psychologically intense abstractions. His career, in which he became a cult figure for the counterculture, was cut short by his early death in a car accident.

PONGE, FRANCIS (1899–1988), was a French poet whose work delineates natural objects precisely to reveal their inner significance. *Things* (New York: Grossman Publishers, 1971) is a volume of translations into English by Cid Corman.

POOR, OLD, TIRED, HORSE ran twenty-two issues, published by Ian Hamilton Finlay's Wild Hawthorne Press in Dunsyre, Lanark, Scotland, 1963–64. The magazine featured concrete poetry but also published Jonathan Williams, Ronald Johnson, and Lorine Niedecker.

PORTER, BERN (1911– ), was the publisher of Bern Porter Books in Berkeley, which published RD's first book, *Heavenly City, Earthly City*. He had a career as an atomic physicist but also wrote concrete and visual poems: *First Poems and Others* (Sausalito, CA: Bern Porter Books, 1954) and *Found Poems* (Millerton, NY: Something Else Press, 1972). He now lives in Maine.

PRIMACK, RONNIE, was a San Francisco poet whose book *For the Late Mayor or Horace Bell of the*

*Los Angeles Rangers* was published by White Rabbit Press (San Francisco, 1963) with illustrations by Graham Mackintosh.

QUARTERLY REVIEW OF LITERATURE was edited by Theodore Weiss and Renée Weiss, first at Bard College, beginning in 1943, and later at Princeton. It published poets from the Pound-Williams line, and in recent years it has taken to publishing several full books by different poets in each issue.

QUASHA, GEORGE (1942– ), is a poet and editor. He was a graduate student at University of Stony Brook, State University of New York, from 1966 to 1971, when he knew DL and edited the literary journal *Stony Brook*. He is the owner and operator of Station Hill Press. His books include: *Soma-poetics: Book One* (Fremont, MI: Sumac Press, 1973), *Giving the Lily Back Her Hands* (Barrytown, NY: Station Hill Press, 1979), and *Ainu Dreams*, with Chie (bunn) Hasegawa (Barrytown, NY: Station Hill Press, 1999). He was co-editor with Jerome Rothenberg of the anthology *America: A Prophecy, A New Reading of American Poetry from Pre-Columbian Times to the Present* (New York: Random House, 1973).

RAGO, HENRY (1915–1969), was a poet, teacher, and editor of the influential journal *Poetry* (Chicago) from 1955 to 1969. DL reviewed his book of poems *A Sky of Late Summer* (New York: Macmillan Co., 1969) as a celebration of "the light of Nature as a reflection of the inner light." During his editorship at *Poetry*, Robert Creeley, RD, DL, and Charles Olson were frequent contributors.

RANSOM, JOHN CROWE (1888–1974), was a poet, critic, teacher, and the powerful editor of *The Kenyon Review*. He was an original member of the Southern Agrarian Movement and a founder of the New Criticism, whose formalist approach and traditional norms dominated literary criticism through the 1940s and provoked the open-form experimentation of the 1950s. His many publications include: *Form and Value in Modern Poetry* (Garden City, NY: Doubleday Anchor Books, 1957), *Selected Poems* (New York: Echo Press, 1969), and *Selected Essays*, ed. Thomas Daniel Young (Baton Rouge: Louisiana State University Press, 1984).

READ, HERBERT (1893–1968), was a prolific writer on literature and art history and a distinguished man of letters. He was one of the new Romantic poets after World War II and an early mentor of DL in England. His books include *Art and Society* (New York: Macmillan Co., 1937), *The Nature of Literature: Collected Essays in Literary Criticism* (New York: Horizon Press, 1956), and *Collected Poems* (London: Faber and Faber, 1966).

REANEY, JAMES (1926– ), is a Canadian playwright and poet whose work is informed by satirical fantasy and surreal wit. His poetry includes: *The Red Heart* (Toronto: McClelland and Stewart, 1949); *A Suit of Nettles* (Erin, ON: Press Porcepic, 1958); *Selected Longer Poems*, ed. Germaine Warkentin (Erin, ON: Press Porcepic, 1976); and *Selected Shorter Poems*, ed. Germaine Warkentin (Erin, ON: Press Porcepic, 1977); his plays include *Killdeer and Other Plays* (Toronto: Macmillan Co., 1962) and *Colours in the Dark* (Vancouver, BC: Talon Plays with Macmillan Co. of Canada, 1970).

REXROTH, KENNETH (1905–1982), was a poet, critic, painter, translator (especially from Chinese and Japanese), and political activist. He moved from Chicago to San Francisco in 1927 and became a patriarchal figure in the San Francisco Renaissance. Marie Rexroth was his second wife (1940–48), Marthe was his third wife (1949–61). He edited *The New British Poets* (1949), in which he first expressed his impassioned advocacy of DL's poetry. His anarchist, pacifist, environmental philosophy and his fusion of Christianity and Buddhism inform the mysticism of his poems about nature poetry and about love. His books include: *The Dragon and the Unicorn* (Norfolk, CT: New Directions, 1952), *In Defense of the Earth* (Norfolk, CT: New Directions, 1956), *Collected Shorter Poems* (New York: New Directions, 1966), *Collected Longer Poems* (New York: New Directions, 1968), *Selected Poems*, ed. Bradford Morrow (New York: New Directions, 1984), and *World outside the Window: Selected Essays* (New York: New Directions, 1987).

REZNIKOFF, CHARLES (1894–1976), was a founding figure in American Jewish poetry ("themes, chiefly Jewish, American, urban") and a member of the Objectivist group of the 1930s, whose spare and factual poems were the basis for Zukofsky's essay defining Objectivist poetics. See *Complete Poems*, ed. Seamus Cooney, 2 vols. (Santa Barbara, CA: Black Sparrow Press, 1976, 1977).

RICH, ADRIENNE (1929– ), is a poet who became a close friend of DL when DL was an honorary scholar at the Radcliffe Institute (1964–66). Rich was at the time moving from an early formalism influenced by Wallace Stevens and W. H. Auden to a poetry more open in form and scope, and her poem "The Roofwalker" is dedicated to DL. Rich moved from Cambridge to New York in the mid-1960s and then to Santa Cruz in the 1980s. She is the most important and influential feminist poet and critic in the United States. Her poetry includes: *Snapshots of a Daughter-in-Law* (New York: Harper and Row, 1963), *The Will to Change: Poems 1968–1970* (New York: W. W. Norton and Co., 1971), *Diving into the Wreck: Poems 1971–1972* (New York: W. W. Norton and Co., 1973), *The Dream of a Common Language: Poems 1974–1977* (New York: W. W. Norton and Co., 1978), *An Atlas of the Difficult World: Poems 1978–1991* (New York: W. W. Norton and Co., 1991); and *Dark Fields of the Republic: Poems 1991–1995* (New York: W. W. Norton and Co., 1995). Her prose books include *Of Lies, Secrecy, and Silence* (New York: W. W. Norton and Co., 1979) and *Blood, Bread and Poetry* (New York: W. W. Norton and Co., 1986).

RICHARDS, M(ARY). C(ATHERINE). (1916–1999), was an artist, potter, and poet who taught literature at Black Mountain College and belonged to an artists' commune, along with David Tudor, John Cage, and others near Stony Point on Long Island in the late 1950s. She was a friend of DL in New York. Her poems appear in the prose books *Centering in Pottery, Poetry and the Person* (Middletown, CT: Wesleyan University Press, 1964) and *The Crossing Point* (Middletown, CT: Wesleyan University Press, 1973) and in *Imagine Inventing Yellow: New and Selected Poems* (Barrytown, NY: Station Hill Press, 1991).

RIVERS, LARRY (1923– ), is a painter associated with New York poets, especially Frank O'Hara and John Ashbery, and painters like Jackson Pollock and Franz Kline. His style moved from Abstract Expressionism to representation.

ROETHKE, THEODORE (1908–1963), was a poet whose tradition included the Romantics and Metaphysicals as well as the Modernists, and whose poems alternated between traditional forms and free verse. Many of his best poems return to his boyhood in Michigan and link him to "confessional" poets such as Robert Lowell and John Berryman. He taught for many years at the University of Washington in Seattle. His books include: *Open House* (New York: Alfred A. Knopf, 1941); *The Far Field* (Garden City, NY: Doubleday and Co., 1961); *Collected Poems* (Garden City, NY: Doubleday and Co., 1966); *Selected Letters*, ed. Ralph J. Mills (Seattle: University of Washington Press, 1968); and *On the Poet and His Craft: Selected Prose*, ed. Ralph J. Mills (Seattle: University of Washington Press, 1965).

ROSELIEP, RAYMOND (1917–1979), was a poet who was ordained a Catholic priest in 1943. His books include: *The Linen Boards*, preface by John Logan (Westminster, MD: Newman Press, 1961); *Love Makes the Air Light* (New York: W. W. Norton and Co., 1965), which was selected for publication by DL; and *A Roseliep Retrospective: Poems and Other Words by and about Raymond Roseliep*, ed. David Dayton (Ithaca, NY: Alembic Press, 1980).

ROSENTHAL, M(ACHA). L(OUIS). (1917–1996), called Mac, was a reviewer, literary critic, poet, and longtime professor at New York University. He preceded DL as poetry editor of *The Nation*. His books include: *As for Love: Poems and Translations* (New York: Oxford University Press, 1987), *The Modern Poets: A Critical Introduction* (New York: Oxford University Press, 1960), *The Modern Poetic Sequence*, with Sally M. Gall (New York: Oxford University Press, 1983), and *The Poet's Art* (New York: W. W. Norton and Co., 1987).

ROTH, WILLIAM (1916– ), was an early collector of Jess's paintings in San Francisco, a patron of the arts, and a friend of both Jess and RD. He made a contribution to maintain the King Ubu Gallery, 1952–53.

ROTHENBERG, JEROME (1931– ), is a poet, translator, teacher. He was active in the New York scene until his move to San Diego in the 1970s. His poetry shows the influence of contemporary experimentation and Native American poetry. His poetry includes: *Poems for the Game of Silence, 1961–1970* (New York: Dial Press, 1971), *Poland* (New York: New Directions, 1974), and *New Selected Poems 1970–1985* (New York: New Directions, 1986). As the editor of *America: A Prophecy* (New York: Random House, 1973), with George Quasha, and *Revolution of the Word: A New Gathering of American Avant Garde Poetry 1914–1945* (New York: Seabury Press, 1974), he brought a multicultural approach to contemporary writing. He edited the journal *Poems from the Floating World* (1953–63).

RUDGE, OLGA (1895–1996), was an American violinist and musicologist who lived most of her life abroad, met Ezra Pound in Paris in the 1920s, and (in addition to his wife Dorothy) became Ezra Pound's life-long and beloved companion, bearing their daughter Mary de Rachewiltz in 1925.

RUKEYSER, MURIEL (1913–1980), was a poet, social and political activist, and translator. She was also an early admirer of RD's poems and was a friend of DL, accompanying her on a peace mission to Hanoi in 1972. *U. S. 1* (New York: Covici, Friede, 1938) is perhaps the most distinguished book of poems about the Depression. Her other books include *A Life of Poetry* (New York: Curnut Books, 1949), *Collected Poems* (New York: McGraw Hill, 1978), and *A Muriel Rukeyser Reader*, ed. Jan Heller Levi, introd. Adrienne Rich (New York: W. W. Norton and Co., 1994).

RUMAKER, MICHAEL (1932– ), is a fiction writer and poet who graduated from Black Mountain College in 1955. His books include: the novel *The Butterfly* (New York: Scribners, 1962), *Gringos and Other Stories* (New York: Grove Press, 1967), *A Day and a Night at the Baths* (Bolinas, CA: Grey Fox Press, 1979), and *Robert Duncan in San Francisco* (Bolinas, CA: Grey Fox Press, 1996).

SANDERS, ED(WARD) (1939– ), is a poet, political and peace activist, and rock musician who moved from his native Missouri to New York in 1958 and became part of the Beat culture there. His poetry, influenced by Charles Olson, includes: *Poems from Jail* (San Francisco: City Lights Books, 1963), *Peace Eye* (Buffalo, NY: Frontier Press, 1967),

*Tales of Beatnik Glory* (Barrytown, NY: Station Hill Press, 1975), *Thirsting for Peace in a Raging Century: Selected Poems 1961–1985* (Minneapolis: Coffee House Press, 1987), *America: A History in Verse 1900–1939*, vol. 1 (Santa Rosa, CA: Black Sparrow Press, 2000), *America: A History in Verse 1940–1961*, vol. 2 (Santa Rosa, CA: Black Sparrow Press, 2000).

SAN FRANCISCO REVIEW, edited by R. H. Miller, June Oppen McKeen, and George Hitchcock, published thirteen issues between Winter 1958 and September 1962, when it became an annual aligned with New Directions. The poets appearing in the review are not thought of as part of the company of RD and DL, though DL did publish "Deaths" in the ninth issue for September 1961.

SAROYAN, ARAM (1943– ), is a writer, editor of the journal *Lines* (1964–65), and son of Armenian-American playwright William Saroyan. His poems are influenced by Robert Creeley's minimalist verse and by the visual effects of concrete poetry: *In* (La Grande, OR: Bear Press, 1965), *Pages* (New York: Random House, 1969), *Genesis Angels: The Saga of Lew Welch and the Beat Generation* (New York: William Morrow, 1979).

SCHEVILL, JAMES (1920– ), is a poet and was the director of the Poetry Center at San Francisco State University from 1961 to 1968. His books include: *American Fantasies: Collected Poems 1948–1980* (Chicago: Swallow Press, 1983) and *Ambiguous Dance of Fame: Collected Poems, 1945–1985* (Chicago: Swallow Press, 1987).

SCHOLEM, GERSHOM (1897–1982), was a German-born Jewish scholar who emigrated to Palestine in 1923 and became a leading expert in Jewish mysticism and the Kabbalah. His books include: *Major Trends in Jewish Mysticism* (Jerusalem: Schocken Publishing House, 1941), *Jewish Mysticism in the Middle Ages* (New York: Judica Press, 1964), *Origins of the Kabbalah*, ed. R. J. Zwi Werblowsky, trans. Allan Arkush (Philadelphia: Jewish Publication Society, 1987), and *Tales of Hasidim*, trans. Olga Marx, 2 vols. (New York: Schocken Books, 1947–1948). He was admired by RD, DL, and Charles Olson.

SCHWERNER, ARMAND (1927–1999), was a Belgian-born New York poet, translator, and professor for many years at the College of Staten Island, City University of New York. His books include: *The Lightfall* (New York: Hawk's Well Press, 1963), *Seaweed* (Los Angeles: Black Sparrow Press, 1968), and the Poundian sequence *The Tablets* (Orono, ME: National Poetry Foundation, 1999).

SET was edited by Gerrit Lansing for two issues in 1961 and 1963. RD's poem "Osiris and Set" appeared in it: *Set* I (Winter 1961–63): 2–3.

SHAYER, MICHAEL (1928– ), is a British poet attracted to the New American Poets by Gael Turnbull's magazine *Migrant*. His books include *Persephone* (Worcester, England: Migrant Press, 1961) and *Poems from an Island* (London: Fulcrum Press, 1970).

SIMPSON, LOUIS (1923– ), is a Jamaican-born poet who taught at the University of California, Berkeley, and later at the University of Stony Brook, State University of New York. With Donald Hall and Robert Pack, he edited the anthology *The New Poets of England and America* (Cleveland: World Publishing Co., 1957); its traditional norms helped to provoke Donald M. Allen's anthology of experimental poetry, *The New American Poetry* (New York: Grove Press, 1960). See his *Collected Poems* (New York: Paragon House, 1988).

SINGER, I(SAAC). B(ASHEVIS). (1904–1991), was a Polish-born writer, playwright, and translator who attended rabbinical seminary in the 1920s and emigrated to New York in 1935. He was awarded the Nobel Prize in Literature in 1978. His books, translated from the Yiddish, include: *Gimpel the Fool and Other Stories*, trans. Saul Bellow and others (New York: Noonday, 1957); *The Magician of Lublin*, trans. Elaine Gottlieb and Joseph Singer (New York: Farrar, Straus and Giroux, 1960); and *Collected Stories* (New York: Farrar, Straus and Giroux, 1982).

SITWELL, EDITH (1887–1964), was a British poet, admired by RD, from a literary family, who gave an exotic air to literary London. Her early poetry is baroque and experimental: *Façade* (Kensington,

England: The Favl Press, 1922), *Troy Park* (London: Duckworth, 1925). Her later poetry is meditative and religious: *The Song of the Cold* (London: Macmillan Co., 1945), *Collected Poems* (London: Papermac, 1982).

SLOMAN, JOEL (1943– ), is a poet whose first book, *Virgil Machines: Poems* (New York: W. W. Norton and Co., 1965), was chosen by DL. He went on to publish *Stops* (Cambridge: Zoland Books, 1979) and *Cuban Journal* (Cambridge: Zoland Books, 2000).

SMART, CHRISTOPHER (1722–1771), was an English religious and mystical poet whose most famous poem is *Jubilate Agno*. See his *Collected Poems*, ed. Norman Callan (London: Routledge and Kegan Paul, 1949).

SNODGRASS, W(ILLIAM). D(EWITT). (1926– ), is a poet and translator who taught at the University of Delaware from 1979 to 1994. His early poems were associated with "confessional" poetry: *Heart's Needle* (New York: Alfred A. Knopf, 1959), which won the Pulitzer Prize; and *After Experience: Poems and Translations* (New York: Harper and Row, 1968). His later poetry includes: Christian Morgenstern's *Gallows Songs*, trans. with Lori Segal (Ann Arbor: University of Michigan Press, 1967); *The Boy Made of Meat* (Concord, NH: William B. Ewert, 1983); and a cycle of dramatic monologues, *The Führer Bunker: The Complete Cycle* (Brockport, NY: Boa Editions, 1995).

SORRENTINO, GILBERT (1929– ), is a New York experimental poet and novelist who taught at Stanford University from 1982 to 1999. He was a key figure in the New York avant-garde in the late 1950s and 1960s. His poetry includes: *The Darkness Surrounds Us* (Highlands, NC: Jonathan Williams, 1960), *Black and White* (New York: Totem Press, 1964), *The Orangery* (Austin: University of Texas Press, 1970), and *Selected Poems* (Santa Barbara, CA: Black Sparrow Press, 1981). His fiction includes: *Mulligan Stew* (New York: Grove Press, 1979), *Aberration of Starlight* (New York: Random House, 1980), and *Odd Number* (San Francisco: North Point Press, 1985).

SPELLMAN, A. B. (1935– ), is a New York poet whose first book is *The Beautiful Days*, introd. Frank O'Hara (New York: Poets Press, 1965).

SPELLMAN, FRANCIS CARDINAL (1887–1967), was the Roman Catholic archbishop of New York who also served as head of the chaplains in the U.S. armed forces.

SPICER, JACK (1925–1965), was a California poet associated with RD and Robin Blaser in Berkeley in the late 1940s and with the San Francisco poetry scene of the 1950s and 1960s. His surreal and antipoetic poems are self-conscious experiments testing the power and limits of language: *Billy the Kid* (Stinson Beach, CA: Enkidu Surrogate, 1959), *The Holy Grail* (San Francisco: White Rabbit Press, 1964), *Language* (San Francisco: White Rabbit Press, 1965), and the *Collected Books of Jack Spicer*, ed. Robin Blaser (Los Angeles: Black Sparrow Press, 1975).

STANISLAVSKY, CONSTANTINE (1863–1938), was a Russian actor and director whose theories about acting were extremely influential in the postwar United States. His books include: *My Life in Art*, trans. J. J. Robbins (Boston: Little, Brown, 1924); *An Actor Prepares*, trans. Elizabeth Reynolds Hapgood (New York: Theater Arts Books, 1936); and *Building a Character*, trans. Elizabeth Reynolds Hapgood (New York: Theater Arts Books, 1949).

STANLEY, GEORGE (1934– ), is a San Francisco–born poet who was part of the Jack Spicer circle. His books include: *The Love Root* (San Francisco: White Rabbit Press, 1958), *Tete Rouge and Pony Express Riders* (San Francisco: White Rabbit Press, 1963), and *Flowers* (San Francisco: White Rabbit Press, 1965).

STILL, CLYFFORD (1904–1980), was born in North Dakota and became a central figure in the Abstract Expressionist movement in New York. Still lived for several years in San Francisco, where he taught at the California School of Fine Arts; Jess was one of his students. His large, intense paintings influenced RD's concept of the open field of composition.

STONY BROOK, edited by George Quasha, had two double issues in 1968 and 1969 and published poets in the Pound-Williams line, including DL and RD.

STRAND, MARK (1934– ), is a Canadian-born poet who came to the United States in 1938 and became part of the New York poetry and art scene after the war. He has taught at a number of American universities and became the U.S. Poet Laureate in 1990–91. Some of his books are: *Sleeping with One Eye Open* (Iowa City, IA: Stone Wall Press, 1964), *Darker* (New York: Antheneum, 1970), *The Story of Our Lives* (New York: Atheneum, 1973), *Selected Poems* (New York: Antheneum, 1980), and *Blizzard of One* (New York: Alfred A. Knopf, 1998).

SUM, edited by Fred Wah, from Albuquerque and Buffalo, ran for five issues from 1963 to 1965 and published mostly younger writers, such as James Koller, Tom Raworth, Ken Irby, and Paul Blackburn.

SWADOS, HARVEY (1920–1972), was a New York leftist intellectual and fiction writer who focused on the social and economic conditions of the working class. See: *On the Line* (Boston: Little, Brown, 1957), *The Will* (Cleveland: World Publishing Co., 1963), and *Standing Fast* (Garden City, NY: Doubleday and Co., 1970).

TALLMAN, WARREN (1921–1994), was a professor at the University of British Columbia and an organizer of the Vancouver Poetry Festival in the summer of 1963. He co-edited, with Donald M. Allen *The Poetics of the New American Poetry* (New York: Grove Press, 1974) and was a critic of American and Canadian writing. See his *Godawful Streets of Man: Essays* (Toronto: Coach House Press, 1976) and *In the Midst: Writings 1962–1992* (Vancouver: Talon Books, 1992). Ellen Tallman was his wife.

TATE, ALLEN (1899–1977), was a poet, critic, and teacher associated with the group of Fugitive poets and Southern Agrarians around John Crowe Ransom at Vanderbilt in the 1920s and with the New Criticism of the 1940s and 1950s. His tight, formal verse about psychological and spiritual anxiety, his literary essays, and his conservative writings on social and religious issues made him a powerful presence in American cultural life. His major collections are: *Collected Poems* (New York: Farrar, Straus and Giroux, 1977), *Essays of Four Decades* (Chicago: Swallow Press, 1968), and *Memoirs and Opinions, 1926–1974* (Chicago: Swallow Press, 1975).

TERKEL, (LOUIS) STUDS (1912– ), is a Chicago-based writer whose interviews with people, especially from the working class, informed his books on American social history of this century, including: *American Dreams, Lost and Found* (New York: Pantheon Books, 1980), *Working People Talk about What They Do All Day and How They Feel about What They Do* (New York: Pantheon Books, 1974), and *Race: How Blacks and Whites Feel about the American Obsession* (New York: New Press, 1992).

THINGS, edited by Emmet Jarrett and Ron Schreiber, ran for three issues, from 1964 to 1966, and published mostly New York writers. DL's "An Admonition" appeared in the first issue.

THOMPSON, VIRGIL (1896–1989), was an American musical composer whose many compositions include the score for Gertrude Stein's opera *Four Saints in Three Acts* (1934).

TIECK, LUDWIG (1773–1853), was a German poet, playwright, writer of fiction and folktales, and a leading figure in German Romanticism. Some books in English include: *Der Gestiefelte Kater. Puss-in-Boots*, ed. and trans. Gerald Gillespie (Austin: University of Texas Press, 1974), and *The Land of Upside Down* [San Francisco], trans. Oscar Mandel, with Maria Kelson Feder (Rutherford, NJ: Fairleigh Dickinson University Press, 1978).

TOLKIEN, J(OHN). R(ONALD). R(EUEL). (1892–1973), was an Oxford philologist and medievalist, a friend of C. S. Lewis and Charles Williams, and the most popular writer of fantasy fiction in English in the twentieth century. The narratives of the imagined world of Middle Earth in *The Hobbit* (London: G. Allen and Unwin, 1951) and the trilogy of *The Lord of the Rings*, 3 vols. (Boston: Houghton Mifflin, 1954–55) invest adventure with historical, moral, and religious significance.

TOMLINSON, CHARLES (1927– ), is a British poet who distinguished himself from his contemporaries by adapting the high Modernist techniques of American poets such as Ezra Pound, William Carlos Williams, and Wallace Stevens to his own sensibility and purposes. During the 1960s and 1970s he published in *Poetry* and in the large and small magazines familiar to RD and DL. His many books include: *Seeing Is Believing* (New York: McDonnell, Obolensky, 1958), *Collected Poems* (New York: Oxford University Press, 1985), and *Some Americans: A Personal Record* (Berkeley: University of California Press, 1981).

TRIEM, EVE (1902–1992), was a Seattle-based poet who was married to Paul Triem, a medical writer. She lived in San Francisco in the 1950s and became a friend of Helen Adam and RD. She was a member of "The Maidens" group in San Francisco in the 1950s and continued to publish after her return to Seattle. Her books include: *Parade of Doves* (New York: E. P. Dutton, 1946), *Poems* (Denver: Poetry and Prose Editions, 1965), and *Nobody Dies in Summer: Selected Poems 1934–1989*, ed. Bernard G. Dack (Seattle: Broken Moon Press, 1993).

TROBAR, edited by George Economou, Joan Kelly, and Robert Kelly, published five issues from New York City between 1960 and 1964. Robert Kelly's essay "Notes on the Poetry of Deep Image" appeared in the second issue. RD published in each of the issues.

TUDOR, DAVID (1926– ), is a pianist and composer who was a participant in the summer sessions at Black Mountain College in the early 1950s and in the artists' commune at Stony Point on Long Island in the late 1950s along with M. C. Richards and John Cage. He wrote and performed experimental and electronic music, sometimes in collaboration with Cage.

TURNBULL, GAEL (1928– ), is a Scottish-born poet and physician who lived for a time in Ventura, California. He edited *Migrant*, a small magazine that introduced new American poets to British readers. His books include: *A Trampoline: Poems 1952–1964* (London: Cape Goliard Press, 1968), *Scantlings: Poems 1964–1969* (London/New York:

Cape Goliard Press/Grossman, 1970), and *A Gathering of Poems* (London: Anvil Press, 1980).

TYLER, HAMILTON (1917–1983), married Mary Campbell in 1942, and they were friends of RD beginning in 1942 in Berkeley. RD lived on their farm in Healdsburg when he returned to California from New York City in 1946. The Tylers maintained contact with Robert Duncan and Jess. Tyler's books combine a scientific and a mythic view of nature: *Pueblo Gods and Myths* (Norman: University of Oklahoma Press, 1964), *Organic Gardening Without Poisons* (New York: Van Nostrand Reinhold, 1970), and *Owls by Day and Night* (Happy Camp, CA: Naturegraph, 1978). See the Tylers' article "In the Beginning, or Recatching *The Years as Catches* with Robert Duncan, in the Years 1942 and 1945–46," in *Scales of the Marvelous*, ed. Robert J. Bertholf and Ian W. Reid (New York: New Directions, 1979): 1–13.

UNGARETTI, GIUSEPPE (1888–1970), was an Italian poet whose work mediated between avant-garde modernists and lyrical traditionalists: in English, *Selected Poems*, ed. and trans. Patrick Creagh (Harmondsworth, Middlesex, England: Penguin Books, 1971).

VIVIN, LOUIS (1861–1936), was a French "primitive" artist noted for scenes and landscapes portrayed with a childlike naïveté.

WAH, FRED(ERICK) (1939– ), is a Canadian poet married to Pauline Buntling. He studied at the University of New Mexico under Robert Creeley and at the University of Buffalo, State University of New York, under Charles Olson and Robert Creeley. He edited the journal *Sum*. His books include: *Tree* (Vancouver, BC: Vancouver Community Press, 1972), *Pictograms From the Interior of British Columbia* (Vancouver, BC: Talon Books, 1975), *Selected Poems: Loki Is Buried at Smoky Creek*, ed. and introd. George Bowering (Vancouver, BC: Talon Books, 1980), and *Diamond Grill* (Edmonton, AL: NeWest, 1996).

WAKOSKI, DIANE (1939– ), is a California-born poet who was associated with Robert Kelly in New York and now teaches and lives in Michigan. Her open-form poems deal with the psychological and emotional drama of her experience as a woman with a sense of archetypal resonance as well as comic irony. Her many books include: *Coins and Coffins* (New York: Hawk's Well Press, 1962), *The George Washington Poems* (New York: Riverrun Press, 1967), *Inside the Blood Factory* (Garden City, NY: Doubleday and Co., 1968), *The Motorcycle Betrayal Poems* (New York: Simon and Schuster, 1971), *Greed Parts 1–13* (Santa Barbara, CA: Black Sparrow Press, 1984), and *Emerald Ice: Selected Poems 1962–1987* (Santa Rosa, CA: Black Sparrow Press, 1988).

WEISS, THEODORE (1916– ), is a poet and long-time Princeton professor who edited *The Quarterly Review of Literature* starting in 1943 at Bard College. His books of poems include: *Outlanders* (New York: Macmillan Co., 1960), *Gunsight* (New York: New York University Press, 1962), and *From Princeton One Autumn Afternoon: Collected Poems* (New York: Macmillan Co., 1987).

WELTY, EUDORA (1909–2001), was a fiction writer from Jackson, Mississippi, whose psychologically subtle and mythically charged stories and novels are set in rural and small-town Mississippi. Her books include: *A Curtain of Green* (New York: Doubleday and Co., 1941), *The Wide Net and Other Stories* (New York: Harcourt, Brace and Co., 1943), *The Golden Apples* (New York: Harcourt, Brace and Co., 1949), *The Optimist's Daughter* (New York: Random House, 1972), and *Collected Stories* (New York: Harcourt, Brace Jovanovich, 1980).

WHALEN, PHILIP (1923– ), is an Oregon-born poet who was associated with Gary Snyder and Lew Welch and became a figure in the San Francisco Renaissance. He was one of the readers at the Six Gallery in 1956. Since 1973, he has been a Zen Buddhist monk in San Francisco. His collections include: *Memoirs of an Interglacial Age* (San Francisco: Auerhahn Press, 1960); *Heavy Breathing: Poems 1967–1980* (San Francisco: Four Seasons Foundation, 1983); *Canoeing Up Cabarga Creek: Buddhist Poems 1955–1986*, ed. Miriam Sagan and Robert Winston (Berkeley: Parallax Press, 1996); and *Overtime: Selected Poems*, ed. Michael Rothenberg, introd. Leslie Scalapino (New York: Penguin Books, 1999).

WIENERS, JOHN (1934–2002), was a Boston-born poet who attended Black Mountain College from 1955 to 1956, studied under Charles Olson at the University of Buffalo, State University of New York, and was influenced by the Beats as well as by the Black Mountain group. He edited the journal *Measure*. Both DL and RD wrote enthusiastic reviews of his early work. His books include: *The Hotel Wentley Poems* (San Francisco: Auerhahn Press, 1958), *Ace of Pentacles* (New York: James F. Carr and Robert A. Wilson, 1964), *Asylum Poems* (New York: Angel Hair Books, 1969), and *Selected Poems: 1958–1984*, ed. Raymond Foye, foreword by Allen Ginsberg (Santa Barbara, CA: Black Sparrow Press, 1986).

WILBUR, RICHARD (1921– ), is a poet and teacher who was the U.S. Poet Laureate from 1987 to 1988. He has translated many of Molière's plays into English couplets. His poems are noted for their formal elegance and for their meditative and religious tenor. His books include: *The Beautiful Changes and Other Poems* (New York: Reynal and Hitchcock, 1947), *Things of This World* (New York: Harcourt, Brace, 1956), *Advice to a Prophet and Other Poems* (New York: Harcourt, Brace and World, 1961), and *New and Collected Poems* (San Diego: Harcourt Brace Jovanovich, 1988).

WILLIAMS, CHARLES (1886–1945), was a British novelist, poet, and playwright whose spiritualist views attracted RD's attention. Some of his books are: *The Greater Trumps* (London: V. Gollancz, 1932), *Witchcraft* (London: Faber and Faber, 1941), *All Hallow's Eve* (London: Faber and Faber, 1945), and *Collected Plays*, intro. John Heath-Stubbs (London: Oxford University Press, 1968).

WILLIAMS, JONATHAN (1929– ), is a poet, photographer, and small press editor. He attended Black Mountain College intermittently from 1951 to 1956 and established the Jargon Society ("a poet's press"), which included among its numerous titles DL's third book, *Overland to the Islands* (1958) and RD's *Letters* (1958). He was influenced by William Carlos Williams and Ezra Pound as well as by Charles Olson and Robert Creeley. His many books include: *Amen, Huzza, Selah: Poems* (Highlands, NC: Jargon Society, 1960), *An Ear in Bartram's Tree: Selected*

*Poems 1957–1967* (Chapel Hill, NC: University of North Carolina Press, 1969), *Elegies and Celebrations*, preface by Robert Duncan (Highlands, NC: Jargon Society, 1962), and *Get Hot or Get Out: A Selection of Poems 1957–1981* (Metuchen, NJ: Scarecrow Press, 1982).

WILSON, ADRIAN (1923–1988), was a San Francisco printer and book designer. He established The Press in Tuscany Alley and set high standards for printing and book design. He wrote *Printing for the Theater* (San Francisco: Adrian Wilson, 1957) and *The Design of Books* (New York: Reinhold Publishing Co., 1967).

WINTERS, (ARTHUR) YVOR (1900–1968), was a poet, critic, and Stanford professor from 1928 to 1966. His early experimental poetry gave way to metered formalism in verse and to vehement criticism of the dangerous egotism and irrationality of Romanticism and Modernism. *Early Poems* (Denver: Allen Swallow, 1966) and *Collected Poems*, introd. Donald Davie (Manchester, England: Carcanet, 1978) represent his work in poetry; *In Defense of Reason* (Denver: Allen Swallow, 1947) and *Forms of Discovery* (Chicago: Allen Swallow, 1967) represent his critical perspective.

WITT-DIAMANT, RUTH (1895–1987), was a professor at San Francisco State University from 1930 to 1962, where she founded and for many years directed the Poetry Center. She edited an anthology of poetry first published in Japan in 1968 as *53 American Poets of Today*, ed. Ruth Witt-Diamant and Rikutaro Fukuda (Folcraft, PA: Folcraft Library Editions, 1971).

WOLFERT, HELEN (1904– ), was a poet and high school teacher in New York City. Her books include: *Nothing Is a Wonderful Thing* (New York: Simon and Schuster, 1946); *The Music* (New York: W. W. Norton and Co., 1965); selected for publication by DL, and *Landlady and Tenant* (New York: Sheep Meadow Press, 1979).

WRIGHT, JAMES (1927–1980,), was an Ohio-born poet, translator, and professor at Hunter College in New York from 1966 to 1980. His poems of alienation and loneliness sought to wring celebration from despair. See: *Saint Judas* (Middletown, CT: Wesleyan University Press, 1959), *The Branch Will Not Break* (Middletown, CT: Wesleyan University Press, 1963), *Shall We Gather at the River* (Middletown, CT: Wesleyan University Press, 1968), and *Above the River: The Complete Poems*, introd. Donald Hall (New York: Farrar, Straus and Giroux, 1992).

YOUNG, AL(BERT JAMES) (1939– ), is an African American poet, novelist, jazz musician, and critic. Born in Mississippi and based in the San Francisco Bay area, he was a close friend of DL and studied in the creative writing program at Stanford. His books of poems include: *Dancing* (New York: Corinth Books, 1969), *The Song Turning Back into Itself* (New York: Holt, Reinhardt and Winston, 1971), and *Heaven: Collected Poems 1956–1990* (Berkeley: Creative Arts Book Co., 1992). His fiction includes: *Snakes: A Novel* (New York: Holt, Reinhardt and Winston, 1970), *Who Is Angelina?* (New York: Holt, Reinhardt and Winston, 1975), and *Sitting Pretty* (New York: Holt, Reinhardt and Winston, 1976).

YUGEN was edited by LeRoi Jones and Hettie Cohen (Jones) in New York and ran for eight issues between 1958 and 1962. The journal featured writers like Robert Creeley, Allen Ginsberg, Joel Oppenheimer, and Paul Blackburn.

ZALMAN, SCHNEOUR, OF LADALY (or LADI) (1745–1813), was a Russian Hasidic scholar of the Talmud and Jewish law and religion. He was also one of DL's great-grandfathers: the maternal grandmother of her father Paul Levertoff, who was himself a Russian-born Hasidic Jew and scholar who converted to Christianity, became an Anglican priest and participated energetically in Jewish-Christian dialogue in England during the years between the World Wars.

ZUKOFSKY, LOUIS (1904–1978), was a poet born in New York of Russian-Jewish parents. He married musician and composer Celia Thaew; their son Paul, born in 1943, is a violinist and musician. Zukofsky was a friend of Ezra Pound and William Carlos Williams and a central figure of the Objectivist group of the 1930s, which also included George Oppen and Charles Reznikoff; he edited *An "Objectivist" Anthology* (1932). His shorter experimental poems were collected in *All* (New York: W. W. Norton and Co., 1966), selected for publication by DL, and then in *Complete Short Poetry*, foreword by Robert Creeley (Baltimore: The Johns Hopkins University Press, 1992). His long poetic sequence *"A"* is influenced by Pound and Williams (Berkeley: University of California Press, 1978). His prose includes: *Bottom: On Shakespeare*, 2 vols. (Austin: University of Texas Press, 1963); *Propositions: Collected Critical Essays* (London: Rapp and Carroll, 1967); *Collected Fiction*, foreword by Gilbert Sorrentino, afterword by Paul Zukofsky (Elmwood Park, IL: Dalkey Archive Press, 1990).

# BRIEF CHRONOLOGY OF
# DUNCAN AND LEVERTOV

## 1919

RD is born in Oakland, California, on January 7 and named Edward Howard Duncan after his father. His mother dies in childbirth, and in August the baby is adopted by Edwin and Minnehaha Symmes of the Oakland Hermetic Brotherhood and given the name Robert Edward Symmes. (In 1941 he takes the name Robert Edward Duncan.) He grows up in Oakland and then in Bakersfield, California, where he goes to high school.

## 1923

DL is born in Ilford, Essex, outside of London. Her father, Paul Levertoff, was a Russian Jew who converted to Christianity, emigrated to England after marriage, became an Anglican clergyman, and as a scholar was active in Christian-Jewish dialogue. DL's Welsh mother, Beatrice Spooner-Jones, had several visionaries as forebears, notably the tailor-preacher Angel Jones of Mold. DL's only sibling, Olga, was born in 1914. Both girls were educated at home and never attended school.

## 1936

RD enters the University of California at Berkeley. He publishes poems in *Occident*; meets Pauline Kael, Virginia Admiral, and Ned Fahs; reads Ezra Pound, and Gertrude Stein; and begins his first literary magazine, *Epitaph*, with Virginia Admiral. RD follows Ned Fahs to the East Coast.

## 1937

RD lives in Philadelphia; publishes poems in *The Phoenix*; moves to Annapolis; and meets Anaïs Nin at Woodstock, New York.

## 1938

RD begins literary magazine *Ritual*, publishes poems in *Ritual* and *The Phoenix*, begins *Experimental Review* with Sanders Russell, breaks with Ned Fahs, begins corresponding with William Everson, and ends the year living in New York.

## 1939

DL's friendship and correspondence with Herbert Read begins. She becomes associated with a group of poets in England called the New Romantics.

## 1940

DL's first published poem, "Listening to Distant Guns," appears in *Poetry Quarterly*.

RD lives with Marjorie McKee in New York. He is drafted, serves at Fort Knox, where he writes "A Spring Memorandum," and is discharged in June. In the summer he visits William Everson in Selma, California, and enrolls again at the University of California at Berkeley.

## 1942–1943

RD lives with Hamilton and Mary Tyler in Berkeley, marries Marjorie McKee, and lives in New York City. He meets Jackson MacLow and works for Dell Publishing Company in Boston.

## 1943–1944

DL works as civilian nurse in London as part of the war effort.

## 1943

RD visits Laura Riding, in Lake Worth, Florida, publishes "The Homosexual in Society" in Dwight

MacDonald's journal *Politics*. His poem "The African Elegy" is accepted and then rejected at *Kenyon Review* by John Crowe Ransom. He lives in Provincetown, Massachusetts.

## 1945–1946

RD moves to a farm in Treesbank, then to Berkeley; he lives at 2029 Hearst Street and enrolls in the University of California at Berkeley to study his medieval history. He begins his friendship with Jack Spicer, Robin Blaser, and James Broughton.

## 1946

DL's first published book, *The Double Image*, appears in England under the name Denise Levertoff.

## 1947

DL serves as a civilian nurse in Paris, meets American writer and ex-G.I. Mitchell Goodman, and marries him in December.

RD publishes *Berkeley Miscellany* (No. 2 1949) and writes "The Venice Poem." He publishes his first book, *Heavenly City Earthly City*, visits Ezra Pound in St. Elizabeth's, and meets Charles Olson in Berkeley. He begins living at the house of Jaime de Angulo and remains there until the fall of 1950.

## 1948

DL and Goodman move to New York City. She begins to remake herself as a poet in response to a new and stimulatingly different cultural and poetic world.

## 1949

Nikolai Goodman is born in June. Kenneth Rexroth includes poems by DL in his anthology *The New British Poets* and begins his enthusiastic advocacy of her work. DL begins friendship with Robert Creeley, a Harvard classmate of Goodman.

## 1950

RD publishes *Medieval Scenes*.

## 1950–1951

The Goodmans live and write in Europe, principally in the countryside near Aix-en-Provence, France.

The Robert Creeleys are neighbors for part of the period. The Goodmans return to New York in 1952. In October 1951 she begins correspondence with William Carlos Williams at Creeley's prompting.

## 1951–1953

RD begins life with his partner, the painter Jess Collins, in San Francisco. He writes poems for *A Book of Resemblances*, the Stein imitations, and *Names of People*.

## 1953

RD admires DL's poems in *Origin*, particularly "The Shifting," writes "Letters for Denise Levertov: An A Muse Ment" in homage, and sends it to her. Their long friendship and correspondence begins.

RD publishes *Faust Foutu*.

DL visits William Carlos Williams at his home in Rutherford, New Jersey, and begins a close association with him until his death in 1963.

## 1955

DL meets RD and Jess Collins in New York on their way to Europe. She arranges for them to meet Robert Creeley in Mallorca, where RD and Jess live for several years.

DL becomes an American citizen.

## 1956

*Here and Now*, DL's second book of poems and the first published in the United States, appears from Lawrence Ferlinghetti's City Lights Books in San Francisco.

RD visits England, writes "Often I Am Permitted to Return to a Meadow," leaves Mallorca, teaches at Black Mountain College, then returns to San Francisco to become Assistant Director of the Poetry Center at San Francisco State until June.

## 1956–1957

The Goodmans live in Mexico, first in Guadalajara and then in Oaxaca.

## 1957

RD wins the Union Civic and Arts Foundation Prize.

1958

The Goodmans visit San Francisco at RD's invitation in January 1958, on their way back from Mexico to New York. DL gives a reading arranged by RD. For the occasion *5 Poems* is published by Joseph Dunn's White Rabbit Press, with illustrations by Jess Collins.

DL's *Overland to the Islands* is published by Jonathan Williams' Jargon Books with a frontispiece by Albert Kresch, a New York painter and friend of DL. The Goodmans begin spending their summers in Maine.

RD and Jess Collins move in March to Stinson Beach in Marin County, just north of San Francisco.

RD publishes *Letters* with "For a Muse Meant" as the first poem.

1959

RD's *Selected Poems* is published by Ferlinghetti's City Light Books. RD begins the readings at colleges and universities in the United States and Canada that would continue until the illness of his last few years.

DL meets Adrienne Rich, whose husband, Alfred Conrad, was a Harvard classmate of Mitchell Goodman, and the two women poets begin a friendship that will remain strong through the sixties.

1960

RD publishes *The Opening of the Field* and begins "The H. D. Book."

DL publishes *With Eyes at the Back of Our Heads* and begins DL's lifelong association with New Directions and with its director, James Laughlin, who becomes a close friend and ardent supporter. The title poem receives the Bess Hokin Prize from *Poetry* (Chicago).

The Goodmans buy a house in Temple, Maine, as their summer place.

1961

DL publishes *The Jacob's Ladder*.

RD receives the Harriet Monroe Memorial Prize. He and Jess Collins move from Stinson Beach to San Francisco in March. His mother dies of a heart attack in December.

1961–1962

DL becomes poetry editor of the politically liberal weekly journal *The Nation*.

1962

DL receives a Guggenheim Fellowship.

1963

Charles Olson, Robert Creeley, RD, and DL attend and participate in the conference on poetry and poetics in Vancouver, British Columbia, in August, the only occasion involving all four of the principal Black Mountain poets.

RD publishes *Writing Writing* and *Roots and Branches*; receives a Guggenheim Fellowship.

1963–1965

DL serves again as poetry editor of *The Nation*.

1964

Olga Levertoff dies of cancer in England in March.

DL publishes *O Taste and See* and receives the Harriet Monroe Memorial Prize.

DL, RD, and Robert Creeley give a joint reading at the Guggenheim Museum in New York on April 16.

1964–1966

DL is an honorary scholar at the Radcliffe Institute (later the Bunting Institute) in Cambridge, Massachusetts, and deepens friendship with Adrienne Rich.

1965

DL teaches at the City University of New York and at Drew University in Madison, New Jersey, and receives the M. D. Zabel Prize from *Poetry* (Chicago).

DL and Goodman begin political activism to protest the Vietnam War.

RD participates in Berkeley Poetry Conference, to which DL is not invited despite his objections.

1966

DL receives an award from the American Academy of Arts and Letters and teaches at Vassar College in 1966–67.

RD publishes *A Book of Resemblances, The Years as Catches,* and *Of the War: Passages 22–27.* His theosophical play *Adam's Way* is produced in Vancouver in February.

## 1967

Goodman teaches in the Voice Project at Stanford University during the spring.

DL publishes *The Sorrow Dance,* which contains the "Olga Poems" and a section of war poems called "Life at War." To benefit the War Resisters League she edits *Out of the War Shadow,* a peace calendar for 1968 with poems, including one by her and one by RD.

RD and Jess Collins buy the house at 3267 20th Street and move in March/April. RD receives a National Endowment for the Arts Grant and the Eunice Tietjens Memorial Prize.

DL and RD participate in "A Meeting of Poets and Theologians to Discuss Parable, Myth, and Language," October 13–15, Washington, DC. The proceedings of the conference, with their contributions, is published in 1968.

## 1968

DL publishes the poem *A Tree Telling of Orpheus,* illustrated with her own line drawings.

Goodman is indicted with Dr. Benjamin Spock and three others and charged with conspiracy against the military draft law; they are convicted, but the conviction will be overturned on appeal the next year.

RD attends a conference on Language and World Order at Central Washington State College, April 18–20.

RD publishes *The Truth and Life of Myth, Names of People,* and *Bending the Bow,* which is his first collection with New Directions and contains the first of the *Passages* sequence. In England *The First Decade* and *Derivations* are published. RD gives the lecture "Changing Perspectives on Whitman" at New York University.

## 1969

DL teaches at the University of California, Berkeley, in the spring semester and participates in the People's Park protests.

The Goodmans move to East Boston.

## 1969–1970

DL teaches at the Massachusetts Institute of Technology.

## 1970

DL publishes *Relearning the Alphabet,* teaches at Kirkham College in Clinton, New York, during the academic year 1970–71, and travels to Moscow at Christmastime, 1970.

RD publishes *Tribunals: Passages 31–35* and teaches in the fall at the University of California, Santa Cruz.

## 1971

DL publishes *To Stay Alive.*

The Goodmans move to Brookline, Massachusetts, in May.

## 1972

DL publishes *Footprints* and travels to Hanoi on a peace mission with Muriel Rukeyser and Jane Hart.

RD teaches a three-week course in Poetic Imagination at Kent State University and gives the Wallace Stevens Memorial Reading at Storrs, Connecticut.

## 1973

RD attends Modern American Poetry Conference at The Polytechnic of Central London, May 25–29.

DL publishes *The Poet in the World,* her first collection of essays.

## 1973–1979

DL teaches at Tufts University in Medford, Massachusetts.

## 1974

DL and Goodman are divorced. DL moves to West Somerville, Massachusetts, and Goodman lives year-round in Temple, Maine.

James Mersmann's *Out of the Vietnam Vortex* is published; a chapter on DL includes a quotation from an interview with RD about DL's political poetry that deepens the break between the two old friends.

RD's *Dante* is published.

1975

RD teaches at the University of California, Riverside, during the winter term.

DL publishes *The Freeing of the Dust*.

1976–1978

DL serves as poetry editor for the radical magazine *Mother Jones*.

1976

RD gives a Library of Congress reading and makes a reading tour of Australia and New Zealand.

DL receives the Lenore Marshall Poetry Prize.

1977

RD participates in the Second Cambridge World Poetry Conference.

1978

DL publishes *Life in the Forest*.

RD attends "Symposium; The Bible and Secular Imagination" at University of Binghamton, State University of New York; participates in the Charles Olson Conference at the University of Iowa in October.

RD delivers Charles Olson Memorial Lectures at Buffalo in March/April, teaches at Alpine Center for Poetry and Literature, Innsbruck, Austria, in July/August.

DL does a reading tour of Australia.

1980

DL is elected to the American Academy of Arts and Letters, attends the World Peace Parliament in Sofia, Bulgaria, as a delegate.

RD is awarded a National Endowment for the Arts Fellowship.

1981–1983

DL teaches at Brandeis University.

1981

DL publishes the book of essays *Light Up the Cave*.

1982–1994

DL teaches in the Creative Writing Program at Stanford University during the winter term.

1982

DL publishes *Candles in Babylon*.

1982–1983

RD teaches at New College, San Francisco.

1984

RD publishes *Ground Work: Before the War*. He is diagnosed with kidney failure.

DL publishes *Oblique Prayers*.

DL and RD are jointly awarded the Shelley Memorial Award from the Poetry Society of America.

1985

RD participates in a conference on H. D. and Marianne Moore at Bryn Mawr College in March; he publishes *Fictive Certainties*, a book of essays.

1986

DL's *Selected Poems* is published in England.

1987

RD publishes *Ground Work: In the Dark*, his final collection.

DL publishes *Breathing the Water*.

1988

RD dies on February 7 in San Francisco of heart and kidney complications.

1989

DL publishes *A Door in the Hive*; moves to Seattle in August while continuing her teaching at Stanford during winter terms.

1990

DL receives the Robert Frost Medal.

1991

DL receives a senior fellowship from the National Endowment for the Arts.

1992

DL publishes *New and Selected Essays* and receives an award from the Lannan Foundation.

**1994**

DL receives the Lifetime Achievement Award from the Conference on Christianity and Literature.

**1995**

DL publishes the prose memoir *Tesserae* and is awarded a fellowship by the Academy of American Poets.

**1996**

DL publishes *Sands of the Well.*

**1997**

DL publishes *The Life around Us*, a selection from her poems about nature, and *The Stream and the Sapphire*, a selection from her poems about faith and religious belief.

Goodman dies of pancreatic cancer, February 1, in Temple, Maine.

DL dies of complications from lymphoma in Seattle, December 20.

**1999**

*This Great Unknowing: Last Poems*, edited by DL's literary executor, Paul Lacey, is published.

# BOOKS IN LETTERS

ROBERT DUNCAN

*Heavenly City, Earthly City. Berkeley:* Bern Porter Books, 1947.
*Poems 1948–49.* Berkeley: Berkeley Miscellany Editions, 1949.
*Medieval Scenes.* San Francisco: Centaur Press, 1950.
*Caesar's Gate: Poems 1949–50.* Palma de Mallorca: The Divers Press, 1955.
*Selected Poems.* San Francisco: City Lights, 1959.
*Faust Foutu.* Stinson Beach, CA: Enkidu Surrogate, 1959.
*The Opening of the Field.* New York: Grove Press, 1960.
*Writing, Writing.* Albuquerque, NM: Sumbooks, 1964.
*As Testimony.* San Francisco: White Rabbit Press, 1964.
*Roots and Branches.* New York: Charles Scribner's Sons, 1964.
*The Sweetness and Greatness of Dante's Divine Comedy.* San Francisco: Open Space, 1965.
*Medea at Kolchis: The Maiden Head.* Berkeley: Oyez Press, 1965.
*Of the War: Passages 22–27.* Berkeley: Oyez Press, 1966.
*The Years as Catches.* Berkeley, CA: Oyez Press, 1966.
*Six Prose Pieces.* Madison, WI: Perishable Press, 1966.
*A Book of Resemblances.* New Haven, CT: Henry Wenning, 1966.
*Epilogos.* Los Angeles: Black Sparrow Press, 1967.
*Bending the Bow.* New York: New Directions, 1968.
*Derivations.* London: Fulcrum Press, 1969.
*The First Decade.* London: Fulcrum Press, 1969.
*Caesar's Gate: Poems 1949–50.* Berkeley: Sand Dollar, 1972.
*A Seventeenth Century Suite.* San Francisco: privately published, 1973.
*Dante.* Canton, NY: The Institute of Further Studies, 1974.
*Ground Work: Before the War.* New York: New Directions, 1984.
*Fictive Certainties.* New York: New Directions, 1985.
*Ground Work: In the Dark.* New York: New Directions, 1987.
*A Selected Prose*, ed. Robert Bertholf. New York: New Directions, 1995.

DENISE LEVERTOV

*The Double Image.* London: The Cresset Press, 1946.
*Here and Now.* San Francisco: City Lights Books, 1956.
*Overland to the Islands.* Ashville, NC: Jargon, 1958.
*5 Poems*, with drawings by Jess. San Francisco: White Rabbit Press, 1958.
*With Eyes at the Back of Our Heads.* New York: New Directions, 1960.
*The Jacob's Ladder.* New York: New Directions, 1961.
*O Taste and See.* New York: New Directions, 1964.

*City Palm.* Berkeley; Oyez Press, 1964. Broadside.

*Psalm Concerning the Castle.* Madison, WI: Perishable Press, 1966.

*The Sorrow Dance.* New York: New Directions, 1967.

*A Tree Telling of Orpheus.* Los Angeles: Black Sparrow Press, 1968.

*Guillevic: Selected Poems,* trans. Denise Levertov. New York: New Directions, 1969.

*Summer Poems.* Berkeley: Oyez Press, 1970.

*Relearning the Alphabet.* New York: New Directions, 1970.

*To Stay Alive.* New York: New Directions, 1971.

*Footprints.* New York: New Directions, 1972.

*Conversation in Moscow.* Cambridge, MA: Hovey Street Press, 1973.

*The Poet in the World.* New York: New Directions, 1973.

*The Freeing of the Dust.* New York: New Directions, 1975.

*Life in the Forest.* New York: New Directions, 1978.

*Collected Earlier Poems 1940–1960.* New York: New Directions, 1979.

*A Door in the Hive.* New York: New Directions, 1989.

*New and Selected Essays.* New York: New Directions, 1992.

# NOTES

LETTER 1    June 1953

1. The correspondence opens with this poem-letter from Robert Duncan to Denise Levertov. The text that appears in Duncan's *Letters* is somewhat revised from this letter.

LETTER 2    June 1953

NOTE: Written on the envelope: "It is as it was in admiration". Annotation from DL: "N.B. This is the envelope for the letter R. D. sent in answer to my mistaken response to 'An a Muse Meant' (Letter #1)".

1. Denise Levertov's letter expressing her puzzlement at the poem in Letter 1 and the identity of her correspondent is lost; this letter is Robert Duncan's explanatory response to that lost letter. Letter 2 was found in the leaves of Denise Levertov's copy of *Letters* given to her by Robert Duncan with an inscription to Denise Levertov and Mitchell Goodman that reads: "from my mother's library for Denny & Mitch Christmas 1962" and is signed "Robert Duncan."

2. "Domestic Scenes" is a series of ten poems written in 1947 and published first in *Quarterly Review of Literature* 6 (Spring 1964): 351–57.

LETTER 3    June–July 1953

1. "The Hands" and "The Rights," printed in *Origin* 1st ser. 10 (Summer 1953): 84–85.

LETTER 4    March 1955

1. The first meeting between the poets took place in New York, Robert Duncan and Jess sailed for Europe on March 8, 1956, and settled in Bañalbufar, Majorca.

2. Levertov had arranged for Duncan and Jess to meet her friend and fellow poet Robert Creeley

and his wife Ann, then also living in Majorca. Blaise Cendrars published *Anthologie nègre* (Paris: Au Sans Pareil, 1927). Robert Duncan published "Early History" (also mentioned in letter #9) with "Africa Revisited" and six other pieces, *Origin* 1st ser. 6 (Summer 1952): 76–87, 122–26.

LETTER 5    April 1955

1. For insight into the relationships mentioned here, see Robert Buckeye, "The Principle, the Demarkation Its Use: Selected Letters of Paul Blackburn in the Abernethy Library," *Credences* new ser. 3 (Spring 1985): 53–90.

LETTER 6    April 1955

1. Reginald Horace Blyth, *Haiku*, 4 vols. (Tokyo: Hokuseido, 1949–52).

2. The fifteenth issue of *Origin* featured Paul Blackburn and Wade Donahoe. The poems "Nocturne"—"Bay Ridge and Book"—"The Consorts"—"The for Icarus"—"Letter"—"The Journey of the King," *Origin* 1st ser. 15 (Winter/Spring 1955): 34–68.

LETTER 7    May 1955

1. Beatrice Levertoff.

2. *The Golden Cushion Story Book* (London: Blackie & Son, 1925).

3. Gertrude Stein, *The World Is Round* (New York: W. R. Scott, 1939).

4. Wade Donahoe's "A Letter," *Origin*, 1st ser. 20 (Winter 1957): 122–27, confirms his position in a poetics much different from Robert Duncan's and Denise Levertov's.

LETTER 8    May 1955

1. Robert Creeley founded the Divers Press in

Palma de Mallorca; it published thirteen books between 1953 and 1955, including: Paul Blackburn, *Proensa* (1954), Robert Creeley, *The Kind of Act of* (1953), Katsue Kitasono, *Black Rain* (1954), and Robert Duncan, *Caesar's Gate* (1955).

## LETTER 9 June 1955

1. Robert Duncan sent a typescript of "The Green Lady"—first published with three other poems in *Botteghe Oscure* 19 (Spring 1957): 339–45—and a typescript of "A Ballad for Helen Adam," unpublished, which he had sent to Helen Adam in April 1955. The "revisited poem" is his earlier poem "Africa Revisited."

2. Gertrude Stein, *How to Write* (Paris: Plain Edition, 1931).

## LETTER 10 June 1955

1. The poem, included below, is also included, under the title "The Lesson," in *Overland to the Islands*.

## LETTER 11 July 1955

1. John Altoon's cover appeared on *The Black Mountain Review* 5 (Summer 1955).

2. Carl Sandburg, *Rootabaga Stories* (New York: Harcourt Brace, 1922) and *Rootabaga Pigeons* (New York: Harcourt Brace, 1923).

3. "Several Poems: In Prose," "Shells," and "From a Notebook," *Black Mountain Review* 5 (Summer 1955): 36–39, 209–12.

4. Published in D. H. Lawrence, *The Woman Who Rode Away* (London: Martin Secker, 1928).

## LETTER 12 July 1955

1. Book 2 of "Asphodel" appeared in *Poetry* 86 (May 1955): 99–107.

## LETTER 13 July 1955

1. The editors have been unable to find this publication.

2. John Livingston Lowes, *The Road to Xanadu: A Study in the Ways of the Imagination* (Boston: Houghton Mifflin, 1927).

3. Katsue Kitasono (1902–1978) was a Japanese poet, founder and editor of *Vou*, a magazine of experimental writing in Japan. His volume, *Black Rain*, with the cover mentioned, was published by the Divers Press (Palma de Mallorca, 1954).

## LETTER 14 August 1955

1. *Poems 1948–49*.

2. The letter is incomplete or missing its conclusion.

## LETTER 15 August 1955

1. See Letter 13.

2. Jonathan Williams published Victor Kalso, with Dan Rice, *The Double Backed Beast* (Highlands, NC: Jargon Society, 1954), as Jargon 4.

3. The translations were published in Richard Seaver and Austryn Wainhouse, trans., *The Marquis de Sade: The Complete Justine, Philosophy in the Bedroom, and Other Writings* (New York: Grove Press, 1965).

## LETTER 16 September 1955

1. James Stephens, *Demi-gods* (London: MacMillan Co., 1914); Virginia Woolf, *The Years* (New York: Harcourt, Brace & Co., 1937).

2. Gertrude Stein, *The Gertrude Stein First Reader, & Three Plays* (Dublin: M. Friberg, 1946); H. D., *The Hedgehog* (London: Brendin Publishing Co., 1936). H. D.'s daughter Perdita was adopted by Bryher.

3. Ruth Plumly Thompson (1891–1976) was a prolific writer who extended the Oz books after Baum's death: among them, *The Cowardly Lion of Oz* (Chicago: The Reilly & Lee Co., 1923) and *The Last King of Oz* (Chicago: The Reilly & Lee Co., 1925).

## LETTER 18 October 1955

1. This letter is incomplete or the conclusion is missing.

## LETTER 19 November–December 1955

1. E. Nesbit is Edith Nesbit Bland (1858–1924) who published many books, including *The House of Arden: A Story of Children* (London: T. F. Unwin, 1908), *The Story of the Amulet*, illus. H. R. Miller (New York: E. P. Dutton Co., 1907), and *The Enchanted Castle* (New York and London: Harper & Brothers, 1908).

2. Robert Duncan met Robert Payne in San Francisco in December 1947. He used Payne's article "A Note on Two Poems of Mao Tse Tung," *Nine* 1 (Oct. 1949): 18–20, in his poem "An Imaginary War Elegy." Payne is a prolific scholar and writer on ancient history, church history, and

China. See his *China Awake* (New York: Dodd, Mead, 1947) and *Revolt of Asia* (New York: Day Co., 1947).

3. Denise Levertov's poem "The Way Through" appeared in *The Black Mountain Review* 6 (Spring 1956), 38–39, and was included in *Overland to the Islands*.

LETTER 20    January 1956

1. The "someone" was John Day. See letter #40.

LETTER 21    February 1956

1. John Davenport (1908–1966) wrote poetry, including *Rock Art Thorns* (Cambridge: W. Heffer, 1927), and articles on Dylan Thomas. G[eorge]. S[utherland]. Fraser (1915– ) is a British man of letters and literary critic; his essays on Pound grew into the book *Ezra Pound* (Edinburgh: Oliver & Boyd, 1960).

LETTER 22    February 1956

1. *The Black Mountain Review* 6 (Spring 1956) contains the following pieces by Duncan: the poem (with drawings) "An Owl Is Only a Bird of Poetry" and two prose pieces, "Notes" and "Notes on Poetics regarding Olson's *Maximus*"; the last was included in *Fictive Certainties*. The issue also contained four collages by Jess and translations of fourteen pieces by the German poet Christian Morgenstern.

2. This is "Homage to Coleridge"; see Letter 25, n. 1.

LETTER 23    April 1956

1. All the poems mentioned here are collected in *Here and Now*.

2. The protagonist in Mozart's opera *The Magic Flute*.

LETTER 24    April 1956

1. Lines from Denise Levertov's "The Lovers," included in *Here and Now*.

2. Lines from Denise Levertov's "The Springtime," included in *Overland to the Islands*.

3. Line from Denise Levertov's "A Song," included in *Overland to the Islands*.

4. Underlined twice in the original letter.

LETTER 25    June 1956

1. "Homage to Coleridge" is a manuscript of

poems that Robert Duncan collected and wrote while living in Majorca. Jess made a cover drawing and some illustrations. The book was not finished and remains unpublished, though the poems were collected in later books.

2. "The Origins of Old Son" is a play written and performed at Black Mountain College in the summer of 1956; it remains unpublished.

LETTER 27    June 1956

1. A typescript of "Often I Am Permitted to Return to a Meadow," "Restore the Hair of the Gods!," and "Black Mountain, North Carolina Poems" accompanied this letter. The final poem is part of "A Poem Beginning with a Line by Pindar." The letter begins below a typescript of the poem "Dream Data."

2. C. K. Ogden, I. A. Richards, and James Wood, *The Foundations of Aesthetics* (New York: International Publishers, 1925).

LETTER 28    July 1956

1. This issue of *The Artist's View* 8 (1956) was devoted to Jess's work.

2. Along with "Tomatlan" these poems were collected in *Here and Now*.

LETTER 29    July 1956

1. This project developed into the play *Medea at Kolchis: The Maiden Head*.

2. The text of "Preface" to "Homage to Coleridge" and the text of "The Structure of Rime III" accompanied this letter.

LETTER 30    July 1956

1. "A Poem Slow Beginning" was collected in Robert Duncan's *The Opening of the Field*.

2. Lawrence Ferlinghetti published Denise Levertov's second book, her first U.S. collection, *Here and Now*, at City Lights Books; Jonathan Williams published her second U.S. collection, *Overland to the Islands*, at Jargon Press.

LETTER 32    September 1956

1. This book of drawings is now in the Levertov papers in Special Collections, Green Library, Stanford University.

2. Konstantin Stanislavsky, *My Life in Art*, trans. J. Robbins (Boston: Little, Brown, 1924).

For Williams's letter to Denise Levertov about *Godot*, see *The Letters of Denise Levertov and William Carlos Williams*, ed. Christopher MacGowan (New York: New Directions, 1998), 40–41.

3. The editors have been unable to find this interview in this periodical.

### LETTER 33    October 1956

1. Marguerite Caetani was the editor and publisher of *Botteghe Oscure*, a literary journal based in Rome.

2. Robert Duncan published the first version of "Often I Am Permitted to Return to a Meadow" and "The Law I Love is Major Mover" in *Ark II / Moby I* (1956/1957): 10–12.

3. Robert Duncan's play *Medea at Kolchis: The Maiden Head.*

### LETTER 36    November 1956

1. Peter Orlovsky (1933– ) was the companion and lover of Allen Ginsberg. Lafcadio is Peter's brother.

2. *Corot* (Milan: Mondadori, 1952).

### LETTER 37    November 1956

1. Jess tells the story (in conversation with the editors) of Allen Ginsberg and his group knocking on the apartment door asking for oregano. Jess put his hand on Ginsberg's breastbone and backed him down the hallway leading to the apartment and then closed the door.

2. Denise Levertov's poem "Scenes from the Life of the Pepper Trees," included in *Overland to the Islands.*

### LETTER 38    December 1956

1. Robert Creeley, *If You* (San Francisco: Porpoise Bookshop, 1956).

2. Robert Lowell, *The Mills of the Kavanaughs* (New York: Harcourt, Brace and World, 1951).

### LETTER 39    December 1956

1. Yvor Winters, "Problems for the Modern Critic of Literature," *Hudson Review* 9 (Autumn 1956): 325–86.

2. Matthew Phipps Shiel (1865–1947) wrote novels and four books of short stories, including *Shapes in the Fire* (London: John Lane, 1896) and

*The Invisible Voices* (New York: The Vanguard Press, 1935). The exact story mentioned has not been identified.

3. The word *heart's* is circled, with the notation: "might delete."

4. A typescript of "3 Poems from a Birthday Book" accompanied this letter.

### LETTER 40    January 1957

1. *Overland to the Islands* (1958).

### LETTER 41    February 1957

1. Robert Duncan was Assistant Director of the Poetry Center at San Francisco State University from September 1956 through June 1957.

2. *Fitzgerald to His Friends: Selected Letters of Edward Fitzgerald*, ed. Althea Hayter (London: Scholar Press, 1979).

3. Elizabeth Madox Roberts, *The Time of Man* (New York: The Modern Library, 1935) and *Black Is My True Love's Hair* (New York: Viking Press, 1938).

4. Robert Duncan, "Three Pages from a Birthday Book" and "Poetry, A Natural Thing," *Folio* 25 (Summer 1960): 2–3.

### LETTER 42    February 1957

1. "Scenes from the Life of the Peppertrees" was included in *Overland to the Islands*; "The Departure," two lines from which are quoted below, was included in *With Eyes at the Back of Our Heads.*

2. "Seven Poems for Marthe, My Wife," *Poetry* 89 (October 1956): 1–8.

### LETTER 43    March 1957

1. Published as *The Special View of History*, ed. Ann Charters (Berkeley: Oyez, 1970).

### LETTER 44    March 1957

1. The new one refers to "The Propositions," which was collected in *The Opening of the Field* along with "The Ballad of the Enamord Mage" and "The Ballad for Mrs. Noah."

2. William's famous dictum, used often, including "A Sort of Song."

### LETTER 45    March 1957

1. Wade Donahoe's "A Letter," *Origin* 1st ser. 20 (Winter 1957): 122–27, confirms his position in a

poetics much different from Robert Duncan's and Denise Levertov's.

2. "For a Muse Meant" was collected in *Letters*.

3. "From 'Book of Friends,'" Hugo von Hofmannsthal, *Selected Prose*, trans. Mary Hottinger, Tania & James Stern, intro. Hermann Broch (New York: Pantheon Books, 1952). Published as Bollingen Series 33.

4. A typescript, headed "Gleanings from Whitman" and containing "A Noiseless Patient Spider," lines from "Starting from Paumanok," and "Sail Out for Good, Eidólon Yacht!" accompanied this letter. Before the last poem Robert Duncan typed: "in 1891-2 Whitman was 72, within the year of his death and I thot of Lawrence's *The Ship of Death*." Pages are missing from this letter. Thus the following text appears out of order, but follows the context of the whole letter.

5. Robert Duncan's "The Spider Song" is part IV of "The Propositions."

## LETTER 47   April 1957

1. Jean Arp and Robert Motherwell, *The Dada Painters and Poets: An Anthology* (New York: Wittenborn, Schultz, 1951).

## LETTER 49   July 1957

1. Aunt Fay was Robert Duncan's mother's sister. She was a collector of books, including a *First Folio* of Shakespeare (1623); she was also a serious theosophist and spiritualist who had a strong influence on the young Robert Duncan.

2. "A Morning Letter," "The Temple of the Animals," "There's Too Much Sea on the Big Sur," "Poem," and "A Ride to the Sea" appeared in *Poetry* 90 (September 1957): 350-55.

## LETTER 50   August 1957

1. "Three Poems in Measure One: An Open Letter," unpublished. Larry Eigner's "Brink" was one of the poems Robert Duncan discussed.

2. John Crowe Ransom wrote in a letter to Robert Duncan dated 14 August 1957: "But I think you have an accurate poetic language; you get some difficult things said poetically. Somehow it seems a little heavy, a little contrived, but you are a good prospect." Robert Duncan quotes the phrase "a little heavy, a little contrived" in his poem "Poetry, a Natural Thing."

## LETTER 52   October 1957

1. "The Lovers" was collected in *Here and Now*; "A Stir in the Air" was collected in *Overland to the Islands*, and "The Departure" was collected in *With Eyes at the Back of Our Heads*.

2. "Marianne Moore, October 11, 1957," *Chicago Review* 45 (1999), 104-6.

3. "In the Sight of a Lyre, Little Spear, a Chair," *Poetry* 91 (January 1958): 256-60.

4. The poems won the Union League Prize.

5. The two poems were collected in *The Opening of the Field*.

## LETTER 53   October 1957

1. "Poetry, a Natural Thing." A holograph copy of "Poetry, A Natural Thing" is dated August 20, 1957, along with a holograph copy of "Keeping the Rhyme," dated August 24, 1957, and signed R. D.

2. The second issue of *The Evergreen Review* in 1957 was called "San Francisco Scene" and contained contributions by (and Harry Redl's photographs of) Kenneth Rexroth, Brother Antoninus, Jack Kerouac, Allen Ginsberg, Robert Duncan, Lawrence Ferlinghetti, Michael McClure, James Broughton, and others. Robert Duncan's poems were "This Place, Rumord To Have Been Sodom . . . ," "The Fear That Precedes . . . ," and seven sections of "The Structure of Rhyme" (21-29).

## LETTER 54   October 1957

1. Robert Duncan's review of Broughton's *True and False Unicorns* was published as "A Risk of Sympathies," *Poetry* 91 (February 1958), 328-32.

2. Creeley's short story "The Dress" was collected in The *Gold Diggers and Other Stories* (London: John Calder, 1965); *The Whip* (Worcester, England Migrant Books, 1957).

3. "The Question" was collected in *The Opening of the Field*.

## LETTER 55   October 1957

1. The letter begins at the end of the typescript of Duncan's poem "The Question."

## LETTER 57   November 1957

1. Frances Toor, *Treasury of Mexican Folkways* (New York: Crown Publishers, 1947).

2. Kenneth Rexroth's review of *Here and Now* is

"The Poetry of Denise Levertov," *Poetry* 91 (November 1957): 120–23.

**LETTER 58    November 1957**

1. A member of the English Department at Mills College in Oakland, California.

**LETTER 59    November 1957**

1. T. S. Eliot, *On Poetry and Poets* (New York: Farrar, Straus and Cudahy, 1957).

2. The letter is unfinished or the remainder lost.

**LETTER 62    December 1957**

1. Werner Wilhelm Jaeger (1888–1961), *Paideia: The Ideals of Greek Culture*, trans. Gilbert Highet (Oxford: Basil Blackwood, 1939).

**LETTER 63    December 1957**

1. The letter resumes by hand after the previous five paragraphs of typed text.

**LETTER 66    December 1957**

1. D. H. Lawrence, *Look, We Have Come Through* (London: Chatto & Windus, 1917). Lawrence's volume was important as Robert Duncan developed his poetics.

2. Jerry van der Wiele was a student at Black Mountain College.

3. The lines are from the first version of "Yes, As a Look Springs to Its Face," collected in *The Opening of the Field*.

**LETTER 67    December 1957**

1. Published as *5 Poems* by Denise Levertov with drawings by Jess (San Francisco: White Rabbit Press, 1958); the poems mentioned below appear in the booklet.

2. Kenneth Rexroth, *The New British Poets: An Anthology* (Norfolk, CT: New Directions, 1949).

**LETTER 69    January 1958**

1. Jack Spicer, *After Lorca* (San Francisco: White Rabbit Press, 1957).

2. This poem appeared under the title "Turning" in Denise Levertov's *Overland to the Islands*.

3. Among Duncan's letters to Levertov is a typescript signed "Robert Duncan / Jan. 19, 1958" and headed "INTRODUCTION FOR DENISE LEVERTOV." It reads:

"Let us turn our minds now to prepare for the poems we are to hear. They are songs of experience that the heart means to share. Where the beautiful thing is achieved we will be aware of a world transformed by the orders of feeling, and in turn of orders of feeling that arise from insight and devotion to the world about us. 'Freedom in art, as in life,' Marianne Moore writes, 'is the result of a discipline imposed by ourselves.' The art of Denise Levertov has grace in freedom for its discipline has been chosen in love. She has, for one thing, no thought of a literature or a performance or an entertainment in writing these poems; they have been written not for us to admire her—so let us not admire her. They have been written not for us to be impressed by her learning or her wit or her passionate vitality—so let us go with her, away from concerns that so often bring us to poetry readings—away to seek ourselves where she has sought, carried by her art that has found the way for her and will for us, to the heart of the reality, to rediscover the world. Overland to the islands of intense feeling, to the moment when the texts of what was outer become inner—to these very streets, rooms, shores where we too can see and hear; can come to have our share in the poetry of an immortalized here and now."

**LETTER 70    January 1958**

1. The last sheet of Letter 69 is written on a page on which is written a holograph draft, in Denise Levertov's hand, of the poem "The Take Off" (included in *With Eyes at the Back of Our Heads*), with a later note in Denise Levertov's hand: "Written on plane leaving Mexico after the 2 years there (leaving Oaxaca, I guess, or did we take the bus to D. F.?)."

**LETTER 72    February 1958**

1. Henry Allen Moe (1894–1975) was Secretary General (now called President) of the John Guggenheim Foundation from 1945 to 1966.

**LETTER 74    February 1958**

1. In Great Neck, Long Island.

**LETTER 75    March 1958**

1. Ruth Witt-Diamant.

2. Denise Levertov's "Notes of Discovery" in Mina Loy, *Lunar Baedecker & Time Tables* (Highlands, NC: Jargon Society, 1958). Published as Jargon 23.

LETTER 76    March 1958

1. The painting is identified as *Majorcan Pastorale* in Denise Levertov's letter of September 22, 1958.

2. Kenneth Rexroth, trans., *One Hundred Poems from the Japanese* (New York: New Directions, 1955) and Kenneth Rexroth, trans., *One Hundred Poems from the Chinese* (New York: New Directions, 1956); Waldo Frank, Lewis Mumford, et al., *America & Alfred Stieglitz* (New York: Doubleday, Doran, 1934).

LETTER 77    March 1958

1. Harry Jacobus (1927– ) was a California painter who met Jess in 1950 at the California School of Fine Arts and remained a close friend of both Jess and Duncan. In January 1955 he accompanied them to New York (where they met Levertov for the first time) on their way to Europe. See Duncan's "Statement on Jacobus for Borregaard's Musum," in Duncan's *A Selected Prose*, ed. Robert J. Bertholf (New York: New Directions, 1995), 194–95.

LETTER 78    March 1958

1. "To the Snake," included in *With Eyes at the Back of Our Heads*.

LETTER 80    April 1958

1. "February Evening in New York," "The Vigil," and "To the Snake," all included in *With Eyes at the Back of Our Heads*.

2. Denise Levertov's "A Happening," included in *With Eyes at the Back of Our Heads*. The phrase quoted in the next sentence is from that poem.

LETTER 81    April 1958

1. A holograph version of the poem "A Storm of White" accompanies this letter. See Appendix.

2. Robert Creeley's poem "Heroes" is collected in *For Love: Poems*.

LETTER 82    April 1958

1. Christina Georgina Rossetti (1830–1894), *Goblin Market* (London: Macmillan, 1893).

2. Heinrich Robert Zimmer, *Philosophies of India*, ed. Joseph Campbell (New York: Pantheon Books, 1951).

3. Louis Comfort Tiffany Exhibition at the Museum of Contemporary Crafts, New York City, January 24–April 6, 1958.

LETTER 83    April 1958

1. This incident happened publicly during her visit to San Francisco in January 1958.

2. *Greek Vases from the Hearst Collection*, Metropolitan Museum of Art, New York City, opened March 27, 1957, and continued indefinitely.

3. Robert Creeley's poems "Going to Bed" and "Saturday Afternoon" are collected in *For Love: Poems 1950–1960* (New York: Charles Scribner's Sons, 1962).

LETTER 86    May 1958

1. Louisa Matthiasdottir at the Tanager Gallery, New York City, May 2–May 22, 1958.

2. "Seurat Paintings and Drawings," Museum of Modern Art, New York City, March 22–May 11, 1958.

LETTER 87    May 1958

1. See Robert Duncan's essay on this poem: "Towards an Open Universe," in *Poets on Poetry*, ed. Howard Nemerov (New York: Basic Books, 1966): 133–46; reprinted in Robert Duncan's *Fictive Certainties*.

2. Kenneth Patchen, *Hurrah for Anything: Poems and Drawings* (Highlands, NC: Jonathan Williams, 1957).

3. "The Room," included in *With Eyes at the Back of Our Heads*.

4. Peter Lum, *The Stars in Our Heaven: Myth and Fable* (New York: Pantheon Books, 1948).

LETTER 88    May 1958

1. M. Raymond, *De Baudelaire au Surrealism* (Paris: J. Corti, 1952).

2. Francisco de Goya's painting *Alegoría del amor (Cupido & Psique?)* is in the collection of Francisco Cambó in Fundación Caja de Barcelona.

3. Levertov wrote below: "Yet a poem can sustain one . . . "

4. "Howl," *Evergreen Review* I.2 (1957): 137–47.

LETTER 89   May 1958

1. Robert Duncan's "Poem of Despondencies" was first published in *The Nation* 191 (19 November 1960): 399. A holograph copy (signed R. D., dated August 1957, and sent to Denise Levertov with an earlier letter, probably close to the date indicated) is followed by this note:

"(August 6, to be exact. Poem follows this entry in my notebook: '*Despondencies*: McClure— that he hated the city, that it was a spider web? What is the web? I askd. (of hypocrisies) superficial friendliness overlying loathing [as in my dream of "audience" as vermin?]—that he had no friends (we, accused, our insufficiency), that the city was ugly, that there were no seasons, that the light was hideous (as we returnd here always longing for the light of home).'

I found out later that the course of the poem did refer to what was actually eating him."

2. Igor Stravinsky, *Poetics of Music in the Form of Six Lessons*, trans. Arthur Knodel and Ingolf Dahl (Cambridge: Harvard University Press, 1947).

LETTER 92   August 1958

1. Collected in *With Eyes at the Back of Our Heads*.

2. "The Communion" was collected in *With Eyes at the Back of Our Heads*.

3. Both poems were collected in *The Opening of the Field*.

LETTER 93   August 1958

1. Among the Duncan letters is a typewritten sheet with the following version of lines from "Often I Am Permitted to Return to a Meadow" (included in *The Opening of the Field*), prefaced by "first writing January 1956" annd followed by "rewritten July 1958":

OFTEN I AM PERMITTED TO RETURN
  TO A MEADOW
That is not mine, but is a made place
—as if the mind made it up—a poem.

Often I am permitted to return to a hall
that is a made place, created by light
wherefrom the shadows that are forms fall.

Wherefrom fall all architectures I am
I say are likenesses of the First beloved
whose flowers are flames lit to the Lady.

Often I am permitted to return to a poem
where I too stirrd may burn however, poor
and turn my face to her shadowless door.

2. Robert Duncan's poem was collected in *The Opening of the Field*.

3. "Manifesto.

"1. We must understand what is really happening.

"2. If the verse makers of our time are to improve on their immediate precursors, we must be vitally aware of the duration of syllables, of melodic coherence, and the tone leading of vowels.

"3. The function of poetry is to debunk by lucidity.

"We, the CLEANERS, D. Simpson, L. C. Flynn, Igon Tan."

(*Four Pages*, (March 1948): [3] The "Manifesto" was first sent to Robert Duncan on a postcard by Dallam Simpson, but presumably the message came from Ezra Pound.

4. Denise Levertov has written next to the Eliot quotation: "same quote as Nov 30 57."

5. In Levertov's hand beneath: "1958."

6. Jeff Rahl appears in Robert Duncan's poem "UnderGround" (*The Opening of the Field*, 80)

> There may be
> here at the center of a chamber cut out
>      of context
> cenotaph for Jeff Rall who
>      in youth fell
> at Dunkirk, . . . .

Robert Duncan and Rall were friends from the Anarchist meetings of the late 1930s and early 1940s in New York City. They corresponded in 1942–43, and then again in 1961–64. Robert Duncan visited Rall during the Vancouver Poetry Conference in the summer of 1963. He was not killed at Dunkirk as Robert Duncan imagined in his poem.

7. Hans Vaihinger, *The Philosophy of "As If,"* trans. C. K. Ogden (London: Routledge & Kegan Paul, 1924).

8. *The Zohar*, trans. Harry Sperlin, Maurice Simon, and Dr. Paul Levertoff, 5 vols. (New York: The Rebecca Bennett Publications, 1958): 2: 13.

LETTER 95   September 1958

1. This letter is incomplete; a typescript of "Often I Am Permitted" (first version) and "Yes,

as a Look Springs to Its Face" (first version, incomplete) is attached. The last page is missing.

2. Jess's show at Dilexi Gallery, San Francisco, was called "Paste-ups and Assemblies," December 12, 1959–January 7, 1960.

3. Jess's paintings are: *Seasons of Astringency, Spring: Rappaccini's Daughter*, 1958; *Seasons of Astringency, Summer: Young Goodman Brown*, 1958; *Seasons of Astringency, Autumn: The Birthmark*, 1958; *Seasons of Astringency, Winter: The Snow Image*, 1958.

### LETTER 96    September 1958

1. Jakob Wasserman (1873–1934) wrote several books, including *My Life as German and Jew*, trans. S. N. Brainin (New York: Coward-McCann, 1933), *The Maurizius Case*, trans. Caroline Newton (New York: H. Liveright, 1929), and *The Dark Pilgrimage*, trans. Cyrus Brooks (New York: Liveright Publishing Co., 1933).

### LETTER 97    September 1958

1. Eloise Mixon (1922–1994) was a student at Black Mountain College. Eloise and Donald (her husband) both acted in the performance of Robert Duncan's play *Medea at Kolchis: The Maiden Head*, August 1956. The Mixons remained friends of Robert Duncan's household after they moved to Mill Valley, California. Later they moved to Australia, where Eloise died.

### LETTER 99    October 1958

1. Louis Ginsberg, *Legends of the Bible* (New York: Simon & Schuster, 1956).

### LETTER 100    October 1958

1. *The New American Poetry*, ed. Donald Allen (New York: Grove Press, 1960).

2. Helen Adam, *The Queen of Crow Castle* (San Francisco: White Rabbit Press, 1958), and Charles Olson, *O'Ryan 2 4 6 8 10* (San Francisco: White Rabbit Press, 1958).

### LETTER 101    October 1958

1. "To The Snake," "A Happening," "The Departure," "Seems Like We Must Be Somewhere Else," and "The Room" appeared in *Poetry* 93 (October 1958): 10–13.

2. Robert Duncan's poems "The Reaper" and "Hero Song" appeared in *The Faber Book of Modern American Verse*, ed. W. H. Auden (London: Faber & Faber, 1956).

### LETTER 102    October 1958

1. Levertov has written beside these phrases: "Here I see a pattern of stress not of pitch."

### LETTER 103    November 1958

1. A page is missing from the letter.

2. Barney Rosset at the Grove Press.

3. M. L. Rosenthal, "In Exquisite Chaos," *The Nation* 187 (November 1958): 324–27.

4. The letter is unfinished, as explained in the following letter.

### LETTER 104    November 1958

1. A. Alvarez, "Poetry Chronicle," *Partisan Review* 25 (Fall 1958): 603–9.

2. The Toltec poem was included as the epigraph to *With Eyes at the Back of Our Heads* in Toltec with a Spanish translation and Denise Levertov's own English translation entitled "The Artist."

3. The completed poem was called "A Ring of Changes" and included in *With Eyes at the Back of Our Heads*.

### LETTER 105    November 1958

1. George L. Trayer and Harry Lee Smith, *An Outline of English Structure* (Washington, D.C.: American Council of Learned Societies, 1957).

2. Francis Alexander Wilson, *W. B. Yeats and Tradition* (London: Gollancz, 1958).

3. This handwritten note appears at the end of a typescript, 3 carbon pages, of "An Open Letter to Friends & Readers," dated Nov. 8, 1958, and signed "Robert Duncan," which is referred to earlier in this letter as being sent with the letter. The "Open Letter" rehearses in detail and with dollar figures Robert Duncan's complaints about the pricing and marketing of *Letters* by Jonathan Williams.

### LETTER 106    November 1958

1. This poem was published as "A Ring of Changes" in *With Eyes at the Back of Our Heads*.

### LETTER 107    December 1958

1. Robert Carlton Brown (1886–1959) had a

varied career as a poet and novelist as well as a journalist in South America. For details of his life see *My Majonary* (Boston: John W. Luce, 1916), *Globe-gliding* (Diessen, Germany: Roving Eye Press, 1930).

2. Jean Cocteau's 1946 film.

LETTER 109    December 1958
1. Arthur Lang, ed. *The Red Fairy Book* (London: Longman, 1890).

2. Arthur Ransome (1884–1967) wrote many books, including *Swallows and Amazons* (Philadelphia: Lippincott, 1931) and *Old Peter's Russian Tales* (New York: Nelson & Sons, 1958).

LETTER 110    January 1959
1. Ingmar Bergman's 1956 film, which was the basis for Robert Duncan's poem "Ingmar Bergman's SEVENTH SEAL."

2. The folder was published as *14 Poets, 1 Artist* (New York: Jonathan Williams, 1958).

LETTER 112    January 1959
1. "Food for Fire, Food for Thought," is the closing poem of *The Opening of the Field*.

LETTER 113    February 1959
1. Hugh Lofting (1886–1947), *The Story of Dr. Doolittle: Being the History of His Peculiar Life at Home and Astonishing Adventures in Foreign Parts* (New York: Frederick A. Stokes, 1920), was the first of a series of books that also included *The Voyages of Dr. Doolittle* (New York: Frederick A Stokes, 1922) and *Dr. Doolittle's Circus* (New York: Frederick A. Stokes, 1924). See Letter 156.

LETTER 114    February 1959
1. *Virgina Quarterly Review* 34 (Summer 1958): [339]–54; *L'Iliustrazione Italiana* 85 (September 1958): 34–39.

2. *Paracelsus: Selected Writings*, ed. Jolande Jacobi, trans. Norbert Guterman (New York: Pantheon Book, 1985). Published as Bollingen Series 28.

3. See his notes in *Chicago Review* 45 (1999): 112–14.

LETTER 118    March 1959
1. Sheri Martinelli (1918–1996) was a model, an artist, and also a companion of Ezra Pound's when he was in St. Elizabeth's. She published a small volume: *La Martinelli*, intro., Ezra Pound (Milan: Officine Grafiche Esparia, 1956). She moved to San Francisco, and was part of the scene in North Beach as a poet and as an editor of the magazine *Anagogic and Paideumic Review* during the 1950s and 1960s. See Letter 359. See Steven Moore, "Sheri Martinelli: A Modernist Muse," *Gargoyle* 41 (1998): 29–54, and *Beerspit Night and Cursing: The Correspondence of Charles Bukowski and Sheri Martinelli, 1960–1967*, ed. Steven Moore (Santa Rosa, CA: Black Sparrow Press, 2001).

2. Philip Lamantia, *Narcotica (I Demand Extinction of Laws Prohibiting Narcotic Drugs)* (San Francisco: Auerhahn Press, 1959).

3. Jacob Böhme, *Six Theosophic Points, and Other Writings*, trans. John Rolleston Earle (Ann Arbor: University of Michigan Press, 1958).

LETTER 119    April 1959
1. The poem was collected as "Apprehensions" in *Roots and Branches*.

2. Jakob Böhme, *The Signature of All Things, with Other Writings* (London, J. M. Dent & Sons Ltd., 1926), and *Of the Incarnation of Jesus Christ*, trans. John Rolleston Earle (London: Constable, 1934).

3. Eugene Debs (1855–1926) was an American Socialist, pacifist, and union activist who helped to organize the Industrial Workers of the World (1905). He went to jail twice, once for strikebreaking and once for speeches opposing American involvement in World War I.

LETTER 120    April 1959
1. Hans Christian Andersen, *Fairy Tales*, trans. Mrs. E. Lucas and Charles Thomas and illus. William Robinson (London: J. M. Dent & Co., 1915), and *Masterpieces of Eilshemius* (New York: Artist's Gallery, 1959).

LETTER 121    April 1959
1. Louis Eilshemius (1864–1941) was an American painter with a sense of abstract style that made his rediscovery in the late 1950s important to the growth of Abstract Expressionism.

2. Jack Bilbo, Hugo Baruch (1907– ), was born in Germany. In England he was known as a

painter and an art critic. See his *Jack Bilbo: An Autobiography* (London: The Modern Art Gallery, 1948).

LETTER 122   May 1959

1. "The Goddess," "The Park," "Relative Figures Reappear," and "With Eyes at the Back of Our Heads" are collected in *With Eyes at the Back of Our Heads.*

2. A typescript of the poem "In Perplexity" is enclosed with Robert Duncan's signature at the bottom and the date May 22, 1959.

LETTER 123   May 1959

1. "Out of the Black," *The Nation* 188 (April 25, 1959): 196–97.

2. The exhibition *Gauguin: Paintings, Drawings, Prints, Sculpture* appeared at the Metropolitan Museum of Art, April 23–May 31, 1959.

3. Barbara Bank and her husband, the New York artist Howard Fussiner, were close friends of the Goodmans.

LETTER 124   June 1959

1. "A Ring of Changes," *Poetry* 94 (July 1959): 240–44. "The Communion" and "A Straw Swan under the Christmas Tree" appeared in the same issue on pp. 245–46. All three poems appeared in *With Eyes at the Back of Our Heads.*

LETTER 125   May–June 1959

1. Daisy Aldan, *A New Folder, Americans: Poems and Drawings*, foreword Wallace Fowlie (New York: Folder Editions, 1959).

2. *Poems in a Floating World.*

3. Paul Eluard, *Dur Désir de Durer*, trans. Stephen Spender and Frances Cornford (Philadelphia: Grey Falcon Press, 1950).

LETTER 126   June 1959

1. Lawrence Campbell, "Blaine Paints a Picture," *Art News* 58 (May 1959): 38–41, 61–62.

2. James Schuyler, "Bell Paints a Picture," *Art News* 57 (Sept 1968): 42–45, 61–62.

3. This sentence, apparently, was left incomplete.

4. *On My Eyes* (Highlands, NC: Jargon Society, 1960), published as Jargon 36.

5. Robert Duncan's review of Edward Dahl-

berg's "*The Sorrows of Priapus*: Against Nature," *Poetry* 94 (April 1959): 369–70.

6. Charlie Chaplin's 1936 film.

LETTER 127   July 1959

1. "Roots and Branches" was included in *Roots and Branches.*

2. "A Ring of Changes," was included in *With Eyes at the Back of Our Heads.* Levertov has written in the margin: "See 58 letter on this poem": see Letter 106.

LETTER 128   July 1959

1. Crunk [Robert Bly], "The Work of Robert Creeley," *The Fifties* 2 (1959): 21.

2. This sentence is marked by lines in both margins, perhaps by Denise Levertov.

LETTER 129   July 1959

1. "A Note on the Poetry of Larry Eigner," *Migrant* 3 (November 1959): 6–8.

2. See the postscript at the end of the letter.

3. "The Five-Day Rain," *Evergreen Review* 3 (Summer 1959): 35, was included in *With Eyes at the Back of Our Heads.*

4. "A Ring of Changes," *Poetry* 94 (July 1959): 240–44.

5. C. H. Kwock and Vincent McHugh, *Why I Live on the Mountain: 30 Chinese Poems from the Great Dynasties* (San Francisco: Golden Mountain Press, 1958).

6. D. H. Lawrence, *The Trespasser*, introd. Richard Aldington (London: Heinemann, 1955).

LETTER 130   July 1959

1. Lawrence Lipton, *The Holy Barbarians* (New York: Messner, 1959).

2. Harry Redl had taken the photographs that had appeared in the "San Francisco Scene" issue of *The Evergreen Review* in 1957.

3. Both poems are collected in *Jacob's Ladder.*

4. "The Wife" is collected in *With Eyes at the Back of Our Heads.*

LETTER 131   July 1959

1. "The Shifting" appeared in Origin 1st ser. 6 (Summer 1952): 114, and was included, under the title "Turning," in *Overland to the Islands.*

2. "Relative Figures Reappear" was included.

LETTER 132    July 1959

1. Robert Duncan's "Nel Mezzo del Camin di Nostra Vita," about the Watts Towers in Los Angeles and its artist-architect, Simon Rodilla, was included in *Roots and Branches*.

LETTER 133    July–August 1959

1. Robert Duncan illustrated *Letters* with several drawings of the Ideal Reader, always wearing a large hat.

2. Robert Duncan's *Selected Poems* (San Francisco: City Lights, 1959).

3. "Three Poems in Measure One: An Open Letter," a typescript sent to several of Robert Duncan's friends, which remains unpublished.

LETTER 134    August 1959

1. Robert Duncan cites the "Manifesto" that he had mentioned in Letter 93 to answer Denise Levertov's question in Letter 133: "whose is / are the quoted line/s on p. 32 of *Poems 1948*—the 'Imaginary Instructions' part of the 'Venice Poem'?" The "Manifesto" was printed in *Four Pages* (March 1948): [3].

2. Published as "Ideas of the Meaning of Form" *4* (1961): 60–74, and included in *Fictive Certainties*.

3. Hugh Kenner, *The Invisible Poet: T. S. Eliot* (New York: McDowell, Obolensky, 1959).

LETTER 135    August 1959

1. Alfred North Whitehead, *Process and Reality: An Essay in Cosmology* (New York: Macmillan Co., 1929). Robert Duncan read this book under Charles Olson's influence.

2. "Come into Animal Presence," included in *The Jacob's Ladder*.

LETTER 136    August 1959

1. "On Reading the Early Poetry of Robert Duncan" was printed as a broadside announcement (Berkeley: Oyez Press, 1966) of Robert Duncan's book *The Years as Catches* and reprinted in *The Poet in the World*.

2. "Dream Data," the first section of "A Sequence of Poems for H. D.'s Birthday," was included in *Roots and Branches*.

3. "The Goddess" was included in *With Eyes at the Back of Our Heads*.

4. Published as "I must wake up into the morning world," the second section of "A Sequence of Poems for H. D.'s Birthday," included in *Roots and Branches*. The poem mentions Herbert and Vaughan.

5. Included in *With Eyes at the Back of Our Heads* under the title "Art."

LETTER 137    August 1959

1. "The Song of the Borderguard" in *The Book of Resemblances*.

2. "A Poem Beginning with a Line by Pindar," included in *The Opening of the Field*.

LETTER 138    August 1959

1. Denise Levertov wrote in the margin: "What were these notes of mine on R D & what became {illegible}."

2. Blaise Cendrars's *L'Anthologie negre*. See Letter 4.

3. *African Folktales and Sculpture*, ed. Paul Radin and James Johnson Sweeney (New York: Pantheon Books, 1952). Published as Bollingen Series 32.

4. Denise Levertov wrote in the margin: "Not of course a dream but a real llama I met."

LETTER 139    August 1959

1. This letter was enclosed with the following letter.

LETTER 140    September 1959

1. "The Boobas and the Bunny Duck" story, by Michael McClure with drawings by Jess, remains unpublished.

2. Robert Creeley, "The Awakening," *Migrant* 2 (September 1959): 1, and Robert Duncan, "A Note" and "Solitude" in the same issue, 22–23.

3. This scholar of Jewish mysticism is mentioned in section 6 of Robert Duncan's "A Sequence of Poems for H. D.'s Birthday."

LETTER 141    September 1959

1. Vladimir Sergeyevich Solovyov (1853–1900), *Lectures on Godmanship*, introd. Peter Peter Zouboff (London, Dennis Dobson, 1948); Robert Duncan belonged to the Mechanics Library, a private subscription library in San Francisco.

2. A typescript of "A Letter," which begins

"Dear Carpenter," accompanied this letter. It was published as "Dear Carpenter" in *J* 2 (October 1959), 10–12, and it was included as "A Letter" in *Roots and Branches*. *J* ran for several mimeographed issues.

LETTER 142    September 1959

1. The Fogg Museum at Harvard.

2. Edward Dorn, *What I See in the Maximus Poems* (Ventura, CA: Migrant Press, 1960).

3. Michael Shayer, "Six Poems": "Hytleby," "Durham Cathedral," "Poem: I Thought . . . As I Sat in Russell Square," "Two Psychological Poems," "Oslo-Dago: 1–10"; *Combustion* 11 September 1959): 7–10. Gael Turnbull published poems in the same issue of *Combustion*: "Les Toits," "A Lamb," "The Priests of Paris": 6–7.

4. This letter is unfinished or the remainder missing.

LETTER 143    October 1959

1. Published as "A Note (on the Work of the Imagination)" in *Migrant* 5 (March 1960): 3–4, and reprinted in *The Poet in the World*.

2. Arthur Rackham (1867–1939) was a well-known and prolific illustrator of many kinds of books. See his Hans Andersen, *Tales, English: Selections, Fairy Tales* (London: Harrap, 1932); Edmund Dulac (1882–1953) was an equally well-known and prolific illustrator; see his Hans Christian Andersen, *Tales. English. Selections. Stories* (London: Hodder & Stoughton, 1911).

3. Denise Levertov wrote in the margin beside this paragraph: "Diff. here seems to be between what connects with what we experience as "laws of Nature" & things "contra naturam" though—not between nice things and nasty things. The Imag. deals with reality, as Stevens says . . . "

4. In Denise Levertov's hand: "(never finished —see Dec. 6, 1960)." It was finally sent with Letter 180 of that date.

LETTER 144    October 1959

1. Seon Givens was an editor at Vanguard Press, and was a friend of Robert Duncan in New York in the early 1940s. She was Irish, and edited *James Joyce: Two Decades of Criticism* (New York: Vanguard Press, 1948). She married Robert Manley.

2. Elfmere is the name of the house Robert Duncan and Jess rented at Stinson Beach.

3. Six poems by Robert Duncan and two poems by Wendell Berry appeared in *Poetry* 91 (March 1958).

LETTER 147    November 1959

1. Robert Duncan's essay "The Homosexual in Society," *Politics* 1 (August 1944): 209–11. Robert Duncan revised the text in 1959 at the request of Seymour Krim. The revised essay was rejected for Krim's anthology, *The Beats* (Greenwich, CT: Fawcett, 1960) and was finally collected in *A Selected Prose*.

2. A typescript of "A Sequence of Poems for H. D.'s Birthday, September 10, 1959" accompanies this letter; page 2 of the typescript is missing.

LETTER 148    January 1959

1. *An Anthology of Spanish Poetry from Garcilaso to Garcia Lorca*, ed. Angel Flores (New York: Anchor Books, Doubleday, 1961). Denise Levertov translated the poem "The House of Alvargonzáles."

2. The paragraph about Nell Blaine is written on the back of the envelope.

LETTER 149    December 1959

1. Andrey Belyi, *St. Petersburg*, trans. John Cournos (New York: Grove Press, 1959).

2. James Reaney, "A Cellar Song" and "The Windyard" in *Poetry* 94 (September 1959): 380–81.

LETTER 150    December 1959

1. Charles Robinson and William Canton, *The True Annals of Fairy-land: The Reign of King Herla* (London: J. M. Dent, 1900).

2. Robert Duncan's biographical statement for *The New American Poetry*, ed. Donald Allen (New York: Grove Press, 1960), appears on pp. 432–36.

3. The last two lines of Emerson's poem "Give All to Love."

LETTER 151    January 1960

1. *With Eyes at the Back of Our Heads*.

2. "The Take Off" is in fact in *With Eyes at the Back of Our Heads*; "The Depths," "The World Outside," "Six Variations," "Son for a Dark Voice,"

and "Come into Animal Presence" would be in Denise Levertov's next collection, *The Jacob's Ladder.*

LETTER 152    January 1960
1. Robert Duncan's 1959 revision of his 1944 essay "The Homosexual in Society."
2. White Rabbit books were published in San Francisco by Joe Dunn and Jack Spicer.
3. Christopher Hill's review of Brown's *Love's Body,* entitled "Luther and Freud," appeared not in *The Observer* but in *The Spectator* 6858 (December 4, 1959): 831.

LETTER 153    January 1960
1. Robert Creeley's reading was on July 16, 1959. See Robert Duncan's "Introduction," *Chicago Review* 45. 2 (1999): 114–18.
2. Robert Creeley, *A Form of Women* (New York: Jargon, 1959).

LETTER 154    January 1960
1. Hubert Crehan, "Clyfford Still: Black Angel in Buffalo," *Art News* (December 1959): 32, 58–60.
2. *Elmer Bischoff: Recent Paintings,* Staempfli Gallery, New York, January 23–February 10, 1960.

LETTER 155    January 1960
1. Denise Levertov's letter begins in her hand below a typed letter from Hubert Crehan, dated January 28, 1960, and finishes on a second sheet. Below the name of Silas Rhodes, publisher of *Proof,* in the letterhead of Crehan's letter, she wrote the exclamation above.

LETTER 156    February 1960
1. Clifford Still's show at the Metart Gallery, 527 Bush Street in San Francisco, lasted from June 17 through July 14, 1950.
2. Hugh Lofting (1886–1947), *Doctor Doolittle in the Moon* (Frederick A. Stokes, 1928). See Letter 115.
3. The words quoted are from Denise Levertov's poem "The Rainwalkers," included in *The Jacob's Ladder.*
4. The poems took the title "Apprehensions" in *Roots and Branches.*

LETTER 157    February 1960
1. Jess Collins, *O* (New York: Hawk's Well Press, 1960); Robert Duncan, *Faust Foutu* (Stinson Beach,

CA: Enkidu Surrogate, 1959); Jack Spicer, *Billy the Kid* (Stinson Beach, CA: Enkidu Surrogate, 1959). Enkidu Surrogate was Robert Duncan's imprint, a surrogate of White Rabbit Press.

LETTER 158    February 1960
1. The poem appared in *Poetry* 96 (April 1960): 5–6, and was collected in *The Jacob's Ladder.*

LETTER 162    February 1960
1. The letter is preceded by a typescript of the first two sections of Robert Duncan's poem "Apprehensions."

LETTER 163    March 1960
1. Richard Ellman, *James Joyce* (New York: Oxford University Press, 1959).

LETTER 166    March 1960
1. Pierre Boulez, *Le Marteu sans maître: Pour voix d'alto et 6 instruments, textes de René Char* (London: Universal Edition, 1957).
2. Karl Shapiro, "T. S. Eliot: The Death of Literary Judgement," *Saturday Review* 43 (27 February 1960): 12–17, 34–36.
3. G. R. S. Mead, *Fragments of a Faith Forgotten: The Gnostic, a Contribution to the Study of the Origins of Christianity* (New Hyde Park, NY: University Books, 1960).

LETTER 167    April 1960
1. The exhibition *Claude Monet: Seasons and Moments* appeared at the Museum of Modern Art in New York City, March 9–May 15, 1960.

LETTER 168    June 1960
1. *Bid Me to Live: A Madrigal* (New York: Grove Press, 1960).
2. *D. H. Lawrence: A Composite Biography,* ed. Edward Nehls, 3 vols. (Madison: University of Wisconsin Press, 1957–59).
3. "Variations on Two Dicta of William Blake," included in *Roots and Branches.*

LETTER 169    June 1960
1. *With Eyes at the Back of Our Heads.*
2. Denise Levertov's review of Zukofsky's 1–12 was published as "A Necessary Poetry," *Poetry* 92 (November 1960): 102–9.

3. Sybille Bedford, *A Legacy* (London: Collins, 1956); Isaac Bashevis Singer, *The Magician of Lublin*, trans. Elaine Gottliebt and Joseph Singer (New York: Farrar, Straus & Giroux, 1960).

4. Jacques Maritain, *Creative Imagination in Art & Poetry* (New York: Pantheon Books, 1953). published as Bollingen Series 35.

LETTER 170   June 1960

1. The letter is incomplete or the conclusion is missing.

LETTER 171   July 1960

1. The phrase and greeting are on a separate sheet that may not be part of this letter.

LETTER 172   August 1960

1. "Five Poems from Mexico," included in *The Jacob's Ladder.*

2. Robert Duncan's "Variations on Two Dicta of William Blake."

3. Evelyn Underhill, *Practical Mysticism* (London: E. P. Dutton, 1919).

LETTER 173   August 1960

1. Denise Levertov's "In Memory of Boris Pasternak," included in *The Jacob's Ladder.*

2. Denise Levertov's "The Jacob's Ladder," the title poem of her 1961 collection.

3. "The Risk" was collected in *Roots and Branches.*

4. H. D., *Bid Me to Live: A Madrigal* (New York: Grove Press, 1960).

5. Randall Jarrell, "Poetry in War and Peace," *Partisan Review* 12 (Winter 1945): 120–26.

6. *The Complete Poems of D. H. Lawrence,* 2 vols. (London: Heinemann, 1957).

LETTER 174   September 1960

1. Jess's show was: "Paste-Ups and Assemblies," Dilexi Gallery, San Francisco, December 12, 1960– January 7, 1961.

2. Robert Kelly, "Notes on the Poetry of Deep Image," *Trobar* 2 (1961): 14–16.

LETTER 175   September 1960

1. "Four Songs the Nightnurse Sang" was collected in *Roots and Branches.*

LETTER 176   October 1960

1. The jazz musician Race Newton and his wife.

LETTER 177   November 1960

1. Denise Levertov was awarded the Bess Hokin Prize by *Poetry* (Chicago) for "With Eyes at the Back of Our Heads"; Robert Creeley was awarded the Levinson Prize for "Ten Poems"; and Robert Duncan was awarded the Harriet Monroe Memorial Prize for poems from *The Opening of the Field.*

2. Ebbe Borregaard converted rooms in a house at 1713 Buchanan Street in San Francisco into a kind of gallery space in April 1960. Jess showed some paintings there in early 1961. Robert Duncan gave a series of lectures there on "The History of Poetry," December 15, 1960–January 26, 1961. The first performances of the songs and ballads of Helen and Pat Adam's *San Francisco's Burning* took place there on Halloween 1960. The gallery lasted through May 1961.

LETTER 178   November 1960

1. Gerrit Lansing was the editor of *Set*, to whom Robert Duncan sent the poem "Osiris and Set," which was collected in *Roots and Branches* (1964).

2. R. T. Rundle Clark, *Myth and Symbol in Ancient Egypt* (London: Thames and Hudson, 1960).

3. Denise Levertov's "Three Meditations," *The Chelsea Review* 8 (October 1960): 20–22, included in *The Jacob's Ladder* (1961).

4. James Wright was awarded the Ohiona Book Award for his book *Saint Judas* (Middletown, CT: Wesleyan University Press, 1959).

LETTER 179   November 1960

1. *The Complete Poems of Emily Dickinson,* ed. Thomas H. Johnson (Boston: Little Brown & Co., 1960).

2. The verso contains the typescript of two Dickinson poems from the Johnson edition: "Going—to—Her" and "Better—than Music! For I—who heard it—."

LETTER 181   December 1960

1. Denise Levertov's letter is written on the back of Nik's linoleum cut showing Santa Claus in a sleigh with sacks of presents under a starry sky with

the hind part of the reindeer disappearing into the left-hand margin. Above the sleigh in Nik's script are the words "Merry Xmas! (& New Year)" and below "from _____" with blank space unfilled.

LETTER 182   January 1961

1. Ed Dorn, "Los Mineros," *Chelsea* 8 (1960): 66–68.

2. "The Argument," *Floating Bear* 11 (1961): [7–8].

3. "An Order That Will Sing," *The Nation* 192 (May 13, 1961): 417–18.

4. James Wright, *Saint Judas*.

5. "A Necessary Poetry," *Poetry* 92 (November 1960): 102–9.

6. See, for example, "Hazards of Sitting for My Portrait," *The Observer* (November 27, 1960): 24.

7. "A Note (on the Work of the Imagination)." See Letter 143, n. 1.

8. *Nineteenth Century German Tales*, ed. Angel Flores (Garden City, NY: Doubleday, 1959). See letter #317 and letter #327.

9. William Kinter was a member of the English Department at Muhlenberg College in Allentown, Pennsylvania. Denise Levertov's poem "A Letter to William Kinter of Muhlenberg" appeared in *The Jacob's Ladder*.

10. The exhibition *Art Nouveau: Art and Design at the Turn of the Century* appeared at the Museum of Modern Art in New York City, June 6–September 6, 1960, and in Pittsburgh, October 13–December 12, 1960.

11. Hector Guimard (1867–1842) was an Art Nouveau architect, best known for Paris Métro entrances made about 1900.

LETTER 183   January 1961

1. "The Fountain," included in *The Jacob's Ladder*.

LETTER 184   January 1961

1. Robert Hatch was the Managing Editor of *The Nation* who wrote to Robert Duncan and Denise Levertov. See Letter 186. The special section was entitled "On the Smashing of Forms," *The Nation* 192 (April 22, 1961).

2. Dame Edith Sitwell's review of A. Alvarez's book *The Shaping Spirit* is "Better Bye and Bye," *Sunday Times* (June 29, 1958): 7.

3. Dame Edith Sitwell, *Alexander Pope* (London: Faber & Faber, 1930).

4. Bruno Bettelheim, "Joey: A Mechanical Boy," *Scientific American* 200 (March 1959): 116–20; Bettelheim's article about the extermination of the Jews by the Nazis appeared in the same issue of Dwight Macdonald's *Politics* as Duncan's article "The Homosexual in Society." See Bettelheim, "Behavior in Extreme Situations," *Politics* 1.7 (August 1944): 199–209.

LETTER 185   January 1961

1. Robert Duncan's poem "Nel Mezzo Del Cammin di Nostra Vita," *National Review* 10 (January 14, 1961): 20.

2. The finished poem is the second part of "Two Presentations," included in *Roots and Branches*.

LETTER 186   January 1961

1. Goodman's novel *The End of It* (New York: Horizon Press, 1961).

2. Denise Levertov's article was not published in the special section, but later as "What Is a Prose Poem?," *The Nation* 193 (December 23, 1961): 518.

3. John Frederick Nims was Visiting Editor of *Poetry* January through September 1961.

4. At this time Hugh Kenner was acting as a Poetry Editor for *The National Review*, but he did not accept any poems by Denise Levertov.

LETTER 187   February 1961

1. Ernst Jünger, *The Glass Bees*, trans. Louise Bogan and Elizabeth Meyer (New York: Noonday Press, 1961).

LETTER 189   November 1961

1. James Wright, "The Few Poets of England and America," *Minnesota Review* 1.2 (Winter 1961): 248–56; Cecil Hemley, "Within a Budding Grove," *Hudson Review* 13.4 (Winter 1960–61): 626–30.

2. John Ashbery, "Europe," *Big Table* 4 (1960): 24–50.

3. Published as "Ideas of the Meaning of Form," but not, as it would turn out, in *The Nation* but in *Kulchur* 4 (1961): 60–74.

LETTER 190   April 1961

1. *The Jacob's Ladder*.

2. The Longview Foundation for Education in World Affairs and International Understanding.

3. C. S. Lewis, *Till We Have Faces: A Myth Retold* (New York: Harcourt Brace, 1957).

4. Michael Rumaker, "The Morning Glory," *Evergreen Review* 5 (March–April 1961): 68–77.

5. Published as *End to Torment* (New York: New Directions, 1979).

## LETTER 191   April 1961

1. The poem was published as "Poem" in *Migrant* 8 (September 1960): 33–34 but collected in *Roots and Branches* as "Come, Let Me Free Myself."

2. "The Effort" in *The Green American Tradition: Essays and Poems for Sherman Paul*, ed. H. Daniel Peck (Baton Rouge: Lousiana State University Press, 1989): 263–79.

3. Ted Enslin, "Seven Poems," *Origin* 2d ser. 1 (April 1961): 35–38.

## LETTER 192   April 1961

1. "Shelley's *Arethusa* Set to New Measures," included in *Roots and Branches*.

2. Jess's painting took the title *Fountain of Arethusa*.

3. "After Reading H. D.'s *Hermetic Definitions*," *Trobar* 4 (1962): 1–3; included in *Roots and Branches*. Robert Duncan consistently mistook the name of H. D.'s poetic sequence *Hermetic Definition*.

## LETTER 193   May 1961

1. *The Nation* 192 (April 22, 1961), 348.

2. Jess's translations from the German of Christian Morgenstern's *Gallows Songs*.

3. Robert Bly's article "Poetry in an Age of Expansion" replaced Robert Duncan's rejected essay in the "Smashing of Forms" issue of *The Nation*, 192 (April 22, 1961): 350–54; Howard Warshaw, "Return of Naturalism as the 'Avant-Garde'" in the same issue of *The Nation*: 344–46.

4. Denise Levertov's "The Well" and "The Illustration," both included in *The Jacob's Ladder*.

5. Satyajit Ray's 1959 film.

6. Jean Renoir's 1934 film.

7. Adolf Eichmann (1906–1961), a German adminstrator, was captured in Argentina and taken to Israel for trial for serious crimes against the Jews during World War II. He was convicted of the slaughter of thousands of Jews and hung. Denise Levertov's sequence "During the Eichmann Trial" appeared in *The Jacob's Ladder*.

## LETTER 194   May 1961

1. "What Is a Prose Poem?," *The Nation* 193 (December 23, 1961): 518.

## LETTER 195   June 1961

1. Robert Duncan's essay "Ideas of the Meaning of Form," rejected by Robert Hatch for *The Nation*, attacks the critic Elizabeth Drew.

2. *Deo volente*, God willing.

3. The Paterson Society, Cambridge, Massachusetts, was a literary society which arranged readings for poets at colleges and universities, made grants to small presses, and distributed their books. It was active from 1959 to 1961. The Society published one-page "Statements" by poets. Denise Levertov wrote one of these.

4. Octavio Paz, "St. John Perse: Poet as Historian," *The Nation* 192 (June 17, 1961): 522–24.

## LETTER 200   August 1961

1. The Perse article was published as "The Poetic Vocation: St. John Perse," *Jubilee* 9 (November 1961): 36–41. See Letter 203 and Letter 220.

2. The second of three sections of H. D.'s *Hermetic Definition*.

## LETTER 201   August 1961

1. Richard Wilbur, "Junk," *The Nation* 193 (September 2, 1966): 126.

2. Charles Olson, *O'Ryan 2 4 6 8 10*, with drawings by Jess (San Francisco: White Rabbit Press, 1958).

3. The man with the house in Cornwall in the novel is, in fact, based on the musician Cecil Gray.

## LETTER 202   August 1961

1. Underlined twice.

## LETTER 203   August 1961

1. Robert Fitzgerald's translation of St. John Perse' *Chroniques* (New York: Pantheon, 1961). Fitzgerald's own poems are collected in *In the Rose of Time* (New York: New Directions, 1956)

and *Spring Shade* (New York: New Directions, 1956).

2. "An Order That Will Sing," *The Nation* 192 (May 13, 1961): 417.

3. United States Information Service is the title used in foreign counties, while United States Information Agency is the title used in the U.S. for this branch of The Fulbright Act.

4. Pheonix Bookstore. Robert Duncan's book was *Heavenly City, Earthly City*.

LETTER 204    September 1961

1. Gilbert Sorrentino, "[Letter]," *Floating Bear* 11 (1961): [2–4].

2. Gilbert Sorrentino reviewed Philip Whalen's *Like I Say* and *Memoirs of an Interglacial Age*, *Kulchur* 3 (1961): 79–81.

LETTER 205    September 1961

1. Richard Stone and Edward Klinà, who lived in Boston, visited Robert Duncan and Jess at Stinson Beach. Klinà purchased two paintings by Jess, "The Breakdown on the Haywain," and "The Earth Is the Fire in the Head."

2. Anon., *Little Thistledown* (London: Cassell Peter Galpin, 1882).

LETTER 208    September 1961

1. Denise Levertov's "September 1961," included in *O Taste and See*.

LETTER 209    October 1961

1. "Poets of the Given Ground," *The Nation* 193 (October 14, 1961): 251–53.

2. Robert Duncan, "Properties and Our Real Estate," and Kay Johnson, "Proximity," *Journal for the Protection of All Beings* 1 (1961): 84–94 and 13–17. The *Journal* was published by City Lights Books.

LETTER 210    October 1961

1. Curzio Malaparte, trans. Caesar Foligno *Kaputt* (New York: E. P. Dutton & Co., 1946), and *The Skin*, trans. David Moore (London: Alvin Redman, 1954).

2. *Modern American and Modern British Poetry*, ed. Louis Untermeyer, with Karl Shapiro and Richard Wilbur (New York: Harcourt, Brace & Co., 1955).

LETTER 211    October 1961

1. "September 1961," included in *O Taste and See*.

LETTER 212    October 1961

1. Robert Creeley's daughter Leslie died October 1, 1961, in New Mexico when a sand bank fell in on her.

2. Both poems are collected in *Roots and Branches*.

LETTER 214    October 1961

1. Mae Belle Beim was a member of the English Department at Mills College, Oakland, California.

LETTER 217    October 1961

1. "Adam's Way" was Robert Duncan's new play, and "The Origins of Old Son" was the play performed at Black Mountain College.

2. Louis Bogan, "Verse," *New Yorker* 20 (October 21, 1944): 91–92, "Briefly Noted," *New Yorker* 21 (December 29, 1945): 68 and "Briefly Noted," *New Yorker* 22 (December 14, 1946): 147. For Jarrell's article see Letter 173, n. 5.

LETTER 218    November 1961

1. Western Union telegram.

LETTER 222    November 1961

1. *Contemporary American Poetry*, ed. Donald Hall (Harmondsworth, Middlesex, England: Penguin Books, 1962).

2. *The Jacob's Ladder*.

LETTER 223    November 1961

1. "The Walls Do Not Fall," the first poem in H. D's *Trilogy*, is dedicated to Bryher.

2. See *Welsh Legends and Folk-Tales*, retold by Gwyn Jones, illus. Joan Kiddell-Monroe (London: Oxford University Press, 1955) and *The Mabinogion*, trans. Gwyn Jones and Thomas Jones (London: J. M. Dent, 1949).

3. The letter breaks off here or the remainder is lost.

LETTER 224    November 1961

1. Robert McAlmon, *Being Geniuses Together* (London: Secker and Warburg, 1938).

2. Erich Heidt and his wife Dori visited Robert

Duncan and Jess at Stinson Beach September 1, 1959. Heidt was H. D.'s primary physician and therapist during her last years in Switzerland.

LETTER 225 November 1961

1. H. Rider Haggard's novel *Ayesha* (New York: Doubleday, 1905).

LETTER 229 December 1961

1. W. S. Merwin, "The Saint of the Upland," *The Nation* 193 (December 6, 1961): 479.

2. Underlined twice.

3. "Song for Ishtar" and "The Ache of Marriage," both included in *O Taste and See.*

LETTER 230 January 1962

1. Rodolphe Bresdin (1822–1885). French printmaker. The print is entitled "The Good Samaritan" (1861).

2. "An Appreciation," *Poetry* 100 (June 1962): 182–86; reprinted in *The Poet in the World.*

3. Grace James, *Green Willow and Other Japanese Fairy Tales* (London: Macmillan, 1923).

4. Tet Borsig, *Designs in Nature* (New York: Viking Press, 1961).

LETTER 231 January 1962

1. Creeley held a teaching position at the University of New Mexico at the time.

2. Robert Duncan's poems are "The Law" and "Two Dicta of William Blake," *Poetry* 99 (December 1961): 168–77.

LETTER 233 February 1962

1. Robert L. Benson at this point was a visiting Professor of Medieval History at Cornell University and author of the book *The Bishop-Elect: A Study in Medieval Ecclesiastical Office* (Princeton: Princeton University Press, 1968). He and Robert Duncan were friends from Berkeley in 1947–49. See Letter 263.

LETTER 234 February 1962

1. "H. D.," *Bryn Mawr Alumnae Bulletin* 42 (Fall 1961): 20; reprinted in *The Complete Prose of Marianne Moore* (New York: Viking Press, 1986).

2. Mimi Goldberg's book *The Lover and Other Poems* (Philadelphia: Kraft Publishing Co., 1961) contained an Introduction by William Carlos Williams.

LETTER 235 February 1962

1. Christina Rosetti and Arthur Hughes, *Speaking Likenesses* (London: Macmillan, 1900).

LETTER 236 February 1962

1. *Odilon Redon, Gustave Moreau, Rodolphe Bresdin,* at the Art Institute of Chicago, March 2–April 15, 1962.

2. *The Chariot: Tarot VII* (1962).

3. "From the Day Book (Excerpts from an Extended Study of H. D.'s Poetry," *Origin* 2d ser. 10 (July 1963): 1–47.

4. Henry Corbin, *Avicenna and the Visionary Recital,* trans. Willard Trask (New York: Pantheon Books, 1960).

LETTER 237 March 1962

1. John Sweeney, Curator of the Woodberry Poetry Room at Harvard.

2. This seeming conclusion to the letter with sign-off is written upside down before the main text of the letter.

3. A. R. Ammons, "Three Poets," *Poetry* 46 (April 1960): 52–55.

LETTER 238 March 1962

1. "A Set of Romantic Hymns," included in *Roots and Branches,* is included in typescript with this letter.

LETTER 239 March 1962

1. The letter is incomplete or the rest is missing.

LETTER 241 April 1962

1. James and Ann Truitt were Robert Duncan's friends from Berkeley in 1947–49.

2. The Delaware Art Museum contains the English Pre-Raphaelite Collection, donated by Samuel and Mary R. Bancroft.

LETTER 242 April 1962

1. Philadelphia Museum of Art contains The Walter and Louise Arensberg Collection. The Rodin Museum is on Benjamin Franklin Parkway in Philadelphia.

LETTER 245 May 1962

1. The poem about John Button was never published by Levertov. The lines quoted in the

poem are from her poem "Clouds," published in *The Jacob's Ladder*. The typescript reproduced here seems to be a later, slightly revised draft of the one sent with this letter. However, since the first draft is missing and since Duncan comments on the text in detail in Letters 246 and 248, this revised version is given here as a guide to his remarks.

LETTER 247 May 1962

1. Elements from the lines about the father-in-law did find their way, much transformed, into the poem "The Old Adam," included in *O Taste and See*.

2. Hyde Soloman (1911–1982) was an American painter known for his abstract paintings and landscape paintings with deep internal structures, and for luminous effects of paint.

3. See Robert Wilson's memoir *Seeing Shelley Plain* (New Castle, DE: Oak Knolls Press, 2001). Larry Walrich later owned a book shop on Queen Street in Toronto.

4. See *Amerikanske Stemmer: Et udvalg af amerikansk lyric fran første halvdel af det tyvende århundrede I dansk gendigtning*, ed. Jens Nyholm (Copenhagen: Arne Frost-Hansens Forlag, 1968).

LETTER 248 May 1962

1. Robert Ambelain, *La Kabbale pratique* (Paris: Niclaus, 1951).

2. Pierre Teilhard de Chardin, *The Phenomenon of Man* (New York: Harper & Row, 1959).

LETTER 249 June 1962

1. "Night Scenes I, II, III," *The Floating Bear* 19 (1962): [1–3].

2. Aleister Crowley, *The Works of Aleister Crowley*, 3 vols. (London: Society for the Propagation of Religious Truths, 1905).

3. "*For Love*, by Robert Creeley," *New Mexico Quarterly* 32 (Autumn/Winter 1962–63): 219–24; reprinted in *A Selected Prose*.

LETTER 252 July 1962

1. Robert Duncan's "Adam's Way," included in *Roots and Branches*.

LETTER 253 July 1962

1. "H. D.: An Appreciation," *Poetry* 100 (June 1962): 182–86.

2. Both poems were collected in *O Taste and See*.

LETTER 254 July 1962

1. All three poems were collected in *O Taste and See*.

2. Published with four other poems as "From *The Mabinogion*," *Quarterly Review of Literature* 12.3 (1963): 184–95.

3. "[Letter]," *Tish* 11 (July 14, 1962): [1]–2, and answering letter by Lionel Kearns, 2–3.

4. Preface by Robert Creeley to George Bowering, *Sticks and Stones: Poems* (Vancouver: Tish Books, 1966).

5. W. H. Auden and Norman Holmes Pearson, *Poets of the English Language* (London: Eyre & Spottiswoode, 1952).

LETTER 255 August 1962

1. The three "Sonnets" were collected in *Roots and Branches*.

LETTER 256 August 1962

1. Samuel Palmer (1805–1881), English painter and follower of William Blake.

2. The poem was collected in *O Taste and See*.

3. The lines of the following fifth stanza are crossed out in Robert Duncan's hand.

4. On separate sheets there is a typescript of "Answering" with this headnote and a postscript and further comment written in Robert Duncan's hand.

LETTER 257 August 1962

1. Published as "Some Notes on Organic Form," *Poetry* 104 (September 1965): 420–25; reprinted in *The Poet in the World* and *New and Selected Essays*.

2. Richard Jefferies, *The Story of My Heart: My Autobiography* (1883; London: Longman, 1922).

3. William Plomer (1903–1973), *Double Lives: An Autobiography* (1943; New York: Noonday Press, 1956); Lilian Bowes-Lyon (1895–1949) was a British poet whose first book was *The Buried Stream* (London: Jonathan Cape, 1929) and last was *Collected Poems* (New York: E. P. Dutton, 1948).

LETTER 258 October 1962

1. Robert Duncan sent Denise Levertov a typescript entitled "Three Songs of the Bard Orpheus,"

with numbered sections about Cyparissus, Gany-
mede, and Hyakinthus. Only "Cyparissus" was
published in *Roots and Branches*.

LETTER 259   October 1962

1. Joseph Campbell, *The Masks of God*, 2 vols.
(London: Secker & Warburg, 1960). Volume 2 is
*Oriental Mythologies*.

LETTER 260   October 1962

1. Robert Duncan's "Cyparissus."

2. George Abbe (1911– ), *Poetry in the Round:
A Poetry Workshop, Narration and Poems* (New
York: Folkways Records, 1961).

3. Ian Hamilton Finlay's poems appeared
under the heading "[23 Poems]," *Origin* 2d ser. 6
(July 1962): 1–22. Denise Levertov's note is "To
the Editors and Readers of *Kulchur*," *Kulchur* 8
(Winter 1962): 29.

LETTER 264   November 1962

1. Robert Duncan's play *Adam's Way*.

LETTER 267   December 1962

1. Ian Hamilton Finlay, *The Dancers Inherit the
Party: Selected Poems*, woodcuts by Zeliko Kujundzic
(Worcester, England/Ventura, CA: Migrant Press,
1960).

LETTER 268   January 1963

1. James Stephens, *Irish Fairy Tales* (London:
Macmillan, 1920).

2. Jazz musician Race Newton, the Goodmans'
neighbor.

3. M. L. Rosenthal, "Seven Voices," *The Re-
porter* 28 (January 3, 1963): 46–49.

LETTER 269   February 1963

1. The letter can be dated from the inscription at
the top in Robert Duncan's hand: "rec. Feb. 9/63."

2. Paul Goodman, *Our Visit to Niagara* (New
York: Horizon Press, 1960), contains a section
entitled "American Stories," which in turn contains
the story "Our Trip to Niagara." In the letter the
word "great" is boxed for emphasis.

3. Perdita Schaffner, H. D.'s daughter (1919–
2002).

4. Thomas B. Swann, *The Classical World of
H. D.* (Lincoln: University of Nebraska Press, 1962).

5. *Genesis West* 1 (Fall 1962): 72.

6. Gordan Lish was the editor of *Genesis West*.

7. "John Button," Kornblee Gallery, New York
City, February 12–March 5, 1963. Bill Berkson
reviewed the show, *Art News* 61 (February 1963): 48.

LETTER 270   February 1963

1. Barney Childs taught at the time in the
English Department of the University of Arizona
and at the Ruth Stephan Poetry Center and was
Associate Editor of *Genesis West* for issues 1–5.

2. Charles Tomlinson, "The Picture of J. T. in
a Prospect of Stone," in *The Poet's Choice*, ed. Paul
Engle and Joseph Langland (New York: The Dial
Press, 1962).

3. John Wieners, "The Acts of Youth," "The
Mermaid"s Song," "An Anniversary Death," *Locus
Solus* 5 (1962): 77–80.

LETTER 271   February 1963

1. Robert Duncan met Robert Haas and Louise
Antoinette Kraus, married graduate students, at
Berkeley, when he was an undergraduate in 1937.
Robert Duncan credits them with directing his
reading to Stein, Pound, Eliot and the authors of
modernism, and so influencing his life as a poet. See
his discussion in "H. D. Book, Part I, Chapter 2,"
*Coyote's Journal* 8 (1967): 27–35.

2. See Robert Duncan's description in ibid.

LETTER 272   March 1963

1. Lines from Robert Duncan's poem "A Part-
Sequence for Change," included in *Roots and
Branches*.

2. Robert Duncan's play *Adam's Way* was
performed at the Tape Music Center on October 1,
1962. Jack Spicer organized a boycott, which in-
volved Stan Persky, Joanne Kyger, George Stanley,
and others.

3. The Scottish poet Robert Dunbar; the Latin
phase means "fear of death."

LETTER 274   March 1963

1. "Tribute to W. C. W.," *The Nation* 196
(March 16, 1963): 230; reprinted in *The Poet in the
World*.

2. "In Abeyance" and "Eros at Temple Stream,"
both included in *O Taste and See*.

3. Muriel Rukeyser, *Body and Waking* (New

York: Harper and Brothers, 1958), contains a section called "Translation: Octavio Paz," that includes "From Sun Stone."

4. Francois Truffault's 1960 film.

**LETTER 275    March 1963**

1. These two pages, dated March 7th, are the copy of the notebook description of Williams's funeral promised in Letter 274.

2. James and Ann Laughlin; and Robert Mac-Gregor, an editor at New Directions, were all at William Carlos Williams's funeral.

**LETTER 276    March 1963**

1. William Stafford was awarded the National Book Award for *Traveling through the Dark* (New York: Harper & Row, 1962).

**LETTER 277    March 1963**

1. "A Part-Sequence for Change," collected in *Roots and Branches*.

2. "Structure of Rime" XIX, XX, and XXI, included in *Roots and Branches*.

3. Geza Roheim (1891–1953), *Eternal Ones of the Dream: A Psychoanalytic Interpretation of Australian Myth and Ritual* (New York: International Universities Press, 1945); *The Riddle of the Sphinx, or Human Origins*, trans. R. Money-Kyrle (London: Hogarth Press, 1934).

4. George Herms (1935– ) is a California artist; "Structure of Rime" XXI is dedicated "(for Louise & George Herms)." See Duncan's article "Of Herms, His Hermes, and His Hermetic Art," in the exhibition catalog for *Selected Works 1960–1973*, Memorial Union Art Gallery, University of California, Berkeley. Reprinted in *A Selected Prose*.

**LETTER 279    March 1963**

1. *Second American Caravan: A Yearbook of American Literature*, ed. Alfred Kreymborg, Lewis Mumford, Paul Rosenfeld (New York: The Maccaulay Co., 1928).

**LETTER 280    March 1963**

1. The poems were sent by Denise Levertov to Robert Duncan with Letter 275, March 13, 1963. See Letter 283.

2. Nancy de Angulo (1890–1972) was the wife of writer Jaime de Angulo.

**LETTER 281    March 1963**

1. *The Sullen Art*, ed. David Ossman (New York: Corinth Books, 1963), is a book of interviews with poets, including Denise Levertov, that originated in a series of radio programs.

**LETTER 284    April 1963**

1. "Sonnet IV," which is the opening poem in *Bending the Bow*; Robert Duncan did not send the text to Denise Levertov until Letter 290, dated May 23, 1963.

2. "Windings (1961–1963)" is the title of the second of the two sections of *Roots and Branches*.

3. *Montana Xibalba: Translations #2*, 1963.

4. "The Continent" appeared in *Poetry* 103 (October–November 1963): 28–32 and was collected in *Roots and Branches*.

**LETTER 285    April 1963**

1. "Two Presentations," included, like the other poems mentioned, in *Roots and Branches*.

2. Willard A. Lockwood was Director of Wesleyan University Press.

**LETTER 286    May 1963**

1. William Morris's utopian novel, *News from Nowhere* (London: Reeves & Turner, 1891).

2. Denise Levertov's review of Paul Goodman's *The Lordly Hudson*: "One of the Lucky," *The Nation* 196 (April 13, 1963): 310–11; reprinted in *The Poet in the World*.

3. Paul Goodman, "The Strike for Peace," *The Village Voice* (November 16, 1961); collected in his *The Society I Live in Is Mine* (New York: Horizon Books, 1962).

4. "Holy Poems," *Locus Solus* 5 (1962): 181–84.

**LETTER 287    May 1963**

1. See Letter 286, n. 2.

2. Maya Deren, *Divine Horseman: Voodoo Gods of Haiti*, pref. Joseph Campbell (New York: Chelsea House, 1970).

**LETTER 288    May 1963**

1. The typescript of a lecture, whose cover sheet reads: "Asking the Fact for the Form" / a lecture by / Denise Levertov / Wabash College / December 6, 1962. The letter to Duncan is written on the cover sheet. The first part of this letter is written on the

title page, and the final bracketed paragraph on the last page of the lecture.

### LETTER 289    May 1963

1. "During the Eichmann Trial." The references in these paragraphs to the stone staircase and to touching the stone allude to Denise Levertov's poem "The Jacob's Ladder," which Oppen discusses in the letter Denise Levertov sent to Robert Duncan.

2. The letter is incomplete and unsent; the following letter resumes the same topics. This letter was then included with Letter 292, dated June 11, 1963.

### LETTER 290    May 1963

1. Daniel B. Aronson, "Robert Duncan," *The Yale Literary Magazine* 131 (April 1963): 15–16.

2. Underlined twice.

### LETTER 293    June 1963

1. Henry Wenning, who died in 1987, owned a company called Henry Wenning Rare Books. He was a dedicated and honest dealer in rare materials. Wenning became the publisher of Robert Duncan's and Jess's *A Book of Resemblances* (1966).

### LETTER 296    June 1963

1. This letter was not actually sent until it was included with Letter 298, dated July 15, 1963.

2. Denise Levertov, "Say the Word," *Harper's Bazaar* 3019 (June 1963): 53, 109–11; reprinted in *O Taste and See*.

3. Denise Levertov's poem "Threshold," included in *O Taste and See*.

4. This interview with Albert Gelpi, Sidney Goldfarb, and Robert Dawson appeared in *The Harvard Advocate* (Spring 1963) and is reprinted in William Everson, *Naked Heart: Talking on Poetry, Mysticism, and the Erotic* (Albuquerque, NM: An American Poetry Book, 1992).

5. The letter has no conclusion and is incomplete, or the conclusion is lost.

### LETTER 297    July 1963

1. *Genesis West* 1 (Fall 1962): 72.

2. Gordan Lish, "Poetry Is the Art of Prejudice: An Interview with Jack Gilbert," *Genesis West* 1 (Fall 1962): 82–94.

3. C. G. Jung, *Memories, Dreams, Reflections*,

ed. Aniela Jaffe (London: Collins, Routledge, & Kegan Paul, 1963).

4. His brother George Kirstein, editor of *The Nation*.

### LETTER 298    July 1963

1. Underlined twice.

### LETTER 300    July 1963

1. Linda Wagner, *Denise Levertov* (New York: Twayne, 1967).

2. Robert Creeley's novel *The Island* (New York: Charles Scribner's Sons, 1963).

### LETTER 301    September 1963

1. Russell Edson, *The Very Thing That Happens: Fables & Drawings* (New York: New Directions, 1964), with "Introduction" by Denise Levertov.

2. Barbara Moraff (1939– ) at this point was a beginning poet, who would publish more in the 1980s, including *Telephone Company Repairman Poems* (West Branch, IA: Tooth Paste Press, 1983) and *Deadly Nightshade* (Minneapolis: Coffee House Press, 1988).

3. Denise Levertov, Robert Duncan, and Robert Creeley read together at the Guggenheim Museum in New York on April 16, 1964.

4. Robert Creeley's *The Island*.

5. An Old Icelandic saga.

6. In the photograph of the Goodmans' house in Temple, sent along with this letter.

### LETTER 303    September 1963

1. Peter Christen Ashjornsen (1812–1885), *East of the Sun and West of the Moon, Old Tales from the North*, illust. Kay Nilsen (Garden City, NY: Garden City Publishing Co., 1932).

2. Andrew Lang, *The Lilac Fairy Book*, illus. H. J. Ford (New York: Longman Green and Co., 1910).

### LETTER 304    September 1963

1. "5th Sonnet," collected in *Bending the Bow*.

2. On September 15, 1965, four black teenage girls were killed in a bomb blast in a Baptist church in Birmingham, Alabama, which was then a center of activity in the Civil Rights Movement.

LETTER 305    September 1963

1. The Putney School in Vermont.

LETTER 306    October 1963

1. The exhibition was "[Six Painters]," at James Alexander's Peacock Gallery, Fall 1963.

2. Robert Duncan's preface to Helen Adam's *Ballads* (New York: Acadia Press, 1964), with illustrations by Jess

3. These poems were collected in Robert Creeley, *For Love.*

LETTER 307    November 1963

1. Ingmar Bergman's 1962 film.

2. Both poems were collected in *O Taste and See.*

LETTER 308    November 1963

1. "Adam's Way."

2. *Roots and Branches*, when published by Scribners in 1964, contained two sections: "Roots and Branches (Poems 1959–60)" and "Windings (Poems 1961–63)."

3. At this time Bernard and Rosemarie Waldrop were graduate students at the University of Michigan, where they edited four issues of the little magazine *Burning Deck* (1963–65).

4. This poem, retitled "Turning," appears in Denise Levertov's *Overland to the Islands.* Phrases from the poem are quoted in this paragraph and the next.

5. "Three Fate Tales" and "Grace" appear in Creeley's collection of stories, *The Gold Diggers* (New York: Scribners, 1965).

6. "An Innocent" I, II, and II (second version) appeared in *Origin* 17; the two versions of "An Innocent" were included in Denise Levertov's *Collected Earlier Poems 1940–1960.*

7. "First Invention on the Theme of Adam," from Robert Duncan's *Letters.*

8. Robert Duncan's misremembering of Denise Levertov's "The Springtime" from *Overland to the Islands.*

9. The "dog one" is Denise Levertov's poem "Overland to the Islands," the title poem of that volume.

10. Denise Levertov's "With Eyes at the Back of Our Heads."

11. Four poems by Creeley, in *For Love.*

12. The envelope is posted with two four-cent stamps with an image of a bearded Abraham Lincoln.

LETTER 309    December 1963

1. Harry Green, husband of Olga Levertoff, who was nine years older than Denise Levertov.

2. "Source" is included in *Letters.*

3. A line is drawn down the left margin of the letter beside the subsequent notes for the reading.

4. Robert Duncan's "From *The Mabinogion,*" offprint from *Quarterly Review of Literature* 12.3 (1963), included in *Roots and Branches.*

5. First titled "Like Dogs in Mexico," but retitled "As It Happens," in *The Sorrow Dance.*

6. Of the many editions of this title, see Nathaniel Hawthorne, *A Wonder-book for Girls and Boys*, illus. Milo Winter (New York: Rand McNally & Co., 1913).

LETTER 310    January 1964

1. Walter Crane, *The Baby's Opera: A Book of Old Rhymes with New Dresses* (London: G. Routledge and Sons, 1876).

2. Published as "Towards an Open Universe," in *Poets on Poetry*, ed. Howard Nemerov (New York: Basic Books, 1966).

3. "Grief Dismissed" is the poem published in *The Sorrow Dance* as "A Lamentation," and the agony poem is, as Levertov noted in the margin, "As It Happens," which is also in *The Sorrow Dance*, along with "Face to Face." "A Psalm Praising the Hair of Man's Body" is in *O Taste and See.*

4. Levertov has written in the margin: "No—the point is the {illegible} with grief *washed* away—is about evasion like laundered money. . . . "

LETTER 311    January 1964

1. John Weiners, *Ace of Pentacles* (New York: James F. Carr and Robert A. Wilson, 1964).

2. Northrop Frye, *Fearful Symmetry: A Study of William Blake* (Princeton: Princeton University Press, 1947).

3. The cat's wet feet had smeared words on the page.

4. Organized by the Museum of Modern Art, the show traveled to nine museums in 1965–66 under the title *American Collages.*

LETTER 312    January 1964
1. Underlined three times.
2. "A Lamentation," included in *The Sorrow Dance*.

LETTER 313    January 1964
1. This poem was collected as "Bending the Bow" in *Bending the Bow*.

LETTER 314    February 1964
1. Olga Levertoff's "The Ballad of My Father," included by Denise Levertov in *The Sorrow Dance*.

LETTER 316    April 1964
1. Betty Olson was killed in an automobile accident on March 28, 1964, in Wyoming County, east of Buffalo, NY.

LETTER 318    June 1964
1. Denise Levertov was serving as a consultant to recommend poets for publication by W. W. Norton.

LETTER 319    June 1964
1. *Trinity's Trine: Translations #5*, 1964.

LETTER 320    June 1964
1. The manuscript for Robert Duncan's *A Book of Resemblances*.
2. The poems were published as "Olga Poems," *Poetry* 106 (April/May 1965): 81–89.
3. The letter is unfinished or the remainder lost.

LETTER 321    June 1964
1. Published with the title *As Testimony* (San Francisco: White Rabbit Press, 1964).

LETTER 322    July 1964
1. The grant to Helen Adam came from the Merrill Foundation.
2. Underlined twice.
3. At the beginning and end of Robert Duncan's "The Fire: Passages 13," included in *Bending the Bow*.

LETTER 323    July 1964
1. W. K. C. Guthrie, *Orpheus and Greek Religion* (London: Methuen, 1952).
2. "Spelling: Passages 14," following "Chords: Passages 14"; both are included in *Bending the Bow*.

LETTER 324    July 1964
1. "These Past Years: Passages 10," in *Bending the Bow*.
2. The letter is incomplete or the remainder lost.

LETTER 325    July 1964
1. In "Spelling: Passages 15." It appears in *Bending the Bow*, as do "The Collage: Passages 6" and "Chords: Passages 14." The reference below is presumably to Samuel Johnson's *Dictionary*.

LETTER 326    August 1964
1. Gwendolyn Bays, *The Orphic Vision: Seer Poets from Novalis to Rimbaud* (Lincoln: University of Nebraska Press, 1964). See Letter 345 and Elizabeth Sewell, *The Orphic Voice: Poetry and Natural History* (New Haven: Yale University Press, 1960).
2. In the eighteenth century Count Nikolaus von Zinzendorf was a patron and protector of the Moravian Brotherhood, a Protestant sect of the inner light. Some migrated to the U.S. and founded a number of communities, including Bethlehem, Pennsylvania, where H. D. was born and raised as a Moravian.

LETTER 327    August 1964
1. Helen Adam, *Ballads*, with illustrations by Jess (New York: Acadia Press, 1964).

LETTER 328    September 1964
1. *Nineteenth-Century German Tales*, ed. Angel Flores (Garden City, NY: Doubleday, 1959).
2. James Dickey, *Two Poems of Air* (Portland, OR: Centicore Press, 1964).
3. *12 Poets & 1 Painter* (San Francisco: Four Seasons Foundation, 1964).
4. Ted Enslin, "Forms III," *Matter* 2 (July 1964): [7–9].
5. Sigrid Undset, *The Master of Hestviken: The Axe, The Snake Pit, In the Wilderness, The Son Avenger* (New York: Alfred A. Knopf, 1934).

LETTER 329    September 1964
1. Bruno Bettelheim, "Joey: A 'Mechanical Boy,'" *Scientific American* 200 (March 1959): 116–20+.
2. *Ace of Pentacles*.

LETTER 330    September 1964
1. Joanne Kyger published three poems, "My

Father Died This Spring," "The Hunt in the Wood: Paolo Uccello," and "These Things We See Are Images of the Past," in *12 Poets & 1 Painter*.

2. Denise Levertov's poem "City Psalm" was published in a portfolio of 10 broadsides (Berkeley: Oyez Press, 1964).

LETTER 331    September 1964
1. "Stepping Westward," included in *The Sorrow Dance*.

LETTER 332    September 1964
1. Michael Rumaker's novel *The Butterfly* (New York: Scribners, 1962).
2. John Wieners, "[*City of Night*] A Review," *The Floating Bear* 27 (1963): [27–29].

LETTER 333    September 1964
1. "Saint Graal: After Verlaine" & "Parsifal: After Wagner & Verlaine," collected in *Bending the Bow*.

LETTER 334    October 1964
1. *Roots and Branches*.

LETTER 335    October 1964
1. "An Admonition," *Things* 1 (Fall 1964): 4–7.
2. See *Coyote's Journal* 1 (1964): 11–43.
3. The letter breaks off here without final signature, or the remainder is lost. In any case it was not mailed until it was included with Robert Duncan's letter of November 19; see Letter 337.

LETTER 336    November 1964
1. Hayden Carruth, "Scales of the Marvellous," *The Nation* 199 (December 7, 1964): 442–44.

LETTER 337    November 1964
1. Larry Eigner's "Murder Talk: The Reception," five poems, and a letter from Robert Duncan constitute the whole of *Duende* 6 (1964).

LETTER 338    November 1964
1. Denise Levertov was a fellow at the Radcliffe Institute from 1964 to 1966.

LETTER 339    November 1964
1. Wallace Stevens, *The Collected Poems* (New York: Alfred A. Knopf, 1954), 296–302.

2. James Dickey, *The Suspect in Poetry* (Madison, WI: Sixties Press, 1964).

3. The prizes listed in *Poetry* for 1964 are as follows: The Levinson Prize to Robert Duncan; The Oscar Blumenthal-Charles Leviton Prize to Robert Creeley; The Eunice Tietjens Memorial Prize to Hayden Carruth; The Harriet Monroe Memorial Prize to Denise Levertov; The Bess Hokin Prize to Gary Snyder; The Union League Civic and Arts Foundation Prize to Louis Zukofsky; The Inez Boulton Prize to Charles Tomlinson; The Morton Zabel Memorial Prize to René Char.

LETTER 340    December 1964
1. The message is written on the back of a postcard of Wassily Kandinsky's gouache "Festival" (ca. 1900) in the Busch-Reisinger Museum, Harvard University.

LETTER 343    January 1965
1. Robert Duncan's review of John Wieners, *Hotel Wentley Poems* and *Ace of Pentacles*: "Taking Away from God His Sound," *The Nation* 200 (May 31, 1965): 595–58
2. Grandin Conover at *The Nation*.
3. SNCC was the Student Non-Violent Coordinating Committee.
4. "To Write Is to Listen," *Poetry* 105 (February 1965): 326–29; reprinted in *The Poet in the World*.

LETTER 344    February 1965
1. The Fogg Museum and Widener Library (referred to later in the letter) are both at Harvard University.
2. "Psalm concerning the Castle," included in *The Sorrow Dance*.
3. Ted Enslin, "Mercury Poems," *El Corno Emplumado* 10 (April 1964): 28–31.
4. Hope Mirrless, *The Counterplot* (London: W. Collins Sons & Co. Ltd, 1914).

LETTER 345    February 1965
1. Denis Saurat, *Literature and the Occult Tradition: Studies in Philosphical Poetry*, trans. Dorothy Bolton (New York: L. MacVeagh, The Dial Press, 1930).

LETTER 346    March 1965
1. Proclus (ca. 410–485), *The Commentaries*

*of Proclus on the Timaeus of Plato in Five Books: Containing a Treasury of Pythagoric and Platonic Physiology*, trans. Thomas Taylor (London: The Author, 1820); see also a new edition, trans. Robert Lamberton (Barrytown, NY: Station Hill Press, 1983); see Letter 230.

LETTER 349   June 1965

1. This notation on a separate sheet is neither in Levertov's hand nor in Duncan's. Perhaps the hand is Jess's.

2. *Sum*, 4 (1965): [1].

3. Robert Lowell declined President Lyndon Johnson's invitation to participate in a "Festival of the Arts" at the White House on June 14, 1965.

4. Lewis Mumford, "Utopia: The City and the Machine," *Daedalus* 94 (Spring 1965): 271–92.

5. Page nine of this letter has been lost.

6. This letter is unfinished or the remainder lost.

LETTER 350   July 1965

1. Underlined twice.

LETTER 351   July 1965

1. *Medea at Kolchis: The Maiden Head* (Berkeley: Oyez Press, 1965). Robert Hawley is the publisher of Oyez Press in Berkeley.

2. David Bromige, *The Gathering: Poems* (Buffalo: Sum Books, 1965).

LETTER 352   July 1965

1. Perhaps Dave Haselwood of the Auerhahn Press.

2. Gaston Bachelard, *The Poetics of Space*, trans. Maria Jolas (New York: Orion Press, 1964). The letter is incomplete or the remainder lost.

LETTER 353   August 1965

1. At the top of the letter Denise Levertov has written: "(Possibly 2 letters mixed?)."

2. Ken Irby (1936– ), from Kansas, had studied at the University of California at Berkeley. *Movement/Sequences* had appeared as *Duende* 8 (1965). His first large book was *Catalpa* (Lawrence, KS: Tansy Press, 1977). Lew Welch (1926–1971) had just published *On Out* (Berkeley: Oyez Press, 1965). Lenore Kandel's (1932– ) first book of note was *The Love Book* (San Francisco: Stolen Paper Review Editions, 1966).

3. There is a break in continuity here. Either a

page or pages of this letter are missing, or what follows is the conclusion of another letter. The pages are consecutive in the Levertov Papers. However, at some point she saw the discrepancy and wrote at the top of the first page: "(Possibly 2 letters mixed?)." See n. 1. Pound often invokes Kung (Confucius) as an authoritative instructor on ethical action.

4. The show was *Jess Translations*, at Rolf Nelson Gallery, Los Angeles.

5. Llyn Foulkes (1934– ) is a California artist known for abstract paintings, assemblages, and collage constructions.

6. Raymond Roseliep, *Love Makes—The Air Light* (New York: W. W. Norton & Co., 1965).

7. Ed Dorn, "The Sense Comes over Me, and the Waning Light of Man, by the 1st National Bank," and "The Problem of the Poem for My Daughter Left Unsolved," *The Paris Review* 35 (Fall 1965): 63–66, 130–36.

8. Robert Duncan means the Berkeley Festival, Summer 1965.

LETTER 354   August 1965

1. Ed Sanders, *Peace Eye* (Buffalo, NY: Frontier Press, 1965).

2. Jake Leed (1924– ) was a friend of Robert Creeley and also a professor at Kent State University. He published several pamphlets of poems, including *In Japan: Poems and Drawings* (Ravenna, OH: Shelley's Press, 1971).

LETTER 355   August 1965

1. Richard Baker worked at the Extension Center of the University of California at Berkeley; he was the primary administrator for the Berkeley Poetry Conference in 1965. He later became head of the Zen Center in San Francisco.

LETTER 357   September 1965

1. "Up Rising," *The Nation* 201 (September 13, 1965): 146–47; collected in *Bending the Bow*.

LETTER 358   October 1965

1. Revisions of the lines below are lines 5 and 6 of "The Soldiers: Passages 26," collected in *Bending the Bow*.

2. Henry Osborn Taylor, *The Medieval Mind: A History of the Development of Thought and Emotion in the Middle Ages* (New York: MacMillan, 1919).

3. See Letter 118.

4. *Residu*, edited by Daniel Richter, published two issues, one in 1965 and one in 1966.

5. The lecture was given at the Dominican College of San Rafael and was published as *The Sweetness and Greatness of Dante's Divine Comedy* (San Francisco: Open Space, 1965).

**LETTER 359    October 1965**

1. "Some Notes on Organic Form," *Poetry* 106 (September 1965): 420–25; reprinted in *The Poet in the World* and in *New and Selected Essays*.

2. In the margin next to this sentence Denise Levertov has written: "See letter of——about early lecture version of essay." See Letters 257, 288, 289, and 292.

3. Frederick Will, "Notes on Robert Duncan," *Poetry* 106 (September 1965): 427–28.

4. Robert Mazzocco, "A Philosophical Poet," *The New York Review of Books* 453 ( June 3, 1965): 20–23.

5. *The Convivio of Dante Alighieri*, ed. Philip Henry Wicksteed (London: J. M. Dent, 1909).

**LETTER 360    October 1965**

1. Henri Bosco, *Malicroix* (Paris: Gallimard, 1949).

2. Robert Wilson was the owner of the Phoenix Book Shop and also the author *of A Bibliography of Denise Levertov* (New York: The Phoenix Book Shop, 1972).

3. *Secant* was a mimeographed magazine, edited by Richard Deutch and Thomas Connors. *Secant* 2.2 (September 1965) contained a review of *O Taste and See*, poems reprinted from *Overland to the Islands*, and poems for Duncan by Ross Feld.

4. Central Park West.

**LETTER 361    December 1965**

1. *The Enamord Mage: Translation #6*, 1965, and *In Praise of Sir Edward: Translation #7*, 1965.

2. The show at Macy's was called "California Here." "Los Angeles Now" was the name of the show at Robert Fraser Gallery (1966).

3. This seems to be a poem that appeared in *Bending the Bow* under the title "An Interlude" between "The Soldiers: Passages 26" and "Transgressing the Real: Passages 27."

4. Rudolph Steiner, *The Four Seasons and the*

*Archangels: Four Lectures Given in Dornach, October 1923* (London: Rudolph Steiner, 1947).

**LETTER 362    January 1966**

1. Written in a hand other than Levertov's or Duncan's, perhaps Jess's.

2. Robert Duncan had sent a handwritten copy of his poem "Earth's Winter Song" with the inscription: "for Mitch, Denise and Nik / with love / Christmas / 1965."

**LETTER 363    January 1966**

1. "Life at War" and "A Vision" were included in *The Sorrow Dance*.

2. "Earth's Winter Song," included in *Bending the Bow*.

3. Linda Welshimer Wagner, "An Interview with Robert Creeley, 1965," *Minnesota Review* 5 (October–December 1965): 309–21, and Walter Sutton, "A Conversation with Denise Levertov," *Minnesota Review* 5 (October–December 1965): 322–41; the second was reprinted in *Conversations with Denise Levertov*, ed. Jewel Spears Brooker (Jackson: University of Mississippi Press, 1998).

4. Louis Z. Hammer, *"How the Poem Speaks," Kayak* 5 (1966): 57–59.

5. Louis Zukofsky, *All the Collected Short Poems, 1923–1958* (New York: Norton, 1965).

6. Peter Weiss's play; published as *Marat/Sade; The Investigation; and The Shadow of the Body of the Coachman*, ed. Robert Cohen (New York: Continuum, 1998).

**LETTER 364    January 1966**

1. Willard Boepple (1945– ) achieved some recognition as a sculptor, with shows at André Emmerick and other galleries.

**LETTER 366    March 1966**

1. The letter was written on a notecard of the stained glass "Peacock Window" by John LaFarge (1835–1910); in Levertov's hand under the identification the reproduction is written: "See L. C. Tiffany Rebel in Glass."

2. The reference here seems to be not to letter #361, dated December 3 and 16, 1965, but to some more recent but lost letter.

3. Charles Robert Leslie, *Memoirs of the Life of John Constable* (London: J. M. Dent, 1941).

4. "Sketches by Constable," Baltimore Museum of Art, January 18–February 13, 1966.

5. The catalog for the exhibition was published as Lawrence Gowing, *Turner: Imagination and Reality* (New York: Museum of Modern Art, 1966).

LETTER 368    April 1966

1. *Audit/Poetry* 4 (1967) featured Robert Duncan's work.

2. *The Sweetness and Greatness of Dante's Divine Comedy*, reprinted in *Fictive Certainties*.

3. Underlined twice.

LETTER 369    April–May 1966

1. Robert Duncan's *Six Prose Pieces*, published by Walter Hamady's Perishable Press in Madison, Wisconsin.

2. *Psalm concerning the Castle*, also published by Walter Hamady's Perishable Press. The poem was collected in *The Sorrow Dance*.

LETTER 370    July 1966

1. Henry Vaughan, *Hermetical Physick or, The Right Way to Preserve, and to Restore Health. By that Famous and Faithfull Chymist, Henry Nollius* (London: Printed for Humphrey Moseley, 1655). Robert Duncan did not finish the introduction.

2. Lama Govinda, *Foundations of Tibetan Mysticism* (London: Rider, 1959).

3. Robert Duncan, "Oriented by Instincts by Stars," *Poetry* 105 (November 1964): 131–33.

LETTER 371    July 1966

1. From "Life at War."

2. William Morris, *The Roots of the Mountains* (London: Reeves and Turner, 1890).

3. "Remembering," "Notebook Pages" (prose), "The Postcards: A Triptych," and "In the Night" (story), *The Chicago Review* 18 (1966): 22–29.

4. Perhaps *Ole* 4 (May 1966), edited by Douglas Blasek; *Wormwood Review* 21 (1966), edited by Marvin Malone; or *Intrepid* 6 (1966), edited by Allen de Loach.

LETTER 372    July 1966

1. Edward Sapir, *Language: An Introduction to the Study of Speech* (New York: Harcourt Brace, 1921).

LETTER 374    July 1966

1. Jess's painting is *A? Year's Darling of a Pig My Size!: Translations #20*, 1968.

2. Being a poet with anarchist views, Robert Duncan was familiar with the trial and execution of Sacco and Vanzetti in 1927. He owned *The Letters of Sacco and Vanzetti*, ed. Marion Denman Frankfurter and Gardner Jackson (New York: Viking Press, 1928).

LETTER 375    August 1966

1. Michael McClure, *The Beard* (San Francisco: The Author, 1965) and *Meat Science Essays* (San Francisco: City Lights Books, 1963).

2. This is Richard Moore's film *Louis Zukofsky*, made as part of the "Poetry USA Series" in San Francisco, 1966, and shown on National Educational Television (NET).

3. Erwin Schrödinger, *What Is Life? The Physical Aspects of a Living Cell* (Cambridge: Cambridge University Press, 1945).

LETTER 376    August 1966

1. "An Interlude," collected in *Bending the Bow*.

2. Both poems appeared in Adrienne Rich, *Necessities of Life* (New York: W. W. Norton, 1966).

3. "On Reading the Earlier Poems of Robert Duncan" was published as a broadside by Oyez Press (Berkeley, 1966) and collected in *The Poet in the World*. See Letter 375.

4. *The Dumbfounding* (New York: W. W. Norton, 1966), one of the books published on Denise Levertov's advice.

LETTER 377    August 1966

1. See Letter 376, n. 3.

2. Three poems, including "The Poetry Shelf," appeared in *Poetry* 108 (July 1966): 217–20.

3. G. R. S. Mead. *Thrice-Greatest Hermes; Studies in Hellenistic Theosophy and Gnosis, Being a Translation of the Extant Sermons and Fragments of the Trismegistic Literature*, 3 vols. (London: The Theosophical Publishing Society, 1906); Hans Jonas, *The Gnostic Religion: The Message of the Alien God and the Beginning of Christianity* (Boston: Beacon Press, 1963); Raymond Klibansky, Erwin Panofsky, and Fritz Saxl, *Saturn and Melancholy: Studies in the History of Natural Philosophy, Religion, and Art* (London: Nelson, 1964); George Gamow,

*Matter, Earth, and Sky* (Englewood Cliffs, NJ: Prentice-Hall, 1958); and John Read, *Through Alchemy to Chemistry: A Procession of Ideas and Personalities* (London: G. Bell, 1957).

4. "The Altars in the Street," in *The Sorrow Dance*.

LETTER 378    September 1966

1. Robert Duncan, *Of the War: Passages 22–27* (Berkeley: Oyez Press, 1966).

2. *Encyclopédie de la Divination* (Paris: Tchou Éditeur, 1965).

3. Maurice Levaillant, *La Crise mystique de Victor Hugo* (Paris: Librairie J. Corti, 1954).

4. Gabriel Gobron, *Histoire et Philosophie du Caodaïsme: Bouddhisme Rénové, Spiritisme Vietnam-ien, Religion Nouvelle en Eurasie* (Paris: Dervy, 1949).

LETTER 379    October 1966

1. "The Seeing" and "The Altars in the Street" were included in *The Sorrow Dance*.

2. *In Praise of Krishna*, trans. Edward C. Di-mock, Jr., and Denise Levertov (New York: Anchor Books, Doubleday, 1967).

LETTER 380    October 1966

1. Robert Duncan no doubt means Robert Peters, see Letter 384.

2. Henry Wenning, who published Duncan's *A Book of Resemblances*.

3. The poem was Denise Levertov's contribu-tion to *1968 Peace Calendar & Appointment Book: Out of the War Shadow*, ed. Denise Levertov (New York: War Resisters League, 1968).

4. H. J. Rose, *A Handbook of Greek Mythology, including Its Extension to Rome* (New York: E. P. Dutton & Co., 1928).

5. Arthur Bernard Cook, *Zeus: A Study in Ancient Religion*, 3 vols. (Cambridge: Cambridge University Press, 1914–40).

LETTER 381    November 1966

1. A student of Denise Levertov, William Bur-ford has not published a book of poems, but his work did appear in magazines, for example: "The Spell," *The Nation* 199 (November 30, 1964): 409.

2. The occasion was a gathering at Albert and Barbara Gelpi's house in Cambridge (while he was teaching at Harvard) after a poetry reading that

Denise Levertov gave at Lowell House at Gelpi's invitation. Lowell and Adrienne Rich were present.

3. Will Grohmann, *Paul Klee*, trans. Norbert Gutermann (New York: M. H. Abrams, 1967).

4. Martin Buber, the Hasidic philosopher.

5. The conclusion to the letter is missing.

LETTER 382    December 1966

1. Peter Schumann (1934– ) is the founder and director of Bread and Puppet Theatre. See Stefan Brecht, *Peter Schumann's Bread and Puppet Theatre*, 2 vols. (New York: Methuen, 1988).

LETTER 383    December 1966

1. *The Years as Catches* (Berkeley: Oyez Press, 1966).

2. Rudolf Karl Bultmann, *Theology of the New Testament*, trans. Kendrick Grobel (London: SCM Press, 1952–55).

3. Levertov has written in above the line: "'The Burning Babe' one? (Advent 1966)." See Letter 382.

LETTER 384    January 1967

1. Blanche (1995) and James Peter Cooney ( –1985) were friends of Robert Duncan from the 1940s. James Peter Cooney was the editor of the magazine *The Phoenix*. Robert Duncan visited them at their farm in North Adams, Massachusetts, where they farmed with horses and lived an independent life. See Blanche Cooney, *In My Own Sweet Time: An Autobiography* (Athens, OH: Swallow Press, 1993).

2. Jim Harrison, "War Suite," in *Locations* (New York: W. W. Norton Co., 1968).

3. "Essay at War" was collected in *Derivations*.

LETTER 385    February 1967

1. Underlined twice.

2. During the week of January 29–February 5, 1967, The Bread and Puppet Theatre staged a series of events under the title "Week of Angry Arts against the War in Vietnam"; one of those events was Robert Nichols's production of "Vietlife (An Act of Respect for the Vietnamese People)."

3. Robert Duncan's *A Book of Resemblances*.

4. The letter is incomplete or the remainder lost.

LETTER 386    February 1967

1. Levertov wrote in the margin next to this first

sentence: "I took refuge in action, & so was less ravaged by the war than he . . . "

2. See G. Parthasarath's review of Rumer Godden's *Two under the Indian Sun* (1966), "Content in Another Country," *Saturday Review* 49 (July/September 1966): 58–59.

3. R. T. Rundle Clark, *Myth and Symbol in Ancient Egypt* (London: Thames and Hudson, 1959).

4. Edna Keough (1901–1992) was Robert Duncan's high school English teacher. See his discussion in "The H. D. Book, Part I, Chapter 2," *Coyote's Journal* 8 (1967): 27–35.

5. Charles B. Wheeler, *The Design of Poetry* (New York: W. W. Norton, 1966).

LETTER 388    February 1967

1. "A Meeting of Poets and Theologians to Discuss Parable, Myth and Language," sponsored by the Advance Program of Washington Cathedral and the Church Society for College Work, with proceedings published in 1969; Denise Levertov and Robert Duncan participated in the symposium.

2. Tony Stoneburner was the organizer of the conference and wrote the introduction to the subsequent publication. He was a Professor at Denison University in Ohio at the time of the conference, 1967.

3. The poem was published as the first section of "Epilogos" and collected in *Bending the Bow*.

4. George Bowering "[Review of Robert Duncan's *Of the War: Passages 22–27*]," *Guerrilla*, 1 (January 1967): 11; revised and reprinted in his *Craft Slices* (Toronto: Oberon Press, 1985).

LETTER 389    March 1967

1. An undated sheet in Duncan's hand says: "Denny, I want to replace some of my Freud volumes with the new standard revised texts, which I believe Norton publishes. If, as editor, you can get them at discount, would you order these for me and have them sent, and I will reimburse you right off. Robert." The following titles are listed: *Psychopathology of Everyday Life, On the History of the Psychoanalytic Movement, Totem and Taboo, Complete Introductory Lectures on Psycho-Analysis*.

LETTER 393    May 1967

1. "The Dishonest Mailman" is a poem in Robert Creeley's *For Love*.

2. George Leite was editor of the ten issues of the magazine *Circle* (1944–48).

LETTER 394    June 1967

1. Leo Frobenius, *African Genesis* (London: Faber & Faber, 1938).

2. See André Mellerio, *Odilon Redon: Peintre, Dessinateur & Graveur* (Paris: H. Floury, Éditeur, 1923), and Klaus Berger, *Odilon Redon: Fantasy and Colour*, trans. Michael Bullock (New York: McGraw-Hill Book Co., 1965).

3. Arthur Bernard Cook, *Zeus* (see Letter 380, n. 5); and Nelson Glueck, *Deities and Dolphins: The Story of Nabataeans* (New York: Farrar, Straus & Giroux, 1965).

LETTER 395    July 1967

1. This form letter was sent to possible and prospective contributors to *1968 Peace Calendar & Appointment Book: Out of the War Shadow*, ed. Denise Levertov with her "Editor's Preface."

LETTER 396    July 1967

1. John Masefield, *The Box of Delights, or, When the Wolves Were Running* (London: W. Heineman, 1935), and Ethel Mary Channon, *The Griffin*, illus. K. Jukes (London: W. Heinemann, 1928).

LETTER 398    July 1967

1. Lawrence S. Dembo was a professor of English at the University of Wisconsin and editor of the journal *Contemporary Literature*. His well-known book of the period was *Conceptions of Reality in Modern American Poetry* (Berkeley: University of California Press, 1966). The interview with L. S. Dembo was not published.

2. "Two Chapters from H. D.," *Triquarterly* 12 (Spring 1968): 67–98, and "Rites of Participation," *Caterpillar* 1 (October 1967): 6–29.

3. Robert Duncan's poem "A Shrine to Ameinias: Parmenides' Dream" appeared in *The Journal of Creative Behavior* 1 (Spring 1967): 129–32. David Posner was the poetry editor.

LETTER 399    July 1967

1. The painters James Rosenquist, Roy Lichtenstein, and Robert Rauschenberg.

LETTER 400 July 1967

1. John Masefield, *Midnight Park: A Novel*
(London: W. Heinemann, 1927).

2. Alain-Fournier, *Le Grand Meaulnes* (Paris:
Emile-Paul Freres, 1913).

3. Elimelekh of Lijensk, "The True Wonder,"
in Martin Buber, *Tales of the Hasidim: The Early
Masters with Eyes* (New York: Schocken Books,
1947).

4. Ezra Pound, *ABC of Reading* (Norfolk, CT:
New Directions, 1951).

5. Theodora Kroeber, *Ishi in Two Worlds: A
Biography of the Last Wild Indian in North America*
(Berkeley: University of California Press, 1961).

6. Rhode Island School of Design.

LETTER 401 July 1967

1. Several typewritten pages from the interview
with L. S. Dembo were sent with this letter, hence
the reference below to "question and answer #1."
See Letter 398.

LETTER 402 August 1967

1. Crunk [Robert Bly], "The Work of Denise
Levertov," *The Sixties* 9 (Spring 1967): 48–65.

2. Louis Simpson, "Dead Horses and Live
Issues," *The Nation* 204 (24 April 1967): 520–22.

3. Robert Duncan, "Notebook Pages," *Chicago
Review* 18 (1966): 26–28.

LETTER 403 August 1967

1. *A Tree Telling of Orpheus*.

LETTER 404 August 1967

1. A typewritten form letter with "Robert,"
"God Spell," and "Denise" written in Levertov's
hand in appropriate spaces.

LETTER 405 November 1967

1. Auguste Viatte, *Les Sources occultes du
Romantisme, Illuminisme—Théosophie, 1770–1820*,
2 vols. (Paris: H. Champion, 1928).

2. Brer Rabbit is a character in the Uncle
Remus stories of Joel Chandler Harris.

3. Paul Blackburn, "Name Cast into the Tree-
Alphabet for Mathew Craig Eshleman born Lima,
Peru, February 22(?), 1966," *Caterpillar* 1 (1967):
1–5; Robert Duncan, "Rites of Participation,"
*Caterpillar* 2 (January 1968): 125–54.

4. Aram Saroyan poems, *Chicago Review* 19
(September 1967): 22–27. This issue had the title
"Anthology of Concretism."

5. "Ought" is underlined twice.

6. "Die Sonate in Urlauten," in *Anthology of
Audio by Visual Poets*, ed. Claudia Gould (New
York: Harvestworks, 1988). Kurt Schwitter
(1887–1948) was a German poet and collagist.

7. Emmett William, *An Anthology of Concrete
Poetry* (New York: Something Else Press, 1967), and
Mary Ellen Slot, *Concrete Poetry: A World View*
(Bloomington: Indiana University Press, 1968).

8. Pierre Garier published two manifestos in
the journal *Les Lettres* (1962): "Manifeste pour une
Poésie Nouvelle, Visuelle et Phonique," 8th Series,
29 (January 1963), 1–8; and "Deuxième Manifeste
pour une Poésie Visuelle," 8th Series, 30 (May 1963),
15–28. Franz Mons (1926– ), a German poet, also
wrote for *Les Lettres*, including two essays: "Articula-
tions," 8th Series, 30 (May 1963), 3–10); and "Textes
dans l'espace," 8th Series, 31 (November 1963), 15–25.

LETTER 407 February 1968

1. Mitchell Goodman was indicted in federal
court in Boston, along with Dr. Benjamin Spock
and three others, for conspiring to counsel draft
evasion; their conviction in spring 1968 was reversed
on appeal in 1969.

2. Published as "From a Notebook: October
'68–May '69" in *Relearning the Alphabet* and ex-
panded into the poem "Staying Alive," published
in *To Stay Alive*.

3. Ary Scheffer (1795–1858) was a Dutch painter,
sculptor, and lithographer, who lived in France and
became an advocate for the Romantic school of
art and who was much admired by Cézanne early
in his career.

4. *Bending the Bow*.

5. *Light from under a Bushel* (Madison, WI:
Perishable Press, 1968).

6. Published as *Guillevic: Selected Poems* (New
York: New Directions, 1969).

LETTER 408 February 1968

1. The Odyssia Gallery in New York City was
owned and operated by Odyssia and Frederico
Quadrani. Jess was then working on the *Trans-
lations*, which were to end with *Narkissos*, but the
final painting of the series remains a pencil drawing.

2. Robert Creeley, *The Finger* (Los Angeles: Black Sparrow Press, 1968).

LETTER 409    March 1968

1. PBL stands for Public Broadcast Lab, a precurser to PBS, Public Broadcast System. The scene appears in Robert Duncan's poem "Santa Cruz Propositions."

2. James Joyce, *Portrait of the Artist as a Young Man* (New York: Huebsch, 1918), chapter 5.

3. Paul Goodman, "The Duty of Professionals," *Liberation* 12 (November 1967): 36–39.

4. *Civil Liberties under Attack*, ed. Henry Steele Commager and C. Wilcox (Philadelphia: University of Pennsylvania Press, 1951).

5. Robert Duncan's lecture was presented at the Seventh Annual Symposium on American Values, entitled "Language and World Order" at Central Washington State College, April 20, 1968; the lecture was published as "Man's Fulfillment in Order and Strife," *Caterpillar* 8/9 (October 1969): 229–49.

6. Dave Dellinger, "Unmasking Genocide," *Liberation* 12 (December 1967 / January 1968): 34–35.

7. *The Scientific American* from January 1964 through March 1968 contains no single article containing the ideas Robert Duncan sets out here; he is probably collecting parts of several articles from the magazine.

8. The remainder of the letter is lost.

LETTER 411    June 1968

1. *The Movement toward a New America*, collated by Mitchell Goodman (Philadelphia: Pilgrim Press, 1970).

2. John Masefield, *The Box of Delights*.

LETTER 413    July 1968

1. "Nights and Days," *Sumac* 1 (Fall 1968): 101–46.

LETTER 418    October 1968

1. This lecture was collected in Rudolph Steiner, *Evil: Selected Lectures*, ed. Michael Kalisch (London: Rudolph Steiner, 1997).

2. See previous reference to Freud's book and Albert Einstein, *Why War?* (Paris; International Institute of Co-operation, League of Nations, 1933).

3. Underlined three times.

LETTER 419    October 1968

1. "He-Who-Came-Forth," included in *Relearning the Alphabet*.

2. "Late June 1968" and "Not to Have," in *The Outsider* 4/5 (1969): 51.

3. "Biafra," *El Corno Emplumado* 29 (January 1969): 77, collected in *Relearning the Alphabet*.

4. Multiply underlined.

5. *The Great Age of Fresco: Giotto to Pontormo*, Metropolitan Museum of Art, New York, September 28–November 19, 1968.

6. "Are" is underlined twice.

LETTER 421    December 1968

1. "From a Notebook: October '68–May '69," in *Relearning the Alphabet*.

2. Multiply underlined.

LETTER 422    December 1968

1. Published as Robert Duncan's "Changing Perspectives in Reading Whitman," in *The Artistic Legacy of Walt Whitman: A Tribute to Gay Wilson Allen*, ed. Edwin Haviland Miller (New York: New York University Press, 1970), reprinted in *Fictive Certainties* and *A Selected Prose*.

LETTER 423    December 1968

1. Spanish for "Such is life."

2. Multiply underlined.

LETTER 424    March 1969

1. Henry Rago, "The Poet in the Poem," *Poetry* 113 (March 1969): 413–20. The lines cited are from Donne's "The Canonization."

2. Stuart Montgomery, "Six and a Single Remorse for the Sky," *Agenda* 7 (Winter 1969): 69–77.

LETTER 425    April 1969

1. "Relearning the Alphabet" was included in *Relearning the Alphabet*. The second poem mentioning Melanie, "Friendship," is unpublished.

2. "Chardin" was collected in *Marcel Proust: On Art and Literature, 1896–1919*, trans. Sylvia Townsend Warner (London: Chatto and Windus Ltd., 1957). Jean-Siéon Chardin (1699–1779) was a French painter.

**LETTER 426    May 1969**

1. "Annotations to Lavater's *Aphorisms on Man*, in *The Complete Poetry and Prose of William Blake*, ed. David Erdman, commentary by Harold Bloom (Garden City, NY: Doubleday, 1965). This letter is unfinished and unmailed.

**LETTER 427    July 1969**

1. Jess's paintings are: *Gastro-Duodenestomy (Kocher): Translations #22*, 1969; *"Handing Me One of the Halves, He Spoke the Simple Word, Drink": Translations #23*, 1969, and *De Macrocosmi Fabrica: Translations #24*, 1969.

2. "Keeping the War Inside," *Journal for the Protection of All Beings* 3 (July 1969): [36].

**LETTER 429    July 1969**

1. Multiply underlined.

**LETTER 431    July 1969**

1. Lines from Robert Duncan's "Come, Let Me Free Myself," in *Roots and Branches*.

2. "Making It New," *The Hudson Review* 31 (Summer 1968): 399–412.

3. The book was published as *Relearning the Alphabet*.

**LETTER 432    July 1969**

1. See Letter 347. For a recent translation, see *On the Cave of the Nymphs*, trans. Robert Lamberton (Barrytown, NY: Station Hill Press, 1983).

2. William Sturgis Thomas (1871–1941), *The Field Book of Common Mushrooms: With Key to Identification of Gilled Mushrooms and Directions for Cooking Those That Are Edible* (New York: Putnam, 1948).

**LETTER 433    July–August 1969**

1. Multiply underlined.

2. Valery Larbaud, *A. O. Barnabooth, His Diary*, trans. Gilbert Cannan (New York: George H. Doran, 1924); William Carlos Williams, *In the American Grain* (New York: Albert & Charles Boni, 1925); Eudora Welty, *The Golden Apples* (New York: Harcourt Brace, 1949).

**LETTER 434    August 1969**

1. Isak Shurin (1945– ) was a student of Denise

Levertov when she taught at Berkeley in January–June 1969.

2. Denise Levertov's review of Robert Creeley's new book *Pieces* appeared in *Caterpillar* 10 (January 1970): 246–248; reprinted in *The Poet in the World*.

**LETTER 436    September 1969**

1. Published not in 1969, but later in *Sulfur* 35 (1994) and reprinted in *A Selected Prose*.

2. William Carlos Williams, *The Wedge* (Cummington, MA: Cummington Press, 1944).

**LETTER 437    October 1969**

1. Denise Levertov held a teaching position at MIT in 1969–70. The Goodmans had moved from New York to 177 Webster Street in East Boston.

**LETTER 438    November 1969**

1. Robert Duncan replaced Charles Olson, who had been diagnosed with cancer, at this International Poetry Festival.

2. *The World's Great Poets Reading at the Festival of Two Worlds, Spoleto Italy: Ezra Pound Reading His Cantos* (New York: Applause Productions, 1968).

3. Ronald Bayes (1932– ) at the time of the letter was a poet teaching at St. Andrews College in Laurinburg, North Carolina. *A Beast in View: Selected Shorter Poems* (Laurinburg, NC: St. Andrews Press, 1985).

4. The lines above by Robert Duncan are unpublished. "An Animadversion" appeared as "Another Animadversion" in *The Opening of the Field*.

**LETTER 439    December 1969**

1. The Child

Beyond their control long they watch its Play:
At times the full existing face
Stands forth from the profile,
clear and complete as a whole Hour,

which raises the beat and strikes to a close.
But the others do not count the strokes,
Gloomy with toil and with living dour;
And they do not mark at all how it endures—

How it endures all, as then, so always,
When weary in the little suit of clothes,
Near by them as in a waiting room
It sits and would await its time.

\*träge full, inert / trägt—endures
wears    wears out (a suite of clothes)

2. *Lament for Icarus: Translations #25*, 1970.

## LETTER 440    February 1970

1. "A Critical Difference of View," *Stony Brook* 3/4 (1969): 360–63.

2. Hayden Carruth, "Making It New," *Hudson Review* 21 (Summer 1968): 399–412.

3. Charles Olson died on January 10, 1970.

## LETTER 441    February–March 1970

1. Robert Duncan wrote about Elizabeth Drew in "Ideas of the Meaning of Form," collected in *Fictive Certainties*, and about Robin Blaser in "Returning to Les Chimères of Gérard de Nerval," *Audit/Poetry* 4 (1967): 41–64.

2. Richard Grossinger, *Solar Journal: Oecological Sections* (Los Angeles: Black Sparrow Press, 1970). Robert Duncan's introduction was inserted inside the book as a separate publication.

3. Edward Dahlberg, *The Leafless American*, ed. Harold Billings (Sausalito, CA: R. Beacham, 1967).

4. Denise Levertov, *Summer Poems* (Berkeley: Oyez Press, 1970).

5. The phrase "revolution or death" is the first line of "From a Notebook," subsequently Part I of "Staying Alive," and recurs as a refrain in the poem and in the subsequent letters between Duncan and Levertov.

6. "Elegies" is the first section of *Relearning the Alphabet*.

7. Carl Sauer, *Land and Life: Selections from the Writings of Carl Ortwin Sauer*, ed. John Leighly (Berkeley: University of California Press, 1963).

## LETTER 443    April 1970

1. "Novella" and "A Defeat in the Green Mtns," published in *Damascus Road* (Summer 1972): [7], were collected in *Footprints*.

2. "At the Justice Dept, Nov 15th 1969" appeared in *Win* 6.8 (May 1, 1970): [2] and was collected in *To Stay Alive*.

3. This poem, titled "A Place to Live," was collected in *Footprints*.

4. Richard W. Edelman's *The Wedding Feast*, introd. Denise Levertov (Berkeley: Oyez Press, 1970); Edelman's following book was *The Nine Finger Image*, introd. Denise Levertov (New York: Barlenmir House, 1979).

## LETTER 444    June 1970

1. Christian Morgenstern, *Gallowsongs/Galgenleider*, trans. Jess (Los Angeles: Black Sparrow Press, 1970).

## LETTER 445    October 1970

1. The Rimer's Club began as a poetry club in Berkeley; David Bromige took the name with him for a new club when he moved to Sebastopol to teach.

2. In a "Cobati scene" houses are individually designed to fit organically into the landscape.

3. First published (with one other poem) as "Santa Cruz Propositions" in *Poetry Review* 62 (Autumn 1971): 237–41 and then collected in *Ground Work: Before the War*.

## LETTER 447    February 1971

1. "Staying Alive"; the "European Section" refers to Part III of "Staying Alive," collected in *To Stay Alive*.

2. Rebecca Mitchell Garnett, a close British friend, who figures in the last poem of Part III of *Staying Alive*.

3. Kirkland College in Clinton, New York, where Denise Levertov was artist in residence.

4. F.B.I. Director J. Edgar Hoover had testified before a Senate subcommittee about an "East Coast Conspiracy to Save Lives," allegedly led by Frs. Daniel & Philip Berrigan with plans to capture a White House aide (Henry Kissinger) and demand an end to U.S. bombing in southeast Asia; the allegations were denied.

5. *Threads* (Los Angeles: Black Sparrow, 1971).

## LETTER 448    September 1971

1. The castle in the mountains above Rapallo where Pound's daughter Mary de Rachewiltz lived and where Pound lived for a time after his release from St. Elizabeth's in 1958.

2. *To Stay Alive*.

3. Robert Duncan's selections of his current writing in a mimeograph edition, *Ground Work*. A "Prospectus" explained the adventure and asked people to send in money to support it.

4. *Translations* (New York: Odyssia Gallery,

1971). Jess's show was at the Odyssia Gallery, May 9–June 12, 1971.

### LETTER 449    October 1971

1. On May 15, 1969, Berkeley Police and California Highway Patrol officers used buckshot against the protesters at the People's Park in Berkeley. Alan Blanshard was blinded and James Rector was killed.

2. The poem was collected in *The Sorrow Dance*.

3. The reference is to the closing lines of Part III of "Staying Alive," in which Denise Levertov's old English friend Bet, Rebecca Garnett, with whom she has been reunited, speaks to Denise Levertov in lines that begin: "Go down into your well." See Denise Levertov's response in Letter 453.

### LETTER 451    October 1971

1. An unidentified U.S. Army major was reported to have said "It became necessary to destroy the town to save it" about the decision to bomb the center of Bên Tre, April 25, 1967. Denise Levertov quotes the major's statement in "Prologue: An Interim," in "Staying Alive." The prose quotations are from the Preface to *To Stay Alive*.

### LETTER 452    October–November 1971

1. In May 1943, Robert Duncan married Marjorie McKee, who was a student at the Hans Hofmann school in Provincetown, Massachusetts.

2. Robert Duncan quotes from Denise Levertov's "Preface" to *To Stay Alive*. See Appendix.

3. Underlined twice.

### LETTER 453    October–November 1971

1. The poem "I Thirst" in the "Entr'acte" between Parts II and III of "Staying Alive." See Appendix for references in this letter.

2. At the time of the Free Speech Movement, Clark Kerr was president of the University of California at Berkeley. He appears in Robert Duncan's poem "The Multiversity: Passages 21" in *Bending the Bow*:

> [Kerr]
> but behind them
> a hidden community,    three thousand
> outside the university in this
> conspiracy for free speech

3. See Emerson's essay "The Poet." In "Projective Verse" Olson had declared that form was never more than an extension of content, and that became an axiom for Black Mountain aesthetics, But in her essay "Some Notes on Organic Form" Levertov had revised the axiom to declare that form was never more than a revelation of content.

4. At this point the typewriter ribbon gives out and Levertov continues by hand. The typewriter resumes with "Notes in Installment 3."

5. Lines from Denise Levertov's "Life at War."

6. Lines from Denise Levertov's "Life at War."

7. Reference to lines in the "Prologue: An Interim" of "Staying Alive."

8. Reference to lines in Part I of "Staying Alive."

9. Reference to Denise Levertov's treatment of People's Park in Part II of "Staying Alive."

10. The U.S. Justice Department in Washington, D.C. See Letter 443.

### LETTER 454    November 1971

1. "Author's Preface" in *To Stay Alive*.

2. Ezra Pound, "How to Read," collected in *Literary Essays of Ezra Pound*, ed. T. S. Eliot (1935; New York: New Directions, 1968).

3. Papus (Gérard Encusse), *The Tarot of the Bohemians: The Most Ancient Book of the World*, ed. A. P. Morton, preface A. E. Waite (New York: Samuel Weiser, 1958).

4. Charles Olson postulated several dates for the beginning of the modern era, 1500 B.C. or 1200 A.D. See his discussions in *The Special View of History*, ed. Ann Charters (Berkeley: Oyez Press, 1970).

5. Jean Danielou is a prolific scholar of biblical history, for example: *The Bible and the Liturgy* (Notre Dame, IN: University of Notre Dame Press, 1956) and *The Dead Sea Scrolls and Primitive Christianity*, trans. Salvator Attanasio (Baltimore, MD: Helicon Press, 1958).

6. For the lines preceding the ones cited in Part II of "Staying Alive," see p. 735, above.

> Robert reminds me *revolution*
> implies the circular: an exchange
> of position, the high
> brought low, the low
> ascending, a revolving,
> and endless rolling of the wheel.
> (*To Stay Alive*: 41)

7. "Author's Preface" to *To Stay Alive.*

8. The lines are from "Tribute to the Angels" 13, in H. D.'s *Trilogy* (New York: New Directions, 1973). It was published separately as *Tribute to the Angels* (London: Oxford University Press, 1945).

9. Underlined twice.

10. Ernst Cassirer, *The Question of Jean-Jacques Rousseau,* trans. Peter Gay (New York: Columbia University Press, 1954).

LETTER 455    November 1971

1. "The Novel" and "Say the Word" are collected in *O Taste and See.*

2. Sigmund Freud, *Psychopathology of Everyday Life,* trans. James Strachey (New York: W. W. Norton, 1965).

LETTER 457    November 1971

1. Underlined twice.

2. The closing lines of Henry Adams, *Mont-Saint-Michel and Chartres* (Boston: Houghton Mifflin Co., 1905).

LETTER 460    January 1972

1. Tolstoy's estate outside Moscow.

LETTER 461    January 1972

1. Published as "Shakespeare's *Romeo and Juliet* as It Appears in the Mysteries of a Late Twentieth Century Poetics," *Fathar* 4 (June 1972): [54–58].

2. *Poems from the Margins of Thom Gunn's Moly* (San Francisco: The Author's Typescript Edition, 1972), collected in *Gound Work: Before the War.*

3. *A Seventeenth Century Suite,* collected in *Ground Work: Before the War.* "The Burning Babe" was printed as Robert Duncan's and Jess's Christmas card for 1971. Denise Levertov had sent "Advent 1966" in December 1966 (see Letter 382); it is collected in *Relearning the Alphabet.*

LETTER 462    March 1972

1. The letter is dated April 26, but the April dates given in the first sentence make it clear that Duncan misdated. So here March 26 is given as what must be the accurate date.

2. George Bowering and Robert Hogg, *Robert Duncan: An Interview* (Toronto: The Coach House Press, 1971).

3. Both the *Moly* sequence and the "Meta-physical Suite" are collected in *Ground Work: Before the War.*

4. Eldridge Cleaver.

LETTER 463    March–April 1972

1. Multiply underlined.

1. The following is a typewritten form letter signed in Denise Levertov's hand.

LETTER 464    August 1972

1. Robert J. Bertholf, then teaching in the English Department at Kent State University.

2. The New Directions book is *Footprints*; the other is *Conversation in Moscow* (Cambridge, MA: Hovey Street Press, 1973), collected in *The Freeing of the Dust.*

3. *The Poet in the World.*

4. Handwritten below typed closing.

LETTER 465    August 1972

1. Paul Goodman's poem appeared with the essay "Politics within Limits," *The New York Review of Books* 19 (August 10, 1972): 32–34.

2. *Caesar's Gate: Poems 1949–50.*

LETTER 466    November 1972

1. Muriel Rukeyser and Jane Hart, wife of Democratic Senator Philip Hart of Michigan.

2. The poem and name are typed, but the inscription and note below are handwritten.

LETTER 467    April 1973

1. *Dante*; Robert Duncan never finished the Vaughan book he goes on to mention.

2. This letter is unfinished and unmailed.

LETTER 469    December 1975

1. "Some Duncan Letters: A Memoir and a Critical Tribute," in *Scales of the Marvelous,* ed. Robert Bertholf and Ian Reid (New York: New Directions, 1979); reprinted in *Light Up the Cave* and in *New and Selected Essays.*

2. *Out of the Vietnam Vortex: A Study of Poets and Poetry against the War* (Lawrence: University Press of Kansas, 1974).

LETTER 470    June 1976

1. The poem is included in *Relearning the Alphabet.*

2. This letter is unfinished and unmailed.

## LETTER 471    August 1976

1. Robert Duncan's trip to Australia took place in September 1976.

## LETTTER 472    November 1978

1. The letter contained the poem "The Torn Cloth," which was collected in *Ground Work: Before the War.* See Appendix.

## LETTER 473    December 1978

1. The text about nuclear energy is printed on the left side of the card on which Denise Levertov wrote her note.

## LETTER 474    February 1979

1. This letter is marked at the top "Not Sent."

2. The poem "The Torn Cloth" accompanied Duncan's letter of November 11, 1978 (see Letter 472); the poem appeared in *Ground Work: Before the War.*

## LETTER 476    March 1984

1. The Shelley Prize was awarded by the Poetry Society of America jointly to Levertov and Duncan.

## LETTER 477    April 1984

1. Jess confirms that this letter was not mailed.

## LETTER 478    September 1985

1. Denise Levertov sent Robert Duncan this letter written to her by Peggy Church, with her note written on the bottom. It was the last communication between them before his death in 1988.

## LETTER 479    April 1988

1. The poem enclosed with this letter, "To R. D., March 4th 1988," reflects on the reasons for the break in the long freiendship of Denise Levertov and Robert Duncan and recounts a dream she had a month after his death. In the dream they meet in the Lady Chapel in the west aisle of a cathedral resonant with organ music, and wordlessly they touch hands in reconciliation. Below the typescript of the poem is written in Levertov's hand: "For Jess from Denny April 1988." "To R. D., March 4th 1988" was published in *A Door in the Hive* (New York: New Directions, 1989). See Appendix for the text of the poem.

# INDEX

This index cites only proper names and titles, with subheadings as appropriate. For the most frequently cited entries, only the more substantive appearances in the letters have been included here.

"A" (Zukofsky), 543
*ABC of Reading* (Pound), 585
Abstract Expressionism, 21
Abulafia, 137
*Ace of Pentacles* (Wieners), 443, 473–74, 477–78, 484
"The Acts of Youth" (Wieners), 383, 473
Adam, Helen, 14, 18, 155, 290, 757; apartment of, 486; "At the Window," 334; *Ballads*, 428, 469; on Hell, 619; illness of, 330, 331–32, 333–34, 417; Merrill Foundation grant for, 460, 823n.1; *The Queen of Crow Castle*, 143, 411; *San Francisco's Burning*, 426, 428
Adams, Henry, Mont-Saint-Michel and Chartres, 695
"Adam's Song" (Duncan), xix
*Adam's Way* (Duncan), 315, 355, 370, 376, 377, 384, 517–18, 819n.2
Admiral, Virginia, 98, 281, 371, 376–77, 409, 411, 416–17, 420–21, 757
"An Admonition" (Levertov), 480
"Advent 1966" (Levertov), xix, 561–62, 700, 701, 712
Aeschylus, 214
"African Elegy" (Duncan), 404
*African Folktales and Sculpture* (Radlin), 206
*African Genesis* (Frobenius), 577
*African Saga* (Cendrars), 7, 799n.2
"Africa Revisited" (Duncan), 14, 204, 207
*After Lorca* (Spicer), 96
*Against the Gnostics* (Plotinus), 298, 299

Ahrimanic process, 619
Aiken, Conrad, 19
*Aion*, 472, 487
Akhmatova, Anna, 757
Alain-Fournier, *Le Grand Meaulnes*, 583
"Alastor" (Shelley), 183
Aldan, Daisy, *A New Folder, Americans*, 177, 178, 189
Aldington, Richard, 186, 757
*Alegoria del amor* (Goya), 118
*Alice in Wonderland* (Carroll), 88
Allen, Donald M., 56, 66, 103, 110, 144–45, 147–48, 279–80, 757; *The New American Poetry*, ix–x
"All in a Day's Work" (Duerden), 455
*Also Sprach Zarathustra* (Nietzsche), 48
"The Altars in the Street" (Levertov), 552–53, 558, 661
Altoon, John, 16, 20–21, 24, 26, 757
Alvarez, A., 149
Ambelain, Robert, *La Kabbale pratique*, 349
"American Collages" (Museum of Modern Art, New York City), 444
American Friends Service Committee, 706
American Humanist Association, 555
*Amers* (Perse), 297, 298, 299, 300
Ammons, A. R., 388, 758; "Catalyst," 392; "Rising," 392; "Saliences," 392; "The Strait," 392; "Three Poets," 338
"An A Muse Ment" (Duncan), xiii, 3–5, 6

*Anabase* (Perse), 297, 299, 300
Andersen, Hans Christian, *Fairy Tales*, 169, 178, 190
Anderson, Lee, 123
*Angel Midnight* (Kerouac), 205
Anger, Kenneth, 530, 758; "Illustration," 444
"An Animadversion" (Duncan), 643
*Anna Karenina* (Tolstoy), 214
"An Anniversary Death" (Wieners), 383
"Another Spring" (Levertov), 359, 378
"The Answer" (Herbert), 90
"Answering" (Duncan), 363–67
Antoninus, Brother (William Everson), 117, 381, 504, 631–32, 758; *Hazards of Holiness*, 382, 413
"Apprehensions" (Duncan), 168, 240, 246–47, 248–49, 374
"The Architecture" (Duncan), 465
Arensberg Collection (Philadelphia Museum of Art), 341, 817n.1
Aristotle, 214
Aronson, Daniel B., 406
Arp, Jean, 19; *The Dada Painters and Poets*, 63
*Art News*, 178, 758
Art Nouveau, 21, 111, 641
*Art Nouveau* (Museum of Modern Art, New York City), 269
Ashbery, John, x, 179, 758
"As in the Old Days" (Duncan), 465, 469
"As I Ponder'd in Silence" (Whitman), 466–67, 553
"As It Happens" (Levertov), 435

"Asking the Fact for the Form" (Levertov), 404, 405, 406, 417–18
"Asphodel, That Greeny Flower" (Williams), 18
As Testimony (Duncan), 460
"Atlantis" (Duncan), 130
"Atlantis" I and II (Blaser), 496–97
"At Sather Gate" (Ginsberg), 50
"At the Justice Dept, Nov 15th 1969" (Levertov), 654, 659
"At the Loom" (Duncan), 463–64
"At the Window" (Adam), 334
Auden, W. H., 758
Audit/Poetry, 525–26
Aunt Fay (Duncan's aunt), 64
Autobiographies (Yeats), 663
"Autumn" (Tomlinson), 222
Avison, Margaret, 758–59; The Dumbfounding, 547
"The Awakening" (Creeley), 208
A? Year's Darling of a Pig My Size!: Translations #20 (Jess), 541

Baker, Richard, 506, 825n.1
"A Ballad for Helen Adam" (Duncan), 14, 16, 18–19, 20, 800n.1
"The Ballad for Mrs. Noah" (Duncan), 59
"The Ballad of My Father" (Levertoff), 450
"The Ballad of the Enamord Mage" (Duncan), 59, 71, 132, 143, 159
Ballads (Adam), 428, 469
Bank, Barbara, 174, 809n.3
Baraka, Amiri. See Jones, Leroi
Barnes, William, 348
Barnstone, Willis, 179, 235
Baudelaire, Charles, "Du Vin," 468–69
Bauhaus, 234
Baum, L. Frank, 29, 759
Bayes, Ronald, 642, 832n.3
Bays, Gwendolyn, The Orphic Vision, 468–69, 488
The Beard (McClure), 542–43
Beats, x, 179
Beauty and the Beast (Cocteau), 156
Bedford, Sybille, 759; The Legacy, 252
"Bee: Flowers" (Duerden), 455
Beim, Maybelle, 76, 104, 313
Bell, Leland, 7, 21, 24, 178, 759

Bell, Louisa Matthiasdottir, 7, 20, 22, 24, 115, 776
Belyi, Andrey, St. Petersburg, 224
"Bending the Bow" (Duncan), 449–50
Bending the Bow (Duncan), 572–73, 574, 580
"Benefice" (Duncan), 492
Benson, Robert L., 334, 817n.1
Berenson, Bernard, 759
Berenson, Betty, 617
Bergé, Carol, 357, 759
Bergman, Ingmar, Winter Light, 430
Berkeley Poetry Conference, 492, 499–501
The Berkeley Review, 176, 199
Berrigan, Daniel, 566, 759, 833n.4
Berrigan, Philip, 759, 833n.4
Berrigan, Ted, 759
Berry, Wendell, 218, 219, 600, 759–60
Berryman, John, 760; Dream Songs, 435, 439
Bertholf, Robert J., 705, 835n.1
Bethlehem (Pennsylvania), 823n.2
Bettelheim, Bruno, 275; "Joey: A 'Mechanical Boy'," 472–73
Between the Acts (Woolf), 487
"Biafra" (Levertov), 621
Bid Me to Live: A Madrigal (H. D.), 256, 262, 263
The Big Table, 205, 240
Bilbo, Jack, 170, 808–9n.2
Birth of Tragedy (Nietzsche), 588, 591
Bischoff, Elmer, 237, 760
Bishop, Gordon, 534, 567
Blackburn, Paul, x, 8, 760; "Death & the Summer Woman," 11; Duncan on, 9; "Here Is a Marriage," 12; Levertov on, 11–12; "Name Cast into the Tree-Alphabet," 594; "Storm," 12
Black Is My True Love's Hair (Roberts), 56
Black Mountain (North Carolina), x
Black Mountain poets, x–xi, 834n.3. See also Creeley, Robert; Duncan, Robert; Levertov, Denise; Olson, Charles
Black Mountain Review, x, 16, 17, 34, 36, 42, 61, 144, 432, 760, 764, 766, 776, 779, 800n.3, 801n.1, 801n.3
Black Rain (Kitasono), 21, 800n.1

Blaine, Nell, 79, 177, 178, 212, 219, 223, 760
Blake, William, 22, 214
Bland, Edith Nesbit, 31, 800n.1
Blanshard, Alan, 661, 686, 834n.1
Blaser, Robin, 56, 123, 355–57, 760; "Atlantis" I and II, 496–97; "The Borrower," 496; Les Chimères, 502–3, 525–26; Cups, 502–3; Duncan on, 384–85, 389, 495–96; The Faerie Queen, 502–3; The Holy Forest, 502–3; "Invisible Pencil," 496–97; Jess on, 495–96; Levertov on, 386, 494–95; "The Medium," 496, 497; The Moth Poems, 444, 496, 502–3; "My Dear," 496; The Park, 502–3; "The Preface," 138, 140; readings by, 502; "Salut," 497; "The Transparencies," 138, 140
Bliss, Donald, 384
Blixen, Karen (Isak Dinesen), 765
Blok, Aleksander, 760
Bloomsbury group, 396
Bloy, Leon, 760–61
Bly, Robert, 175, 177, 182–83, 203, 761; "Poetry in the Age of Expansion," 290; "The Work of Denise Levertov," 588–90, 591
Blyth, Reginald Horace, Haiku, 9, 799n.1
Boehme, Jacob, 188–89; The Incarnation of Christ, 199, 211; Mysterium Magnum, 528–29, 539–40; The Signature of All Things, 168; Six Theosophic Points, 168–69
Boepple, Willard, 826n.1; "The Fear that Precedes Changes of Heaven," 521
Bogan, Louise, 315, 761
Bombadil, Tom, 531
A Book of Resemblances (Duncan), 66, 111, 204, 207, 288, 458–61, 462, 567
"The Border Line" (Lawrence), 17
Borregaard, Ebbe, 125, 444, 761; gallery of, 262, 270, 281, 813n.2; "Wapitis," 129–30, 132, 133, 135
"The Borrower" (Blaser), 496
Borsig, Tet, Designs in Nature, 329
Bosco, Henri, Malicroix, 513
The Bostonians (James), 87–88
Boston Museum of Fine Arts, 185

*Botteghe Oscure*, 49, 802n.1
*Bottom* (Zukofsky), 543
Boulez, Pierre, *Le Marteu sans Maître*, 249
Bowering, George, 383, 573
Bowes-Lyon, Lilian, 369, 761
*The Box of Delights* (Masefield), 579, 581, 583
Boyce, Jack, 501
Brancusi, Constantin, 582–83
Brautigan, Richard, 761
Bread and Puppet Theatre, 566, 601, 828n.1, 828n.2
Brecht, Bertolt, 673
Bresdin, Rodolphe, "The Good Samaritan," 328–29
*Breton Village Under Snow* (Gauguin), 170
"Brink" (Eigner), 66
Brinnin, John Malcolm, 761
"Broken Glass" (Levertov), 433
Bromige, David, 626, 656, 761, 833n.1; *The Gathering*, 498; *Threads*, 659
Brooke, Rupert, 217
Broughton, James, 64, 70, 74–75, 145, 388, 761; *True and False Unicorns*, 71
Brown, Lynne, 204
Brown, Norman O., 151–52, 172, 193, 761–62; *Love's Body*, 235
Brown, Robert Carlton, 155, 807–8n.1
"Brown Study" (Guest), 290
Bryher (*pseud. of* Annie Winnifred Ellerman), xxix, 762; Duncan on, 321–22, 324; *Heart to Artemis*, 391; Levertov on, 318–19, 322, 323–24; McAlmon on, 320–21; politics of, 322; "A Small Grain of Worship," 305
Buber, Martin, 139, 140, 271, 418, 561, 762; *Tales of the Hasidim*, 140–41
Bueno, William de la Torre (Bill), 461
"Bullfrogs to Fireflies to Moths" (Levertov), 712
Bultmann, Rudolf Karl, *Theology of the New Testament*, 562–63
Bunting, Basil, 762
Burford, William, 560, 762, 828n.1
Burke, Edmund, 80
Burlington (Vermont), 22–23
"The Burning Babe" (Southwell), 700, 749–52

Burroughs, William, 762; *Naked Lunch*, 205
Burton, David, 762
Burton, Hilda, 384, 762
*The Butterfly* (Rumaker), 476, 477
Button, John, 284, 342, 345, 346, 347–48, 381, 762, 819n.7
Butts, Mary, 21

Caballa. See *Zohar*
*Caesar's Gate* (Duncan), 18, 28, 66, 110–11, 708
Caetani, Marguerite, 48, 49, 802n.1
Cage, John, x, 123, 762
Camus, Albert, 676; *The Rebel*, 663
*The Cantos* (Pound), xii, 81, 125, 131, 163–64, 213, 534
Cardenal, Ernesto, 540, 541, 545–46, 762
Carlyle, Thomas, 282–83
*Carnival Night* (Rousseau), 30
"The Carpenter" (Duncan), 210, 212
Carroll, Lewis, *Alice in Wonderland*, 88
Carroll, Paul, 93, 762–63
Carruth, Hayden, xxx, 543, 557, 637, 742, 763; Duncan on (*see* "A Critical Difference of View"); illness of, 645; Levertov on, 645–47; "Making It New," 638, 646; "Scales of the Marvellous," 479, 481, 482; on William Carlos Williams, 648, 649, 729–30, 731, 732, 733
"Casa Felice I & II" (Levertov), 659
Cassirer, Ernst, *The Question of Jean-Jacques Rousseau*, 690
Castro, Fidel, 630
"Catalyst" (Ammons), 392
*Caterpillar*, 581, 763
"A Cellar Song" (Reaney), 224
Cendrars, Blaise (*pseud. of* Frederic Sauser-Hall), 763; *African Saga*, 7, 799n.2
Central Park West (New York City), 516
Cernovich, Nicola, 763
Cézanne, Paul, 605, 830n.3
*Cézanne's Garden* (Vuillard), 112
Chagall, Marc, 19
"Changing Perspectives in Reading Whitman" (Duncan), 625

"Chardin" (Proust), 632
Chardin, Jean-Siéon, 831n.2
*The Chariot: Tarot VII* (Jess), 336
Chicago Cadre, 600
*Chicago Review*, 185, 763
"The Child" (Duncan), 643–44, 832–33n.1
"Childhood" (Vaughn), 200
Childs, Barney, 383, 819n.1
*Les Chimères* (Blaser), 502–3, 525–26
"Chinese Nightingale" (Lindsay), 262
"Chocorua to Its Neighbor" (Stevens), 483
"Chords: Passages 14" (Duncan), 463, 466
Christian Caballa. See *Zohar*
Church, Peggy Pond, 718, 763
*Circle*, 829n.2
"*[City of Night]* A Review" (Rumaker), 476, 478
"City Psalm" (Levertov), 474
*Civilization and Its Discontents* (Freud), 619
Civil Rights Movement, 821n.2
"Claritas" (Levertov), 363, 370
Clark, R. T. Rundle, *Myth and Symbol in Ancient Egypt*, 567
Clark Institute (Williamstown), 515
*Claude Monet: Seasons and Moments* (Museum of Modern Art, New York City), 249, 812n.1
Cleaver, Eldridge, 702
"Clyfford Still" (Crehan), 237
Cobati scene, 656, 833n.2
"Cocaine" (Wieners), 473
Cocteau, Jean, 14; *Beauty and the Beast*, 156
Coleridge, Samuel Taylor, 14, 46, 514
"The Collage: Passages 6" (Duncan), 464, 466, 469–70
"The Collar" (Herbert), 95
*Collected Poems 1942–1952* (Duncan), 460
Collins, Burgess. See Jess
*Combustion*, 212, 763
"Come, Let Me Free Myself" (Duncan), 637
"Come into Animal Presence" (Levertov), 200, 202, 231
*Come into Animal Presence* (Levertov), 285
*Commedia* (Dante), 516–17

*The Commentaries on the Timaeus of Plato in Five Books* (Proclus), 490

"The Communion" (Levertov), 130

*The Complete Poems of D. H. Lawrence* (Lawrence), 256–57

*The Complete Poems of Emily Dickinson* (Dickinson), 264, 265

Confucius, 5, 501, 595, 825n.3

Connors, Thomas, 826n.3

Conover, Grandin, 506–7, 515

Constructivism, 21

*Contact*, 185, 240, 763

*Contemporary American Poetry*, 317–18

"The Continent" (Duncan), 399–400, 401–3

"Continuing" (Levertov), 231

*Conversation in Moscow* (Levertov), 705

"A Conversation with Denise Levertov" (Sutton), 521

*Convivio* (Dante), 509, 511, 512

*The Convivio of Dante Alighieri* (Wicksteed), 512

Cook, Arthur Bernard, *Zeus: A Study in Ancient Religion*, 559, 577–78

Cooney, Blanche, 564, 828n.1

Cooney, James Peter, 564, 828n.1

Corman, Cid (Sidney), x, 36, 49, 61, 63, 763

*El Corno Emplumado*, 764

Corot, Jean Baptiste Camille, *Le Pont de Mantes*, 50

*Correspondences*, 14, 17–18

Corso, Gregory, 49–50, 103, 179, 764; "I Married the Pig's Daughter," 51

Cosimo, Piero di, *A Forest Fire*, xviii–xix, xxi

*Cosmographie* (Heylin), 12

*The Counterplot* (Mirrlees), 487

*Coyote's Journal*, 480

Craig, Edward Henry Gordon, 47, 764

*Creative Imagination in Art & Poetry* (Maritain), 252

Creeley, Ann, 7–8, 10–11, 17, 25–27, 799n.2

Creeley, Leslie, 312, 816n.1

Creeley, Robert, 17, 764; "The Awakening," 208; at Black Mountain, x; at *Black Mountain Review*, x; Bly on, 182–83; children of, 26–27; "The Cri-

sis," 432; "The Crow," 432; Divers Press founded by, 13, 799–800n.1; "The Dress," 71, 181; and Duncan, 51–52, 81, 120–23, 235–36, 330–31, 587–88; "The Fate Tales," 432; *The Finger*, 606; "The Flower," 236–37; "A Folk Song," 236–37; "For Leslie," 428; *For Love*, 354; "A Form of Women," 236, 425, 433; "For the New Year," 236–37; "Le Fou," 432; "Going to Bed," 113, 121, 122; "The Gold Diggers," 432; "Grace," 432; "The Hero," 236–37, 433; "Heroes," 107, 109, 113, 121–23, 236–37; "The Hill," 236–37; *If You*, 52; *The Island*, 416, 424; and Jess, 51, 235; and Levertov, x, 234–35, 235; in Majorca, 7–8, 799n.2; "The Messengers," 428; "My Love," 157; and Olson, Charles, x, xii; *Pieces*, 640, 641; "Please," 236–37; readings by, 109, 452–53; and Marthe Rexroth, 38–39, 41–42, 43, 45–46, 51; Rexroth on, 20; "The Rose," 234, 235; "Saturday Afternoon," 113, 122; at the State Department, 526; "They Say," 433; "The Three Ladies," 433; *The Whip*, 71; "A Wicker Basket," 236–37; "The Women, 221; on writing a poem, 548

Crehan, Hubert, 233–34, 235, 238–39, 764; "Clyfford Still," 237

*Le Crise mystique de Victor Hugo* (Levaillant), 553–54

"The Crisis" (Creeley), 432

"A Critical Difference of View" (Duncan), xxx, 645–49, 651–53, 729–33

"Crosses of Harmony & Disharmony" (Duncan), 65, 70

"The Crow" (Creeley), 432

Crowley, Aleister, 354

Cubism, 21

cummings, e. e., 9, 145, 240

Cunningham, Merce, x

"Cunt Poem One" (Moraff), 493

*Cups* (Blaser), 502–3

"The Curve" (Duncan), 548, 551

"Cyparissus" (Duncan), 372–73, 374

*D. H. Lawrence: A Composite Biography*, 250

Dada, 119

*The Dada Painters and Poets* (Arp and Motherwell), 63

Dahlberg, Edward, 8, 205, 764; *The Leafless American*, 649; *Sorrows of Priapus*, 105

Damballah, 401–2

"The Dance" (Duncan), 48, 65

"The Dancers: Passages 27" (Duncan), 517, 545

*The Dancers Inherit the Party* (Finlay), 378

Dante Alighieri, 214–15, 609; *Commedia*, 516–17; *Convivio*, 509, 511, 512

Darwin, Charles, 111, 542, 691; *Origin of Species*, 31

Davenport, John, 33; *Ezra Pound*, 801n.1

*David Copperfield* (film), 374–75

Da Vinci, Leonardo, 41

Dawson, Fielding, 764

Day, John, 32

"The Dead" (Levertov), 433

de Angulo, Jaime, 558, 764

"Death & the Summer Woman" (Blackburn), 11

Debs, Eugene, 168, 808n.3

"A Defeat in the Green Mountains" (Levertov), 653

De Kooning, Willem, 24, 765

Dellinger, Dave, 609

*De Macrocosmi Fabrica: Translations #24* (Jess), 633

Dembo, Lawrence S., 581, 829n.1

De Niro, Robert (painter), 765

"The Departure" (Levertov), 57, 59, 68, 433

"The Depths" (Levertov), 231

De Rachewiltz, Mary, 765, 833n.1

*Derivations* (Duncan), 64

*The Design of Poetry* (Wheeler), 569

*Designs in Nature* (Borsig), 329

Deutch, Richard, 826n.3

Dickey, James, 462, 765; "The Fire-bombing," 470, 695–96; Levertov on, 536–37; "Reincarnation," 470–71; *The Suspect in Poetry*, 483; *Two Poems of the Air*, 470, 530, 536

Dickinson, Emily, 267, 273, 440, 447, 560; *The Complete Poems of Emily Dickinson*, 264, 265

Dinesen, Isak (*pseud. of* Karen Blixen), 765

di Prima, Diane, 451, 513–14, 765
"The Directive" (Duncan), 242
"Discipline" (Herbert), 90
Divers Press, 13, 18, 799–800n.1
*Doctor Faustus* (Mann), 186
*Doctor Zhivago* (Pasternak), 173
"Domestic Scenes" (Duncan), 6, 432
Donahoe, Wade, 12; "A Letter," 61, 63, 799n.4, 802–3n.1
Donne, John, 21
Dorfman, Elsa, 765
Dorn, Edward, x, 16, 138, 212, 765; *Georgraphy*, 502; *Measure #1*, 116; "Los Mineros," 266; "The Problem of the Poem for My Daughter Left Unsolved," 502; "The Sense Comes over Me," 502
Dorn, Helène, 16
*The Double Image* (Levertov), 448, 449, 712
Douglas, Gavin, 63
"Doves" (Duncan), 310, 312, 316
*The Dragon and the Unicorn* (Rexroth), 24–25, 732
"Dream" (Levertov), 231
"Dream Data" (Duncan), 202
*Dreaming of Temptation* (Eilshemius), 170
*Dream Songs* (Berryman), 435, 439
"The Dress" (Creeley), 71, 181
Drew, Elizabeth, 648, 833n.1
Duerden, Richard, 77–78, 456–57, 461, 462, 464–65, 765; "All in a Day's Work," 455; "Bee: Flowers," 455; "In Spite of It All," 455; "Mr. Boswell & Dr. Johnson," 455; "Poem: Completely Naked," 455; "Poems 1958–1961," 455; "Right Now," 455; "The Sonata," 455; "3 AM Black," 455
Dugan, Alan, 765
*Duino Elegies* (Rilke), 270–71
Dull, Harold, 200, 201–2, 765
"Dullness" (Herbert), 92
*The Dumbfounding* (Avison), 547
Dunbar, Robert, 385
Duncan, Robert, anarchism of, 827n.2; Australia trip of, 712–13, 836n.1; birth/adoption of, 791; at Black Mountain, x; and Creeley, 51–52; death of, xxvii, 795; drafting of, 791; Harriet Monroe Memorial

Prize won by, 793; health of, 528; illness of, xxvii, 717–18, 795; and Jess, xiv; and Levertov, first meeting with, xiv, 7, 799n.1; and Levertov, personal meetings with, x, xiv, 99–100, 108, 316, 317, 325, 426, 575, 613–14, 620; in Majorca, 7, 799n.1; marriage to Marjorie McKee, 791, 834n.1; and Olson, Charles, x, 61; at the Poetry Center, 48, 52–53, 56, 57, 802n.1; projection by, 662, 663, 665; religious background of, xv–xvii, xx–xxii, xxv, 243; San Francisco house of, 563–64, 571; at San Francisco State University, 489; Shelley Memorial Award received by, 717, 795; surgery of, 633, 634, 635–36, 638–39; Union Civic and Arts Foundation Prize won by, 792; at University of California at Berkeley, 791, 792
Duncan, Robert, letters to Levertov, admiration for Levertov in, 5, 68, 80–81; on cats, 48, 105, 106, 109, 136–37, 265, 325; on effort, 5; on finances, 18, 33–34, 35, 111, 220, 270, 334, 367, 392; first letter, xiii–xiv, 5–6; on Guggenheim Fellowships, 99, 111, 160, 391, 395, 804n.1; handwriting, samples of, 724–26; on imagination, xv; importance/scope of correspondence, ix, xiv–xv; on income taxes, 393–94; on Levertov, Denise, 665; on Levertov, love for, xxviii–xxx, 107–8, 325, 481, 713–14; on Levertov, readings by, 77, 79, 83, 93–94, 96, 99, 106, 109, 312–14, 804n.3; on Levertov's friendship, 107, 624, 699–700, 701–2, 707 (see also Duncan/Levertov rupture); on love, 34–35, 225, 325; poetic explorations in, generally, xv–xvi; on publication/prestige, 220–21; on reading his poems, 162, 166–67, 172, 241, 243–44, 246, 294–95, 297, 334–35, 431, 507; reading recommendations in, 28–29; on smoking, 371; on titles of poems, 5

Duncan, Robert, works of, "Adam's Song," xix; *Adam's Way*, 315, 355, 370, 376, 377, 384, 517–18, 819n.2; "African Elegy," 404; "Africa Revisited," 14, 204, 207; "An A Muse Ment," xiii, 3–5, 6; "An Animadversion," 643; "Answering," 363–67; "Apprehensions," 168, 240, 246–47, 248–49, 374; "The Architecture," 465; "As in the Old Days," 465, 469; *As Testimony*, 460; "Atlantis," 130; "At the Loom," 463–64; "A Ballad for Helen Adam," 14, 16, 18–19, 20, 800n.1; "The Ballad of Mrs. Noah," 59; "The Ballad of the Enamord Mage," 59, 71, 132, 143, 159; *Bending the Bow*, 572–73, 574, 580; "Bending the Bow," 449–50; "Benefice," 492; *A Book of Resemblances*, 66, 111, 204, 207, 288, 458–61, 462, 567; *Caesar's Gate*, 18, 28, 66, 110–11, 708; "The Carpenter," 210, 212; "Changing Perspectives in Reading Whitman," 625; "The Child," 643–44, 832–33n.1; "Chords: Passages 14," 463, 466; "The Collage: Passages 6," 464, 466, 469–70; *Collected Poems 1942–1952*, 460; "Come, Let Me Free Myself," 637; "The Continent," 399–400, 401–3; "A Critical Difference of View," xxx, 645–49, 651–53, 729–33; critical reception of, 384–85, 511–12; "Crosses of Harmony & Disharmony," 65, 70; "The Curve," 548, 551; "Cyparissus," 372–73, 374; "The Dance," 48, 65; "The Dancers: Passages 27," 517, 545; *Derivations*, 64; "The Directive," 242; "Domestic Scenes," 6, 432; "Doves," 310, 312, 316; "Dream Data," 202; "Early History," 7; "Earth Song," 517; "Earth's Winter Song," xviii, 519–20, 522, 650, 734–35; "The Effort," 287; "Epilogos," 572, 577–78, 580; "The Essay at War," 204, 565; *Faust Foutu*, 100; "The Fear That Precedes Changes of Heaven," 65; "5th Sonnet,"

427; "The Fire: Passages 13," xviii, 461, 462, 463, 572–73; "Fire Dying," 289; "First Invention on the Theme of Adam," 433; *First Poems*, 518; "Food for Fire, Food for Thought," 161–62; "For a Muse Meant," xiii–xiv, 61, 432–33; "Four Songs the Nightnurse Sang," 260; "God Spell," 580; "The Green Lady," 14, 16, 18–19, 20, 65, 800n.1; *Ground Work: In the Dark*, xxiii, 660, 700, 833n.3; The H. D. Book, xxix; "The Heart," 548, 551; *Heavenly City, Earthly City?* xiii, 142, 370; "Hero Song," 65; "Homage," 35, 60; "Homage to Coleridge," 35, 38, 48, 801n.1; "The Homosexual in Society," 217–18, 221, 222, 225; "The Horns of Artemis," 204; "Ideas of the Meaning of Form," 196, 283, 293, 648; "An Imaginary War Elegy," 800n.2; "I must wake up into the morning world," 202, 208; "In Perplexity," 174, 176, 189–90; "An Interlude," 545, 557; "Keeping the Rhyme," 69, 70; "Keeping the War Inside," 634; "Lassitude," 431; "The Law," 238; "The Law I Love Is Major Mover," xxii, 802n.2; *Letters*, 52, 61, 62, 66, 68, 90, 140, 150–51, 154–55, 169, 193, 807n.3; "The Little Day Book," 294, 295–96, 297, 301–3, 389–91, 395–96, 458, 472–73, 492; "The Lost Cat," 232–33; "The Maiden," 65; "Man's Fulfillment in Order and Strife," xxii, 609, 618–19; *Medea at Kolchis: The Maiden Head*, 44, 48, 49, 58, 63, 497, 801n.1; *Medieval Scenes*, 431–32, 449; "The Message," 326, 328; "Metaphysical Suite," 701; "The Moon," 464; "The Multiversity," 572–73, 673, 834n.2; "The Museum," 711; "My Mother Would Be a Falconess," 470, 472; "Nel Mezzo del Camin di Nostra Vita," 194; "Night Scenes I, II, III," 353, 357, 371; "Often I Am Permitted to Re-

turn to a Meadow," 131, 136, 802n.2, 806n.1; "Of the Art," 65; "Of the War," xxi–xxii; *Of the War: Passages 22–27*, xviii, 553; *The Opening of the Field*, 48, 90, 111, 126, 131, 134–35, 137, 169, 194, 220; "Oriented by Instincts by Stars," 530; "The Origins of Old Son," 38, 315, 801n.2; "Out of the Black," 173; "Parsifal: Afer Wagner & Verlaine," 478; "A Part-Sequence for Change," 384; "Passages," xvi, xviii; "Play with Masks," 525; "A Poem Beginning with a Line by Pindar," 204–5; "A Poem of Despondencies," 121, 806n.1; *Poems 1948–49*, 22, 90; "A Poem Slow Beginning," 46, 48, 131–32; "The Poetic Vocation: St. John Perse," 297, 299, 316–17; "Poetry, a Natural Thing," 56, 66, 70, 803n.2; "The Propositions," 58, 59, 61, 65; "The Question," 72, 74; "Reflections on the Mode of Literary Polemics," 649; "Risk," 262, 264, 267; "Rites of Participation," 581; *Roots and Branches*, 430–31, 458, 479–80, 615; "Roots and Branches," 165–66, 181; "Saint Graal: After Verlaine," 478; "Salvages," 431; "Santa Cruz Propositions," xxi, 656, 663, 701, 711, 740–41, 831n.1; *Selected Poems*, 110, 160, 162, 196, 199, 201; "The Self in Postmodernist Poetry," xxii; "A Set of Romantic Hymns," 338–39; "Shadows," 465, 468; "Shakespeare's *Romeo and Juliet*," 699; "Shelley's *Arethusa* Set to New Measures," 288, 291; "A Shrine to Ameinias," 581; "The Soldiers: Passages 26," 507–8, 517, 525, 527, 528, 531, 572–73; "Song of Fair Things," 69, 70; "A Song of the Old Order," 178; "The Song of the Borderguard," 204; "Songs for an Evening's Singing," 70; "Sonnet IV," 394, 409, 415; "Source," 433, 434; "Spelling: Passages 14," 463, 464, 466, 469–70; "The Spider Song," 62; Stein period

of, 204; "A Storm of White," 109, 114–15, 117, 130, 728–29; "Strains of Sight," 312, 316; "The Structure of Rime," 48, 65, 390–91; "Structure of Rime XXIII," 465; "Such Is the Sickness of Many a Good Thing," 442–43, 446; "Taking Away from God His Sound," 484, 485, 489–90; "The Temple of the Animals," 202, 207; "These Past Years: Passages 10," 463; "This Place, Rumord to be Sodom," 65; "Three Pages from a Birthday Book," 56; "Three Poems in Measure One," 66; "Three Songs of the Bard Orpheus," 370–71; "To Pumpkin-Cat," 54; "The Torn Cloth," xxvii, 716, 752–54; "Towards an Open Universe," 439; "Tribal Memories," 463–64; "The Truth and Life of Myth: An Essay in Essential Autobiogrpahy," 617; "Two Poems for the Jews," 204; "Two Presentations," 277; "Under Ground," 130, 806n.6; "Upon Taking Hold," 432–33; "Up Rising: Passages 25," xviii, xx, 505, 506–7, 515, 528, 563, 572–73, 612, 666, 679, 695, 738–39; "Variations on Two Dicta of William Blake," 251, 255, 262; "The Venice Poem," 195–96, 197–98, 199, 384, 431; "What I Saw," 464, 467; "Where It Appears," 464, 467–68, 478–79, 550; *Windings*, 430; *Writing Writing*, 52, 66, 462–63, 469; *The Years as Catches*, 562; "Yes, As a Look Springs to Its Face," 94, 139
Duncan/Levertov rupture, xiii–xv, xx–xxi, xxv–xxviii, 794; Duncan on Levertov's antiwar activism/neglect of her work, 490, 607–8, 611–12, 661–62; Duncan's criticisms of Levertov/her responses, 664–74, 686–91, 693–98, 701, 707, 714; Levertov on Duncan's criticisms/her criticisms of him, 662, 674–86, 693; Levertov on Duncan's quote in Mersmann, 711, 715–17. *See also* "To R. D., March 4th, 1988"

Dunn, Joe, 94, 156, 766
*Dur Désir de Durer* (Eluard), 177–78
"During the Eichmann Trial" (Levertov), 404–5, 407, 410, 821n.1
Durrell, Gerald, 766
Dusenberry, Gail, 566, 626, 766
"The Duty of Professionals" (Goodman), 608
"Du Vin" (Baudelaire), 468–69

"Early History" (Duncan), 7
"Earth Psalm" (Levertov), 448–49
"Earth Song" (Duncan), 517
"Earth's Winter Song" (Duncan), xviii, 519–20, 522, 650, 734–35
"East Coast Conspiracy to Save Lives," 658, 833n.4
Eberhart, Richard, 766
Economou, George, 766
Edelman, Richard W.; *The Wedding Feast*, 655
Edson, Russell, 766; *The Very Thing That Happens*, 423
"The Effort" (Duncan), 287
*The Egoist*, 261
Eichmann, Adolf, 290, 404, 815n.7
Eigner, Larry, x, 70, 87, 110, 766; "Brink," 66; disability/illness of, 75, 76, 138, 184, 187, 191; "Murder Talk: The Reception," 481; *Poems*, 190
Eilshemius, Louis, 169–70, 173, 808n.1; *Dreaming of Temptation*, 170; *Malaga Beach*, 170
Einstein, Albert, *Why War?* 619
Elimelekh of Lijensk, "The True Wonder," 584
Eliot, George, 41
Eliot, T. S., 196–97; *On Poetry and Poets*, 77; "The Three Voices of Poetry," 132–33; *The Waste Land*, 197, 270
Elkinton, Dave, 600
Ellerman, Annie Winnifred. *See* Bryher
Ellingham, Lewis, 494, 497, 498, 513, 766
Ellmann, Richard, *James Joyce*, 247
Elmslie, Kenward, 179, 766
Eluard, Paul (pseud. of Eugene Grindel), 766; *Dur Désir de Durer*, 177–78
"The Elves" (Levertov), 326
"Elysium" (Lawrence), 258–59

Emerson, Ralph Waldo, 684; "Give All to Love," 227; "The Poet," xxiv, 406, 680, 834n.3; "Poetry and Imagination," xxii; Romanticism of, xxii–xxiii
*Encyclopédie de la Divination*, 553
*The End of It* (Goodman), 253, 278, 279–80, 310
*End to Torment* (H. D.), 285
Engle, Paul, 766–67
"Enquiry" (Levertov), 666–67
Enslin, Theodore, 234, 767; "Forms III," 471; "Landscape with Figures," 292; "Mercury Poems," 487; "Seven Poems," 287–88
"Enter with Riches" (Levertov), 448
*Epilegomena* (Harrison), 68, 70
"Epilogos" (Duncan), 572, 577–78, 580
Ernst, Max, 17, 19
Eshleman, Clayton, 508, 566, 581, 615, 767
"The Essay at War" (Duncan), 204, 289, 565
*The Evergreen Review*, 71, 143–45, 174, 185, 204–5, 232, 234, 767, 803n.3
Expressionism, 21
*Ezra Pound* (Davenport), 801n.1

Fabilli, Mary, 767
"Face to Face" (Levertov), 435, 440–41, 444, 447–48
*The Faerie Queen* (Blaser), 502–3
Fahs, Ned, 791
"The Fair-Haired Eckbert" (Tieck), 280
*Fairy Tales* (Andersen), 169, 178, 190
Farmington Fair (Maine), 427–28
"The Fate Tales" (Creeley), 432
*Faust Foutu* (Duncan), 100
*Fearful Symmetry: A Study of William Blake* (Frye), 443
"The Fear That Precedes Changes of Heaven" (Duncan), 65, 521
Ferlinghetti, Lawrence, 30, 46, 49, 77–78, 767, 801n.2
"Festival" (Kandinsky), 483
Field, Edward, 179, 767
"5th Sonnet" (Duncan), 427
"A Figure of Time" (Levertov), 358
*The Finger* (Creeley), 606
Finlay, Ian Hamilton, 543, 595,

767; *The Dancers Inherit the Party*, 378; "[23 Poems]", 373
"The Fire: Passages 13" (Duncan), xviii, 461, 462, 463, 572–73
"The Fire-bombing" (Dickey), 470, 695–96
"Fire Dying" (Duncan), 289
"First Invention on the Theme of Adam" (Duncan), 433
*First Poems* (Duncan), 518
Fitts, Dudley, 768
Fitzgerald, Edward, 56, 768
Fitzgerald, F. Scott, 478
Fitzgerald, Robert, 303
"The Five-Day Rain" (Levertov), 185
*5 Poems* (Levertov), 95
Flaubert, Gustave, *Letters*, 255; *Madame Bovary*, 256; *Salambo*, 256; *St. Julian*, 256; *The Temptation of St. Anthony*, 256
*The Floating Bear*, 768
"The Flower" (Creeley), 236–37
"The Flower" (Herbert), 90, 91–92
"A Folk Song" (Creeley), 236–37
"Food for Fire, Food for Thought" (Duncan), 161–62
*Foot*, 232, 768
*Footprints* (Levertov), 705
"For a Muse Meant" (Duncan), xiii–xiv, 61, 432–33
Ford, David, 423
*A Forest Fire* (Cosimo), xviii–xix, xxi
"For Leslie" (Creeley), 428
*For Love* (Creeley), 354
"Formal Reply" (Levertov), 231
"A Form of Women" (Creeley), 236, 425, 433
"Forms III" (Enslin), 471
"For the New Year" (Creeley), 236–37
"Le Fou" (Creeley), 432
Foulkes, Lyn, 501, 825n.5
*The Foundations of Aesthetics* (Ogden, Richards, and Wood), 41
*Foundations of Tibetan Mysticism* (Govinda), 529–30
*Found Objects* (Zukofsky), 729, 732–33
*Fountain of Arethusa* (Jess), 288
*The Four Seasons and the Archangels* (Steiner), 517
"Four Songs the Nightnurse Sang" (Duncan), 260

*Fragments of a Faith Forgotten* (Mead), 249
Franco, Francisco, 629
Fredericks, Claude, 150–51, 556–57, 768
Freilicher, Jane, 768
Freud, Sigmund, 80, 225, 442, 501, 551–52, 610, 696; *Civilization and Its Discontents*, 619
Frobenius, Loe, *African Genesis*, 577
"From a Notebook: October '68–May '69" (Levertov), 544–45, 591, 604, 623, 650, 656, 672, 742
*From Baudelaire to Surrealism* (Raymond), 118
"From the Roof" (Levertov), 589
Frye, Northrop, *Fearful Symmetry: A Study of William Blake*, 443
Fuller, Buckminster, x
Fussiner, Howard, 809n.3

*Gallowsongs/Galgenleider* (Morgenstern), 655
Garcia Lorca, Federico, "Puñal," 420
Garier, Pierre, 830n.8
Garnett, Rebecca Mitchell ("Bet"), 658, 683, 833n.2, 834n.3
Garth, Midi, 103, 768
*Gastro-Duodenestomy (Kocher): Translations #22* (Jess), 633
*The Gathering* (Bromige), 498
Gaudier-Brzeska, Henri, 768
Gauguin, Paul, *Breton Village Under Snow*, 170
Gelpi, Albert, 638, 828n.2
Gelpi, Barbara, 828n.2
*Genesis West*, 768
*Georgraphy* (Dorn), 502
"Ghandi's Gun & Brecht's Vow" (Levertov), 659
"Giant" (Richards), 141, 149
Gilbert, Jack, 381, 382–83, 414–15, 768
Gilhain, Bob, 601
Ginsberg, Allen, x, 49–51, 55–56, 156, 768, 802n.1; "At Sather Gate," 50; "Howl," 49, 103, 119, 131, 172, 284–85, 287, 408, 509; "Ignu," 178; "Kaddish," 234, 284–85, 287; readings by, 170–71, 172, 500; "Xbalba," 119
Ginsberg, Louis, *Legends of the Bible*, 142

"Girlhood of Jane Harrison" (Levertov), 95
"Give All to Love" (Emerson), 227
Givens, Seon (Mrs. Robert Manley), 215, 224, 255, 279, 454, 811n.1
*The Glass Bees* (Jünger), 280
Gleason, Madeline, 51, 102, 155, 159, 431, 768–69
*Goblin Market* (Rossetti), 110
Gobron, Gabriel, *Histoire et Philosophie du Caodaïsme*, 554
Godden, Rumer, 567
"The Goddess" (Levertov), 202, 433
"God Spell" (Duncan), 580
"Going to Bed" (Creeley), 113, 121, 122
Goldberg, Mimi, *The Lover and Other Poems*, 335
"The Gold Diggers" (Creeley), 432
*The Golden Apples* (Welty), 640
*The Golden Cushion Story Book* (Levertov), 10
Goldman, Michael, 515
Goodman, Mitchell ("Mitch"; Levertov's husband), 7, 769; death of, 796; divorce from Levertov, xxviii, 711, 794; *The End of It*, 253, 278, 279–80, 310; at Hofstra, 485; indictment/trial of, xx, 603–4, 605–6, 677–78, 794, 830n.1; *Light from under a Bushel*, 605; marriage to Levertov, xiv, 33, 55, 398–99, 792; *Movement*, 655; *The Movement toward a New America*, 613
Goodman, Nik (Levertov's son); arrest of, 642–43; Biafran poster by, 622; birth of, 792; book report on *Ayesha*, 332; at camp, 187, 368; childhood of, 11, 13, 40, 69–70, 95, 100–101, 108, 180; at Haystack, 535; linoleum cut by, 265, 813–14n.1; poetry writing of, 284; at Putney School, 372, 427, 429, 486; at Rhode Island School of Design, 586–87, 621–22, 655
Goodman, Paul, 401, 707–8, 730, 769; "The Duty of Professionals," 608; *The Lordly Hudson*, 397–98; *Our Visit to Niagara*,

380; "The Strike for Peace," 397
"The Good Samaritan" (Bresdin), 328–29
Govinda, Lama, *Foundations of Tibetan Mysticism*, 529–30
Goya, Francisco de, *Alegoria del amor*, 118
"Grace" (Creeley), 432
*La Grande Jatte* (Seurat), 115
*Le Grand Meaulnes* (Alain-Fournier), 583
Grass, Günther, 219, 220
Greek play, chorus of, 27
*Greek Vases from the Hearst Collection* (Metropolitan Museum of Art, New York City), 112, 805n.2
Green, Harry (Levertov's brother-in-law), 434, 676
Greene, Jonathan, 341, 769
"The Green Lady" (Duncan), 14, 16, 18–19, 20, 65, 800n.1
Gresser, Seymour ("Sy"), 16, 769
"Grief, have I denied thee?" (Levertov), 435, 440–42
"Grief Dismissed" (Levertov), 435, 440–42
*The Griffin* (Masefield), 579, 581, 583
Grindel, Eugene. See Éluard, Paul
Grossinger, Richard, *Solar Journal*, 649
"The Ground Mist" (Levertov), 412
*Ground Work: In the Dark* (Duncan), xxiii, 660, 700, 833n.3
Grove Press, 52, 65, 66, 110, 224, 226
Guadalajara, 35, 60
Guest, Barbara, 179, 375, 457–58, 459, 460, 769; "Brown Study," 290
Guggenheim Museum (New York City), 223–24
*Guillevic: Selected Poems* (Levertov), 606
Guimard, Hector, 269, 814n.11
Gurdjieff, G. I., 769
Guston, Philip, 769
Guthrie, W. K. C.; *Orpheus and Greek Religion*, 463
Guy Fawkes' Day, 73

H. D., 176, 251; *Bid Me to Live: A Madrigal*, 256, 262, 263; critical reception of, 310, 315; death of, xxix, 309, 318–19;

*End to Torment*, 285; fears of traveling, 321; *Helen in Egypt*, 294; *Hermetic Definition*, 289; illness of, 295, 296, 309, 318–19, 458; and Levertov, xxix, "Prisoners," 262; *Sagesse*, 207; *Selected Poems*, 68, 71; "Tributes," 396; "Tributes to the Angels," 689; *Trilogy*, xxii; *Vale Ave*, 207; "The Walls Do Not Fall," 256

"H. D.: An Appreciation" (Levertov), 358

The H. D. Book (Duncan), xxix, *see also* "The Little Day Book"

Haas, Robert, 383, 819n.1

*Haiku* (Blyth), 9

Hall, Donald, 317–18, 423, 769–70

*Hamlet* (Shakespeare), 671; Hammer, Louis Z.; "How the Poem Speaks," 521

Hammond, Mac, 770

*A Handbook of Greek Mythology* (Rose), 558–59

"Handing Me One of the Halves, He Spoke the Simple Word, Drink": Translations #23 (Jess), 633

"The Hands" (Levertov), 432, 433, 589–90

Hanson, Kenneth O., 770

Hardenberg, Frederick von. *See* Novalis

Hardy, Thomas, 90, 214

Harris, Joel Chandler, 830n.2

Harrison, Jane, 770; *Epilegomena*, 68, 70; *Reminiscences of a Student's Life*, 494

Harrison, Jim, 471, 543, 546, 770; "War Suite," 565

Hart, Jane, 708

Haselwood, Dave, 770

Hassidism, 142, 621

Hatch, Robert, 293, 308

Hawkes, John, 770

Hawley, Robert, 770

*The Hazards of Holiness* (Antoninus), 382, 413

"The Heart" (Duncan), 548, 551

*Heart to Artemis* (Bryher), 391

"Heaven" (Herbert), 90

*Heavenly City, Earthly City* (Duncan), xiii, 142, 370

Hebrew Caballa. See *Zohar*

Hecht, Anthony, 305, 770

Heidt, Dori, 816–17n.2

Heidt, Erich, 321, 816–17n.2

*Helen in Egypt* (H. D.), 294

Hemley, Cecil, 162, 223, 282

"Henry Purcell" (Hopkins), 275–76

Heraclitus, 191

Herbert, George, "The Answer," 90; "The Collar," 95; "Discipline," 90; "Dullness," 92; "The Flower," 90, 91–92; "Heaven," 90; "Holy Baptism," 92; "Hope," 90; "Jordan," 90; "The Odor," 90; "Sighs and Groans," 90; *The Temple*, 90–93; "Time," 90; "A True Hymn," 90

*Here and Now* (Levertov), 55, 2, 74–75, 76–77, 83, 87, 89, 107, 111

"Here Is a Marriage" (Blackburn), 12

Herman, John, 35–36

"Hermaphoroditic Telephones" (Williams), 119

*Hermetical Physick* (Vaughan), 528

*Hermetic Definition* (H. D.), 289

Herms, George, 390, 820n.4

"The Hero" (Creeley), 236–37, 433

"Heroes" (Creeley), 107, 109, 113, 121–23, 236–37

"Hero Song" (Duncan), 65

Herrmann, John, 46, 770

Hesiod, *Theogony*, 559; *Works and Days*, 508

"He-Who-Came-Forth" (Levertov), 620

Heylin, Peter, *Cosmographie*, 12

"The Hill" (Creeley), 236–37

Hiroshima Day demonstration (New York City), 601

Hirschman, Jack, 771

*Histoire et Philosophie du Caodaïsme* (Gobron), 554

Hochman, Sandra, 338, 771

Hodes, Ida, 102, 501, 771

Hofmann, Hans, 771

Hofmannstahl, Hugo von, 61–62

Holabird, Donna, 600

"Holy Baptism" (Herbert), 92

*The Holy Barbarians* (Lipton), 189

*The Holy Forest* (Blaser), 502–3

"Holy Poems" (Richards), 398

"Homage" (Duncan), 35, 60

"Homage to Coleridge" (Duncan), 35, 38, 48, 801n.1

Homer, 214

"The Homeric Hymn to Mercury" (Shelley), 730

"The Homosexual in Society" (Duncan), 217–18, 221, 222, 225

Hoover, J. Edgar, 658, 833n.4

"Hope" (Herbert), 90

Hopkins, Gerard Manley, xvi; "Henry Purcell," 275–76

"The Horns of Artemis" (Duncan), 204

Housman, A. E., 369

"Howl" (Ginsberg), 49, 103, 119, 131, 172, 284–85, 287, 408, 509

"How the Poem Speaks" (Hammer), 521

*How to Write* (Stein), 14, 24

Hoyem, Andrew, 378

*The Hudson Review*, 771

Hugo, Victor, *La Légende des Siècles*, 487–88; "Pleine Mer," 487–88, 489

Hulme, T. E., 435, 439, 771

Humphrey, Hubert, 519–20, 522, 546, 620

Humphries, Rolfe, 144

"The Hunt in the Wood: Paolo Uccello" (Kyger), 474

Hutter, Donald, 394–95, 569, 572–73

"Hymn to Eros" (Levertov), 504, 590

Ibsen, Henrik, 17

"The Ice Eagle" (Wakoski), 566

"Ideas of the Meaning of Form" (Duncan), 196, 283, 293, 648

"If John Button" (Levertov), 342–46, 347, 348–53

*If You* (Creeley), 52

Ignatow, David, 771

"Ignu," (Ginsburg), 178

"Illustration" (Anger), 444

"Illustrious Ancestors" (Levertov), 433

"An Imaginary War Elegy" (Duncan), 800n.2

Imagism, x, 569, 732

"I Married the Pig's Daughter" (Corso), 51

"I must wake up into the morning world" (Duncan), 202, 208

*The Incarnation of Christ* (Boehme), 199, 211

*In Cold Hell in Thicket* (Olson), 431

"Indochina Summer," 706

*Industrial Worker*, 216

Industrial Workers of the World, 808n.3
"In Memory of Boris Pasternak" (Levertov), 255
"An Innocent" I, II (Levertov), 231, 432
"In Obedience" (Levertov), 432
"In Perplexity" (Duncan), 174, 176, 189–90
*In Praise of Krishna* (Levertov), 556
"In Spite of It All" (Duerden), 455
"An Interlude" (Duncan), 545, 557
International Poetry Festival (Austin, Texas), 642, 832n.1
"An Interview with Robert Creeley, 1965" (Wagner), 521
"In Thai Bihn (Peace) Province" (Levertov), 709
"In the Night" (Levertov), 544
"Into the Interior" (Levertov), 412
*Intrepid*, 537, 827n.4
"Invisible Pencil" (Blaser), 496–97
*The Invisible Poet: T. S. Eliot* (Kenner), 196–97
Irby, Ken, 499–500, 825n.2
Isabella Gardner Museum (Boston), 185–86
*Ishi in Two Worlds* (Kroeber), 586
*The Island* (Creeley), 416, 424
"I Thirst" (Levertov), 659
Izzo, Carlo, 180, 771

*J*, 232, 771
*Jacob and His Brothers*, 360–62
"The Jacob's Ladder" (Levertov), 255–56
Jacobus, Harry, 105, 805n.1
Jaege, Werner Wilhelm, 80
James, Henry, 510; *The Bostonians*, 87–88
James, William, 503
*James Joyce* (Ellmann), 247
Jargon Society, 771
Jarrell, Randall, 256, 315, 771
Jarrett, Emmett, 514, 534, 541
Jefferies, Richard, 771; *The Story of My Heart*, 369
Jess (Burgess Collins; Duncan's life partner), 8, 763; *A? Year's Darling of a Pig My Size!: Translations #20*, 541; background of, 226; "The Boobas and the Bunny Duck" draw-

ings, 208, 810n.1; *A Book of Resemblances* illustrations, 339, 346, 460–61, 462, 518; *The Chariot: Tarot VII*, 336; collages by, 17–18, 23, 34, 259–60, 801n.1; and Creeley, 51, 235; *De Macrocosmi Fabrica: Translations #24*, 633; and Duncan, beginning of life partnership with, 792; exhibition at Borregaard's Museum, 281, 286; exhibition at Dilexi Gallery, 137, 259, 262, 807n.2, 813n.1; exhibition at Gumps, 86, 161, 164; exhibition at Rolf Nelson Gallery, 501, 516; exhibition at the Museum of Modern Art, 444; exhibition at the Odyssia Gallery, 660, 833–34n.4; *Fountain of Arethusa*, 288; *Gastro-Duodenestomy (Kocher): Translations #22*, 633; and Ginsberg, 51, 802n.1; *"Handing Me One of the Halves, He Spoke the Simple Word, Drink": Translations #23*, 633; on imagination/fancy, 213; *Lament for Icarus: Translations #25*, 644; and Levertov, 29, 323, 719; on *Measure*, 67; *Montana Xibalba: Translations #2*, 395; *The Nasturtium that Dissolved the World*, 12–13; *O!* 241; at the Odyssia Gallery, 606, 830n.1; *The Opening of the Field* drawing, 244–45, 247; poems of, 101; *San Francisco's Burning* illustrations, 426; on sexuality, 227; on Spicer, 57; translations by, 289; *Trinity's Trine: Translations #5*, 458, 516; *12 Poets & 1 Painter* illustrations, 471; works in *The Artist's View*, 42, 801n.1
"Jess Translations" (Rolf Nelson Gallery, Los Angeles), 501
"Joey: A 'Mechanical Boy'" (Bettleheim), 472–73
"John Button" (Kornblee Gallery, New York City), 381, 819n.7
John Guggenheim Foundation, 804n.1
John Jay Whitney Foundation, 78
"John Smith" (Olson), 178–79
Johnson, Kay, 310
Johnson, Lyndon B., 519, 541, 546, 552, 558, 685, 696
Johnson, Ronald, 547, 569, 772;

"Still Life," 480; "When Men Will Lie Down As Gracefully & As Ripe," 480–81
Jonas, Stephen, 94, 116, 119, 772
Jones, Angel, 791
Jones, David, 698, 772
Jones, Leroi (*later* Amiri Baraka), 234, 401–2, 492–93, 772
"Jordan" (Herbert), 90
Joseph, Barbara, 500, 563
Joyce, James, 214, 247, 304, 416; *Portrait of the Artist as a Young Man*, 608
Judeo-Christian experience/tradition, xvi, xvii, 210
*Jugend*, 538
Jung, C. G., 699; *Memories, Dreams, Reflections*, 415, 419
Jünger, Ernst, *The Glass Bees*, 280
"Junk" (Wilbur), 290, 300

*La Kabbale pratique* (Ambelain), 349
"Kaddish" (Ginsberg), 234, 284–85, 287
Kalish, Donald, 772
Kalos, Victor, 25
Kandel, Lenore, 500, 825n.2
Kandinsky, Vasily, 239–40; "Festival," 483
Kantorowicz, Ernst, 772
Karnes, Karen, 123
*Kayak*, 772
Keats, John, 197, 271, 382
"Keeping the Rhyme" (Duncan), 69, 70
"Keeping the War Inside" (Duncan), 634
Kees, Weldon, 10, 30, 548, 772–73
Kelley, Betty, 713
Kelley, Bryan, 713
Kelly, Robert, 773; "Notes on the Poetry of Deep Image," 260, 269, 300; "115 Weeks," 510
Kennedy, John F., 558
Kenner, Hugh, 279, 280, 424, 773, 814n.4; *The Invisible Poet: T. S. Eliot*, 196–97
*Kenyon Review*, 396
Keough, Edna, 568
Kerkam, Earl, 46, 773
Kerouac, Jack, x, 119; *Angel Midnight*, 205; *On the Road*, 73, 103, 116; *The Subterraneans*, 116
Kerr, Clark, 679, 834n.2
King, Martin Luther, Jr., 541

Kinnell, Galway, 514, 773; "The Poetry Shelf," 548
Kinter, William, 268
Kirkland College (Clinton, N.Y.), 658, 674
Kirstein, George, 503, 515, 773
Kirstein, Lincoln, 415–16, 425, 773
Kitasono, Katsue, *Black Rain*, 21, 800n.3
Kizer, Carolyn, 773
Klee, Paul, 239, 560
Klinà, Edward, 307, 816n.1
Kline, Franz, x, 23, 24, 119, 773
"The Knot" (Rich), 547
Koch, Kenneth, 179, 773
Koven, David, 564
Kramer, Bernard, 583–84
Kraus, Louise Antionette, 383, 819n.1
Kray, Elizabeth, 234, 295, 450, 487, 773
Kresch, Albert, 46, 103, 123, 208, 373, 705, 773
Kresch, Pat, 208, 373, 705
Krim, Seymour, 217, 221, 236
Kroeber, Theodorea, *Ishi in Two Worlds*, 586
*Kulchur*, 306, 373, 774
*Kultur*, 308
Kung (Confucius), 501, 825n.3
Kwock, C. H.; *Why I Live on the Mountain*, 186
Kyger, Joanne, 444, 501, 774, 819n.2; "The Hunt in the Wood: Paolo Uccello," 474; "My Father Died This Spring," 474; "These Things We See Are Images of the Past," 474

Lagherlof, Selma, 774; *Wonderful Adventures of Nils*, 70
Lamantia, Philip, 161, 167, 774
"A Lamentation" (Levertov), 440–42, 444–46
*Lament for Icarus: Translations #25* (Jess), 644
"Landscape with Figures" (Enslin), 292
*Language* (Sapir), 538–39
"Language and World Order" (Central Washington State College, 1968), 609
Lansing, Gerrit, 813n.1
Laos invasion, 658
Larbaud, Valery, 774
"Lassitude" (Duncan), 431

Laughlin, James, 52, 100, 158, 219, 220, 399, 581, 774
"Laughter" (Lawrence), 64
"The Law" (Duncan), 238
"The Law I Love Is Major Mover" (Duncan), xxii, 802n.2
Lawrence, D. H., 65; "The Border Line," 17; *The Complete Poems of D. H. Lawrence*, 256–57; "Elysium," 258–59; "Laughter," 64; *Look, We Have Come Thru*, 90, 804n.1; "Paradise Re-Entered," 257–58; *The Trespasser*, 186, 369; "Two Wives," 250–51
Lax, Robert, 774
"Laying the Dust" (Levertov), 41, 42
*The Leafless American* (Dahlberg), 649
*Leaves of Grass* (Whitman), 61, 90, 625–26
*Lectures on Godmanship* (Solovyev), 209
Leed, Jake, 504–5, 825n.2
*The Legacy* (Bedford), 252
*La Légende des Siècles* (Hugo), 487–88
*Legends of the Bible* (Ginsberg), 142
Leger, Alexis. *See* Perse, Saint-John
Leite, George, 576, 829n.2
Leonardo, 41
Leontief, Wassily, 775
"The Lesson" (Levertov), 15
"A Letter" (Donahoe), 61, 63, 799n.4, 802–3n.1
*Letters* (Duncan), 52, 61, 62, 66, 68, 90, 140, 150–51, 154–55, 169, 193, 807n.3
"Let the heart's pain slack off" (Wieners), 473
Lettrist Movement, 596
"Let Us Sing Unto the Lord a New Song" (Levertov), 659
Levaillant, Maurice, *Le Crise mystique de Victor Hugo*, 553–54
Levertoff, Beatrice (Levertov's mother), 10, 12, 23, 254, 284, 621, 791
Levertoff, Olga (Levertov's sister), 434, 675–76, 791, 822n.1; "The Ballad of My Father," 450
Levertoff, Paul (Levertov's father), 791

Levertov, Denise, x; background of, 95–96; Bess Hokin Prize won by, 261; birth of, 791; and Creeley, x; dancing of, 29, 47, 96, 97; and Day, 32; death of, xxx, 796; at Drew University, 513; and Duncan, first meeting with, xiv, 7, 799n.1; and Duncan, personal meetings with, x, xiv, 99–100, 108, 316, 317, 325, 426, 575, 613–14, 620; England visit by, 655; and H. D., xxix; in Hanoi, 708; illness of, 148–49; and Jess, 29, 323, 719; at Kirkland College, 658, 674; Lifetime Achievement Award received by, 796; marriage to Mitch (*see* Goodman, Mitchell); at MIT, 642–43, 645, 832n.1; at *The Nation*, xxix, 283, 289–90, 425, 430; at Norton, xxx; at the Radcliffe Institute, 482, 824n.1; religious background of, xvi, xvii, xxv; Robert Frost Medal received by, 795; in Russia, 698–99; at the School of Visual Arts, 304, 306; Shelley Memorial Award received by, 717, 795; at Vassar College, 554, 569–70
Levertov, Denise, letters to Duncan, admiration for Duncan in, 6, 59–60; on cats, 73, 149, 203, 223, 292, 430, 555; on Christmas, 158; on drug use, 50; on Duncan, love for, xxviii–xxix, 715–16; on Duncan's attack on Carruth, 645–47; on Duncan's first letter, misunderstanding about, 6; on Duncan's friendship, 106, 622–23, 693, 706, 712, 715–17 (see also Duncan/Levertov rupture); on Duncan's readings, 451–54; on finances, 184–85, 284; on Guggenheim Fellowships, 392–93, 394; handwritten, samples of, 721–23; on imagination, xv; importance/scope of correspondence, ix, xiv–xv; on parenthood, 471; poetic explorations in, generally, xv–xvi; on reading her poems, 75–76, 79, 88–89, 95, 156, 248, 311–12, 314–15, 452; on "Revolution or death," 629, 660–61, 681–82

Levertov, Denise, works of, "An Admonition," 480; "Advent 1966," xix, 561–62, 700, 701, 712; "The Altars in the Street," 552–53, 558, 661; "Another Spring," 359, 378; "As It Happens," 435; "Asking the Fact for the Form," 404, 405, 406, 417–18; "At the Justice Dept, Nov 15th 1969," 654, 659; "Biafra," 621; "Broken Glass," 433; "Bullfrogs to Fireflies to Moths," 712; "Casa Felice I & II," 659; "City Psalm," 474; "Claritas," 363, 370; *Come into Animal Presence*, 285; "Come into Animal Presence," 200, 202, 231; "The Communion," 130; "Continuing," 231; *Conversation in Moscow*, 705; "The Dead," 433; "A Defeat in the Green Mountains," 653; "The Departure," 57, 59, 68, 433; "The Depths," 231; *The Double Image*, 448, 449, 712, 792; "Dream," 231; "During the Eichman Trial," 404–5, 407, 410, 821n.1; "Earth Psalm," 448–49; "The Elves," 326; "Enquiry," 666–67; "Enter with Riches," 448; "Face to Face," 435, 440–41, 444, 447–48; "A Figure of Time," 358; "The Five-Day Rain," 185; *5 Poems*, 95; *Footprints*, 705; "Formal Reply," 231; "From a Notebook: October '68–May '69," 604, 623, 650, 656, 672–3, 675, 686, 742; "From the Roof," 589; "Ghandi's Gun & Brecht's Vow," 659; "Girlhood of Jane Harrison," 95; "The Goddess," 202, 433; "Grief Dismissed," 435, 440–42; "The Ground Mist," 412; *Guillevic: Selected Poems*, 606; "H. D.: An Appreciation," 358; "The Hands," 432, 433, 589–90; *Here and Now*, 55, 62, 74–75, 76–77, 83, 87, 89, 107, 111; "He-Who-Came-Forth," 620; "Hymn to Eros," 504, 590; "If John Button," 342–46, 347, 348–53; "Illustrious Ancestors," 433; "In Memory of Boris Pasternak," 255; "The Innocent Cat," 9; "An Innocent" I, II, 231, 432; "In

Obedience," 432; *In Praise of Krishna*, 556; "In Thai Bihn (Peace) Province," 709; "In the Night," 544; "Into the Interior," 412; "I Thirst," 659; "The Jacob's Ladder," 255–56; *The Jacob's Ladder*, 284; "A Lamentation," 440–42, 444–46; "Laying the Dust," 41, 42; "The Lesson," 15; "Let Us Sing Unto the Lord a New Song," 659; "Life at War," xviii, xix, xxv–xxvi, 519, 530, 532–33, 588–89, 666–67, 678, 684, 735–36; *Life in the Forest*, xxvii, 713; "Like Dogs in Mexico," 435, 444; "Lonely Man," 433; "Looking for the Devil Poems," 659; "The Lost Black-and-White Cat," 231; "The Lovers," 37, 40–41, 42, 68; "A Map of the Western Part of the County of Essex in England," 242; "Merritt Parkway," 432, 433; "Metamorphic Journal," 714; "Mrs. Cobweb," 171–72, 433; "The Muse," 242; "A Necessary Poetry," 252, 266–67; "A Night," 432; "Notebook Pages," 544–45, 591; "Note of A Scale," 231, 433; "A Note on the Poetry of Larry Eigner," 184, 190–91; "A Note on the Work of the Imagination," 213; "Notes of Discovery," 102; "A Note to Olga, 1966," 742; "The Novel," 692; "Novella," 653; "Novices," 412; "October," 429, 434–35; "The Old Adam," 520, 818n.1; "Olga Poems," 459, 461–62, 469, 471, 491–92, 493, 553, 557, 667, 670–71, 675–76, 690; "One of the Lucky," 397–98, 401; "On Reading the Early Poems of Robert Duncan," 201, 206–8, 547–48; *O Taste and See*, 435, 691–92; *Overland to the Islands*, 55, 67–68, 76–77, 87, 107, 111, 400–401; "The Park," 171, 231, 433; "The Path," 289; "A Place to Live," 654–55; *The Poet in the World*, xxiii; "A Poet's View," xvii, xxiv–xxv; "The Postcards," 544; "Prologue: An Interim," 663, 684, 834n.1; "Psalm concerning the

Castle," 486, 487; "A Psalm Praising the Hair of Man's Body," 430, 434–35, 440–41; "Puñal," 412, 413, 419–20; "The Rabbits," 433; "Relative Figures," 171, 181, 202; "Relative Figures Reappear," 433; *Relearning the Alphabet*, 638, 650–51, 657, 712; "Relearning the Alphabet," 631, 634, 650, 692; "A Ring of Changes," 149, 152–54, 175, 181–82, 186, 231, 433, 590; "The Risk," 256; "Say the Word," 411, 421, 435, 692; "Scenes from the Life of the Pepper Trees," 51, 57, 171, 231, 433; "A Secret," 354, 358; "Seedtime," 430, 434–35; "Seems Like We Must Be Somewhere Else," 95; "September 1961," 309, 310; "Shalom," 358, 363; "The Sharks," 68, 171, 433, 589; "The Shifting," xiii, 97, 193, 714; "Six Variations," 191, 231; "Some Duncan Letters—A Memoir and a Critical Tribute," xxvi; "Some Notes on Organic Form," xvi, xxii, xxiv, 368, 510, 834n.3; "Something to Wear," 35, 433; "A Song," 37; "Song for a Dark Voice," 191, 231, 448; *The Sorrow Dance*, 533, 556, 742; "The Springtime," 37, 40–41, 171, 231; "Staying Alive," xxi, 604, 682–83, 743–48, 834n.3, 834n.6; "Stepping Westward," 474–75; "A Stir in the Air," 65, 68, 374, 455; "Sunday Afternoon," 65; "The Take Off," 231, 804n.1; "Tenebrae," xix, 666–67, 668, 672, 678, 685, 737; "Three Meditations," 263, 266; "Threshold," 412; "Today," 659; "Today's Saint," 231; "To Death," 449; "Tomatlan," 35, 42, 43–45; "To R. D., March 4th, 1988," xxx–xxxi, 719, 754–55, 836n.1; "To Robert: a letter," 523–25, 526; *To Stay Alive*, xix, 662, 663–65, 679, 742–43; "To the Muse," 359; "To the Snake," 105; "To Write Is to Listen," 485; translations by, 223, 811n.1; "The Tree," 544; *A Tree Telling of Orpheus*, 592–93, 606–7, 657; "Turn-

ing," 431, 589–90; "A Vision,"
519, 531; "The Way Through,"
32; "What Is a Prose Poem?",
278–79, 291; "What Were
They Like?", 535–36, 666–67;
"Who Is at My Window," 412;
"The Wife," 191–92; "The
Willow of Massachusetts,"
435; "The Willows," 412;
"Wine," 468–69; *With Eyes
at the Back of Our Heads*, 231,
327; "With Eyes at the Back of
Our Heads," 171, 175, 231, 433,
589; "The World Outside,"
231; "Xmas Trees on the Bank's
Facade," 432; "The Year One,"
659

Levinsohn, Florence, 600

"Levity" (Richards), 141

Levy, G. Rachel, 775

Lewis, C. S., 775; *Till We Have
Faces*, 284, 288

Lewis, John, 600

Lichtenstein, Roy, 582–83

"Life at War" (Levertov), xviii,
xix, xxv–xxvi, 519, 530, 532–33,
588–89, 666–67, 678, 684,
735–36

*Life in the Forest* (Levertov), xxvii,
713

*Life Studies* (Lowell), 283

*Light from under a Bushel* (Good-
man), 605

"Like Dogs in Mexico" (Lever-
tov), 435, 444

*Lilith* (MacDonald), 18

Lindbloom, Nancy, 575

Lindsay, Vachel, "Chinese
Nightingale," 262

Linenthal, Mark, 774

Lipton, Lawrence, *The Holy
Barbarians*, 189

Lish, Gordon, 381, 819n.6

*Literature and the Occult Tradi-
tion* (Saurat), 488

"The Little Day Book" (Duncan),
294, 295–96, 297, 301–3,
389–91, 395–96, 458, 472–73,
492

Litz, Katy, 775

Living Theatre (New York City),
243–44, 245

Lockwood, Willard A., 459–60,
461

*Locus Solus*, 775

Loewinsohn, Ron, 574, 775

Lofting, Hugh, 239

Logan, John, 775

"Lonely Man" (Levertov), 433

*Look, We Have Come Thru*
(Lawrence), 90, 804n.1

"Looking for the Devil Poems"
(Levertov), 659

Lopes, Michael, 632

*The Lordly Hudson* (Goodman),
397–98

"Los Angeles Now" (Robert
Fraser Gallery, London), 516

"The Lost Black-and-White Cat"
(Levertov), 231

"The Lost Cat" (Duncan), 232–33

Louis XI, king of France, 671

*Louis Zukofsky* (film), 543, 827n.2

Lourie, Dick, 514, 534, 567

*Love Makes—The Air Light*
(Roseliep), 502

*The Lover and Other Poems*
(Goldberg), 335

"The Lovers" (Levertov), 37,
40–41, 42, 68

*Love's Body* (Brown), 235

Lowell, Robert, 494, 509, 560,
775, 825n.3, 828n.2; *Life
Studies*, 283; *The Mills of the
Kavanaughs*, 52–53

Loy, Mina, 101, 775–76

"Lucerific and Ahrimanic Powers
Wrestling for Man" (Steiner),
619

Lum, Peter, 118

MacDonald, George, 31, 46, 75,
167, 288, 776; *Lilith*, 18; *Mal-
colm*, 18; *Phantasies*, 18; *Robert
Falconer*, 30; "Works of Fancy
and the Imagination," 214

MacFarland, Arthur, 127–28, 184

Machado, Antonio, 776

Mackintosh, Graham, 581, 776

MacLow, Jackson, 543, 776

Macmillan, 201, 215–16, 226

*Madame Bovary* (Flaubert), 256

*The Magician of Lublin* (Singer),
252

"The Maiden" (Duncan), 65

"Making It New" (Carruth), 638,
646

*Malaga Beach* (Eilshemius), 170

Malanga, Gerard, 534, 776

*Malcolm* (MacDonald), 18

*Malicroix* (Bosco), 513

"The Man in the Moon" (Zukof-
sky), 450

Manley, Mrs. Robert. *See* Givens,
Seon

Manley, Robert, 215

Mann, Thomas, 498–99; *Doctor
Faustus*, 186

Mansfield, Katherine, 776

"Man's Fulfillment in Order and
Strife" (Duncan), xxii, 609,
618–19

"A Map of the Western Part
of the County of Essex in
England" (Levertov), 242

*Marat/Sade* (Weiss), 521

Maritain, Jacques, *Creative Imag-
ination in Art & Poetry*, 252

Marlowe, Alan, 513–14

Marshall, Edward, 116, 119, 776

*Le Marteu sans Maître* (Boulez),
249

Martin, Frances, 776; *Nine Tales
of Raven*, 74

Martin, John, 580–81, 632, 776

Martinelli, Sheri, 167, 808n.1

Marx, Karl, 118

Masefield, John, *The Box of
Delights*, 579, 581, 583; *The
Griffin*, 579, 581, 583; *Mid-
night Park*, 583

*The Master of Hestviken* (Undset),
472

Matisse, Henri, 21–22

*Matter*, 776

Matthei, Chuck, 600–601

Matthiasdottir, Louisa. *See* Bell,
Louisa Matthiasdottir

*The Maximus Poems* (Olson), 81,
385

Mazzocco, Robert, "A Philosoph-
ical Poet," 512

McAlmon, Robert, 320, 322, 324,
777; *Being Geniuses Together*,
320–21, 322

McCarroll, Tolbert H., 555

McCarthy, Eugene, 619–20

McClure, Joanne, 113

McClure, Michael, 47, 55, 77–78,
236, 777; *The Beard*, 542–43;
"The Boobas and the Bunny
Duck," 208, 810n.1; *Meat
Science Essays*, 542–43; "Ode
to Jackson Pollock," 149

McHugh, Vincent, *Why I Live on
the Mountain*, 186

McKee, Marjorie (Duncan's
wife), 665, 791, 834n.1

Mead, G. R. S.; *Fragments of a
Faith Forgotten*, 249

*Measure*, 65, 67, 71, 181, 777

*Measure #1* (Dorn), 116

*Meat Science Essays* (McClure),
542–43

*Medea at Kolchis: The Maiden
    Head* (Duncan), 44, 48, 49,
    58, 63, 497, 801n.1
Medical Report of Vietnam, 597
*The Medieval Mind* (Taylor), 508
*Medieval Scenes* (Duncan), 431–32,
    449
"The Medium" (Blaser), 496, 497
"A Meeting of Poets and Theolo-
    gians to Discuss Parable, Myth
    and Language" (Washington,
    D.C., 1967), 570–71, 576, 595
*Memories, Dreams, Reflections*
    (Jung), 415, 419
"Mercury Poems" (Enslin), 487
"The Mermaid's Song"
    (Wieners), 383
"Merritt Parkway" (Levertov),
    432, 433
Mersmann, James, *Out of the
    Vietnam Vortex*, xxv–xxvii,
    711, 715–16, 749, 794
Merwin, W. S., 777; "The Saint
    of the Upland," 327
"The Message" (Duncan), 326,
    328
"The Messengers" (Creeley), 428
"Metamorphic Journal" (Lever-
    tov), 714
"Metaphysical Suite" (Duncan),
    701
Michoacan (Mexico), 49
*Midnight Park* (Masefield), 583
*Migrant*, 232, 777
Miles, Josephine, 777
Miller, Henry, 21, 119
Miller, Jason, 514–15, 534
*The Mills of the Kavanaughs*
    (Lowell), 52–53
"Los Mineros" (Dorn), 266
"The Mines at Falun" (Hoffman),
    470
*Minnesota Review*, 777
Mirrlees, Hope, *The Counterplot*,
    487
MIT, 642–43, 645, 832n.1
Mitchell, David, 39
Mixon, Donald, 807n.1
Mixon, Eloise, 139, 280, 807n.1
Modernism, xi, xxii–xxiv, 582–83
Moe, Henry Allen, 99, 804n.1
Mondrian, Piet, 19
Monet, Claude, 249, 812n.1
Mons, Franz, 596, 830n.8
Montaigne, Michel Eyquem de,
    119
*Montana Xibalba: Translations #2*
    (Jess), 395

Montgomery, Stuart, 777; "Six
    and a Single Remorse for the
    Sky," 631
Montreal Poetry Conference, 592
*Mont-Saint-Michel and Chartres*
    (Adams), 695
"The Moon" (Duncan), 464
Moore, Marianne, 52–53, 68, 80,
    93, 99, 114
Moore, Richard, 827n.2
Moraff, Barbara, 423; "Cunt
    Poem One," 493
Moravian Brotherhood, 823n.2
Morgenstern, Christian, 777;
    *Gallowsongs/Galgenleider*, 655
"The Morning Glory" (Rumaker),
    284
Morris, William, *News from
    Nowhere*, 397; *The Roots of the
    Mountains*, 533–34
Mosley, Jim, 416
Motherwell, Robert, *The Dada
    Painters and Poets*, 63
*The Moth Poems* (Blaser), 444,
    496, 502–3
*The Movement toward a New
    America* (Goodman), 613
"Mr. Boswell & Dr. Johnson"
    (Duerden), 455
"Mrs. Cobweb" (Levertov),
    171–72, 433
"The Multiversity" (Duncan),
    572–73, 673, 834n.2
Mumford, Lewis, 777–78;
    "Utopia: The City and the
    Machine," 494, 499
"Murder Talk: The Reception"
    (Eigner), 481
"The Muse" (Levertov), 242
"The Museum" (Duncan), 711
Muste, A. J., 778
"My Dear" (Blaser), 496
"My Father Died This Spring"
    (Kyger), 474
"My Love" (Creeley), 157
"My Mother Would Be a Fal-
    coness" (Duncan), 470, 472
*Mysterium Magnum* (Boehme),
    528–29, 539–40
*Myth and Symbol in Ancient
    Egypt* (Clark), 567
*Mythologies* (Yeats), 215

*Naked Lunch* (Burroughs), 205
"Name Cast into the Tree-
    Alphabet" (Blackburn), 594
*The Nasturtium that Dissolved
    the World* (Jess), 12–13

*The Nation*, 273, 276, 280, 778
*The National Review*, 276, 279,
    280
"A Necessary Poetry" (Levertov),
    252, 266–67
Neiland, Dr., 599
"Nel Mezzo del Camin di Nostra
    Vita" (Duncan), 194
Nemerov, Howard, 778
Neruda, Pablo, 778
Nesbitt, Gogo, 46–47
*The New American Poetry* (Allen),
    ix–x
New Criticism, ix–x, 111
*New Directions*, 52, 178, 180, 200,
    399, 406, 581, 587, 593, 605
*A New Folder, Americans* (Aldan),
    177, 178, 189
*The New Freewoman*, 261
*The New Republic*, 280
*News from Nowhere* (Morris), 397
New Testament, 611
Newton, Race, 261
*New World Writing*, 149, 778
New York City, 21, 24, 29–30,
    98, 108
New York school, 179
New York University, 248
Nichols, Robert, 778; "Vietlife
    (An Act of Respect for the
    Vietnamese People)", 566,
    828n.2
Nietzsche, Friedrich Wilhelm,
    596; *Also Sprach Zarathustra*,
    48; *Birth of Tragedy*, 588, 591
"A Night" (Levertov), 432
"Night Scenes I, II, III" (Dun-
    can), 353, 357, 371
Nims, John Frederick, 279
*Nine Tales of Raven* (Martin), 74
Nixon, Richard, 620, 661, 685,
    696
*Noonday Review*, 162, 778
Norbert Schimmel Collection
    (Fogg Museum, Harvard
    University), 486
Norman, Itzak, 326–27
"Note of A Scale" (Levertov), 231,
    433
"A Note on the Poetry of Larry
    Eigner" (Levertov), 184,
    190–91
"A Note on the Work of the Ima-
    gination" (Levertov), 213
"Notes of Discovery" (Levertov),
    102
"Notes on Robert Duncan"
    (Will), 511

"Notes on the Poetry of Deep Image" (Kelly), 260, 269, 300

"A Note to Olga, 1966" (Levertov), 742

Novalis (*pen name of* Frederick von Hardenberg), 778

"The Novel" (Levertov), 692

"Novella" (Levertov), 653

"Novices" (Levertov), 412

Nyholm, Jens, 348

*O!* (Jess), 241

Oaxaca (Mexico), 74

Objectivism, x, 582

"October" (Levertov), 429, 434–35

"Ode to Jackson Pollock" (McClure), 149

*Odilon Redon, Gustave Moreau, Rodolphe Bresdin* (Art Institute of Chicago), 336

"The Odor" (Herbert), 90

Odyssia Gallery (New York City), 606, 660, 830n.1, 833–34n.4

"Often I Am Permitted to Return to a Meadow" (Duncan), 131, 136, 802n.2, 806n.1

"Of the Art" (Duncan), 65

"Of the War" (Duncan), xxi–xxii

*Of the War: Passages 22–27* (Duncan), xviii, 553

Ogden, C. K.; *The Foundations of Aesthetics*, 41

O'Gorman, Ned, 305, 310, 778

O'Hara, Frank, x, 179, 778–79

Okamura, Arthur, 779

"The Old Adam" (Levertov), 520, 818n.1

Old Testament, 539, 611

*Ole*, 537, 827n.4

"Olga Poems" (Levertov), 459, 461–62, 469, 471, 491–92, 493, 553, 557, 667, 670–71, 675–76, 690

Olson, Betty, 454, 823n.1

Olson, Charles, 779; at Black Mountain, x; and Creeley, x, xii; death of, xi, 833n.3; and Duncan, x, 61, 582; health of, 422; illness of, 646, 832n.1; *In Cold Hell in Thicket*, 431; "John Smith," 178–79; Levertov on, 86, 138, 504; *The Maximus Poems*, 81, 385; on the modern era, beginning of, 834n.4; at the Poetry Center, 78; "La Préface," 550–51; "Projective Verse," x, xi, xii, 282, 733, 834n.3; readings by,

500–501; *The Special View of History*, 58

"115 Weeks" (Kelly), 510

"One of the Lucky" (Levertov), 397–98, 401

*On Poetry and Poets* (Eliot), 77

"On Reading the Early Poems of Robert Duncan" (Levertov), 201, 206–8, 547–48

*On the Cave of the Nymphs* (Porphyry), 639

*On the Road* (Kerouac), 73, 103, 116

*The Opening of the Field* (Duncan), 48, 90, 111, 126, 131, 134–35, 137, 169, 194, 220

*Open Space*, 444, 518

Oppen, George, x, 397, 401, 405, 407, 779

Oppenheimer, Joel, 155, 447, 779

"Oriented by Instincts by Stars" (Duncan), 530

*Origin*, x, 9, 396, 538, 779, 799n.2

*Origin of Species* (Darwin), 31

"The Origins of Old Son" (Duncan), 38, 315, 801n.2

Orlovsky, Lafcadio, 49–50, 802n.1

Orlovsky, Peter, 49–50, 103, 420, 802n.1

*Orpheus and Greek Religion* (Guthrie), 463

*The Orphic Vision* (Bays), 468–69, 488

Orvino, Jennie, 601

Osborne, Ken, 703

*O Taste and See* (Levertov), 435, 691–92

Our Visit to Niagara (Goodman), 380

"The Outer Banks" (Rukeyser), 486

*An Outline of English Structure* (Trayer and Smith), 150

"Out of the Black" (Duncan), 173

*Out of the Vietnam Vortex* (Mersmann), xxv–xxvii, 711, 715–16, 749, 794

*Outsider*, 779

*Overland to the Islands* (Levertov), 55, 67–68, 76–77, 87, 107, 111, 400–401

Oyez, 574, 581

Palmer, Samuel, 363

*Paracelsus: Selected Writings*, 164

"Paradise Re-Entered" (Lawrence), 257–58

"The Park" (Levertov), 171, 231, 433

*The Park* (Blaser), 502–3

Parkinson, Thomas, 166–67, 176, 181, 193–94, 197–98, 205, 232, 276–77, 779–80

"Parsifal: Afer Wagner & Verlaine" (Duncan), 478

*Partisan Review*, 100, 169, 396, 780

"A Part-Sequence for Change" (Duncan), 384

"Passages" (Duncan), xvi, xviii

Pasternak, Boris, 251–52; *Doctor Zhivago*, 173

Patchen, Kenneth, 85–86, 118

*Paterson* (Williams), xii, 431, 656–57

Paterson Society, 312–13

"The Path" (Levertov), 289

Payne, Robert, 32, 800–801n.2

Paz, Octavio, 780

*Peace Eye* (Sanders), 504

Pearson, Norman Holmes, 310, 335, 410, 780

People's Park, 672–73, 675, 686

People's Park protest (Berkeley, Calif.), 661, 672–73, 675, 685–86, 834n.1

"Perpetual revolution," 630

Perse, Saint-John (*pseud. of* Alexis Leger), 299, 303, 304–5, 780; *Amers*, 297, 298, 299, 300; *Anabase*, 297, 299, 300

*Personae* (Pound), 90

Peters, Robert, 557, 569, 780

"A Philosophical Poet" (Mazzocco), 512

*Philsophies of India* (Zimmer), 110

Physicians for Social Responsibility, 597

"The Picture of J. T. in a Prospect of Stone" (Tomlinson), 383

*Pieces* (Creeley), 640, 641

"A Place to Live" (Levertov), 654–55

Plato, xvii, 64, 214, 299

"Play with Masks" (Duncan), 525

Pleasant Point (Maine), 126–27

"Please" (Creeley), 236–37

"Pleine Mer" (Hugo), 487–88, 489

Plomer, William, 780

Plotinus, *Against the Gnostics*, 298, 299

"Poem: Completely Naked" (Duerden), 455

"A Poem Beginning with a Line by Pindar" (Duncan), 204–5
"A Poem of Despondencies" (Duncan), 121, 806n.1
Poems 1948–49 (Duncan), 22, 90
"Poems 1958–1961" (Duerden), 455
Poems in a Floating World, 177, 205
"A Poem Slow Beginning" (Duncan), 46, 48, 131–32
"The Poet" (Emerson), xxiv, 406, 680, 834n.3
Poetics of Music in the Form of Six Lessons (Stravinsky), 121
"The Poetic Vocation: St. John Perse" (Duncan), 297, 299, 316–17
"The Poet in the Poem" (Rago), 630
The Poet in the World (Levertov), xxiii
Poetry, 65, 68, 232, 483, 780, 824n.3
"Poetry, a Natural Thing" (Duncan), 56, 66, 70, 803n.2
"Poetry and Imagination" (Emerson), xxii
Poetry Center (San Francisco), 33, 35, 48, 52–53, 56, 57, 77, 78, 802n.1
Poetry Collection (University of California), 508
"Poetry in the Age of Expansion" (Bly), 290
"The Poetry Shelf" (Kinnell), 548
"A Poet's View" (Levertov), xvii, xxiv–xxv
Pollock, Jackson, 119, 780
Ponge, Francis, 780
Le Pont de Mantes (Corot), 50
Poor, Old, Tired, Horse, 780
Poor Clares, 601–2
Porphyry, On the Cave of the Nymphs, 639
Porter, Bern, 780
Portland State College, 196
Portrait of the Artist as a Young Man (Joyce), 608
Posner, David, 581
"The Postcards" (Levertov), 544
Postmodernism, xi, xxii–xxiv
Pound, Ezra, x; ABC of Reading, 585; on awareness, 19; at Brunnenburg, 659, 833n.1; The Cantos, xii, 81, 125, 131, 163–64, 213, 534; Duncan on, 582; as a

fad, 21; Levertov on, 86; at the Montreal Poetry Conference, 592; Personae, 90; readings by, 642; "A Retrospect," 441; Rock Drill, 33–34; "The Serious Artist," 404, 406; Thrones, 236; "We, the CLEANERS, D. Simpson, I. C. Flynn, Igon Tan," 132, 195; on William Carlos Williams, 388–89; and Yeats, 533–34
Pound, Mary de Rachewiltz, 380, 389
Practical Mysticism (Underhill), 255
"The Preface" (Blaser), 138, 140
"La Préface" (Olson), 550–51
"Prelude" (Wordsworth), 367, 369
The Prelude (Wordsworth), 39–40, 367, 369
Pre-Raphaelite Collection (Delaware Art Museum), 341, 817n.2
Primack, Ronnie, 780–81
"Prisoners" (H. D.), 262
"The Problem of the Poem for My Daughter Left Unsolved" (Dorn), 502
"Problems for the Modern Critic of Literature" (Winters), 53
Process and Reality (Whitehead), 199
Proclus, The Commentaries on the Timaeus of Plato in Five Books, 490
"Projective Verse" (Olson), x, xi, xii, 282, 733, 834n.3
"Prologue: An Interim" (Levertov), 663, 684, 834n.1
Prometheus, 210
"The Propositions" (Duncan), 58, 59, 61, 65
Proust, Marcel, "Chardin," 632
"Psalm Concerning the Castle" (Levertov), 486, 487
"A Psalm Praising the Hair of Man's Body" (Levertov), 430, 434–35, 440–41
"Puñal" (Garcia Lorca), 420
"Puñal" (Levertov), 412, 413, 419–20
Putney School (Vermont), 372, 427, 429, 486

Quarterly Review of Literature, 781
Quasha, George, 635, 781
The Queen of Crow Castle (Adam), 143

"The Question" (Duncan), 72, 74
The Question of Jean-Jacques Rousseau (Cassirer), 690

"The Rabbits" (Levertov), 433
Rackham, Arthur, 213, 811n.2
Radlin, Paul, African Folktales and Sculpture, 206
Rago, Henry, 65, 143, 781; "The Poet in the Poem," 630
Rall, Jeff, 134, 217, 219, 806n.6; Industrial Worker, 216
Rankin Brigade protest (Washington, D.C.), 607
Ransom, John Crowe, 66, 781, 803n.2
Ransome, Arthur, 158–59, 808n.2
Rauschenberg, Robert, 582–83
Raymond, M.; From Baudelaire to Surrealism, 118
Read, Herbert, 32, 781, 791
Read, John, Through Alchemy to Chemistry, 548
Reading for the Defense of the Presidio 27, 630–31
Reaney, James, 781; "A Cellar Song," 224; "The Windyard," 224
The Rebel (Camus), 663
Rector, James, 661, 686, 834n.1
Redl, Harry, 189, 809n.2
"Reflections on the Mode of Literary Polemics" (Duncan), 649
"Reincarnation" (Dickey), 470–71
"Relative Figures" (Levertov), 171, 181, 202
"Relative Figures Reappear" (Levertov), 433
"Relearning the Alphabet" (Levertov), 631, 634, 650, 692
Relearning the Alphabet (Levertov), 638, 650–51, 657, 712
Rembrandt, 41
Reminiscences of a Student's Life (Harrison), 494
Residu, 508–9, 826n.4
Resist, 597–603, 611, 703–5
The Resistance, 598
"A Retrospect" (Pound), 441
Rexroth, Kenneth, 10, 781; on Creeley, 20; The Dragon and the Unicorn, 24–25, 732; Duncan on, 53, 77–78, 84–85, 93, 113–14; and Levertov, 79, 83, 88–89, 97, 112; marriage to Marthe, 38–39, 41–42, 43, 45, 48, 51, 85, 112; on Moore, 93,

114; "Seven Poems for Marthe, My Wife," 57–58; translations by, 102

Rexroth, Marthe, 38–39, 41–42, 43, 45–46, 48, 51, 85, 112

Reznikoff, Charles, 781–82

Rhode Island School of Design, 586–87, 621–22, 655

Rich, Adrienne, xxx, 543, 729, 732–33, 782, 793; Duncan on (see "A Critical Difference of View"); "The Knot," 547; "Spring Thunder," 547

Richards, I. A.; *The Foundations of Aesthetics*, 41

Richards, M. C., x, 7, 112, 123, 147, 173–74, 782; "Giant," 141, 149; "Holy Poems," 398; "Levity," 141

Richter, Daniel, 826n.4

"Right Now" (Duerden), 455

Rigney, Warren ("Rhonda"), 713

Rilke, Rainer Maria, 399, 530, 536, 644, 657; *Duino Elegies*, 270–71

Rimbaud, Arthur, 469, 543

Rimer's Club, 656, 833n.1

*The Ring* (Wagner), 280–81

"A Ring of Changes" (Levertov), 149, 152–54, 175, 181–82, 186, 231, 433, 590

Riordan, Dennis, 600–601, 604

"Rising" (Ammons), 392

"The Risk" (Levertov), 256

"Risk" (Duncan), 262, 264, 267

*Ritual*, 791

Rivers, Larry, 177, 782

*Robert Falconer* (MacDonald), 30

Roberts, Elisabeth Madox, *Black Is My True Love's Hair*, 56; *The Time of Man*, 56

Robinson, Charles, 190

*Rock Drill* (Pound), 33–34

Rodin Museum (Philadelphia), 341, 817n.1

Roethke, Theodore, 782

Romanticism, xi, xii–xiii, xxii–xxiv

*Romeo and Juliet* (Shakespeare), 699–700

*Rootabaga Pigeons* (Sandburg), 28

*Rootabaga Stories* (Sandburg), 16, 28

"Roots and Branches" (Duncan), 165–66, 181

*Roots and Branches* (Duncan), 430–31, 458, 479–80, 615

*The Roots of the Mountains* (Morris), 533–34

*Rosa Alchemica* (Yeats), 215

"The Rose" (Creeley), 234, 235

Rose, H. J.; *A Handbook of Greek Mythology*, 558–59

Roseliep, Raymond, 546–47, 782; *Love Makes—The Air Light*, 502

Rosenqust, James, 582–83

Rosenthal, M. L., 355, 380, 782

Ross, Dacharina ("Dickie"), 713

Ross, Don, 713

Rosset, Barney, 148, 224

Rossetti, Christiana Georgina, *Goblin Market*, 110

Roth, William, 78, 782

Rothenberg, Jerome, 177, 193, 782–83

Rousseau, Henri Julien Félix, *Carnival Night*, 30

Rousseau, Jean-Jacques, 690

Rudge, Olga, 783

Rukeyser, Muriel, 305, 386–87, 486, 606, 708, 783; "The Outer Banks," 486

Rumaker, Michael, 100, 116, 138, 163, 223, 260–61, 279, 783; *The Butterfly*, 476, 477; "[City of Night] A Review," 476, 478; "The Morning Glory," 284

"The Runnenberg" (Tieck), 280

Sacco, Nicola, 827n.2

*Sagesse* (H. D.), 207

"Saint Graal: After Verlaine" (Duncan), 478

*Saint Judas* (Wright), 264, 813n.4

"The Saint of the Upland" (Merwin), 327

*Salambo* (Flaubert), 256

"Saliences" (Ammons), 392

"Salut" (Blaser), 497

"Salvages" (Duncan), 431

Sandburg, Carl, *Rootabaga Pigeons*, 28; *Rootabaga Stories*, 16, 28

Sanders, Ed, 783; *Peace Eye*, 504

San Francisco Renaissance, xiv

*San Francisco Review*, 185, 783

*San Francisco's Burning* (Adam), 426

"Santa Cruz Propositions" (Duncan), xxi, 656, 663, 701, 711, 740–41, 831n.1

Sapir, Edward, *Language*, 538–39

Saroyan, Aram, 119, 594, 605, 783

"Saturday Afternoon" (Creeley), 113, 122

Saurat, Denis, *Literature and the Occult Tradition*, 488

Sauser-Hall, Frederic. *See* Cendrars, Blaise

Sawbridge, Keith, 17

Sawyer, Paul, 500

"Say the Word" (Levertov), 411, 421, 435, 692

"Scales of the Marvellous" (Carruth), 479, 481, 482

"Scenes from the Life of the Pepper Trees" (Levertov), 51, 57, 171, 231, 433

Schaffner, Perdita, 380

Scheffer, Ary, 605, 830n.3

Schevill, James, 783

Scholem, Gershom, 137, 140, 327; *Major Trends in Jewish Mysticism*, 783

School of Visual Arts, 304, 306

Schrödinger, Erwin, 544

Schub, Phyllis, 534

Schumann, Peter, 562, 601, 828n.1

Schweitzer, Byrd, 598

Schwerner, Armand, 269, 784

Schwitters, Kurt, "Die Sonate in Urlauten," 595

*Scientific American*, 609, 831n.7

Scribners, 396, 399, 430–31, 458–59, 574

Seaver, Richard, 243, 244–45

*Secant*, 826n.3

"A Secret" (Levertov), 354, 358

"Seedtime" (Levertov), 430, 434–35

"Seems Like We Must Be Somewhere Else" (Levertov), 95

*Selected Poems* (Duncan), 110, 160, 162, 196, 199, 201

*Selected Poems* (H. D.), 68, 71

"The Self in Postmodernist Poetry" (Duncan), xxii

"The Sense Comes over Me" (Dorn), 502

"September 1961" (Levertov), 309, 310

"The Serious Artist" (Pound), 404, 406

*Set*, 263, 784

"A Set of Romantic Hymns" (Duncan), 338–39

Seurat, Georges Pierre, *La Grande Jatte*, 115

"Seurat Paintings and Drawings" (Museum of Modern Art, New York City), 115

"Seven Poems" (Enslin), 287–88
"Seven Poems for Marthe, My Wife" (Rexroth), 57–58
"Shadows" (Duncan), 465, 468
"The Shadow Song" (Zukofsky), 450
Shakespeare, William, 81, 213–14; Hamlet, 671; Romeo and Juliet, 699–700
"Shalom" (Levertov), 358, 363
"The Sharks" (Levertov), 68, 171, 433, 589
Shayer, Michael, 212, 784
Shelley, Percy Bysshe, 288, 291; "Alastor," 183; "The Homeric Hymn to Mercury," 730; "Witch of Atlas," 183
"Shelley's Arethusa Set to New Measures" (Duncan), 288, 291
Shiel, Matthew Phipps, 53, 802n.2
"The Shifting" (Levertov), xiii, 97, 193, 714
"A Shrine to Ameinias" (Duncan), 581
Shurin, Isak, 640, 832n.1
"Sighs and Groans" (Herbert), 90
The Signature of All Things (Boehme), 168
Simpson, Louis, 205, 283, 293, 784
Singer, I. B., 784; The Magician of Lublin, 252
Sitwell, Edith, 21, 59, 61, 267, 273–74, 440, 784
"Six and a Single Remorse for the Sky" (Montgomery), 631
Six Theosophic Points (Boehme), 168–69
"Six Variations" (Levertov), 191, 231
"Sketches by Constable" (Baltimore Museum of Art), 522
Sloman, Joel, 546, 784
"A Small Grain of Worship" (Bryher), 305
Smart, Christopher, 21, 49, 784
Smith, Harry Lee, An Outline of English Structure, 150
Snodgrass, W. D., 282, 283, 784
Socrates and His Physician (Valéry), 84
Solar Journal (Grossinger), 649
"The Soldiers: Passages 26" (Duncan), 507–8, 517, 525, 527, 528, 531, 572–73
Solomon, Hyde, 348
Solovyev, Vladimir Sergeyevich, 208; Lectures on Godmanship, 209
Solt, Mary Ellen, 596
"Some Duncan Letters—A Memoir and a Critical Tribute" (Levertov), xxvi
"Some Notes on Organic Form" (Levertov), xvi, xxii, xxiv, 368, 510, 834n.3
"Something to Wear" (Levertov), 35, 433
Some Time (Zukofsky), 543
"The Sonata" (Duerden), 455
"Die Sonate in Urlauten" (Schwritters), 595
"A Song" (Levertov), 37
"Song for a Dark Voice" (Levertov), 191, 231, 448
"Song of Fair Things" (Duncan), 69, 70
"Song of Myself" (Whitman), 188
"The Song of the Borderguard" (Duncan), 204
"A Song of the Old Order" (Eluard), 178
"Songs for an Evening's Singing" (Duncan), 70
"Sonnet IV" (Duncan), 394, 409, 415
Sorrentino, Gilbert, 306, 784
The Sorrow Dance (Levertov), 533, 556, 742
Sorrows of Priapus (Dahlberg), 105
"Source" (Duncan), 433, 434
Les Sources occultes du Romantisme, Illuminisme (Viatte), 594
Southwell, Robert, "The Burning Babe," 700, 749–52
The Special View of History (Olson), 58
"Spelling: Passages 14" (Duncan), 463, 464, 466, 469–70
Spellman, A. B., 566, 785
Spellman, Francis Cardinal, 785
Spenser, Edmund, 324
Spicer, Jack, 57, 94, 109, 785; Adam's Way boycotted by, 384, 819n.2; After Lorca, 96; death of, 505; and Duncan, 505–6, 509, 625; influence of, 505; style of, 537–39
Spicer, Jim, 242
"The Spider Song" (Duncan), 62
Spock, Benjamin, xx, 638, 794, 830n.1
Spring and All (Williams), 270–71, 272
"Spring Thunder" (Rich), 547
"The Springtime" (Levertov), 37, 40–41, 171, 231
St. Augustine, xvii
St. Julian (Flaubert), 256
St. Petersburg (Belyi), 224
St. Teresa's College (Winona, Minn.), 601–2
Stafford, William, 389; Traveling through the Dark, 389
Stanislavsky, Constantine, 785
Stanley, George, 156, 200, 201–2, 785, 819n.2
"Staying Alive" (Levertov), xxi, 604, 682–83, 743–48, 834n.3, 834n.6
Stein, Chuck, 472, 487
Stein, Gertrude, xiii–xiv, 21; How to Write, 14, 24; The World Is Round, 11
Steiner, Rudolph, The Four Seasons and the Archangels, 517; "Lucerific and Ahrimanic Powers Wrestling for Man," 619
"Stepping Westward" (Levertov), 474–75
Stevens, Wallace, "Chocorua to Its Neighbor," 483
Still, Clyfford, 239, 785, 812n.1
"Still Life" (Johnson), 480
"A Stir in the Air" (Levertov), 65, 68, 374, 455
Stone, Richard, 307, 816n.1
Stoneburner, Tony, 571, 829n.2
Stony Brook, 785
"Storm" (Blackburn), 12
"A Storm of White" (Duncan), 109, 114–15, 117, 130, 728–29
The Story of My Heart (Jefferies), 369
"Strains of Sight" (Duncan), 312, 316
"The Strait" (Ammons), 392
Strand, Mark, 785
Stravinsky, Igor, Poetics of Music in the Form of Six Lessons, 121
"The Strike for Peace" (Goodman), 397
"The Structure of Rime" (Duncan), 48, 65, 390–91
"Structure of Rime XXIII" (Duncan), 465
Student Peace Association (Tucson), 598–99
The Subterraneans (Kerouac), 116
"Such Is the Sickness of Many a Good Thing" (Duncan), 442–43, 446

*The Sullen Art*, 393

*Sum*, 493, 785

Summerfield, Geoffrey, 658

"Sunday Afternoon" (Levertov), 65

Surrealism, 21, 177–78

*The Suspect in Poetry* (Dickey), 483

Sutton, Walter, "A Conversation with Denise Levertov," 521

Swados, Harvey, 785

Sweeney, John, 337

Symmes, Edwin (Duncan's adoptive father), 791

Symmes, Minnehaha (Duncan's adoptive mother), 791

"The Take Off" (Levertov), 231, 804n.1

"Taking Away from God His Sound" (Duncan), 484, 485, 489–90

*Tales of the Hasidim* (Buber), 140–41

Tallman, Warren, 297, 360, 785

Tate, Allen, 592, 785–86

Taylor, Henry Osborn, *The Medieval Mind*, 508

Temple (Maine), 422

*The Temple* (Herbert), 90–93

"The Temple of the Animals" (Duncan), 202, 207

*The Temptation of St. Anthony* (Flaubert), 256

"Tenebrae" (Levertov), xix, 666–67, 668, 672, 678, 685, 737

Terkel, Studs (Louis), 600–601, 786

*The Double Image* (Levertov), 792

*The Jacob's Ladder* (Levertov), 284

*Theogony* (Hesiod), 559

*Theology of the New Testament* (Bultmann), 562–63

"These Past Years: Passages 10" (Duncan), 463

"These Things We See Are Images of the Past" (Kyger), 474

"They Say" (Creeley), 433

Thich Nhat Hanh, 534, 535, 536, 537

*Things*, 480, 786

"This Compost" (Whitman), 199, 203

"This Place, Rumord to be Sodom" (Duncan), 65

Thomas Jefferson College, 710

Thompson, Ruth Plumly, 29, 800n.3

Thompson, Virgil, 786

*Threads* (Bromige), 659

"3 AM Black" (Duerden), 455

"The Three Ladies" (Creeley), 433

"Three Meditations" (Levertov), 263, 266

"Three Pages from a Birthday Book" (Duncan), 56

"Three Poems in Measure One" (Duncan), 66

"Three Poets" (Ammons), 338

"Three Songs of the Bard Orpheus" (Duncan), 370–71

"The Three Voices of Poetry" (Eliot), 132–33

"Threshold" (Levertov), 412

*Thrones* (Pound), 236

*Through Alchemy to Chemistry* (Read), 548

Tieck, Ludwig, 786; "The Fair-Haired Eckbert," 280; "The Runnenberg," 280; "The Trusty Eckbert," 280

Tiffany, Louis Comfort, 111

*Till We Have Faces* (Lewis), 284, 288

"Time" (Herbert), 90

*The Time of Man* (Roberts), 56

"Today" (Levertov), 659

"Today's Saint" (Levertov), 231

"To Death" (Levertov), 449

Tolkien, J. R. R., 526, 786

Tolstoy, Leo, *Anna Karenina*, 214; *War and Peace*, 214

"Tomatlan" (Levertov), 35, 42, 43–45

Tomlinson, Charles, 729, 730, 732, 786; "Autumn," 222; "The Picture of J. T. in a Prospect of Stone," 383

Toor, Frances, *Treasury of Mexican Folkways*, 74

"To Pumpkin-Cat" (Duncan), 54

"To R. D., March 4th, 1988" (Levertov), xxx–xxxi, 719, 754–55, 836n.1

"The Torn Cloth" (Duncan), xxvii, 716, 752–54

*To Stay Alive* (Levertov), xix, 662, 663–65, 679, 742–43

"To the Muse" (Levertov), 359

"To the Snake" (Levertov), 105

"To thine own self be true," 671

"Towards an Open Universe" (Duncan), 439

"To Write Is to Listen" (Levertov), 485

*Translations* (Odyssia Gallery, N.Y.C), 660, 833–34n.4

"The Transparencies" (Blaser), 138, 140

*Traveling through the Dark* (Stafford), 389

Trayer, George L.; *An Outline of English Structure*, 150

*Treasury of Mexican Folkways* (Toor), 74

"The Tree" (Levertov), 544

*A Tree Telling of Orpheus* (Levertov), 592–93, 606–7, 657

"Tribal Memories" (Duncan), 463–64

"Tributes" (H. D.), 396

"Tributes to the Angels" (H. D.), 689

Triem, Eve, 331–32, 414, 786

*Trinity's Trine: Translations #5* (Jess), 458, 516

*Trobar*, 266, 786

"A True Hymn" (Herbert), 90

"The True Wonder" (Elimelekh of Lijensk), 584

Truitt, Anne, 341, 817n.1

Truitt, Jim, 341, 817n.1

"The Trusty Eckbert" (Tieck), 280

Tucson (Arizona), 377–78, 597–99

Tudor, David, 112, 123, 786

Turnbull, Gael, 138, 416, 543, 547, 566, 786–87; "20 Words 20 Days," 460

"Turning" (Levertov), 431, 589–90

*12 Poets & 1 Painter*, 471

"[23 Poems]" (Finlay), 373

"20 Words 20 Days" (Turnbull), 460

"Two Poems for the Jews" (Duncan), 204

*Two Poems of the Air* (Dickey), 470, 530, 536

"Two Presentations" (Duncan), 277

"Two Wives" (Lawrence), 250–51

Tyler, Hamilton, 787

Tyler, Mary, 93, 99

"Under Ground" (Duncan), 130, 806n.6

Underhill, Evelyn, *Practical Mysticism*, 255

Undset, Sigrid, *The Master of Hestviken*, 472

Ungaretti, Giuseppe, 787

Union College (Barbourville, Kentucky), 599–600, 602

University of Arizona, 597–98, 599, 602

University of California at Berkeley, 77

University of Kentucky (Lexington), 600

"Upon Taking Hold" (Duncan), 432–33

"Up Rising: Passages 25" (Duncan), xviii, xx, 505, 506–7, 515, 528, 563, 572–73, 612, 666, 679, 695, 738–39

"Utopia: The City and the Machine" (Mumford), 494, 499

Vaihinger, Hans, 134, 806

*Vale Ave* (H. D.), 207

Valéry, Paul, *Socrates and His Physician*, 84

Vandenbroek, André, 46–47

*Vanity Fair*, 707

Vanzetti, Bartolomeo, 542, 568, 629, 632–33, 827n.2

"Variations on Two Dicta of William Blake" (Duncan), 251, 255, 262

Vassar College, 554, 569–70

Vaughan, Henry, "Childhood," 200; *Hermetical Physick*, 528

"The Venice Poem" (Duncan), 195–96, 197–98, 199, 384, 431

*The Very Thing That Happens* (Edson), 423

Veterans for Peace, 519

Viatte, August, *Les Sources occultes du Romantisme, Illuminisme*, 594

"Vietlife (An Act of Respect for the Vietnamese People)" (Nichols), 566, 828n.2

Vietnam War, xv, xvii–xviii; arguing against vs. knowing what's happening, 619; draft resistence, 597–98, 601, 608, 830n.1; Duncan on, xix–xxii, 552, 558, 563, 565, 567, 608–9, 661; Duncan on conscription, 568, 612, 629; Duncan on image/drama of, 529–30; Duncan on protest/Protestantism, 619; Duncan on U.S. refusal to negotiate, 487–88; Duncan on wearing black armbands/bearing witness, 563, 564, 568, 608; Duncan's antiwar poetry, xviii, 546, 572–73 (*see also specific poems*); Duncan's outrage at, 546; as evil, 541, 558, 608–9; Levertov in march against, 515; Levertov's activism against, xviii–xix, xx, xxi, 556, 592, 597–603, 619, 621, 742–43, 828–29n.1; Levertov's antiwar poetry, xxv–xxvi, 546 (*see also specific poems*); Levertov's outrage at, 546; the Movement, 629–31, 632, 681–82; Resist and Conscientious Resistance Statements, 598; student demonstrations against, 597–98, 742–43. *See also under* Duncan/Levertov rupture

"A Vision" (Levertov), 519, 531

*Vision* (Yeats), 535

Vivin, Louis, 30, 787

*Voice of America*, 439, 446

Vuillard, Édouard, *Cezanne's Garden*, 112

W. W. Norton, 457, 458–59, 823n.1

Wagner, Linda, 421; "An Interview with Robert Creeley, 1965," 521

Wagner, Richard, *The Ring*, 280–81

Wah, Fred, 787

Wainhouse, Austryn, 26

Wakoski, Diane, 787; "The Ice Eagle," 566

Waldrop, Bernard, 431, 822n.3

Waldrop, Rosemarie, 822n.3

Wallace, George, 492

"The Walls Do Not Fall" (H. D.), 256

Walrich, Larry, 348, 818n.3

Walter and Louise Arensberg Collection (Philadelphia Museum of Art), 341, 817n.1

"Wapitis" (Borregaard), 129–30, 132, 133, 135

*War and Peace* (Tolstoy), 214

War Resisters' League, 578, 579

"War Suite" (Harrison), 565

Wasserman, Jakob, 807n.1

*The Waste Land* (Eliot), 197, 270

"The Way Through" (Levertov), 32

"We, the CLEANERS, D. Simpson, I. C. Flynn, Igon Tan" (Pound), 132, 195

*The Wedding Feast* (Edelman), 655

*The Wedge* (Williams), 641

"Week of Angry Arts against the War in Vietnam," 828n.2

Weiss, Peter, *Marat/Sade*, 521

Weiss, Theodore, 486, 787

Welch, Lew, 499–500, 825n.2

Welty, Eudora, 787; *The Golden Apples*, 640

Wenning, Henry, 410, 567, 821n.1

Wesleyan Poetry series, 423, 458–59

"We Won't Go" movement, 592

Whalen, Philip, 429, 787

"What Is a Prose Poem?" (Levertov), 278–79, 291

"What I Saw" (Duncan), 464, 467

"What Were They Like?" (Levertov), 535–36, 666–67

Wheeler, Charles B.; *The Design of Poetry*, 569

"When Men Will Lie Down As Gracefully & As Ripe" (Johnson), 480–81

"Where It Appears" (Duncan), 464, 467–68, 478–79, 550

*The Whip* (Creeley), 71

Whitehead, Alfred North, 83, 84; *Process and Reality*, 199

*White Rabbit Press*, 94

Whitman, Walt, 49, 62, 632–33; "As I Ponder'd in Silence," 466–67, 553; idealism of, 271; *Leaves of Grass*, 61, 90, 625–26; "Song of Myself," 188; "This Compost," 199, 203

"Who Is at My Window" (Levertov), 412

*Why I Live on the Mountain* (Kwock and McHugh), 186

*Why War?* (Einstein), 619

"A Wicker Basket" (Creeley), 236–37

Wicksteed, Philip Henry, *The Convivio of Dante Alighieri*, 512

Wiele, Jerry van der, 93, 804n.2

Wieners, John, 65, 71, 181, 381, 415, 447, 462, 616–17, 788; *Ace of Pentacles*, 443, 473–74, 477–78, 484; "The Acts of Youth," 383, 473; "An Anniversary Death," 383; "Cocaine," 473; drug use by, 474, 475–76; "Let the heart's pain slack off," 473; "The Mermaid's Song," 383

"The Wife" (Levertov), 191–92

Wilbur, Richard, 327, 788; "Junk," 290, 300

Will, Frederick, "Notes on Robert Duncan," 511
Williams, Charles, 788
Williams, Emmett, 595–96
Williams, Flossie, 388–89
Williams, Jonathan, x, 16, 30, 49, 788; Duncan on, 58, 151, 152, 167; Levertov on, 55, 154–55, 159
Williams, William Carlos, x, "Asphodel, That Greeny Flower" 18; Bly on, 589; death of, 385; Duncan on, 582–83 (see also "A Critical Difference of View"); funeral of, 387–89; "Hermaphoroditic Telephones," 119; on ideas, xxiv, 59, 802n.2; illness of, 148, 294, 381; influence of, xii, 431–32; *Paterson*, xii, 431, 656–57; on poetry, 240; *Spring and All*, 270–71, 272; *The Wedge*, 641; and Yeats, 533–34
"The Willow of Massachusetts" (Levertov), 435
"The Willows" (Levertov), 412
Wilson, Adrian, 10, 13, 788
Wilson, Robert, 348, 515, 826n.2
"Windings" (Duncan), 430
"The Windyard" (Reaney), 224
"Wine" (Levertov), 468–69
*Winter Light* (Bergman), 430
Winters, Yvor (Arthur), 788; "Problems for the Modern Critic of Literature," 53

"Witch of Atlas" (Shelley), 183
"With Eyes at the Back of Our Heads" (Levertov), 171, 175, 231, 433, 589
*With Eyes at the Back of Our Heads* (Levertov), 231, 327
Witt-Diamant, Ruth, 77–78, 93, 98, 102, 151, 414, 788
Wolfert, Helen, 546, 788
Wolff, Kurt, 218
"The Women (Creeley), 221
*Wonderful Adventures of Nils* (Lagherlof), 70
Wood, James, *The Foundations of Aesthetics*, 41
Woolf, Virginia, 28, 32, 416, 487; *Between the Acts*, 487
Wordsworth, William, 37, 541–42; *Prelude*, 39–40; "Prelude," 367, 369
"The Work of Denise Levertov" (Bly), 588–90, 591
*Works and Days* (Hesiod), 508
"Works of Fancy and the Imagination" (MacDonald), 214
*The World Is Round* (Stein), 11
"The World Outside" (Levertov), 231
*Wormwood Review*, 537, 827n.4
Wright, Frank Lloyd, 246
Wright, James, 266, 282, 788–89; *Saint Judas*, 264, 813n.4
*Writing Writing* (Duncan), 52, 66, 462–63, 469

"Xbalba" (Ginsberg), 119
"Xmas Trees on the Bank's Facade" (Levertov), 432

"The Year One" (Levertov), 659
*The Years as Catches* (Duncan), 562
Yeats, W. B., 150, 533–34, 541; *Autobiographies*, 663; *Mythologies*, 215; *Rosa Alchemica*, 215; *Vision*, 535
"Yes, As a Look Springs to Its Face" (Duncan), 94, 139
York, Ruth Lansdorff, 179
Young, Al (Albert James), 789
*Yugen*, 149, 205, 234, 236, 789

Zalman, Schneour, of Ladaly, 224, 789
*Zeus: A Study in Ancient Religion* (Cook), 559, 577–78
Zimmer, Heinrich Robert, *Philsophies of India*, 110
Zinzendorf, Count Nikolaus von, 469, 823n.2
*Zohar*, 327, 539–40, 545
Zukofsky, Celia, 129
Zukofsky, Louis, x, 125–26, 129, 252, 582, 789; "A," 543; *Bottom*, 543; *Found Objects*, 729, 732–33; "The Man in the Moon," 450; "The Shadow Song," 450; *Some Time*, 543